The Papers of Andrew Jackson

Guide and Index to the Microfilm Editions

From life by Wm. H Brown

Lith of E.B.&E.C.Kellogg

ANDREW JACKSON.

THE PAPERS OF
Andrew Jackson

GUIDE AND INDEX TO THE MICROFILM EDITIONS

Harold D. Moser
Sharon Macpherson
John H. Reinbold
Daniel Feller
Editors

Philip Lucas   Julie Macpherson   Wyatt Wells
Editorial Associates

SR Scholarly Resources Inc.
Wilmington, Delaware

Publication of
the Microfilm Supplement
of The Papers of Andrew Jackson
was assisted by grants from
The Ladies' Hermitage Association
The University of Tennessee
The National Historical Publications
and Records Commission
The Tennessee Historical Commission
The National Endowment for the Humanities,
an independent federal agency

First published 1987
Printed and bound in the United States of America

Library of Congress Cataloging-in-Publication Data

The papers of Andrew Jackson.
Bibliography: p.
Includes index.
1. Jackson, Andrew, 1767–1845—Archives—Indexes. 2. United States—Politics and government—1829–1837—Sources—Indexes. I. Moser, Harold D. II. Jackson, Andrew, 1767–1845. Works. 1986.
Z6616.J18P36 1986 [E337.8.J3] 973.5′6 86-33831
ISBN 0-8420-4007-2

Advisory Board

Contents

Introduction

The years of Andrew Jackson's life spanned more than seven crucial decades in the history of the American nation, from the early days of the revolutionary era to the eve of Texas annexation. During these years the British colonies won their independence, established a republic, and expanded across the continent to the Oregon country. Large increases in population and rapid expansion altered the character of the nation, provoking sectional tensions, Indian conflicts, and social disharmony. Revolutions in industry and transportation transformed business, labor, and professional organizations and structures. The economic life of the country advanced through unsettling cycles of expansion and contraction, affecting varied interests in different ways. Money, banking, internal improvements, the tariff, public land disposition, and moral questions, including slavery and Indian removal, became commonplace subjects of politics. Party structure, practices, and procedures changed drastically, a new style of electioneering emerged, and voter participation rose as the first American party system succumbed to the second.

Following the War of 1812, nationalism emerged as a dominant mood, but sectionalism and slavery soon reached crisis proportions, threatening the young republic. It was an age when such leaders as Thomas Jefferson, James Madison, Daniel Webster, Henry Clay, John C. Calhoun, and Andrew Jackson guided the nation through revolutionary economic, political, social, and cultural changes that tested the mettle of men and the organic nature of the Union. The same period marked the origin of the modern American state and the modern American presidency and the entry of the young republic as a full-fledged member in the international family of nations.

Andrew Jackson was one of a handful of Americans who dominated the first half of the nineteenth century. He had made his political debut as delegate to the Tennessee constitutional convention in 1796. Subsequently he served as congressman and senator, state superior court judge, state militia officer, and territorial governor of Florida. He rose to national fame, however, as a military officer, defeating the Creeks at Horseshoe Bend and the British at New Orleans. Jackson's popularity carried him to Washington in 1829, where as seventh president of the United States he made his mark, lending his name both to a movement, Jacksonian Democracy, and to an era, the Age of Jackson. He was the only occupant of the White House between James Monroe and Abraham Lincoln returned to office. As president, Jackson redefined and strengthened the office, he altered the role of the federal government in the nation's development, and he championed the concept of a united nation in the face of rising threats of disunion. In retirement, he remained the figurehead and spokesman for the coalition and party that had elected him to office.

By all accounts, Andrew Jackson was one of this nation's strongest presidents, but he was also one of its most controversial. Though a beloved hero and leader to many, opponents denounced him as a ruffian and tyrant who violated accepted political norms and arrogantly asserted his own will. His controversial character revealed itself in his private as well as his public life. Strong-willed and ever sensitive to honor, Jackson punctuated his entire life with quarrels and disputes. His duels have become the stuff of legend. And yet, Jackson revealed another side, filled with generosity, tenderness, paternal care, and a courtly manner. Loyal to friends, unyielding to foes, Jackson was both honored and despised, loved and hated. Self-styled spokesman of the "common" man, he was nevertheless a most uncommon man.

The documents in this microfilm edition of the papers of Andrew Jackson portray both the man and the period. The personal, public, and official letters, speeches, memoranda, legal papers and opinions, receipts, accounts, and deeds collected here and published for the first time chronicle his life as he reacted to people, issues, and events. They document every phase in his complex life and the course of a nation in transition. With the publication of this microfilm, a supplement to the microfilms of Jackson papers in the Library of Congress and the National Archives, the complete body of Jackson papers is now available for the study and reevaluation of Jackson and the period which bears his name.

Acknowledgments

The objective of the Papers of Andrew Jackson--to conduct an exhaustive worldwide search for extant Jackson documents and to publish them in complementary microfilm and letterpress editions--is far beyond the ability of any single individual to accomplish; and in achieving its goal, the staff of the Jackson Papers has been most fortunate in having the assistance of thousands of individuals and institutions. The list would be too long to name each separately, but to all who responded to our requests for documents, to those archivists and curators who made available and searched collections, and to those who provided funds and moral support, we are indeed grateful.

Chief among those organizations which have provided financial and moral support has been the Ladies' Hermitage Association. More than fifteen years ago there was wide interest in founding a scholarly enterprise to collect, edit, and publish the papers of Andrew Jackson, but it was the creative leadership of the Ladies' Hermitage Association that translated interest into accomplished deed. With the strong support of the Association's regent, Mrs. Fred Russell; executive board member, Mrs. Harry A.J. Joyce; and its trustees, the Association undertook in 1971 to support the project with an annual stipend and housing on the Hermitage grounds.

Generous encouragement and support of the project has continued under the succeeding regents, Mrs. Cawthon A. Bowen, Jr., Mrs. Allen Steele, Mrs. Robert W. Sturdivant, Mrs. Walter Morgan, Jr., Mrs. James H. Reed III, and Mrs. Charles E. Wells. For their continued nurturing over the years, indispensable to our success, we are and will remain deeply indebted to the LHA's trustees, regents, board, and membership.

Several institutions deserve special mention, mainly for the magnitude of their contributions. Chief among these are the Library of Congress, the National Archives, and the Tennessee State Library and Archives. At the Library of Congress, John McDonough, Manuscript Historian, has assisted the project at every turn: he has made the Library's extensive Jackson collection readily available, he has answered innumerable questions, and he continues to share with us his broad knowledge. At the National Archives, the research staff of the National Historical Publications and Records Commission, and particularly Mary A. Giunta, now Assistant Director of the Commission's Publications Program, Sara Dunlap Jackson and Timothy Connelly, Archivists, have been indefatigable in unearthing documents and answering difficult questions. Our demands at the Tennessee State Library and Archives have been incessant, but Jean Waggener, State Archivist, and her staff, Marylin Bell Hughes, John Thweatt, and Ann Alley; and Fran Schell, Reference Librarian, have cheerfully made their collections available and serviced our research requests. The staffs of the Vanderbilt University and the University of Tennessee libraries, like those of Houghton Library at Harvard University, the Chicago Historical Society, the Historic New Orleans Collection, the New York Public Library, Perkins Library at Duke University, Alderman Library at the University of Virginia, and Baker Library at Dartmouth College have far exceeded our expectations with their cooperation and assistance. The hundreds of other institutions and individuals who have answered our queries and provided us with documents and information are noted in the Repository Symbols list and in the provenance notes appended to each document. We sincerely appreciate their assistance.

We are also deeply obligated to several individuals who have assisted us far beyond any normal expectations: Debbie Cooney, research assistant; Leland Johnson, freelance historian; Kenneth C. Thomson, Jr., a Donelson descendant; Fletch Coke and Angie C.M. Donelson, members of the Board of the Ladies' Hermitage Association; Robert V. Remini, Chairman of the project's Advisory Board, who shared with us his knowledge of Jackson and assisted in our search for documents; Col. James S. Corbitt, who shared his collection and gave moral support; and Mary-Jo Kline, who gave us the benefit of her experience in documentary editing. To each of them, we offer our sincere thanks.

Among those to whom we are most indebted are Harriet Chappell Owsley and Sam B. Smith, former editors. They bequeathed to the project they guided from 1971 until 1979 a strong base from which the search for documents and their editing for microfilm and letterpress publications might proceed.

Our sponsors have seen to it that the work continued, and our indebtedness to them is great and our appreciation sincere: to John Cooney, former Resident Director of The Hermitage, and particularly to Ann Harwell Wells, now Regent of the LHA and liaison to the project, for more than seven years of continuous support and encouragement; to the National Historical Publications and Records Commission and its staff, Frank G. Burke, Acting Archivist of the United States, and Richard A. Jacobs, Acting Executive Director, Richard N. Sheldon, Assistant to the Director, Roger A. Bruns, Director of the Publications Program, and George L. Vogt, Director of the Records Program; to the National Endowment for the Humanities, Research Programs, for funding which made this microfilm publication possible, and especially to Richard Ekman,

Director, and to staff associates Margot Backas, Kathy Fuller, David Nichols, and Helen Aguera, who have monitored our grant applications and our progress, and advised us when asked; to the Tennessee Historical Commission: Herbert L. Harper, Executive Director, Russell H. Hippe, Chairman, and Linda T. Wynn, Administrative Assistant; and finally, to our fiscal agent and sponsor, the University of Tennessee at Knoxville. At the University, we are fortunate to have the encouragement and support of Edward J. Boling, President, John W. Prados, Vice President for Academic Affairs, Jack E. Reese, Chancellor, and George W. Wheeler, Provost; but we are particularly appreciative of the Office of the Dean, College of Liberal Arts--Deans Lorman A. Ratner, Charles O. Jackson, and Mary P. Richards, and Phyllis Cole, Administrative Services Assistant--for their patience, understanding, and guidance in the day-to-day administration of the project.

The supporting staff of the Jackson papers has made the work easier and more pleasant. Volunteers Elizabeth King Folger, Mary Hathcock, and Maria Kieltyka helped us when there was no one else, and they have continued to help as the staff and work increased. Charles F. Bryan, Jr., former Assistant Editor and now Director of the Mercantile Library, St. Louis, helped us get the work started; and Linda Keeton, Susan Doughty, and Rosemarie Stinemetz not only assisted with the microfilm editing but also relieved the editors of other duties which would have fallen to them.

My own greatest appreciation and thanks is to those staff members listed on the title page. They, more than any others, are responsible for making available, finally, a comprehensive edition of the papers of Andrew Jackson and this Guide and Index to the Microfilm Editions.

Harold D. Moser

Chronology

1767 March 15	Andrew Jackson, third son of Andrew Jackson and Elizabeth Hutchinson, born in the Waxhaws of South Carolina
1767	Andrew Jackson, Sr., died
1774 Sept 5	First Continental Congress convened in Carpenter's Hall, Philadelphia
1775 May 20	Mecklenburg Declaration of Independence reputedly adopted
c1775-80	Attended schools conducted by William Humphries and James White Stephenson
1776 July 4	Continental Congress approved Declaration of Independence
1779 June 20	Battle of Stono Ferry
cJune 22	Hugh Jackson, Andrew's oldest brother, died
1780 Feb	Charleston occupied by British army
Aug 6	Participated in Battle of Hanging Rock
Aug 16	Battle of Camden
Oct 7	Battle of King's Mountain
1781 April	Captured and wounded by British; imprisoned along with brother Robert at Camden; contracted smallpox
cMay	Released from Camden jail; Robert died shortly thereafter
Fall	Elizabeth Jackson contracted cholera and died in Charleston
1782	Resumed education and visited Charleston
1784-86	Studied law under Spruce McCay in Salisbury, N.C.
1786-87	Continued study of law under John Stokes
1787 May 25	Constitutional Convention formally organized in Philadelphia
1787 July 13	Northwest Ordinance adopted
Sept 26	Licensed to practice law in North Carolina

1788	May 12	Licensed to practice law in Washington County
	Oct	Settled in Nashville; appointed North Carolina attorney in Mero District
	Nov 3	Licensed to practice law in Davidson County
1789	Feb 4	Electoral college selected George Washington as president under the new Constitution
	March 4	First meeting of Congress
1790	May 26	Territory South of the River Ohio created; William Blount confirmed as governor, July 8
	Dec 15	Licensed to practice law in territory
1791	Feb 15	Commissioned Mero District attorney under territorial government
	cAug	Married Rachel Donelson Robards for the first time
	Dec 15	Bill of Rights ratified
1792	Feb 23	Bought Poplar Grove farm in Davidson County; sold October 18, 1797
	Sept 10	Commissioned judge advocate for the Davidson County militia
1794	Jan 18	Remarried Rachel
	May 12	Formed land partnership with John Overton
	Nov 19	Jay's Treaty signed; ratified on June 24, 1795
1795	May-June	Made first trip to Philadelphia and commenced general merchandising in Nashville in partnership with Samuel Donelson
	Dec 19	Elected a delegate to Tennessee constitutional convention
1796	Jan 11	Took seat in constitutional convention; served until February 6
	March 10	Purchased Hunter's Hill farm
	June 1	Tennessee admitted as a state
	July 5	Licensed to practice law in Tennessee
	Sept 19	Washington's Farewell Address published
	Oct 22	Elected to United States House of Representatives from Tennessee
	Dec 5	Took seat in Congress
	Dec 7	John Adams and Thomas Jefferson elected president and vice president
	Dec 29	Delivered first speech before the House of Representatives in Philadelphia

1797	May	Quarreled with John McNairy and John Sevier
	Sept 26	Elected to United States Senate from Tennessee
	Nov 22	Took Senate seat
	Dec 6	Exposed Glasgow land frauds
1798	April 7	Mississippi Territory created
	April 16	Took leave of absence from Senate; probably resigned in June
	Sept 20	Commissioned interim Tennessee Superior Court judge
	Dec 20	Elected judge of the Superior Court of Tennessee by joint houses of the legislature
1799		Rode circuit as judge of the Superior Court through April 1804
	Dec 14	Washington died
1800	May 7	Indiana Territory created
1801	March 4	Thomas Jefferson inaugurated as president; Aaron Burr, vice president
	Sept 29	Endorsed William Dickson as Republican candidate for Congress
	cNov 17	Rachel Stockley Donelson, Rachel Jackson's mother, died
1802	Feb 5	Elected major general of the Tennessee militia
	Feb 16	Formed mercantile partnership with Thomas A. Watson and John Hutchings
1803	May	Purchased goods in Philadelphia for Jackson, Watson & Hutchings
	May 2	Treaty of cession signed for the purchase of Louisiana
	July 19	Accused John Sevier of land fraud
	Aug 6	Dissolved partnership of Jackson, Watson & Hutchings, effective July 10
	Aug 7	Petitioned Thomas Jefferson re arrest of Thomas Butler
	Aug 23	Formed partnership with John Hutchings
	Oct 2	Challenged Sevier to a duel
1804	March 26	Orleans Territory created; Jackson sought governorship
	April 19	Received license for the operation of a retail store, Andrew Jackson & Co.
	cJune	Took John Coffee into the Jackson & Hutchings partnership
	July 6	Sold Hunter's Hill farm

	July 11	Aaron Burr killed Alexander Hamilton in duel in New Jersey
	July 23	Resigned Superior Court judgeship
	Aug 23	Purchased Hermitage property
	Dec 5	Thomas Jefferson reelected president; George Clinton, vice president
1805	Jan 11	Michigan Territory created
	March 3	Louisiana-Missouri Territory created
	May 11	Purchased stud horse Truxton
	May 29	Aaron Burr made first visit to the Hermitage
	July 26	Served as Thomas J. Overton's second in Overton's duel with John Dickinson
	Nov 28	Race between Ploughboy and Truxton cancelled
1806	Jan 13	Caned Thomas Swann in Nashville
	cMarch 3	Duel between Jackson and Nathaniel McNairy aborted
	April 3	Race between Ploughboy and Truxton
	May 23	Challenged Charles Dickinson to duel
	May 30	Killed Dickinson in duel; Jackson wounded
	Sept 24	Burr again visited Nashville and the Hermitage
	Oct 4	Ordered militia to state of readiness in event of war with Spain
	Nov 10	Captain John A. Fort visited Jackson at the Hermitage and revealed nature of Burr's plans
	Nov 15	First non-importation act took effect
	Nov 27	Jefferson issued proclamation re conspiracy against Spanish possessions
	Dec 13	Burr returned to Nashville; departed December 22
1807	Jan 2	Placed militia on alert to counteract Burr expedition
	May 12	Departed for Richmond to testify before grand jury in Burr hearing
	June 22	British ship *Leopard* fired upon the *Chesapeake*
	June 25	Testified before Burr grand jury in Richmond
	Dec	Sold Clover Bottom store to Samuel Pryor
1808	April	Campaigned in behalf of James Monroe
	Dec 4	Andrew Jackson Donelson, son of Severn and Elizabeth Rucker Donelson, born; "adopted" by the Jacksons
	Dec 7	James Madison elected president; George Clinton, vice president

1809	Jan 16	Addressed citizens of Nashville on administration policy and relations with Great Britain
	Feb 3	Illinois Territory created
	Sept 20	Willie Blount succeeded John Sevier as governor of Tennessee
1810	Jan	Sought judgeship in Mississippi Territory
	Fall	Formed partnership with Joseph Coleman and Horace Green
1811	Nov 7	General William Henry Harrison engaged Indians at Tippecanoe
	Nov 29	Departed for Natchez to salvage investment in slaves of Coleman, Green & Jackson
	Dec 16	Severe earthquakes, centered about New Madrid, began along the Mississippi Valley
1812	Feb 6	President authorized to accept twelve-month volunteers to a maximum of 50,000 men
	March 7	Issued call for volunteers
	April 8	Louisiana admitted to the Union
	April 10	Congress authorized the president to call up 100,000 detached militia for six months' service
	June 18	United States declared war on Great Britain
	June 25	Tendered service of Tennessee volunteers to Governor Blount and the president
	Nov 1	Ordered by Governor Blount to mobilize 1,500 men for a southern expedition
	Dec 10	James Madison reelected president; Elbridge Gerry elected vice president
	Dec 10	Second Division troops mustered in Nashville for expedition to New Orleans
1813	Jan 8	Troops under Jackson departed Nashville
	Feb 6	Secretary of war ordered Jackson's troops dismissed
	Feb 16	Troops arrived in Natchez
	March 15	Received the secretary of war's orders of February 6
	March 24	Jackson's volunteers began return march to Tennessee
	June 14	Served as William Carroll's second in Carroll's duel with Jesse Benton
	Aug 30	Creek Indians massacred settlers at Fort Mims
	Sept 4	Wounded in fight with Jesse and Thomas Hart Benton in Nashville
	Sept 24	Second Division troops mustered in Nashville for departure to the Creek country
	Oct 5	Tecumseh killed in the Battle of the Thames

	Oct 24	Joined troops at Fort Deposit
	Nov 3	General John Coffee destroyed Creek town of Tallushatchee; Lyncoya found and later sent to the Hermitage
	Nov 7	Major General Thomas Pinckney ordered to take command of the Creek campaign
	Nov 9	Defeated Creeks at Talladega
	Nov 18	James White's brigade of East Tennessee Volunteers destroyed Hillabee towns
	Nov 29	Georgia militia under John Floyd attacked Creeks at Autosse
	Dec 13	Ordered 1st Brigade, West Tennessee Volunteers, to return home for discharge
1814	Jan 22	Battle of Emuckfaw
	Jan 24	Battle of Enotochapco
	March 14	Ordered execution of John Woods for mutiny
	March 27	Battle of Horseshoe Bend
	May 28	Commissioned major general of the United States Army by President Madison
	Aug 9	Treaty of Fort Jackson sealed Creek capitulation
	Aug 22	Occupied Mobile and garrisoned Fort Bowyer
	Nov 7	Seized Pensacola
	Dec 1	Arrived in New Orleans
	Dec 16	Imposed martial law on New Orleans
	Dec 23	Attacked advance force of the invading British army
	Dec 24	Treaty of Ghent signed
1815	Jan 8	Battle of New Orleans
	Jan 22	Approved decision of court martial condemning six militiamen to death for mutiny
	March 5	Arrested Judge Dominick A. Hall
	March 31	Fined for contempt of U.S. District Court, New Orleans
	April 6	Left New Orleans for Nashville
	May 22	Attended banquet in his honor in Nashville
	May 22	Informed of appointment as major general, Division of the South, in the reduced peacetime army
	Sept 5	John Reid's proposed Life of Andrew Jackson announced
	cOct 13	Left Nashville for Washington accompanied by Rachel Jackson and John Reid
1816	Jan 18	John Reid died
	Feb 1	Arrived in Nashville on return trip from Washington
	Aug 14	Ordered William O. Butler to survey the route for a military road from Nashville to New Orleans

	Sept 20	Concluded Chickasaw treaty
	Oct 4	Concluded Cherokee treaty
	Dec 11	Indiana admitted as a state
1817	cFeb 22	Ralph E.W. Earl painted his first portrait of Jackson
	March 3	Alabama Territory created
	July 8	Concluded Cherokee treaty
	Dec 10	Mississippi admitted as a state
	Dec 26	Issued orders to suppress the Seminoles
1818	Jan 1	Copyright notice for Reid's Life of Andrew Jackson, completed and revised by John Henry Eaton, registered
	April 7	Seized St. Marks in Spanish Florida
	April 29	Ordered execution of Robert Ambrister and Alexander Arbuthnot
	May 24	Occupied Pensacola
	Oct 19	Concluded Chickasaw treaty
	Dec 3	Illinois admitted as a state
1819	Jan 23	Arrived in Washington to defend his action in the Seminole campaign
	Feb	Toured Maryland, Pennsylvania, and New York
	Feb 8	Censure of Seminole campaign defeated in House of Representatives
	Feb 22	Adams-Onis Treaty ceding Florida to the United States signed; Senate ratified treaty on February 24
	Feb 24	Senate committee condemned AJ's conduct of Seminole campaign
	March 2	Arkansas Territory created
	Summer	Began construction of new house on the Hermitage property
	Dec 14	Alabama admitted as a state
1820	Feb 23	Defense of Seminole campaign presented to the Senate
	Oct 18	Concluded Choctaw treaty
	Oct 24	Spain ratified Adams-Onis Treaty
1821	Feb 19	Senate reratified Adams-Onis Treaty
	March 10	Commissioned governor of Florida
	June 1	Resigned commission as major general
	July 17	Received Florida for the United States from Spanish authorities
	Aug 10	Missouri admitted as a state
	Nov 13	Resigned as governor of Florida
1822	March 30	Florida Territory created
	July 20	Nominated for president by the Tennessee legislature

1823	March 4	Declined appointment as minister to Mexico
	Oct 1	Elected to the United States Senate
1824	March 4	Nominated for president by Pennsylvania convention
	March 16	Received medal voted by Congress for victory at New Orleans
	July 4	Attended Independence Day celebration in Nashville
	Nov	Received popular and electoral plurality in presidential election
1825	Feb 9	House of Representatives elected John Quincy Adams president
	Feb 11	Adams offered State Department to Henry Clay
	Feb 14	Denounced Adams-Clay "corrupt bargain"
	May 5	Entertained the Marquis de Lafayette at the Hermitage
	Oct 12	Resigned Senate seat
	Oct 14	Renominated for president by the Tennessee legislature
1826	Feb 6	United States Telegraph, edited by Duff Green, commenced publication in Washington
	March 3	Wrote John Branch of his opposition to the Panama mission
	July 4	Thomas Jefferson and John Adams died
	July 4-6	Attended Independence Day celebrations in Pulaski, Fayetteville, and Shelbyville, Tenn.
	Nov 18	Henry Lee announced his intention to write biography of Jackson
	Nov 23	Went to Florence, Ala., to oversee the affairs of Andrew Jackson Hutchings, his ward
	Dec	Nashville Central Committee began collecting affidavits concerning Jackson's marriage
1827	Jan 5	Opened correspondence and quarrel with Samuel L. Southard
	March	Nashville Central Committee replied to John Binns's "Coffin Handbill"
	June	Nashville Central Committee completed report on Jackson's marriage
	Aug 22	Amos Kendall joined the Jackson campaign forces
	May	Henry Lee arrived at the Hermitage to work on biography
1828	Jan 8	Attended New Orleans anniversary celebration
	June 1	Lyncoya died

	Nov	Elected president; John C. Calhoun, vice president
	Dec 22	Rachel Jackson died
1829	Jan 19	Departed Nashville for Washington
	Feb 11	Arrived in Washington
	Feb 26	Cabinet appointees announced in the _United States Telegraph_
	March 4	Inaugurated as seventh president
	March	Controversy over Peggy Eaton began
	Oct 10	Instructed Anthony Butler to purchase Texas from Mexico
	Dec 8	Sent first annual message to Congress
1830	Jan	Cabinet confrontation over the Eaton affair
	April 13	Offered toast "Our Federal Union" at Jefferson Birthday dinner
	May 13	Letter to Calhoun initiated Seminole campaign correspondence and resulted in break with the vice president
	May 27	Vetoed Maysville Road bill
	May 28	Signed Indian removal bill
	June 17	Left Washington for Tennessee; returned September 25
	Aug	Oversaw Indian removal negotiations in Tennessee
	Oct 5	Proclaimed opening of the British West Indian trade
	Dec 7	Washington _Globe_ commenced publication
	Dec 7	Sent second annual message to Congress
1831	Feb 17	Calhoun published Seminole correspondence
	April	Cabinet secretaries John Henry Eaton, Martin Van Buren, John Branch, and Samuel D. Ingham resigned
	July 4	Signed treaty with France settling American spoliation claims
	Aug 1	Appointed Martin Van Buren minister to Great Britain
	Nov 24	Andrew Jackson, Jr., and Sarah Yorke married in Philadelphia
1832	Jan 9	Bank of the United States memorialized Congress for recharter
	Jan 25	Senate rejected nomination of Van Buren as minister to Great Britain
	March 3	Supreme Court ruled in _Worcester_ v. _Georgia_
	July 10	Vetoed Bank recharter bill
	July 14	Signed tariff act of 1832
	July 23	Left Washington for the Hermitage; returned October 19

	Nov	Defeated Henry Clay in presidential election
	Nov 1	Rachel Jackson, granddaughter, born
	Nov 24	South Carolina nullified tariff of 1832
	Dec 4	Sent fourth annual message to Congress
	Dec 10	Issued proclamation against nullification
1833	Jan 16	Requested tariff enforcement legislation from Congress
	March 2	Signed force bill and compromise tariff
	March 4	Pocket-vetoed distribution bill
	March 4	Inaugurated for second term
	March 15	South Carolina rescinded nullification ordinance
	April 12	John Overton died
	May 6	Assaulted by Robert B. Randolph
	June 6	Left on northeastern tour; returned July 4
	June 26	Ordered preparations for removing federal deposits from the Bank of the United States
	July 7	John Coffee died
	July 10	Treasury Secretary William J. Duane declined to order removal of the deposits
	Sept 18	Announced to the Cabinet his decision to remove the deposits
	Sept 23	Dismissed Duane and appointed Roger B. Taney secretary of the treasury
	Sept 26	Taney ordered removal of federal deposits from the Bank of the United States
	Dec 3	Sent fifth annual message to Congress
	Dec 12	Refused Senate call for the Cabinet paper of September 18
	Dec 31	Andrew Jackson, Jr., purchased Hunter's Hill farm
1834	March 28	Censured by the Senate for conduct in removing the deposits
	April 4	Andrew Jackson III, grandson, born
	April 17	Sent to the Senate his protest of censure
	June 16	Louis McLane resigned as secretary of state
	June 24	Senate rejected nomination of Taney as treasury secretary
	June 24	Appointed John Forsyth and Mahlon Dickerson as secretaries of state and navy
	July 8	Departed Washington for the Hermitage; returned September 30
	Oct 13	Hermitage partially destroyed by fire
	Dec 1	Recommended reprisals for French failure to fulfill claims treaty of 1831
1835	Jan 1	National debt extinguished
	Jan 30	Thwarted assassination attempt by Richard Lawrence

	May 1	Appointed Amos Kendall postmaster general
	May 22	Democratic convention at Baltimore nominated Martin Van Buren for president
	Oct 17	Tennessee legislature nominated Hugh Lawson White for president
	Dec 7	Recommended, in seventh annual message, prohibiting circulation of abolitionist literature through Southern mails
	Dec 18	Second Seminole War began
	Dec 28	Nominated Roger B. Taney for Chief Justice of the United States
	Dec 29	Cherokee removal treaty signed at New Echota, Ga.
1836	Jan 15	Announced diplomatic rupture with France and recommended reprisals and military preparations
	Feb 3	Accepted British offer of mediation in French dispute
	Feb 22	Announced resolution of French dispute
	March 2	Texas declared independence
	March 3	Federal charter of the Bank of the United States expired
	April 20	Territory of Wisconsin created
	April 21	Battle of San Jacinto
	May 23	Proclaimed Cherokee removal treaty in force
	June 15	Arkansas admitted as a state
	June 23	Signed Deposit Act
	July 2	Signed Post Office Act
	July 8	Ordered the issuance of the Specie Circular
	July 10	Departed Washington for the Hermitage; returned October 1
	July 11	Specie Circular issued by the Treasury Department
	Aug 23	Traveled to Alabama
	Nov	Martin Van Buren defeated Whig candidates in presidential election
	Dec 21	Sent message on Texas to Congress
1837	Jan 16	Censure of AJ expunged from Senate journal
	Jan 26	Michigan admitted as a state
	March 3	Recognized independence of Texas
	March 3	Pocket-vetoed bill rescinding the Specie Circular
	March 4	Martin Van Buren inaugurated as eighth president
	March 7	Left Washington
	March 25	Arrived at Hermitage
	May	Panic of 1837 began
	June 9	Grandson, Samuel Jackson, born

	Aug 16	*Madisonian*, newspaper established by the Conservative Democrats, commenced publication in Washington
	Sept 4	President Van Buren recommended Independent Treasury
1838	May 31	Congress rescinded Specie Circular
	July 15	Joined Presbyterian church
	Sept 16	Ralph E.W. Earl died
	Oct 19	Amos Kendall arrived for visit at the Hermitage
	Nov 20	Andrew Jackson, Jr., purchased Halcyon plantation in Mississippi
1839	Oct 14	James K. Polk inaugurated as governor of Tennessee
1840	Jan 8	Attended Battle of New Orleans 25th anniversary celebration
	March 5	Democratic convention in Baltimore renominated Martin Van Buren for president
	July 4	Independent Treasury bill signed into law
	July 14	Sold Hunter's Hill plantation to pay family debts
	Oct 8	Delivered speech in Jackson, Tenn., on behalf of the Democratic candidates
	Nov	William Henry Harrison defeated Van Buren in presidential contest
1841	Jan 15	Andrew Jackson Hutchings died
	April 4	Death of Harrison and accession of John Tyler as president
	Aug 13	Independent Treasury Act repealed
	Aug 18	Thomas J. Jackson, grandson, died
	Aug	Polk defeated in gubernatorial election
	Sept 11	Tyler's Cabinet, with the exception of Daniel Webster, resigned
	Dec 21	Received loan of $7,000 from Jean B. Plauche of New Orleans
1842	April 25	Van Buren arrived at the Hermitage for a visit
	May 23	Received loan of $10,000 from Francis P. Blair
	Oct	Injured in carriage accident
	cDec 12	James A. McLaughlin, nephew of Amos Kendall, arrived at Hermitage to examine papers for Kendall's proposed biography of Jackson
1843	Feb 12	Espoused annexation of Texas in subsequently published letter to Aaron V. Brown
	Feb 22	Kendall announced that his biography of Jackson would be issued in fifteen or more numbers

	June 7	Revised last will and testament
	Aug	Polk again defeated in bid for governor
	Oct 21	Kendall forwarded to Jackson the first number of his biography; only seven numbers published
	Nov 11	Robert Armstrong Jackson, grandson, died
1844	Feb 16	Congress refunded AJ's New Orleans fine of 1815
	April 27	Henry Clay and Martin Van Buren's letters opposing annexation of Texas published in Washington newspapers
	May 16	Published letter in the Nashville Union on Van Buren as presidential candidate
	May 29	News of Polk's nomination for president by the Democratic convention in Baltimore reached Washington via telegraph
	Nov	Polk defeated Henry Clay in the presidential contest
1845	Jan 30	Conferred with Polk at the Hermitage on the selection of his cabinet
	March 27	Declined Commodore Jesse Duncan Elliott's offer of a sarcophagus
	May 20	Wrote Blair that his papers, including those in Kendall's hands, were to go to Blair for safekeeping
	June 8	Died at the Hermitage at seventy-eight years of age
	June 10	Buried in the Hermitage garden

Genealogy

#1

Andrew Jackson
(1767-1845)
m 1791/1794
Rachel Donelson
(1767-1828)

1 m 1785
Lewis Robards
divorced 1793
no issue

Andrew, Jr. (adopted)
(1808-65)
m 1831
Sarah Yorke
(1805-87)

Rachel	Andrew	Samuel	Thomas Jefferson	Robert Armstrong
(1832-1923) m 1853 John M. Lawrence (1823-82) 9 children	(1834-1906) m 1877 Amy A. Rich (1851-1921) 2 children	(1837-63) unmarried	(b&d 1841 Aug 18)	(1843 June 18-Nov 11)

#2

John Donelson
(c1718-86)
m c1749
Rachel Stockley
(c1730-1801)

Alexander	Catherine	John	Mary	William	Stockley
(1751-1834) unmarried	(c1752-1834) see #3	(1755-1830) see #4	(c1756-1823) see #5	(1758-1820) see #6	(c1759-1805) m 1797 Elizabeth (Glasgow) Martin (1772-1847) no issue

Jane	Rachel	Samuel	Severn	Leven
(1766-1834) see #7	(1767-1828) see #1	(c1770-1804) see #8	(1773-1818) see #9	(1776-1833) unmarried

#3

Thomas Hutchings (1750-1804) m 1772 Catherine Donelson (c1752-1834)

- Mary (1775-1846) m Daniel Small (1772-1830)
  - 6 children
- John (c1776-1817) m 1810 Mary Smith (d 1813)
  - Andrew Jackson (1811-41) m 1833 Mary D. Coffee (1812-39)
    - 4 children
- Christopher (c1783-1854) m 1829 Louisa A. Edwards (d 1884)
  - 9 children
- Rachel Donelson (b 1784) m 1806 James S. Rawlings (1784-1820)
  - John Hutchings (1807-59) m 1833 Sarah Jane Hays (1814-60)
- Stockley Donelson (d 1821) m 1816 Elizabeth Atwood (c1794-1854)
  - Elizabeth Atwood (b 1822) m 1839 Andrew J. Coffee (1819-91)
- Lemuel 1 m 1821 Elizabeth Owen 2 m Miss ? Owen
- Thomas (d 1830) unmarried
- Jean "Jennie" unmarried
- Elizabeth m _____ Bryant

#4

John Donelson (1755-1830) m 1779 Mary Purnell (1763-1848)

- Chesed (b&d 1780)
- Tabitha (1781-1854) m George Smith (1776-1849)
  - 5 children
- Alexander (1784-1814) unmarried
- John (1787-1840) m 1823 Eliza E. Butler (1791-1850)
  - 2 children
- Lemuel (1789-1832) m 1819 Eliza Whyte (1802-32)
  - 2 children
- Rachel (1791-1822) m 1809 William Eastin (1784-1829) see #11
- Mary (1793-1871) m 1809 John Coffee (1772-1833) see #12
- William (1795-1864) 1 m 1822 Rachel Donelson (1803-24) 2 m 1827 Elizabeth Anderson (1809-41) 3 m 1845 Martha Anderson
- Elizabeth (1796-1836) m 1815 John C. McLemore (1790-1864)
  - 4 children
- Catherine (1799-1836) m 1815 James G. Martin (1791-1849) see #10
- Chesed Purnell (b&d 1801)
- Stockley (1805-88) m 1828 Phila Ann Lawrence (1809-51)
  - 6 children
- Emily Tennessee (1807-36) m 1824 Andrew Jackson Donelson (1799-1871) see #8

#5

John Caffery
(1756-1811)
m 1775
Mary Donelson
(c1756-1823)

- Rachel (c1776-1812) m 1791 John George Walker
  - 10 children
- Sarah (b c1783) m 1800 John Walker (1774-1838)
- Eliza (c1784-1823) m 1801 Abraham Green
  - children
- Donelson (1786-1835) m 1818 Lydia Murphy (1802-81)
  - 8 children
- Mary (b c1788) m 1805 John Knox (d c1815)
  - Sarah "Sally" (c1807-91)
  - William L. (1814-81)
- Nancy (b c1789) m 1806 John Jenkins
- Sophia (b 1792) m 1811 Peter A. Van Dorn
  - 6 children
- John (b c1795) m Catherine Smith
- Catherine (b c1797) m 1814 John George Walker
  - Rachael
  - George Wythe
- Jane (c1801-19) m 1818 Ralph E.W. Earl (1788-1838) no issue
- Jefferson (b c1804) m 1824 Alix de Maret

#6

William Donelson
(1758-1820)
m 1796
Charity Dickinson
(1778-1827)

- Severn (b 1797) m 1821 Mary H. Sampson
  - 3 children
- Mary C. (1799-1819) m 1818 John M.A. Hamblen
  - Mary Eliza Overton (b 1819)
- Jacob (b 1801) m 1825 Agnes P. Sampson
- Rachel (b 1804)
- Milbery M. (1806-36) m 1825 John McGregor (d 1835)
  - children
- Martha H. (1809-73) 1 m 1820 Robert M. Burton (1800-43) 2 m Paul Anderson
- William T. (1810-27) unmarried
- Andrew Jackson (1815-61) 1 m 1835 Katherine J. Nelson (d 1837) 2 m 1841 Sarah Nelson
- Alexander S. (b 1817)
- Elizabeth Hays (1819-50) m 1837 Robert A. Burton

#7

Robert Hays (1758-1819) m 1786 Jane Donelson (1766-1834)

- Rachel (b 1786) m 1808 Robert Butler (1786-1860)
  - Robert (b c1809)
  - Thomas (b c1810)
  - Jane (b c1811) m ? Patton
  - Andrew Jackson (c1819-26)
  - Rachel Jackson (1824-1918) m 1851 Peter P. Lewis
- Stockley Donelson (1788-1831) m 1811 Lydia Butler (b 1789)
  - Sarah Jane (1814-60) m 1833 John H. Rawlings (1807-59)
  - Richard J. (1822-99)
- Martha Thompson (1790-1857) m 1811 William E. Butler (1790-1882)
  - children
- Narcissa (b c1795) unmarried
- Mary S. (1798-1815)
- Samuel Jackson (1800-66) m 1829 Frances P. Middleton (1813-65)
  - 13 children
- Elizabeth (1805-41) m 1825 Robert J. Chester (1793-1892)
  - 4 children

#8

Samuel Donelson (c1770-1804) m 1796 Mary Ann Michie Smith (1781-1857)

- John Samuel (1797-1817) unmarried
- Andrew Jackson (1799-1871) 1 m 1824 Emily T. Donelson (1807-36)
  - Andrew Jackson (1826-59) unmarried
  - Mary Emily (1829-1905) m 1852 John A. Wilcox
  - John Samuel (1832-63) unmarried
  - Rachel Jackson (1834-88) m 1860 William B. Knox
- Andrew Jackson 2 m 1841 Elizabeth A. (Martin) Randolph (c1817-71)
  - Daniel Smith (1842-64)
  - Martin (b 1847)
  - William Alexander (1849-1900)
  - Catherine (1850-68)
  - Vinet (b 1854)
  - Lewis Randolph (b 1856)
  - Rosa Elizabeth (1858-61)
  - Andrew Jackson (b 1860)
- Daniel Smith (1801-63) m 1830 Margaret Branch (b 1811)
  - 11 children

#9

Severn Donelson (1773-1818) m c1802 **Elizabeth Rucker** (1782-1828)

- Rachel (1803-24) m 1822 William Donelson (1795-1864)
- James Rucker (1805-29)
- John (b c1807) 1 m 1833 Laura M. Lawrence (1815-44) 2 m Delia C. Waters
- Andrew Jackson (1808-65) m 1831 Sarah Yorke (1805-87) see #1
- Thomas Jefferson (1808-95) m 1832 Emma Y. Farquhar (d 1880)
  - Andrew Jackson (1833-37)
  - Eliza Yorke (c1835-98) m Bernard A. Hoopes
  - Emma L. (1837 May-Aug)
  - Isabella (1844-47)
  - Sarah Polk (1845-75)
  - Frances (d 1912) m Edward Gratz
- Samuel Rucker (b c1811) 1 m 1838 Elizabeth D. Eastin (1817-39) 2 m Jane Royster
- Lucinda Rucker (1812-37) m 1830 George W. Martin (1792-1854) see #10
- Alexander (1816-87) m 1841 Sarah K. Royster

#10

John Martin m 1790 **Elizabeth Glasgow** (1772-1847) — 2 m 1797 Stockley Donelson (c1759-1805) no issue; 3 m 1808 John Anderson

- (with John Anderson)
  - Elizabeth (1809-41) m 1827 William Donelson (1795-1864)
  - Martha m 1845 William Donelson (1795-1864)
- James Glasgow (1791-1849) m 1815 Catherine Donelson (1799-1836)
  - Elizabeth Anderson (c1817-71) 1 m 1835 Lewis M. Randolph (1811-37); 2 m 1841 Andrew Jackson Donelson (1799-1871) see #8
    - Andrew Jackson (1836-41)
  - Mary D. (1818-60) m 1847 Robert B. Currey
  - James Glasgow (b c1824) m 1851 Mary ?
  - Emily D. (1825-92) m 1846 George W. Currey
  - Rachel Jackson (1827-48)
  - John (c1829-62) m Rosa ?
  - Andrew Jackson (b c1830)
  - Catherine (b c1832)
  - Anna Handy (1834-38)
- George Washington (1792-1854) m 1830 Lucinda R. Donelson (1812-37)
  - Andrew Jackson (b 1831)
  - Elizabeth

#11

William Eastin
(1784-1829)
m 1809
Rachel Donelson
(1791-1822)

- Mary Ann (1810-47) m 1832 Lucius J. Polk (1802-70)
- Susanna (1812-24)
- Tabitha Smith (1814-16)
- Elizabeth Donelson (1817-39) m 1838 Samuel R. Donelson (b c1811)
- John Donelson (b 1820) m 1848 Amanda Calloway
- Rachel Jackson (b 1822) m 1842 Richard O. Currey (1816-65)

#12

John Coffee
(1772-1833)
m 1809
Mary Donelson
(1793-1871)

- Mary Donelson (1812-39) m 1833 Andrew J. Hutchings (1811-41)
- John Donelson (1815-37) m 1836 Mary N. Brahan (1817-93)
- Elizabeth Graves (1817-38) unmarried
- Andrew Jackson (1819-91) m 1839 Elizabeth A. Hutchings (b 1822)
- Alexander Donelson (1821-1901) 1 m 1844 Ann Eliza Sloss (1824-71) 2 m 1876 Camilla (Madding) Jones (1842-1928)
- Rachel Jackson (1823-92) m 1856 Alexander J. Dyas (1815-1900)
- Katherine (1826-81)
- Emily (1828-29)
- William (1830-1902) m Virginia Malone (1840-91)
- Joshua (1832-79)

The Papers

Andrew Jackson felt a deep obligation to history and, over the four decades he spent in public life, took particular care to preserve his papers so that his legacy to the American republic might be justly appraised. There were, however, unfortunate gaps in his collection. Jackson did not always keep copies of his extensive outgoing correspondence and much of that had been lost. The Hermitage fire in 1834 had also consumed some of his personal letters and, more important for posterity, he had ordered the private and confidential letters and memoranda of his two presidential terms destroyed in 1836. Yet, there remained a massive archives; and on August 7, 1842, and again on April 9, 1845, Jackson specifically entrusted all his papers to the custody of his longtime friend and adviser, Francis P. Blair, to be used at his discretion.

When Jackson died in 1845, Andrew Jackson, Jr., and Amos Kendall, a former member of Jackson's "Kitchen Cabinet," had possession of the papers. The larger body was housed at the Hermitage, Jackson's home. Kendall's collection, however, consisted of the more important documents, having been carefully selected by Jackson and his son, and by Kendall's nephew, James A. McLaughlin, in 1842 and 1843 and sent to Kendall for his use in a proposed serial biography of Jackson. Although projected for fifteen numbers, only seven subsequently appeared, beginning with the first in October 1843 and ending with the last in mid-1844. By July 1845, Jackson's closest friends conceded that Kendall would not likely complete his study.

After Jackson's death, Blair sought to claim the papers Jackson had promised him. Pursuant to Blair's request, in July 1845, Andrew, Jr., immediately forwarded the papers at the Hermitage, as Blair acknowledged in October. At the same time, Jackson fulfilled the second of Blair's requests and urged Kendall to turn over his papers to Blair. Kendall initially refused, however, and it was not until mid-1849 that he finally relinquished the bulk of the papers. According to the best available evidence, Kendall delivered part of the papers to Blair personally and part to Jackson Hall, the old Globe offices on Pennsylvania Avenue in Washington. But he withheld his personal correspondence with Jackson. Thus, within four years, Jackson's stated wishes for the disposition of his papers had been fulfilled. Blair had both the Kendall and Hermitage collections, the latter stored at his country residence in Silver Springs, Maryland. (For a more detailed discussion of the Blairs and the Jackson papers, see John McDonough's excellent essay in Index to the Andrew Jackson Papers, Washington, 1967.)

The Jackson papers attracted little public attention in the 1850s and 1860s, and the collection became somewhat reduced. Occasionally, Blair or his sons published an important Jackson document relating to a campaign issue, and they sometimes honored solicitations for Jackson autographs. In 1850 they extracted a large portion of Martin Van Buren's letters and sent them to him, at his request. They also destroyed a number of what they regarded as unimportant papers. They allowed Missouri Senator Thomas Hart Benton access to both sets of papers for his Thirty Years' View (1854-56), but denied James Parton the use of the collection for his three-volume Life of Jackson (1859-60).

Parton's study preempted the field and produced a hiatus in the efforts of Jackson's friends to commission a new biography of the "sage of the Hermitage." George Bancroft, whom many favored for the task, had never shown any real commitment to it, and even Francis P. Blair abandoned his fleeting notions of writing one. With Kendall's death in 1869, all hopes for a new and complete study vanished; and, upon Francis P. Blair's death in 1875, custody of the papers passed to his son Montgomery.

The last quarter of the nineteenth century marked a rekindling of interest in the Jackson archives. This change, which had a lasting impact on the Blair collection, grew out of the efforts of William Goodson Terrell (1829-1900), an Indiana-born, Kentucky-based newspaper editor, publisher, and correspondent of the Cincinnati Commercial, to collect materials for a proposed history of Kentucky. In the course of his research, he became particularly interested in Amos Kendall as an early Kentucky journalist and Kendall's relationships with Henry Clay and Andrew Jackson.

In the late 1870s, Terrell sought out in Washington Kendall's son-in-law William Stickney, who in 1872 had published the Autobiography of Amos Kendall. Stickney loaned Terrell a copy of the work and at the same time produced for Terrell's examination a large bundle of Kendall-Jackson papers and correspondence. Terrell immediately requested and received permission to publish the documents in the Cincinnati Commercial.

While transcribing the papers, Terrell's interests switched altogether from the Kentucky history to Jackson. According to his own account, he had long admired Jackson and, as a lad of twelve, had read Kendall's serialized Life. With his discovery of the Kendall-Jackson papers, he developed a preliminary outline for a late nineteenth-century life and letters and began to search for the remainder of Jackson's correspondence. Through Stickney he located the long-forgotten Kendall portion at the Globe office and through Montgomery Blair he gained access to the Blairs' collection, which they brought to Washington for his examination.

Once he resolved his personal affairs in Kentucky, Terrell settled in Washington and began to devote his free time to the Jackson papers, which in his initial publication he described as a "mass of Jacksonia never before published." Over the next five years, until 1883, he published documents and articles dealing with virtually every controversial subject in Jackson's long life. At the same time, he contacted and consolidated his friendship with the Jackson descendants. He also gained the confidence of descendants of several of Jackson's associates, who loaned him their collections for research and publication.

Terrell's publications in the Cincinnati Commercial and elsewhere established beyond doubt the significance and value of the Jackson collection. They also induced the Jackson descendants to claim the papers, arguing that President Jackson had loaned the documents to Kendall and to Blair for the limited purpose of writing biographies. Whereas Kendall had partially fulfilled the agreement, Blair had not. The papers, they therefore argued, were rightfully theirs. Terrell supported these contentions and represented the Jacksons before the Senate Committee on the Library in March and April 1884. Although the Committee examined the Jackson papers and heard the evidence, it did not concur. A year later, the Jackson family sought to prove their ownership in the Supreme Court of the District of Columbia, but this effort also failed and the Jackson descendants allowed the case to drop in 1890.

Terrell, meanwhile, had amassed a large collection of Jackson papers, including copies and originals from the Kendall and Blair collections, from the collections of some of Jackson's contemporaries, and perhaps from the Jackson descendants themselves. Though he was authorized only to make copies from the Blair holdings and had been requested to return borrowed collections, he apparently violated these arrangements. At his death in 1900, he still had the large group of papers he had accumulated over a quarter century.

Terrell's destruction of the integrity of the Blair collection has made the history of the Jackson papers in the twentieth century much more difficult to trace. Jackson scholars and editors of Jackson have long expressed concern that a significant portion of the Jackson archives has not been found. Those documents published by Terrell, for which manuscripts were missing, led some to conclude that Kendall retained his portion and that it was consumed in the Washington fire of 1894 that purportedly claimed his papers. Others have suggested that significant documents may have been intentionally destroyed, or perhaps retained by Jackson descendants. This concern has been heightened by increased autograph market activity and intermittent transfers of Jackson items to repositories and private collectors around the country in recent decades.

The first major breakthrough in public access to the Jackson papers came in 1903, when the Blairs donated their holdings to the Library of Congress. Almost immediately, the Jackson descendants renewed their claim to ownership, assisted by John Wesley Gaines, congressman from Tennessee. Their efforts again came to nothing, but, in 1909, in the course of his investigation and negotiations for the return of the Jackson papers, Gaines located a Terrell collection, then held by a Washingtonian who had received it in payment for a debt Terrell owed. According to Gaines, he purchased the collection and returned it to Rachel Jackson Lawrence, Jackson's granddaughter. Conflicting reports of the transaction make it difficult to establish the size of the purchase, but the selection of documents printed in the Nashville Tennessean in April and May 1909 confirm that the documents were indeed from the Terrell holdings. While the Lawrences retained these documents for some time, the descendants of Andrew Jackson III, Rachel Lawrence's brother, sold a portion of their collection, approximately 2,000 manuscripts, to the Library of Congress in 1911.

These acquisitions by the Library led to efforts in 1919 to publish an edition of the writings and correspondence of Andrew Jackson. Jackson was one of the few prominent figures in America for whom there was no printed collection beyond the official papers in James D. Richardson's Compilation of the

Messages and Papers of the Presidents, 1787-1897 (10 vols., Washington, 1899). The Carnegie Institution of Washington agreed to sponsor the work and J. Franklin Jameson persuaded John Spencer Bassett, who had published his Life of Andrew Jackson in 1911, to undertake it. Bassett labored at the task for eight years, editing the six volumes of the Correspondence of Andrew Jackson but publishing only three before his death in 1928.

For its time, Bassett's Correspondence set a high standard for documentary publications. His search for documents was thorough and exhaustive. Though forced by financial constraints to conduct his search mainly by mail and to rely upon the assistance of others to identify and often to transcribe documents, he managed to acquire copies of most of the Jackson papers then in the major repositories. His selection of documents, sometimes excerpted and generally emphasizing Jackson's military career, was on the whole sound, and his transcriptions, fairly accurate. Annotations and explanations, however, were sparse.

Shortly before the publication of the last of the edited volumes of the Correspondence in 1933, new discoveries diminished the completeness of the edition. While working on his biography of Andrew Jackson in 1931, Marquis James located a large collection of Jackson papers not previously available. This collection of almost 1,200 letters passed to the Library of Congress in late 1931; and from it, Jameson, Bassett's successor, selected approximately 100 items for inclusion in Volume 6. About the same time, roughly 600 items in the Charles F. Gunther Collection at the Chicago Historical Society became available, and one was included in the final volume of the Bassett series.

Over the next three decades, additional significant collections of Jackson correspondence and other papers surfaced in scattered repositories. The Jackson descendants' residual collection went on the market in the early 1920s and began to filter into repositories in the late 1930s. The Tennessee Historical Society and the State Library and Archives acquired through purchase and gifts a significant body of documents. The Library of Congress acquired, in 1943, approximately 600 fragments, and in 1964, from the Kendall descendants, the small but important group of Jackson-Kendall letters that Terrell had published in the Cincinnati Commercial. Other institutions--Princeton University, the Cincinnati Historical Society, Duke University, the University of Virginia, and Morristown National Historical Park--also accessioned important Jackson materials.

This explosion in the number of Jackson papers known to be held in widely scattered repositories prompted the establishment of the Papers of Andrew Jackson at the Hermitage in 1971 with the objective of searching for and publishing the Jackson papers in complementary microfilm and letterpress series. The microfilm edition, in conjunction with earlier microfilm series, is comprehensive, including all documents found in an exhaustive search. The printed-volume series, of which two have been published, is intended to be a highly selective and carefully annotated edition of fifteen volumes of papers, one volume of legal papers, and a comprehensive index.

This current search for Jackson papers has been the most thorough to date. It has been conducted by dozens of staff members and hundreds of cooperative archivists, curators, and librarians. The search has been carried into barns, attics, jails, and banks, as well as libraries, and has required an untold number of letters and telephone calls, and miles of travel in the United States, France, England, Scotland, and Spain. Staff members have visited and searched Jackson collections and those of Jackson's contemporaries in every major repository in the country. In the absence of evidence to warrant a visit, the staff contacted either by letter or telephone most other institutions that might conceivably hold

Jackson papers: state and county archives; state and local historical societies; county, municipal, and private libraries; and historic sites. In one manner or another, the staff has contacted worldwide in excess of 6,000 institutions and 600 individuals--private collectors, autograph dealers, Jackson and Donelson descendants, and descendants of many of Jackson's contemporaries--seeking copies of their materials. The staff and its consultants have also searched the massive collections of autograph dealer catalogs at the American Antiquarian Society, Yale University, the Grolier Club, and the Huntington Library; and have scanned great numbers of published works: newspapers of Washington, New York, Cincinnati, and Nashville; nineteenth- and twentieth-century popular and scholarly periodicals; historical journals; diaries; reminiscences; printed collections of letters, monographs, and biographies; the Congressional Serial Set and American State Papers. And finally, the staff has searched dozens of unfilmed record groups in the National Archives and hundreds of rolls of film issued by the National Archives and Records Service. The results of this search are now made available on the accompanying thirty-nine rolls of microfilm.

This Scholarly Resources microfilm is a supplement to the 1967 Library of Congress microfilm publication of the Andrew Jackson Papers and to the NARS microfilm series. The collection, about half the size of that in the Library of Congress, consists of 14,000 new documents from approximately 335 repositories. A large portion of the Jackson papers published here was originally a part of the Kendall collection, retained by Terrell, and since dispersed throughout the country. This Microfilm Supplement, in bringing together all these documents, restores in large measure the integrity of the Blair collection and makes readily available--and in many instances for the first time--literally thousands of other items which illuminate the life and times of Andrew Jackson.

Editorial Method

This Microfilm Supplement to the Library of Congress Andrew Jackson Papers and the National Archives microfilm series comprises all Jackson documents found in the project's search not included on those two publications. It includes all additional copies of Jackson documents; variant copies or drafts; a typewritten or printed copy in the absence of a manuscript; documents from the Library of Congress Andrew Jackson Papers, Series 10 and 12, which have not been filmed; documents from the National Archives not available on film; documents from the Library of Congress and National Archives films incorrectly dated or identified; and all Jackson documents in collections other than the Jackson Papers in the Library of Congress, whether previously filmed or not. Spurious documents, in so far as they could be identified, have not been filmed.

In an effort to assist readers and researchers, targets have been filmed with each document. The target at the top of each document, beginning with that document's first page, carries the date of the letter and the full name of the writer, recipient, or subject of the item; and if the document is an enclosure or a cover letter, the target will so state. Square brackets around names and dates on these targets indicate information supplied by the editors. Targets filmed at the bottom of the first page of each document identify the type of document and the location of the original. Frame numbers appear below the documents.

With two exceptions--a series of early account books and addenda (acquisitions too late to interfile) appearing on Rolls 38 and 39--the documents have been filmed in chronological sequence. In those instances where there is more than one item on a particular date, the documents have been filmed in alphabetical order according to the last name of the addressee or recipient. Undated documents for which only an approximate date could be established precede dated items, but documents with ascribed dates are filed sequentially with dated ones. Accounts have been placed at the earliest date in the document rather than when rendered; undated Jackson endorsements on correspondence between other parties have been filmed according to the date of the letter; and treaties, pardons, and other such official documents have been arranged according to the date on which Jackson affixed his signature.

The Index provides access to this Microfilm Supplement and to the Library of Congress Andrew Jackson Papers series and the National Archives microfilm series. For the convenience of the user, this Guide and Index and the Index to the Andrew Jackson Papers, Library of Congress, have been reproduced on Roll 39.

Document Symbols

Abstract	Summary of document contents
AD	Autograph document
AD draft	Autograph document, draft
ADS	Autograph document signed
ADS copy	Autograph document signed, copied by author
ADS draft	Autograph document signed, draft
AL	Autograph letter
AL copy	Autograph letter, copied by author
AL draft	Autograph letter, draft
ALS	Autograph letter signed
ALS copy	Autograph letter signed, copied by author
ALS draft	Autograph letter signed, draft
AN	Autograph note
ANS	Autograph note signed
Copy	Copy, not in author's hand
DS	Document signed
Draft	Draft, not in author's hand
Extract	Copy of a portion of a document
Facsimile	Photographic or engraved exact copy
LC	Letterbook copy
LS	Letter signed
Note	Note in third person, not in author's hand

Repository Symbols

The symbols below are those designed by the Library of Congress and published in Symbols of American Libraries, 11th Edition (Washington, D.C., 1976).

A-Ar	Alabama Department of Archives and History, Montgomery
ABAU	University of Alabama in Birmingham
AFLau	Lauderdale County Archives, Florence
AFlT	University of North Alabama, Florence
AH	Huntsville Public Library, Huntsville
AHAB	First Alabama Bank of Huntsville
AMob	Mobile Public Library, Mobile
Ar-Hi	Arkansas History Commission, Little Rock
ArU	University of Arkansas, Fayetteville
C-S	California State Library, Sutro Branch, San Francisco
CCamarSJ	St. John's Seminary, Camarillo
CLCM	Los Angeles County Museum of Natural History, Los Angeles
CLU-C	University of California, Los Angeles, William Andrews Clark Memorial Library
CLU-URL	University of California, Los Angeles, University Research Library
CSaT	San Francisco Theological Seminary, San Anselmo
CSmH	Henry E. Huntington Library, San Marino
CSt	Stanford University, Stanford
CU-BANC	University of California, Berkeley, Bancroft Library
CoCC	Colorado College, Colorado Springs
CoHi	Colorado State Historical Society, Denver
Ct	Connecticut State Library, Hartford
CtHi	Connecticut Historical Society, Hartford
CtLHi	Litchfield Historical Society, Litchfield
CtNlCG	United States Coast Guard Academy, New London
CtW	Wesleyan University, Middletown
CtY	Yale University, New Haven
CtY-A	Yale University, School of Fine Arts, New Haven
DGU	Georgetown University, Washington
DLC	United States Library of Congress, Washington
DNA	United States National Archives, Washington
	RG 11 General Records of the United States Government

RG 15 Records of the Veterans' Administration
RG 21 Records of the District Courts of the United States
RG 23 Records of the Coast and Geodetic Survey
RG 26 Records of the United States Coast Guard
RG 28 Records of the Post Office Department
RG 36 Records of the Bureau of the Customs
RG 39 Records of the Bureau of Accounts (Treasury)
RG 42 Records of the Office of Public Buildings and Grounds
RG 45 Naval Records Collection of the Office of Naval Records and Library
RG 46 Records of the United States Senate
RG 48 Records of the Office of the Secretary of the Interior
RG 49 Records of the Bureau of Land Management
RG 50 Records of the Treasurer of the United States
RG 56 General Records of the Department of the Treasury
RG 59 General Records of the Department of State
RG 60 General Records of the Department of Justice
RG 75 Records of the Bureau of Indian Affairs
RG 76 Records of Boundary and Claims Commissions and Arbitrations
RG 77 Records of the Office of the Chief of Engineers
RG 84 Records of the Foreign Service Posts of the Department of State
RG 92 Records of the Office of the Quartermaster General
RG 94 Records of the Adjutant General's Office
RG 98 Records of the United States Army Commands
RG 99 Records of the Office of the Paymaster General
RG 104 Records of the Bureau of the Mint
RG 107 Records of the Office of the Secretary of War
RG 108 Records of the Headquarters of the Army
RG 112 Records of the Office of the Surgeon General (Army)

	RG 125 Records of the Office of the Judge Advocate General-Navy
	RG 127 Records of the United States Marine Corps
	RG 153 Records of the Office of the Judge Advocate General-Army
	RG 156 Records of the Office of the Chief of Ordnance
	RG 192 Records of the Office of the Commissary General of Subsistence
	RG 206 Records of the Solicitor of the Treasury
	RG 217 Records of the United States General Accounting Office
	RG 233 Records of the United States House of Representatives
	RG 391 Records of the United States Regular Army Mobile Units, 1821-1942
	RG 393 Records of the United States Army Continental Commands
DNDAR	Daughters of the American Revolution, Washington
DSC	Scottish Rite of Freemasonry, Southern Jurisdiction U.S.A., Supreme Council Library, Washington
DeGE	Eleutherian Mills Historical Library, Greenville
DeHi	Historical Society of Delaware, Wilmington
DeU	University of Delaware, Newark
F	Florida State Library, Tallahassee
FHi	Florida Historical Society, Tampa
FPeE	Escambia County Historical Documents Section, Pensacola
FPeU	University of West Florida, Pensacola
FU	University of Florida, Gainesville
FWpR	Rollins College, Winter Park
FrN	Bibliotheque Municipale, Nantes
G	Georgia State Library, Atlanta
G-Ar	Georgia State Department of Archives and History, Atlanta
GHi	Georgia Historical Society, Savannah
GU	University of Georgia, Athens
I	Illinois State Library, Springfield
I-Ar	Illinois State Library, Archives Division, Springfield
ICHi	Chicago Historical Society, Chicago
ICN	Newberry Library, Chicago
ICU	University of Chicago, Chicago
ICarbS	Southern Illinois University, Carbondale

IEN	Northwestern University, Evanston
IGK	Knox College, Galesburg
IHi	Illinois State Historical Library, Springfield
IU	University of Illinois, Urbana
Ia-HA	Iowa State Department of History and Archives, Des Moines
IaDaM	Davenport Public Museum, Davenport
IaU	University of Iowa, Iowa City
InHi	Indiana Historical Society, Indianapolis
InU	Indiana University, Bloomington
InU-Li	Indiana University, Lilly Library, Bloomington
KHi	Kansas State Historical Society, Topeka
KU-S	University of Kansas, Kenneth Spencer Research Library, Lawrence
KyBgW	Western Kentucky University, Bowling Green
KyClHi	Hickman County Archives, Clinton
KyCTa	Taylor County Archives, Campbellsville
KyHMer	Mercer County Archives, Harrodsburg
KyLoF	Filson Club, Louisville
KyPBo	Bourbon County Archives, Paris
KyStLi	Lincoln County Archives, Stanford
L-M	Louisiana State Museum, New Orleans
LN	New Orleans Public Library, New Orleans
LNHiC	Historic New Orleans Collection, New Orleans
LNT	Tulane University, New Orleans
LU	Louisiana State University, Baton Rouge
LU-Ar	Louisiana State University, Department of Archives and Manuscripts, Baton Rouge
MA	Amherst College, Amherst
MB	Boston Public Library, Boston
MBAt	Boston Atheneum, Boston
MBU	Boston University, Boston
MGrS	Groton School, Groton
MH	Harvard University, Cambridge
MH-Ar	Harvard University Archives, Cambridge
MH-H	Harvard University, Houghton Library, Cambridge
MHi	Massachusetts Historical Society, Boston
MLexM	Museum of Our National Heritage, Lexington
MNS	Smith College, Northampton
MSaE	Essex Institute, Salem
MWalA	American Jewish Historical Society, Waltham
MWalK	John F. Kennedy Library, Boston
MWiW-C	Williams College, Chapin Library, Williamstown
MdAA	Hall of Records Commission, Annapolis
MdBJ	Johns Hopkins University, Baltimore
MdBSAr	Sulpician Archives, Baltimore
MdHi	Maryland Historical Society, Baltimore
MeB	Bowdoin College, Brunswick

MeHi	Maine Historical Society, Portland
MeSaco	Dyer Library, Saco
MeWC	Colby College, Waterville
MiD	Detroit Public Library, Detroit
MiDbEI	Edison Institute, Henry Ford Museum, and Greenfield Village Library, Dearborn
MiU-C	University of Michigan, William L. Clements Library, Ann Arbor
MiU-H	University of Michigan, Michigan Historical Collection, Ann Arbor
MnHi	Minnesota Historical Society, St. Paul
MoHi	Missouri State Historical Society, Columbia
MoIT	Harry S. Truman Library, Independence
MoSHi	Missouri Historical Society, St. Louis
MoSM	Saint Louis Mercantile Library Association, St. Louis
MoStgA	Ste. Genevieve Archives, Ste. Genevieve
MoSW	Washington University, St. Louis
Ms	Mississippi State Library, Jackson
Ms-Ar	Mississippi Department of Archives and History, Jackson
MsClaCoa	Coahoma County Archives, Clarksdale
MsSM	Mississippi State University, State College
N	New York State Library, Albany
NAlI	Albany Institute of History of Art, Albany
NBuHi	Buffalo and Erie County Historical Society, Buffalo
NCanHi	Ontario County Historical Society, Canandaigua
NHC	Colgate University, Hamilton
NHi	New-York Historical Society, New York City
NHpR	Franklin D. Roosevelt Library, Hyde Park
NIC	Cornell University, Ithaca
NN	New York Public Library, New York City
NNC	Columbia University, New York City
NNFoM	Forbes Magazine, Inc., New York City
NNM	American Museum of Natural History, New York City
NNMAI	Museum of the American Indian, New York City
NNMus	Museum of the City of New York, New York City
NNPM	Pierpont Morgan Library, New York City
NNS	New York Society Library, New York City
NPV	Vassar College, Poughkeepsie
NRU	University of Rochester, Rochester
NUt	Utica Public Library, Utica
NUtM	Munson-Williams-Proctor Institute, Utica
NWM	United States Military Academy, West Point
NbO	Omaha Public Library, Omaha
Nc	North Carolina State Library, Raleigh
Nc-Ar	North Carolina State Department of Archives and History, Raleigh
NcD	Duke University, Durham

NcGM	Greensboro Historical Museum, Greensboro
NcMHi	Historical Foundation of the Presbyterian and Reformed Churches, Montreat
NcSal	Rowan Public Library, Salisbury
NcU	University of North Carolina, Chapel Hill
Nh-Ar	New Hampshire Department of Administration and Control, Division of Archives and Records Management, Concord
NhD	Dartmouth College, Hanover
NhHi	New Hampshire Historical Society, Concord
NjGbS	Glassboro State College, Glassboro
NjHi	New Jersey Historical Society, Newark
NjMHi	Madison Historical Society, Madison
NjMoHP	Morristown National Historical Park, Morristown
NjP	Princeton University, Princeton
NjR	Rutgers-The State University, New Brunswick
OCHP	Cincinnati Historical Society, Cincinnati
OCX	Xavier University, Cincinnati
OClWHi	Western Reserve Historical Society, Cleveland
OFH	Rutherford B. Hayes Library, Fremont
OGK	Kenyon College, Gambier
OHi	Ohio Historical Society, Columbus
OMC	Marietta College, Marietta
OO	Oberlin College, Oberlin
OkChicW	Oklahoma College of Liberal Arts, Chickasha
OkTG	Thomas Gilcrease Institute of American History and Art, Tulsa
OrU	University of Oregon, Eugene
PBL	Lehigh University, Bethlehem
PCarlD	Dickinson College, Carlisle
PHC	Haverford College, Haverford
PHi	Historical Society of Pennsylvania, Philadelphia
PJo	Cambria County Library System, Johnstown
PMA	Allegheny College, Meadville
PMCHi	Crawford County Historical Society, Meadville
PP	Free Library of Philadelphia, Philadelphia
PPAmP	American Philosophical Society, Philadelphia
PPFRC	Federal Archives and Records Center, Philadelphia
PPPrHi	Presbyterian Historical Society, Philadelphia
PPRF	Rosenbach Foundation, Philadelphia
PPiU	University of Pittsburgh, Pittsburgh
PSC	Swarthmore College, Swarthmore
PSt	Pennsylvania State University, University Park
PU	University of Pennsylvania, Philadelphia
PWbH	Wyoming Historical and Geological Society, Wilkes-Barre
PWbW	Wilkes College, Wilkes-Barre

PWcHi	Chester County Historical Society, West Chester
PYHi	Historical Society of York County, York
RHi	Rhode Island Historical Society, Providence
RP	Providence Public Library, Providence
RPB	Brown University, Providence
RPB-JH	Brown University, John Hay Library of Rare Books and Special Collections, Providence
Sc	South Carolina State Library, Columbia
ScCleU	Clemson University, Clemson
ScHi	South Carolina Historical Society, Charleston
ScU	University of South Carolina, Columbia
Sp	Biblioteca Nacional, Madrid
Sp-Ar	Archivo General de Indias, Seville
SpS	Archivo Nacional, Seville
SwSKM	Kungliga Biblioteket, Stockholm
T	Tennessee State Library and Archives, Nashville
TBHay	Haywood County Archives, Brownsville
TCAn	Anderson County Archives, Clinton
TCMau	Maury County Archives, Columbia
TCMon	Montgomery County Archives, Clarksville
TCSm	Smith County Archives, Carthage
TDRh	Rhea County Archives, Dayton
TFLi	Lincoln County Archives, Fayetteville
TFWi	Williamson County Archives, Franklin
TGSum	Sumner County Archives, Gallatin
THer	Ladies' Hermitage Association, Hermitage
THi	Tennessee Historical Society, Nashville
TJoS	East Tennessee State University, Johnson City
TKKn	Knox County Archives, Knoxville
TKL	Public Library of Knoxville and Knox County, Knoxville
TKRo	Roane County Archives, Kingston
TLOv	Overton County Archives, Livingston
TLWil	Wilson County Archives, Lebanon
TM	Memphis Public Library, Memphis
TMM	Memphis State University, Memphis
TMRu	Rutherford County Archives, Murfreesboro
TMSh	Shelby County Archives, Memphis
TNDa	Davidson County Archives, Nashville
TNJ	Vanderbilt University Library, Nashville
TPHen	Henry County Archives, Paris
TSBe	Bedford County Archives, Shelbyville
TSRob	Robertson County Archives, Springfield
TU	University of Tennessee, Knoxville
TWFr	Franklin County Archives, Winchester
TWHu	Humphreys County Archives, Waverly
Tx	Texas State Library and Historical Commission, Austin

TxGR	Rosenberg Library, Galveston
TxHSJM	San Jacinto Museum of History Association, Deer Park
TxHU	University of Houston, Houston
TxHuT	Sam Houston State University, Huntsville
TxSjM	San Jacinto Museum of History Association, San Jacinto Monument
TxU	University of Texas, Austin
TxWasRM	Star of the Republic Museum, Washington
UPB	Brigham Young University, Provo
Uk	British Library, London
UkENL	National Library of Scotland, Edinburgh
UkLPR	Public Record Office, London
Vi	Virginia State Library, Richmond
ViHi	Virginia Historical Society, Richmond
ViL	Jones Memorial Library, Lynchburg
ViMtvL	Mount Vernon Ladies' Association of the Union, Mount Vernon
ViRVal	Valentine Museum, Richmond
ViU	University of Virginia, Charlottesville
ViW	College of William and Mary, Williamsburg
ViWC	Colonial Williamsburg, Inc., Williamsburg
WHi	State Historical Society of Wisconsin, Madison
WaU	University of Washington, Seattle

National Archives Microfilm Publications

The following abbreviations have been used in the Index to identify the large body of Jackson documents published in the National Archives Microfilm Publication Program. For additional information on the microfilm and the program, see Microfilm Resources for Research: A Comprehensive Catalog (Washington, 1986).

M6 Letters Sent by the Secretary of War Relating to Military Affairs, 1800-1889
M7 Confidential and Unofficial Letters Sent by the Secretary of War, 1814-47
M9 Despatches from United States Consuls in Cap Haitien, Haiti, 1797-1906
M10 Despatches from United States Ministers to Chile, 1823-1906
M15 Letters Sent by the Secretary of War Relating to Indian Affairs, 1800-1824
M16 Letters Sent by the Superintendent of Indian Trade, 1807-23
M21 Letters Sent by the Office of Indian Affairs, 1824-81
M22 Registers of Letters Received by the Office of the Secretary of War, Main Series, 1800-1870
M23 Despatches from United States Consuls in Algiers, Algeria, 1785-1906
M25 Miscellaneous Letters Sent by the General Land Office, 1796-1889
M30 Despatches from United States Ministers to Great Britain, 1791-1906
M31 Despatches from United States Ministers to Spain, 1792-1906
M34 Despatches from United States Ministers to France, 1789-1906
M35 Despatches from United States Ministers to Russia, 1808-1906
M37 Records of the Department of State, Communications from Special Agents, 1794-1906
M38 Notes from the Department of State to Foreign Ministers and Consuls in the United States, 1793-1834
M39 Notes from the Russian Legation in the United States to the Department of State, 1809-1906
M40 Domestic Letters of the Department of State, 1784-1906
M42 Despatches from United States Ministers to the Netherlands, 1794-1906
M46 Despatches from United States Ministers to Turkey, 1818-1906

M49 Notes from the Brazilian Legation in the United States to the Department of State, 1824-1906
M50 Notes from the British Legation in the United States to the Department of State, 1791-1906
M51 Notes from the Colombian Legation in the United States to the Department of State, 1810-1906
M52 Notes from the Danish Legation in the United States to the Department of State, 1801-1906
M53 Notes from the French Legation in the United States to the Department of State, 1789-1906
M54 Notes from the Mexican Legation in the United States to the Department of State, 1821-1906
M55 Notes from the Legation of the Kingdom of the Two Sicilies to the Department of State, 1826-60
M56 Notes from the Netherlands Legation in the United States to the Department of State, 1784-1906
M59 Notes from the Spanish Legation in the United States to the Department of State, 1790-1906
M60 Notes from the Swedish Legation in the United States to the Department of State, 1813-1906
M64 Letters Sent by the Director of the United States Mint at Philadelphia, 1795-1817
M73 Notes from the Chilean Legation in the United States to the Department of State, 1811-1906
M77 Diplomatic Instructions of the Department of State, 1801-1906
M78 Consular Instructions of the Department of State, 1801-34
M84 Despatches from United States Consuls in La Guaira, Venezuela, 1810-1906
M91 Records Relating to the United States Military Academy, 1812-67
M97 Despatches from United States Ministers to Mexico, 1823-1906
M101 Despatches from United States Consuls in Canton, China, 1790-1906
M116 State Department Territorial Papers, Florida, 1777-1824
M121 Despatches from United States Ministers to Brazil, 1809-1906
M124 Letters Received by the Secretary of the Navy: Miscellaneous Letters, 1801-84
M125 Letters Received by the Secretary of the Navy: Captains' Letters, 1805-61, 1866-85
M127 Letters Sent to the President by the Secretary of War, 1800-1863
M146 Despatches from United States Consuls in Valparaiso, Chile, 1812-1906
M179 Miscellaneous Letters of the Department of State, 1789-1906
M183 Despatches from United States Consuls in Veracruz, Mexico, 1822-1906

M199 Despatches from United States Consuls in Santa Fe, New Mexico, 1830-46
M200 Territorial Papers of the United States Senate, 1789-1873
M205 Correspondence of the Secretary of the Navy Relating to African Colonization, 1819-44
M208 Records of the Cherokee Indian Agency in Tennessee, 1801-35
M209 Miscellaneous Letters Sent by the Secretary of the Navy, 1798-1886
M219 Despatches from United States Ministers to Central America, 1824-1906
M220 Reports to Congress from the Secretary of War, 1803-70
M221 Letters Received by the Secretary of War, Registered Series, 1801-70
M222 Letters Received by the Secretary of War, Unregistered Series, 1789-1861
M234 Letters Received by the Office of Indian Affairs, 1824-81
M235 Miscellaneous Treasury Accounts of the First Auditor (Formerly the Auditor) of the Treasury Department, September 6, 1790-July 15, 1840
M236 A Microfilm Supplement to the Territorial Papers of the United States: Wisconsin, 1836-48
M271 Letters Received by the Office of the Secretary of War Relating to Indian Affairs, 1800-1823
M273 Records of General Courts-Martial and Courts of Inquiry of the Navy Department, 1799-1867
M281 Despatches from United States Consuls in Matamoros, Mexico, 1826-1906
M286 Despatches from United States Consuls in Campeche, Mexico, 1820-80
M296 Despatches from United States Consuls in Mexico City, Mexico, 1822-1906
M303 Despatches from United States Consuls in Tabasco, Mexico, 1832-74
M370 Miscellaneous Letters Sent by the Secretary of War, 1800-1809
M371 Records of the District of Columbia Commissioners and of the Offices Concerned with Public Buildings, 1791-1867
M415 Letters Sent to the President by the Secretary of the Treasury, 1833-78
M439 Letters of Application and Recommendation during the Administration of James Monroe, 1817-25
M472 Letters Sent by the Secretary of the Navy to the President and Executive Agencies, 1821-86
M477 Letters Sent by the Surveyor General of the Territory Northwest of the Ohio River, 1797-1854
M478 Letters Received by the Secretary of the Treasury and the Commissioner of the General Land Office from the Surveyor General of the Territory Northwest of the Ohio River, 1797-1849

M531 Letters of Application and Recommendation during the Administration of John Quincy Adams, 1825-29
M565 Letters Sent by the Office of the Adjutant General (Main Series), 1800-1890
M566 Letters Received by the Office of the Adjutant General, 1805-21
M567 Letters Received by the Office of the Adjutant General (Main Series), 1822-60
M601 Letters Sent by the Postmaster General, 1789-1836
M625 Area File of the Naval Records Collection, 1775-1910
M639 Letters of Application and Recommendation during the Administration of Andrew Jackson, 1829-37
M640 Records of the Southern Superintendency of Indian Affairs, 1832-70
M664 Notes from Foreign Consuls in the United States to the Department of State, 1789-1906
M668 Ratified Indian Treaties, 1722-1869
M687 Letters of Application and Recommendation during the Administrations of Martin Van Buren, William Henry Harrison, and John Tyler, 1837-45
M688 United States Military Academy Cadet Application Papers, 1805-66
M699 Letters Sent by the Department of Justice: General and Miscellaneous, 1818-1904
M733 Letters Sent by the Secretary of the Treasury Relating to Public Lands (N Series), 1801-78
M735 Circular Letters of the Secretary of the Treasury (T Series), 1789-1878
M749 Correspondence of the Secretary of the Treasury Relating to the Administration of Trust Funds for the Chickasaw and Other Tribes (S Series), 1834-72
M858 The Negro in the Military Service of the United States, 1639-1886
M873 Letters of Application and Recommendation during the Administrations of James Polk, Zachary Taylor, and Millard Fillmore, 1845-53

T1 Despatches from United States Consuls in Paris, France, 1790-1906
T20 Despatches from United States Consuls in Havana, Cuba, 1783-1906
T33 Despatches from United States Ministers to Colombia, 1820-1906
T34 Notes from Central American Legations in the United States to the Department of State, 1823-1906
T55 Despatches from United States Consuls in Santiago de Cuba, Cuba, 1799-1906
T61 Despatches from United States Consuls in Tangier, Morocco, 1797-1906
T168 Despatches from United States Consuls in London, United Kingdom, 1790-1906

T172 Despatches from United States Consuls in Rio de Janeiro, Brazil, 1811-1906
T185 Despatches from United States Consuls in Bristol, United Kingdom, 1792-1906
T194 Despatches from United States Consuls in Constantinople, Turkey, 1820-1906
T203 Despatches from United States Consuls in Fayal, Azores, 1795-1897
T206 Despatches from United States Consuls in Gibraltar, Spain, 1791-1906
T212 Despatches from United States Consuls in Havre, France, 1789-1906
T224 Despatches from United States Consuls in Naples, Italy, 1796-1906
T229 Despatches from United States Consuls in Puerto Cabello, Venezuela, 1823-1906
T238 Despatches from United States Consuls in Smyrna, Turkey, 1802-1906
T239 Despatches from United States Consuls in Southampton, United Kingdom, 1790-1906
T303 Despatches from United States Consuls in Tunis, Tunisia, 1797-1906
T330 Despatches from United States Consuls in Aux Cayes, Haiti, 1797-1874
T339 Despatches from United States Consuls in Matanzas, Cuba, 1820-99
T357 Despatches from United States Consuls in Alicante, Spain, 1788-1905
T412 Opinions of the Attorney General, 1817-32
T431 Despatches from United States Consuls in St. Pierre, Martinique, French West Indies, 1790-1906
T494 Documents Relating to the Negotiation of Ratified and Unratified Treaties with Various Indian Tribes, 1801-69
T690 Despatches from United States Consuls in Tenerife, Canary Islands, 1795-1906
T802 Notes from the Peruvian Legation in the United States to the Department of State, 1827-1906
T809 Notes from the Texan Legation in the United States to the Department of State, 1836-45
T953 Notes from Miscellaneous Foreign States to the Department of State, 1817-1906
T967 Copies of Presidential Pardons and Remissions, 1794-1893
T1223 Presidential Proclamations 1-2160 (1789-1936)

Select Bibliography

In addition to the highly selective list of monographs and primary sources below, the following journals carry a number of articles on or related to Andrew Jackson: American Historical Magazine (AHM), American Historical Review (AHR), East Tennessee Historical Society's Publications (ETHSP), Journal of Southern History (JSH), Louisiana Historical Quarterly (LHQ), Pennsylvania Magazine of History and Biography (PMHB), Tennessee Historical Magazine (THM), and Tennessee Historical Quarterly (THQ).

Abernethy, Thomas P. From Frontier to Plantation in Tennessee. University, Ala., 1967.

Aderman, Ralph M., ed. The Letters of James Kirke Paulding. Madison, 1962.

Bassett, John Spencer. The Life of Andrew Jackson. Hamden, Conn., 1967.

Bassett, John Spencer, ed. Correspondence of Andrew Jackson. 7 vols. Washington, 1926-35.

Belohlavek, John M. Let the Eagle Soar: The Foreign Policy of Andrew Jackson. Lincoln, Nebr., 1985.

Bond, Octavia Louise Zollicoffer. The Family Chronicle and Kinship Book. Nashville, 1928.

Brady, Cyrus Townsend. The True Andrew Jackson. Philadelphia, 1906.

Brown, William G. Andrew Jackson. Boston, 1900.

Buell, Augustus C. History of Andrew Jackson, Pioneer, Patriot, Soldier, Politician, President. 2 vols. New York, 1904.

Burke, Pauline Wilcox. Emily Donelson of Tennessee. 2 vols. Richmond, 1941.

Caldwell, Mary French. General Jackson's Lady. Nashville, 1936.

Campbell, Tom W. Two Fighters and Two Fines: Sketches of the Lives of Matthew Lyon and Andrew Jackson. Little Rock, 1941.

Carter, Clarence Edwin, et al., eds. Territorial Papers of the United States. 28 vols. Washington, 1934-75.

Cobbett, William. Life of Andrew Jackson, President of the United States. New York, 1837.

Colyar, Arthur St. Clair. Life and Times of Andrew Jackson. 2 vols. Nashville, 1904.

Curtis, James C. Andrew Jackson and the Search for Vindication. Boston, 1976.

Davis, Burke. Old Hickory: A Life of Andrew Jackson. New York, 1977.

Doherty, Herbert J., Jr. Richard Keith Call: Southern Unionist. Gainesville, 1961.

Drury, Clifford Merrill. William Anderson Scott, "No Ordinary Man." Glendale, Calif., 1967.

Duane, William John. Narrative and Correspondence Concerning the Removal of the Deposits. Philadelphia, 1838.

Dusenbery, Benjamin M. Monument to the Memory of General Andrew Jackson. Philadelphia, 1846.

Ely, Ezra Stiles. The Duty of Christian Freemen to Elect Christian Rulers. Philadelphia, 1828.

Fitzpatrick, John C., ed. The Autobiography of Martin Van Buren. New York, 1969.

Galloway, Linda Bennett. Andrew Jackson, Jr., Son of a President: A Biographical Study. New York, 1966.

Goodwin, Philo A. Biography of Andrew Jackson, President of the United States. Hartford, 1832.

Green, Michael D. The Politics of Indian Removal: Creek Government and Society in Crisis. Lincoln, Nebr., 1982.

Hamilton, James A. Reminiscences of James A. Hamilton. New York, 1869.

Hamilton, Stanislaus M., ed. Writings of James Monroe. 7 vols. New York, 1898-1903.

Heiskell, Samuel Gordon. Andrew Jackson and Early Tennessee History. 2 vols. Nashville, 1918.

__________. Andrew Jackson and Early Tennessee History. 3 vols. Nashville, 1921.

Herd, Elmer Don, Jr. Andrew Jackson, South Carolinian: A Study of the Enigma of His Birth. Lancaster, S.C., 1963.

Horn, Stanley F. The Hermitage, Home of Old Hickory. Nashville, 1950.

Hunt, Charles Havens. Life of Edward Livingston. New York, 1864.

Jackson, Andrew IV. Andrew Jackson, President of the United States of America. Los Angeles, c1926.

Jackson, Joseph Abram. Masonry in Alabama: A Sesquicentennial History, 1821-1971. Montgomery, 1970.

James, Marquis. Andrew Jackson: The Border Captain. Indianapolis, 1933.

__________. Andrew Jackson: Portrait of a President. Indianapolis, 1937.

Jenkins, John Stilwell. The Life and Public Services of Andrew Jackson. Philadelphia, 1880.

Johnson, Gerald W. Andrew Jackson, an Epic In Homespun. New York, 1927.

Jordan, Weymouth T. George Washington Campbell of Tennessee, Western Statesman. Tallahassee, 1955.

Kendall, Amos. Life of Andrew Jackson, Private, Military and Civil. New York, 1843-44.

Klingberg, Frank J., and Andrew Jackson IV. "The Americanism of Andrew Jackson," South Atlantic Quarterly, 21(April 1922):127-143.

__________. "Personal Traits of President Andrew Jackson," Historical Outlook, 14(January 1923):10-14.

Latner, Richard B. The Presidency of Andrew Jackson: White House Politics, 1829-1837. Athens, Ga., 1979.

Linn, Elizabeth A., and Nathan Sargent. The Life and Public Services of Dr. Lewis F. Linn. New York, 1857.

Manning, William R., ed. Diplomatic Correspondence of the United States, 1831-1860. 12 vols. Washington, 1932-39.

Mayo, Robert. Political Sketches of Eight Years in Washington. Baltimore, 1839.

__________. The Affidavit of Andrew Jackson Taken by the Defendants in the Suit of Robert Mayo vs. Blair and Rives, for a Libel. Washington, 1840.

McGovern, James R., ed. Andrew Jackson and Pensacola. Pensacola, 1974.

Meriwether, Robert L., et al., eds. The Papers of John C. Calhoun. 16 vols. to date. Columbia, S.C., 1959- .

Moser, Harold D., et al., eds. The Papers of Andrew Jackson. 2 vols. to date. Knoxville, Tenn., 1980- .

Nicolay, Helen. Andrew Jackson, the Fighting President. New York, 1929.

Ogg, Frederic A. The Reign of Andrew Jackson: A Chronicle of the Frontier in Politics. New Haven, 1919.

Owsley, Frank Lawrence, Jr. Struggle for the Gulf Borderlands: The Creek War and the Battle of New Orleans, 1812-1815. Gainesville, 1981.

Parton, James. Life of Andrew Jackson. 3 vols. New York, 1860.

Reid, John, and John Henry Eaton. The Life of Andrew Jackson. Edited by Frank Lawrence Owsley, Jr. University, Ala., 1974.

Remini, Robert V. Andrew Jackson. New York, 1966.

__________. Andrew Jackson and the Bank War: A Study in the Growth of Presidential Power. New York, 1968.

__________. Andrew Jackson and the Course of American Empire, 1767-1821. New York, 1977.

__________. Andrew Jackson and the Course of American Freedom, 1822-1832. New York, 1981.

__________. Andrew Jackson and the Course of American Democracy, 1833-1845. New York, 1984.

__________. The Election of Andrew Jackson. Philadelphia, 1963.

Rogin, Michael Paul. Fathers and Children: Andrew Jackson and the Subjugation of the American Indian. New York, 1975.

Rowland, Dunbar, ed. Official Letter Books of W. C. C. Claiborne, 1801-1816. 6 vols. New York, 1972.

Royall, Anne Newport. Letters from Alabama, 1817-1822. Edited by Lucille Griffith. University, Ala., 1969.

Satz, Ronald N. American Indian Policy in the Jacksonian Era. Lincoln, Nebr., 1975.

Snelling, William Joseph. A Brief and Impartial History of the Life and Actions of Andrew Jackson, President of the United States. Boston, 1831.

Sumner, William Graham. Andrew Jackson as a Public Man. Boston, 1882.

__________. Andrew Jackson. Boston, 1899.

Syrett, Harold C. Andrew Jackson: His Contribution to the American Tradition. Indianapolis, 1953.

Tyler, Lyon Gardiner. The Letters and Times of the Tylers. 3 vols. Richmond and Williamsburg, 1884-96.

Waldo, Samuel Putnam. Memoirs of Andrew Jackson. Hartford, 1818.

Ward, John William. Andrew Jackson: Symbol for an Age. New York, 1962.

Watson, Thomas E. The Life and Times of Andrew Jackson. Thomson, Ga., 1912.

Williams, Amelia W., and Eugene C. Barker, eds. The Writings of Sam Houston. 8 vols. Austin, 1938-43.

Williams, Emma Inman. Historic Madison: The Story of Jackson and Madison County, Tennessee. Jackson, Tenn., 1946.

Yoakum, Henderson K. History of Texas from Its First Settlement in 1685 to Its Annexation to the United States in 1846. 2 vols. New York, 1855.

Roll List

1. 1770 December 17-1804 December 18
2. 1805-1813 January 7
3. 1813 January 7-1814 August 24
4. 1814 August 24-1816 April 1
5. 1816 April 1-1818 February 9
6. 1818 February 10-1818 November 24
7. 1818 November 28-1820 November 23
8. 1820 November 29-1822 January 22
9. 1822 January 22-1824 January 19
10. 1824 January 19-1825 September 19
11. 1825 September 27-1828 May 12
12. 1828 May 12-1829 April 17
13. 1829 April 18-1829 September 30
14. 1829 October-1830 January 21
15. 1830 January 22-1830 June 30
16. 1830 July 8-1830 December 25
17. 1830 December 27-1831 June 12
18. 1831 June 13-1831 December 2
19. 1831 December 3-1832 March 28
20. 1832 March 28-1832 September 15
21. 1832 September 16-1833 January 19
22. 1833 January 19-1833 June 7
23. 1833 June 7-1833 December 2
24. 1833 December 3-1834 March 8
25. 1834 March 9-1834 June 30
26. 1834 June 30-1834 December 24
27. 1834 December 24-1835 April 8
28. 1835 April 8-1835 September 7
29. 1835 September 7-1836 January 12
30. 1836 January 13-1836 May 12
31. 1836 May 13-1836 October 2
32. 1836 October 3-1837 January 17
33. 1837 January 17-1837 October 27

34. 1837 October 28-1840 September 7
35. 1840 September 10-1843 October 30
36. 1843 November 11-1845 March 18
37. 1845 March 18-1845 August 4
    Additional papers, nd-1843
38. General store account books
39. General store account books
    Guides and indexes

PROPERTY RIGHTS

The user is cautioned that the publication of the contents of this microfilm may be construed as constituting a violation of literary property rights. These rights derive from the principle of common law that the writer of an unpublished letter or other manuscript has the sole right to publish the contents thereof, unless he affirmatively parts with the right; the right descends to his legal heirs regardless of the ownership of the physical manuscript itself. It is the responsibility of an author or his publisher to secure the permission of the owner of literary rights in unpublished writings. Any citation of or bibliographical reference to a manuscript in this microfilm should include identification of its owner or depository.

INDEX

This index directs the user to papers of Andrew Jackson in three microfilm editions. Sample entries:

DLC-66	Library of Congress 1967 film, roll 66
M639-27	National Archives and Records Service film publication M639, roll 27
18-1192	Microfilm Supplement 1986, roll 18, frame 1192

Although essentially a listing of recipient and writer names, the index also includes a few subject headings, used only in instances (such as memoranda) where no personal name can be attached to the document. The user is cautioned that listings such as Bank of the United States by no means embrace all items concerning this subject.

Symbols and Abbreviations

* indicates a variant copy of the item preceding

# indicates an item not written by or to Andrew Jackson

add	address, speech
chk	check
fin	financial document (e.g., invoice, receipt, bill of sale, promissory note)
leg	legal document (e.g., minutes and records of courts, deposition, subpoena, power of attorney, agreement)
lnd	land record (e.g., deed, survey)
mem	memorandum
par	presidential pardon or remission

AB			
	To 1816 Aug 31	chk	DLC-21
AB and Lady			
	To 1806 Oct 05		2-0362
Abbot J			
	Fr 1834 Nov 21#	fin	DLC-45
Abbot J Mrs			
	To 1833 Jan 12	chk	DLC-41
Abbott E			
	Fr 1824 Oct 27#	fin	DLC-33
	Fr 1825 Jan 04	fin	DLC-33
Abbott Edward			
	Re 1832 Apr 19	par	20-0256
Abd ar-Rahman Sultan of Morocco			
	To 1831 Aug 23		18-0580
	To 1832 Jul 02		20-0856
Abert John James			
	Fr 1832 Aug 13#		M567-66
	Fr 1834 Mar 03#		M567-102
	Fr 1834 Dec 16		M234-241
	Fr 1834 Dec 16*		26-1520
	Fr 1836 Sep 30#		M687-1
	Fr 1836 Oct 01		31-1567
	Fr 1836 Oct 11#		32-0133
	Fr 1836 Oct 24#		M567-117
Abner Randal et al			
	Fr 1830 Dec 27		M234-832
	Fr 1830 Dec 27*		17-0002
Ackland Samuel			
	Re 1801 Oct 09	mem	DLC-60
Acklen Alsander J			
	Fr 1813 Oct 27		DLC-7
	Fr 1813 Oct 30		DLC-7
	Fr 1813 Dec 12		DLC-7
	To 1813 Dec 15		DLC-61
	Fr 1813 Dec 19		DLC-7
	Fr 1813 Dec 19*		DLC-61
Acklen Thomas			
	Fr 1836 Jan 05		M639-5
Acre Samuel			
	Fr 1816 Apr 05		DLC-20
	Fr 1821 Sep		8-1117
	Fr 1829 Nov 02		M639-1
Adair G W			
	Fr 1836 Aug 30		DLC-48
Adair John			
	Fr 1814 Jun 22		DLC-11
	To 1814 Dec 21		DLC-62
	To 1814 Dec 26		DLC-15
	Fr 1815 Mar 20		DLC-17
	To 1815 Apr 02		DLC-62
	To 1817 Jul 23		DLC-71
	Fr 1817 Oct 21		5-1111
	Re 1830		DLC-72
	Fr 1832		19-0509
	Re 1832 Jul 13		20-1060
Adam Adelaide			
	Re 1830 Mar 20	par	15-0404
Adams Ann			
	Fr 1836 Jul 20		31-1132
Adams David			
	Fr 1823 Jan 20		M439-18
Adams Isaac Hull			
	Fr 1836 cJul 07		31-0906
Adams James			
	Fr 1794 Sep 14	fin	DLC-71
	Re 1833 Feb 06	par	22-0271
	Re 1833 Feb 06*	par	T967-1
Adams John			
	Fr 1797 Dec 01		1-0551
	To 1798 Mar 05		1-0631
	To 1798 Mar 22		1-0642
	Fr 1798 Jul 16		DLC-71
Adams John Quincy			
	Re 1798 cMar 14	mem	DLC-58
	To 1817 Sep 15		M439-5
	Fr 1818 Jul 02		6-1097
	Fr 1818 Jul 02*		M40-15
	To 1819 Jan 25		7-0190
	Fr 1819 Jul 02		7-0566
	Fr 1819 Jul 09		M40-15
	To 1819 Jul 14#		M439-11
	Fr 1821 Mar 12		DLC-30
	Fr 1821 Mar 12*		DLC-63
	Fr 1821 Mar 12*		M221-88
	Fr 1821 Mar 12*		8-0188
	Fr 1821 Mar 20		DLC-72
	Fr 1821 Mar 20*		DLC-63
	Fr 1821 Mar 20*		8-0246
	Fr 1821 Mar 23		DLC-30
	Fr 1821 Mar 23*		DLC-63
	Fr 1821 Mar 23*		8-0254
	To 1821 Apr 02		M116-5
	To 1821 Apr 02*		8-0281
	To 1821 Apr 02*		DLC-63
	To 1821 Apr 10		M116-5
	To 1821 Apr 10*		DLC-63
	To 1821 Apr 10*		8-0289
	To 1821 Apr 12		M116-5
	To 1821 Apr 12*		8-0314
	To 1821 Apr 12*		DLC-63
	Re 1821 Apr 22		M116-5
	To 1821 Apr 24		M116-5
	To 1821 Apr 24*		DLC-63
	To 1821 Apr 24*		8-0361
	To 1821 May 01		M179-51
	To 1821 May 01*		M116-6
	To 1821 May 01*		DLC-63
	To 1821 May 01*		8-0405
	To 1821 May 07		M116-5
	To 1821 May 07*		DLC-63
	To 1821 May 07*		8-0428
	To 1821 May 07		M116-5
	To 1821 May 07*		M116-6
	To 1821 May 07*		DLC-63
	To 1821 May 07*		8-0429
	To 1821 May 19		M116-6
	To 1821 May 19*		DLC-63
	To 1821 May 19*		8-0482
	To 1821 May 21		M116-5
	To 1821 May 21*		M116-6
	To 1821 May 21*		DLC-63
	To 1821 May 21*		8-0489
	Fr 1821 May 22		DLC-30
	Fr 1821 May 22*		8-0502
	Fr 1821 May 23		DLC-30
	Fr 1821 May 23*		8-0507
	To 1821 May 30		M116-5
	To 1821 May 30*		M116-6
	To 1821 May 30*		DLC-63
	To 1821 May 30*		8-0532
	To 1821 Jun 08		M116-5
	To 1821 Jun 08*		DLC-63
	To 1821 Jun 08*		8-0551
	To 1821 Jun 09		M116-5
	To 1821 Jun 09*		DLC-63
	To 1821 Jun 09*		8-0552

Adams John Quincy (cont)
To 1821 Jun 10 M116-5
To 1821 Jun 10* 8-0560
To 1821 Jun 11 M116-5
To 1821 Jun 11* M116-6
To 1821 Jun 11* 8-0571
To 1821 Jun 11* DLC-63
To 1821 Jun 13 M116-5
To 1821 Jun 13* DLC-63
To 1821 Jun 13* 8-0599
Fr 1821 Jun 22 8-0646
Fr 1821 Jun 27 DLC-30
Fr 1821 Jun 27* M40-17
Fr 1821 Jun 27* 8-0696
Fr 1821 Jun 27 M40-17
Fr 1821 Jun 27* 8-0701
To 1821 Jun 29 8-0727
To 1821 Jun 29* DLC-63
To 1821 Jun 29 M116-5
To 1821 Jun 29* M116-6
To 1821 Jun 29* DLC-63
To 1821 Jun 29* 8-0730
Fr 1821 Jul 06 DLC-30
Fr 1821 Jul 06* M40-17
Fr 1821 Jul 06* 8-0773
To 1821 Jul 16 M116-5
To 1821 Jul 16* DLC-63
To 1821 Jul 17 M116-6
To 1821 Jul 17* DLC-63
To 1821 Jul 17* 8-0848
To 1821 Jul 17 DLC-30
To 1821 Jul 18 M116-5
To 1821 Jul 18* DLC-63
To 1821 Jul 18* 8-0858
To 1821 Jul 30 M116-6
To 1821 Jul 30* DLC-63
To 1821 Jul 30* 8-0920
To 1821 Jul 30 mem DLC-30
To 1821 Aug 8-0986
To 1821 Aug 04 M116-7
To 1821 Aug 04* DLC-63
to 1821 Aug 15 M116-7
To 1821 Aug 20 8-1074
To 1821 Aug 20 M116-7
Fr 1821 Aug 20 DLC-30
Fr 1821 Aug 20* M40-17
Fr 1821 Aug 20* 8-1076
To 1821 Aug 26 M116-7
To 1821 Aug 26* DLC-30
To 1821 Aug 26* DLC-63
Re 1821 Sep mem DLC-30
To 1821 Sep 01 M116-7
To 1821 Sep 01* DLC-63
To 1821 Sep 02 8-1139
To 1821 Sep 17 8-1162
To 1821 Sep 20 8-1183
To 1821 Sep 30 M116-7
To 1821 Sep 30* DLC-63
To 1821 Oct M116-8
To 1821 Oct 04 M116-8
To 1821 Oct 04* DLC-63
To 1821 Oct 06 M116-8
To 1821 Oct 06* DLC-63
To 1821 Oct 06* 8-1278
Fr 1821 Oct 26 DLC-31
Fr 1821 Oct 26* M116-8
Fr 1821 Oct 26* M40-17
Fr 1821 Oct 26* 8-1301
To 1821 Nov 13 M116-9
To 1821 Nov 13* DLC-63
To 1821 Nov 14 M116-9
To 1821 Nov 22 M116-9
To 1821 Nov 22* DLC-63
To 1821 Dec 12 M179-52
To 1821 Dec 12* DLC-63
Fr 1821 Dec 26 DLC-31
Fr 1821 Dec 26* M40-17
Fr 1822 Jan 01 DLC-31
Fr 1822 Jan 01* M40-17
To 1822 Jan 05 M116-10
To 1822 Jan 05* DLC-63
To 1822 Jan 22 M116-10
To 1822 Jan 22* 8-1404
To 1822 Jan 22* DLC-63
To 1822 Jan 31 M116-10
To 1822 Jan 31* DLC-63
To 1822 Jan 31* 9-0018
To 1822 Feb 13 M116-10
Fr 1822 Feb 22 DLC-31
Fr 1822 Feb 22* M40-17
To 1822 Mar 08 M116-10
To 1822 Mar 08* DLC-31
To 1822 Mar 19 M116-10
To 1822 Mar 19* DLC-63
To 1822 Apr 23 M116-10
To 1822 May 19 M116-10
Fr 1823 Feb 19 DLC-32
Fr 1823 Feb 19* 9-0457
To 1823 Mar 15 9-0496
To 1823 Mar 15* DLC-32
To 1823 Dec 20 9-0814
To 1823 Dec 23 M439-13
To 1824 Jan 29 M439-12
To 1824 Mar 09 10-0538
To 1824 May 20 M439-12
To 1824 May 24 M439-10
To 1824 Dec 25 10-1000
To 1829 Feb 09# 12-0488
To 1829 Feb 19# 12-0534
Re 1838 Jul mem DLC-51
To 1838 Jul 21 DLC-51
Adams Joseph H
Fr 1829 Jul 07 M639-1
Adams Littleton et al
Fr 1832 Mar 26 19-1546
Adams Louisa Catherine (Johnson)
To 1823 Dec 20 9-0814
To 1824 Dec 25 10-1000
Adams Martha
Fr 1818 Oct 27 fin DLC-26
Fr 1821 Apr 14 fin DLC-30
Fr 1824 Apr 29 fin DLC-33
Adams Matilda
Fr 1827 Sep 23# fin DLC-34
Adams Sally
To 1821 Apr 07# fin DLC-30
Adams & McKibben
Fr 1844 Feb 21 fin DLC-57
Fr 1845 Feb 21# fin DLC-57
Adams County MS Superior Court
To 1813 Mar 25 leg 3-0356
To 1813 Sep 25 leg 3-0477
To 1814 Mar 25 leg 3-0923
Addison A E
Fr 1842 Mar 14# fin DLC-54
Adjutant Juniata
Fr 1829 Aug 23 M124-120
Adkins James
Re 1832 Feb 10 par 19-1029

Adlum John
Fr 1829 M639-1
Africans shipwrecked
Re 1829 Jul 03 mem 13-0809
Agshire D R
Fr 1814 Mar 02 DLC-9
Aguirre Maximo de
Fr 1833 Feb 17 M639-6
Re 1833 Apr 29 22-1196
Aignon _____
Fr 1836 Sep 11 DLC-49
Aiken James
To 1803 Feb 1-1077
Aikman _____ (Ens)
Re 1814 Jan 04 DLC-8
Aine Ozanne
Re 1831 Sep 19 par 18-0830
Re 1831 Sep 19 par 18-0846
Aisquith William E
Re 1832 May 22 20-0549
Re 1833 Apr 15 22-1031
Fr 1836 May 28 M567-116
Aker Andrew et al
Fr 1834 Dec M639-22
Akin James
Fr 1829 Mar 13 M639-1
Fr 1829 Apr 16 M639-1
Alabama General Assembly
Fr 1836 Jan 09 29-1515
Fr 1836 Jan 09* M234-80
Fr 1837 Jan 02 32-1473
Alabama land purchase
Re 1818 Mar 02 leg 6-0064
Alabama legislators
Fr 1831 Feb 24 M22-27
Alabama public lands
Re 1830 Mar 06 T1223-1
Re 1830 Mar 06* 15-0305
Alabranche _____ (Col)
Fr 1815 Feb 27 4-0795
Alaman Lucas
Fr 1829 Dec 31 M54-1
Alba Peter
Fr 1832 Jan 15 M639-9
Fr 1832 Feb M124-131
Alberti Edwin R et al
Fr 1831 Dec 31 19-0467
Alcock Edward J
Fr 1835 Oct 25 M124-149
Fr 1836 Nov 17 32-0544
Aldrich James
Re 1831 Mar 03 par 17-0781
Re 1831 Mar 23 par 17-0934
Aldrich Timothy
Re 1829 Dec 18 par 14-1061
Alexander (pseudonym)
Fr 1837 Mar 06 33-1068
Alexander Adam Rankin
Fr 1825 May 30 DLC-33
To 1825 Jun 18 add 10-1312
Fr 1834 Aug 09 DLC-44
To 1834 Aug 10 26-0304
Alexander Charles
Fr 1842 Sep 28 DLC-54
Alexander D
Fr 1828 Dec 02 12-0295
To 1828 Dec 13 12-0324
Alexander Francis
Fr 1820 Jun 14 fin 7-1113
Alexander James
Fr 1818 Mar 13 DLC-24
Alexander John
Fr 1840 Dec 15 DLC-53
Alexander John et al
Fr 1837 Feb 01 33-0342
Alexander Lucy
Fr 1835 Oct 08 DLC-47
Alexander Robert J et al
Fr 1832 Dec 13 M639-27
Alexander Samuel
Re 1813 Oct 29 DLC-61
Alexander William
Fr 1824 Dec 10-0959
Fr 1828 Jun 04 DLC-35
To 1828 Jun 04 DLC-35
Fr 1828 Dec 26 DLC-36
Re 1832 mem 19-0511
Alexander William A
To 1813 Oct 10 DLC-61
To 1813 Nov 15 3-0601
Alexander William J et al
Fr 1844 Jun 15 36-0616
To 1844 Jul 36-0677
Alexandria (schooner)
Re 1835 Jul 17 fin DLC-46
Alexis Louis
To 1814 Dec 28 DLC-62
Fr 1814 Dec 28 DLC-15
Fr 1819 Aug 13 DLC-27
To 1819 cAug 30 DLC-27
To 1819 Sep 21 7-0671
Alfred (slave)
Re 1839 Jan 28 leg 34-0607
Algerian government
To 1830 Oct 26 16-0538
Algiers Dey of
To 1829 May 13 13-0310
To 1830 Apr 03 15-0574
Alix Gaud
Re 1831 Oct 08 par 18-0941
Allcorn John
Fr 1813 Dec 19 DLC-7
Fr 1813 Dec 19* DLC-61
To 1813 Dec 20 DLC-61
Fr 1813 Dec 29 DLC-8
Fr 1816 Aug 18 DLC-21
Allegheny County PA citizens
Fr 1832 Apr 03 M22-29
Allen E H
Fr 1841 Jul 27 DLC-53
Allen Heman
Fr 1831 Apr 11 17-1115
Allen Ira H
Fr 1829 Apr 18 13-0001
Allen J D
Fr 1840 Jun 06 DLC-52
Allen James
Fr 1814 Jan 09 DLC-8
To 1814 Mar 07 DLC-62
Fr 1827 Mar 22 DLC-72
To 1827 Mar 31 11-0519
To 1827 Mar 31* DLC-72
Fr 1836 Jul 08 M234-189
Allen James et al
Fr 1830 Jan 04 M639-21
Allen John
Re 1803 Feb 28 mem 1-1088
Fr 1814 Dec 19 DLC-14
Fr 1814 Dec 20 DLC-14

Allen John & Robert
Fr 1803 Jul 05 DLC-2
Allen John A
Fr 1814 Nov 10 DLC-14
Fr 1816 Jun 08 DLC-20
Fr 1816 Jun 08* M221-70
Fr 1816 Jul 25 DLC-21
To 1816 Jul 28 5-0335
Allen John B et al
Re 1835 May 16 M273-31
Allen John James
Fr 1835 Nov 12 M639-18
Allen John L
Fr 1829 Feb 03 M639-13
Fr 1829 Oct 19# M234-135
Fr 1830 Jan 23 M234-136
Fr 1833 Feb 11 DLC-42
Allen John W P
Re 1836 Mar 19 30-0823
Allen Jonathan
Fr 1836 Sep 30 31-1531
Allen Jonathan et al
Fr 1833 Sep 04 23-0617
Allen Lewis
Fr 1814 Mar 07 DLC-9
Allen M W
Fr 1818 Jun 12 fin 6-1043
Allen Matthew
Fr 1838 Aug 01 fin DLC-51
To 1840 Jul 21 chk DLC-53
Allen Paul
Fr 1824 Jul 08 DLC-33
Fr 1825 Mar 01 DLC-33
To 1825 cMar 05 DLC-33
Allen Richard C
To 1831 May 28# 17-1463
Fr 1831 Sep 25# M639-7
Allen Robert
Re 1803 Feb 28 mem 1-1088
To 1813 Oct 11 3-0523
To 1833 Jan 21-1258
Fr 1834 Aug 09 DLC-44
To 1834 Aug 10 26-0304
Allen Robert et al
Fr 1828 May 12 11-1244
To 1828 May 19 12-0014
Allen Samuel
Fr 1789 Jul 18 lnd 1-0066
Allen Samuel A
Fr 1814 Feb 09 DLC-8
To 1814 Feb 14 DLC-61
Allen Samuel Clesson
Fr 1836 Jun 11 M639-5
Allen Samuel M
Fr 1842 Dec fin DLC-54
Allen Stephen
Fr 1835 Feb 17 27-0541
Allen Stephen et al
Fr 1833 Dec 27 M639-7
Allen Sutton F
Fr 1821 May 10 DLC-30
Allen Waters
Fr 1814 Sep 21 DLC-12
Fr 1814 Oct 19 DLC-13
Fr 1814 Oct 19 DLC-13
Fr 1814 Oct 26 DLC-13
Fr 1814 Nov 15 DLC-14
Fr 1814 Dec 04 DLC-14
To 1814 Dec 23 DLC-62
Allen William
Fr 1827 Jun 02 fin DLC-34
To 1839 Dec 12# chk DLC-52
To 1839 Dec 24# fin DLC-52
To 1840 Jul 21 chk DLC-53
Allen William (1803-1879)
Fr 1833 Sep 30 M639-21
Fr 1835 Jan 13 M639-27
Fr 1835 Jan 21 M639-3
Fr 1835 Dec 31 M639-27
Fr 1837 Feb 05 M124-156
Allen William H
Fr 1830 Feb M222-28
Allen William Oliver
Fr 1810 Jan 10 DLC-4
Fr 1810 Jan 10* M222-4
Fr 1812 May 09 DLC-5
Alley Saul
Fr 1834 Jun 12 25-1320
Alley Saul et al
Fr 1829 Mar 26 12-1135
Re 1834 May 01 mem DLC-44
Allinson Samuel
Fr 1829 Jul 01 M639-16
Re 1831 Mar 02 17-0715
Allison Alexander
To 1820 Jun 04 7-1110
Allison Alexander et al
Fr 1812 Aug 03 lnd 2-1217
Allison David
Fr 1790 Nov 08 mem DLC-1
Fr 1795 May 13 fin 1-0255
Fr 1795 May 13# 1-0256
Re 1795 May 14 leg DLC-1
To 1795 May 14 lnd 1-0258
To 1795 May 14 lnd 1-0267
To 1795 May 14 lnd 1-0277
To 1795 cMay 14 lnd 1-0287
Re 1795 Aug fin DLC-1
Fr 1796 Jun 08 fin 1-0412
To 1796 Jun 11 lnd 1-0413
Fr 1796 Jun 11 leg DLC-1
Fr 1796 Jun 11 fin 1-0437
Re 1807 Jul 22 leg 2-0519
Re 1820 Jun 03 lnd 7-1106
Allison David (seaman)
Re 1832 Apr 24 M273-27
Allison J S
Fr 1829 Feb 16 M639-10
Allison James
Fr 1813 Oct 30 DLC-7
Allison John
To 1820 Jun 04 7-1110
Allison John et al
Re 1810 Dec 17 leg 2-0973
Allison John Stadler
Fr 1818 Mar 02 DLC-24
Alliston Joseph T
To 1814 Jun 21 chk DLC-10
Alpuente Francisco Bonaventura
To 1815 Feb 10 DLC-16
Alrick Herman
Fr 1834 Aug 26 M639-4
Alsbury Thomas J
Fr 1839 Apr 24 DLC-52
Re 1839 Nov 10 mem DLC-52
Re 1844 cMay leg 36-0462
Alsop Richard et al
Fr 1829 Mar 09 M639-17

Alston Robert West
To 1812 Nov 12 2-1273
Fr 1829 Jun 30 M639-16
Alston Willis
Fr 1826 Apr 26 DLC-33
To 1826 May 18 DLC-33
Alton Samson et al
Fr 1831 Feb 17 17-0567
Alva H Henry
Fr 1844 May 11 DLC-56
Amans Jacques
Fr 1840 Jan 10 DLC-52
Ambrister Robert
Re 1818 Apr 26 6-0460
Re 1818 Apr 28 DLC-24
Re 1818 Apr 28* 6-0510
Re 1818 Apr 29 5-0514
Re 1818 Apr 29* DLC-71
Fr 1819 Jan 12 7-0138
Amelung Ferdinand Louis
Fr 1816 Jun 04 DLC-20
Fr 1816 Jun 04* 5-0124
Fr 1816 Jun 04* M221-70
Ament George
Fr 1829 Jan 17 fin DLC-36
Ament Henry
Fr 1843 Jan 05 fin DLC-56
American Board of Commissioners for Foreign Missions
Fr 1831 Nov 03 M234-775
Fr 1831 Nov 03* 18-1184
To 1832 Sep 20-1446
Ames Ellis et al
Fr 1835 Mar 26 M639-5
Amicus Patria (pseudonym)
Fr 1830 Nov 29 DLC-38
Amonheizer John
Re 1831 Jan 03 par 17-0136
Amory Nathaniel
Fr 1829 cJun 13-0517
Anderson Alexander
Fr 1834 Mar 29 M179-77
Anderson Alexander Outlaw
Fr 1821 Mar 27 DLC-30
Fr 1841 Mar 30 DLC-53
Anderson Alfred et al
Fr 1838 May 20 DLC-51
Anderson Andrew
Re 1834 Apr 02 par 25-0556
Re 1834 Apr 02* par T967-1
Anderson Andrew et al
Fr 1831 Oct 12 M639-2
Anderson Branch H
Fr 1811 May 25 DLC-5
Anderson Charles E
To 1836 Oct 04 32-0048
Anderson Edmund
Fr 1844 Nov 18 DLC-57
Anderson Elizabeth (Glasgow) see also Donelson E G
Re 1826 Jun 08 leg 11-0226
To 1837 Oct 19 DLC-74
Anderson H J
Fr 1837 Jul 01 DLC-50
Anderson Henry
Re 1831 Aug 05 par 18-0421
Anderson Isaac
Fr 1829 May 18 13-0347
To 1829 May 28 13-0460
Anderson J J
Fr 1836 cNov M22-41
Anderson James J
Fr 1830 Jun 21 M567-49
Anderson James W
Fr 1829 Apr 09 M639-1
Fr 1829 Jul 25 M639-1
Anderson John (FL) et al
Fr 1832 Jan 24 19-0823
Anderson John (ME)
Fr 1829 Mar 06 M639-6
Fr 1829 Mar 07 12-0879
Fr 1829 May 04 M639-4
Anderson John (ME) et al
Fr 1833 Mar 02 M639-23
Fr 1837 Feb 03 M687-20
Anderson John (OH)
Fr 1844 Dec 04 DLC-57
Anderson John (TN)
To 1813 Mar 21 DLC-6
To 1813 Mar 21* DLC-61
Fr 1814 Oct 07 DLC-13
Fr 1814 Nov 25 DLC-14
Fr 1814 Dec 23 DLC-14
Anderson John W
Re 1830 Jan 06 M205-1
Anderson Joseph (Nashville)
Fr 1840 May 30 fin DLC-52
To 1842 Jan 22 DLC-74
To 1842 May 26 35-0743
Fr 1845 Feb 14 DLC-57
Anderson Joseph Inslee
Fr 1795 Dec 03 DLC-1
Fr 1796 Aug 04 DLC-1
Fr 1798 Apr 26 DLC-71
Fr 1802 Mar 20 1-0957
Fr 1806 Jan 05 DLC-3
Fr 1806 Jan 13 DLC-3
Fr 1806 Mar 24 DLC-4
Fr 1806 Oct 27 DLC-4
Fr 1806 Nov 08 lnd 2-0380
Fr 1807 Jan 28 DLC-4
Fr 1808 Jan 12 2-0604
Fr 1822 Aug 20 DLC-31
Fr 1822 Aug 20* 9-0254
To 1825 Feb 12 fin 10-1106
Fr 1825 Mar 26 DLC-33
Fr 1829 Feb 25 12-0581
Fr 1829 Apr 24 M639-16
Fr 1829 Sep 23 13-1404
Fr 1829 Oct 15 DLC-75
Fr 1831 17-0065
Fr 1831 Mar 02 M639-11
Fr 1832 Apr 13 20-0199
Fr 1832 Apr 17 M22-29
To 1833 Mar 22 22-0851
Fr 1834 Mar 14# 25-0208
To 1834 Apr 10# 25-0663
Fr 1836 Jun 13 31-0440
Anderson Martha J
Fr 1839 Mar 30 fin DLC-52
Anderson Nathaniel et al
Fr 1839 Dec 31 DLC-52
To 1840 Jan 01 34-1125
Anderson P C & Co
Fr 1818 Mar 06 fin DLC-24
Anderson Patton
Fr 1804 Sep 21 DLC-3
Fr 1805 Feb 16 DLC-71

Anderson Patton (cont)
Fr 1806 May 25# 2-0250
Re 1814 Aug leg 3-1209
Anderson Pleasant
Re 1813 Mar 13 DLC-61
Anderson Samuel
Fr 1832 Nov 06 DLC-41
Anderson Samuel Read
Fr 1845 Feb 24 DLC-57
Anderson Samuel T
Fr 1831 Apr 06 M221-111
Fr 1831 Nov 21 M179-71
Fr 1835 May 28 M124-147
Fr 1835 May 30 M124-147
Anderson William
Re 1794 Jan leg 1-0182
Anderson William et al
Fr 1831 Jun M639-7
Fr 1844 Feb 24 DLC-56
Anderson William E
Fr 1829 Apr 07 M639-4
Fr 1832 Oct 30 M639-4
Fr 1833 Aug 25 M639-3
Fr 1836 Feb 20 M639-9
Anderson William Preston
Fr 1802 Apr 29 DLC-2
Fr 1803 Sep 26 1-1172
To 1803 cNov 20 1-1251
Fr 1803 Dec 10 1-1253
Fr 1804 Sep 18 DLC-3
To 1805 Feb 16 fin 2-0012
Re 1805 Mar 15 mem 2-0023
To 1805 Jun 27 2-0068
Fr 1806 Feb 08 2-0156
Re 1806 Apr 08 leg 2-0208
Fr 1806 May 07 2-0233
Fr 1806 Jun 13 2-0271
Fr 1806 Jun 13 37-0489
To 1806 Sep 25 2-0344
Fr 1806 Dec 31 2-0415
Fr 1807 ___ 14 2-0420
To 1807 Jan 03 2-0431
Fr 1807 May 10 DLC-4
To 1807 Jun 16 2-0502
Fr 1808 DLC-75
Fr 1809 Jun 25 DLC-75
Fr 1810 cJul 01 DLC-4
Fr 1810 Nov 17 DLC-5
Fr 1811 Nov 16 DLC-5
Re 1812 Mar 11 mem DLC-5
Fr 1812 Jun 06 2-1094
To 1812 Jun 07 2-1096
To 1812 Aug 05 chk DLC-5
Re 1813 Jan 18 mem DLC-6
Fr 1813 Jul 15 3-0408
Fr 1814 Aug 19 DLC-11
Fr 1814 Aug 19 DLC-11
Fr 1814 Aug 19 DLC-11
Fr 1814 Aug 19 DLC-11
Fr 1814 Aug 20 DLC-11
Fr 1814 Sep 08 DLC-12
Fr 1814 Sep 14 DLC-12
Fr 1814 Oct 05 DLC-13
To 1814 Oct 17 DLC-62
Fr 1814 Nov 04 DLC-13
Fr 1814 Dec 02 DLC-14
Fr 1814 Dec 16 DLC-14
Fr 1815 Mar 31 DLC-17
Fr 1815 Apr 03 DLC-18
Fr 1815 Oct 17 DLC-71
Fr 1828 Oct 24 12-0246

Anderson & Hagan
To 1842 Mar 12 fin DLC-54
Anderson & Hamilton
Fr 1840 Dec 04 fin DLC-54
Fr 1840 Dec 04 fin DLC-53
Fr 1841 Jan 16# fin DLC-54
Fr 1842 Jan 01 fin DLC-56
Fr 1842 Jan 06 DLC-54
Fr 1842 Jan 08 DLC-54
To 1842 Jan 12 chk DLC-54
Anderson & Knox
Fr 1824 Jun 23 fin DLC-32
Fr 1825 Apr 22 fin DLC-35
Andrew Thomas et al
Fr 1831 Oct 12 M639-21
Andrew William R
Fr 1834 Nov 14 DLC-45
Andrews Christopher
Fr 1829 Jun 03 M639-11
To 1830 Feb 20# DLC-37
Andrews Henry et al
Fr 1829 Apr 24 M179-67
Andrews John
Fr 1837 Oct 05# fin DLC-53
To 1842 Jan 28 chk DLC-54
Andrews Philo
To 1821 Jul 19 M179-51
To 1821 Jul 24 M179-51
Andrews Robert
To 1813 Jan 05 DLC-5
To 1813 Jan 05* 2-1322
To 1813 Mar 03 DLC-61
To 1813 Mar 04 DLC-61
To 1813 Mar 04 DLC-61
To 1813 Mar 14 DLC-61
To 1813 Mar 14* 3-0306
To 1813 Mar 14 DLC-61
To 1813 Mar 14* 3-0308
To 1813 Mar 15 3-0309
To 1813 Mar 23 DLC-61
To 1813 Mar 23 3-0354
Fr 1813 Mar 23 DLC-61
To 1813 Mar 24 DLC-6
To 1813 Mar 24* DLC-61
To 1813 Mar 24 DLC-6
To 1813 Mar 24* DLC-61
Fr 1813 Mar 24 DLC-61
To 1813 Mar 25 M221-50
Fr 1813 May 25 DLC-75
To 1813 Jul 04 DLC-6
To 1813 Jul 12 DLC-6
Fr 1813 Jul 20 3-0418
Andrews Timothy Patrick
To 1831 Aug 02 chk DLC-39
Andrews William W
Re 1834 Oct 07 26-0528
Andrus & Judd
To 1833 Jun 17 23-0044
Fr 1833 Jun 17 23-0042
Anduze _____ (Abbe)
Fr 1840 Jan 08 add 34-1143
Angus Samuel
Fr 1829 Mar 23 M124-117
To 1829 Sep 29 13-1454
To 1829 Sep 29* DLC-60
To 1829 Sep 29* DLC-37
Fr 1829 Oct 15 M124-121
Anna Maria (schooner)
Re 1829 May 23 par 13-0382

Re 1829 May 23* par DLC-60
Re 1829 May 23* par T967-1
Anthony Burrington
Fr 1834 Jan 02 M639-9
Anthony Joseph
Fr 1803 May 05 fin 1-1120
To 1813 Dec 20 DLC-61
To 1813 Dec 20 DLC-61
Fr 1813 Dec 27 DLC-8
Fr 1813 Dec 28 DLC-8
Fr 1814 Jan 02 DLC-8
Fr 1814 Jan 31 DLC-8
To 1814 Mar 05 DLC-9
Fr 1814 Mar 05 DLC-9
Fr 1814 Mar 05 DLC-9
Re 1814 Mar 05 DLC-9
Re 1814 Mar 05 3-0898
Fr 1814 Sep 24 DLC-12
Anthony Joseph Biles
Fr 1833 Jun 08 M639-6
Anthony Michael H & Thomas
Fr 1814 Aug 29 fin DLC-66
Apenoose
Fr 1834 Sep 22 M234-729
Apenoose et al
Fr 1834 Aug 26 M234-729
Appalachicola treaty
Re 1833 Feb 13 M668-7
Re 1834 Apr 12 M668-7
Apperson Richard
Re 1811 May 18 2-1002
Re 1811 May 18 fin DLC-5
Applegate Amiah et al
Fr 1830 cNov M567-51
Appleton John C
Fr 1838 May 25 DLC-51
Appling Daniel
Fr 1816 Apr 18 DLC-20
Appointments and removals
Re c1829 mem 12-0354
Re 1829 Apr mem 12-1204
Re 1829 cMay mem 13-0212
Re 1829 cMay 18 mem 13-0349
Re 1830 mem DLC-38
Re 1830 cFeb mem 15-0083
Re 1830 Mar mem 15-0266
Re 1831 cDec 05 mem 19-0073
Appropriations and estimates
Re 1829 cJun mem 13-0520
Arabian horses
Re 1836 Aug 28 fin DLC-74
Arbuckle Mathew
Fr 1814 Jun 27 DLC-11
To 1814 Jul 24 DLC-62
Fr 1814 Aug 17 DLC-11
To 1814 Aug 23 DLC-62
Fr 1814 Aug 24 DLC-11
Fr 1814 Sep 08 DLC-12
Fr 1814 Sep 19 DLC-12
To 1814 Sep 30 DLC-62
Fr 1814 Oct 03 DLC-13
Fr 1814 Oct 25 DLC-13
Fr 1814 Dec 12 DLC-14
Fr 1815 Jan 24 4-0608
To 1815 Mar 05 DLC-62
Fr 1815 Mar 05 4-0816
To 1815 Mar 05 DLC-62
To 1815 Mar 05 DLC-62
Fr 1817 Dec 19 DLC-23
Fr 1818 Jan 06 DLC-23
Fr 1818 Jan 12 DLC-23
Fr 1818 Jan 12* 5-1245
To 1818 Jan 20 5-1297
Fr 1818 Feb 12 6-0017
Fr 1818 Feb 13 DLC-24
Fr 1818 Mar 05 6-0067
Fr 1818 Mar 06 DLC-24
Fr 1818 Mar 07 DLC-24
Fr 1818 Apr 28 DLC-24
Fr 1818 Jul 03 6-1105
Fr 1818 Jul 16 6-1126
To 1818 Sep 02 6-1276
Fr 1821 Feb 03 DLC-29
Fr 1821 Feb 15 DLC-29
Fr 1836 Aug 02 31-1215
Fr 1836 Aug 02* M234-236
To 1839 Oct 12# DLC-52
Arbuckle Sally Anne
To 1825 Feb 16 10-1118
Arbuthnot Alexander
Re 1818 Apr 26 6-0460
Re 1818 Apr 28 DLC-24
Re 1818 Apr 28* 6-0510
Re 1818 Apr 29 6-0514
Re 1818 Apr 29* DLC-71
Fr 1819 Jan 12 7-0138
Archer John
To 1807 Jan 12 fin DLC-4
To 1807 Feb 16 fin DLC-4
Archer Richard T
Fr 1833 Nov 16 23-1239
Fr 1834 Jun 30 25-1615
Archer Samuel et al
Fr 1829 Oct M639-27
Arfwedson Charles D
Re 1836 Nov 11 32-0478
Argenbright George
Fr 1813 Dec 17 DLC-7
To 1813 Dec 18 DLC-61
Fr 1816 Jan 20 DLC-20
Arkansas Territory General Assembly
Fr 1829 Nov 02 M222-26
Fr 1829 Nov 02 M222-26
Fr 1829 Nov 02 M222-26
Fr 1829 Nov 05 M222-26
Fr 1831 Nov 03 M234-29
Fr 1831 Nov 03* 18-1192
Armistead Henry M
Fr 1834 Oct 25 M625-62
Armistead Samuel
Fr 1810 Jul 16 DLC-4
Armistead W A
Fr 1834 Apr 21 M688-95
Armistead Walker Keith
Fr 1820 May 12 7-1092
Arms William et al
Fr 1841 Nov 26 DLC-54
To 1841 Dec 13 DLC-54
To 1841 Dec 13* 35-0530
Armstrong Alexander et al
Fr 1832 Apr 29 20-0408
Armstrong Andrew
Re 1831 cJan mem 17-0104
Fr 1833 Sep 09 M639-1
Armstrong Ellen
Re 1840 Aug 24 mem DLC-53
Armstrong Francis W
Fr 1815 Apr 06 DLC-18

Armstrong Francis W (cont)		
Fr 1815 Jun 22		DLC-18
Fr 1815 Jun 22		DLC-18
Fr 1815 Jun 22		4-1086
To 1816 Feb 22		DLC-20
Fr 1817 Mar 17#		5-0779
Fr 1826 May 07		DLC-33
Fr 1829 May 25		M639-11
Fr 1831 May 22		DLC-39
Fr 1831 May 24		DLC-39
Fr 1832 Sep 07		20-1500
Fr 1834 Sep 19#		DLC-44
Armstrong J N		
Fr 1842 Jan 13		DLC-54
Fr 1843 Nov 24		36-0019
Armstrong James Loudon		
Fr 1813 Nov 04		3-0562
Fr 1813 Nov 07		DLC-7
Fr 1813 Nov 07*		DLC-61
Fr 1813 Nov 07		DLC-7
Fr 1814 Nov 23		DLC-14
Re 1819 Sep 26	mem	DLC-27
Armstrong James Trooper		
To 1844 Jan 28		36-0153
Armstrong John (1758-1843)		
Fr 1813 Feb 06		DLC-6
Fr 1813 Feb 06*		DLC-61
Fr 1813 Feb 06*		M6-6
Fr 1813 Feb 06*		DLC-5
Fr 1813 Feb 06*		3-0267
Fr 1813 Feb 16		M6-6
Fr 1813 Feb 16*		DLC-61
Fr 1813 Feb 16*		DLC-6
To 1813 Mar 01		M221-54
To 1813 Mar 01*		DLC-61
To 1813 Mar 07		M221-54
To 1813 Mar 07*		DLC-61
To 1813 Mar 15		DLC-6
To 1813 Mar 15*		DLC-61
Fr 1813 Mar 22		3-0351
Fr 1813 Mar 22*		M6-6
Fr 1813 Mar 22*		DLC-6
To 1813 Mar 22		DLC-6
To 1813 Mar 22*		DLC-61
To 1813 Mar 22*		M221-54
To 1813 Mar 30		M221-54
To 1813 Mar 30*		DLC-61
To 1813 Apr 08		M22-7
Fr 1813 Apr 10		M6-6
Fr 1813 Apr 10*		3-0372
Fr 1813 Apr 10*		DLC-6
To 1813 Apr 21		M22-7
To 1813 Apr 24		3-0377
To 1813 May 10		DLC-6
To 1813 May 10*		M221-54
Fr 1813 Jun 21		M6-6
Fr 1813 Jun 21*		3-0404
Fr 1813 Jun 21*		DLC-75
To 1813 Nov 20		M221-54
To 1813 Nov 20*		DLC-7
To 1813 Dec 16		M221-54
To 1813 Dec 16*		DLC-7
To 1813 Dec 16*		DLC-61
To 1813 Dec 16*		3-0679
Fr 1813 Dec 28		DLC-8
Fr 1813 Dec 28*		3-0723
Fr 1813 Dec 28*		M6-7
To 1813 Dec 30		M221-54
To 1813 Dec 30*		DLC-61
To 1813 Dec 30*		3-0743

To 1814	3-0776
Fr 1814 Jan 13	DLC-8
Fr 1814 Jan 13*	M6-7
To 1814 Jan 31	3-0832
To 1814 Jan 31*	DLC-8
To 1814 Jan 31*	DLC-61
Fr 1814 Feb 04	DLC-8
Fr 1814 Feb 04*	3-0850
Fr 1814 Feb 04*	M6-7
Fr 1814 Feb 28	DLC-9
To 1814 Apr 02	M221-54
To 1814 Apr 02*	DLC-10
To 1814 Apr 07	DLC-66
To 1814 Apr 25	M221-54
To 1814 Apr 25*	DLC-10
To 1814 Apr 25*	3-0988
To 1814 May 08	3-1005
To 1814 May 08*	DLC-10
Fr 1814 May 22	DLC-10
Fr 1814 May 22*	M6-7
Fr 1814 May 22*	3-1042
Fr 1814 May 24	DLC-10
Fr 1814 May 24*	3-1052
Fr 1814 May 28	DLC-10
Fr 1814 May 28	DLC-10
Fr 1814 May 28*	3-1074
Fr 1814 May 31	DLC-10
Fr 1814 May 31*	M15-3
Fr 1814 May 31*	3-1080
To 1814 Jun 08	M221-63
To 1814 Jun 08*	DLC-10
To 1814 Jun 08*	3-1084
To 1814 Jun 13	M221-63
To 1814 Jun 13*	DLC-62
To 1814 Jun 13*	DLC-10
To 1814 Jun 13*	3-1093
To 1814 Jun 13	M221-63
To 1814 Jun 13*	DLC-62
To 1814 Jun 20	3-1098
To 1814 Jun 20*	DLC-10
To 1814 Jun 25	M221-63
To 1814 Jun 25*	DLC-62
To 1814 Jun 25*	3-1105
Fr 1814 Jun 25	DLC-11
Fr 1814 Jun 25*	M6-7
To 1814 Jun 27	M221-63
To 1814 Jun 27*	M200-9
To 1814 Jun 27*	DLC-62
To 1814 Jun 27*	3-1114
Fr 1814 Jul 02	DLC-11
Fr 1814 Jul 02*	M6-7
Fr 1814 Jul 02*	3-1117
Fr 1814 Jul 12	DLC-11
Fr 1814 Jul 12*	M6-7
Fr 1814 Jul 12*	3-1120
To 1814 Jul 14	M221-63
To 1814 Jul 14*	DLC-62
To 1814 Jul 14*	3-1136
Fr 1814 Jul 18	DLC-11
Fr 1814 Jul 18*	3-1145
To 1814 Jul 24	M221-63
To 1814 Jul 24*	DLC-11
To 1814 Jul 24*	3-1161
To 1814 Jul 25	3-1169
To 1814 Jul 25*	DLC-62
To 1814 Jul 26	DLC-62
To 1814 Jul 26*	3-1171
To 1814 Jul 30	M221-63
To 1814 Jul 30*	DLC-62

To 1814 Jul 30*		M200-9
To 1814 Jul 31		M221-63
To 1814 Jul 31*		DLC-62
To 1814 Jul 31*		3-1193
Fr 1814 Aug 10		DLC-11
Fr 1814 Aug 10*		M6-7
To 1814 Aug 10		M221-63
To 1814 Aug 10*		DLC-62
To 1814 Aug 10*		3-1271
To 1814 Aug 10		M221-63
To 1814 Aug 10*		DLC-62
To 1814 Aug 10*		3-1273
Fr 1814 Aug 20		DLC-11
Fr 1814 Aug 20*		M6-7
Fr 1814 Aug 20*		3-1305
To 1814 Aug 23		3-1308
To 1814 Aug 23*		DLC-62
To 1814 Aug 23*		M200-9
To 1814 Aug 25		3-1344
To 1814 Aug 25		M221-63
To 1814 Aug 25*		M200-9
To 1814 Aug 25*		DLC-62
To 1814 Aug 25*		DLC-11
To 1814 Aug 30		M221-63
To 1814 Aug 30*		DLC-62
To 1814 Aug 30*		M200-9
To 1814 Sep 05		4-0174
To 1814 Sep 05*		DLC-62
To 1814 Sep 05*		M200-9
To 1814 Sep 08		M221-63
To 1814 Sep 08*		DLC-62
To 1814 Sep 08*		M200-9
To 1814 Sep 09		M221-63
To 1814 Sep 09*		DLC-62
To 1814 Sep 09*		M200-9
To 1814 Sep 16		M221-63
To 1814 Sep 16*		DLC-62
To 1814 Sep 17		M221-63
To 1814 Sep 17*		DLC-62
To 1814 Sep 17		M221-63
To 1814 Sep 17*		DLC-62
To 1814 Sep 20		M221-63
To 1814 Sep 20*		DLC-62
To 1814 Sep 20*		DLC-12
To 1814 Sep 20*		M200-9
Fr 1824 Jun 06		DLC-32
To 1824 Jun 29		DLC-32
Fr 1829 Mar 30		M639-9
Armstrong John (VA)		
Fr 1804 Oct 22		1-1399
Armstrong John M		
To 1813 Aug 09		DLC-6
To 1813 Aug 09*		DLC-8
Fr 1813 Aug 23		DLC-71
Fr 1816 Feb 08		DLC-20
To 1816 Feb 13		DLC-62
Armstrong Margaret D		
Fr 1833 Aug 17		23-0357
Fr 1833 Dec 10		24-0431
Armstrong Martin		
Fr 1796#		1-0335
Fr 1796 May 09	lnd	1-0382
Fr 1796 May 09	lnd	1-0384
Re 1801 Jan 08	leg	1-0832
Fr 1801 Jan 08	leg	1-0834
Re 1803 Feb 28	leg	1-1090
Fr 1803 Aug 29		DLC-3
Armstrong R & W		
Fr 1822 cMay	fin	DLC-58
Armstrong Robert		
Fr 1826 Jan	fin	DLC-33
Fr 1826 Jul 16	fin	DLC-34
Fr 1831 Mar 07		DLC-39
Fr 1833 Aug 15		M639-3
Fr 1834 Oct 14		DLC-44
Fr 1834 Oct 20		DLC-44
Fr 1834 Nov 04		DLC-45
Fr 1835 Jun 01		DLC-46
Fr 1835 Jul 31		DLC-46
Fr 1835 Jul 31#		DLC-49
Fr 1835 Aug 13		DLC-46
To 1835 Aug 13#	fin	DLC-46
To 1835 Sep 15		DLC-47
Fr 1835 Sep 29		DLC-47
Fr 1835 Oct 28		DLC-47
Fr 1835 Nov 08		DLC-47
Fr 1835 Nov 14		DLC-47
To 1835 Nov 25#		DLC-47
Fr 1835 Nov 27		DLC-47
Fr 1835 Dec 07		DLC-47
Fr 1835 Dec 19		DLC-47
Fr 1835 Dec 29		DLC-47
Fr 1836 Feb 03		DLC-47
Fr 1836 Mar 26		DLC-47
Fr 1836 Apr 25		DLC-48
To 1836 Apr 25#	fin	DLC-48
Fr 1836 May 06		DLC-48
Fr 1836 May 27		DLC-48
Fr 1836 May 28#		DLC-48
Fr 1836 Jun 24#		DLC-48
Fr 1836 Jun 27		DLC-48
Fr 1836 Jul 22		DLC-48
Fr 1836 Aug 15		DLC-48
Fr c1837 Aug		37-0364
Fr c1837 Aug		37-0366
Fr 1837 Aug 12		33-1419
Fr 1837 Oct 07		33-1511
Fr 1837 Oct 10		DLC-50
Fr 1837 Oct 12		DLC-50
Fr 1837 Nov 14		DLC-50
Fr 1838 Jan		34-0155
To 1838 Jan 09		34-0174
Fr 1838 Jan 11		DLC-51
To 1838 Oct 29#		DLC-51
Fr 1838 Dec 07		34-0551
Fr 1839 Jan 07		DLC-51
Fr 1839 Feb 20		34-0656
To 1839 Feb 20	fin	DLC-53
To 1839 Jul 01	chk	DLC-52
Fr 1839 Aug 26		34-0874
Fr 1839 Sep 26		34-0955
Fr 1839 Nov 06		34-1046
Fr 1839 Dec 10		34-1078
Fr c1840		37-0392
To 1840 Jan 12#	fin	DLC-52
Fr 1840 Apr 25		DLC-52
To 1840 Jun 26		DLC-74
Fr 1840 Jul 13		DLC-53
To 1840 Jul 21	chk	DLC-53
Fr 1840 Aug 14		DLC-53
Fr 1840 Sep 23		DLC-53
Fr 1840 Oct 18		35-0058
Fr 1841 Feb 19		DLC-53
Fr 1841 May 26		35-0308
To 1841 Aug 02#		DLC-53
To 1842 Feb 14		35-0625
Fr 1842 Apr 02		35-0669
Fr 1842 Aug 11		DLC-54

Armstrong Robert (cont)
Fr 1843 cApr DLC-55
To 1843 Apr 08 35-1300
To 1843 May 26 35-1356
To 1843 Aug 07# DLC-55
Fr 1843 Sep 02 DLC-55
Fr 1843 Oct 06 DLC-55
Fr 1843 Oct 07 DLC-55
To 1843 Nov 11 DLC-74
To 1843 Dec 12# DLC-56
Fr 1844 Jan 22 DLC-56
Fr 1844 Feb 28 DLC-56
Fr 1844 May 08 DLC-56
To 1844 May 23# DLC-56
Fr 1844 May 25 DLC-56
Fr 1844 Jun 01 DLC-57
Fr 1844 cJun 02 36-0571
To 1844 Oct 17 36-0951
To 1844 Oct 22 36-0954
To 1844 Oct 30 36-0968
Fr 1844 Oct 31 36-0969
Fr 1844 Dec 13 M873-6
Fr c1845 Jan 36-1282
Fr 1845 Jan 22 M873-13
Fr 1845 Feb 03 M873-32
Fr 1845 Feb 03 M873-65
Fr 1845 Mar 31 37-0114
Re 1845 May 16 37-0210
Armstrong Robert et al
Fr 1834 Dec 26-1106
Armstrong Samuel T
Fr 1841 Nov 09 DLC-54
Armstrong William
Fr 1829 Mar M639-20
Fr 1833 Feb 11 22-0336
Arndt John P et al
Fr 1832 Jul 09 M234-315
Arnold Robert
Re 1833 Mar 22 par T967-1
Re 1833 Mar 22* par 22-0853
Re 1833 Jun 13 par 23-0007
Re 1833 Aug 28 23-0479
Re 1833 Sep 27 par 23-0884
Arnold Thomas D
Fr 1826 Oct 24 11-0387
Arnold William Thomas
Fr 1832 Mar 12 19-1394
Arthur William
Fr 1819 May 08 fin 7-0507
Artillery improvements
Re 1829 Apr mem 12-1205
Ash Michael Woolston
Fr 1833 Apr 20 M639-20
Fr 1834 Oct 17 M639-20
Fr 1836 Jan 25 M639-27
Fr 1836 Jan 27 M639-3
Fr 1836 Mar 22 30-0860
Fr 1836 Jun M639-18
Fr 1836 Jun 30 M567-122
Fr 1836 Dec 25 32-1314
Fr 1836 Dec 27 32-1349
Ash Samuel
To 1798 Jan 17 1-0584
To 1798 Feb 10 1-0610
Ashby James A
Fr 1842 Dec 01 DLC-54
Ashley William Henry
Fr 1831 Mar 15 M234-883
Fr 1832 Jun 17 20-0763
Fr 1836 Jun 20 M567-127
Ashmead William
Fr 1829 Feb 25 12-0585
Ashton Henry
Fr 1829 Apr 14 M639-1
Fr 1829 Apr 24 M639-16
Fr 1830 cJan 29 15-0061
Fr 1830 Nov 01 M639-17
Fr 1830 Nov 10 M639-17
Fr 1831 Jan 24 17-0341
Fr 1831 May 29 M124-128
Fr 1833 Feb 18 M639-5
Ashton Henry et al
Re 1830 Mar 24 15-0445
Re 1830 Mar 24 15-0446
Ashton James
Re 1831 Mar 31 par 17-1016
Ashton John H
Fr 1835 May 20 DLC-46
Ashton Leonard
Re 1833 Feb 02 par 22-0242
Fr 1840 May 09 DLC-52
Aspinwall Thomas
Re 1831 Aug 27 mem 18-0606
Fr 1834 Oct 12# T168-14
Assereto de Seravalle Stephen
Fr 1834 Dec 14 T357-1
Aston Alexander
Fr 1839 Nov 23 34-1057
Astor John Jacob et al
Fr 1829 Jun M639-20
Astor William Backhouse
Fr 1833 May 27# M179-76
Atchison Daniel D
Fr 1844 Mar 30 DLC-56
Atkins James
Re 1832 Jan 04 par 19-0603
Atkins Joseph
To 1796 Oct 24 lnd 1-0453
Fr 1810 Jan 24 DLC-4
Atkins Joseph Jr
Fr 1806 Dec 13 mem DLC-4
Atkinson Henry
Fr 1819 Apr 17 DLC-26
Fr 1819 May 04 DLC-27
To 1819 May 15 DLC-63
Fr 1819 May 16 DLC-27
Fr 1819 May 23 DLC-27
Re 1819 Jun 01 7-0540
Fr 1819 Jun 07 DLC-27
Fr 1819 Jun 19 DLC-27
Fr 1819 Jul 30 DLC-27
Fr 1819 Sep 06 DLC-27
Fr 1819 Oct 03 DLC-27
Fr 1819 Nov 23 DLC-28
Fr 1819 Nov 23* M221-86
Fr 1819 Dec 05 DLC-28
Fr 1819 Dec 08 DLC-28
Fr 1819 Dec 15 M221-86
To 1819 Dec 30 DLC-63
To 1820 Feb 21 DLC-63
To 1820 Feb 21* M221-86
Fr 1820 Apr 28 7-1081
To 1820 Jun 26 DLC-63
To 1820 Sep 06 DLC-63
To 1820 Nov 11# DLC-63
Fr 1820 Nov 14 7-1414
Fr 1820 Nov 17 M221-89
To 1820 Dec 08 DLC-63
Fr 1820 Dec 08 8-0011
To 1821 Feb 08 DLC-63

Atkinson John
Re 1830 May 04 par 15-0878
Atkinson Richard
Fr 1814 Jul 19 DLC-11
Fr 1814 Jul 29 DLC-11
Fr 1814 Jul 31 DLC-11
Fr 1814 Aug 08 DLC-11
Fr 1814 Aug 08 DLC-11
Atlee Samuel Yorke
Fr 1836 Dec 24 DLC-49
To 1837 Jan 17 32-1591
Atwater Caleb
Fr 1824 Jun 24 DLC-72
Fr 1824 Nov 01 DLC-33
Fr 1827 Sep 04 DLC-34
Fr 1827 Sep 20 DLC-34
Fr 1827 Nov 30 11-0936
Fr 1828 Feb 29 DLC-35
Fr 1829 Jan 29 DLC-72
Fr 1829 Feb 16 M639-1
Fr 1829 Feb 28 DLC-36
Fr 1830 Jan 13 DLC-37
Fr 1831 Mar 11 M22-27
Atwood Henry C
Fr 1843 Jul 20 DLC-55
Auburns John
Fr 1836 Sep 10 M221-117
Fr 1836 Sep 10* 31-1436
Auld James
Re 1832 Jul 21 par 20-1199
Austin Charles et al
Fr 1831 Jul 21 M639-14
Austin Daniel P
Fr 1836 Oct 18 M687-1
Austin James et al
Re 1814 Dec 03 4-0379
Austin John
Fr 1821 Apr 29 fin DLC-70
Fr 1821 May 01 fin DLC-70
Fr 1821 May 01 fin DLC-30
Fr 1821 May 07 fin DLC-70
Fr 1821 May 07 fin DLC-70
Austin John W et al
Re 1835 May 16 M273-32
Austin Stephen Fuller
Fr 1836 Apr 15 DLC-48
Fr 1836 Apr 15* 30-1179
Fr 1836 Jul 04 31-0784
Fr 1836 Jul 04* M221-116
Fr 1836 Jul 04* M179-82
Fr 1836 Dec 14# DLC-49
Austin Thomas
Fr 1813 Nov 03 DLC-7
Austria shipping
Re 1829 May 11 T1223-1
Re 1829 May 11* 13-0276
Re 1829 Jun 03 T1223-1
Re 1829 Jun 03* 13-0557
Austria treaty
Re 1830 Feb 11 15-0123
Re 1831 Feb 10 17-0486
Avery Cyrus H
Fr 1831 Dec 10# M567-58
Avery Latham B
To 1831 Dec 19 19-0351
Avery Waightstill
To 1788 Aug 12 1-0043
Awl William Maclay
Fr 1835 Feb 17 DLC-45
Axim Micajah
Fr 1804 Apr 12 fin DLC-3
Ayer Ebenezer H et al
Fr 1837 Feb 17 M687-20
Ayer Eli et al
Fr 1837 Feb M687-20
Ayer Lewis M
Fr 1814 Jul 20 DLC-11
Ayer Richard A et al
Fr 1836 Jan 23 M639-5
Ayer Thomas J
Fr 1820 Nov 01 DLC-29
Ayers William L
Fr 1844 Sep 08 DLC-57
Aymar Benjamin & Co
Fr 1834 Feb 11 T690-1

Babbidge Perez et al
Fr 1837 Feb 14 M687-20
Babbitt Jacob et al
Fr 1835 Sep 16 M639-21
Babcock John C
Fr 1840 Jun 26 DLC-52
Baber A W
Fr 1818 Mar 06 DLC-24
Baber James
Fr 1842 Dec 13 DLC-54
Bacharie J & Co
Fr 1835 Jun 25 28-0775
Backman L Augustus
To 1838 Aug 06 34-0419
Backus Christopher
Fr 1815 Feb 08 DLC-16
Bacon L C
Fr 1834 Nov 30 DLC-45
Bacon Samuel
Fr 1835 Aug 13 fin DLC-46
Bagby Arthur Pendleton
Fr 1839 Jan 30 DLC-51
To 1840 Feb 20 DLC-52
Bagby Arthur Pendleton et al
Fr 1840 Sep 19 35-0009
Bailey Benjamin
Fr 1829 Apr 06 M639-22
Fr 1829 Apr 06* 12-1275
Fr 1829 Jun 26 M639-20
Fr 1829 Jul 02 13-0792
Fr 1831 Feb 23 17-0634
Fr 1831 cSep M639-18
Bailey Benjamin et al
Fr 1831 Apr 29 17-1262
Bailey Edward B
Fr 1835 Sep 19 M639-18
Bailey John
Re c1835 mem 27-0052
Bailey S T
Fr 1831 Mar 24 17-0940
Bailey William L et al
Fr 1831 Jan 29 M639-1
Bailey & Kitchen
Fr 1833 Apr 30# fin DLC-43
Bailey Keeler & Remsen
Fr 1833 Apr 23 M639-16
Bain George M
Fr 1829 Jul 31 M124-119
Bain J R
Fr 1842 May 11# fin DLC-54

Bainbridge Allen
Fr 1840 Jun 24 34-1441
Bainbridge Henry
Fr 1837 Jan M22-41
Bainbridge William et al
Fr 1831 Jan 11 17-0229
Baird Felix W et al
Fr 1832 Nov 05 DLC-41
Baird Henry S et al
Fr 1834 Nov 17 26-0941
Baird John
Fr 1806 cFeb 01 2-0133
Fr 1811 Jan 01 fin DLC-5
Fr 1817 Aug 21# fin DLC-23
Baird Robert
Re 1835 Jan 22 27-0274
Baird Thomas
Fr 1830 Dec 22 16-1538
Baird Timothy
Re 1806 Jan 27 leg 2-0124
Baker Artemas et al
Fr 1833 Feb 13 22-0360
Baker B F
To 1843 Nov 27# fin DLC-56
Baker Baxter
Fr 1815 Aug 22 DLC-19
Baker Charlotte (Lewis)
Fr 1820 Sep 10 lnd 7-1315
Baker D D
Fr 1831 Sep 01 M639-6
Baker D F
Fr 1831 Aug 06 M688-78
Baker David Jewett
Fr 1830 Dec 31 17-0047
Fr 1831 May 10 M222-29
Fr 1836 Mar 12 30-0751
Baker Isaac Lewis
To 1814 Sep 04 DLC-62
Fr 1814 Sep 06 DLC-12
Fr 1814 Sep 07 DLC-12
Fr 1815 Feb 25 DLC-17
Fr 1815 Jun 30 DLC-18
Fr 1815 Sep 03 DLC-19
To 1815 Sep 12 DLC-19
Fr 1815 Sep 12 DLC-19
Fr 1815 Nov 09 DLC-19
Fr 1816 Apr 02 DLC-20
Fr 1816 Jun 02 M221-70
Fr 1816 Jun 08 DLC-20
Fr 1816 Nov 06 DLC-21
Fr 1817 Apr 16 DLC-22
Fr 1818 Dec 28 DLC-26
Fr 1819 Apr 07 DLC-26
Fr 1819 Jun 07 M566-123
Fr 1820 Sep 10 lnd 7-1315
Fr 1820 Oct 24 DLC-75
Fr 1820 Oct 24* DLC-72
Fr 1821 Feb 18 DLC-29
To 1821 Dec 14 lnd 8-1365
Fr 1823 Feb 14 DLC-32
Fr 1823 Feb 26 DLC-32
Fr 1823 May 03 DLC-32
Fr 1825 Mar 21 DLC-33
Fr 1826 Aug 20 DLC-34
Fr 1827 Apr 21 DLC-34
Fr 1827 Sep 01 DLC-34
Baker J
Re 1845 May mem 37-0167
Baker Jacob
Fr 1834 Oct 14 DLC-44
Re 1835 May 07 par 28-0301
Baker James McCutcheon
Re 1837 Jan 26 par 33-0165
Baker John
To 1813 Nov 23 3-0622
Fr 1840 Dec 23# fin DLC-53
Baker John H et al
Fr 1829 cJun M639-4
Fr 1830 cSep 28 M639-25
Baker John Martin
Re 1831 Oct 20 18-1065
Baker Joshua (d 1816)
Fr 1814 Dec 27 DLC-15
Fr 1814 Dec 28 DLC-15
Fr 1815 Jan 02 DLC-15
Fr 1815 Jan 27 DLC-16
Fr 1815 Feb 02 DLC-16
Baker Joshua
Fr 1820 Sep 01 M688-14
Baker Nathaniel B
Fr 1835 Mar 01 DLC-45
Baker Paul
Fr 1835 Apr fin 27-1398
Baker William
Fr 1807 Aug 26 fin DLC-4
Bakewell Benjamin
To 1825 Mar 08# 10-1220
Bakewell Page & Bakewell
Fr 1832 Feb 02 fin DLC-42
Balch Alfred
Fr 1823 Mar 11 DLC-32
Fr 1823 Mar 20 DLC-72
Fr 1826 Oct 12 DLC-34
Fr 1827 Jan 11-0454
Fr 1827 Jun 25 11-0713
Fr 1827 Nov 26 DLC-35
Fr 1828 Sep 03 DLC-35
Fr 1830 Jan 08 DLC-37
Fr 1831 May 07 DLC-39
Fr 1831 cJun 25 18-0102
Fr 1831 Jul 21 DLC-39
Fr 1831 Sep 14 DLC-40
Fr 1833 Nov 29 23-1325
Re 1834 Oct 03 mem DLC-44
Fr 1834 Oct 30 DLC-44
Fr 1834 Dec 19 DLC-45
Fr 1835 Feb 03 DLC-45
Fr 1835 Feb 12 DLC-45
To 1835 Feb 16 DLC-45
Fr 1835 Apr 04 DLC-46
Fr 1835 Aug 12 DLC-46
Fr 1835 Aug 26 DLC-46
To 1835 Sep 06 DLC-46
Re c1835 Nov mem 29-0402
To 1835 Nov 05 DLC-47
Fr 1836 Aug 06 DLC-48
Fr 1837 Jan 17 DLC-49
Fr 1837 Dec 22 DLC-50
Fr 1843 Apr 06 DLC-55
To 1843 Dec 08 36-0046
Balch L P W
Fr 1831 Feb 08 M22-27
Balch S B
Fr 1829 Jun 17 M639-16
Baldridge Josiah W
Fr 1840 Dec 28 DLC-53

Baldwin Benjamin
Fr 1818 Jun 12 fin DLC-69
Fr 1818 Jun 12* fin 6-1044
Baldwin Cornelius C
Fr 1835 Dec 28 M639-21
Baldwin Ebenezer
Fr 1829 Jun 23 M639-2
Baldwin Eli
Fr 1829 Aug 14 13-1129
Baldwin Ethan
To 1832 Jul 06 chk DLC-41
Baldwin Frederick
Fr 1821 Mar 01 DLC-29
Baldwin Henry
Fr 1823 Jan 02 DLC-31
To 1823 Jan 24 9-0425
To 1823 Jan 24* DLC-32
To 1824 May 20 10-0736
Fr 1824 Oct 10 DLC-33
To 1825 Apr 28 10-1251
To 1825 Apr 30 10-1254
To 1826 Mar 29 11-0178
Fr 1828 Apr 01 DLC-35
Fr 1828 Apr 11 DLC-35
Fr 1828 Nov 16 DLC-35
Fr 1829 Feb 15 DLC-36
Fr 1829 Nov 23 14-0549
To 1830 Feb 01# M639-3
Fr 1831 Jul 24# DLC-39
Fr 1831 Jul 26 M179-70
Fr 1831 Oct 18 DLC-40
To 1831 Oct 31 18-1160
To 1831 Oct 31* DLC-40
Fr 1831 Nov 03 DLC-40
To 1831 Nov 07 18-1216
Fr 1831 Nov 20 18-1325
Fr 1831 Dec# DLC-43
To 1832 Jan 26 19-0865
To 1832 Jan 26 19-0866
To 1832 Feb 27 DLC-40
To 1832 Mar 06 19-1323
To 1832 Mar 07 chk DLC-40
Fr 1832 Apr 13 20-0203
To 1832 Apr 27 20-0393
Fr 1832 May 13 DLC-40
To 1832 May 28 20-0606
To 1832 May 28* DLC-40
Fr 1832 Jun 23 M22-29
Fr 1832 Nov 15 DLC-41
Fr 1835 Oct 26 29-0351
Baldwin Henry et al
Fr 1828 Nov 24 DLC-35
To 1828 cNov 12 DLC-36
Fr 1830 Oct 28 M639-14
Fr 1831 Jan 10 M639-11
Baldwin Henry Jr
Fr 1833 Dec 26# lnd DLC-43
Fr 1843 Jan 30 DLC-55
Baldwin Loammi
To 1833 Dec 20# DLC-43
Fr 1835 Jul 11# M124-154
Baldwin Marion Augustus et al
Fr 1844 Jul 08 DLC-57
Baldwin Roger Sherman
Fr 1833 Dec 27 24-0595
Balestier Joseph
Re 1833 Oct 11 23-1002
Ball Miriam
To 1831 Oct 17 chk DLC-40
Ball R M
Fr 1820 Jan 05 DLC-28
Ball William
Fr 1839 Feb 11 DLC-51
Ballagh James et al
Fr 1834 Oct 06 26-0508
Ballance Charles
Fr 1834 Mar 25 25-0355
Ballant Henry S
Fr 1837 Feb 16# DLC-50
Ballard Charles
Fr 1831 Aug 15 M22-28
Ballard Christopher
Fr 1810 Dec 19 lnd 2-0974
Ballard David G
Fr 1821 Sep 24 fin DLC-70
Ballard Riland
Re 1836 cJul 01 par 31-0731
Ballard William
Fr 1807 Mar 24 DLC-4
Fr 1808 Jan 03 fin DLC-4
Baltimore Hannah
Re 1830 Feb 02 par T967-1
Baltimore & Potomac Steam Packet Co
Fr 1834 Aug 11 fin DLC-44
Fr 1834 Dec 22# fin DLC-45
Baltimore citizens
To 1819 Mar 01 add 7-0391
Fr 1829 Nov 03 M179-67
To 1830 Oct 14 DLC-73
Baltimore conspiracy
Re 1834 Apr mem 25-0518
Baltimore Jackson Committee
To 1828 Dec 25 12-0333
Baltzell Thomas
Fr 1835 Sep 05 28-1522
Bancroft Benjamin
Fr 1841 Feb 11 DLC-53
Bancroft George
Fr 1839 Jun 10 34-0815
To 1839 Jun 25 34-0831
Fr 1841 Nov 11 DLC-54
To 1841 Dec 09 35-0526
To 1844 Jun 24 36-0640
To 1844 Nov 16 36-1023
Banger Timothy
Fr 1815 Aug 10 DLC-19
Fr 1815 Aug 10* 4-1156
Bangs Benjamin et al
Fr 1836 Oct M687-12
Fr 1836 Oct* M639-9
Bank deposits
Re 1833 Dec 26 mem DLC-43
Bank national
Re c1829 mem 12-0356
Bank note circulation act
Re 1836 Apr 14 DLC-48
Bank of Tennessee
Re 1821 Apr 14 mem DLC-30
Fr 1840 Jul 03# fin DLC-53
To 1842 Jun 01 chk DLC-54
Bank of the Metropolis
To 1837 cMar 01 mem 33-0946a
Fr 1837 Aug 01 fin DLC-50
Bank of the United States
Re 1829 Nov 14-0297
Re 1830 Nov mem 16-0618
Re c1832 DLC-75
Re 1832 cJan mem 19-0529

Bank of the United States (cont)
Re 1832 Nov mem 21-0242
Re 1832 Nov mem 21-0246
Re c1833 21-1229
Re c1833 mem 37-0302
Re 1833 cMar mem 22-0565
Re 1833 May mem 22-1247
Re 1833 Sep 03 mem 23-0603
Re 1833 Sep 10 mem 23-0673
Re 1833 Sep 19 mem 23-0786
Bankhead ______
Re 1836 Nov mem DLC-49
Bankhead James
To 1815 Dec 23 DLC-62
Fr 1829 Mar 16 12-1015
Bankhead Thomas Mann Randolph
Fr 1844 Dec 30 DLC-57
Bankruptcy laws
Re 1829 cSep mem 13-1220
Banks Cuthbert
To 1806 Mar 2-0184
To 1810 Jun 18 2-0958
Banks Ephraim et al
Fr 1831 Jan 21 17-0325
Banks Henry
Fr 1826 Feb 10 DLC-33
Fr 1826 Mar 02 DLC-33
Fr 1826 May 28 DLC-33
Fr 1826 May 29 DLC-34
Fr 1826 Jul 10 DLC-34
Fr 1827 May 18 DLC-34
Fr 1827 Jun 04 DLC-34
Fr 1827 Oct 12 DLC-34
Fr 1828 Sep 11 DLC-35
Fr 1828 Sep 30 DLC-35
Banks J
Fr 1831 Aug 02 DLC-39
Banks Linn et al
Fr 1832 Jan 19 19-0769
Banks William et al
Fr 1821 Apr 12 DLC-30
Bantz Henry Jr
Fr 1828 Sep 06 DLC-35
Baptiste John
Re 1818 May 07 6-0659
Barbee Gabriel T
Fr 1840 Jun 05 34-1392
Fr 1843 Dec 13 DLC-56
Barber Noyes et al
Fr 1829 Feb 26 12-0590
Barbour James
To 1825 cMar 09 M22-17
To 1825 Apr 24 M688-38
To 1825 Jun 10 M22-17
To 1825 Aug 06 10-1403
Fr 1825 Sep 03 M91-1
To 1825 Nov 16 M688-38
Fr 1826 Apr 18 DLC-33
To 1826 May 06 M688-38
To 1826 Jul 22 DLC-34
To 1826 Jul 22* M22-17
To 1826 Jul 22 M221-103
To 1826 Jul 22* DLC-34
Fr 1826 Oct 11 M6-12
To 1827 Apr 28 11-0569
Fr 1827 May 18 M565-2
Barbour John Strode
Fr 1828 Oct 04 DLC-35
Fr 1829 Mar 04 M639-24
Fr 1829 Jun 03 M639-11
Fr 1829 Sep 02 13-1231
Fr 1829 Dec 20 M639-8
Fr 1829 Dec 20# 14-1075
Fr 1830 Apr 05 M273-25
Fr 1830 Oct 09 16-0347
Fr 1831 Feb 14 DLC-39
Barbour Philip Pendleton
To 1822 Jan 22 DLC-63
Fr 1822 Feb 09 DLC-31
Fr 1829 Sep 04 13-1255
Fr 1829 Dec 20 M639-8
Fr 1830 Aug 20 DLC-38
Re 1830 Oct 08 16-0336
Fr 1833 Jul 11 M688-105
Fr 1836 Mar 18# 30-0807
Re 1836 Mar 22 30-0878
Fr 1836 Mar 23# 30-0880
Barclay George Y
Fr 1834 Sep 13 M639-13
Barclay James T
Fr 1836 Jan 09 29-1520
Barclay John D et al
Fr 1836 cApr M687-28
Barclay Salkeld & Co
Fr 1805 Nov 09 DLC-2
Bard Isaac
To 1826 Mar 08 chk 11-0155
Bard Samuel et al
Fr 1832 Jan 19 19-0772
Barker Abraham et al
Fr 1835 Mar 02 27-0684
Barker George
Fr 1838 Jan 20 34-0202
Barker George W
Fr 1837 Feb 27 33-0909
Barker Harriet
Fr 1835 Sep 02 M179-80
Barker Jacob
Fr 1829 Mar 16 M639-10
Fr 1833 Aug 19 M639-2
Fr 1836 Jan 23 M639-4
Fr 1836 Aug 16 M687-1
Barker James Nelson
Fr 1829 Mar 23 M639-17
Fr 1830 Mar 11 15-0338
Fr 1831 Feb 09 M639-14
Fr 1831 Mar 16 17-0902
Fr 1833 Mar 26 M688-89
Fr 1833 May 10 DLC-43
Fr 1833 Jul 12 23-0103
Fr 1834 Oct 03 26-0479
Fr 1834 Dec 10 M688-93
Fr 1835 Jan 02# M639-10
Fr 1835 Jan 28 DLC-45
Fr 1835 Feb 23 M688-98
Fr 1836 Oct 03 M639-19
Fr 1836 Oct 13 M639-9
Fr 1836 Oct 15 M687-12
Fr 1836 Dec 13 M639-15
Barker James Nelson et al
To 1832 Jan 08 19-0642
Barker Mary (Rogers)
Fr 1834 Oct 14 DLC-44
Fr 1834 Dec 25 DLC-45
To 1834 Dec 29 DLC-45
Fr 1836 Nov 28 DLC-49
To 1837 Jan 03# 32-1480
Barker S A et al
Fr 1833 Oct 02 M639-24

Barker Thomas H
Fr 1833 Feb 05 M639-2
Re 1833 Sep 12 23-0698
To 1836 Aug 31 31-1388
Barker William et al
Fr 1813 Dec 26 DLC-61
Barksdale Alex
Fr 1823 Jan 08 fin DLC-31
Barlow Joseph
Fr 1831 May 30 17-1483
Re 1831 Aug par 18-0333
Barlow Stephen
Fr 1829 Mar 05 M639-2
Barlow Thomas
Fr 1844 Mar 23 DLC-56
Barnard Edward
Re 1837 Feb 25 par 33-0881
Barnard Isaac Dutton
Fr 1829 Mar 18 M639-18
Fr 1829 Mar 24 12-1092
Fr 1829 Mar 25 12-1100
Fr 1829 May 26 13-0433
To 1830 Apr 03# DLC-38
Fr 1830 May 28 M639-17
Fr 1831 Feb 24 17-0647
Barnard J D
Fr 1837 Feb 06 33-0408
Barnard William
Fr 1830 Oct 09 M234-774
Barnes Erastus
Fr 1833 Dec 26 M639-24
Barnes Francis
Fr 1833 Feb 08 M124-136
Fr 1833 Feb 11# M124-136
Barnes George
Re 1832 Aug 17 par 20-1310
Barnes Henry H
Fr 1840 Feb 26 DLC-52
Barnes John
Fr 1831 Jun 10 M22-28
Barnes Loring B
Fr 1841 Sep 09 DLC-53
Barnes Sidney M
Fr 1843 Aug 29 DLC-55
Fr 1843 Aug 29 DLC-55
Barnet Charles
Re 1830 Jun 15 15-1448
Barnet Isaac Cox
Re 1830 Aug 28 T1-6
Fr 1833 Feb 03# T1-7
Barnett Joel et al
Fr 1834 May 22 M234-188
Barnett John
Fr 1820 Feb 03 fin DLC-1
Barnett Robert
Re 1791 May 21 lnd DLC-1
To 1803 Aug 05 fin 1-1140
Re 1806 Sep 25 leg 2-0345
Barnett Thomas
Fr 1820 fin 7-0962
Barnett William
Fr 1815 Jul 30 4-1137
To 1815 Aug 08 DLC-62
To 1821 Jul 24 DLC-63
Barneville Edward
Re 1830 Jan 11 par 14-1373
Re 1830 May 08 par 15-0951
Barney ______
Fr c1844 Feb 36-0154
Fr c1844 Jun 36-0567
Barney Eliakim
Re 1833 May 04 par 22-1279
Barney John
To 1824 Dec 23 10-0995
Barney Joshua
Fr 1832 Jun 19 M567-67
Barney Mary (Chase)
Fr 1829 Jun 13 DLC-37
Fr 1834 May 27 M688-92
Barney William Jr
Fr 1833 Jan 12 M639-2
Barnum D
Fr 1825 Mar 11 fin DLC-72
Baron D
Fr 1830 Jul 17 M124-124
Barr James
Re 1814 Apr 01 DLC-9
Barr James et al
Fr 1835 cJan DLC-59
Barr R M et al
Fr 1844 Jun 13 36-0607
Barr Robert
Fr 1808 Feb 28 DLC-4
Barragan Miguel
Fr 1836 Jan 19 M54-2
Barrell George
Fr 1830 Dec 04 DLC-38
Barrett Andrew
Fr 1815 Feb 24 DLC-17
Barrett D C et al
Fr 1834 May 22 25-1120
Barringer Daniel Laurens et al
Fr 1832 Jun 19 M639-27
Barrister Samuel et al
Fr 1836 May 30-1430
Barron James
To 1824 Sep 14 10-0892
To 1828 Nov 14 12-0267
Fr 1829 May 13-0214
Fr 1829 Oct 09 14-0126
Fr 1830 May 15 15-1012
Fr 1830 Nov 30 M124-125
Fr 1830 Dec 19 M124-125
To 1833 May 03 22-1270
Barron Thomas & Co
Fr 1823 Apr 01# fin DLC-32
Barrott Thomas
Re 1804 Sep 21 leg 1-1371
Barrow Alexander
Fr 1829 Jan 31 M639-21
Fr 1829 May 23# M639-10
Barrow Washington
Fr 1829 Apr 06 M639-2
Barrows Stephen et al
Fr 1837 Feb 03 M687-20
Barry John Waller
Re 1834 Jan 27 24-1066
Fr 1836 Nov 20 M567-118
Barry Mary
Fr 1831 Jun 10 M124-128
Barry Patrick
Re 1834 Mar 10 par 25-0010
Fr 1835 Aug 14 28-1279
Barry Redmond Dillon
Re 1808 Sep 15 leg 2-0722
Barry Richard H
Fr 1833 Apr 14 DLC-42
Barry Thomas
Fr 1834 Nov 06 26-0833

Barry William Taylor			
	Fr 1821 Apr 15		M439-15
	Fr c1829		37-0277
	Fr 1829 Feb 19		M639-21
	Fr 1829 Feb 27		M639-11
	To 1829 Apr 15#		DLC-36
	Fr 1829 Apr 30		13-0187
	To 1829 Jul 03		DLC-37
	Fr 1829 Jul 15		M179-67
	To 1829 Oct 21		14-0223
	To 1829 Oct 31		14-0278
	Fr 1829 Nov 24		14-0558
	Fr 1830 Jul 10		DLC-38
	To 1830 Oct 23		16-0469
	To 1830 Oct 23		16-0472
	To 1830 Oct 29		16-0573
	Fr 1830 Nov 12		16-0713
	Fr 1830 Nov 30		16-0900
	Fr 1831 Jan 31		M601-47
	Fr 1831 Jun 17		DLC-39
	Fr 1831 Jul 13		M601-47
	Re 1831 Sep 08	mem	18-0701
	Fr 1831 Nov 28		18-1505
	Fr 1832 Jan 19		19-0775
	To 1832 Mar 06#		DLC-40
	Fr 1832 May 05		20-0656
	Fr 1832 May 05*		M601-47
	Fr 1832 Nov 30		21-0617
	Fr 1833 Jan 28		22-0087
	Fr 1833 Jan 31		M124-136
	To 1833 Feb 25	chk	DLC-42
	Fr 1833 cApr		DLC-42
	Fr 1833 Oct 12		DLC-43
	Fr 1833 Oct 16		23-1043
	Fr 1833 Nov 07		M601-48
	Fr 1833 Nov 20		23-1262
	Fr 1833 Nov 30		23-1376
	To c1834#		37-0327
	To 1834 Jun 16		25-1386
	Fr 1834 Aug 28		DLC-44
	Fr 1834 Oct 03		26-0482
	Fr 1834 Oct 11		M601-49
	Fr 1834 Nov 29		26-1053
	Fr 1834 Nov 29*		DLC-77
	Fr 1835 Mar 22#		DLC-45
	Fr 1835 Apr 01		M601-49
	Fr 1835 Apr 08		27-1565
	To 1835 Apr 11		DLC-46
	To 1835 Apr 11*		M601-49
	Fr 1835 Apr 11#		DLC-46
	Fr 1835 Apr 15		DLC-46
	Fr 1835 Apr 15*		M601-49
	Fr 1835 Apr 17		28-0095
	Fr 1835 Apr 27		M601-49
	Fr 1835 Jul 24		DLC-46
Barry William Taylor et al			
	Fr 1828 Nov 17		DLC-35
	To 1828 Nov 28		DLC-35
Barry & Krickbaum			
	Fr 1837 Feb 09	fin	DLC-50
	Fr 1837 Feb 16	fin	DLC-50
Barstow George			
	Fr 1843 Oct 20		DLC-55
	To 1844 Feb 19		DLC-56
	To 1844 Feb 19*		36-0297
Bartle Andrew			
	Fr 1836 May 09		M124-153
Bartlet William et al			
	Fr 1830 Nov 20		16-0806

Bartlett Amasa et al			
	Fr 1835 Mar 27		M639-16
Bartlett George et al			
	Fr 1836 Jul 07		M567-125
Bartlett Isaac			
	Fr 1831 May 25		17-1419
	To 1834 Mar 04	chk	DLC-44
	Fr 1834 Apr 24	fin	DLC-44
	Fr 1834 Oct 29	fin	DLC-44
	To 1834 Nov 01	chk	DLC-44
	Fr 1835 May 18	fin	DLC-47
	Fr 1836 Jun 27	fin	DLC-48
	To 1836 Jul 02	chk	DLC-48
Bartlett William			
	Re 1830 Jan 16	par	14-1434
Barton _____			
	To 1803 Jul 17	fin	DLC-2
Barton _____ (Mr and Mrs)			
	Re 1828 Jan 15		DLC-35
Barton Cora (Livingston)			
	To 1833 Jun 04		22-1561
	Fr 1834 Oct 21		26-0668
Barton Thomas Pennant			
	Fr 1833 May 06		DLC-42
	Re 1833 May 29		22-1476
	Re 1835 Sep 14	mem	DLC-46
Baskerville James			
	Fr 1815 May 30		DLC-18
Baskerville John			
	To 1814 Feb 01		DLC-62
	To 1814 Feb 01*		DLC-8
	Fr c1830		14-1226
Bass John Meredith			
	Fr 1844 Jun 29		DLC-74
	Fr 1845 May 05		37-0194
Bass Jordan			
	To 1813 Aug 10	chk	DLC-6
	Fr 1813 Aug 10	fin	DLC-6
Bassett Horace et al			
	Fr 1830 cNov 08		16-0679
Bassett Jared et al			
	Fr 1836 May 27		M687-17
Bateman Isaac			
	Fr 1797 Jul 11	fin	1-0525
Bates Barnabas			
	Fr 1833 Jun 15#		23-0035
Bates Martin Waltham			
	Fr 1829 Nov 18		M639-10
Bates Martin Waltham et al			
	Fr 1829 Nov		M639-10
Bathurst Matthew et al			
	Fr 1833 Sep 02		M639-20
Baxley Joseph M			
	Fr 1836 Jun		M567-118
Baxter Edward			
	Fr 1834 Feb		M639-2
Baxter James			
	To 1813 Dec 27		DLC-61
	Fr 1814 Jan 14		DLC-8
	To 1814 Jan 29		DLC-61
	To 1814 Jan 31		DLC-8
	To 1814 Feb 05		DLC-62
	To 1814 Feb 11		DLC-61
	Fr 1814 Feb 22		DLC-9
	To 1814 Feb 23		DLC-61
	To 1814 Feb 28		DLC-61
	To 1814 Feb 28		DLC-61
	To 1814 Mar 02		DLC-61
	To 1814 Mar 22		DLC-9

	To 1814 Mar 23		DLC-9
	Fr 1814 Mar 30		DLC-9
	To 1814 Apr 01		DLC-9
	To 1814 Apr 05		DLC-10
	Fr 1814 Jul 21		DLC-11
	To 1815 Jun 27		DLC-18
	Fr 1815 Jul 02		DLC-18
Bay Elihu Hall			
	Fr 1829 Jun 05		DLC-72
Bayard James Asheton			
	Fr 1834 Jan 30		M179-77
Bayard Samuel J			
	Fr 1832 Apr 03#		20-0115
Baylies Francis			
	Fr 1829 Nov 17		14-0481
Baylor Henry Weidner			
	Fr 1845 Jan 28		DLC-57
Baylor John Walker			
	Re 1833 May 20		M567-79
Bayly Thomas Monteagle			
	Fr 1807 cJun 20		DLC-60
	To 1807 Jun 27		2-0507
Beach Amos et al			
	Fr c1836		29-1378
Beach Israel			
	Fr 1829		M222-28
Beale George			
	Fr 1829 Oct 06#		DLC-75
Beale James Madison Hite			
	Fr 1836 Apr 28		M687-28
	Fr 1836 Jul 04		M687-28
Beale John			
	To 1817 Feb 18		DLC-22
Beale Robert			
	Fr 1831 Aug 08		DLC-39
	Fr 1835 Feb 05		M124-146
	Fr 1835 Apr 06		DLC-46
	To 1839 Nov 16		34-1056
Beale Thomas			
	To 1815 Mar 06		DLC-62
	Fr 1815 Mar 06		DLC-17
	To 1818 Jan 01		DLC-23
Beale Thomas et al			
	Fr 1815 Mar 31	add	DLC-17
	Fr 1815 Mar 31*	add	M221-63
	To 1815 Mar 31	add	4-0916
Beales Ezra et al			
	Fr 1829 cMar		12-0614
Beall G et al			
	Fr 1829 Mar 09		12-0893
Beall Reasin			
	Fr 1829 Feb 11		M639-17
Beall Reasin et al			
	Fr 1840 Feb 24		34-1248
Beall W T			
	Fr 1845 Jan 23		DLC-57
Beam B			
	Fr 1825 Mar 16	fin	DLC-72
Bean Benning Moulton			
	Fr 1835 Apr 28		M639-26
Bean Jesse			
	To 1814 Apr 01		DLC-9
	Fr 1835 Feb 24		M567-103
Bean Peter E			
	Fr 1835 Sep 11		29-0026
	Fr 1835 Sep 11*		M234-435
Bean Robert			
	Fr 1829 Nov 23		M222-25
Beard Andrew			
	Re 1787 Oct 28	leg	1-0029
Beard Caroline Ada			
	Fr 1843 Jul 05		DLC-55
Beard David			
	Re 1813 Apr 22		3-0374
Beard William C			
	Fr 1818 Sep 03		DLC-25
	Fr 1820 Jan 04		DLC-28
	To 1820 Feb 04#		DLC-63
Beardsley Samuel			
	Fr 1833 Oct 05		M639-13
Bears Asa			
	Re 1835 Jun 09	par	28-0612
Bears Asa Jr			
	Re 1835 Feb 19	par	27-0553
Bears Patrick			
	Re 1834 Jan 16	par	24-0905
Beasley Isham			
	To 1843 Jun 10		DLC-74
Beatty Francis G			
	Re 1830 Dec 10		M273-25
Beatty Horatio			
	Fr 1829 Jul 04		M124-119
Beatty William H			
	Fr 1829 Mar 14		M124-117
Beaty John			
	Fr 1818 Sep 27		DLC-25
Beaty & Grieves			
	Fr 1821 May 23#	fin	DLC-30
Beaubien John B			
	Fr 1829 Sep 04		M234-315
Beauchamp M			
	Fr 1844 Jun 25		36-0644
Beaumont Augustus			
	Fr 1835 Sep 08		M179-80
Beaumont William			
	Fr 1833 Dec 30		24-0685
Beck Gideon			
	Fr 1830 Jun 23		DLC-38
Beck John E			
	Fr 1814 Apr 09		DLC-10
	Fr 1814 Apr 09		DLC-10
Beckcom Andrew Jackson			
	Fr 1841 Jul 28		DLC-53
Beckwith George C			
	Fr 1845 Mar 20		DLC-57
Bedford G A			
	Fr 1815 Sep 16	fin	DLC-69
	Fr 1815 Sep 28		DLC-68
Bedford John Robertson			
	Fr 1809 Oct 26	fin	DLC-5
	Fr 1824 Apr 22	fin	10-0673
	Fr 1842 Dec 10		DLC-54
Bedford Matilda (Smith)			
	Fr 1829 Sep 10	fin	13-1289
Bedford & Co			
	Fr 1817 Feb 21	fin	DLC-22
Bedford & Mackey			
	Fr 1824 Jan 30	fin	DLC-32
Bedford County TN			
	Re 1808 Jul 20	lnd	2-0691
	Re 1808 Oct 17	lnd	2-0736
	Re 1809 Aug 15	lnd	2-0854
	Re 1816 Aug 16	lnd	5-0360
	Re 1816 Aug 18	lnd	5-0362
Bedinger Henry			
	Fr 1827 Nov 19		DLC-35
Bee William			
	Fr 1833 Nov 27		23-1316

Beecher Sylvester et al
Fr 1830 Jan 08 M639-14
Beedle Alexander
Re 1836 Dec 30 par 32-1404
Beekman James
Fr 1840 Sep 07 DLC-53
Beekman Theophilus E
Fr 1828 Dec 18 DLC-36
Beeler Henry
Re 1801 Nov leg 1-0942
Beeson Henry White
Fr 1836 Mar 03 M639-5
Beeson Richard
Fr 1835 Mar 21 DLC-45
Beirne Andrew
Fr 1836 Feb 15 DLC-47
Belgium treaty
Re 1833 Feb 15 22-0380
Bell A W
Fr 1822 Nov 15 fin 9-0305
Bell Abraham & Co et al
Fr 1831 Feb 09 M639-10
Bell Caroline S (Butler)
Fr 1818 Apr 20# DLC-24
Fr 1818 May 24# DLC-25
Fr 1821 Mar 04 DLC-29
Fr 1840 Jan 17 34-1179
To 1843 Jan 05 35-1090
Fr 1843 Nov 27 DLC-56
Fr 1845 Jan 04 M873-63
Bell Charles et al
Fr 1831 Jan 24 M639-1
Bell David H
Fr 1820 Feb 18 fin DLC-28
Bell George
Fr 1819 Aug 23 DLC-27
Fr 1819 Aug 23* DLC-28
Bell James
To 1837 Jan 31 chk DLC-49
Bell John
Fr 1829 Feb 11 add 12-0501
Fr 1831 Jul 29 18-0312
Fr 1832 Feb 10 M234-136
Fr 1832 Feb 10* 19-1033
Fr 1833 Dec 08 M639-3
Re 1834 Oct 03 mem DLC-44
Re 1835 cAug mem DLC-73
Re c1838 Jan# DLC-74
Re 1839 cJul 34-0833
Bell John (Chickasaw surveyor)
Fr 1836 Mar 11 M234-436
Bell John (OH)
Fr 1845 Jan 08 DLC-57
Bell John A et al
Fr 1833 May 11 DLC-43
Fr 1836 Feb 25 M234-80
Bell John H
Re 1830 Mar 06 M273-22
Re 1830 Mar 06* 15-0307
Bell John R
Fr 1814 Jul 05 DLC-11
Fr 1814 Jul 16 DLC-11
Fr 1814 Jul 22 DLC-11
Fr 1814 Jul 26 DLC-11
Fr 1814 Jul 28 DLC-11
Fr 1814 Jul 28 DLC-11
Fr 1814 Jul 28* M565-5
Fr 1814 Aug 01 DLC-11
Fr 1814 Aug 04 DLC-11
Fr 1814 Aug 04 DLC-11
Fr 1814 Aug 06 DLC-11
Fr 1814 Oct 01 M565-5
Fr 1814 Nov 01 M565-5
Fr 1821 Aug 04 DLC-30
To 1821 Aug 09 M116-7
To 1821 Aug 13 M116-10
To 1821 Aug 13* DLC-63
To 1821 Aug 13* 8-1045
Fr 1821 Aug 14 M221-93
Fr 1821 Aug 14* M221-92
Fr 1821 Aug 14* M222-22
Fr 1821 Aug 14* 8-1051
To 1821 Aug 24 M221-94
To 1821 Sep 01 M116-10
To 1821 Sep 01* M116-7
To 1821 Sep 01* M116-9
To 1821 Sep 01* DLC-63
To 1821 Sep 01* 8-1125
To 1821 Oct 01 8-1246
Fr 1821 Oct 08 M221-93
To 1821 Dec 12 DLC-63
Bell Levi et al
Fr 1835 cJan DLC-59
Bell Richard Hales
Fr 1831 Jul 29 M567-59
Bell Robert
To 1816 Jun 28 chk DLC-21
Fr 1817 Oct 21 DLC-23
Re 1843 Jan 05 mem DLC-55
Bell Samuel
Re 1820 Sep 20 leg 7-1362
Bell William
Fr 1836 Nov 13 M234-770
Bellair Lewis and Mariette
Fr 1834 Jun 25-1206
Bellamy Abraham
Fr 1831 Jan 05 17-0198
Fr 1831 Jan 19 17-0288
Fr 1831 Sep 25 M639-7
Fr 1833 Jan 24 M639-2
Bellamy Abraham et al
Fr 1829 Oct 24 M639-23
Fr 1831 Jan 05 17-0202
Bellamy John
Fr 1830 Jul 10 M234-433
Bellevue Francis Barbin de
Fr 1816 Mar 26 DLC-20
Bellmyden & Montz
Fr 1838 Mar 15# DLC-51
Belser James E
Fr 1836 Jun 12 M234-243
Belt Richard G
Fr 1831 Nov 22 M22-28
Fr 1832 Jun 25 M22-29
Belton Francis Smith
Fr 1831 Aug 17 M221-111
Re 1831 Aug 27 DLC-60
Fr 1834 Aug 07# DLC-44
Belton Francis Smith et al
Fr 1836 Feb 22 M567-127
Fr 1836 Feb 22* M567-117
Bender George
Fr 1834 Jan 06 24-0753
Benkard James
Fr 1833 Apr 23 M639-16
Bennett Caleb Prew et al
Fr 1834 Dec M639-19

Bennett E H			
	Fr 1837 Jul 29#	fin	DLC-50
Bennett James			
	Fr 1829 Jul 29		M639-2
Bennett James Gordon			
	Fr 1833 Mar 05		M688-88
	Fr 1833 Sep 10		23-0676
	To 1833 Sep 12		23-0699
	Fr 1833 Sep 14		DLC-43
	Fr 1833 Sep 21		DLC-43
	Fr 1833 Dec 04		24-0330
Bennett James H			
	Fr 1829 Jun 29		M639-2
Bennett John			
	Fr 1830 Jun 23		DLC-38
Bennett Joseph			
	Re 1832 Dec 17	par	21-1072
Bennett Thomas			
	Fr 1816 Jul 18		DLC-21
	Fr 1821 Mar 08		DLC-30
Bennett Victor			
	Fr 1814 Aug 31		DLC-11
Benson Joseph			
	Fr 1839 Jun 24		DLC-52
Benson Nimrod E			
	Fr 1835 Sep 14		M639-4
Benson Nimrod E et al			
	Fr 1840 Jun 19		34-1429
Benson Samuel			
	Fr 1835 Jan 14#		M124-146
Benson Sylvanus E			
	Fr 1839 May 18#	fin	DLC-52
	To 1839 Dec 12#	fin	DLC-52
	Fr 1840 Dec 01		DLC-53
Benson William R			
	Re 1834 Jun 04	par	25-1239
Benson Hunt & Co			
	Fr 1834 Jun 23#	fin	DLC-51
Bentham Jeremy			
	Fr 1830 Jun 14		15-1368
Benton James			
	Fr 1816 Dec 17		DLC-22
Benton Jesse			
	Fr 1824 Sep		10-0864
	Fr 1824 Sep*		DLC-33
	Re 1824 Oct 12		10-0915
Benton John F			
	Fr 1832 Nov 03		DLC-41
Benton Nathaniel S			
	Fr 1834 Jun 23		25-1489
Benton Thomas Hart			
	Fr 1812 Jan 30		DLC-5
	Fr 1812 Jul 04		DLC-5
	To 1812 Dec 28		DLC-5
	To 1812 Dec 28*		DLC-61
	To 1812 Dec 30		DLC-5
	To 1812 Dec 30*		DLC-61
	To 1813 Jan 02		DLC-61
	To 1813 Jan 04		DLC-61
	To 1813 Jan 07		DLC-5
	To 1813 Jan 07*		DLC-61
	Fr 1813 Jan 09		3-0238
	Fr 1813 Feb 01		DLC-6
	To 1813 Feb 25		DLC-61
	Fr 1813 Feb 27		DLC-6
	Fr 1813 Jun 15		DLC-6
	Fr 1813 Jul 09		DLC-71
	Re 1813 Jul 09	mem	DLC-71
	To 1813 Jul 19		DLC-6
	Fr 1813 Jul 25		DLC-6
	To 1813 Aug 04		3-0429
	Fr 1813 Sep 10#		3-0472
	Fr 1814 Jul 05		DLC-11
	To 1814 Aug 20		DLC-62
	Fr 1814 Aug 23		3-1313
	Fr 1814 Sep 02		DLC-12
	Fr 1814 Sep 11		DLC-12
	Fr 1814 Sep 13		4-0217
	To 1814 Sep 20		DLC-62
	Fr 1814 Sep 21		DLC-12
	To 1814 Sep 23		DLC-62
	To 1814 Sep 23		DLC-62
	Fr 1814 Sep 28		DLC-12
	Fr 1814 Oct 16		DLC-13
	Fr 1814 Oct 16		DLC-13
	To 1814 Oct 28		DLC-13
	Fr 1829 Mar 14		12-1005
	Fr 1829 Dec 17#		DLC-37
	Fr 1831 Mar 03		17-0797
	Fr 1832 Jul 05		M639-14
	Fr 1833 May 11		M639-11
	Fr 1834 Jun 01		25-1219
	Fr 1835 Mar 03#		27-0702
	Fr 1835 Dec 28		M567-107
	Fr 1836 Mar 11		M639-6
	Fr 1836 May 02		M639-25
	Re 1836 cJun 07	mem	31-0364
	To 1837 Jan 17		DLC-49
	Fr 1837 Feb 18		M687-23
	Fr 1837 Nov 10		DLC-50
	To 1837 Nov 29		34-0050
	Fr 1837 Dec 12		DLC-50
	Fr 1838 Feb 20		DLC-51
	Fr 1838 Apr 06		DLC-51
	Fr 1839 Apr 03		DLC-52
	Fr 1839 Oct 14		DLC-52
	Fr 1840 Apr 24		DLC-52
	Fr 1840 Apr 28		DLC-52
	Fr 1840 Sep 25		DLC-74
	Fr 1842 Mar 10		DLC-54
	Fr 1842 Mar 31		DLC-54
	Fr 1844 May 03		36-0475
	To 1844 May 16		36-0547
	Fr 1844 May 28		DLC-56
	Fr 1844 May 28*		36-0564
	Fr 1844 Aug 10		36-0783
	Fr 1844 Aug 10		36-0786
Benton Thomas Hart et al			
	Fr 1844 May 29		DLC-56
Bergen Cornelius			
	Fr 1837 Oct 16		33-1527
Bernard H			
	To 1839 Mar 30#	fin	DLC-52
Bernard John			
	Fr 1826 Sep 19	fin	DLC-34
Bernard Simon			
	Fr 1831 Jul 08		18-0162
	To 1831 Jul 09		18-0169
	Fr 1835 Apr 19#		DLC-46
Bernay Auguste			
	Fr 1830 Mar 09	fin	15-0313
Berns James			
	Fr 1815 Feb 08		4-0713
Berrien John Macpherson			
	Fr 1829 Mar 28		M699-1
	Fr 1829 Mar 28*		M699-2
	To 1829 Mar 30		12-1180
	To 1829 Apr 06		12-1276
	To 1829 Apr 06*		DLC-60

Berrien John Macpherson (cont)
Fr 1829 Apr 09 DLC-36
To 1829 Jun 11 13-0624
To 1829 Jun 13 13-0649
To 1829 Jun 13* DLC-60
Fr 1829 Jun 15 M179-67
Fr 1829 Jun 15* T412-3
Fr 1829 Jun 18 T412-3
Fr 1829 Jul 18 T412-3
Fr 1829 Jul 18* 13-0862
Fr 1829 Jul 21 13-0988
Fr 1829 Jul 21* T412-3
Fr 1829 Aug 17 T412-3
Fr 1829 Sep 10 M179-67
Fr 1829 Sep 10* T412-3
Fr 1829 Sep 15 12-1044
Fr 1829 Sep 15* M699-1
Fr 1829 Sep 15* M699-2
Fr 1829 Oct 12 T412-3
Fr 1829 Nov 03 14-0352
Fr 1829 Nov 03* T412-3
Fr 1829 Nov 03 14-0360
Fr 1829 Nov 27 DLC-37
Fr 1829 cDec 01 14-0740
Re 1830 Jan 29 mem 15-0063
To 1830 Feb 19 15-0197
Fr 1830 Mar 17 T412-3
Fr 1830 Apr 16 T412-3
Fr 1830 Apr 16* 15-0729
Fr 1830 May 22# 15-1069
To 1830 Jun 02 15-1257
To 1830 Jun 03 15-1273
Fr 1830 Jun 08 T412-3
To 1830 Jun 16 15-1468
Fr 1830 Jun 25 M234-74
Fr 1830 Aug 10 16-0090
Fr 1830 Sep 27 M639-9
Fr 1830 Oct 02 T412-3
Fr 1831 Feb 22 M179-70
Fr 1831 Mar 02 T412-3
Fr 1831 Mar 25 M179-70
Fr 1831 Mar 25* T412-3
Fr 1831 May 17 M222-29
Fr 1831 Jun 15 DLC-39
Fr 1831 Jun 15* 18-0020
To 1831 Jun 15 18-0024
To 1831 Jun 15* DLC-39
Fr 1831 Jun 22 DLC-39
Fr 1831 Jun 22* 18-0071
To 1831 Jun 22 18-0073
To 1831 Jun 22* DLC-39
Fr 1831 Jul 15 DLC-39
To 1831 Jul 15 DLC-39
Berry John
Fr 1819 Mar 01 add DLC-26
Berry Samuel H
Fr 1829 Aug 05 M124-120
Berry William W
Fr 1839 Jan 01# fin DLC-53
To 1840 Jul 21 chk DLC-53
Fr 1843 Jan 09# fin DLC-56
Berryhill William McLean
Fr 1820 May 05 7-1084
Fr 1829 Apr 08 M639-2
To 1832 Dec 25 21-1160
Fr 1835 Jan 17 M639-9
Berryhill & McKee
Fr 1816 Aug 21 fin DLC-22
Fr 1820 Mar 22 fin DLC-28
Bertrand A
Fr 1827 Jul 29 fin DLC-34
Bertrand Henri Gratien
Fr 1843 Oct 07 DLC-55
Bertrand Madelaine
Re 1829 Apr 13 12-1323
Bertrand P G et al
Fr 1833 Jul 12 M639-27
Besson L & Son
Fr 1835 Apr 16# fin DLC-46
Bethell J P
Fr 1844 Apr 17 DLC-56
Bettner & Wright
Fr 1833 Apr 25 M639-16
Betton Turbutt R
Fr 1832 Dec 15 M639-26
Betts Samuel Rossiter
Fr 1833 Dec 13 24-0464
Fr 1835 Nov 25 M639-25
Fr 1836 May 28 leg 31-0170
Betts Zachariah
Fr 1816 Dec 14 fin DLC-22
Bevan Matthew L et al
Fr 1831 Aug 23 M639-21
Bevans Lorenzo
Fr 1839 May 12 DLC-52
Beveridge Robert
Fr 1830 Jun 25 15-1525
Beverley Carter
To 1827 Jun 05 11-0683
Fr 1827 Jun 09 11-0690
Fr 1827 Jun 27 DLC-34
Fr 1827 Nov 01 DLC-34
Fr 1827 Nov 05 DLC-34
Fr 1828 Jan 20 DLC-35
Fr 1831 Feb 04 DLC-39
Beverley Peter R
Fr 1838 Dec 18 DLC-51
Fr 1838 Dec 18 37-0384
Beverley Robert
Fr 1830 Sep 11 16-0232
Beyerbach Edward
Re 1835 Nov 17 29-0520
Bibb Charles Scott
Fr 1828 Dec 05 DLC-36
Fr 1829 Apr 22 M639-22
Fr 1829 Jun 11 M639-2
Bibb George Mortimer
Fr 1832 cMay M639-16
Bibb John B
Fr 1818 Jan 24 DLC-24
Bibb Thomas
Fr 1814 Nov 10 DLC-14
Fr 1816 Dec 20 DLC-22
Bibb William Wyatt
Fr 1818 May 19 6-0760
Fr 1818 May 19* M116-4
Fr 1818 May 19* M271-2
Fr 1818 Oct 01 DLC-25
Bickham George
Fr 1805 Aug 18 DLC-3
Re 1807 Jul 29 leg 2-0521
Re 1809 Oct 17 leg 2-0858
Bickham & Reese
Fr 1805 Jan 31 DLC-3
To 1805 cSep 10 DLC-60
Fr 1805 Nov 29 DLC-3
To 1806 Jul 29 DLC-4

Biddle Charles
    Fr 1829 Jun 25 M639-8
    Fr 1832 Jan 11 DLC-40
    Fr 1834 Feb 09 M688-87
    Fr 1834 Mar 29 M688-87
    Fr 1835 Jan 27# DLC-45
    Fr 1835 May 03 28-0243
    Fr 1835 Nov 14 M625-12
Biddle James
    Fr 1830 Jun 08 M46-3
    Fr 1830 Jun 08* 15-1318
    Fr 1830 Jun 15 15-1449
    Fr 1830 Jun 15* M46-3
    Fr 1833 Jul 12 23-0106
Biddle John
    Fr 1830 Jan 24# M639-14
    Fr 1830 Dec 14 16-1421
    Fr 1834 Apr 09 M639-9
    Fr 1835 May 21 M179-80
    Fr 1835 May 21# M179-80
    Fr 1835 Jun 17# 28-0722
    Fr 1835 Nov 24 29-0557
Biddle Nicholas
    Re 1829 cSep 20 mem 13-1387
Bidlack Benjamin Alden
    Fr 1843 Feb 11 DLC-55
    Fr 1844 Feb 26 DLC-56
Bigelow Timothy
    Fr 1815 Feb 28 DLC-17
Big Kettle
    Fr 1831 Jan 11 M234-808
    Fr 1831 Jan 11* 17-0231
Bigler John
    Fr 1834 Oct 24 26-0718
Bigley Patrick Mrs
    To 1815 Aug 15 chk DLC-19
    Fr 1815 Aug 15 fin DLC-19
Biglow Horatio
    Fr 1821 Sep 21 mem M116-7
Big Warrior
    Fr 1814 Apr 3-0943
    Fr 1814 Aug 06 DLC-11
    Fr 1814 Aug 06* DLC-62
    To 1814 Aug 07 DLC-11
    To 1814 Aug 07* DLC-62
    Fr 1816 Apr 16 M221-69
    Fr 1816 Apr 16* DLC-20
    To 1816 Aug 30 DLC-62
    To 1816 Aug 30* M668-4
    To 1816 Aug 30* 5-0444
    Fr 1818 Feb 26 DLC-24
Bihler R
    Fr 1837 Mar# fin 33-0943
    Fr 1837 Mar 02# fin DLC-50
Bill Alexander T F
    Re 1833 Mar 30 par 22-0913
Billings A
    Fr 1844 Aug 27 36-0827
Billings A & Son
    Fr 1844 Mar 19# fin DLC-57
Billings Eleazar Brackham
    Fr 1814 Nov 17 DLC-14
Billings John Jr
    Fr 1830 Jul 05 M221-110
Billings S C
    Fr 1833 Jul 02 DLC-43
Bills Price B
    Fr 1836 Sep M22-41
Bingey John W
    Fr 1836 Jan 30 30-0224
Bingham Joseph
    Fr 1835 Feb 17 27-0544
Bininger Abraham & Son
    Fr 1832 Nov 20# fin DLC-41
Binkley William
    Fr 1839 Aug 03 DLC-52
    Fr 1839 Oct 14# fin DLC-52
    Re 1844 Jul 29 mem 36-0758
Binney C J F
    Re 1835 Jun 09 par 28-0612
Binney Horace
    Fr 1830 Oct 09 M234-808
    Fr 1830 Oct 09* 16-0350
Binney John et al
    Fr 1835 Feb 10 27-0462
    Fr 1835 Aug 22 M639-21
Binns William A
    Fr 1845 Jan 15 36-1333
Bioren Benjamin T
    Fr 1829 Mar 16 M639-2
Bird William et al
    Fr 1829 May 13-0215
Birdsall Benjamin
    Fr 1834 Jan 04 M639-18
Bishop S W
    Fr 1844 Mar 02 DLC-56
Bissell Daniel
    To 1807 Jan 02 M221-9
    Fr 1807 Jan 05 2-0433
    To 1807 Jan 09 DLC-4
    Fr 1815 Jun 09 DLC-18
    Fr 1815 Jul 02 M221-59
    Fr 1815 Jul 15 M221-59
    Fr 1815 Aug 05 4-1142
    Fr 1815 Aug 27 DLC-19
    To 1815 Sep 04 M221-101
    To 1815 Sep 04* DLC-62
    Fr 1816 Jan 08 4-1321
    Fr 1816 Jan 08* M221-101
    Fr 1816 Jan 15 DLC-20
    To 1816 Feb 03 DLC-62
    Fr 1818 Apr 10 DLC-24
    Fr 1818 May 03 DLC-24
    Fr 1818 Aug 19 DLC-25
    To 1819 Aug 19# DLC-63
    Fr 1819 Dec 23 DLC-28
    Fr 1820 Jan 07 M221-86
    To 1820 Jan 08 DLC-63
    To 1820 Jan 31 DLC-63
    To 1820 Jan 31* M221-86
    Fr 1820 Feb 09 DLC-28
    Fr 1820 Feb 14 DLC-28
    Fr 1820 Feb 14* M221-86
    To 1820 Feb 28 M221-86
    To 1820 Feb 28* DLC-63
    Fr 1820 Mar 14 DLC-28
    To 1820 Apr 12 DLC-63
    Fr 1820 Apr 22 DLC-29
    Fr 1820 May 08 DLC-29
    Fr 1820 May 10 DLC-29
    Fr 1820 May 10* M221-21
    To 1820 May 15 DLC-63
    To 1820 May 20# DLC-63
    To 1820 May 22# DLC-63
    Fr 1820 Jun 04 DLC-29
    Fr 1820 Jun 04 DLC-29
    To 1820 Jun 21# DLC-63

Bissell Daniel (cont)

To 1820 Jun 23		DLC-63
Fr 1820 Jul 26		DLC-29
To 1820 Aug 18		DLC-63
Fr 1820 Sep 01		DLC-29
Fr 1820 Sep 01		DLC-29
Fr 1820 Sep 20		DLC-29
To 1820 Oct 20#		DLC-63
To 1820 Nov 13		DLC-63
Fr 1820 Nov 30		DLC-29
To 1820 Dec 20#		DLC-63
Fr 1820 Dec 24		DLC-29
To 1821 Jan 14#		DLC-63
Fr 1821 Jan 18		DLC-29
Fr 1821 Jan 20		DLC-29
To 1821 Feb 08		DLC-63
Fr 1821 Feb 22		DLC-29
Fr 1821 Feb 27		DLC-29
Fr 1821 Feb 27*		8-0145
To 1821 Mar 10#		DLC-63
Fr 1821 Mar 14		M221-89
To 1821 Mar 26		DLC-63
To 1821 Mar 26*		M221-89
Fr 1821 Mar 27		8-0267
Fr 1821 Apr 23		DLC-30
To 1821 May 13#		DLC-63
Fr 1821 Jun 16		DLC-30
Black John		
Fr 1834 Jan 10		M639-23
Black John et al		
Fr 1829		M639-11
Black M		
Fr 1835 Apr 06#		M639-11
Black Samuel et al		
Fr 1831 Sep 16		M567-61
Black William		
Re 1835 Aug 28	par	28-1446
Blackburn George		
Fr 1835 Sep 10		29-0010
Blackburn Gideon		
To 1812 Dec 11		2-1292
Fr 1813 Nov 20		DLC-7
Fr 1813 Nov 20*		DLC-61
To 1813 Dec 03		3-0633
To 1813 Dec 03*		DLC-61
To 1814 Jan 11		DLC-61
Blackburn William et al		
Fr 1835 Jan 03		M639-27
Black Hoof et al		
Fr 1830 Jan 30		M234-669
Blackman E et al		
Fr 1835 Apr		27-1400
Blacksmith		
Re 1828		DLC-36
Blackson & Ford		
Fr 1832 Mar 20		M22-29
Blaine Ephraim A		
Fr 1821 May	fin	DLC-70
Fr 1821 May*		8-0402
Fr 1821 Jul 17	fin	DLC-70
Fr 1821 Aug 20	fin	DLC-70
Blair Eliza (Gist)		
To 1837 Mar 06		33-1069
Blair Francis Preston		
Fr 1828 Dec 05		DLC-36
Fr c1830		DLC-38
Fr 1830 Aug 17		DLC-38
To 1830 Aug 24		DLC-38
Fr 1831 Jul 11		18-0175
To 1832 Apr		DLC-73
To 1832 Nov 15#		DLC-41
Fr c1833		37-0305
To 1833 Mar 14		22-0753
To 1833 Apr 01		DLC-42
Fr 1833 cMay		DLC-42
To 1833 Jun 25#		DLC-43
Fr 1833 cAug 05		DLC-43
To 1833 Oct 18		DLC-43
Fr 1833 Oct 24		DLC-43
To 1833 Nov 30		DLC-43
To 1833 Dec 13#		DLC-43
Fr 1834 Jan 07		DLC-44
To 1834 Jan 13		24-0874
To 1834 Jan 17		DLC-41
Fr 1834 cApr		25-0520
To 1834 Apr 22#		DLC-73
To 1834 Apr 25		DLC-41
To 1834 Aug 07		DLC-44
Fr 1834 Aug 18		DLC-44
Fr 1834 Aug 26		DLC-44
To 1834 Aug 30		DLC-44
To 1834 Sep 06		DLC-44
To 1834 Oct 29		26-0759
Fr 1834 Oct 29		DLC-44
Fr 1834 Dec 14		DLC-45
To 1835 Apr 03		DLC-46
Fr 1835 May 19		DLC-46
To 1835 May 19		DLC-46
Fr 1835 Jun 10#		DLC-46
To 1835 Aug 16#	fin	DLC-46
To 1835 Oct 05#		29-0196
To 1835 Oct 22		DLC-47
Fr 1836 May 07		DLC-48
To 1836 Jun 20#		31-0516
Fr 1836 Jul 14		DLC-48
Fr 1836 Jul 30		DLC-48
Fr 1836 Aug 01		DLC-46
To 1836 Aug 12		DLC-48
To 1836 Aug 15#		31-1290
To 1836 Aug 22		DLC-48
Fr 1836 Aug 24		DLC-49
Fr 1836 Aug 25		DLC-49
Fr 1836 Oct 20		32-0248
To c1837		32-1448
To 1837 Jan	mem	DLC-50
To 1837 Feb 25		DLC-50
To 1837 Mar 11		DLC-50
To 1837 Apr 02		DLC-50
Fr 1837 Apr 05		DLC-50
To 1837 Apr 06		DLC-50
Fr 1837 Apr 10		DLC-50
To 1837 Apr 18		DLC-50
Fr 1837 Apr 23		DLC-50
To 1837 Apr 24		DLC-50
Fr 1837 May 01		33-1203
Fr 1837 May 01		33-1207
To 1837 May 11		DLC-50
To 1837 May 11		DLC-50
To 1837 May 16		DLC-50
Fr 1837 May 26		DLC-50
To 1837 Jun 05		DLC-50
To 1837 Jun 13		DLC-50
Fr 1837 Jun 25		DLC-50
To 1837 Jul 09		DLC-50
Fr 1837 Jul 21		DLC-50
To 1837 Jul 23		DLC-50
Fr 1837 Aug 10		DLC-50
To 1837 Aug 16		DLC-50
To 1837 Aug 20		DLC-50

To 1837 Sep 06	33-1466
Fr 1837 Sep 09	DLC-50
To 1837 Sep 15	DLC-50
To 1837 Sep 27	DLC-50
Fr 1837 Oct 01	DLC-50
Fr 1837 Oct 13	DLC-50
Fr 1837 Oct 15	DLC-50
To 1837 Oct 31	DLC-50
To 1837 Nov 29	DLC-50
Fr 1837 Nov 29	DLC-50
To 1837 Dec 14	DLC-50
Fr 1837 Dec 20	DLC-50
To 1838 Jan 01	DLC-50
Fr 1838 Jan 08	DLC-51
To 1838 Jan 16	DLC-51
Fr 1838 Jan 16	DLC-51
To 1838 Feb 08	DLC-51
Fr 1838 Feb 11	DLC-51
To 1838 Feb 12	34-0238
Fr 1838 Feb 24	DLC-51
To 1838 Feb 26	DLC-51
To 1838 Mar 06	DLC-51
Fr 1838 Mar 11	DLC-51
Fr 1838 Mar 20	DLC-51
To 1838 Mar 26	DLC-51
To 1838 Apr 04	DLC-51
Fr 1838 Apr 17	DLC-51
To 1838 May 01	DLC-51
Fr 1838 May 28	DLC-51
To 1838 Jun 04	DLC-51
Fr 1838 Jun 16	DLC-51
Fr 1838 Jul 07	DLC-51
To 1838 Jul 19	DLC-51
Fr 1838 Jul 30	DLC-51
Fr 1838 Aug 02	DLC-51
To 1838 Aug 09	DLC-51
To 1838 Aug 14	34-0424
Fr 1838 Aug 23	DLC-51
Fr 1838 Sep 15	DLC-51
To 1838 Sep 27	DLC-51
Fr 1838 Oct 19	DLC-51
To 1838 Nov 12	DLC-51
To 1838 Dec 08	34-0561
To 1838 Dec 08*	DLC-74
Fr 1838 Dec 23	DLC-51
To 1839 Jan 05	DLC-51
To 1839 Jan 29	DLC-51
To 1839 Feb 07	34-0628
Fr 1839 Feb 08	DLC-51
Fr 1839 Feb 16	DLC-52
Fr 1839 Mar 28	DLC-52
Fr 1839 Apr 14	DLC-52
To 1839 Apr 20	34-0755
Fr 1839 Apr 26	DLC-52
To 1839 May 02	DLC-52
To 1839 May 15	DLC-52
Fr 1839 May 20	DLC-52
Fr 1839 May 26	DLC-52
To 1839 Jun 05	DLC-52
Fr 1839 Jul 27	DLC-52
Fr 1839 Aug 20	DLC-52
Fr 1839 Aug 28	DLC-52
To 1839 Sep 05	DLC-52
To 1839 Sep 23	DLC-52
Fr 1839 Oct 04	DLC-52
To 1839 Nov 08	DLC-52
Fr 1839 Dec 03	DLC-52
Fr 1839 Dec 15	DLC-52
Fr 1839 Dec 22	DLC-52
To 1840 Feb 15	DLC-52
To 1840 Feb 15*	34-1202
Fr 1840 Mar 17	DLC-52
Fr 1840 Mar 17*	34-1259
To 1840 Apr 09	DLC-52
To 1840 Apr 09*	34-1294
Fr 1840 Apr 15	34-1308
To 1840 May 22	DLC-52
To 1840 May 22*	34-1376
Fr 1840 Jun 17	DLC-52
Fr 1840 Jun 17*	34-1414
To 1840 Jun 27	DLC-53
To 1840 Jun 27*	34-1451
Fr 1840 Jul 12	DLC-53
Fr 1840 Jul 12*	34-1471
To 1840 Jul 28	34-1513
To 1840 Jul 28*	DLC-74
To 1840 Aug 04#	DLC-74
Fr 1840 Sep 10	DLC-53
Fr 1840 Sep 10*	35-0001
Fr 1840 Sep 10	35-0004
To 1840 Sep 26	DLC-53
To 1840 Sep 26*	35-0026
Fr 1840 Oct 21	DLC-53
Fr 1840 Oct 21*	35-0060
Fr 1840 Nov 07	DLC-53
Fr 1840 Nov 07*	35-0092
To 1840 Dec 18	35-0121
Fr 1840 Dec 28	DLC-53
Fr 1840 Dec 28*	35-0146
To 1841 Jan	35-0162
To 1841 Jan 05	DLC-53
To 1841 Jan 05*	35-0192
Fr 1841 Jan 30	DLC-53
Fr 1841 Jan 30*	35-0222
To 1841 Feb 19	DLC-53
To 1841 Feb 19*	35-0230
Fr 1841 Apr 04	DLC-53
Fr 1841 Apr 04*	35-0273
Fr 1841 Apr 11	DLC-53
Fr 1841 Apr 11*	35-0285
To 1841 Apr 19	DLC-53
To 1841 Apr 19*	35-0287
Fr 1841 May 16	DLC-53
Fr 1841 May 16*	35-0306
To 1841 May 31	DLC-53
To 1841 May 31*	35-0315
Fr 1841 Jun 17	35-0328
To 1841 Jul 17	DLC-53
To 1841 Jul 17*	35-0340
Fr 1841 Aug 02	DLC-53
Fr 1841 Aug 02*	35-0358
To 1841 Aug 12	DLC-53
To 1841 Aug 12*	35-0366
Fr 1841 Aug 26	DLC-53
Fr 1841 Aug 26*	35-0391
Fr 1841 Sep 29	DLC-53
Fr 1841 Sep 29*	35-0417
To 1841 Oct 11	DLC-53
To 1842 Jan 01	DLC-54
To 1842 Jan 01*	35-0576
Fr 1842 Jan 01	35-0577
Fr 1842 Jan 18	DLC-54
Fr 1842 Jan 18*	35-0605
To 1842 Feb 03	DLC-54
To 1842 Feb 03*	35-0613
Fr 1842 Feb 16	DLC-74
To 1842 Feb 24	DLC-54
To 1842 Feb 24*	35-0633

Blair Francis Preston (cont)

Re	1842 Mar 04	fin	DLC-54
Fr	1842 Mar 11		DLC-74
Fr	1842 Mar 11*		35-0645
To	1842 Mar 29		DLC-54
Re	1842 Mar 29	mem	DLC-54
To	1842 Mar 31		DLC-54
To	1842 Apr 04#		DLC-54
To	1842 Apr 23		DLC-54
To	1842 Apr 23*		35-0680
Fr	1842 May 03		DLC-54
Fr	1842 May 03*		35-0688
To	1842 May 23		DLC-54
To	1842 May 23*		35-0722
Fr	1842 May 24		DLC-54
Fr	1842 May 24*		35-0737
To	1842 Jun 04		DLC-54
To	1842 Jun 04*		35-0775
To	1842 Jun 09		35-0777
To	1842 Jun 09		DLC-74
To	1842 Jun 09*		35-0780
To	1842 Jun 16		DLC-54
To	1842 Jun 16*		35-0797
Fr	1842 Jun 17		DLC-54
Fr	1842 Jun 17*		35-0805
To	1842 Jun 28		35-0818
Fr	1842 Jun 30		DLC-54
Fr	1842 Jun 30*		35-0827
To	1842 Jul 02		DLC-54
To	1842 Jul 02*		35-0833
To	1842 Jul 08		DLC-54
To	1842 Jul 08*		35-0844
Fr	1842 Jul 14		DLC-54
Fr	1842 Jul 14*		35-0849
To	1842 Jul 25		DLC-54
To	1842 Jul 25*		35-0853
Fr	1842 Jul 25		DLC-54
Fr	1842 Jul 25*		35-0855
To	1842 Aug 01		DLC-54
To	1842 Aug 07		DLC-54
To	1842 Aug 07*		35-0873
Fr	1842 Aug 12		DLC-54
Fr	1842 Aug 12*		35-0875
To	1842 Sep 09		DLC-74
Fr	1842 Sep 12		DLC-54
Fr	1842 Sep 12*		35-0941
To	1842 Sep 23		DLC-54
To	1842 Sep 23*		35-0950
To	1842 Sep 26		35-0951
To	1842 Sep 26		DLC-54
To	1842 Sep 28		DLC-54
To	1842 Sep 28*		35-0957
To	1842 Oct 03		DLC-54
To	1842 Oct 03*		35-0961
Fr	1842 Oct 06		DLC-54
Fr	1842 Oct 06*		35-0966
Fr	1842 Oct 14		DLC-54
Fr	1842 Oct 14*		35-0970
To	1842 Oct 19		DLC-54
To	1842 Oct 19*		35-0974
To	1842 Oct 29		DLC-54
To	1842 Oct 29*		35-0984
Fr	1842 Nov 13		DLC-54
Fr	1842 Nov 13*		35-0991
Fr	1842 Nov 20		DLC-54
Fr	1842 Nov 20*		35-0993
To	1842 Nov 25		DLC-54
To	1842 Nov 25*		35-1004
To	1842 Dec 02		DLC-54
To	1842 Dec 02*		35-1019
To	1842 Dec 23		DLC-75
To	1842 Dec 31		DLC-54
To	1842 Dec 31*		35-1071
Fr	1843 Jan 01		DLC-54
Fr	1843 Jan 01*		35-1083
Fr	1843 Jan 07		DLC-55
Fr	1843 Jan 07*		35-1100
To	1843 Jan 11		DLC-55
To	1843 Jan 11*		35-1106
To	1843 Jan 13		DLC-55
To	1843 Jan 13*		35-1114
To	1843 Jan 17		DLC-55
To	1843 Jan 17*		35-1125
Fr	1843 Jan 22		DLC-55
Fr	1843 Jan 22*		35-1138
To	1843 Jan 26		DLC-55
To	1843 Jan 26*		35-1148
To	1843 Feb 04		DLC-55
To	1843 Feb 06		35-1164
To	1843 Feb 07		DLC-55
To	1843 Feb 07*		35-1188
Fr	1843 Feb 07		DLC-55
Fr	1843 Feb 07*		35-1190
To	1843 Feb 08		DLC-55
To	1843 Feb 08*		35-1193
Fr	1843 Feb 09		DLC-55
Fr	1843 Feb 09*		35-1202
Fr	1843 Feb 12		DLC-55
Fr	1843 Feb 12*		35-1213
Fr	1843 Feb 18		DLC-55
Fr	1843 Feb 18*		35-1236
To	1843 Feb 20		DLC-55
To	1843 Feb 20*		35-1238
To	1843 Feb 21		DLC-55
To	1843 Feb 21*		35-1250
Fr	1843 Feb 22		DLC-55
Fr	1843 Feb 22*		35-1251
To	1843 Feb 27		DLC-55
To	1843 Feb 27*		35-1257
To	1843 Mar 02		DLC-55
To	1843 Mar 02*		35-1270
To	1843 Mar 20		DLC-55
To	1843 Mar 20*		35-1284
Fr	1843 Mar 22		DLC-55
Fr	1843 Mar 22*		35-1288
Fr	1843 Apr 14		DLC-55
Fr	1843 Apr 14*		35-1305
To	1843 May 17		DLC-55
To	1843 May 20		DLC-55
Fr	1843 May 21		DLC-55
To	1843 Jun 01		DLC-55
Fr	1843 Jun 22		DLC-55
Fr	1843 Jun 22*		35-1387
To	1843 Jun 27		DLC-55
Fr	1843 Jun 29		DLC-55
Fr	1843 Jun 29*		35-1391
Fr	1843 Jul 04		DLC-55
Fr	1843 Jul 04*		35-1398
To	1843 Jul 14		DLC-55
To	1843 Jul 14*		35-1415
Fr	1843 Jul 18		DLC-55
Fr	1843 Jul 18*		35-1420
Fr	1843 Jul 30		DLC-55
Fr	1843 Jul 30*		35-1437
To	1843 Aug 11		DLC-55
To	1843 Aug 11*		35-1450
To	1843 Aug 18		DLC-55
To	1843 Aug 18*		35-1467
To	1843 Sep 07		DLC-55

To 1843 Sep 07*	35-1478
Fr 1843 Sep 10	DLC-55
Fr 1843 Sep 26	DLC-55
Fr 1843 Sep 26*	35-1512
To 1843 Oct 09	DLC-55
To 1843 Oct 09*	35-1532
Fr 1843 Oct 26	DLC-55
Fr 1843 Oct 26*	35-1565
To 1843 Oct 31	DLC-56
To 1843 Oct 31*	35-1574
To 1843 Nov 02	DLC-56
To 1843 Nov 02*	35-1581
Fr 1843 Nov 11	DLC-56
Fr 1843 Nov 11*	36-0001
To 1843 Nov 17	DLC-56
To 1843 Nov 17*	36-0009
To 1843 Nov 22	DLC-56
To 1843 Nov 22*	36-0016
Fr 1843 Nov 26	DLC-56
Fr 1843 Nov 26*	36-0022
Fr 1843 Nov 30	DLC-74
To 1843 Dec 05	DLC-56
To 1843 Dec 05*	36-0041
Fr 1843 Dec 06	DLC-56
Fr 1843 Dec 06*	36-0044
To 1843 Dec 15	36-0051
Fr 1843 Dec 16	DLC-56
Fr 1843 Dec 16*	36-0061
Fr 1843 Dec 18	DLC-56
Fr 1843 Dec 18*	36-0066
Fr 1843 Dec 25	DLC-56
Fr 1843 Dec 25*	36-0073
To 1844 Jan 05	DLC-56
To 1844 Jan 05*	36-0112
Fr 1844 Jan 09	DLC-56
Fr 1844 Jan 09*	36-0115
To 1844 Jan 19	DLC-56
To 1844 Jan 19*	36-0139
To 1844 Feb 06	DLC-56
To 1844 Feb 06*	36-0157
Fr 1844 Feb 14	DLC-56
Fr 1844 Feb 14*	36-0256
To 1844 Feb 24	DLC-56
To 1844 Feb 24*	36-0334
To 1844 Feb 24	DLC-56
To 1844 Feb 24*	36-0336
To 1844 Feb 29	DLC-56
To 1844 Feb 29*	36-0353
Fr 1844 Mar 02	DLC-56
Fr 1844 Mar 02*	36-0360
Fr 1844 Apr 02	36-0416
To 1844 Apr 05	36-0417
To 1844 Apr 12	DLC-56
To 1844 Apr 12*	36-0438
Fr 1844 May 02	DLC-56
Fr 1844 May 02*	36-0472
To 1844 May 03	DLC-56
To 1844 May 03*	36-0478
To 1844 May 07	DLC-56
To 1844 May 07*	36-0498
To 1844 May 11	DLC-56
To 1844 May 11*	36-0509
To 1844 May 11	DLC-56
To 1844 May 11*	36-0512
To 1844 cMay 11	36-0516
To 1844 May 18	DLC-56
To 1844 May 18*	36-0555
Fr 1844 May 19	DLC-56
Fr 1844 May 19*	36-0558
To 1844 Jun 07	DLC-57
To 1844 Jun 07*	36-0590
To 1844 Jun 25	DLC-57
To 1844 Jun 25*	36-0646
Fr 1844 Jul 07	DLC-57
Fr 1844 Jul 07*	36-0680
To 1844 Jul 12	DLC-57
To 1844 Jul 12*	36-0697
To 1844 Jul 26	DLC-57
To 1844 Jul 26*	36-0745
Fr 1844 Aug 04	DLC-57
Fr 1844 Aug 04*	36-0765
To 1844 Aug 15	DLC-57
To 1844 Aug 15*	36-0790
To 1844 Aug 29	DLC-57
To 1844 Aug 29*	36-0831
Fr 1844 Sep 09	DLC-57
Fr 1844 Sep 09*	36-0846
To 1844 Sep 19	DLC-57
To 1844 Sep 19*	36-0891
Fr 1844 Sep 28	DLC-57
Fr 1844 Sep 28*	36-0912
To 1844 Oct 17	DLC-57
To 1844 Oct 17*	36-0952
To 1844 Oct 24	DLC-57
To 1844 Oct 24*	36-0959
Fr 1844 Oct 27	DLC-57
Fr 1844 Oct 27*	36-0962
Fr 1844 Nov 07	DLC-74
Fr 1844 Nov 13	DLC-57
Fr 1844 Nov 13*	36-1020
To 1844 Nov 18	DLC-57
To 1844 Nov 18*	36-1027
Fr 1844 Nov 24	36-1048
To 1844 Nov 29	DLC-57
To 1844 Nov 29*	36-1071
Fr 1844 Nov 30	DLC-57
Fr 1844 Nov 30*	36-1079
Fr 1844 Dec 08	DLC-74
To 1844 Dec 14	DLC-57
To 1844 Dec 14*	36-1207
To 1844 Dec 21	DLC-57
To 1844 Dec 21*	36-1232
Fr 1844 Dec 22	DLC-57
Fr 1844 Dec 22*	36-1244
Fr 1844 Dec 25	DLC-57
Fr 1844 Dec 25*	36-1266
To 1845 Jan 01	DLC-57
To 1845 Jan 01*	36-1284
Fr 1845 Jan 03	DLC-57
Fr 1845 Jan 03	36-1295
To 1845 Jan 04	DLC-57
To 1845 Jan 04*	36-1300
Fr 1845 Jan 04	DLC-57
Fr 1845 Jan 04*	36-1301
Fr 1845 Jan 13	DLC-74
Fr 1845 Jan 19	DLC-57
Fr 1845 Jan 19*	36-1373
To 1845 Jan 21	DLC-57
To 1845 Jan 21*	36-1384
Fr 1845 Jan 30	DLC-57
Fr 1845 Jan 30*	36-1424
To 1845 Feb 08	36-1463
Fr 1845 Feb 09	DLC-57
Fr 1845 Feb 09*	36-1469
Fr 1845 Feb 21	36-1504
To 1845 Feb 28	DLC-57
To 1845 Feb 28*	36-1514
Fr 1845 Feb 28	DLC-57

Blair Francis Preston (cont)
Fr 1845 Feb 28* 36-1517
To 1845 Mar 03 DLC-57
To 1845 Mar 03* 36-1530
To 1845 Mar 10 DLC-57
To 1845 Mar 10* 36-1558
To 1845 Mar 18 DLC-57
To 1845 Mar 18* 36-1584
Fr 1845 Mar 24 DLC-57
Fr 1845 Mar 24* 37-0025
Fr 1845 Mar 30 DLC-57
Fr 1845 Mar 30* 37-0059
To 1845 Apr 04 DLC-58
To 1845 Apr 04* 37-0115
To 1845 Apr 07 DLC-58
To 1845 Apr 07* 37-0116
To 1845 Apr 09 37-0124
To 1845 Apr 10 DLC-58
To 1845 Apr 10* 37-0135
Fr 1845 Apr 17 DLC-58
Fr 1845 Apr 17* 37-0147
Fr 1845 Apr 19 37-0150
To 1845 Apr 20 DLC-58
To 1845 Apr 28 DLC-58
To 1845 Apr 28* 37-0160
Fr 1845 Apr 30 DLC-58
Fr 1845 Apr 30* 37-0162
To 1845 May 03 37-0182
Fr 1845 May 03 37-0184
To 1845 May 26 DLC-58
To 1845 May 26* 37-0219
Fr 1845 Jun 08 DLC-74
Blair George
Fr 1832 Apr 02 20-0089
Fr 1834 Dec 14 26-1497
Blair J C et al
Fr c1836 29-1380
Blair James
Fr 1830 May 01 DLC-72
Fr 1831 Nov 07 M639-6
Fr 1832 Jun 02 M639-11
Fr 1832 Jun 13 M639-7
Blair John
Fr 1825 Mar 30 DLC-33
Fr 1829 Apr 14 M639-11
Fr 1831 Mar 18 DLC-39
Fr 1834 Feb 04 M567-95
Fr 1837 Apr 19 33-1163
Fr 1837 Apr 21 DLC-74
Blair Montgomery
Fr 1836 Jan 26# 30-0203
Fr 1843 Nov 20 DLC-56
Fr 1843 Nov 20* 36-0011
To 1843 Nov 27 36-0025
Fr 1844 Mar 16 DLC-56
Fr 1844 Dec 23 DLC-57
Fr 1845 Jan 16 36-1349
Blair Samuel
Fr 1831 Oct 12 M639-2
Blair & Rives
Re 1839 May 15 leg DLC-52
Re 1839 May 15* leg 34-0791
Fr 1841 Apr 15 DLC-53
To 1843 Apr 12 DLC-55
Fr 1843 May 11 35-1350
Fr 1845 Mar 12 fin 36-1560
Fr 1845 Apr 01 DLC-58
Blake Francis et al
Fr 1836 Jun 04 31-0309
Blake James et al
Fr 1840 Jun 24 34-1443
Blake James H
Fr 1815 Nov 21 4-1257
To 1815 Nov 21 4-1258
Blake James H et al
Fr 1815 Nov 25 add DLC-19
To 1815 Nov 25 add 4-1259
Blake John B
Fr 1830 Feb 20# DLC-37
Blake John S
Re 1829 Nov par 14-0301
Blake Thomas Holdsworth
Fr 1829 Mar 09 12-0897
Blakeley Josiah
To 1814 Jul 26 DLC-62
Blakeley Josiah et al
Fr 1814 Jul 20 DLC-11
Blakemore George
Fr 1808 Mar 22 DLC-71
Blakemore Thomas
Re 1809 Mar 25 leg 2-0794
Blalock Charles
Fr 1807 Nov 05 2-0590
Blanchard Albert Gallatin
Fr 1833 Sep 11 M567-85
Blanchard Charles K
Fr 1815 Mar 20 DLC-17
Blanckenship Joel
To 1829 Feb 14 12-0510
Bland Theodorick
Fr 1829 Feb 14 DLC-36
Fr 1834 May 28 M124-142
Bland Theodorick Mrs
To 1831 Jan 02 17-0133
Blaney George
Fr 1819 Jan 14 DLC-26
Fr 1819 Jan 14* 7-0183
Bledsoe Jesse
Fr 1826 Jan 02 DLC-33
To 1826 Jan 18 DLC-33
Fr 1828 Sep 22 DLC-35
Fr 1828 Dec 27 DLC-36
Bleecker James W
Fr 1830 Feb 24 15-0239
Blennerhassett R S
Fr 1844 Mar 18 DLC-56
Blennerhassett v Burr
Re 1813 Mar 25 leg 3-0356
Re 1813 Sep 25 leg 3-0477
Re 1815 Apr 21 leg 4-1012
Bliss Henry
Fr 1835 Apr 20 DLC-46
Bliss Horace
Fr 1836 Mar 25 M567-117
Blockberger Christopher
Fr 1829 May 26 M124-118
Bloodgood Francis
To 1833 Jun 30 23-0083
Bloodworth James
To 1815 Feb 26 DLC-62
Blount John Gray
Fr 1815 Sep lnd DLC-19
Blount Thomas M et al
Fr 1835 Jan 29 M639-1
Blount William
Fr 1792 Sep 10 DLC-1
Fr 1795 Sep 02 DLC-1
To 1796 Feb 29 1-0341
Re 1796 Mar 09 mem DLC-1
Re 1796 Mar 09* mem DLC-60

Fr 1796 Jun 11 fin DLC-1
Fr 1798 Jul 06# 1-0670
Fr 1798 Jul 12 fin DLC-2
Blount William (steersman)
Fr 1812 Jul 24 fin DLC-5
Blount William Grainger
Fr 1813 Apr 22 3-0375
To 1813 Apr 22 3-0376
Fr 1813 Oct 12 DLC-6
Fr 1813 Oct 12* DLC-61
Fr 1814 Feb 08 DLC-8
Fr 1814 Jul 05 DLC-11
Fr 1814 Dec 26 DLC-15
Blount Willie
Fr 1796 Apr 24 DLC-1
Fr 1796 Jul 05# 1-0440
Fr 1797 Jun 23 DLC-2
To 1797 Dec 15 1-0556
To 1798 Feb 21 1-0620
Fr 1799 Oct 08 DLC-2
Fr 1801 Dec 07 DLC-2
Fr 1804 Jul 28 1-1359
Fr 1809 Dec 28 DLC-4
Fr 1810 Jan 10 DLC-75
To 1810 Feb 15 DLC-4
Fr 1810 Mar 15 DLC-4
Fr 1810 Nov 18 DLC-5
Fr 1811 Feb 26 2-0992
Fr 1811 Dec 04 2-1021
To 1812 Jan 25 M221-42
Fr 1812 Feb 10 2-1049
Fr 1812 Mar 20 DLC-5
Fr 1812 Mar 22 DLC-5
Fr 1812 Apr 17 DLC-5
Fr 1812 Apr 18 2-1070
To 1812 Apr 23 2-1072
To 1812 May 09 2-1090
Fr 1812 Jun 04 DLC-5
To 1812 Jun 05 DLC-5
Fr 1812 Jun 12 DLC-5
Fr 1812 Jun 12 DLC-5
Fr 1812 Jun 14 DLC-5
Fr 1812 Jun 17 2-1105
To 1812 Jun 17 DLC-5
Fr 1812 Jun 18 DLC-5
Fr 1812 Jun 23 DLC-5
Fr 1812 Jun 25 DLC-5
To 1812 Jul 03 DLC-5
Fr 1812 Jul 04 DLC-5
Fr 1812 Jul 07 DLC-5
To 1812 Jul 08 DLC-5
To 1812 Jul 10 DLC-5
Fr 1812 Jul 13 DLC-5
Fr 1812 Jul 21 DLC-5
Fr 1812 Jul 24 DLC-5
Fr 1812 Jul 24 DLC-5
Fr 1812 Jun 30 DLC-5
Fr 1812 Aug 07 DLC-5
To 1812 Aug 22 DLC-5
To 1812 Sep 08 2-1241
To 1812 Nov 10 DLC-61
To 1812 Nov 11 DLC-5
Fr 1812 Nov 11 DLC-5
Fr 1812 Nov 11* DLC-61
Fr 1812 Nov 11* M222-5
Fr 1812 Nov 23 DLC-5
Fr 1812 Nov 23* DLC-61
Fr 1812 Nov 23* M222-5
To 1812 Nov 27 2-1277
To 1812 Dec 13 DLC-5
To 1812 Dec 13* DLC-61
Fr 1812 Dec 13 DLC-5
Fr 1812 Dec 13* DLC-61
Fr 1812 Dec 15 DLC-61
Fr 1812 Dec 17 DLC-5
Fr 1812 Dec 17* DLC-61
Fr 1812 Dec 17* 2-1297
To 1812 Dec 21 DLC-61
To 1812 Dec 21* DLC-5
To 1812 Dec 21* 2-1306
Fr 1812 Dec 24 DLC-5
Fr 1812 Dec 27 DLC-5
Fr 1812 Dec 27 DLC-5
Fr 1812 Dec 31 DLC-5
Fr 1812 Dec 31* DLC-61
Fr 1812 Dec 31 DLC-5
Fr 1812 Dec 31* DLC-61
Fr 1812 Dec 31 DLC-5
Fr 1812 Dec 31* DLC-61
Fr 1812 Dec 31* M221-50
Fr 1813 Jan 01 DLC-5
Fr 1813 Jan 02 DLC-5
Fr 1813 Jan 02* DLC-61
To 1813 Jan 03 DLC-5
To 1813 Jan 03* DLC-61
Fr 1813 Jan 03 DLC-5
To 1813 Jan 04 DLC-5
To 1813 Jan 04* M221-50
To 1813 Jan 04* DLC-61
To 1813 Jan 09 DLC-6
To 1813 Jan 09* DLC-61
Fr 1813 Jan 09 DLC-6
Fr 1813 Jan 10 DLC-6
Fr 1813 Jan 13 fin 3-0244
To 1813 Feb 21 DLC-6
Fr 1813 Mar 05 DLC-61
Fr 1813 Mar 08 DLC-6
Re 1813 Mar 10 DLC-5
To 1813 Mar 15 DLC-61
To 1813 Mar 15* DLC-6
Fr 1813 Apr 27 DLC-6
To 1813 Jul 31 M200-20
Fr 1813 Aug 14 DLC-6
Fr 1813 Sep 24 DLC-6
Fr 1813 Sep 24* M222-7
Fr 1813 Sep 24* DLC-61
Fr 1813 Sep 24* DLC-64
Fr 1813 Sep 24 M222-7
Fr 1813 Sep 24* DLC-64
Fr 1813 Oct 04 DLC-6
Fr 1813 Oct 04* DLC-61
Fr 1813 Oct 04* M221-50
To 1813 Oct 11 DLC-71
To 1813 Oct 13 DLC-6
To 1813 Oct 14 DLC-7
Fr 1813 Oct 15 DLC-7
Fr 1813 Oct 15* DLC-61
Fr 1813 Oct 18 DLC-7
To 1813 Oct 20 DLC-7
To 1813 Oct 20* M222-7
Fr 1813 Oct 21 DLC-7
Fr 1813 Oct 21* DLC-61
To 1813 Oct 24 DLC-61
To 1813 Oct 28 DLC-61
To 1813 Oct 28* M222-7
To 1813 Nov 01 DLC-61
Fr 1813 Nov 03 DLC-7
Fr 1813 Nov 03* M222-7

Blount Willie (cont)

To 1813 Nov 04	DLC-7
Fr 1813 Nov 09	DLC-7
To 1813 Nov 11	DLC-61
To 1813 Nov 11*	M221-50
Fr 1813 Nov 12	DLC-7
Fr 1813 Nov 12	DLC-7
To 1813 Nov 12	3-0583
To 1813 Nov 14	DLC-7
To 1813 Nov 15	DLC-61
To 1813 Nov 15	DLC-61
Fr 1813 Nov 17	DLC-7
Fr 1813 Nov 17*	DLC-61
Fr 1813 Nov 19	DLC-7
Fr 1813 Nov 19	DLC-7
To 1813 Nov 20	M221-50
Fr 1813 Nov 20	DLC-7
Fr 1813 Nov 20*	DLC-61
To 1813 Nov 21	3-0619
To 1813 Nov 22	DLC-61
Fr 1813 Nov 23	DLC-7
Fr 1813 Nov 24	DLC-7
To 1813 Nov 29	3-0623
To 1813 Nov 29	DLC-7
Fr 1813 Dec 07	DLC-7
Fr 1813 Dec 07*	DLC-61
To 1813 Dec 12	DLC-6
To 1813 Dec 13	DLC-61
Fr 1813 Dec 15	DLC-7
Fr 1813 Dec 15*	DLC-61
To 1813 Dec 15	3-0671
To 1813 Dec 18	DLC-61
Fr 1813 Dec 22	DLC-7
Fr 1813 Dec 22*	3-0696
Fr 1813 Dec 22*	M221-56
Fr 1813 Dec 22	DLC-7
Fr 1813 Dec 22*	M221-56
Fr 1813 Dec 22*	3-0698
Fr 1813 Dec 26	DLC-8
To 1813 Dec 26	DLC-8
To 1813 Dec 28	DLC-8
To 1813 Dec 29	DLC-61
To 1813 Dec 29*	3-0733
To 1814 Jan 02	DLC-61
To 1814 Jan 04	DLC-61
Fr 1814 Jan 05	DLC-8
To 1814 Jan 07	DLC-61
Fr 1814 Jan 23	DLC-8
Fr 1814 Jan 23	DLC-8
Fr 1814 Jan 25	DLC-8
To 1814 Jan 29	DLC-61
To 1814 Jan 31	3-0833
To 1814 Feb 08	DLC-61
To 1814 Mar 07	DLC-61
To 1814 Mar 10	DLC-61
To 1814 Mar 10*	M221-60
Fr 1814 Mar 13	DLC-9
Fr 1814 Mar 20	DLC-9
To 1814 Mar 23	DLC-9
To 1814 Mar 31	3-0937
To 1814 Apr 02	3-0951
To 1814 Apr 02*	DLC-10
To 1814 Apr 18	DLC-10
To 1814 Apr 18*	M221-60
To 1814 Apr 25	3-0993
To 1814 May 01	DLC-10
Fr 1814 May 03	DLC-10
Fr 1814 May 04	DLC-10
Fr 1814 May 05	DLC-10
Fr 1814 May 05	DLC-10
Fr 1814 May 05	DLC-10
Fr 1814 May 05*	M221-62
To 1814 May 08	3-1008
To 1814 May 10	M221-62
To 1814 May 10	3-1022
To 1814 May 19	DLC-10
To 1814 May 19*	M221-62
Fr 1814 May 20	DLC-10
Fr 1814 May 20*	M221-62
Fr 1814 May 20*	3-1038
Fr 1814 Jul 11	DLC-11
To 1814 Jul 22	DLC-62
To 1814 Aug 05	DLC-62
To 1814 Aug 06	3-1230
To 1814 Aug 09	DLC-62
To 1814 Aug 27	DLC-62
To 1814 Aug 27*	M221-59
To 1814 Aug 27*	DLC-12
Fr 1814 Sep 08	4-0191
Fr 1814 Sep 11	DLC-12
Fr 1814 Sep 16	DLC-12
Fr 1814 Sep 20	DLC-12
To 1814 Oct 07	DLC-62
Fr 1814 Oct 08	DLC-13
To 1814 Oct 10	4-0262
To 1814 Oct 11	DLC-62
Fr 1814 Oct 13	DLC-13
Fr 1814 Oct 19	DLC-13
Fr 1814 Oct 21	DLC-13
Fr 1814 Oct 23	DLC-13
Fr 1814 Oct 25	DLC-13
To 1814 Oct 27	4-0297
To 1814 Oct 27*	DLC-62
Fr 1814 Oct 28	DLC-13
To 1814 Nov 14	DLC-14
To 1814 Nov 14*	4-0329
Fr 1814 Nov 18	DLC-14
Fr 1814 Nov 24	DLC-14
Fr 1814 Nov 26	DLC-14
To 1814 Dec 12	DLC-62
Fr 1814 Dec 16	DLC-14
To 1814 Dec 17	4-0407
To 1814 Dec 26	4-0463
Fr 1814 Dec 29	DLC-15
Fr 1815 Jan	4-0480
Fr 1815 Jan 08	DLC-71
To 1815 Jan 27	4-0625
Fr 1815 Feb 06	DLC-71
Fr 1815 Feb 10	DLC-16
Fr 1815 Feb 14	DLC-16
To 1815 Mar 01	4-0806
Fr 1815 Mar 07	DLC-17
Fr 1815 Mar 08	DLC-17
Fr 1815 Apr 13	DLC-18
To 1819 Apr 08	7-0467
Fr 1819 Apr 18	DLC-26
Fr 1819 Apr 18	DLC-26
To 1823 May 29	9-0578
To 1825 Feb 15	10-1117
To 1825 Feb 17	10-1120
To 1829 May 22	13-0371
Fr 1829 Jul 04	13-0814
Fr 1829 Oct	14-0005
Fr 1830 Jan 04	14-1311
Fr 1830 Jan 04	14-1315
Fr 1830 Oct	DLC-73
To 1831 Aug 29	DLC-40
Fr 1831 Sep	DLC-40
Fr 1831 Sep 30	DLC-40

Fr 1833 Feb 08		DLC-42
Fr 1833 Jun		22-1540
Fr 1833 Jun 27		DLC-73
Fr 1834 Jan 28		DLC-73
Fr 1834 Aug 06		DLC-44
Fr 1834 Sep 01		DLC-44
Fr 1835 Apr		27-1403
Blue Uriah		
Fr 1814 Oct 25		DLC-13
Fr 1814 Nov 14		M221-63
To 1814 Nov 16		DLC-62
Fr 1814 Dec 07		DLC-14
Fr 1814 Dec 18		DLC-14
Fr 1814 Dec 27		DLC-15
Fr 1815 Jan 10		4-0510
Fr 1815 Jan 10*		M221-16
Fr 1815 Jan 29		DLC-16
Fr 1815 Mar 18		DLC-17
Fr 1815 Apr 26		DLC-18
Blue & Shomo		
Fr 1821 May 31	fin	DLC-70
Blue Jacket James		
Fr 1836 Jul 04		M234-422
Blue Jacket James Jr		
Fr 1836 Jul 04		M234-422
Blum John C		
Fr 1833 Sep 05		23-0629
Blunt Edmund March		
Fr 1829 May 15		M124-118
Blunt John		
Fr 1827 Oct 28		11-0903
Blunt John et al		
Fr 1830 Aug 01		M234-287
Blythe Calvin		
Fr 1829 Mar		12-0620
Fr 1829 Jun 06		13-0581
Fr 1834 Jul 19		26-0235
Fr 1836 Jan 20		M221-116
Blythe Calvin et al		
Fr 1828 Dec 09		DLC-36
Blythe Samuel K		
Re 1825 May 10	leg	DLC-33
Boardman Elijah		
Re 1831 Oct 14		18-0987
Boat building		
Re 1803 Nov 23	fin	DLC-3
Re 1803 Dec 07	fin	DLC-3
Re 1804 Feb 10	fin	1-1279
Re 1804 Feb 17	fin	1-1281
Re 1804 Feb 18	mem	DLC-3
Re 1804 Apr 28	fin	1-1318
Re 1804 Jul 19	fin	1-1347
Boatner Mark		
Fr 1836 Aug 12		DLC-48
Fr 1839 Jun 14		DLC-52
Boddie Elijah et al		
To 1841 Sep 07		35-0393
Bodley Thomas		
Fr 1821 Apr 12		M439-15
Bogardus Evert		
Fr 1814 Jul 20		DLC-11
Fr 1814 Aug 23		DLC-11
Fr 1814 Sep 16		DLC-12
Fr 1814 Oct 14		DLC-13
Bogardus Robert		
Fr 1831 Sep 22		M639-18
Bogert Cornelius		
Fr 1831 Apr 13		DLC-39
Bogert James		
Fr 1839 Aug 22		DLC-52
Boggs James		
Re 1807 Jul 29	leg	2-0522
Boggs Lilburn W		
Fr 1837 Jun 20		DLC-50
Boggs William M et al		
Fr 1829 Jul 20		M639-2
Boggs & Davidson		
Fr 1803 Aug 02		DLC-3
To 1803 Sep 02		DLC-3
Fr 1803 Sep 19		DLC-3
Fr 1803 Oct 07		DLC-3
To 1804 Jul 31		DLC-3
To 1806 Nov 30		DLC-71
Bohan & Magruder		
Fr 1833 Mar 10#	fin	DLC-42
Bohrer Benjamin F		
To 1835 Jan 21		27-0264
Fr 1835 Feb 26#		DLC-45
Boissiere Joseph S		
Re 1830 Mar 29	par	15-0480
Boker John G		
Re 1829 Nov 30		14-0627
Bolivar Simon		
To 1829 Jun 09		13-0602
Fr 1829 Nov 28		DLC-37
Fr 1830 Feb 12		15-0136
Bolles James G et al		
Fr 1836 May		M687-17
Bolles Lucius		
Fr 1829 May 09		M234-774
Fr 1832 Mar 08		M234-775
Bolton Joel		
Fr 1806 Oct 25	fin	DLC-4
Bolton W C		
Fr 1845 Feb 25#		36-1510
Bomford George		
Fr 1816 Jan 15		DLC-20
Fr 1816 Jul 30		DLC-21
Fr 1816 Jul 30*		5-0336
Fr 1816 Oct 15		DLC-21
To 1816 Nov 01		DLC-21
Fr 1824 Apr 01		10-0619
Fr 1830 Nov 08#		M567-56
To 1833 Sep 27		23-0888
Fr 1835 Feb 11		27-0491
Re 1835 cMar	mem	27-0668
Fr 1835 Mar 30		27-1392
To 1835 Jul 25		28-1156
Fr 1835 Jul 30		M22-36
Fr 1836 cOct		M221-126
Fr 1837 Sep 13		33-1475
Fr 1837 Sep 14		33-1476
Bonaparte Joseph		
To 1831 May 23		17-1409
Bondstreet N C		
Fr 1842 Jan 07		DLC-54
Bondurant Edward		
Fr 1811 Dec 14		DLC-5
Bondurant Jacob		
To 1842 Jan 08		35-0591
Bones John		
Fr 1844 Sep 17		DLC-57
Bonifaul John		
Re 1835 Dec 22	fin	DLC-47
Bonsall Benjamin S		
Fr 1833 May 09		DLC-42
Fr 1834 Nov 10		M639-10

Name / Date		Note	Source
Bonsall Benjamin S (cont)			
	Fr 1835 Oct 25		DLC-47
	Fr 1836 Jan 25		M639-3
Bonsall Benjamin S et al			
	Fr 1829 Apr 11		M639-13
	Fr 1832 Dec 22		M639-7
Bonsall William			
	Fr 1841 Jun 17		35-0333
Booby Francis			
	Re 1817 Oct 06		5-1100
Booge Aaron Jordan			
	Fr 1818 Apr 04		DLC-24
Booker Peter R			
	To 1822 Jan 26	fin	9-0005
	Fr 1823 Jan 30	fin	9-0437
Booker W B et al			
	Fr 1829 Apr		M639-15
Boon Hampton L			
	Fr 1830 Jan 01		14-1257
Boon Ratliff			
	Fr 1832 Jan 23		19-0816
	Fr 1832 Apr 13		M22-29
	Fr 1832 Dec 01		21-0645
	Fr 1835 Dec 21		M639-11
	Fr 1836 Mar 07		DLC-47
Boon Ratliff et al			
	Fr 1829 Feb 05		M639-16
	Fr 1836 Feb		M234-355
Boone Samuel			
	Fr 1839 Jul 29		DLC-52
Booraem H & Co			
	Fr 1833 Apr 23		M639-16
Boorman Johnston & Co et al			
	Fr 1833 Aug 31		M639-20
Booth John P			
	Fr 1833 Jan 24		M639-2
Booth Junius Brutus (pseudonym)			
	Fr 1835 Jul 04		DLC-46
Booth William et al			
	Fr 1836 Nov		M639-9
Boott Kirk			
	To 1833 Jul 01#		23-0091
Bordelau Valere			
	Fr 1815 Feb 15		4-0743
	To 1815 Feb 18		DLC-62
Border William			
	Re 1836 Jan 27	par	30-0204
	Re 1836 Feb 10	par	30-0341
Borgan J J			
	Fr 1829 Jun 20		M639-20
Borland Euclid			
	Re 1834 Oct 15		M273-31
Borner ______ (Capt)			
	To 1828 Dec 13		12-0323
Bosley John			
	Fr 1808 May 15	fin	DLC-4
Bosque Felicite			
	Fr 1815 Feb 16	fin	4-0749
Bosque Joseph			
	Fr 1815 Mar 12		4-0841
Bostick ______ (Dr)			
	To 1813 Dec 15		DLC-61
Bostick John G			
	Fr 1836 Feb 15		DLC-47
Boston Young Men			
	Fr 1840		DLC-53
Boswell William			
	Re 1829 Jun 27	par	13-0720
Bosworth Jacob			
	Fr 1831 Apr 03		M22-27
	Fr 1831 Sep 15		18-0793

Name / Date		Note	Source
Bosworth W			
	Fr 1839 Mar 20#	fin	DLC-52
Boteler & Beck et al			
	Fr 1832 Feb 18		M639-6
Botsford Joseph E et al			
	Fr 1832 Dec 26		M639-16
Botts George W			
	To 1825 Feb 05		10-1097
Bouchaud Joseph			
	Fr 1833 Apr 25		M639-16
Bouck C W			
	Fr 1844 Mar 20		DLC-56
Bouck William C			
	Fr 1843 Dec 30		DLC-56
	Fr 1844 Jan 12		DLC-56
Bouis Amedee Theod			
	Fr 1842 Sep 01		DLC-54
Boulanger Joseph			
	Fr 1833		21-1234
	To 1833 May 02	chk	DLC-42
	To 1833 Jun 03	chk	DLC-43
	To 1833 Jun 13	chk	DLC-43
	To 1833 Jul 05	chk	DLC-43
	To 1833 Aug 02	chk	DLC-43
	To 1833 Sep 12	chk	DLC-43
	To 1833 Oct 02	chk	DLC-43
	To 1833 Nov 02	chk	DLC-43
	To 1833 Nov 20	chk	DLC-43
	To 1833 Dec 03	chk	DLC-43
	To 1833 Dec 16	chk	DLC-43
	To 1834 Jan 03	chk	DLC-43
	To 1834 Feb 03	chk	DLC-44
	To 1834 Feb 03	chk	DLC-44
	To 1834 Feb 10	chk	DLC-44
	To 1834 Feb 17	chk	DLC-44
	To 1834 Feb 24	chk	DLC-44
	To 1834 Mar 04	chk	DLC-44
	To 1834 Mar 04	chk	DLC-44
	To 1834 Apr 01	chk	DLC-44
	To 1834 Apr 24	chk	DLC-44
	To 1834 May 01#	fin	DLC-44
	To 1834 May 06	chk	DLC-44
	To 1834 May 08#	fin	DLC-44
	To 1834 May 19	chk	DLC-44
	To 1834 May 29	chk	DLC-44
	To 1834 Jun 03	chk	DLC-44
	To 1834 Jul 02	chk	DLC-44
	To 1834 Jul 10#	fin	DLC-44
	To 1834 Jul 15	chk	DLC-44
	To 1834 Aug 05	chk	DLC-44
	To 1834 Aug 11#	fin	DLC-44
	To 1834 Sep 15#	fin	DLC-44
	To 1834 Oct 04	chk	DLC-44
	To 1834 Nov 03	chk	DLC-45
	To 1834 Nov 04#	fin	DLC-45
	To 1834 Nov 17	chk	DLC-45
	To 1834 Dec 01#	fin	DLC-45
	To 1834 Dec 02	chk	DLC-45
	To 1835 Jan 01#	fin	DLC-45
	To 1835 Jan 02	chk	27-0078
	To 1835 Mar 31#	fin	DLC-46
	To 1835 Apr 01#	fin	DLC-46
	To 1835 May 01	chk	28-0208
	To 1835 Jun 01#	fin	DLC-46
	To 1835 Jun 15#	fin	DLC-46
	To 1835 Jul 01#	fin	DLC-46
	To 1835 Aug 11#	fin	DLC-46
	To 1835 Sep#	fin	DLC-47
	To 1835 Oct 01	chk	DLC-47

To 1835 Oct 02# fin DLC-47
To 1835 Oct 07 chk DLC-47
To 1835 Nov 02 chk DLC-47
To 1835 Nov 04# fin DLC-47
To 1835 Nov 18# fin DLC-47
To 1835 Dec 03# fin DLC-47
To 1836 Jan 04 chk DLC-47
To 1836 Jan 07# fin DLC-47
To 1836 Jan 29# fin DLC-47
To 1836 Feb 01# fin DLC-47
To 1836 Feb 02 chk DLC-47
To 1836 Feb 11# fin DLC-47
To 1836 Mar 03 chk DLC-47
To 1836 Apr 02 chk DLC-47
To 1836 May 04 chk DLC-48
To 1836 May 17 chk DLC-48
To 1836 Jul 04 chk DLC-48
To 1836 Aug 01 chk DLC-48
To 1836 Oct 01 chk DLC-49
To 1836 Oct 03 chk DLC-49

Bourgeau Antoine
To 1815 Feb 16 DLC-16

Bourke Walter
Fr 1814 Apr 24 DLC-10
Fr 1816 Mar 11 DLC-20

Bourne George S
Fr 1832 Dec 16# M639-2

Boutard Joseph
Fr 1836 Dec 25 32-1315

Boutineff A
Fr 1835 Apr 10 M46-9

Bouton Nathaniel
To 1833 Jun 29 23-0072

Bowen Ephraim
Fr 1831 Apr 08 M179-70
Fr 1831 Sep 04 T339-1

Bowen Henry et al
Fr 1835 cJan DLC-59

Bowen James
Re 1803 Sep 29 leg 1-1173

Bowen John Arthur (slave)
Re 1836 Feb 25 par 30-0520
Re 1836 Feb 25* par T967-1
Re 1836 Jun 03 par 31-0273
Re 1836 Jun 27 par 31-0587
Re 1836 Jun 27* par T967-2

Bowen John D
Fr 1838 Jan 07 DLC-51
Fr 1841 May 15 DLC-53

Bowen John H
To 1816 Jun 17 lnd 5-0169

Bowen M
Fr 1833# fin 21-1235
Fr 1834# fin DLC-45
Fr 1836 May 07# fin DLC-48

Bowen Mary H
Fr 1826 Dec 21 DLC-34

Bowen William
Fr 1793 Jan 03 fin 1-0137
Fr 1793 Jan 03* fin DLC-71
Re 1793 Jun 15 leg DLC-1

Bower John et al
Fr 1830 Dec 22 16-1540

Bowers William Pitt
Re 1796 Feb 19 leg DLC-1

Bowie George
To 1821 Jul 19 DLC-63
To 1821 Sep 22 DLC-63
Fr 1821 Sep 27 DLC-63

Bowker Leonard
Re 1834 Jan 16 par 24-0929

Bowman James H
Fr 1828 Dec 27 DLC-36

Bowne Samuel Smith et al
Fr 1834 Jan 08 M639-7

Bowne Walter
To 1829 Apr 04 12-1266
Fr 1829 Oct 24 M222-27
Fr 1830 Dec 01 16-0920
Fr 1831 Mar 22 17-0923
Fr 1831 Sep 08 M639-18

Bowne Walter et al
Fr 1829 Feb 23 12-0570
Fr 1829 Dec 01 M639-21
Fr 1830 Jun 24 M639-3
Fr 1831 Jul 30 M639-11
Fr 1831 Aug 12 M639-18
Fr 1831 Oct 14 M639-24

Bowyer John M
Re 1829 Nov 03 14-0395

Boyce William H et al
Fr 1842 Dec 07 35-1020
To 1842 Dec 18 DLC-74

Boyce William M
Fr 1836 Oct 31 M567-118

Boyd George
Fr 1835 Aug 15 28-1288
Fr 1835 Dec 07# 29-0775

Boyd George C
Fr 1840 Apr 09 DLC-52
Fr 1841 Jan 25 DLC-53
Fr 1841 May 03 DLC-53

Boyd John
To 1796 Apr 08 fin 1-0374
To 1807 Apr 11 fin DLC-4
Fr 1807 Oct 17 lnd DLC-4
Fr 1807 Oct 17* lnd 2-0580
Re 1808 Mar 12 DLC-71
Fr 1830 Sep 06 M234-433

Boyd John Wallace
Fr 1835 cMay 14 28-0377

Boyd Joseph B
Fr 1837 Oct 12 DLC-50

Boyd Joseph K
Fr 1843 Sep 16 DLC-55
To 1843 Oct 02 35-1522

Boyd Robert B
Fr 1843 Dec 30 DLC-56

Boyd Thomas G et al
Fr 1835 Sep 25 M639-18

Boyd William A
Fr 1836 Nov 18 32-0553

Boyden James W
Fr 1841 Sep 27 DLC-53

Boyer Jacob K
Re 1829 Jun 20 par DLC-60
Re 1831 Apr 01 par 17-1037

Boyer Joseph
To 1806 Nov 24 fin DLC-4

Boyes Anson
Re 1831 Jun 07 par 17-1554

Boykin F M
Fr 1835 Aug 16 fin 28-1291
Fr 1835 Aug 16 fin DLC-46
Fr 1835 Aug 16# fin DLC-46

Boyle Edward R
Fr 1842 Jul 02 DLC-54
To 1842 Sep 14 DLC-54

Boyle John	
To 1831 Mar 19	DLC-73
To 1831 Mar 19*	17-0909
Fr 1831 Mar 21	M472-1
Fr 1831 Mar 24	M472-1
Fr 1831 Mar 24	M472-1
To 1831 Mar 25	M124-127
To 1831 Mar 26	M124-127
Fr 1831 Mar 26	M472-1
To 1831 Mar 31	M124-127
Fr 1831 Mar 31	M472-1
Fr 1831 Apr 07	M472-1
To 1831 Apr 11	M124-127
Fr 1831 Apr 11	M472-2
Fr 1831 Apr 11	M472-2
To 1831 Apr 12	M124-127
Fr 1831 Apr 12	M472-2
Fr 1831 May 12	M472-2
To 1831 May 12	DLC-73
To 1831 May 12*	17-1355
Fr 1831 May 17	M472-2
Fr 1831 May 18	M472-2
To 1831 Jun 16	DLC-73
To 1831 Jun 16*	18-0031
Fr 1831 Jun 20	M472-2
To 1831 Aug 10	DLC-73
To 1831 Aug 10*	18-0491
Fr 1831 Aug 12	M472-2
Fr 1831 Aug 18	M472-2
Fr 1831 Aug 25	M472-2
Fr 1831 Aug 27	M472-2
Fr 1831 Sep 02	M472-2
Fr 1831 Sep 08	M472-2
To 1831 Sep 17	M124-129
Fr 1832 Jun 21	DLC-40
Re 1832 Jul 23	DLC-73
Re 1832 Jul 23*	20-1223
To 1833 Jan 28#	DLC-42
To 1833 Mar 28	DLC-73
To 1833 Mar 28*	22-0905
Fr 1833 Apr 03	M472-2
Fr 1833 Apr 04	M472-2
Fr 1833 Apr 08	M472-2
Fr 1833 Apr 09	M472-2
To 1833 Apr 11	M124-137
Fr 1833 Apr 11	M472-2
Fr 1833 Apr 16	M472-2
To 1833 Apr 19	M124-137
Fr 1833 Apr 20	M472-2
Fr 1833 Apr 24	M472-2
Fr 1833 Apr 25	M124-137
Fr 1833 Apr 25*	M472-2
To 1833 Apr 29	M124-137
Fr 1833 Apr 29	M472-2
To 1833 Apr 30	M124-137
Fr 1833 May 02	M472-2
Fr 1833 May 03	M472-2
Fr 1833 May 04	M472-2
Fr 1833 May 08	M472-2
Fr 1833 May 11	M472-2
To 1833 May 13	M124-138
Fr 1833 May 13	M472-2
Fr 1833 May 16	22-1365
Fr 1833 May 16*	M472-2
Fr 1833 May 17	M472-2
Fr 1833 May 20	M472-2
Fr 1833 May 21	M472-2
Fr 1833 May 21	M472-2
To 1833 May 25	M124-138
Fr 1833 May 25	M472-2
Fr 1833 May 27	DLC-43
To 1833 Jun 05	22-1570
Fr 1833 Aug 02	M124-139
Fr 1833 Aug 02*	M472-2
Fr 1833 Aug 09	M472-2
Fr 1833 Aug 24	M472-2
Fr 1833 Aug 26	M472-2
Fr 1833 Aug 27	M472-2
Re 1834 Jul 05	26-0152
Fr 1835 Mar 27	M472-2
Fr 1835 May 07	DLC-46
Fr 1835 May 07*	M472-2
To 1835 May 07	28-0315
To 1835 May 09	M124-147
Fr 1835 May 09	M124-147
Fr 1835 May 09*	M472-2
Fr 1835 May 22	M472-2
Fr 1835 May 22	M472-2
Fr 1835 May 25	M472-2
Fr 1835 May 30	M472-2
Fr 1835 Jun 01	M472-2
To 1835 Jun 03	M124-148
Fr 1835 Jun 04	M472-2
To 1835 Jun 09	28-0628
Fr 1835 Jun 10	M472-2
Fr 1835 Jun 12	M472-2
To 1835 Jul 07#	M124-148
To 1836 Jul 09	31-0994
Fr 1838 Jul 26#	DLC-51
Boyle John et al	
To 1835 Mar 15	27-1223
Boyle Matthew James	
Fr 1833 Aug 01	M234-776
Boyle Stuart & Co et al	
Fr 1835 Oct 15	M639-11
Boyles Thomas H	
Fr 1815 Mar 22	DLC-17
Fr 1819	DLC-26
Boynton Nehemiah	
Fr 1837 Feb 06	M639-14
Braberton John	
Re 1813 Apr 07	3-0370
Bracken Charles et al	
Fr 1835 Nov 15	29-0517
Brackenridge A et al	
Fr 1836 Dec 23	DLC-49
To 1837 Jan 04	DLC-49
Brackenridge Alexander	
Fr 1830 Feb 01#	M639-3
Brackenridge Henry Marie	
Fr 1821 May 07	M116-5
Fr 1821 May 07*	M116-6
Fr 1821 May 07*	DLC-63
Fr 1821 May 07*	8-0436
Fr 1821 May 15	DLC-30
Fr 1821 Jul 04	DLC-30
To 1821 Jul 08	8-0777
Fr 1821 Jul 08	DLC-30
To 1821 Jul 17	DLC-63
To 1821 Jul 17	DLC-63
Fr 1821 Jul 26	M116-6
Fr 1821 Jul 26*	8-0898
Fr 1821 Jul 30	M116-6
To 1821 Aug 21	DLC-63
Fr 1821 Aug 21	DLC-63
Fr 1821 Aug 22	M116-7
Fr 1821 Aug 22*	DLC-63
Fr 1821 Aug 23	M116-7

Fr 1821 Aug 23* DLC-63
To 1821 Aug 23 DLC-30
Fr 1821 Aug 24 M116-7
Fr 1821 Aug 24* DLC-63
Fr 1821 Aug 24 fin DLC-70
To 1821 Sep 22 DLC-63
Fr 1821 Sep 27 DLC-63
Fr 1821 Sep 30 8-1244
To 1821 Oct 08 8-1293
Fr 1821 Oct 22 M116-9
Fr 1821 Oct 22* DLC-63
To 1821 Nov 8-1319
Fr 1821 Nov 04 DLC-31
Fr 1823 Dec 22 DLC-32
Fr 1824 Feb 04 DLC-32
Fr 1824 Aug 17 DLC-33
Fr 1829 Feb 04 DLC-36
Fr 1829 Aug 03 M124-120
Re 1832 mem 19-0512
Brackenridge Robert
Fr 1831 Jan 24 M234-354
Brackett Luther
Fr 1837 Jan 19 M687-20
Brackin William
To 1812 Apr 14 lnd DLC-31
To 1812 Apr 14* lnd 2-1068
Fr 1823 Jul 15 DLC-32
Fr 1826 Sep 18 DLC-34
Fr 1827 Feb 20 DLC-34
Bradbury Bion
Fr 1837 Jan 19 M687-20
Bradbury Jabez et al
Fr 1835 Mar 12 27-1112
Bradbury Jeremiah
Fr 1837 Feb 18 M687-16
Bradford Alden
Fr 1830 Mar 04 15-0292
Bradford Benjamin
Fr 1808 fin 2-0601
Fr 1812 cJun 10 DLC-5
Fr 1812 cJun 15 DLC-5
Fr 1812 Aug 01 DLC-5
Fr 1812 Aug 07 DLC-5
Bradford Benjamin J
To 1803 Jul 19 1-1135
To 1806 May 03 2-0231
To 1806 Jul 10# 2-0295
To 1806 Jul 26# 2-0305
Fr 1806 Aug 22 2-0314
Bradford Daniel
Fr 1839 Sep 15 DLC-52
Fr 1839 Sep 29 DLC-52
Bradford James
Fr 1829 Jun 06 M639-3
Fr 1842 Jul 04 35-0836
Fr 1842 Jul 05 35-0837
Bradford James Andrew John
Fr 1829 May 28 13-0463
Fr 1834 Aug 21 DLC-44
Bradford James M
Fr 1828 Sep 14 DLC-35
Fr 1829 Jan 30 M639-21
Bradford John O
Fr 1837 Nov 10 34-0017
Fr 1838 Jan 01 DLC-50
Fr 1838 Mar 30 DLC-51
Fr 1839 Oct 08 DLC-52
Fr 1844 Sep 16 36-0868
Bradford Richard H
Re 1829 Apr 08 mem 12-1302
Fr 1829 Apr 24 M472-1
Fr 1829 Apr 27 M472-1
Fr 1829 Apr 28 M472-1
Fr 1829 May 02 M472-1
To 1829 May 04 DLC-60
Fr 1829 May 04 M472-1
Re 1829 Jul 08 13-0826
Re 1829 Jul 08 mem 13-0828
Fr 1829 Jul 20 M124-119
Fr 1829 Jul 20* M472-1
Fr 1829 Jul 20* 13-0904
Bradford Samuel D
Fr 1836 Sep 06# DLC-49
Fr 1837 Feb 16 DLC-50
To 1837 Feb 21 DLC-50
Fr 1839 Apr 19 DLC-52
Bradford Samuel D et al
Fr 1833 Sep 02 M639-20
Bradford Samuel F
Fr 1829 May 05 M124-118
Fr 1829 Oct 10 DLC-75
Fr 1831 Aug 23 DLC-40
To 1831 Aug 25 18-0586
Fr 1832 Feb 28# DLC-40
Bradford Theodoric F
Re 1819 Sep 26 mem DLC-27
Bradford Thomas G
Fr 1811 Sep 07 DLC-5
To 1812 Mar 30 2-1059
To 1812 Jun 10 2-1102
Fr 1812 Oct 08 M222-5
Fr 1834 Mar 31 DLC-44
Bradford Thomas M
Fr 1821 Jun 02 DLC-30
Bradford William
To 1806 Feb 18# fin DLC-3
Fr 1815 Jul 29 4-1136
Fr 1815 Sep 29 DLC-19
Fr 1816 Apr 27 DLC-20
Fr 1816 Jun 12 DLC-20
Fr 1816 Jul 03 DLC-21
Fr 1818 Jan 01 DLC-23
Fr 1819 Feb 04 7-0227
Fr 1819 Apr 21 DLC-26
Fr 1819 Nov 02 M221-86
Fr 1819 Dec 06 DLC-28
Fr 1819 Dec 07 M221-86
Fr 1820 Mar 04 M221-86
Bradford & Cooch et al
Fr 1829 Mar 12-0623
Bradford & Stacker
Fr 1827 Mar 13 fin DLC-34
Bradlee Joseph P et al
Fr c1836 M687-28
Bradlee Josiah & Co et al
Fr 1836 May 10 30-1576
Bradley Abraham
Fr 1829 Oct 14-0009
Fr 1834 May 10 25-1002
Fr 1834 Jun 01 25-1221
Fr 1834 Jul 10 26-0208
Fr 1834 Jul 15 26-0221
Bradley Edward
To 1813 Jan 07 3-0001
To 1813 Jan 07* DLC-61
To 1813 Jan 07 DLC-61
To 1813 Feb 25 DLC-61

Bradley Edward (cont)
- Fr 1813 Dec 03 DLC-7
- Fr 1813 Dec 03* DLC-61
- To 1813 Dec 03 DLC-61
- Fr 1813 Dec 04 DLC-7
- Fr 1813 Dec 04* 3-0640
- Fr 1813 Dec 04* DLC-61
- To 1813 Dec 05 DLC-61
- To 1814 Feb 13 DLC-61

Bradley James
- To 1813 Oct 10 DLC-61

Bradley John
- Fr 1814 Feb 09 DLC-8
- To 1814 Feb 11 DLC-62
- Fr 1814 Feb 15 DLC-9
- To 1814 Feb 22 DLC-62
- To 1814 Feb 23 DLC-61
- Fr 1814 Feb 24 DLC-9
- Fr 1814 Mar 01 DLC-9
- To 1814 Mar 03 DLC-62
- Fr 1814 Mar 03 DLC-9
- Fr 1814 Mar 03 DLC-9
- Fr 1814 Mar 03 DLC-9
- Fr 1814 Mar 13 DLC-9
- To 1814 Mar 14 DLC-9
- Fr 1814 Mar 16 DLC-9
- Fr 1814 Mar 24 DLC-9
- Fr 1814 Apr 05 DLC-10
- Fr 1814 Apr 07 DLC-10

Bradley Thomas
- Fr 1805 Dec 24 leg DLC-3
- Fr 1813 Jun 05 lnd 3-0403
- Re 1818 Oct 6-1325
- Re 1818 Oct 6-1331

Bradley William
- To 1814 Jan 03 DLC-61
- Fr 1814 Jan 03 DLC-8
- Fr 1814 Jan 03* DLC-61
- Fr 1814 Jan 04 DLC-8
- Fr 1814 Jan 04* DLC-61

Bradley William A
- Fr 1834 Dec 03 26-1344
- Fr 1835 Nov 30 M639-24

Bradley William Czar
- Fr 1837 Feb M687-2

Bradley & Catlett
- Fr 1834 Jul 05 fin DLC-44
- To 1834 Oct 09 chk DLC-44
- Fr 1834 Oct 09 fin DLC-44
- Fr 1834 Dec 19# fin DLC-45
- Fr 1835 Mar 18# fin DLC-45
- Fr 1836 Jan 01# fin DLC-49

Bradley & Catlett et al
- Fr 1833 Sep 10 M639-23

Bradshaw William
- Fr 1830 Feb 11 15-0125

Bradstreet John
- Fr 1817 May 03 DLC-22
- To 1817 May 26 5-0874

Bradstreet Martha
- Fr 1819 7-0105

Brady Benjamin
- Fr 1834 Dec 19 M179-79
- Fr 1834 Dec 26 M639-11

Brady Freeman
- Fr 1829 Jun 13 M222-25
- Fr 1835 Jun 20 M22-36

Brady Hugh
- Fr 1836 Feb 02# 30-0261

Brady Nathaniel
- Re 1830 Dec 02 16-0962

Brady Peter
- Fr 1829 Sep 16# DLC-75
- Fr 1837 Jul 06 DLC-50

Brady William
- Fr 1823 Sep 20 DLC-32
- To 1823 Sep 27 DLC-32
- To 1825 Oct 12 11-0019
- To 1825 Oct 12* DLC-58
- Fr 1825 Oct 14 add 11-0028
- Fr 1825 Oct 14* add DLC-33
- Fr 1834 Oct 07 DLC-44

Bragg John
- Fr 1844 Feb 14 DLC-56

Bragg Talbot
- Fr 1831 Nov 28 M639-18

Bragg Thomas
- Re 1831 Aug 26 par 18-0592

Brahan John
- Fr 1806 Mar 08# 2-0188
- Fr 1808 Nov 01 DLC-4
- Fr 1813 Aug 29 M221-50
- Fr 1813 Oct 07 DLC-6
- Fr 1813 Oct 07* DLC-61
- Fr 1813 Nov 15 DLC-7
- To 1813 Nov 20 DLC-61
- Fr 1813 Nov 24 DLC-7
- Fr 1813 Nov 29 DLC-7
- Fr 1813 Nov 29 DLC-7
- To 1813 Dec 15 DLC-61
- To 1813 Dec 18 DLC-61
- Fr 1814 Jan 09 DLC-8
- To 1814 Jan 13 DLC-61
- Fr 1814 Jan 14 DLC-8
- Fr 1814 Feb 12 DLC-9
- Fr 1814 Feb 23 DLC-9
- Fr 1814 Mar 22 DLC-9
- Fr 1814 Apr 04 DLC-10
- Fr 1814 Oct 31 DLC-13
- Fr 1814 Dec 22 DLC-14
- To 1815 Jun 13 DLC-62
- Fr 1824 Feb 01 M688-28
- To 1827 Feb 13 11-0486
- Fr 1829 Mar 22 M639-16
- Fr 1829 May 29 M639-20

Brahan Robert Weakley
- Fr 1836 Mar 15 30-0775

Brahan & Hutchings
- Fr 1817 Oct 29 fin 5-1123
- Re 1820 Jan 12 mem 7-0991

Branch John
- Fr 1825 Jul 30 DLC-33
- To 1826 Mar 03 11-0150
- Fr 1827 Dec 11 DLC-35
- Fr 1828 May 23 DLC-35
- To 1828 Jun 24 DLC-35
- Fr 1829 Mar 16 M472-1
- To 1829 Mar 16 M124-117
- To 1829 Mar 16* DLC-60
- To 1829 Mar 16 DLC-60
- Fr 1829 Mar 17 M472-1
- To 1829 Mar 17 M124-117
- To 1829 Mar 17* DLC-60
- Fr 1829 Mar 17 M472-1
- Fr 1829 Mar 19 M472-1
- Fr 1829 Mar 20 M472-1
- Fr 1829 Mar 23 M472-1
- To 1829 Mar 27 DLC-60
- Fr 1829 Mar 28 M472-1
- Fr 1829 Mar 31 M472-1

Fr	1829	Apr	03		12-1257
Fr	1829	Apr	03*		M472-1
Fr	1829	Apr	06		12-1280
Fr	1829	Apr	06*		M472-1
Fr	1829	May	13		M472-1
To	1829	May	18		M124-118
Fr	1829	May	20		M472-1
Fr	1829	May	21		13-0365
Fr	1829	May	21*		M472-1
Fr	1829	May	23		M472-1
Fr	1829	May	27		M472-1
Fr	1829	May	27		M472-1
Fr	1829	Jun	04		M472-1
Fr	1829	Jun	04*		13-0566
Fr	1829	Jun	08		M472-1
To	1829	Jun	13#		M124-119
To	1829	Jun	30		M124-119
To	1829	Jun	30*		DLC-37
Fr	1829	Jul	02		M472-1
Fr	1829	Aug	10		M472-1
To	1829	Aug	20		M124-120
Fr	1829	Aug	26		DLC-37
Fr	1829	Sep	10		M472-1
To	1829	Sep	12		M77-162
Fr	1829	Sep	22		M472-1
Fr	1829	Oct	02		M472-1
Fr	1829	Oct	03		M472-1
Fr	1829	Oct	06		M472-1
Fr	1829	Oct	17		M472-1
To	1829	Oct	27#		M179-67
Fr	1829	Oct	28		M472-1
To	1829	Nov	06		14-0419
To	1829	Nov	10		M124-121
Fr	1829	Nov	13		M472-1
Fr	1829	Nov	19		M472-1
Fr	1829	Dec	01		14-0743
Fr	1829	Dec	12		M472-1
To	1829	Dec	31		14-1165
To	1830	Jan	05#		M124-122
Fr	1830	Jan	06		M472-1
Fr	1830	Jan	07		14-1351
Fr	1830	Jan	16		M472-1
To	1830	Jan	18#		14-1460
To	1830	Jan	23		M124-122
Fr	1830	Jan	25		M472-1
To	1830	Jan	26		15-0026
Fr	1830	Jan	27		15-0058
To	1830	Jan	27#		M124-122
Re	1830	Jan	29	mem	15-0063
Fr	1830	Feb	05		M472-1
To	1830	Feb	19		15-0203
Fr	1830	Feb	26		M472-1
Fr	1830	Feb	27		M472-2
To	1830	Mar	10#		15-0324
Fr	1830	Mar	12		M472-1
Fr	1830	Mar	17		15-0383
Fr	1830	Mar	17*		M472-1
Fr	1830	Mar	25		15-0450
Fr	1830	Mar	25*		M472-1
Fr	1830	Mar	30		M472-1
Fr	1830	Apr	01		M472-1
To	1830	Apr	07		M124-123
Fr	1830	Apr	09		15-0647
Fr	1830	Apr	09*		M472-1
Fr	1830	Apr	16		M179-68
Fr	1830	Apr	16*		M472-1
Fr	1830	Apr	26		M472-1
Fr	1830	May	04		M472-1
To	1830	May	07#		M124-124

Fr	1830	May	11	15-0981
Fr	1830	May	11*	M472-1
Fr	1830	May	12	15-0985
Fr	1830	May	12*	M472-1
Fr	1830	May	14	M472-1
Fr	1830	May	18	M472-1
To	1830	May	22	15-1071
Fr	1830	May	26	15-1095
Fr	1830	May	26*	M472-1
Fr	1830	May	29	15-1199
Fr	1830	May	29*	M472-1
To	1830	Jun	01	M124-124
Fr	1830	Jun	03	M472-1
To	1830	Jun	04	M124-124
Fr	1830	Jun	04	M472-1
To	1830	Jun	05	M625-405
To	1830	Jun	07	15-1308
Fr	1830	Jun	09	M472-1
To	1830	Jun	11	15-1338
Fr	1830	Jun	15	M472-1
Fr	1830	Aug	14	DLC-38
Fr	1830	Oct	02	M472-1
Fr	1830	Oct	05	M472-1
Fr	1830	Oct	14	M472-1
Fr	1830	Oct	23	16-0475
Fr	1830	Oct	23*	M472-1
To	1830	Oct	23	M124-125
To	1830	Oct	28	M124-125
To	1830	Oct	28*	DLC-38
Fr	1830	Oct	29	M472-1
Fr	1830	Nov	03	M472-1
Fr	1830	Nov	06	M472-1
Fr	1830	Nov	06	M472-1
Fr	1830	Nov	12	M472-1
Fr	1830	Nov	15	M472-1
Fr	1830	Nov	18	M472-1
Fr	1830	Nov	20	M472-1
To	1830	Nov	23	M124-125
Fr	1830	Nov	26	16-0877
Fr	1830	Nov	26*	M472-1
Fr	1830	Dec	01	M472-1
Fr	1830	Dec	06	16-1303
To	1830	Dec	24	M124-125
Fr	1830	Dec	31	M472-1
Fr	1831	Jan	05	17-0205
Fr	1831	Jan	05*	M472-1
Fr	1831	Jan	13	M472-1
Fr	1831	Jan	14	17-0255
Fr	1831	Jan	14*	M472-1
Fr	1831	Jan	14*	M205-1
Fr	1831	Jan	15	17-0257
Fr	1831	Jan	15*	M472-1
To	1831	Jan	17	M124-126
Fr	1831	Jan	18	M472-1
Fr	1831	Jan	20	M472-1
Fr	1831	Jan	24	17-0342
Fr	1831	Jan	24*	M472-1
Fr	1831	Jan	25	M472-1
To	1831	Jan	25	17-0346
Fr	1831	Feb	07	17-0448
Fr	1831	Feb	07*	M472-1
Fr	1831	Feb	10	17-0489
Fr	1831	Feb	10*	M472-1
To	1831	Feb	20	M124-126
Fr	1831	Feb	23	M472-1
Fr	1831	Mar	01	17-0693
Fr	1831	Mar	01*	M472-1
Fr	1831	Mar	01*	M124-153
To	1831	Mar	01#	M124-127

Branch John (cont)			
Fr	1831 Mar 03		M472-1
Fr	1831 Mar 10		M472-1
Fr	1831 Mar 16		M472-1
Fr	1831 Apr 19		DLC-39
To	1831 Apr 19		DLC-39
Fr	1831 Apr 19		DLC-39
Fr	1831 Apr 19		M472-2
To	1831 Apr 20		17-1200
Fr	1831 Apr 27		M472-2
Fr	1831 May 01		M472-2
Fr	1831 May 02		M472-2
Fr	1831 May 04		M472-2
To	1831 May 10		17-1337
Fr	1831 May 11		M472-2
Fr	1831 May 12		DLC-39
Fr	1831 May 12*		M472-2
Re	1831 Sep	mem	18-0636
Branch Robert			
Fr	1813 Oct 30		DLC-7
Brand William			
Fr	1821 May	fin	DLC-70
Fr	1821 May 16#	fin	DLC-30
To	1821 May 17#	fin	DLC-30
To	1821 May 23#	fin	DLC-30
To	1821 May 23#	fin	DLC-30
To	1821 May 25	fin	DLC-30
To	1821 May 25#	fin	DLC-30
To	1821 May 25#	fin	DLC-30
To	1821 May 25#	fin	DLC-30
Fr	1821 Jun 05	fin	DLC-70
Fr	1821 Sep 03	fin	DLC-70
To	1822 Jan 16		8-1399
To	1822 May 15		9-0162
To	1828 Apr 01		11-1199
To	1840 Jan 14#	fin	DLC-52
Fr	1840 Jan 15		DLC-52
Fr	1840 Aug 14		DLC-53
Branden George			
To	1813 Oct 29		DLC-61
To	1813 Oct 29*		3-0552
Brandon Byrd			
Fr	1829 Aug 11		M639-16
Fr	1836 Jul 26		31-1160
Fr	1836 Aug 18		31-1305
Fr	1836 Oct 15		32-0179
Brandon Gerard Chittocque			
To	1830 Aug 31		16-0185
Brandon Gerard Chittocque et al			
Fr	1830 Jan 05		M639-3
Fr	1830 Feb 07		M639-19
Brandon Logan D			
Fr	1829 Jun 27		M639-21
Brandon Thomas et al			
Fr	1826 Jun 26		DLC-34
To	1826 Jun 30		DLC-34
Brandt John			
To	1813 Mar 19		DLC-61
Fr	1813 Mar 19		DLC-61
To	1813 Mar 22		DLC-61
Fr	1814 Sep 04		DLC-12
Fr	1814 Oct 18		DLC-13
Fr	1814 Dec 21		DLC-14
Fr	1814 Dec 23		DLC-14
Fr	1815 Jan 16		DLC-15
Fr	1815 Jan 26		DLC-15
Fr	1816 Jul 03		DLC-21
Fr	1816 Jul 06		DLC-21
Brannon Thomas			
Fr	1831 Jul 13		18-0206
Brashears Eden			
Fr	1820 Nov 10		M222-21
Brashears Turner			
Fr	1816 Sep		5-0449
Brasseur J			
Fr	1830 Dec 15		M639-3
Brawley John et al			
Fr	1835 Jan		DLC-45
Brawner Peter			
Fr	1804 Oct 19		DLC-3
Bray James			
To	1801 Oct 24	lnd	1-0940
Brazeal Henry			
To	1799 Oct 06#	lnd	37-0401
Brazil Provisional Regency			
To	1831 Sep 13		18-0718
Brazil treaty			
Re	1829 Mar 18		12-1024
Brearley David			
To	1817 Mar 17#		5-0779
Fr	1818 Feb 20		DLC-24
Fr	1818 Feb 21		DLC-24
Fr	1818 Feb 24		DLC-24
Fr	1818 Feb 27		DLC-24
Fr	1819 Feb 28		DLC-26
Fr	1819 Oct 20		DLC-28
Fr	1819 Oct 20		DLC-28
Fr	1819 Oct 20*		M221-84
Fr	1819 Oct 23		DLC-28
To	1819 Nov 16		DLC-63
Fr	1819 Dec 01		DLC-28
Fr	1819 Dec 03		DLC-28
Brearley David et al			
Fr	1818 Feb 10		6-0009
Fr	1830 Oct 27		16-0560
Breathitt Edward			
Fr	1825 Jul 04	add	10-1340
To	1825 Jul 04	add	10-1342
To	1835 Mar 30		DLC-45
Breathitt George			
Fr	1832 Mar 19#		DLC-40
Fr	1832 Oct 01#		DLC-41
To	1832 Nov 07		DLC-41
To	1833 Apr 29	chk	DLC-42
Breathitt John			
Fr	1818 Jan 25		DLC-24
Fr	1828 Sep 23		12-0214
Fr	1832 Aug 23		DLC-41
Fr	1832 Dec 12		M567-68
To	1833 Jan 18		21-1568
Brecht George W et al			
Fr	1835 cJan		DLC-59
Breckinridge James Douglas et al			
Fr	1829 Feb 18		M639-2
Breckinridge John Cabell			
Fr	1821 Apr 15		M439-15
Breckinridge Robert et al			
Fr	1825 Mar 31		DLC-33
To	1825 Mar 31		DLC-33
Fr	1828 Dec 19		DLC-36
To	1829 Jan 03		12-0430
Bredin John			
Fr	1832 Sep 18		M639-9
Breedlove James Waller			
Fr	1835 Apr 20		M567-105
Fr	1836 Jan 23		M639-4
Fr	1836 Mar 23		30-0882
Fr	1836 Jun 12#		31-0438
Fr	1836 Aug 08		31-1261

Fr 1836 Aug 13 M639-26
Fr 1837 Jun 21 DLC-50
Fr 1838 May 31 DLC-51
To 1838 Sep 20 34-0475
To 1838 Dec 11 34-0569
Fr 1839 Apr 18 34-0749
Fr 1839 May 15 DLC-52
To 1841 Dec 04 35-0521
Fr 1842 Jul 18 DLC-54
To 1842 Aug 01 35-0864
Fr 1842 Aug 16 DLC-54
Fr 1842 Aug 18 DLC-54
To 1842 Oct 03 35-0963
Fr 1842 Oct 20 DLC-54
Fr 1842 Dec 07 DLC-54
To 1843 Jan 11 35-1108
Fr 1843 Jan 27 DLC-55
Fr 1843 Feb 02 DLC-55
To 1843 Feb 17 35-1234
To 1843 Feb 27 35-1258
Fr 1843 Mar 03 DLC-55
Re 1843 Mar 13 mem DLC-55
Fr 1843 May 04 DLC-55
To 1843 May 08 35-1344
Fr 1843 May 25 DLC-55
To 1843 Jul 25 35-1430
Fr 1844 Jan 17 DLC-56

Breedlove James Waller et al
Fr 1835 May 04 28-0254

Breese Sidney
Fr 1844 Apr 27 36-0449

Breese Sidney et al
Fr 1832 Dec M639-12

Brenan Thomas H
Fr 1829 Jun 11 13-0629

Brent Daniel
Fr 1821 Sep 11 DLC-30
Fr 1821 Sep 11* M40-18
Fr 1821 Sep 11* M116-7
Fr 1821 Sep 11* 8-1158
Fr 1821 Sep 18 DLC-30
Fr 1821 Sep 18* M40-18
Fr 1821 Sep 18* M116-7
Fr 1821 Sep 18* 8-1181
Fr 1821 Sep 24 DLC-30
Fr 1821 Sep 24* M40-18
Fr 1821 Sep 24* 8-1208
Fr 1822 Apr 18 DLC-31
To 1829 Jul 30 DLC-60
Fr 1829 Dec 21# M40-21
Fr 1830 Jan 14# M40-21
To 1830 Mar 15# M179-68
To 1830 Apr 13# M179-68
To 1830 May 25# M179-73
Fr 1831 Feb 08# 17-0888
Fr 1831 Feb 08* M40-22
Re 1831 Aug 10 18-0492
Re 1831 Aug 10* M78-3
Re 1831 Aug 10* M221-111
Fr 1831 Aug 15 M40-22
To 1831 Aug 22 18-0578
To 1831 Aug 27 M179-71
To 1831 Aug 27* M78-3
To 1831 Aug 27* DLC-60
To 1831 Aug 31 M179-71
To 1831 Sep 05 M179-71
Fr 1832 Jan 14# M40-22
To 1832 Feb 14# M179-72
Fr 1832 Feb 14# M40-23
To 1832 Jul 21 20-1211
To 1833 Mar 07 22-0680
To 1833 Apr 12# M179-76
Re 1833 Jun 05 22-1574
Re 1833 Jun 13 23-0017
Re 1833 Aug 08 23-0293
Fr 1833 Aug 14 M40-24
To 1833 Aug 17 M179-77
Fr 1834 Jan 07# T1-7
Fr 1834 Aug 21 DLC-44

Brent Robert
Fr 1816 Jul 16 5-0303
To 1816 Aug 02 5-0340
Fr 1816 Nov 18 DLC-22
Fr 1817 May 07 5-0845
Fr 1817 Jun 26 DLC-23
Fr 1817 Jul 25 5-0945
To 1817 Aug 12 5-0961
Fr 1817 Sep 09 5-1011
Fr 1817 Dec 12 5-1174
Fr 1818 Mar 06 6-0071
Fr 1818 Apr 20 6-0402
To 1818 Jun 04 6-1022
Fr 1818 Jun 12 6-1045
Fr 1818 Jun 17 DLC-25
Fr 1818 Jun 17* 6-1060

Brent William
Fr 1830 Mar 15 M273-25

Brent William Jr
Fr 1836 Oct 29 M567-118

Brevoort Henry B
Fr 1830 Sep 03 M234-433
Fr 1831 Jan 04 M22-27

Brewster William et al
Fr 1835 May 12 DLC-46

Briant G A
Fr 1843 Sep 29 DLC-55

Brice Benjamin William
Fr 1831 Aug 18# M567-59

Brickelew Frederick
Fr 1843 Aug 14 DLC-55

Bridge E T
Fr 1837 Feb 26 M687-16

Bridges Otis L et al
Fr 1835 Jun 20 28-0747

Bridges Thomas
Fr 1834 Dec 12 M639-3
Fr 1835 May 23 DLC-46

Bridgham Rowland H
Fr 1835 Mar 23 27-1312
Fr 1836 cDec 32-0600

Bridport Rachel
Fr 1834 Dec 18# fin DLC-45

Briggs Benjamin
Fr 1835 Dec 24 M639-5

Briggs George Nixon
Fr 1832 Feb 01 M22-29

Briggs George Nixon et al
Fr 1835 Jun 28 M639-25
Fr 1836 Oct M639-9

Bright James
Fr 1826 Jun 10 DLC-34
To 1826 Jun 15 DLC-34

Bright Thomas G et al
Fr 1832 Feb 06 19-0972

Brightwell John L
Re 1833 May 11 22-1337
Fr 1835 Apr 13 fin DLC-46
To 1835 Jun 06 chk 28-0591

Briscoe Richard S et al
Fr 1831 Jan 26 M639-1
Bristol William
Fr 1832 Jan 19-0532
British colonial trade
Re 1830 Oct 05 T1223-1
Re 1830 Oct 05* M735
Re 1830 Oct 05* 16-0316
Re 1830 Oct 05* M179-69
British prisoners of war
Re 1815 Jan 17 DLC-15
Re 1815 Jan 17* M222-16
Re 1815 Jan 17* 4-0555
Re 1815 cJan 17 mem 4-0557
Britton William et al
Fr 1833 Sep 25 M639-21
Broad Philander R
Re 1837 Feb 18 par 33-0753
Broadhead Daniel M
Re 1835 Nov mem 29-0403
Brocchus Perry E
Fr 1844 Jul 09 DLC-57
Brockenbrough William Henry
Fr 1835 Feb 16 M688-96
Brockman John
Fr 1814 Jul 16 DLC-11
Brodhead Daniel D
Re 1830 Mar mem 15-0268
Brodhead John
Fr 1830 Aug 27 M639-10
Brodie Charles D
Fr 1836 Jan 16 M124-151
Fr 1836 Jan 16* 30-0118
Fr 1836 Jun 23 M124-149
Brodnax John H
Fr 1832 Jan 19 M234-434
Fr 1832 Jan 19* 19-0777
Bronaugh James C
Re 1818 5-1220
Fr 1818 Jun 04 fin DLC-25
Fr 1819 DLC-59
Fr 1819 Jul 29 DLC-27
Fr 1819 Aug 24 DLC-27
Fr 1819 Sep 16 DLC-27
Fr 1819 Nov 29 DLC-28
Fr 1820 7-0964
To 1820 Feb 12 DLC-28
Fr 1820 Sep 13 7-1353
Fr 1820 Sep 13* M221-90
Fr 1821 Feb 11 DLC-29
Fr 1821 Feb 17 M439-8
Fr 1821 May 07 M116-5
Fr 1821 May 07* M116-6
Fr 1821 May 07* DLC-63
Fr 1821 May 07* 8-0436
To 1821 Jun 09 DLC-30
To 1821 Jul 03 DLC-30
To 1821 Jul 06 DLC-30
Fr 1821 Jul 09 DLC-30
To 1821 Jul 11 DLC-30
To 1821 Jul 15 DLC-30
To 1821 Jul 19 DLC-63
To 1821 Aug 03 DLC-30
To 1821 Aug 03* M116-6
To 1821 Aug 03* DLC-63
To 1821 Aug 03* 8-0998
Fr 1821 Aug 03 DLC-30
Fr 1821 Aug 03* M116-6
Fr 1821 Aug 03* DLC-63
Fr 1821 Aug 03* 8-1001
To 1821 Aug 22 M116-7
To 1821 Aug 22* DLC-63
Fr 1821 Aug 22 M116-7
Fr 1821 Aug 22* DLC-63
Fr 1821 Aug 23 DLC-30
Fr 1821 Sep 02 8-1140
Fr 1821 Sep 03 M116-7
Fr 1821 Sep 03* DLC-63
Fr 1821 Sep 03* M116-9
Fr 1821 Sep 28 8-1235
Fr 1821 Dec 02 DLC-72
Fr 1821 Dec 11 DLC-72
Fr 1821 Dec 19 DLC-31
Fr 1821 Dec 26 DLC-31
Fr 1821 Dec 30 DLC-72
Fr 1822 Jan 07 DLC-31
To 1822 Jan 10 DLC-72
Fr 1822 Jan 30 DLC-31
Fr 1822 Feb 08 DLC-31
Fr 1822 Feb 16 DLC-31
Fr 1822 Feb 23 DLC-31
Fr 1822 Apr 16 DLC-31
To 1822 May 29 DLC-31
To 1822 Jun 01 DLC-31
To 1822 Jul 18 DLC-31
To 1822 Aug 01 DLC-31
To 1822 Aug 27 9-0255
Re 1822 Sep 20 leg DLC-31
Bronaugh Jeremiah W
Fr 1829 Jun 12 M639-15
To 1830 Jun 03 chk DLC-38
Bronaugh Rebecca
Fr 1823 Mar 07 DLC-32
Fr 1825 Jan 05 10-1029
Bronaugh Sarah
To 1830 Jan 20 14-1479
Bronson Birdsey
Fr 1838 Mar 19 DLC-51
Bronson Greene Carrier
Fr 1835 Dec 04 29-0741
Bronson Greene Carrier et al
Fr 1835 Dec 09 M639-8
Brook Samuel
Fr 1822 Jun 05 fin DLC-31
Fr 1827 Nov 23 DLC-35
Brooke George Mercer
Fr 1818 Jul 02 6-1099
Fr 1818 Sep 15 DLC-25
To 1821 Apr 02# DLC-63
To 1821 May 07 DLC-63
Re 1821 May 10 DLC-63
To 1821 Jul 10 M116-6
To 1821 Jul 10* DLC-63
To 1821 Jul 10* 8-0782
To 1821 Aug 22 DLC-63
To 1821 Aug 22 DLC-63
To 1821 Aug 24 DLC-63
To 1821 Aug 29 DLC-63
Fr 1821 Sep 01 8-1136
To 1821 Oct 06 DLC-63
Fr 1835 Sep 01 M688-90
Fr 1835 Dec 07# 29-0775
Brookhart D
Fr 1825 Mar 15 fin DLC-72
Brooks Cotton B et al
Fr 1829 May 04 13-0253
Brooks Edward E
Fr 1830 Jan 12 14-1385

Brooks Gerard
Fr 1815 Sep 05 DLC-19
To 1815 Sep 19 DLC-62
Brooks Henry M
Fr 1840 Aug 26 DLC-53
Brooks Jacob R
Fr 1818 May 03 6-0558
Fr 1818 May 03* DLC-24
Brooks James Gordon
Fr 1830 Nov 07 16-0665
Brooks Jehiel
Fr 1829 Apr 01 12-1221
Fr 1829 Jun 06 M639-3
Fr 1836 Jun 09 M234-31
Fr 1836 Jun 20 DLC-48
Brooks John
Re 1822 May 13 leg 9-0147
Brooks John S
Fr 1835 Aug 02 28-1224
Brooks Maria
Fr 1829 Dec 22 M688-72
Fr 1836 Jul 18 M567-118
Fr 1836 Aug 24 M567-118
Brooks Peter Chardon et al
Fr 1829 Oct 16 14-0172
Brooks W Mrs
Fr 1836 Sep M22-41
Broom Ann
Fr 1832 Jun 30 20-0841
Broom Jacob
Fr 1836 Jun 08 M639-3
Fr 1837 May 12 DLC-50
Brown ______
To 1842 Aug 20# 35-0890
Re 1845 Jan 24 mem DLC-57
Brown ______ (paymaster agent)
To 1814 May 26 DLC-10
Brown Aaron Venable
Fr 1826 Jul 04 add 11-0264
To 1826 Jul 04 add 11-0265
Fr 1841 Aug 08 DLC-53
Fr 1843 Jan 23 35-1141
To 1843 Feb 12 35-1215
To 1843 Feb 12* DLC-74
Fr 1843 Dec 12# DLC-56
Fr 1845 Jan 21 36-1387
Brown Addison
Re 1833 May 04 par 22-1290
Brown Alexander & Sons et al
Fr 1834 Dec M639-8
Brown B F
Fr 1843 Oct 18 DLC-55
Brown Bedford
Fr 1835 Jan 09 M639-27
Fr 1836 Jun M687-15
To 1836 Jun 24 31-0565
Fr 1836 Jun 29 31-0639
Fr 1837 Feb 15 M687-17
Brown Bedford et al
Fr 1836 Jun M687-15
Fr 1836 Jun 20 M687-30
Brown Benjamin et al
Fr 1837 Feb M687-20
Brown Edmund F et al
Fr 1831 Oct M179-72
Brown Elias
Fr 1829 Mar 17 M639-3
Brown Ethan Allen
Fr 1829 Jan 13 M639-25
Fr 1832 Jan 01 19-0566
Fr 1833 Sep 27 M121-11
Fr 1835 Mar 09 DLC-45
Fr 1835 Jun 28 28-0828
To 1835 Jul 24 28-1127
Fr 1835 Sep 19 29-0083
Fr 1835 Oct 31 29-0393
Fr 1835 Oct 31* M25-30
Fr 1835 Nov 13 M25-30
To 1835 Nov 22# 29-0545
Fr 1835 Dec 05 29-0742
Fr 1835 Dec 12 29-1092
Fr 1835 Dec 18 DLC-73
Fr 1835 Dec 22 29-1278
Fr 1835 Dec 22 mem 29-1282
Fr 1835 Dec 31 29-1363
Fr 1835 Dec 31* M234-136
Fr 1836 Jan 07 29-1490
Fr 1836 Jan 18 30-0133
To 1836 Jan 18# 30-0139
Fr 1836 Jan 21 30-0154
Fr 1836 Jan 23 30-0185
Fr 1836 Feb 30-0250
Fr 1836 Feb 02 30-0265
Fr 1836 Feb 02 30-0266
Fr 1836 Feb 02 30-0267
Fr 1836 Feb 04 30-0286
Fr 1836 Feb 04* M25-30
Fr 1836 Feb 11 M25-30
To 1836 Feb 13# 30-0384
Fr 1836 Feb 15 30-0387
Fr 1836 Feb 15# 30-0392
Fr 1836 Feb 20 30-0422
Fr 1836 Feb 20 30-0423
Fr 1836 Feb 20* M234-189
Fr 1836 Mar 04 30-0669
Fr 1836 Mar 18 M25-30
Fr 1836 Mar 19 30-0831
Fr 1836 Mar 22 30-0863
To 1836 Mar 24# 30-0888
Fr 1836 Apr 04 30-0987
Fr 1836 Apr 09 DLC-48
Fr 1836 Apr 13# 30-1146
Fr 1836 Apr 20 30-1265
Fr 1836 Apr 20 30-1268
Fr 1836 Apr 20 30-1271
Fr 1836 Apr 21 30-1278
Fr 1836 Apr 22 30-1308
Fr 1836 Apr 25 30-1334
Fr 1836 Apr 25 30-1336
Fr 1836 Apr 25 30-1341
Fr 1836 Apr 27 30-1368
Fr 1836 Apr 28 30-1403
To 1836 Apr 30 30-1423
Fr 1836 Apr 30 30-1425
To 1836 May 02 mem 30-1483
Fr 1836 May 02 30-1484
Fr 1836 May 03 30-1488
Fr 1836 May 04 30-1497
Fr 1836 May 11 30-1599
Fr 1836 May 17 M200-6
Fr 1836 May 17* 31-0037
Fr 1836 May 28 31-0180
Fr 1836 May 30 31-0195
Fr 1836 Jun 08 31-0403
Fr 1836 Jun 14 31-0468
Fr 1836 Jun 18 31-0504
Fr 1836 Jun 18 31-0506
To 1836 Jun 21# M21-19

Brown Ethan Allen (cont)		
Fr 1836 Jun 25		31-0577
Fr 1836 Jul 08		31-0957
Fr 1836 Jul 09		31-0997
Fr 1836 Jul 09		31-0998
Fr 1836 Jul 11		31-1057
To 1836 Aug 23		31-1350
Fr 1836 Oct 03		32-0002
Fr 1836 Oct 03		32-0007
Fr 1836 Oct 03		32-0010
Fr 1836 Oct 03		32-0014
Fr 1836 Oct 03		32-0018
Fr 1836 Oct 03		32-0022
Fr 1836 Oct 03		32-0026
Fr 1836 Oct 03		32-0029
Fr 1836 Oct 03		32-0033
Fr 1836 Oct 03		32-0036
Fr 1836 Oct 06		32-0082
Fr 1836 Oct 13		32-0167
Fr 1836 Oct 14		32-0174
Fr 1836 Oct 18		32-0219
Brown G M		
To 1838 cApr		34-0297
Fr 1840 Jan 01		DLC-52
Brown George		
Re 1807 Oct 11	leg	2-0565
Fr 1824 Jan 19	chk	DLC-32
Fr 1833 Feb 15		22-0382
Brown George et al		
Fr 1835 Apr 24		M639-14
Brown George J		
Fr 1821 Sep 24		DLC-30
Fr 1821 Oct		M116-8
Brown H G		
Fr 1837 Mar 08#	fin	DLC-50
Brown Jacob Jennings		
To 1815 Aug 08		4-1146
To 1815 Aug 08*		DLC-62
To 1815 Aug 08*		M222-16
Fr 1815 Aug 20		4-1162
To 1815 Dec 23		4-1300
Fr 1816 Jan 03		4-1320
Fr 1816 Jan 06		DLC-20
Fr 1816 Apr 01		DLC-20
Fr 1816 Apr 01*		4-1419
To 1816 May 08		5-0072
Fr 1820 Feb 14		7-1026
To 1824 Apr 22		10-0675
Brown James		
Re 1829 Nov	par	14-0308
Re 1833 Sep 05	par	23-0633
Brown James (Cherokee)		
Fr 1814 Feb 27		DLC-9
Fr 1814 Feb 27		DLC-9
Brown James (LA)		
Fr 1814 Sep 26		DLC-12
Fr 1814 Oct 29		DLC-13
Fr 1814 Dec 05		DLC-19
Fr 1814 Dec 14		DLC-14
Fr 1815 Jan 03		DLC-15
To 1815 Jan 26		4-0616
To 1815 Feb 04		4-0686
To 1815 Feb 04*		DLC-16
Fr 1815 Feb 20		DLC-16
Fr 1815 Mar 03		DLC-17
To 1816 Jan 23		DLC-20
To 1816 Sep 06		5-0453
Fr 1816 Oct 06		DLC-21
Fr 1816 Oct 24		DLC-21
To 1829 Dec 08		14-0979
Brown James F		
Fr 1834 Dec 20		M639-6
Brown Jeremiah		
Re 1832 Aug 17	par	20-1310
Fr 1836 Jun 01		M687-17
Brown John (Cherokee)		
Fr 1813 Dec 28		DLC-8
Fr 1814 Jun 25		DLC-11
Re 1817 Jul 01		M222-23
Fr 1817 Dec 29		DLC-23
Fr 1836 Dec 14		32-1143
Brown John (KY)		
Fr 1819 Feb 20		DLC-26
Brown John (TN)		
Fr 1814 Jan 09		DLC-8
Fr 1814 Jan 21		DLC-8
To 1814 Jan 31		DLC-61
To 1814 Feb 02		DLC-62
To 1814 Feb 04		DLC-61
Fr 1814 Feb 04		3-0851
Fr 1814 Feb 05		DLC-8
Fr 1814 Feb 13		DLC-9
Fr 1814 Feb 15		DLC-9
To 1814 Feb 17		DLC-61
Fr 1814 Feb 19		DLC-9
Fr 1814 Feb 22		DLC-9
Fr 1814 Mar 15		DLC-9
Fr 1819 Sep 25		DLC-27
To 1819 Oct 08		DLC-27
Fr 1819 Oct 16		DLC-28
Fr 1829 Mar 27		M639-3
Fr 1844 Mar 07		DLC-56
Brown John (VA)		
Fr 1829 Mar 10		DLC-36
Brown John A		
Fr 1834 Mar 14		DLC-44
To 1834 Mar 17		DLC-44
Brown John L		
Fr 1839 Jul 03		DLC-52
Fr 1842 Dec 10	lnd	DLC-54
Brown John Porter		
Fr 1836 Feb 05		M639-3
Brown John T		
To 1833 Nov 14	chk	DLC-43
Brown John Thomas et al		
Fr 1829 Jul 29		M639-19
Brown Joseph		
Re 1830 Dec 16	leg	16-1456
Brown Lucinda		
Fr 1843 Aug 29		DLC-55
To 1843 Sep 14		35-1490
Brown Morgan		
Fr 1794 Oct 30		1-0239
Fr 1795 Sep 02		1-0311
Re 1799 Apr 19	leg	1-0703
Brown Morgan W		
Fr 1829 Apr 06		M639-3
Fr 1833 Aug 15		M639-3
Brown Nicholas et al		
Fr 1829 Nov 13		14-0455
Brown Obadiah B		
Fr 1829 Sep 03		DLC-75
Brown Richard		
Fr 1814 Feb 02		DLC-8
To 1814 Feb 18		DLC-61
Fr 1814 Mar 01		DLC-9
Fr 1814 Apr 19		DLC-10
Fr 1814 Jun 08		DLC-10
Fr 1814 Jun 09		DLC-10

Fr 1814 Oct 12 DLC-13
To 1814 Oct 22 DLC-62
To 1815 Aug 10 DLC-19
To 1816 Feb 4-1368
Fr 1817 Mar 01 DLC-22
Fr 1817 Jul 03 DLC-23
Fr 1817 Aug 01 DLC-23
Fr 1817 Dec 21 DLC-23
Brown Richard C S
Fr 1832 Sep 07 20-1502
Brown Richmond et al
Fr 1830 Feb 18 M639-21
Brown Robert
Fr 1833 cApr 22-0923
Brown Robert et al
Fr 1835 Feb 04 DLC-45
Brown Sam
Fr 1817 Aug 23 DLC-23
Fr 1821 Apr 04 M439-15
Brown Thomas
Fr 1832 Dec 16 M639-26
Fr 1844 May 05 36-0490
Fr 1845 Mar 14 M873-10
Brown Thomas B
Fr 1833 Aug 10# DLC-43
Brown Thomas H
Re 1840 Oct 24 DLC-53
Brown W
Fr 1821 Mar 30 DLC-30
Brown Weber D
Fr 1833 Sep 12 M124-139
Brown William
Re 1791 Apr 18 leg DLC-1
Re 1806 Sep 24 leg 2-0343
Fr 1831 May M639-12
Fr 1837 Jan 17 M687-20
Brown William et al
Fr 1832 Jan 30 19-0907
Brown William Gay et al
Fr 1829 Aug M639-6
Brown William Henry
Fr 1843 Aug 17 DLC-55
Brown William Little
Fr 1829 Apr 06 M639-7
Fr 1829 Apr 06 M639-5
Brown William T
Fr 1837 Oct 03 M567-147
Fr 1844 Dec 22 M873-69
Brown Brothers & Co et al
Fr 1832 Jan 03 M639-15
Fr 1834 Jan 27 M639-5
Browne Fielding A et al
Fr 1831 Nov 14 18-1271
Browne Thomas
Fr 1829 Nov 14 M179-67
Browne William
Fr 1829 Mar 20 M639-3
Browning Leven
Fr 1828 Dec 20 DLC-36
Brownlow Isaac
To 1813 Oct 19 DLC-7
Fr 1813 Oct 20 DLC-7
To 1813 Oct 28 DLC-61
Fr 1814 Feb 02 DLC-8
Bruce James
Re 1835 Nov 03 par 29-0404
Bruce John
Fr 1845 Jan 25 36-1402
Brutus (brig)
Re 1830 Jan 13 par 14-1391
Brutus (pseudonym)
Fr 1834 May 07 25-0980
Bryan Henry H
Fr 1829 Jun 29 13-0739
Bryan John A
Fr 1833 Oct 13 DLC-43
Fr 1835 Jan 10 M639-27
Fr 1843 Oct 16 DLC-55
To 1843 Oct 27 DLC-55
Bryan Joseph
Fr 1837 Jan 03 fin DLC-49
To 1837 Jan 07 chk DLC-49
Fr 1837 Feb 06 fin 33-0410
Bryan Joseph Hunter
Fr 1826 Apr 03 DLC-33
Bryan & Wood
Fr 1834 Dec 26 fin DLC-45
Bryant Nathan
To 1807 Jan 06 fin DLC-4
Bryant William
Fr 1840 Nov 28 DLC-53
Bryant Zophar W
Fr 1840 May 09 34-1340
Bryce J G
Fr 1835 Dec 08 M639-8
Bryce John
To 1840 May 09 34-1341
Fr 1840 Jun 23 34-1435
Bryson David et al
Fr 1835 Feb 19 mem 27-0565
Buchanan ______
To 1826 Nov 06 11-0390
Buchanan Andrew
Fr 1836 Feb 29 M639-8
Fr 1836 Apr 08 M639-5
Buchanan George
Fr 1816 Mar 11 add DLC-20
Buchanan George Washington
Fr 1829 Sep 19 M639-3
Fr 1829 Oct 01 M639-3
Buchanan J M
Fr 1830 Nov 23# 16-0838
Buchanan James
Fr 1825 May 29 DLC-32
Fr 1825 May 29 10-1287
To 1825 Jun 25 10-1319
Fr 1826 Mar 08 DLC-33
Fr 1826 Mar 08* 11-0156
To 1826 Apr 08 11-0184
Fr 1826 Sep 21 DLC-34
Fr 1826 Sep 21* 11-0369
To 1826 Oct 15 11-0381
To 1827 Jan 29 11-0480
To 1827 Jul 15 11-0748
To 1827 Jul 15* DLC-35
Fr 1827 Aug 10 11-0785
Fr 1829 Aug 08 M639-7
To 1831 Jan 04# 17-0187
To 1831 Jan 13# 17-0252
Fr 1831 Sep 10 18-0713
To 1831 Sep 14 18-0755
Fr 1832 May 14 DLC-40
Fr 1832 Jun 22 DLC-40
Fr 1832 Jun 22* 20-0793
Fr 1832 Oct 13 DLC-41
Fr 1832 Oct 13* 21-0085
Fr 1832 Dec 20 DLC-41

Buchanan James (cont)		
Fr 1832 Dec 20*		21-1098
To 1833 Mar 21		22-0847
To 1833 Mar 21*		DLC-42
Fr 1833 May 29		DLC-43
Fr 1833 May 29*		22-1478
Fr 1833 Sep 21		DLC-43
To 1833 Nov 18		23-1250
Fr 1834 Jan 18		DLC-44
Fr 1834 Jan 18*		24-0987
Fr 1834 Jul 15		26-0222
Fr 1834 Nov 05		M639-10
To 1835 Jan 14		27-0227
Fr 1835 Nov 06		M639-27
Fr 1836 Jan 30		M567-127
To 1836 Feb 02#		30-0261
Fr 1836 Apr 02		M639-18
Fr 1836 Jun 04		31-0311
Fr 1836 Jun 14		31-0469
Fr 1836 Jul 03		31-0782
Fr 1836 Jul 08		DLC-48
To 1836 Jul 11		31-1058
Fr 1836 Oct 03		32-0037
Fr 1837 Feb 03		33-0379
Fr 1837 Jul 28		DLC-50
Fr 1837 Jul 28*		33-1391
To 1837 Aug 24		33-1438
Fr 1837 Oct 26		DLC-50
To 1837 Dec 26		34-0141
Fr 1838 Jul 21		DLC-74
Fr 1839 Apr 09		DLC-52
Fr 1839 Apr 09*		34-0734
Fr 1839 Jul 02		34-0843
Fr 1843 Feb 28		DLC-55
To 1843 Mar 20		35-1285
Fr 1844 Apr 10		DLC-56
Fr 1844 Apr 29		36-0450
Buchanan James et al		
Fr c1835		37-0329
Buchanan James (TN)		
Fr 1790 Nov 08	leg	DLC-1
Fr 1810 Jun 06	fin	DLC-4
Buchanan James Madison		
Fr 1829 Jul 16		M639-3
Buchanan John		
Fr 1820 Sep 27	fin	DLC-29
Buchanan R		
Fr 1820 Oct 28	fin	DLC-29
Buchanan Thomas J et al		
Fr 1840 Feb 17		34-1222
Buchanan Thomas McKean		
Re 1832 Oct 20		M273-28
Buchanan & Spraule		
Fr 1827 Oct 24	fin	11-0893
Buck C N		
Fr 1832 Feb 01		M664-2
Buck Daniel Azro Ashley et al		
Fr 1835 Oct 22		M639-22
Buckingham William		
To 1791 Aug 22	fin	DLC-1
Buckler Henry		
Fr 1803 Aug 01	fin	DLC-3
Buckman Bowen		
Fr 1838 Sep 24		DLC-51
Buckner Alexander		
Fr 1832 Feb 02		M639-14
Fr 1832 Apr 23		20-0345
Budd George Knight		
Fr 1829 Aug 18		M179-67
Budd William		
Fr 1836 Jan 12		29-1556
Buddy & Colvin		
Fr 1830 Jun 05	fin	DLC-73
Buegrus ______		
Fr 1815 Jan 26		DLC-15
Buford Simeon		
Fr 1806 Aug 22		2-0316
Buford William		
Fr 1814 Sep 19		DLC-12
Bulfinch B S		
Fr 1818 Jan 10		DLC-23
Bulfinch Thomas		
Fr 1833 Nov 01		23-1170
Bulkley Ichabod		
Fr 1836 Mar 15		M687-17
Bullard Christopher		
Fr 1808 Jul 28		2-0718
Bullitt George		
Fr 1808 Jul 13		DLC-4
To 1808 Aug 06		DLC-4
Bullock George W et al		
Fr 1834 cJan		24-0709
Bullock Nathaniel		
Fr 1836 Jun 28		31-0622
Bullock W B et al		
Fr 1835 Jan 26		M124-146
Bullock Waller		
Fr 1837 Jan		M22-41
Bumstead Susan		
Fr 1836 Oct		31-1539
Bunch Samuel		
To 1814 May 18		DLC-10
Fr 1819 Sep 23		DLC-27
Fr 1819 Sep 23*		7-0673
Fr 1837 cFeb 04		M22-41
Fr 1837 cFeb 17		M22-41
Bunker Frederick E		
Fr 1830 Mar 15		M639-3
Bunner J C		
Fr 1844 Dec 24		36-1256
Bunner Rudolph		
Fr 1829 Mar 24		M639-7
Bunting J S		
Fr 1802 Jul 05	fin	DLC-2
Burbank Robert J		
Fr 1840 Sep 04		DLC-53
Burbank Sullivan et al		
Fr 1833 Dec 16		M567-78
Burch ______		
Re c1836 Jul	mem	37-0350
Burch Daniel E		
Fr 1819 Dec 05	leg	DLC-28
Fr 1821 Jul 07		DLC-30
Burch S		
Fr 1836 Mar 16	par	30-0797
Burchan Waide et al		
Fr c1835 Jan		M639-10
Burchard Matthew		
Re 1836 Oct 03		32-0041
Burd George		
Fr 1832 Dec 28		M639-27
Burd George et al		
Fr 1831 cDec		M639-22
Fr 1834 Jan 15		24-0888
Burden Jesse R		
Fr 1830 Feb 28		M639-23
Fr 1831 Feb 24		M22-27

Burden Jesse R et al
Fr 1833 Jan 10 M639-7
Burdgess Peter et al
Fr 1835 cJan DLC-59
Bureau ______ (Mr and Mrs)
Fr 1833 Sep 15 DLC-43
Burford David
Fr 1831 Jul 03 DLC-39
To 1831 Jul 28 18-0294
To 1831 Jul 28* DLC-39
Fr 1831 Dec 04 DLC-40
Fr 1831 Dec 04* 19-0063
Fr 1832 Sep 10 DLC-41
Fr 1832 Sep 10* 20-1506
To 1832 Sep 10 DLC-41
Fr 1833 Sep 27 M639-3
Burgess Thomas
Re 1802 May 05 leg 1-0993
Burke Edmund
Re 1830 Jun 16 M273-24
Burke John R
Fr 1832 Sep 07 DLC-41
To 1832 Sep 10 20-1509
To 1832 Sep 10* DLC-41
Burke Thomas
Re 1831 Oct 03 M273-27
Fr 1832 Jul 18 20-1130
Burke William
To 1825 Mar 06 10-1216
Fr 1829 Mar 06 12-0864
Fr 1829 Mar 28 12-1159
To 1831 Nov 09 18-1231
Fr 1835 Jan 10 DLC-45
Fr 1835 Mar 21 M639-1
Fr 1836 Feb 10 M639-12
Fr 1840 Jun 19 DLC-52
Fr 1840 Nov 18 DLC-53
Burke William et al
Fr 1829 Feb 09 M639-16
Fr 1837 Jan 27 DLC-49
Re 1837 Jan 27 33-0187
Burnet David Gouverneur
Fr 1836 Jun 02 T809-1
Burnett Charles A
Fr 1815 Nov 21 fin DLC-19
Burnett James
Fr 1832 Jan 11 19-0661
Burnett John et al
Re 1832 Mar 27 19-1558
Burnett Rebecca
Fr 1836 Jun 06 31-0342
Burnham Andrew Jackson
Fr 1845 Apr 14 DLC-58
Burnham Frederick G
Fr 1843 Dec 13 DLC-56
Burnham John
Fr 1837 Jan 02 M687-3
Burnham John et al
Fr 1830 Feb 04 M639-22
Burnham Michael
Fr 1831 Oct 14 M639-24
Burns ______
To 1835 Oct 12# fin DLC-47
Burns Michael
Fr 1841 Jan 06 fin 35-0194
Burr Aaron
Fr 1805 Jun 02 2-0058
Fr 1806 Mar 24 2-0194
Fr 1806 Apr 05 2-0206
Re 1806 Sep 27 add 2-0350
To 1806 Oct 04 fin 2-0352
Re 1807 Jun 25 leg 2-0506
Re 1807 Aug 21 leg 2-0542
Re 1828 Aug 12-0063
Burr Jonathan
Fr 1837 Feb 07 M687-20
Burrough Marmaduke
Fr 1834 May 30 M639-3
Fr 1834 Jun 28 M639-3
Burrows Albert et al
Fr 1831 May 01 M639-12
Burrows Silas Enoch
Fr 1831 Aug 17 DLC-39
Fr 1831 Dec 07 19-0216
Fr 1831 Dec 07 DLC-40
To 1831 Dec 08 DLC-40
Fr 1831 Dec 26 19-0416
Fr 1832 Feb 10 19-1053
Fr 1836 May 02 DLC-48
Burrows Silas Enoch et al
Fr 1832 Feb 11 19-1060
To 1832 Feb 11 19-1061
Burrows Stephen
Fr 1828 Nov 25 DLC-35
Fr 1829 Jun 10 M639-3
Burton Frank N W et al
Fr 1823 Jul 09 add 9-0608
To 1823 Jul 09 add 9-0610
To 1823 Jul 10 add 9-0612
Burton Martha H (Donelson)
To 1843 Dec 22 36-0070
Fr 1843 Dec 26 36-0078
To 1844 Oct 01 fin 36-0920
Burton Robert A
To 1839 Dec# fin 34-1066
Fr 1840 Feb 17 fin DLC-52
Burton Robert Minns
Fr 1826 May 09 DLC-33
To 1830 May 29 15-1201
Fr 1830 Oct 16 DLC-38
To 1830 Nov 06 16-0649
To 1830 Nov 06* DLC-38
Fr 1831 Oct 05 DLC-40
To 1831 Oct 19 18-1024
To 1831 Oct 20 18-1067
To 1831 Nov 24 18-1483
Fr 1833 Jan 13 DLC-42
To 1833 Jan 30 22-0110
Fr 1833 Feb 16 DLC-42
Fr 1834 Apr 23 DLC-44
To 1834 Apr 27 25-0904
Fr 1835 Feb 01# DLC-45
To 1835 Apr 09 28-0005
Fr 1835 May 13 DLC-46
To 1835 May 14 28-0379
To 1835 May 31 28-0541
To 1835 Jul 23 28-1121
Fr 1836 Apr 05 DLC-48
Fr 1836 Sep M22-41
Fr 1838 Apr 14 DLC-51
To 1838 Apr 23 DLC-51
Fr 1838 Apr 30 DLC-51
To 1838 Dec 17 34-0574
Fr 1838 Dec 22 DLC-51
Fr 1839 Mar 27 DLC-52
To 1839 Apr 01 34-0699
Fr 1839 Oct 25 fin DLC-52
Fr 1840 Feb 10 DLC-52

Burton Robert Minns (cont)			
	Fr 1840 Mar 15		DLC-52
	To 1840 Sep 28		35-0029
	To 1840 Oct 27		35-0074
	Fr 1842 Sep 25		DLC-54
	To 1843 Sep 15		35-1491
Burwell David			
	Fr 1816 May 20		DLC-20
Burwell John et al			
	Fr 1832 Apr 24		20-0383
Burwell N			
	Fr 1834 Mar 17		M688-87
Busbee Perrin			
	To 1844 Apr 29		36-0452
Bush Chauncey			
	To 1835 Oct 22		29-0333
Bush William			
	Re 1812 Jul 24	leg	2-1133
Bushnell Charles			
	Fr 1815 Mar 14		DLC-17
Bussard William			
	Fr 1830 May 14#		M639-3
Bustamante Anastasio			
	To 1830 Oct 07		16-0326
	To 1831 Jun 06		17-1526
Bute G H			
	Fr 1835 Mar 09		DLC-45
Butler Anthony			
	Fr 1811 Sep 28		2-1009
	Fr 1811 Oct 12		DLC-5
	Fr 1811 Oct 29		DLC-5
	Fr 1812 Nov 22		DLC-5
	Fr 1813 May 23		DLC-6
	Fr 1815 Nov 07		DLC-19
	Fr 1818 Jan 21		DLC-24
	Fr 1818 Jan 24		DLC-24
	Fr 1819 Nov 07		7-0841
	Fr 1826 Sep 04		DLC-34
	Fr 1827 Jan 04		DLC-34
	Fr 1827 May 17		DLC-34
	Fr 1829 Aug 11		13-1073
	To 1829 Oct 10		14-0130
	To 1829 Oct 10*		DLC-60
	Re 1829 Oct 12		14-0146
	To 1829 Oct 18		14-0193
	To 1829 Oct 19		14-0194
	To 1829 Oct 19*		DLC-37
	To 1830 Mar 23		15-0434
	To 1830 Mar 23*		DLC-72
	Fr 1830 Apr 15		M97-6
	Fr 1830 Apr 15*		15-0712
	Fr 1830 May 24		DLC-38
	To 1830 Oct 06		16-0322
	To 1830 Oct 06*		DLC-73
	To 1830 Oct 07		16-0330
	To 1831 Feb 15		17-0520
	Fr 1831 May 25		M97-6
	Fr 1831 Jun 23		DLC-39
	Fr 1831 Jul 22		18-0244
	To 1831 Aug 17		18-0555
	To 1831 Aug 17*		DLC-39
	To 1831 Aug 24		18-0582
	Fr 1831 Oct 06		18-0929
	To 1831 Dec 09		19-0273
	Fr 1831 Dec 23		M97-6
	Fr 1832 Jan 02		DLC-40
	Fr 1832 Feb 19		19-1155
	Fr 1832 Feb 23		DLC-40
	To 1832 Feb 25		19-1241
	Fr 1832 Feb 27		DLC-40
	To 1832 Mar 06		19-1325
	To 1832 Apr 19		20-0295
	To 1832 Apr 19*		DLC-40
	Fr 1832 Jun 21		DLC-40
	Fr 1832 Jul 18		DLC-41
	Fr 1832 Aug 02		DLC-41
	Fr 1832 Aug 12		DLC-41
	Fr 1832 Aug 30		DLC-41
	To 1832 Sep 04		20-1481
	Fr 1832 Oct 09		DLC-41
	Fr 1832 Oct 10		DLC-41
	To 1832 Oct 29		21-0205
	To 1832 Nov 04#		DLC-41
	To 1832 Dec 04		21-0832
	Fr 1832 Dec 20		DLC-41
	Fr 1832 Dec 22		DLC-41
	Fr 1833 Jan 02		DLC-41
	Fr 1833 Feb 10		M97-7
	To 1833 Feb 14		22-0374
	Fr 1833 Apr 19		M97-7
	Fr 1833 Sep 26		DLC-43
	To 1833 Oct 01		23-0924
	Fr 1833 Oct 02		DLC-43
	Fr 1833 Oct 28		DLC-43
	To 1833 Oct 30		23-1119
	To 1833 Nov 27		23-1318
	To 1833 Nov 27*		DLC-43
	Re 1834 Jan 16		24-0957
	Fr 1834 Feb 06		DLC-44
	Fr 1834 Mar 07		DLC-44
	Fr 1834 Jun 06		DLC-44
	To 1834 Jun 21		25-1453
	Fr 1834 Jul 02		DLC-44
	Fr 1834 Oct 20		DLC-44
	Fr 1834 Nov 21		DLC-45
	Fr 1834 Dec 24		DLC-45
	Fr 1835 Feb 26		27-0631
	Fr 1835 Jun 06		M97-7
	Fr 1835 Jun 17#		M97-7
	Fr 1835 Nov		DLC-47
	Fr 1835 Dec 19		DLC-47
	Fr 1836 Jan 15#		M97-7
	To 1841 Mar 15		DLC-74
	Fr 1843 Jul 28		DLC-55
Butler Anthony Wayne			
	Re 1813 Jan 18	mem	DLC-6
	Fr 1818 Dec 21		DLC-26
	Fr 1819 Mar 10		DLC-75
	Fr 1819 May 06		DLC-27
	Fr 1822 Dec 09		9-0341
	To 1823 Jan 13		9-0403
	Fr 1823 Mar 15		DLC-32
	To 1823 May 18		9-0559
	To 1823 Jun 02		9-0582
	Fr 1823 Jul		9-0601
	To 1823 Aug 14		9-0633
	To 1823 Nov 10		9-0751
	To 1824 Jan 31		10-0421
	Fr 1824 Mar 23		10-0575
	To 1824 Apr 21		10-0667
Butler Benjamin Franklin			
	Fr 1833 Nov 12		23-1225
	Re 1833 Nov 15		23-1236
	Fr 1833 Nov 20		DLC-43
	Fr 1834 Feb 03		24-1143
	To 1834 Feb 24		DLC-75
	Fr 1834 Mar 08		DLC-75
	Fr 1834 Mar 12		25-0124
	Fr 1834 Mar 29		25-0489

Fr 1834 May 19#	25-1087
Fr 1834 Jun 25	DLC-44
To 1834 Jun 26	25-1550
To 1834 Jul 07	26-0174
Fr 1834 Jul 23	M222-32
Fr 1834 Oct 28	DLC-44
Fr 1834 Nov 06	26-0839
To 1835 Jan 22	27-0275
Fr 1835 Feb 09#	DLC-45
To 1835 cMar 17	27-1224
Fr 1835 Mar 21	27-1246
Fr 1835 Apr 07#	DLC-46
To 1835 Jun 11	28-0637
Fr 1835 Jun 15	M699-4
Fr 1835 Sep 02	M179-80
To 1835 Oct 29	29-0363
Fr 1836 Jan 10	29-1535
Fr 1836 Feb 26#	M234-225
Fr 1836 Mar 25	30-0897
Fr 1836 Mar 25*	M699-4
Fr 1836 Mar 25*	T412-2
Fr 1836 Apr 11	30-1126
Fr 1836 May 17	M179-82
Fr 1836 May 17*	31-0045
To 1836 cJun 20	31-0517
Fr 1836 Jul 04	31-0794
Fr 1836 Jul 07	31-0916
Fr 1836 Aug 16	M687-1
To 1836 Oct 04	32-0049
To 1836 Oct 25	32-0343
To 1836 Nov 01	32-0375
To 1836 Nov 02	32-0387
Fr 1836 Nov 03	32-0391
To 1836 Nov 05	32-0405
To 1836 Nov 05	32-0406
Fr 1836 Nov 08	32-0411
To 1836 Nov 09#	M567-118
Fr 1836 Nov 16	32-0536
Fr 1836 Nov 16*	M127-3
Fr 1836 Nov 16*	M21-20
To 1836 Nov 16#	32-0540
Fr 1836 Dec 03	32-0624
Fr 1836 Dec 03*	M127-3
Fr 1836 Dec 19	M127-3
To 1836 Dec 19	32-1191
Fr 1836 Dec 20	32-1197
Fr 1836 Dec 20*	M21-20
Fr 1836 Dec 20*	M127-3
Fr 1836 Dec 20	32-1202
Fr 1836 Dec 20*	M21-20
Fr 1836 Dec 20*	M127-3
Fr 1836 Dec 24	32-1294
To 1836 Dec 28	M221-117
Fr 1836 Dec 29	32-1386
Fr 1836 Dec 29*	M21-20
Fr 1836 Dec 29*	M127-3
Fr 1836 Dec 29	32-1388
Fr 1836 Dec 29*	M21-20
Fr 1836 Dec 29*	M127-3
Fr 1836 Dec 29	32-1390
Fr 1836 Dec 29*	M21-20
Fr 1836 Dec 29*	M127-3
Fr 1836 Dec 29	32-1392
Fr 1836 Dec 29*	M127-3
Fr 1836 Dec 29	32-1395
Fr 1836 Dec 29*	M127-3
To 1836 Dec 31	M221-117
To 1837 Jan 07	M22-41
Fr 1837 Jan 09	32-1550
Fr 1837 Jan 09*	M127-3
To 1837 cJan 10	M22-41
To 1837 Jan 16	M221-117
To 1837 Jan 16*	M22-41
Fr 1837 Jan 18	33-0011
Fr 1837 Jan 18*	M127-3
Fr 1837 Jan 19	33-0030
Fr 1837 Jan 19	M127-3
Fr 1837 Jan 19	33-0032
Fr 1837 Jan 19	M127-3
Fr 1837 Jan 20	33-0065
Fr 1837 Jan 25	33-0137
Fr 1837 Jan 30	33-0208
Fr 1837 Jan 30*	M221-117
Fr 1837 Feb 02	M127-3
Fr 1837 Feb 02	33-0356
Fr 1837 Feb 02*	M127-3
To 1837 Feb 11	33-0604
Fr 1837 Feb 11	33-0607
Fr 1837 Feb 11*	M127-3
Fr 1837 Feb 11	33-0608
Fr 1837 Feb 11*	M127-3
To 1837 Feb 14	M221-117
To 1837 Feb 14*	33-0686
To 1837 Feb 14	33-0698
Fr 1837 Feb 14	33-0697
Fr 1837 Feb 14*	M127-3
Fr 1837 Feb 17	33-0737
To 1837 Feb 17#	M234-225
To 1837 Feb 18	33-0766
To 1837 Feb 18	M221-117
To 1837 Feb 20#	33-0780
Fr 1837 Feb 21	33-0795
Fr 1837 Feb 21*	M127-3
Fr 1837 Feb 21	M127-3
To 1837 Feb 21	M22-41
To 1837 Feb 21	M22-41
To 1837 Feb 23	33-0838
Fr 1837 Feb 24	33-0852
Fr 1837 Feb 24*	M127-3
Fr 1837 Feb 24	33-0853
Fr 1837 Feb 24*	M127-3
To 1837 Feb 25	M234-244
Fr 1837 Mar 02	33-0970
Fr 1837 Mar 03	33-1010
Fr 1837 Mar 03	33-1024
To 1837 Mar 03	33-1030
To 1837 Mar 07#	M567-143
Fr 1837 Jun 10	DLC-50
To 1837 Jun 24	33-1334
To 1838 Feb 15	34-0246
Fr 1839 Mar 16	DLC-52
To 1839 Apr 04	34-0715
Fr 1840 Jul 07	DLC-53
Fr 1841 Aug 18	35-0378
Fr 1841 Sep 06	DLC-53
To 1841 Sep 22	35-0399
Fr 1841 Oct 05	DLC-53
To 1842 Jul 12	35-0846
To 1843 Oct 05	35-1529
Fr 1844 Feb 10	DLC-56
To 1844 Feb 22	36-0328
Fr 1844 Apr 06	DLC-56
To 1844 Apr 29	36-0454
To 1844 May 06	36-0492
Fr 1844 May 10	DLC-56
To 1844 May 14	36-0534
To 1844 Jun 26	36-0651
Fr 1844 Jul 13	36-0704

Butler Benjamin Franklin (cont)			
	Fr 1844 Nov 08		DLC-57
	To 1845 Jan 04		36-1303
	Fr 1845 May 06		37-0196
Butler Carlos P			
	Fr 1835 Mar 09		M639-3
Butler Caroline Swanwich			
	Fr 1843 Mar 15		DLC-55
Butler Edward estate			
	Re 1804 Oct 07	leg	DLC-58
	Re 1809 Oct 07	leg	2-0855
Butler Edward George Washington			
	Re 1813 Jan 18	mem	DLC-6
	Re 1813 Apr 26		DLC-6
	Fr 1815 Feb 12		DLC-16
	To 1816 Aug 19	chk	DLC-21
	Fr 1817 Sep 10	fin	DLC-23
	Re 1817 Sep 10	mem	DLC-29
	Fr 1817 Sep 16#	fin	DLC-23
	Fr 1818 Jul 22		DLC-25
	Fr 1820 Apr 27		DLC-29
	Fr 1820 Jun 05		DLC-29
	To 1821 Jan 08		8-0049
	Fr 1821 May 26		DLC-30
	Fr 1821 Sep 20		DLC-30
	Fr 1821 Dec 17		DLC-31
	To 1822 Jan 08		8-1387
	Fr 1822 Jan 22		9-0001
	To 1823 Mar 03		9-0472
	To 1823 May 01		9-0541
	To 1824 Jan 20		10-0381
	Fr 1824 Feb 24		DLC-75
	To 1824 Apr 27		10-0684
	Fr 1824 May 24		10-0749
	Fr 1824 Aug 18		DLC-72
	To 1824 Dec 12		10-0974
	To 1825 Mar 25		10-1228
	To 1825 Apr 28		10-1252
	To 1825 Jul 25		10-1366
	To 1825 Nov 10		11-0056
	To 1825 Dec 08		11-0069
	Fr 1826		DLC-75
	To 1826 Jan 24		11-0118
	To 1826 Feb 02		11-0122
	To 1826 Mar 09		11-0163
	To 1826 May 28		11-0222
	To 1826 Jun 22		11-0261
	Fr 1826 Jul		DLC-75
	Fr 1826 Jul 14		DLC-34
	Fr 1826 Dec 11		DLC-75
	To 1826 Dec 22		11-0436
	Fr 1827 Jan 11		DLC-72
	Fr 1827 Apr 27		DLC-72
	To 1827 May 21		11-0604
	Fr 1827 Sep 04		DLC-34
	Fr 1828 Dec 23		DLC-72
	To 1829 Feb 12		12-0505
	To 1830 Mar 15#		15-0362
	To 1831 Oct 13	chk	DLC-40
	Fr 1831 Oct 17		DLC-40
	To 1838 Sep 19		34-0459
	Fr 1841 Apr 10		35-0276
	Fr 1842 Jul 17		DLC-54
	To 1842 Aug 17		35-0879
	Fr 1843 Mar 15		DLC-55
	To 1843 Oct 04		35-1526
	Fr 1844 Jan 17		36-0128
	To 1844 Feb 09		36-0241
	Fr 1844 Nov 27		DLC-57
	To 1844 Dec 20		36-1221
	Fr 1845 Mar 27		DLC-75
Butler Edward George Washington Jr			
	To 1844 Jul 19		36-0711
Butler Eleanor Angela Isabella			
	Fr 1843 Mar 15		DLC-55
Butler Eliza Eleanor			
see also Donelson E E B			
	To 1809 Oct 09	leg	2-0857
Butler Frances Parke (Lewis)			
	To 1826 Jun 22		11-0261
Butler George G			
	Fr 1843 Dec 14		DLC-56
Butler Harriet (Allen)			
	To 1837 Jun 24		33-1342
Butler Isaac			
	Re 1833 Dec 14	par	24-0496
Butler Isabella (Fowler)			
see also Vinson I F			
	Fr 1803 Aug 03		DLC-71
Butler J P			
	Fr 1835 Dec 12#	fin	DLC-47
Butler James			
	Re 1813 Jan 20		DLC-61
	Re 1834 Feb 15	par	24-1344
Butler Percival			
	Fr 1806 Jan 10		DLC-3
Butler Philip S			
	Fr 1829 Apr 23		13-0104
Butler Pierce (KY)			
	Fr 1807 Dec 09		DLC-4
Butler Pierce (1744-1822)			
	Re 1798 May 17	leg	1-0661
Butler Pierce Mason			
	Re 1843 Oct 14	mem	35-1544
Butler Richard			
	Fr 1815 Jun 30		DLC-18
	To 1816 Jun 04		5-0131
	Fr 1817 Apr 20		DLC-22
	To 1817 Dec 06		5-1165
Butler Richard et al			
	Fr 1832 Jan		19-0535
Butler Robert			
	Fr 1805 Nov 02		DLC-3
	Fr 1806 Feb 03		2-0141
	Re 1809 Mar 04	leg	DLC-4
	Fr 1810 Dec 20	fin	DLC-5
	Fr 1813 Jul 28		DLC-6
	Fr 1813 Jul 31		DLC-6
	Fr 1813 Aug 18		DLC-6
	Fr 1813 Oct 10		DLC-6
	Fr 1813 Nov 26		DLC-7
	Fr 1814 May 31		DLC-66
	Fr 1814 Aug 26		DLC-11
	To 1814 Aug 27		DLC-11
	To 1814 Aug 28		DLC-11
	To 1814 Sep 04		4-0170
	To 1814 Sep 07		DLC-62
	To 1814 Sep 08		DLC-12
	Fr 1814 Sep 12		DLC-12
	To 1814 Sep 15		DLC-62
	To 1814 Sep 17		DLC-12
	Fr 1814 Sep 22		DLC-12
	To 1815 Jan 31#		4-0664
	To 1815 Jul 15		4-1115
	To 1815 Jul 18	mem	DLC-18
	To 1815 Jul 20		4-1120
	To 1815 Jul 31	mem	4-1139
	To 1815 Aug 21		DLC-19
	To 1815 Aug 27		4-1173
	To 1815 Oct 18		DLC-19

Fr	1815	Oct 18		DLC-19
Fr	1815	Oct 27		DLC-19
Fr	1815	Nov 02		DLC-19
Fr	1815	Nov 08		DLC-19
Fr	1815	Nov 09		DLC-19
To	1815	Dec 31		DLC-20
To	1816	Feb 18		DLC-62
Fr	1816	Mar 12		DLC-20
Fr	1816	Mar 19		DLC-20
To	1816	Mar 20		DLC-20
Fr	1816	Mar 26		DLC-20
Fr	1816	Apr 07		DLC-20
To	1816	Apr 22		5-0039
To	1816	Aug 19	chk	DLC-21
To	1816	Sep 05		DLC-21
To	1816	Oct 24	chk	DLC-21
To	1817	Feb 17		DLC-22
To	1817	May 07		DLC-22
To	1817	cMay 08		DLC-22
To	1817	May 22		DLC-22
To	1817	Jun 21		DLC-23
Fr	1817	Jul 22	fin	5-0932
Fr	1817	Jul 23		5-0938
To	1817	cAug 17		5-0989
To	1817	Dec 06#		DLC-23
To	1817	Dec 19		5-1192
To	1817	Dec 29		DLC-23
To	1817	Dec 31		DLC-23
Fr	1818	Jun 29	fin	6-1088
To	1818	Aug 03		DLC-25
To	1818	Aug 12		6-1225
To	1818	Aug 18		6-1236
To	1818	Sep 01		DLC-25
To	1818	Sep 17		6-1308
To	1818	Nov 01		DLC-25
Fr	1818	Dec 15		DLC-26
To	1819			DLC-28
Fr	1819	Jan 30		M221-80
Fr	1819	Mar 03	leg	7-0393
To	1819	Mar 07		DLC-26
Fr	1819	Apr 25		DLC-26
To	1819	Apr 29#		DLC-26
Fr	1819	Aug 23		DLC-27
To	1819	Nov 12		DLC-28
To	1819	Nov 19		DLC-28
To	1820	Jan 20#		7-1001
Fr	1820	Feb 27		DLC-28
To	1820	Jun 19		DLC-29
Fr	1820	Aug 03		7-1184
Fr	1821	Jan 15		DLC-29
Fr	1821	Feb 16		DLC-29
To	1821	Apr 12		DLC-63
Re	1821	Apr 12		DLC-63
Fr	1821	May 17		DLC-30
Fr	1821	May 20		DLC-30
To	1821	Jun 02		DLC-63
Fr	1821	Jun 07		DLC-30
To	1821	Jun 13		M116-5
To	1821	Jun 26		DLC-63
Fr	1821	Jul 12	fin	DLC-70
Fr	1821	Jul 24		DLC-30
To	1821	Jul 27		DLC-30
To	1821	Aug 08		DLC-63
Fr	1821	Aug 08		M116-7
Fr	1821	Aug 08*		DLC-63
Fr	1821	Aug 08	fin	DLC-70
Fr	1821	Aug 08	mem	DLC-70
To	1821	Aug 12		DLC-63
Fr	1821	Aug 16	mem	DLC-63
To	1821	Aug 22		M116-7
To	1821	Aug 22*		DLC-63
To	1821	Aug 22		8-1082
Fr	1821	Aug 22		M116-7
Fr	1821	Aug 22*		DLC-63
Fr	1821	Aug 22		M116-7
Fr	1821	Aug 22*		DLC-63
Fr	1821	Aug 26	fin	DLC-70
Fr	1821	Sep 19		DLC-30
Fr	1822	Jan 19		DLC-31
Fr	1822	Jan 21		M116-10
Fr	1822	Jan 21*		8-1402
Fr	1822	Jan 21*		DLC-63
Fr	1822	Oct 12		M688-19
Re	1824	Jan 09		DLC-32
To	1824	Jul 17		10-0832
To	1824	Jul 19		10-0834
To	1824	Aug 13		10-0849
Fr	1825	Nov 09	fin	DLC-33
Fr	1826	Jun 30		DLC-34
Fr	1826	Sep 15		DLC-34
Fr	1827	Jun 06		DLC-34
Fr	1827	Aug 14		11-0788
Fr	1828	Feb 21		DLC-75
Fr	1828	Apr 23		11-1216
Fr	1828	Sep 15		12-0198
Fr	c1829			12-0360
Fr	1829	Jun 02		M639-21
Fr	1830	May 31		DLC-38
Fr	1830	Nov 08		DLC-38
Fr	1830	Nov 28		M222-27
Fr	1831	Feb 03		DLC-39
Fr	1831	Jun 09		DLC-39
Fr	1833	Jan 16#		21-1442
Fr	1833	Dec 10		24-0438
Fr	1834	Apr 29#		25-0910
Fr	1834	cMay 01		DLC-75
Fr	1835	May 13		DLC-46
Fr	1835	Dec 04		DLC-47
Fr	1837	Apr 05		DLC-74
Fr	1838	Sep 15		DLC-74
Fr	1841	Aug 14		DLC-74
Fr	1841	Oct 25		DLC-74
To	1841	Nov 16		35-0489
Fr	1842	Jan 01		DLC-74
To	1842	Jan 24		DLC-74
Fr	1842	Feb 28		DLC-74

Butler Samuel

Fr	1813	May 10		DLC-6

Butler Thomas (1754-1805)

Fr	c1804	Aug 01		DLC-58
Fr	1804	Aug 04		DLC-3
Fr	1804	Aug 23		DLC-3
To	1804	Aug 25		DLC-3
Fr	1804	Oct 15		DLC-71
Fr	1804	Oct 21		DLC-71
Fr	1804	Nov 05		DLC-71
Fr	1804	Nov 20		DLC-71
Fr	1804	Dec 17		DLC-71
Fr	1804	Dec 24		DLC-71
Fr	1804	Dec 31		DLC-71
Fr	1805	Jan 28		DLC-71
Fr	1805	Feb 18		DLC-71
Fr	1805	Mar 04		DLC-3
Fr	1805	Apr 17		DLC-71
Fr	1805	May 21		2-0039
Fr	1805	May 27		DLC-71
Fr	1805	Jun 09		DLC-71
Fr	1805	Jul 08		DLC-71

Butler Thomas (cont)
Fr 1805 Jul 15 DLC-71
Re 1805 Aug 12 2-0078
Fr 1805 Aug 26 DLC-71
Fr 1805 Aug 26 DLC-71
Butler Thomas (1785-1847)
To 1823 Mar 21 9-0499
To 1828 Nov 23 12-0285
Fr 1829 May 25 M639-10
To 1832 Jul 17# 20-1114
Butler Thomas Langford
Fr 1814 Sep 01 M566-38
Fr 1814 Sep 03 DLC-18
To 1814 Dec 25 DLC-62
Fr 1815 Jan 13# 4-0527
Fr 1815 Mar 20 DLC-71
Fr 1816 Feb 02 DLC-20
Fr 1829 Feb 06 M639-3
Butler Thomas Ryan
Fr 1807 Jan 08 fin DLC-4
Butler William
Re 1813 Jan 20 DLC-61
Fr 1829 Nov 27 fin DLC-37
Butler William Edward
Fr 1808 Dec 22 2-0752
Fr 1814 Sep 28 DLC-12
To 1819 Nov 15 lnd 7-0850
Re 1824 Jan 09 DLC-32
Fr 1831 Jul 25 DLC-39
Fr 1838 Sep 18 DLC-51
Fr 1842 Jul 21 DLC-54
Fr 1842 Jul 21 DLC-54
Fr 1843 Sep 21 DLC-55
Butler William Orlando
Fr 1815 Jun 15 DLC-18
To 1816 Aug 14 5-0353
Fr 1816 Sep 06 DLC-21
Fr 1816 Oct 08 M221-74
Fr 1817 Jan 12 5-0680
Fr 1817 Apr 01 DLC-22
Fr 1830 Jun 12 15-1340
Buybee William et al
Fr 1835 Oct 01 29-0162
Bybee J N et al
Fr c1836 Dec M687-14
Byler John
Fr 1814 Mar 14 DLC-9
Byrn John W
Fr 1828 Jan 15 fin 11-1061
Fr 1831 Sep 23 M234-185
Fr 1831 Sep 23* 18-0873
Byrne David
Fr 1828 May 05 DLC-35
Byrne Edmund
Fr 1830 May 29 M124-124

Cabaniss Charles
To 1811 Feb 06 fin DLC-5
Cabell John J
Fr 1824 Feb 08 M688-33
To 1828 Dec 09 12-0305
Fr 1829 Feb 22 M639-25
Cabinet
Re 1830 cJan mem 14-1247
To 1833 Sep 18 DLC-42
To 1833 Sep 18* 23-0735
To 1833 Sep 18* DLC-77
Cabinet members
To 1829 Feb 23 DLC-60
To 1829 Feb 23* 12-0573
To 1829 Dec 02 14-0795
To 1832 Jun 05 20-0700
To 1832 Jun 05* M124-133
To 1833 Mar 19 DLC-42
To 1833 Mar 19* 22-0815
To 1833 Mar 31 22-0919
Fr 1833 Apr 12 22-0983
To 1834 Feb 12 24-1292
To 1837 Feb 02 33-0358
Cabot Joseph S
Re 1833 Apr 02 22-0925
Fr 1834 Dec 23 26-1559
Cabot Joseph S et al
Fr 1830 M639-6
Caddo treaty
Re 1836 Feb 02 M668-8
Cadle Joseph
Re 1830 Apr 02 15-0564
Cadwalader Thomas
To 1819 Feb 19 add 7-0285
Fr 1819 Feb 19 add 7-0288
Fr 1828 Jun 21 DLC-35
Fr 1828 Oct 15 DLC-35
To 1828 Nov 16 DLC-35
Caffery Donelson
Fr 1806 Aug 25 2-0321
Fr 1810 May 20 DLC-4
Fr 1810 Jun 10 DLC-4
Fr 1810 Jul 20 DLC-4
Fr 1810 Aug 15 DLC-4
Fr 1810 Nov 28 DLC-5
Fr 1810 Dec 05 DLC-5
Fr 1811 Oct 23 DLC-5
Fr 1813 Feb 22 DLC-6
Fr 1814 Dec 28 DLC-15
Fr 1815 Jan 09 DLC-15
To 1816 Feb 24 4-1410
Fr 1818 Nov 26 DLC-26
Fr 1828 Feb 18# 11-1124
Fr 1830 Jul 14 DLC-38
Fr 1834 Aug 13 DLC-44
Caffery John (1756-1811)
Re 1796 May 18 mem DLC-1
Fr 1797 cMay DLC-1
Fr 1802 Jun 21 lnd 1-1006
Fr 1803 Jul 05 leg 1-1129
Fr 1805 Sep 24 leg DLC-3
Re 1807 Jan 17 lnd 2-0461
Fr 1808 Sep 23 DLC-4
Caffery John (b c1795)
To 1816 Jul 15 chk DLC-21
Caffery Mary (Donelson)
To 1812 Feb 08 DLC-5
Fr 1819 Jan 19# 7-0184
Fr 1819 Mar 03# DLC-26
Fr 1823 Aug 13# DLC-32
Cage Harry
Fr 1815 Mar 17 DLC-17
To 1833 Dec 23# M639-23
Cage James
Fr 1806 Nov 30 DLC-4
Fr 1808 Dec 19 DLC-4
Fr 1815 Jul 13 DLC-18
Fr 1815 Nov 06 M179-32
Fr 1816 Jun 20 5-0183
Fr 1819 Jun 10 7-0547
Fr 1833 Dec 23# M639-23
Cage Reuben
Fr 1806 May 29 lnd 2-0251

Cage Wilson		
Fr 1810 Aug 18		DLC-4
Cage & Black		
Re 1806 Aug 19	leg	DLC-71
Cahoon Reuben		
Fr 1836 Oct		M22-41
Caicedo Domingo		
To 1831 Jun 09		17-1572
Calderon de la Barca Angel		
Fr 1837 Mar 04		33-1061
Caldwell Alexander M et al		
Fr 1840 Sep 10		DLC-53
Caldwell Charles		
Fr 1824 Jul 12		10-0823
Caldwell D		
Fr 1820 Dec 16		DLC-29
Caldwell John		
Fr 1808 Apr 25	fin	DLC-4
Fr 1838#	fin	DLC-51
Caldwell Samuel		
Fr 1803 Jul 28		DLC-3
Caldwell W E		
Fr 1841 Sep 07		DLC-53
Calhoon Julin C et al		
Fr c1836		29-1384
Calhoun John Caldwell		
Fr 1817 Dec 11		DLC-23
Fr 1817 Dec 11*		M15-4
Fr 1817 Dec 12		DLC-23
Fr 1817 Dec 12*		M6-9
Fr 1817 Dec 17		DLC-23
Fr 1817 Dec 17*		M15-4
Fr 1817 Dec 17*		M271-2
Fr 1817 Dec 19		DLC-23
Fr 1817 Dec 19*		M6-9
Fr 1817 Dec 24		DLC-23
Fr 1817 Dec 24*		M15-4
Fr 1817 Dec 26		DLC-23
Fr 1817 Dec 26*		M6-9
Fr 1817 Dec 26*		M271-2
Fr 1817 Dec 26*		5-1198
To 1817 Dec 27		M22-10
Fr 1817 Dec 27		DLC-23
Fr 1817 Dec 27*		M15-4
Fr 1817 Dec 29		DLC-23
Fr 1817 Dec 29*		M6-9
Fr 1817 Dec 29		DLC-23
Fr 1817 Dec 29*		M6-9
To 1817 Dec 30		5-1212
Fr 1817 Dec 30		DLC-23
Fr 1817 Dec 30*		M15-4
To 1818 Jan 06		5-1226
To 1818 Jan 06		DLC-75
To 1818 Jan 09		M22-11
Fr 1818 Jan 10		DLC-23
To 1818 Jan 12		5-1254
To 1818 Jan 13		5-1280
Fr 1818 Jan 17		DLC-23
Fr 1818 Jan 17*		M6-9
To 1818 cJan 19		5-1287
To 1818 Jan 20		5-1298
To 1818 Jan 21		M221-78
To 1818 Jan 27		5-1340
Fr 1818 Jan 29		DLC-24
Fr 1818 Jan 29*		M15-4
Fr 1818 Jan 29*		5-1400
Fr 1818 Feb 06		M6-10
Fr 1818 Feb 06*		5-1439
To 1818 Feb 10		M221-78
To 1818 Feb 10*		6-0001
Fr 1818 Feb 12		M15-4
To 1818 Feb 14		M221-78
To 1818 Feb 14*		6-0022
Fr 1818 Feb 19		DLC-24
Fr 1818 Feb 19*		M6-10
Fr 1818 Feb 23		DLC-24
Fr 1818 Feb 23*		M6-10
To 1818 Feb 26		M221-78
To 1818 Feb 26*		6-0050
Fr 1818 Mar 02		DLC-24
Fr 1818 Mar 02*		M6-10
To 1818 Mar 09		M222-21
Fr 1818 Mar 14		DLC-24
Fr 1818 Mar 14*		M6-10
Fr 1818 Mar 17		DLC-24
To 1818 Mar 25		M221-78
To 1818 Mar 25*		6-0089
To 1818 Apr 08		M221-78
To 1818 Apr 08*		6-0308
To 1818 Apr 09		6-0331
Fr 1818 Apr 11		DLC-24
Fr 1818 Apr 11*		M6-10
To 1818 Apr 20		6-0405
Fr 1818 Apr 22		DLC-24
Fr 1818 Apr 22*		M6-10
To 1818 Apr 26		6-0466
Fr 1818 May 02		DLC-24
Fr 1818 May 02*		M271-2
Fr 1818 May 02*		M15-4
Fr 1818 May 02*		6-0537
To 1818 May 05		M221-78
To 1818 May 05*		6-0592
To 1818 May 06		6-0658
To 1818 May 07		M271-2
To 1818 May 07*		M221-78
To 1818 May 07*		6-0661
To 1818 Jun 02		M221-78
To 1818 Jun 02*		6-0951
To 1818 Jun 02		6-0962
To 1818 Jun 27		M22-11
To 1818 Jun 28		6-1085
To 1818 Jun 28*		DLC-25
To 1818 Jul 08		6-1113
To 1818 Jul 08		M221-78
To 1818 Jul 13		6-1121
Fr 1818 Jul 13		M6-10
Fr 1818 Jul 21		DLC-25
Fr 1818 Jul 21*		M6-10
Fr 1818 Jul 27		DLC-25
Fr 1818 Jul 27*		M6-10
Fr 1818 Jul 27*		6-1157
Fr 1818 Jul 28		DLC-25
Fr 1818 Jul 28*		M6-10
Fr 1818 Jul 28*		6-1160
Fr 1818 Jul 30		DLC-25
Fr 1818 Jul 30*		M15-4
Fr 1818 Jul 30*		6-1165
To 1818 Jul 31		M271-2
To 1818 Aug		M22-11
To 1818 Aug 09		M221-78
To 1818 Aug 10		M221-78
To 1818 Aug 10*		6-1209
Fr 1818 Aug 11		M6-10
Fr 1818 Aug 14		DLC-25
Fr 1818 Aug 14*		6-1227
Fr 1818 Aug 14*		M6-10
To 1818 Aug 18		6-1237
Fr 1818 Aug 18		6-1240

Calhoun John Caldwell (cont)

Fr 1818 Aug 18*	M15-4
To 1818 Aug 22	DLC-25
Fr 1818 Aug 22	DLC-25
Fr 1818 Aug 22*	M6-10
Fr 1818 Aug 28	DLC-25
Fr 1818 Aug 28*	M6-10
Fr 1818 Sep 01	M6-10
To 1818 Sep 02	6-1279
Fr 1818 Sep 02	DLC-25
Fr 1818 Sep 02*	M6-10
Fr 1818 Sep 08	DLC-25
Fr 1818 Sep 08*	M6-10
Fr 1818 Sep 08*	DLC-71
Fr 1818 Sep 08*	6-1286
Fr 1818 Sep 10	DLC-25
Fr 1818 Sep 10*	M6-10
To 1818 Sep 11	M221-78
Fr 1818 Sep 11	M15-4
Fr 1818 Sep 11*	DLC-25
To 1818 Sep 20	M221-81
To 1818 Sep 20*	DLC-59
To 1818 Sep 21	6-1316
Fr 1818 Sep 24	DLC-25
Fr 1818 Sep 24*	M6-10
Fr 1818 Sep 29	DLC-25
Fr 1818 Sep 29*	M6-10
To 1818 Oct 23	M222-20
To 1818 Oct 23	T494-1
To 1818 Oct 30	M271-2
To 1818 Oct 30*	6-1388
To 1818 Oct 30	M271-2
Fr 1818 Nov 13	DLC-26
Fr 1818 Nov 13*	M15-4
To 1818 Nov 25	M222-20
To 1818 Nov 25*	DLC-63
To 1818 Nov 28	M221-81
To 1818 Nov 28*	7-0001
To 1818 Nov 30	DLC-63
Fr 1818 Dec 15	M15-4
Fr 1818 Dec 15*	M271-2
Fr 1818 Dec 15*	7-0060
Fr 1818 Dec 28	DLC-26
Fr 1818 Dec 28*	M7-1
Fr 1818 Dec 28*	7-0074
Fr 1818 Dec 28	DLC-26
Fr 1818 Dec 28*	M7-1
Fr 1818 Dec 28*	7-0081
To 1818 Dec 30	M221-81
Fr 1819 Jan 05	7-0117
Fr 1819 Jan 05*	M7-1
Fr 1819 Jan 05*	DLC-26
To 1819 Feb 01	M221-81
Fr 1819 Feb 05	DLC-26
Fr 1819 Feb 05*	DLC-24
Fr 1819 Feb 05*	M6-10
Fr 1819 Feb 05*	7-0234
To 1819 Feb 05	7-0235
To 1819 Feb 05*	DLC-24
To 1819 Mar 12	M688-10
Fr 1819 Mar 06	DLC-26
Fr 1819 Mar 06*	7-0401
Fr 1819 Mar 06*	M6-10
To 1819 Mar 09	M22-12
To 1819 Mar 12	M688-10
Fr 1819 Mar 13	DLC-26
Fr 1819 Mar 29	DLC-26
Fr 1819 Mar 29*	M6-10
To 1819 Apr 14#	DLC-63
To 1819 Apr 14*	M221-80

To 1819 Apr 16#	DLC-63
To 1819 Apr 16*	M221-80
To 1819 May 10#	M221-81
To 1819 May 10*	DLC-63
To 1819 Jul 05	M221-87
To 1819 Jul 14#	M566-123
Fr 1819 Jul 19	DLC-27
Fr 1819 Jul 19*	M6-10
To 1819 Jul 24	M221-86
To 1819 Jul 24*	DLC-63
Fr 1819 Jul 31	DLC-27
Fr 1819 Jul 31*	M6-10
To 1819 Aug 02#	M221-86
To 1819 Aug 02*	DLC-63
Fr 1819 Aug 10	M7-1
To 1819 Aug 20	7-0622
To 1819 Aug 24	M271-2
Fr 1819 Aug 27	DLC-27
Fr 1819 Aug 27*	M6-10
To 1819 Sep 07	7-0639
To 1819 Sep 07*	DLC-63
To 1819 Sep 07	DLC-63
To 1819 Sep 30	DLC-27
To 1819 Oct 02	M22-13
To 1819 Oct 02#	M221-86
To 1819 Oct 04	M22-13
To 1819 Oct 08	DLC-63
To 1819 Oct 17#	DLC-28
To 1819 Nov 15	M221-86
To 1819 Nov 15*	DLC-63
To 1819 Nov 15*	7-0852
To 1819 Nov 15	7-0855
To 1819 Nov 22	M221-21
To 1819 Nov 22*	DLC-63
To 1819 Nov 30	M566-123
To 1819 Dec 05	M221-86
To 1819 Dec 05*	DLC-63
To 1819 Dec 11	DLC-63
Fr 1819 Dec 24	DLC-28
Fr 1819 Dec 24*	M7-1
Fr 1819 Dec 24*	7-0935
Fr 1819 Dec 24	DLC-28
Fr 1819 Dec 24*	M6-10
To 1819 Dec 27	DLC-63
To 1819 Dec 27*	M221-86
To 1819 Dec 28	DLC-63
To 1819 Dec 28*	7-0942
To 1819 Dec 30	7-0952
To 1819 Dec 31	M566-124
To 1819 Dec 31	DLC-63
To 1819 Dec 31*	M221-86
Fr 1819 Dec 31	M7-1
Fr 1819 Dec 31*	DLC-28
Fr 1819 Dec 31*	7-0958
To 1820 Jan 10	M221-86
To 1820 Jan 10*	DLC-63
To 1820 Jan 17	M221-86
To 1820 Jan 17*	DLC-63
To 1820 Jan 17	M271-3
To 1820 Jan 18	7-0997
To 1820 Jan 21	7-1003
To 1820 Jan 21*	DLC-63
Fr 1820 Jan 22	DLC-28
Fr 1820 Jan 22*	M6-10
Fr 1820 Jan 23	DLC-28
To 1820 Jan 27	7-1012
To 1820 Jan 29#	M221-86
Fr 1820 Feb 05	DLC-28
Fr 1820 Feb 05*	M6-10

To 1820 Feb 11	M221-15
Fr 1820 Feb 17	M6-10
To 1820 Feb 27	M221-86
To 1820 Feb 28	DLC-63
To 1820 Mar 02	M221-86
To 1820 Mar 02*	DLC-63
To 1820 Mar 02	M566-130
To 1820 Mar 09	M221-86
To 1820 Mar 09*	DLC-63
Fr 1820 Mar 15	DLC-28
Fr 1820 Mar 15*	M6-11
To 1820 Mar 25	M221-86
To 1820 Mar 25*	DLC-63
Fr 1820 Mar 27	7-1061
To 1820 Mar 31	M221-86
To 1820 Mar 31*	DLC-63
To 1820 Apr 07#	M221-86
To 1820 Apr 07*	DLC-28
Fr 1820 Apr 13	M6-11
Fr 1820 Apr 25	M6-11
To 1820 Apr 27	DLC-63
To 1820 Apr 30	M221-86
To 1820 May 12	M221-89
To 1820 May 15	7-1093
Fr 1820 May 16	DLC-29
Fr 1820 May 16*	M6-11
Fr 1820 May 16	DLC-29
Fr 1820 May 16*	M15-4
To 1820 May 17	M221-89
Fr 1820 May 24	DLC-29
Fr 1820 May 24*	DLC-39
Fr 1820 May 24*	M15-4
Fr 1820 Jun 01	DLC-29
To 1820 Jun 15	M221-89
To 1820 Jun 15*	DLC-63
To 1820 Jun 19	7-1115
To 1820 Jun 19*	DLC-63
Fr 1820 Jun 19	DLC-29
Fr 1820 Jun 19*	M6-11
To 1820 Jun 21#	M221-89
To 1820 Jun 26	DLC-63
To 1820 Jun 26*	7-1127
To 1820 Jul 08	M221-89
To 1820 Jul 08*	DLC-63
To 1820 Jul 08	DLC-63
To 1820 Jul 09	7-1141
Fr 1820 Jul 12	DLC-29
Fr 1820 Jul 12*	M15-4
Fr 1820 Jul 12*	7-1149
Fr 1820 Jul 12	DLC-29
Fr 1820 Jul 12*	M15-4
Fr 1820 Jul 12*	7-1150
To 1820 Jul 18	M688-15
Fr 1820 Jul 20	DLC-29
Fr 1820 Jul 20*	M6-11
Fr 1820 Jul 21	DLC-29
Fr 1820 Jul 21*	M6-11
To 1820 Jul 24	DLC-63
To 1820 Jul 26	DLC-63
Fr 1820 Jul 31	DLC-29
Fr 1820 Jul 31*	M6-11
To 1820 Aug 02	M221-89
To 1820 Aug 02*	DLC-63
To 1820 Aug 05	M221-89
To 1820 Aug 05*	DLC-63
To 1820 Aug 07	M221-89
To 1820 Aug 07*	DLC-29
To 1820 Aug 09	M221-89
To 1820 Aug 09*	DLC-63
To 1820 Aug 09*	7-1191
To 1820 Aug 10	M221-89
To 1820 Aug 10*	DLC-63
Fr 1820 Aug 10	DLC-29
Fr 1820 Aug 10*	7-1202
To 1820 Aug 19	DLC-63
To 1820 Aug 25	DLC-63
To 1820 Sep 02	M271-3
To 1820 Sep 02*	DLC-63
To 1820 Sep 14	7-1358
To 1820 Sep 14*	M221-90
To 1820 Sep 15	M221-89
To 1820 Sep 15*	DLC-63
To 1820 Sep 17#	M221-89
Fr 1820 Oct 04	DLC-29
Fr 1820 Oct 04*	M6-11
To 1820 Oct 11	M221-89
Fr 1820 Oct 14	DLC-29
Fr 1820 Oct 14*	M208-8
Fr 1820 Oct 14*	M15-5
To 1820 Oct 16	M221-89
To 1820 Oct 19	T494-1
Fr 1820 Oct 25	DLC-29
Fr 1820 Oct 25*	M15-5
Fr 1820 Nov 06	DLC-29
Fr 1820 Nov 06*	M6-11
To 1820 Nov 13	DLC-63
To 1820 Nov 13*	M221-89
Fr 1820 Nov 23	DLC-63
Fr 1820 Nov 25	DLC-29
Fr 1820 Nov 25*	M6-11
Fr 1820 Nov 25	DLC-29
Fr 1820 Nov 25*	M6-11
To 1820 Nov 30	8-0003
To 1820 Nov 30*	DLC-63
Fr 1820 Nov 30	DLC-29
Fr 1820 Nov 30*	M6-11
To 1820 Dec 08	M221-89
To 1820 Dec 08*	DLC-63
Fr 1820 Dec 14	DLC-29
Fr 1820 Dec 14*	M6-11
To 1820 Dec 15	DLC-63
Fr 1820 Dec 16	DLC-29
To 1820 Dec 21	M221-89
To 1820 Dec 28	M221-89
To 1821 Jan 01	M22-14
To 1821 Jan 04	DLC-63
Fr 1821 Jan 05	M6-11
Fr 1821 Jan 11	M6-11
To 1821 Jan 13	DLC-29
Fr 1821 Jan 13*	M6-11
Fr 1821 Jan 16	DLC-29
Fr 1821 Jan 16*	M6-11
To 1821 Jan 18	M221-89
To 1821 Jan 18*	DLC-63
To 1821 Jan 18*	8-0081
To 1821 Jan 21	M221-89
To 1821 Jan 21	M221-89
To 1821 Jan 21*	DLC-63
Fr 1821 Jan 21	DLC-29
Fr 1821 Jan 22	DLC-29
Fr 1821 Jan 22*	M6-11
Fr 1821 Jan 25	DLC-29
To 1821 Feb 08	M221-89
To 1821 Feb 08*	DLC-63
To 1821 Feb 18	8-0140
To 1821 Mar 01	M221-89
Fr 1821 Mar 03	8-0153
Fr 1821 Mar 03*	M6-11

Calhoun John Caldwell (cont)

Fr	1821 Mar 07	DLC-29
To	1821 Mar 17	8-0231
Fr	1821 Mar 19	DLC-30
Fr	1821 Mar 19*	M6-11
Fr	1821 Mar 22	DLC-30
Fr	1821 Mar 22*	DLC-63
Fr	1821 Mar 22*	M6-11
Fr	1821 Mar 22*	M116-5
Fr	1821 Mar 24	M6-11
To	1821 Mar 26	8-0266
To	1821 Mar 27	M221-89
To	1821 Mar 27*	DLC-63
Fr	1821 Mar 31	DLC-30
Fr	1821 Mar 31*	M15-5
Fr	1821 Mar 31*	M116-5
Fr	1821 Apr 08	DLC-30
To	1821 Apr 10	M221-89
To	1821 Apr 10*	DLC-63
To	1821 Apr 10	8-0292
To	1821 Apr 10*	DLC-63
Fr	1821 Apr 13	DLC-30
Fr	1821 Apr 13*	M6-11
To	1821 Apr 14	M221-89
To	1821 Apr 14*	M222-22
To	1821 Apr 14*	DLC-63
Fr	1821 May 01	M116-5
Fr	1821 May 01*	M6-11
Fr	1821 May 14	DLC-30
Fr	1821 May 14*	M6-11
Fr	1821 May 14*	M116-5
To	1821 May 19	DLC-63
Fr	1821 May 19	DLC-29
To	1821 May 22	DLC-30
Fr	1821 May 24	8-0517
Fr	1821 May 24*	DLC-29
Fr	1821 May 24*	M15-4
To	1821 May 26	M221-89
Fr	1821 Jun 19	DLC-30
Fr	1821 Jun 19*	M6-11
Fr	1821 Jul 04	DLC-30
To	1821 Jul 17	M221-93
To	1821 Jul 29	DLC-63
To	1821 Jul 29	DLC-63
To	1821 Aug 28	M22-15
To	1821 Sep 02	M221-93
To	1821 Sep 02*	DLC-63
To	1821 Sep 02*	8-1141
To	1821 Sep 17	M221-93
To	1821 Sep 17*	DLC-63
To	1821 Sep 17*	8-1164
To	1821 Sep 20	M221-93
To	1821 Sep 20*	DLC-63
To	1821 Sep 20*	8-1185
To	1821 Oct 02	M221-93
Fr	1821 Oct 19	DLC-31
Fr	1821 Oct 19*	M6-11
Fr	1821 Oct 28	DLC-31
To	1821 Nov 02	M221-93
Fr	1821 Nov 16	DLC-31
Fr	1821 Nov 16*	M15-5
Fr	1821 Nov 16	DLC-31
To	1821 Nov 22	8-1357
To	1821 Nov 22*	DLC-63
To	1821 Dec 06	DLC-63
To	1821 Dec 12	M221-93
To	1821 Dec 12*	DLC-63
To	1822 Jan 05	DLC-63
To	1822 Jan 05	M221-93
To	1822 Jan 05*	DLC-63
To	1822 Jan 12	DLC-72
To	1822 Jan 12*	M221-96
To	1822 Jan 26	9-0007
To	1822 Feb 28	9-0039
Fr	1822 Apr 06	M6-11
To	1822 May 02	M221-93
To	1822 Jun 28	DLC-31
To	1822 Jul 25	9-0222
Fr	1822 Oct 31	DLC-31
Fr	1822 Oct 31*	M91-1
To	1823 Feb 08	M688-22
To	1823 Mar 23	DLC-32
Fr	1823 Mar 30	DLC-32
Fr	1823 Jun 19	M91-1
Fr	1823 Jun 27	M91-1
To	1823 Jul 14	M221-97
Fr	1823 Jul 31	DLC-32
To	1823 cAug 10	9-0625
To	1823 Aug 31	9-0645
To	1823 Aug 31*	M221-97
To	1823 Aug 31*	DLC-32
Fr	1823 Sep 25	M6-11
To	1823 Oct 14	M688-28
To	1823 Dec 14	M22-17
To	1824 Jan 15	M221-97
Fr	1824 Jan 16	9-0935
Fr	1824 Jan 16*	M220-1
To	1824 Jan 18	9-0942
To	1824 Jan 19	9-0944
To	1824 Jan 25	M221-97
To	1824 Feb	10-0425
To	1824 Feb 01	M222-23
To	1824 Feb 06	M22-17
Fr	1824 Feb 06	M220-1
To	1824 Feb 09	M22-17
To	1824 Feb 10	M22-17
Fr	1824 Feb 10	M15-6
To	1824 Feb 11	M22-17
To	1824 Feb 11	M22-17
To	1824 Feb 11	M22-17
To	1824 Feb 12	M22-17
To	1824 Feb 14	M22-17
To	1824 Feb 16	M22-17
Fr	1824 Feb 16	M220-1
To	1824 Feb 22	M22-17
To	1824 Feb 22	M22-17
To	1824 Feb 24	M22-17
To	1824 Feb 26	M221-97
Fr	1824 Feb 27	M220-1
Fr	1824 Mar 04	M220-1
To	1824 Mar 06	10-0521
To	1824 Mar 06*	M221-97
Fr	1824 Mar 08	10-0536
To	1824 Mar 10	M221-97
Fr	1824 Mar 13	10-0549
Fr	1824 Mar 13*	M220-1
To	1824 Mar 14	10-0553
To	1824 Mar 15	M688-29
To	1824 Mar 22	M688-35
To	1824 Mar 26	10-0595
To	1824 Apr 12	M688-32
Fr	1824 Apr 23	M6-12
To	1824 May 10	10-0717
To	1824 Jun 08	M221-107
Fr	1824 Jun 10	DLC-32
Fr	1824 Jun 10*	10-0773
Fr	1824 Jun 25	10-0814
Fr	1824 Jun 25*	M6-12
Fr	1824 Dec 30	DLC-33

Fr 1824 Dec 30*	10-1016
To 1825 Jan 04	M688-38
To 1825 Jan 05	M221-99
Fr 1825 Jan 10	M220-1
Fr 1825 Jan 10*	10-1055
Fr 1825 Jan 10	10-1061
Fr 1825 Jan 10*	M220-1
To 1825 Feb 15	M688-34
Fr 1825 Feb 25	M21-1
Fr 1826 Jun 04	DLC-34
To 1826 Jul 26	DLC-34
Fr 1827 Jan 24	DLC-34
Fr 1827 Feb 25	DLC-34
Fr 1828 Apr 30	DLC-35
To 1828 May 25	DLC-35
Fr 1828 Jul 10	DLC-35
To 1829 Mar 02	12-0817
To 1829 Mar 02*	DLC-60
Fr 1829 Mar 18	M639-6
Re c1830 mem	14-1229
To 1830 May 13	DLC-72
Fr 1830 May 13	DLC-38
Fr 1830 May 29	DLC-38
To 1830 May 30	DLC-73
Fr 1830 Jun 01	DLC-38
To 1830 Jun 07	DLC-38
Fr 1830 Jun 22	DLC-38
To 1830 Jul 19	DLC-73
Fr 1830 Aug 25	DLC-38
To 1830 Oct 02#	DLC-38
To 1832 May 28	DLC-40
To 1832 May 28*	20-0610
Fr 1832 May 31	20-0683
To 1837 Feb 07	33-0465
Call G W	
Fr 1826 Jul 06	DLC-34
Fr 1827 Jul 11	DLC-34
To 1827 Jul 20	DLC-34
Call Jacob	
To 1824 Oct 09	10-0912
Call Mary Letitia (Kirkman)	
Fr 1826 Mar 24#	DLC-33
To 1830 Feb 04	15-0101
Call Richard Keith	
To 1814 Jan 30	3-0827
To 1818 Aug 05	6-1181
To 1818 Aug 17	6-1233
To 1819	7-0108
To 1819*	DLC-75
Fr 1819 Apr 14#	DLC-63
Fr 1819 Apr 14*	M221-80
Fr 1819 Apr 16#	DLC-63
Fr 1819 Apr 16*	M221-80
Fr 1819 May 10#	M221-81
Fr 1819 May 10*	DLC-63
Fr 1819 Jul 30	DLC-27
Fr 1819 Aug 02#	M221-86
Fr 1819 Aug 02*	DLC-63
Fr 1819 Aug 17#	DLC-63
Fr 1819 Aug 17	DLC-63
Fr 1819 Aug 17#	DLC-63
Fr 1819 Aug 19#	DLC-63
Fr 1819 Aug 27	DLC-27
Fr 1819 Aug 27*	DLC-28
To 1819 Sep 09	7-0648
Fr 1819 Oct 02#	M221-86
Fr 1819 Nov 15	M221-86
Fr 1819 Dec 11#	DLC-63
Fr 1819 Dec 12#	M221-86
Fr 1819 Dec 12*	DLC-63
Fr 1819 Dec 13#	DLC-63
To 1820	7-0966
Fr 1820 Jan 29#	M221-86
Fr 1820 Jan 30#	DLC-63
Fr 1820 Feb 04#	DLC-63
Fr 1820 Apr 07#	M221-86
Fr 1820 Apr 07*	DLC-28
Fr 1820 Apr 12#	DLC-63
To 1820 May 03#	DLC-29
To 1820 May 03*	M565-6
To 1820 May 08#	DLC-29
To 1820 May 08*	M565-6
Fr 1820 May 20#	DLC-63
Fr 1820 May 20#	DLC-63
Fr 1820 May 22#	DLC-63
Fr 1820 Jun 14#	DLC-63
Fr 1820 Jun 21#	DLC-63
Fr 1820 Jun 21#	M221-89
Fr 1820 Jun 23#	DLC-63
Fr 1820 Jun 27#	DLC-29
Fr 1820 Jun 27*	DLC-29
Fr 1820 Jun 28#	M208-8
Fr 1820 Jun 28*	DLC-63
Fr 1820 Jun 29#	DLC-63
Fr 1820 Jun 30#	DLC-63
To 1820 Jul 01	7-1131
Fr 1820 Jul 08	DLC-29
Fr 1820 Jul 12	DLC-29
Fr 1820 Jul 16	DLC-29
Fr 1820 Jul 23	DLC-29
To 1820 Jul 31	7-1180
To 1820 Aug 06	7-1185
Fr 1820 Aug 17	DLC-29
Fr 1820 Aug 19#	DLC-63
Fr 1820 Aug 29	DLC-29
Fr 1820 Sep 17#	M221-89
Fr 1820 Sep 17	M221-89
To 1820 cOct	7-1371
To 1820 Oct 03#	7-1379
Fr 1820 Oct 20#	DLC-63
Fr 1820 Nov 11#	DLC-63
To 1821 Feb 13	8-0110
Fr 1821 Feb 26#	M208-9
Fr 1821 Mar 10#	DLC-63
To 1821 Apr 12	DLC-63
To 1821 May 11	8-0466
Fr 1821 May 21	M116-5
Fr 1821 May 21*	M116-6
Fr 1821 May 21*	8-0499
Fr 1821 May 21*	DLC-63
To 1821 Jun 11	8-0577
To 1821 Jun 12	M116-5
To 1821 Jun 12*	M116-6
To 1821 Jun 12*	DLC-63
To 1821 Jun 12*	8-0588
To 1821 Jun 20	8-0626
Fr 1821 Jun 23	M116-6
Fr 1821 Jun 23*	8-0658
To 1821 Jun 24	8-0671
Fr 1821 Sep 30	M221-93
To 1821 Oct 10	8-1297
Fr 1821 Oct 14	DLC-30
Fr 1821 Oct 14	DLC-30
Fr 1821 Oct 30	DLC-31
To 1821 Nov 04	8-1328
To 1821 Nov 15	DLC-31
Fr 1821 Nov 19	DLC-31
Fr 1821 Nov 26	DLC-31

Call Richard Keith (cont)
To 1821 Dec 15# 8-1367
To 1822 Jan 05 8-1383
Fr 1822 Feb 02# DLC-31
To 1822 Mar 25 9-0074
To 1822 May 20 DLC-31
To 1822 Jun 29 9-0195
To 1822 cSep 29 9-0276
To 1822 Oct 15 9-0289
To 1822 Nov 27 9-0322
To 1822 Dec 9-0333
To 1823 Feb 03 9-0442
Fr 1823 Oct 02 DLC-32
To 1825 May 07 10-1260
To 1825 May 26 10-1279
To 1825 Jun 24 10-1315
To 1825 Jul 24 10-1365
Fr 1825 Sep 23 DLC-33
To 1825 cDec 11-0063
To 1826 Mar 09 DLC-33
To 1826 Apr 09 11-0189
To 1826 Jul 26 11-0325
To 1826 Sep 05 11-0365
Fr 1826 Nov 08 DLC-34
To 1826 Nov 21 11-0393
To 1827 Jan 18 11-0471
To 1827 May 03 11-0571
To 1827 Jul 01 11-0721
To 1827 Oct 02 11-0886
Fr 1827 Dec 24 DLC-35
To 1828 Feb 05 11-1094
Fr 1828 Mar 11 DLC-72
To 1828 Mar 20 11-1177
To 1828 May 12 12-0001
To 1828 May 18 12-0011
To 1828 Aug 14 12-0135
Fr 1828 Aug 25 DLC-72
To 1828 Oct 18 DLC-35
To 1828 Dec 12-0293
To 1828 Dec 22 12-0330
To 1829 Mar 05 chk DLC-36
To 1829 Apr 03 12-1263
Fr 1829 Apr 03 M639-3
Fr 1829 Apr 28 DLC-37
Fr 1829 Apr 28 M639-6
Fr 1829 May 05 M639-4
To 1829 May 18 DLC-37
Fr 1829 Jun 02 M639-21
Fr 1829 Jun 02 M639-7
Fr 1829 Jun 12 13-0633
To 1829 Jun 13 DLC-37
Fr 1829 Jun 29 M639-1
To 1829 Jul 05 DLC-37
Fr 1829 Jul 18 13-0883
Fr 1829 Jul 23 DLC-72
To 1829 Jul 31 13-1019
Fr 1830 Mar 09 DLC-72
Fr 1830 Oct 26 16-0540
Fr 1831 Mar 24 M567-64
Fr 1831 Sep 24 M639-7
To 1832 Mar 20 chk DLC-40
Fr 1832 Mar 28 M639-27
Fr 1832 Mar 28 19-1568
Fr 1833 Feb 21 M688-90
Fr 1833 cMar 22-0567
Fr 1833 May 23 22-1429
To 1833 Jul 14 23-0129
Fr 1833 Aug 28 M639-25
Fr 1834 Mar 07 24-1581
Fr 1834 Aug 25 26-0359
To 1834 Oct 16 26-0651
Fr 1835 Mar 19 M688-101
Fr 1835 Mar 22 27-1305
Fr 1835 Mar 22* M234-800
Fr 1835 Dec 22 M567-106
Fr 1835 Dec 22* 29-1284
Fr 1836 Jan 09 M567-119
Fr 1836 Jan 09* 29-1523
To 1836 Mar 17 30-0803
Fr 1836 May 12 M567-119
Fr 1836 May 12* 30-1605
To 1836 May 16# 31-0027
To 1836 May 25 31-0094
Fr 1836 May 26# 31-0131
Fr 1836 May 30 M567-120
Fr 1836 May 30* 31-0198
Fr 1836 Jun DLC-75
Fr 1836 Jun 01 31-0254
Fr 1836 Jul 09 DLC-48
Fr 1836 Sep 22 M567-120
Fr 1836 Sep 22* 31-1484
Fr 1836 Oct 22 DLC-49
Fr 1836 Oct 29 M567-121
Fr 1836 Oct 29* 32-0359
Re 1836 Nov mem DLC-49
To 1836 Nov 01 32-0377
Fr c1837 32-1449
Fr 1837 Feb 28 M687-27
Fr 1837 Mar 27 DLC-50
To 1842 Aug 20 35-0891
Fr 1842 Sep 05 DLC-54
Fr 1842 Sep 08 35-0925
To 1842 Oct 03 35-0965
Fr 1842 Oct 03 DLC-54
Fr 1842 Oct 18 35-0972
Call Richard Keith et al
Fr 1830 Nov 16 M639-1
Fr 1837 Feb 13 M687-9
Callaghan Charles
Fr 1830 Mar 03 M639-12
Fr 1836 Jan 11 29-1538
Callaghan Charles et al
Fr 1832 Jun 13 M84-2
Callahan Dennis
Re 1835 Jan 13 par 27-0208
Callahan John
Re 1836 Jul 09 par 31-1000
Callan Nicholas
Fr 1834 Nov 06 26-0841
Callan Nicholas et al
Fr 1833 Jan M639-4
Callava Jose
To 1821 Apr 30 M116-6
To 1821 Apr 30* DLC-63
To 1821 Apr 30* 8-0379
To 1821 Apr 30 M116-6
To 1821 Apr 30* DLC-63
To 1821 Apr 30* 8-0387
Fr 1821 May 04 M116-5
Fr 1821 May 04* DLC-63
Fr 1821 May 04* 8-0416
To 1821 May 11 DLC-63
To 1821 May 11* M116-6
To 1821 May 11* 8-0468
To 1821 May 11 M116-5
To 1821 May 11* M116-6
To 1821 May 11* DLC-63
To 1821 May 11* 8-0469
Fr 1821 May 16 DLC-63

Fr 1821 May 16*		M116-6
Fr 1821 May 16*		8-0479
Fr 1821 Jun 10		M116-5
Fr 1821 Jun 10*		M116-6
Fr 1821 Jun 10*		DLC-63
Fr 1821 Jun 10*		8-0563
To 1821 Jun 12		M116-10
To 1821 Jun 12*		DLC-63
To 1821 Jun 12*		8-0592
To 1821 Jun 16		DLC-63
To 1821 Jun 16*		M116-6
To 1821 Jun 16*		8-0605
Fr 1821 Jun 16		M116-6
Fr 1821 Jun 16*		DLC-63
Fr 1821 Jun 16*		8-0607
To 1821 Jun 17		M116-6
To 1821 Jun 17*		DLC-63
To 1821 Jun 17*		8-0615
Re 1821 Jun 17	mem	DLC-30
To 1821 Jun 19		M116-6
To 1821 Jun 19*		DLC-63
To 1821 Jun 19*		8-0619
Fr 1821 Jun 19		M116-6
Fr 1821 Jun 19*		DLC-63
Fr 1821 Jun 19*		8-0620
Fr 1821 Jun 19		DLC-63
Fr 1821 Jun 19*		M116-6
Fr 1821 Jun 19*		8-0624
To 1821 Jun 20		M116-6
To 1821 Jun 20*		DLC-63
To 1821 Jun 20*		8-0627
Fr 1821 Jun 20		M116-6
Fr 1821 Jun 20*		DLC-63
Fr 1821 Jun 20*		8-0635
Fr 1821 Jun 22		M116-6
Fr 1821 Jun 22*		DLC-63
Fr 1821 Jun 22*		8-0647
Fr 1821 Jun 22		M116-6
Fr 1821 Jun 22*		DLC-63
Fr 1821 Jun 22*		8-0652
To 1821 Jun 23		M116-6
To 1821 Jun 23*		DLC-63
To 1821 Jun 23*		8-0661
To 1821 Jun 25		M116-6
To 1821 Jun 25*		DLC-63
To 1821 Jun 25*		8-0675
Fr 1821 Jun 25		M116-6
Fr 1821 Jun 25*		DLC-63
Fr 1821 Jun 25*		8-0680
To 1821 Jun 26		M116-6
To 1821 Jun 26*		DLC-63
To 1821 Jun 26*		8-0691
Fr 1821 Jun 26		M116-6
Fr 1821 Jun 26*		DLC-63
Fr 1821 Jun 26*		8-0694
Fr 1821 Jun 28		M116-6
Fr 1821 Jun 28*		DLC-63
Fr 1821 Jun 28*		8-0707
Fr 1821 Jun 28		M116-6
Fr 1821 Jun 28*		DLC-63
Fr 1821 Jun 28*		8-0709
Fr 1821 Jun 28		M116-6
Fr 1821 Jun 28*		DLC-63
Fr 1821 Jun 28*		8-0711
Fr 1821 Jun 28		M116-6
Fr 1821 Jun 28*		DLC-63
Fr 1821 Jun 28*		8-0715
Fr 1821 Jun 28		M116-6
Fr 1821 Jun 28*		8-0723

To 1821 Jun 28#	8-0725
Fr 1821 Jun 28	M116-6
Fr 1821 Jun 28*	DLC-63
To 1821 Jun 29	M116-6
To 1821 Jun 29*	DLC-63
To 1821 Jun 29*	8-0738
To 1821 Jun 29	M116-6
To 1821 Jun 29*	DLC-63
To 1821 Jun 29*	8-0739
Fr 1821 Jun 30	M116-6
Fr 1821 Jun 30*	DLC-63
Fr 1821 Jun 30*	8-0743
Fr 1821 Jun 30	M116-6
Fr 1821 Jun 30*	DLC-63
To 1821 cJul	DLC-59
To 1821 Jul 01	M116-6
To 1821 Jul 01*	DLC-63
To 1821 Jul 01*	8-0748
To 1821 Jul 01	M116-6
To 1821 Jul 01*	DLC-63
To 1821 Jul 01*	8-0750
To 1821 Jul 03	M116-6
To 1821 Jul 03*	DLC-63
To 1821 Jul 03*	8-0753
Fr 1821 Jul 03	M116-6
Fr 1821 Jul 03*	DLC-63
Fr 1821 Jul 03*	8-0755
Fr 1821 Jul 03	M116-6
Fr 1821 Jul 03*	DLC-63
Fr 1821 Jul 03*	8-0756
Fr 1821 Jul 04	M116-6
Fr 1821 Jul 04*	DLC-63
Fr 1821 Jul 04*	8-0765
To 1821 Jul 04	M116-6
To 1821 Jul 05	M116-6
To 1821 Jul 05*	DLC-63
To 1821 Jul 05*	8-0771
To 1821 Jul 09	M116-6
To 1821 Jul 09*	DLC-63
To 1821 Jul 09*	8-0780
Fr 1821 Jul 10	M116-6
Fr 1821 Jul 10*	DLC-63
Fr 1821 Jul 10*	8-0789
Fr 1821 Jul 11	M116-6
Fr 1821 Jul 11*	DLC-63
Fr 1821 Jul 11*	8-0791
To 1821 Jul 12	M116-6
To 1821 Jul 12*	DLC-63
To 1821 Jul 12*	8-0793
To 1821 Jul 13	M116-6
To 1821 Jul 13*	DLC-63
To 1821 Jul 13*	8-0799
To 1821 Jul 13	M116-6
To 1821 Jul 13*	DLC-63
To 1821 Jul 13*	8-0802
Fr 1821 Jul 13	M116-6
Fr 1821 Jul 13*	DLC-63
Fr 1821 Jul 13*	8-0805
Fr 1821 Jul 13	M116-6
Fr 1821 Jul 13*	DLC-63
Fr 1821 Jul 13*	8-0808
Fr 1821 Jul 14	M116-6
Fr 1821 Jul 14*	DLC-63
Fr 1821 Jul 14*	8-0817
Fr 1821 Jul 14	M116-6
Fr 1821 Jul 14*	DLC-63
Fr 1821 Jul 14*	8-0818
To 1821 Jul 15	M116-6
To 1821 Jul 15*	DLC-63

Callava Jose (cont)
To 1821 Jul 15* 8-0821
To 1821 Jul 15 M116-6
To 1821 Jul 15* 8-0823
To 1821 Jul 15* DLC-63
To 1821 Jul 15 M116-6
To 1821 Jul 15* DLC-63
To 1821 Jul 15* 8-0825
Fr 1821 Jul 15 M116-6
Fr 1821 Jul 15* DLC-63
Fr 1821 Jul 15* 8-0829
To 1821 Jul 16 M116-6
To 1821 Jul 16* 8-0836
Fr 1821 Jul 16 M116-6
Fr 1821 Jul 16* DLC-63
Fr 1821 Jul 16* 8-0839
Fr 1821 Jul 16 DLC-63
To 1821 Jul 16 DLC-63
Fr 1821 Jul 17 DLC-70
Fr 1821 Jul 17* M116-6
To 1821 Aug 03 DLC-30
To 1821 Aug 03* M116-6
To 1821 Aug 03* DLC-63
To 1821 Aug 03* 8-1006
Re 1821 Aug 22 mem DLC-63
Re 1821 Aug 22 M116-7
Re 1821 Aug 22* DLC-63
Re 1821 Aug 22 M116-7
Re 1821 Aug 22* DLC-63
Re 1821 Aug 23 M116-7
Re 1821 Aug 23* DLC-63
Re 1821 Aug 23 leg M116-7
Re 1821 Aug 23* leg DLC-63
Re 1821 Oct mem DLC-31
Fr 1821 Oct 03 DLC-30
Fr 1821 Oct 03* 8-1249
Callender James T
Re 1797 1-0467
Callender William
Fr 1835 May 12 DLC-46
Callicot Theodore C
Fr 1844 Sep 06 DLC-57
Callis Otho W
Fr 1829 Aug 03 M222-29
Cally J M
Fr 1829 Jul 21 M639-2
Calvert Caroline
Re 1833 May 30 par 22-1519
Calvert Catherine
Fr 1836 Mar 29 M567-119
Camble Alex
Re 1813 Mar 11 DLC-61
Cambreleng Churchill Caldom
Fr 1829 Apr 14 M639-22
Fr 1829 Apr 14* 12-1338
Fr 1829 Apr 15 12-1354
Fr 1831 Feb 14 M639-10
Fr 1831 Dec 23 M22-28
Fr 1832 Feb 25# M179-72
Fr 1833 Jan 18 M639-22
Fr 1833 May 11 22-1339
Fr 1833 Sep 19 M639-2
Fr 1834 Mar 07 M639-18
Fr 1834 May 09 25-1000
Fr 1834 Dec 11 M639-10
Fr 1834 Dec 25 M639-2
Fr 1836 May 05 DLC-48
Fr 1836 Sep 16 M567-120
To 1837 Feb 11 33-0610
Fr 1843 Aug 24 DLC-55
Cambreleng Churchill Caldom et al
Fr 1832 Feb 25 19-1245
Fr 1832 Jun 11 20-0734
Fr 1836 Feb 27 30-0592
Fr 1836 Apr 25 M687-18
Cameron John A
Re 1831 Mar 02 17-0716
Fr 1832 Jan 25 M183-2
Fr 1832 Feb 02 M183-2
Fr 1832 Feb 06 M183-2
Fr 1832 Feb 25 M183-2
Fr 1834 Nov 05 M124-145
Fr 1835 Jul 03 DLC-46
Fr 1837 Jan 23 M687-9
Fr 1837 Feb M687-9
Cameron Simon
Fr 1830 Feb 24 M639-23
Cameron Simon et al
Fr 1829 Oct 10 add 14-0139
Cameron Thomas N
Fr 1820 Oct 05# fin DLC-29
Cammack Chris
Fr 1835 Apr 01 fin DLC-46
Camp James
Fr 1814 Oct 08 DLC-13
Fr 1814 Oct 12 DLC-13
To 1814 Oct 27 DLC-62
To 1814 Oct 27* M222-10
To 1816 Oct 23 chk DLC-21
Camp James W
Fr 1809 Nov 18# 2-0861
Fr 1829 Jul 07 M639-4
Camp John H
To 1808 Jul 12 lnd 2-0686
Fr 1820 Apr 14 7-1068
Fr 1820 May 16 DLC-29
Camp John H et al
Fr 1826 May 10 11-0211
To 1826 May 14 DLC-33
Camp Thomas
Fr 1814 Aug 30 DLC-11
Fr 1814 Oct 22 DLC-13
Fr 1814 Nov 19 DLC-14
Campau Francois
Fr 1829 May 06 13-0262
Campbell Alexander
Fr 1829 Aug 13 M639-6
Campbell Allan
Fr 1827 Feb 04 DLC-34
To 1827 Mar 31 11-0548
Campbell Allan D
Fr 1824 Apr DLC-32
Fr 1827 Jun 14 DLC-34
Fr 1829 Feb 25 DLC-36
Re 1829 Apr 13 12-1330
To 1833 Apr 08 chk DLC-42
Fr 1835 Oct 01 DLC-47
Fr 1836 Apr 23 DLC-48
Fr 1837 Mar 14 DLC-50
Fr 1837 Mar 15 DLC-50
Campbell Anthony
Fr 1814 Jul 21 DLC-11
Fr 1814 Jul 21 DLC-11
Fr 1835 Jul 08 28-0990
To 1835 Jul 29 28-1194
Campbell Argyle
Fr 1832 Nov 05 DLC-41
Campbell Arthur Lee
To 1826 Apr 10 11-0191
To 1826 Jun 12 11-0248

Fr 1829 Mar 09		M639-4
Fr 1837 Mar 20		DLC-50
Campbell Charles et al		
Fr 1835 cJan		DLC-59
Campbell David		
To 1802 Apr 07	lnd	1-0969
To 1804 Jan 20		DLC-71
Fr 1808 Oct 15		2-0734
Fr 1818 Jun 13	fin	DLC-69
Fr 1818 Jun 13*	fin	6-1048
Fr 1823 Oct 25		DLC-32
Fr 1837 Jan 28		DLC-49
Campbell David (1750-1812)		
To 1797 Dec 29		1-0560
To 1798 Jan 11		1-0577
Campbell David (1753-1832)		
Fr 1801 Dec 19		DLC-2
Fr 1802 Jan 25		DLC-2
To 1803 Oct 12		1-1234
Fr 1811 Oct 19		DLC-5
Fr 1814 Jan 19		DLC-8
To 1818 Dec 11		7-0046
Re 1823 May 19		9-0565
Fr 1829 May 29		13-0492
Campbell David (1779-1859)		
Fr 1817 Apr 16		DLC-22
To 1823 Dec 06		9-0786
Fr 1826 Sep 18		DLC-34
Fr 1828 Dec 01		DLC-35
To 1828 Dec 12		12-0317
To 1829 Feb 14		12-0511
To 1830 Jun 14		15-1383
To 1835 Sep 07		28-1579
To 1836 Jul 07		31-0922
Fr 1843 Jun 29		35-1394
To 1843 Jul 13		35-1413
Campbell George Washington		
Fr 1803 Oct 29		DLC-3
To 1804 Apr 13		1-1310
To 1804 Apr 28		1-1322
Fr 1804 Dec 06		DLC-71
Fr 1805 Jan 17		DLC-3
Fr 1805 Jul 18		DLC-3
To 1805 Aug 05		2-0073
To 1807 Jan 15		2-0454
Fr 1807 Feb 06		DLC-4
To 1809 Nov 30		2-0866
To 1811 Aug 05		2-1006
Fr 1811 Dec 24		DLC-5
Fr 1812 Apr 10		DLC-5
Fr 1812 Jul 17		2-1131
To 1812 Oct 15		2-1256
To 1812 Oct 15*		DLC-5
To 1812 Nov 29		M222-5
Fr 1813 Jun 25		DLC-71
Fr 1813 Jul 19		3-0416
Fr 1814 Jan 28		3-0819
Fr 1814 May 15		DLC-10
Fr 1814 May 29		DLC-10
To 1814 Jul 22		DLC-62
Fr 1815 Dec		4-1268
Fr 1816 Feb 18		DLC-20
To 1816 Dec 22		M221-73
Fr 1816 Dec 27		5-0639
Fr c1817		5-0651
Fr 1817 Feb 18		5-0734
To 1818 Oct 05		6-1343
Fr 1819 Sep 08		DLC-75
Fr 1828 Feb 12		DLC-35
To 1828 Feb 14		11-1115
Fr 1828 Apr 03		11-1202
Fr 1831 Jan 14		DLC-38
Fr 1835 Jun 25		M22-36
Fr 1836 Feb 21		30-0450
Fr 1836 May 28		DLC-48
Fr 1836 Aug 04	add	31-1225
Campbell George Washington et al		
To 1836 Aug 04	add	31-1226
Campbell Harriet (Stoddert)		
Fr 1829 Oct 12		M688-65
Campbell Hugh		
Fr 1798 Sep 17		DLC-2
Campbell J Mason		
Fr 1838 Aug 13		DLC-51
Campbell James et al		
Fr 1829 May 18		13-0343
Fr 1831 Oct 17		M639-8
Campbell James H		
Fr 1814 Dec 09		DLC-14
Campbell James M		
Fr 1831 Jul 11		M22-28
Campbell James W		
Fr 1813 Oct 06		DLC-6
Fr 1813 Oct 06*		DLC-61
Campbell John		
Fr 1805 Jun 02		2-0060
Re 1813 May	leg	3-0382
To 1814 Jan 31		DLC-62
Fr 1815 Oct 25		4-1220
To 1815 Oct 25		4-1221
Campbell John (TN)		
Fr 1829 May 10		M639-4
Fr 1831 Mar 02		M234-236
Fr 1831 Jul 02		M22-28
Campbell John (VA)		
Re 1829 May 26		13-0435
To 1829 Jun 04#	fin	13-0570
To 1829 Jul 06#	fin	13-0820
Fr 1830 May 21		15-1063
Fr 1831 Mar 03		17-0799
To 1831 Mar 12#		DLC-39
To 1831 Jun 22		18-0075
To 1831 Jun 22*		DLC-39
Fr 1831 Jun 22		18-0077
To 1831 Sep 08#	fin	18-0702
Fr 1831 Dec 12		19-0288
To 1832 Feb 09		19-1025
Fr 1832 Dec 05		21-0868
Fr 1833 Jan 16		21-1445
To 1833 Mar 25#	fin	22-0893
To 1833 Apr 06#	fin	22-0959
Fr 1833 Dec 04		24-0331
To 1834 Jul 08#	fin	26-0202
Fr 1834 Dec 03		26-1361
Fr 1835 Jul 03		28-0887
Fr 1835 Dec 09		29-1043
Fr 1836 Mar		M639-6
Fr 1836 Oct 03		32-0042
Campbell John Archibald		
Fr 1835 Sep 22		M639-4
Campbell John K		
Re 1831 Nov 17		18-1321
Campbell John N		
Re 1829 Sep 03	mem	13-1235
Re 1829 Sep 03*	mem	DLC-75
Fr 1829 Sep 05		DLC-75
To 1829 Sep 05		13-1257
To 1829 Sep 05*		DLC-75

Campbell John N (cont)
Fr 1829 Sep 05 DLC-75
To 1829 Sep 10 13-1291
To 1829 Sep 10* DLC-75
Re 1829 Sep 10 mem DLC-75
To 1829 Sep 12# DLC-75
Fr 1829 Sep 12# DLC-75
To 1829 Sep 16# DLC-75
Fr 1829 Oct 19 14-0198
Fr 1829 Oct 19# DLC-75
To 1829 Oct 19# DLC-75
To 1829 Oct 23# 14-0238
Campbell John Wilson
Fr 1831 Sep 05# DLC-40
To 1831 Nov 01 37-0510
To 1831 Nov 01* DLC-40
Campbell Joshua
Re 1790 May leg 1-0075k
Campbell Maria Hamilton (Campbell)
Fr 1837 Jun 09 33-1289
To 1837 Jun 29 33-1348
Campbell Mary
Fr 1821 Jan 10 DLC-29
Campbell Patrick
To 1800 Mar 27# leg 1-0760
To 1801 Jul 21 lnd 1-0901
To 1801 Oct 05 lnd 1-0924
To 1801 Oct 05 lnd 37-0403
Campbell Patrick et al
Fr 1803 Oct 07 DLC-3
Campbell Robert & Co
Fr 1797 Jan 07 fin DLC-1
Campbell S et al
Fr 1835 Dec 25 M234-883
Campbell Thomas J
Re 1816 Jun 21 leg 5-0187
Campbell William
To 1803 Oct 17 fin DLC-3
Fr 1829 Mar 11 12-0939
Fr 1831 Mar 03 M234-749
Fr 1831 Mar 24 M22-27
Fr 1832 Jun 17 M234-750
Fr 1832 Jul 20-0849
Re c1835 mem 27-0052
Campbell William R
Fr 1835 Nov 20 29-0534
Camper Francis
Fr 1827 Jun 14 fin 11-0699
Fr 1827 Jun 14 fin 11-0701
Campino Joaquin
Fr 1829 May 29 M73-1
Canada boundary
Re 1830 cMar mem 15-0269
Canby Israel Thompson
Fr 1828 May 19 DLC-35
To 1828 Jun 02 DLC-35
Canesse ______
Fr 1815 Feb 20 DLC-16
Canfield Robert T
Fr 1834 Feb 17 24-1402
Cannon Elias B
Fr 1832 Oct 01 fin DLC-41
Cannon Newton
Fr 1813 Dec 29 DLC-8
Fr 1816 Nov 03 DLC-21
To 1816 Nov 06 DLC-21
Fr 1836 Feb 23 M567-119
Fr 1836 Feb 23* 30-0486
Fr 1836 Jul 29 DLC-48
To 1836 Aug 03 DLC-48
Fr 1836 Aug 04 DLC-48
To 1836 Aug 05 DLC-48
Cannon Newton et al
Fr 1813 Nov 12 DLC-7
Fr 1813 Nov 12* DLC-61
Canton Joseph
To 1807 Jan 12 fin DLC-4
To 1807 Feb 16 fin DLC-4
Cantrell Stephen
Fr 1811 Jul 13 DLC-5
Fr 1814 Jun 23 DLC-11
Cantrell & Read
To 1812 Nov 25 DLC-5
To 1812 Dec 20 DLC-5
To 1812 Dec 20* DLC-61
To 1812 Dec 31 DLC-61
Fr 1812 Dec 31 DLC-61
To 1813 Jan 07 DLC-61
To 1813 Jan 13 DLC-61
To 1813 Jan 14 3-0248
Re 1813 Apr 23 fin DLC-6
Capers Legrand G
Fr 1839 Nov 17 DLC-52
Capes Joseph S
Fr 1845 Jan 11# 36-1325
Caplan William F
Fr 1835 Aug 06 M22-36
Caplinger S
To 1838 Nov 03# DLC-51
Carbery James
Fr 1837 Mar 03 33-1036
To 1837 Mar 03 33-1037
To 1837 Mar 03* DLC-50
Carbery Thomas
Fr 1824 Jan 26 M439-12
Re 1831 Mar 02 17-0717
Re 1832 Mar 13 19-1417
Fr 1832 Mar 22 M179-72
Fr 1833 Jan 18 21-1569
Fr 1834 Jan 25 24-1056
Fr 1836 Jan 27 30-0215
Fr 1837 Jan 18 33-0012
Carbery Thomas et al
Fr 1831 Jan 24 M639-1
Carey Mathew
To 1815 Aug 28 4-1175
To 1815 Aug 28* DLC-71
To 1818 Aug 03 6-1179
Fr 1831 Feb 09 M639-14
Carey Patrick
Fr 1816 Aug 08 DLC-21
Cargill Abraham et al
Fr 1831 Jan 25 17-0347
Carithers John G
Fr 1830 Nov 01 fin 16-0630
Carleton Henry
Fr 1829 Apr 15 12-1361
Fr 1830 Jan 23 M639-4
Fr 1834 May 05# M179-78
Fr 1835 Oct 10 29-0265
Fr 1836 Apr 02 30-0980
Fr 1845 Mar 02 36-1525
Carlisle William W
Fr 1835 Apr 10 28-0008
Fr 1835 Apr 10* M234-242
Carmichael William
Fr 1829 Apr 10 M639-23
Carmick Daniel
Fr 1815 Feb 17 DLC-16
Fr 1816 Apr 07 DLC-20

Carnahan James
    To 1833 Oct 05   23-0962
Carnes George A
    Fr 1845 Mar 01   DLC-57
Carnes John
    Re 1834 Apr 08   mem   25-0638
Carnes Peter A
    Fr 1831 Jul 18   M234-77
    Fr 1831 Jul 28   M567-58
    Fr 1831 Jul 28*   M222-29
Carnes Thomas P
    Fr 1816 Nov 08   DLC-21
Carney John
    Fr 1829 Feb 13   M639-25
Caro Joseph
    Fr 1821 Aug 23   DLC-30
Caro Sebastian
    Fr 1821 Aug 23   DLC-30
Caroline Marion (schooner)
    Re 1831 Apr 22   par   17-1204
Carpenter Benjamin E et al
    To 1837 Apr 13   33-1160
Carpenter Joshua
    Fr 1834 Mar 01   24-1517
Carpenter Miles N et al
    Fr 1844 Dec 11   DLC-57
Carr Anderson B
    Fr 1824 May 24   M221-99
Carr Anthony V
    Fr 1829 Sep 07   M222-26
Carr Anthony V et al
    Fr 1829 Jul   M222-25
Carr Benjamin
    Fr 1837 Feb 21   M687-20
Carr Dabney Smith
    Fr 1829 Mar 19   M639-3
    Fr 1829 Apr 03   M639-20
    Fr 1829 Jun 23   M639-4
    Fr 1835 Jan 21   27-0266
    Fr 1836 Nov 12   32-0486
    Fr 1841 Aug 18   DLC-53
    Fr 1841 Oct 07   DLC-53
Carr Samuel et al
    Fr 1831 Dec 11   M639-19
Carr Samuel J
    Re 1831 Aug 10   18-0494
Carradine Parker
    Fr 1815 Aug 29   DLC-19
Carrick Addison
    Fr 1811 Apr 24   fin   DLC-5
Carriel John D
    Fr 1832 Sep 15   DLC-41
    To 1832 Oct 01#   DLC-41
Carrol Joseph et al
    Fr 1829 cMar 25   12-1102
Carroll Charles
    Fr 1829 Feb 13   M639-26
    Fr 1829 Jun 14   DLC-37
    To 1829 Jun 16   DLC-37
    Re 1832 Nov 15   DLC-41
Carroll Charles et al
    Fr 1829 Feb 18   M639-11
Carroll James G
    Fr 1829 Mar 20   M639-4
    Fr 1829 Jun 30   M639-4
Carroll Nathaniel
    Fr 1813 Jun   3-0402
    Fr 1813 Nov 21   DLC-7
Carroll Thomas
    Fr 1814 Nov 16   DLC-14
Carroll Thomas King
    Fr 1832 Mar 03   M639-18
Carroll William
    Fr nd   DLC-75
    Fr 1811 Aug 08   DLC-5
    Re 1812 Jul 04   2-1122
    To 1812 Dec 09   DLC-5
    To 1812 Dec 09*   DLC-61
    To 1812 Dec 14   DLC-61
    To 1812 Dec 14*   DLC-5
    To 1812 Dec 15   DLC-61
    To 1812 Dec 20   DLC-5
    To 1812 Dec 20*   DLC-61
    To 1812 Dec 20   DLC-58
    To 1812 Dec 20*   DLC-61
    To 1812 Dec 20*   DLC-5
    To 1812 Dec 20*   2-1305
    Fr 1813 Jan 01   2-1318
    To 1813 Jan 07   DLC-61
    Fr 1813 Apr 29   DLC-6
    Fr 1813 Aug 08   3-0439
    Fr 1813 Sep 06   3-0452
    Fr 1813 Nov 20   DLC-7
    Fr 1813 Nov 22   DLC-7
    To 1813 Dec 03   DLC-61
    Fr 1813 Dec 09   DLC-7
    Fr 1813 Dec 15   DLC-7
    Fr 1813 Dec 16   DLC-7
    Fr 1813 Dec 17   DLC-7
    To 1813 Dec 23   DLC-61
    To 1813 Dec 23*   3-0702
    Fr 1813 Dec 23   DLC-8
    To 1813 Dec 27   DLC-8
    Fr 1813 Dec 29   DLC-8
    To 1814 Jan 11   DLC-61
    Fr 1814 Jan 11   DLC-8
    To 1814 Feb 04   DLC-62
    To 1814 Feb 05   DLC-61
    To 1814 Feb 08   DLC-61
    Fr 1814 Feb 09   DLC-8
    Fr 1814 Feb 11   DLC-8
    Fr 1814 Feb 14   DLC-9
    Fr 1814 Feb 14   DLC-9
    Fr 1814 Feb 16   DLC-9
    To 1814 Feb 17   DLC-61
    Fr 1814 Feb 17   DLC-9
    Fr 1814 Feb 18   DLC-9
    Fr 1814 Feb 20   DLC-9
    Fr 1814 Feb 22   DLC-9
    To 1814 Feb 23   DLC-61
    Fr 1814 Feb 24   DLC-9
    Fr 1814 Feb 26   DLC-9
    To 1814 Feb 28   DLC-61
    Fr 1814 Feb 28   DLC-9
    To 1814 Mar 05   DLC-61
    Fr 1814 Mar 05   DLC-9
    Fr 1814 Mar 10   3-0909
    Fr 1814 Jun 13   DLC-10
    Fr 1814 Jun 24   DLC-11
    Fr 1814 Jul 24   DLC-11
    Fr 1814 Sep 23   DLC-12
    Fr 1814 Oct 14   DLC-13
    Fr 1814 Oct 18   DLC-71
    Fr 1814 Oct 21   DLC-71
    Fr 1814 Oct 25   DLC-71
    Fr 1814 Oct 28   DLC-13
    To 1814 Oct 31   DLC-62

Carroll William (cont)			
	Fr 1814 Nov 01		DLC-13
	Fr 1814 Nov 15		4-0339
	Fr 1814 Nov 18		DLC-14
	Fr 1814 Nov 26		DLC-14
	Fr 1814 Nov 28		DLC-14
	Fr 1814 Dec 09		DLC-14
	Fr 1814 Dec 14		DLC-14
	To 1814 Dec 16		DLC-62
	To 1814 Dec 19		4-0421
	Fr 1814 Dec 20		4-0429
	Fr 1814 Dec 20*		DLC-71
	To 1814 Dec 21		DLC-62
	Fr 1814 Dec 21		DLC-14
	Fr 1815 Jan 25		DLC-15
	Fr 1815 Feb 07		DLC-16
	Fr 1815 Feb 11		DLC-16
	Fr 1815 Feb 28		DLC-17
	Fr 1815 Mar 04		DLC-17
	Fr 1815 Mar 04		4-0811
	Fr 1815 Mar 16		DLC-17
	Fr 1815 Apr 01		DLC-17
	Fr 1815 May 22		DLC-18
	Fr 1815 Jun 20		DLC-71
	Fr 1815 Oct 04		DLC-19
	Fr 1815 Dec 05		DLC-19
	Fr 1817 Sep 11		DLC-23
	Fr 1822 Jul 04	add	9-0209
	To 1822 Jul 04	add	9-0210
	Fr 1823 Oct 04		9-0677
	Fr 1823 Dec 31		9-0862
	Fr 1824 Oct		10-0905
	Fr 1824 Oct 04#		DLC-33
	To 1824 Nov 02		DLC-33
	Fr 1824 Nov 06		DLC-32
	To 1825 Feb 08		10-1101
	Fr 1825 Apr 27		DLC-33
	Fr 1828 Aug 15		DLC-35
	Fr 1829 May 11		M639-2
	Fr 1829 May 21		DLC-37
	Fr 1829 May 24		13-0415
	Fr 1829 May 25		DLC-37
	Fr 1829 Jun 29		M234-113
	Fr 1829 Jun 29*		13-0743
	Fr 1830 Jul 07		DLC-38
	Fr 1831		17-0076
	Fr 1831 Apr 08#		DLC-39
	Fr 1831 Apr 11#		17-1117
	Fr 1831 May 06		DLC-73
	Fr 1831 Jun 13		18-0001
	Fr 1831 Sep 01		DLC-73
	Fr 1831 Sep 27		DLC-73
	Fr 1831 Nov 13		DLC-40
	Fr 1831 Dec 26		DLC-73
	Fr 1832 Feb 14		DLC-40
	Fr 1832 Feb 20		DLC-73
	Fr 1832 Aug 18		M234-185
	Fr 1832 Dec 02		21-0648
	Fr 1832 Dec 18		DLC-73
	Fr 1832 Dec 22		DLC-75
	Fr c1833		DLC-75
	Fr 1833 Jan 07		21-1336
	To 1833 Jul 15		DLC-43
	Fr 1833 Aug 04		DLC-73
	Fr 1833 Aug 09		DLC-43
	Fr 1833 Sep 12		DLC-75
	Fr 1833 Dec 03		DLC-43
	Fr 1834 Dec 15		26-1505
	Fr 1834 Dec 15*		DLC-73
	Fr c1835		DLC-75
	Fr 1835 cJan		DLC-75
	Fr 1835 Jan 19		M639-9
	Fr 1835 Mar 12		DLC-75
	Fr 1835 cApr		DLC-75
	Fr 1835 May 03		DLC-73
	Fr 1835 May 29		DLC-47
	Fr 1835 Jun 28		DLC-73
	Fr 1835 Oct 16		29-0303
	Fr 1836 Aug 13		DLC-48
	Fr 1836 Aug 27#		DLC-49
	Fr 1836 Oct 07#		M234-137
	Re 1837 Jun 30		33-1351
	Fr 1837 Nov 20		34-0030
	Fr 1838 Dec 14		34-0572
	Fr 1842 Dec 28		DLC-74
Carroll William et al			
	Fr 1811 May 08		M221-38
Carron Josette et al			
	Fr 1830 Oct 08		M234-315
	Fr 1830 Oct 08*		M234-316
Carson Charles S			
	Fr 1804 May 26	mem	DLC-3
	Fr 1806 Feb 08		2-0160
Carson James et al			
	Fr 1837 Jan 27		M639-15
Carson Joseph			
	Fr 1814 Aug 29		DLC-11
	Fr 1814 Sep 06		DLC-12
	To 1814 Sep 14		DLC-62
	Fr 1814 Sep 18		DLC-12
	Fr 1814 Sep 22		DLC-12
	Fr 1814 Sep 23		DLC-12
	To 1814 Sep 26		DLC-62
	To 1814 Sep 26		DLC-62
	Fr 1814 Sep 30		DLC-12
	Fr 1814 Oct 06		DLC-13
	Fr 1814 Oct 12		DLC-13
	Fr 1814 Dec 22		DLC-14
	Fr 1815 Mar 27		4-0910
	Fr 1815 Jun 01		DLC-18
Carson Joseph H			
	Fr 1808 Nov 18	fin	DLC-4
Carson William			
	Fr 1814 Jul 23		DLC-11
Carson William et al			
	Fr 1832 Jan 19		19-0779
Carswell Samuel			
	To 1813 May 19		3-0396
	To 1813 Jul 08		3-0407
	Fr 1814 Aug 05		DLC-11
	Fr 1815 Jun 26		DLC-18
	To 1817 Jan 12		5-0683
	To 1817 Feb 23		5-0735
	To 1817 Dec 17		5-1179
	Fr 1819 May 26		DLC-27
Carswell Samuel & Co			
	Fr 1804 May 12	fin	1-1333
Cart William J			
	Fr 1823 May 06		9-0553
Carter Charles			
	Fr 1794 Jul 08	fin	1-0236
	Fr 1794 Jul 08*	fin	DLC-71
Carter Hill			
	Fr 1836 Oct 15		32-0181
Carter John P			
	Fr 1830 Dec 14#	fin	DLC-38
Carter Landon			
	To 1796 May 14	fin	1-0411
Carter Landon F			
	Fr 1836 Feb 29		30-0619

Carter Madison
Re 1837 Mar 01 par 33-0947
Carter Nathaniel
To 1840 Jul 18 chk DLC-53
Carter R B
Re 1833 Dec 16 par 24-0531
Carter Reuben A
Fr 1824 Nov 15 DLC-33
Carter Richard M
Fr 1835 Jul 02 M639-4
Carter William
Fr 1834 Mar 10 25-0019
Carter William Blount
Fr 1834 Aug 13 DLC-44
To 1834 Aug 13 DLC-73
Carthage TN citizens
To 1828 Jul 04 add 12-0042
Cartwright Samuel A
Fr 1834 Nov 15 26-0926
Carusi Gaetano
Fr 1834 May M639-4
Caruthers Robert Looney
Fr 1829 Apr 17# M639-15
Carvalho Jose da Costa
To 1831 Oct 24 18-1119
Carvalho Paer d'Andrade Manuel de
Fr 1832 Jul 22 M639-19
Carver Hartwell
Fr 1831 Dec 26 DLC-40
Carvill G & C
Fr 1827 Jan 04 fin DLC-34
Cary Shepard et al
Fr 1836 Dec M687-3
Cary William M
Fr 1842 Jun 14 35-0787
Case Eliphalet
Fr 1834 Dec 23 26-1561
Fr 1835 Mar 30 M639-16
Casey John
To 1813 Jan 09 DLC-61
Casey Thomas
Fr 1813 Oct 20 DLC-7
Caso y Luengo Francisco
To 1818 Apr 06 6-0189
To 1818 Apr 07 6-0217
To 1818 Apr 07 6-0235
Fr 1818 Apr 07 6-0251
Fr 1818 Apr 07* DLC-24
Fr 1818 Apr 07 6-0286
Fr 1818 Apr 07* DLC-24
Fr 1818 Apr 09 DLC-24
Fr 1818 Apr 09* 6-0337
Cass George Washington
Fr 1834 Dec 17 DLC-45
Cass Lewis
To 1817 May 29 5-0880
Fr 1829 Mar 06 M222-25
Fr 1831 Feb 01# 17-0394
Fr 1831 Feb 25 17-0654
Re 1831 Aug 01 18-0390
Re 1831 Aug 01* M6-13
Fr 1831 Aug 10 M567-62
To 1831 Aug 18# M567-59
Fr 1831 Aug 20 M567-65
Fr 1831 Aug 26 M221-111
To 1831 Aug 27 18-0607
To 1831 Aug 29 18-0618
To 1831 Aug 30 18-0625
Fr 1831 Sep 02 M21-7
Fr 1831 Sep 02* 18-0651
To 1831 Oct 05 M688-77
To 1831 Oct 18 M234-136
To 1831 Oct 18* 18-1019
Fr 1831 Nov 06 M127-2
Fr 1831 Nov 06 18-1206
Fr 1831 Nov 12 18-1246
Fr 1831 Nov 12* M127-2
Fr 1831 Nov 21 18-1333
Fr 1831 Nov 21* M127-2
Fr 1831 Nov 21* DLC-76
To c1831 Dec DLC-40
Fr 1831 Dec 05 19-0074
Fr 1831 Dec 07 19-0224
To 1831 Dec 12 M221-111
Fr 1831 Dec 16 19-0318
Fr 1831 Dec 17 19-0320
Fr 1831 Dec 17* M127-2
Fr 1831 Dec 17 19-0323
Fr 1831 Dec 21 M179-71
Fr 1831 Dec 21 19-0371
Fr 1831 Dec 31 19-0472
Fr 1832 Jan 05 M127-2
Fr 1832 Jan 11 M127-2
Fr 1832 Jan 12 M127-2
Fr 1832 Jan 12 M127-2
To 1832 Jan 20 M234-434
To 1832 Jan 20* 19-0798
Fr 1832 Jan 20 M127-2
Fr 1832 Jan 21 19-0807
Fr 1832 Jan 21* M127-2
Fr 1832 Jan 24 M127-2
Fr 1832 Jan 24 19-0832
Fr 1832 Jan 24* M127-2
Fr 1832 Feb 02 M127-2
Fr 1832 Feb 02 M127-2
Fr 1832 Feb 08 19-1000
Fr 1832 Feb 08* M127-2
Fr 1832 Feb 08 19-1001
Fr 1832 Feb 08* M127-2
Fr 1832 Feb 08 19-1018
Fr 1832 Feb 08* M127-2
Fr 1832 Feb 16 19-1089
Fr 1832 Feb 16* M21-8
Fr 1832 Feb 16 19-1143
Fr 1832 Feb 16* M127-2
To 1832 Feb 29# 19-1254
Fr 1832 Mar 08 19-1342
Fr 1832 Mar 09 19-1366
Fr 1832 Mar 09* M127-2
Fr 1832 Mar 10 19-1388
Fr 1832 Mar 10* M127-2
Fr 1832 Mar 12 19-1398
Fr 1832 Mar 12* M127-2
Fr 1832 Mar 12 19-1400
Fr 1832 Mar 12* M127-2
Fr 1832 Mar 13 19-1419
Fr 1832 Mar 26 19-1551
Fr 1832 Mar 26* M127-2
Fr 1832 Mar 31 20-0067
Fr 1832 Apr 16 M127-2
Fr 1832 Apr 20 20-0309
Fr 1832 Apr 20* M127-2
Fr 1832 Apr 28 M127-2
To 1832 May 01 M22-29
To 1832 May 16# 20-0529
Fr 1832 May 17 20-0540
Fr 1832 May 22 20-0556
Fr 1832 May 22* M127-2

Cass Lewis (cont)

Fr 1832 May 22*	M21-8
To 1832 May 29	M234-78
Fr 1832 Jun 05	20-0702
Fr 1832 Jun 05*	M127-2
Fr 1832 Jun 19	20-0767
Fr 1832 Jun 19*	M127-2
To 1832 Jun 22#	M688-79
Fr 1832 Jun 26	M21-8
Fr 1832 Jun 27	M127-2
Fr 1832 Jul 02	20-0857
Fr 1832 Jul 04	M127-2
Fr 1832 Jul 05	20-0884
Fr 1832 Jul 05*	M21-9
To 1832 Jul 06	20-0886
Fr 1832 Jul 07	20-0890
Fr 1832 Jul 07*	M127-2
Fr 1832 Jul 09	20-0906
Fr 1832 Jul 09	20-0908
Fr 1832 Jul 09	20-0911
Fr 1832 Jul 10	20-1006
Fr 1832 Jul 10*	M127-2
Fr 1832 Jul 14	20-1079
Fr 1832 Jul 14*	M21-9
Fr 1832 Jul 14	20-1081
Fr 1832 Jul 14*	M127-2
Fr 1832 Jul 14	20-1083
Fr 1832 Jul 14*	M21-9
To 1832 Jul 19	M22-30
To 1832 Aug 16#	DLC-41
To 1832 Aug 19#	DLC-41
To 1832 Aug 20	20-1364
To 1832 Sep 04	M22-32
To 1832 Oct 25	21-0148
To 1832 Oct 29	21-0209
To 1832 Oct 29*	DLC-41
Fr 1832 Oct 31	M127-2
To 1832 Nov 01	M22-32
Fr 1832 Nov 05	M127-2
Fr 1832 Nov 21	M127-2
To 1832 Nov 22	M22-32
Fr 1832 Nov 25	21-0498
Fr 1832 Nov 25*	M127-2
Fr 1832 Nov 25*	M234-434
Fr 1832 Dec 04	21-0836
Fr 1832 Dec 04*	M127-2
Fr 1832 Dec 04	21-0845
Fr 1832 Dec 04*	M21-9
Fr 1832 Dec 10	M127-2
Fr 1832 Dec 11	M127-2
To 1832 Dec 12	M222-31
To 1832 Dec 12*	DLC-41
To 1832 Dec 17	DLC-41
To 1832 Dec 19#	M222-31
Fr 1832 Dec 22	M127-2
Fr 1832 Dec 27	M567-74
Fr 1832 Dec 27	21-1176
To 1832 Dec 30	21-1206
Fr 1833 Jan 02	21-1298
Fr 1833 Jan 02*	M127-2
Fr 1833 Jan 03	21-1306
Fr 1833 Jan 03*	M21-9
Fr 1833 Jan 05	21-1327
Fr 1833 Jan 05*	M127-2
To 1833 Jan 07	21-1342
Fr 1833 Jan 09	21-1380
Fr 1833 Jan 09*	M127-2
Fr 1833 Jan 09	M127-2
To 1833 Jan 10	21-1395
Fr 1833 Jan 11	M127-2
Fr 1833 Jan 12	M127-2
Fr 1833 Jan 12	M127-2
Fr 1833 Jan 16	M127-2
Fr 1833 Jan 24	22-0042
Fr 1833 Jan 24*	M127-2
To 1833 Jan 24#	M222-31
Fr 1833 Feb 01	22-0230
Fr 1833 Feb 11	M127-2
Fr 1833 Feb 12	22-0337
Fr 1833 Feb 12*	M127-2
Fr 1833 Feb 14	M127-2
Fr 1833 Feb 26	22-0482
Fr 1833 Feb 26*	M127-2
To 1833 Feb 27	M22-32
Fr 1833 Feb 28	22-0535
Fr 1833 Feb 28	22-0539
Fr 1833 Mar 09	M127-2
To 1833 Mar 09#	22-0710
Fr 1833 Mar 23	M21-10
Fr 1833 Mar 23*	22-0866
Fr 1833 Mar 23*	M222-31
Fr 1833 Mar 23*	M749-1
Fr 1833 Mar 29	M21-10
Fr 1833 Mar 29*	22-0910
To 1833 Apr 10	M22-32
To 1833 Apr 25	22-1167
Fr 1833 May 20	M127-3
Fr 1833 May 20*	23-0635
To 1833 May 21#	DLC-43
To 1833 May 27#	M179-76
Fr 1833 May 29	22-1490
Fr 1833 May 29*	M234-437
Fr 1833 Jul 24	23-0211
Fr 1833 Aug 02	23-0637
Fr 1833 Aug 02*	M127-3
Fr 1833 Aug 07	23-0292
Fr 1833 Aug 14	23-0331
To 1833 Sep 05	M22-33
Fr 1833 Sep 06	23-0661
Fr 1833 Sep 06*	M127-3
Fr 1833 Sep 06*	M21-11
To 1833 Sep 10	23-0679
To 1833 Oct 19	23-1062
To 1833 Oct 23#	M234-136
To 1833 Oct 25	23-1086
Fr 1833 Oct 29	M127-3
Fr 1833 Oct 29*	23-1112
Fr 1833 Oct 31	M127-3
Fr 1833 Nov 09	M127-3
To 1833 Nov 19#	23-1252
Fr 1833 Nov 20	M127-3
Fr 1833 Nov 22	23-1266
Fr 1833 Nov 22*	M127-3
Fr 1833 Nov 28	M21-11
Fr 1833 Nov 29	23-1328
Fr 1833 Nov 29*	M127-3
Fr 1833 Nov 29	23-1370
Fr 1833 Nov 29*	M127-3
Fr 1833 Nov 29*	M472-2
To 1833 Nov 29#	M234-75
Fr 1833 Dec 04	24-0332
Fr 1833 Dec 04*	M127-3
Fr 1833 Dec 05	24-0383
Fr 1833 Dec 05*	M127-3
Fr 1833 Dec 06	24-0406
Fr 1833 Dec 06*	M127-3
Fr 1833 Dec 14	M127-3
Fr 1833 Dec 18	M21-11
To 1833 Dec 23	24-0573

Fr 1833 Dec 23		M127-3
Fr 1833 Dec 23*		M21-11
Fr 1833 Dec 28		M127-3
Fr 1833 Dec 28*		M21-11
To 1834		M234-416
Fr 1834 Jan 02		24-0736
To 1834 Jan 04		24-0747
Fr 1834 Jan 09		T494-3
Fr 1834 Jan 09*		M127-3
Fr 1834 Jan 09*		M21-12
Fr 1834 Jan 17		M127-3
Fr 1834 Jan 17*		M21-12
Fr 1834 Jan 18		24-0993
Fr 1834 Jan 18*		M127-3
To 1834 Jan 30		24-1104
Fr 1834 Jan 30		24-1107
Fr 1834 Jan 30*		M127-3
To 1834 Feb 12		M22-34
Fr 1834 Feb 13		24-1303
Fr 1834 Feb 13*		M127-3
Fr 1834 Feb 17		M21-12
Fr 1834 Feb 17		M127-3
Fr 1834 Feb 17*		M21-12
Fr 1834 Feb 17		M127-3
Fr 1834 Feb 17*		M21-12
To 1834 Feb 28		24-1500
To 1834 Mar 02#		M234-921
Fr 1834 Mar 03		24-1522
To 1834 Mar 03#		M567-102
To 1834 Mar 04		M234-76
To 1834 cMar 05#		24-1575
Fr 1834 Mar 07		M234-288
Fr 1834 Mar 07*		M127-3
Fr 1834 Mar 07*		24-1583
To 1834 Mar 10		25-0021
Fr 1834 Mar 18		25-0265
Fr 1834 Mar 18		M127-3
Fr 1834 Mar 19		25-0270
To 1834 Mar 19		M22-34
Fr 1834 Mar 21		25-0313
Fr 1834 Mar 22		M567-98
Fr 1834 Mar 22*		M127-3
Fr 1834 Apr 02		25-0564
Fr 1834 Apr 02*		M127-3
To 1834 Apr 03		M22-34
To 1834 Apr 23		25-0866
To 1834 Apr 30		25-0925
Fr 1834 May 03		M567-100
Fr 1834 May 03*		M127-3
Fr 1834 May 07		25-0984
To 1834 May 07		M234-236
To 1834 May 08		25-0990
Fr 1834 May 10		25-1009
To 1834 May 14		M688-92
To 1834 May 15		25-1052
Fr 1834 May 27		25-1158
Fr 1834 May 27		25-1160
Fr 1834 May 27*		M21-12
Fr 1834 May 27*		M127-3
To 1834 Jun 02		25-1224
To 1834 Jun 03		25-1236
To 1834 Jun 03*		M22-35
Fr 1834 Jun 09		25-1277
To 1834 Jun 14		25-1359
To 1834 Jun 16		25-1387
Fr 1834 Jun 16		M567-93
Fr 1834 Jun 16*		M127-3
Fr 1834 Jun 16*		M21-13
Fr 1834 Jun 25		25-1530
Fr 1834 Jun 30		25-1620
Fr 1834 Jul 03		26-0079
Fr 1834 Jul 03*		M21-13
Fr 1834 Jul 07		26-0175
Fr 1834 Jul 07*		M21-13
Fr 1834 Jul 07		M21-13
To 1834 Jul 08		26-0185
To 1834 Oct 03		M567-101
To 1834 Oct 16		M22-35
To 1834 Nov 03		26-0813
To 1834 Nov 06		M567-94
To 1834 Nov 06*		26-0843
To 1834 Nov 06		26-0845
Fr 1834 Nov 06		M127-3
Fr 1834 Nov 07		M127-3
Fr 1834 Nov 27		26-0993
Fr 1834 Nov 27*		M127-3
Fr 1834 Dec 03		26-1362
Fr 1834 Dec 10		M127-3
Fr 1834 Dec 10*		M21-14
Fr 1834 Dec 10		M668-7
Fr 1834 Dec 10*		M127-3
Fr 1834 Dec 10*		M21-14
Fr 1834 Dec 20		M127-3
Fr 1834 Dec 20*		M21-14
Fr 1834 Dec 22		M234-136
Fr 1834 Dec 22*		26-1534
To 1834 Dec 22		26-1552
Fr 1835 Jan 07		27-0114
Fr 1835 Jan 07*		M21-14
Fr 1835 Jan 12		27-0181
To 1835 Jan 12#		M221-115
Fr 1835 Jan 13		27-0214
To 1835 Jan 28		27-0301
Fr 1835 Jan 28		27-0303
To 1835 Jan 28	mem	M234-31
Fr 1835 Jan 29		M127-3
Fr 1835 Jan 30		M639-13
Fr 1835 Jan 30*		M127-3
Fr 1835 Feb 05		27-0400
Fr 1835 Feb 05*		M127-3
Fr 1835 Feb 05*		M21-15
To 1835 Feb 09		M221-115
Fr 1835 Feb 09		27-0445
Fr 1835 Feb 09*		M21-15
Fr 1835 Feb 10		M127-3
Fr 1835 Feb 10		M127-3
Fr 1835 Feb 12		M127-3
Fr 1835 Feb 13		27-0509
Fr 1835 Feb 17		T494-8
Fr 1835 Feb 17*		M21-15
Fr 1835 Feb 18		27-0549
Fr 1835 Feb 18*		M21-15
Fr 1835 Feb 18*		M127-3
Fr 1835 Feb 20		T494-3
Fr 1835 Feb 20*		M127-3
Fr 1835 Feb 24		27-0597
Fr 1835 Feb 24*		M127-3
To 1835 Feb 26	mem	T494-3
Fr 1835 Feb 27		27-0637
Fr 1835 Feb 27		M127-3
Fr 1835 Mar 02		M567-152
Fr 1835 Mar 02*		M221-116
Fr 1835 Mar 02		M127-3
Fr 1835 Mar 12		27-1114
To 1835 Mar 12		27-1131
To 1835 Mar 12*		M567-109
To 1835 Mar 23		27-1316
To 1835 Mar 24		DLC-45

Cass Lewis (cont)

Fr 1835 Mar 24		M127-3
Fr 1835 Mar 25		M127-3
Fr 1835 Apr 01		M127-3
To 1835 Apr 25#		28-0130
Fr 1835 Apr 28		28-0150
Fr 1835 Apr 28*		M127-3
To 1835 Apr 30		28-0193
To 1835 May 08		28-0320
To 1835 May 13		37-0525
To 1835 May 25		M221-115
Fr 1835 Jul 11		DLC-46
To 1835 Aug 21#		M567-112
Fr 1835 Aug 28		M567-110
Fr 1835 Aug 28*		M127-3
Fr 1835 Aug 28*		M567-146
To 1835 Aug 31		M22-37
Fr 1835 Sep 08		M21-17
Fr 1835 Sep 08*		M127-3
To 1835 Sep 10		M22-37
To 1835 Oct 05		29-0189
Fr 1835 Oct 15		29-0291
Fr 1835 Oct 15*		M21-17
Fr 1835 Oct 15*		M127-3
Fr 1835 Oct 16		29-0307
Fr 1835 Oct 16*		M21-17
Fr 1835 Oct 16*		M127-3
Fr 1835 Nov 04		29-0438
To 1835 Nov 24		29-0597
Fr 1835 Nov 30		29-0629
Fr 1835 Nov 30*		M127-3
Fr 1835 Dec 02		M127-3
To 1835 Dec 08		29-1032
Fr 1835 Dec 10		29-1070
Fr 1835 Dec 10*		M127-3
Fr 1835 Dec 10*		M200-6
To 1835 Dec 16	mem	29-1182
Fr 1835 Dec 17		29-1194
Fr 1835 Dec 18		29-1215
Fr 1835 Dec 19		29-1228
Fr 1835 Dec 19		29-1230
Fr 1835 Dec 19*		M127-3
Fr 1835 Dec 23		M234-242
Fr 1835 Dec 28		29-1346
Fr 1835 Dec 28*		M21-17
Fr 1835 Dec 28*		M127-3
Fr 1835 Dec 31		29-1364
Fr 1835 Dec 31*		M21-17
Fr 1835 Dec 31*		M127-3
Fr 1835 Dec 31*		M234-242
Fr 1836 Jan 05		29-1461
Fr 1836 Jan 05*		M21-17
Fr 1836 Jan 05*		M127-3
Fr 1836 Jan 05		29-1462
Fr 1836 Jan 05*		M565-9
Fr 1836 Jan 05*		M127-3
Fr 1836 Jan 06		29-1467
Fr 1836 Jan 06*		M124-151
Fr 1836 Jan 06*		M565-9
Fr 1836 Jan 06*		M127-3
Fr 1836 Jan 08		29-1505
Fr 1836 Jan 08*		M127-3
Fr 1836 Jan 11		29-1541
Fr 1836 Jan 11*		M21-17
Fr 1836 Jan 11*		M127-3
Fr 1836 Jan 12		29-1560
Fr 1836 Jan 12		29-1563
Fr 1836 Jan 12*		M21-17
Fr 1836 Jan 12*		M127-3
Fr 1836 Jan 15		30-0048
To 1836 Jan 18		DLC-47
To 1836 Jan 18*		30-0136
To 1836 Jan 18*		M234-76
To 1836 Jan 21		30-0159
To 1836 Jan 23		30-0189
To 1836 Jan 25#		M234-355
To 1836 Jan 26#		30-0203
Fr 1836 Jan 27		30-0217
Fr 1836 Jan 27*		M565-9
Fr 1836 Jan 27*		M127-3
To 1836 Jan 30		M567-127
To 1836 Feb 01#		30-0255
Fr 1836 Feb 02		30-0269
Fr 1836 Feb 05		30-0288
Fr 1836 Feb 05		30-0291
Fr 1836 Feb 09		30-0337
Fr 1836 Feb 09*		M565-9
Fr 1836 Feb 09*		M127-3
To 1836 Feb 09#		M234-80
Fr 1836 Feb 10		30-0346
Fr 1836 Feb 10*		M21-18
Fr 1836 Feb 10*		M127-3
Fr 1836 Feb 11		30-0358
Fr 1836 Feb 11*		M127-3
To 1836 Feb 16	mem	30-0399
Fr 1836 Feb 22		30-0451
Fr 1836 Feb 23		30-0487
Fr 1836 Feb 23*		M127-3
To 1836 Feb 25		30-0573
To 1836 Feb 25		M22-38
Fr 1836 Feb 26		30-0589
Fr 1836 Feb 26*		M21-18
Fr 1836 Feb 26*		M127-3
To 1836 Feb 26#		M234-225
Fr 1836 Mar 04		30-0674
Fr 1836 Mar 04*		M21-18
Fr 1836 Mar 04*		M127-3
Fr 1836 Mar 07		M21-18
To 1836 Mar 11#		DLC-47
Fr 1836 Mar 17#		M7-2
To 1836 Mar 17		M22-39
To 1836 Mar 23		30-0885
To 1836 Mar 23	mem	M234-80
Fr 1836 Apr 01		30-0965
Fr 1836 Apr 01*		M21-18
Fr 1836 Apr 01*		M127-3
Fr 1836 Apr 07		M127-3
Fr 1836 Apr 07*		30-1026
To 1836 Apr 08	mem	M234-80
Fr 1836 Apr 12		30-1142
Fr 1836 Apr 12*		M21-18
Fr 1836 Apr 12*		M127-3
To 1836 Apr 18#		M567-125
Fr 1836 Apr 22		30-1315
Fr 1836 Apr 26		M127-3
Fr 1836 Apr 26*		30-1351
Fr 1836 Apr 26		30-1354
Fr 1836 Apr 27		30-1370
Fr 1836 Apr 27*		M21-18
Fr 1836 Apr 27*		M127-3
Fr 1836 Apr 27		30-1373
Fr 1836 Apr 27*		M21-18
Fr 1836 Apr 27*		M127-3
Fr 1836 Apr 29		M127-3
To 1836 May 03		30-1491
Fr 1836 May 07#		30-1551
Fr 1836 May 09		30-1571
Fr 1836 May 09		30-1573
Fr 1836 May 09*		M21-18

Fr 1836 May 09* M127-3
Fr 1836 May 14 M179-82
Fr 1836 May 14* M127-3
Fr 1836 May 14 31-0012
Fr 1836 May 14* M127-3
Fr 1836 May 14 31-0014
Fr 1836 May 14* M21-8
Fr 1836 May 14* M127-3
Fr 1836 May 16# 31-0027
To 1836 May 20# M234-422
Fr 1836 May 21 31-0069
Fr 1836 May 21* M21-18
Fr 1836 May 21* M127-3
Fr 1836 May 25 31-0098
Fr 1836 May 25* M127-3
Fr 1836 May 25 31-0108
Fr 1836 May 26 31-0116
Fr 1836 May 26* M127-3
Fr 1836 Jun 06 31-0347
Fr 1836 Jun 13# DLC-48
Fr 1836 Jun 15 31-0487
To 1836 Jun 15# 31-0488
Fr 1836 Jun 16 M127-3
To 1836 Jun 17# 31-0498
Fr 1836 Jun 18 31-0509
To 1836 Jun 20 DLC-48
To 1836 Jun 20* M124-153
Fr 1836 Jun 21 M21-19
Fr 1836 Jun 21* M127-3
Fr 1836 Jun 23 31-0551
Fr 1836 Jun 23* M127-3
Fr 1836 Jun 25 mem M127-3
Fr 1836 Jun 25* mem 31-0579
To 1836 Jun 25# M567-122
To 1836 Jun 25# M567-125
Fr 1836 Jun 27 M21-19
Fr 1836 Jun 27* M127-3
Fr 1836 Jun 27* M640-1
Fr 1836 Jun 27* M234-189
Fr 1836 Jun 28 31-0624
Fr 1836 Jun 28* M127-3
Fr 1836 Jun 28* M21-19
Fr 1836 Jul 01 31-0738
Fr 1836 Jul 01* M127-3
Fr 1836 Jul 01* M21-19
To 1836 Jul 01 mem M234-225
Fr 1836 Jul 02 31-0750
To 1836 Jul 05# M234-145
Fr 1836 Jul 06 M127-3
Fr 1836 Jul 06* M21-19
To 1836 Jul 07 31-0925
Fr 1836 Jul 07 31-0928
Fr 1836 Jul 07* M127-3
Fr 1836 Jul 07* M21-19
Fr 1836 Jul 09# 31-1005
To 1836 Jul 10 31-1036
To 1836 Jul 11 31-1060
To 1836 Aug 09 31-1268
Fr 1836 Aug 22 M127-3
Fr 1836 Aug 22* 31-1336
Fr 1836 Aug 22 M127-3
Fr 1836 Aug 22* 31-1337
To 1836 Aug 26 M234-189
To 1836 Aug 31 31-1389
To 1836 Sep 05 M179-82
To 1836 Sep 05* 31-1425
To 1836 Sep 30# M687-1
To 1836 Oct 04 DLC-74
To 1836 Oct 04* 32-0053
To 1836 Oct 04* M221-117
Fr 1836 Oct 04 DLC-74
Fr 1836 Oct 04* M127-3
Fr 1836 Oct 04 M179-82
Fr 1836 Oct 04 M567-134
Fr 1836 Oct 09 M221-117
Re 1836 Nov 15 mem 32-0507
Fr 1837 Feb 21 33-0796
Fr 1837 Mar 06 DLC-50
Fr 1843 May 26 DLC-55
To 1843 Jul 08 35-1406
Fr 1843 Aug 11 DLC-55
Fr 1844 Dec 02 M873-26

Casseday A A
Fr 1841 Oct 15# fin DLC-53

Cassedy Charles
To 1814 Aug 10 3-1285
Fr 1814 Sep 21 DLC-12
Fr 1814 Sep 23 DLC-12
Fr 1814 Sep 28 DLC-12
Fr 1814 Oct 15 DLC-13
Fr 1814 Nov 20 DLC-14
Fr 1814 Dec 12 DLC-14
Fr 1819 Dec 27 DLC-28
Fr 1821 Mar 04 DLC-29
Fr 1826 Sep 07 DLC-34
Fr 1830 Oct 20 16-0454
Fr 1833 Aug 01 DLC-43
Fr 1834 Feb 25# DLC-44
Fr 1838 Feb 04 DLC-51
Fr 1838 Feb 05 DLC-51
Fr 1840 May 25 DLC-52

Cassedy Samuel
Fr 1834 Feb 09 DLC-44

Cassel Ephraim
Fr 1835 Apr 28 M22-36

Cassine Washington
Re 1831 May 18 par 17-1377

Castleman Henry
To 1807 Feb 21 fin DLC-4

Castleman John
To 1807 Jan 03 fin DLC-4
To 1807 Jan 03 fin DLC-4
To 1807 Jan 09 fin DLC-4
To 1807 Feb 14 fin DLC-4
To 1807 Mar 11 fin DLC-4
Re 1809 Mar 20 mem 2-0782

Castleman Robert B
Fr 1845 Jul# leg DLC-58

Castner & Co
To 1833 May 02 22-1263

Cates Richard
To 1815 Aug 01 DLC-62

Cathcart Charles W
Fr 1836 Jan 25# M234-355
Fr 1836 Aug 29 M234-355

Cathcart James Leander
Fr 1829 May 01 13-0228
Fr 1833 Oct 30 23-1123

Cathey John A
Fr 1802 Aug 09 fin DLC-71
Re 1808 Sep 22 leg 2-0724

Catlet Hanson
Fr 1806 Jun 20 2-0275
Fr 1806 Jun 25 2-0279

Catlett Thomas K
Fr 1835 May 09 28-0328

Catlin Lynde et al
Fr 1829 Aug 28 M639-21

Caton John et al
Fr 1831 cJan 28 M639-1
Caton Mary (Carroll)
To 1831 Jun 22 18-0079
Fr 1832 cFeb# 19-0924
Catron John
Fr 1825 Aug 08 DLC-33
Fr 1828 Dec 08 DLC-36
Fr 1829 Mar 21 M639-1
Fr 1833 Jan 02 DLC-41
Fr 1833 Sep 20 M639-3
Fr 1835 Mar 21 DLC-45
Fr 1835 May 25 DLC-46
Fr 1836 Jun 08 DLC-48
Fr 1836 Aug 08 DLC-48
Fr 1836 Sep 22 DLC-49
Fr 1837 Jun 21 33-1321
Fr 1837 Aug 16 DLC-50
Fr 1837 Nov 22 DLC-50
Fr 1838 Jan 04 DLC-51
Fr 1838 Feb 05 DLC-51
Fr 1838 Mar 17 DLC-51
Fr 1838 Dec 23 34-0580
To 1839 Sep 12 fin DLC-53
Fr 1839 Dec 21 DLC-52
To 1840 Jul 21 chk DLC-53
Fr 1841 Jan 03 DLC-53
Fr 1841 Jul 23 35-0342
Fr 1841 Dec 03 35-0516
Fr 1844 Jan 12 36-0117
Fr 1844 Nov 13 DLC-57
Fr 1844 Dec 09 DLC-57
Fr 1845 Mar 01 DLC-57
Fr 1845 Mar 09 DLC-57
Fr 1845 May 19# DLC-58
Causin Nathaniel Pope
Fr 1829 Mar 06 M639-4
To 1834 Feb 12 chk DLC-44
Fr 1834 Jul 03 26-0091
Fr 1844 Dec 11 36-1141
Causten James H
Fr 1829 cNov 01 14-0342
Causten James H Jr
Fr 1836 Dec 28 DLC-49
Cavaille Pierre
Fr 1815 Mar 4-0801
Cavitt Richard et al
Re 1808 Apr 13 leg 2-0635
Cazenove Arthur Charles
Fr 1837 Jul 01 DLC-50
Cebra John Yates
Fr 1829 Mar 25 12-1104
Cebra John Yates et al
Fr 1833 Nov 14 M639-25
Fr 1834 Jan 07 M639-18
Chabaud H
Fr 1815 Feb 10# 4-0716
Chabaud John
Fr 1815 Feb 15 DLC-16
Chabowawa et al
Fr 1834 Oct 15 M234-421
Fr 1834 Oct 15* 26-0648
Chadbourne Israel
Fr 1837 Feb 22 M687-16
Chain Hugh et al
Fr 1815 Feb 27 DLC-17
Chamberlain Denmark
Re 1791 Aug leg 1-0098
Chamberlain Ebenezer Mattoon et al
Fr 1835 Dec 29-0694
Chamberlain Jeremiah
Re 1791 Aug leg 1-0099
Fr 1829 Feb 03 M639-21
Chambers Ezekiel Forman et al
To 1832 Feb 21 19-1197
Chambers George W
Fr 1836 Jun 02 M567-120
Chambers Henry
Fr 1815 Jun 13 DLC-18
Chambers Latitia
To 1824 Aug 12# 10-0845
Fr 1844 Jan 15 DLC-56
Chambers William
Fr 1827 Aug 05 DLC-34
Fr 1844 Mar 23 36-0396
To 1844 Apr 10 36-0435
Champlain Samuel
To 1814 Jul 27 DLC-62
Fr 1815 Jun 05 M566-20
Fr 1815 Nov 14 DLC-71
To 1815 Nov 22 DLC-62
Champlin Christopher Grant et al
Fr 1831 Sep 10 M639-11
Fr 1834 Dec 01 26-1118
Chancellor George
Fr 1834 Sep 29 fin DLC-73
Chanche John Mary Joseph
Fr 1833 Feb 16 22-0394
Chandler Anson G
Fr 1837 Jan 18 M687-20
Chandler Edward
Fr 1829 Sep 30 M639-4
Fr 1832 May 21 M639-17
Fr 1833 May 31 M639-4
Fr 1834 Aug 15 26-0315
Chandler John
Fr 1829 Feb 28 12-0603
Re 1829 Apr 21 mem 13-0086
Fr 1833 Jan 24 M639-1
Fr 1835 May 08 DLC-46
Fr 1837 Feb 13 M687-28
Chandler Joseph Ripley
Fr 1835 Sep 15 DLC-47
To 1835 Sep 18 DLC-47
Chandler L H et al
Fr 1837 Jan 26 33-0181
Chandler William
Fr 1822 Jan 24 fin DLC-31
Fr 1823 Jan 03 fin DLC-31
Fr 1823 Jan 28 fin DLC-32
Fr 1824 Jul 05 fin DLC-33
Fr 1825 Feb 19 fin DLC-34
Fr 1832 Mar 05# fin DLC-40
Re 1834 Oct 15 M273-31
Re 1835 Apr 03 mem 27-1513
Chandler & Howard
Fr 1831 Oct 15 M22-28
Chaney Thomas
Fr 1837 Jun 08# fin DLC-50
Chapin Benjamin
Fr 1829 Feb 10 M639-27
Chapin Cyrenius
Fr 1830 Dec 10 M234-433
Chapin Graham Hurd et al
Fr c1835 27-0054
Chapin S
Fr 1830 Oct 15 16-0386
Fr 1844 Dec 11 36-1147

Name	Date	Note	Location
Chaplin Jonathan E et al			
	Fr 1833 Oct 16		M639-21
Chapman B F			
	Fr 1842 Jan 29		DLC-54
	Fr 1844 May 16		DLC-56
Chapman George			
	Fr 1812 Jul 12		DLC-5
Chapman J			
	Fr 1824 Jun 30	fin	DLC-32
Chapman Reuben			
	Fr 1836 Jun 28		31-0630
	Fr 1836 Dec 13		M687-33
Chapman S F			
	Fr 1833 Jan 06		DLC-41
Chapman Thomas			
	To 1801 Jul 15	lnd	1-0896
Chapman Thomas P			
	Fr 1815 May 01		DLC-18
	Fr 1815 May 05		DLC-18
	Fr 1815 Sep 12		DLC-19
Chappell William			
	To 1826 Nov 07	fin	DLC-34
Chappell William D			
	Fr 1824 Nov#		DLC-33
Charles Abraham			
	Fr 1836 May 30		31-0201
	Fr 1836 Jun 03		31-0291
Charles Stephen et al			
	Fr 1831 Feb 22		17-0605
	To 1831 Mar 08		17-0822
Charles William			
	Re 1834 Oct 15		M273-31
Charles X King of France			
	To 1829 Jun 10		13-0611
	Fr 1830 Apr 25		15-0810
	Fr 1830 Apr 25*		M53-8
	Fr 1830 Apr 25		15-0812
	Fr 1830 Apr 25*		M53-8
Charles John King of Sweden			
	Fr 1829 Jan 22		M60-2
	Fr 1829 Mar 18		M60-2
	To 1829 May 28		13-0465
	To 1829 May 29		13-0496
	Fr 1830 Apr 24		M60-2
	To 1830 Oct 26		16-0542
	To 1831 Nov 11		18-1240
Chartier Haycinth et al			
	Fr 1836 Aug 19		M234-422
Chase George M			
	Fr 1837 Jan 18		M687-20
Chase George M et al			
	Fr c1836 Jan		29-1420
Chase William Henry			
	Fr 1836 Jan 14		M124-151
	Fr 1844 May 16		DLC-56
Chauncey Charles et al			
	Fr 1829 Mar 28		M639-3
Chauveau Louis			
	Fr 1815 Oct 06		DLC-19
Cheatham Archer			
	Fr 1825 Nov 26	fin	11-0061
	Fr 1826 May 13	fin	11-0214
	Fr 1826 Nov 24	fin	11-0405
	Fr 1827 May 14	fin	11-0584
	Fr 1828 cMay 15	fin	12-0008
Cheatham George W			
	Fr 1839 May 13		DLC-52
Cheatham John A			
	Re 1814 Mar 14		DLC-62
Cheatham Leonard Pope			
	Fr 1824 Jul 22		DLC-33
	To 1838 Mar 26		DLC-51
	Fr 1838 Nov 12		DLC-51
	Fr 1839 Jan 18		DLC-51
	To 1841 Apr 10		35-0281
	Fr 1841 Apr 10		35-0283
	Fr 1842 May 14		DLC-54
	To 1842 May 17		DLC-54
	To 1842 Nov 25		35-1006
	Fr 1843 Apr 24		DLC-55
	To 1843 Aug 11		35-1454
	To 1843 Oct 09		DLC-55
	Re 1843 Dec 08	mem	DLC-56
Cheatham Richard			
	Fr 1833 May 24		22-1439
	To 1833 Jun 06		22-1591
	Fr 1833 Oct 06		M639-3
Cheegepinquay			
	Fr 1831 Oct 03		M234-775
	Fr 1831 Oct 03*		18-0916
Cheegepinquay et al			
	Fr 1835 Dec		29-0698
	Fr 1835 Dec*		M234-133
Chehaw Indians			
	To 1818 May 07		M271-2
	To 1818 May 07*		M221-78
	To 1818 May 07*		6-0665
Chennabee			
	To 1813 Oct 19		DLC-7
Cherbonnier Jean			
	Fr 1816 Mar 26		DLC-20
Cherbonnier Pierre			
	Fr 1815 Jan 22		DLC-15
Cherokee Indians			
	Re 1814 Mar 04		DLC-66
	Re 1814 May 05		DLC-10
	To 1814 Aug 05		DLC-11
	To 1814 Aug 05*		3-1212
	To 1814 Aug 05*		DLC-62
	Re 1816 Oct 08		5-0532
	Fr 1817 Apr 18		DLC-22
	To 1817 Jun 28		DLC-23
	Fr 1817 Jun 29		DLC-23
	To 1817 cJul 02		5-0901
	Fr 1817 Jul 02		DLC-23
	Fr 1817 Jul 02*		5-0905
	To 1817 Jul 04		DLC-23
	To 1817 Jul 04*		T494-1
	Re 1820 Feb 26		DLC-28
	Fr 1821 Jan 03		M221-89
	Fr 1821 Jan 03*		8-0039
	To 1821 Jan 08		M221-89
	Fr 1821 Jan 08		M221-89
	Fr 1821 Jan 08*		8-0052
	Re 1821 Jan 17		8-0075
	Fr 1831 Jun 02		M22-28
	Fr 1832 Mar 26		M22-29
	To 1835 Mar 16		M21-15
Cherokee lands intruders			
	To 1820 May 29		DLC-29
Cherokee Nation v. Georgia			
	Re 1831 Mar 19		DLC-39
	Re 1831 Mar 19	mem	17-0910
Cherokee treaty			
	Re 1816 Aug 19		5-0372
	Re 1816 Oct 04		DLC-62
	Re 1816 Oct 04*		M668-4
	Re 1816 Oct 04		M668-4

Cherokee treaty (cont)
Re 1817 Jun 20 DLC-23
Re 1817 Jul 08 5-0909
Re 1817 Jul 08 mem 5-0912
Re 1817 Jul 08 M668-4
Re 1817 Jul 08* DLC-23
Re 1834 Apr 12 M668-7
Re 1836 May 23 M668-8
Cherry Daniel
To 1811 Mar 26 lnd 2-1000
To 1819 Aug 28 lnd 7-0636
Re 1820 Sep 12 leg 7-1325
Chesapeake (steamboat)
Fr 1834 Nov 19 fin DLC-45
Chesapeake & Ohio Canal
Re c1829 mem 12-0362
Re c1833 mem 37-0302
Chester John P
Fr 1836 Dec 30 32-1412
Fr 1836 Dec 30* M234-81
Chester Robert Johnstone
To 1827 Jan 16 11-0467
To 1828 Nov 13 12-0265
To 1829 Nov 30 14-0628
To 1829 Dec 11 14-1003
To 1830 Nov 07 16-0669
To 1830 Nov 25 16-0869
To 1831 Feb 14 17-0513
Fr 1831 Apr 03# DLC-39
To 1831 Apr 06 17-1069
To 1832 Jul 20 20-1167
To 1833 Mar 03 22-0663
To 1833 Aug 08 23-0294
To 1834 Oct 16 26-0652
To 1836 Dec 31 32-1428
To 1837 Jul 15 33-1376
Fr 1838 May 07 DLC-51
Fr 1838 Jul 25 DLC-51
To 1839 May 02 DLC-75
To 1839 Jun 07 34-0810
To 1839 Sep 04 34-0905
To 1839 Sep 09 34-0929
Fr 1839 Dec 02 DLC-52
To 1840 Apr 09 34-1296
To 1840 Apr 23 34-1318
To 1840 Oct 21 35-0062
Fr 1841 Nov 22 DLC-54
To 1841 Nov 26 35-0508
To 1842 Jan 20 35-0608
To 1843 Jan 16 35-1118
Fr 1844 Jun 06 DLC-57
Fr 1844 Dec 22 M873-69
Chesterman & Caney
Fr 1833 Apr 24 M639-16
Chestoo ("Rabbit")
Re 1836 May 27 par 31-0135
Chevers George W
Fr 1836 Sep 13 M567-120
Cheves Langdon
To 1821 Aug 15 8-1063
Fr 1821 Sep 29 8-1238
Chew Beverly
Fr 1821 Apr 26 M116-5
Fr 1821 Apr 26* 8-0372
Chew Beverly et al
Fr 1835 May 14 28-0392
Chew William W et al
To 1836 Oct 22 32-0318
Chickasaw Indians
Re 1816 Aug 17 fin DLC-69
To 1818 Oct 12 6-1353
To 1818 Oct 12* DLC-62
To 1818 Oct 12* T494-1
To 1830 Aug 23 add DLC-38
To 1830 Aug 23* add 16-0137
To 1830 Aug 23* add T494-2
To 1830 Aug 26 16-0162
Fr 1830 Aug 27 add 16-0180
Fr 1830 Aug 27* add T494-2
Re 1837 Jan 23 mem 33-0108
Chickasaw treaty
Re 1816 Aug 19 5-0372
Re 1816 Sep 08 DLC-62
Re 1816 Sep 08* 5-0464
Re 1816 Sep 08* M668-4
Re 1816 Sep 12 DLC-62
Re 1816 Sep 12* 5-0473
Re 1816 Sep 12* M668-4
Re 1816 Sep 20 M668-4
Re 1818 Sep 29 DLC-62
Re 1818 Sep 29* T494-1
Re 1818 Sep 29* DLC-25
Re 1818 Oct 19 M668-5
Re 1818 Oct 19* 6-1365
Re 1833 Mar 01 M668-7
Re 1834 Jul 01 M668-7
Re 1834 Jul 01* 26-0050
Child Asa et al
Fr 1831 Dec 19 M639-2
Child Ezra et al
Fr 1829 Jan 22 M639-13
Child James L
Fr 1829 May M639-24
Child John
Fr 1835 Aug 26 M567-105
Child T
Fr 1829 Jul 11 M234-185
Childress Edwin H
Re 1841 Jan 15 leg 35-0201
Childress George C
Fr 1832 Oct 28 M639-4
Fr 1833 Aug 21 M639-3
Fr 1834 Nov 16 DLC-45
Fr 1836 Jun 22 T809-1
Childress Joel
To 1814 Jun 27 mem DLC-11
Fr 1814 Jun 29 fin DLC-11
Childress John
Fr 1805 Aug 06 DLC-3
To 1811 Oct 02 chk DLC-5
Fr 1812 Mar 25 DLC-5
To 1813 Mar 31 fin DLC-6
To 1813 Jun 02 fin DLC-6
To 1813 Aug 04 fin DLC-6
To 1814 Oct 05 fin DLC-13
Childress John et al
To 1814 May 14 add DLC-10
Fr 1814 May 14 add DLC-10
Childress Lemuel
Fr 1814 Sep 27 DLC-12
Childress Thomas
Fr 1811 Sep 12 fin DLC-5
Fr 1812 Mar 10 fin 2-1054
Fr 1815 May DLC-18
Fr 1820 Jan 12 DLC-28
Childress William G
Fr 1815 Mar 17 DLC-17
Childress & Martin
Fr 1815 Aug 08 fin DLC-68
Childress Hotel
Fr 1838 Nov 24 fin DLC-51

Childs H H			
Fr	1836 Oct 27		32-0354
Chile treaty			
Re	1834 Apr 26		25-0894
Re	1834 Apr 29		25-0915
Chiles John			
Fr	1814 Jan 21		DLC-8
To	1814 Jan 31		DLC-61
Fr	1814 Feb 18		DLC-9
Fr	1814 Jun 17		DLC-10
Fr	1814 Oct 28		DLC-13
Fr	1814 Nov 13		DLC-14
Chilton Robert S			
Fr	1841 Jul 22		DLC-53
Fr	1841 Aug 23		DLC-53
Chilton Thomas			
Fr	1828 Nov 14		DLC-35
Fr	1829 Feb 20		M639-2
Fr	1829 Mar 07		M639-6
Chinn Joseph William			
Fr	1833 Mar		M179-75
Fr	1833 Dec 12		24-0458
Chinn Thomas Withers			
Fr	1829 Feb 04		M639-21
Chinoweth Gideon D			
Fr	1841 Apr 14		DLC-53
Chippewa treaty			
Re	1830 Jan 02		M668-6
Re	1836 May 25		M668-8
Chippewa Ottawa and Potawatomi treaty			
Re	1835 Feb 21		M668-7
Chissolm John			
To	1814 Mar 05		DLC-9
Chitta			
Re	1834 Nov 01		26-0794
Chitton Joseph			
Fr	1829 Apr 21		M639-5
Chitty Charles			
Re	1829 Mar 19	par	12-1037
Re	1829 Mar 19*	par	T967-1
Choctaw Indians			
Re	1819 Mar 29		DLC-26
Re	1820 Aug 08	mem	DLC-29
To	1820 Oct 03		7-1380
To	1820 Oct 03*		T494-1
To	1820 Oct 10		T494-1
To	1820 Oct 13		T494-1
To	1820 Oct 17		T494-1
Re	1820 Oct 18		M668-5
To	1830 Aug 26	add	16-0166
Re	1831 May 26		M21-7
Re	1831 May 26*		17-1443
Re	1831 May 26*		M234-184
Re	c1835		37-0331
Re	1836 Jan 22		DLC-47
Choctaw reservations			
Re	1834 Apr 15		M234-188
Re	1834 Oct 13		M21-14
Re	1834 Oct 13*		26-0613
Choctaw treaty			
Re	1820 Aug 31		7-1222
Re	1820 Aug 31*		T494-1
Re	1821 Apr 05	fin	DLC-70
Re	1831 Feb 24		M668-6
Choctaw-Chickasaw boundary			
Re	1836 Apr 08		DLC-73
Chotard ______			
Fr	1797 Oct 25	mem	DLC-2
Chotard Henry			
Fr	1815 Mar 27		DLC-17
Fr	1815 Jun 15		DLC-18
Chouteau August			
Fr	1815 Jul 11		DLC-18
Christian William			
Fr	1815 Apr 21		DLC-18
Fr	1821 Oct 08		DLC-30
Christy William			
Fr	1816 Mar 28		DLC-20
Fr	1839 Feb 05		DLC-51
Chulea			
Fr	1814 Jan 31		DLC-8
Fr	1814 Mar 24		DLC-9
Chuning Richard			
To	1807 Jan 02	fin	DLC-4
Church Rodney S			
Fr	1835 Apr 23		DLC-46
To	1835 Apr 27		DLC-46
Fr	1836 Jan 30		M567-119
Fr	1837 Oct 16		33-1527
Churchill Henry			
Fr	1815 Oct 14		DLC-19
Churchill Samuel			
Fr	1844 Mar 09		DLC-56
Churchill William C et al			
Fr	1836 Sep 19		31-1459
Churchwell George Wellington			
Fr	1829 May 29		M639-4
Cilley Jonathan			
Fr	1837 Feb 23		M687-28
Cissell Julianna			
Re	1832 Dec 28	par	21-1191
Cist Charles			
Fr	1835 Jan 20		DLC-45
Cist Lewis Jacob			
Fr	1837 Apr 20		DLC-50
Fr	1837 Jun 15		DLC-50
Fr	1838 Mar 24		DLC-51
To	1838 Mar 30		34-0295
To	1841 Feb 10		35-0226
Citizen (pseudonym)			
Fr	1819 May 16		DLC-27
Citizens' Union Line			
Fr	1834 Sep 18	fin	DLC-44
City Samuel G			
Re	1835 May 02		M273-31
Clack John H			
Re	1830 Nov 23	mem	16-0841
Re	1830 Nov 23		M273-24
Fr	1831 Mar 02		17-0720
Clagett Darius et al			
Fr	1835 Nov 25		M639-24
Clagett Darius & Co			
Fr	c1832#	fin	DLC-58
Fr	c1832#	fin	DLC-58
Fr	c1832#	fin	DLC-58
To	1832 Aug 02	chk	DLC-41
To	1833 Jan 12	chk	21-1406
To	1833 Jun 01	chk	DLC-43
To	1833 Oct 02	chk	DLC-43
Fr	1834 Nov 28#	fin	DLC-45
To	1835 Jan 02	chk	27-0079
Fr	1835 Jan 21#	fin	DLC-45
Fr	1835 Feb 14#	fin	DLC-45
Fr	1835 Mar 12#	fin	DLC-45
Fr	1835 May 26#	fin	DLC-46
Fr	1835 Jun 06		M179-80
Fr	1835 Aug 16	fin	DLC-47

Clagett Darius & Co (cont)
Fr 1835 Oct 10# fin DLC-47
Fr 1835 Nov 09# fin DLC-47
Fr 1835 Nov 28# fin DLC-47
To 1836 Jan 04 chk DLC-47
Fr 1836 Mar 03# fin DLC-48
Fr 1836 Mar 07# fin 30-0704
To 1836 Apr 22 chk DLC-48
Fr 1836 Apr 29# fin DLC-48
To 1837 Feb 11 chk DLC-50
Clagett & Norris
Fr 1824 Dec 29# fin DLC-33
Claggett William
Fr 1829 Feb 14 M639-27
Fr 1829 Nov 24 M639-6
Claiborne F L
Fr 1834 Jun 16 25-1390
Claiborne Ferdinand Leigh
To 1813 Mar 06 3-0292
To 1813 Mar 25 37-0407
Fr 1813 Nov 12 DLC-7
Fr 1813 Nov 12* 3-0584
Fr 1813 Nov 12* DLC-61
Fr 1813 Nov 29 DLC-7
Fr 1813 Nov 29* 3-0624
Fr 1813 Dec 05 DLC-7
To 1813 Dec 18 DLC-61
To 1814 DLC-59
Fr 1814 Nov 20 DLC-14
Fr 1814 Dec 18 DLC-14
Claiborne Guilford G
Fr 1842 May 11 DLC-54
To 1842 May 21 DLC-54
Claiborne Henry L et al
Fr 1844 Jul 16 DLC-57
Claiborne John
Fr 1839 Jul 29# fin DLC-52
Fr 1840 Mar 29 DLC-52
Fr 1840 Apr 23 DLC-52
Fr 1840 Jul 08 DLC-53
Fr 1840 Oct 02 DLC-53
Fr 1841 Jan 16 DLC-53
Fr 1841 May 21 DLC-53
Fr 1841 Dec 09 DLC-54
Fr 1842 Jun 23 DLC-54
Fr 1842 Oct 22 DLC-54
Fr 1845 May 03 37-0190
Claiborne John Francis Hamtramck
Fr 1835 Sep 15 29-0045
Fr 1836 Jan 21# DLC-47
Fr 1836 Mar 11 M234-189
Fr 1836 Apr 11 M639-8
Fr 1836 May 16 31-0031
Fr 1836 Jun 17 31-0496
Fr 1837 Feb 23 M687-9
Fr 1844 Aug 17 36-0796
Claiborne M G L
Fr 1830 Mar 15 M273-25
Fr 1844 Jul 04 DLC-57
Claiborne Nathaniel Herbert
Fr 1797 Dec 16 1-0558
Fr 1829 Mar 01 M639-25
Claiborne Nathaniel Herbert et al
Fr 1832 Mar 14 M639-9
Claiborne Thomas
To 1812 Sep 10 DLC-5
Fr 1815 May 14 DLC-18
Fr 1818 Dec 23 DLC-26
Fr 1831 Mar 28 M639-2
Fr 1832 Nov 24 M688-84
Claiborne Thomas et al
Fr 1809 Jun mem 2-0821
Fr 1830 Jul 08 16-0003
To 1830 Jul 08 16-0006
Fr 1830 Nov 27 16-0891
Claiborne Thomas Augustine
Fr 1803 Jul 14 DLC-2
Fr 1806 Feb 01 2-0135
Fr 1806 Jul 10# 2-0295
Fr 1806 Jul 26# 2-0305
Fr 1811 Jun 26 DLC-5
Fr 1814 Nov 07 DLC-13
Claiborne W M
Fr 1843 Jul 05 DLC-55
Claiborne William Charles Cole
Fr 1796 Aug 01 1-0443
Fr 1797 Jul 20 DLC-2
Fr 1798 Apr 30 DLC-71
Fr 1800 Mar 20 DLC-2
Fr 1800 Apr 26 DLC-2
To 1801 Jul 04 1-0883
Fr 1801 Dec 09 DLC-2
Fr 1801 Dec 23 DLC-2
Fr 1802 Jan 09 DLC-2
Fr 1802 Jan 20 DLC-2
Fr 1802 Feb 04 DLC-2
Fr 1802 Mar 06 DLC-2
Fr 1802 Mar 20 DLC-2
Fr 1803 Oct 09 DLC-3
Fr 1805 Apr 18 2-0030
To 1806 Nov 12 2-0384
To 1806 Nov 12* DLC-4
Fr 1806 Dec 05 M221-9
To 1807 Jan 08 2-0440
To 1807 Jan 08* DLC-4
Fr 1807 Mar 27 DLC-4
Fr 1807 Dec 03 DLC-4
To 1813 Jan 05 2-1324
Fr 1813 Mar 15 3-0310
To 1814 Jul 21 DLC-62
To 1814 Aug 05 DLC-62
Fr 1814 Aug 08 DLC-71
Fr 1814 Aug 08 3-1236
Fr 1814 Aug 12 DLC-71
Fr 1814 Aug 16 DLC-11
Fr 1814 Aug 21 DLC-71
To 1814 Aug 22 DLC-62
Fr 1814 Aug 24 DLC-11
To 1814 Aug 27 DLC-62
Fr 1814 Aug 29 DLC-11
To 1814 Aug 30 DLC-62
Fr 1814 Sep 08 DLC-71
Fr 1814 Sep 10 DLC-71
To 1814 Sep 17 4-0219
Fr 1814 Sep 19 DLC-12
Fr 1814 Sep 20 DLC-12
Fr 1814 Sep 20 DLC-71
To 1814 Sep 21 DLC-62
Fr 1814 Sep 21 DLC-12
To 1814 Sep 30 DLC-62
Fr 1814 Oct 02 4-0253
Fr 1814 Oct 03 DLC-12
Fr 1814 Oct 11 DLC-13
To 1814 Oct 15 DLC-62
Fr 1814 Oct 17 DLC-13
Fr 1814 Oct 17 DLC-13
To 1814 Oct 23 DLC-62
Fr 1814 Oct 24 DLC-13
Fr 1814 Oct 24 DLC-13

Fr 1814 Oct 28 DLC-13
Fr 1814 Oct 28 DLC-13
To 1814 Oct 31 DLC-62
To 1814 Oct 31 DLC-62
Fr 1814 Nov 04 DLC-13
Fr 1814 Nov 05 DLC-13
Fr 1814 Nov 05 DLC-13
Fr 1814 Nov 07 DLC-13
To 1814 Nov 16 DLC-62
Fr 1814 Nov 16 DLC-14
Fr 1814 Nov 19 DLC-14
Fr 1814 Nov 20 DLC-14
To 1814 Dec 10 DLC-62
Fr 1814 Dec 16 DLC-14
To 1814 Dec 18 DLC-62
Fr 1814 Dec 20 DLC-14
To 1814 Dec 21 DLC-62
To 1814 Dec 21 4-0436
Fr 1814 Dec 21 DLC-14
Fr 1814 Dec 22 DLC-14
Fr 1814 Dec 22 DLC-14
Fr 1814 Dec 22 DLC-14
To 1814 Dec 23 DLC-62
To 1814 Dec 24 DLC-62
Fr 1814 Dec 24 DLC-15
Fr 1814 Dec 26 DLC-15
Fr 1814 Dec 31 DLC-15
To 1815 Jan 03 DLC-15
To 1815 Jan 03 4-0486
Fr 1815 Jan 04 DLC-15
Fr 1815 Jan 06 DLC-15
Fr 1815 Jan 06 DLC-15
Fr 1815 Jan 06 DLC-71
Fr 1815 Jan 06 DLC-71
To 1815 Jan 07 DLC-62
Fr 1815 Jan 07 4-0494
Fr 1815 Jan 07 DLC-15
Fr 1815 Jan 07 DLC-71
Fr 1815 Jan 07 DLC-71
Fr 1815 Jan 09 DLC-15
Fr 1815 Jan 09 DLC-15
Fr 1815 Jan 12 DLC-15
Fr 1815 Jan 12 4-0523
Fr 1815 Jan 13 DLC-71
Fr 1815 Jan 13 DLC-71
Fr 1815 Jan 14 4-0543
Fr 1815 Jan 15 DLC-15
To 1815 Jan 16 DLC-62
Fr 1815 Jan 16 DLC-15
Re 1815 Jan 16 mem 4-0554
To 1815 Jan 17 DLC-62
To 1815 Jan 17 DLC-15
To 1815 Jan 17* DLC-62
Fr 1815 Jan 17 DLC-15
Fr 1815 Jan 17 DLC-15
Fr 1815 Jan 17 DLC-15
To 1815 Jan 18 DLC-15
To 1815 Jan 18* DLC-62
Fr 1815 Jan 18 DLC-15
Fr 1815 Jan 20 DLC-15
Fr 1815 Jan 21 DLC-15
Fr 1815 Jan 21 DLC-15
Fr 1815 Jan 21 4-0585
To 1815 Jan 22 DLC-15
Fr 1815 Jan 22 DLC-15
Fr 1815 Jan 22 DLC-15
Fr 1815 Jan 23 4-0602
Fr 1815 Jan 25 4-0613
To 1815 Jan 26 DLC-15
Fr 1815 Jan 26 4-0618
Fr 1815 Jan 28 4-0641
To 1815 Jan 28 4-0642
Fr 1815 Jan 28 DLC-16
Fr 1815 Jan 30 4-0644
Fr 1815 Jan 31 DLC-16
Fr 1815 Feb 01 DLC-16
To 1815 Feb 01# DLC-17
Fr 1815 Feb 01 DLC-16
To 1815 Feb 01 DLC-16
To 1815 Feb 01 DLC-16
To 1815 Feb 03 DLC-16
Fr 1815 Feb 03 DLC-16
To 1815 Feb 03 DLC-16
Fr 1815 Feb 03 DLC-75
Fr 1815 Feb 04 DLC-16
To 1815 Feb 05 DLC-16
Fr 1815 Feb 05 DLC-16
To 1815 Feb 05 DLC-16
Fr 1815 Feb 06 DLC-16
To 1815 Feb 06 DLC-16
To 1815 Feb 06 4-0709
Fr 1815 Feb 06 DLC-16
To 1815 Feb 06 DLC-16
Fr 1815 Feb 06 DLC-16
Fr 1815 Feb 07 DLC-16
Fr 1815 Feb 07 DLC-16
To 1815 Feb 08 DLC-16
Fr 1815 Feb 08 DLC-16
Fr 1815 Feb 08 DLC-16
To 1815 Feb 08 DLC-16
Fr 1815 Feb 09# DLC-16
To 1815 Feb 10# 4-0716
Fr 1815 Feb 13 DLC-16
Fr 1815 Feb 13 DLC-16
Fr 1815 Feb 15 DLC-16
Fr 1815 Feb 16 DLC-16
Fr 1815 Feb 16 DLC-16
Fr 1815 Feb 16* 4-0750
Fr 1815 Feb 17 DLC-16
Fr 1815 Feb 20 DLC-16
Fr 1815 Feb 24 DLC-17
To 1815 Feb 25 DLC-62
To 1815 Feb 25* DLC-59
Fr 1815 Apr 05 DLC-18
Fr 1816 Apr 14 DLC-20

Claiborne William Ferdinand
Re 1821 Mar 07 leg 8-0160

Clampet Ezekiel
To 1807 Jan 22 fin DLC-4

Clark Edwin T
Fr 1832 Mar 20 M639-18

Clark Gasaway
To 1835 Sep 12 chk DLC-46
To 1835 Oct 02 chk DLC-47

Clark James
Fr 1832 Apr 16 M688-84

Clark James P
Fr 1829 Apr 05 M639-4
Fr 1833 Aug 22 M639-3

Clark James P et al
Fr 1836 Aug 16 31-1300
Fr 1839 Jun 24 DLC-52
To 1839 Jun 25 DLC-52

Clark John
To 1819 Apr 20 7-0486
To 1819 Apr 20* DLC-26
Fr 1819 May 24 DLC-27
To 1819 Jul 13 DLC-27

Clark John (cont)
To 1819 Jul 13* 7-0576
To 1819 Aug 18 7-0616
Fr 1819 Aug 18 DLC-27
Fr 1819 Nov 02 DLC-28
To 1819 Nov 23 DLC-28
Fr 1819 Nov 29 DLC-28
To 1820 Jan 06 7-0977
Fr 1820 May 23 DLC-29
To 1820 Jun 21 7-1126
To 1820 Jul 06 7-1137
To 1820 Nov 23 7-1420
Fr 1821 Mar 14 DLC-30
To 1821 Apr 09 8-0288
Clark John D
Re 1833 Mar 16 22-0775
Clark Lardner
Re c1790 leg 1-0075a
Clark M et al
Fr 1827 Aug 27 11-0822
To 1827 Sep 04 DLC-34
Clark Nathan
To 1835 May 25 28-0499
Clark Nathaniel
Fr 1837 Feb 11 M687-16
Clark Nathaniel et al
Fr 1837 cJan 32-1462
Clark Peter J et al
Fr 1833 Feb 06 22-0284
Clark Samuel
Fr 1831 May 09 M22-28
Clark Solomon
Fr 1833 Sep 13 M639-3
Clark Thomas
Fr 1805 Jul 09 fin DLC-3
Clark Thomas Norris
To 1802 Oct 10 fin DLC-2
Fr 1805 Jan 18 DLC-3
To 1811 Feb 19 2-0991
To 1816 Jun 25 lnd 5-0238
Fr 1816 Aug 18 DLC-21
Clark William (1770-1838)
Fr 1815 Jun 26 DLC-18
To 1815 Jun 27 DLC-62
Fr 1815 Jul 11 DLC-18
Fr 1815 Jul 16 DLC-18
Fr 1815 Jul 16* M222-16
Fr 1815 Jul 20 DLC-19
To 1815 Jul 25 DLC-62
Fr 1815 Aug 06 DLC-19
To 1815 Aug 21 DLC-62
To 1815 Aug 21* M222-16
Fr 1815 Sep 10 DLC-19
Fr 1815 Sep 23 DLC-19
To 1817 Jul 29 5-0946
Fr 1830 Jan 18 14-1450
Fr 1830 Jul 21 M222-27
Fr 1831 Aug 12 DLC-39
Fr 1835 Apr 08# M234-300
Clark William (1774-1851)
To 1829 Mar 13# fin 12-0997
To 1829 Apr 11# fin 12-1319
Clarke Egbert M
Fr 1837 Jan 02 M22-41
Clarke James
Fr 1834 Aug 09 M639-13
Clarke John
Re 1832 Jul 20 par 20-1182
Clarke Joshua et al
Fr 1830 cFeb M639-27
Clarke Robert
Re 1831 May 26 17-1445
Clarke Robert et al
Fr 1831 cJan 28 M639-1
Clarke Russell
Fr 1837 Feb 17 33-0740
Clarke Samuel J
Fr 1835 Oct 20# M873-87
Clarke Thomas C
Fr 1814 Jan 31 DLC-8
Fr 1814 Feb 05 DLC-8
Fr 1814 Feb 16 DLC-9
To 1814 Feb 17 DLC-61
Fr 1814 Feb 20 DLC-9
Fr 1814 Feb 21 DLC-9
Fr 1814 Feb 22 DLC-9
To 1814 Feb 23 DLC-61
Fr 1814 Mar 08 DLC-9
Fr 1815 Feb 01 DLC-16
Fr 1816 Jan 26 DLC-20
Fr 1816 Nov 08 DLC-21
Fr 1817 Feb 25 DLC-22
Clarke W C
Fr 1825 Mar 25 fin DLC-72
Clarke William
Re 1834 Jul 04 par 26-0135
Clarke Beecher & Co
Fr 1835 Oct 20# M179-81
Clary Ethan A
Fr 1837 Nov 14 DLC-50
Claxton Alexander
Fr 1830 Apr 14 15-0694
Clay Clement Comer
Fr 1829 Jul 07 M639-4
Fr 1830 Apr 08# M179-68
Fr 1832 cFeb 22 DLC-40
Fr 1832 Feb 27 DLC-40
Fr 1835 Feb 24 M234-242
Fr 1835 Sep 22 M639-4
Fr 1836 Jan 07 M639-14
Fr 1836 Jan 11 DLC-47
Fr 1836 Jul 18 31-1127
Fr 1836 Dec 31 DLC-49
Fr 1837 Nov 15 M687-7
Fr 1839 Jul 06 DLC-52
Fr 1842 Jul 18 DLC-54
Fr 1844 Feb 05 DLC-56
Fr 1844 Nov 23 DLC-57
Clay Henry
To 1808 Oct 27 DLC-4
Re 1827 Jul 18 11-0754
To 1828 11-0996
Re 1828 DLC-36
Fr 1840 Aug 20# 34-1570
Clay Henry M
Re 1841 Mar 08# leg 35-0244
Clay John Randolph
Re 1830 Jun 04 15-1288
Fr 1831 Jul 24 18-0260
Fr 1836 Mar 08 M35-13
Clay John W
To 1810 Mar 05 DLC-4
Clay Joseph
To 1839 Aug 05 DLC-52
Claybrooke John
To 1831 Jun 04# 17-1520
Claybrooke John Samuel
To 1833 May 23 22-1432

Clayton Alexander M			
	Fr 1829 Apr 21		M639-5
	Fr 1832 Oct 31		M639-4
	Fr 1834 Feb 25		24-1468
	Fr 1834 Mar 03		24-1524
	Fr 1834 Mar 04		24-1554
Clayton George R			
	Fr 1818 Apr 11		DLC-24
Clayton John Middleton			
	To 1835 Jan 17#		27-0245
Clayton Richard C			
	Fr 1839 Aug 07#	fin	DLC-52
	Fr 1839 Aug 07#	fin	DLC-52
Cleaveland Parker			
	Fr 1833 Jun 24		23-0053
Cleland Horatio			
	Fr 1816 Jun 02	fin	DLC-22
Clem George P			
	Fr 1842 Feb 10		DLC-54
Clement Adam			
	Fr 1807 Apr 18		DLC-4
Clement J M et al			
	Fr 1835 Jun 30		28-0838
Clement Joseph W et al			
	Fr 1833 Jan 04		M639-7
Clement Samuel			
	Fr 1815 Jan 26		4-0620
Clements _____ (Capt)			
	To 1814 Dec 19		DLC-62
Clements _____ et al			
	Fr 1832 Mar 03		M22-29
Clements Benjamin			
	To 1828 Mar 17		11-1173
	Fr 1829 May 25		M124-118
Clemson Eli B			
	Re c1816	mem	4-1312
Clench Robert			
	Re 1835 Dec 12	par	29-1097
	Re 1836 Jan 06	par	29-1469
Clendinen Alexander			
	Fr 1835 Nov 26		M179-81
Clephane Lewis			
	Fr 1830 Apr 22		M234-433
	Fr 1830 Apr 27		M234-433
Cleveland A P			
	Fr 1843 May 08		DLC-55
Cleveland Chauncey Fitch			
	Fr 1835 Feb 10		DLC-45
	Fr 1836 Mar 15		M687-17
	Fr 1842 Dec 16		DLC-54
	To 1843 Jan 13		DLC-55
Cleveland Jesse Franklin			
	Fr 1837 cJan 12		M22-41
Cleveland Jesse Franklin et al			
	Fr 1836 Jun 04		31-0312
	Fr 1836 Jun 04*		M234-113
Clew William			
	Re 1830 Mar 23	par	15-0439
	Re 1830 Apr 14	par	15-0696
	Re 1830 May 10	par	T967-1
Clifford Thomas & John			
	Fr 1798 Mar 26	fin	1-0648
	Fr 1804 Jun 26		DLC-75
	To 1804 Jul 24		1-1353
	To 1804 Nov 23		1-1411
	Fr 1804 Dec 14		1-1425
	To 1805 Mar 03		2-0020
	To 1805 Mar 25		2-0027
	Fr 1806 Feb 26		DLC-3
	To 1807 Aug 17#		2-0538
	To 1807 Sep 25#		2-0559
Clinch Duncan Lamont			
	Fr 1815 Aug 30		DLC-19
	To 1816 Sep 06		5-0454
	Fr 1816 Oct 28		DLC-21
	Fr 1816 Nov 15		DLC-22
	Fr 1821 Sep 17		DLC-30
	Re c1836 Jan		29-1422
	Fr 1836 Apr 26		M567-119
Clinton Charles A			
	Fr 1829 Apr 14		12-1341
	Fr 1829 Apr 28		M124-118
	Fr 1829 Jun 02		M639-4
Clinton Charles A et al			
	Fr 1834 Jan		M639-18
Clinton DeWitt			
	Fr 1831 Nov 21		M222-29
	Fr 1831 Nov 24		M222-29
Clinton DeWitt (1769-1828)			
	Re 1819 Feb 21	add	7-0308
	Fr 1821 Oct 02		DLC-30
	Fr 1823 Aug 02		9-0623
	To 1823 Aug 31		DLC-32
	Fr 1823 Sep 20		9-0671
	To 1824 Aug 18		10-0851
	Fr 1824 Dec 02		10-0964
	Fr 1827 Mar 22		11-0508
	Fr 1827 Nov 22		11-0930
	Re 1828 Mar 15		11-1167
Clinton Franklin			
	Fr 1836 Apr		30-0964
Clinton George W			
	Fr 1829 Jun 12		M124-119
	Fr 1842 Aug 03		DLC-54
Clopton John H			
	Fr 1827 Jan 16	fin	DLC-34
	To 1834 May 07#	fin	DLC-44
Clossey M Franklin			
	Fr 1833 Mar 07		M639-4
Cloud Joseph			
	Fr 1835 Dec 01		29-0707
Coatney John			
	Re 1790 May 06	leg	1-0075m
Cobb Jeremiah et al			
	Fr 1831 Aug 29		M221-111
Cobbs Robert L			
	Fr 1814 Dec 20		DLC-14
	Fr 1829 Apr 28		M639-5
	Re 1839 Apr 01		34-0703
Cobbs Waddy Vine			
	Fr 1816 Mar 26		DLC-20
	Fr 1838 May 08		DLC-51
Coburn John			
	Fr 1833 Jan 05		DLC-41
	Fr 1834 May 03	fin	DLC-44
	Fr 1834 Aug 12	fin	DLC-44
	Fr 1834 Oct 01	fin	DLC-44
	Fr 1834 Oct 09	fin	DLC-44
	Fr 1834 Oct 18	fin	DLC-44
	Fr 1834 Oct 25	fin	DLC-44
	Fr 1834 Nov 08	fin	DLC-45
	Fr 1834 Nov 15	fin	DLC-45
	Fr 1834 Nov 21	fin	DLC-45
	Fr 1834 Dec 03	fin	DLC-45
	Fr 1834 Dec 08	fin	DLC-45
	Fr 1834 Dec 15	fin	DLC-45
	Fr 1834 Dec 24	fin	DLC-45
	Fr 1834 Dec 26	fin	DLC-45

Name	Dir	Date		Source
Coburn John (cont)				
	Fr	1835 Jan 02	fin	DLC-45
	Fr	1835 Jan 02	fin	DLC-45
	Fr	1835 Jan 08	fin	DLC-45
	Fr	1835 Jan 15	fin	DLC-45
	Fr	1835 Jan 20	fin	DLC-45
	Fr	1835 Jan 22	fin	DLC-45
	Fr	1835 Jan 26	fin	DLC-45
	Fr	1835 Apr 01	fin	DLC-46
	Fr	1835 Apr 01	fin	DLC-46
	Fr	1835 Apr 11	fin	DLC-46
	Fr	1835 Apr 16	fin	DLC-46
	Fr	1835 Apr 27	fin	DLC-46
	Fr	1835 Jun 02	fin	DLC-46
	Fr	1835 Jun 10	fin	DLC-46
	Fr	1835 Jul 02	fin	DLC-46
	Fr	1835 Jul 04	fin	DLC-46
	Fr	1835 Jul 06	fin	DLC-46
	Fr	1835 Jul 15	fin	DLC-46
	Fr	1835 Jul 24	fin	DLC-46
	Fr	1835 Aug 01	fin	DLC-46
	Fr	1835 Aug 01	fin	DLC-46
	Fr	1835 Oct 01	fin	DLC-47
	Fr	1835 Oct 01	fin	DLC-47
	Fr	1835 Oct 09	fin	DLC-47
	Fr	1835 Oct 17	fin	DLC-47
	Fr	1835 Oct 24	fin	DLC-47
	Fr	1835 Nov 02	fin	DLC-47
	Fr	1835 Nov 02	fin	DLC-47
	Fr	1835 Nov 09	fin	DLC-47
	Fr	1835 Nov 16	fin	DLC-47
	Fr	1835 Nov 23	fin	DLC-47
	Fr	1835 Dec 07	fin	DLC-47
	Fr	1835 Dec 16	fin	DLC-47
	Fr	1835 Dec 22	fin	DLC-47
	Fr	1836 Feb 03	fin	DLC-47
	Fr	1836 Feb 09	fin	DLC-47
	Fr	1836 Feb 19	fin	DLC-47
	Fr	1836 Apr 01	fin	DLC-47
	Fr	1836 Apr 04	fin	DLC-47
	Fr	1836 Apr 05	fin	DLC-48
	Fr	1836 Apr 08	fin	DLC-48
	Fr	1836 Apr 16	fin	DLC-48
	Fr	1836 Apr 22	fin	DLC-48
	Fr	1836 May 02	fin	DLC-48
	Fr	1836 May 02	fin	DLC-48
	Fr	1836 May 09	fin	DLC-48
	Fr	1836 May 16	fin	DLC-48
	Fr	1836 May 23	fin	DLC-48
Cochran A et al				
	Fr	1835 Dec		M639-3
Cochran Andrew et al				
	Fr	1835 cJan		DLC-59
Cochran George				
	Fr	1790 Nov 03		DLC-75
	Fr	1791 Oct 21		DLC-1
	Fr	1796 Nov 18		DLC-1
	Fr	1797 Apr 15		DLC-1
	Fr	1801 Mar 26		DLC-2
Cochran John				
	Fr	1835 Feb 03		DLC-45
Cochran John C et al				
	Fr	1837 Jan 31		M687-20
Cochran Robert et al				
	Fr	1835 cJan		DLC-59
Cochran William				
	Fr	1839 Aug 21		DLC-52
Cochran William & Brothers				
	Fr	1802 May 17	fin	DLC-2
Cochrane Alexander				
	Fr	1815 Feb 12		DLC-16
	Fr	1815 Feb 13		DLC-16
	To	1815 Feb 20		4-0767
	To	1815 Feb 20*		DLC-16
	To	1815 Feb 21		4-0774
	To	1815 Feb 21*		DLC-62
Cochrane Alexander Fulton				
	Fr	1816 Aug 05		DLC-21
Cocke John				
	Fr	1809 Jun 05		2-0833
	Fr	1813 Oct 02		DLC-61
	To	1813 Oct 10		DLC-15
	To	1813 Oct 10*		DLC-61
	To	1813 Oct 23		DLC-61
	To	1813 Oct 23*		3-0540
	To	1813 Oct 31		DLC-61
	To	1813 Oct 31*		3-0556
	To	1813 Nov 03		DLC-7
	To	1813 Nov 03*		M222-7
	Fr	1813 Nov 14		DLC-61
	To	1813 Nov 16		DLC-61
	To	1813 Nov 17		DLC-61
	To	1813 Nov 18		DLC-61
	Fr	1813 Nov 20		DLC-61
	Fr	1813 Nov 27		DLC-61
	To	1813 Dec 02		DLC-61
	Fr	1813 Dec 03		DLC-61
	Fr	1813 Dec 05		DLC-61
	To	1813 Dec 06		DLC-61
	To	1813 Dec 12		DLC-61
	To	1813 Dec 12		DLC-61
	Fr	1813 Dec 13		DLC-61
	Fr	1813 Dec 13*		M221-56
	To	1813 Dec 14		DLC-61
	To	1813 Dec 15		DLC-61
	To	1813 Dec 15*		3-0675
	To	1813 Dec 21		DLC-61
	To	1813 Dec 21*		DLC-8
	To	1813 Dec 24		DLC-61
	To	1813 Dec 27		DLC-61
	To	1813 Dec 28		DLC-8
	Fr	1814 Jan 16		DLC-8
	To	1814 Jan 31		3-0838
	To	1814 Jan 31*		DLC-61
	To	1814 Feb 02		DLC-61
Cocke Stephen				
	Fr	1835 Sep 14		29-0036
	Fr	1835 Dec 20		DLC-73
Cocke Stephen et al				
	Fr	1836 Jan 14		M639-26
Cocke William				
	Fr	1797 Apr 18		DLC-1
	To	1797 Nov 09		DLC-2
	To	1798 Jun 24		DLC-2
	To	1798 Jun 24		DLC-2
	To	1798 Jun 25		DLC-2
	Fr	1798 Jun 25		DLC-2
	Fr	1798 cJul		1-0669
	Fr	1802 Mar 26		DLC-2
	To	1814 Jan 28		DLC-8
	To	1814 Jan 28*		3-0820
	Fr	1814 Jan 28		DLC-8
	Fr	1814 Feb 07		DLC-8
	Fr	1814 Feb 09		DLC-8
	Fr	1814 Feb 14		DLC-9
	Fr	1814 Feb 15		DLC-9
	To	1814 Feb 17		DLC-61
	Fr	1814 Feb 22		DLC-9

Fr 1814 Feb 24 DLC-9
Fr 1814 Mar 05 DLC-9
Fr 1814 Mar 12 DLC-9
Fr 1814 Mar 14 DLC-9
Fr 1814 Mar 23 DLC-71
Fr 1814 Apr 06 DLC-10
Fr 1814 Apr 12 DLC-10
Fr 1814 May 20 DLC-10
Fr 1814 Nov 22 DLC-14
Fr 1815 Aug 18 DLC-19
To 1815 Aug 22 DLC-62
Fr 1815 Aug 27 DLC-19
To 1815 Sep 04 DLC-62
Fr 1816 Mar 25 DLC-20
Fr 1816 Jun 12 DLC-20
Fr 1816 Jul 09 DLC-21
Fr 1816 Jul 22 DLC-21
Fr 1816 Jul 27 DLC-21
Fr 1816 Jul 30 DLC-21
Fr 1816 Aug 03 DLC-21
Fr 1816 Oct 19 DLC-21
Fr 1817 Jan 15 5-0704
Fr 1817 May 24 DLC-22
Fr 1817 Aug 25 DLC-23
Fr 1820 May 01 M221-89
Fr 1824 Jul 10 DLC-33

Cockfighting
Re 1779 Mar 22 mem DLC-1

Cockrill John
Re 1806 Feb 01 leg 2-0137

Coddington David L
Fr 1843 Mar 22 DLC-55

Coddington Jonathan J
Fr 1829 Mar 13 M639-5
Fr 1844 Sep 17 36-0878

Codwise D
Fr 1837 Feb 24 M687-6

Coe Alvan
To 1829 Mar 19 12-1050

Coffee Alexander Donelson
Fr 1841 May 30 DLC-53
Fr 1843 Feb 16 35-1231
To 1843 Feb 22 35-1253

Coffee Andrew Jackson
Fr 1831 Nov 06 DLC-40
Re 1836 Jan 20 mem 30-0153
Fr 1840 Jan 12 DLC-52
To 1840 Apr 25 34-1322
Fr 1840 Nov 25 DLC-53
To 1841 Jan 22 35-0210
Fr 1843 Mar 11 DLC-55
Fr 1844 Sep 07 36-0844
To 1844 Sep 11 36-0861
Fr 1844 Sep 20 DLC-57
Fr 1845 Feb 10 DLC-57
To 1845 Feb 17 36-1494

Coffee John
To nd 37-0271
To 1801 May 29# 1-0878
To 1803 Jan 06 fin DLC-2
Fr 1803 Dec 29 DLC-3
To 1804 Jan 07 1-1270
To 1804 Jan 07 1-1272
To 1804 Feb 28 1-1288
To 1804 Mar 04 1-1290
To 1804 Mar 07 1-1292
To 1804 Apr 09 1-1304
To 1804 Apr 13 1-1312
Fr 1804 Apr 23 DLC-3
To 1804 Apr 28 1-1325
To 1804 May 03 1-1329
To 1804 May 13 1-1334
To 1804 Jun 21 1-1342
Fr 1804 Oct 02 DLC-3
To 1805 Feb 04 leg DLC-3
Fr 1805 Mar 11 DLC-3
Fr 1806 Feb 05 2-0148
Re 1806 Apr 08 leg 2-0208
To 1806 cJun 14 2-0272
Fr 1806 Jul 04 DLC-4
To 1806 Jul 20 2-0300
Fr 1807 Mar 21 2-0477
To 1807 Apr 01 DLC-4
To 1807 Apr 20# 2-0490
Fr 1807 May 16# fin 2-0495
Fr 1807 cSep 01# fin 2-0552
Fr 1808 Nov DLC-75
To 1808 Dec 24 2-0754
Fr 1809 Feb 21 2-0774
To 1809 Mar 17 2-0780
Fr 1810 May 14 DLC-4
To 1810 Dec 24 lnd 2-0976
To 1811 Nov 29 2-1019
To 1812 Mar 25 DLC-5
To 1812 Mar 26 DLC-5
Fr 1812 Mar 30 2-1060
To 1812 Apr 03 2-1063
Fr 1812 Aug 24 DLC-5
To 1812 Sep 15 2-1247
To 1812 Dec 13 DLC-61
To 1812 Dec 19 DLC-61
To 1812 Dec 19* DLC-5
To 1812 Dec 19* 2-1303
To 1813 Jan 01 DLC-61
To 1813 Jan 01* DLC-65
To 1813 Jan 01 DLC-5
To 1813 Jan 07 DLC-5
To 1813 Jan 07* DLC-61
To 1813 Feb 16 DLC-6
To 1813 Feb 16 DLC-6
To 1813 Mar 04 3-0287
To 1813 Mar 06 DLC-6
Fr 1813 Mar 13 DLC-65
To 1813 Mar 14 DLC-6
To 1813 Mar 20 DLC-61
To 1813 Mar 20* 3-0339
To 1813 Mar 20 DLC-61
To 1813 Mar 20* 3-0340
To 1813 Mar 20* DLC-75
To 1813 Mar 24 DLC-61
Fr 1813 Mar 25 leg 3-0359
Fr 1813 Mar 26 3-0362
Fr 1813 Mar 28 3-0364
Fr 1813 Apr 04 DLC-6
Fr 1813 Apr 05 DLC-6
Fr 1813 Apr 11 DLC-6
Fr 1813 Apr 19 DLC-6
To 1813 Sep 19 DLC-61
To 1813 Sep 25 DLC-6
To 1813 Sep 25* DLC-61
To 1813 Sep 26 DLC-6
To 1813 Sep 26* DLC-61
To 1813 Sep 26* DLC-64
To 1813 Sep 26 DLC-61
To 1813 Sep 27 DLC-6
To 1813 Sep 28 DLC-6
To 1813 Sep 28 DLC-65
To 1813 Sep 29 3-0492

Coffee John (cont)

Fr 1813 Oct 04	DLC-6
Fr 1813 Oct 04*	DLC-61
Fr 1813 Oct 04	DLC-6
Fr 1813 Oct 04*	DLC-61
Fr 1813 Oct 06	DLC-6
Fr 1813 Oct 06	DLC-6
To 1813 Oct 07	DLC-6
To 1813 Oct 09	DLC-6
To 1813 Oct 09	DLC-61
Fr 1813 Oct 22	DLC-7
Fr 1813 Oct 22*	DLC-61
Fr 1813 Oct 29	3-0554
To 1813 Oct 30	DLC-7
To 1813 Nov 02	3-0561
To 1813 Nov 02*	DLC-7
Fr 1813 Nov 02	DLC-7
To 1813 Nov 06	DLC-7
Fr 1813 Nov 23	DLC-7
To 1813 Dec 05	DLC-7
To 1813 Dec 09	DLC-7
Fr 1813 Dec 10	DLC-7
To 1813 Dec 11	DLC-7
To 1813 Dec 12	DLC-7
Fr 1813 Dec 12	DLC-7
To 1813 Dec 13	DLC-7
To 1813 Dec 16	DLC-7
Fr 1813 Dec 17	DLC-7
Fr 1813 Dec 17*	DLC-61
Fr 1813 Dec 17	DLC-7
To 1813 Dec 18	DLC-7
To 1813 Dec 18*	DLC-61
Fr 1813 Dec 18	DLC-7
Fr 1813 Dec 18*	DLC-61
Fr 1813 Dec 20	DLC-7
To 1813 Dec 21	DLC-61
Fr 1813 Dec 22	DLC-7
To 1813 Dec 22	DLC-7
To 1813 Dec 23	DLC-8
To 1813 Dec 23*	DLC-61
Fr 1813 Dec 23	DLC-8
Fr 1813 Dec 23	DLC-8
To 1813 Dec 24	DLC-8
To 1813 Dec 25	DLC-8
To 1813 Dec 25*	3-0718
To 1813 Dec 27	DLC-8
To 1813 Dec 27*	DLC-61
Fr 1813 Dec 27	DLC-8
To 1813 Dec 27	DLC-8
To 1813 Dec 27*	DLC-61
Fr 1813 Dec 28	DLC-8
To 1813 Dec 29	DLC-8
Fr 1813 Dec 29	DLC-8
Fr 1813 Dec 30	DLC-8
To 1813 Dec 31	DLC-8
To 1814 Jan 02	DLC-8
To 1814 Jan 04	DLC-8
Fr 1814 Jan 07	DLC-8
Fr 1814 Jan 07	DLC-8
Fr 1814 Jan 07*	DLC-61
Fr 1814 Jan 14	DLC-8
Fr 1814 Jan 14*	DLC-61
Fr 1814 Jan 15	DLC-8
Fr 1814 Jan 15*	DLC-61
To 1814 Jan 30	DLC-8
Fr 1814 Feb 03	DLC-8
To 1814 Feb 08	DLC-8
To 1814 Feb 08*	DLC-61
To 1814 Feb 17	DLC-9
Fr 1814 Feb 17	DLC-9

Fr 1814 Mar 12	DLC-9
To 1814 Mar 17	DLC-9
Fr 1814 Apr 01	3-0944
Fr 1814 Apr 01*	M221-56
To 1814 Apr 15	DLC-10
Fr 1814 May 01	DLC-10
To 1814 May 01	DLC-10
To 1814 Jul 17	DLC-11
To 1814 Aug 10	DLC-71
Fr 1814 Oct 04	DLC-13
Fr 1814 Oct 04*	4-0254
Fr 1814 Oct 14	DLC-13
To 1814 Oct 20	DLC-13
To 1814 Oct 20	DLC-13
To 1814 Oct 20*	4-0279
Fr 1814 Oct 23	DLC-13
Fr 1814 Nov 08	M221-63
Fr 1814 Nov 08*	DLC-14
Fr 1814 Nov 18	DLC-14
Fr 1814 Nov 21	DLC-14
To 1814 Dec 11	DLC-14
To 1814 Dec 11*	4-0391
Fr 1814 Dec 13	DLC-14
Fr 1814 Dec 13*	4-0393
Fr 1814 Dec 15	DLC-14
Fr 1814 Dec 15	DLC-14
Fr 1814 Dec 15*	4-0400
To 1814 Dec 16	DLC-14
To 1814 Dec 16*	4-0405
Fr 1814 Dec 17	DLC-14
To 1814 Dec 17	DLC-14
To 1814 Dec 17*	DLC-62
To 1814 Dec 17*	4-0408
To 1814 Dec 19	DLC-14
To 1814 Dec 19*	4-0422
Fr 1815 Jan 22	DLC-15
Fr 1815 Feb 02	DLC-16
Fr 1815 Mar 05	DLC-17
To 1815 Mar 18	DLC-17
To 1815 Mar 18*	DLC-62
Fr 1815 Mar 26	DLC-17
Fr 1815 Apr 01	4-0923
Fr 1815 Apr 05	DLC-18
Fr 1815 Apr 06	4-0976
To 1815 Apr 24	DLC-71
Fr 1815 Apr 27	4-1015
To 1815 Jul 28	DLC-19
To 1815 Dec 04	4-1272
Fr 1815 Dec 27	DLC-20
Fr 1816 Jan 21	DLC-20
To 1816 Feb 02	4-1372
Fr 1816 Feb 08	DLC-20
To 1816 Feb 13	4-1392
To 1816 Feb 13*	DLC-20
To 1816 Feb 13	4-1396
To 1816 Feb 13*	DLC-62
To 1816 Feb 13	4-1398
Fr 1816 Feb 18	DLC-20
To 1816 Feb 21	4-1408
To 1816 Apr 13	5-0032
To 1816 May 08	5-0073
To 1816 Jul 19	5-0312
To 1816 Jul 21	5-0321
Fr 1816 Jul 24	DLC-21
To 1816 Jul 26	5-0327
Fr 1816 Aug 29	5-0443
To 1816 Aug 31	5-0447
To 1816 Sep 19	5-0489
To 1816 Dec 26	5-0636

Fr	1816 Dec 29		DLC-22
To	1817 Mar 29		5-0796
To	1817 Apr 08		5-0804
To	1817 May 20		5-0862
To	1817 May 24		5-0868
To	1817 Jun 21		5-0898
To	1817 Jul 13		5-0928
To	1817 Aug 12		5-0964
To	1817 Aug 21		5-0993
To	1817 Sep 28		5-1023
To	1817 Sep 29		5-1026
To	1817 Sep 30		5-1030
To	1817 Oct 06		5-1101
To	1818 Jan 14		5-1281
To	1818 Jan 27		5-1344
Fr	1818 Feb 12		DLC-24
To	1818 Mar 26		6-0170
To	1818 Dec 08	fin	7-0044
To	c1819		7-0110
To	1819 Jan 04		7-0114
To	1819 Apr 03		7-0453
To	1819 May 04		7-0505
To	1819 Aug 20		7-0629
To	1819 Nov 09	fin	7-0847
Fr	1820 Jan 12		DLC-28
To	1820 Jul 19		7-1169
To	1820 Dec 13		8-0021
To	1821 Jan 05		8-0046
To	1821 Feb 06		8-0099
To	1821 Mar 01		8-0149
To	1821 Apr 11		8-0302
To	1821 Apr 14		8-0320
To	1821 May 01		8-0412
To	1821 May 11		8-0472
To	1821 Jun 27		8-0703
To	1821 Jul 04		8-0767
To	1821 Jul 18		8-0870
To	1821 Jul 21		8-0882
Fr	1821 Jul 25		DLC-30
To	1821 Jul 26		8-0906
To	1821 Aug 10		8-1040
To	1821 Aug 18#		8-1069
To	1821 Aug 26		8-1105
To	1822 Feb 25		9-0035
To	1822 Feb 28		9-0040
To	1822 Mar 14		9-0048
To	1822 Mar 20		9-0066
To	1822 Mar 30		9-0086
Fr	1822 Aug 05	leg	9-0232
To	1822 Sep 29		9-0277
To	1822 Oct 04		9-0280
To	1822 Nov 20		9-0311
To	1822 Nov 27		9-0326
To	1822 Dec 21		9-0364
To	1822 Dec 27		9-0374
Re	1823 Jan 08	add	9-0386
To	1823 Jan 10		9-0397
To	1823 Jan 24		9-0428
To	1823 Jan 27	fin	9-0432
To	1823 Feb 17		9-0451
To	1823 Feb 21		9-0462
To	1823 Mar 01		9-0467
To	1823 Mar 10		9-0486
Fr	1823 Apr 06		9-0515
To	1823 Apr 15		9-0524
To	1823 Apr 28		9-0533
To	1823 May 24		9-0569
To	1823 Jul 03		9-0604
To	1823 Aug 15		9-0637
To	1823 Aug 22		9-0642
To	1823 Sep 12		9-0656
To	1823 Oct 05		9-0680
Fr	1823 Oct 19		DLC-32
To	1823 Oct 24		9-0709
To	1823 Nov 08		9-0735
To	1823 Nov 09		9-0747
To	1823 Dec 31		9-0868
Fr	1824 Jan		9-0875
To	1824 Jan 05		9-0891
To	1824 Feb 15		10-0457
To	1824 Feb 22		10-0464
To	1824 Mar 04		10-0512
To	1824 Mar 28		10-0604
To	1824 May 07		10-0708
Fr	1824 Jun 08		DLC-32
To	1824 Jun 18		10-0791
To	1824 Jun 21		10-0802
To	1824 Jul 01		10-0818
To	1824 Sep 20		10-0894
To	1824 Sep 23		10-0899
To	1824 Dec 27		10-1001
To	1825 Jan 05		10-1032
To	1825 Jan 06		10-1042
To	1825 Jan 23		10-1081
To	1825 Feb 19		10-1129
To	1825 Mar 02		10-1201
Fr	1825 Apr 23		DLC-33
To	1825 Apr 24		10-1242
To	1825 May 08		10-1264
To	1825 May 19		10-1275
Fr	1825 Jun 02		DLC-33
To	1825 Jun 06		10-1303
To	1825 Jun 07		10-1307
To	1825 Jul 09		10-1351
To	1825 Jul 23		10-1361
To	1825 Aug 02		10-1399
Fr	1825 Aug 31	mem	10-1411
To	1825 Oct 12		11-0013
To	1825 Oct 12		11-0017
To	1825 Oct 30		11-0051
To	1825 Dec 01		11-0065
To	1825 Dec 28		11-0077
Fr	1826	lnd	11-0088
To	1826 Feb 02		11-0125
To	1826 May 02		11-0201
Fr	1826 Jun 10		11-0242
To	1826 Jun 19		11-0253
To	1826 Jun 21		11-0257
To	1826 Jul 31		11-0335
To	1826 Aug 20		11-0341
To	1826 Sep		11-0349
To	1826 Sep 02		11-0353
To	1826 Sep 25		11-0371
Fr	1826 Oct 01		DLC-34
To	1826 Oct 05		11-0375
Fr	1826 Oct 11		DLC-34
Fr	1826 Dec 14		DLC-34
To	1826 Dec 20		11-0432
Fr	1827 Jan 20	fin	11-0473
To	1827 Feb 15	fin	11-0488
To	1827 Mar 16		11-0504
To	1827 Apr 03		11-0552
To	1827 Apr 08		11-0559
To	1827 Apr 13		11-0564
Fr	1827 May 12	fin	11-0582
To	1827 May 19		11-0597
To	1827 Jun 02	fin	11-0677
Fr	1827 Jun 21		DLC-34

Coffee John (cont)		
To 1827 Jul 01		11-0725
To 1827 Jul 30		11-0780
To 1827 Sep 29		11-0880
Fr 1827 Nov 20	fin	11-0926
To 1827 Nov 27		11-0933
To 1827 Dec 05		11-0946
To 1827 Dec 17		11-0960
To 1827 Dec 22		11-0974
Fr 1828 Jan 19	fin	11-1063
To 1828 Jan 23		11-1070
Fr 1828 Feb 06		11-1098
To 1828 Feb 16		11-1119
To 1828 Feb 26		11-1145
To 1828 Apr 08		11-1204
Fr 1828 Apr 11		11-1210
Fr 1828 Apr 13		11-1211
To 1828 Apr 24		11-1220
Fr 1828 May 01		11-1226
To 1828 May 12		12-0005
To 1828 Jun 20		12-0021
Fr 1828 Jul 02		DLC-35
To 1828 Aug 04		12-0116
To 1828 Aug 11		12-0128
To 1828 Oct 29		12-0247
To 1828 Nov 11		12-0261
To 1828 Nov 24		12-0286
To 1828 Nov 24		12-0288
To 1828 Dec 11		12-0313
To 1828 Dec 30	leg	12-0345
To 1828 Dec 30	leg	12-0347
To 1829 Jan 17		12-0457
Fr 1829 Jan 21	fin	12-0468
To 1829 Mar 19		12-1052
To 1829 Mar 22		12-1074
Fr 1829 Apr 03#		DLC-36
Fr 1829 May 25		M639-20
To 1829 May 30		13-0499
To 1829 Jun 13		13-0651
To 1829 Jul 21		13-0906
To 1829 Sep 21		13-1393
To 1829 Oct 04		14-0099
To 1829 Oct 19#	fin	14-0200
To c1829 Nov 19		37-0297
Fr 1829 Nov 28		DLC-37
Fr 1830 Mar 02		DLC-37
Fr 1830 Mar 02		DLC-37
To 1830 Apr 10		15-0656
To 1830 May 08		15-0959
To 1830 May 31		15-1232
To 1830 Jun 14		15-1385
To 1830 Jul 09		16-0007
To 1830 Jul 20		16-0031
To 1830 Aug 15		16-0108
To 1830 Aug 27		16-0182
Fr 1830 Sep 29		DLC-38
To 1830 Oct 03		16-0304
To 1830 Oct 16		16-0394
To 1830 Dec 06		16-1343
Fr 1830 Dec 12		16-1410
To 1830 Dec 28		17-0023
Fr 1830 Dec 29		DLC-38
Fr 1831	fin	17-0081
Fr 1831 Jan 01		DLC-38
To 1831 Jan 19		17-0291
Fr 1831 Feb 06		DLC-39
Fr 1831 Feb 16		DLC-39
To 1831 Apr 24		17-1220
Fr 1831 Apr 28		DLC-39
Fr 1831 May 03		DLC-39
To 1831 May 13		17-1359
To 1831 May 26		17-1446
To 1831 May 29		17-1469
Fr 1831 May 30		DLC-39
To 1831 Jun 19		18-0042
Fr 1831 Jul 09		DLC-39
To 1831 Sep 06		18-0682
To 1831 Sep 07		18-0693
Fr 1831 Sep 11		DLC-40
Fr 1831 Sep 23		M234-185
Fr 1831 Sep 23*		18-0874
To 1831 Oct 03		18-0911
To 1831 Oct 04#		18-0920
To 1831 Oct 23		18-1102
To 1831 Nov 20		18-1327
To 1831 Nov 21		18-1462
Fr 1831 Dec 03		M234-169
To 1832 Jan 21		19-0808
To 1832 Jan 26#		19-0867
To 1832 Jan 27		19-0881
Fr 1832 Feb 06		19-0974
To 1832 Feb 19		19-1161
Fr 1832 Feb 24		DLC-40
To 1832 Mar 09		19-1367
To 1832 Mar 13		19-1429
To 1832 Mar 26		19-1552
Fr 1832 Mar 30		DLC-38
Fr 1832 Apr 01		DLC-40
To 1832 Apr 07		20-0160
To 1832 Jul 17		20-1109
To 1832 Aug 18		20-1324
To 1832 Sep 17	lnd	21-0024
To 1832 Oct		21-0060
To 1832 Nov 06		21-0343
To 1832 Nov 26		21-0576
Fr 1832 Nov 30		DLC-41
Fr 1832 Dec 05		DLC-41
Fr 1832 Dec 12		21-1002
To 1832 Dec 14		21-1046
To 1832 Dec 17		21-1079
To 1833 Mar 16		22-0776
To 1833 Mar 16		22-0780
To 1833 Mar 17		22-0791
Fr 1833 Mar 25		DLC-42
To 1833 Apr 09		22-0971
To 1833 May 03		22-1272
To 1833 May 11		22-1341
Fr 1833 May 26		M567-80
Fr 1833 Jul 03		M639-26
Re 1834 Dec 24		26-1576
Coffee John et al		
Fr 1814 May 10		DLC-10
Coffee John & Co		
Re 1803 Feb 25	leg	1-1085
Fr 1804 Feb 10	fin	DLC-3
Coffee John (GA)		
Fr 1830 Jul 10		M234-237
Fr 1834 Mar 04		24-1557
Coffee John (GA) et al		
Fr c1836		29-1387
Coffee John Donelson		
To nd		37-0270
To nd		37-0272
To 1831 Dec 26#		19-0418
To 1832 Aug 25		20-1379
To 1833 Feb 23#		22-0454
Fr 1833 Aug 17		DLC-43
To 1833 Aug 31		23-0558
To 1833 Dec 17#		24-0549

To 1833 Dec 30 24-0686
To 1834 Feb 25# DLC-44
To 1834 Apr 06 25-0599
Fr 1834 Sep 02 DLC-44
Fr 1834 Nov 02 DLC-45
To 1834 Nov 14 26-0902
Fr 1834 Dec 10 DLC-45
To 1834 Dec 24 26-1578
Fr 1835 Jan 17 DLC-45
Fr 1835 May 17 DLC-46
To 1835 Jun 01 28-0549
To 1835 Nov 27 29-0602
Fr 1836 Jan 31 DLC-47
To 1836 Apr 11 30-1132
To 1836 Apr 16# 30-1193
To 1837 Jul 13 33-1373

Coffee Mary (Donelson)
To 1822 Mar 20 9-0068
To c1829 Jul 28 37-0292
To 1833 Jul 22 23-0189
To 1834 Oct 20 26-0663
To 1843 Feb 10 35-1206

Coffee Mary Donelson
see also Hutchings M D C
Fr 1833 Feb 23# 22-0454
Fr 1833 Apr 29 22-1197
To 1833 May 29 22-1495
To 1833 Aug 15 23-0334
To 1833 Sep 15 23-0711

Coffee Rice
To 1812 Dec 23 lnd 2-1309

Coffey James
Fr 1826 Jul 04 DLC-34

Coffin Charles
Fr 1821 Mar 08 DLC-30
Fr 1829 Jan 21 DLC-36

Cogdell John Stevens
Fr 1831 Mar 25 17-0971

Cohens M I
To 1837 Mar 04 33-1062

Coke Thomas William
To 1834 Oct 01 26-0464

Colbert George
To 1812 Jun 05 DLC-5
Fr 1814 Jan 10 DLC-8
To 1816 Feb 13 DLC-20
Fr 1816 Mar 01 DLC-20
To 1818 Oct 17 DLC-62
To 1818 Oct 17* T494-1

Colbert George et al
Fr 1833 Jan 14 21-1414
Fr 1834 Apr 21 T494-3

Colbert James
Fr 1814 Jan 10 DLC-8
Fr 1814 Sep 29 DLC-12
Fr 1816 Jul 17 5-0305
Fr 1816 Sep 5-0449
Fr 1818 Jul 17 M271-2
Fr 1818 Jul 17* 6-1138
To 1818 Jul 24 DLC-25
To 1818 Jul 24* 6-1153
To 1818 Aug 04 DLC-25
Fr 1818 Aug 08 M271-2

Colbert James et al
Fr 1836 May 18 M234-145

Colbert Levi
Fr 1817 Jul 23 M221-74
To 1818 Oct 17 DLC-62
To 1818 Oct 17* T494-1
Fr 1818 Oct 20 DLC-25
Fr 1832 Feb 23 M234-136
Fr 1832 Feb 23* 19-1203
Fr 1834 Mar 31 M234-136
Fr 1834 Mar 31* 25-0509

Colbert Levi et al
Fr 1832 Nov 22 M234-136
Fr 1833 Dec 27 24-0597

Colbert Pitman
Fr 1835 Aug 27 28-1411
Fr 1835 Aug 27 28-1415

Colbert Susan
Fr 1831 Mar 28 M234-136
Fr 1831 Mar 28* 17-0995

Colclozer Jacob
Fr 1835 Aug 22 fin DLC-46
Fr 1835 Sep 16 fin DLC-47
Fr 1835 Sep 22 fin DLC-47
Fr 1835 Sep 22 fin DLC-47
Fr 1835 Sep 23 fin DLC-47
Fr 1835 Sep 23 fin DLC-47
Fr 1835 Sep 24 fin DLC-46
Fr 1835 Sep 25 fin DLC-47
Fr 1835 Sep 28 fin DLC-47
Fr 1836 Oct 03# DLC-49
Fr 1836 Oct 11# fin DLC-49
Fr 1836 Oct 26# DLC-49

Colden Cadwallader David
To 1819 Feb 23 add 7-0310
Fr 1819 Feb 23 add 7-0309

Cole ______ (Capt) et al
Fr 1835 Jan 01 27-0063

Cole Abner Womick
Fr 1815 Feb 10 DLC-16

Cole Henry et al
Fr 1835 Jan 07 DLC-45

Cole James C
Fr 1834 Jun 10 25-1297

Cole John
Fr 1844 Jun 04 36-0573

Cole Joseph
To 1805 Oct 15 leg 2-0087
Re 1806 Sep leg 2-0324

Cole Joseph G et al
Fr 1837 Jan M687-16

Cole Mathew M
Fr 1833 Mar 15 M639-5
Re 1833 Apr 11 22-0982

Cole William H
Fr 1836 Nov 17 32-0548

Colebridge Samuel K
Fr 1829 May 03 M639-20

Coleman Blackman
Fr 1830 Dec 03 16-0978
Fr 1831 Jul 13 M22-28
Fr 1837 Sep 20 DLC-50

Coleman Blackman et al
Fr 1837 Jun 25 33-1343

Coleman Daniel
Fr 1843 Sep 17 DLC-55

Coleman Hannah
Fr 1830 Apr 27 M124-123

Coleman James
Fr 1841 Feb 06 fin DLC-55

Coleman John H et al
Fr 1824 Nov 17 10-0957
To 1824 Nov 17 10-0958

Coleman Joseph
To 1811 Oct 23 chk DLC-5
Fr 1815 Sep 24 DLC-68

Coleman Joseph (cont)
Fr 1815 Oct 02 DLC-19
Fr 1815 Oct 07 DLC-19
Fr 1815 Nov 17 DLC-19
Coleman & Stewart
Fr 1838 May 23# fin DLC-51
Coles Charles W
Fr 1843 Jun 16 DLC-55
Coles Walter
Fr 1836 May 01 M639-25
Colhoun James et al
Fr 1833 Feb 22 M222-31
Colhoun William & Hugh et al
Fr 1833 Sep 02 M639-20
Collier George R
Fr 1842 Jun 07 DLC-54
Collier Henry Watkins et al
Fr 1844 Mar 30 DLC-56
Collins ______
To 1839 Oct 19# fin DLC-52
Collins Antoine
Fr 1821 Sep 20 fin DLC-70
Collins Bradbury
Fr 1836 Nov 29 M687-3
Collins Ela
Fr 1830 Jan 26 M639-15
Collins John W
Fr 1815 Jan 27# 4-0627
Collins Joseph S
Re c1831 mem 17-0085
Collins Mathew
Fr 1835 cFeb M567-105
Collins Robert
Fr 1845 Feb 08 DLC-57
Collins Stephen et al
Fr 1829 Mar 12 M639-5
Collins William
Re 1834 Jun 26 par 25-1552
Re 1834 Jul 05 par 26-0153
Collinsworth James
Fr 1829 Apr 04 M639-5
Fr 1835 Jan 25 27-0291
Colman Jesse
Fr 1818 Jun 09 fin DLC-69
Fr 1818 Jun 09* fin 6-1038
Colman Littleton H
Fr 1824 Apr 21 10-0670
To 1824 Apr 26 10-0681
To 1824 May 15 10-0726
Colson John Baptiste
To 1815 Feb 10 DLC-16
Coltman Charles L
Fr 1835 Jan fin DLC-45
Fr 1837 Feb 11 33-0611
Coltman Charles L et al
Fr 1834 Jun 14 25-1361
Colton Henry
Re 1830 cAug mem 16-0074
Re 1831 Oct 15 DLC-73
Colton Walter
Fr 1829 Mar 02 12-0820
Fr 1830 Oct 26 16-0543
Fr 1831 Sep 08 M639-27
Comanche and Wichita treaty
Re 1836 May 19 M668-8
Combs Charles
Re 1834 Oct 15 M273-31
Combs George
Re 1801 Oct 09 mem DLC-60
Combs Leslie
Fr 1828 Oct 14 DLC-72
Fr 1828 Nov 15 12-0269
Fr 1828 Nov 20 12-0279
Combs Martin B
Fr 1842 Jan 19 DLC-54
Commerford John
Fr 1844 Apr DLC-56
Compberry Francis
Re 1807 Jun leg 2-0497
Compere Lee
Fr 1830 Oct 09 M234-774
Compton William
Fr 1814 Mar 15 DLC-9
Comstock Taft et al
Fr 1837 Jan 30 33-0214
Conchattemcko
Fr 1821 Dec 24 M116-10
Condict Edward et al
Fr 1829 Jan 12 M639-6
Condict Lewis et al
Fr 1830 May 22 M639-11
Condon James
Fr 1813 Aug 14 fin DLC-11
To 1814 Jun 21 chk DLC-10
Fr 1815 Jan 28 fin DLC-19
To 1815 Aug 03 chk DLC-19
Fr 1815 Oct 02 fin 4-1204
Fr 1815 Oct 07 fin DLC-23
Fr 1816 Feb 24 fin DLC-22
Condy Thomas D
Fr 1834 Apr 30# M179-78
Fr 1835 Feb 03 M688-101
Fr 1836 Nov 07 M687-6
Cone Peter
Fr 1818 May 03 6-0558
Fr 1818 May 03* DLC-24
Conn John M
Fr 1829 May 05 M688-68
Conn Josephus H
To 1813 Dec 26 DLC-61
Fr 1814 Jan 24 DLC-8
Connell Rebecca
Fr 1834 Nov 08 fin DLC-45
Conner Henry
Fr 1829 Jun 04 13-0568
Conner James
Fr 1829 May 23 13-0395
Conner James et al
Fr 1844 Dec 02 DLC-57
Conner John H
Fr 1837 Feb 04 33-0390
Conner Mary
Fr 1829 Mar 10 M567-42
Conner William
Re 1836 Jul 05 par 31-0856
Re 1836 Dec 23 par 32-1275
Re 1836 Dec 31 par 32-1432
Connor Henry W
Fr 1836 Jun 20 31-0518
Fr 1836 Jun 29 31-0639
Fr 1837 Jan 06 32-1503
Connor John Coppinger
Fr 1821 Sep 04 mem DLC-63
Fr 1821 Sep 27 fin DLC-70
Fr 1821 Nov 26 DLC-31
Fr 1822 Jan 28 DLC-31
Fr 1822 Feb 03 DLC-31
Connor McAlister & Co
Fr 1835 Nov 18# fin DLC-48

Conrad Francis D
Fr 1834 May 14 | | 25-1041
Conrad John
Fr 1829 Mar 05 | | M639-13
Fr 1829 Mar 31 | | 12-1187
Conrad John & Co
Fr 1805 Sep 09 | | DLC-3
Conrad Nicholas
Re 1799 Apr 19 | leg | 1-0703
Constant J
To 1814 Dec 22 | | DLC-62
Fr 1814 Dec 28 | | DLC-15
Fr 1814 Dec 29 | | DLC-15
Contee Hannah
Re 1834 Apr 30 | par | 25-0928
Contee John
Fr 1836 Nov 09 | | M567-134
Converse Erasmus D
Fr 1834 Mar | | M639-5
Conway Charles
Fr 1835 Jul 05 | | M124-148
Conway Elizabeth
Fr 1835 Jul 05 | | M124-148
Conway Henry
Re 1791 Feb 18 | leg | 1-0092
Fr 1816 Jan 20 | | DLC-20
Conway James Sevier
Re 1830 Jun 08 | | 15-1322
Fr 1832 Oct 17 | | 21-0100
Fr 1836 Oct 08 | | M567-121
Fr 1836 Oct 19 | | 32-0229
Conway William B
Fr 1831 Mar 31 | | DLC-39
To 1831 Apr 04 | | DLC-39
Fr 1834 Jan 10 | | M873-75
Fr 1837 Nov 22 | | DLC-50
Conwell Henry
Fr 1829 Jan 01 | | 12-0423
To 1829 Apr 25 | | 13-0150
Fr 1832 May 04 | | M688-83
Conwell Henry et al
Fr 1830 Mar | | M639-15
Coody William
Re 1834 Jan 20 | | 24-1003
Cook Alexander
Fr 1829 Feb 24 | | 12-0576
Cook Alexander et al
Fr 1829 | | 12-0364
Cook Elisha M et al
Fr 1835 Jan 10 | | DLC-45
Cook George K
Fr 1815 Jul 11 | | DLC-18
Cook Harvey et al
Fr 1830 Mar | | M639-20
Cook Henry
Fr 1815 Aug 20 | | DLC-19
Cook J C
Fr 1823 May 18 | | M688-32
Cook James H
To 1839 Jul 31 | | DLC-52
To 1840 Sep 05 | | DLC-53
To 1840 Sep 07 | | DLC-53
Cook Joseph
To 1806 Nov 20 | | 2-0390
To 1808 Jul 19 | lnd | 2-0687
Fr 1808 Nov | fin | DLC-4
Cook Samuel
Fr 1835 Jan 08 | | DLC-45
Cook William A
Fr 1829 Apr 05# | | M639-5
Fr 1829 Apr 06 | | M639-5
Fr 1833 Aug 15 | | M639-3
Fr 1833 Aug 15# | | M639-3
Cooke ______ (Gen)
Fr 1825 Sep 27 | add | 11-0002
To 1825 Sep 27 | add | 11-0004
Cooke John W
Fr 1833 Sep 26 | | M639-3
Cooke William W
Fr 1812 Nov 08 | | DLC-5
Cool Simon
To 1803 Sep 30 | fin | DLC-3
Cooley B M
Fr 1840 Sep 18 | | DLC-53
Cooley Ebenezer
Fr 1814 Oct 24 | | DLC-13
Fr 1814 Nov 05 | | DLC-13
Coolidge Ellen W (Trist)
Fr 1839 Nov 29 | | DLC-52
Coons David
Fr 1828 Nov 19 | | DLC-72
Cooper Benjamin B
Fr 1831 Jun 15 | | DLC-39
To 1831 Jul | | DLC-39
Fr 1831 Oct 15 | | DLC-40
To 1831 Oct 21 | fin | 18-1089
To 1831 Oct 21* | fin | DLC-40
To 1831 Nov 07 | | DLC-40
Fr 1831 Nov 30 | | DLC-40
Fr 1831 Dec 01 | | 18-1533
Fr 1831 Dec 22 | | DLC-40
Fr 1831 Dec 27 | | DLC-40
Fr 1832 Feb 08 | | DLC-40
Fr 1832 Mar 12 | | DLC-40
To 1832 Mar 20 | | DLC-40
Fr 1832 Aug 29 | | DLC-41
To 1832 Sep 15 | | DLC-41
Fr 1832 Nov 01 | | DLC-41
Fr 1833 Jan 29 | | DLC-42
Fr 1833 Mar 29 | | DLC-42
Fr 1833 Nov 02 | | DLC-43
To 1833 Nov 06 | | DLC-43
Cooper Edmond
To 1811 Feb 13 | fin | DLC-5
Fr 1819 Sep 16 | fin | 7-0662
Cooper Isaac
Fr 1833 Oct 15 | fin | DLC-50
Cooper James Fenimore
Fr 1832 Mar 08 | | M639-9
Fr 1832 Mar 08* | | 19-1345
Cooper Samuel
Fr 1835 Aug 21# | | M567-112
Cooper Samuel et al
Fr 1829 cNov | | 14-0310
Cooper Samuel T
Re 1835 cApr 28 | mem | 37-0340
Fr 1835 Apr 29 | | 28-0176
Cooper Thomas
To 1818 Aug 24 | | 6-1259
Cooper William
Fr 1818 Jun 21 | fin | DLC-69
Fr 1818 Jun 21* | fin | 6-1069
Copeland Richard
To 1813 Dec 29 | | DLC-8
Copeland Solomon
Fr 1840 Apr 05 | | 34-1283
Copeland Thomas
Re 1844 May 22 | mem | DLC-56

Copes Joseph S et al		
Fr 1840 Jan 18		34-1183
Coplan William F		
Fr 1836 Apr 02		M639-5
Copp Daniel		
To 1821 Jul 19		8-0876
Coppage Thomas L		
To 1844 Sep 20#		DLC-57
Coppel Charles		
Fr 1815 Feb 15		4-0743
To 1815 Feb 18		DLC-62
Coppinger Joseph		
Fr 1818 Nov 18		DLC-26
Corbin Abel Rathbone		
Fr 1836 Aug 22		31-1338
Corcoran Thomas Jr		
Fr 1829 Apr 20		M639-16
Cordova Vicente et al		
Fr 1838 Aug 10#		DLC-51
Cornell Thomas F		
Fr 1831 Nov 08		M639-5
Corner James et al		
Fr 1834 Dec		M639-8
Cornplanter		
Fr 1830 Aug 02		M234-808
Cornstick et al		
Fr 1829 Oct 15		14-0161
Fr 1830 Sep 22		M234-669
Fr 1830 Sep 22*		16-0256
Fr 1831 Mar 14		17-0841
Cornwell Richard		
Fr 1830 Apr 20		M124-123
Fr 1837 Oct 16		33-1527
Corro Jose Justo		
Fr 1836 Mar 11		M54-2
To 1836 Jun 07		31-0379
Coryell Lewis S		
To 1831 Jan 27		17-0370
Cosby James		
Fr 1814 Apr 13		DLC-10
Coster John G et al		
Fr 1829 Nov		14-0313
Cott Mary (Shields)		
Re 1835 Jul 16	lnd	28-1027
Cott Stephen		
Re 1835 Jul 16	lnd	28-1027
Cotten Henry		
Fr 1826 Jul 13		11-0311
Cotten Spencer D		
Fr 1828 Jul 17		DLC-35
Cotter Thomas		
Fr 1833 Jun 15		DLC-43
Cotton A J		
Fr 1841 Sep 03		DLC-53
To 1841 Sep 29		35-0420
Cotton Godwin B		
To 1815 Feb 21		DLC-62
To 1815 Mar 06		4-0820
Cotton John		
Re 1789 Oct	leg	1-0069
Cotton John Winslow		
Fr 1835 Dec 03		29-0732
Cotton Lazarus		
Re 1808 Sep 22	leg	2-0725
Cotton gin committee		
Fr 1802 Jul 13		1-1014
Coulter Asia		
To 1839 May 03	chk	DLC-52
To 1840 Jan#	fin	DLC-52
Fr 1840 Jan 12#	fin	DLC-52
Coulter Richard		
Fr 1829 Mar 06		M639-14
Fr 1829 Mar 10		M639-12
Counterfeiting		
Re 1829 cApr	mem	12-1207
Coutant Gilbert		
Fr 1831 cSep		M639-18
Covington Richard		
Fr 1815 Jun 28		DLC-18
Cowan David		
To 1821 Jun 29#		8-0742
Fr 1821 Jul 13		DLC-30
Fr 1821 Aug 13		DLC-30
Cowan Eliza		
Re 1830 Jan 18	par	14-1452
Cowan James		
To 1814 Mar 07		DLC-9
To 1814 Apr 02		DLC-10
Fr 1814 Apr 09		DLC-10
Fr 1829 Jun 15		M234-73
Cowan Samuel M		
Fr 1845 Feb 02		36-1437
Cowardin Collin M		
Fr 1832 Oct 07	fin	DLC-41
Cowell Benjamin		
Fr 1834 Jan 01		M639-9
Cowell Son & Evans		
Fr 1836 Nov 03#	fin	DLC-50
Fr 1837 Feb 18	fin	DLC-50
Cowgill Elisha		
To 1825 Nov 16	fin	DLC-33
Cowgill Henry		
To 1807 Jan 17	fin	DLC-4
To 1807 Feb 05	fin	DLC-4
Cowgill John		
To 1806 Dec 04	fin	DLC-4
To 1807 Jan 12	fin	DLC-4
To 1807 Jan 12	fin	DLC-4
Cowgill Thompson		
To 1839 Jun 28	chk	DLC-52
Cowles G J		
Fr 1833 Jul 08		DLC-43
Cowper Lewis M et al		
Fr 1831 Feb 26		17-0656
To 1831 Mar 08		17-0823
Cowperthwaite Thomas S		
Re 1834 Jan 09	par	24-0806
Re 1834 Mar 04	par	24-1561
Cowsar Mary		
Fr 1828 Aug 19		12-0167
Cox Caleb et al		
Fr 1815 Feb		4-0670
Cox Edward		
Fr 1794 Jan 15	lnd	1-0184
Fr 1794 Jan 15*	lnd	DLC-1
Cox George		
Fr 1814 Jan 04		DLC-8
To 1814 Jan 13		DLC-61
Cox Henry Bainbridge		
Re 1831 Jun 21	par	18-0056
Cox Horatio J		
Fr 1821 Mar 25		DLC-30
Cox John		
Fr 1836 Feb 10		M639-11
Cox John et al		
Fr 1833 Jan 20		M639-4
Fr 1834 Apr 19		M639-9
Cox Joshua		
Fr 1812 Jun 19		DLC-75

Cox Moses et al			
	Fr 1815 Jan		4-0482
Cox William			
	Fr 1829 Jun 08		M639-11
Cox Zachariah			
	Fr 1797 Apr 27		DLC-1
Coxe Francis L			
	Fr 1815 Jan 07		DLC-15
Coxe John R Jr			
	Re 1837 cFeb 20		33-0778
Coxe Richard S			
	Fr 1833 Jan 25		M124-136
Coyle ______ (Capt)			
	Fr 1829 Sep 08		13-1265
Coyle A			
	Fr c1836#	fin	29-1388
	Fr 1836 Feb 18#	fin	DLC-47
	Fr 1836 Mar 23#	fin	DLC-47
	To 1836 Dec 15	chk	DLC-49
Coyle Randolph			
	Fr 1843 Aug 26		35-1473
Crabb Henry			
	Fr 1813 Oct 08		DLC-6
	Fr 1814 Aug 02		DLC-11
Crabb Henry S			
	Fr 1832 Nov 06		DLC-41
Crabb Horatio N			
	Fr 1836 Oct 24		T172-6
Crabb Thomas D			
	Fr 1814 Mar 24		DLC-9
Crabtree James			
	Fr 1805 Feb 22	fin	DLC-3
Cracheron Jacob			
	Fr 1831 Oct 07		M639-18
Crafford John			
	Fr 1812 May 31		DLC-5
Craig Amanda P			
	Fr 1838 Aug 22		DLC-51
Craig Hector			
	Fr 1825 Mar 02		10-1204
	To 1825 Mar 02		10-1206
	To 1825 Mar 02*		DLC-33
	Fr 1828 Sep 26		DLC-35
	Fr 1831 Jul 16		DLC-39
Craig James C			
	To 1821 Jul 19		DLC-63
	To 1821 Aug 28		8-1111
Craig John D			
	Fr 1831 Mar 09		17-0828
	Fr 1835 Jan 07#		M639-15
Craig Robert			
	Fr 1794 Sep 24	fin	DLC-71
	Fr 1831 Dec 08		M639-18
	Fr 1836 Dec 31		M688-112
Craig William			
	Fr 1829 Oct 02		M639-27
	Fr 1830 Mar 03		M639-12
	Fr 1830 Nov 16		M639-5
	Fr 1831 Feb 11		M639-5
	Fr 1831 Aug 23		M639-21
	Fr 1833 Sep 03		M639-20
	Fr 1835 Jan 03		M639-9
Craig William et al			
	Fr 1830 Feb 24		M639-12
	Fr 1836 Aug 31		M687-1
Craighead David			
	Fr 1829 Apr 05		M639-5
Craighead Elizabeth			
	Fr 1826 Dec 02		DLC-34
	Fr 1826 Dec 02*		11-0411
Craighead Thomas B			
	Fr 1803 Jan 14		DLC-2
	Fr 1814 Dec 12		DLC-14
	Fr 1815 Nov 24		DLC-19
	Fr 1816 Aug 12	fin	DLC-21
	Fr 1823 Apr 25		DLC-32
Cram John P			
	Fr 1845 Mar 01		DLC-57
Cram Thomas Jefferson			
	Fr 1836 May 05#		30-1520
Cramer John			
	Fr 1839 Aug 18		DLC-52
Crane Ichabod Bennet et al			
	Fr 1835 Dec		M567-127
Crane Isaac W			
	Fr 1831 Nov 07		M639-5
	Fr 1833 Dec 05#		DLC-43
Crane James et al			
	Fr 1835 cJan		DLC-59
Crane William Montgomery			
	Fr 1829 Mar 08		M46-2
	Fr 1829 Mar 17		M46-2
	Fr 1829 Mar 17*		12-1022
	Fr 1829 Sep 02		M46-2
Crary Isaac Edwin			
	Fr 1835 Dec 09		M200-6
	Fr 1836 Feb 05		M639-26
	Fr 1836 Apr 20		M639-6
	Fr 1837 Jan 27		M234-422
Crary Mary			
	Fr 1832 Mar 08		19-1348
Crary Susan H			
	Fr 1837 Aug 08		DLC-50
Cravens Robert			
	Fr 1828 Feb 24		DLC-35
Crawford Andrew Jackson			
	Fr 1823 Jul 23#		9-0619
	Fr 1831 Jul 11		DLC-39
	To 1833 May 01		22-1249
	To 1833 May 01*		DLC-40
	Fr 1838 Mar 07		34-0266
	Fr 1838 Mar 08		34-0269
	Fr 1841 Jan 03		DLC-53
	Fr 1844 Dec 28		36-1267
	Fr 1845 Jan 15		M873-79
Crawford Edward			
	Fr 1843 May 22		DLC-55
Crawford Ingoldsby W			
	Fr 1829 Feb 20		M639-26
	Fr 1836 Mar 15		M687-17
Crawford Ingoldsby W et al			
	Fr 1831 Nov 08		M179-71
Crawford James			
	To 1784 Dec 04	fin	1-0015
	To 1792 Nov 28	leg	1-0134
	Re 1804 Jul 28	leg	DLC-3
	To 1806 Mar 05		DLC-4
	Fr 1812 May 04	lnd	2-1088
Crawford John			
	Fr 1802 Dec 28		DLC-2
	Fr 1814 Feb 12		DLC-9
Crawford Samuel			
	To 1809 Aug 09	lnd	2-0853
Crawford Thomas Hartley			
	Fr 1830 Feb 16		15-0149
	To 1830 Feb 19		15-0205
	Fr 1830 Apr 05		15-0582
	To 1830 Apr 05		15-0583
	Fr 1835 Apr 21		28-0106

Crawford Thomas Hartley (cont)

Fr	1843	May	29		DLC-55
To	1844	Jan	19		36-0141

Crawford William

To	1783	Dec	12	fin	1-0009
Fr	1815	Nov	16	fin	DLC-68
Fr	1815	Nov	19		DLC-71
To	1818	Oct	25	lnd	6-1385

Crawford William Harris

Fr	1815	Aug	15	DLC-19
Fr	1815	Aug	15*	M6-8
To	1815	Aug	18	DLC-71
To	1815	Aug	22	4-1169
To	1815	Aug	22*	DLC-62
To	1815	Sep	04	DLC-62
To	1815	Sep	04	M221-63
To	1815	Sep	04*	DLC-62
To	1815	Sep	04*	4-1182
To	1815	Sep	30	M22-8
To	1815	Sep	30*	DLC-62
To	1815	Nov	18	DLC-19
To	1815	Nov	20	4-1246
To	1815	Nov	24	DLC-19
To	1815	Nov	25	4-1262
To	1815	Nov	25	DLC-62
To	1815	Dec	07	4-1274
To	1815	Dec	07*	DLC-19
To	1815	cDec	08	M22-8
To	1815	Dec	15	4-1280
To	1815	Dec	15*	DLC-62
To	1815	Dec	15*	DLC-19
To	1815	Dec	15*	DLC-71
To	1815	Dec	16	DLC-62
To	1815	Dec	16*	M221-63
To	1815	Dec	17	M221-63
To	1815	Dec	17*	DLC-62
To	1815	Dec	18	4-1290
To	1815	Dec	20	4-1293
To	1815	cDec	20	M22-8
To	1815	Dec	23	DLC-71
To	1816			4-1313
Fr	1816	Jan	12	DLC-20
Fr	1816	Jan	17	DLC-20
Fr	1816	Jan	27	M21-11
Fr	1816	Jan	27*	M6-8
Fr	1816	Jan	27*	4-1364
Fr	1816	Jan	27*	DLC-20
Fr	1816	Jan	29	DLC-20
Fr	1816	Jan	29*	M6-8
To	1816	Feb	02	M221-70
To	1816	Feb	02*	DLC-62
To	1816	Feb	10	M221-70
To	1816	Feb	11	DLC-62
To	1816	Feb	13	4-1402
To	1816	Feb	13*	DLC-62
To	1816	Feb	19	M221-70
To	1816	Feb	19*	DLC-62
To	1816	Mar		M22-8
Fr	1816	Mar	08	DLC-20
Fr	1816	Mar	08*	M6-8
Fr	1816	Mar	12	DLC-20
Fr	1816	Mar	12*	M6-8
To	1816	Mar	15	M221-70
Fr	1816	Mar	15	DLC-20
Fr	1816	Mar	15*	M6-8
Fr	1816	Mar	15	DLC-20
Fr	1816	Mar	15*	M6-8
Fr	1816	Mar	15*	4-1413
Fr	1816	Mar	21	DLC-20
Fr	1816	Mar	21*	M6-8
To	1816	Mar	25	4-1416
To	1816	Mar	27	4-1418
To	1816	Mar	28	M566-89
To	1816	Mar	29	M221-70
To	1816	Apr	05	M22-8
To	1816	Apr	11	M22-8
To	1816	Apr	12	5-0029
To	1816	Apr	15	M22-8
To	1816	Apr	19	M221-70
To	1816	Apr	23	5-0042
To	1816	Apr	24	M221-70
To	1816	Apr	24	M221-70
To	1816	Apr	24*	5-0065
Fr	1816	May	07	M6-9
To	1816	May	08	M22-8
To	1816	May	12	M221-70
To	1816	May	12*	5-0078
To	1816	May	16	5-0085
To	1816	May	16*	M22-8
Fr	1816	May	20	DLC-20
Fr	1816	May	20*	M6-9
Fr	1816	May	20	M15-3
Fr	1816	May	21	DLC-20
Fr	1816	May	21*	M15-3
Fr	1816	May	21	DLC-20
Fr	1816	May	21*	M6-9
Fr	1816	May	24	M15-3
To	1816	Jun	02	M221-70
To	1816	Jun	03	M221-70
To	1816	Jun	04	5-0133
Fr	1816	Jun	04	5-0144
Fr	1816	Jun	07	DLC-20
Fr	1816	Jun	07*	M6-9
To	1816	Jun	09	M221-70
To	1816	Jun	10	5-0150
To	1816	Jun	10	5-0152
To	1816	Jun	10	M22-9
Fr	1816	Jun	11	DLC-20
Fr	1816	Jun	11*	M6-9
To	1816	Jun	13	M221-70
To	1816	Jun	13#	DLC-20
To	1816	Jun	13	5-0157
To	1816	Jun	15	M221-70
To	1816	Jun	15*	5-0166
Fr	1816	Jun	15	DLC-21
Fr	1816	Jun	15*	M15-3
To	1816	Jun	16	DLC-21
To	1816	Jun	18	M221-70
To	1816	Jun	18	5-0172
Fr	1816	Jun	19	M15-3
Fr	1816	Jun	19*	5-0174
To	1816	Jun	20	M221-70
To	1816	Jun	24	5-0236
To	1816	Jun	29	5-0244
Fr	1816	Jul	01	DLC-21
Fr	1816	Jul	01*	5-0246
Fr	1816	Jul	01*	M15-3
Fr	1816	Jul	01	DLC-21
Fr	1816	Jul	01*	M6-9
To	1816	Jul	04	5-0260
Fr	1816	Jul	05	DLC-21
Fr	1816	Jul	05*	M15-3
Fr	1816	Jul	05	5-0262
Fr	1816	Jul	05*	M15-3
Fr	1816	Jul	05	5-0263
Fr	1816	Jul	05*	M668-4
Fr	1816	Jul	05*	M15-3
Fr	1816	Jul	05	5-0283
Fr	1816	Jul	05*	M668-4

Fr 1816 Jul 05* M15-3
Fr 1816 Jul 09 DLC-21
Fr 1816 Jul 09* M7-1
To 1816 Jul 13 M22-9
To 1816 Jul 17 M221-70
To 1816 Jul 19 5-0316
To 1816 Jul 20 5-0317
To 1816 Jul 24 M221-70
To 1816 Jul 31 M221-70
To 1816 Aug 06 5-0346
Fr 1816 Aug 09 M15-3
To 1816 Aug 18 5-0363
Fr 1816 Sep 02 DLC-21
Fr 1816 Sep 02* M6-9
To 1816 Sep 04 DLC-62
To 1816 Sep 04* 5-0450
To 1816 Sep 04* M668-4
To 1816 Sep 07 5-0460
Fr 1816 Sep 10 M15-3
Fr 1816 Sep 10* 5-0468
Fr 1816 Sep 12 M15-3
Fr 1816 Sep 12* 5-0477
To 1816 Sep 20 5-0494
To 1816 Sep 20* DLC-62
To 1816 Sep 20* M668-4
To 1816 Sep 20 M22-9
Fr 1816 Sep 24 M6-9
Fr 1816 Sep 24* 5-0516
Fr 1816 Sep 27 5-0518
Fr 1816 Sep 27* DLC-21
Fr 1816 Sep 27* M7-1
Fr 1816 Oct 02 M7-1
Fr 1816 Oct 02* 5-0527
To 1816 Oct 04 DLC-62
To 1816 Oct 04* M668-4
Fr 1816 Oct 04 DLC-21
Fr 1816 Oct 04* M6-9
To 1816 Oct 18 5-0538
To 1816 Oct 18 M221-74
Fr 1816 Oct 20 DLC-21
To 1816 Nov 12 DLC-21
To 1816 Nov 16 M222-19
To 1816 Nov 16* 5-0584
Re 1822 cFeb 9-0022
Fr 1822 Mar 31 9-0089
Fr 1822 Jun 30 9-0204
Fr 1830 Oct 02# DLC-38
Fr 1834 Sep 01 DLC-44

Crawford William W
Fr 1818 Sep 15 fin 6-1298
Fr 1819 Dec 03 DLC-28
Fr 1821 Mar 11 DLC-30
Fr 1822 Mar 14 fin DLC-31
Fr 1822 Nov 15 fin DLC-31
Fr 1827 Jan 30 fin 11-0482
Fr 1832 Dec 21 DLC-41

Crawley John
Re 1808 Dec 17 leg 2-0748

Creath A G et al
Fr 1832 cJan 19-0539

Creath Jacob
Fr 1821 Apr 03 DLC-30

Creek Indians
Re 1814 Apr 08 mem DLC-61
To 1814 Aug 05 DLC-11
To 1814 Aug 05* 3-1212
To 1814 Aug 05* DLC-62
Fr 1814 Aug 08 3-1238
Fr 1814 Aug 08* T494-1
Fr 1814 Aug 08* M221-62
To 1815 Sep 04 DLC-19
To 1829 Mar 23 12-1080
To 1829 Mar 23* DLC-60
To 1829 Mar 23* M21-5
Fr 1830 Jun 12 15-1348
Re 1831 cSep mem 18-0644
Re 1833 Nov 23-1150
Re 1835 Dec 23 29-1312
Re 1836 May 23 mem 31-0080
Re 1836 Jul mem 31-0711

Creek treaty
Re 1832 Apr 04 M668-6
Re 1834 Apr 12 M668-7

Creel Thomas W
Fr 1823 Mar 25 fin DLC-32

Creighton John Orde
Re 1831 Apr M273-26

Creighton William et al
Fr 1833 Sep 27 M639-21

Crenshaw William
Re 1805 Oct 15 mem DLC-4
Fr 1806 Dec 14 fin 2-0397

Crews Micajah
Fr 1788 Nov 17 fin 1-0054

Crim John
Fr 1813 Nov 28 DLC-7

Crittenden Alexander Parker
Re 1834 Mar 09 25-0001

Crittenden John Jordan
Fr 1821 Apr 14 M439-15

Crittenden Robert
To 1824 Mar 03 10-0508

Crocker J P
Fr 1835 Jun 03 M179-80

Crocker Roland R et al
Fr 1833 Jun 03 22-1560
To 1833 Jun 13 23-0018

Crocker William H
Fr 1821 May 25# fin DLC-30

Crocker Brothers & Co
Fr 1837 Sep 11# fin DLC-50

Crocket George F
Fr 1840 Apr 13 DLC-52

Crockett David
Fr 1829 Dec 29 14-1134

Crockett George
Fr 1823 Oct 20 fin DLC-32
Fr 1824 Apr 03 fin DLC-32

Crockett Granville Smith et al
Fr 1834 Aug 19 26-0335
To 1834 Aug 23 26-0347

Crockett William
Fr 1814 Jun 11 DLC-10
Fr 1824 Dec 07 DLC-33
Re 1838 Jan 01 leg DLC-51

Crockett William & Co
Fr 1836 Sep 17# fin DLC-50

Crockett & Adams
Fr 1816 Nov 18# fin DLC-22
Fr 1823 Jan 27 fin DLC-32
Fr 1823 Jun 16 fin DLC-32

Crockett & Bankhead
To 1836 Apr 25 fin DLC-48

Crockett & Park
To 1836 Feb 19 chk DLC-47

Croggins Isaac
Re 1831 Dec 09 par 19-0277

Croghan George
Fr 1815 Apr 08 4-0980
Fr 1815 Sep 24 DLC-19
Fr 1815 Sep 24 DLC-71
Fr 1815 Oct 14 DLC-19
Fr 1815 Oct 14* 4-1212
To 1815 Oct 18 4-1216
To 1815 Oct 18* DLC-62
Fr 1815 Nov 09 DLC-19
Fr 1815 Nov 09* 4-1226
Fr 1815 Nov 17 4-1234
Fr 1815 Nov 20 4-1248
Fr 1815 Nov 24 DLC-19
Fr 1815 Dec 11 4-1277
Fr 1816 Jan 01 DLC-20
Fr 1816 Jan 01* 4-1314
Fr 1816 Feb 02 DLC-20
Fr 1816 Feb 02* 4-1376
Fr 1816 Mar 27 DLC-20
Fr 1816 Mar 29 DLC-20
Fr 1816 Apr 08 DLC-20
To 1816 Apr 11# DLC-20
Fr 1816 Apr 12 DLC-20
Fr 1816 Apr 18 DLC-20
To 1816 Apr 24 5-0067
Fr 1816 Apr 30 DLC-20
Fr 1816 Apr 30* 5-0070
Fr 1816 May 02 DLC-20
Fr 1816 May 13 DLC-20
Fr 1816 May 13* 5-0083
To 1816 May 15 DLC-75
Fr 1816 May 22 DLC-20
Fr 1816 May 22* 5-0086
Fr 1816 Jun 04 DLC-20
Fr 1816 Jul 22 DLC-21
Fr 1816 Jul 22* 5-0325
Fr 1816 Aug 06 DLC-21
Fr 1834 Dec 22 DLC-45
Fr 1835 Sep 04 28-1519
Crook James W et al
Fr 1835 Apr 01 M639-16
Crooker Isaiah Jr et al
Fr 1831 Feb 13 17-0506
Crosman George Hampton
Fr 1837 Jan M22-41
Cross Edward
Fr 1836 Sep 16 31-1452
Cross George Warren et al
Fr 1831 Jul 19 M639-9
Cross Henry L
Fr 1832 Jan 07 fin DLC-40
Fr 1833 Feb 23 fin DLC-42
Cross Maclin
Fr 1804 Aug 31 fin DLC-3
Cross Trueman
Fr 1818 May 23 DLC-25
Fr 1820 Oct 26 DLC-29
Fr 1822 Jan 04 M221-93
Fr 1824 Dec 09 10-0967
Fr 1834 Oct 10 M222-32
Fr 1834 Dec 23 26-1563
Fr 1836 May 27 M221-116
Fr 1836 May 27* 31-0156
Re 1836 Jul 23 31-1151
Cross William C
Fr 1830 Aug 31 M639-5
Crosthwait Shelton et al
Fr 1815 May 24 DLC-18
Croswell Edwin
To 1839 Oct 17 34-1002
Crouch Martha Ann
Fr 1829 May 04 M567-42
Crouisle Henry
Fr 1832 Jul 10 20-1017
Crouse David et al
Fr 1836 Feb 09 DLC-47
Crow Isaac L
Fr 1816 Nov 16 fin DLC-22
Crow Mansfield W
Re 1813 Mar 11 3-0298
Crowe David
Re 1792 Jan 12 leg 1-0121
Crowell John
Fr 1829 Mar 25 M222-25
Fr 1830 Jun 30# M234-222
Re 1831 Oct 05 mem 18-0927
Fr 1833 Jan 22 M234-223
Crowly Charles E
Fr 1844 Feb 19 DLC-56
Crowninshield Benjamin Williams
To 1815 Dec 24 4-1306
Croxall Daniel Carroll
Fr 1829 May 14 M873-19
Re 1829 Jul 27 13-0940
Croxall Morris
Fr 1829 Nov 20 M639-1
Fr 1834 Oct 06 DLC-44
Croxall Morris et al
Fr 1829 Nov 18 M639-17
Crozier John
Fr 1814 Oct 24 DLC-13
Crozier John et al
Fr 1823 Nov 17 add 9-0760
To 1823 Nov 17 add 9-0761
To 1823 Nov 17 add 9-0762
Fr 1828 Dec 12 12-0320
To 1828 Dec 20 12-0329
Crumby & Draper
Fr 1833 Apr 25 M639-16
Crume Marks et al
Fr 1833 Jan 22 M639-6
Crump George William
Re 1831 Mar 02 17-0738
Re 1836 Jul 09 31-1007
Crutcher Thomas
Fr 1829 Apr 04 M639-2
Fr 1829 Apr 04 M639-5
Fr 1829 Apr 04 M639-2
Fr 1836 Dec 12 32-1093
To 1842 Jan 05 chk DLC-54
Crutchfield A M et al
Fr 1836 Mar 21 M639-6
Crutchfield J M
Fr 1844 May 18 DLC-56
Crutchfield O F
Fr 1837 Apr 08# fin DLC-51
Crutchfield Peter Tinsley
Fr 1832 Nov 05 21-0307
Fr 1836 Sep 17 31-1454
Cryer Hardy M
Fr 1823 Jun 10 DLC-32
Re 1825 May 10 leg DLC-33
Fr 1825 Jul 21 DLC-33
To 1826 Dec 20 chk 11-0435
Fr 1827 May 19 DLC-34
To 1827 Aug 18 11-0799
Fr 1827 Aug 22 fin DLC-34

To 1828 Mar 06 11-1160
To 1828 Mar 22 11-1184
To 1828 May 05 11-1237
To 1828 May 11 11-1241
Fr 1829 Jan 05 fin DLC-36
To 1829 May 16 13-0336
Fr 1829 Dec 26 DLC-37
To 1830 Jan 10 14-1366
To 1830 Feb 28 15-0262
Fr 1830 Mar 04 DLC-37
To 1830 Aug 11 16-0096
Fr 1831 Apr 03 DLC-39
To 1831 Apr 25 17-1228
To 1831 May 10 17-1338
To 1831 Aug 18 18-0561
To 1832 Jan 17 19-0732
To 1833 Feb 20 22-0426
Fr 1833 Mar 17 DLC-42
To 1833 Apr 07 22-0963
To 1833 Oct 29 23-1115
To 1834 Feb 10 24-1275
To 1835 May 10 28-0333
To 1836 Oct 24# DLC-49
Fr 1836 Oct 29# DLC-49
Fr 1836 Oct 30 DLC-49
To 1836 Nov 13 32-0488
To 1840 Feb 05 34-1195
Fr 1843 May 28 DLC-74
To 1843 cMay 30 DLC-74
Fr 1844 May 15 DLC-56

Cryer Hardy M et al
To 1840 May 09 34-1342

Cudliff F
Fr 1835 Jul 02# fin DLC-46

Cullen Joseph
Re 1835 Mar 24 27-1375

Culpeper John
Fr 1833 Sep 12 M124-139

Cumberland Bank of Portland (ME)
Re 1835 Nov 12 29-0502

Cumberland College
To 1811 Jul 17 chk DLC-5
Re 1826 Oct 11 11-0379

Cumberland College students
Fr 1815 May 15 add 4-1033
To 1815 May 15 add 4-1034

Cumberland Road
Re 1835 cApr mem 27-1406
Re 1835 cApr mem 27-1408
Re 1836 DLC-49

Cumming William
Fr 1820 Jan 18 fin DLC-28

Cummings James
To 1814 Nov 15 DLC-14

Cummings John et al
Fr 1833 Jun 06 M639-6

Cummins David
Re 1816 May 23 leg 5-0088
Re 1817 Jan 27 leg 5-0713

Cummins Ebenezer H
Fr 1815 Feb 28 DLC-17
Fr 1826 Aug 10 DLC-34
To 1826 Sep 04 11-0357
To 1826 Sep 04* DLC-34

Cummins John
Fr 1791 Mar 27# DLC-1
Fr 1796 Mar 21 fin DLC-1

Cummins William
Fr 1827 Jul 04 fin DLC-34
Fr 1828 Apr 23 fin DLC-35

Cunard S & Co
Fr 1833 Feb 22 M639-16

Cunningham A
Fr 1829 Feb 26 M639-17

Cunningham George
To 1813 Sep DLC-61
Fr 1813 Oct 10 fin DLC-61

Cunningham Joshua
To 1837 Dec 21 34-0140
To 1838 Dec 08 34-0564

Cunningham Robert
Re 1834 Feb 26 par 24-1484
Re 1834 Oct 08 par 26-0543

Cunningham Robert M
Fr 1838 Oct 17 DLC-51

Cunningham Thomas S et al
Fr 1833 Jan 14 21-1422

Cupples William
Re 1787 Oct 28 leg 1-0029
Fr 1795 Aug 19 DLC-1
Fr 1795 Oct 31 DLC-1

Currath James T
Fr 1829 Jan 06 fin DLC-36

Currency issue
Re 1837 cJul add 33-1357
Re 1837 cJul add 33-1359

Currey Benjamin Franklin
Fr 1829 Jan 06 fin DLC-36
Fr 1831 Aug 11 DLC-39
Fr 1833 May 25 22-1445
Fr 1834 Apr 09# 25-0647
To 1834 Sep 03 DLC-44
To 1834 Sep 03* M208-9
To 1834 Sep 03* 26-0413
Fr 1834 Nov 10 M234-76
Fr 1834 Nov 27 26-1049
Fr 1834 Nov 27 M234-113
Fr 1835 Feb 02 DLC-45
Fr 1835 Mar 23 DLC-45
Fr 1835 Apr 30 28-0195
To 1835 May 18 28-0450
Fr 1835 Jun 16 28-0688
Fr 1835 Oct 20 M567-109
Fr 1835 Dec 29 29-1355
Fr 1836 Jan 19# DLC-47
Fr 1836 Feb 09# M234-80
Fr 1836 Aug 30 DLC-49
To 1836 Sep 07 31-1429
Fr 1836 Oct 24 32-0331
Fr 1836 Oct 24* M234-80
Fr 1836 Nov 20# 32-0567

Currey Richard Owen
Fr 1844 Mar 09 DLC-56
Fr 1845 Feb 06 DLC-57
Fr 1845 Apr 24 DLC-58

Currey Robert Brownlee
Fr 1815 Jun 24 fin 4-1091
Fr 1815 Aug 12 fin DLC-70
Fr 1817 Jul 30# DLC-23
Fr 1822 Feb 08 DLC-70
Fr 1822 Jul 17 fin DLC-31
To 1824 Nov 06 10-0951
Fr 1825 May 04 fin DLC-33

Currier Jacob
Re 1835 Aug 02 M22-36
Fr 1835 Aug 27 M22-37

Currier Jacob M et al
Fr 1832 19-0513

Currin Robert P
Fr 1838 Apr 06 DLC-51
Curtin William
Re 1829 Oct 14 par 14-0154
Re 1829 Oct 14* par T967-1
Curtis Jeremiah
Fr 1837 Feb 02 M687-20
Curtis John
Re 1831 Sep 19 par 18-0819
Cushing Abel
Fr 1835 cMar 03 M639-5
Fr 1836 Jun 04 31-0313
Cushing Caleb
To 1835 cDec 24 29-1337
Cushing Courtland et al
Fr 1835 Jul 24 M639-23
Cushing Thomas P
Fr 1836 May 08 30-1566
Cushman John W
To 1824 Feb 22 10-0469
Fr 1829 Apr 29 13-0182
Cushman Jonathan et al
Fr 1828 Nov 29 DLC-35
Cushman Samuel
Fr 1832 Feb 03 19-0936
Fr 1837 Feb 33-0340
Cushman Samuel et al
Fr 1835 Jan 11 M639-13
Fr 1835 Dec M639-17
Cusselan Micco
Fr 1818 Mar 19 DLC-24
Custice Caleb
Re 1788 Sep leg 1-0045
Custis Eliza Parke
Fr 1825 Feb 22 10-1142
To 1825 Feb 22 10-1143
Fr 1828 Dec 25 12-0334
Customs service
Re 1829 cOct 10 mem DLC-37
Re 1829 cOct 10 mem DLC-37
Cutbush James
Fr 1815 Aug 01 DLC-19
Cuthbert Alfred
Fr 1836 Feb 29 30-0623
Fr 1836 Feb 29* M234-436
Cuthbert James
Fr 1836 Jul 14 DLC-48
To 1836 Oct 10 chk DLC-49
To 1836 Oct 10 chk DLC-49
To 1836 Oct 18 chk DLC-49
To 1836 Oct 21 chk DLC-49
To 1836 Oct 24 chk DLC-49
To 1836 Oct 25 chk 32-0344
To 1836 Oct 27 chk DLC-49
To 1836 Nov 01 chk DLC-49
To 1836 Nov 09 chk DLC-49
To 1836 Nov 16 chk DLC-49
To 1836 Nov 25 chk DLC-75
To 1836 Dec 02 chk DLC-49
To 1836 Dec 02 chk DLC-49
To 1836 Dec 06 chk DLC-49
To 1836 Dec 15 chk 32-1145
To 1836 Dec 24 chk DLC-49
To 1837 Jan 04 chk DLC-49
To 1837 Jan 07 chk DLC-49
To 1837 Jan 11 chk DLC-49
To 1837 Jan 17 chk DLC-49
To 1837 Jan 21 chk DLC-49
To 1837 Jan 28 chk DLC-49
To 1837 Feb 04 chk DLC-50
To 1837 Feb 04 chk DLC-50
To 1837 Feb 08 chk DLC-50
To 1837 Feb 13 chk DLC-50
To 1837 Feb 20 chk DLC-50
To 1837 Mar 03 chk DLC-50
To 1837 Mar 06 chk DLC-50
Re 1837 Mar 08 mem DLC-50
Cuthbert John
Re 1831 Mar 02 17-0739
Cutler Enos
Fr 1818 Apr 27 DLC-24
Fr 1818 Aug 13 6-1226
Cutting John Browne
Fr 1825 Oct 24 DLC-33
Fr 1829 Dec 18 14-1066
Cutts L Henry Mrs
To 1835 Aug 18 28-1294
Cutts Richard
Fr 1815 Jul 14 DLC-18
Cutts Walter C
Re 1832 Dec 29 M273-28

Dabb John R
Fr 1839 Oct 12# fin DLC-52
Dabney Charles W
Fr 1830 Sep 04 T203-1
Dabney John L
Fr 1830 Sep 05 T203-1
D'Acre Samuel et al
To 1814 Oct 04 DLC-62
Dade Francis Langhorne
To 1821 Aug 22 8-1084
To 1821 Aug 22* DLC-63
To 1821 Aug 22 8-1087
To 1821 Aug 22* DLC-63
Fr 1821 Sep 25 M116-9
Fr 1835 cMay M22-36
Dade Lawrence T
Fr 1830 Aug 24 DLC-38
Fr 1831 Mar 07# 17-0814
Fr 1833 Sep 29 M124-140
Dade Lawrence T et al
Fr 1829 Feb 13 M639-24
Fr 1830 Sep 24 16-0258
To 1830 Sep 24 16-0259
Fr 1832 Jan 19 19-0781
Dade Townshend Stuart
Fr 1802 Apr 12 DLC-2
Fr 1829 Feb 25 DLC-36
Daggart John
Fr 1836 May 22 M234-243
Daggett David
Fr 1829 Feb 12 12-0506
Dailey Samuel C
Fr 1840 Nov 02 DLC-53
Dakan John
Fr 1843 Mar 13 DLC-55
Dalahite James
Re 1835 Sep 30 par 29-0141
Dale Adam
Fr 1825 Aug 18 DLC-33
Dallas Alexander James
Fr 1815 Mar 14 DLC-17
Fr 1815 Mar 14* 4-0845
Fr 1815 Mar 14* M7-1
To 1815 Mar 20 M221-63
To 1815 Mar 20* DLC-62

To 1815 Mar 22 M221-63
To 1815 Mar 30 DLC-17
To 1815 cMar 30 mem 4-0913
To 1815 Apr 01 M22-8
Fr 1815 Apr 08 4-0982
Fr 1815 Apr 12 DLC-18
Fr 1815 Apr 12* M6-8
Fr 1815 Apr 14 DLC-18
Fr 1815 Apr 14* M6-8
Fr 1815 Apr 17 4-0999
Fr 1815 Apr 22 DLC-18
Fr 1815 Apr 22* M6-8
To 1815 May 16 M221-63
To 1815 May 16* DLC-62
Fr 1815 May 22 DLC-18
Fr 1815 May 22* M6-8
Fr 1815 May 22* M271-1
To 1815 May 23 4-1050
To 1815 May 23* DLC-62
To 1815 May 25 M221-63
To 1815 May 25* DLC-62
Fr 1815 May 26 DLC-18
Fr 1815 May 26* M6-8
To 1815 May 27 DLC-18
To 1815 May 27* M221-63
Fr 1815 May 29 DLC-18
Fr 1815 May 29* M6-8
Fr 1815 Jun 03 DLC-18
Fr 1815 Jun 03* M6-8
To 1815 Jun 10 DLC-62
Fr 1815 Jun 12 DLC-18
Fr 1815 Jun 12* M6-8
To 1815 Jun 13 M221-63
To 1815 Jun 13* DLC-62
To 1815 Jun 13 M221-63
To 1815 Jun 13* DLC-62
Fr 1815 Jun 17 DLC-18
Fr 1815 Jun 17* M6-8
To 1815 Jun 20 M221-63
To 1815 Jun 20* DLC-18
To 1815 Jun 20* DLC-62
Fr 1815 Jun 21 DLC-18
Fr 1815 Jun 21* M6-8
To 1815 Jun 22 M221-63
To 1815 Jun 22* DLC-62
To 1815 Jun 28 4-1097
To 1815 Jun 28* DLC-62
Fr 1815 Jun 30 DLC-18
Fr 1815 Jun 30* M6-8
Fr 1815 Jul 01 DLC-18
Fr 1815 Jul 01* M6-8
To 1815 Jul 03 M221-63
To 1815 Jul 03* DLC-62
Fr 1815 Jul 05 DLC-18
Fr 1815 Jul 05* M15-3
To 1815 Jul 11 4-1107
To 1815 Jul 11* DLC-62
To 1815 Jul 11 4-1112
To 1815 Jul 11* DLC-62
To 1815 Jul 11 DLC-62
To 1815 Jul 11* M221-63
To 1815 Jul 17 4-1116
To 1815 Jul 17* DLC-62
To 1815 Jul 18 M221-63
To 1815 Jul 18* DLC-62
To 1815 Jul 18 M221-63
To 1815 Jul 18* DLC-62
Fr 1815 Jul 24 DLC-19
Fr 1815 Jul 24* M6-8
To 1815 Jul 25 DLC-62
To 1815 Jul 25 DLC-62
To 1815 Jul 25* 4-1131
Fr 1815 Jul 26 DLC-19
To 1815 Jul 31 DLC-62
To 1815 Aug 01 DLC-62
To 1815 Aug 01 M221-63
To 1815 Aug 01* DLC-62
To 1815 Aug 01 M221-63
To 1815 Aug 01* DLC-62
To 1815 Sep 05 M221-63
To 1815 Sep 05* DLC-62
To 1815 Sep 05* DLC-20
Fr 1815 Dec 20 DLC-19
To 1816 Feb 04 DLC-62

Dallas George Mifflin
Fr 1829 Mar 14 M639-6
Re 1829 Apr 07 12-1294
Fr 1829 May 04 M639-17
Fr 1830 Apr 20# M179-68
Fr 1830 Jun 07# 15-1310
Fr 1831 Mar 16 17-0902
Fr 1831 Nov 26 18-1504
Fr 1831 Dec 15 M639-15
Fr 1831 Dec 31 M222-31
Fr 1832 Jan 13 M639-15
Fr 1832 Dec 05 DLC-41
Fr 1833 Jul 12 23-0109
Fr 1833 Aug 20 M639-27
Fr 1833 Aug 23 M639-1
Fr 1834 Oct 29 26-0765
Fr 1836 Oct M22-41
Fr 1836 Oct 26 32-0346
Fr 1836 Nov 10# 32-0476

Dallas George Mifflin et al
Fr 1830 Mar 15 M639-9
Fr 1832 cFeb 25 19-1247
To 1836 Jan 06 29-1475
To 1837 Feb 11 DLC-50

Dalrymple James
Fr 1834 Jan 23 24-1034

Dalzell Francis
Fr 1815 Oct 22 fin 4-1219

Damberville Rosalie
Fr 1819 Aug 23 DLC-27

D'Ambrugeac Countess
Fr 1832 Mar 12 M34-29
Fr 1832 Mar 12* 19-1401
Fr 1834 Dec 09 26-1441
Fr 1834 Dec 09* M179-79
Fr 1835 May 02 M179-80
Fr 1835 May 02* 28-0214
Fr 1836 Dec 25 M179-82

Dameron George B
Re 1834 May 20 mem DLC-44

Dana Judah
Fr 1837 Feb 33-0340

Dana Judah et al
Fr 1836 Dec 27 M639-11

Dancy Charles F M
To 1840 Jul 03 34-1465

Dancy John Winfield Scott et al
Fr 1844 Apr 18 DLC-56

Danforth Joshua N
Fr 1829 Jun 16 DLC-37
To 1829 Jun 17 DLC-37
Fr 1829 Jun 23 DLC-37
Re 1832 Apr 20 mem 20-0316
Fr 1832 Apr 30 20-0411

Danforth Walter R
Fr 1831 Jun 27 DLC-39
Fr 1836 Sep 26 M687-13
Daniel Alexander
Fr 1844 Jan 31 DLC-56
Daniel Harrison et al
Fr 1830 Mar M639-21
Daniel Henry
Fr 1827 Jun 09 DLC-34
To 1827 Jun 25 11-0715
To 1827 Jun 25* DLC-34
Fr 1829 Mar 22 M639-10
Daniel John L et al
Fr 1835 Nov 27 M639-9
Daniel Peter Vivian
Fr 1832 Jan 17 19-0736
Fr 1833 Jan 25 22-0066
Fr 1833 Sep 08 DLC-43
Re 1833 Oct 22 23-1076
Fr 1834 Dec 07 DLC-45
Fr 1835 Feb 08 M639-3
Fr 1835 Jul 01 M22-36
Fr 1835 Aug 18 DLC-46
Fr 1836 Jan 02 M639-3
To 1836 Nov 29 32-0590
Fr 1837 Jul 11 DLC-50
To 1843 Jul 06 35-1404
Fr 1844 Dec 29 36-1275
Daquin Louis
Fr 1815 Feb 25 4-0786
Darby D
To 1815 Jan 27 DLC-16
Darby Patrick Henry
Re 1821 Apr 13 leg 8-0316
Re 1821 Apr 13* leg DLC-30
To 1821 Apr 18 leg 8-0356
Fr 1821 Jul 04 DLC-30
Fr 1822 Apr 07 9-0104
Fr 1822 Nov 24 DLC-31
To 1822 Nov 25 9-0316
Fr 1827 May 24 DLC-34
Darby Thomas
Fr 1826 Dec 06 fin 11-0421
Darby William
Fr 1815 Feb 05 DLC-16
Fr 1815 Feb 08 DLC-16
Fr 1815 Feb 09 DLC-16
To 1815 Feb 10 DLC-16
Re 1815 Apr 05 4-0967
Fr 1819 Feb 27 7-0372
Fr 1821 Mar 19 DLC-30
To 1821 Apr 10 8-0300
Fr 1821 Jun 30 M639-3
Fr 1823 Oct 18 DLC-32
To 1827 Sep 07 11-0851
Fr 1836 May 24 31-0088
Darjou Concheta
Fr 1815 Feb 23 DLC-17
Darling Enoch G
Fr 1836 Jul 19 M234-948
Darling Noyes et al
Fr 1831 May 12 M639-17
Darmon David
Fr 1836 Apr 15 T194-1
Darnell Benjamin
Re 1813 Mar 13 DLC-61
Darras Mozel
Fr 1835 Jul 15 T212-2
Darst Thomas J
To 1832 Mar 29 chk DLC-40
Dashiell Arthur
Fr 1836 Jul 25 par 31-1154
Fr 1836 Aug 31 par 31-1391
Daudet A
Fr 1815 Mar 08 DLC-71
Daughty Joseph T
Fr 1831 Sep 24 M22-28
Davault Jacob
To 1807 Jan 02 fin DLC-4
Daveiss Joseph Hamilton
Fr 1808 Sep 28 DLC-71
To 1810 May 15 2-0921
Davenport H I Mrs
To 1828 Feb 25# 11-1141
Davenport Stephen
Re 1830 Jan 13 par 14-1400
Davenport William
To 1818 May 04 6-0585
To 1819 Mar 18 7-0425
Davezac Auguste Genevieve Valentin
Fr 1815 Jan 07 DLC-15
Fr 1815 Apr 06 DLC-18
Fr 1824 Dec 01 DLC-33
Fr 1825 Apr 11 DLC-33
To 1826 Feb 27 11-0149
Fr 1827 May 08 DLC-34
To 1827 Sep 02 11-0840
Fr 1828 Jan 08 add 11-1011
To 1828 Jan 08 add 11-1014
Fr 1828 Feb 14 DLC-35
Fr 1829 Jan 03 12-0431
Fr 1829 Jan 27 M639-4
Fr 1829 Jan 28 M639-4
Re 1829 Aug 11 13-1103
Fr 1831 Jan 15 17-0260
Re 1831 Oct 15 18-1005
Fr 1840 Nov 07 35-0094
Fr 1841 Jan 08 DLC-53
Fr 1841 Feb 09 DLC-53
To 1841 Feb 20 35-0232
Fr 1841 Jun 27 35-0336
Fr 1843 Aug 07 DLC-55
To 1844 cJan 36-0090
Fr 1844 Jan 08 DLC-56
Fr 1844 Mar 16 DLC-56
Fr 1844 Jun 20 36-0635
Fr 1845 Mar 02 36-1525
Fr 1845 Mar 15 36-1573
Fr 1845 Apr 24 DLC-58
Davezac Gaston
Fr c1829 Oct 08 37-0295
Davidson Ephraim B
Fr 1808 Jul 26 lnd 2-0716
Fr 1808 Oct DLC-71
Fr 1808 Oct 07 lnd 2-0730
Davidson John
Fr 1798 Aug 18# fin DLC-2
Davidson John A
Fr 1815 Feb 18 DLC-16
Davidson John E
Fr 1815 Jan 24 DLC-15
Davidson Nathan
To 1803 Apr 18 DLC-3
Fr 1803 Jun 03 DLC-2
Fr 1804 Jul 14 DLC-3
To 1804 Aug 25 DLC-3
Re 1807 Jul 29 leg 2-0522
Fr 1825 Mar 10-1192

Davidson Nelson
Fr 1829 Apr 02 fin DLC-72
To 1830 May 15 chk DLC-38
Fr 1830 Oct 02 fin DLC-73
To 1830 Nov 12 chk DLC-38
Fr 1831 May 23 DLC-73
To 1831 May 24 DLC-73
Fr 1831 May 24 DLC-73
Fr 1831 May 27 fin 17-1461
Davidson Thomas Green
Fr 1829 Nov 04 M639-4
Fr 1830 Dec 08 16-1352
Davidson County TN Court
Fr 1808 Jul DLC-4
To 1829 Jan 20 leg 12-0466
Davies Charles
Fr 1830 Oct 16# M222-27
Davies Edgar W
Fr 1838 Oct 08 DLC-51
Davies Jacob G
Fr 1836 Nov 11 32-0479
Davies Jacob G et al
Fr 1835 Feb M639-27
Daviess Samuel
Fr 1829 Apr 22 M639-15
Davis Charles Augustus
Fr 1833 Mar 12# DLC-42
Davis Charles W
Re 1832 Nov 14 21-0400
Davis E S
Fr 1831 Dec 15 M639-6
Fr 1832 Nov 22 DLC-41
To 1833 May 13 DLC-43
Fr 1833 Oct 18 23-1058
Fr 1834 Jan 29 DLC-44
Fr 1834 May 15 M639-6
Fr 1834 Jul 23 DLC-44
Fr 1835 Mar 18 DLC-45
Fr 1838 Mar 13 DLC-51
Davis Edmund Vaughan
Fr 1838 Jul 06 DLC-51
Davis Fielding
To 1841 May 13 DLC-53
Re 1841 cOct 35-0431
To 1841 Oct 22 35-0456
Davis George M
Fr 1835 Apr 10 fin DLC-46
Davis George W
Fr 1838 Jan 08 DLC-51
Fr 1838 Feb 05 DLC-51
Davis Hiram et al
Fr c1836 29-1389
Davis Ira
Fr 1828 May 24 DLC-35
Davis Isham F
To 1803 Mar 10 fin DLC-2
To 1804 Feb 23 fin 1-1286
Davis James
Fr 1813 Oct 03 DLC-6
Fr 1813 Oct 03* DLC-61
Fr 1831 Oct 20 M199-1
Davis Jane
Re 1836 Jan 22 par 30-0160
Davis John
To 1803 Mar 10 fin DLC-2
To 1804 Feb 23 fin 1-1286
Fr 1829 Mar 09 12-0899
Fr 1831 Jul 13 18-0206
Fr 1836 Apr 13 M687-28
Fr 1838 Apr 06# lnd DLC-51
Davis John M
Fr 1814 Sep 19 DLC-12
Fr c1815 4-0477
Fr 1815 Mar 29 DLC-17
Fr 1815 Jun 22 DLC-18
Fr 1818 Mar 6-0061
To 1818 May 07 DLC-24
To 1818 May 07* M271-2
To 1818 May 07* M221-77
To 1818 May 07* 6-0669
Fr 1818 May 08 DLC-25
Fr 1818 May 08 6-0684
Fr 1818 May 30 DLC-25
Fr 1818 Jul 22 6-1148
Fr 1818 Sep 09 DLC-25
Fr 1819 Jan 19 DLC-26
Fr 1819 Oct 02 DLC-27
Fr 1821 Feb 24 DLC-29
Fr 1821 Sep 22 DLC-30
Fr 1823 Jul 26 DLC-32
Fr 1827 Feb 01 DLC-34
Fr 1828 Oct 06 DLC-35
Fr 1829 Mar 05 M639-6
Fr 1829 Mar 28 M639-6
Fr 1829 Sep 08 M639-3
Fr 1830 Feb 03 M639-3
Fr 1830 Feb 10 M234-433
Fr 1838 Mar 06 DLC-51
Fr 1840 Feb 01 DLC-52
To 1844 Jun 24 DLC-74
Fr 1844 Jul 30 DLC-57
Fr 1844 Sep 09 36-0852
Davis John Wesley
Fr 1836 Dec 22 M687-8
Davis Joseph et al
Fr 1829 Jul 25 M639-2
Davis Joseph H
To 1840 Oct 29# leg DLC-53
Davis Levi
Fr 1843 May 29 DLC-55
Davis Nathan
To 1814 Jan 01 DLC-61
Fr 1814 Jan 29 DLC-66
To 1814 Apr 05 DLC-10
Davis Richard
Fr 1834 Jul 07 fin DLC-73
Davis Richard David
Fr 1829 Apr 15 12-1364
Davis Richard W
Re 1836 Nov 01 par 32-0381
Davis Robert C
Fr 1815 May 23 lnd 4-1054
Fr 1815 Jul 20 4-1123
Fr 1815 Nov 07 4-1224
Fr 1816 Jul 20 5-0318
Davis Saint Colombe
Fr 1840 Jan 09 34-1161
Davis Samuel
Re 1833 Aug 08 23-0298
To 1841 Oct 01 fin DLC-54
Davis Samuel B
Fr 1829 Jul 27 M873-19
Fr 1835 Apr 15 M639-10
Davis Samuel B et al
Fr 1831 Jan 22 17-0331
Fr 1831 Jan 22 M639-3
Davis Sarah
Re 1832 May 04 par 20-0468

Davis Thomas D
Fr 1828 Nov 14 DLC-35
Davis Thomas Terry
Fr 1805 Feb 20 DLC-3
Davis Thomas W
Fr 1828 Nov 09 DLC-35
Davis W B
Fr 1834 Oct 25# M179-78
Fr 1835 Sep 10 M124-149
Fr 1835 Sep 10 M124-149
Fr 1836 Nov 16 M124-155
Davis Warren Ransom
Fr 1829 Oct 20# 14-0203
Davis William
Fr 1834 Jun 24 25-1523
Re 1836 May 19 par 31-0052
Davis William G
Fr 1830 Aug 22 M688-79
Davis William George
Fr 1829 Dec 16 DLC-37
Davis William M
Fr 1834 Apr 15 M234-76
Davison Charles A
Fr 1838 Mar 27 DLC-51
Fr 1838 Nov 22 DLC-51
Davison S C
Fr 1834 Oct 21 fin DLC-44
Fr 1834 Nov 21 fin DLC-45
Fr 1834 Dec 22 fin DLC-45
Fr 1835 Apr 22 fin DLC-46
Fr 1835 Jun 22 fin DLC-46
Fr 1835 Jul 22 fin DLC-46
Fr 1835 Aug 21 fin DLC-46
Fr 1835 Oct 21 fin DLC-47
Davison William
Fr 1822 Nov 29 M439-5
Davison & Cheyney
To 1798 Mar 21 fin DLC-2
Davy J
Fr 1821 May fin DLC-70
Dawes William
Re 1830 May 15 par 15-1013
Dawns ______
To 1838 Apr 14 34-0319
Dawson Henry Barton
Fr 1844 Aug 20 36-0801
Dawson Jesse
Fr 1802 Feb 15 DLC-2
Dawson John Bennett
Fr 1829 May 20 M639-10
Fr 1834 Dec 09 M639-10
Fr 1845 Jan 18 36-1366
Dawson Moses
Fr 1828 Nov 24# DLC-35
Fr 1829 Mar 26 12-1137
Fr 1829 Mar 28 12-1159
Fr 1829 Sep 29 M639-21
To 1829 Oct 01 14-0063
Fr 1829 Nov 15# 14-0468
Fr 1829 Dec 20# DLC-37
Fr 1830 Jul 05 DLC-38
To 1830 Jul 17 16-0022
To 1830 Jul 17* DLC-38
Fr 1833 Nov 22 23-1291
To 1833 Dec 27 24-0601
To 1834 Mar 04 24-1568
Fr 1835 Jan 07 DLC-45
Fr 1836 Mar 16 DLC-47
Fr 1836 May 01 DLC-48
To 1837 May 26 33-1251
To 1837 Aug 31 33-1455
Fr 1837 Dec 04 DLC-50
To 1837 Dec 17 34-0093
Fr 1837 Dec 26 DLC-50
To 1838 Apr 10 34-0316
Fr 1838 Aug 28 DLC-51
To 1839 Nov 25 34-1061
To 1839 Dec 09 34-1074
To 1840 Jan 07# 34-1141
To 1840 Apr 01 34-1266
To 1840 Apr 22 34-1315
To 1840 Jun 19 34-1431
To 1840 Aug 10 34-1557
Fr 1841 Sep 20 DLC-53
To 1841 Sep 28 35-0410
Fr 1841 Dec 10 DLC-54
To 1841 Dec 16 35-0532
Fr 1842 Mar 16 DLC-54
To 1842 Mar 22 35-0652
Fr 1842 Jun 10 DLC-54
To 1842 Jun 21 35-0810
To 1842 Oct 26 35-0981
To 1842 Nov 24 35-1000
Fr 1842 Dec 05 DLC-54
Fr 1843 Jan 22 DLC-55
Fr 1843 Aug 02 DLC-55
To 1843 Aug 12 35-1463
To 1843 Oct 19 35-1546
To 1844 Jan 23 36-0149
To 1844 Aug 28 36-0829
Fr 1844 Sep 20 DLC-57
To 1844 Sep 27 36-0908
Fr 1844 Oct 14 DLC-57
Fr 1844 Oct 18 DLC-57
Fr 1844 Nov 07 DLC-57
Fr 1844 Nov 12 DLC-57
Fr 1844 Nov 13 DLC-57
To 1844 Nov 16 36-1024
Dawson Thomas
Fr 1844 Dec 19 DLC-57
To 1845 Jan 02 36-1294
Day Alexander Hamilton
Fr 1832 May 16 M179-73
Day Lewis
Fr 1844 Apr 29 DLC-56
Day Samuel W
Fr 1829 Feb 10 12-0495
Fr 1829 Nov 03 14-0396
Day & Brothers
Fr 1838 Jan 13 DLC-51
To 1838 Jan 18 34-0200
Day & Hubbell
To 1832 Aug 21# fin DLC-41
Dayan Charles
Fr 1830 Jan 26 M639-15
Dayne J
Fr 1832 Jan 11 M22-29
Dayton Aaron
To 1824 Dec 30 10-1017
Dayton John Kean
Fr 1830 Mar 09 M639-6
Daze Joseph
Fr 1829 Jun 15 13-0660
Deaderick David
Fr 1803 Nov 09 leg 1-1249
Deaderick David Samuel
To 1813 Jan 07 DLC-61
Fr 1813 Oct 06 DLC-6

Fr 1813 Oct 06* DLC-61
Fr 1813 Oct 10 DLC-6
To 1813 Nov 15 DLC-61
To 1814 Jan 31 DLC-62
Fr 1814 Oct 04 4-0256

Deaderick George Michael
Fr 1800 Jan 02 DLC-75
Fr 1802 Jan 21 DLC-2
Fr 1802 Jul 31 DLC-2
Fr 1802 Sep 10 DLC-2
Fr 1802 Sep 14 DLC-2
Fr 1806 Jul 20 2-0301
Re 1807 Apr leg DLC-60
Fr 1807 Apr 25 DLC-4
Fr 1808 Jan 15 DLC-4
Fr 1809 Mar 05 DLC-4
Fr 1810 Jun 04 fin DLC-4
Fr 1815 May 14 DLC-18
Fr 1815 Nov 16 DLC-19

Deaderick George Michael et al
Fr 1815 May 22 DLC-18

Deaderick George Michael & John
Fr 1796 May 30 fin DLC-1

Deaderick Mary
Re 1807 Apr leg DLC-60

Deaderick Thomas
Fr 1804 Apr 23 fin DLC-3
Fr 1819 Jul 03 fin DLC-27

Deaderick & Sittler
Fr 1804 Aug fin DLC-3

Deaderick & Tatum
Fr 1802 Jan 15 DLC-2
Fr 1802 Feb 10 DLC-2
Fr 1802 May 12 fin 1-0996
Fr 1802 May 12 fin DLC-2
To 1802 May 17 fin DLC-2
Fr 1802 Aug 07 fin DLC-2
Fr 1803 Dec 11 DLC-3

Dean John
Fr 1829 May 09 M639-6
Re 1829 Jun 06 13-0584

Dean Nicholas
Fr 1829 Mar 14 12-1007
Fr 1829 Mar 24 12-1094

Dean Samuel
Fr 1829 Dec 05 M22-28

Dearborn Henry
To 1803 cAug 01 M22-2
Fr 1803 Oct 31 M370-2
To 1803 Nov 12 DLC-3
Fr 1803 Dec 06 1-1252
Fr 1803 Dec 06* DLC-3
To 1803 Dec 17 M22-2
Fr 1804 Jan 11 1-1274
Fr 1804 Jan 11* M370-2
To 1804 Jan 13 DLC-3
To 1804 Jan 22 1-1276
To 1804 Mar 08 M22-2
To 1804 Apr 05 M22-2
To 1804 Jul 04 M22-2
To 1804 Nov 24 M22-2
To 1804 Nov 24 M22-2
Fr 1804 Dec 13 M370-2
Fr 1806 Dec 19 M370-2
To 1807 Jan 04 M221-9
To 1807 Jan 08 DLC-4
To 1807 Jan 08* M221-9
To 1807 cJan 17 DLC-4
To 1807 Mar 17 DLC-4
To 1807 Apr 24 M22-3
To 1807 Aug 01 2-0528
To 1807 Aug 01* M22-3

Deason Enoch
To 1818 Nov 10 lnd 6-1414

DeBast B
Fr 1836 Oct 12 32-0160

DeBree J B
Fr 1815 Nov 23 DLC-19

Debtors insolvent
Re 1831 cAug mem 18-0379

Debuys Gaspard M
Fr 1815 Jan 13 DLC-15
Fr 1815 Jan 13 DLC-15

DeCala Manuel
Re 1829 Jul 29 par 13-0954
Re 1829 Jul 29* par T967-1

DeCalo Angelus
Fr 1835 Mar 25 DLC-45

Decatur John Pine
Fr 1829 Mar 10 M639-9
Fr 1831 Oct 30 M567-60

Decatur Susan (Wheeler)
Fr 1828 Jan 22 11-1068
Fr 1829 Mar 07 M639-20
To 1829 Apr 02 DLC-36
Fr 1829 May 26 DLC-37
Fr 1829 Dec 31 DLC-37
To 1830 Jan 02 14-1294
To 1830 Jan 02* DLC-37
Fr 1830 Mar 19 DLC-38
Fr 1831 May 25 17-1421
Fr 1831 Jun 10 DLC-39
To 1831 Jun 24 18-0095
Fr 1832 Feb 09 M22-29
Fr 1833 May 13 DLC-43
Fr 1833 May 18 22-1392
To 1833 May 18 chk DLC-43
Fr 1833 May 19 22-1398
Fr 1833 May 22 22-1424

Decker Benjamin
To 1820 Oct 02# fin DLC-29

Decker John
Fr 1822 Mar 10 fin DLC-32

Decker & Black
Fr c1817 leg 37-0492
Fr c1817* leg 5-0652

Decker & Dyer
Fr 1824 Apr 10 fin DLC-32
Fr 1824 May 18 fin DLC-32
Fr 1824 Jun 24 fin DLC-32
Fr 1826 Jul 19 fin DLC-34
Fr 1826 Nov 15 fin DLC-34
Fr 1827 Jun 05 fin DLC-34
Fr 1832 Sep 17 fin DLC-41

DeClouet Charles
Fr 1815 Feb 15 DLC-16

DeCluny _____
Fr 1815 Feb 10 DLC-16

DeCluny _____ (Capt)
Fr 1815 Jan 06 DLC-15

DeCluny _____ (Gen)
Fr 1815 Jan 16 DLC-15

DeCoin R L
Fr 1836 Dec 08 32-1061

Dedham MA citizens
Fr 1836 May 06 30-1523

DeForest Benjamin et al
Fr 1837 Feb 23 M687-24

DeForest & Son et al
Fr 1832 Apr 02 M639-2
DeGraff John Isaac
Fr 1831 Feb 15 M124-126
Degraffenried Mathew F
Fr 1816 Jul 28 DLC-21
DeGroot Henry
Fr 1833 Apr 23 M639-16
DeKay George Coleman
Fr 1843 Apr 26 DLC-55
DeKay James Ellsworth
Fr 1833 Mar 01 M688-88
Fr 1833 Mar 26 M688-88
DeKoster Peter Frederic William
Fr 1831 Jan 05 M639-6
DeKrafft Edward
To 1830 May 24 15-1074
Fr 1832 Mar 05 M179-72
DeKrafft Edward et al
Fr 1833 cMay 25 22-1454
To 1833 May 29# 22-1499
DeLacy John Devereux
Fr 1818 Jan 31 DLC-24
Fr 1829 Jul 17 M221-110
Delaffite ______ et al
Fr 1815 Mar 08 DLC-17
DeLagnel Adolphus H
Fr 1845 Mar 03 DLC-57
DeLagnel Julius Adolphus
Fr 1830 Apr 17# M124-123
Fr 1836 Sep 26 M22-40
Fr 1836 Oct 01 31-1568
Delaplaine John F
Re 1832 Mar 08 par 19-1350
Delaplaine Joseph
Fr 1815 Mar 25 DLC-17
Fr 1818 Dec 31 DLC-26
Delarue Dupuis
Fr 1829 Nov 18 DLC-37
Delasserriere A
Fr 1833 Jul 29 M688-90
Delaunay David
Fr 1815 Jul 17 DLC-18
Delaunay Luuyt Burgy & Co
Fr 1833 Apr 25 M639-16
Delavan Benjamin
Fr 1820 Sep 14 DLC-29
Delavan Edward C
Fr 1838 Jul 30 DLC-51
Delaware treaty
Re 1830 Jan 02 M668-6
Re 1831 Mar 24 M668-6
DeLesdernier William
Fr 1837 Jan 18 M687-20
Delintosh James & Co
To 1837 May 11 33-1214
Dell James et al
Fr 1829 cOct 01 14-0069
Delle Vidue T
Fr 1831 Oct 13 M664-2
Fr 1831 Oct 13* 18-1012
Deloach Simon
Fr 1831 Jul 15 DLC-39
Delony Edward
Fr 1840 Jan 10# 34-1163
Delotch John
Re 1802 Jul 15 leg 1-1029
Demick Prelate
Fr 1839 Jan 24 DLC-51
To 1839 Feb 06 34-0624
DeMiollis Charles E
Fr 1843 Jun DLC-55
Fr 1844 Nov 18 DLC-57
Democrat (pseudonym)
Fr 1834 Feb 08 24-1254
Fr 1834 cMar 24-1516
Democratic Hickory Club No. 1
To 1832 Jan 04 DLC-73
Democratic Review
Re 1844 mem 36-0087
Demonbreun Timothy
Re 1792 Jan 12# leg 1-0121
Dempsy Andrew et al
Fr 1829 Mar 12-0630
Denison Conain & Co
Fr 1837 Feb 28 fin DLC-51
Denman Samuel
Re 1807 Jul 29 leg 2-0523
Denmark claims convention
Re 1830 Jun 02 15-1263
Re 1830 Jun 05 15-1290
Denney John
Fr 1829 Mar 26 M234-432
Dennison Gilbert
Re 1831 Feb 01 17-0397
Denny Harmar
To 1830 May 06# DLC-38
Denson Jesse
Fr 1814 Nov 05 DLC-13
Dent Hatch
Fr 1815 Jan 06 DLC-15
To 1815 Jan 07 DLC-62
Fr 1815 Jan 11 DLC-15
Dent Lewis
Fr 1829 Aug 24 13-1197
DePauw John
Fr 1832 Jan 16 19-0698
Deposit bill
Re 1836 Jun mem 31-0228
Re 1836 Jun mem 31-0237
Derbigny Pierre et al
Fr 1814 Dec 29 4-0473
Derby John B
Fr 1829 Jul 02 DLC-37
DeRham Iselin & Moore et al
Fr 1829 Jul M639-14
Derickson Joseph
Re 1814 Jan 31 DLC-62
DeRome Charles H
Fr 1832 May 01 20-0448
Fr 1834 Jan 24-0712
DeRussy Rene Edward
Fr 1821 Sep 05 DLC-30
Fr 1833 Nov 04# M688-89
Fr 1834 Oct 09# M688-94
Fr 1836 Jan 12 29-1567
DeSaternand A
Fr 1832 Jan 12 M22-29
Deserters
Re 1813 Nov 29 DLC-7
Re 1814 Jan 31 DLC-62
Desforges Louis
Fr 1843 Aug 35-1441
To 1843 Oct 30 35-1571
Desha Benjamin
Fr 1829 Jul 01# 13-0772
Desha Joseph
Fr 1825 Jun 08 DLC-33
To 1825 Jun 24 DLC-33

Fr 1829 Feb 23 M639-2
Fr 1829 Feb 24 M639-2
Fr 1829 Feb 24 M639-21
Fr 1834 May 31 25-1192
Fr 1840 Oct 18 DLC-53

Desha Robert
To 1816 Jun 17 lnd 5-0170
Fr 1828 Jan 21 DLC-35
Fr 1828 Dec 05 DLC-36
Fr 1829 Mar 03 M639-18
Fr 1830 Apr 08 M567-51
Fr 1830 May 25 15-1082

Deshon C Mrs
Fr 1834 Oct 04 DLC-44

DeSoto Bernardo
Re 1835 Jun 05 par 28-0571
Re 1835 Jul 06 par 28-0954

DeSoto Jose
Fr 1814 Nov 14 4-0336
To 1814 Nov 15 DLC-62
To 1814 Nov 15* 4-0344

Desporter Mahe Madame
Fr 1815 Jul 07 DLC-18

Detrahuit
Fr 1831 May 28 M234-31

Detray William R et al
Fr 1832 Jul 10 20-1008

Deutsche Edouard
Re 1831 Oct 19 par 18-1028

Devereux James
Re 1830 mem DLC-38

Devereux James et al
Fr 1829 cJun 01 13-0531

Devers Margaret
Fr 1834 Jan 12 24-0862

Dew John Howell
Fr 1837 Jun 16 33-1305
Fr 1840 May 15 DLC-52

Dewees M
Fr 1829 Mar 10 12-0924

Dewees William et al
Fr 1831 Jan 25 M639-1

Dewey William
Re 1833 May 31 22-1534

DeWitt Charles Gerrit
Fr 1831 Mar 14 M639-6
Fr 1831 Jul 20 DLC-39
Fr 1832 Feb 06 DLC-40
Fr 1833 Feb 04 M219-2

DeWolf James
Fr 1829 Jul 10 M639-6

DeWolf John et al
Fr 1831 Sep 10 M639-11

Dexter Samuel et al
Fr 1829 Mar 12 12-0971

Dey Anthony
Fr 1830 Jan 22 DLC-37

Dezong Dirk Ary
Re 1832 Sep 15 par 20-1528

Diana (mare)
Re 1834 Aug 16 26-0321

Dibble Orange H
Fr 1834 Feb 01 DLC-44
Fr 1834 Mar 15 25-0218
Fr 1834 Jul 10 26-0209

Dick William et al
Fr 1832 Sep 01 20-1472

Dickerson Mahlon
Fr 1829 Mar 24 M639-17
Fr 1829 Jun 10 M124-120
Fr 1829 Jul 31 M639-14
Fr 1829 Aug 01 M873-19
Fr 1829 Dec 15 M639-21
Fr 1831 May 26 M639-12
Fr 1831 Aug 10 M179-71
Fr 1834 Jun 30 26-0002
Fr 1834 Jul 03 M472-2
Fr 1834 Jul 03 M472-2
To 1834 Jul 03# M37-10
To 1834 Jul 07 26-0178
Fr 1834 Jul 07 M472-2
Fr 1834 Oct 02 M472-2
Fr 1834 Oct 20 M472-2
Fr 1834 Oct 30 26-0773
Fr 1834 Oct 30* M472-2
Fr 1834 Oct 30 M472-2
Fr 1834 Nov 01 M472-2
Fr 1834 Nov 03 M472-2
Fr 1834 Nov 04 M472-2
Fr 1834 Nov 12 M472-2
Fr 1834 Nov 12 M472-2
Fr 1834 Nov 13 M472-2
Fr 1834 Nov 15 26-0928
Fr 1834 Nov 15* M472-2
Fr 1834 Nov 25 M472-2
Fr 1834 Nov 29 26-1069
Fr 1834 Nov 29* DLC-77
Fr 1834 Dec 01 M472-2
Fr 1834 Dec 16 M472-2
Fr 1834 Dec 19 M472-2
Fr 1834 Dec 27 M472-2
To 1835 M124-146
Fr 1835 Jan 08 27-0133
Fr 1835 Jan 08* M472-2
Fr 1835 Jan 14 M472-2
To 1835 Jan 14# M124-146
To 1835 Jan 19 27-0255
Fr 1835 Jan 21 M472-2
Fr 1835 Jan 22 M472-2
To 1835 Jan 24 M124-146
Fr 1835 Feb 06 M472-2
To 1835 Feb 09 M124-146
To 1835 Feb 09* 27-0449
Fr 1835 Feb 16 M472-2
To 1835 Feb 20 M124-146
Fr 1835 Feb 24 M472-2
To 1835 Feb 25 M124-146
Fr 1835 Feb 27 M472-2
Fr 1835 Mar 02 M472-2
Fr 1835 Mar 04 M472-2
Fr 1835 Mar 09 M472-2
Fr 1835 Mar 12 M472-2
Fr 1835 Mar 27 M472-2
Fr 1835 Mar 30 M472-2
Fr 1835 Mar 31 M472-2
Fr 1835 Apr 03 M472-2
Fr 1835 May 04 28-0257
Fr 1835 May 05 28-0289
Fr 1835 Jun 23 M124-148
Fr 1835 Jun 23* M472-2
Fr 1835 Jun 24 M124-148
Fr 1835 Jun 24* M472-2
Fr 1835 Jun 27 M472-2
To 1835 Jun 29 M124-148
To 1835 Jul 11# M124-154
Fr 1835 Jul 22 M472-2
Fr 1835 Jul 24 M472-2
Fr 1835 Jul 24* 28-1130
Fr 1835 Jul 25 M472-2

Dickerson Mahlon (cont)

Fr 1835 Aug 04		M472-2
Fr 1835 Aug 28		M472-2
To 1835 Sep 09		29-0006
Fr 1835 Sep 15		M472-2
Fr 1835 Sep 25		M124-149
Fr 1835 Sep 28		M639-8
Fr 1835 Sep 29		DLC-73
Fr 1835 Sep 29*		M472-2
Fr 1835 Oct 08		M472-2
Fr 1835 Nov 28		M472-2
Fr 1835 Nov 30		M639-9
Fr 1835 Dec 05		29-0746
Fr 1835 Dec 05*		DLC-77
Fr 1835 Dec 08		M472-2
Fr 1835 Dec 11		M472-2
Fr 1835 Dec 16		M472-2
Fr 1835 Dec 18		M472-2
Fr 1835 Dec 21		M205-2
Fr 1835 Dec 21*		M205-1
Fr 1835 Dec 21		M472-2
Fr 1835 Dec 23		M472-2
To c1836#		29-1391
Fr 1836 Jan 07		M472-2
To 1836 Jan 09		29-1529
Fr 1836 Jan 15		M472-2
Fr 1836 Jan 16		M472-2
To 1836 Jan 19#		M124-151
Fr 1836 Jan 28		M472-2
Fr 1836 Feb 08		M472-2
Fr 1836 Feb 24		30-0496
Fr 1836 Feb 24*		M472-2
Fr 1836 Feb 24		M472-2
To 1836 Feb 26		M124-151
Fr 1836 Mar 09		M472-2
Fr 1836 Mar 11		M472-2
Fr 1836 Mar 12		M472-2
Fr 1836 Mar 25		M472-2
Fr 1836 Mar 30		M472-2
Fr 1836 Mar 31		M472-2
Fr 1836 Mar 31*		30-0948
Fr 1836 Apr 15		M472-2
Fr 1836 Apr 20		M472-2
Fr 1836 Apr 25		M472-2
Fr 1836 Apr 26		M472-2
Fr 1836 May 03		M472-2
Fr 1836 May 03		M472-2
Fr 1836 May 05		M472-2
Fr 1836 May 07		M472-2
Fr 1836 May 12		M472-2
Fr 1836 May 17		31-0049
Fr 1836 May 17*		M472-2
Fr 1836 May 19		M472-2
Fr 1836 May 19		M273-33
Fr 1836 May 19*		M472-2
Fr 1836 May 19		M472-2
Fr 1836 May 19		M273-33
Fr 1836 May 19*		M472-2
Fr 1836 May 21		M472-2
Fr 1836 Jun 03		M472-2
Fr 1836 Jun 03		M472-2
Fr 1836 Jun 15		M472-2
To 1836 Jun 18#		M124-153
To 1836 Jun 20		M124-153
To 1836 Jun 20*		DLC-48
Fr 1836 Jun 20		M124-153
Fr 1836 Jun 21		M472-2
Fr 1836 Jul 02		M472-2
To 1836 Jul 05		31-0868
To 1836 Jul 07		31-0931
Fr 1836 Jul 07		M472-2
To 1836 Jul 09		31-1008
To 1836 Jul 09#		31-1005
Fr 1836 Aug 23		DLC-49
Fr 1836 Oct 03		M472-3
Fr 1836 Oct 04		M472-3
Fr 1836 Oct 05		M472-3
Fr 1836 Oct 06		M472-3
Fr 1836 Oct 07		M472-3
Fr 1836 Oct 08		M472-3
To 1836 Oct 10		32-0122
Fr 1836 Oct 31		M472-3
To 1836 Nov 10#		32-0476
Fr 1836 Nov 11		M472-3
Fr 1836 Nov 12		M472-3
Fr 1836 Dec 03		32-0796
Fr 1836 Dec 12		M472-3
Fr 1836 Dec 14		M472-3
Fr 1836 Dec 28		32-1370
Fr 1837 Jan 03		M472-3
Fr 1837 Jan 05		M472-3
Fr 1837 Jan 20		M472-3
To 1837 Feb 02		M124-156
Fr 1837 Feb 06		33-0411
Fr 1837 Feb 06*		M472-3
Fr 1837 Feb 07		M472-3
To 1837 Feb 20		33-0779
Fr 1837 Mar 02		M124-153
Fr 1837 Mar 02*		M472-3
Fr 1837 Mar 02		M472-3
Fr 1837 Mar 03		M472-3
To 1837 Aug 29		33-1453
To 1838 Jan 10		34-0178
Fr 1838 Feb 07		DLC-51

Dickerson Mahlon et al

Fr 1833 Oct 24		M639-6
Fr 1834 Feb 26		M639-3

Dickey John

Fr 1827 Mar 30	fin	11-0517

Dickins Asbury

To 1829 Apr 24		13-0131
To 1829 Apr 24*		DLC-60
Fr 1829 Apr 24		13-0134
To 1829 Nov 21		14-0541
To 1831 Jun 21		18-0070
To 1831 Jul 28#		DLC-39
Fr 1831 Aug 03		18-0411
To 1831 Aug 06		18-0448
To 1831 Oct 18		18-1020
To 1832 Mar 17		19-1499
Fr 1832 Mar 19#		19-1503
Fr 1832 Mar 19*		M733-1
Fr 1832 Mar 21		19-1517
Fr 1832 Mar 21*		M733-1
To 1832 Jul 18		20-1135
To 1832 Nov 08		21-0350
Fr c1833		37-0308
Re 1833 May 06		22-1304
Re 1833 May 29		22-1498
Re 1833 Aug 10		23-0309
To 1833 Nov 11		23-1216
To 1834 Apr 29#		M179-78
Re 1834 Jul 08		26-0186
To 1834 Oct 03		26-0487
To 1834 Oct 14#		26-0643
Fr 1834 Oct 15		26-0650
To 1835 Jan 07#		27-0116
To 1835 Jan 20#		M639-7
Fr 1835 Feb 10#		M639-3

To 1835 Feb 10# M639-3
To 1835 Feb 26# M179-79
To 1835 May 02 28-0220
To 1835 May 16# M639-9
To 1835 Jun 08# 28-0607
To 1835 Jul 06 28-0959
To 1835 Aug 31 28-1464
To 1835 Sep 10 29-0015
To 1835 Sep 28 29-0133
To 1835 Oct 03 29-0175
To 1835 Oct 12 29-0277
To 1836 May 12 M179-82
Re 1836 May 19 31-0057
Re 1836 Jul 07 31-0933
Fr 1836 Aug 01 31-1181
Fr 1836 Aug 01 31-1182
Fr 1836 Aug 05 DLC-48
Fr 1836 Aug 10 M179-82
Fr 1836 Aug 10* M40-26
To 1836 Aug 17 31-1303
To 1836 Aug 17* DLC-48
To 1836 Aug 21 M179-82
Fr 1836 Aug 24 DLC-49
Fr 1836 Oct 03 32-0044
Fr 1836 Oct 04 32-0055
To 1836 Oct 20 32-0250
To 1836 Dec 12# 32-1096
To 1837 Jan 31 33-0271

Dickinson Charles Henry
Fr 1806 Jan 10 DLC-71
Fr 1806 Jan 10* 2-0118
Fr 1806 May 21# 2-0243
Re 1806 May 23 2-0246
Re 1806 cJun mem 2-0257

Dickinson David W
Fr 1833 Sep 27 M639-3

Dickinson John (ME)
Fr 1837 Feb 02 M687-20
Fr 1837 Feb 02 33-0360

Dickinson John (ME) et al
Fr 1836 Jan 07 29-1492

Dickinson John (TN)
Re 1805 cJul 28 mem DLC-60
To 1806 Jul 21 lnd 2-0303
To 1810 Jul 18 fin DLC-4

Dickson David
Fr 1836 Jan 20 M639-27

Dickson Ephraim D
Fr 1834 Jul 14 M234-79

Dickson James
Fr 1814 Dec 29 DLC-15

Dickson John
Fr 1807 Apr 06 fin DLC-4

Dickson William
To 1801 Sep 01 1-0913
Fr 1801 Sep 16 1-0917
Fr 1802 Mar 04 DLC-2
Fr 1802 Apr 17 DLC-2
Fr 1802 Sep 29 DLC-2
Fr 1802 Dec 10 DLC-2
Fr 1803 Oct 31 DLC-3
Fr 1803 Nov 20 DLC-3
Fr 1803 Nov 21 DLC-3
Fr 1803 Dec DLC-3
Fr 1803 Dec 06 DLC-3
Fr 1804 Jan 08 DLC-3
Fr 1804 Dec 22 DLC-3
Re 1805 Oct 01 leg 2-0086
To 1806 Nov 17 DLC-4
Fr 1806 Dec 15 2-0398
Fr 1806 Dec 21 2-0411

Didenhover Benjamin W
Re 1830 May 04 par 15-0883

Dietz Louis
Fr 1832 Nov 21 M639-26

Digges Edward
Fr 1829 Mar 24 12-1096

Dill Benjamin F et al
Fr 1840 Aug 18 34-1565

Dill James
Fr 1831 Nov 05 M639-16
Fr 1831 Nov 05 M639-16
Fr 1831 Nov 05 M639-16

Dill John
Fr 1829 Apr 20 M234-237
Fr 1830 Jul 10 M234-433

Dillahunty Lewis
Fr 1815 Jun 20 DLC-71

Dillard L
Fr 1838 Mar 18 DLC-51

Diller Adam
Fr 1832 Dec 28 M221-113

Dillingham James
Re 1834 Jan 17 par 24-0965

Dillingham Lucy Elizabeth
Fr 1837 Feb 11 33-0617

Dillon Edward
To 1802 Jun 28 lnd 1-1007
To 1802 Jun 28 lnd 1-1012

Dillon George D
Fr 1829 Aug 10 M179-67

Dimock Davis et al
Fr 1829 Mar 12 M639-19

Dineur ______
Fr 1836 May 31 DLC-48
Fr 1836 May 31* 31-0214

Dingee Henry Augustus
Fr 1833 Oct 28 add 23-1096
Fr 1834 Mar 04 DLC-44

Dingee William H
Fr 1830 Oct 05 M639-6

Dinkins James Edward
Fr 1814 Sep 09 DLC-12
To 1814 Sep 15 DLC-62
Fr 1814 Sep 18 DLC-12
Fr 1814 Sep 21 DLC-12
Fr 1814 Sep 24 DLC-12
Fr 1814 Sep 30 DLC-12
Fr 1814 Oct 03 DLC-13
Fr 1814 Oct 08 DLC-13
Fr 1814 Oct 12 DLC-13
Fr 1814 Nov 21 M566-41
Re 1819 Jun 10 7-0552
To 1819 Nov 22 DLC-63
Fr 1820 Jan 20# 7-1001

Dinsmoor Samuel
Fr 1832 Feb 18 19-1151
Fr 1833 Jun 29 add 23-0074

Dinsmoor Silas
Fr 1815 Jan 26 DLC-15
Fr 1815 Jan 27 DLC-16
To 1815 Jan 30 DLC-16
Fr 1815 Feb 10 DLC-16
Fr 1815 Feb 11 DLC-16

Diplomatic dress
Re 1829 May 18 mem 13-0346
Re 1829 Jun 15 M179-67

Disbrow Henry et al
Fr 1834 Jul 22 M639-27

Disney David Tiernan
    Fr 1834 Dec 12   M639-1
    Fr 1835 Mar 20   M639-1
Disney David Tiernan et al
    Fr 1832 Dec 12   21-1014
Disosway Gabriel P
    Fr 1829 Jul 02   DLC-37
Distillery
    Re 1801 Jan 03   leg   DLC-2
    Re 1803 Aug 07   mem   DLC-71
District of Columbia banks
    Re 1836 May 25   mem   DLC-48
Ditto James
    Fr 1813 Nov 10   DLC-7
Ditty Samuel
    Fr 1830 Jan 06#   fin   DLC-38
    Fr 1830 Nov 12#   fin   DLC-38
Dix John Adams
    Re 1829 Nov   mem   14-0316
    Fr 1829 Nov 10   M639-6
    Fr 1834 Dec 12   M688-96
    Fr 1835 Dec 07   29-0779
Dix John Adams et al
    Fr 1832 May 26   20-0604
Dixon Ann L
    Fr 1842 Feb 09   DLC-54
Dixon Jacob
    Re 1831 Mar 24   par   17-0945
Dixon Samuel
    Fr 1844 Jun 24   36-0641
Dixon Tilman
    Fr 1805   DLC-2
Doak John
    Fr 1812 Aug 21   DLC-5
Dobbs Richard
    To 1824 Jan 27   fin   10-0399
Dodd Jesse
    Fr 1836 Aug 07   DLC-48
Dodds Ebenezer
    Fr 1832 Jul 22   fin   DLC-41
Dodge Henry
    To 1836 Apr 30   M236-14
Dodge Jeremiah et al
    Fr 1834 Jan   M639-18
Dodge John Wood
    Re 1842 Apr 28   35-0687
Dodge Joshua
    Re 1833 Apr 30   22-1213
Dodson Timothy
    Re 1839 Jan 23   leg   34-0605
Dodson Timothy F et al
    Fr 1844 Dec 24   36-1259
Doggett John L
    Fr 1831 Oct 20   M639-6
Doherty George
    To 1814 Feb 03   DLC-61
    To 1814 Feb 11   DLC-61
    To 1814 Feb 14   DLC-61
    Fr 1814 Feb 22   DLC-75
    To 1814 Feb 28   DLC-61
    To 1814 Feb 28   DLC-61
    To 1814 Mar 02   DLC-61
    Fr 1814 Mar 02   DLC-61
    Fr 1814 Mar 06   DLC-9
    Fr 1814 Mar 06*   M221-56
    To 1814 Mar 10   DLC-61
    Fr 1814 Mar 22   DLC-9
    To 1814 Apr 24   DLC-10
    To 1814 Apr 25   DLC-10
Doherty James
    To 1814 Feb 11   DLC-61
    To 1814 Mar 01   DLC-61
    To 1814 Mar 14   DLC-61
    To 1814 Mar 23   DLC-29
Dolbear Rufus
    Fr 1844 Oct 14#   fin   DLC-57
Donahoe ______
    Fr 1835 May 20   M567-107
Donaldson John J et al
    Fr 1832 Nov 15   21-0405
    To 1832 Nov 15   21-0406
Donelson Alexander (1751-1834)
    To 1797 Oct 18   lnd   1-0532
    Fr 1798   fin   1-0564
    Fr 1815 Sep 01   4-1180
    Re 1823 Mar 03   9-0474
Donelson Alexander (1784-1814)
    Fr 1811 Oct 09   DLC-5
Donelson Alexander (1816-1887)
    To 1836 Mar 15   chk   30-0792
    Fr 1841 Apr 28   DLC-53
Donelson Andrew Jackson (1799-1871)
    To 1817 Jan 12   5-0685
    To 1817 Feb 23   5-0736
    To 1817 Feb 24   5-0739
    Fr 1817 Apr 05   5-0801
    To 1817 Apr 29   5-0842
    To 1817 Aug 04   5-0953
    To 1817 Oct 20   5-1108
    To 1817 Dec 04   5-1161
    To 1817 Dec 16   5-1175
    To 1818 Feb 05   5-1428
    To 1818 Jul 14   6-1122
    To 1818 Aug 03   6-1180
    To 1818 Sep 07   6-1285
    To 1818 Sep 20   6-1314
    To 1818 Oct 19#   6-1372
    Fr 1818 Nov 23   DLC-26
    To 1818 Nov 24   6-1438
    Fr 1818 Nov 29   DLC-71
    To 1818 Dec 28   7-0085
    Fr 1819   DLC-59
    To 1819 Jan 31   7-0220
    To 1819 Feb 15   7-0273
    Fr 1819 May 05   DLC-27
    To 1819 May 17   7-0524
    To 1819 Jul 23   7-0585
    To 1819 Aug 06   7-0595
    To 1819 Sep 17   7-0667
    To 1819 Oct 12   7-0712
    To 1819 Nov 16   7-0863
    To 1819 Nov 21   7-0873
    To 1819 Dec 03   7-0904
    To 1819 Dec 30   7-0953
    To 1820 Jan 31   7-1018
    To 1820 Feb 09   7-1024
    To 1820 Feb 29   7-1036
    To 1820 Mar 21   7-1050
    To 1820 Mar 21   7-1053
    To 1820 cApr 16   7-1073
    To 1820 May 06   7-1086
    To 1820 May 15   7-1094
    To 1820 Jul 14   7-1153
    To 1820 Aug 19   7-1211
    Fr 1820 Dec 20#   DLC-63
    Fr 1821 Jan 14#   DLC-63
    Fr 1821 Jan 14#   DLC-63
    To 1821 Feb 18   DLC-63

To 1821 Feb 28		8-0146
Fr 1821 Mar 03		DLC-29
To 1821 Mar 10		8-0176
To 1821 Mar 31		8-0274
Fr 1821 Apr 29#		DLC-63
Fr 1821 May 07#		DLC-63
Fr 1821 May 10#		DLC-63
Fr 1821 May 12#		DLC-63
Fr 1821 May 12#		DLC-63
Fr 1821 May 13#		DLC-63
Fr 1821 May 13#		DLC-63
Fr 1821 May 13#		DLC-63
To 1821 Jul 03		8-0758
To 1821 Jul 22		DLC-63
Fr 1821 Aug 16	mem	DLC-63
To 1821 Aug 25		8-1097
Fr 1821 Oct 08	mem	DLC-70
Fr 1821 Oct 08	fin	DLC-70
Fr 1821 Nov 12		M116-9
Fr 1821 Nov 12*		DLC-63
To 1822 Mar 15		9-0052
To 1822 Mar 21		9-0070
To 1822 Apr 01		9-0091
To 1822 Apr 12		9-0110
To 1822 Apr 22		9-0133
To 1822 Apr 26		9-0137
To 1822 May 02		9-0142
To 1822 May 16		9-0164
To 1822 May 19		9-0165
To 1822 May 20		9-0167
To 1822 Jun 02		9-0184
Fr 1822 Jun 05		DLC-31
To 1822 Jun 28		9-0191
To 1822 Jul 05		9-0213
To 1822 Jul 16		9-0217
To 1822 Jul 25		9-0224
To 1822 Aug 06		9-0239
Fr 1822 Aug 19		DLC-31
Fr 1822 Aug 27		DLC-31
To 1822 Aug 28		9-0259
To 1822 Sep 06		9-0263
To 1822 Sep 27		9-0273
To 1822 Oct 11		9-0285
To 1822 Oct 23		9-0297
Fr 1822 Nov 09		9-0301
To 1822 Nov 27		9-0329
To 1822 Dec 13		9-0353
Fr 1822 Dec 14		9-0357
To 1822 Dec 16		9-0359
To 1822 Dec 23		9-0368
Fr 1822 cDec 30		9-0379
To 1823 Jan 08		9-0387
To 1823 Jan 21		9-0409
To 1823 Feb 08		9-0448
To 1823 Feb 22		9-0465
To 1823 Mar 05		9-0480
To 1823 Mar 08		9-0484
To 1823 Mar 10		9-0490
To 1823 Jun 04		9-0587
To 1823 Nov 16		DLC-32
To 1823 Dec 05		DLC-72
Fr 1824 Jan 06		9-0895
To 1824 Jan 14		DLC-32
To 1824 Jan 16		DLC-32
To 1824 Jan 18		DLC-32
To 1824 Jan 21		DLC-32
To 1824 Feb 12		10-0449
To 1824 Feb 26		10-0483
To 1824 Mar 01		10-0500

To 1824 Mar 06		10-0526
To 1824 Mar 07		10-0531
To 1824 Mar 07		10-0534
To 1824 Mar 13		10-0551
To 1824 Mar 16		10-0557
To 1824 Mar 19		10-0567
To 1824 Mar 27		10-0597
To 1824 Mar 27		10-0600
To 1824 Apr 04		10-0626
To 1824 Apr 11		10-0639
To 1824 Apr 15	chk	10-0643
To 1824 Apr 16		10-0645
To 1824 Apr 17		10-0649
To 1824 Apr 23		10-0679
To 1824 Apr 27		10-0687
To 1824 Apr 28		10-0695
To 1824 May 14		10-0723
To 1824 May 18	chk	10-0729
To 1824 May 21		10-0744
Re 1824 Jun	fin	10-0760
Fr 1824 Jun	mem	10-0769
To 1824 Jun 11	mem	10-0783
To 1824 Jun 11	chk	10-0785
To 1824 Jun 14	chk	37-0497
To 1824 Jun 20	chk	10-0800
To 1824 Jun 30	chk	10-0816
To 1824 Sep 04	chk	10-0890
To 1824 Oct 04#		DLC-33
Re 1824 Oct 11	lnd	10-0913
To 1824 Oct 21	chk	10-0945
Fr 1825 Mar 16	fin	DLC-72
To 1825 Jun 29		10-1329
To 1827 Feb 22	lnd	DLC-34
Fr 1827 Feb 22	lnd	DLC-34
To 1828 Jun 26	chk	12-0031
To c1829#		37-0284
To 1829 Jan 24#		M639-26
To 1829 Feb 14#		M639-8
To 1829 Feb 16#		M639-2
To 1829 Feb 17#		M639-10
To 1829 Feb 18#		M639-10
To 1829 Feb 23#		DLC-36
To 1829 Feb 23#		M639-16
To 1829 Feb 23#		M639-2
To 1829 Feb 25#		M639-2
Fr 1829 Mar#		12-0676
To 1829 Mar 01#		DLC-36
To 1829 Mar 02#		M639-11
Fr 1829 Mar 06#		DLC-60
Fr 1829 Mar 06#		DLC-60
To 1829 Mar 07#		M639-11
To 1829 Mar 09#		M639-22
To 1829 Mar 11#		M639-20
To 1829 Mar 14#		M639-12
To 1829 Mar 18	chk	DLC-36
Fr 1829 Mar 20#		DLC-60
Fr 1829 Mar 20#		DLC-60
To 1829 Mar 25#		M639-21
To 1829 Mar 29#		12-1177
To 1829 Apr 04	chk	DLC-36
To 1829 Apr 05#		M639-5
To 1829 Apr 06#		M639-2
To 1829 Apr 08#		M639-15
To 1829 Apr 09#		M639-4
To 1829 Apr 11	chk	DLC-36
Fr 1829 Apr 14#		M23-13
To 1829 Apr 14#		12-1343
To 1829 Apr 14*		37-0499
Fr 1829 Apr 15#		DLC-36

Donelson Andrew Jackson (cont)

To 1829 Apr 17#		M639-15
To 1829 Apr 20#		DLC-72
To 1829 Apr 21		DLC-72
To 1829 Apr 22#		13-0098
To 1829 May 05	chk	DLC-37
Fr 1829 May 14#		M639-5
To 1829 May 14#		13-0321
To 1829 May 22#	fin	DLC-37
To 1829 May 23#		M639-10
To 1829 May 23#		M639-26
To 1829 cMay 31		13-0513
To 1829 Jun 04#		13-0572
To 1829 Jun 05#		M639-22
Fr 1829 Jun 09	mem	DLC-60
Fr 1829 Jun 11#		13-0631
To 1829 Jun 25#		M639-8
To 1829 Jul 06	chk	DLC-37
To 1829 Jul 16#		M639-15
To 1829 Jul 23#		M639-21
To 1829 Aug 04#		M639-14
To 1829 Aug 06	chk	DLC-37
Fr 1829 Aug 08#		13-1042
Fr 1829 Aug 13	mem	13-1116
To 1829 Aug 13#		37-0503
Fr 1829 Aug 15#		M179-67
To 1829 Aug 18#		M639-10
Fr 1829 Aug 19#		M179-67
To 1829 Aug 20		13-1178
To 1829 Aug 21#		13-1181
To 1829 Aug 22		13-1193
Fr 1829 Sep#		DLC-37
To 1829 Sep 03		13-1239
Fr 1829 Sep 03	mem	DLC-37
Fr 1829 Sep 03*	mem	DLC-72
To 1829 Sep 05	chk	DLC-37
Fr 1829 Sep 05#		13-1258
To 1829 Sep 08#		M25-24
To 1829 Sep 08		13-1267
Fr 1829 Sep 15#		DLC-37
Fr 1829 Sep 25	mem	DLC-37
To 1829 Oct 05	chk	DLC-37
To 1829 Oct 05	chk	DLC-37
To 1829 Oct 05#		14-0106
To 1829 Oct 06#		M639-1
To 1829 Oct 12#		M124-121
To 1829 Oct 15#		M639-11
Fr 1829 Oct 17#		M273-27
To 1829 Oct 20#		14-0203
Fr 1829 Oct 23#		14-0238
Fr 1829 Oct 23#		14-0239
To 1829 Nov 04	chk	DLC-37
To 1829 Nov 24#		14-0594
To 1829 Dec 04#		14-0796
To 1829 Dec 05	chk	DLC-37
Fr 1829 Dec 05#		14-0801
To 1829 Dec 06#		DLC-72
To 1829 Dec 07#		M639-14
To 1829 Dec 08	chk	DLC-37
To 1829 Dec 14#		DLC-36
To 1829 Dec 17#		DLC-37
Fr 1829 Dec 18#		M179-67
To 1829 Dec 20#		14-1075
To 1829 Dec 21#		M40-21
Fr 1829 Dec 22#		14-1088
To 1829 Dec 30#		DLC-37
To 1830 Jan 01#	fin	14-1263
To 1830 Jan 06	chk	DLC-37
To 1830 Jan 07#		DLC-37
To 1830 Jan 12#		M639-3
To 1830 Jan 14#		M40-21
Fr 1830 Jan 27	mem	DLC-60
Fr 1830 Jan 27#		M124-122
To 1830 Jan 30	chk	DLC-37
Fr 1830 Feb 03	mem	DLC-60
Fr 1830 Feb 04	mem	DLC-60
Fr 1830 Feb 18#		M639-4
To 1830 Mar 06	chk	DLC-37
To 1830 Mar 06	chk	DLC-37
Fr 1830 Mar 06	mem	15-0308
Fr 1830 Mar 09		M639-10
To 1830 Mar 15	chk	DLC-37
Fr 1830 Mar 15#		M179-68
Fr 1830 Mar 15#		15-0362
To 1830 Apr 07	chk	DLC-38
Fr 1830 Apr 13#		M179-68
To 1830 Apr 17#		M124-123
To 1830 May 05	chk	DLC-38
Fr 1830 May 07#		M124-124
Fr 1830 May 25#		M179-73
To 1830 May 29	chk	DLC-38
To 1830 Jun 05#		M567-55
Fr 1830 Jun 06	mem	15-1303
Fr 1830 Jun 12#		15-1357
Fr 1830 Jun 15#		15-1455
Fr 1830 Sep 05#		M179-69
Fr 1830 Sep 07#		16-0211
Fr 1830 cOct		16-0286
Fr 1830 Oct 08#		16-0338
To 1830 Oct 16#		M222-27
Fr 1830 Oct 25		16-0518
Fr 1830 Oct 25*		DLC-73
To 1830 Oct 26		DLC-73
To 1830 Oct 27		16-0563
Fr 1830 Oct 27		DLC-73
To 1830 Oct 27		DLC-73
To 1830 Oct 29#		16-0580
To 1830 Oct 30		16-0583
Fr 1830 Oct 30		DLC-73
To 1830 Oct 30		16-0588
Fr 1830 Oct 31		16-0613
Fr 1830 Nov 09		DLC-73
Fr 1830 Nov 10	mem	DLC-73
To 1830 Nov 16		16-0735
To 1830 Nov 23#		16-0838
Fr 1830 Dec 18#		M179-69
Fr 1830 Dec 18#		M221-111
To 1830 Dec 21		16-1519
To c1831#		17-0090
Fr 1831 Jan 04#		17-0187
Fr 1831 Jan 15#		M639-15
Fr 1831 Jan 29#		17-0375
To 1831 Jan 31#		17-0387
Fr 1831 Feb 04#		17-0433
Fr 1831 Feb 10#		M179-70
To 1831 Feb 18	chk	DLC-39
To 1831 Feb 22#		17-0607
Fr 1831 Mar 01#		M124-127
To 1831 Mar 07#		17-0814
To 1831 Mar 08		17-0824
To 1831 Mar 10		17-0830
To 1831 Mar 24		17-0952
Fr 1831 Mar 31		17-1022
To 1831 Apr 03#		DLC-39
To 1831 Apr 19		17-1194
To 1831 Apr 20		17-1201
To 1831 Apr 24#		17-1225
To 1831 May 05		17-1281
Fr 1831 May 21#		M567-63

Fr 1831 May 21		DLC-73
Fr 1831 May 26#		17-1450
Fr 1831 May 28#		17-1463
To 1831 Jun 14		18-0010
To 1831 Jun 14	chk	18-0016
Fr 1831 Jun 18		18-0034
To 1831 Jun 23		18-0084
To 1831 Jul 10		18-0171
To 1831 Jul 11		18-0178
Fr 1831 Jul 23		DLC-30
To 1831 Jul 27		18-0280
To 1831 Aug 06		18-0451
Fr 1831 Sep 07#		18-0698
To 1831 Sep 19	chk	DLC-40
To 1831 Sep 25#		M639-7
To 1831 Sep 26#		37-0507
Fr 1831 Oct 04#		18-0920
To 1831 Oct 14#		M639-24
Fr 1831 Oct 16#		18-1006
Fr 1831 Oct 20#		18-1070
To 1831 Oct 24	chk	DLC-40
Fr 1831 Dec 03#		19-0001
To 1831 Dec 03#		19-0008
Fr 1831 Dec 03#		19-0002
To 1831 Dec 14	chk	DLC-40
Fr c1832#		19-0516
Fr 1832 Jan 04#		19-0611
Fr 1832 Jan 05#		M179-70
Fr 1832 Jan 13#		19-0678
To 1832 Jan 14#		M40-22
Fr 1832 Jan 26#		19-0867
To 1832 cFeb#		19-0924
Fr 1832 Feb 03#		M124-131
Fr 1832 Feb 06#		M179-72
To 1832 Feb 10#		19-1054
Fr 1832 Feb 14#		M179-72
To 1832 Feb 14#		M40-23
Fr 1832 Feb 29#		19-1254
To 1832 Mar 02#		19-1297
To 1832 Mar 05#		19-1306
To 1832 Mar 12	chk	DLC-40
To 1832 Mar 13#		19-1433
To 1832 Mar 14#		19-1469
To 1832 Mar 18#		19-1501
To 1832 Mar 23	chk	DLC-40
To 1832 Mar 29#		20-0038
Fr 1832 Apr#		M124-132
To 1832 Apr 03#		20-0115
To 1832 Apr 16	chk	DLC-40
Fr 1832 May 16#		20-0529
To 1832 Jul 11	chk	DLC-41
Fr 1832 Jul 17#		20-1114
Fr 1832 Jul 17#		M688-83
To 1832 Jul 19#		20-1151
Fr 1832 Jul 21#		M179-74
Fr 1832 Jul 21*		M221-112
To 1832 Jul 30	chk	DLC-41
To 1832 Aug 04	chk	DLC-41
To 1832 Aug 09		20-1256
To 1832 Aug 16		20-1298
To 1832 Aug 17		20-1316
To 1832 Aug 19		20-1338
To 1832 Aug 26#		20-1392
To 1832 Aug 30		20-1416
Fr 1832 cSep 02		20-1479
To 1832 Sep 13		20-1518
To 1832 Sep 17		21-0009
To 1832 Sep 18		21-0033
To 1832 Sep 22	chk	DLC-41
To 1832 Sep 28	chk	DLC-41
To 1832 Oct 05		21-0063
To 1832 Oct 10		21-0073
To 1832 Oct 16	chk	DLC-41
To 1832 Oct 18	chk	DLC-41
Fr 1832 Nov 15#		DLC-41
To 1832 Dec 10	chk	21-0934
Fr 1832 Dec 20#		M179-74
To 1832 Dec 21#		21-1108
To 1832 Dec 27	chk	DLC-41
Fr 1833 Jan 07#		M179-72
Fr 1833 Jan 24#		M222-31
Fr 1833 Jan 24#		M124-136
Fr 1833 Feb 03#		22-0256
To 1833 Mar 02#	fin	DLC-42
To 1833 Mar 02#		M639-24
To 1833 Mar 07#		M40-23
Fr 1833 Mar 07#		22-0682
Fr 1833 Mar 09#		22-0710
To 1833 Mar 12	chk	22-0744
To 1833 Mar 20		22-0834
To 1833 Apr 01#		DLC-42
Fr 1833 Apr 12#		M179-76
To 1833 Apr 12#		M639-20
To 1833 Apr 19#		M639-27
Fr 1833 Apr 27#		22-1190
To 1833 Apr 27#		M639-27
To 1833 May 01#		M639-27
To 1833 May 07#	fin	DLC-43
To 1833 May 16#		22-1367
Fr 1833 May 28#		M639-16
Fr 1833 May 29#		22-1499
Fr 1833 Jun 13#		23-0019
To 1833 Jun 13#		37-0517
To 1833 Jun 13*		23-0027
Fr 1833 Jun 14#		23-0032
To 1833 Jun 15#		23-0035
To 1833 Jun 22#		23-0051
Fr 1833 Jun 25#		DLC-43
Fr 1833 Jun 29#		23-0075
Fr 1833 Jul 01#		23-0091
To 1833 Jul 15#		DLC-73
Fr 1833 Jul 16#		M179-76
To 1833 Jul 25		23-0219
To 1833 Aug 05		23-0272
To 1833 Aug 15#		M639-3
To 1833 Sep 05#		23-0655
To 1833 Sep 10#		23-0684
Fr 1833 Sep 20		DLC-73
To 1833 Oct 31		23-1141
Fr 1833 Dec 17#		24-0549
To 1833 Dec 24#	fin	DLC-43
To 1833 Dec 27#		24-0615
Fr c1834#		24-0694
Re 1834 Jan	mem	24-0716
To 1834 Jan 09	chk	24-0823
Fr 1834 Jan 19#		24-0996
To 1834 Feb 25#		24-1475
Fr 1834 cMar 05#		24-1575
To 1834 Mar 14#		25-0208
Fr 1834 Mar 29#		M179-77
Fr 1834 Apr 07#		M179-78
To 1834 Apr 09#		25-0647
Fr 1834 Apr 10#		25-0663
Fr 1834 Apr 22#		DLC-73
Fr 1834 Apr 23#		25-0868
Fr 1834 Apr 29#		M179-78
To 1834 May 16#		25-1072
To 1834 May 17#		T20-6

Donelson Andrew Jackson (cont)

To	1834 Jun 05	fin	25-1266
Fr	1834 Jul 04#		M179-78
Fr	1834 Jul 08#		26-0187
Fr	1834 Jul 08#		26-0190
To	1834 Aug 07#		DLC-44
To	1834 Aug 29	lnd	26-0381
Fr	1834 Aug 29	lnd	26-0383
To	1834 Sep 19#		DLC-44
To	1834 Sep 20#		26-0448
Fr	1834 Oct 03#		26-0488
To	1834 Oct 13#		26-0621
To	1834 Oct 18#		DLC-44
To	1834 Oct 31	chk	26-0791
To	1834 Nov 10#		26-0873
To	1834 Nov 13#	fin	DLC-45
To	1834 Dec 05#	fin	DLC-45
To	1834 Dec 09#	fin	DLC-45
Fr	1834 Dec 24#		M179-79
To	1834 Dec 29#		27-0032
Fr	1835 Jan 05	mem	M124-146
Fr	1835 Jan 07#		27-0116
To	1835 Jan 08#		M179-79
To	1835 Jan 12#	fin	DLC-45
Fr	1835 Jan 17#		27-0245
Fr	1835 Jan 20#		M639-7
Fr	1835 Jan 27		27-0297
To	1835 Feb 01#		DLC-45
To	1835 Feb 02#		27-0370
To	1835 Feb 09#		DLC-45
To	1835 Feb 10#		M639-3
Fr	1835 Feb 10#		M639-3
Fr	1835 cFeb 25#		27-0623
Fr	1835 Feb 26#		M179-79
To	1835 Mar 01#		27-0672
To	1835 Mar 03#	fin	DLC-45
To	1835 Mar 17#		27-1227
To	1835 Apr		37-0339
To	1835 Apr 06#		M639-11
To	1835 Apr 10	chk	28-0016
To	1835 Apr 23		28-0113
To	1835 Apr 24		28-0119
To	1835 Apr 28		28-0159
To	1835 May 02		28-0222
To	1835 May 04		28-0259
To	1835 May 11		28-0337
To	1835 May 12		28-0344
To	1835 Jun 11#		28-0663
To	1835 Jul 07		28-0977
Fr	1835 Jul 07#		M124-148
To	1835 Jul 20		28-1060
To	1835 Jul 22		28-1112
To	1835 Jul 24		28-1136
To	1835 Jul 24#		M179-80
To	1835 Jul 25		28-1160
Fr	1835 Jul 25#		28-1167
To	1835 Jul 30		28-1212
Re	1835 cAug	fin	37-0341
To	1835 Aug 01		28-1221
To	1835 Aug 12		28-1274
To	1835 Sep 05#		DLC-51
Fr	1835 cSep 16#		37-0343
To	1835 Sep 22#		DLC-73
Fr	1835 Nov 07#		M179-81
To	1835 Nov 07#		29-0472
Fr	1835 Nov 09#		29-0476
To	1835 Nov 14#		DLC-47
To	1835 Nov 28#	fin	DLC-47
To	1835 Dec 12#	fin	DLC-47
To	1835 Dec 22#		29-1295
Fr	c1836#		29-1391
To	1836 cJan #		29-1424
To	1836 Jan 01#		DLC-47
Fr	1836 Jan 19#		M124-151
Fr	1836 Feb 01#		30-0255
To	1836 Feb 08#		DLC-47
To	1836 Mar 03#		30-0663
To	1836 Mar 17#		M7-2
Fr	1836 Mar 17#		M22-39
Fr	1836 Mar 24#		30-0888
To	1836 Apr 07		30-1108
To	1836 Apr 13#		30-1146
To	1836 May 09#		30-1575
To	1836 May 09	chk	DLC-48
To	1836 May 14	chk	DLC-48
To	1836 Jun 04#		31-0330
To	1836 Jul 06#		31-0898
To	1836 Jul 10#		DLC-48
To	1836 Jul 14#		31-1074
To	1836 Jul 20#		31-1136
Fr	1836 Aug 03#		DLC-48
To	1836 Aug 06#		31-1236
Fr	1836 Aug 15#		31-1290
To	1836 cAug 15		31-1292
To	1836 Aug 23#		DLC-49
Fr	1836 Sep 20#	leg	31-1473
Fr	1836 Sep 20#	leg	DLC-56
To	1836 Sep 23		DLC-74
To	1836 Oct 02		31-1587
To	1836 Nov 09#		32-0426
To	1836 Nov 30	chk	32-0595
Fr	1836 Dec 02		32-0615
To	1836 Dec 06		32-1025
To	1836 Dec 06		32-1027
To	1836 Dec 10		32-1070
To	1836 Dec 13		32-1133
To	1836 Dec 14#		DLC-49
To	1836 Dec 16		32-1166
To	1836 Dec 17		32-1181
Fr	1836 Dec 23		DLC-49
To	1836 Dec 27		32-1352
To	1836 Dec 29		32-1399
To	1836 Dec 31		32-1436
Fr	1836 Dec 31		DLC-49
Re	c1837	mem	37-0354
To	1837 Jan 01		32-1470
Fr	1837 Jan 01		DLC-49
To	1837 Jan 02		32-1474
To	1837 Jan 09		32-1556
To	1837 Jan 11		32-1568
Fr	1837 Jan 20		DLC-49
To	1837 Jan 20#		DLC-49
Fr	1837 Jan 22		33-0107
To	1837 Jan 24		33-0124
To	1837 Jan 31		33-0272
To	1837 Feb 23		33-0839
Re	1837 cMar	mem	33-0944
Fr	1837 Mar 07#		M567-143
To	1837 Mar 18#		DLC-50
To	1837 Mar 19		33-1090
To	1837 Mar 20		33-1093
To	1837 Mar 29		33-1123
To	1837 Apr 04		33-1144
To	1837 Apr 10		33-1158
To	1837 Apr 22		33-1167
To	1837 Apr 24		33-1177
To	1837 May		33-1196
To	1837 May 30		33-1258
Fr	1837 Jun 01		33-1268

To 1837 Jun 20 33-1319
Fr 1837 Jun 23 33-1330
To 1837 cJul 33-1366
Fr 1837 Jul 02 DLC-74
To 1837 Jul 18 33-1379
To 1837 Jul 18 33-1382
To 1837 cJul 21 mem DLC-74
To 1837 Sep 27 33-1491
Fr 1837 Nov 13# DLC-50
Fr 1837 Nov 23 34-0039
To 1838 Jan 12 34-0186
To 1838 Feb 04# DLC-51
To 1838 cMar 01 DLC-74
To 1838 Mar 22 34-0285
To 1838 Aug 02 34-0408
To 1838 Aug 12 34-0422
Re 1838 Sep 01 fin 34-0449
To 1838 Nov 15# 34-0516
To 1838 Dec 07 34-0554
To 1838 Dec 08 DLC-74
Fr c1839 34-0597
To 1839 Mar 04 34-0668
To 1839 Mar 28 34-0697
To 1839 Apr 26 chk DLC-52
To 1839 Apr 29 34-0761
To 1839 May 13 34-0790
To 1839 Jul 24 34-0849
To 1839 Aug 08 34-0855
To 1839 Aug 28 34-0876
To 1839 Sep 08 34-0920
To 1839 Sep 14 34-0936
To 1839 Sep 28 34-0963
To 1839 Dec 10 34-1082
To 1839 Dec 14 34-1085
To 1839 Dec 21 34-1102
To 1840 Jan 10# 34-1163
To 1840 Feb 15 34-1205
To 1840 Feb 19 34-1241
Fr 1840 Mar 04 DLC-52
Re 1840 Apr 03 34-1271
To 1840 May 18 34-1358
To 1840 Jun 18 34-1423
To 1840 Jun 28 34-1457
To 1840 Jul 09 34-1469
To 1840 Jul 17 34-1487
To 1840 Aug 02 DLC-74
Fr 1840 Aug 04# DLC-74
To 1840 Aug 10 mem DLC-53
To 1840 Aug 18 DLC-74
To 1840 Aug 18 34-1569
To 1840 Oct 08 35-0044
To 1840 Dec 29# 35-0148
Fr 1841 Mar 04 35-0235
To 1841 Mar 15 DLC-74
To 1841 Apr 21 35-0294
To 1841 Jul 12 35-0339
To 1841 Sep 07 35-0394
To 1841 Sep 09 35-0396
To 1842 Jun 01 35-0749
To 1842 Jun 02 35-0755
To 1842 Jun 02 DLC-74
To 1842 Jun 09 DLC-74
Re 1842 Jul 18 fin 35-0851
Re 1842 Aug 23 35-0897
Re 1842 Aug 25 fin 35-0901
To 1842 Sep 07 35-0923
To 1842 Sep 08 35-0931
Re 1842 Oct 01 fin 35-0959
To 1842 Dec 18 35-1041
To 1842 Dec 19 35-1044
To 1843 cFeb 09 35-1204
To 1843 cApr 13 DLC-74
To 1843 cMay 30 DLC-74
To 1843 Aug 21 35-1470
To 1843 Aug 22 35-1471
To 1843 Oct 13 35-1541
To 1843 Oct 15 mem DLC-74
To 1843 Oct 23 35-1554
To 1843 Oct 27 35-1568
To 1843 Nov 13 36-0004
To 1843 Dec 16 36-0064
To 1843 Dec 31 36-0081
To 1844 Jan 02 36-0103
Fr 1844 Jan 02 36-0105
To 1844 Jan 03 36-0107
To 1844 Jan 04 36-0109
To 1844 Feb 20 36-0321
To 1844 May 09# 36-0507
Fr 1844 May 14 36-0540
Fr 1844 May 29 DLC-56
To 1844 Jul 11 36-0695
Re 1844 Oct 08 mem 36-0943
Re 1844 Oct 18 mem DLC-57
Fr 1844 Nov 07 DLC-57
To 1844 Nov 18 36-1030
To 1844 Dec 02 36-1108
To 1844 Dec 11 36-1158
Fr 1844 Dec 24 DLC-57
Fr 1844 Dec 28 DLC-57
To 1845 Jan 17 36-1360
To 1845 Feb 04 36-1450
To 1845 Feb 10 36-1471
To 1845 cFeb 10 DLC-74
To 1845 Feb 25# 36-1510
Fr 1845 Mar 01 fin DLC-57
Fr 1845 Mar 07 36-1551
Fr 1845 Mar 09 36-1554
To 1845 Mar 12 36-1562
Fr 1845 Mar 20 37-0003
To 1845 May 24 37-0214
Fr 1845 May 24 DLC-58
Fr 1845 May 28 37-0230

Donelson Andrew Jackson (1799-1871) et al
Re 1834 Oct 02 mem 26-0473

Donelson Andrew Jackson (1815-1861)
To 1833 Oct 20 23-1069
To 1834 Jun 14 25-1364

Donelson Andrew Jackson (1826-1859)
To 1830 Aug 30 fin DLC-73
To 1835 Apr 06 27-1522
To 1836 Apr 22 30-1320
To 1836 Dec 01 32-0608
Re 1843 Jun 08 mem 35-1385
To 1843 Jul 19 35-1423
To 1844 Jun 30 36-0664
To 1844 Oct 16 36-0947

Donelson Daniel Smith
Fr 1822 Nov 20 9-0314
Fr 1823 Sep 27 DLC-32
Fr 1824 Jun 22 DLC-32
To 1830 Apr 24 chk DLC-38

Donelson Edward Butler
To 1844 cDec 20 36-1224

Donelson Eliza Eleanor (Butler) see also Butler E E
To 1840 Jul 14 lnd 34-1475
Fr 1840 Jul 19 DLC-53

Donelson Elizabeth A (Martin)
see also Martin E A
and Randolph E A M
To 1842 Aug 12 35-0876
To 1844 Jan 17 36-0130
To 1844 Nov 14 36-1022
To 1844 Nov 16 36-1026
To 1844 Nov 26 36-1055
To 1844 Dec 09 36-1136
To 1845 Jan 16 36-1350

Donelson Elizabeth (Glasgow)
see also Anderson E G
Fr 1799 Nov 08 DLC-75
To 1801 Jun 28 1-0881
Fr 1802 Jan 26 DLC-2
Fr 1806 2-0107
Fr 1806 Aug 06 DLC-4

Donelson Elizabeth (Rucker)
To 1822 Feb 02 fin DLC-31
Fr 1823 Jan 23 fin DLC-31

Donelson Emily Tennessee (Donelson)
To 1830 Mar 10# fin DLC-39
To 1830 Sep 07# 16-0211
To 1830 Nov 28 DLC-73
To 1831 Jan 20 17-0302
To 1831 Feb 04# 17-0433
To 1831 Mar 10 17-0833
To 1831 May 25 17-1424
To 1831 Nov 07 chk DLC-40
To 1832 Nov 02 chk 21-0264
Re 1834 Jan 09 fin DLC-44
To 1835 May 26 chk 28-0503
To 1836 Jul 02 31-0757
To 1836 Oct 21 32-0306
To 1836 Oct 31 32-0361
To 1836 Nov 27 32-0588
To 1836 Nov 27 37-0353
To 1836 Dec 01 32-0610

Donelson James Rucker
Fr 1823 Jun 09 fin DLC-32
Fr 1829 Jan 02 fin DLC-36

Donelson John (c1718-86)
Fr 1785 Feb 09# leg 1-0021
Re 1791 Jan 28 leg 1-0084
Re 1805 Nov 12 leg 2-0090
Re 1815 Oct 05 leg 4-1206

Donelson John (1755-1830)
Fr 1792 Feb 23 lnd 1-0123
Fr 1792 Oct 03 fin 1-0132
Fr 1794 Mar 24 fin 1-0223
To 1798 Jan 18 DLC-71
Fr 1798 Mar 20# fin DLC-2
To 1801 Feb 18 1-0843
Fr 1803 fin 1-1066
Fr 1803 Feb 14 fin 1-1083
To 1807 Jan 02 fin DLC-4
Fr 1807 Dec 01 fin 2-0595
Fr 1808 Aug 13 fin DLC-4
Fr 1809 Jun 15 lnd 2-0835
To 1812 Jul 06 lnd 2-1123
Fr 1821 Jan 11 fin 8-0059
Fr 1821 Mar 21 fin DLC-30
To 1821 Jul 03 8-0761
To 1821 Aug 25# 8-1102
To 1821 Sep 02 8-1144
To 1823 Jan 31 9-0439
To 1824 Feb 09 10-0440
To 1824 Jul 24 37-0421
To 1824 Oct 22 10-0946
Fr 1825 Apr 25 mem 10-1246
Fr 1825 May 19 DLC-33
Fr 1826 Feb 02 fin 11-0128
Fr 1829 May 19 13-0353
To 1829 Jun 07 13-0589

Donelson John (1787-1840)
To 1815 May 28 DLC-18
Fr 1815 Jun 22 4-1088
Fr 1815 Jul 23 DLC-19
To 1818 Jan 14 5-1285
Fr 1820 Jan 13 DLC-28
Fr 1827 Feb 26 DLC-34
Fr 1828 Mar 22 DLC-35
Fr 1829 Apr 27 M639-15
Fr 1831 May 12 DLC-39
Fr 1831 Aug 09 DLC-39
Fr 1831 Oct 31 DLC-40
Fr 1832 Mar 14 DLC-40
Fr 1833 May 08 22-1320
Fr 1833 May 28 22-1466
Fr 1833 Jul 08 DLC-43
Fr 1834 May 04 DLC-44
Fr 1838 Mar 24 DLC-51
Fr 1838 Dec 25 DLC-51
Re 1843 cAug mem 35-1444

Donelson John (b c1807)
To 1839 Jun 15# 34-0822

Donelson Leven
To 1806 Aug 12 fin DLC-4
To 1807 Mar 02 fin DLC-4
Fr 1810 Feb 02 leg 2-0870
Fr 1812 Feb 01 DLC-5

Donelson Mary Emily
To 1834 Jan 27 24-1079
To 1836 May 22 31-0076
Re 1843 Jun 08 mem 35-1385
To 1845 Feb 18 36-1503

Donelson Mary (Purnell)
To 1825 Jan 27# 10-1086

Donelson Mary Rachel
To 1832 Apr 16 fin 20-0231

Donelson Mary (Smith)
see also Sanders M S
Fr 1804 Apr 22# fin 1-1317
Re 1805 Mar 18 leg 2-0026

Donelson Rachel Jackson
Re 1843 Jun 08 mem 35-1385

Donelson Samuel
To 1792 Jan 01 DLC-71
Fr 1795 Jun 29 DLC-1
To c1796 Jun DLC-2
To 1799 DLC-2
Re 1804 Sep 19 leg 1-1367
Re 1804 Sep 19 leg 1-1368
Re 1804 Oct 1-1396
Re 1804 Nov 01 leg DLC-3
Re 1804 Nov 01 leg 1-1404
Re 1805 Jun 17 leg 2-0065
Re 1805 Sep 23 fin DLC-3
Re 1805 Dec 16 leg 2-0101
Re 1805 Dec 16 leg 2-0103
Re 1805 Dec 20 leg DLC-3
Re 1805 Dec 24 leg DLC-3

Donelson Samuel et al
Fr 1802 Jul 27 lnd 1-1031

Donelson Samuel Rucker
Fr 1831 May 02# DLC-39
Fr 1838 Dec 03# DLC-51

Donelson Severn (1773-1818)
To 1806 Feb 11 lnd 2-0175
Fr 1812 Feb 01 DLC-5
Donelson Severn (b 1797) et al
Fr 1821 Apr 22 lnd 8-0359
Donelson Stockley (c1759-1805)
Re 1791 Aug leg 1-0099
Fr 1792 Aug 03 DLC-1
Fr 1792 Sep 10 leg DLC-1
Fr 1794 Mar 02 DLC-71
Fr 1795 Jun 09 lnd DLC-1
Fr 1796 May 09 mem DLC-1
Fr 1796 May 09 lnd 1-0382
Fr 1796 May 09 lnd 1-0384
Fr 1796 May 09 lnd 1-0385
Fr 1796 May 09 lnd 1-0387
Fr 1796 May 09 lnd 1-0393
Fr 1796 May 09 lnd 1-0401
Fr 1796 Jun 16 DLC-71
Fr c1798 DLC-60
Fr 1799 Oct 06# lnd 37-0401
Fr 1800 Mar 07 lnd 1-0756
Fr 1800 Mar 27# leg 1-0760
Fr 1800 Oct 02 1-0785
Fr 1801 Mar 15 DLC-2
Fr 1801 Dec 22 DLC-4
Fr 1802 Jan 17 DLC-2
Fr 1802 Mar 26 DLC-2
Fr 1802 Mar 27 lnd 1-0964
Fr 1802 Jun 14 DLC-2
Donelson Stockley (1805-1888)
Fr c1828 37-0275
To 1829 Mar 29# 12-1173
Fr 1834 Oct 14 DLC-44
Fr 1834 Nov 11# fin DLC-45
Fr 1837 Jan 08# DLC-49
Fr 1837 Jan 16# 37-0531
To 1839 Feb 28 34-0666
Fr 1839 Mar 02 DLC-52
Fr 1839 Mar 05 34-0680
Fr 1839 Mar 09 34-0684
Fr 1840 Jul 14 34-1477
Fr 1842 Aug 22 DLC-54
Re 1843 Jun 06 mem DLC-55
Fr 1843 Aug 24 DLC-55
To 1843 Aug 28 DLC-55
Re 1843 Sep 12# leg 35-1489
Re 1844 Oct 07 mem 36-0938
Re 1845 May 30 leg 37-0235
Re 1845 Jun 02 leg 37-0241
Donelson Thomas Jefferson
To 1831 May 02# DLC-39
Fr 1834 Jan 29 24-1097
Fr 1834 Nov 04 DLC-45
To 1839 Feb 06# fin DLC-52
To 1839 Aug 09# fin DLC-52
Fr 1839 Dec# fin 34-1066
Fr 1842 Jan 07 fin DLC-54
Donelson William (1756-1820)
Re 1789 Jun 25 leg DLC-75
Fr 1795 Feb 24 lnd 1-0252
Fr 1803 Aug 23 fin DLC-3
Fr 1804 Aug 20# fin DLC-3
Fr 1806 Dec 11 lnd 2-0396
To 1808 Mar 10 fin DLC-4
Re 1820 mem DLC-70
Donelson William (1795-1864)
Fr 1826 Jan 21 fin 11-0110
Fr 1829 Jan 11 fin DLC-36
To 1829 Mar 22 12-1078
To 1829 Oct 08 14-0115
Fr 1829 Dec 20 14-1077
To 1830 Jan 30 15-0075
Fr 1831 Apr 10 17-1112
To 1831 Sep 09# 37-0425
To 1831 Oct 08# 37-0429
To 1831 Nov 05 18-1201
To 1832 Feb 06# 37-0433
To 1832 Mar 26# 37-0513
To 1832 Jul 19 chk DLC-41
To 1833 Jan 21-1261
Fr 1833 Mar 26 DLC-42
Fr 1833 Aug 28 DLC-43
Fr 1834 fin DLC-50
To 1834 Nov 02 26-0808
To 1834 Nov 11# fin DLC-45
Re 1834 Dec 09 lnd DLC-73
To 1836 Dec 13 32-1139
To 1837 Dec 12 DLC-50
Fr 1838 Feb fin DLC-52
To 1839 Feb 28 34-0666
To 1842 Nov 29 35-1012
Re 1844 Oct 07 mem 36-0938
Donnelly (slave)
Re 1832 Mar 01 par 19-1285
Re 1832 Apr 13 par 20-0221
Donnelly John
To 1830 Aug 04# DLC-38
Donoho Sanders
Fr 1818 Mar 24 DLC-24
Donoho Thomas
Fr 1824 Dec 02 fin DLC-33
Dorfeuille J
Fr 1815 Feb 07 DLC-16
Dorman James
Fr 1818 Jan 13 DLC-23
To 1818 Aug 14 6-1229
Fr 1818 Sep 10 DLC-25
Fr 1818 Sep 12 DLC-25
Fr 1818 Nov 02 DLC-26
Fr 1819 Jan 08 DLC-26
Dorr Joseph et al
Fr 1832 Oct 29 M639-24
Dorsett Nancy
To 1825 Nov 11 fin DLC-33
Dorsey Allen
Fr 1825 Mar 13 fin DLC-72
Dos Amigos (brig)
Re 1832 Jun 04 par 20-0691
Doty Baron S
Fr 1834 Dec 03 26-1364
Fr 1835 Dec 03# 29-0734
Fr 1836 Jun 22# 31-0547
Doty Baron S et al
Fr 1833 Oct 30 23-1125
Doty James Duane
Fr 1830 Sep 18 16-0248
Fr 1830 Dec 02 16-0963
Fr 1831 Aug 11 18-0508
Re 1835 Feb 16 mem DLC-45
Doty William et al
Fr 1835 cJan DLC-59
Doubleday Ulysses Freeman et al
Fr 1833 Sep 28 M639-7
Dougharty George
Fr 1833 Nov 16 23-1239
Dougherty Charles H
Fr 1838 Nov 10 DLC-51

Dougherty John
Fr 1829 Aug 31 DLC-37
Dougherty Nathaniel E
Fr 1831 Oct 12 18-0974
Dougherty Robert
Re 1793 Nov 06 leg 1-0165
Dougherty William
Fr 1836 Oct 17 M234-243
Doughty James H et al
Fr 1836 Nov M22-41
Douglas L
Fr 1829 Mar 12-0620
Fr 1831 Jan 25 17-0358
Douglas L A Mrs
To 1825 Apr 15# 10-1235
Douglas Thomas
Fr 1832 Apr 21 20-0335
Fr 1834 Sep 05 26-0421
Douglas Thomas et al
Fr 1831 Dec 03 19-0003
Douglass Edward
Re 1794 Apr leg 1-0224
To 1805 Feb 08 lnd 2-0009
To 1809 May 15 lnd 2-0807
Douglass Ezekiel
Re 1794 Feb 09 leg 1-0192
To 1797 Jun 14 fin 1-0514
Douglass George & Co et al
Fr 1834 Oct T55-1
Douglass George L
Fr 1832 Apr 14 M234-170
Douglass Henry L
Fr 1813 Nov 14 DLC-7
Fr 1813 Nov 14* DLC-61
Fr 1816 Aug 28 DLC-21
Douglass William
Re 1811 Oct 16 leg 2-1012
Re 1816 Apr 01 leg 4-1420
Fr 1826 May 27# DLC-33
To 1827 May 30 11-0608
Fr 1828 Sep 21 12-0211
Fr 1831 Jun 23 M22-28
Dourel S W
Fr 1839 Mar 14 DLC-52
Dousman Hercules Louis
Fr 1836 May M200-6
Dover NH citizens
Re 1842 Jan 28 mem DLC-54
Dow Ezra A
Fr 1842 Jun 25 DLC-54
Dow J E
Fr 1836 Jul 06 DLC-48
Dowles B
To 1840 Jan 10 34-1166
Dowling William Henry
Re 1834 Jul 05 par 26-0159
Downer & Co
Fr 1833 Apr 22 M639-16
Downes John
Fr 1830 Nov 01 16-0631
Downes William
Re 1830 Nov 20 par 16-0818
Downing B
Fr 1829 Jul 25 DLC-37
Downing Charles et al
Fr 1829 Oct 14-0024
Fr 1835 Apr 25 M639-15
Downing Joseph
Re 1830 Jan 19 par 14-1464
Re 1832 Nov 12 par 21-0376
Re 1832 Nov 20 par 21-0469
Downing Nicholas
Fr 1829 May 30 DLC-37
Downing Samuel W
Re 1834 cApr M273-29
Re 1837 Feb 17 M273-33
Downs ______
Fr 1840 Jan 08 add 34-1145
To 1840 Jan 08 add 34-1147
Doxey Jeremiah
Re 1816 Dec 07 5-0597
Doyle ______ et al
To 1838 Dec 29 37-0388
Doyle D J M
To 1840 Dec 26 35-0136
To 1840 Dec 27 35-0145
To 1840 cDec 28 chk DLC-53
To 1841 Jan 12 35-0196
Fr 1844 Jan 24 DLC-56
Fr 1844 Mar 02 DLC-56
Doyle D J M Mrs
To 1840 Dec 26 35-0136
Doyle Edmund
Fr 1818 May 02 6-0539
Fr 1818 May 02* DLC-24
Fr 1821 Dec 05 M221-93
Fr 1821 Dec 05* M221-96
Doyle N
Fr 1835 Apr 07 27-1554
Fr 1835 Apr 07* M234-242
Drake Andrew Jackson
Fr 1837 Jul 22 DLC-50
Drake Edwin A
Fr 1839 Aug 18 DLC-52
Drake James
To 1826 Mar 15 11-0167
Drake James P
Fr 1833 Apr 11 M234-354
Fr 1835 Aug 14 M639-16
Drake Zephaniah et al
Fr 1833 Jul 31 M639-12
Draper William
Fr 1836 Oct 24 32-0334
Draper & Baker
Fr 1833 Apr 22 M639-16
Drayer Barend
Re 1832 Nov 05 par 21-0311
Drayton William
Fr 1830 Dec 28 M124-125
Fr 1831 Dec 13 19-0290
Fr 1833 Mar 01 DLC-42
Drayton William et al
Fr 1831 Dec 30 M22-28
Drennen John
Fr 1832 Feb 07 M567-69
Fr 1832 Nov 12 M567-69
Drew Elisha A
Re 1835 Jul 20 par 28-1062
Driggs John F
Fr 1838 Nov 27 DLC-51
Fr 1842 Aug 14 DLC-54
Dromgoole George Coke
Fr 1836 Mar 21 M687-33
Fr 1837 Feb 14 M687-9
Drown Daniel P
Fr 1829 Mar 17 M639-4
Drum August et al
Fr 1837 Feb 22 DLC-50
To 1837 Mar 03 DLC-50

Drum Simon
Fr 1831 Feb 08 17-0464
Drummond Eliza (Clark)
Fr 1845 Apr 09 DLC-58
Drummond Richard
To 1829 Jul 28 13-0947
To 1835 Aug 03 28-1229
To 1835 Aug 13 28-1276
Fr 1836 Feb 29 30-0626
Drury E N
Fr 1840 Mar 17 DLC-52
Drury Samuel
To 1836 Nov 17 32-0552
Drury Samuel et al
Fr 1833 Aug 28 M639-14
Duane William
Fr 1830 Jan 25# DLC-37
Fr 1833 Aug 24 M639-18
Duane William John
Fr 1829 Mar 20 12-1065
Fr 1830 Oct 27 M639-14
Fr 1833 Jan 30# DLC-42
Re 1833 May 29 22-1502
To 1833 Jun 26 DLC-64
To 1833 Jun 26* DLC-42
To 1833 Jun 26 DLC-64
To 1833 Jun 26* DLC-43
Fr 1833 Jul 10 DLC-42
To 1833 Jul 12 23-0111
To 1833 Jul 12* DLC-43
Fr 1833 Jul 12 23-0115
Fr 1833 Jul 13 23-0122
To 1833 Jul 17 DLC-64
To 1833 Jul 17* DLC-43
Fr 1833 Jul 19 23-0155
Fr 1833 Jul 20 M415-1
To 1833 Jul 22 DLC-64
To 1833 Jul 22* DLC-43
Fr 1833 Jul 22 DLC-43
Fr 1833 Jul 22 M415-1
Re 1833 Jul 22 mem 23-0190
To 1833 Jul 23 DLC-64
To 1833 Jul 23* DLC-43
To 1833 Jul 23 DLC-43
Fr 1833 Jul 23 23-0197
Fr 1833 Aug 10 23-0312
Fr 1833 Aug 24 23-0460
Fr 1833 Aug 24* M415-1
Fr 1833 Sep 05 23-0648
Fr 1833 Sep 05* M415-1
Fr 1833 Sep 09 23-0672
Fr 1833 Sep 12 23-0700
Fr 1833 Sep 13 M415-1
Fr 1833 Sep 13* 23-0707
Fr 1833 Sep 17 M415-1
Fr 1833 Sep 21 23-0813
To 1833 Sep 21 DLC-64
To 1833 Sep 21* DLC-43
Fr 1833 Sep 21 23-0814
Fr 1833 Sep 21 23-0815
Fr 1833 Sep 21 23-0816
Fr 1833 Sep 23 M733-1
Fr 1833 Sep 23* 23-0837
To 1833 Sep 23 DLC-43
Dubois Barent
Fr 1835 Aug 21# 28-1341
Dubose John
To 1821 Jul 19 M116-6
DuBourg Pierre Francois
Fr 1815 Jan 30 DLC-16
Fr 1815 Feb 08 DLC-16
DuBourg William
To 1815 Jan 19 DLC-15
To 1815 Jan 19* DLC-62
Fr 1815 Jan 20 DLC-15
To 1815 Jan 23 add 4-0603
Fr 1815 Jan 23 add 4-0604
Fr 1815 Feb 14 DLC-16
Fr 1815 Mar 26 4-0907
Dubs Martin
Fr 1834 Jan 18 M639-7
Dubuclet Joseph
Fr 1814 Dec 18 4-0416
Fr 1815 Feb 14 DLC-16
Fr 1815 Feb 26 DLC-17
Fr 1815 Mar 01 DLC-17
Dubuclet Joseph et al
Fr 1815 Feb 11 DLC-16
Duck River massacre
Re 1812 cJul 07 add 2-1125
Ducker Benjamin
Fr 1821 Feb 14 leg DLC-29
Duckworth J H
Fr 1845 Mar 01 DLC-57
Duclos Francis
Fr 1831 Nov 02 M22-28
Duclozel Oliver
Fr 1815 Feb 25 DLC-17
Dudley Charles Edward
Fr 1829 Mar 12 M639-13
Fr 1830 Dec 15 DLC-38
To 1830 Dec 18 DLC-38
Fr 1833 Dec 27 M639-7
Fr 1833 Dec 27* 24-0604
To 1836 Nov 26 32-0586
To 1836 Nov 26* DLC-74
Dudley Edward Bishop
To 1831 May 23 17-1410
Dudley J
Fr 1844 Nov 21 DLC-57
Duffield George
To 1802 Jun 25 DLC-2
Fr 1814 Oct 18 DLC-13
Fr 1815 Feb 26 DLC-17
Duffy Francis
Fr 1845 Jan 17 36-1364
Duffy Francis et al
Fr 1838 Oct 15 34-0487
To 1838 Nov 04 34-0508
Duffy Moses
Fr 1815 Mar 04 DLC-17
Dufour Vincent
To 1825 Jun 03 10-1301
Dugan Frederick I
To 1831 Oct 20 18-1083
Dugan Jane Mary
Fr 1844 Mar 14 DLC-56
Duggett Elijah A
Fr 1837 Feb M687-20
Dulany Henry Rozer
Fr 1829 Mar 07# M639-11
Re 1830 Apr 24 par 15-0781
Dulany Thomas
Re 1830 May 04 par 15-0891
Dumartrait C
Fr 1815 Mar 04 DLC-17

Dumas Hypolite
Fr 1816 Jul 10 DLC-21
Dumas John F
Fr 1829 Apr 18 13-0058
Dumond A G et al
Fr 1835 Aug 07 28-1260
Fr 1835 Aug 07* M234-355
Dun Walter
Fr 1830 Feb 16 M639-16
Dunbar Peter
Fr 1836 Apr 25 30-1347
Dunbar William et al
Fr 1834 Jul 16 M639-9
Duncan Abner L
Fr 1815 cMar 27 DLC-17
Fr 1815 Jun 02 DLC-18
Fr 1815 Jun 23 DLC-18
Fr 1815 Jun 26 DLC-18
Fr 1816 Apr 23 DLC-20
Fr 1816 Jun 09 DLC-20
To 1816 Jul 09 DLC-21
Fr 1816 Sep 05 DLC-21
Fr 1817 Jan 27 DLC-22
Fr 1819 Apr 28 DLC-26
Fr 1821 Apr 24 DLC-30
Fr 1821 Dec 12 DLC-31
To 1823 Mar 11 9-0491
Fr 1823 Jul 06 DLC-32
Duncan Abner L et al
Fr 1821 DLC-31
Duncan Evan E
Fr 1840 Jun 21 34-1432
Duncan John
To 1820 Sep 06 7-1306
Duncan John B
Fr 1829 Nov 05 M234-135
Duncan Joseph
Fr 1829 Mar 09 M639-15
Fr 1829 Mar 09 M639-26
Fr 1832 Mar 01 M234-728
Fr 1832 Mar 01* 19-1290
Duncan Lucius C
Fr 1828 Jan 08 DLC-35
Fr 1833 Mar 01 22-0583
Duncan Silas
Fr 1833 Mar 06 M179-75
Duncan Thomas
Fr 1821 Mar 03 DLC-29
Duncan Thomas A
Fr 1829 Apr 06# M639-2
Duncan William
Fr 1829 Mar 12 M639-11
Fr 1829 May 25 M873-19
Fr 1831 Feb 26 17-0657
Fr 1834 Mar 03 M639-3
Fr 1834 Nov 08 M639-10
Fr 1836 Dec 07 M639-15
Duncan William et al
Fr 1829 Nov 20 M639-1
Fr 1835 Aug M639-15
Duncan & Jackson
Fr 1805 Aug 10 DLC-3
Fr 1807 Apr 17 DLC-4
Fr 1807 Jul 09 DLC-4
Duncombe Eli
Fr 1834 Jan 10 DLC-44
Dunham Jeremiah
Fr 1835 Apr 14 M234-355
Dunlap Alexander
Fr 1829 Apr 09 M639-7
Dunlap Augusta
Fr 1835 Mar 14 DLC-45
Dunlap James A
Fr 1831 Jul 28 DLC-39
Re 1831 Oct 17 18-1008
Re 1831 Oct 17 18-1010
Dunlap James A et al
Fr 1831 Jul 25 DLC-39
Dunlap Mary (Crawford)
To 1831 Oct 13 DLC-40
Fr 1831 Dec 13 DLC-40
Dunlap Richard Gilliam
Fr 1819 Mar 30 DLC-26
Fr 1819 Mar 30* 7-0444
Fr 1823 Jul 02 DLC-32
Fr 1823 Oct 16 DLC-32
Fr 1827 Mar 24 11-0511
Fr 1827 May 12 DLC-34
To 1827 May 23 DLC-34
Fr 1827 Jun 04 11-0679
Fr 1828 Apr 23 DLC-35
Fr 1828 Jun 10 DLC-35
To 1828 Jun 21 DLC-35
Fr 1828 Nov 30 M639-14
Fr 1828 Dec 22 DLC-36
Fr 1829 Apr 23 M222-25
Fr 1829 Apr 23 M222-25
Fr 1829 Jul 12 DLC-37
Fr 1831 Jun 30 18-0138
To 1831 Jul 18 18-0235
Fr 1831 Aug 10 DLC-39
To 1831 Aug 29 DLC-40
Fr 1832 Sep 06 20-1484
Fr 1833 Aug 25 M234-75
Fr 1835 Mar 11 27-1079
Fr 1835 Mar 11* M234-76
Fr 1836 May 04 DLC-48
Fr 1836 Jul 19 DLC-48
To 1836 Jul 30 DLC-48
Fr 1836 Aug 06 DLC-48
Fr 1839 Feb 27 DLC-52
Dunlap Robert Pinckney
Fr 1836 Apr 22 30-1327
Fr 1836 Jun 30 31-0653
Fr 1836 Dec 01 M687-3
Dunlap Robert Pinckney et al
Fr 1835 Jul 27 M639-3
Dunlap W C et al
Fr 1829 Apr 16 M639-5
Dunlop James
Re 1831 Mar 02 17-0717
Fr 1832 Jan 30 19-0910
Re 1832 Mar 13 19-1417
Fr 1835 Jan 09 27-0161
Dunlop James et al
Fr 1831 Jan 26 M639-1
Dunn Michael C
Re 1808 Oct 24 mem 2-0737
To c1811 chk DLC-58
Fr 1811 Jun 26 lnd 2-1003
To 1812 Mar 07 chk DLC-5
To 1813 Jul 13 chk DLC-6
Dunn William
Fr 1836 Feb 12 30-0364
Fr 1836 Dec 06 M687-3
Dunning Clement S
Re 1829 Oct 14-0028

Dunscomb Daniel L
Fr 1831 Apr 28 M688-70
Duplessis Pierre LeBreton
Fr 1814 Oct 17 DLC-13
Fr 1814 Oct 18 DLC-13
Fr 1814 Oct 29 DLC-13
Fr 1815 Jan 02 DLC-15
To 1815 Jan 09 DLC-62
Fr 1815 Jan 30 DLC-16
Fr 1815 Feb 21 DLC-17
Fr 1815 Apr 04 DLC-18
To 1815 Apr 14 4-0986
Fr 1817 May 31 5-0884
DuPont Charles H
Fr 1836 May 16 M567-122
Dupres J H
Fr 1821 Aug 18 DLC-73
Dupuy Charles M
Fr 1832 Oct 30 21-0219
Durand John & Co
Fr 1833 Apr 26 M639-16
Durand William Jr
Fr 1834 Jun 14 M639-24
Durand & Dupre et al
Fr 1829 Jul M639-14
Durant Latchlan
Fr 1829 Sep 13 DLC-37
Durell Daniel Meserve
Fr 1830 Sep 04 M639-7
Duryee Richard
Fr 1834 May 16 25-1060
Dusong Pierre
To 1814 Dec 15 DLC-62
Dutch jewels
Re 1831 cAug mem 18-0380
Re 1831 Nov 09 M179-71
Re 1831 Nov 09 mem 18-1233
Re 1832 Jan 13 M179-72
Dutcher William
Re 1835 Oct 29 par 29-0366
Dutillet Charles Daubeville
Fr 1816 Jan 15 DLC-20
Fr 1829 Dec 22 M688-56
DuVal Samuel H
Fr 1836 Jan 08 M639-19
Duval William
Fr 1831 Jul 28 M567-58
Fr 1831 Jul 28* M222-29
Duval William Pope
To 1822 Jun 01 9-0179
Fr 1823 Aug 26 DLC-32
To 1824 Nov 01 10-0948
Fr 1825 Jul 05 DLC-33
To 1825 Jul 25 10-1373
To 1825 Aug 06 10-1405
Fr 1827 Jun 12 DLC-34
Fr 1828 Jun 23 DLC-35
Fr 1829 Apr 21 M639-1
Fr 1829 Apr 21 M179-67
Fr 1829 Jun 02 M639-2
Fr 1830 Dec 20 M639-22
Re 1831 Apr 18 17-1188
Fr 1831 Jul 15 DLC-39
Fr 1831 Jul 21 M639-14
Fr 1831 Oct 04 DLC-40
Fr 1833 Aug 17 23-0358
Re c1834 mem 24-0695
Fr 1835 May 17 DLC-46
Fr 1836 Jun 25# M567-122
Fr 1837 Feb 28# M687-9
Duval William Pope et al
Fr 1829 Oct 26 M639-23
Duvall Benjamin F
Fr 1840 Jan 07 DLC-52
Duvall Gabriel
Fr 1835 Jan 12 27-0182
Duvimont Desvaux
Fr 1836 Mar 12 M124-152
Dwight Henry Williams
Fr 1830 Dec 28 M124-125
Fr 1831 Jan 19 17-0294
Dwight Serano Edwards
Fr 1835 Dec 12 M179-81
Dwyer J H
Fr 1843 Feb 12 DLC-55
Dyer David H
Re 1830 Apr 06 par 15-0588
Dyer E
Fr 1836 Jun 16 fin DLC-48
Dyer Henry
To 1814 Feb 18 DLC-62
To 1814 Mar 07 DLC-62
Dyer James S
Fr 1839 Jul 01 DLC-52
Dyer Nichols et al
Fr 1832 Dec 26 M639-16
Dyer Robert Henry
Fr 1812 Aug 22 DLC-5
Fr 1812 Sep 15 DLC-5
To 1814 Feb 23 DLC-61
Fr 1814 Dec 26 4-0465
Fr 1819 May 21 7-0528
Fr 1823 Jun 19 DLC-32
Dyer Robert Henry et al
To 1818 Jan 11 5-1242
Dyer Robert Henry Jr
To 1829 Sep 21 DLC-37
Dyer Susan
Fr 1827 Sep 18 11-0864
Fr 1829 Sep 18 13-1356

Eads James D
Fr 1840 Apr 07 34-1289
Eakin Constant Mathieu
Fr 1831 Jul 13 M567-60
Fr 1832 Jan 16 19-0701
Eakin James
Fr 1818 Sep 02 6-1281
To 1829 Oct 31 14-0279
To 1829 Dec 23 14-1101
To 1830 Apr 17 15-0739
To 1830 Jun 16 15-1470
To 1831 May 04 17-1276
To 1831 Jul 29 18-0309
To 1831 Nov 22 18-1471
To 1832 Jul 20 20-1186
To 1833 Apr 02 22-0927
Re 1834 Apr 03 25-0574
To 1834 Jul 08 26-0192
To 1834 Oct 27 26-0742
To 1835 Apr 13 28-0041
To 1835 Nov 19 29-0533
To 1836 Jan 16 30-0123
To 1836 Jul 09 31-1012
Earl Ralph Eleazar Whitesides
Fr 1818 Nov 05# 6-1400
To 1819 Feb 23# DLC-26
To 1819 Mar 09# DLC-26

Earl Ralph Eleazar Whitesides (cont)
To 1819 Jul 03# DLC-24
To 1821 Jan 10 8-0054
To 1821 cFeb 8-0097
Fr 1827 Feb 14 DLC-34
Fr 1827 Jun 12 fin DLC-34
To 1827 Jul 02 11-0729
To 1828 cApr 20 11-1215
To 1828 Jul 10 12-0044
Fr 1828 Jul 17 DLC-35
To 1828 Aug 24 12-0175
To 1828 Sep 13 12-0194
Fr 1829 Jan 17 fin DLC-36
To 1829 Mar 16 12-1017
Fr 1829 Apr 03 12-1265
To 1829 Jul 19 13-0903
Fr 1830 Apr 05 15-0578
Fr 1830 Apr 05* DLC-38
To 1830 Aug 13 16-0104
To 1831 Jul 28 chk DLC-39
To 1832 Apr 16 chk DLC-40
To 1832 Aug 02 chk DLC-41
To 1833 Sep 24 chk DLC-43
To 1835 Jan 27# DLC-45
To 1836 Jun 02 chk DLC-48
To 1836 Jul 04 chk DLC-48
To 1836 Jul 05# fin DLC-48
Fr 1836 Jul 29 DLC-48
Fr 1836 Jul 31 DLC-48
To 1836 Aug 01 31-1186
To 1836 Sep 06# DLC-49
To 1836 Sep 12 31-1442
To 1836 Sep 23 31-1490
Re 1837 mem 32-1452
To 1837 Feb 16# DLC-50
To 1838 May 24# fin DLC-53

Earles James
Fr 1821 Jun 15 fin DLC-70

Earll Jonas Jr
Fr 1831 Sep 26 M639-23

Early Lemuel
Fr 1815 Jun 22 DLC-18

Early Peter
Fr 1814 Oct 26 4-0292
To 1814 Oct 31 4-0304
To 1814 Oct 31* DLC-62
To 1814 Nov 16 4-0354
Fr 1814 Dec 12 DLC-14

Easter Richard Ivy
Fr 1818 Dec DLC-26
Fr 1818 Dec 08 DLC-26
Fr 1819 Apr 21 DLC-26
Fr 1819 Apr 21* 7-0490
Fr 1819 Apr 21 DLC-26
Fr 1819 Jul 14# M439-11
Fr 1819 Jul 14# M566-123
Fr 1819 Aug 27 DLC-27
Fr 1819 Sep 07 DLC-27
Fr 1819 Sep 30 DLC-27
Fr 1819 Nov 25 DLC-28
Fr 1820 Sep 11 7-1325
To 1820 Sep 11 DLC-63
Fr 1821 Feb 28 M221-89
Fr 1821 Apr 08 DLC-30
Fr 1821 May 03 DLC-30
Fr 1821 May 10 DLC-30
Fr 1821 Jun 08 DLC-30
Fr 1821 Jun 25 DLC-30
Fr 1821 Jun 29 DLC-30
Fr 1822 Jan 31 DLC-31
Fr 1822 Feb 02 DLC-31
To 1822 May 14 9-0160
Fr 1823 Feb 25 DLC-72
Fr 1823 Apr 23 DLC-32
Fr 1823 Jul 21 DLC-32
Re 1824 May 27 leg 10-0753
Fr 1824 Oct 22 DLC-33

Easter Charco Micco et al
Fr 1829 Aug 14 M234-237

Eastin Mary Ann
see also Polk M A E
To 1830 Oct 24 16-0509
Fr 1830 Dec 05 16-0983
To 1831 Jan 01 17-0120
To 1831 Feb 17 17-0571
To 1831 May 10 17-1341
Fr 1831 Jun 12 DLC-39
To 1831 Jul 08 18-0164
To 1831 Nov 07 chk DLC-40
Fr 1831 Dec 03 DLC-40

Eastin Thomas
To 1806 Feb 07 2-0155
To 1806 Feb 10 2-0164
To 1806 Feb 15# 2-0178
To 1806 Feb 21# 2-0180
To 1806 Mar 06# 2-0187
To 1806 May 20# 2-0240
To 1806 May 21# 2-0243
To 1806 May 25# 2-0250
To 1806 cJun 2-0258
To 1806 Jun 06 2-0270
To 1806 Jun 28 2-0281
To 1806 Jul 03# 2-0291
Fr 1814 Jul 14 DLC-11
Fr 1814 Sep 06 DLC-12
Re 1832 Sep 12 20-1512
Fr 1834 Dec 29# 27-0032
Fr c1837 37-0355
Fr 1839 Sep 25 DLC-52

Eastin William
Fr 1810 Nov 27 DLC-5
To 1811 Jul 24 chk DLC-5
Fr 1815 May 02 DLC-18
Fr 1818 Aug 30 DLC-25
Re 1818 Aug 30 leg DLC-25
Fr 1821 Jul 31 DLC-30
Fr 1822 Oct 22 fin 9-0295
Fr 1828 Aug 29 DLC-72

Eastland Thomas
To 1816 Sep 20 chk DLC-21
Fr 1818 Jan 27 DLC-24
Fr 1819 Aug 23 leg DLC-27
Fr 1819 Aug 23* leg DLC-28

Eastman Henry W
Fr 1844 Feb 19 DLC-56

Eastman Philip
Fr 1837 Feb M687-16

Easton B G
Fr 1837 Jun 03# fin DLC-50

Easton Robert
Re 1832 Nov 01 par 21-0252

Easton PA Hickory Club
To 1829 Dec 15 DLC-37
To 1829 Dec 15* DLC-72

Eaton John Henry
Fr 1817 Feb 04 DLC-71
Fr 1817 Mar 20 DLC-22
Fr 1817 Sep fin DLC-31
To 1817 Sep 10 5-1012

To 1818 Feb 05		DLC-24
Fr 1818 Feb 12		DLC-24
Fr 1818 Nov 20		DLC-26
Fr 1818 Dec 14		DLC-26
To 1819 Feb 10		7-0245
To 1819 Feb 10*		DLC-28
Fr 1819 Jul 26		DLC-27
To 1819 Nov 29		DLC-28
Fr 1819 Dec 25		DLC-28
To 1819 Dec 28		7-0950
Fr 1820 Jan 13		DLC-75
Fr 1820 Feb#	mem	DLC-28
Fr 1820 Feb 23		DLC-75
Fr 1820 Mar 11		DLC-28
Fr 1820 Mar 15		DLC-28
Fr 1820 Apr 02		DLC-28
Fr 1820 Apr 16		DLC-29
Fr 1821 Jan 27		DLC-29
Fr 1821 Mar 03		DLC-29
Fr 1821 Mar 09		DLC-72
Fr 1821 Dec 30		DLC-31
Fr 1822 Jan		DLC-72
Fr 1822 Feb 12		DLC-31
Fr 1822 Dec 03		DLC-31
Fr 1823 Jan 11		DLC-72
Fr 1823 Jan 15		DLC-72
To 1823 Jan 21		9-0413
To 1823 Feb 01		DLC-32
Fr 1823 Feb 23		DLC-72
Fr 1823 Dec 18#		DLC-32
Re 1824		DLC-58
Fr 1824 Feb 08#		DLC-32
Fr 1824 Jun 22		10-0806
To 1825 Mar 23		10-1227
Fr 1826 Mar 29		DLC-72
Fr 1826 cMay 03		11-0203
Fr 1826 May 05		DLC-72
To 1826 Aug 13		DLC-34
Fr 1826 Sep 12		11-0367
To 1826 Oct 23		11-0385
Fr 1826 Dec 22		DLC-72
Fr 1827 Jan 05		DLC-72
Fr 1827 Jan 27		DLC-72
Fr 1827 Feb 04		DLC-72
Fr 1827 Feb 05		11-0483
Fr 1827 Feb 08		DLC-34
Fr 1827 cAug		DLC-72
Fr 1828 Jan 05		DLC-72
Fr 1828 Jan 21		DLC-35
To 1828 Mar		11-1151
Fr 1828 Mar 04		DLC-72
To 1828 Mar 28		DLC-35
Fr 1828 Apr 22		DLC-75
Fr 1828 Apr 22		DLC-72
To 1828 May 06		DLC-35
Fr 1828 Jul 04		12-0043
Fr 1828 Aug 21		DLC-35
Fr 1828 Sep 25		DLC-72
Fr 1828 Dec 07		12-0301
Fr 1828 Dec 07#		DLC-36
Fr 1828 Dec 08		DLC-29
To 1829		12-0365
Fr 1829 Mar 10		M127-2
Fr 1829 Mar 11		12-0941
Fr 1829 Mar 11*		M127-2
To 1829 Mar 11		12-0943
To 1829 Mar 17		DLC-60
To 1829 Mar 28		12-1162
To 1829 Mar 28*		DLC-60
To 1829 Mar 28*		M221-109
Fr 1829 cApr 01		M639-22
Fr 1829 Apr 13		12-1333
Re 1829 Apr 22		M234-808
To 1829 Apr 28		M222-24
To 1829 May 01		M22-24
To 1829 May 24#		DLC-37
To 1829 Jun 04	chk	DLC-37
To 1829 Jun 17		M222-26
Fr 1829 Jul		13-0765
To 1829 Jul 18		M688-63
Fr 1829 Sep 07		DLC-37
To 1829 Sep 08		13-1268
Fr 1829 Sep 12#		DLC-75
To 1829 Sep 12#		DLC-75
To 1829 Sep 15#		DLC-75
Fr 1829 Sep 16#		DLC-75
To 1829 Sep 16#		DLC-75
To 1829 Sep 22#		DLC-75
Fr 1829 Sep 23		13-1406
To 1829 Sep 23		13-1410
To 1829 Sep 24		M22-25
To 1829 Sep 25		M688-60
To 1829 cOct		14-0059
To 1829 Oct 06#		DLC-75
To 1829 Oct 09#		DLC-75
To 1829 Oct 19#		M234-135
Fr 1829 Oct 21		14-0224
To 1829 Oct 23#		14-0239
Fr 1829 Oct 27		14-0249
Fr 1829 Oct 27*		M127-2
Fr 1829 Oct 28		14-0253
Fr 1829 Nov		14-0317
To 1829 Nov 19		DLC-37
Fr 1829 Nov 30		14-0631
Fr 1829 Nov 30*		M127-2
To 1829 Nov 30#		DLC-75
Fr 1829 Dec 12		14-1026
Fr 1829 Dec 12*		M127-2
Fr 1829 Dec 14#		DLC-36
Fr 1829 Dec 28		M127-2
Fr 1829 Dec 29		14-1135
Fr 1829 Dec 29*		M127-2
Fr 1829 Dec 31		14-1167
Fr 1829 Dec 31		14-1169
Fr 1829 Dec 31		14-1178
Fr 1829 Dec 31		14-1183
To 1830		M234-74
Fr 1830 Jan 02		14-1297
Fr 1830 Jan 14		14-1424
To 1830 Jan 14		DLC-37
To 1830 Jan 25#		DLC-37
Fr 1830 Feb 04		M127-2
Fr 1830 Feb 05		15-0104
Fr 1830 Feb 05*		M127-2
To 1830 Feb 07		M22-25
Fr 1830 Feb 10		15-0118
Fr 1830 Feb 12		M21-6
Fr 1830 Feb 16		15-0143
To 1830 Feb 17		M222-27
Fr 1830 Mar 01		15-0277
Fr 1830 Mar 01		15-0280
Fr 1830 Mar 17		15-0385
To 1830 Mar 19		M221-110
Fr 1830 Mar 30		15-0533
Fr 1830 Mar 30*		M127-2
Fr 1830 Apr 01		15-0561
Fr 1830 Apr 01*		M127-2
Fr 1830 Apr 06		15-0619

Eaton John Henry (cont)

Fr	1830 Apr 07		15-0632
Fr	1830 Apr 09		15-0649
Fr	1830 Apr 09		15-0651
Fr	1830 Apr 13		15-0688
To	1830 Apr 16		M222-26
To	1830 Apr 17#		15-0751
Fr	1830 Apr 20		15-0756
Fr	1830 Apr 22		15-0767
Fr	1830 Apr 22*		M127-2
Fr	1830 Apr 22		15-0769
Fr	1830 Apr 23		15-0776
Fr	1830 Apr 23*		M127-2
To	1830 Apr 24		M222-27
Fr	1830 Apr 24		15-0803
Fr	1830 Apr 27		15-0820
To	1830 May 07		M22-26
Fr	1830 May 14		15-1009
Fr	1830 May 14*		M127-2
To	1830 May 20		15-1053
To	1830 May 21		15-1065
Fr	1830 May 24		15-1075
Fr	1830 May 24*		M127-2
To	1830 May 24		15-1076
Fr	1830 May 28		15-1180
Fr	1830 May 28*		M222-27
To	1830 Jun 12		15-1358
To	1830 Jun 30#		M234-222
To	1830 Jul 18		M567-55
To	1830 Jul 19		DLC-38
To	1830 cJul 25		16-0047
To	1830 Aug 03		DLC-38
Fr	1830 Aug 04#		DLC-38
Fr	1830 Aug 05#		DLC-38
To	1830 Aug 11#		DLC-38
To	1830 Aug 15		16-0108
Fr	1830 Aug 15		DLC-38
To	1830 Aug 27		16-0182
Fr	1830 Sep 01		DLC-73
Fr	1830 Sep 18		M234-169
To	1830 Nov 08#		M567-56
To	1830 Nov 09		M221-111
Fr	1830 Nov 15		DLC-75
To	1830 Nov 17		M567-54
To	1830 Nov 18		M234-113
To	1830 Nov 18*		16-0799
To	1830 Nov 20#		16-0809
Fr	1830 Dec 01		16-0923
Fr	1830 Dec 01*		M127-2
To	1830 Dec 03		16-0980
To	1830 Dec 10#		16-1377
To	1830 Dec 14		M234-315
To	1830 Dec 14*		16-1423
Fr	1830 Dec 14		16-1425
Fr	1830 Dec 16		16-1461
Fr	1830 Dec 16*		M127-2
Fr	1830 Dec 17		16-1464
Fr	1830 Dec 17*		M127-2
To	1830 Dec 18#		M221-111
To	1830 Dec 21		16-1520
Fr	1830 Dec 23		16-1545
To	1830 Dec 27		M222-27
Fr	1830 Dec 27		17-0016
Fr	1830 Dec 27*		M21-7
Fr	1830 Dec 27*		M234-433
Fr	1831 Jan 04		17-0190
Fr	1831 Jan 04*		M127-2
To	1831 Jan 12		M222-30
Fr	1831 Jan 18		DLC-73
Fr	1831 Jan 22		17-0333

To	1831 Feb 01		T494-2
To	1831 Feb 01*		17-0398
To	1831 Feb 01#		17-0394
To	1831 Feb 03		17-0416
Fr	1831 Feb 04		M21-7
To	1831 Feb 07		M234-808
To	1831 Feb 07*		17-0454
To	1831 Feb 11		M22-27
Fr	1831 Feb 18		17-0576
Fr	1831 Feb 18*		M127-2
Fr	1831 Feb 21		17-0600
Fr	1831 Feb 21*		M127-2
Fr	1831 Feb 23		17-0637
Fr	1831 Feb 25		M21-7
Fr	1831 Feb 26		17-0659
Fr	1831 Feb 26*		M127-2
To	1831 Feb 28		M124-126
Fr	1831 Mar 01		17-0695
Fr	1831 Apr 07		DLC-39
To	1831 Apr 08		17-1086
To	1831 Apr 08*		DLC-39
To	1831 Apr 15#		DLC-39
To	1831 May 21#		M567-63
Fr	1831 May 28		DLC-39
To	1831 Jun 02#		M234-77
Fr	1831 Jun 15		18-0027
To	1831 Jun 16#		M567-62
Fr	1831 Jul 01		DLC-73
To	1831 Jul 14		DLC-39
Fr	1831 Sep 06		DLC-75
Fr	1831 cSep 28		18-0881
Fr	1831 Oct		DLC-73
To	1831 Oct 23		18-1108
Fr	1831 Nov 05		DLC-73
Fr	1831 Nov 05		18-1204
Fr	1831 Dec 03		M234-169
Fr	1832 Jan 05		DLC-73
Fr	1832 Mar 13		DLC-40
Fr	1832 Apr 16		DLC-73
Fr	1832 May 30		DLC-73
To	1832 Sep 17	lnd	21-0024
Fr	1832 Dec 28		DLC-41
To	1833 Feb 19#		22-0412
Fr	1833 Mar 23		DLC-42
Fr	1833 Sep 07		DLC-75
Fr	1833 Sep 11		DLC-75
Fr	1833 Oct 23#		M234-136
Fr	1833 Nov 25		M639-3
To	1833 Dec 18	chk	DLC-43
Fr	1834 Jan		DLC-75
Fr	1834 Jun 05		M22-35
Fr	1834 Jul 22		DLC-44
Fr	1834 Aug 27		DLC-44
Fr	1835 Feb 05		M639-11
Fr	1835 Mar 29		27-1388
Fr	c1836 Jan		29-1430
Fr	c1836 Jan		DLC-75
Fr	1836 Feb 20		DLC-75
Fr	1836 Apr 10		DLC-48
Fr	1836 Apr 12		DLC-48
Fr	1836 Nov 17		DLC-75
Fr	1837		32-1455
Fr	1837		DLC-75
Fr	1837 Apr		33-1135
Fr	1837 Jun		33-1262
Fr	1839 cJul		34-0837
Fr	1840 Feb 15		34-1208
Fr	1841 Nov 15		DLC-54
Re	1842 Aug 23	mem	35-0898

Eaton Lewis et al			
	Fr 1837 Jan		M687-23
Eaton Margaret (O'Neale)			
	To 1829 Apr 18#		DLC-75
	Fr 1830 Jun 09		15-1328
Eaton Nathaniel Jackson			
	Fr 1836 Oct 02		31-1591
Eaton Zelora			
	Fr 1836 Sep 21		31-1481
Eaton affair			
	Re 1830 cJan	mem	14-1247
	Re 1830 Jan 24	mem	15-0009
Eauckson James			
	Fr 1829 Dec 27		14-1132
Echofixeca			
	Fr 1818 Mar 13		DLC-24
Eckert J C			
	Fr 1840 Sep 07		DLC-53
Eckford Henry			
	Fr 1830 Apr 07		M124-123
	Fr 1831 Apr 19		DLC-39
	To 1831 Apr 20		DLC-39
Eckloff Christian			
	Fr 1830 Jan 20#	fin	DLC-38
	Fr 1830 Jan 20	fin	DLC-38
	Fr 1830 May 29#	fin	DLC-38
	Fr 1831 Mar 07	fin	DLC-39
	Fr 1833 Apr 30		22-1214
	Fr 1835 Dec 12#	fin	DLC-47
Eddy Caleb			
	Fr 1836 May 13		31-0001
Eddy Henry et al			
	Fr 1832 Jul 01		M567-69
Eden Catharine E			
	Fr 1835 Jun 17		M639-10
Edgar John Todd			
	Fr 1840 May 14		DLC-52
	To 1845 Jan 11#		36-1325
Edgar Samuel Miller Jr			
	To 1844 Mar 02		36-0363
Edgerton Bela et al			
	Fr 1831 Apr 23		M639-1
Edgerton Luther et al			
	Fr 1836 Nov 01		M567-131
Edmiston William			
	Fr 1826 Jun 10		DLC-34
	To 1826 Jun 15		DLC-34
Edmondson James			
	Fr 1825 Mar 29	fin	DLC-72
	Fr 1825 Apr 05	fin	DLC-72
	Fr 1839 Sep 09		DLC-52
Edmonson B B			
	Fr 1836 Sep 15		DLC-49
	To 1836 Sep 15		DLC-49
Edmonston Theophilus			
	Re 1829 Sep 03	par	13-1240
	Re 1829 Sep 03*	par	T967-1
Edrington Edmond G Mrs			
	Fr 1833 Mar 01		DLC-42
Edwards Abraham			
	Fr 1844 Jun 12		36-0604
Edwards Amos			
	Fr 1818 Jan 24		DLC-24
Edwards Andrew			
	Re 1814 Mar 15		DLC-9
Edwards Haden			
	Fr 1821 Jul 24		M116-6
	To 1821 Jul 27		M116-6
Edwards Henry Waggaman			
	Fr 1832 Jan		19-0532
Edwards James L			
	Fr 1824 Feb 04		10-0430
	Fr 1824 Mar 29		10-0609
	Fr 1824 May 03		10-0699
	Fr 1825 Jan 05		10-1036
	Fr 1825 Jan 18		10-1076
	To 1829 Oct 05#		DLC-75
	Fr 1829 Oct 05#		DLC-75
	Fr 1829 Oct 09#		DLC-75
	Fr 1833 May 16#		22-1367
	Fr 1834 Oct 13#		26-0621
	Fr 1834 Nov 10#		26-0873
	Fr 1836 Oct 20		32-0251
	Fr 1843 Oct 19		35-1549
Edwards John Cummins			
	Fr 1835 Feb 09		DLC-45
Edwards Ninian			
	Re 1799 Nov 14	leg	1-0740
	Fr 1806 Nov 28		DLC-71
	To 1815 Jun 11		DLC-62
	To 1815 Jun 27		DLC-62
	Fr 1815 Jun 27		DLC-18
	Fr 1815 Jul 11		DLC-18
	Fr 1815 Jul 16		DLC-18
	To 1815 Jul 25		DLC-62
	Fr 1815 Aug 09		DLC-68
	To 1815 Aug 21		DLC-62
	Fr 1815 Sep 17		DLC-19
	To 1824 Mar 04		10-0515
	Fr 1829 cOct 01		14-0077
	To 1829 cNov 01		14-0350
Edwards Penelope			
	Fr 1844 Dec 12		DLC-57
Edwards Presley			
	Fr 1830 Sep 01		M234-433
Edwards Rebecca			
	Fr 1830 May 07		M567-51
Edwards Samuel M			
	Fr 1845 Jan 27		36-1413
Edwards Thomas			
	Fr 1807 Feb 09	fin	DLC-4
Edwards William			
	Re c1805	mem	DLC-60
	To 1810 Apr 21		2-0898
	Re 1813 Sep 07	leg	3-0454
Efar Emarthlar			
	Re 1834 Oct 25		26-0721
Efar Tustennugga			
	Fr 1834 Feb 25		M234-241
Egerton Alice			
	Fr 1842 Oct 10		35-0968
	To 1842 Oct 25		35-0980
Eggleston Elizabeth			
	Re 1830 Aug 08	mem	DLC-38
Ehringhaus John C			
	Fr 1833 Jan 22		DLC-42
Eichbaum William A			
	Fr 1837 Jun 22#	fin	DLC-50
	Fr 1839 Jan 05#	fin	DLC-52
Eldred Nathaniel B			
	Fr 1832 Nov 16		DLC-41
Eldridge James S			
	Fr 1823 Apr 20		DLC-32
Eldridge Thomas			
	Fr 1814 Feb 09		DLC-8
	To 1814 Feb 13		DLC-62

Elgar Joseph
To 1829 Jun 20 DLC-60
Fr 1832 Oct 26 21-0153
Fr 1832 Oct 26* M371-5
Fr 1833 Apr 01 M371-5
Eliason William A
To 1836 Sep 20# leg 31-1473
To 1836 Sep 20* leg DLC-56
To 1836 Sep 20 leg DLC-74
To 1836 Sep 20* 37-0526
Eliott H et al
Fr 1824 Jun 28 DLC-32
Elkins Jeremiah
Re 1831 Jul 13 18-0203
Ellery Charles
Re 1830 Nov 23 16-0843
Ellicott Thomas
Fr 1833 Apr 06 DLC-42
To 1833 Apr 09 22-0974
Fr 1833 Apr 10 22-0980
Elliot Jonathan
To 1834 May 17 25-1074
Elliot William P
Fr 1834 Apr 09 M639-7
Elliott Andrew et al
Fr 1835 cJan DLC-59
Elliott George
Fr 1815 Aug 01 DLC-19
Fr 1822 Mar 04 fin DLC-31
Elliott Jesse Duncan
Fr 1831 Apr 30 M22-28
Fr 1832 Jun 09# M179-73
To 1832 Sep 06# 20-1486
Fr 1835 Jan 31 M179-79
To 1835 Apr 19# DLC-46
Fr 1835 Apr 23 DLC-46
Fr 1835 Jun 22 DLC-46
Fr 1835 Jul 22 DLC-46
Fr 1835 Aug 10 28-1269
Fr 1835 Aug 18 28-1295
Fr 1835 Sep 03 28-1517
Fr 1835 Sep 03 DLC-46
Fr 1836 Apr 21 30-1280
Fr 1836 Jul 05 M179-82
Fr 1836 Aug 23 M179-82
Fr 1836 Oct 11 DLC-49
Fr 1844 Dec 22 36-1249
Re 1845 Mar 17 add DLC-57
Fr 1845 Mar 18 DLC-57
Fr 1845 Mar 18 37-0001
To 1845 Mar 27 37-0030
Fr 1845 Jun 04 DLC-58
Elliott John
Fr 1816 Dec 21 DLC-22
Fr 1818 Jun 14 fin DLC-69
Fr 1818 Jun 14* fin 6-1049
Fr 1845 Feb 03 36-1440
Elliott Moses H
Fr 1817 Feb 15 5-0726
Elliott Myles
Fr 1835 Mar 17 27-1225
Elliott Robert
To 1815 Aug 15 DLC-62
Fr 1828 Jan 29 DLC-35
Elliott William et al
Fr 1828 Dec 08 M639-25
Ellis Daniel H et al
Fr 1829 Mar 27 M873-19
Ellis Leonard
Re 1830 Oct 19 par 16-0443
Ellis Powhatan
To 1830 Apr 11# 15-0673
To 1832 Feb 02 19-0934
Fr 1832 Jun 07 20-0708
Fr 1833 Jul 02 DLC-43
Fr 1836 Aug 26 M97-8
Fr 1839 Oct 15 DLC-52
Fr 1840 Aug 01 DLC-53
Ellis William H
Fr 1832 Jan 19-0543
Fr 1833 Jul 13 23-0123
Fr 1834 Jun 14 M639-24
Fr 1836 May 08 M687-17
Fr 1837 Feb 15 DLC-50
Ellis William H et al
Fr 1831 Jan 15 M639-5
Ellsworth Henry Leavitt
Re 1831 Dec 21 19-0375
Fr 1832 Jan 19 19-0784
Fr 1832 Jul 21 M222-31
Fr 1836 Feb 23 M639-26
Fr 1836 Mar 31# M639-7
Fr 1836 Jun 07 M639-26
Fr 1836 Jun 13 M687-17
Elting William H
Fr 1829 May 05 M567-47
Elton Romeo
Fr 1843 Jul 31 35-1439
Elwyn Elizabeth Langdon
Fr 1829 Jun 05 M124-119
Elwyn John Langdon
Fr 1829 Dec 07 14-0802
Ely Ezra Stiles
Fr 1819 Oct 22# DLC-28
To 1823 Apr 21 9-0529
To 1824 Jan 01 9-0880
To 1824 Feb 24 10-0478
Fr 1825 Mar 02 10-1208
To 1825 cMar 05 10-1215
Fr 1825 Jun 04 DLC-33
To 1827 May 19 11-0600
To 1827 Jul 12 11-0746
To 1828 Dec 10 12-0310
Fr 1829 Jan 28 DLC-36
Fr 1829 Feb 02 M639-1
Fr 1829 Mar 04 12-0841
Fr 1829 Mar 14 M639-7
Fr 1829 Mar 18 DLC-75
To 1829 Mar 23 DLC-75
Fr 1829 Apr 04 DLC-75
To 1829 Apr 10 DLC-75
Fr 1829 Apr 11 M639-14
Fr 1829 May 02 DLC-75
Fr 1829 May 07 M124-118
Fr 1829 May 30 DLC-75
To 1829 Jun 29 13-0746
Fr 1829 Jul 03 DLC-37
Fr 1829 Aug 19 13-1175
To 1829 Sep# DLC-37
To 1829 Sep 03 DLC-37
Fr 1829 Nov 23 14-0551
To 1830 Jan 12 DLC-37
Fr 1830 Jan 15 DLC-37
Fr 1830 Feb 10 DLC-37
Fr 1831 Jul 18 M22-28
Ely Hugh et al
Fr 1829 Mar M639-3
Ely Samuel Carswell
Fr 1838 Jan 08 DLC-51

Emerson John et al
Fr 1837 Feb 14 M687-20
Emerson Seth
Fr 1837 Jan 20 M687-20
Emerson Thomas
To 1833 Jun 13 23-0020
Emerson Thomas et al
Fr 1835 Dec 28 DLC-73
Emery Daniel
Fr 1837 Feb 20 M687-16
Emery Nicholas
Fr 1836 Apr 18 30-1224
Emmerson Arthur et al
Fr 1829 Jul 10 13-0833
Emmerson Thomas
Fr 1816 Feb 15 DLC-20
Emmit William C
Fr 1826 Jun 18 11-0252
To 1826 Jun 26 11-0262
Fr 1828 Jan 29 fin DLC-35
Fr 1828 May 26 DLC-35
To 1828 May 26 fin DLC-35
Emmons William
Fr 1828 Jan 29 DLC-35
Fr 1828 Mar 10 DLC-35
Fr 1844 Oct 06# 36-0934
Fr 1844 Oct 31# 36-0972
Fr 1844 Nov 05# 36-0989
Fr 1844 Nov 09# 36-1010
Fr 1844 Nov 24# 36-1052
Fr 1845 Jan 04 36-1307
Emory Robert
Fr 1833 Nov 13 23-1230
Emuckfaw (battle)
Re 1814 Jan 31 add DLC-8
Re 1814 Jan 31* add DLC-62
Eneix Joseph
Fr 1831 Dec 27 M22-28
England John
Fr 1829 Sep 26 M179-67
Engles Aaron C et al
Fr 1831 Aug 20 M639-5
English James T
Re 1832 Feb 21 par 19-1198
Enirault L
Fr 1829 Nov 13 M639-10
Enochs Enoch
To 1806 Nov 27 fin DLC-4
To 1807 May 16# fin 2-0495
To 1809 May 14 lnd 2-0804
Enochs Gabriel
Re 1808 Jul 28 leg 2-0720
Enos Truman et al
Fr 1830 Jan 08 M639-14
Ensign Silas et al
Fr 1836 Oct 31-1542
Ernenputsch J C
Fr 1833 Apr 22 M639-16
Ervin William
Fr c1831 Dec 03 19-0005
Erving George William
Fr 1829 Dec 17 DLC-37
Fr 1832 Feb 05 DLC-40
Fr 1832 Feb 05* 19-0968
Fr 1835 Sep 25 DLC-47
Erwin Andrew
To 1820 Feb 16 7-1028
Re 1823 mem 9-0383
Re 1823 Sep 19 leg 9-0660
Erwin Andrew et al
Re 1824 Jan 19 leg 9-0946
To 1824 Feb 11 lnd 10-0444
Erwin Hugh
Fr 1824 Mar 30 fin DLC-32
Erwin James
Fr 1839 Apr 09# fin DLC-53
To 1840 Jul 21 chk DLC-53
Erwin John
Fr 1806 Feb 13 2-0177
Erwin Joseph
Fr 1804 Oct 14 fin DLC-71
Fr 1804 Oct 18 1-1397
Re 1806 Jan 04 2-0113
Fr 1806 Jun 21 2-0276
Re 1809 Oct 20 leg 2-0860
Erwin K I
Fr 1817 Sep 15 fin DLC-31
Erwin William H
Fr 1815 Feb 13 DLC-16
Esery William
To 1803 Oct 04 fin 1-1192
Eskridge Thomas P
Fr 1832 Nov 12 21-0380
Espocokoke Hadjo
Re 1814 Aug 11 3-1300
Esselman John N
Fr c1841 35-0156
Re 1841 Jan 16# leg 35-0203
To 1841 Oct 23 fin DLC-53
To 1842 Jan 12 chk DLC-54
Fr 1843 Aug 07# fin DLC-58
Fr 1844 Dec 30 M873-32
Fr 1845 Jun 02 DLC-58
Essex R
Fr 1833 Oct 04 23-0943
Estabrook Nathan
Fr 1835 Feb 02 27-0368
Etting E J et al
Fr 1830 May 10 15-0969
Eustis Abraham
Fr 1821 Oct 01 DLC-30
Fr 1821 Oct 09 M221-93
To 1821 Dec 12 DLC-63
Eustis George
Fr 1840 Jan 10 add DLC-52
Eustis William
To 1811 May 10 M221-38
Fr 1811 May 29 M6-5
Evans ____
Fr c1837 37-0357
Evans Clarissa
Fr 1826 Sep 10 DLC-34
Evans Estwick
Fr 1830 Jan 11 14-1378
Evans French S
Fr 1829 Aug 07 M639-13
Fr 1832 Jul 26 DLC-41
Fr 1832 Oct 23 21-0134
Fr 1834 Nov 15 DLC-45
Fr 1835 Jan 31 DLC-45
Fr 1844 Oct 23 DLC-57
Evans French S et al
Fr 1836 Nov M639-6
Evans John B
Re 1800 Nov 24 leg 1-0824
Evans John B & Co
Fr 1796 Jan 04 1-0337
Re 1801 cJul 15 mem 1-0898

Evans Joshua Jr
To 1833 Mar 06 22-0670
Fr 1833 Mar 06 22-0673
Evans Lewis
Fr 1816 Sep 03 DLC-21
Fr 1817 Sep 18 5-1019
Evans Robert
To 1813 Dec 22 DLC-61
Fr 1816 Aug 01 DLC-21
Evans Samuel
Fr 1835 Dec 16 M639-8
Evans William
Re 1835 Jun 30 par 28-0849
Evans & Smith
Fr 1844 Jan 24 DLC-56
Evens Benjamin
Fr 1829 Mar 14 M639-7
Fr 1829 Jul 14 M639-7
Fr 1829 Jul 14 M639-7
Fr 1829 Sep 07 M639-7
Fr 1831 Mar 12 M639-7
Everett Edward
To 1829 Dec 22 14-1092
To 1831 Jan 18 17-0283
To 1833 Jan 17 21-1565
Fr 1833 Jun 24 add 23-0055
To 1834 Jan 07 24-0772
To 1835 Jan 09 27-0163
Fr 1836 Mar 18 30-0809
Everett John F
Fr 1831 Nov 17 M639-3
Everett John F et al
Fr 1829 Apr 25 M639-5
Everett Silas K
Re 1829 Oct 15 14-0163
Ewell James
Fr 1828 Oct 18 DLC-35
To 1828 Oct 19 12-0236
To 1828 Oct 19* DLC-35
Fr 1830 Mar 14 M639-7
Ewing Alexander
Fr 1808 Mar 13 lnd 2-0619
Ewing Andrew
Re 1795 Jan 16 leg 1-0248
To 1839 Apr 01 34-0705
To 1841 Mar 08 35-0246
Fr 1841 Apr 14 DLC-53
Fr 1843 Jun 26 DLC-55
Fr 1843 Dec 20 DLC-56
To 1843 Dec 25 36-0075
Ewing Edwin Hickman
To 1839 Apr 01 34-0705
To 1841 Mar 08 35-0246
Fr 1841 Apr 14 DLC-53
Fr 1842 Feb 23 DLC-54
To 1842 Feb 24 DLC-54
Ewing Finis
Fr 1813 Nov 24 DLC-7
Fr 1828 Oct 04 DLC-35
To 1828 Nov 17 DLC-35
To 1828 Nov 17* 12-0275
Fr 1833 Sep 26 23-0865
Ewing Henry
Fr 1823 Dec 22 fin DLC-32
Fr 1826 May 05 DLC-33
Fr 1826 May 12 fin 11-0212
Fr 1826 Nov 25 fin 11-0407
Fr 1827 Nov 12 fin 11-0919
Fr 1828 Jul 14 fin 12-0049
Fr 1828 Dec 30 fin 12-0349
Ewing Juliet C
Fr 1829 Oct 03 M688-58
Ewing Mary Jane
Fr 1844 Feb 29 DLC-56
Ewing Nathan
Fr 1829 Apr 06 M639-2
Ewing O & Co
Fr 1838 Jul 04 fin DLC-51
Ewing Robert et al
To 1825 May 06 DLC-33
Ewing Thomas and Sarah
Fr 1770 Dec 17 lnd 1-0003
Ewing W G et al
Fr 1830 Oct 19 16-0448
Ewing William Lee Davidson
Fr 1831 Sep 24 18-0875
Fr 1836 Mar 30 30-0912
Fr 1836 Mar 30 30-0916
Fr 1836 Oct 01 31-1572
Fr 1837 Feb 06 33-0417
Fr 1837 Feb 18 M687-23
Fr 1837 Apr 18 33-1161
Fr 1840 Mar 14 DLC-52
Ewing William Lee Davidson et al
Fr 1832 Dec M639-12
Fr 1836 Apr M639-7
Ewing Young
Fr 1815 Jan 21 DLC-15
Executive policy
Re 1829 cFeb mem DLC-36
Expunging resolution
Re 1835 Nov 13 mem DLC-47
Re 1837 Jan DLC-49
Re 1837 Jan 16 DLC-49
Re 1837 Jan 16 DLC-74
Exum James W
Fr 1835 Feb 26 M639-7
Eynaud Paul
Re 1830 Jun 15 15-1457
Ezell Lewis
Fr 1827 Apr 15 fin 11-0567

Fahnestock Levi
Fr 1836 Jan 09 29-1531
Fr 1838 Feb 09 DLC-51
Fain Nicholas
Fr 1828 Dec 02 12-0295
To 1828 Dec 13 12-0324
Fairchild Robert
Fr 1831 May 23 M639-27
Fairchild William B
Fr 1843 Jan 15 DLC-55
Fairfield John
Fr 1836 Dec 21 M639-5
Fr 1837 Jan 21 M687-28
Fr 1844 May 04 36-0487
To 1844 May 16 36-0551
Fales ______
Fr 1835 Jun 01 M124-148
Fall G R
Fr 1836 Aug 02 31-1190
Fannin Abraham B
Fr 1814 Aug 19 DLC-11
Fanning Alexander Campbell Wilder
Fr 1818 Jan 20 fin 5-1317
To 1818 Apr 29 6-0528
Fr 1818 May 11 DLC-25
Fr 1818 Jul 12 DLC-25

Fr 1818 Jul 13 DLC-25
Fr 1819 Apr 21 M221-86
Fr 1820 Sep 03 DLC-29
To 1820 Nov 13 DLC-63
To 1821 May 22 DLC-63
To 1821 May 22* M116-6
Fr 1821 Jun 27 M116-6
To 1821 Jul 10 DLC-63
Fr 1832 Jan 24 19-0834
Fr 1832 Apr 06 20-0153

Fanning Edmund
Fr c1836 29-1394
Fr 1836 Mar 27 M179-81

Fanning Tolbert
Fr 1843 May 18 DLC-55
Fr 1845 May 30 DLC-58

Farewell Address
Re 1837 Mar 04 add DLC-64
Re 1837 cMar 04 add 33-1064

Farnsworth E et al
Fr 1835 cNov M639-9

Farnsworth Thomas J et al
Fr 1836 May 14 31-0016

Farragut David Glasgow
Fr 1833 Apr 09 22-0976

Farragut George
Fr 1815 Mar 24 DLC-17
Fr 1816 Mar 30 DLC-20

Fatio Francis Philip
Fr 1818 Jun 15 DLC-25

Faucett Joseph
Fr 1839 Nov 22 DLC-52

Fauche Jonas
Fr 1832 Jul 30 M234-223

Faulkner James
Fr 1828 Aug 18 12-0164

Faulkner Samuel
Fr 1837 Jul 24 DLC-50

Faulkner William
To 1827 Aug 28 11-0828

Fauntleroy Thomas Turner
Fr 1836 Aug 15 M567-128

Favor H S
Fr 1844 Nov 18 DLC-57

Favre Bartelemy
Fr 1815 Mar 11 DLC-17

Faygart Arthur et al
Fr 1833 Apr 03 22-0928

Fearn Thomas
Fr 1813 Dec 24 DLC-61
To 1814 Feb 01 DLC-62
To 1814 Mar 08 DLC-61
Fr 1814 Mar 15 DLC-9
Fr 1815 Aug 08 DLC-19

Fearson Charles L
Re 1830 Dec 13 par 16-1414

Fearson J N
Fr 1838 May 19 DLC-51

Federal Seminary
Re 1799 Feb 19 mem 37-0486
Re 1799 Feb 19* mem 1-0697

Feemster Lucien J
Fr 1829 Feb 14# M639-8

Feeny Hugh F et al
Fr 1832 Jan 29 M639-21
Fr 1834 Feb M639-27

Fegely Samuel et al
Fr 1843 Feb 15 DLC-55

Feijo Diogo Antonio
Fr 1835 Oct 25 M49-2
To 1836 Mar 14 30-0762

Felder Gabriel et al
Fr 1834 Sep 06 M234-188

Felker Joseph
Fr 1831 Jun 04 M22-28

Fellows Elizabeth
Fr 1833 Jun 14 M124-138

Female Friend (pseudonym)
Fr 1827 Jun 10# 11-0694

Fenner James
Fr 1829 Feb 26 M639-7
Fr 1830 Jan 08 14-1356
Fr 1830 Apr 30 15-0861
Fr 1831 Jun 18 M639-10
Fr 1831 Nov 01 M639-20
Fr 1833 Feb 16 22-0400
Re 1844 Apr 05 mem 36-0423

Fenner Robert
Fr 1828 Dec 18 DLC-36

Fennon _____ (Capt)
To 1821 Feb 20 8-0142

Fenwick John Roger
Fr 1821 Aug 04 DLC-30

Fenwick Robert W
Re 1837 Jan 07 par 32-1516

Ferdinand II King of the Two Sicilies
Fr 1830 Nov 09 16-0701
Fr 1830 Nov 09* M55-1
To 1831 Mar 01 17-0698
Fr 1832 Apr 07 20-0164
To 1832 Aug 11 20-1275
Fr 1832 Nov 30 21-0641
Fr 1832 Dec 30 21-1210
To 1833 Jan 30 22-0112
To 1833 Jan 30 22-0113
To 1833 Apr 20 22-1061
Fr 1833 Jun 07 22-1605
To 1833 Dec 27 24-0610
Fr 1834 Apr 22 25-0854
Fr 1836 Jan 16 30-0124
Fr 1836 Jan 31 30-0243
To 1836 Mar 28 30-0906
To 1836 May 24 31-0090

Ferdinand VII King of Spain
Fr 1820 Oct 24 DLC-19
To 1829 Jun 01 13-0534
To 1829 Oct 01 14-0085
To 1829 Nov 19 14-0498
Fr 1829 Dec 25 14-1119
To 1830 Mar 22 15-0429
Fr 1830 Oct 15 16-0388
To 1831 Mar 01 17-0699
Fr 1832 Feb 03 19-0939
Fr 1832 Jun 20 20-0774
To 1832 Jun 22 20-0799
Fr 1832 Jul 20 20-1187
To 1832 Oct 23 21-0136
To 1832 Oct 31 21-0221
To 1833 Apr 12 22-0988
Fr 1833 Jun 07 23-0001
Fr 1833 Jun 07* M59-13
Fr 1833 Aug 20 23-0426
To 1833 Aug 29 23-0486

Ferguson A Jr
Fr 1826 Oct 08 DLC-34

Ferguson James B
Fr 1837 Dec 07 fin DLC-50
Fr 1838 Oct 20 DLC-51

Ferguson James B (cont)
To 1839 Jan 18# fin DLC-52
Fr 1839 Feb 04 fin DLC-51
Fr 1842 Jan 05 fin DLC-54
Ferguson John
Fr 1831 Oct 17 M639-8
Ferguson T L
Fr 1809 Mar 31 DLC-4
Ferguson William D
Fr 1830 Jun 10 15-1336
Ferguson William D et al
Fr 1836 Sep 15 31-1447
Ferraire Felix
Fr 1815 Mar DLC-17
Fr 1815 Mar* 4-0803
Ferrell Larken
To 1814 Mar 09 DLC-9
Ferris Charles Goadsby et al
Fr 1835 Jan 01 M639-20
Ferry Charles
Fr 1815 Jan 31 DLC-16
Ferry Hiram
Fr 1845 Jan 22 DLC-57
Fessenden Stephen
Fr 1829 Mar 18 M639-8
Fetterman A T et al
Fr 1835 Nov 14 M639-27
Fetterman Nathaniel P et al
Fr 1830 Feb 27 M639-23
Fickle Abram B
Re 1829 Jul 29 par 13-0963
Re 1829 Jul 29* par T967-1
Re 1830 Jan 13 par 14-1409
Ficklin Joseph
Fr 1821 Apr 28 DLC-30
Fr 1821 Apr 30 DLC-30
Fr 1827 Sep 18 DLC-34
Fr 1829 Feb 16 DLC-36
Fr 1829 Feb 16# M639-2
Fr 1829 Feb 25# M639-2
Fr 1829 Mar 05 M639-11
Fr 1830 Mar 18 M639-21
Fr 1844 Dec 07 DLC-57
Fr 1844 Dec 11 36-1162
Ficklin Joseph et al
Fr 1830 Mar 18 M639-21
Field Alexander P
Fr 1829 Feb 17 M639-3
Field Alexander P et al
Fr 1833 cFeb M639-27
Field R H
Fr 1830 May 31 15-1235
Field Thomas Jefferson et al
Fr 1836 Nov 24 M234-355
Field Timothy B
Re 1830 Dec 10 M273-25
Re 1831 Jan 25 M273-25
Field William
Fr 1824 Nov 14 DLC-33
Fr 1828 Nov 14 DLC-35
Fr 1829 May 09 M234-432
Fr 1829 May 14 13-0315
Fr 1832 Nov 01 21-0257
Fr 1836 Feb 10 DLC-47
Fields Balaam D
Fr 1830 May 20 DLC-38
Fields John
To 1814 Jan DLC-8
Fields L N
Fr 1831 Jan 26# M222-29
Fields Robert
Re 1832 Jul 19 par 20-1140
Fife James
Re 1814 Aug 10 3-1287
To 1820 Dec 11 8-0015
Fife James et al
Re 1814 May 01 mem DLC-61
Figures M
Fr 1803 Feb 02 fin 1-1082
Files David
Fr 1815 Feb 11 DLC-16
Fr 1815 Mar 17 DLC-17
Fr 1815 Mar 19 DLC-17
Fr 1815 Apr 14 DLC-18
Fillebrown Thomas Jr
Fr 1829 Sep 15# DLC-75
Fr 1829 Sep 16# DLC-75
Fr 1829 Sep 22# DLC-75
Finch Aaron
Fr 1832 Jan 25 19-0843
Finch Aaron et al
Fr 1832 Dec M639-24
Finch William
To 1809 May 15 lnd 2-0814
Finch William B
Fr 1831 Feb 05 17-0444
Findlay James
Re 1829 Nov mem 14-0324
Findlay James et al
Fr 1834 Sep 18 M639-13
Findlay William
Re 1830 Sep 30 16-0275
Fr 1831 Jun 17 M639-13
To 1834 Aug 20 DLC-44
Findley John
Fr 1829 Feb 23 M639-8
Finley Ann
Fr 1834 Nov 29# fin DLC-45
Fr 1835 Jul 02# fin DLC-46
Fr 1836 Apr 27# fin 30-1374
Finley William
Fr 1829 Mar 02 M639-9
Finsh Richard et al
Fr 1836 Jul 04 M234-355
Fio Francis
Fr 1815 Jan 16 DLC-15
First Presbyterian Church (DC)
Fr 1831 Oct 07 fin DLC-40
Fr 1834 Mar 31 fin DLC-44
To 1834 Apr 04 chk DLC-44
Fr 1834 Sep 30 fin DLC-44
To 1834 Oct 03 chk DLC-44
Fr 1835 Apr 02 fin DLC-46
Fr 1835 Jul 06 fin DLC-46
Fr 1836 Jan 02 fin DLC-49
To 1836 Jan 02 chk DLC-47
Fr 1836 Apr 04 fin DLC-47
To 1836 Apr 04 chk DLC-47
Fr 1836 Jul 01 fin DLC-48
To 1836 Jul 01 chk DLC-48
Fr 1837 Jan 03 fin DLC-49
To 1837 Jan 03 chk DLC-49
Fish Preserved
Fr 1829 Nov 05 14-0410
Fr 1833 Apr 09 M639-20
Fish Preserved et al
Fr 1830 Nov 08 16-0689
Fr 1831 Sep 13 M639-4
Fr 1834 Oct 15 M639-14

Fish Grinnell & Co et al		
Fr 1833 Apr 09		M639-20
Fr 1833 Sep 07		M639-10
Fishell Michael		
Fr 1831 Aug 10		M22-28
Fisher Elisha & Co		
Fr 1803 May 03	fin	DLC-3
Fr 1804 Mar 31	fin	DLC-3
Fisher Henry J et al		
Fr 1829 May		M639-10
Fisher John et al		
Fr 1814 May 14	add	3-1025
Fisher Samuel Rhoads		
Fr 1829 Jun 10		M639-8
Fr 1829 Jun 10*		13-0612
Fr 1835 Feb 13		M639-3
Fisher William		
Re 1831 Nov 29	par	18-1514
Fisher William et al		
Fr 1835 Oct		29-0159
Fisk Alvarez		
Fr 1815 Feb 02		DLC-16
Fiske Francis N et al		
Fr 1829 Jul 02		13-0800
Fitch A Jr		
Fr 1835 Jan 12		27-0185
Fitch Augustus		
Fr 1833 Mar 16		22-0784
Fite Leonard B		
To 1840 Jul 22	chk	DLC-53
Fitz Gideon		
Re 1835 Feb 02	mem	DLC-45
Fitzgerald Aaron		
Fr 1831 Apr 24#		17-1225
Fitzgerald Edward		
Fr 1829 Dec 15		M22-28
Fitzgerald John		
Fr 1828 Oct 20		12-0243
To 1828 Oct 31		12-0256
Fitzgerald William		
Fr 1840 Jul 02		34-1459
Fitzpatrick Benjamin		
Fr 1835 Sep 20		M639-4
Fitzpatrick Catherine		
Fr 1829 Apr 27		M179-67
Flagg Azariah Cutting		
Fr 1844 Nov 07		36-0999
Flannagan Josias		
Fr 1829 Sep 06		M222-25
Fleaugeac Garrigues de		
Fr 1815 Feb 06		4-0710
Fleming George		
Fr 1829 Apr 13		M234-432
Fr 1836 Jul 28		M688-106
Fleming John		
Fr 1828 Oct 10		DLC-35
Re 1844 Jun 17	mem	DLC-57
Fleming John S		
Re 1834 May 23	mem	25-1142
Flenniken Robert P		
Fr 1835 Mar 21		DLC-45
Fletcher Ephraim et al		
Fr 1829 May		M639-24
Fletcher John		
Fr 1829 Mar 06		M639-6
Fletcher John Calvin		
Fr 1831 Dec 18		M688-79
Fletcher Madison		
Fr 1831 Jan 12		M688-60
Fletcher Thomas H		
Fr 1813 Aug 11		DLC-6
To 1816 Aug 08	fin	DLC-21
Fr 1829 Apr 07		12-1295
Fr 1839 Aug 18		DLC-52
To 1840 Jul 22	chk	DLC-53
Fr 1840 Jul 22	fin	DLC-53
Fr 1842 Jul 08		DLC-54
To 1844 Mar 18		DLC-56
Fr 1844 Aug 03		DLC-57
Fletcher William Asa		
Fr 1835 Dec 03		M639-9
Flint Horace K		
Fr 1838 Jan 19		DLC-51
Flood ______ (Miss)		
Fr 1839 Nov 25#	fin	DLC-52
Fr 1840 Sep 29#	fin	DLC-53
Flood George H		
Fr 1835 Jan 08		M639-27
Fr 1835 Dec 30		M639-27
Fr 1836 Apr 29		M687-31
Fr 1840 Feb 14		34-1200
Fr 1841 Jan 17		DLC-53
Flood Thomas		
Fr 1832 Jun 28#		DLC-41
Flood Thomas et al		
Fr 1833 Oct		M639-24
Flood William		
To 1821 Feb 15		8-0113
Flores Juan Jose		
Fr 1832 Jan 13		M179-72
Florida		
Re 1818 May 28		M125-58
Re 1819 Jan		DLC-59
Re 1821 Mar 10		DLC-30
Re 1821 Mar 10*		DLC-63
Re 1821 Mar 10*		8-0179
Re 1821 Mar 10		DLC-63
Re 1821 Mar 10*		8-0181
Re 1821 Mar 20		DLC-63
Re 1821 Mar 20*		8-0251
Re 1821 Mar 20*		DLC-30
To 1821 Apr 14	fin	DLC-70
Re 1821 Apr 14	fin	8-0323
Re 1821 Apr 22	fin	DLC-70
Re 1821 Jun 25		DLC-30
Re 1821 Jun 25*		DLC-63
Re 1821 Jun 25*		8-0687
Re 1821 Jul	leg	DLC-59
Re 1821 Jul*	leg	DLC-63
Re 1821 Jul*	leg	M116-6
Re 1821 Jul	mem	DLC-31
Re 1821 Jul 17	leg	8-0851
Re 1821 Jul 17		M116-6
Re 1821 Jul 17*		DLC-63
Re 1821 Jul 17		DLC-70
Re 1821 Jul 21		M116-6
Re 1821 Jul 21*		DLC-63
Re 1821 Jul 21*		8-0889
Re 1821 Jul 21		DLC-63
Re 1821 Jul 21*		8-0885
Re 1821 Jul 26		M116-6
Re 1821 Jul 26*		DLC-63
Re 1821 Jul 26*		8-0910
Re 1821 Aug 20	fin	DLC-70
Re 1821 Sep 09		DLC-30
Re 1821 Sep 22	add	8-1203
Re 1821 Oct	mem	DLC-59
Re 1821 Oct 06		8-1288

Florida (cont)
Re 1821 Oct 31 mem DLC-31
Re 1822 mem DLC-31
Re 1822* mem DLC-59
Re 1822 cMar 16 mem DLC-63
Re 1822 Aug 16 9-0248
Re 1822 Aug 19 9-0251
Florida citizens
To 1821 Oct 06 add 8-1289
Florida Indians
To 1821 Sep 20 M221-93
To 1821 Sep 20* DLC-63
To 1821 Sep 20* 8-1190
Flotard Thomas et al
Fr 1832 Jan 26 M639-9
Flournoy Alfred
Re 1817 Aug 12 5-0968
Flournoy Francis
Fr 1834 Jul 04 26-0144
Flournoy George Washington
Fr 1844 Jul 25 36-0743
Flournoy John J
Fr 1831 Nov 28 M179-71
Flournoy Mathew et al
Fr 1837 Mar 13 DLC-50
To 1837 Apr 01 DLC-50
Flournoy Thomas
To 1813 Oct 24 DLC-61
Fr 1813 Nov 09 DLC-7
Fr 1813 Nov 09* DLC-61
Fr 1813 Nov 09* 3-0579
To 1814 Jul 22 DLC-62
Flowers Hardy
To 1807 Jan 23 fin DLC-4
To 1807 Jan 26 fin DLC-4
Flowers Henry
To 1807 Jan 21 fin DLC-4
Floyd Gabriel J
Fr 1837 Jan 17 32-1592
Floyd John (1769-1839)
Fr 1813 Dec 18 DLC-7
To 1813 Dec 27 M222-8
To 1813 Dec 27* DLC-61
Fr 1814 Jan 02 DLC-8
Fr 1814 Jan 24 DLC-8
To 1814 Jan 29 3-0822
To 1814 Jan 29* DLC-61
To 1814 Jan 30 DLC-8
Fr 1814 Feb 04 DLC-8
To 1814 Feb 10 DLC-61
Floyd John (1783-1837)
Fr 1827 May 27 DLC-35
Fr 1829 Mar 12 M639-24
Fr 1829 Mar 12 12-0972
Fr 1830 May 07 M639-23
Fr 1832 May 14 M179-73
Flugel Johann Gottfried
Fr 1841 Feb 15 35-0228
To 1841 Sep 22 35-0403
Foelikel L V
Fr 1815 Jan 08 DLC-71
Fr 1815 Feb 02 DLC-16
Fogg Francis Brinley
Fr 1832 Oct 30 M639-4
Fogg Mary Middleton (Rutledge)
Fr 1829 cJan 01 12-0426
To 1829 Jan 17 12-0461
Folch Vincente
Fr 1814 Jul 22 DLC-11
Foley James B
Fr 1841 Dec 05 DLC-54
Follett Frederick
Fr 1844 Sep 14 DLC-57
Folsom David
Fr 1830 Mar 18 15-0391
Folsom Edmond
Fr 1820 Sep 13 M271-3
Fr 1820 Sep 13* 7-1355
Fr 1820 Oct 06 M271-3
Fr 1820 Nov 02 M221-89
Folsom Isaac
Fr 1836 Aug 10 31-1275
Fonseca Antonio da Silveira Pinto da
To 1831 Mar 25 17-0975
Fontenilles Marquis de
Fr 1832 Sep 12 M179-74
Foot George
Fr 1845 Apr 23 DLC-58
Foote Rensselaer W
Fr 1835 Aug 28-1217
Forbert John
Fr 1829 Aug 17 M639-10
Forbes Hugh
Fr 1785 Oct 24 fin 1-0024
Forbes J et al
Fr 1833 Nov 04 23-1182
Forbes James Grant
Fr 1821 May 07 M116-5
Fr 1821 May 07* M116-6
Fr 1821 May 07* DLC-63
Fr 1821 May 07* 8-0460
Fr 1821 Jun 09 M116-5
Fr 1821 Jun 09* M116-6
Fr 1821 Jun 09* 8-0555
To 1821 Jun 11 M116-5
To 1821 Jun 11* M116-6
To 1821 Jun 11* DLC-63
To 1821 Jun 11* 8-0581
Fr 1821 Jun 11 M116-5
Fr 1821 Jun 11* M116-6
Fr 1821 Jun 11* 8-0585
Fr 1821 Jun 15 M116-6
Fr 1821 Jun 21 M116-6
Fr 1821 Jun 21* 8-0643
To 1821 Jun 24 M116-6
To 1821 Jun 24* DLC-63
To 1821 Jun 24* 8-0673
Fr 1821 Jun 25 M116-6
Fr 1821 Jun 25* 8-0689
Forbes John et al
Fr 1829 Apr 23 M639-16
Fr 1835 Sep 11 M234-435
Forbes Sardinia
Fr 1831 Mar 17-0686
Forbes grant
Re 1835 mem DLC-47
Force Peter
Fr 1827 Apr 27 fin DLC-34
To 1827 cJun 11-0612
To 1829 Dec 05# 14-0801
Fr 1837 Mar 03 33-1036
To 1837 Mar 03 33-1037
To 1837 Mar 03* DLC-50
Ford Athanasius
Fr 1842 Mar 08 DLC-54
Ford Elias
Fr 1836 Aug 08 M221-116

Ford J B
Fr 1836 Dec 29# fin DLC-50
Ford James
Fr 1829 Sep 01 M639-14
Ford John
Fr 1815 Jan 02 DLC-15
Fr 1815 Jan 14 DLC-15
Fr 1818 Aug 13 M221-78
Ford Mary Duncan
Fr 1837 Feb 28 33-0923
Ford Thomas
To 1843 Jan 24 35-1142
Fore Greene P
Fr 1815 Jan 03 DLC-15
Foreign ministers
To 1829 Apr 06 add DLC-60
To 1837 Mar 04 add 33-1063
Forman William P
Fr 1835 Jun 01 M567-107
Forney Daniel Munroe
Fr 1823 Dec 25 M439-16
Forrest French
Fr 1836 Nov 03 32-0395
Forrest Henry
Fr 1824 Jan 04 9-0889
Forrest Henry et al
Fr 1831 Jan 28 M639-1
Forrest Joseph
Fr 1831 Dec 05 19-0075
Forrest Joseph et al
Fr 1832 Feb M639-6
Forstall B et al
Fr 1832 May 08 M639-19
Forster John M
Fr 1835 Apr 22 DLC-46
Forster Thomas
Fr 1835 Mar 06 DLC-45
Fr 1835 Mar 06 DLC-45
Re 1835 cMay mem DLC-47
Forsyth John
Fr 1829 Mar 11 M234-222
Fr 1829 Mar 11* 12-0946
Fr 1829 Jun 23 13-0699
Fr 1829 Jun 23* DLC-37
To 1829 Aug 06 DLC-60
Fr 1829 Aug 14 DLC-37
Fr 1829 Aug 14* 13-1130
Fr 1830 May 18 DLC-72
Fr 1830 Jun 02 DLC-38
To 1830 Jun 07 DLC-38
Fr 1830 Jun 17 DLC-38
To 1831 Feb 28# DLC-39
Fr 1831 Jun 20 DLC-39
Fr 1833 Mar 20 M124-137
To 1834 Jan 07 24-0774
Fr 1834 Apr 18# DLC-44
Fr 1834 Jul 03 26-0092
To 1834 Jul 04# M179-78
To 1834 Jul 07 26-0180
Fr 1834 Jul 07 M40-24
Fr 1834 Jul 11 DLC-44
Fr 1834 Jul 11* M40-24
Fr 1834 Jul 12 DLC-44
Fr 1834 Jul 14 M40-24
Fr 1834 Jul 15 M40-24
Fr 1834 Jul 17 DLC-52
Fr 1834 Jul 27 DLC-44
Fr 1834 Jul 31 M40-24
Fr 1834 Aug 11 DLC-44
Fr 1834 Aug 18 M40-25
To 1834 Aug 20# M30-38
Fr 1834 Sep 01 M40-25
Fr 1834 Oct 01 26-0465
To 1834 Oct 11# 26-0597
To 1834 Oct 12# 26-0600
To 1834 Oct 12# T168-14
To 1834 Oct 25# M179-78
Fr 1834 cNov DLC-45
Fr 1834 Nov 11 26-0882
To 1834 Dec 04 M639-14
To 1834 Dec 06# M639-14
Fr 1834 Dec 11 26-1472
Fr 1834 Dec 15 26-1507
Fr 1834 Dec 15 M179-79
Fr 1834 Dec 15* 26-1510
Fr 1834 Dec 16 26-1521
To 1834 Dec 24# M179-79
Fr 1834 Dec 27 27-0019
Fr 1834 Dec 27 27-0023
To 1834 Dec 27# T20-6
Fr 1835 Jan 05 27-0083
Fr 1835 Jan 05 27-0085
Fr 1835 Jan 06 27-0103
Fr 1835 Jan 07 27-0118
To 1835 Jan 07# M639-15
Fr 1835 Jan 08# M179-79
Fr 1835 Jan 09 27-0164
Fr 1835 Jan 09 27-0165
Fr 1835 Jan 12 27-0191
To 1835 Jan 12# 27-0197
To 1835 Jan 24# M179-79
Fr 1835 Jan 29 27-0313
To 1835 Jan 31 mem M179-79
Fr 1835 Feb 05 27-0403
Fr 1835 Feb 10 27-0466
To 1835 Feb 13 M179-79
Fr 1835 Feb 13 M639-10
Fr 1835 Feb 13* M40-25
Fr 1835 Feb 13 27-0512
To 1835 Feb 16 M179-79
Fr 1835 Feb 19 27-0571
Fr 1835 Feb 21 M46-7
Fr 1835 Feb 25 27-0609
To 1835 Feb 26 M179-79
Fr 1835 Feb 27 27-0639
Fr 1835 Feb 27 M179-79
Fr 1835 Feb 28 DLC-45
To 1835 Mar 05# 27-1018
To 1835 Mar 05# 27-1020
To 1835 Mar 05# 27-1022
To 1835 Mar 06# 27-1035
To 1835 Mar 06# 27-1030
To 1835 Mar 09# DLC-45
To 1835 Mar 11# M179-79
To 1835 Mar 18# 27-1231
To 1835 Mar 20# 27-1238
To 1835 Mar 22# DLC-45
To 1835 Apr 01 27-1504
Fr 1835 Apr 02# 27-1510
Fr 1835 Apr 06 27-1528
To 1835 Apr 11# DLC-46
Fr 1835 Apr 14 28-0071
To 1835 Apr 19 28-0100
Fr 1835 Apr 29 M40-26
To 1835 Apr 30# M179-80
To 1835 Apr 30# M179-80
Fr 1835 May 02 28-0234
To 1835 May 13 M179-80

Forsyth John (cont)

To	1835 May 21#		M179-80
To	1835 Jun 17#		M97-7
To	1835 Jun 17#		28-0722
Fr	1835 Jun 18		28-0732
Fr	1835 Jun 18		28-0738
To	1835 Jun 30		28-0842
To	1835 Jul 04		28-0898
Fr	1835 Aug 09		DLC-46
Fr	1835 Aug 18		28-1298
Fr	1835 Aug 29		28-1452
To	1835 Aug 31#		M639-24
To	1835 Sep 02		28-1507
Fr	1835 Sep 04		DLC-46
To	1835 Sep 06		DLC-46
To	1835 Sep 14#		M50-18
Fr	1835 Sep 17		29-0057
To	1835 Sep 26#		29-0113
Fr	1835 Oct 20		DLC-47
Fr	1835 Oct 20*		M40-26
To	1835 Oct 20#		M873-87
To	1835 Oct 20#		M179-81
Fr	1835 Nov 02		M179-81
Fr	1835 Nov 02*		M40-26
To	1835 Nov 07#		M179-81
To	1835 Nov 12		29-0505
Fr	1835 Dec 09		29-1049
To	1835 Dec 09#		T330-1
Fr	1835 Dec 16		29-1188
Fr	1835 Dec 16*		M37-12
To	1835 Dec 19	mem	29-1263
To	1835 Dec 20#		M281-1
To	1835 Dec 20#		M639-16
Fr	1836 Jan 04		M179-81
Fr	1836 Jan 04*		29-1451
Fr	1836 Jan 06		29-1477
Fr	1836 Jan 11		29-1543
Fr	1836 Jan 13		30-0001
To	1836 Jan 15#		M97-7
Fr	1836 Jan 16		30-0127
To	1836 Jan 16#		30-0128
Fr	1836 Feb 03		30-0275
Fr	1836 Feb 04		DLC-47
Fr	1836 Feb 13		30-0369
To	1836 Feb 16	mem	M179-81
Fr	1836 Feb 17		30-0401
Fr	1836 Feb 24		30-0507
Fr	1836 Feb 27		30-0593
Fr	1836 Feb 27		30-0603
Fr	1836 Feb 27		M639-17
Fr	1836 Mar 09		30-0736
To	1836 Mar 09#		M687-27
To	1836 Mar 10#		DLC-47
Fr	1836 Mar 17		30-0804
To	1836 Mar 23#		30-0880
To	1836 Mar 30#		30-0932
To	1836 Mar 31#		M639-7
To	1836 Apr 01		30-0966
Fr	1836 Apr 06		30-1020
To	1836 Apr 10		M179-82
Fr	1836 Apr 11		M179-82
Fr	1836 Apr 11*		30-1136
Fr	1836 May 02		30-1406
Fr	1836 May 02		30-1485
Fr	1836 May 02		30-1486
Fr	1836 May 06		30-1525
To	1836 May 10	mem	M179-82
Fr	1836 May 13		31-0003
Fr	1836 May 16		31-0032
To	1836 May 19		31-0059
To	1836 May 21	mem	M179-82
To	1836 May 25		31-0110
To	1836 May 25		31-0111
To	1836 Jun 06		M179-82
Fr	1836 Jun 13		31-0442
Fr	1836 Jun 14		31-0471
To	1836 Jun 18	mem	M179-82
Fr	1836 Jun 23		31-0553
To	1836 Jun 28	mem	M179-82
Fr	1836 Jun 29		31-0641
Fr	1836 Jul 02		31-0758
Fr	1836 Jul 07		M40-26
Fr	1836 Jul 08		31-0958
Fr	1836 Jul 08*		DLC-48
Fr	1836 Jul 08		M40-26
Fr	1836 Jul 09		31-1013
Fr	1836 Jul 09		31-1014
Fr	1836 Jul 15		DLC-48
Fr	1836 Aug 30		31-1375
To	1836 Sep 05		M179-82
Fr	1836 Sep 27		DLC-49
To	1836 Oct 06#		32-0093
To	1836 Oct 18#		M121-12
To	1836 Nov 02		32-0390
To	1836 Nov 12		M179-82
Fr	1836 Nov 19		32-0562
To	1836 Dec 02#		32-0618
Fr	1836 Dec 14		M179-82
Fr	1836 Dec 14*		32-1141
Fr	1836 Dec 16		M179-82
Fr	1836 Dec 16*		32-1178
Fr	1836 Dec 20		32-1204
To	1836 Dec 22#		M179-82
To	1836 Dec 23	mem	M179-82
To	1836 Dec 26	mem	32-1338
To	1836 Dec 26	mem	32-1340
Fr	1836 Dec 28		32-1371
Fr	1836 Dec 30		32-1413
Fr	1837 Jan 02		M179-83
To	1837 Jan 05		M179-83
To	1837 Jan 06		32-1505
Fr	1837 Jan 07		32-1520
To	1837 Jan 09		M179-83
To	1837 Jan 17		M179-83
Fr	1837 Jan 21		33-0086
Fr	1837 Jan 25		33-0148
Fr	1837 Jan 30		DLC-49
Fr	1837 Jan 30		33-0216
To	1837 Feb 01		33-0344
Fr	1837 Feb 03		33-0381
Fr	1837 Feb 06		33-0422
To	1837 Feb 07	mem	M179-83
Fr	1837 Feb 11		33-0622
Fr	1837 Feb 13		33-0649
Fr	1837 Feb 16		33-0715
Fr	1837 Feb 22		33-0820
Fr	1837 Mar 02		33-0980
To	1837 Mar 03		33-1038
Fr	1837 Mar 06		M687-17
Fr	1837 Mar 06*		33-1071
Fr	1837 Mar 17		DLC-50
Fr	1837 Aug 08		DLC-50
Fr	1837 Oct 06		DLC-50
To	1837 Nov 22		M687-32
Fr	1837 Dec 05		34-0077
Fr	1837 Dec 19		M179-85
To	1838 Jan 06		M179-85
To	1838 Jan 23		M179-85
Fr	1838 Feb 14		DLC-51

To 1838 Mar 06 DLC-51
Fr 1839 Mar 14 DLC-52
Fr 1839 Mar 14* M40-28
Fr 1841 Jan 09 DLC-53

Forsyth John et al
Fr 1834 Jun 10# M639-15

Fort Read
Fr 1820 Jul 21 7-1172

Fort Tomlinson
Fr 1829 Jun 01 13-0536

Ft Bowyer commanding officer
To 1819 Nov 22 DLC-63
To 1819 Nov 22* 7-0877

Ft Jackson treaty
Re 1814 Aug 09 M688-4
Re 1814 Aug 09 DLC-11
Re 1814 Aug 09* DLC-62
Re 1814 Aug 09* 3-1251

Ft Strother
Re 1813 Dec 11 3-0656
Re 1813 Dec 26 DLC-61
Re 1814 Mar 13 DLC-62

Ft Williams
Re 1814 Mar 15 DLC-9
Re 1814 Mar 23 DLC-9

Ft Winnebago
Re 1835 cFeb 09 27-0450

Fortier Michael
Fr 1815 Jan 19 DLC-15
Fr 1815 Feb 28# DLC-17

Fortson John T
Fr 1836 Feb 11 M234-189

Forzen Jose
Fr 1815 Feb 13 DLC-16

Foscue Lewis
Fr 1815 Aug 22 DLC-19

Foster Anthony
Fr 1797 Sep 03 fin DLC-2
To 1805 Apr 19 lnd DLC-3
To 1805 Apr 19* lnd 2-0031
Fr 1808 Aug 13 lnd DLC-4
Fr 1808 Aug 13* lnd 2-0721
Fr 1809 Jan 02 2-0760

Foster Ephraim Hubbard
Fr 1819 Apr 05 DLC-26
Fr 1823 Jan 07 9-0385
Fr 1823 Jan 08 add 9-0391
To 1823 Jan 08 add 9-0393
To 1826 May 26 chk 11-0218
Fr 1830 Dec 10 DLC-38
To 1832 Jun 22 DLC-40
Fr 1832 Oct 30 M639-4
Fr 1832 Dec 18 DLC-41

Foster Ephraim Hubbard et al
Fr 1830 Sep M567-51

Foster Henry
Re 1835 Nov 06 par 29-0461

Foster Henry Allen et al
Fr 1832 Jan M639-24

Foster Ira R
Fr 1836 Jun 20 M567-123

Foster Joshua H
Fr 1839 Feb 15 DLC-51

Foster Moses
Fr 1823 Sep 04 DLC-32
Fr 1834 Mar 27 25-0432

Foster Nathan L
Fr 1836 Dec 27 DLC-49
To 1837 Jan 06 DLC-49

Foster Robert Coleman
To 1825 Oct 12 11-0019
To 1825 Oct 12* DLC-58
Fr 1825 Oct 14 add 11-0035
Fr 1825 Oct 14* add DLC-33
Fr 1831 Mar 26 17-0979

Foster Robert Coleman & Son
Fr 1828 Nov 13 DLC-35

Foster William
Fr 1835 May 14 mem M124-147

Foster William B
Fr 1830 Apr 12 M639-3

Foster & Giraud et al
Fr 1832 Apr 20 M639-26

Foucher Pierre et al
Fr 1814 Sep 18 DLC-12
Fr 1814 Sep 18* M221-63
To 1814 Oct 01 DLC-62

Foulkes John E
Fr 1835 Aug 31 fin DLC-46
Fr 1835 Dec 04 fin DLC-47

Fourage W E
Fr 1814 Dec fin 4-0378

Fourth of July
see Independence Day

Fowler Charles S
Fr 1831 Dec 29 fin DLC-42
To 1833 Feb 11 chk DLC-42

Fowler James
Re 1832 Dec 04 par 21-0846

Fowler John
Fr 1826 Jan 02 DLC-33
Fr 1829 Jun 23 M688-59

Fowler John et al
Fr 1838 Nov 06 34-0513
To 1838 Dec 24 34-0589

Fowler Thomas
Re 1830 Apr 17 par 15-0740

Fowler William et al
Fr 1834 Dec M639-6

Fox (Indian)
Re 1834 Nov 01 26-0796

Fox Henry Stephen
Fr 1836 Mar 14 add 30-0764

Fox Thomas
Re 1834 May 05 par 25-0963

Foy Benjamin
Fr 1812 May 08 fin DLC-5

Foy Bernard
Re 1830 May 18 par 15-1037

Foy Mordecai
Fr 1834 Jul 05 fin DLC-44
Fr 1834 Nov 19 fin DLC-45
Fr 1835 Feb 14 leg DLC-73
Fr 1835 Apr 25 fin DLC-48
Fr 1835 Jul 26 fin DLC-46
Fr 1835 Aug 26 fin DLC-47
To 1835 Dec 02 chk 29-0731
Fr 1835 Dec 19 fin DLC-47

France indemnity controversy
Re 1829 Apr mem 12-1208
Re 1830 cMar mem 15-0270
Re 1834 Mar 27 M179-80
Re 1834 Mar 27* 25-0435
Re 1834 May 01 DLC-44
Re c1835 mem DLC-47
Re 1835 Mar 29 DLC-45
Re 1835 Dec 21 DLC-47

France trade
Re 1833 mem DLC-73

France treaty
Re 1832 Feb 02 19-0935
Re 1832 Jul 13 20-1065
Francis John Brown
Fr 1834 Jan 03 M639-9
Fr 1834 Dec 09 26-1444
Fr 1835 Sep 22 DLC-47
Fr 1835 Sep 24 M688-86
Francis Michael
To 1837 Oct 12 33-1518
Francis & Boardman
To 1833 Mar 20 chk DLC-42
Fr 1833 Mar 20 fin DLC-42
Francis I King of the Two Sicilies
Fr 1829 Sep 28 13-1436
Fr 1829 Sep 28* DLC-37
To 1830 Jan 23 15-0007
Franklin Jesse
Fr 1816 cSep 15 5-0482
Fr 1816 Oct 11 DLC-21
Franklin County TN
Re 1809 Mar 22 lnd 2-0786
Franklin TN citizens
To 1825 Jul 04 add 10-1343
Fraser Andrew F
Fr 1818 May 03 DLC-24
Fr 1818 May 03* 6-0563
Fraser Anthony R
Fr c1834 Feb 10 fin DLC-33
Fraser Donald
Fr 1819 Jun 04 fin DLC-27
Fraser John
Fr 1836 Apr 16 M124-152
Frazee John
Fr 1833 Aug 16 23-0342
Fr 1836 Sep 14 M567-120
Frazier David
Fr 1834 Oct 20 M639-1
Frederick VI King of Denmark
To 1830 Jun 29 15-1553
Fr 1831 Apr 09 17-1092
To 1831 Sep 06 18-0692
Fredericksburg VA citizens
Fr 1837 cFeb 14 DLC-50
Freelon Thomas W
Re 1830 Jan 09 M273-22
Fr 1830 Mar 11 M273-25
Freeman Constant
Fr 1834 Mar 01 M688-93
Freeman Frederick
Fr 1837 Jul 24 DLC-50
Freeman Isaac P
Fr 1833 Jan 22 DLC-42
Freeman Margaret
Fr 1833 Nov 19 M688-93
Freeman O K
Fr 1836 Nov 05 M567-123
Freeman Thomas
Fr 1815 Jan 07 DLC-15
To 1815 Aug 08 4-1154
Fr 1816 Apr 12 DLC-20
Fremon Charles
Fr 1814 May 20 fin DLC-10
Fremon J C
To 1814 Jun 20 chk DLC-10
French Francis M
Re 1835 Jun 13 par 28-0667
French John
Re 1833 Aug 30 par 23-0492
Re 1833 Aug 30* par T967-1
Re 1833 Sep 20 par 23-0792
Re 1833 Sep 20* par T967-1
Frey George H
Fr 1843 Sep 30 DLC-55
Freymuth Benjamin E
To 1834 Dec 03 chk 26-1380
Frick Jacob et al
Fr 1831 Nov M639-20
Friend (pseudonym)
Fr 1821 Oct 29 DLC-72
Fr 1821 Oct 29* 8-1311
Friend of Fatherless
and Widow (pseudonym)
Fr 1831 Feb 20 17-0597
Friend to the Union (pseudonym)
Fr 1833 Oct 03 M234-223
Frisby Richard
Fr 1829 Aug 20 M688-64
Frohm Louis and Margaret
Fr 1834 Jun 28 25-1591
Fromentin Eligius
To 1821 Aug 23 8-1090
Fr 1821 Aug 23 M116-7
To 1821 Aug 23 DLC-63
Fr 1821 Aug 24 8-1095
To 1821 Aug 25 M116-7
Fr 1821 Aug 25 DLC-63
To 1821 Sep 03 M116-7
To 1821 Sep 03* DLC-63
To 1821 Sep 03* M116-9
To 1821 Sep 03 M116-7
To 1821 Sep 03* M116-9
Fr 1821 Sep 03 DLC-30
Fr 1821 Sep 03* DLC-63
Fr 1821 Sep 03* M116-7
Fr 1821 Sep 03* M116-9
Fr 1821 Sep 03 DLC-30
Fr 1821 Sep 03* DLC-63
Fr 1821 Sep 03* M116-7
Fross Abijah
Fr 1835 Mar 06 leg DLC-45
Frost Elizabeth
Fr 1830 Nov 06 M124-125
Frost John
Re 1829 Jun 12 par 13-0635
Re 1829 Jun 12* par T967-1
Frost Oliver
Fr 1837 Feb 24 M687-16
Fry Henry
Fr 1834 Jun 25-1211
Fry Jacob Jr et al
Fr 1836 Jul 31-0728
Frye Nathaniel
Fr 1818 Aug 05 DLC-25
Fr 1818 Aug 05* 6-1184
To 1835 Sep 11 29-0030
Fullarat Antoine
Re 1821 Aug 22 M116-7
Re 1821 Aug 22* DLC-63
Re 1821 Aug 22 M116-7
Re 1821 Aug 22* DLC-63
Re 1821 Aug 23 M116-7
Re 1821 Aug 23* DLC-63
Fuller A B
Fr 1835 Jun M567-107
Fuller John
Re 1832 May 23 par 20-0564
Fr 1835 Dec 22 M639-8
Fuller John et al
Fr 1829 Mar 12-0678

Fuller Peter			
	Fr 1837 Jan 30		33-0232
Fuller Thomas James Duncan			
	Fr 1837 Jan 17		M687-20
Fuller Walden & Co			
	Fr 1822 Jan 08	fin	8-1393
Fuller William Kendall et al			
	Fr 1835 Feb 09		M639-8
Fulton Archibald et al			
	Fr 1815 cJan 31		4-0652
Fulton David			
	Fr 1822 Dec 30		DLC-31
	Fr 1839 Feb 18		DLC-52
Fulton John Hall et al			
	Fr 1835 Sep 29		M639-18
Fulton Lyle			
	Fr 1828 Dec 09		DLC-36
Fulton Samuel			
	Fr 1814 Sep 20		DLC-12
Fulton Samuel et al			
	Fr 1829 Feb		M639-16
Fulton William Savin			
	Fr 1818 Jan 14		DLC-23
	Fr 1818 Jun 30	fin	DLC-69
	To 1823 Apr 04		9-0509
	Fr 1823 Jun 22		DLC-32
	To 1823 Dec 21		9-0817
	To 1824 Jul 04		DLC-32
	Fr 1829 Feb 21	lnd	12-0562
	Re 1829 Apr 08		12-1303
	To 1829 Apr 11		12-1317
	Fr 1829 Sep 07		13-1260
	To 1830 Dec 10		M179-88
	To 1830 Dec 10*		16-1365
	To 1830 Dec 10*		DLC-52
	Fr 1831 Aug 03		DLC-39
	Fr 1831 Aug 03		18-0413
	Fr 1831 Aug 27		M22-28
	Fr 1832 Apr 25		DLC-40
	Fr 1832 Nov 03		21-0294
	Fr 1834 Dec 17		DLC-45
	Fr 1835 Aug 11		M567-112
	Fr 1835 Aug 22		DLC-46
	Fr 1836 Feb 09		DLC-47
	Fr 1836 Feb 19		DLC-47
	Fr 1836 Sep		M22-41
	Fr 1836 cSep		M22-40
	Fr 1836 cSep		M22-40
	Fr 1836 Sep 13		31-1443
	Fr 1836 Dec 07		M639-10
	To 1837 Jun 27		33-1344
	Fr 1837 Aug 07		DLC-50
	To 1837 Aug 22		33-1429
	Fr 1837 Dec 24		DLC-50
	To 1837 Dec 26		34-0144
	Fr 1838 Jan 11		DLC-51
	To 1838 Jan 23		DLC-51
	To 1838 Jan 25		34-0214
	To 1838 Jan 29		34-0225
	Fr 1838 Feb 17		DLC-51
	Fr 1838 Apr 01		DLC-51
	Fr 1838 Jul 10		DLC-51
	Fr 1839 Jan 26		DLC-51
	To 1839 Feb 15		34-0641
	Fr 1839 Aug 21		DLC-52
	Fr 1839 Dec 27		DLC-52
Fuqua S & B			
	Fr 1822 Aug 28	fin	DLC-31
Furgerson Gracy			
	To 1835 Aug 22#	fin	DLC-46
	To 1835 Dec 12#	fin	DLC-47
Gadsby John			
	To 1825 Jan 05	chk	10-1037
	Fr 1825 Jan 11	fin	10-1067
	Fr 1825 Jan 22	fin	DLC-72
	Fr 1825 Feb 18	fin	DLC-33
	To 1829 Mar 12		12-0974
	To 1829 Nov 21	chk	DLC-37
Gadsden James			
	Fr 1816 May 11		DLC-20
	To 1816 May 30		DLC-20
	Fr 1816 Jun 11		DLC-20
	Fr 1816 Jun 29		DLC-21
	Fr 1816 Jul 02		DLC-21
	To 1816 Aug 19		DLC-62
	To 1816 Aug 19*		M668-4
	To 1816 Aug 19*		5-0435
	Fr 1816 Nov 17		DLC-22
	Fr 1817 Mar 22		DLC-22
	Fr 1817 Apr 08		DLC-22
	Fr 1817 May 08		DLC-22
	Fr 1817 Jun 08		DLC-22
	Fr 1818 May 03		DLC-24
	Fr 1818 May 03*		6-0566
	Fr 1818 May 03*		M222-20
	To 1818 Jun 30		6-1089
	Fr 1818 Aug 01		6-1168
	Fr 1818 Aug 06		DLC-25
	Fr 1818 Aug 07		DLC-25
	Fr 1818 Sep 28		DLC-25
	Fr 1818 Dec 01		DLC-26
	Fr 1819 Jan 04		DLC-26
	Fr 1819 Jan 17		DLC-26
	Fr 1819 Feb 18		DLC-26
	Fr 1819 Feb 25		DLC-26
	Fr 1819 cApr 01		DLC-75
	Fr 1819 Apr 15		DLC-26
	Fr 1819 Apr 18		DLC-26
	Fr 1819 Apr 22		DLC-26
	Fr 1819 May 03		DLC-72
	Fr 1819 Jun 05		DLC-27
	Fr 1819 Jun 06		7-0542
	Fr 1819 Jun 26		DLC-27
	Fr 1819 Jun 28		DLC-27
	Fr 1819 Jul 06		DLC-27
	To 1819 Aug 01		DLC-59
	Fr 1819 Sep 27		DLC-27
	Fr 1819 Oct 10		DLC-27
	Fr 1819 Oct 28		DLC-28
	Fr 1819 Nov 06		DLC-28
	Fr 1819 Nov 06*		M221-86
	Fr 1819 Nov 08		DLC-28
	Fr 1819 Nov 20		M221-86
	Fr 1819 Nov 21		DLC-28
	Fr 1819 Dec 03		DLC-28
	Fr 1819 Dec 15		DLC-28
	Fr 1820 Jan 08		7-0985
	Fr 1820 Jan 17		DLC-28
	Fr 1820 Feb 05		DLC-28
	Fr 1820 Feb 06		DLC-28
	Fr 1820 Apr 15		DLC-28
	Fr 1820 Apr 30		DLC-29
	Fr 1820 Jul 06		DLC-29
	Fr 1820 Sep 25		DLC-29
	Fr 1820 Dec 08		DLC-29

Gadsden James (cont)

Fr 1820 Dec 24	DLC-29
To 1821 May 21	DLC-63
To 1821 May 21*	M116-5
To 1821 May 21*	M116-6
Re 1821 May 21	DLC-63
Fr 1821 May 24	8-0518
To 1821 Jun 26	DLC-63
Fr 1821 Jun 28#	8-0725
Fr 1821 Aug 15	8-1065
Fr 1821 Sep 05	8-1149
Fr 1821 Sep 14	DLC-30
Fr 1821 Nov 08	DLC-31
Fr 1821 Nov 14	8-1349
Fr 1821 Nov 20	DLC-31
Fr 1821 Dec 03	DLC-31
To 1821 Dec 06	DLC-31
Fr 1822 Mar 02	9-0044
To 1822 Mar 13	9-0046
To 1822 Mar 13*	M221-93
Fr 1822 Apr 10	DLC-31
Fr 1822 Apr 13	DLC-31
To 1822 May 02	DLC-31
Fr 1822 Jul 16	DLC-75
To 1822 Aug 09	DLC-31
Fr 1822 Nov 20	DLC-31
Fr 1822 Dec	DLC-75
To 1823 Mar 01	9-0471
Fr 1823 Apr 09	DLC-32
Fr 1823 Jun 08	DLC-32
Fr 1823 Jun 12	DLC-32
Fr 1823 Jun 30	DLC-32
Fr 1823 Jul 30	DLC-32
Fr 1824 May 26	DLC-32
Fr 1824 May 27	DLC-32
Fr 1824 Jun 05	10-0771
Fr 1824 Jul 08	DLC-33
Fr 1824 Aug 06	DLC-33
Fr 1825 Mar 31	DLC-75
Fr 1825 Jul 07	10-1345
Fr 1825 Jul 08	10-1347
Fr 1825 Sep 15	DLC-33
Fr c1826	11-0091
Fr 1826 Aug 18	11-0340
Fr 1827 May 12	DLC-34
Fr 1827 Aug 19	DLC-75
Fr 1827 Sep 05	11-0843
Fr 1829 Apr 17	12-1370
Fr 1829 May 25	M639-4
Fr 1829 Jun 03	13-0560
Fr 1829 Jun 20	M639-9
Fr 1829 Jun 27	M639-9
Fr 1829 Jul 13	M639-6
Fr 1829 Aug 09	M688-63
Fr 1829 Sep 08	13-1270
To 1829 Oct 12	DLC-37
Fr 1829 Nov 14	M234-806
Fr 1830 Oct 20	16-0460
Fr 1831 Jun 11	DLC-39
To 1831 Jul 21	DLC-39
Fr 1831 Sep 23	M639-4
Fr 1831 Sep 26	M639-7
Fr 1831 Oct 11	M639-2
Fr 1831 Oct 16	M639-2
To c1832#	19-0516
Fr 1833 Jan 22	M639-2
Fr 1833 Feb 12	M234-288
Fr 1833 Mar 16	22-0787
Fr 1833 May 03	22-1275
Fr 1833 Jun 24	DLC-43
Fr 1833 Aug 30	M179-77
Fr 1833 Sep 01	M639-25
Fr 1834 Sep 22	M639-16
Fr 1835 Jun 01	DLC-46
Fr 1836 Jan 09	M567-123
Fr 1836 Jan 14	DLC-47
Fr 1836 Apr 09	DLC-48
Fr 1836 Apr 15	DLC-48
Fr 1836 Jun 12	DLC-48
Fr 1836 Jul 16	31-1096
Fr 1836 Jul 24	DLC-48
Fr 1836 Aug 25	31-1352
Fr 1836 Aug 25	DLC-49
To 1836 Nov	DLC-74
Fr 1836 Nov 02	DLC-49
Fr 1837 Aug	DLC-75
Fr 1840 Aug 14	DLC-53
Fr 1842 Jul 20	DLC-54
Fr 1842 Dec 06	DLC-54
Fr 1844 May 03	36-0479
Fr 1844 May 15	36-0543
Fr 1844 Jul 08	36-0685
To 1844 Jul 19	36-0717
Fr 1844 Aug 01	DLC-57
Fr 1844 Aug 05	36-0770
Fr 1844 Aug 24	36-0821
Fr 1844 Aug 30	36-0834
Fr 1844 Nov 18	36-1034
Fr 1845 Jan 16	36-1352
Fr 1845 Mar 04	DLC-57

Gadsden Thomas

Fr 1822 Oct 29	DLC-31

Gage Ann Maria

Fr 1830 Jun 06	15-1305

Gaines Edmund Pendleton

Fr 1815 Feb 04	DLC-16
Fr 1815 Feb 21	DLC-17
Fr 1815 Feb 27	DLC-17
Fr 1815 Mar 06	DLC-17
To 1815 Mar 17	DLC-62
To 1815 Mar 17*	4-0882
To 1815 cMar 17	4-0888
Fr 1815 Mar 25	DLC-17
Fr 1815 Mar 26	4-0909
Fr 1815 Mar 28	DLC-17
Fr 1815 Apr 07	4-0978
Fr 1815 Apr 14	DLC-18
To 1815 Apr 20	DLC-18
Fr 1815 Apr 28	4-1017
Fr 1815 May 14	M221-61
Fr 1815 May 22	M221-61
Fr 1815 Jun 02	M221-61
Fr 1815 Jun 08	DLC-18
Fr 1815 Jun 08*	M221-61
Fr 1815 Jun 20	DLC-18
Fr 1815 Jun 20*	M221-61
Fr 1815 Jun 20	M221-61
To 1815 Jun 24	DLC-62
To 1815 Jun 24*	M222-16
To 1815 Jun 28	DLC-62
To 1815 Jul 03	DLC-18
To 1815 Jul 03*	DLC-62
To 1815 Jul 24	DLC-62
Fr 1815 Jul 29	DLC-75
To 1815 Aug 08	DLC-62
Fr 1815 Aug 30	4-1179
Fr 1815 Sep 12	DLC-19
Fr 1815 Sep 12*	M222-16
To 1815 Sep 20	DLC-62

To 1815 Sep 30	M222-16
To 1815 Sep 30*	DLC-62
Fr 1815 Oct 03	DLC-19
Fr 1815 Oct 08	DLC-19
Fr 1815 Oct 14	DLC-19
Fr 1815 Oct 26	DLC-19
Fr 1815 Oct 26	DLC-19
Fr 1815 Oct 31	DLC-19
Fr 1815 Nov 02	DLC-19
Fr 1815 Nov 04	DLC-19
Fr 1815 Nov 14	DLC-19
To 1815 Nov 22	DLC-62
Fr 1815 Dec 12	DLC-19
Fr 1815 Dec 14	DLC-19
Fr 1815 Dec 17	M221-70
To 1815 Dec 31	DLC-62
Fr 1816 Feb 16	DLC-69
Fr 1816 Feb 20	DLC-20
To 1816 Mar 12	M221-69
Fr 1816 Mar 12	DLC-20
Fr 1816 Mar 15	DLC-20
Fr 1816 Mar 20	DLC-20
Fr 1816 Mar 20*	M221-70
Fr 1816 Mar 20*	4-1415
To 1816 Apr 08	M221-70
To 1816 Apr 08*	5-0025
Fr 1816 Apr 18	DLC-20
Fr 1816 Apr 21	DLC-20
Fr 1816 May 14	DLC-20
Fr 1816 May 15	DLC-20
Fr 1816 May 18	DLC-20
Fr 1816 May 18*	M221-70
Fr 1816 May 27	M221-70
Fr 1816 May 27*	DLC-20
Fr 1816 Jun 03	DLC-20
Fr 1816 Jun 03*	M221-70
Fr 1816 Jul 21	DLC-21
Fr 1816 Dec 08	DLC-22
Fr 1817 Feb 08	DLC-22
Fr 1817 Feb 14	DLC-22
Fr 1817 Mar 06	DLC-22
Fr 1817 Apr 02	DLC-22
Fr 1817 Apr 06	DLC-22
Fr 1817 May 08	DLC-22
Fr 1817 May 08	DLC-22
Fr 1817 Jun 01	DLC-22
Fr 1817 Jun 01	DLC-22
Fr 1817 Jun 30	DLC-23
Fr 1817 Jul 10	DLC-23
Fr 1817 Aug 25	DLC-23
Fr 1817 Aug 31	DLC-23
Fr 1817 Oct 01	DLC-23
Fr 1817 Oct 23	DLC-23
Fr 1817 Nov 09	DLC-23
Fr 1817 Nov 09*	M222-19
Fr 1817 Nov 09*	5-1132
Fr 1817 Nov 21	DLC-23
Fr 1817 Nov 21*	M222-19
Fr 1817 Nov 21*	5-1136
Fr 1817 Nov 26	DLC-23
Fr 1817 Dec 02	DLC-23
Fr 1818 Jan	5-1221
Fr 1818 Jan 12	DLC-23
Fr 1818 Jan 12*	5-1264
Fr 1818 Jan 12	DLC-23
Fr 1818 Jan 12*	5-1273
Fr 1818 Jan 19	DLC-24
Fr 1818 Jan 19*	5-1289
To 1818 Jan 20	5-1319
Fr 1818 Jan 24	DLC-24
Fr 1818 Jan 24*	5-1335
Fr 1818 Jan 31	DLC-24
Fr 1818 Jan 31*	5-1403
Fr 1818 Feb 01	DLC-24
Fr 1818 Feb 01*	5-1421
Fr 1818 Feb 05	DLC-24
Fr 1818 Feb 05*	5-1431
Fr 1818 Feb 08	DLC-24
Fr 1818 Feb 22	DLC-24
Fr 1818 Feb 22*	6-0044
To 1818 Mar 24	6-0087
Fr 1818 Mar 24	DLC-24
Fr 1818 Mar 24*	6-0088
To 1818 Mar 25	6-0145
Fr 1818 Mar 25	6-0147
Fr 1818 Mar 25	6-0150
Fr 1818 Apr 03	6-0180
Fr 1818 Apr 03*	DLC-24
Fr 1818 Apr 20	DLC-24
Fr 1818 Apr 20*	6-0449
Fr 1818 Apr 20	DLC-24
Fr 1818 Apr 20*	6-0452
Fr 1818 May 04	6-0587
To 1818 May 05	6-0636
To 1818 May 07	6-0673
Fr 1818 May 07	M271-2
To 1818 May 10	6-0686
Fr 1818 May 17	DLC-25
Fr 1818 May 17*	6-0698
Fr 1818 May 17	DLC-25
Fr 1818 May 17*	6-0708
To 1818 May 30	6-0944
To 1818 Jun 02	6-1003
Fr 1818 Jun 06	DLC-25
Fr 1818 Jun 06*	6-1024
Fr 1818 Jun 06	6-1036
Fr 1818 Jun 18	DLC-25
Fr 1818 Jun 18*	6-1061
Fr 1818 Jul 17	DLC-25
Fr 1818 Jul 17*	6-1140
To 1818 Aug 07	6-1186
To 1818 Aug 07*	M221-81
Fr 1818 Aug 08	6-1201
Fr 1818 Sep 08	DLC-25
Fr 1818 Sep 08*	6-1288
Fr 1818 Sep 16	DLC-25
Fr 1818 Sep 16*	6-1301
Fr 1818 Sep 24	DLC-25
Fr 1818 Sep 24*	6-1319
Fr 1818 Oct 14	DLC-25
Fr 1818 Oct 14*	6-1357
Fr 1818 Oct 22	DLC-25
Fr 1818 Oct 22*	6-1382
Fr 1818 Nov 07	DLC-26
Fr 1818 Nov 07*	6-1402
Fr 1818 Nov 14	DLC-26
Fr 1818 Nov 14*	6-1416
Fr 1818 Nov 20	DLC-26
Fr 1818 Nov 20*	6-1435
Fr 1818 Nov 24	DLC-26
Fr 1818 Nov 28	DLC-26
Fr 1818 Nov 28*	7-0006
Fr 1818 Nov 30	DLC-26
Fr 1818 Nov 30*	7-0013
Fr 1818 Nov 30*	M221-81
Fr 1818 Dec 26	DLC-26
Fr 1818 Dec 26*	7-0071
Fr 1818 Dec 29	DLC-26

Gaines Edmund Pendleton (cont)
Fr 1818 Dec 29* 7-0089
Fr 1819 Jan 02 DLC-26
Fr 1819 Jan 02* 7-0113
Fr 1819 Jan 12 DLC-26
Fr 1819 Jan 12* 7-0129
Fr 1819 Jan 16 DLC-26
Fr 1819 Jan 19 DLC-26
Fr 1819 Jan 19* 7-0187
Fr 1819 Jan 26 DLC-26
Fr 1819 Jan 26* 7-0201
Fr 1819 Feb 13 DLC-26
Fr 1819 Feb 13* 7-0267
Fr 1819 Feb 27 DLC-26
Fr 1819 Feb 27* 7-0375
Fr 1819 Feb 27 DLC-26
Fr 1819 Feb 27* 7-0380
Fr 1819 Mar 07 7-0410
Fr 1819 Mar 12 DLC-26
Fr 1819 Mar 12* 7-0420
Fr 1819 Mar 23 DLC-26
Fr 1819 Mar 23* 7-0431
To 1819 Apr 15 DLC-63
To 1819 Apr 15* 7-0479
To 1819 Apr 24 7-0499
Fr 1819 May 16 7-0521
Fr 1819 Aug 14 DLC-27
Fr 1819 Aug 14 7-0608
To 1819 Aug 17# DLC-63
Fr 1819 Aug 20 DLC-27
Fr 1819 Aug 20* 7-0632
Fr 1819 Sep 04 DLC-27
Fr 1819 Sep 16 DLC-27
Fr 1819 Sep 16* 7-0664
Fr 1819 Oct 04 DLC-27
Fr 1819 Oct 04 DLC-27
Fr 1819 Oct 04* 7-0703
To 1819 Oct 12 7-0716
To 1819 Oct 12* DLC-27
Fr 1819 Oct 17# DLC-28
Fr 1819 Nov 07 DLC-28
Fr 1819 Nov 07* M221-21
Fr 1819 Nov 07* 7-0845
To 1819 Nov 22 DLC-63
Fr 1819 Dec 05 7-0911
To 1819 Dec 11# DLC-63
Fr 1819 Dec 15 7-0929
Fr 1819 Dec 26 M221-86
Fr 1820 Jan 01 M221-89
To 1820 Jan 04 7-0975
Fr 1820 Jan 18 DLC-28
Fr 1820 Jan 25 DLC-28
Fr 1820 Feb 20 7-1032
To 1820 Feb 28 DLC-63
Fr 1820 Mar 19 DLC-28
Fr 1820 Jun 03 DLC-29
Fr 1820 Jun 03 DLC-29
To 1820 Aug 19# DLC-63
Fr 1820 Sep 01 DLC-29
Fr 1820 Sep 02 DLC-29
Fr 1820 Sep 24 DLC-29
Fr 1820 Dec 31 DLC-29
Fr 1821 Jan 03 M221-89
To 1821 Apr 02 DLC-63
To 1821 Apr 02 DLC-63
To 1821 Apr 10 DLC-63
To 1821 Apr 13 DLC-63
Fr 1821 Apr 27 DLC-30
Fr 1823 Jan 01 DLC-31
Fr 1828 cOct 12-0221
Fr 1828 Nov 22 DLC-35
To 1828 Dec 04 DLC-36
Fr 1829 Apr 27 13-0160
Fr 1830 Mar 20 M222-27
Fr 1830 Jul 12 16-0012
Fr 1831 Aug 10 DLC-39
Fr 1834 Aug 20 DLC-44
Fr 1836 Jul 20 31-1134
Fr 1836 Jul 28 M221-116
Fr 1836 Aug 11 M221-116
Fr 1836 Aug 11* M179-82
To 1836 Sep 04 DLC-49
To 1836 Sep 04* M179-82
To 1836 Sep 04* M221-116
To 1836 Sep 04* 31-1406
To 1836 Sep 04 M179-82
To 1836 Sep 04* M221-116
To 1836 Sep 04* 31-1410
Gaines Edmund Pendleton et al
Re 1836 Aug mem 37-0351
Gaines George Strother
Fr 1814 Jul 17 DLC-11
To 1814 Jul 22 DLC-62
Fr 1814 Aug 19 DLC-11
To 1814 Aug 23 DLC-11
Fr 1814 Sep 16 DLC-12
Fr 1814 Sep 17 DLC-12
Fr 1814 Nov 17 DLC-14
Gaines Richard M
Fr 1834 Jun 12 M639-27
Fr 1834 Jun 12# M639-27
Fr 1834 Oct 16 DLC-44
To 1834 Nov 05 DLC-45
Fr 1842 Jan 06# DLC-54
Fr 1842 Jan 20 DLC-54
Fr 1842 Apr 14# DLC-54
Fr 1844 Dec 03 M873-26
Gaines William D
Fr 1821 Jun 26 DLC-30
Gaisser John D
Fr 1825 Jan 05 fin 10-1038
Fr 1826 Jan 05 fin 11-0100
Fr 1827 Jan 02 fin 11-0456
Fr 1827 Dec 21 fin 11-0969
Gaither Greenbury
Fr 1834 Mar 13 fin DLC-44
Gaither Greenbury et al
Fr 1831 Jan 26 M639-1
Galaspie A
Fr 1802 Oct 09# fin DLC-2
Galbraith John
Fr 1835 Feb 24 DLC-45
Fr 1835 Jul 22 28-1114
Fr 1837 Apr 07 DLC-50
Gale James H
Re 1831 Jul 28 18-0304
Fr 1831 Jul 28# M567-61
Gale John
Fr 1839 Aug 22 DLC-52
To 1839 Sep 04 34-0908
Gales Edward
Re 1834 Jul 01 par 26-0057
Gales Joseph
To 1824 Mar 11 10-0547
Gales Thomas
Fr 1814 Jul 08 DLC-11
Fr 1814 Dec 16 DLC-14
To 1814 Dec 17 4-0409
Fr 1815 Feb 01 DLC-16

Fr 1815 Feb 01 4-0674
Fr 1815 Mar 07 DLC-17
Fr 1815 Mar 15 DLC-17
Fr 1815 Jun 27 DLC-18
Galladay George S
Fr 1844 Mar 12 DLC-56
Gallaher Thomas
To 1801 Mar 26 lnd 1-0851
Gallatin Albert
Fr 1806 Dec 19 2-0404
To 1821 Apr 24 8-0367
Gambell Benjamin et al
Fr 1840 Sep 13 DLC-53
Gamble Edmund A
Fr 1796 Apr 30 DLC-1
Gamble James H
Fr 1811 May 24 fin DLC-5
Gamble James H et al
Fr 1813 Jan 10 DLC-6
Gamble Robert
Fr 1807 Jul 03 2-0501
Gamble William
Fr 1832 Nov 27 M639-9
Ganett William A
Fr 1840 Jan 14# fin DLC-52
Gannaway John Jr
Fr 1807 Mar 18 2-0475
Gannon John F
Fr 1840 Jul 24 DLC-53
Gansevoort Peter et al
Fr 1830 Feb 24 15-0235
Gantt Edward
Fr 1814 Mar 19 DLC-9
Gantt John
Fr 1836 Oct M22-41
Gantt Thomas John
Fr 1821 Aug 25 DLC-30
Gard Benjamin Franklin
Fr 1829 Jul 15 M222-25
Gard Timothy et al
Fr 1829 Jan 22 12-0473
Garden Alexander
To 1823 Mar 11 9-0492
Fr 1823 Apr 11 DLC-32
Garden Andrew
Fr 1832 Apr 18 20-0252
Gardiner J
Fr 1844 Feb 19 DLC-56
Gardiner James B
Fr 1830 Oct 28# DLC-38
Fr 1831 Mar 22 DLC-39
Fr 1831 Apr 02 DLC-39
Fr 1831 Jul 24 18-0265
To 1832 Feb 04# M234-601
Gardiner James B et al
Fr 1829 Feb 17 M639-10
Gardiner John
Fr 1830 Apr 22 M234-433
Fr 1830 Apr 27 M234-433
Gardner Charles Kitchel
Fr 1829 Mar 13 M639-22
Fr 1830 Oct 26 M601-47
Fr 1830 Oct 26* 16-0546
Fr 1830 Oct 26 M601-47
Fr 1831 Apr 06 17-1071
Fr 1832 Jul 21 M601-47
Fr 1833 May 01# M639-27
To 1834 Nov 08 26-0847
Gardner George W & Co
Re 1820 Oct 01 7-1374
Gardner James
Fr 1833 Apr 22 22-1108
Gardner John
Re 1802 Jul 15 leg 1-1029
Gardner William A et al
Re 1831 Dec 07 par 19-0231
Fr 1832 Feb 13 M179-72
Gardner William N et al
Fr 1837 Feb 08 33-0564
Garesche V M
Re 1834 Oct 13 26-0623
Fr 1836 Jun 09 31-0413
Fr 1837 May 04 33-1212
Garland Hudson M
Fr 1833 Apr 15 M639-9
Fr 1835 Jan 06 M639-9
Garland James
Fr 1836 Apr 29 M639-25
Garland Rice
Fr 1836 May 27 31-0159
Garner Brice M
Fr 1814 Mar 28 DLC-9
Garner John
Fr 1812 Dec 18 fin DLC-5
Garner Preston et al
Fr 1832 cJan 19-0546
Garnett Robert Selden
Fr 1831 Feb 07 DLC-39
Garnier John
To 1821 Jul 19 DLC-63
To 1821 Jul 24 8-0896
To 1821 Sep 18 DLC-63
Fr 1821 Oct 06 fin DLC-70
Garnsey Daniel Greene
Fr 1834 Jul 10 M639-9
Garrard Henry
Fr 1824 Aug 28 fin 10-0862
Fr 1826 fin 11-0093
Fr 1827 fin 11-0451
Garrard John M
Re 1811 Mar 05 mem 2-0995
Re 1812 Jan leg 2-1034
Garrard John M Jr
Fr 1805 Feb 12 fin DLC-3
Re 1805 May 01 fin DLC-3
Fr 1805 Jul 02 DLC-3
Garrett Lewis
Fr 1839 Aug 28 DLC-52
Fr 1843 Sep 26 DLC-55
Garrett Nathan
Fr 1818 Jun 21 fin DLC-69
Fr 1818 Jun 21* fin 6-1070
Garrett Phineas et al
Fr 1836 Sep 25 31-1510
Garrett R P
Fr 1818 Aug 24 fin DLC-25
Fr 1820 May 16# fin DLC-29
Garrett Thomas L
Fr 1826 Dec 06 DLC-34
Garrison Daniel
Fr 1831 May M639-12
Garrison John
Fr 1830 Apr 20 M124-123
Garrison M Jr
Fr 1834 Dec 20 M639-6
Garrison Samuel
Fr 1834 M273-31

Name	Date	Note	Reference
Garrison Samuel (cont)			
	Re 1834 Oct 15		M273-31
	Fr 1835 Dec		M273-31
Garrison William et al			
	Fr 1829 Aug 10		M639-18
Garrow Nathaniel et al			
	Fr 1829 Mar 04		M639-23
Garrow Samuel H			
	Fr 1834 Jul 21#		DLC-44
	Fr 1837 Oct 20		M687-7
Garvey Dennis et al			
	Fr 1829 Mar 04		12-0842
Garvin & Paterson			
	Fr 1843 Nov 16		DLC-56
	To 1843 Dec 12		DLC-56
Gaskell Thomas Penn			
	Fr 1834 Sep 06		M639-10
Gaskell Thomas Penn et al			
	Fr 1834 Sep 04		M639-10
Gaskill John et al			
	Fr 1844 Feb 28		DLC-56
Gaskin Robert			
	Re 1835 Jun 26	par	28-0809
Gasperi L			
	Fr 1829 Mar 29		12-1170
Gassaway Hanson			
	Fr 1832 Nov 12		21-0384
	Fr 1832 Dec 11		M222-31
	Fr 1832 Dec 11*		21-0991
Gates Cornelius			
	Fr 1830 Feb 04		M221-110
Gates John et al			
	Fr 1836 Jun 03		31-0278
Gates William			
	Fr 1834 Nov 27		M567-97
Gatewood William			
	Fr 1834 Oct 02#		DLC-44
	Fr 1834 Dec 03		26-1381
Gatlin John			
	Re 1794 Feb 09	leg	1-0192
Gaubert Annie			
	Fr 1835 Jan 16#	fin	DLC-46
	Fr 1835 Dec 28#	fin	DLC-47
Gault William W			
	Fr 1829 Apr 06		M639-9
	Fr 1829 Apr 27		M639-9
Gault William W et al			
	Fr 1830 Jan 26		15-0027
Gauthier Joseph			
	Re 1835 Jan	mem	M234-421
Gauthier Peter			
	Fr 1815 Apr 03		DLC-18
Gay Gamaliel			
	Fr 1835 Jan 23		27-0278
	To 1835 Jan 26		27-0296
Gay George W			
	Re 1832 Nov 27		M273-28
Gay Payton			
	Fr 1829 Oct 28		M639-9
	Fr 1832 May 22		M639-9
	Fr 1832 Jun 19		M639-9
	Fr 1834 Dec 18		T690-1
	Fr 1836 Jul 04		M687-12
Gayle John et al			
	Fr 1832 Aug 22		20-1377
	To 1832 Sep 01		20-1475
Gayoso de Lemos Fernando			
	Fr 1816 May 20		DLC-20
Gearhart Jacob			
	Fr 1834 Jul 23		M639-4
Geddes John			
	Fr 1824 Jan 17		9-0940
	To 1824 Jan 27		10-0400
Geisse George W & Co et al			
	Fr 1832 Aug 25		M639-15
Geisse & Korckhauss et al			
	Fr 1831 Jan 20		M639-3
	Fr 1834 Dec 27		M639-9
Gelston John M			
	Fr 1803 Dec 07		DLC-3
Genet Edmond Charles			
	Fr 1831 Dec 21		19-0377
	To 1832 Jan 02		19-0580
Genois Charles			
	Fr 1840 Jan 08	add	34-1148
	To 1840 Jan 08	add	34-1149
George (slave)			
	Re 1804	mem	DLC-1
George James Bascom Jr			
	Fr 1840 Jul 30		DLC-53
George IV King of Great Britain			
	To 1829 Jun 10		13-0618
Georgetown citizens			
	To 1815 Nov 28	add	4-1266
	To 1815 Nov 28	add	4-1267
Georgetown Metropolitan editors			
	Fr 1836 Aug 03		DLC-48
Georgia General Assembly			
	To 1818 Nov 09		6-1405
Gerard Jean Batiste			
	Re 1831 Sep 19	par	18-0830
Gerding George F			
	Fr 1837 Feb 07		33-0467
	Fr 1838 Nov 04		34-0510
Germann Anthony			
	Fr 1842 Jun 08		DLC-54
	To 1842 Jun 21		DLC-54
Getty Robert			
	Re 1829 May 26		13-0438
	Fr 1835 May 16#		M639-9
	Re 1835 May 30		28-0528
Gevelot N			
	Fr 1833 Dec 28		24-0617
Ghent John B			
	Fr 1844 Nov 13		DLC-57
Gholson Benjamin			
	Fr 1834 Jul 26		M567-97
Gibbon John H			
	Fr 1836 Dec 28		32-1374
Gibbs Daniel			
	Re 1831 Sep 17	par	18-0802
Gibbs George			
	Fr 1835 Oct 27		29-0353
Gibbs George W			
	Fr 1812 Nov 21		DLC-5
	To 1813 Jan 07		3-0002
	To 1813 Jan 07*		DLC-61
	Fr 1813 Oct 14		DLC-7
	Fr 1813 Oct 14*		DLC-61
Gibbs V			
	Fr 1833 Apr 12	fin	DLC-42
Gibbs William Channing et al			
	Fr 1831 Sep 15		M639-11
Gibbs & Coyle			
	Fr 1834 Oct 07	fin	DLC-44
Gibert Pedro et al			
	Re 1835 Mar 03	par	27-0704
Gibson Alexander			
	Re 1830 Apr 13		M273-23
	Fr 1831 Sep 29		18-0899

Name / Date	Note	Reference
Gibson Caledonia M		
Fr 1837 Aug 05		33-1407
Fr 1837 Aug 05*		DLC-50
To 1837 Oct 28		34-0001
Gibson George		
Re 1788 Nov	leg	1-0048
Re 1804 May 12	fin	DLC-3
Gibson George (d 1861)		
Fr 1816 Dec 15		DLC-22
To 1816 Dec 17		5-0631
To 1817		5-0653
To 1817		5-0655
To 1817		5-0657
To 1817		5-0659
To 1817 Jan 07		5-0666
Fr 1817 Jan 14		DLC-22
Fr 1817 Mar 20		DLC-22
Fr 1817 Apr 14		M221-73
Fr 1817 May 13		DLC-22
To 1818 Jan 19#		5-1294
Fr 1818 Jan 20		DLC-24
Fr 1818 Feb		5-1420
Fr 1818 Feb 02		DLC-24
Fr 1818 Feb 12		DLC-24
Fr 1818 Mar 28		DLC-24
Fr 1818 Mar 28		DLC-24
Fr 1818 Mar 29		DLC-24
Fr 1818 Apr 04		DLC-24
To 1818 Apr 09		6-0338
Fr 1818 Apr 12		DLC-24
Fr 1819 Mar 24		DLC-26
Fr 1819 May 10		DLC-27
Fr 1819 May 10*		7-0510
To 1819 May 13		7-0515
Fr 1819 Aug 02		DLC-27
Fr 1819 Aug 18		DLC-27
To 1819 Sep 07		7-0642
To 1819 Sep 08		7-0646
Fr 1819 Nov 25		DLC-28
Fr 1820 Jan 03		DLC-28
To 1820 Jan 10		7-0989
To 1820 Feb 01		7-1022
Fr 1820 Feb 14		DLC-28
To 1820 Mar 15		7-1045
Fr 1820 Mar 20		DLC-28
Fr 1820 Mar 29		DLC-28
Fr 1820 Apr 01		DLC-28
Fr 1820 Apr 20		DLC-29
Fr 1820 May 03		DLC-29
Fr 1820 May 06		DLC-29
Fr 1820 Jun 19		DLC-29
To 1820 Jul 10		7-1145
Fr 1821 Feb 26		DLC-29
To 1822 Jan 29		9-0008
To 1822 Oct 15		9-0293
Fr 1828 Nov 21		DLC-36
To 1828 Dec 08		DLC-36
To 1830 Oct 24		16-0515
Fr 1830 Oct 25		16-0525
Fr 1832 Apr 23		20-0347
Fr 1832 Jun 22		20-0800
To 1835 Jan 17#		27-0248
Fr 1835 Oct 09		29-0240
Fr 1836 Apr 18#		M567-125
Fr 1836 Jun 15#		31-0488
To 1838 Jun 27		34-0389
Gibson George (d 1861) et al		
Fr 1836 Apr 04		M687-28
Fr 1836 Oct 22		32-0320
Gibson Henry		
Fr 1835 Jul 31		M124-148
Gibson J F		
Fr 1833 Dec 24#	fin	DLC-43
Gibson Jacob		
Fr 1842 Jul 19		DLC-54
To 1842 Aug 01		DLC-54
To 1842 Aug 01*		35-0866
Gibson James		
Fr 1840 Jun 13		34-1413
Gibson John		
Fr 1831 Oct 20		M639-2
Gibson John Jr		
Re 1831 Apr 13	par	17-1159
Gibson John Bannister		
Fr 1829 Mar 14		M639-6
Fr 1830 Jun 16		M639-17
Gibson John Bannister et al		
Re 1829 Nov	mem	14-0325
Gibson John H		
To 1814 Apr 18		DLC-10
Fr 1818 Jan 12		DLC-23
Fr 1821 Apr 22		DLC-30
Gibson Robert		
Fr 1839 Aug 09#	fin	DLC-53
To 1840 Jul 22	chk	DLC-53
Gibson Samuel		
To 1810 Sep 20	lnd	2-0963
Gibson Samuel R		
Fr 1831 Dec 12		M639-6
Gibson Thomas W		
Re 1835 Oct 10		M273-31
Gibson William		
Fr 1823 Apr 06		DLC-32
Gibson William & Robert		
Fr 1825 May 09	fin	DLC-35
Giesey Valentine et al		
Fr 1825 Feb 26		DLC-33
Fr 1825 Oct 10		DLC-33
To 1825 Oct 31		DLC-33
Gilbert (slave)		
Re 1822 Apr 24		9-0136
Re 1824 Sep		10-0881
Gilbert Algernon Sidney et al		
Fr 1834 Apr 10		25-0666
Gilbert Garrit		
Fr 1841 Aug 28		DLC-53
To 1841 Sep 11		35-0398
Gilbert H		
Fr c1835 Aug		DLC-46
Gilbert Walker		
Fr 1815 Jan 24		DLC-15
Fr 1815 Jan 27		DLC-16
Fr 1815 Feb 01		DLC-16
Fr 1815 Feb 23		DLC-17
Gilchrist M		
Fr 1835 Jan 09		27-0166
Gilchrist Robert Budd		
Fr 1831 Jul 19		M639-9
Fr 1835 Nov 07		M639-9
Gilchrist William et al		
Fr 1834 Nov 04		M639-27
To 1836 Aug 20		31-1320
Giles William Branch		
Fr 1802 Feb 18	add	DLC-2
Fr 1803 Sep 23		1-1169
Fr 1829 Oct 09		DLC-37
Fr 1829 Oct 22		14-0227
To 1829 Nov 21		DLC-37

Giles William Branch (cont)
Fr 1830 Mar 02 15-0284
To 1830 Mar 13 15-0355
Gill A B
Fr 1836 Jun 03 31-0281
Gill Richard
Fr 1800 Oct 01 lnd DLC-2
Fr 1800 Oct 01* lnd 1-0780
Fr 1800 Oct 02 lnd DLC-2
Fr 1800 Oct 02 lnd DLC-2
Fr 1800 Oct 02* lnd 1-0789
Fr 1802 Oct 26# leg 1-1046
Gill Samuel
Fr 1835 Jan 08 DLC-45
Gillaspey George et al
Fr 1829 Mar 26 M873-19
Gillchrest Robert et al
Fr 1837 Feb 01 33-0346
Gillenwater ______ (Capt)
To 1814 Jan 07 DLC-61
Gillespie D H et al
Fr c1836 29-1395
Gillespie George
Fr 1804 Jul 20 DLC-3
Fr 1829 Aug 14 M234-432
Fr 1831 Sep 20 M22-28
Gillespie James S
Fr 1833 Sep 13 M688-93
Gillespie Thomas
Fr 1829 Jan 26 M639-25
Fr 1829 Feb 18 M639-9
Fr 1829 Feb 20 M639-4
Gillespy John F
Fr 1836 Dec 20 32-1207
Gillet Ransom Hooker
To 1834 May 18# 25-1079
Gilliam Charles estate
Fr 1803 Feb 02 fin 1-1082
Gilliam Janet (Colquhoun)
Fr 1844 Feb 07 DLC-56
Gilliam William
To 1839 Dec 24# fin 34-1112
Gilliam & Aston
Fr 1841 Mar 23 fin DLC-53
Gilliss George
Fr 1831 Apr 01 fin DLC-39
Gilliss Thomas H
To 1829 Jul 29 13-0991
To 1829 Dec 07 14-0806
To 1831 May 02 17-1270
To 1831 May 02* M124-128
To 1832 May 30 20-0677
To 1833 Feb 21 22-0444
To 1833 Apr 08 22-0966
To 1833 May 04 22-1293
To 1833 Jul 25 23-0222
To 1834 Jul 07 26-0181
To 1835 Oct 03 29-0176
Gillium Charles
Re 1801 Jan 08 leg 1-0832
Gillmer John Smith
Fr 1836 Oct 24 M639-9
Gilman ______ (Maj)
To 1841 Oct 23 DLC-53
Gilman Warren et al
Fr 1835 Jun 20 28-0752
Gilmer George Rockingham
Fr 1829 Dec 29 M234-73
Fr 1829 Dec 29* 14-1138
Fr 1830 Jun 17 M234-74
Fr 1830 Jun 17* 15-1483
Fr 1830 Oct 29 M222-27
Fr 1830 Oct 29* 16-0576
Fr 1831 Mar 22 M179-70
Fr 1831 Mar 22* 17-0927
Fr 1831 Jun 04 M234-222
Fr 1831 Jun 04* 17-1518
Fr 1831 Jun 20 M234-113
Fr 1831 Jun 20* 18-0045
To 1831 Jul 15 18-0220
Gilmore James
Fr 1817 Jul 11 DLC-23
Gilmore John
Fr 1830 Apr 12 M639-3
Fr 1831 Jan 22 17-0334
Fr 1831 Dec 16 M639-1
Gilmore John et al
Fr 1831 Mar 01 17-0700
Gilpin Henry Dilworth
To 1833 Mar 01 22-0586
Fr 1833 Apr 08 DLC-42
To 1833 Apr 14 22-1022
To 1833 Apr 14* DLC-42
Fr 1833 Apr 22 22-1110
To 1833 Aug 03 DLC-43
To 1833 Aug 03* 23-0262
Fr 1833 Aug 13 DLC-43
Fr 1833 Aug 13* 23-0329
Fr 1833 Aug 20 DLC-43
Fr 1833 Aug 20* 23-0434
Fr 1833 Aug 24 M639-18
Fr 1833 Aug 27 23-0462
To 1833 Aug 29 23-0487
Fr 1833 Sep 17 DLC-43
Fr 1833 Sep 17* 23-0731
Fr 1833 Dec 16 24-0522
Fr 1834 May 22 25-1123
Re 1834 Nov 05 26-0817
Fr 1834 Nov 08 DLC-45
Fr 1835 Apr 24 28-0122
Fr 1835 Jun 16 M124-148
Fr 1836 Nov 16 32-0538
Fr 1837 Jan 08 M639-18
Fr 1837 Jan 26 M687-30
To 1837 Feb 14 33-0699
Fr 1837 Mar 25 33-1114
Fr 1840 Mar 17 DLC-52
Gilpin Henry Dilworth et al
Fr 1833 Aug 19 23-0382
Fr 1833 Sep 03 23-0605
Gilpin Joshua
Fr 1829 Nov 15 14-0473
Gilpin Thomas William
Re 1830 Jun 15 15-1458
Girod Nicholas
Fr 1814 Dec 21 DLC-14
Fr 1814 Dec 25 DLC-15
Fr 1815 Jan 02 DLC-15
Fr 1815 Jan 14 DLC-15
To 1815 Jan 16 DLC-62
Fr 1815 Jan 16 DLC-15
Fr 1815 Jan 25 DLC-15
To 1815 Jan 27 4-0630
Fr 1815 Feb 18 DLC-16
Fr 1816 Nov 5-0558
Giusta Michael Anthony
To 1830 Feb 06 chk DLC-37
To 1830 Jul 30 chk DLC-38
To 1830 Sep 16 chk DLC-38

To 1831 Jan 06 chk 17-0210
To 1831 Mar 07 chk DLC-39
To 1831 Apr 07 chk DLC-39
To 1831 May 05 chk DLC-39
To 1831 May 26 17-1452
To 1831 May 26 chk DLC-39
To 1831 Jun 06 chk DLC-39
To 1831 Jul 06 chk DLC-39
Fr 1831 Aug 18-0382
To 1831 Aug 09 chk DLC-39
To 1831 Sep 05 chk DLC-40
To 1831 Oct 06 chk DLC-40
To 1831 Nov 07 chk DLC-40
To 1831 Dec 06 chk DLC-40
To 1831 Dec 21 chk DLC-40
To 1832 Jan 07 chk DLC-40
To 1832 Feb 04 chk DLC-40
To 1832 Mar 06 chk DLC-40
To 1832 May 06 chk DLC-40
To 1832 Jul 05 chk DLC-41
To 1832 Aug 06 chk DLC-41
To 1832 Sep 08 chk DLC-41
To 1832 Nov 05 chk DLC-41
To 1832 Dec 05 chk DLC-41
To 1833 Feb 05 chk DLC-42
To 1833 Mar 05 chk DLC-42
To 1833 Apr 04 chk DLC-42
To 1833 May 01 chk DLC-42
Fr 1836 Feb 11# fin DLC-47

Given George
Fr 1844 Sep 20 36-0895

Givens Thomas et al
Fr 1828 Dec 29 M639-12

Glascock Thomas
To 1818 Jan 20 5-1322
Fr 1818 Feb 25 DLC-24
Fr 1818 Apr 18 DLC-24
Fr 1818 Apr 30 DLC-24
Fr 1818 Apr 30* M271-2
Fr 1818 Apr 30* M221-78
Fr 1818 Apr 30* 6-0531
To 1818 May 07 6-0675
Fr 1818 May 11 DLC-25
Fr 1823 Jan 04 M439-18

Glascock Thomas et al
Fr 1818 Apr 20 DLC-24

Glass (Indian)
Fr 1817 Sep 30 M222-19

Glasscock Spencer
Re 1806 Dec 01 mem DLC-4
To 1807 Feb 03 fin DLC-4

Glassell James McMillan
To 1817 Mar 27 DLC-22
To 1817 May 29 DLC-22
To 1817 May 29* DLC-23
To 1817 Jul 24 5-0942
Re 1817 Jul 30 fin DLC-23
To 1817 Oct 03# DLC-23
To 1817 Oct 16# DLC-23
To 1817 Oct 16* M565-5
Fr 1818 Jan 07# M221-78
To 1818 Apr 08 6-0330
Fr 1820 DLC-60
Fr 1822 Oct 10 DLC-31
To 1823 Mar 11 9-0494
To 1823 Apr 30 9-0538
Fr 1823 Jul 18 DLC-32
Fr 1824 Feb 13 DLC-32
Fr 1824 Aug 01 DLC-33
Re 1830 Nov 30 16-0906

Gleason C K
Fr 1843 May 04# DLC-55

Gleason R H
To 1843 May 04# DLC-55

Gleaves F R
Fr 1839 Oct 01 fin DLC-52

Gleaves Michael
Re 1793 Nov 06 leg 1-0165
To 1798 Mar 20# fin DLC-2
Fr 1800 Jun 15 leg DLC-2
To 1808 Jul 19 lnd 2-0688

Gleaves Thomas
Fr 1800 Jun 15 leg DLC-60
Fr 1826 Apr 19 fin DLC-33

Gleim Jacob
Fr 1831 Oct 11 18-0949

Glenn Elias
Fr 1829 May 19 M639-24
Fr 1836 Apr 01 30-0968

Glenn S
Fr 1826 Jan 09 fin 11-0104
Fr 1843 Dec 05 fin DLC-55
Fr 1844 Nov 04 fin DLC-57

Glover John
Re 1807 Jul 09 leg 2-0514

Goddard Charles B
Fr 1832 Mar 24 M688-86

Goddard Joseph
Re 1833 Jan 05 par T967-1

Goddard Samuel A
To 1835 Oct 13 29-0279

Goddard William et al
Fr 1829 Mar M639-1

Godde de Liancourt
Calixte-Auguste de
Fr 1834 Aug 15 DLC-44

Godfroy Richard et al
Fr 1834 May 31 25-1194

Goentgen Samuel George
Fr 1832 Jan 22 M179-72

Gohagen Thomas
Re 1829 Mar 18 par 12-1027
Re 1829 Mar 18* par T967-1

Gold Joseph
Fr 1836 Mar 31 30-0950

Gold circulation
Re 1836 cJul mem DLC-48

Golder Robert
Fr 1835 Apr 02# fin DLC-46
Fr 1836 May 30# fin DLC-48

Goldsborough Charles W
Fr 1834 Dec 03 26-1344
Fr 1837 Mar 03 33-1036
To 1837 Mar 03 33-1037
To 1837 Mar 03* DLC-50

Goldsborough John
Fr 1844 Jan 25 DLC-56

Gondree P
Re 1829 Mar 19 par 12-1037
Re 1829 Mar 19* par T967-1

Gonzales Diego
Fr 1815 Jan 31 DLC-16

Gonzalez Manuel
Fr 1821 Jul 11 fin DLC-70

Gooch Claiborne W
Fr 1835 Nov 28 DLC-47

Gooch James
Fr 1832 Apr 16 20-0234

Name	Date	Type	Source
Good John			
	Fr 1827 Mar 08		DLC-34
	To 1827 Mar 29		DLC-34
	Fr 1829 Jul 10		DLC-37
	Fr 1829 Aug 12		M639-18
Goode Samuel			
	Re 1808 Sep 17	fin	DLC-4
	Re 1813 Jan 02		DLC-61
	To 1813 Mar 28		3-0365
Goodenow John Milton			
	Fr 1828 Feb 22		11-1128
	Fr 1830		14-1235
	Fr 1833 Sep 27		M639-9
	Fr 1835 Dec 31		M639-27
Goodenow John Milton et al			
	Fr 1829 Feb 18		M639-17
	Fr 1830 Mar		M639-2
Goodenow R K et al			
	Fr 1837 Jan		M687-16
Goodhue & Co et al			
	Fr 1834 May 26		M639-24
Goodin Benjamin			
	Fr 1815 Feb 27		DLC-17
Goodlett Adam Gibbs			
	Fr 1815 Jan 25		DLC-15
	Fr 1817 Apr 07		DLC-22
	Fr c1837		37-0358
	Fr 1844 Mar 07		DLC-56
	To 1844 Mar 12		DLC-56
Goodloe Robert			
	Fr 1807 Mar 25	fin	DLC-4
Goodlow John M			
	Re 1814 Oct 17	leg	4-0267
Goodman B L			
	Fr 1830 Jul 27#		DLC-38
Goodman Duke			
	Re 1831	mem	DLC-40
Goodman George			
	Fr 1810 Sep 20	fin	DLC-4
Goodman J R			
	Fr 1835 Sep 23		29-0099
Goodrich Archibald W			
	Fr 1829 Apr 05		M639-9
	Fr 1836 May 16		31-0036
Goodrich James et al			
	Fr 1829 Nov 09		14-0426
Goodwin J et al			
	Fr 1829 Aug 19		M639-14
Goodwin Jeremiah			
	Fr 1827 Nov 12		DLC-35
	Fr 1827 Nov 12		DLC-35
	To 1827 Dec 06		DLC-35
Goodwin S W			
	Re 1838 cJun	mem	34-0356
Goodwin Simeon S			
	Fr 1831 Jun 06		17-1527
	Fr 1833 Feb 08#		M221-113
Gordon Bolling			
	Fr 1833 Sep 24		M639-3
	Fr 1843 May 19		DLC-55
Gordon Bowling			
	Fr 1823 Jun 01		DLC-32
	To 1823 Jun 12		9-0594
Gordon Dolley			
	Fr 1822 Sep 03		DLC-31
Gordon George			
	To 1802 Oct 26#	leg	1-1046
	Fr 1808 Mar 03		2-0615
Gordon James			
	Fr 1829 Jan 19		M639-6
Gordon James H			
	Fr 1815 Jan 04		DLC-15
	Fr 1815 Jan 11		DLC-15
Gordon John			
	Re 1793 Mar 10#	leg	1-0154
	Fr 1804 Feb 22		DLC-3
	Re 1805 May 24	leg	2-0050
	Re 1806 Jul	leg	2-0287
	Fr 1812 Sep 26		M222-5
	Re 1813 Jan 18	mem	DLC-6
	To 1813 Dec 22		DLC-61
	To 1814 Jan 31		DLC-62
	To 1814 Feb 17		DLC-61
	Re 1814 Apr 01		DLC-9
	To 1814 May 07		DLC-10
	Fr 1814 Jul 29		DLC-11
	Fr 1814 Jul 29*		M200-9
	Fr 1814 Jul 29*		M221-63
	Fr 1815 Feb 10		DLC-16
	Fr 1815 Feb 27		DLC-17
	Fr 1816 Jun 04		DLC-20
	To 1819 Apr 03		7-0458
Gordon Joseph			
	To 1813 Dec 16		DLC-61
Gordon Louis			
	Re 1834 Oct 03	par	26-0490
Gordon Martin			
	Fr 1828 Jun 20		DLC-35
	To 1828 cJun 30		DLC-35
	To 1828 Aug 12		DLC-35
	Fr 1829 Mar 07		M639-15
	Fr 1829 Mar 10		M639-14
	Fr 1829 Apr 13		M639-21
	To 1829 May 11		DLC-60
	Fr 1829 Dec 10		14-0985
	Fr 1831 Dec 17		M639-16
	Fr 1832 Feb 17		M179-72
	Fr 1832 Mar 03		M179-72
	Fr 1832 Mar 03*		M124-132
	To 1833 Apr 09		DLC-42
	To 1833 Nov 23#		23-1308
	Fr 1833 Dec 13#		DLC-43
	Fr 1833 Dec 14		24-0501
	Fr 1833 Dec 16#		DLC-43
	Fr 1835 Jan 08		DLC-45
	Fr 1835 Feb 23		M688-98
	Fr 1835 Oct 02		29-0167
	Fr 1836 Mar 22		30-0873
	Fr 1836 Apr 05		M639-14
	Fr 1844 Dec 11		36-1165
	Fr 1845 Jan 07		DLC-57
Gordon Martin et al			
	Fr 1821 Apr 22		DLC-30
	Fr 1821 Apr 22*		DLC-35
	Fr 1829 Mar 07		M639-17
	Fr 1829 Apr		M639-21
Gordon Martin Jr			
	Fr 1836 Mar 22		30-0868
	Fr 1836 Mar 22#		30-0871
Gordon O			
	To 1823 Oct 31		DLC-32
Gordon Robert			
	Fr 1832 Feb 10		M234-136
	Fr 1832 Feb 10*		19-1033
Gordon Robert C			
	To 1803 Sep 22	lnd	1-1168

Gordon William
Fr 1829 Aug 16 M222-25
Fr 1836 Aug 22 31-1346
Gordon William Fitzhugh
Fr 1830 Aug 22 DLC-38
Fr 1832 Dec 05 M639-4
Gordon & Barnett
Fr 1839 Dec 28 fin 34-1114
Gordon & Walker
Fr 1819 Mar 03 fin DLC-26
Goree Marchioness de la
Fr 1832 Mar 12 M34-29
Fr 1832 Mar 12* 19-1401
Fr 1834 Dec 09 26-1441
Fr 1834 Dec 09* M179-79
Fr 1835 May 02 M179-80
Fr 1835 May 02* 28-0214
Fr 1836 Dec 25 M179-82
Gorman George
Fr 1835 Oct 22 29-0334
Goss John D
Fr 1837 Dec 23 fin DLC-50
Fr 1840 Jan 06# fin DLC-53
Goss Mary
Re 1832 May 21 par 20-0544
Goss William
Re 1831 Apr 09 par 17-1098
Re 1831 Apr 18 par 17-1190
Re 1832 Nov 09 par 21-0370
Gouge William M
Fr 1836 Aug 16 DLC-48
Gouin Charles
Fr 1829 Aug 26 13-1203
Gouin Pierre
Fr 1829 Aug 26 13-1203
Gouin Therese
Fr 1829 Aug 26 13-1203
Gould Sarah A
Fr 1844 Aug 17 36-0798
Gould William et al
Fr 1832 Feb 11 19-1062
Gourlay Robert
Fr 1829 Dec 24 14-1104
Gouverneur Samuel L
Fr 1837 Jan 06 32-1508
Fr 1838 Jul 30 DLC-51
To 1845 Jan 04 36-1310
To 1845 Jan 04* DLC-57
Fr 1845 Jan 16 DLC-57
Fr 1845 Jan 16* 36-1356
Gove Moses M
Re 1830 Feb 10 par 17-0880
Re 1830 Feb 10* par M40-21
Re 1831 Mar 16 par 17-0869
Gowen James
Fr 1830 Jul 03 DLC-38
To 1830 Jul 22 16-0041
Fr 1830 Aug 13 16-0105
Gowyer Henry
To 1803 Dec 22 fin DLC-3
Re 1804 Sep 01 leg DLC-60
Grace Jacob
Re 1804 May 11 fin DLC-3
Gracie William
Fr 1830 Oct 18 M639-9
Graebe Charles
Fr 1834 Jun 03 M639-9
Fr 1834 Jun 03* M687-13
Gragroy William
Fr 1829 Sep 12 13-1310
Graham Daniel
Re 1824 Jul 14 leg 10-0827
Graham Edward
Fr 1831 Dec 21 M22-28
Graham George
Fr 1815 Mar 27 DLC-17
Fr 1815 Mar 27* M7-1
Fr 1815 May 19 DLC-18
Fr 1815 May 19* M6-8
Fr 1815 Jun 03 DLC-18
Fr 1815 Jun 03* M6-8
Fr 1815 Jun 09 DLC-18
Fr 1815 Jun 09* M6-8
To 1815 Jun 10 M221-63
To 1815 Jun 10* DLC-18
To 1815 Jun 10* DLC-62
Fr 1815 Jun 12 DLC-18
Fr 1815 Jun 12* M6-8
Fr 1815 Jun 20 DLC-18
Fr 1815 Jun 22 M6-8
Fr 1815 Jun 24 DLC-18
Fr 1815 Jun 24* M6-8
Fr 1815 Jun 26 DLC-18
Fr 1815 Jun 26* M6-8
Fr 1815 Jun 27 DLC-18
Fr 1815 Jun 27* M6-8
Fr 1815 Jul 02 DLC-18
Fr 1815 Jul 02* M6-8
Fr 1815 Jul 15 DLC-18
Fr 1815 Jul 15* M6-8
Fr 1815 Jul 21 DLC-19
Fr 1815 Jul 21* M6-8
Fr 1815 Jul 27 DLC-19
Fr 1815 Jul 27* M6-8
Fr 1815 Jul 28 DLC-19
Fr 1815 Jul 28* M6-8
Fr 1815 Jul 29 DLC-19
Fr 1815 Jul 29* M6-8
Fr 1815 Aug 05 DLC-19
Fr 1815 Aug 05* M6-8
To 1815 Aug 08 DLC-62
Fr 1815 Aug 10 DLC-19
Fr 1815 Aug 10* M6-8
Fr 1815 Aug 23 DLC-19
Fr 1815 Aug 25 DLC-19
Fr 1815 Aug 25* M6-8
To 1815 Aug 29 M221-63
To 1815 Aug 29* DLC-62
To 1815 Aug 29* DLC-19
To 1815 Aug 29* 4-1177
Fr 1815 Sep 04 DLC-19
Fr 1815 Sep 04* M6-8
Fr 1815 Sep 05 DLC-19
Fr 1815 Sep 05* M6-8
Fr 1815 Sep 05 DLC-19
Fr 1815 Sep 05* M6-8
Fr 1815 Sep 09 DLC-19
Fr 1815 Sep 09* M6-8
Fr 1815 Sep 11 DLC-19
Fr 1815 Sep 11* M6-8
To 1815 Sep 12 DLC-62
To 1815 Sep 19 4-1186
To 1815 Sep 19* DLC-62
To 1815 Sep 20 M221-63
To 1815 Sep 20* DLC-62
Fr 1815 Sep 21 M6-8
Fr 1815 Sep 27 DLC-19
Fr 1815 Sep 27* M6-8
Fr 1815 Oct 02 M6-8

Graham George (cont)

Fr 1815 Oct 07	DLC-19
Fr 1815 Oct 07*	M6-8
Fr 1815 Oct 10	DLC-19
Fr 1815 Oct 10*	M6-8
To 1815 Oct 18	DLC-62
Fr 1815 Oct 25	DLC-19
Fr 1815 Oct 25*	M6-8
Fr 1815 Oct 31	DLC-19
Fr 1815 Nov 16	DLC-19
Fr 1816 Apr 13	M6-8
Fr 1816 Jun 21	DLC-21
Fr 1816 Jun 21*	M6-9
Fr 1816 Jul 11	DLC-21
Fr 1816 Jul 11*	M6-9
Fr 1816 Jul 16	DLC-21
Fr 1816 Jul 16*	M6-9
To 1816 Jul 30	M221-70
Fr 1816 Aug 03	5-0341
Fr 1816 Aug 03*	M6-9
Fr 1816 Aug 05	5-0343
Fr 1816 Aug 05*	DLC-21
Fr 1816 Aug 05*	M15-3
Fr 1816 Aug 09	5-0350
Fr 1816 Aug 15	DLC-21
Fr 1816 Aug 15*	M6-9
Fr 1816 Oct 26	5-0549
Fr 1816 Oct 26*	M15-3
To 1816 Oct 30	M22-9
Fr 1816 Oct 31	DLC-21
Fr 1816 Oct 31*	M7-1
Fr 1816 Oct 31*	5-0552
Fr 1816 Oct 31	DLC-21
Fr 1816 Oct 31*	5-0557
Fr 1816 Oct 31*	M15-3
Fr 1816 Nov 04	M6-9
Fr 1816 Nov 05	DLC-21
Fr 1816 Nov 05*	M7-1
Fr 1816 Nov 05*	5-0564
Fr 1816 Nov 07	DLC-21
Fr 1816 Nov 07*	M15-3
Fr 1816 Nov 07*	5-0568
Fr 1816 Nov 07	DLC-21
Fr 1816 Nov 07*	M6-9
To 1816 Nov 12	M221-60
To 1816 Nov 12	5-0570
To 1816 Nov 12*	M668-4
To 1816 Nov 13	M22-9
To 1816 Nov 20	M22-9
To 1816 Dec 03	5-0589
To 1816 Dec 04	M222-19
Fr 1816 Dec 04	DLC-22
Fr 1816 Dec 04*	M15-3
Fr 1816 Dec 04*	5-0590
Fr 1816 Dec 04	DLC-22
Fr 1816 Dec 04*	M15-3
Fr 1816 Dec 04*	5-0592
To 1816 Dec 11	M221-74
Fr 1816 Dec 20	DLC-22
Fr 1816 Dec 20*	M6-9
To 1816 Dec 21	5-0635
To 1816 Dec 21	M221-74
Fr 1816 Dec 28	DLC-22
Fr 1816 Dec 28*	M6-9
Fr 1816 Dec 28*	M15-3
Fr 1816 Dec 28*	5-0647
To 1817 Jan 06	M221-74
To 1817 Jan 09	5-0667
To 1817 Jan 09	M22-10
To 1817 Jan 12	5-0686
Fr 1817 Jan 13	DLC-22
Fr 1817 Jan 13*	M15-4
Fr 1817 Jan 13	DLC-22
Fr 1817 Jan 13*	M15-4
Fr 1817 Jan 13*	5-0696
To 1817 Jan 14	5-0697
To 1817 Jan 19	M221-74
Fr 1817 Jan 23	DLC-22
Fr 1817 Jan 23*	M6-9
Fr 1817 Jan 25	DLC-22
Fr 1817 Jan 25*	M6-9
Fr 1817 Feb 01	DLC-22
Fr 1817 Feb 01*	M6-9
Fr 1817 Feb 01*	5-0715
To 1817 Feb 12	M221-73
To 1817 Feb 12*	5-0722
To 1817 Feb 17	DLC-71
To 1817 Feb 17*	5-0728
Fr 1817 Feb 21	DLC-22
Fr 1817 Feb 21*	M6-9
To 1817 Feb 26	M221-74
To 1817 Feb 26*	5-0743
Fr 1817 Mar 22	DLC-22
Fr 1817 Mar 22*	M15-4
Fr 1817 Mar 22*	5-0785
Fr 1817 Mar 22*	M208-7
Fr 1817 Mar 25	DLC-22
Fr 1817 Mar 25*	M15-4
Fr 1817 Mar 25*	5-0793
To 1817 Mar 31	M221-74
Fr 1817 Apr 03	DLC-22
Fr 1817 Apr 03*	M6-9
Fr 1817 Apr 05	DLC-22
Fr 1817 Apr 05*	M6-9
Fr 1817 Apr 07	M6-9
To 1817 Apr 11	5-0806
Fr 1817 Apr 11	DLC-22
Fr 1817 Apr 11*	M6-9
To 1817 Apr 22	M221-74
To 1817 Apr 29	M221-74
To 1817 Apr 29*	5-0843
To 1817 May	M22-10
Fr 1817 May 09	DLC-22
Fr 1817 May 09*	M15-4
Fr 1817 May 09*	M6-9
To 1817 May 13	5-0852
Fr 1817 May 14	5-0855
Fr 1817 May 14*	M15-4
Fr 1817 May 14*	DLC-22
Fr 1817 May 16	DLC-22
Fr 1817 May 16*	M15-4
Fr 1817 May 16*	T494-1
Fr 1817 May 16*	5-0857
Fr 1817 May 20	DLC-22
Fr 1817 May 20*	M6-9
Fr 1817 May 21	5-0865
Fr 1817 May 21*	M6-9
To 1817 May 26	M22-10
Fr 1817 May 26	M15-4
To 1817 May 27	5-0877
To 1817 May 31	5-0886
Fr 1817 Jun 06	DLC-22
Fr 1817 Jun 06*	M15-4
To 1817 Jun 11	5-0889
To 1817 Jun 23	M22-10
To 1817 Jul 08	DLC-23
To 1817 Jul 09	DLC-23
To 1817 Jul 09	M221-74
To 1817 Jul 09*	5-0914

To 1817 Jul 09 5-0916
To 1817 Jul 09 M222-19
To 1817 Jul 09 5-0917
To 1817 Jul 09 5-0920
To 1817 Jul 10 M221-74
To 1817 Jul 10 5-0925
Fr 1817 Jul 12 DLC-23
Fr 1817 Jul 12* M6-9
Fr 1817 Jul 17 DLC-23
Fr 1817 Jul 17* M6-9
To 1817 Jul 22 M221-74
To 1817 Jul 22* 5-0935
Fr 1817 Jul 30 DLC-23
Fr 1817 Jul 30* M15-4
Fr 1817 Aug 01 DLC-23
Fr 1817 Aug 01* M15-4
Fr 1817 Aug 01* M208-7
Fr 1817 Aug 01* 5-0952
Fr 1817 Aug 09 DLC-23
Fr 1817 Aug 09* M15-4
Fr 1817 Aug 09* M208-7
Fr 1817 Aug 09* 5-0960
Fr 1817 Aug 14 5-0977
Fr 1817 Aug 14* DLC-23
Fr 1817 Aug 14* M15-4
Fr 1817 Aug 14* M208-7
Fr 1817 Aug 16 5-0988
Fr 1817 Aug 16* M15-4
To 1817 Aug 19 5-0991
To 1817 Aug 19* M22-10
Fr 1817 Aug 28 5-1001
Fr 1817 Aug 28* M15-4
To 1817 Sep 02 M22-10
Fr 1817 Sep 29 M15-4
Fr 1817 Oct 11 DLC-23
Fr 1817 Oct 11* M6-9
To 1817 Oct 17 5-1105
Fr 1817 Oct 25 DLC-23
Fr 1817 Oct 25* M15-4
Fr 1817 Oct 25* M271-2
Fr 1817 Oct 27 DLC-23
Fr 1817 Oct 27* M15-4
Fr 1817 Oct 27* 5-1122
Fr 1817 Oct 30 DLC-23
Fr 1817 Oct 30* M6-9
Fr 1817 Oct 30 M6-9
Fr 1817 Nov 06 DLC-23
Fr 1817 Nov 06* M15-4
Fr 1817 Nov 13 DLC-23
Fr 1817 Nov 13* M6-9
Fr 1817 Nov 24 DLC-23
Fr 1817 Nov 24* M6-9
Fr 1817 Nov 26 DLC-23
Fr 1817 Nov 27 M6-9
To 1817 Dec 01 5-1149
Fr 1817 Dec 06# DLC-23
To 1817 Dec 16 M221-78
To 1817 Dec 16* 5-1177
Fr 1829 Feb 23 M25-23
Fr 1829 Feb 28 M25-23
Fr 1829 Mar 05 M25-23
Fr 1829 Mar 09 12-0901
Fr 1829 Mar 09* M25-23
Fr 1829 Apr 10 12-1311
Fr 1829 Apr 10* M25-23
Fr 1829 Apr 28 M25-23
Fr 1829 May 15 M25-23
Fr 1829 Jun 29 M25-24
To 1829 Jul 01# 13-0772
Fr 1829 Jul 16 M25-24
Fr 1829 Jul 16* 13-0849
Fr 1829 Jul 29 M124-119
Fr 1829 Jul 29* M25-24
Fr 1829 Sep 08# M25-24
Fr 1829 Oct 20 14-0205
To 1829 Oct 31# 14-0282
To 1829 Nov 09 14-0430
To 1829 Nov 09* DLC-37
Fr 1829 Nov 17 M25-25
Fr 1830 Mar 05 M25-25
To 1830 Apr 15-0552
Fr 1830 Apr 06 M25-25
To 1830 Apr 06# 15-0625
To 1830 Apr 15# 15-0721
To 1830 Apr 16 15-0737
Fr 1830 Jun 02 15-1264
Fr 1830 Jun 02* M25-25

Graham George Taylor
Re 1829 Nov 20 par 14-0504
Re 1829 Dec 29 par 14-1151

Graham James
Fr 1837 Jan 28 33-0195
Fr 1837 Feb 17 33-0743
Fr 1837 Feb 17* M234-114

Graham John
Fr 1815 Nov 29 DLC-19

Graham John Andrew
Fr 1828 May 24 DLC-35
To 1828 Jun 19 DLC-35
Fr 1829 Jun 02 M639-4
Re 1835 May 27 M22-36

Graham Joseph
To 1814 Apr 17 DLC-10
To 1814 May 08 3-1009
Fr 1814 Jul 11 DLC-11

Graham William M
Fr 1820 Jun 23 DLC-29
To 1820 Jun 27# DLC-29
To 1820 Jun 27* DLC-63

Gramvenstand John
Fr c1798 fin 1-0567

Grant Abijah
Fr 1844 Dec 02 DLC-57

Grant James
Fr 1795 Aug 13 DLC-71
Fr 1795 Sep 03 DLC-1
Fr 1795 Nov 16 DLC-1

Grant Reuben
Re 1836 Apr 18 par 30-1240

Grant Reuben H
Fr 1834 May 03 M234-188
Fr 1834 Oct 01 DLC-44
Fr 1844 May 10 DLC-56

Grant Squire
Fr 1793 Nov 07 DLC-2
Fr 1796 May 19 DLC-1
Fr 1797 Nov 07 DLC-2
Fr 1799 Jun 07 1-0719
Fr 1799 Nov 25 1-0743
To 1825 Feb 18 10-1122

Grant T P
Fr 1835 Jan 08 DLC-45

Gratiot Charles
To 1832 Jul 14 20-1085
To 1832 Oct 26 21-0157
Fr 1832 Oct 27 21-0164
Fr 1832 Dec 24 21-1151
To 1834 Feb 08 DLC-44

Gratiot Charles (cont)		
Fr 1834 Feb 10		24-1279
To 1834 Apr 23#		25-0868
To 1834 Oct 09#		M688-94
To 1834 Nov 11		26-0883
Fr 1834 Nov 11		26-0884
To 1835 Jun 12		M688-75
Fr 1835 Jun 12		M688-75
Fr 1835 Jun 12*		28-0664
Fr 1835 Jul 23		M22-36
To 1835 Nov 09#		29-0476
Fr 1838 Mar 31		34-0296
Graves Francis		
Fr 1804 Aug 10		DLC-3
Graves John James et al		
Fr 1836 Nov 15		32-0503
Graves Michael		
To 1807 Jan 02	fin	DLC-4
Graves Samuel		
Re 1788 Mar	leg	1-0035
Gray Alexander et al		
Fr 1839 Aug 24		DLC-52
Gray Alexander T		
Fr 1845 Mar 19		DLC-57
Gray Andrew et al		
Fr 1829 Nov 23		M639-27
Gray Andrew Jackson		
Fr 1839 Feb 01		DLC-51
Gray Edgar A M		
Fr 1831 Nov 26		M688-79
Gray James		
Fr 1823 Apr 11	fin	DLC-32
Fr 1829 Sep 13		M639-3
Fr 1830 Jan 22#		M639-3
Gray John Jr et al		
Fr 1832 cApr		20-0081
Gray John B		
Re 1833 Apr 25	par	22-1168
Gray John T		
Fr 1831 Aug 02		DLC-39
Fr 1831 Aug 03		DLC-39
Gray Thomas		
Fr 1801		1-0830
Gray Thomas R		
Re 1836 Aug 09		31-1270
Gray Vincent		
Fr 1826 Dec 30		DLC-34
Fr 1827 Feb 14		DLC-34
Gray William W		
To 1831 May 02		17-1271
Grayson Edward B		
Fr 1823 Dec 20		M688-25
Fr 1834 Oct 27		26-0745
Grayson John		
To 1829 Jan 09		12-0454
Fr 1829 Apr 02		M639-6
Grayson Peter W		
Fr 1815 Feb 09		DLC-16
Great Britain		
Re 1807 Jul 29		2-0525
Greaves Thomas		
Fr 1829 Nov 12		M234-432
Gredy George		
Fr 1830 Dec 25		16-1558
Greeley John		
Fr 1844 Aug 06		36-0778
Green ______		
Re 1843 Dec 15	mem	DLC-56
Green Abraham		
To 1800 Dec 27	fin	1-0828
Fr 1801 Jan 17	fin	1-0837
To 1811 Dec 27	fin	2-1027
Green Ashbel Jr		
Fr 1841 Jul 02		DLC-53
Green Duff		
Fr 1825 Jun 09		DLC-33
Fr 1826 Aug 09		DLC-34
To 1826 cAug 30		DLC-34
Fr 1827 Apr 26	fin	DLC-34
Fr 1827 Jun 09		DLC-34
Fr 1827 Jul 08		DLC-34
Fr 1827 Jul 18		DLC-34
To 1827 Aug 13		DLC-34
Fr 1827 Aug 29		DLC-34
Fr 1827 Aug 29*		11-0831
Fr 1827 Oct 22		DLC-34
Fr 1828 Nov 12		DLC-35
Fr 1829 Feb 04		12-0480
Fr 1829 Mar 09		M639-15
Fr 1829 Apr 23		13-0105
Fr 1829 May 01		13-0236
Fr 1829 Jun 14		DLC-37
Fr 1829 Jun 24		13-0706
To 1829 Aug 08#		13-1042
Fr 1829 Aug 31		M639-1
Fr 1829 Sep 03		13-1245
To 1829 Oct 19#		DLC-75
Fr 1829 Oct 19#		DLC-75
Fr 1829 Dec 06		DLC-72
Fr 1830 Jan 04		14-1318
To 1830 Oct 28#		DLC-38
To 1830 Nov 11		16-0709
To 1831 Dec 03#		19-0001
Fr 1831 Dec 03#		19-0008
To 1831 Dec 03#		19-0002
Green Horace		
Re 1812 Feb 29		DLC-5
Green Isaac H		
Fr 1818 Jun 21	fin	DLC-69
Fr 1818 Jun 21*	fin	6-1071
Green James S		
Fr 1831 Jun 27		M567-59
Green John et al		
Fr 1830 Feb 01		15-0088
Green Joseph		
Re 1814 Apr 26	leg	3-0997
Green Joseph K		
Fr 1813 Nov 28		DLC-7
Green Ruth C		
Fr 1836 Mar 23		DLC-47
Green Samuel		
Fr 1820 May 13	fin	DLC-29
Fr 1823 Feb 26	fin	DLC-32
Fr 1829 Nov		14-0326
Fr 1830 Aug 05		M639-7
Green Samuel R		
To 1815 Jan 19	chk	DLC-15
Green Thomas		
Fr 1789 Aug 26	leg	1-0068
Green Thomas Jefferson		
Fr 1829 Jun 09		M639-17
Fr 1836 Mar 11		M567-123
Fr 1836 Mar 11*		M234-436
Fr 1840 Jan 08		34-1151
Fr 1840 Jan 16		34-1176
Green Willis		
To 1785 Feb 09#	leg	1-0021
Greene Benjamin		
Fr 1829 Sep 15		M179-67

Greene Daniel A et al
    Fr 1837 Jan 24   DLC-49
Greene H W
    Fr 1841 Feb 28   DLC-53
Greene Nathaniel
    Fr 1829 Mar 18   12-1033
    Fr 1829 Apr 11   M639-6
Greene Pardon C
    Fr 1832 May 31   M639-17
    Fr 1833 May 31   M179-76
Greene Pardon C et al
    Fr 1832 May 21   M639-17
Greene Richard W
    Fr 1833 Dec 18   M639-9
Greenfield H
    Fr 1830 Jun 13   M124-124
Greenhow Robert
    Fr 1835 Nov 10   29-0489
Greenleaf Abner
    To 1828 May 06   DLC-75
    To 1833 Jun 30   23-0086
Greenleaf James
    Fr 1834 Apr 10   25-0668
Greer A
    Fr 1832 May 24   20-0590
Greer Andrew
    Re 1791 Feb 15   leg   1-0090
    Fr 1803 Oct 23#   leg   1-1241
Greer David
    Re c1790   leg   1-0075a
Greer Jacob
    Fr 1836 May 01   30-1471
    Fr 1836 Oct 01   31-1574
Greer John
    Fr 1844 Nov 20   DLC-57
Greer Thomas
    Fr 1818 Jun 11   fin   DLC-69
    Fr 1818 Jun 11*   fin   6-1042
Greer Vance
    To 1813 Sep 25   DLC-61
    Fr 1813 Oct 01   DLC-6
    To 1814 May 24   DLC-10
Gregg Andrew & Co et al
    Fr 1831 Dec 27   M639-15
Gregory E N
    Fr 1832 May 28   M639-12
Gregory Edmund D
    To 1814 Jan 31   DLC-62
Gregory George
    Fr 1839 Jan 08   DLC-51
Gregory Henry
    To 1839 May 23#   chk   DLC-52
Gregory John
    To 1813 Dec 22   DLC-61
Gregory Shirlock S
    Fr 1835 Jun 27   DLC-46
Grier Robert Cooper
    Fr 1833 Jun 06   M639-6
Grier Robert Cooper et al
    Fr 1836 Jan   M639-8
Grierson Robert
    Fr 1813 Nov 13   3-0593
    Fr 1813 Nov 13*   DLC-61
    Fr 1813 Nov 13*   DLC-7
    To 1813 Nov 17   DLC-61
    Fr 1814 Feb 11   DLC-8
Grieve Robert
    Re 1833 Oct 17   23-1054
Griffin J
    Fr 1823 Jan 08#   fin   9-0395
Griffin John
    Fr 1808 May 09   fin   DLC-4
    Fr 1811 Feb 16   fin   2-0989
Griffin T
    To 1831 Oct 12   DLC-40
Griffin Thomas B
    Fr 1825 Jan 05   fin   DLC-33
    To 1831 Dec 01   chk   DLC-40
    Fr 1835 Feb 15#   fin   DLC-46
Griffin William
    Fr 1820 Oct 03   fin   7-1383
    Fr 1821 Jan 04   fin   8-0042
    Fr 1822 Nov 16   fin   DLC-31
Griffith Andrew C et al
    Fr 1836 Jan 13   M639-26
Griffith Camillus
    To 1818 Jun 01   fin   DLC-69
Griffith L C et al
    Fr 1815 Apr 14   DLC-18
Griffith Thomas W
    To 1823 May 24   9-0574
Griggs Jane S
    Fr 1832 Mar 10   19-1389
Griggs John H
    Fr 1832 Mar 10   19-1389
Griggs William et al
    Fr 1835 Mar 03   M234-242
Grignon Lewis et al
    Fr 1835 Sep 14   29-0040
Grigsby Joseph
    Fr 1835 May 20   DLC-46
Grimes William et al
    Fr 1833 Oct 11   M639-24
Grinnell Clark S et al
    Fr 1834 Mar   M639-7
Grinnell Joseph
    Fr 1829 May 23#   M639-26
Griswold Daniel S et al
    Fr 1831 Nov 12   18-1248
    Fr 1831 Dec 31   19-0474
Griswold George et al
    Fr 1836 cJun 24   31-0566
Griswold Nathaniel L et al
    Fr 1829 Sep 24   M639-27
    Fr 1831 Nov 01   M639-7
Grizzard Jeremiah
    To 1804 Aug 31   fin   DLC-3
Grochamps Adelaide de Grasse de
    Fr 1834 Oct 03   26-0484
Groesbeck John H
    Fr 1835 Mar 21   M639-1
Grotjan Thomas Jefferson
    To 1833 Jun 09   DLC-43
Groton Nathaniel
    Fr 1837 Feb 04   M687-16
Groundie G H
    Fr 1835 May 13   M639-9
Grubb Thomas P et al
    Fr 1835 cJan   DLC-59
Grubbs William
    Fr 1844 May 31   DLC-56
Grundy Felix
    To 1810 Jun 06   fin   2-0957
    Fr 1810 Jun 13   fin   DLC-4
    Fr 1810 Jun 16   fin   DLC-4
    Fr 1811 Mar 19   DLC-5
    Fr 1811 Nov 28   DLC-5

Grundy Felix (cont)		
Fr 1811 Dec 24		DLC-5
Fr 1812 Feb 12		DLC-5
Fr 1812 Jun 05		DLC-59
To 1813 Mar 15		3-0312
To 1813 Jul 15		DLC-71
Fr 1813 Jul 26		DLC-6
Fr 1815 May 15	add	4-1035
To 1815 May 15	add	4-1036
To 1817 Jan 23		M221-117
Fr 1819 Jan 02		DLC-72
Fr 1819 Apr 05		DLC-26
Fr 1822 Jun 27		DLC-31
To 1826 May 30		11-0223
To 1827 Nov 15		11-0921
Fr 1827 Nov 15		11-0922
To 1828 Aug 15		12-0140
To 1828 Aug 23		12-0173
Fr 1828 Nov 20		DLC-35
Fr 1829 May 22		DLC-37
Fr 1829 Oct 22		DLC-37
Fr 1830 Jan 09		14-1359
Fr 1830 Apr 03		15-0575
Fr 1830 Jul 31		DLC-38
Fr 1830 Sep 01		M639-27
Fr 1831		17-0086
Fr 1831 Sep 30		DLC-40
Fr 1832 Feb 04		DLC-40
To 1832 Mar 21		DLC-73
Fr 1832 Jun 15		DLC-73
To 1832 Aug 20		20-1368
To 1833 Feb 07		22-0297
To 1833 Feb 13		22-0364
Fr 1833 Feb 22	add	22-0445
Fr 1833 May 06		22-1305
Fr 1833 May 06		DLC-42
To 1833 May 19		DLC-43
To 1833 May 19*		22-1401
Fr 1833 Aug 06		23-0284
Fr 1833 Aug 07		DLC-43
Fr 1834 Aug 29		26-0396
Fr 1835 Mar 28		DLC-45
Fr 1835 May 30		28-0529
Fr 1835 Jun 06		DLC-46
To 1835 Jun 10#		DLC-46
To 1835 Jun 11		DLC-74
To 1835 Jun 11*		28-0646
Fr 1835 Jun 17		DLC-46
To 1835 Sep 24		29-0103
To 1835 Oct 05		29-0192
Fr 1835 Nov 05		29-0459
Fr 1836 Feb 08		M639-9
Fr 1836 Feb 08*		30-0327
To 1836 Feb 17		30-0404
Fr 1836 Aug 08		31-1264
Fr 1836 Dec 31		32-1444
Fr 1837		32-1457
Fr 1837 cJan 03		M22-41
Fr 1837 Jan 04		DLC-49
Fr 1837 May 11		33-1217
Fr 1837 Oct 02		DLC-50
To 1837 Dec 16		34-0090
Fr 1838 Jan 18		DLC-51
Fr 1838 Feb 09		DLC-51
To 1838 Aug 23		34-0432
To 1838 Sep 12#		DLC-51
Fr 1838 Nov 13		DLC-51
Fr 1838 Nov 15#		34-0516
To 1839 Feb 20		34-0658
Fr 1839 Apr 14		DLC-52
To 1839 May 01		34-0773
To 1839 Jun 28		34-0832
To 1839 Sep 26		34-0958
Grundy Felix et al		
Fr c1830		14-1237
Fr 1836 Aug 10		M567-120
Grundy James P		
Fr 1835 Jan 16		M639-9
Grymes John Randolph		
To 1821 Feb 15		8-0115
Fr 1827 Nov 03		DLC-34
Fr 1828 Jan 08	add	11-1020
To 1828 Jan 08	add	DLC-36
To 1828 Jan 08*	add	11-1021
To 1829 Mar 23		12-1084
Fr 1829 May 11		M639-9
Fr 1834 Jun 02		25-1227
To 1843 Jan 27		DLC-55
Fr 1843 Feb 15		DLC-55
Gue Francis et al		
Fr 1831 Oct 12		M639-21
Guerrero Vicente		
Fr 1829 Apr 06		M54-1
To 1829 Oct 12		14-0147
To 1829 Oct 17		14-0185
To 1829 Oct 18		DLC-37
To 1829 Oct 20		14-0220
Fr 1829 Nov 17		M54-1
Guild Curtis Jr		
Fr 1844 Oct 30		DLC-57
Fr 1845 Apr 15		DLC-58
Guild James		
Fr 1831 Jan 04		17-0193
Guild Josephus Conn		
Fr 1835 Apr 11		DLC-46
To 1835 Apr 24		DLC-46
Fr 1836 Jun 07		M688-105
Guilford Nathan		
Fr 1817 Aug 03		DLC-23
To 1817 Aug 18		5-0990
Guill John H		
Fr 1822 Dec 06	fin	DLC-31
Guillemard Arnaldo		
Fr 1814 Sep 16		DLC-12
Guinness W S		
Fr 1831 Jul 21		M688-77
Guion John Isaac et al		
Fr 1835 Nov 24		M639-4
Guion Walter Burling		
Fr 1833 May 21#		DLC-43
Gunnell J S		
Fr 1829 Jun 07	fin	DLC-72
Gunter John Jr		
Fr 1834 Jul 26		26-0245
Gunton William		
Fr 1836 Oct 10		DLC-49
Gurley Henry Hosford		
Fr 1829 Mar 04		M639-18
Fr 1829 Aug 04		M639-10
Gurley Ralph Randolph		
Fr 1829 Jun 24		M124-119
Gurley W H H		
Fr 1843 Dec 22		DLC-56
Gurney Harris		
Re 1834 Oct 10	par	26-0550
Re 1835 cJan 08	par	27-0141
Guthrie James		
Fr 1834 Jul 09		26-0204

Gwin James
Re 1825 May 10 leg DLC-33
Fr 1830 Oct 10 DLC-38
Fr 1830 Dec 18 DLC-38
To 1835 Feb 23 27-0588
Fr 1835 May 16 28-0444
To 1835 Aug 08 28-1262
To 1835 Aug 12 DLC-46
Fr 1836 Dec 32-0602

Gwin Samuel
To 1831 Aug 09 chk DLC-39
Re 1831 Oct 03 18-0914
Re 1832 Jul 21 20-1212
Fr 1832 Dec 13 21-1035
To 1835 cApr mem 27-1410
Fr 1835 Apr 06 DLC-46
To 1835 Apr 25 28-0125
Fr 1835 May 07# M234-136
Fr 1835 Jun 27 DLC-46
Fr 1835 Sep 23 DLC-47
Re 1835 Sep 26 mem DLC-47
Fr 1836 Oct 07 32-0103

Gwin Smedley & Co
Fr 1839 Dec 28 fin DLC-52

Gwin William McKendree
To 1834 Jul 03 26-0109
Fr 1834 Aug 08 DLC-44
Fr 1834 Aug 09 DLC-44
Fr 1835 Feb 20 M639-9
Fr 1836 Jan 21# DLC-47
To 1836 Feb 06 mem DLC-47
Fr 1839 Nov 30 DLC-52
To 1840 Jan 20# fin DLC-52
To 1840 Jan 20# fin DLC-52
To 1840 Dec 25 35-0132
To 1841 Jan 27 35-0214
Fr 1841 May 11 DLC-53
Fr 1841 May 31 DLC-53
To 1841 Jun 15 35-0325
Fr 1841 Dec 25 DLC-54
To 1842 Jan 11 35-0594
Fr 1842 Feb 10# DLC-54
Fr 1842 Feb 16 DLC-54
Fr 1842 Feb 16 DLC-54
Fr 1842 Mar 14 DLC-54
Fr 1842 Mar 14 DLC-54
To 1842 May 17 35-0716
Fr 1843 Jan 03 DLC-55
To 1843 Jan 16 35-1121
Fr 1844 Jul 11 DLC-57
Fr 1845 Jan 22 36-1393
Fr 1845 Apr 28 DLC-58
To 1845 May 09 37-0198

Gwinn Hall & Co
Fr 1819 Jan 23 fin DLC-26
Fr 1819 Feb 24 fin DLC-28

Gwynn William
To 1829 Oct 20# DLC-37
To 1829 Dec 16# DLC-37
Fr 1837 Feb 21 33-0800

Gwynne David
Fr 1829 Feb 16 M639-17

Hadden D & Co et al
Fr 1830 May 21 M639-5

Hadley Joshua
Re c1790 leg 1-0075a
Fr 1797 Oct 22 DLC-2

Hadley William
Re 1820 Sep 12 leg 7-1328

Hagan James
Re 1837 Mar 02 33-0982

Hagner Peter
Fr 1816 Oct 30 DLC-21
Fr 1816 Oct 30* 5-0551
Fr 1816 Nov 02 DLC-21
Fr 1816 Nov 02* 5-0563
Fr 1816 Nov 07 DLC-21
Fr 1816 Nov 07* 5-0569
Fr 1816 Nov 12 DLC-21
Fr 1816 Nov 12* 5-0583
To 1816 Dec 04 5-0593
Fr 1816 Dec 11 5-0601
Fr 1816 Dec 18 DLC-22
Fr 1816 Dec 18* 5-0632
Fr 1816 Dec 20 DLC-22
Fr 1816 Dec 20* 5-0633
Fr 1816 Dec 20 DLC-22
Fr 1816 Dec 20* 5-0634
Fr 1817 Jan 11 DLC-22
Fr 1817 Jan 11* 5-0679
Fr 1817 Oct 21 5-1114
Fr 1817 Nov 06 5-1125
To 1818 Jan 06 5-1227
To 1818 Jan 22 fin 5-1327
Fr 1818 Jan 22 fin 5-1329
Fr 1818 Jan 22 fin 5-1331
Fr 1818 Feb 05 5-1436
Fr 1818 May 15 6-0691
Fr 1818 May 15 fin 6-0692
Fr 1818 May 22 6-0783
Fr 1818 Jul 28 6-1162
To 1818 Aug 18 6-1243
Fr 1818 Sep 03 6-1283
Fr 1818 Oct 02 6-1336
Fr 1819 Apr 29# DLC-26
Fr 1819 Apr 29* 7-0502
Fr 1819 Jun 17 7-0555
Fr 1820 Mar 17 DLC-28
Fr 1820 Mar 17* 7-1049
To 1820 Apr 06 7-1065
To 1820 Apr 20 7-1078
Fr 1820 Apr 24 7-1080
To 1820 May 15 7-1096
Fr 1820 Nov 10 DLC-29
Fr 1820 Nov 10* 7-1406
Fr 1821 Jan 10 8-0057
Fr 1821 Apr 11 8-0306
To 1821 May 26 8-0530
To 1821 Nov 14 8-1350
To 1821 Nov 14* DLC-63
Fr 1821 Dec 18 DLC-31
Fr 1821 Dec 18* 8-1369
To 1822 Jan 11 8-1396
Fr 1823 Dec 23 9-0832
Fr 1824 Jan 01 9-0882
Fr 1824 Jan 07 9-0900
To 1824 Jan 19 10-0377
Fr 1824 Jan 19 10-0378
Fr 1824 Jan 31 10-0424
Fr 1824 Feb 02 10-0428
Fr 1824 Feb 07 10-0439
Fr 1824 Feb 12 10-0453
To 1824 Feb 20 10-0461
Fr 1824 Feb 21 10-0463
Fr 1824 Mar 01 10-0504
Fr 1824 Mar 01 M222-23

Hagner Peter (cont)
Fr 1824 Mar 01* 10-0505
Fr 1824 Apr 19 10-0659
Fr 1824 Apr 22 10-0677
Fr 1824 Apr 29 10-0698
Fr 1824 May 13 10-0721
Fr 1824 May 19 10-0730
Fr 1825 Jan 07 10-1045
To 1825 Jan 17 10-1074
Fr 1825 Jan 18 10-1077
Fr 1825 Feb 25 10-1156
Fr 1830 Jan 06# M222-27
To 1832 Sep 17 21-0025
Fr 1832 Oct 20 21-0111
Haight John H
Re 1831 Apr 28 par 17-1242
Re 1831 May 09 par 17-1314
Haight Samuel
Re 1835 Mar 24 27-1376
Haile Christopher Mason
Fr 1835 Oct 12 M688-86
Haile Robert
Fr 1829 Jan 30 M639-21
Haile William
Fr 1835 Sep 27 29-0131
Haines Thomas
To 1814 Dec 21 DLC-62
Halberstadt John
Fr 1835 Apr 04 M639-10
Fr 1835 Jul 13 M639-10
Halcyon plantation
Re 1839 Mar fin DLC-52
Re 1839 Jun 01 fin DLC-52
Hale John A
Fr 1844 May 08 DLC-56
Haley David W
To 1829 Sep 18# 13-1360
To 1829 Sep 18# M222-26
Fr 1829 Oct 08 M234-432
To 1829 Oct 15 DLC-37
Fr 1830 Jul 13 M234-185
Fr 1830 Jul 24 M234-185
Fr 1830 Sep 12 M234-169
Fr 1831 Mar 10 M234-169
Fr 1831 Apr 15 M234-169
Fr 1831 Apr 15* 17-1167
Fr 1831 May 29 M234-169
Fr 1831 May 29* 17-1473
Haley Elisha
Fr 1836 Jun M687-17
Hall Allen A
Fr 1828 Oct 20 12-0243
To 1828 Oct 31 12-0256
Fr 1833 Aug 28 M639-3
Fr 1833 Oct 30 M639-3
Fr 1834 Aug 17 DLC-44
Hall Bolling
Fr 1829 Jul 01 M234-237
Hall Charles Henry et al
Fr 1832 May 29 M639-12
Fr 1832 Jun 11 M639-12
Hall Charles M
Re 1805 Mar mem DLC-3
Re 1810 Jan 15 leg 2-0869
Fr 1811 Nov 26 fin DLC-71
Hall Dominick Augustin
To 1815 Mar 05# leg DLC-17
Fr 1815 Mar 06 leg 4-0821
To 1815 Mar 11 DLC-62
Re 1842 cJun 09 mem 35-0782
Re 1842 cJun 09 mem 35-0784
Re 1842 Jul 35-0829
Hall Elihu S
To 1813 Jul 22 chk DLC-6
Hall Elijah
Fr 1829 Apr 30 M625-405
Hall Elijah et al
Fr 1829 Mar 13 M639-4
Hall Elisha T
Fr 1814 Sep 10 DLC-12
Fr 1815 Feb 01 DLC-16
Fr 1815 Feb 06 DLC-16
Fr 1815 Feb 17 DLC-16
Fr 1816 Jun 26 DLC-20
Hall Francis
Re 1805 May 22 leg 2-0044
Hall George et al
Fr 1834 Oct 30 26-0774
Hall James
Fr c1829 M639-22
Fr 1832 Aug 29 20-1404
Hall James C
Fr 1832 Jan 01 fin DLC-40
To 1832 Jan 09 chk DLC-40
To 1833 Sep 14 chk DLC-43
Fr 1833 Sep 14 fin DLC-43
Fr 1834 Jun 09 fin DLC-44
To 1834 Jun 09 chk DLC-44
Fr 1835 Mar 01 fin DLC-47
Fr 1835 Apr 06 fin DLC-46
To 1835 Apr 06 chk DLC-46
To 1836 Jan 11 29-1546
Hall John
Fr 1808 Nov 22 fin DLC-4
To 1816 Jun 13 chk DLC-20
Hall John H
Fr 1829 Jun 08 M222-25
Hall Jonathan Prescott
Fr 1829 Apr 18# 13-0064
Hall Joseph
Fr 1835 Apr 23 M639-26
Fr 1835 Jun 29 28-0836
Fr 1836 Feb 08 M639-2
Fr 1836 Feb 22 30-0452
Fr 1837 Jan M687-28
Fr 1837 Feb 24 M687-16
Fr 1844 Nov 18 DLC-57
Hall Joseph et al
Fr 1829 May M639-24
Hall Joshua et al
Fr 1830 Feb 16 M639-22
Hall Luther
Fr 1837 Feb 09 M687-20
Hall Peter
Fr 1831 Jan 28 DLC-38
Hall Richard
Re 1832 Jan 05 par 19-0621
Hall Samuel
Fr 1844 Dec 02 DLC-57
Hall William
Re 1805 Mar mem DLC-3
Fr 1807 Mar 25 fin DLC-4
Re 1812 Jun 15 2-1103
Re 1812 Jun 15* DLC-5
To 1812 Nov 11 DLC-5
To 1812 Nov 11* DLC-61
To 1812 Dec 28 DLC-5
To 1812 Dec 28* DLC-61
To 1812 Dec 30 DLC-61

To 1813 Jan 11 DLC-61
To 1813 Nov 15 DLC-61
To 1813 Nov 15 DLC-61
To 1813 Nov 17 3-0618
To 1813 Dec 13 3-0661
To 1813 Dec 21 3-0692
To 1813 Dec 21* DLC-61
To 1813 Dec 24 3-0706
To 1813 Dec 24* DLC-61
Fr 1813 Dec 28 DLC-8
Fr 1813 Dec 28* 3-0724
Fr 1829 Jul 12 M639-9
Hall William et al
Fr 1832 Jan 10 M639-14
Fr 1834 Aug 16 26-0322
To 1834 Aug 18 26-0331
Fr 1844 Jul 26 36-0749
Hallet John
Fr 1833 Apr 23 22-1147
Halsey Robert
Fr 1844 Sep 02 DLC-57
Halsey Thomas Lloyd
Fr 1833 Jun 20 23-0045
Ham Yancey B
Re 1814 Jan 11 DLC-61
Hamblen John M A
To 1822 Jun 29 9-0202
Fr 1823 Jun 13 DLC-32
To 1824 Jun 13# 10-0788
Fr 1827 Jun 29 11-0716
Hambly William
Fr 1818 May 02 6-0539
Fr 1818 May 02* DLC-24
To 1825 Sep 08 10-1414
Hambright Frederick
Fr 1830 Feb 26 M639-23
Hambright Frederick et al
Fr 1835 cFeb 13 M639-17
Hambright John
To 1802 Apr 09 lnd 1-0977
Hambro Charles J
Re 1833 Sep 12 23-0701
Hamer Thomas Lyon
Fr 1830 Feb 03 M639-2
Fr 1830 Jul 15 16-0021
Fr 1834 Jan 10 24-0849
Fr 1836 Jun 25 DLC-48
Fr 1837 Jan 14 DLC-49
To 1837 Jan 17 32-1596
Fr 1837 Feb 18 DLC-50
Fr 1837 Feb 18* 33-0769
Hamer Thomas Lyon et al
Fr 1836 Feb 17 M639-12
Hamersley Thomas S
Re 1830 Mar 06 M273-25
Re 1830 Apr 09 M273-25
Hamilton Alexander
Fr 1829 Jul 04 M639-10
Hamilton Andrew
To 1843 Sep 02 35-1477
Fr 1845 Feb 28# fin DLC-57
Hamilton Andrew & Co
To 1842 Jan 06# fin DLC-54
Hamilton Andrew (VA)
To 1807 Jul 02 2-0510
To 1807 Aug 01 2-0531
Hamilton Archibald W
Fr 1829 Mar 23 M639-10
Fr 1829 Mar 23* M222-27
Hamilton Elias et al
Fr 1831 Nov M639-1
Hamilton Elizabeth (Schuyler)
Fr 1834 Jun 06 25-1271
Hamilton George P
Fr 1843 Aug 11 DLC-55
To 1843 Aug 22 35-1472
To 1843 Aug 22* DLC-55
Hamilton James
Re 1791 Apr 18 leg DLC-1
Re 1791 Aug leg 1-0098
Fr 1793 Nov 06 fin 1-0170
Hamilton James Jr
Fr 1821 Mar 07 8-0174
To 1824 Mar 10 10-0542
Fr 1824 Mar 10 10-0545
Fr 1827 Feb 16 DLC-34
Fr 1828 Mar 04 DLC-35
Fr 1828 May 25 DLC-35
To 1828 Jun 29 DLC-35
Fr 1828 Nov 15 DLC-35
Fr 1829 Feb 11 add 12-0501
Fr 1830 May 13 M688-70
Fr 1830 Nov 14 DLC-38
Fr 1831 Jan 07 M221-111
Fr 1832 Nov 16 M221-113
Fr 1844 May 22 36-0563
Hamilton James Alexander
To 1828 Jan 08 add 11-1025
Fr 1828 Jan 08 add 11-1039
Fr 1828 Feb 17 DLC-35
To 1828 Mar 11-1153
To 1828 Apr 29 DLC-35
Fr 1828 May 29 DLC-35
Fr 1828 Oct 03 DLC-35
Fr 1828 Nov 24 DLC-35
Fr c1829 12-0366
To 1829 Mar 04 12-0847
To 1829 Mar 04* DLC-60
Fr 1829 Mar 05 12-0855
Fr 1829 Mar 09 12-0903
Fr 1829 Mar 09 12-0909
Fr 1829 Mar 09 12-0911
Fr 1829 Mar 16 M124-117
To 1829 Mar 17 DLC-60
To 1829 Mar 19 12-1056
Fr 1829 Mar 26 12-1139
To 1829 Apr 24 13-0135
Fr 1829 May 16 13-0340
To 1829 Jul 15 13-0847
To 1829 Sep 11 13-1302
Re 1829 cDec mem 14-0712
To 1829 Dec 19 14-1072
Fr 1829 Dec 22 DLC-37
To 1830 Jan 01 14-1260
Fr 1830 Jan 04 DLC-37
Fr 1830 Mar 16 DLC-37
To 1830 May 03 15-0876
To 1830 May 13 15-0989
To 1830 May 18 15-1043
To 1830 May 29 15-1205
To 1830 Jun 03 15-1276
Fr 1830 Jun 03 DLC-38
Fr 1830 Jun 05 DLC-38
Fr 1830 Jun 07 15-1312
Fr 1830 Jun 27 DLC-38
To 1830 Jul 12 16-0015
Fr 1830 Jul 13 DLC-38
Fr 1830 Jul 23 16-0045

Hamilton James Alexander (cont)

Fr 1830 Jul 29 DLC-38
To 1830 Oct 05 16-0319
Fr 1830 Oct 16 16-0398
Fr 1830 Nov 09 DLC-38
Fr 1830 Dec 24# DLC-38
Fr c1831 DLC-40
Fr 1831 Feb 03 17-0418
Fr 1831 Feb 22 17-0606
Fr 1831 Feb 24 17-0650
To 1831 Apr 06 17-1073
To 1831 Apr 06* DLC-39
Fr 1831 Apr 09 17-1107
To 1831 Apr 12 17-1147
Fr 1831 Apr 14 DLC-39
Fr 1831 Apr 17 17-1185
To 1831 Apr 23 17-1207
Fr 1831 May 03 17-1274
Fr 1831 May 03 17-1275
To 1831 May 04 17-1277
To 1831 May 04* DLC-39
Fr 1831 May 05 17-1296
Fr 1831 May 18 17-1384
To 1831 May 22 17-1405
Fr 1831 May 22 17-1408
Fr 1831 May 23 M179-70
Fr 1831 Jun 28# DLC-39
Fr 1831 Jul 17 DLC-39
To 1831 Jul 23 18-0248
Fr 1831 Jul 28 DLC-39
Fr 1831 Aug 15 DLC-39
Fr 1831 Sep 01 DLC-40
To 1831 Sep 03 18-0661
Fr 1831 Sep 18 DLC-40
Fr 1831 Oct 12 M179-71
To 1831 Oct 23 18-1112
To 1831 Nov 12 18-1252
Fr 1831 Nov 24 18-1485
Fr 1831 Nov 25 18-1486
To 1831 Dec 12 19-0289
Fr 1832 Jan 12 DLC-40
Fr 1832 Jan 14 DLC-40
To 1832 Jan 18 19-0756
To 1832 Jan 27 19-0885
Fr 1832 Jan 29 19-0903
To 1832 Mar 28 19-1570
Fr 1832 Mar 31 DLC-40
To 1832 Apr 16 20-0247
Fr 1832 May 07 DLC-40
Fr 1832 Jun 15 20-0760
Fr 1832 Oct 20 DLC-41
To 1832 Nov 02 21-0265
To 1832 Nov 20# fin DLC-41
To 1832 Nov 26 21-0579
To 1832 Dec 06 21-0881
Fr 1832 Dec 13 DLC-41
Fr 1833 Jan 22 DLC-42
Fr 1833 Feb 18# DLC-42
To 1833 Feb 23 22-0458
Fr 1833 Feb 28 22-0542
Fr 1833 Apr 16# 22-1032
Fr 1833 Aug 13 DLC-43
Fr 1833 Aug 31 DLC-43
To 1833 Sep 08 23-0664
To 1833 Sep 13 23-0710
Fr 1833 Sep 13 DLC-43
Fr 1833 Sep 15 DLC-43
Fr 1833 Sep 16 DLC-43
Fr 1833 Sep 25 DLC-43
Fr 1833 Nov 18 DLC-43
Fr 1833 Dec 09 DLC-43
Fr 1833 Dec 13 DLC-43
To 1833 Dec 24 24-0582
Fr 1833 Dec 28 24-0618
To 1834 Feb 02 24-1138
Fr 1834 Feb 13# DLC-44
Fr 1834 Feb 24 DLC-44
Fr 1834 Jul 28 DLC-44
Fr 1834 Aug 01 26-0272
Fr 1834 Nov 29 26-1101
Fr 1835 Feb 16 DLC-45
To 1835 Sep 17 29-0062
Fr 1836 Aug 25 DLC-49
To 1836 Oct 11 32-0146
Fr 1837 Feb 24 33-0859
Fr 1837 Mar 11 DLC-50
Fr 1838 Feb 03 DLC-51
To 1838 Feb 23 34-0248

Hamilton John

Fr 1812 Feb 12 DLC-5

Hamilton Robert

Fr 1836 Jun 22 T809-1

Hamilton Samuel

Fr 1835 Feb 04 27-0387

Hamilton Samuel C

Fr 1836 Aug 06 M567-120

Hamilton Samuel S

Fr 1829 Apr 20# DLC-72

Hamilton Thomas

Fr 1829 Mar 02 M639-10

Hamilton William

Fr 1813 Dec 17 DLC-7
To 1813 Dec 18 DLC-61
Fr 1829 Apr 30 M222-25

Hamilton William Southerland

Fr 1816 Oct 08 DLC-21
Re 1829 Sep 08 13-1273

Hamilton William Stephen

Fr 1836 Jan 08 M639-11

Hamilton William Stephen et al

Fr 1836 Jan 12 M687-3
Fr 1836 Jan 14 M639-23
Fr 1836 cFeb 37-0346

Hamlin Hannibal

Fr 1837 Feb M687-20

Hamm John

Fr 1830 May 28 15-1183
Fr 1830 Jun 19 M639-23
Fr 1832 May 31 M10-3
Fr 1836 Jan 01 M639-27

Hamm John et al

Fr 1835 May 04 DLC-46

Hammett Alexander

Fr 1833 Dec 15 T224-2

Hammond Charles

Re 1827 DLC-59

Hammond Eli

To 1791 Mar 27# DLC-1
Re 1805 Jul 10 mem DLC-3
To 1805 Sep 23 fin DLC-3
Fr 1806 May 13 fin DLC-3
To 1807 Jan 05 fin DLC-4
To 1807 Mar 08 fin 2-0471
To 1808 May 16 DLC-4
To 1812 Jun 27 fin DLC-5
Fr 1812 Oct 08 leg DLC-5
To 1814 Feb 01 DLC-62
To 1814 Feb 08 DLC-62
To 1814 Feb 18 DLC-62

To 1814 Feb 22 DLC-62
Fr 1814 Feb 23 DLC-9
To 1814 May 05 DLC-10
Fr 1814 Jun 10 DLC-10
Fr 1814 Aug 28 DLC-11
To 1817 Nov 21 5-1145

Hammond J C P
Fr 1844 Nov 27 DLC-57

Hammond James Henry
Fr 1842 Dec 22 35-1056
To 1843 Jan 13 35-1116
To 1843 Jan 13* DLC-55

Hammond Samuel
Fr 1831 Dec 15 M639-6
Fr 1832 Dec 24 M179-74

Hammond William
Fr 1837 Jan 12 M688-103

Hammons Joseph et al
Fr 1831 M639-5

Hammons Leroy
Fr 1814 Nov 08 DLC-13
Fr 1814 Nov 30 DLC-14

Hamot Peter S V
Fr 1835 Oct 05# 29-0196

Hamot Peter S V et al
Fr 1835 Feb 04 DLC-45

Hampson James
Fr 1830 Jun 19 M639-23

Hampton John
Fr 1814 Mar 11 DLC-9
Fr 1814 Mar 11 DLC-66
Fr 1814 Mar 19 DLC-9
To 1814 Mar 23 DLC-9

Hampton Wade
Fr 1810 Jun 03 DLC-71
Fr 1810 Dec 02 DLC-71
Fr 1810 Dec 09 DLC-5

Hampton Wade Jr
Fr 1815 Nov 14 4-1231
To 1815 Nov 22 DLC-62

Hampton William et al
Fr 1833 Sep 29 M639-21

Hamretson James Jr et al
Fr 1832 Oct 23 DLC-41

Hancock & Co
Fr 1836 Dec 26# fin DLC-50

Hand John H
Fr 1830 Jul 26 M222-28

Hand Thomas
To 1836 Oct 31 chk DLC-49

Handy S W
Fr 1834 Jun 21 fin DLC-44

Handy Samuel
Re 1836 Sep 30 leg 31-1533

Haney William S
Fr 1845 Mar 22 37-0017

Hanham James R
Fr 1821 Jul 12 DLC-30
To 1821 Jul 28 8-0917
Fr 1821 Aug 13 DLC-30

Hankins Daniel et al
Fr 1831 Jan 31 DLC-39

Hankins William
To 1806 Nov 03 DLC-4

Hanna James
Fr 1794 Jul 01 fin DLC-1
Fr 1814 Jul 29 fin DLC-68

Hanna James J
Fr 1820 Jan 30 DLC-28
To 1820 Oct 05# fin DLC-29
Fr 1821 fin DLC-60
Fr 1821 Mar 01 DLC-29

Hanna Samuel
Fr 1829 Oct 24 14-0244

Hannah Eneas
To 1795 Jan 01 fin 1-0247

Hannah John
To 1803 ___ 12 fin 1-1070

Hannan Thomas L
Fr 1816 Aug 10 DLC-21

Hannegan Edward Allen
Fr 1833 Dec 03 24-0176
Fr 1833 Dec 03 24-0192
Fr 1835 Feb 19 27-0576
Fr 1835 Aug 26 M639-26

Hannegan Edward Allen et al
Fr 1835 Dec 12 M639-11

Hannum Richard M
Fr 1833 May 13 M234-530
Fr 1833 May 13* 22-1357

Hannum Washington L
Fr 1818 Jan 27 DLC-24
To 1821 Jul 24 DLC-63
Fr 1821 Oct 15 M116-9
Fr 1821 Oct 15 DLC-63
Fr 1829 Apr 06 M639-10

Hannum Washington L et al
Fr 1815 Feb 03 add DLC-16

Hanson Ellen M
Fr 1835 Mar 12 DLC-45
To 1835 Mar 25 DLC-45

Hanson J Thomas
Re 1836 Dec 31 mem 32-1445

Haralson Archibald
Fr 1829 Aug 18# M639-10

Haralson Lea
To 1831 Aug 06 lnd 18-0465

Harbert William
Fr 1844 Feb 06 DLC-56

Hardeman Nicholas Perkins
Fr 1795 Dec 08 lnd 1-0330
Fr 1801 Nov 18 lnd DLC-2
Fr 1801 Nov 18* lnd 1-0945

Hardeman Thomas
To 1797 Nov 28 1-0548

Hardeman William
Fr 1831 Apr 01 fin DLC-39

Hardia William
Fr 1833 Feb 04 22-0258

Hardin Amos
To 1802 Jun 05 lnd 1-1001

Hardin Benjamin
Fr 1835 Sep 22# DLC-47

Hardin Gibson
To 1802 Apr 09 lnd 1 0979

Hardin James
To 1802 Apr 09 lnd 1-0983
Fr 1813 Nov 17 DLC-7
To 1823 Nov 01 9-0727
Fr 1825 Apr 20 mem DLC-33

Hardin Joseph
To 1802 Apr 09 lnd 1-0984

Hardin Martin
To 1807 Jan 09 fin DLC-4

Hardin Martin Davis
Fr 1815 Feb 16 DLC-16

Harding Betsey
Re 1806 Feb 01 leg 2-0137

Harding J W Q
Fr 1831 Apr 02 DLC-39

Harding James
Fr 1815 Feb 13 DLC-16
Harding Joshua
Re 1829 Sep 08 par 13-1274
Re 1829 Sep 08* par T967-1
Harding Stephen
Re 1830 Oct 04 par 16-0308
Hardwicke Jonathan P
Fr 1841 Dec 10 DLC-54
To 1841 Dec 13 DLC-54
Hardwicke Jonathan P et al
Fr 1841 Oct 19 35-0453
To 1841 Oct 20 35-0454
Hardy James G et al
Fr 1829 Jan 26 M639-21
Hardy Sullivan
Fr 1831 Sep 08 M22-28
Hare Elizabeth
Fr 1833 Jul 14 M567-84
Hargrave John
Re 1834 Mar 24 par 25-0322
Re 1834 Apr 05 par 25-0593
Harker Samuel
Fr 1829 Aug 17 M639-10
Fr 1837 Mar 02 DLC-50
Fr 1837 Jun 28 DLC-50
Fr 1841 Oct 15 DLC-53
Harker Samuel et al
Fr 1835 Feb 04 M639-27
Harkins George W
Fr 1834 24-0696
Harlan Thomas
Fr 1816 Aug 08 DLC-21
Fr 1816 Dec 03 fin DLC-22
Harland Henry
Fr 1828 Jan 10# 11-1051
Harman Thomas et al
Fr 1833 Jan M639-16
Harman Thomas D
To 1814 Dec 11 DLC-62
Fr 1815 Jan 28 DLC-16
Harmeson Nathaniel
Fr 1839 Nov 13 DLC-52
Harney Benjamin Franklin
Fr 1816 Apr 30 DLC-20
Fr 1829 Sep 03 13-1248
Harney Robert B et al
Fr 1813 Dec 16 DLC-7
Fr 1813 Dec 16* DLC-61
To 1813 Dec 17 DLC-61
Harney Thomas
Re 1807 Oct 27 leg 2-0581
Fr 1808 Nov 05 DLC-4
Re 1814 Jun 07 leg 3-1082
Harney William Selby
Fr 1825 Jan 03 DLC-33
To 1836 Aug 15 M567-130
To 1836 Aug 15* M567-125
Harper _____
Fr 1836 May 01 30-1480
Harper Charles Carroll
Re 1829 Jun 01 13-0543
Harper Francis Jacob et al
Fr 1835 cFeb 13 M639-17
Harper James P
Fr 1844 Mar 15 36-0383
Harper Joseph Morrill
Fr 1830 Aug 30 M639-10
Fr 1835 Apr 28 M639-26
Harper Joseph Morrill et al
Fr 1833 Jan 23 M639-1
Harper Robert
Fr 1831 Oct 07 M639-10
Harper Samuel H
Fr 1829 Feb 21 M639-10
Fr 1829 Feb 26 M639-10
Fr 1829 Mar 07 M639-15
Harrington Jubal
Fr 1836 Apr 27 30-1375
Fr 1836 May 30-1432
Harrington Jubal et al
Fr 1830 Feb 16 M639-21
Harris Alfred M
Fr 1815 Jan 13 DLC-15
Harris Arnold
Re 1833 May 30 22-1525
Harris Carey A
To 1835 Jan 17 27-0247
To 1835 May 18 28-0458
Re 1835 cJun mem 28-0544
To 1835 Jun 16 28-0693
To 1835 Jun 16* M234-242
Fr 1835 Jun 17 M127-3
Fr 1835 Jul 03 M127-3
Fr 1835 Jul 09 M221-115
Fr 1835 Jul 09* M127-3
Fr 1835 Jul 28 M127-3
Fr 1835 Aug 10 M127-3
Fr 1835 Aug 11 M567-114
Fr 1835 Aug 11* M127-3
To 1835 Oct 23 29-0337
To 1836 Apr 29 30-1414
To 1836 May 27 31-0162
Fr 1836 May 31 M221-116
Fr 1836 May 31* 31-0219
Fr 1836 May 31* M127-3
Fr 1836 May 31 31-0221
Fr 1836 May 31* M127-3
Fr 1836 May 31* M21-18
Fr 1836 Jun 01 31-0256
Fr 1836 Jun 02 31-0271
Fr 1836 Jun 02* M127-3
Fr 1836 Jun 03 31-0285
Fr 1836 Jun 03* M127-3
Fr 1836 Jun 03* M21-19
Fr 1836 Jul 05# M234-145
Fr 1836 Jul 07 31-0934
Re 1836 Jul 18 31-1130
Fr 1836 Jul 20# 31-1136
Fr 1836 Jul 26 DLC-48
To 1836 Aug 07 31-1239
To 1836 Aug 07* DLC-48
Re 1836 Sep 08 31-1434
Re 1836 Oct 05 32-0061
To 1836 Oct 07# M234-137
To 1836 Oct 11# 32-0133
To 1836 Oct 11# 32-0158
Fr 1836 Oct 17 32-0209
Fr 1836 Oct 17* M127-3
Fr 1836 Oct 19 32-0231
Fr 1836 Oct 19* M127-3
To 1836 Oct 24# M567-117
Fr 1836 Nov 03 32-0397
Fr 1836 Nov 03 M234-244
Fr 1836 Nov 16# 32-0540
To 1836 Nov 20# 32-0567
Fr 1837 Feb 17# M234-225
Fr 1837 Feb 20# 33-0780

	Fr 1837 Jun 14		33-1299
	Fr 1838 Sep 15		DLC-51
Harris Clabon			
	Fr 1816 Jan 14		DLC-20
Harris Edwin L			
	Fr 1815 Feb 06		DLC-16
Harris Egbert			
	Fr 1822 Mar 27	fin	DLC-37
	To 1822 Apr 13		9-0114
	Fr 1822 Jul 27		DLC-31
	Fr 1822 Aug 13		DLC-31
	Fr 1822 Aug 24		DLC-31
	To 1822 Sep 30#	fin	DLC-31
	Fr 1823 Mar 28		DLC-32
Harris Elisha B			
	Fr 1834 Dec 12		26-1475
Harris J W			
	Fr 1817 Apr 07		DLC-71
Harris James			
	Fr 1814 Feb 03		DLC-61
Harris James et al			
	To 1814 Feb 19		DLC-62
Harris Jeremiah George			
	To c1839		37-0390
	To 1839 Apr		DLC-74
	Fr 1840 Jun 10		DLC-52
	Fr 1840 Jun 13		DLC-52
	To 1840 Jun 23		34-1439
	To 1840 cJun 30		DLC-52
	To 1840 Aug 18		DLC-74
	To 1840 Aug 21		34-1574
	Fr 1842 Sep 23		DLC-54
	To 1842 Sep 27		35-0953
	Fr 1842 Dec 12		35-1026
	To 1842 Dec 14		35-1030
	To 1842 Dec 23		35-1057
	Fr 1843 Jan 06		DLC-55
	Fr 1843 May 21		DLC-55
	Fr 1843 Jun 01		DLC-55
	Fr 1845 Feb 28		DLC-57
Harris John			
	Fr 1815 Jan 15		4-0547
	Fr 1830 Aug 05		M639-7
Harris John L			
	Fr 1829 Jun 26		M873-19
Harris Leavitt			
	Fr 1834 Aug 23		DLC-44
	Fr 1835 Apr 30#		M179-80
Harris Ludd			
	Fr 1821 Jun 13	fin	DLC-30
Harris Mark			
	Fr 1836 Apr 27		30-1378
Harris Reuben			
	Fr 1829 Sep 18#		13-1360
Harris Simpson			
	To 1805 Jul 29	fin	2-0071
Harris Thomas K			
	Fr 1804 Oct 10		DLC-3
Harris Thomson S			
	Fr 1831 Jan 11		M234-808
	Fr 1831 Jan 11*		17-0231
	Fr 1836 cApr 15		30-1183
Harris William			
	Fr 1814 Jan 04		DLC-8
	Fr 1818 Jun 25	fin	DLC-69
	Fr 1818 Jun 25*	fin	6-1078
	Fr 1818 Jun 27	fin	DLC-69
	To 1818 Jul 10		6-1120
Harrisburg PA citizens			
	To 1833 Jun		22-1544
Harrison Albert Galliton			
	Fr 1829 Feb 17#		M639-10
	Fr 1834 Feb 24		24-1458
	Fr 1836 Apr 27		M639-7
	Fr 1836 May 14		M639-21
	Fr 1836 May 23		M639-19
	Fr 1836 Jun 17		M639-20
	Fr 1836 Jun 20		M567-127
	Fr 1836 Jun 30		M234-931
	To 1837 Feb 23#		33-0845
	Fr 1838 Aug 15		DLC-51
Harrison Albert Galliton et al			
	Fr 1836 cSep		M22-41
Harrison Alexander			
	To 1833 Jun 16		23-0039
Harrison B J			
	Fr 1835 Jul 25		M124-148
Harrison Edward Augustus			
	Fr 1835 Feb 04		27-0392
	Fr 1835 Aug 06		28-1244
Harrison Landon			
	To 1845 Feb 11	lnd	36-1481
Harrison Micajah			
	Fr 1829 Feb 10		M639-10
Harrison P			
	Fr 1811		DLC-5
	Fr 1811 Nov 18		DLC-5
Harrison Richard			
	Fr 1797 Jan 17		DLC-1
	Fr 1832 Mar 19		19-1506
	Fr 1832 May 05		20-0476
	Fr 1836 Oct 05		32-0062
Harrison Robert Monroe			
	Fr 1829 Apr 07		M639-10
	Re 1831 Feb 03		17-0420
Harrison Thomas			
	Fr 1837 Jan 19		33-0034
Harrison Thomas T			
	Fr 1831 Nov 14	fin	DLC-40
	Fr 1833 Mar 14		DLC-42
	To 1836 Mar 05#	lnd	DLC-47
	Fr 1838 Feb 22	lnd	DLC-51
	To 1838 Feb 23	lnd	34-0252
	Fr 1839 Sep 02#	fin	DLC-52
Harrison Timothy J			
	Fr 1833 Jan 30		M688-93
Harrison William			
	Fr 1806 Jun 30		2-0283
Harrison William A			
	Fr 1829 Jun 15		M639-10
	Fr 1834 Jan 04		24-0750
	Fr 1835 Nov 10		M639-18
Harrison William Henry			
	To 1811 Nov 28		M221-44
	To 1811 Nov 28*		DLC-5
	Fr 1815 Apr 20		4-1003
	To 1824 Aug 18		10-0853
	Re 1829 Jun 09	mem	13-0603
Harrison & Sterett			
	Fr 1829 Jun 19		13-0684
Harryman Charles			
	To 1806 May 01	lnd	2-0229
	Fr 1829 Jan 29		DLC-36
Hart James			
	Fr 1810 Aug 26		DLC-4
	Fr 1810 Oct 23		DLC-4
Hart John			
	Fr 1840 Apr 18		DLC-52

Hart John D
Fr 1833 Jan 03 21-1312
Hart Joseph C
Fr 1829 Oct 12 M639-10
Hart R W
Fr 1814 Sep 04 DLC-12
Fr 1814 Oct 17 DLC-13
Fr 1814 Nov 19 DLC-14
Hart Simeon
Fr 1829 Jun 23 13-0701
Hartsher J C
Fr 1835 Aug 15 M639-15
Hartshorn J
Fr 1837 Oct 05# fin DLC-51
Hartsill ______ (Lt)
Re 1813 Dec 29 DLC-61
Harttell Thomas
Fr 1837 Jan 16 DLC-49
Hartwell Calvin
Fr 1842 Jan 19 DLC-54
Harvey John et al
Fr 1829 Dec 24 M639-17
Harvey Jonathan
To 1828 May 06 11-1240
Fr 1829 Feb 26 12-0591
Fr 1831 Feb 28 17-0670
Harvey Jonathan et al
Fr 1829 Feb 24 12-0579
Fr 1829 Dec 11 14-1006
Fr 1829 Dec 17 14-1057
Fr 1832 Feb 16 M639-18
Harvey L S
Fr 1834 Aug 21 fin DLC-45
Harvey Louisa
Re 1830 Jan 02 par 14-1300
Harvey Matthew
Fr 1829 Sep 21 M639-6
Re 1830 Nov 02 16-0642
Harvey Reuben Jr
Re 1831 Feb 15 17-0532
Harvey William
Fr 1821 Apr 19 fin DLC-30
Fr 1821 Sep 13 DLC-30
Harvey William P
Fr 1832 Mar 20 DLC-40
Harwell Buckner Jr
Fr 1814 Apr 04 DLC-10
Harwell William T L
To 1823 Jun 11 fin DLC-32
Fr 1823 Jun 11 DLC-32
Fr 1823 Aug 31 fin DLC-32
Harwood Richard
Fr 1829 Dec 31 M567-44
Haskell Jesse
Fr 1829 Jul 15 M639-10
Haskell Joshua
Fr 1814 Feb 09 DLC-8
Fr 1814 Feb 09 DLC-8
Fr 1814 Feb 11 DLC-8
Fr 1814 Feb 11 DLC-8
To 1814 Feb 13 DLC-62
Fr 1814 Feb 15 DLC-9
To 1814 Feb 16 DLC-62
Fr 1814 Feb 18 DLC-9
To 1814 Feb 19 DLC-61
Fr 1814 Feb 19 DLC-9
Fr 1814 Feb 20 DLC-9
Fr 1814 Feb 22 DLC-9
To 1814 Feb 28 DLC-61
Fr 1814 Feb 28 DLC-9
Fr 1814 Mar 02 DLC-9
Fr 1815 Jan 10 DLC-16
Fr 1825 May 28 add DLC-33
Fr 1825 May 30 DLC-33
To 1825 Jun 18 add 10-1312
Haskins Francis J
Re 1836 Oct 20 par 32-0253
Hasnell Nathan B
Fr 1837 Feb 27 M687-20
Hassert Luke
Fr 1830 Jan 18 M688-68
Hassinger David S
Fr 1829 Aug 25 M639-23
Hassler Ferdinand Rudolph
Fr 1834 Apr 03 25-0575
Fr 1834 Apr 06 25-0603
Fr 1834 Oct 25 26-0722
Fr 1835 Feb 05 27-0407
Fr 1835 May 14 mem 28-0396
To 1836 Aug 02# 31-1193
Hastings Mathew et al
Fr 1835 Jun 22 28-0758
Haszard Albert Arnold
Fr 1844 Oct 25 DLC-57
Hatch Elizabeth et al
Fr 1831 Nov 18-1165
To 1831 Dec 05 19-0077
Hattum John
Re 1806 Sep 23 leg 2-0342
Hauck John
Fr 1842 Jun 08 DLC-54
To 1842 Jun 21 DLC-54
Haugh J H
To 1840 Jul 22 chk DLC-53
Haughan John
To 1838 Jun 07# fin DLC-51
Re 1840 Jun 08# leg 34-1399
Re 1842 Sep# leg 35-0913
Haughey James C
Re 1830 Jun 12 par 15-1360
Havenor Charles
Fr 1831 Sep 26 M22-28
Havens Joseph
Fr 1834 Dec 19 DLC-45
Hawes William
Fr 1814 Jan 07 DLC-8
Fr 1814 Jan 23 DLC-8
Hawkes Gilbert
Fr 1843 Dec 29 DLC-56
Hawkins Benjamin
To 1814 Jun 13 DLC-62
To 1814 Jul 11 DLC-62
Fr 1814 Aug 06 DLC-11
Fr 1814 Aug 06* DLC-62
Fr 1814 Aug 06* M221-63
To 1814 Aug 10 DLC-62
Fr 1814 Aug 30 DLC-11
To 1814 Sep 12 M221-65
To 1814 Sep 19 4-0230
Fr 1814 Oct 02 DLC-12
To 1814 Oct 13 DLC-62
To 1814 Oct 22 DLC-62
Fr 1814 Oct 23 DLC-75
To 1814 Oct 31 DLC-62
Fr 1814 Nov 04 DLC-13
Fr 1814 Nov 11 DLC-14
To 1814 Nov 15 DLC-62
To 1814 Nov 16 4-0355

	Fr 1814 Dec 13		4-0396
	Fr 1814 Dec 27		DLC-15
	Fr 1815 Feb 27		DLC-17
	To 1815 Mar 20		M221-62
	Fr 1815 Mar 24		DLC-17
	Fr 1815 May 05		DLC-18
	Fr 1815 May 05*		M221-62
	Fr 1815 May 26		DLC-18
	Fr 1815 May 26*		4-1058
	Fr 1815 Jul 17		DLC-18
	Fr 1815 Aug 04		DLC-19
	Fr 1815 Aug 04*		M221-62
	Fr 1815 Aug 12		DLC-19
	To 1815 Aug 14		4-1157
	To 1815 Aug 14*		DLC-62
	To 1815 Sep 04	mem	DLC-62
	Fr 1815 Dec 01		DLC-19
	Fr 1815 Dec 08		DLC-19
	Fr 1816 Mar 21		DLC-20
	Fr 1816 Apr 21		DLC-20
Hawkins Benjamin (Creek)			
	Fr 1830 Feb 25		M234-236
	Fr 1830 Feb 27		M234-236
	Fr 1830 Mar 22		M234-236
Hawkins Edgar			
	To 1821 May 05		DLC-63
Hawkins Joseph C			
	To 1830 Dec 21#		DLC-73
Hawkins Joseph H			
	Fr 1811 Feb 18		DLC-5
	Fr 1811 Jun 09		DLC-5
Hawkins Olney et al			
	Fr 1835 Nov		M639-9
Hawkins Pleasant			
	Re 1813 Oct 29		DLC-61
Hawkins Richard			
	Re 1836 Nov 22	par	32-0575
Hawkins Richard C			
	Fr 1832 Nov 02		21-0267
Hawkins Samuel			
	Fr 1816 Oct 04		M221-60
Hawkins William G			
	Fr 1831 Jan		17-0106
Hawkins William G et al			
	Fr 1832 Apr 14		M22-29
Hawley Betsey			
	Fr 1829 Mar 19		T229-1
	Fr 1829 Apr 04		T229-1
	Fr 1829 Apr 30		T229-1
	Fr 1833 Jul 27		T229-1
	Fr 1833 Sep 10		T229-1
	Fr 1833 Nov 14		T229-1
	Fr 1834 Feb 20		T229-1
	Fr 1836 May 24		M179-82
Hawley William			
	Fr 1831 Jul 20		DLC-39
Haxtun Washington M			
	Re 1833 Oct 17		23-1055
	Fr 1835 Sep 12		M639-10
Hay Ann			
	Fr 1797 Aug 25#	fin	DLC-1
Hay David			
	Re 1793 May	leg	1-0159
Hay George			
	To 1829 Apr 19		13-0072
Hay James S			
	Fr 1828 Dec 27		DLC-36
Hayden Chester et al			
	Fr 1832 Dec 26		M639-16
Hayden William			
	Re 1830 Jun 05	par	15-1293
Hayden William Jr			
	Fr 1824 Mar 29		DLC-32
	To 1824 Mar 30		10-0610
	To 1824 Mar 30*		DLC-32
Haydon Mary A			
	Fr 1839 Feb 04		34-0620
Hayes Isaac Austin			
	Re 1829 Jun 08		13-0593
Hayes Oliver Bliss			
	Fr 1843 Jun 23		DLC-55
	Fr 1844 Jun 06		DLC-57
Hayes R P			
	Fr 1825 Aug 13		DLC-33
	To 1825 Aug 14		DLC-33
Hayes Thomas S			
	Re 1830 Dec 02	par	16-0964
Hayes William A et al			
	Fr 1837 Feb		M687-16
Hayman William			
	Fr 1834 Apr 07	fin	DLC-44
	Fr 1834 Aug 05	fin	DLC-44
	Fr 1834 Oct 13	fin	DLC-45
	Fr 1835 Apr 07	fin	DLC-46
	Fr 1835 Jun 09	fin	DLC-46
	Fr 1835 Jul 07	fin	DLC-46
	Fr 1835 Aug 01	fin	DLC-46
	Fr 1835 Oct 10	fin	DLC-47
	Fr 1835 Nov 03	fin	DLC-47
	Fr 1836 May 19	fin	DLC-48
Hayne Arthur Peronneau			
	Fr 1814 Sep 05		M222-16
	Fr 1814 Oct 17		DLC-13
	Fr 1814 Oct 20		DLC-13
	Fr 1814 Oct 23		DLC-13
	Fr 1814 Oct 25		DLC-13
	Fr 1814 Dec 01		DLC-14
	Fr 1814 Dec 10		DLC-14
	Fr 1814 Dec 15		DLC-14
	Fr 1815 Jan 10		M221-63
	Fr 1815 Jan 13		M221-16
	Fr 1815 Jan 20		DLC-15
	Fr 1815 Jan 20		DLC-15
	To 1815 Jan 25		M222-16
	To 1815 Jan 25*		DLC-15
	Fr 1815 Mar 24		DLC-17
	Fr 1815 Sep 16		DLC-19
	Fr 1815 Sep 20		DLC-19
	Fr 1815 Dec 20		4-1296
	Fr 1816 Jan 24		DLC-15
	Fr 1816 Mar 27		DLC-20
	Fr 1816 May 31		DLC-20
	Fr 1816 Jul 11		DLC-21
	Fr 1816 Nov 27		DLC-22
	Fr 1817 Jan 10		DLC-22
	Fr 1817 Jun 11#		DLC-22
	Fr 1817 Jul 19		DLC-23
	Fr 1817 Aug 05		DLC-23
	To 1818 Jan 21		M221-78
	To 1818 Jan 21		M221-78
	Fr 1818 Feb 01		DLC-24
	To 1818 Feb 11		6-0015
	Fr 1818 Feb 13		DLC-24
	Fr 1818 Feb 22		DLC-24
	Fr 1818 Mar 09		DLC-24
	Fr 1818 Mar 09*		M221-78
	Fr 1818 Mar 10		DLC-24
	Fr 1818 Mar 10*		M221-78

Hayne Arthur Peronneau (cont)		
Fr 1818 Mar 19		DLC-24
Fr 1818 Mar 19*		M221-78
Fr 1818 Mar 29		DLC-24
Fr 1818 Apr 01		DLC-24
Fr 1818 Sep 16		DLC-25
Fr 1819 Jan 21		DLC-26
Fr 1819 Jan 21		DLC-26
Fr 1819 Mar 06		DLC-26
Fr 1819 Jun 04		DLC-27
Fr 1819 Jun 12		DLC-27
Fr 1819 Jun 12		DLC-27
Fr 1819 Jul 07		DLC-27
Fr 1819 Aug 18		DLC-27
To 1819 Dec 04		7-0907
Fr 1819 Dec 15		DLC-28
Fr 1820 Mar 04		DLC-28
Fr 1820 Apr 03		DLC-28
Fr 1820 Jun 10		DLC-29
Fr 1820 Jun 10*		M222-21
Fr 1820 Aug 06		DLC-29
Fr 1820 Aug 06		7-1187
To 1820 Aug 10		DLC-63
Fr 1821 Jun 24		DLC-30
Fr 1823 Oct 07		DLC-32
Fr 1824 Apr 16		DLC-32
Fr 1824 Sep 18		DLC-33
Fr 1825 Jan 11		DLC-33
Fr 1825 Sep 05		DLC-33
Fr 1825 Nov 15		DLC-33
Fr 1826 Jan 14		DLC-33
Fr 1826 Apr 06		DLC-33
Fr 1826 Jul 20		DLC-59
Fr 1826 Oct 26		DLC-34
Fr 1827 Mar 28		DLC-34
To 1827 May 03		DLC-34
Fr 1827 Oct 15		DLC-34
Fr 1827 Dec 27		DLC-35
Fr 1828 Mar 12		DLC-35
Fr 1828 Sep 20		DLC-35
Fr 1828 Nov 15		DLC-35
Re c1829		12-0368
Fr 1829 May 03		M639-10
Fr 1829 Nov 03		DLC-37
Fr 1830 Apr 17		15-0747
To 1830 Apr 27		DLC-38
Fr 1830 May 22		M124-124
Fr 1831 Jan 07		DLC-38
Fr 1834 Feb 15		24-1397
Fr 1835 Mar 31		DLC-46
Fr 1835 Apr 07		DLC-46
Fr 1835 Apr 13		28-0042
Fr 1835 Nov 11		DLC-47
Fr 1835 Nov 13		DLC-47
To 1835 Nov 13		DLC-47
Fr 1835 Nov 13		DLC-47
Fr 1835 Dec 15		DLC-47
To 1836 Feb 15		30-0394
Fr 1836 Feb 23		DLC-47
Fr 1836 Apr 11		DLC-48
To 1836 Apr 17		30-1220
Fr 1836 Apr 28		DLC-48
Fr 1836 Aug 12		DLC-48
Fr 1836 Aug 15		DLC-48
Fr 1836 Oct 25#		M567-125
Fr 1836 Dec 11		DLC-49
Fr 1837 Sep 07		DLC-50
To 1837 Sep 28		33-1492
Fr 1838 Feb 09		DLC-51
Fr 1838 May 21		DLC-51
Fr 1838 Jun 01		DLC-51
Fr 1838 Jun 08		DLC-51
Fr 1838 Jul 29		DLC-51
Fr 1839 Mar 02		DLC-52
Fr 1840 Jun 21		DLC-52
Fr 1843 Dec 25#		DLC-56
Fr 1844 Jul 23		DLC-57
Fr 1845 Jan 14		DLC-57
Fr 1845 Feb 18		M873-38
Fr 1845 Mar 05		DLC-57
Hayne Elisa		
Fr 1829 Dec 01		DLC-37
Hayne Frances D		
Fr 1818 Aug 13#		DLC-25
Fr 1819 Feb 14#		DLC-26
Hayne James M et al		
Fr 1835 Feb 14		M124-146
Hayne Robert Young		
To 1819 Oct 02		7-0698
Fr 1819 Nov 10		DLC-72
Fr 1827 Jun 05		DLC-34
To 1827 Jul 09		11-0737
Fr 1828 Sep 03		DLC-35
Fr 1828 Dec 18		DLC-36
Fr 1829 May 11		13-0308
To 1830 Mar 06		15-0309
To 1830 Apr 26		DLC-38
Fr 1830 May 28		15-1184
Fr 1830 Dec 28		M124-125
Fr 1831 Feb 04		DLC-39
To 1831 Feb 08		17-0466
To 1831 Feb 08*		DLC-39
Fr 1831 Feb 14		DLC-39
Fr 1837 Nov 20		34-0032
Haynes James		
To 1803 Dec 05	fin	DLC-71
Haynes John D et al		
Fr 1836 May		30-1435
Haynes William Scott		
Fr 1841 Jan 20#		37-0540
Hays ______		
Fr 1831 Apr 05		17-1068
Hays A A B		
Fr 1829 May 22		13-0375
Hays Aizea		
Re 1813 May 04		3-0392
Hays Andrew		
To 1807 Feb 18	lnd	2-0468
Fr 1829 Apr 04		M639-2
Fr 1829 Apr 04		M639-2
To 1842 Sep 08		35-0933
Hays Andrew et al		
Fr 1811 Mar 15	lnd	DLC-5
Fr 1811 Mar 15*	lnd	2-0996
Hays Andrew C		
Fr 1821 Mar 07		DLC-29
Hays D A		
To 1802 Oct 09#	fin	DLC-2
Hays Elizabeth		
To 1793 Nov 30	fin	DLC-1
Hays Harmon A		
Fr 1815 Jun 09		DLC-18
Fr 1815 Jul 14		DLC-18
To 1828 Aug 13		12-0130
Fr 1828 Sep 25		DLC-35
Hays Jane (Donelson)		
Fr 1825 May 10#		37-0422
Hays John		
To 1797 Apr 01	lnd	1-0502

Hays John B			
	Fr 1828 Aug 01		DLC-35
Hays Joseph			
	Fr 1806 Nov 19	fin	DLC-4
Hays Martha Thompson			
	To 1802 Jul 13	lnd	1-1016
Hays Nathaniel			
	Fr 1804 Aug 20#	fin	DLC-3
	Fr 1804 Aug 23	lnd	DLC-3
	Fr 1804 Aug 23*	lnd	1-1362
	To 1808 Jul 19	lnd	DLC-4
	Re 1808 Sep 30	fin	2-0726
	Fr 1809 Jun 07		DLC-4
Hays Rachel			
	To 1802 Jul 13	lnd	1-1016
Hays Richard Jackson			
	To 1843 Feb 10		35-1211
Hays Robert			
	To 1790 Mar 04#		1-0075g
	To 1794 Dec 12	leg	1-0244
	Fr 1795 Jul 25		DLC-75
	Fr 1796 Nov 07	leg	DLC-1
	To 1796 Dec 06		1-0457
	To 1796 Dec 16		DLC-71
	To 1797 Jan		1-0469
	To 1797 Jan 08		DLC-1
	To 1797 Feb 17		DLC-71
	To 1797 Nov	fin	DLC-2
	To 1797 Nov 02		DLC-2
	To 1798 Jan 12		DLC-2
	To 1798 Jan 25		DLC-2
	To 1798 Mar 02		DLC-2
	To 1798 Aug 18#	fin	DLC-2
	To 1799 Sep		DLC-2
	To 1800 Feb 18		DLC-2
	To 1800 Mar 03		DLC-2
	To 1800 Jul 13		DLC-2
	To 1800 Jul 13		1-0776
	To 1800 Aug 10		DLC-2
	To 1800 Sep 05		1-0778
	To 1800 Sep 26		DLC-71
	To 1801 Aug 24		DLC-71
	To 1801 Sep 09		DLC-2
	To 1801 Sep 23		DLC-2
	Fr 1802 Jul 13	lnd	1-1020
	Fr 1802 Jul 13*	lnd	DLC-2
	To 1803 Jul 04		1-1127
	Fr 1803 Dec 15		DLC-3
	To 1804 Nov 18#	fin	DLC-3
	Re 1806	mem	2-0108
	Fr 1806 Feb 03		2-0144
	To 1807 Mar 09#		2-0472
	Re 1807 May	mem	DLC-75
	Re 1807 Sep 15	mem	DLC-4
	Re 1807 Oct 17		DLC-4
	Re 1807 Nov 25	leg	2-0594
	To 1807 Dec 07		2-0596
	To 1808 Feb 05		2-0611
	Fr 1808 Feb 13#		DLC-4
	Re 1812 Sep		DLC-1
	To 1812 Dec 04		2-1279
	Fr 1813 Oct 26		DLC-7
	Fr 1813 Nov 02		DLC-7
	To 1814 Jan 04		3-0781
	To 1814 Feb 22#		3-0889
	Fr 1814 Feb 25		DLC-9
	Fr 1814 Mar 06		DLC-9
	To 1814 Sep 16		DLC-12
	Fr 1814 Dec 20		DLC-14
	To 1814 Dec 23		DLC-14
	To 1814 Dec 26		4-0468
	Fr 1814 Dec 29		DLC-15
	To 1815 Jan 26		DLC-15
	To 1815 Feb 04		DLC-16
	To 1815 Feb 09		DLC-16
	To 1815 Feb 09		DLC-71
	To 1815 Feb 17		DLC-16
	To 1815 Mar 05#		DLC-71
	To 1815 Mar 06		DLC-71
	Fr 1815 Mar 10		DLC-17
	To 1815 Dec 15		4-1289
	To 1816 Jan 02		DLC-15
Hays Samuel Jackson			
	Fr 1829 Mar 29#		12-1173
	To 1829 Oct 09	chk	DLC-37
	To 1829 Oct 30	chk	DLC-37
	To 1830 Apr 08	chk	DLC-38
	To 1830 Apr 19		15-0753
	Fr 1830 May 05		DLC-38
	To 1830 May 31		15-1239
	Fr 1830 Sep 12		DLC-38
	To 1830 Oct 02		16-0299
	To 1830 Nov 21		16-0825
	To 1830 Dec 07		16-1348
	Fr 1831 Jan 03		DLC-38
	To 1831 Apr 23		17-1210
	To 1831 Dec 06		19-0168
	Fr 1831 Dec 13		DLC-40
	Fr 1832 Aug 21#	fin	DLC-41
	Fr 1834 Jun 23		DLC-44
	To c1835		27-0056
	To 1835 Mar 11		27-1081
	Fr 1836 Dec 26		DLC-49
	Fr 1837 May 31		DLC-50
	Fr 1839 Jun 09		DLC-52
	To 1839 Jun 16		34-0824
	To 1839 Dec 20		34-1099
	Fr 1840 May 02		DLC-52
	Fr 1840 Dec 23		DLC-53
	Fr 1841 Apr 23		DLC-53
	To 1841 May 04		35-0297
	Fr 1841 Oct 20		DLC-53
	Fr 1844 May 20		DLC-56
	To 1845 May 27		37-0228
Hays Stockley Donelson			
	Fr 1807 Apr 20		DLC-71
	Fr 1807 Apr 20#		2-0490
	Fr 1808 Nov 06		DLC-4
	Fr 1809 Jan 28		2-0769
	Fr 1809 Jun 17		DLC-4
	To 1811 Mar 18	lnd	2-0998
	Fr 1812 Mar 09		DLC-5
	To 1813 Nov 22		DLC-75
	To 1813 Nov 22*		DLC-61
	Fr 1813 Nov 26		DLC-7
	To 1813 Dec 13		DLC-61
	To 1813 Dec 21		DLC-61
	To 1813 Dec 21		DLC-7
	Fr 1813 Dec 27		DLC-8
	Fr 1813 Dec 29		DLC-8
	Fr 1813 Dec 29		DLC-8
	To 1814 Jan 27		DLC-62
	To 1814 Jan 31		DLC-62
	To 1814 Feb 02		DLC-62
	To 1814 Feb 05		DLC-62
	To 1814 Feb 08		DLC-62
	To 1814 Feb 09		DLC-62
	To 1814 Feb 09		DLC-62

Hays Stockley Donelson (cont)

To 1814 Feb 10 DLC-62
To 1814 Feb 11 DLC-62
Fr 1814 Feb 15 DLC-9
To 1814 Feb 19 DLC-61
Fr 1814 Feb 25 DLC-9
To 1814 Mar 01 DLC-9
To 1814 Mar 13 DLC-62
To 1814 Mar 14 DLC-9
Fr 1814 Mar 22 DLC-9
Fr 1814 Apr 12 DLC-10
Fr 1814 Apr 17 DLC-10
Fr 1814 Apr 21 DLC-10
Fr 1814 May 21 DLC-10
To 1814 Aug 31 DLC-62
Fr 1814 Sep 04 DLC-12
Fr 1814 Nov 20 DLC-14
Fr 1815 Jan 06 DLC-15
To 1815 Dec 16 chk DLC-19
Fr 1819 Oct 20 M221-21
Fr 1819 Oct 27 DLC-28
Fr 1820 Nov 12 DLC-29
Fr 1820 Nov 12* 7-1407
To 1821 May 18 DLC-63
Fr 1830 Sep 21 M234-136
Fr 1830 Sep 21* 16-0254
Re 1830 Dec 20 mem 16-1504
Re 1830 Dec 23 mem DLC-38
Re 1831 Mar 08 mem DLC-73
Fr 1831 Jun 13 18-0005

Hayward Elijah

Fr 1829 Apr 01 12-1225
Fr 1830 Feb 12 15-0138
Re 1830 Sep 30 16-0276
Fr 1830 Oct 27 M25-26
Fr 1830 Nov 26 M25-26
Fr 1830 Dec 10 16-1369
Fr 1830 Dec 10* M25-26
Fr 1830 Dec 10# 16-1377
Fr 1831 Jan 19 17-0295
Fr 1831 Jan 19* M25-26
Fr 1831 Mar 17 M25-26
Fr 1831 Mar 23 M25-26
Fr 1831 May 19 17-1391
Fr 1831 Jul 15 M25-26
To 1831 Sep 05# DLC-40
Fr 1831 Sep 30 M25-26
To 1831 Oct 14 18-0993
Fr 1831 Oct 19 M25-26
Fr 1831 Oct 26 M25-26
To 1831 Oct 26# 18-1136
Fr 1831 Dec 27 M25-27
Fr 1832 Jan 07 19-0633
Fr 1832 Jan 12 19-0665
Fr 1832 Jan 12* M25-27
Fr 1832 Jan 16 M25-27
Fr 1832 Jan 16* 19-0703
Fr 1832 Jan 21 19-0813
Fr 1832 Jan 21* M25-27
Fr 1832 Jan 30 M25-27
Fr 1832 Feb 07 DLC-40
Fr 1832 Feb 29 19-1256
Fr 1832 Feb 29* M25-27
Fr 1832 Feb 29 19-1260
Fr 1832 Feb 29* M25-27
Fr 1832 Mar 14 19-1462
Fr 1832 Mar 14* M25-27
Fr 1832 Mar 20 M25-27
Fr 1832 Mar 26 19-1553
Fr 1832 Mar 26* M25-27
Fr 1832 Apr 28 20-0398
Fr 1832 Jun 11 M25-27
Fr 1832 Jun 12 M25-27
Fr 1832 Jun 16 M25-27
Fr 1832 Jun 18 M25-27
Fr 1832 Jul 11 20-1025
Fr 1832 Jul 11 20-1027
Fr 1832 Jul 11 20-1029
Fr 1832 Jul 11 20-1031
Fr 1832 Jul 11 20-1033
Fr 1832 Jul 11 20-1035
Fr 1832 Jul 11 20-1037
Fr 1832 Jul 11 20-1039
Fr 1832 Jul 11 20-1041
Fr 1832 Jul 11 20-1043
Fr 1832 Jul 11 20-1045
Fr 1832 Oct 22 M25-28
To 1832 Nov 03 21-0297
Fr 1832 Nov 08 21-0351
Fr 1832 Nov 08* M25-28
Fr 1832 Dec 24 M639-24
To c1833# 37-0310
Fr 1833 Jan 04 21-1318
Fr 1833 Jan 04* M25-28
To 1833 Jan 16# 21-1442
Fr 1833 Jan 22# 22-0019
Fr 1833 Jan 22* M733-1
Fr 1833 Jan 23 22-0026
Fr 1833 Jan 23* M25-28
Fr 1833 Jan 24 22-0043
Fr 1833 Jan 24* M25-28
Fr 1833 Jan 24 22-0046
Fr 1833 Jan 24* M25-28
Fr 1833 Jan 24 22-0049
Fr 1833 Jan 24* M25-28
Fr 1833 Jan 24 22-0052
Fr 1833 Jan 24* M25-28
Fr 1833 Feb 01 M25-28
Fr 1833 Feb 04 22-0260
Fr 1833 Feb 15# 22-0388
Fr 1833 Feb 15* M733-1
Fr 1833 Feb 21 M25-28
Fr 1833 Feb 26 22-0484
Fr 1833 Feb 26 22-0503
Fr 1833 Feb 26 22-0508
Fr 1833 Feb 26 22-0511
Fr 1833 Feb 26 22-0515
Fr 1833 Feb 27 22-0526
Fr 1833 Feb 28 M25-28
To 1833 Mar 02 22-0594
Fr 1833 Mar 09 22-0712
Fr 1833 Mar 09 22-0716
Fr 1833 Mar 09 22-0720
Fr 1833 Mar 09 22-0724
Fr 1833 Mar 09 22-0725
Fr 1833 Mar 11 22-0732
Fr 1833 Mar 11 22-0735
Fr 1833 Mar 11 22-0738
Fr 1833 Mar 11 22-0739
Fr 1833 Mar 13 22-0750
Fr 1833 Mar 20 22-0835
Fr 1833 May 15 22-1362
Fr 1833 May 15 22-1363
Fr 1833 May 28 22-1467
Fr 1833 May 28* M25-28
Fr 1833 May 29 22-1507
Fr 1833 May 29 M25-28
To 1833 Jul 20 23-0163
Fr 1833 Aug 08 M25-28

To 1833 Aug 10# DLC-43
Fr 1833 Aug 24 M25-28
To 1833 Oct 08 23-0991
Fr 1833 Oct 14 23-1034
Fr 1833 Oct 15 M25-28
Fr 1833 Oct 16 23-1045
Fr 1833 Oct 16* M25-28
Fr 1833 Oct 16 23-1047
Fr 1833 Oct 26 23-1088
Fr 1833 Oct 26* M25-28
Fr 1833 Oct 29 M25-28
Fr 1833 Nov 11 M25-28
To 1833 Nov 28# 23-1323
Fr 1833 Dec 19 M25-28
Fr 1834 Jan 14 24-0879
Fr 1834 Jan 29 24-1098
Fr 1834 Feb 06 24-1245
Fr 1834 Feb 10 M25-28
Fr 1834 Feb 18 24-1411
Fr 1834 Feb 18 24-1414
Fr 1834 Feb 24 24-1460
Fr 1834 Feb 26 24-1488
Fr 1834 Mar 10 25-0023
Fr 1834 Mar 11 25-0035
To 1834 Mar 12 25-0135
Fr 1834 Mar 13 25-0146
Fr 1834 Mar 22 25-0317
Fr 1834 Mar 25 25-0348
Fr 1834 Mar 25 25-0352
Fr 1834 Apr 07 25-0613
Fr 1834 Apr 07 25-0617
Fr 1834 Apr 07 25-0620
Fr 1834 Apr 07 25-0623
Fr 1834 Apr 07 25-0627
Fr 1834 Apr 07* M25-29
Fr 1834 Apr 08 25-0639
Fr 1834 Apr 09 25-0648
Fr 1834 Apr 29 25-0921
To 1834 Apr 29# 25-0910
Fr 1834 May 16 25-1064
Fr 1834 Jun 02 M25-29
Fr 1834 Jun 18 25-1421
Fr 1834 Jun 23 M639-10
Fr 1834 Jun 23* M25-29
Fr 1834 Jun 26 25-1566
Fr 1834 Jun 26* M25-29
Fr 1834 Jun 27 25-1571
Fr 1834 Jun 30 26-0008
To 1834 Jul 03 26-0121
Fr 1834 Jul 03 26-0123
Fr 1834 Jul 07 M25-29
Fr 1834 Oct 10 26-0573
Fr 1834 Nov 07 M25-29
Fr 1834 Nov 07 M25-29
Fr 1834 Nov 20 M25-29
Fr 1834 Nov 21 M25-29
Fr 1834 Nov 24 26-0980
Fr 1834 Nov 24 DLC-45
Fr 1834 Dec 05 26-1420
Fr 1834 Dec 08 26-1435
Fr 1834 Dec 19 26-1532
Fr 1835 Jan 05 27-0089
Fr 1835 Jan 13 M25-29
To 1835 Jan 27# 27-0297
Fr 1835 Jan 28 M25-29
Fr 1835 Jan 29 M25-29
Fr 1835 Feb 09 27-0453
Fr 1835 Feb 09 M25-29
Fr 1835 Feb 17 27-0546
Fr 1835 Feb 26 27-0634
Fr 1835 Mar 11 27-1087
Fr 1835 Mar 11 27-1092
Fr 1835 Mar 11 27-1095
Fr 1835 Mar 11 27-1099
Fr 1835 Mar 11 27-1104
Fr 1835 Mar 11 27-1109
Fr 1835 May 02 M25-30
To 1835 May 07# M234-136
Fr 1835 May 23 M25-30
Fr 1835 May 29 28-0512
Fr 1835 May 29* M234-136
Fr 1835 May 29# 28-0518
Fr 1835 May 30 M25-30
Fr 1835 Jun 20 28-0753
Fr 1835 Jul 24# M179-80
Fr 1835 Aug 01 M25-30
Re 1836 Jan 17 mem DLC-47
Fr 1836 Mar 05 DLC-78
To 1836 Oct 24 32-0337
Fr 1839 Oct 16 DLC-52
Haywood John
Fr 1818 Jan 27 DLC-24
Fr 1821 Feb 16 M439-8
Re 1832 Apr 18 M273-27
Haywood William Henry Jr
Fr 1834 Feb 22 DLC-44
Fr 1844 May 29 36-0565
Fr 1845 Jan 02 DLC-57
Hazard Sylvester R
Fr 1834 Apr 18 25-0833
Head William H
Fr 1843 Mar 23 DLC-55
Heap Samuel Davies
Fr 1829 Aug 27 M639-7
Heard Morgan A
Fr 1818 Jun 04 fin DLC-69
Heath Asa
Fr 1837 Feb M687-20
Heath Richard K
Fr 1819 Mar 01 DLC-26
To 1819 Mar 01 DLC-26
Heath Robert et al
Fr 1835 Jan 08 DLC-45
Heath Upton S
Fr 1835 Mar 18# 27-1231
Heath Upton S et al
Fr 1829 Jun 18 M639-11
Fr 1835 Jan 15 27-0233
Heaton Johnson F
Fr 1843 Nov 20 DLC-56
Hebb William
To 1833 Jan 29 chk DLC-42
To 1833 Feb 12 chk DLC-42
Heck John H
Fr 1829 Jun 12 13-0647
Heckaton
Fr 1833 Jul 09 M234-530
Fr 1833 Jul 09* 23-0096
Heckaton et al
Fr 1831 Jul 10 M234-530
Heckscher Charles A & Edward et al
Fr 1836 Aug M687-29
Hedden Josiah
Fr 1831 Sep 27 M639-18
Hedges Hannah
Re 1833 Jun 04 par 22-1562
Hedges Joseph H
Fr 1841 Dec 12 DLC-54

Hedges Josiah			
	Fr 1832 Apr 07#		20-0168
Heermann Lewis			
	Fr 1815 Jan 26		DLC-15
	To 1815 Jan 27		4-0636
	To 1815 Jan 27*		DLC-16
Heiskell Henry Lee			
	Fr 1828 Oct 21	fin	12-0245
	Fr 1831 Jan 31		M22-27
Heiss James			
	Fr 1841 Aug 16		DLC-53
Heiss John P			
	To 1844 May 03		36-0483
	To 1844 May 13		36-0528
Helfenstein John P			
	Fr 1828 Sep 19		12-0204
Helm George			
	Fr 1815 Aug 15		DLC-19
Helm Henry Pope			
	To 1815 Feb 05		DLC-16
	Fr 1815 May 29		4-1071
Helm James J			
	Fr 1840 Aug 25		34-1577
Hemphill James			
	Fr 1829 Jun 24		13-0707
Hemphill Joseph			
	To c1830		DLC-40
	Fr 1830 Oct 02		16-0302
Hemphill Joseph et al			
	Fr c1830		14-1239
HeMulluka			
	Fr 1835 Nov 10		29-0490
Hendel Jacob et al			
	Fr 1829 May 19		M639-11
Henderson Archibald			
	Fr 1829 Apr 09		M639-11
	To 1835 Dec 07		29-0780
	To 1835 Dec 07*		M472-2
	Fr 1836 May 27		31-0163
Henderson Archibald et al			
	Fr 1836 May 28		M124-153
Henderson Bennett H			
	Fr 1805 Dec 20	leg	DLC-3
	Fr 1832 Jun 12		M567-71
Henderson James			
	Fr 1811 Dec 23		2-1024
	Fr 1811 Dec 23*		DLC-5
	Fr 1812 Apr 11		2-1064
	To 1813 Jan 06		DLC-5
	To 1813 Jan 06*		DLC-61
	To 1813 Jan 07		DLC-61
	To 1813 Mar 15		DLC-61
	Fr 1813 Oct 04		DLC-6
	Re 1818 cJan 10		5-1237
	Re 1827 Oct 01	add	11-0885
Henderson James Pinckney			
	Fr 1844 May 01		36-0465
	To 1844 May 11		36-0520
Henderson James R			
	Fr 1814 Sep 20		DLC-12
Henderson John			
	Fr 1813 Jun 15		DLC-6
	To 1813 Jul 04		DLC-6
Henderson John C			
	Re 1804 Sep 21	leg	1-1378
	Re 1805 Jun 17	leg	2-0065
	Re 1806 Apr 25	leg	2-0211
	Re 1808 Nov	leg	2-0739
Henderson Joseph			
	Fr 1834 cSep		26-0408
	Re 1835 cFeb	mem	27-0360
Henderson Joseph et al			
	Fr 1835 Jan		M639-18
	Fr 1836 cFeb		M639-8
Henderson Lawson			
	Fr 1815 Mar 12		DLC-17
Henderson Pleasant			
	Fr 1828 Apr 29		DLC-35
Henderson Robert			
	To 1812 Nov		DLC-61
Henderson Thomas			
	Fr 1802 Apr 02		DLC-2
	Fr 1827 Jul 28		DLC-34
	Fr 1836 Mar 02		30-0658
Hendrick Elijah			
	Re 1799 Aug 06	leg	1-0724
Hendrick Jeremiah			
	Re 1799 Aug 06	leg	1-0724
Hendrick Joseph			
	Fr 1796 Feb 18	lnd	DLC-1
	To 1797 Jan 20	lnd	1-0480
	Fr 1797 Feb 18	lnd	1-0492
	Fr 1797 Feb 18*	lnd	DLC-1
	Re 1799 Aug 06	leg	1-0724
Hendrick Mycajah et al			
	Fr 1820 May 31		M221-89
Hendrick Obadiah			
	Re 1799 Aug 06	leg	1-0724
Hendricks William			
	Fr 1829 Feb 28		M639-25
	Fr 1829 Feb 28		M639-13
	Fr 1829 Feb 28		M639-15
	Fr 1829 Mar 04		M639-25
	Fr 1829 Mar 05		12-0856
	Fr 1829 Mar 05		M639-22
	Fr 1829 Mar 05		M639-15
	Fr 1829 Mar 05		M639-6
	Fr 1829 Mar 06		12-0866
	Fr 1829 Oct 22		14-0231
	Fr 1831 Feb 28		M124-126
	Fr 1831 Mar 05		DLC-39
	Fr 1831 Aug 30		M639-13
	Fr 1833 Nov 01		23-1174
	Fr 1833 Dec 06		24-0407
	Fr 1835 Mar 09		27-1075
	Fr 1836 Apr 25		M639-6
	Fr 1836 Aug		31-1178
	Fr 1837 Jan 18		33-0014
Hendrix Thomas			
	Re 1788 Nov	leg	1-0049
Henley David			
	To 1797 Feb 17		1-0489
Henley John D			
	To 1815 Jan 23		DLC-15
	Fr 1815 Feb 02		DLC-16
	Fr 1815 Feb 03		DLC-16
Hennen Alfred			
	Fr 1821 May 26#	fin	DLC-30
	Fr 1825 Nov 08		DLC-33
	Fr 1830 Jan 18		M639-4
	Fr 1836 Feb 06		M639-13
	Fr 1843 May 13	leg	DLC-55
	Fr 1845 Mar 11		DLC-57
Hennen R			
	Fr 1816 May 31		DLC-69
Hennen & Dickson			
	Fr 1802 Feb 10	fin	DLC-2

Heno P Jr
    Fr 1814 Aug 13   DLC-11
Henrion Sebastian
    Fr 1835 Nov 03   fin DLC-47
    Fr 1836 Jan 29#   fin DLC-47
Henry Bernard
    Re 1832 Nov 09   T206-4
Henry Ezekiel
    Re 1815 Mar 25   leg 4-0895
Henry Lemuel
    Fr 1803 Jun 14   DLC-2
Henry Louis D
    Fr 1837 Feb 08   33-0567
Henry Patrick
    Fr 1829 Jun 16   M688-60
Henry Robert Pryor et al
    Fr 1825 Feb 22   DLC-33
    To 1825 Feb 22   DLC-33
Henry Thomas
    Fr 1818 Sep 05   DLC-25
Henry William
    Fr 1814 Sep 03   DLC-12
    Fr 1814 Dec 06   DLC-14
    Fr 1814 Dec 22   DLC-14
    Fr 1815 May 10   DLC-18
Henry County TN militia
    To 1825 Sep 27   add 11-0004
Henshaw Charles et al
    Fr 1836 Oct 01   M687-22
Henshaw David
    Fr 1829 Aug 10   13-1059
    To 1830 May 03   15-0877
    Fr 1835 Jun 16#   28-0720
    Fr 1836 Jan 16#   30-0128
    Fr 1841 Dec 03   DLC-54
    Fr 1841 Dec 03#   DLC-54
    Fr 1843 Aug 25   DLC-55
    To 1843 Sep 15   DLC-55
Henshaw David et al
    Fr 1829 Jul 22   M639-6
    Fr 1830 Feb 22   M639-21
    Fr 1834 May 24   M873-15
Henshaw J P K
    Fr 1829 Jun 23   M124-119
Henshaw J P K et al
    Fr 1829 Jun 19   M124-119
Henton Peter
    Fr 1835 Oct 09   29-0262
Hepburn Burton et al
    Fr 1835 Mar 02   27-0688
Herbert John Carlyle
    Fr 1830 Mar 19   M273-25
Hereford William
    Fr 1802 Jan 08   DLC-2
    Fr 1802 Oct 06   DLC-2
Heriot Benjamin D
    Fr 1814 Mar 22   DLC-9
Hermitage plantation
    Re 1804 Jul 23   leg 1-1352
    Re 1829 Apr   mem 12-1209
    Re 1831   DLC-78
    Re c1836   fin DLC-49
    Re 1836 Mar 18   mem DLC-47
    Re 1836 Jun 01   fin DLC-48
    Re 1836 cAug 02   fin DLC-48
    Re 1841 Jan 01   35-0169
    Re 1843 Jun 20   35-1386
Hermitage church
    Re 1838 Aug 25   fin 34-0437
    Re 1838 cSep   mem 34-0448
Hermitage TN citizens
    To 1815 May 16   add 4-1045
Herrick Benjamin J
    Fr 1837 Feb 21   M687-16
Herrick Samuel et al
    Fr 1829 Jan 03   12-0432
Herrill Barney
    Re 1832 Jul 20   par 20-1192
Herring Charles
    Fr 1831 cDec   M50-16
Herring Elbert
    Fr c1832   DLC-43
    To 1835 Apr 08#   M234-300
    Fr 1835 Jul 25   DLC-46
    Fr 1835 Oct 05   29-0199
    To 1835 Dec 07#   29-0775
    Fr 1836 Jan 18   30-0139
    Fr 1836 May 20#   M234-422
    Fr 1836 Jun 21#   M21-19
    Fr 1836 Jul 02   31-0759
Herrington James C
    Fr 1845 Apr 11   DLC-58
Herron James
    Fr 1829 May 25   M639-11
Herttell Thomas
    Fr 1844 Mar 18   DLC-56
Herttell Thomas et al
    Fr 1834 Jan   M639-18
Hess William R
    Fr 1813 Nov 17   DLC-7
    Fr 1813 Dec 28   DLC-8
    To 1814 Jan 14   DLC-61
    Fr 1825 Sep 19   add 10-1423
    To 1825 Sep 19   add 10-1425
Heustis Jabez W
    Fr 1814 Dec 25   DLC-15
    Fr 1815 Feb 06   DLC-16
Hewes Maria
    Fr 1837 Feb   M22-41
Hewes William G
    Fr 1838 Jun 08   DLC-51
Hewes William G et al
    Fr 1833 Jul 12   M639-27
Hewitt Benjamin
    Re 1813 Mar 01   DLC-64
Hewitt J M
    Fr 1829 Apr 22   M639-15
Hewlett Edmond
    To 1814 Jun 26   chk DLC-11
Hewlett George
    To 1814 Jun 26   chk DLC-11
    Fr 1821 Apr 14   fin DLC-30
Hewlett E & G
    Fr 1813 Oct 04   DLC-11
    To 1815 Jul 18   chk DLC-18
    Fr 1815 Sep 30   fin DLC-68
Hewlett & Harper
    Fr 1816 Jul 08   fin DLC-69
Hibbard Billy
    Fr 1833 Jan 30   22-0114
Hickey Thomas M
    Fr 1827 Sep 18   DLC-34
    To 1827 Sep 25   DLC-34
    Fr 1835 Nov 28   M639-24
Hickey Thomas M et al
    Fr 1836 Mar 24   par 30-0890
Hickman Edwin
    Re 1788 Mar 30   fin 1-0040
Hickman George et al
    Fr 1831 Dec 19   M222-31

Hickman John Pryor			
	Fr 1814 Mar 13		DLC-66
	Fr 1814 Mar 13*		DLC-62
	Fr 1814 Mar 17		DLC-9
	To 1814 Mar 21		DLC-9
	Fr 1814 Mar 22		DLC-9
	Fr 1814 Mar 30		DLC-9
	Fr 1814 Apr 04		DLC-10
	Fr 1814 Apr 21		DLC-10
	To 1814 Jul 16		DLC-62
	Fr 1814 Jul 24		DLC-11
	To 1814 Aug 02		DLC-62
	Fr 1815 May 16		DLC-18
	Fr 1829 Aug 23		M639-17
	Fr 1837 Nov 29		DLC-50
	To 1837 Dec 26		34-0147
	To 1837 Dec 26*		DLC-50
Hickman John Pryor et al			
	Re 1814 Aug	leg	3-1202
Hickman Thomas			
	Re 1793 May	leg	1-0159
	Fr 1796 Apr 13	lnd	1-0375
	Fr 1818 Dec 16	fin	7-0063
	Fr 1820 Sep 08	fin	7-1311
	Fr 1831 Jul 25		M22-28
	Fr 1831 Sep 08		M22-28
	Fr 1833 Feb 13		M221-113
Hickman William			
	Fr 1805 Feb 28		DLC-3
Hicks Charles			
	To 1813 Oct 23		DLC-61
	To 1813 Oct 23*		3-0543
	To 1817 Jul 02		DLC-23
Hicks Charles R			
	Fr 1815 Jan 18		DLC-15
	Fr 1815 Jan 22		DLC-15
Hicks John C			
	To 1816 Jul 06	chk	DLC-21
	Fr 1818 Jun 12	fin	6-1046
	Fr 1818 Jun 12	fin	6-1043
Hicks Nehemiah			
	Re 1836 Dec 07	par	32-1049
Hicks Samuel			
	Fr 1833 Feb 02		22-0250
Hicks Ewing & Co			
	Fr 1835 Oct 15#	fin	DLC-51
Hickson James			
	To 1816 Oct 19	chk	DLC-21
Hicky Philip			
	Fr 1836 Nov 07		M567-128
Hicky Philip et al			
	Fr 1828 Jan 05		DLC-35
	To 1828 Jan 05		DLC-35
Hiester Joseph			
	Fr 1829 Feb 12		12-0508
Higgerson Samuel D			
	Re 1840 Feb 17		34-1226
Higgins P			
	Fr 1836 Apr 25#	fin	DLC-48
	Fr 1836 Jun 17	fin	DLC-48
Higgins William Y			
	To 1814 Jan 29		DLC-62
Higinbotham Eliza			
	Fr 1835 Aug 31#		M639-24
Hilbus Jacob			
	Fr 1836 Jan 16	fin	DLC-47
Hill A S			
	Fr 1831 Mar 26		DLC-39
Hill Ann			
	Fr c1835 Aug 22#	fin	28-1345
	Fr 1835 Sep 26#	fin	DLC-47
	Fr 1836 May 12#	fin	DLC-48
Hill E B			
	Fr 1839 Oct 12	fin	DLC-52
	Fr 1844 Nov 25		DLC-57
Hill Elias et al			
	Fr 1832 Jun 21		20-0781
Hill Harry R W			
	Fr 1833 Dec 31#	lnd	DLC-45
	Fr 1833 Dec 31*	lnd	24-0690
	To 1834 May 06#	fin	DLC-44
	Fr 1834 Sep 20#		26-0448
	Fr 1834 Nov 01	fin	26-0799
	Fr 1835 Aug 08		28-1263
Hill Harry R W et al			
	Fr 1835 Jan 16		M639-9
Hill Harry R W & Co			
	To 1835 Nov 11#	fin	DLC-47
Hill Henry Jr			
	Fr 1840 May 15		34-1352
Hill Henry M			
	Fr 1837 Jun 04		DLC-50
Hill Isaac			
	Fr 1829 Mar 02		12-0822
	Fr 1829 Mar 10		M639-9
	Fr 1829 Mar 18		12-1033
	Re 1829 Mar 21		12-1069
	Fr 1829 May 12		DLC-37
	Fr 1829 May 14		13-0319
	To 1830 Jan 06#		M222-27
	Fr 1832 Jul 10		20-1012
	Fr 1835 Mar 08		27-1072
	Fr 1835 Apr 23		M639-26
	Fr 1835 Sep 05		DLC-46
	Fr 1836 Apr 13		M687-28
	Fr 1837 Jan 30		33-0234
	Fr 1839 Sep 06		DLC-52
	To 1839 Oct 31		34-1030
	Fr 1845 Mar 18		DLC-57
	To 1845 Apr 23#		37-0155
Hill Isaac et al			
	Fr 1829 Mar		M639-9
	Fr 1832 Jan 27		M22-29
Hill Isaac (Delaware Indian)			
	Fr 1831 cOct		M234-601
	Fr 1831 cOct*		18-0908
Hill J J			
	Fr 1835 Jun 03#	fin	DLC-51
Hill Jesse			
	Fr 1823 Dec 31	fin	DLC-32
Hill John W			
	To 1818 May 05		6-0642
	Fr 1818 Jun 21	fin	DLC-69
	Fr 1818 Jun 21*	fin	6-1072
	Fr 1818 Jun 21	fin	DLC-69
	Fr 1818 Jun 21*	fin	6-1073
Hill Joseph A			
	To 1831 May 23		17-1410
Hill Susanna (Ayer)			
	To 1845 Mar 03		36-1533
Hill Thomas			
	Fr 1842 Aug 17	fin	DLC-54
Hill Will K			
	Fr 1825 Sep 05	add	DLC-33
Hill William			
	Fr 1817 Dec 29	fin	DLC-69

Hill William P			
	Fr 1845 May 05#		DLC-58
	To 1845 Jun 04#		37-0248
Hillhouse David P			
	Fr 1817 Nov 06		DLC-23
Hilliard Isaac H			
	Re 1832 Oct		21-0062
Hilliard Robert C			
	Fr 1845 Jan 10		DLC-57
Himebaugh Matthias			
	Fr 1835 Jan 08		DLC-45
Himes George W			
	Fr 1844 Apr 09		DLC-56
Hindman Thomas Carmichael			
	Re 1814 Apr 01		DLC-9
	Fr 1816 Mar 26		DLC-20
	Fr 1816 May 16		DLC-20
	Fr 1818 Jun 21	fin	DLC-69
	Fr 1818 Jun 21*	fin	6-1074
Hinds How			
	Fr 1841 Oct 13		DLC-53
Hinds John			
	Fr 1796 Jul 23		DLC-1
Hinds Thomas			
	Fr 1815 Jan 25		DLC-15
	Fr 1816 Aug 10		DLC-21
	Re 1820 Sep 02		7-1227
	Re 1820 Sep 02*		T494-1
	Fr 1829 Mar 23		M639-6
	Fr 1830 May 24		M639-24
	Fr 1831 Feb 15		17-0533
	Fr 1834 Mar 08		M179-78
	Fr 1834 Dec 03		26-1382
	Fr 1838 May 13		DLC-51
	To 1839 Sep 21		34-0945
Hinds Thomas et al			
	Fr 1832 cJan		19-0549
	To 1839 Dec 17		34-1088
Hines C & M			
	Fr 1824 Dec 15	fin	10-0985
Hines Harmon			
	Fr 1831 Nov 30		M639-18
Hinkley Watson S			
	Fr 1835 Oct 29		M688-99
Hinkson B			
	Fr 1835 Jan 05		M639-27
Hinman Joel et al			
	Fr 1836 May		M687-17
Hinman R R			
	Fr 1836 May 30		M687-17
Hinman Walter			
	Re 1833 Apr 12	par	22-0989
Hinton Joseph B			
	Fr 1831 Feb 16		DLC-39
	Fr 1831 Mar 25		DLC-39
Hinton William R			
	Fr 1830 Oct 23		16-0487
Hipple Henry			
	Fr 1828 Oct 20		DLC-35
	Fr 1844 Nov 27		36-1056
Hird Reuben			
	Fr 1815 Feb		DLC-17
Hiriart Samuel			
	Fr 1829 Feb 12		M639-4
Hiriart Samuel et al			
	Fr 1830 Jan 23		M639-4
Hitchcock J J			
	To 1834 Feb 15		24-1399
Hitchcock Luther A			
	Fr 1821 Oct 16		DLC-31
Hitchcock M			
	Fr 1832 Apr 06		M688-83
Hitchcock Roswell			
	Fr 1837 Feb 14		M687-20
Hite Isaac R			
	Fr 1836 Sep		M22-41
Hitt Jackey Spencer			
	Fr 1825 Apr 22		DLC-33
	Fr 1829 Dec 31		M688-70
	Fr 1830 Jan 01		M688-70
Hoagland Moses T			
	Fr 1814 Sep 14		DLC-12
	Fr 1814 Sep 16		DLC-12
	Fr 1814 Oct 11		DLC-13
Hobbie Selah Reeve			
	Fr 1835 Jul 13		M639-18
Hobbs Edward			
	Fr 1835 Aug 13#	fin	DLC-46
	Fr 1835 Aug 26#		DLC-46
Hobbs Henry			
	Fr 1835 Feb 11		M639-11
Hobbs Warren			
	Fr 1825 Jul 14	fin	10-1356
Hobby William			
	Fr 1829 Nov 20		14-0510
	Fr 1829 Nov 29		14-0625
Hoch Augustus			
	Fr 1829 Jun 18		13-0673
Hockley George W			
	Fr 1824 Jan 16		M439-17
Hodgden John			
	Fr 1837 Feb 06		M687-20
Hodge Andrew Jr			
	Fr 1844 Feb 12#	lnd	36-0249
Hodge Andrew & Co			
	Re 1844 cFeb 12	mem	36-0248
Hodge Samuel			
	Fr 1820 May 30#		DLC-29
	To 1823 Nov 08		DLC-32
Hodgson William Brown			
	Fr 1830 Mar 16		M179-68
	Fr 1834 Aug 25		M124-142
	Fr 1835 Jun 12		M179-80
	Fr 1836 Apr 28		30-1404
	Fr 1837 Mar 01		M687-16
Hoffman Beekman V			
	Re 1830 Apr 13		M273-23
Hoffman George et al			
	Fr 1829 Oct 10		M639-27
Hoffman Michael et al			
	Fr 1830 May 31		M639-2
Hoffman Ogden			
	Fr 1829 Mar 25		12-1106
	Fr 1829 Apr 17#		12-1374
Hog Peter			
	Fr 1815 Mar 04		DLC-17
Hogan Catherine Boyd			
	Fr 1843 Oct 21		DLC-55
Hogan Daniel			
	Fr 1828 Oct 27		DLC-35
	Fr 1840 Jul 24		DLC-53
Hogan John B			
	Fr 1818 Jun 25		DLC-25
	Fr 1818 Jun 25*		6-1079
	Fr 1818 Jun 26	fin	DLC-69
	To 1818 Jun 28		6-1087
	To 1818 Jul 01		6-1095
	Fr 1818 Jul 01	fin	DLC-70
	Fr 1818 Jul 02		6-1103

Hogan John B (cont)
Fr 1818 Jul 02 fin DLC-70
Fr 1818 Jul 06 DLC-25
Fr 1818 Jul 07 DLC-25
To 1819 Aug 17# DLC-63
To 1834 Jul 21# DLC-44
Fr 1835 Mar 06 27-1027
To 1835 Aug 21# 28-1341
Fr 1835 Sep 28-1470
Fr 1835 Sep* M234-242
Fr 1835 Sep 27 DLC-47
Fr 1835 Oct 25 M234-242
Fr 1835 Oct 27 M234-242
Fr 1835 Nov 03 29-0420
Fr 1835 Nov 03* M234-242
Fr 1836 Jan 08 M234-243
Fr 1836 Apr 22 M234-243
Fr 1836 Jul 15 DLC-48
Fr 1837 Nov 05 M687-12
Fr 1844 Feb 13 DLC-56
Fr 1844 Dec 20 36-1225
Hogan Maria S (Barbour)
Fr 1844 Nov 29 36-1074
Hogan Michael
Fr 1833 Mar 21 M146-2
Hogan Thomas
To 1844 May 03 36-0483
Hogg Jane
Fr 1832 Mar 16# fin DLC-40
Hogg Samuel
Fr 1815 Mar 26 DLC-17
Fr 1823 Apr 20 DLC-32
To 1823 Jul 01 fin DLC-72
To 1823 Jul 01 fin DLC-72
Fr 1825 Nov 25 fin DLC-72
Fr 1829 Apr 07 M639-2
Re 1830 cDec mem 16-0909
Fr 1833 Jul 08 DLC-43
Fr 1833 Aug 23 M639-3
Fr 1836 Jan 25 DLC-47
Fr 1836 Jul 01 31-0739
Fr 1836 Oct 15 DLC-49
To 1839 Dec 17 34-1089
Re 1841 cNov 08 leg 35-0482
Hogg Samuel et al
Fr 1834 Aug 06 26-0279
To 1834 Aug 06 26-0280
Hoggatt James W
Fr 1836 Mar 05# lnd DLC-47
Hoggatt John
Fr 1805 Feb 16 fin 2-0012
Fr 1806 Jun 24 2-0278
Fr 1820 Sep 12 fin DLC-70
Hoggatt & Overton
Fr 1821 Jan 11 fin DLC-31
Hoghland Jacob
Fr 1837 Jan M22-41
Hointen E
Fr 1838 Feb 01 fin DLC-51
Holabird William S
Fr 1836 May 30 M687-17
Holata Emathla et al
Fr 1836 Feb 07 30-0298
Holbrook Amory
Fr 1840 Jul 03 DLC-53
Fr 1841 Jan 19 DLC-53
Holbrook Benjamin
Fr 1833 Aug 23 23-0442
Fr 1835 Sep 01 M179-80
Holcomb Theodore M et al
Fr 1829 Feb 23 M639-6
Holdredge William
Fr 1845 Jan 09 DLC-57
Holladay John C
To 1839 Jan 03# fin DLC-51
Holland Elijah
Fr 1840 Jun 26 34-1445
Holland James H
Fr 1844 Dec 13 36-1189
Holley Horace
To 1822 Feb 27 9-0038
Holley Robert C
Fr 1841 Aug 23 DLC-53
Fr 1842 Jul 09 DLC-54
Holleyman Hermon
Fr 1841 Feb 13 DLC-53
Holliday D S
Fr 1845 Feb 20 DLC-57
Hollinger Adam C
Fr 1836 Jun 14 31-0474
Hollingsworth Benjamin et al
Fr 1834 Dec 04 M234-242
Hollister Charles
Re 1832 Nov 29 par 21-0595
Re 1833 Mar 08 par 22-0685
Holly George
Re 1833 Sep 26 par 23-0869
Holman James T
Fr 1836 Oct 10 M688-104
Holman Jesse Lynch
To 1835 Sep 16 29-0056
Fr 1836 May 03 30-1493
Holmead A
Fr 1837 Feb 24# fin DLC-50
Fr 1837 Feb 24# fin DLC-50
Holmes David
To 1813 Jan 05 2-1325
Fr 1813 Feb 22 3-0281
To 1813 Mar 16 3-0323
To 1813 Mar 16* DLC-61
To 1813 Mar 16* DLC-6
Fr 1813 Mar 16 DLC-61
Fr 1813 Mar 16* 3-0326
To 1813 Apr 14 3-0373
To 1813 Apr 24 DLC-6
To 1813 Sep 26 3-0480
To 1813 Sep 26* DLC-6
Fr 1813 Oct 05 DLC-6
Fr 1813 Oct 05* 3-0497
Fr 1813 Oct 05* DLC-61
To 1813 Oct 17 3-0532
To 1813 Nov 04 DLC-61
To 1813 Nov 04* 3-0565
To 1814 Apr 18 3-0974
To 1814 Apr 18* DLC-10
Fr 1814 Jun 19 DLC-10
Fr 1814 Jun 19* 3-1097
To 1814 Aug 05 DLC-62
Fr 1814 Aug 15 DLC-11
Fr 1814 Aug 15* 3-1303
To 1814 Aug 31 DLC-62
Fr 1814 Sep 07 DLC-12
Fr 1814 Sep 07* 4-0181
Fr 1814 Sep 19 DLC-12
Fr 1814 Sep 29 DLC-12
Fr 1814 Sep 29 DLC-12
Fr 1814 Sep 29* 4-0247
To 1814 Sep 30 DLC-62
To 1814 Sep 30* 4-0249
To 1814 Oct 31 4-0306

	To 1814 Oct 31*		DLC-62
	To 1814 Dec 21		4-0439
	To 1814 Dec 21*		DLC-62
	To 1814 Dec 24		4-0452
	To 1814 Dec 25		4-0457
	To 1814 Dec 26		DLC-62
	Fr 1814 Dec 27		DLC-15
	Fr 1814 Dec 28		4-0472
	Fr 1814 Dec 30		DLC-15
	Fr 1814 Dec 30*		4-0474
	Fr 1815 Jan 06		DLC-15
	Fr 1815 Jan 06*		4-0491
	Fr 1815 Jan 06		DLC-15
	To 1815 Jan 17		4-0558
	To 1815 Jan 18		4-0568
	To 1815 Jan 18*		DLC-62
	To 1815 Jan 18*		DLC-15
	To 1815 Jan 20		4-0581
	To 1815 Jan 20*		DLC-15
	To 1815 Jan 21		4-0586
	Fr 1815 Jan 24		DLC-15
	Fr 1815 Jan 24*		4-0609
	Fr 1815 Feb 04		DLC-16
	Fr 1815 Feb 04*		4-0690
	To 1815 Feb 04		4-0692
	To 1815 Feb 04*		DLC-16
	Fr 1815 Feb 09		DLC-16
	Fr 1815 Feb 09*		4-0715
	To 1815 Feb 10		4-0718
	To 1815 Feb 10*		DLC-16
	To 1815 Feb 14		4-0740
	To 1815 Feb 14*		DLC-16
	Fr 1815 Feb 18		DLC-16
	Fr 1815 Feb 18*		4-0764
	Fr 1815 Feb 20		DLC-16
	Fr 1815 Feb 20*		4-0771
	To 1815 Feb 21		4-0777
	To 1815 Feb 21*		DLC-17
	Fr 1815 Mar 01		DLC-17
	Fr 1815 Mar 01*		4-0808
	To 1815 Apr 22	fin	DLC-68
	Fr 1815 May 05		4-1023
	To 1815 May 24		DLC-18
	To 1815 Dec 23		4-1302
	To 1817 May 29		5-0882
	To 1817 Dec 02		5-1151
	Fr 1819 Aug 07		DLC-27
	Fr 1821 Jan 19		DLC-29
	Fr 1821 May 19		DLC-30
	Re 1828 Jan 04	add	11-1005
	Fr 1828 Sep 05		12-0182
Holmes Ephraim			
	Fr 1832 Apr 24		M639-5
Holmes Gabriel			
	Fr 1834 Mar 29		M179-77
Holmes George			
	Re 1837 Jan 30	par	33-0239
Holmes L			
	Fr 1840 Dec 15		DLC-53
Holmes Owen			
	To 1831 May 23		17-1410
Holmes Reuben			
	Fr 1833 Sep		M567-82
Holmes Thomas G			
	Fr 1814 Sep 28		DLC-12
	Fr 1815 Mar 29		DLC-17
	Fr 1815 Dec 13		DLC-19
	To 1816 Feb 09		DLC-20
Holt Henry			
	Re 1829 Apr 27	par	13-0164
	Re 1829 Apr 27*	par	T967-1
Holt Jesse			
	Re 1821 Mar 27	leg	DLC-30
Holt John E			
	Fr 1829 Jul 10		13-0834
Holt Joseph			
	To 1835 May 26		28-0504
Holt Orrin et al			
	Fr 1836 May 09		M687-17
Holt Robert			
	To 1801 Jul 11	lnd	1-0889
Holt Thaddeus			
	Re 1816 Jun 03	leg	5-0121
Holtzclaw Burnard W			
	Fr 1833 Mar 06		DLC-42
	Fr 1833 Oct 21		DLC-43
Holtzman Samuel et al			
	Fr 1833 Jan 22		M639-4
Homans James T			
	Fr 1830 Mar		M273-25
	Re 1833 Apr 02		M273-28
Homer Jonathan			
	Fr 1834 Mar 11		DLC-44
Homes William C			
	Re 1831 Sep 22		M273-26
Hone Henry			
	Fr 1834 Nov 29		DLC-45
Hood Charles et al			
	Fr 1829 May 11		13-0278
Hood John McClellan			
	Fr 1834 Mar 26		25-0368
	Fr 1836 Feb 03		DLC-47
Hood Washington			
	To 1834 Oct 21	chk	DLC-44
Hood William S			
	Fr 1831 May 29		17-1475
Hood & Walker			
	To 1815 Sep 11	chk	DLC-19
Hooe Robert Emmet			
	Re 1830 Jun 16		M273-24
Hooglereik Henry			
	Fr 1828 Aug 12		DLC-35
Hook James Harvey			
	To 1829 Mar#		12-0676
	Fr 1829 Oct 05#		14-0106
	Fr 1830 Mar 15		15-0364
	Fr 1832 Apr 17		M22-29
	Fr 1835 Jun 15		DLC-46
	Fr 1836 Jul 04		DLC-48
	Fr 1836 Aug 05		DLC-48
	Fr 1836 Oct 01		31-1576
	Fr 1836 Oct 12		32-0163
Hook John			
	Fr 1826 Aug 14	fin	11-0338
Hooper Benjamin			
	To 1807 May 11	lnd	2-0493
Hooper G			
	Re 1836 cMay 07	mem	30-1562
Hooper James			
	Fr 1823 Oct 03		DLC-32
Hooper John			
	Re 1829 Oct 15		14-0164
Hooper John Locke			
	Fr 1836 Oct 07		M567-125
Hooper Joshua Jr et al			
	Fr 1834 Mar 10		25-0026
Hoover Andrew			
	To 1803 Nov 01	fin	DLC-3

Hoover Benjamin
Re 1804 May 11 fin DLC-3
Hoover C L
Fr 1843 Mar 23 DLC-55
Hoover John
To 1811 Nov 23 lnd 2-1017
Hoover M C
Fr 1827 Apr 17 fin DLC-34
Hope P R & J W
Fr 1840 Feb 18# fin DLC-52
Hope Thomas
To 1835 Aug 13# M567-112
Hope William
Fr 1835 Aug 13# M567-112
Hopiaskitenah et al
Fr 1831 Apr 01 M234-169
Fr 1831 Apr 01* 17-1060
Hopkins George Washington
Fr 1837 cFeb 14 M22-41
Hopkins John
Fr 1833 May 23 22-1434
Hopkins Samuel
Fr 1815 Jan 07 DLC-15
Hopkins Stephen A
Fr 1815 Jan 07 DLC-15
Fr 1815 Feb 12 DLC-16
To 1815 Feb 18 DLC-16
Fr 1815 Feb 22 DLC-17
To 1815 Feb 25 DLC-17
To 1815 Feb 25* DLC-62
To 1815 Feb 25* 4-0788
To 1815 Mar 04 DLC-62
Hopkins William
Fr 1834 Oct 20 M639-1
Hopkinson Joseph
Fr 1831 Mar 16 17-0902
Hopony
Fr 1818 Mar 13 DLC-24
Hopson Joshua B
Fr 1813 Oct 07 DLC-6
Hord Eldridge et al
Fr 1830 Sep 11 16-0236
To 1830 Sep 11 16-0238
Horn Harriett M
Fr 1840 Mar 06 DLC-52
Horn Henry
Fr 1829 Jun 06 M639-19
Fr 1831 Jul 21 18-0242
Fr 1832 Nov 01 M639-18
Fr 1833 Apr 01 M639-20
Fr 1833 Apr 15 M639-4
Fr 1833 Jul 12 23-0117
Fr 1833 Aug 24 M639-18
Fr 1834 Feb 16 DLC-44
Fr 1834 Feb 17 DLC-44
Fr 1834 Mar 19 M688-89
Fr 1834 Aug 14 DLC-44
Fr 1834 Oct 01 26-0467
Fr 1834 Nov 01 DLC-44
To 1834 Dec 16 chk 26-1522
To 1835 Jan 25 DLC-45
Fr 1835 Mar 31 DLC-46
Fr 1835 Apr 21 M639-15
Fr 1835 Apr 30 M639-18
Fr 1835 Jun 25 28-0785
To 1835 Jul 21 28-1098
Fr 1835 Dec 02 M639-17
To 1836 Jun 29 31-0642
Fr 1836 Oct 22 M124-155
Fr 1836 Dec 15 M687-21
To 1837 May 18 33-1229
Fr 1839 May 13 DLC-52
Fr 1839 Nov 06 DLC-52
Fr 1841 Apr 09 DLC-53
To 1841 Apr 19 35-0290
Fr 1841 May 01 DLC-53
Fr 1844 May 14 36-0541
Fr 1844 Oct 31 36-0974
Fr 1844 Nov 08# 36-1006
Horn Henry et al
Fr 1829 Feb M639-18
Fr 1829 Feb 17 12-0523
Fr 1829 Mar M639-7
Fr 1831 Feb 10 M639-5
Fr 1832 Jun 22 M22-29
Fr 1832 Aug 22 M639-18
Fr 1833 Oct 05 M124-140
Fr 1834 Nov 13 M179-79
Fr 1835 cFeb 13 M639-17
Fr 1835 cFeb 13 M639-17
Fr 1835 Apr 06 M639-18
Horn James et al
Fr 1834 Jan M234-288
Fr 1834 Jan* 24-0717
Horn Lawrence
Re 1798 Oct 05 leg 1-0682
Horn Lewis
Fr 1836 Apr 25 fin DLC-48
Fr 1836 Jun 17 fin DLC-48
Horner James
Fr 1835 Sep 04 M639-15
Horner John Scott
To 1835 Sep 08 29-0005
Fr 1837 Mar 22 DLC-50
Re 1837 Nov 22 34-0034
Fr 1838 Jan 25 DLC-51
Fr 1838 Apr 19 DLC-51
Horses and horseraces
see also names of
individual horses
Re 1807 Dec 31 fin DLC-58
Re 1810 Oct 18 2-0969
Re 1812 cSep 01 mem 2-1238
Re 1819 Jan fin DLC-72
Horton Joseph W
Fr 1825 Jun 28 fin 10-1327
Fr 1826 Jun 13 fin DLC-34
Fr 1828 Feb 28 fin DLC-35
Fr 1835 Jan 19 M639-9
Fr 1836 Oct 29 M688-104
Horton William D
Fr 1836 Oct 09 M688-104
Fr 1837 Jan M687-16
Horwitz Jonas
Fr 1829 Mar 30 M639-11
Hosack David
To 1832 Mar 19 DLC-40
Hoss John F et al
Fr 1825 Mar 10 DLC-33
To 1825 Mar 10 add DLC-33
Hotchkiss Calvin et al
Fr 1835 Mar 28 M567-108
Hotz Peter Jr
Re 1830 Mar 11 mem 15-0340
Houghland Jacob C
To 1831 Mar 28 17-0998
Houghton Samuel S
Fr 1834 Mar 15 M567-102

Houk George W
Fr 1843 Dec 30 DLC-56
House George
Fr 1831 Oct 03 M639-10
House George et al
To 1831 Oct 01 18-0910
Houston J W
Fr 1834 Oct 18# DLC-44
Houston James
Fr 1819 Sep 24 DLC-27
Fr 1819 Nov 17 DLC-28
Houston James B
Fr 1814 May 20 fin 3-1040
Fr 1816 Jun 25 fin DLC-69
Fr 1819 Feb 24 fin DLC-70
Fr 1820 Sep fin DLC-30
Houston John A
Fr 1829 Oct 14 DLC-75
Houston John H
Fr 1829 Feb 23# DLC-36
Fr 1829 Apr 14# 37-0499
Fr 1829 Apr 14* 12-1343
Fr 1837 Jan 04 32-1483
Houston R M et al
To 1834 Apr 07 25-0634
Fr 1834 Apr 07 25-0637
Houston Robert
Fr 1801 Apr 13 lnd 1-0865
Fr 1815 Dec 12 DLC-19
Houston Samuel Sr
Re 1804 Apr 05 leg 1-1299
Houston Samuel
Fr 1817 Jan 10 5-0674
To 1817 Jul 30# DLC-23
Fr 1817 Dec 18 5-1184
Fr 1818 Dec 06 7-0019
Fr 1822 Mar 11 M221-93
Fr 1822 Aug 03 DLC-72
Fr 1823 Jan 19 DLC-41
Fr 1824 Jul 20 DLC-33
To 1824 Jul 21 DLC-33
To 1824 Jul 21* 10-0836
Fr 1825 Aug 08 DLC-33
To 1825 Aug 11 DLC-33
To 1825 Dec 08 11-0072
To 1826 Mar 08 11-0159
To 1826 Mar 20 11-0175
To 1826 Apr 15 11-0195
Fr 1826 Jul 16 11-0322
To 1826 Oct 23 DLC-72
To 1826 Oct 23 DLC-72
To 1826 Nov 22 DLC-34
Fr 1826 Dec 13 DLC-72
To 1826 Dec 15 DLC-34
Fr 1826 Dec 18 DLC-75
To 1827 Jan 05 DLC-72
Fr 1827 Jan 05 DLC-34
To 1827 Jan 08 DLC-72
Fr 1827 Jan 13 DLC-72
To 1827 Jan 27 DLC-34
Fr 1827 Jan 28 DLC-34
To 1827 Feb 04 DLC-72
Fr 1827 Feb 04 DLC-72
Fr 1827 Feb 07 DLC-72
To 1827 Feb 15 DLC-72
Fr 1827 Feb 15 DLC-72
To 1827 Nov 07 11-0914
Fr c1828 11-0998
To 1828 Feb 13 11-1113
To 1828 Apr 02# DLC-72
To 1828 Jun 28 12-0033
To 1828 Dec 27# DLC-36
Fr 1829 Feb 12 M639-18
Fr 1829 May 11 DLC-72
Re 1829 May 21 mem 13-0367
To 1829 Jun 21 13-0696
Fr 1829 Jun 24 M234-236
Fr 1829 Jun 25 M234-236
Fr 1829 Sep 19 DLC-37
Fr 1830 cFeb M234-433
Fr 1830 cFeb* 15-0085
Fr 1830 Mar 22 M234-774
Fr 1830 May 18 DLC-72
Fr 1830 Dec 15 M234-631
Fr 1830 Dec 15* 16-1440
Fr 1833 Feb 13 22-0366
Fr 1833 Jul 30 DLC-43
Fr 1834 Apr 20 25-0839
Re 1834 Jul 03 par 26-0127
Fr 1835 Dec 17 DLC-73
Fr 1836 Apr 20 30-1273
Fr 1836 Aug 09 M179-82
To 1836 Sep 04 DLC-49
Fr 1836 Nov 20 32-0571
Fr 1836 Nov 20 DLC-49
To 1837 Jul 19 33-1384
Fr 1838 Jan 04 34-0160
To 1838 Aug 10# DLC-51
Fr 1838 Aug 11 DLC-74
To 1840 Jan 03 34-1137
Fr 1840 May 15 DLC-52
To 1841 Dec 12 35-0528
To 1842 May 25 35-0739
Fr 1842 Jul 26 35-0858
To 1842 Aug 17 35-0886
Fr 1843 Jan 31 DLC-55
Fr 1843 Jan 31* 35-1154
Fr 1843 Jul 24 35-1428
To 1844 Jan 18 36-0132
To 1844 Jan 19 36-0142
To 1844 Jan 23 36-0152
Fr 1844 Feb 16 36-0258
Fr 1844 Feb 17 DLC-56
Fr 1844 Feb 17 36-0290
To 1844 Mar 15 36-0386
Fr 1844 Apr 29 36-0457
To 1844 Jul 19 36-0723
Fr 1844 Dec 13 DLC-74
To 1845 Mar 12 36-1566
Fr 1845 Jun 08# DLC-58
Houston Samuel et al
Fr 1835 Sep 11 29-0031
Houston Samuel (VA)
Fr 1836 Jul 30 DLC-48
Houston William A
Fr 1833 Jan 04 M567-83
Hovey William et al
Fr 1836 Jun 04 31-0319
How Hall J
Fr 1836 Oct 13# 32-0172
Howard Benjamin
Fr 1818 Jan 26 DLC-24
Howard Benjamin Chew
Fr 1828 Nov 12 DLC-36
To 1828 Dec 04 12-0296
To 1828 Dec 04* DLC-36
Fr 1829 Mar 05 M639-15
To 1829 Mar 23 12-1086

Howard Benjamin Chew (cont)
Fr 1829 Apr 06 M639-20
Fr 1831 Feb 24 M688-77
To 1831 Aug 04 DLC-73
Fr 1832 Mar 27 M639-18
Fr 1832 Mar 31 20-0071
Fr 1835 Oct 24 M124-149
Fr 1836 Feb 16 M639-17
Fr 1836 Mar 14 M687-15
To 1837 Feb 02 33-0362
To 1837 Feb 02* DLC-50
Fr 1838 Jul 23 DLC-51
To 1838 Aug 02 34-0410
To 1838 Aug 02* DLC-51
Fr 1838 Aug 29 DLC-51
To 1838 Sep 13 34-0451
Howard Edward
Fr 1839 Jan 19 DLC-51
Howard Flodoardo
Fr 1834 May 01 fin DLC-44
Fr 1834 Aug 07 fin DLC-44
Fr 1834 Oct 01 fin DLC-44
Fr 1834 Nov 05 fin DLC-45
Fr 1834 Nov 30 fin DLC-45
Fr 1835 Jun 01 fin DLC-46
Fr 1835 Jul 07 fin DLC-46
Fr 1835 Aug 08 fin DLC-46
Fr 1835 Oct 04 fin DLC-47
Fr 1835 Dec 03 fin DLC-47
Howard Frances
Fr 1829 Jun 04 M567-43
Howard Jacob
Fr 1829 Apr 25 M639-11
Howard John
Re 1833 Sep par 23-0574
Re 1834 May 22 par 25-1129
Howard John E
Fr 1819 Mar 01 add DLC-26
Howard John H
Fr 1834 Jun 17 M234-241
Howard Joseph H
Fr 1834 Feb 01 M234-241
Fr 1834 Feb 01* 24-1127
Howard Joseph H et al
Fr 1835 May 19 28-0481
Fr 1835 May 19* M234-242
Howard Richard
Fr 1832 Mar 27 M688-84
Howard Robert
Fr 1844 Mar 26 DLC-56
Howard Tilghman Ashurst
Fr 1831 Nov 11 DLC-40
Fr 1833 Jul 27 DLC-43
To 1833 Aug 20 DLC-43
Fr 1835 Dec 03 DLC-47
Howe James B
Fr 1844 Dec 29 DLC-57
Howe John et al
Fr 1815 Feb 28 add DLC-17
Howe P G et al
Fr 1836 Apr 04 M687-28
Howell Aaron B
Fr 1831 Sep 16 M639-11
Howell Asher M
Fr 1834 Jan 02 M639-9
Fr 1845 Mar 22 DLC-57
Howell Hugh
Fr 1830 Oct 14 16-0377
Howell Joshua B et al
Fr 1835 Dec 21 M639-8
Howerton James
To 1839 May 12# fin DLC-52
Fr 1840 Mar 04 fin DLC-53
Fr 1840 Oct 21# DLC-53
Re c1841 mem 35-0158
Re c1841 mem 35-0159
To 1841 Jan 14 fin DLC-54
Re 1841 cMar 08 mem DLC-53
Fr 1841 Apr 05 DLC-53
Howerton William J
Fr 1839# fin DLC-52
To 1840 May 22# fin DLC-52
To 1840 Nov 01# fin DLC-53
Fr 1841 Jul 19# DLC-53
Howland Gardiner Greene
Fr 1833 Apr 24 M639-16
Howland G G & S et al
Fr 1829 Mar 26 M639-13
Fr 1830 May 19 15-1050
Fr 1832 Mar 08 M639-5
Fr 1832 May 08 M84-2
Hubbard Adolphus F
Fr 1829 Feb 14 M639-11
Hubbard David
Fr 1826 Apr 22 fin 11-0199
Fr 1844 Aug 22 36-0818
Hubbard Edward B
Fr 1842 Mar 19 DLC-54
Hubbard Henry
Fr 1832 Jan 27 M639-5
Fr 1836 Apr 18# 30-1227
Fr 1836 Dec 21 M639-5
Fr 1843 Jun 21 DLC-55
Hubbard Henry et al
Fr 1830 Apr 02 M639-7
Fr 1834 Dec 22 26-1553
Fr 1835 Jan 03 DLC-45
To 1835 Jan 07 DLC-45
Fr 1836 Apr 11 M639-17
Hubbard Henry G
Fr 1842 Mar 19 DLC-54
Hubbard James Mrs et al
Fr 1840 Oct 01 DLC-53
To 1840 Oct 05 DLC-53
Hubbard Simeon
Fr 1836 Jan 08 DLC-47
Fr 1836 Apr 09 DLC-48
Hubbell Horatio
Fr 1829 Feb 21 M639-11
Fr 1829 Aug 25 M639-11
Hubbell William Spring
Fr 1844 Mar 25 DLC-56
Hudry John
Re 1815 Mar 21 4-0894
Hudson Cuthbert
Fr 1814 Feb 16 DLC-9
Hudson David
Re 1831 Apr 15 par 17-1170
Hudson Thomas B
Fr 1843 Dec 07 DLC-56
Fr 1844 Mar 18 DLC-56
Huey John et al
Fr 1831 Feb 08 17-0472
Huey Joseph
To 1840 Sep 04 DLC-53
Huey Joseph et al
Fr 1840 Aug 01 DLC-53
Huger Francis Kinloch
Fr 1833 Dec 26# M124-141

Huges John
Re 1835 Feb 11 par 27-0492
Huggins ______ (Dr)
To 1844 May 03 DLC-56
Hughes Daniel
Fr 1814 Aug 11 DLC-11
Fr 1814 Dec 19 DLC-14
Fr 1814 Dec 20 DLC-14
Fr 1815 Jan 17 DLC-15
Fr 1815 Jan 17 DLC-15
Fr 1815 Jan 19 DLC-15
Fr 1815 Feb 17 DLC-16
Fr 1815 Mar 02 DLC-17
Fr 1815 Mar 02 DLC-17
Fr 1815 Mar 03 DLC-17
Fr 1815 Mar 03 DLC-17
To 1815 Mar 04 DLC-17
Fr 1815 Mar 06 DLC-17
Fr 1815 Mar 07 DLC-17
Fr 1815 Mar 09 DLC-17
Fr 1815 Mar 12 DLC-17
Fr 1815 Mar 12 DLC-17
Fr 1815 Mar 13 DLC-17
Fr 1818 Mar 08 DLC-24
Fr 1818 Mar 15 DLC-24
Fr 1826 May 06 DLC-33
Hughes George Wurtz
Fr 1834 Nov 11 M639-19
To 1835 Dec 08# 29-1033
Fr 1836 Sep M22-40
Re 1845 Mar 17 add DLC-57
Hughes Joseph
Re 1828 Sep 15 DLC-35
Fr 1835 Nov 28# fin DLC-47
Hughes Samuel
Fr 1807 Mar 26 2-0480
Hughes Sarah (alias Catherine)
Re 1836 May 18 par T967-2
Hughes William
Re 1836 Jan 22 par 30-0160
Hughey James
Fr 1839 May 12# fin DLC-52
Hulbert E N
Fr 1834 Dec 29 leg DLC-45
Huling David Watts
Fr 1829 Oct 20 M639-11
Fr 1829 Oct 20* 14-0221
Huling Frederick Watts
Fr 1829 Apr 12 M639-5
Fr 1833 Aug 16 M639-3
Hull Isaac
Fr 1841 Oct 24 DLC-53
To 1841 Nov 06 35-0479
To 1841 Nov 06* DLC-53
Hull James F
Fr 1814 Dec 23 DLC-14
Fr 1821 Dec 15 DLC-31
Hull John
Fr 1820 Oct 15 M222-21
Fr 1821 Feb 24 DLC-29
Hull William S
Fr 1842 Nov 29 DLC-54
Hull & Townsend
Fr 1823 Dec 15 DLC-32
To 1823 Dec 20 DLC-32
Fr 1823 Dec 24 DLC-32
Hulse Isaac
Fr 1834 Dec 24 26-1582
Hulsey Nicoll
Fr 1835 Jun 29 M639-18
Hulshart John
Re 1836 Apr 16 par 30-1195
Re 1836 Apr 27 par 30-1380
Humbert Jean Joseph Amable
Fr 1815 Jan 31 DLC-16
Fr 1815 Jan 31* 4-0659
To 1815 Feb 01 4-0675
To 1815 Feb 01* DLC-16
Fr 1815 Feb 05 DLC-16
Fr 1815 Feb 14 DLC-16
Fr 1815 Feb 15 DLC-16
Fr 1815 Feb 16 DLC-16
Fr 1815 Feb 16 DLC-16
Fr 1815 Feb 17 DLC-16
Fr 1815 Feb 22 DLC-67
Fr 1815 Feb 24 DLC-67
Fr 1815 Feb 28 DLC-17
Fr 1815 Mar 02 DLC-67
Fr 1815 Mar 03 DLC-17
Fr 1815 Mar 09 DLC-17
Fr 1815 Mar 17 DLC-17
Fr 1815 Mar 20 DLC-17
Fr 1815 Mar 23 DLC-17
To 1815 Apr 15 4-0990
Fr 1815 Jun 03 4-1074
Fr 1815 Jun 03* DLC-18
Re 1816 Apr 15 5-0035
Fr 1821 Jul 17 DLC-30
Fr 1821 Aug 04 DLC-30
Hume Ebenezer James
To 1830 Mar 11 chk DLC-37
Fr 1833 Jun 03 DLC-43
Fr 1839 Nov 02 DLC-52
Fr 1839 Nov 19 DLC-52
Hume Joseph
Fr 1839 Oct 15 34-0997
To 1840 Apr 04 34-1279
Hume William
Fr 1813 Jul 20 fin 3-0422
Fr 1813 Jul 20* fin DLC-7
Fr 1814 Mar 31 fin DLC-9
Fr 1814 May 14 3-1026
Fr 1816 Oct 15 fin 5-0534
Fr 1829 Jul 13 13-0844
Fr 1830 Aug 24 16-0143
Humphrey Enoch
Fr 1814 Sep 05 DLC-12
To 1814 Dec 21 DLC-62
Fr 1816 May 02 DLC-20
Humphreys Carlisle
Re 1816 Jun 21 leg 5-0187
Humphreys David
Fr 1812 Aug 29 DLC-5
Fr 1813 Dec 08 DLC-7
Fr 1813 Dec 08* DLC-61
Fr 1813 Dec 08 DLC-61
To 1813 Dec 08 DLC-61
To 1813 Dec 08 DLC-61
Fr 1816 Aug 28 DLC-21
Humphreys Moses
Fr 1801 Mar 30 leg 1-0854
Humphreys Parry Wayne
Fr 1830 Sep 10 M639-10
Humphreys Reuben
Fr 1818 Jun 23 fin DLC-69
Fr 1818 Jun 23* fin 6-1077
Fr 1819 May 30 DLC-27
To 1820 Jan 08 DLC-63
To 1820 Jan 08* M221-86
Fr 1820 Mar 04 DLC-28

Humphreys Reuben (cont)
Fr 1820 Mar 04* M221-86
To 1820 Apr 12 DLC-63
To 1820 May 20# DLC-63
To 1820 Jun 14# DLC-63
Fr 1820 Jun 28 DLC-29
To 1820 Jun 29# DLC-63
Fr 1820 Aug 04 DLC-29
To 1820 Aug 12 DLC-63
Fr 1820 Aug 20 DLC-29
To 1820 Aug 24 DLC-63
Fr 1820 Aug 27 DLC-29
Hunt Andrew M
Fr 1834 Mar 25 25-0355
Hunt Charlton
Fr 1827 Aug 29 DLC-34
To 1827 Sep 11 DLC-34
Fr 1829 Feb 23 M639-2
Hunt Fielding S
To 1842 Feb 10# DLC-54
Hunt James S
Re 1832 Oct 29 par 21-0212
Hunt Jesse
Fr 1832 Dec 26 DLC-41
Hunt John Wesley
Fr 1808 Oct 06 DLC-75
Hunt Memucan
Fr 1837 Feb 08 33-0571
Fr 1837 Mar 03 DLC-50
Hunt Philip D
Fr 1831 Mar 15 M222-29
Hunt Samuel & Co
Fr 1838 May 24# fin DLC-53
Fr 1838 Jul 02 fin DLC-53
To 1840 Jul 22 chk DLC-53
Fr 1841 May 13 fin DLC-55
Hunt Sylvester
Fr 1840 Jul 10 DLC-53
Hunt Thomas F
Fr 1818 Jun 19 DLC-25
Fr 1819 Apr 05 7-0460
Fr 1821 Apr 21 DLC-30
Re 1829 Mar 27 DLC-60
To 1835 Sep 02 28-1511
To 1835 Nov 07 29-0471
Re 1836 May 20 31-0061
Hunt W Hasell
Fr 1836 Feb 10 M179-81
Hunt W W & Co
Fr 1839 Oct 26 fin DLC-52
Hunt William Gilles
To 1826 May 03 DLC-33
Hunt William Gilles et al
Fr 1824 Oct 09 DLC-33
To 1824 Oct 10 DLC-33
Hunter Alexander
Fr 1829 Apr 27 M639-11
Fr 1829 Oct 15# M639-11
Fr 1831 Jul 25 18-0267
To 1835 Feb 26# DLC-45
Fr 1835 Aug 14 M221-115
Hunter Baldwin M
Fr 1835 Dec 15 29-1109
Hunter David
Fr 1833 Sep M567-82
Hunter Henry et al
Fr 1815 Feb 04 DLC-16
To 1815 Feb 17 DLC-62
Hunter Henry D
Fr 1836 Feb 17 30-0407
Hunter John
Fr 1831 Nov 28 M124-130
Hunter Robert
To 1835 May 08 28-0322
Hunter Robert R
Fr 1833 Jan 01 T239-3
Hunter Thomas
To 1814 Aug 03 DLC-62
Hunter William
Fr 1818 Jun 14 fin DLC-69
Fr 1818 Jun 14* fin 6-1050
To 1829 Jan 09 12-0454
Fr 1835 Aug 06 28-1247
Fr 1836 Jan 12 M121-12
Fr 1836 Oct 18# M121-12
Fr 1836 Oct 20 M121-12
Hunter's Hill farm
Re 1838 Apr 07 DLC-51
Re 1840 Mar 30 34-1265
Huntington Abel et al
Fr 1836 Feb 17 M639-8
Huntington Warren W
Fr 1838 Feb 18 DLC-51
Fr 1838 Apr 15 DLC-51
Hunton Charles et al
Fr 1836 Mar 21 M639-6
Hunton William E
Fr 1829 Mar 30 12-1181
Huntsman Adam
To 1830 Dec 16-0911
Fr 1835 Dec 31 M234-76
Fr 1836 Feb 15 DLC-47
Fr 1837 Jan 01 DLC-49
Fr 1837 Jan 01* DLC-74
To 1837 Jan 02 DLC-49
To 1837 Jan 02* DLC-74
Fr 1838 Jan 04 34-0162
Huntsman Adam et al
Fr 1830 cNov 25 16-0872
Fr 1837 May 29 DLC-50
To 1837 Jun 10 DLC-50
Fr 1842 Sep 09 DLC-54
Huntt Henry
Fr 1832 Jan fin DLC-73
Fr 1833 Mar 27# fin DLC-42
To 1833 Mar 27 chk DLC-42
Fr 1833 Apr 27# M639-27
Fr 1833 Oct 11 fin 23-1003
Fr 1836 Jan 01 fin DLC-47
To 1836 Jan 02 chk DLC-47
Fr 1837 Jan 02 fin 32-1475
To 1837 Jan 03 chk DLC-49
Huntzelman R B
Fr 1842 Jun 27 DLC-54
Hurst Edward
Fr 1841 Jun 17 35-0333
Husbands John
To 1807 Aug 19 fin DLC-4
Huse Nathaniel
Fr 1844 Jan 30 DLC-56
Hussey Ebenezer et al
Fr 1837 Feb M687-20
Huston John Jr et al
Fr 1836 cFeb M639-8
Huston Robert
Fr 1814 Aug 23 DLC-11
To 1814 Aug 25 DLC-62
Fr 1814 Aug 25 DLC-11
Hutchings ______ (soldier)
Fr 1821 Oct 07 fin DLC-70

Hutchings Stockley Donelson
Fr 1819 Sep 09 fin 7-0653
To 1819 Nov 09 fin 7-0847
Fr 1820 Nov 03 7-1399
Fr 1821 Feb 27 DLC-29
To 1821 Jul 19 DLC-63
Hutchings Thomas
Re 1791 Feb 18 leg 1-0092
Fr 1791 Oct 02 DLC-1
Re c1802 fin DLC-2
Re 1806 Oct leg 2-0351
Re 1807 Jan leg 2-0422
Re 1807 Jan 27 leg DLC-4
Re 1807 Apr leg 2-0482
Re 1808 Apr 13 leg 2-0635
Re 1813 May leg 3-0382
Hutchings William Jr et al
Fr 1829 May 29 M639-24
Hutchins Lewis
Re 1833 Dec 28 par 24-0621
Re 1833 Dec 28* par T967-1
Re 1834 Jan 24 par 24-1046
Hutchins Samuel A
Re 1831 Apr 28 par 17-1248
Hutchinson Anderson
Fr 1845 Apr 22 DLC-58
Hutchinson Archibald
Re 1832 Oct 31 par 21-0222
Hutchison James H
Fr 1835 Sep 17 M639-14
Hutchison Susan D (Nye)
Fr 1836 Feb 26 M688-97
Huttleson Henry
Re 1834 Oct 06 par 26-0510
Hutto Henry
Fr 1831 Jun 20 M22-28
Hutton Benjamin V L
Re 1837 Mar 02 par 33-0994
Hutton James
Fr 1836 Nov 14 32-0492
Hutton John B
Fr 1833 Mar 02# fin DLC-42
To 1834 Jul 01 chk DLC-44
Fr 1835 Mar 03# fin DLC-45
Huygens Roger Bangeman
To 1830 Jun 09 chk DLC-38
To 1832 Jan 13# M38-5
Huyler George
Fr 1831 Jul 30 M639-11
Fr 1831 Dec 30 M639-11
Fr 1833 Feb 23 M639-11
Re 1833 Mar 26 22-0896
Hyatt Noah et al
Fr 1832 Jun 12 20-0739
Hyde Archibald W
Fr 1837 Feb 26 M687-20
Hyde James N
Fr 1821 May 25# fin DLC-30
Hyde John E
To 1829 Nov 22# DLC-75
Fr 1829 Nov 26# DLC-75
Hynes Andrew
Re 1812 Dec 24 DLC-8
Re 1812 Dec 24* DLC-61
To 1813 Jan 16 fin 3-0250
To 1813 Mar 21 DLC-6
To 1813 Mar 21* DLC-61
Fr 1813 Apr 15 DLC-6
Fr 1813 Jul 16 DLC-6
Fr 1813 Aug 28 DLC-75
Fr 1813 Sep 01 3-0446
Fr 1813 Sep 09 DLC-6
Fr 1813 Dec 08 DLC-7
Fr 1814 Mar 26 DLC-9
Fr 1814 Aug 23 DLC-11
To 1814 Aug 27 4-0154
To 1814 Aug 30 4-0163
To 1814 Sep 17 4-0223
To 1814 Sep 17 4-0225
To 1814 Sep 19 4-0232
To 1814 Sep 26 4-0240
Fr 1814 Oct 04 DLC-13
Fr 1814 Oct 11 DLC-13
Fr 1814 Oct 14 DLC-13
To 1814 Oct 21 4-0284
To 1814 Oct 21* DLC-62
Fr 1814 Nov 14 4-0332
Fr 1814 Nov 15 DLC-14
Fr 1815 Jul 26 DLC-19
Fr 1815 Oct 24 DLC-19
Fr 1815 Nov 06 DLC-19
Fr 1815 Nov 18 4-1244
Fr 1816 Jun 19 DLC-21
Re 1817 Jan 09 5-0669
Hynes & Fletcher
Fr 1814 Jun 14 fin DLC-19
Hynes Knowles & Wood
Fr 1827 Aug 27 fin DLC-36

Idler Jacob
Fr 1833 Oct 30 23-1128
Ienari Shogun of Japan
To 1832 Jun 06 20-0705
To 1835 Mar 20 M37-10
Illinois Bank
Re c1833 mem DLC-43
Inaugural address
Re 1829 Mar 04 DLC-36
Re 1833 Mar 04 DLC-42
Re 1833 Mar 04* 22-0665
Re 1833 Mar 04* DLC-77
Re 1833 Mar 04* DLC-43
Independence Day
Re 1805 cJul 01 DLC-71
Re 1805 Jul 04 2-0070
Indian Affairs Commissioner
Re 1833 May 10 22-1331
Re 1836 Nov 08 32-0419
Re 1836 Nov 08* M21-19
Re 1836 Nov 08* M234-436
Indian removal
Re 1835 cDec add DLC-47
Indian reserves
Re 1836 Feb 12 30-0366
Indian traders British
Re 1829 cApr mem 12-1210
Indiana General Assembly
Fr 1834 Jan 06 M234-354
Fr 1836 Jan 23 30-0191
Ingalls E A
Fr 1843 Jun 22 DLC-55
Ingalls Theodore et al
Fr 1830 Jan 27 M639-9
Ingalls William
Fr 1829 Mar 17 M639-27
Fr 1829 Mar 23 M639-1
Fr 1829 Aug 09 13-1048

Fr 1829 Aug 09 13-1053
Fr 1829 Oct 14 M639-1

Ingersol E K
To 1825 Jan 31 10-1096

Ingersoll Charles Jared
Fr 1831 Feb 28# DLC-39
Fr 1833 Jul 04 DLC-43
Fr 1834 May 30 M688-94
Fr 1844 Feb 15 DLC-56
To 1844 Feb 26 DLC-56
Fr 1844 Nov 21 DLC-57
Fr 1844 Dec 28 DLC-57

Ingersoll Charles Jared et al
To 1830 Oct 12 16-0371
Fr 1835 Jan 12 M639-21

Ingersoll Ralph Isaacs
Fr 1833 Apr 19# M639-27

Ingham Samuel Delucenna
Fr 1826 Mar 08 DLC-33
To 1826 Apr 08 11-0187
To c1829 12-0371
To 1829 Mar 06# DLC-60
Fr 1829 Mar 13# fin 12-0997
To 1829 Mar 20# DLC-60
To 1829 Mar 28 12-1166
To 1829 Apr 04 12-1267
Fr 1829 Apr 11# fin 12-1319
To 1829 Apr 18 13-0067
To 1829 Apr 20 13-0074
Fr 1829 Apr 21 M639-11
To 1829 Apr 22 13-0097
To 1829 Apr 23 DLC-60
To 1829 Apr 23 13-0109
To 1829 cMay 13-0219
Fr 1829 May 08 M639-5
To 1829 May 30 13-0507
Fr 1829 Jun 04# fin 13-0570
Fr 1829 Jul 06# fin 13-0820
To 1829 Jul 18 13-0889
Fr 1829 Aug 03 13-1034
Fr 1829 Aug 03* M733-1
To 1829 Aug 06 13-1040
To 1829 Aug 06* M733-1
Fr 1829 Aug 12 13-1106
To 1829 Sep 16 13-1317
Fr 1829 Sep 21 13-1397
To 1829 Sep 24 13-1421
To 1829 Oct 03 14-0095
To 1829 Oct 03 14-0098
Fr 1829 Oct 10 14-0140
Fr 1829 Oct 10 DLC-37
Fr 1829 cOct 10 14-0143
To 1829 Oct 12 14-0148
To 1829 Oct 20 M625-405
To 1829 Oct 23 14-0242
To 1829 Oct 28 14-0255
To 1829 Oct 28* M127-2
Fr 1829 Nov 09 14-0437
To 1829 Nov 14 14-0460
Fr 1829 Nov 14 14-0461
To 1829 Nov 18 DLC-37
Fr 1829 Nov 18 14-0487
To 1829 Nov 19 14-0501
To 1829 Nov 19 14-0502
To 1829 Nov 20 14-0524
Fr 1829 Nov 24 DLC-37
Fr 1829 Nov 24 14-0579
Fr 1829 Nov 24 14-0585
Fr 1829 Nov 26 DLC-37
Fr 1829 Nov 27 DLC-37
Fr 1829 Dec 01 14-0789
To 1829 Dec 11 14-1009
To 1830 14-1243
Fr 1830 mem DLC-38
Fr 1830 Jan 04 14-1320
Fr 1830 Jan 08 DLC-37
To 1830 Jan 18 14-1458
Fr 1830 Jan 20 14-1480
Re 1830 Jan 29 mem 15-0063
To 1830 Feb 09 15-0117
To 1830 Feb 17 15-0164
To 1830 Feb 25 M179-68
Fr 1830 Mar 05 DLC-75
To 1830 Mar 06 DLC-75
To 1830 Mar 08 15-0312
Fr 1830 Mar 09 15-0315
Fr 1830 Mar 13 M639-3
To 1830 Mar 16 15-0376
Fr 1830 Mar 23 DLC-38
To 1830 Mar 23 DLC-38
To 1830 Mar 23 15-0444
To 1830 Mar 29 15-0528
To 1830 Mar 30 15-0534
Fr 1830 Apr 26 15-0814
To 1830 Apr 26 15-0815
To 1830 Apr 27 15-0826
Fr 1830 May 01 15-0873
To 1830 May 15 15-1028
Fr 1830 May 15 15-1030
To 1830 May 15 15-1032
To 1830 May 18 15-1045
To 1830 May 20 15-1055
Fr 1830 May 28 15-1186
To 1830 Jun 03 15-1280
To 1830 Jun 09 15-1333
Fr 1830 Jul 17 DLC-38
Fr 1830 cJul 20 DLC-38
Fr 1830 Jul 25 DLC-38
To 1830 Jul 31 DLC-38
To 1830 Aug 07 16-0075
Fr 1830 Oct 08 16-0345
To 1830 Oct 08 16-0346
To 1830 Oct 11 16-0360
To 1830 Oct 11 16-0362
To 1830 Oct 13 16-0374
To 1830 Oct 16 16-0400
To 1830 Oct 18 16-0434
To 1830 Oct 19 16-0453
To 1830 Oct 27 16-0566
To 1830 Nov 06 16-0653
Fr 1830 Nov 08 16-0693
To 1830 Nov 13 16-0719
To 1830 Nov 14 16-0731
Fr 1830 Dec 03 16-0982
To 1830 Dec 20 DLC-38
Fr 1830 Dec 27 17-0017
To 1831 Jan 28# DLC-73
Fr 1831 Feb 01 17-0399
Fr 1831 Feb 02 17-0411
To 1831 Mar 11 17-0840
To 1831 Mar 18 17-0904
To 1831 Apr 04 17-1064
To 1831 Apr 07 M221-111
Fr 1831 Apr 08 M688-82
Fr 1831 Apr 18 DLC-39
Re 1831 Apr 18 mem DLC-39
Fr 1831 Apr 19 DLC-39
To 1831 Apr 20 DLC-39

Entry	Note	Reference
Ingham Samuel Delucenna (cont)		
To 1831 Apr 22		DLC-39
To 1831 Jun 06		17-1531
Fr 1831 Jun 07		DLC-39
To 1831 Jun 08		DLC-39
Fr 1831 Jun 09		DLC-39
Fr 1831 Jun 20		DLC-39
Fr 1831 Jun 21		DLC-39
To 1831 Jun 23		DLC-39
Fr 1831 Jun 30		DLC-39
To 1831 Jul 07#		DLC-39
Fr 1831 Jul 26		18-0272
Ingraham Edward Duffield		
Fr 1834 Oct 29		26-0767
Fr 1835 Dec 02		M639-17
Fr 1836 May 26		31-0120
Ingraham Edward Duffield et al		
To 1834 Oct 14		26-0641
To 1834 Oct 14*		DLC-73
Ingram John J		
Fr 1834 Jul 25		DLC-44
Ingram & Lloyd		
Fr 1821 Apr 03	fin	DLC-30
Fr 1821 Nov 24	fin	DLC-70
Innerarity James		
To 1815 Apr 20		4-1005
Innerarity John		
Fr 1818 May		6-0536
To 1821 Aug 23		8-1091
Fr 1821 Sep		8-1120
Fr 1821 Sep		8-1117
Re 1821 Sep 06	leg	8-1156
Re 1821 Sep 17	leg	8-1174
Re 1821 Sep 25	mem	8-1211
Re 1821 Sep 25		8-1216
To 1821 Sep 27		DLC-63
Fr 1821 Sep 27		8-1225
Fr 1821 Sep 27		8-1228
Re 1821 Oct 08	leg	8-1285
Re 1821 Dec 10	leg	DLC-31
Inskeep A H & Co		
To 1821 May 16#	fin	DLC-30
Inskeepe John		
Fr 1806 Jul 19		DLC-4
Instone John		
Re 1805 Feb 11	mem	DLC-3
Ioway and Sac and Fox treaty		
Re 1837 Feb 21		M668-8
Irby John K		
Fr 1818 Jun 09	fin	DLC-69
Fr 1818 Jun 09*	fin	6-1039
Iredell James		
Fr 1829 Mar 04		M639-3
Irion Robert Anderson		
Fr 1838 Nov 30		DLC-51
Irons John		
Fr 1836 Oct 03		M688-104
Irons Joseph Fenley		
Fr 1836 Oct 03		M688-104
Irvin David		
Fr 1835 Feb 27		27-0646
Fr 1836 Apr 01		30-0970
Irvin Robert		
Fr 1829 Jul 26		13-0932
Irvin William W		
Fr 1829 Feb 18		M639-11
Fr 1829 Feb 18		M639-10
To 1832 Apr 07#		20-0168
Irvine Clementina		
Fr 1835 Dec 26		M688-104
Irvine Robert		
Fr 1818		37-0493
Irving Levin G et al		
Fr 1835 Jan 10		M639-8
Irving Washington		
Re 1829 Jun 01		13-0544
Fr 1830 Oct 10		16-0357
Fr 1831 Feb 13		M639-16
To 1833 Jun 13#		23-0019
Irwin David		
To 1814 Feb 22		DLC-61
Fr 1816 Jul 09	fin	DLC-23
Irwin Hayes		
Re 1804 May 08	fin	DLC-3
Irwin James		
Fr 1804 Nov 09		1-1408
Fr 1805 Jan 25		DLC-71
Fr 1805 Feb 09		DLC-71
Fr 1805 Oct 14		DLC-3
Fr 1814 Sep 19		DLC-12
Irwin John		
To 1796 Jul 13#	fin	1-0442
Fr 1801 May 29#		1-0878
Irwin Joseph		
To 1842 Jan 22		DLC-74
Irwin Thomas		
Fr 1829 Mar		12-0679
Fr 1829 Mar 21		M639-6
Re 1831 Apr 14		17-1164
Fr 1833 May 20		22-1413
Fr 1835 Dec 01		M639-8
Isacks Jacob C		
Fr 1829 Mar 07		M639-13
Ish William		
Fr 1838 Oct 08		DLC-51
Ishtahotapa et al		
Fr 1834 Mar 07		24-1585
Fr 1834 Mar 07		T494-3
Fr 1834 Mar 07*		24-1591
Fr 1835		M234-136
Fr 1835 Jul 24		28-1144
Fr 1836 Jun 10		31-0422
Fr 1836 Jun 10*		M234-145
Fr 1837 Feb 17		M234-137
Islands James et al		
Re 1836 Apr 16	lnd	30-1191
Isler Nathaniel et al		
Fr 1832 cMay		20-0416
Ivey Thomas		
Fr 1828 Feb 25	fin	DLC-35
Fr 1829 Jan 02	fin	DLC-36
Fr 1829 Jan 06	fin	DLC-36
Iyacherhopia et al		
Fr 1833 Feb 06		M234-170
Fr 1833 Feb 06*		22-0287
J M L		
Fr 1831 Oct 31		DLC-40
J W		
To 1815 Jan 11	chk	DLC-15
Jack Charles J		
Fr 1829 Jan		M639-12
Fr 1829 Feb 24		M639-7
Fr 1829 Mar 14#		M639-12
Fr 1829 Mar 29#		12-1177
Fr 1829 Apr 17		12-1378
Fr 1829 Aug 20		M639-12
Fr 1835 Dec 21		M639-18

Jack John
    Fr 1829 Apr 06   M639-10
Jackson Andrew
--accounts military
    Re 1812 Dec 10   2-1281
    Re 1813 Feb 01   3-0265
    Re 1813 Feb 10   3-0269
    Re 1813 Sep 26   3-0484
    Re 1813 Sep 26*   DLC-10
    Re 1814 Jun 08   3-1089
    Re 1814 Sep 07   4-0184
    Re 1815 Jun 01   4-1073
    Re 1815 Aug 01   4-1141
    Re 1815 Oct 01   DLC-19
    Re 1815 Oct 01*   4-1201
    Re 1816 Jan 01   4-1316
    Re 1816 Jul 01   5-0251
    Re 1816 Oct 01   5-0524
    Re 1816 Nov 01   5-0561
    Re 1817 Jun 01   5-0887
    Re 1817 Jul 14   DLC-23
    Re 1818 Jan 01   5-1222
    Re 1818 Jul 01   6-1096
    Re 1818 Oct 01   6-1335
    Re 1819 Jan 26   7-0197
    Re 1819 Feb 16   7-0278
    Re 1819 Feb 19   7-0289
    Re 1819 Apr 01   7-0446
    Re 1819 Jun 17   7-0557
    Re 1819 Oct 01   7-0696
    Re 1820 Jan   7-0968
    Re 1820 Jan 01   7-0972
    Re 1820 Mar 13   7-1040
    Re 1820 Dec 31   DLC-29
    Re 1821 Mar 14   DLC-30
    Re 1821 Apr 11   8-0307
    Re 1821 Oct 01   DLC-70
    Re 1821 Dec 18   8-1371
    Re 1821 Dec 18*   DLC-31
--accounts personal and White House
    Re 1803 Nov 8   fin   DLC-3
    Re c1804   mem   DLC-60
    Re 1810 cJan 02   mem   DLC-4
    Re 1812 Feb 19   chk   DLC-5
    Re 1812 Mar 18   chk   DLC-5
    Re 1812 Dec   mem   DLC-13
    Re 1813 Jul 07   chk   DLC-6
    Re 1813 Jul 21   chk   DLC-6
    Re 1819   mem   7-0112
    Re 1822 Sep   mem   DLC-78
    Re 1829 Jan   mem   12-0415
    Re 1833 May 02   mem   22-1262
    Re 1836 Aug 10   fin   31-1277
    Re 1836 Aug 10*   fin
    Re 1837 Feb 22   fin   33-0822
    Re 1837 Mar 23   fin   33-1099
    Re 1842 Jan 05   mem   DLC-54
    Re 1842 Jan 11   mem   DLC-54
--bank books
    Re 1810 May 26   2-0923
    Re 1829 Feb 12   DLC-78
    Re 1829 Feb 12   DLC-78
    Re 1833 Apr 02   DLC-78
    Re 1833 Dec 18   DLC-78
    Re 1835 Nov 27   DLC-78
    Re 1839 Mar 09   DLC-78
    Re 1840 Jul 16   DLC-78
--biography
    Re 1843   mem   35-1075
    Re 1843 cJan   mem   DLC-74
    Re 1843 cMay 05   mem   35-1341
    Re c1844 Jan   mem   36-0091
--checks to self
    To 1811 Jul 24   DLC-5
    To 1811 Oct 09   DLC-5
    To 1811 Oct 23   DLC-5
    To 1812 Mar 11   DLC-5
    To 1813 Aug 24   DLC-6
    To 1813 Sep 04   DLC-6
    To 1813 Sep 14   DLC-6
    To 1814 Jun 21   DLC-10
    To 1814 Jun 21   DLC-10
    To 1815 Jul 18   DLC-18
    To 1816 Feb 26   DLC-20
    To 1816 Feb 26   DLC-20
    To 1816 Aug 02   DLC-21
    To 1816 Aug 19   DLC-21
    To 1816 Aug 20   DLC-21
    To 1816 Oct 14   DLC-21
    To 1826 Oct 22   11-0384
    To 1827 Dec 26   11-0982
    To 1828 Sep 02   12-0181
    To 1830 Jan 07   DLC-37
    To 1830 Dec 27   DLC-38
    To 1831 Apr 01   DLC-39
    To 1831 May 05   DLC-39
    To 1831 Jun 08   17-1565
    To 1831 Jul 27   DLC-39
    To 1831 Aug 29   DLC-40
    To 1831 Sep 17   DLC-40
    To 1831 Oct 06   DLC-40
    To 1831 Nov 17   DLC-40
    To 1831 Dec 12   DLC-40
    To 1831 Dec 14   DLC-40
    To 1832 Jan 07   DLC-40
    To 1832 Jan 14   DLC-40
    To 1832 Jan 30   DLC-40
    To 1832 Mar 26   DLC-40
    To 1832 Mar 29   DLC-40
    To 1832 Apr 02   DLC-40
    To 1832 Apr 10   DLC-40
    To 1832 Apr 14   20-0230
    To 1832 Apr 18   DLC-40
    To 1832 May 30   DLC-40
    To 1832 Jul 19   DLC-41
    To 1832 Nov 01   DLC-41
    To 1832 Nov 12   DLC-41
    To 1832 Nov 29   DLC-41
    To 1832 Dec 24   DLC-41
    To 1833 Feb 16   DLC-42
    To 1833 Mar 27   DLC-42
    To 1833 Apr 02   DLC-42
    To 1833 May 06   DLC-42
    To 1833 Jun 05   DLC-43
    To 1833 Sep 07   DLC-43
    To 1833 Oct 02   DLC-43
    To 1833 Oct 07   DLC-43
    To 1833 Oct 09   DLC-43
    To 1833 Nov 16   DLC-43
    To 1833 Nov 27   DLC-43
    To 1833 Dec 19   DLC-43
    To 1834 Jan 04   24-0752
    To 1834 Apr 19   DLC-44
    To 1834 May 08   DLC-44
    To 1834 Jun 26   DLC-44
    To 1834 Jun 28   DLC-44
    To 1834 Jul 07   DLC-44
    To 1834 Jul 07   DLC-44

Jackson Watson & Co			
	To 1802	fin	1-0949
	Fr 1802 Jun 30	fin	DLC-2
	Re c1803	fin	DLC-2
	Fr 1803	fin	DLC-71
	Re 1803 Sep	fin	DLC-3
	Re c1804	mem	1-1269
Jackson Andrew (VA)			
	Fr 1843 Sep 05		DLC-55
Jackson Andrew Jr			
	Fr 1814 Apr 08		DLC-10
	To 1824 Jan 05		9-0894
	To 1824 Jan 15		9-0927
	To 1824 Feb 12		10-0454
	To 1824 Apr 05		10-0630
	To 1824 Nov#		DLC-33
	To c1827		11-0453
	To 1827 Jan 31		DLC-34
	To 1827 Nov 27		DLC-35
	To 1828 May 15		12-0010
	Re 1829	mem	DLC-78
	To 1829 Mar 10	chk	DLC-36
	To 1829 Mar 26	chk	DLC-36
	To 1829 Apr 20	chk	DLC-37
	To 1829 Jun 03	chk	DLC-37
	To 1829 Jun 23	chk	DLC-37
	To 1829 Jul 04		DLC-37
	To 1829 Jul 20		DLC-37
	To 1829 Jul 22		DLC-37
	To 1829 Jul 26		13-0935
	To 1829 Aug 18	chk	DLC-37
	To 1829 Aug 18		DLC-37
	To 1829 Aug 19		DLC-37
	To 1829 Aug 20		DLC-37
	To 1829 Sep 21		DLC-37
	Fr 1829 Oct 19#	fin	14-0200
	To 1829 Dec 10#	fin	DLC-72
	To 1829 Dec 17	chk	DLC-37
	To 1829 Dec 22	chk	14-1093
	To 1830 Jan 06#	fin	DLC-38
	To 1830 Jan 11#	fin	14-1382
	To 1830 Jan 15	chk	DLC-37
	To 1830 Jan 20#	fin	DLC-38
	To 1830 Apr 08#	fin	DLC-40
	To 1830 Apr 15	chk	DLC-38
	To 1830 May 11#	fin	DLC-38
	To 1830 May 18	chk	15-1046
	To 1830 May 29#	fin	DLC-38
	To 1830 Jun 12	chk	DLC-38
	To 1830 Oct 19	chk	DLC-38
	To 1830 Nov 12#	fin	DLC-38
	To 1830 Nov 25#		DLC-38
	To 1830 Dec 14#	fin	DLC-38
	To 1830 Dec 18	chk	DLC-38
	To 1830 Dec 30	chk	DLC-38
	To 1831 Jan 03	chk	DLC-38
	To 1831 Feb 01	chk	DLC-39
	To 1831 Feb 02#	fin	DLC-39
	To 1831 Feb 02#	fin	DLC-40
	To 1831 Feb 24	chk	DLC-39
	To 1831 Mar 07	chk	DLC-39
	To 1831 May 14		17-1370
	To 1831 May 14	chk	DLC-39
	To 1831 May 16		17-1374
	To 1831 May 18		17-1387
	To 1831 Jun 23		DLC-39
	Fr 1831 Jun 27#	fin	DLC-39
	To 1831 Jul 03		18-0147
	To 1831 Jul 09		DLC-39

Fr 1831 Aug 27#		18-0608
Fr 1831 Sep 09#		37-0425
To 1831 Sep 10	chk	DLC-40
To 1831 Sep 16		DLC-40
Fr 1831 Sep 26#		37-0507
Fr 1831 Oct 08#		37-0429
To 1831 Oct 10	chk	DLC-40
To 1831 Oct 26	chk	DLC-40
To 1831 Oct 27		18-1140
To 1831 Nov 17	chk	DLC-40
Re 1831 Nov 25	leg	18-1487
To 1831 Dec 20	chk	DLC-40
To 1832 Jan 11	chk	19-0664
To 1832 Jan 23#	fin	DLC-43
Fr 1832 Feb 06#		37-0433
To 1832 Feb 07#	fin	DLC-40
To 1832 Mar 19#		DLC-40
To 1832 Mar 22#	fin	DLC-40
To 1832 Mar 23	chk	DLC-40
To 1832 Mar 23	chk	DLC-40
Fr 1832 Mar 26#		37-0513
To 1832 cMar 31		DLC-40
To 1832 Apr 12		DLC-40
To 1832 Apr 23		20-0349
To 1832 Apr 25		DLC-40
To 1832 May 06		20-0479
To 1832 May 06		20-0481
To 1832 May 13		DLC-40
To 1832 May 15		20-0527
To 1832 May 19		DLC-40
To 1832 May 24		DLC-40
To 1832 May 31		20-0685
To 1832 Jun 09		DLC-40
To 1832 Jun 10#		20-0732
To 1832 Jun 13		DLC-40
To 1832 Jun 21		20-0785
To 1832 Jun 27		20-0829
To 1832 Jul 19		DLC-41
To 1832 Jul 22		20-1218
To 1832 Jul 29		DLC-41
To 1832 Aug 10		DLC-41
To 1832 Sep 17	lnd	21-0024
To 1832 Sep 23		DLC-41
To 1832 Sep 30		21-0055
To 1832 Oct 21		DLC-41
To 1832 Oct 22		21-0132
To 1832 cNov 01		21-0261
To 1832 Nov 08		DLC-41
To 1832 Nov 12		21-0392
To 1832 Nov 16		21-0410
To 1832 Nov 25		DLC-41
To 1832 Dec 08		21-0927
To 1832 Dec 19		DLC-41
To 1832 Dec 24		DLC-41
Fr c1833#		37-0310
To 1833 Jan 08		21-1374
To 1833 Jan 15	chk	DLC-42
To 1833 Jan 21		DLC-42
To 1833 Mar 10#	fin	DLC-42
To 1833 Mar 15	chk	DLC-42
To 1833 Mar 27#	fin	DLC-42
To 1833 Mar 27#	fin	DLC-42
To 1833 Mar 29		22-0912
To 1833 Apr 02		DLC-42
To 1833 Apr 05		DLC-42
To 1833 Apr 08		DLC-42
To 1833 Apr 16		DLC-42
To 1833 Apr 20		22-1062
To 1833 Apr 30#	fin	DLC-43

Jackson Andrew Jr (cont)

To	1833 May 07#	fin	DLC-43
To	1833 Jun 05	leg	22-1577
To	1833 Jun 05	chk	22-1578
To	1833 Jun 06		DLC-43
To	1833 Jun 10		DLC-43
To	1833 Jun 14		DLC-43
To	1833 Jun 17		DLC-43
To	1833 Jun 28#		23-0066
To	1833 Jul 02	chk	DLC-43
To	1833 Aug 10		23-0313
Fr	1833 Aug 17#		23-0362
To	1833 Aug 27#		DLC-43
To	1833 Aug 31		DLC-43
To	1833 Sep 02		23-0587
To	1833 Sep 24		23-0856
To	1833 Sep 27	chk	DLC-43
To	1833 Oct		23-0922
Fr	1833 Oct 04		DLC-43
To	1833 Oct 06		23-0982
To	1833 Oct 08		DLC-43
To	1833 Oct 09#		23-1000
To	1833 Oct 11		DLC-43
To	1833 Oct 11		23-1004
To	1833 Oct 19		23-1063
To	1833 Oct 20		23-1071
To	1833 Oct 20#	fin	DLC-43
To	1833 Oct 26		DLC-43
To	1833 Oct 27		DLC-43
To	1833 Oct 28		DLC-43
To	1833 Oct 31#	fin	DLC-44
To	1833 Nov		23-1161
To	1833 Nov 01		DLC-43
To	1833 Nov 13		DLC-43
To	1833 Nov 16		DLC-43
To	1833 Nov 23		23-1298
To	1833 Nov 25		DLC-43
To	1833 Dec 03		DLC-43
To	1833 Dec 08		DLC-43
To	1833 Dec 15		DLC-43
To	1833 Dec 22		DLC-43
To	1833 Dec 26#	lnd	DLC-43
To	1833 Dec 31#	lnd	DLC-45
To	1833 Dec 31*	lnd	24-0690
Fr	1834	fin	DLC-78
To	1834 Jan 11		24-0856
Fr	1834 Jan 25		DLC-44
To	1834 Jan 26		DLC-44
Fr	1834 Jan 30#		DLC-44
To	1834 Feb 05		DLC-44
To	1834 Feb 08		DLC-44
To	1834 Feb 08		24-1255
To	1834 Feb 12		DLC-44
To	1834 Feb 16		DLC-44
To	1834 Mar 02		24-1521
To	1834 Mar 09		DLC-44
To	1834 Mar 16		DLC-44
To	1834 Mar 24		DLC-44
To	1834 Mar 26		DLC-44
To	1834 Apr 06		DLC-44
To	1834 Apr 15		DLC-44
To	1834 Apr 15*		25-0708
To	1834 Apr 20		DLC-44
To	1834 Apr 27		DLC-44
To	1834 May 01		25-0950
To	1834 May 02		DLC-44
Fr	1834 May 06#	fin	DLC-44
Fr	1834 May 07#	fin	DLC-44
To	1834 May 16		DLC-44
Fr	1834 May 19	fin	25-1090

To	1834 May 25		DLC-44
Fr	1834 May 25		DLC-73
To	1834 Jun 02		DLC-44
To	1834 Jun 05		DLC-44
To	1834 Jun 18		DLC-44
To	1834 Jun 23#	fin	DLC-51
To	1834 Jul 15		DLC-44
To	1834 Jul 26		DLC-44
To	1834 Aug 29		DLC-44
To	1834 Sep 10		DLC-44
To	1834 Sep 11		DLC-44
To	1834 Oct 01		DLC-44
To	1834 Oct 11		DLC-44
To	1834 Oct 12		DLC-44
To	1834 Oct 15		DLC-44
To	1834 Oct 20#	fin	DLC-50
To	1834 Oct 21		DLC-44
To	1834 Oct 23		DLC-44
To	1834 Oct 25		DLC-44
To	1834 Oct 30		DLC-44
To	1834 Oct 30		26-0777
To	1834 Nov 02		DLC-45
To	1834 Nov 11		26-0894
To	1834 Nov 12		DLC-45
To	1834 Nov 14#	fin	DLC-51
To	1834 Nov 15		DLC-45
To	1834 Nov 19		DLC-45
Fr	1834 Nov 20#		DLC-73
To	1834 Nov 26		DLC-45
To	1834 Nov 27		DLC-45
To	1834 Nov 29		DLC-45
To	1834 Dec 01		DLC-43
To	1834 Dec 04		26-1409
Fr	1834 Dec 06#		DLC-73
To	1834 Dec 07		26-1431
To	1834 Dec 09		DLC-45
Fr	1834 Dec 14#		DLC-73
To	1834 Dec 15#	fin	DLC-45
To	1834 Dec 19#	fin	DLC-45
To	1835 Jan 01	mem	DLC-45
To	1835 Jan 11#	fin	DLC-45
To	1835 Jan 21#	fin	DLC-47
To	1835 Mar 06#		DLC-45
To	1835 Mar 17#	fin	DLC-45
To	1835 Apr 02#	fin	DLC-46
To	1835 Apr 04		DLC-46
To	1835 Apr 05		DLC-46
To	1835 Apr 07		27-1559
To	1835 Apr 09		28-0006
To	1835 Apr 14		DLC-46
To	1835 Apr 15		DLC-46
To	1835 Apr 17		DLC-46
To	1835 Apr 21		DLC-46
To	1835 Apr 23		DLC-46
To	1835 Apr 25		DLC-46
Fr	1835 Apr 25#		DLC-73
To	1835 Apr 29		DLC-46
To	1835 May 01		DLC-46
To	1835 May 02		DLC-46
To	1835 May 02		DLC-46
To	1835 May 03		DLC-46
To	1835 May 04		DLC-46
To	1835 May 07		DLC-46
Fr	1835 May 08#		28-0326
To	1835 May 09		DLC-46
To	1835 May 11		DLC-46
To	1835 May 16		DLC-46
To	1835 May 20		28-0483
To	1835 May 20*		DLC-73

To	1835	May	21		28-0489
To	1835	May	22		DLC-46
To	1835	May	31		DLC-46
To	1835	Jun	01		DLC-46
To	1835	Jun	03		DLC-46
To	1835	Jun	03#	fin	DLC-51
Fr	1835	Jun	18#	fin	DLC-53
To	1835	Jul	01#	fin	DLC-47
To	1835	Jul	29#	fin	DLC-46
To	1835	Jul	31#		DLC-49
To	1835	Aug	26#		DLC-46
To	1835	Aug	30		DLC-46
To	1835	Sep	01#	fin	DLC-46
To	1835	Sep	02		DLC-46
To	1835	Sep	04		28-1520
To	1835	Sep	06		DLC-46
To	1835	Sep	09		DLC-46
To	1835	Sep	12		DLC-46
To	1835	Sep	12	chk	DLC-46
To	1835	Sep	22	chk	DLC-47
To	1835	Sep	27		DLC-47
To	1835	Sep	29		DLC-47
To	1835	Oct	01		DLC-47
To	1835	Oct	01		DLC-47
To	1835	Oct	05		DLC-47
To	1835	Oct	07		29-0230
To	1835	Oct	08		DLC-47
To	1835	Oct	09	fin	29-0247
To	1835	Oct	10		DLC-47
Fr	1835	Oct	11#		DLC-73
To	1835	Oct	12		DLC-47
To	1835	Oct	15		DLC-47
To	1835	Oct	15#	fin	DLC-51
To	1835	Oct	17		DLC-47
To	1835	cOct	20		29-0319
To	1835	Oct	25		DLC-47
To	1835	Oct	30		DLC-47
To	1835	Nov	02		DLC-47
To	1835	Nov	18#	fin	DLC-48
Fr	1835	Nov	19#	fin	DLC-47
Fr	1835	Dec	08#		29-1033
To	1835	Dec	10	chk	DLC-47
To	1835	Dec	12#	fin	DLC-47
To	1835	Dec	28	chk	DLC-47
To	1836	Jan	01#	fin	DLC-49
To	1836	Jan	01#	fin	DLC-47
To	1836	Jan	02#	fin	DLC-47
To	1836	Jan	26#	fin	DLC-47
To	1836	Feb	13#	fin	DLC-47
To	1836	Mar	01		DLC-47
To	1836	Mar	02	chk	DLC-47
To	1836	Mar	15		DLC-47
To	1836	Mar	17		DLC-47
To	1836	Mar	25		30-0899
To	1836	Mar	29		DLC-47
To	1836	Apr	02		DLC-47
Fr	1836	Apr	10#		DLC-73
Fr	1836	Apr	16#		30-1193
To	c1836	Apr	16#	fin	30-1216
To	1836	Apr	25#	fin	DLC-48
Re	1836	Apr	25#	fin	30-1350
To	1836	May	14	chk	DLC-48
To	1836	May	28#		DLC-48
To	1836	May	30#	fin	DLC-48
To	1836	Jun	02	chk	DLC-48
To	1836	Jun	04#	fin	DLC-49
Fr	1836	Jun	18#		M124-153
To	1836	Jun	20		DLC-48
To	1836	Jun	22		DLC-48
To	1836	Jun	24		DLC-48
To	1836	Jun	24		DLC-48
To	1836	Jun	24#		DLC-48
To	1836	Jun	27		DLC-48
To	1836	Jun	29#	fin	DLC-48
To	1836	Jun	30		DLC-48
Fr	1836	Jun	30	fin	DLC-48
To	1836	Jul	04		DLC-48
To	1836	Jul	05#		DLC-48
To	1836	Jul	10		DLC-48
To	1836	Jul	16#	fin	DLC-50
To	1836	Jul	17		DLC-48
To	1836	Jul	18#	fin	DLC-48
To	1836	Jul	23		DLC-48
To	1836	Jul	30		DLC-48
To	1836	Aug	01		31-1187
Fr	1836	Aug	05#		31-1234
To	1836	Aug	17#		DLC-48
To	1836	Aug	23		DLC-49
To	1836	Aug	26		DLC-49
To	1836	Sep	09		DLC-49
To	1836	Sep	14		31-1445
To	1836	Sep	17		DLC-49
To	1836	Sep	17#	fin	DLC-50
To	1836	Sep	19		DLC-49
Fr	1836	Sep	20#	leg	31-1473
Fr	1836	Sep	20*	leg	DLC-56
To	1836	Sep	22		DLC-49
To	1836	Sep	23		DLC-49
To	1836	Oct	21	chk	DLC-49
To	1836	Oct	31#	fin	DLC-50
To	1836	Nov	02#	fin	DLC-50
To	1836	Nov	03#	fin	DLC-50
Fr	1836	Nov	03	fin	32-0399
To	1836	Nov	04		DLC-49
To	1836	Nov	05		DLC-49
To	1836	Nov	06		DLC-49
To	1836	Nov	09#	fin	DLC-50
To	1836	Nov	09#	fin	32-0474
To	1836	Dec	02		32-0617
Fr	1836	Dec	02#		32-0618
Fr	1836	Dec	12#		32-1096
To	1836	Dec	21	chk	DLC-49
To	1836	Dec	26#	fin	DLC-50
To	1836	Dec	29#		DLC-49
To	1836	Dec	29#	fin	DLC-50
Fr	1837	Jan#			DLC-49
To	1837	Jan	08#		DLC-49
To	1837	Jan	16		37-0530
To	1837	Jan	16#		37-0531
Fr	1837	Jan	23#		33-0109
To	1837	Jan	23#	fin	DLC-51
To	1837	Jan	28	chk	DLC-49
To	1837	Feb	06#		DLC-50
To	1837	Fcb	07#		M567-149
To	1837	Feb	08	chk	DLC-50
To	1837	Feb	09#		DLC-50
To	1837	Feb	11#		DLC-50
To	1837	Feb	17	chk	DLC-50
To	1837	Feb	22#		DLC-74
To	1837	Feb	24#	fin	DLC-50
To	1837	Feb	24#	fin	DLC-50
To	1837	Feb	25#		33-0898
To	1837	Feb	28#		M687-9
Fr	1837	Mar	04#		33-1065
To	1837	Mar	06	chk	DLC-50
To	1837	Mar	06#	fin	DLC-50
Fr	1837	cMar	06#		33-1072
Fr	1837	Mar	06#	mem	33-1074

Jackson Andrew Jr (cont)

To	1837 Mar 08#	fin	DLC-50
Re	1837 Mar 16	fin	33-1078
To	1837 Apr 08#	fin	DLC-51
To	1837 Apr 22#	fin	DLC-51
Fr	1837 May 14#		33-1226
To	1837 Jun 03#	fin	DLC-50
To	1837 Jun 08#	fin	DLC-50
To	1837 Jun 22#	fin	DLC-50
To	1837 Jul 04	mem	DLC-50
To	1837 Jul 07#		DLC-50
To	1837 Jul 29#	fin	DLC-50
Fr	1837 Aug#		33-1402
To	1837 Sep 11#	fin	DLC-50
To	1837 Oct 04		DLC-50
To	1837 Oct 05#	fin	DLC-53
To	1837 Oct 05#	fin	DLC-51
To	1837 Oct 26#		DLC-50
To	1837 Nov 02#		DLC-50
To	1837 Nov 09#	fin	DLC-50
To	1837 Nov 13#		DLC-50
Fr	1837 Dec 01#		34-0066
To	1838 Mar 12		DLC-51
To	1838 Mar 15#		DLC-51
To	1838 Mar 19#	fin	DLC-51
To	1838 Apr 05		DLC-51
To	1838 Apr 06#	lnd	DLC-51
To	1838 Apr 07#	fin	DLC-51
To	1838 Apr 10#	fin	DLC-51
To	1838 Apr 11		34-0318
To	1838 Apr 19#	fin	DLC-51
To	1838 Apr 30#		DLC-51
To	1838 May 23#	fin	DLC-51
To	1838 May 29#	fin	DLC-51
Fr	1838 Jun 07#	fin	DLC-51
Fr	1838 Jun 07#		DLC-51
Fr	1838 Jul 20#	fin	DLC-51
Fr	1838 Nov 01#	fin	DLC-51
To	1838 Nov 11		DLC-51
To	1838 Dec 03#		DLC-51
To	1839#	fin	DLC-52
To	c1839	mem	DLC-52
To	1839 Jan 01#	fin	DLC-53
Fr	1839 Jan 03#	fin	DLC-51
To	1839 Jan 05#	fin	DLC-52
To	1839 Jan 07#	fin	DLC-52
To	1839 Jan 09#	fin	DLC-52
Fr	1839 Jan 18#	fin	DLC-52
Re	1839 Jan 23	leg	34-0605
To	1839 Jan 27#		DLC-51
Fr	1839 Jan 30#	chk	DLC-52
Fr	1839 Feb 06#	fin	DLC-52
To	1839 Feb 20		DLC-52
To	1839 Mar 14	chk	DLC-52
To	1839 Mar 20#	fin	DLC-52
Fr	1839 Mar 30#	fin	DLC-52
Fr	1839 Apr		DLC-52
To	1839 Apr 09#	fin	DLC-53
To	1839 Apr 10#	fin	DLC-52
To	1839 Apr 17	chk	DLC-52
To	1839 cApr 18	mem	34-0750
Fr	1839 Apr 18#	fin	DLC-52
To	1839 Apr 18#	fin	DLC-52
Fr	1839 Apr 25#	fin	DLC-52
To	1839 Apr 26#	fin	DLC-51
To	1839 May 18#	fin	DLC-52
To	1839 May 23#	fin	DLC-52
Fr	1839 May 23#	chk	DLC-52
Fr	1839 May 28#	fin	DLC-54
Fr	1839 Jun 15#		34-0822
Fr	1839 Jul 03#		DLC-52
To	1839 Jul 29#	fin	DLC-52
To	1839 Aug 07#	fin	DLC-52
To	1839 Aug 07#	fin	DLC-52
To	1839 Aug 08#	fin	DLC-52
To	1839 Aug 09#	fin	DLC-53
Fr	1839 Aug 09#	fin	DLC-52
To	1839 Aug 31#	fin	DLC-52
Re	1839 Sep#	leg	34-0894
Re	1839 Sep#	leg	34-0896
Re	1839 Sep#	leg	34-0901
Re	1839 Sep#	leg	34-0903
To	1839 Sep 02#	fin	DLC-52
To	1839 Sep 06#	fin	DLC-52
Re	1839 Oct 07#	leg	34-0989
To	1839 Oct 12#	fin	DLC-52
To	1839 Oct 14#	fin	DLC-52
To	1839 Oct 15#	fin	DLC-52
Fr	1839 Oct 19#	fin	DLC-52
Fr	1839 Dec#	fin	34-1066
Fr	1839 Dec 12#	chk	DLC-52
Fr	1839 Dec 12#	fin	DLC-52
To	1839 Dec 24	mem	DLC-52
Fr	1839 Dec 24#	fin	DLC-52
Fr	1839 Dec 24#	fin	DLC-53
Fr	1839 Dec 24#	fin	DLC-53
Fr	1839 Dec 24#	fin	DLC-53
Fr	1839 Dec 24#	fin	34-1112
To	1839 Dec 27		DLC-52
To	1839 Dec 31		34-1116
Fr	1840 Jan 01#	fin	DLC-52
To	1840 Jan 03		DLC-74
To	1840 Jan 06#	fin	DLC-53
Fr	1840 Jan 07#		34-1141
Fr	1840 Jan 08#	fin	DLC-52
To	1840 Jan 12#	fin	DLC-52
To	1840 Jan 20#	fin	DLC-52
To	1840 Jan 20#	fin	DLC-52
Fr	1840 Jan 20#	fin	DLC-52
Fr	1840 Jan 20#	fin	DLC-52
To	1840 Jan 22#		DLC-52
Fr	1840 Jan 27#	chk	DLC-52
To	1840 Jan 28#	fin	DLC-52
Fr	1840 Jan 29#	fin	DLC-52
Fr	1840 Feb 04#	mem	DLC-52
To	1840 Feb 06#	fin	DLC-53
To	1840 Feb 18#	fin	DLC-52
Re	1840 Mar 12#	leg	34-1225
To	1840 Apr 21#		DLC-52
Fr	1840 May 14#	fin	DLC-55
Fr	1840 May 18#	fin	DLC-53
Fr	1840 May 22#	fin	DLC-52
Fr	1840 May 27	fin	DLC-52
Re	1840 Jun 08#	leg	34-1399
Re	1840 Jun 08#	leg	34-1402
To	1840 Jul 03#	fin	DLC-53
Fr	1840 Jul 11#	fin	DLC-53
Fr	1840 Jul 11#	fin	DLC-53
Fr	1840 Jul 17#	fin	DLC-53
Re	1840 Jul 20#	leg	34-1489
Re	1840 Jul 22	mem	DLC-53
To	1840 Sep 28		DLC-53
To	1840 Oct 05		35-0035
To	1840 Oct 05		35-0038
To	1840 Oct 05		37-0539
To	1840 Oct 21#		DLC-53
Fr	1840 Nov 10		DLC-74
To	1840 Dec 23#	fin	DLC-53
Fr	1840 Dec 29#		35-0148

To	1841 Jan 16#	fin	DLC-54
Re	1841 Jan 16#	leg	35-0203
To	1841 Jan 20#		37-0540
Re	1841 Mar 08#	leg	35-0244
To	1841 Mar 18	leg	DLC-53
To	1841 Apr 29#		DLC-53
Fr	1841 May#		35-0296
To	1841 May 23#	fin	DLC-53
To	1841 Jul 19#		DLC-53
Fr	1841 Aug 12#		35-0371
Fr	1842 Jan 06#	fin	DLC-54
To	1842 Jan 06#		DLC-54
To	1842 Feb 10	chk	DLC-54
To	1842 Feb 10#	fin	DLC-54
Fr	1842 Mar 13		35-0647
To	1842 Mar 14#	fin	DLC-54
To	1842 Mar 31		DLC-54
To	1842 Apr 14#		DLC-54
To	1842 Apr 18#	fin	DLC-54
Fr	1842 Aug 20#		35-0890
Re	1842 Sep#	leg	35-0913
To	1843 Jan 09#	fin	DLC-56
To	1843 Aug 07#	fin	DLC-58
Re	1843 Sep 12#	leg	35-1489
To	1843 Sep 19	fin	DLC-55
Re	1843 Nov 02	leg	DLC-56
Fr	1843 Nov 27#	fin	DLC-56
To	1844 Jan 09	mem	DLC-56
To	1844 Feb 12#	lnd	36-0249
To	1844 Mar 19#	fin	DLC-57
Fr	1844 May 09#		36-0507
Fr	1844 Sep 20#		DLC-57
To	1844 Oct 14#	fin	DLC-57
To	1844 Dec 01	mem	36-1100
To	1845 Feb 21#	fin	DLC-57
To	1845 Feb 28#	fin	DLC-57
Re	1845 Mar 27#		37-0034
Re	1845 Mar 30	fin	37-0061
To	1845 Apr 11#		DLC-58
Fr	1845 Apr 23#		37-0155
To	1845 May	mem	37-0169
To	1845 May 05#		DLC-58
Re	1845 May 12#	leg	37-0201
Fr	1845 Jun 04#		37-0248
Fr	1845 Jun 30#		37-0261
To	1845 Jul#	leg	DLC-58
Fr	1845 Oct 10#		DLC-58
Jackson Andrew L			
Fr	1829 Jun 12		M688-60
Jackson Andrew McD			
Fr	1832 Mar 29#		20-0038
Jackson Craven			
Fr	1821 Apr 14	fin	DLC-30
Jackson Daniel			
Fr	1831 Oct 14		M639-24
Fr	1831 Oct 22		M639-9
Fr	1833 Dec 26		M303-1
Fr	1835 Mar 06#		DLC-45
Fr	1837 Apr 28		DLC-50
To	1842 Jul 12		DLC-74
Jackson Daniel et al			
Fr	1831 Oct 14		M639-9
Fr	1835 cOct 27		29-0358
To	1835 Oct 27		29-0362
Fr	1835 Dec 23		29-1315
To	1837 Feb 22		DLC-50
Jackson Daniel Mrs			
To	1837 Feb 19		33-0776
Jackson E O			
Fr	1844 Feb 22		DLC-56
Jackson Elizabeth			
Fr	1819 Apr 06		DLC-26
Jackson Frances H			
Fr	1842 Aug 20		DLC-54
Jackson George			
Fr	1830 May 28		15-1188
Jackson George et al			
Fr	1830 May		15-0866
Jackson Henry			
Fr	1829 Mar 10		M639-12
To	1834 Mar 10#		M688-94
Jackson J J			
Fr	1821 Sep 22	leg	DLC-63
Fr	1823 Apr 12		DLC-32
Jackson James			
Fr	1831 Dec 23		19-0402
Fr	1833 Jan 12		DLC-41
Fr	1833 Aug 20		M234-421
Jackson James (1782-1840)			
To	c1805	mem	2-0002
To	1805 Aug 10		DLC-3
Fr	1805 Sep 21		DLC-3
Fr	1808 Feb 04		DLC-71
Fr	1808 Mar 18		DLC-4
Fr	1808 Apr 10		DLC-4
Fr	1809 Nov 22		2-0865
Fr	1810 Aug 03		DLC-4
Fr	1810 Oct 27		2-0970
To	1812 Mar 11	chk	DLC-5
Fr	1812 Aug 22		DLC-5
To	1812 Dec 30	fin	DLC-5
Re	1813 Jan 09	leg	3-0240
To	1813 Mar 03	fin	DLC-6
To	1813 Jul 21	fin	DLC-6
To	1813 Sep 22	fin	DLC-6
To	1813 Oct 06	fin	DLC-6
To	1813 Oct 27	fin	DLC-7
Fr	1813 Nov 21		DLC-71
To	1813 Nov 24	fin	DLC-7
To	1813 Dec 08	fin	DLC-7
To	1813 Dec 29	fin	DLC-8
To	1814 Jan 26	fin	DLC-8
To	1814 Feb 09	fin	DLC-8
To	1814 Mar 02	fin	DLC-9
To	1814 Mar 30	fin	DLC-9
To	1814 May 04	fin	DLC-10
To	1814 Jun 01	fin	DLC-10
To	1814 Jun 25	chk	DLC-11
To	1814 Jul 06	fin	DLC-11
To	1814 Jul 23	chk	DLC-11
To	1814 Aug 28		4-0161
To	1814 Sep 19		4-0234
Fr	1814 Oct 10		DLC-71
Fr	1814 Nov 27		DLC-14
Fr	1814 Dec 16		DLC-71
To	1815		4-0478
Fr	1815 Jan 10	fin	4-0513
To	1815 Jan 11	fin	DLC-15
To	1815 Jan 11	fin	DLC-15
Fr	1815 Jan 13		DLC-15
Fr	1815 Jan 26		DLC-71
Fr	1815 Feb 21		DLC-71
To	1815 Mar 15	fin	DLC-17
To	1815 Mar 15	fin	DLC-17
To	1815 May 17	fin	DLC-18
Re	1816 Jan 12		4-1325
To	1816 Aug 24	chk	DLC-21
To	1816 Sep 21	chk	DLC-21
Fr	1818 Feb 12		6-0018

Jackson James (cont)
To 1819 Aug 25 DLC-27
Fr 1820 Mar 21 fin 7-1056
To 1820 Nov 20 7-1417
To 1821 Jan 29 8-0095
Fr 1821 Mar 01 DLC-29
Fr 1821 Mar 18 DLC-30
Re 1821 Apr 13 leg 8-0316
Re 1821 Apr 13* leg DLC-30
To 1821 Aug 02 8-0990
Fr 1821 Sep fin 8-1123
Fr 1821 Sep 15 8-1160
Fr 1821 Nov 19 DLC-31
To 1822 Apr 20 lnd 9-0128
To 1822 Apr 20 lnd 9-0131
Fr 1822 Jul 24 DLC-31
Fr 1822 Sep 30 DLC-31
Fr 1823 May 04 DLC-32
Fr 1823 Jun 30 DLC-32
Fr 1823 Oct 19 DLC-32
Fr 1823 Oct 21 DLC-32
Fr 1823 Oct 28 DLC-32
To 1823 Nov 06 leg 9-0734
Fr 1824 Jul 20 fin DLC-33
To 1825 Jun 30 DLC-33
To 1825 Aug 30 DLC-33
Jackson James & Co
Fr 1818 Jan 01 fin DLC-26
Re 1819 Jan 05 mem DLC-26
Fr 1819 Apr 18 fin 7-0483
Jackson James & Washington
Fr 1804 Jul 16 fin DLC-4
Fr 1804 Nov 23 fin DLC-3
Fr 1805 Jul 10 fin DLC-3
Fr 1806 fin DLC-3
Re 1806 Mar 21 mem DLC-4
Fr 1806 Dec 17 fin 2-0401
Fr 1806 Dec 30 fin DLC-4
Fr 1807 Jan 10 fin DLC-4
Fr 1807 Jan 31 fin DLC-3
Fr 1807 Jan 31 fin DLC-4
Fr 1808 Mar 05 fin DLC-4
Fr 1808 Apr 12 fin 2-0623
Fr 1808 Nov 09 fin DLC-4
Fr 1809 Mar 10 fin DLC-4
Fr 1809 May 07 fin DLC-4
Fr 1810 Feb 15 fin DLC-4
To 1810 May 16 fin DLC-4
Jackson James Jr
Fr 1820 Jan 12 DLC-28
Jackson Jesse
To 1811 Apr 23 fin DLC-5
Fr 1836 Jan 18 M639-26
Jackson John (NC)
Re 1829 Jul 27 13-0941
Fr 1829 Aug 01 M639-12
Jackson John (PA)
Re 1804 May mem DLC-3
Re 1804 Jul 16 mem DLC-4
Fr 1805 Mar 29 DLC-3
Fr 1805 Jun 14 DLC-3
To 1805 Jun 18 DLC-3
Fr 1819 Apr 05 DLC-26
Fr 1819 Apr 30 DLC-26
Fr 1820 Jan 13 DLC-28
Fr 1821 Nov 03 DLC-31
Jackson John H
Fr 1840 Oct 21 DLC-53
Jackson Joseph et al
Fr 1829 Feb 18 M222-25
To 1829 Jun 15 13-0663
To 1829 Jun 15* DLC-37
Jackson N
Fr 1843 Feb 07 DLC-55
Jackson Nathan
Fr 1828 Nov 23 DLC-35
Fr 1835 May 23 DLC-46
Jackson Obadiah
Fr 1812 Dec 08 fin DLC-5
Jackson Rachel (Donelson)
Re 1785 Mar 01# leg 1-0023
Re 1790 Dec 20 leg 1-0079
To 1792 Jan 24 leg 1-0122
Re 1793 Sep 27 leg 1-0163
Re 1794 Jan 17 leg 1-0187
Re 1794 Jan 18 leg 1-0188
To 1796 May 09 1-0407
To 1796 May 09 37-0397
To 1798 Jan 26 1-0596
To 1799 Sep 17 DLC-71
To 1803 Mar 22 1-1114
To 1803 May 26 1-1122
Fr 1804# 1-1267
To 1804 Feb 06 1-1277
To 1804 Apr 06 1-1301
Fr 1806 Jul 31 2-0309
Fr 1806 Sep 10# 2-0336
Fr 1806 Oct 21# 2-0366
To 1811 Dec 17 2-1022
To 1813 Jan 08 3-0233
Fr 1813 Feb 08 DLC-71
To 1813 Feb 15 3-0273
To 1813 Feb 22 DLC-6
Fr 1813 Feb 28 DLC-6
To 1813 Mar 01 3-0283
To 1813 Mar 07 DLC-6
To 1813 Mar 15 DLC-6
To 1813 Mar 21 3-0344
Fr 1813 Apr 05 3-0368
To 1813 Oct 11 3-0524
To 1813 Oct 13 3-0527
To 1813 Oct 18 3-0535
To 1813 Oct 31 3-0558
To 1813 Nov 04 3-0566
To 1813 Nov 12 3-0588
To 1813 Nov 21 3-0620
To 1813 Dec 09 3-0651
To 1813 Dec 14 DLC-7
To 1813 Dec 19 3-0684
To 1813 Dec 29 3-0737
To 1814 3-0777
To 1814 Jan 28 DLC-8
To 1814 Feb 01 3-0847
Fr 1814 Feb 10 DLC-8
To 1814 Feb 13 3-0867
To 1814 Feb 17 DLC-9
To 1814 Feb 20# DLC-9
To 1814 Feb 21 3-0883
To 1814 Feb 23 DLC-9
To 1814 Mar 04 3-0897
To 1814 Mar 08 3-0905
Fr 1814 Mar 11 DLC-9
To 1814 Mar 12 DLC-9
Fr 1814 Mar 21 DLC-9
To 1814 Apr 01 DLC-9
To 1814 Apr 06 3-0956
Fr 1814 Apr 07 DLC-10
Fr 1814 Apr 12 DLC-10
To 1814 Apr 14 3-0966

To 1814 Apr 25		3-0995
To 1814 May 08		3-1011
To 1814 Jul 16		3-1142
To 1814 Jul 22#		DLC-11
To 1814 Jul 31		3-1199
To 1814 Aug 05		3-1227
To 1814 Aug 10		3-1289
To 1814 Aug 23		3-1316
To 1814 Aug 28		DLC-60
To 1814 Sep 22		4-0236
To 1814 Oct 07		4-0259
To 1814 Oct 11		DLC-13
To 1814 Oct 17		4-0268
To 1814 Oct 20		4-0281
To 1814 Oct 21		DLC-71
To 1814 Nov 01#		DLC-13
To 1814 Nov 15		4-0350
To 1814 Nov 17		4-0360
To 1814 Nov 21		4-0364
To c1815#		4-0479
To 1815 Jan 25	chk	DLC-15
To 1815 Feb 28#		DLC-17
Fr 1815 Mar 05#		DLC-71
Fr 1815 Apr#		DLC-71
To 1815 May 05#		DLC-18
To 1815 Dec 01#	fin	DLC-19
Fr 1815 Dec 21#	fin	DLC-68
To 1815 Dec 21#	fin	DLC-19
To 1815 Dec 24#	fin	DLC-68
To 1816 Mar 13		DLC-20
Fr 1816 Apr 27#		DLC-71
To 1816 Sep 12		5-0480
To 1816 Sep 18		5-0485
To 1816 Nov 18#	fin	DLC-22
To 1817 May 29		5-0883
To 1817 Jun 11		5-0892
To 1817 Jun 11#		DLC-22
To 1817 Aug 21#	fin	DLC-23
Fr 1818 Jan 19#		5-1294
To 1818 Jan 27		5-1346
To 1818 Feb 05		5-1437
To 1818 Feb 10		DLC-24
To 1818 Feb 14		6-0043
To 1818 Mar 26		6-0173
To 1818 Apr 08		DLC-24
To 1818 Apr 10		6-0344
To 1818 Apr 10		6-0346
To 1818 Apr 20		DLC-24
To 1818 Apr 20#		DLC-24
To 1818 May 04		6-0591
To 1818 May 24#		DLC-25
To 1818 May 27#	fin	DLC-26
To 1818 Jun 02		6-1011
To 1818 Jun 02		DLC-25
To 1818 Aug 13#		DLC-25
Fr 1818 Oct 19#		6-1372
To 1818 Nov 05#		6-1400
Fr 1819#		7-0111
To 1819 Jan 15#	fin	DLC-26
To 1819 Jan 15#	fin	DLC-28
To 1819 Jan 19#		7-0184
To 1819 Jan 25		7-0192
To 1819 Jan 30		7-0210
To 1819 Feb 06		7-0243
To 1819 Feb 14#		DLC-26
Fr 1819 Feb 23#		DLC-26
To 1819 Mar 03#		DLC-26
Fr 1819 Mar 09#		DLC-26
Fr 1819 Mar 18		7-0425
Fr 1819 Mar 18		7-0428
To 1819 Mar 26		7-0441
Fr 1819 Jul 03#		DLC-24
To 1819 Aug 30#	fin	DLC-27
To 1819 Oct 22#		DLC-28
To 1820 May 16#	fin	DLC-29
To 1820 May 30#		DLC-29
To 1820 Aug 08#	fin	DLC-29
To 1820 Sep 30		7-1364
Fr 1820 Oct 03#		7-1379
To 1820 Oct 28	fin	DLC-29
To 1821 Mar 31#	fin	DLC-30
Re 1821 Apr 07#	fin	DLC-30
Fr 1821 Apr 27#		8-0377
To 1821 May 15#		DLC-30
Fr 1821 Jun 21#		8-0644
Fr 1821 Jun 29#		8-0742
Fr 1821 Jul 23#		8-0893
Fr 1821 Aug 25#		8-1102
To 1821 Aug 28#	fin	DLC-30
Fr 1821 Dec 15#		8-1367
To 1822 Feb 02#		DLC-31
Fr 1823 May 18#		9-0562
To 1823 Jul 23#		9-0619
To 1823 Aug 13#		DLC-32
To 1823 Nov 16		9-0756
To 1823 Nov 19		DLC-32
To 1823 Nov 23		9-0764
To 1823 Nov 28		9-0766
To 1823 Dec 03		9-0780
To 1823 Dec 07		DLC-32
To 1823 Dec 10		DLC-32
To 1823 Dec 11		9-0798
To 1823 Dec 18#		DLC-32
To 1823 Dec 21		DLC-32
To 1823 Dec 28		9-0854
To 1824 Jan		9-0876
To 1824 Jan 05		DLC-32
To 1824 Jan 10		DLC-32
To 1824 Jan 15		DLC-32
To 1824 Jan 21		10-0388
To 1824 Jan 29		10-0415
To 1824 Feb 06		10-0436
To 1824 Feb 08#		DLC-32
To 1824 Feb 20		37-0417
To 1824 Feb 27		10-0491
To 1824 Mar 02		DLC-32
To 1824 Mar 06		DLC-32
To 1824 Mar 16		10-0559
To 1824 Mar 19		DLC-32
To 1824 Mar 27		DLC-32
To 1824 Apr 02		10-0622
To 1824 Apr 05		DLC-32
To 1824 Apr 07		DLC-32
To 1824 Apr 08		DLC-32
To 1824 Apr 08		10-0631
To 1824 Apr 12		DLC-32
To 1824 Apr 23		DLC-32
To 1824 Apr 27		DLC-32
To 1824 May 05		10-0700
To 1824 May 13		DLC-32
To 1824 cMay 15		10-0728
To 1824 May 19		10-0732
Fr 1824 Jun 13#		10-0788
Fr 1824 Aug 12#		10-0845
To 1824 Aug 22#		10-0858
To 1824 Oct 20#	fin	DLC-33
To 1824 Oct 27#	fin	DLC-33
To 1824 Dec 02#	fin	DLC-33

Jackson Rachel (cont)

To	1824 Dec 15#	fin	DLC-33
Fr	1824 Dec 23#		10-0996
To	1824 Dec 29#	fin	DLC-33
To	1825 Jan 04#	fin	DLC-33
To	1825 Jan 08	fin	DLC-33
Fr	1825 Jan 27#		10-1086
To	1825 Jan 28	fin	DLC-33
Fr	1825 Mar 08#		10-1220
Fr	1825 Apr 15#		10-1235
To	1825 May 10#		37-0422
Fr	1825 May 18#		10-1271
Fr	c1826#		11-0095
To	1826 Mar 24#		DLC-33
To	1826 May 27#		DLC-33
To	1826 Sep 15#	fin	DLC-33
To	1827 May 11#	fin	DLC-34
Re	1827 Jun		11-0613
To	1827 Jun 10#		11-0694
To	1827 Sep 23#	fin	DLC-34
To	1828 Jan 10#		11-1051
To	1828 Jan 13#		11-1057
Fr	1828 Jan 13#		11-1058
To	1828 Feb 18#		11-1124
Fr	1828 Feb 25#		11-1141
Fr	1828 Mar#		11-1155
To	1828 May 24#		DLC-35
Fr	1828 Jul 18#		12-0055
Fr	1828 Oct 29#		12-0252
To	1828 Nov 24#		DLC-35
To	1828 Dec 04#	fin	DLC-36
To	1828 Dec 07#		DLC-36

Jackson Rachel (1832-1923)

Re	1834 Jun 13	fin	25-1329
To	1836 Mar 30		30-0928

Jackson Robert

Fr	1822 Dec 06		DLC-31
Fr	1837 Sep 07		DLC-50

Jackson Samuel

Fr	1838 Mar 11		DLC-51

Jackson Samuel Dorsey

Fr	1799 Sep 14		DLC-2
Fr	1802 Jun 09		DLC-2
Fr	1802 Oct 25		1-1043
Re	1806	mem	2-0108
Fr	1806 Jan 27	lnd	2-0125
Fr	1806 Mar 17		DLC-4
Fr	1807 Feb 13		DLC-4
Fr	1807 Feb 15		DLC-71
Fr	1807 Mar 09#		2-0472
Re	1807 Aug 01	leg	2-0535
Re	1807 Nov 09	leg	2-0592
To	1808 Mar 10		DLC-71
Re	1808 Jul 22	leg	2-0713
Re	1809 May 18	leg	2-0818
Re	1810 Sep 10	leg	2-0961
Re	1810 Sep 12	leg	2-0962
Fr	1823 Jan 01		M688-26

Jackson Sarah (Yorke)

Re	1831 Nov 25	leg	18-1487
To	c1832#	fin	DLC-58
To	c1832#	fin	DLC-58
To	c1832#	fin	DLC-58
To	c1832#	fin	DLC-58
To	c1832#	fin	19-0524
To	1832 Mar 16#	fin	DLC-40
To	1832 Apr 25		20-0390
To	1832 Apr 30		DLC-40
To	1832 May 06		20-0483
To	1832 May 19		20-0542
To	1832 Jun 10		20-0728
To	1832 Jun 13		DLC-40
To	1832 Jun 21		20-0788
To	1832 Jul 11		20-1047
To	1832 Jul 17		20-1117
To	1832 Jul 19		20-1149
To	1832 Sep 23		21-0048
To	1832 Oct 05		21-0066
To	1832 Oct 21		21-0126
To	1832 Oct 21		21-0128
To	1832 Dec 16		21-1063
To	1833#	fin	21-1235
To	1833 Jan 26		22-0079
To	1833 Oct 02#	fin	DLC-43
To	1833 Oct 06		23-0986
To	1833 Oct 11		23-1009
To	1833 Oct 13		23-1030
To	1833 Nov 08		23-1206
To	1833 Dec 02		DLC-43
To	1833 Dec 15		24-0506
To	1833 Dec 16		DLC-43
To	1833 Dec 22		24-0572
To	1834#	fin	DLC-45
To	1834 Jan 02		DLC-41
To	1834 Jan 05		DLC-43
Fr	1834 Jan 19		24-0999
To	1834 Jan 23		24-1038
To	1834 Feb 18		24-1419
To	1834 Mar 25		25-0361
To	1834 Apr 20		25-0844
Fr	1834 May 02		DLC-42
To	1834 May 05		DLC-44
To	1834 May 16		25-1069
To	1834 May 19		25-1091
To	1834 Jul 26		26-0249
To	1834 Oct 01		26-0469
To	1834 Oct 10		26-0574
To	1834 Oct 25		26-0724
To	1834 Nov 20#		DLC-73
To	1834 Nov 21#	fin	DLC-45
To	1834 Nov 28#	fin	DLC-45
To	1834 Nov 29#	fin	DLC-45
To	1834 Dec#	fin	DLC-45
To	1834 Dec 03#	fin	DLC-45
To	1834 Dec 06#		DLC-73
To	1834 Dec 08#	fin	DLC-45
To	1834 Dec 14#		DLC-73
To	1834 Dec 18#	fin	DLC-45
To	1835#	fin	DLC-47
To	1835 Jan 16#	fin	DLC-46
To	1835 Jan 16#	fin	DLC-45
To	1835 Jan 21#	fin	DLC-45
To	1835 Feb 14#	fin	DLC-45
To	1835 Feb 15#	fin	DLC-46
To	1835 Feb 24#	fin	DLC-46
To	1835 Feb 26#	fin	DLC-45
To	1835 Mar 12#	fin	DLC-45
To	1835 Mar 18#	fin	DLC-45
To	1835 Apr 01#	fin	DLC-46
To	1835 Apr 14		28-0074
To	1835 Apr 15		28-0086
To	1835 Apr 16#	fin	DLC-46
To	1835 Apr 21		28-0108
To	1835 Apr 25#		DLC-73
To	1835 Apr 27		28-0137
To	1835 Apr 29		28-0178
To	1835 May 02		28-0239
To	1835 May 02		28-0237
To	1835 May 07		28-0319

To 1835 May 09 28-0331
To 1835 May 26# fin DLC-46
To 1835 Jun 19# fin DLC-46
To 1835 Jun 29# fin DLC-46
To 1835 Jul 02# fin DLC-46
To 1835 Jul 02# fin DLC-46
To 1835 Aug 21# fin DLC-46
To 1835 Aug 22# fin DLC-46
To c1835 Aug 22# fin 28-1345
To 1835 Sep# fin DLC-47
To 1835 Sep 03# fin DLC-46
To 1835 Sep 06 28-1578
To 1835 Sep 08# fin DLC-46
To 1835 Sep 09 29-0008
To 1835 Sep 26# fin DLC-47
To 1835 Oct 01 chk DLC-47
To 1835 Oct 03# fin DLC-47
To 1835 Oct 03 chk DLC-47
To 1835 Oct 09 chk DLC-47
To 1835 Oct 10# fin DLC-47
To 1835 Oct 11# DLC-73
To 1835 Oct 20# fin 29-0331
To 1835 Nov 09# fin DLC-47
To 1835 Nov 28# fin DLC-47
To 1835 Nov 28# fin DLC-47
To 1835 Dec 10# fin DLC-47
To 1835 Dec 28 chk DLC-47
To 1835 Dec 28# fin DLC-47
To 1835 Dec 31# fin DLC-47
To c1836# fin 29-1388
To 1836 Jan 18# fin DLC-47
To 1836 Feb# fin DLC-47
To 1836 Feb 15# fin DLC-47
To 1836 Feb 18# fin DLC-47
To 1836 Mar 03# fin DLC-48
To 1836 Mar 07# fin 30-0704
To 1836 Mar 23 chk DLC-47
To 1836 Mar 23# fin DLC-47
To 1836 Apr 10# DLC-73
To 1836 Apr 27# fin 30-1374
To 1836 Apr 29# fin DLC-48
To 1836 May 07# fin DLC-48
To 1836 May 12# fin DLC-48
To 1836 May 18# fin DLC-48
To c1836 May 28# fin 31-0185
To 1836 Jun 18# fin DLC-48
To 1836 Jun 22 DLC-48
To 1836 Sep 22 31-1486
To 1836 Nov 12# fin DLC-49
To 1836 Dec 29# fin DLC-49
Fr 1837 Jan 03# 32-1480
To 1837 Feb 21# fin DLC-50
To 1837 Feb 21# fin DLC-50
To 1837 Feb 24# fin DLC-50
To 1837 Feb 24# fin DLC-50
To 1837 Mar# fin 33-0943
To 1837 Mar 02# fin DLC-50
To 1837 Mar 04# fin DLC-50
Fr 1837 May 23# 33-1246
To 1839 Nov 25# fin DLC-52
To 1840 Jan 04 DLC-52
To 1840 Sep 29# fin DLC-53
To 1840 Oct 05 35-0035
To 1841 Oct 15# fin DLC-53
To 1842 May 11# DLC-54
To 1843 Nov 24# 37-0544
To 1845 May 19# DLC-58

Jackson Selena
Fr 1836 Mar 19 M22-39

Jackson Washington
Fr 1805 Mar 07 DLC-3
Re 1805 Sep 07 mem 2-0082
Fr 1806 Mar 24 mem 2-0202
Fr 1806 Jun 19 DLC-4
Fr 1809 Dec 20 DLC-4
To 1813 Jan 05 DLC-61
To 1813 Feb 12 3-0270
To 1818 Dec 28 DLC-26
Fr 1821 Mar 13 DLC-30

Jackson Washington J
Fr 1844 Jan 08 DLC-55
Fr 1844 Feb 07 DLC-56
Fr 1844 Mar 14 DLC-56

Jackson William
Fr 1831 Oct 20 M22-28
Re 1835 Aug 27 par 28-1423

Jackson William Murphy
Fr 1829 Apr 26 M639-12

Jackson William W
Fr 1830 Apr 20 M124-123

Jackson TN
Re 1825 Sep 19 add 10-1427

Jackson TN citizens
To 1840 Oct 08 add 35-0051

Jacob (slave)
Re 1839 Jan 28 leg 34-0607

Jacobs Cyrus S
Fr 1835 Apr 23# DLC-46

Jacobs Edmond
Fr 1805 Feb 01 fin DLC-3

Jacobs Philip
Fr 1831 May 28 M22-28

Jacobs Solomon D
Fr 1832 Mar 17 M22-29

Jacobs Thomas H
Fr 1834 Apr 14 fin DLC-44
Fr 1834 Jun 30 fin DLC-44
Fr 1834 Oct 01 fin DLC-44
Fr 1834 Nov 06 fin DLC-45
Fr 1834 Nov 06 fin DLC-45
Fr 1835 Jun 30 fin DLC-46
Fr 1835 Jul 01 fin DLC-46
Fr 1835 Aug 17 fin DLC-46
Fr 1835 Nov 04 fin DLC-47
Fr 1836 Mar 01 fin DLC-47
Fr 1836 Apr 07 fin DLC-48
Fr 1836 May 10 fin DLC-48
Fr 1836 May 31 fin DLC-48
Fr 1836 Jun 02 fin DLC-48
Fr 1836 Jul 05 fin DLC-48

Jacocks John H
Fr 1833 Jul 13 23-0126
Fr 1833 Nov 08 23-1209
Fr 1835 Dec 31 29-1366
Fr 1836 Jan 09 DLC-73

Jacques Henry et al
Fr 1832 May 22 M234-601

Jamerson James
Re 1804 Jul 25 leg 1-1357

James Amanda M
Fr 1845 May 30 DLC-58

James Daniel
Fr 1790 Dec 07 lnd 1-0078

James E H & C H
Fr 1833 May 03 fin DLC-43
Fr 1833 May 07# fin DLC-43
Fr 1833 May 07# fin DLC-43
Fr 1833 Oct 08 fin DLC-45

James E H & C H (cont)
Fr 1835 Jan 12# fin DLC-45
Fr 1835 Apr 04 fin DLC-47
To 1835 Apr 09 chk 28-0007
To 1835 Oct 03 chk DLC-47
Fr 1835 Oct 06 fin DLC-47
To 1836 Jan 02 chk DLC-47
To 1836 Jul 08 chk DLC-48
Fr 1836 Oct 01 fin DLC-50
To 1837 Mar 01 chk DLC-50
James Jeremiah
Fr 1829 Jun 20 fin DLC-37
James John W
Fr 1829 Mar 18 12-1033
James John W et al
Fr 1827 DLC-35
Fr 1836 May 30-1440
Fr 1836 Jun 01 31-0259
James Roberson
Fr 1836 Jun 23 M234-145
Re 1836 cJul 11 mem M234-145
James Thomas
Fr 1834 Feb 21 M234-883
Fr 1834 Feb 21* 24-1439
James Vannelia
Fr 1845 May 30 DLC-58
James William Dobein
Fr 1824 Aug 10-0839
Jameson David
Re 1834 Jun 25 par 25-1535
Jameson George W
To 1834 Jun 16 chk DLC-44
Janney Samuel McPherson
Fr 1829 May 25 13-0416
Jansen Benjamin G
To 1829 Oct 22 14-0234
Janvier Thomas
Re 1830 Oct 30 par 16-0591
Janvrot Francis
Fr 1834 Jul 10# fin DLC-44
Jarrett William et al
Fr 1829 Aug 07 M639-13
Jarvis J G Jr
Fr 1842 Aug 01 DLC-54
Fr 1842 Aug 15 DLC-54
Jarvis Leonard
Fr 1834 Mar 16 25-0245
Fr 1835 Dec 17 29-1195
Fr 1835 Dec 22 29-1287
Fr 1836 Feb 27 30-0606
Fr 1836 Jun 20 31-0520
Fr 1837 Jan M687-28
Jarvis Russell
Fr 1836 Mar 12 M687-17
Jaudon Samuel
Re 1833 Feb 07 22-0299
Jefferds William et al
Fr 1832 Mar 03 M639-5
Jeffers William N
Fr 1831 Jun 08 M639-12
Re 1831 Jun 14 18-0017
Fr 1831 Sep 05 M219-2
Re 1831 cSep 10 mem 18-0715
Fr 1831 Sep 12 M219-2
To 1831 Sep 22# M77-9
Fr 1831 Nov 19# M219-2
Jefferson F et al
Fr 1831 Jan 26 M639-1
Jefferson Robert
Re 1831 May 25 par 17-1427
Jefferson Thomas
To 1802 Jun 16 1-1004
To 1802 Aug 18 1-1033
To 1803 Aug 07 1-1142
To 1803 Aug 07* DLC-3
Fr 1803 Sep 19 1-1167
Fr 1803 Sep 19* DLC-3
To 1803 Oct 17 1-1239
To 1804 Aug 03 DLC-3
To 1804 cDec 1-1415
To 1805 Sep 23 2-0084
To 1806 cNov 05 2-0379
Fr 1806 Dec 03 2-0394
Fr 1807 Mar 21 DLC-4
Fr 1807 Mar 21* M370-2
To 1808 Apr 20 M221-24
To 1808 Apr 20* DLC-4
To 1808 May 14 2-0653
Fr 1819 Nov 22 7-0878
To 1822 Feb 06 DLC-31
To 1823 Oct 04 9-0679
To 1823 Dec 08 9-0794
Fr 1823 Dec 18 9-0810
To 1825 May 31 10-1297
Jefferson Academy students
Fr 1815 Jun 01 add DLC-18
Jeffries L C
Fr 1845 May 13 DLC-58
Jenkins Alexander M
Fr 1836 Mar 30 30-0916
Jenkins Charles J
Fr 1821 Jul 20 DLC-30
Jenkins Joseph E
Fr 1831 Jul 12 M179-70
Jenkins William et al
Fr 1836 Mar 21 M639-8
Jennette Matthew
Fr 1836 Jan 26 M124-151
Jennings Jonathan
Fr 1831 Sep 24 M639-13
Jennings Thomas Reid
Fr 1838 Sep 15 fin DLC-52
Jeremiah Thomas
Fr 1834 Apr 24 25-0870
Jesup Thomas Sidney
Fr 1815 May 31 DLC-18
To 1816 Jun 06 5-0146
Fr 1816 Jun 06 5-0148
Fr 1816 Jun 06* M221-70
Fr 1816 Jun 13 DLC-20
Fr 1816 Jun 13* 5-0164
Fr 1816 Jun 25 DLC-21
Fr 1816 Jun 25* 5-0240
Fr 1816 Jul 02 DLC-21
Fr 1816 Jul 02* 5-0254
Fr 1816 Jul 02* M221-70
Fr 1816 Jul 09 DLC-21
Fr 1816 Jul 09* 5-0295
To 1816 Jul 17 5-0307
To 1816 Jul 30 5-0338
Fr 1816 Aug 12 DLC-21
Fr 1816 Aug 17 DLC-21
Fr 1816 Aug 17* 5-0361
Fr 1816 Aug 18 DLC-21
Fr 1816 Aug 18* M222-19
Fr 1816 Aug 21 DLC-21
Fr 1816 Aug 21* 5-0436
Fr 1816 Sep 05 DLC-21
To 1816 Sep 06 5-0455

Fr 1816 Sep 09 DLC-21
Fr 1816 Sep 09* 5-0466
Fr 1816 Sep 11 DLC-21
Fr 1816 Sep 11* 5-0469
Fr 1816 Sep 23 DLC-21
Fr 1816 Oct 28 DLC-21
Fr 1816 Oct 28* 5-0550
Fr 1816 Dec 02 5-0588
Fr 1818 Jul 28 DLC-25
Fr 1818 Jul 28* 6-1163
Fr 1818 Jul 30 DLC-25
Fr 1818 Jul 30* 6-1166
To 1818 Aug 18 6-1245
Fr 1818 Aug 27 DLC-25
Fr 1818 Aug 27* 6-1270
Fr 1818 Sep 12 DLC-25
Fr 1818 Sep 12* 6-1297
Fr 1818 Sep 16 DLC-25
Fr 1818 Sep 16* 6-1307
Fr 1820 Aug 18 DLC-29
Fr 1836 Jun 20# 31-0516
Fr 1836 Jul 19 DLC-48
Fr 1836 Jul 23 DLC-48
To 1836 Aug 02 DLC-48
To 1836 Aug 02* M567-126
To 1836 Aug 02* 31-1207
To 1836 Aug 03 DLC-48
To 1836 Aug 03* M567-126
Fr 1836 Oct 08 32-0112
To 1836 Nov 05 32-0407
To 1836 Nov 05* DLC-74
Fr 1836 Dec 24 DLC-49
To 1837 Oct 13 33-1521
Fr 1837 Oct 24 DLC-50
Fr 1845 May 30 37-0237
To 1845 Jun 03 37-0246
Jetton Robert
Fr 1813 Dec 22 DLC-61
Fr 1818 Sep 29 DLC-25
Jewell R G W
Fr 1840 Aug 29 DLC-53
Jewell William
Fr 1824 Jan 26 fin DLC-32
Jewett Albert Gallatin
Fr 1844 Nov 30 36-1081
Fr 1845 Feb 04 DLC-57
Jewett Nathaniel G
Fr 1836 Apr 21 30-1282
Jimeson George
Fr 1836 cApr 15 30-1183
Joachim Lelevel et al
Fr 1832 May 09 20-0494
Jobson Samuel Jr
Fr 1834 Jan 18 DLC-44
John Gideon
Fr 1836 Jan 05 M639-5
John (Negro boy)
Re 1834 Feb 25 par 24-1470
John the Barber
To 1813 Oct 04 chk DLC-6
Johns Henry Van Dyke
Fr 1830 Oct 11 16-0364
Johns Leonard S
Fr 1833 Jan 14 21-1426
Johns Thomas
Fr 1835 Jun 16 M179-80
Johns William et al
Fr 1835 cJan DLC-59
Johnson ______
Fr 1828 Jan 08 add 11-1048
Johnson Absalom et al
Fr 1840 Jun 03 34-1388
Johnson Alexis L
Fr 1833 Aug 05 DLC-43
Johnson Alfred Jr et al
Fr 1829 May M639-24
Johnson Andrew et al
Fr 1844 Jul 23 DLC-57
Johnson Ann
Fr 1815 Dec 21# fin DLC-68
Johnson Anthony W
Fr 1820 Dec 10 fin DLC-32
Re 1840 Jun 08# leg 34-1402
Johnson Benjamin
Fr 1830 Dec 06 M639-19
Fr 1836 Feb 10 DLC-47
Fr 1836 Oct 01 31-1578
Johnson Cave
Fr 1827 May 23 DLC-34
Fr 1831 Dec 17 19-0325
Fr 1832 Oct 30 M639-4
Fr 1835 Jan 28 M639-3
To 1835 Sep 22# DLC-47
Fr 1837 cJan 30 M22-41
Fr 1838 Aug 28 DLC-51
Fr 1838 Sep 09 DLC-51
Fr 1841 Oct 07 DLC-53
To 1842 Nov 25 35-1009
Fr 1842 Dec 08 DLC-54
To 1843 Feb 09 DLC-74
Fr 1843 Feb 18 DLC-55
Fr 1843 Apr 12 DLC-55
To 1843 Nov 22 DLC-74
Fr 1843 Nov 30 DLC-56
Fr 1843 Dec 07 DLC-56
To 1843 Dec 11 DLC-74
Re c1844 mem 36-0088
Fr 1844 Mar 15 DLC-56
Fr 1845 Jan 22 36-1395
Johnson Cave et al
Fr 1812 Aug 17 2-1230
To 1812 Aug 17 2-1232
Johnson Chauncey P E
Fr 1844 Nov 11 DLC-57
Johnson E S
Fr 1842 Nov 29 DLC-54
Johnson Edward
To 1819 Feb 27 add 7-0384
Fr 1819 Feb 27 add 7-0386
Johnson Elisha
Fr 1836 Aug 10 M234-777
Johnson George Washington
Fr 1840 Feb 01 DLC-52
Johnson H M
Fr 1823 Apr 18 DLC-32
Fr 1823 Apr 27 DLC-32
Johnson Henry (DC) et al
Fr 1833 Aug 28 M639-14
Johnson Henry (KY)
Fr 1835 Aug 10 28-1270
Johnson Henry (LA)
Fr 1827 Mar 31 DLC-34
To 1827 Apr 18 DLC-34
Fr 1827 Aug 19 DLC-34
Fr 1828 Jan 08 add 11-1045
To 1828 Jan 08 add 11-1046
To 1828 Jan 13# 11-1057
To 1828 Feb 09 11-1102
Fr 1836 May 27 31-0166

Johnson Homer
Fr 1829 Feb 23# M639-16
Fr 1829 Apr 22# 13-0098
Johnson Isaac
Fr 1829 Feb 06 M639-21
Johnson Israel
Fr 1831 Jul 13 18-0204
Johnson James
Fr 1816 Apr 17 DLC-20
Fr 1817 Feb 12 DLC-22
Fr 1819 Dec 14 DLC-28
To 1840 Oct 05 35-0039
To 1840 Oct 05* DLC-53
Johnson James et al
Fr 1840 Sep 24 DLC-53
Johnson James Jr
Fr 1829 Jun 15 13-0665
Johnson Jeremiah
Fr 1831 Sep 27 M222-29
Johnson Jeromus
Fr 1829 Jun 18 13-0676
Fr 1833 Feb 20# DLC-42
Johnson Jeromus et al
Fr 1834 Dec 26 M639-2
Johnson Jimmy et al
Fr 1831 Dec 25 M234-832
Johnson John
Fr 1829 cAug 10 13-1064
Fr 1829 Oct 09 14-0128
Johnson John Telemachus
Fr 1825 Oct 20 DLC-33
To 1825 Oct 30 DLC-33
Fr 1828 Aug 08 DLC-35
Fr 1830 Feb 18 M639-16
Fr 1831 Nov 18 M639-3
Fr 1832 Dec 02 21-0653
Johnson Joseph H
Fr 1834 Oct 20# fin DLC-50
Johnson Lewis
Fr 1835 Mar 17# fin DLC-45
Johnson Lewis et al
Fr 1836 Apr 04 M687-28
Johnson Oliver
Fr 1804 Sep 24 DLC-3
Fr 1834 Jul 22 M639-27
Johnson Philip C
Fr 1837 Feb 21 M687-16
Johnson Richard Mentor
Fr 1814 Nov 21 DLC-14
Fr 1817 Jan 20 DLC-22
Fr 1819 Apr 26 DLC-26
Fr 1819 Jun 27 DLC-27
Fr 1819 Aug 04 DLC-27
Fr 1821 Mar 31 DLC-30
Fr 1821 Mar 31 DLC-30
Fr 1823 Oct 12 DLC-32
Fr 1825 Dec 02 DLC-33
To 1825 Dec 22 DLC-33
Fr 1826 Sep 16 DLC-34
Fr 1826 Oct 27 DLC-34
Fr 1828 Mar 10 DLC-35
Fr 1828 Aug 22 DLC-35
To 1828 cSep 09 DLC-35
Fr 1829 Mar 04 12-0849
Fr 1829 Mar 09 DLC-36
Fr 1830 Dec 10 16-1380
Fr 1831 Feb 13 DLC-39
Fr 1831 Mar 03 17-0797
Fr 1831 Aug 11 18-0510
Fr 1832 Apr 23 20-0350
Fr 1832 May 18 M22-29
Fr 1833 Aug 02 M234-776
Fr 1833 Aug 09 23-0307
Re 1834 Oct 03 mem DLC-44
Fr 1834 Dec 26 27-0017
Fr 1835 Jan 02 M639-5
Fr 1835 Jan 09 27-0170
Fr 1835 Feb 10 M639-15
Fr 1836 Feb 18 M639-12
Fr 1836 Mar 04 M639-3
Fr 1836 Apr 04 M639-5
Fr 1836 cApr 10 M124-152
Fr 1836 Jun M639-3
Fr 1836 Jun 21 DLC-48
Fr 1836 Aug 18 31-1316
Fr 1836 Aug 24 M234-416
Fr 1836 Sep M22-40
Fr 1837 Jan 18 33-0014
Fr 1837 Feb 22 DLC-50
Fr 1837 cMar 01 33-0954
Johnson Richard Mentor et al
Fr 1824 Jan 9-0878
Fr 1829 Feb 18 M639-2
Fr 1829 Feb 19 M639-16
Johnson Samuel
Fr 1815 Dec 11 fin 4-1279
Fr 1815 Dec 23 fin 4-1303
Johnson Thomas
Fr 1800 Nov 19 DLC-2
Fr 1801 May 10 DLC-2
Fr 1805 Dec 21 DLC-3
To 1806 Jan 01 DLC-3
Fr 1807 Jan 15 2-0460
Fr 1808 May 07 2-0643
Fr 1808 May 13 2-0651
Fr 1812 Apr 22 DLC-75
Fr 1812 May 02 DLC-5
Fr 1812 May 27 2-1091
Fr 1812 Jun 08 2-1098
Fr 1812 Jun 25 2-1109
Fr 1812 Jul 20 2-1132
Fr 1812 Jul 27 DLC-5
Fr 1812 Aug 31 DLC-5
Fr 1814 Jan 28 DLC-8
To 1814 Feb 01 DLC-62
Fr 1814 Feb 02 DLC-8
Fr 1814 Feb 04 DLC-8
To 1814 Feb 08 DLC-61
Fr 1814 Feb 09 DLC-8
To 1814 Feb 11 DLC-62
Fr 1814 Feb 11 DLC-8
Fr 1814 Feb 15 DLC-9
To 1814 Feb 16 DLC-61
Fr 1814 Feb 19 DLC-9
Fr 1814 Feb 19 DLC-9
To 1814 Feb 19 DLC-62
Fr 1814 Feb 21 DLC-9
To 1814 Feb 22 DLC-61
Fr 1814 Feb 22 DLC-9
Fr 1814 Feb 25 DLC-9
Fr 1814 Feb 25 DLC-9
To 1814 Feb 28 DLC-62
Fr 1814 Mar 02 DLC-9
Fr 1814 Mar 03 DLC-9
To 1814 Mar 05 DLC-9
To 1814 Mar 05 DLC-9
Fr 1814 Mar 07 DLC-9
Fr 1814 Mar 09 DLC-9

To 1814 Mar 10		DLC-9
To 1814 Mar 14		DLC-9
Re 1814 Mar 21		DLC-9
To 1814 Mar 22		DLC-9
Fr 1814 Mar 23		DLC-9
Fr 1814 Apr 01		DLC-9
Fr 1814 Apr 02		DLC-10
To 1814 Apr 07		3-0958
To 1814 Apr 14		DLC-10
Fr 1814 Apr 16		DLC-10
Fr 1814 Apr 16		DLC-10
Fr 1814 Apr 17		DLC-10
Fr 1814 Apr 19		DLC-10
Fr 1814 Apr 20		DLC-10
Fr 1814 Apr 22		DLC-10
Fr 1814 Apr 23		DLC-10
Fr 1814 Apr 25		DLC-66
Fr 1814 Apr 26		DLC-10
Fr 1814 May 08		DLC-10
Fr 1814 Jul 06		DLC-11
Fr 1815 Dec 21	fin	4-1298
Fr 1816 Jul 18		DLC-21
Johnson Thomas B		
To 1815 Feb 28		4-0798
Johnson William		
Fr 1824 Aug 16		DLC-33
Fr 1824 Sep 22		DLC-72
Fr 1828 May 27		DLC-35
Fr 1837 Jan 23		DLC-49
Johnson William K et al		
Fr 1835 Apr 24		DLC-46
Johnson & Weaver		
Fr 1844 Dec 17	fin	DLC-57
Johnson Rayburn & Co		
Fr 1837 Apr 22#	fin	DLC-51
Fr 1837 Jul 17	fin	DLC-50
Fr 1838 Apr 07#	fin	DLC-51
To 1839 Apr 18#	fin	DLC-52
Fr 1839 Apr 26#	fin	DLC-53
Re 1840 Apr 24		34-1320
Fr 1840 Jul 22	fin	34-1492
To 1842 Jan 06	chk	DLC-54
Fr 1842 Jan 06	fin	DLC-54
Johnston Alexander		
Fr 1834 Sep 13		M639-13
Johnston Anna		
To 1833 Jun 15		23-0037
Johnston Benjamin W		
Fr 1823 Jun 28		DLC-32
Fr 1823 Aug 12		DLC-32
Johnston E H		
Fr 1840 Jun 26		DLC-52
Johnston J		
Fr 1829 Apr 04		M639-6
Johnston James C		
Fr 1829 Feb 18#		M639-10
Fr 1829 Feb 25		M639-18
Fr 1831 Feb 22#		17-0607
Johnston Job		
Fr 1827 Sep 18		DLC-34
Johnston John		
Fr 1829 Feb 26		12-0594
Johnston Joseph		
To 1813 Dec 16		DLC-61
Johnston Peter		
Fr 1829 Jan 05		12-0445
Johnston Robert		
Fr 1793 Oct 14	lnd	1-0164
Johnston Stroder		
Re 1832 Jun 07	par	20-0710
Johnston Thomas		
To 1801 Oct 21	lnd	1-0936
Johnston William		
Re 1807 Jul 17	leg	2-0518
To 1813 Aug 06	chk	DLC-6
Johnstone Thomas		
Fr 1835 Jun 01		M124-148
Jolly John		
To 1829 cSep		13-1221
Fr 1829 Dec 03		M222-26
Fr 1831 Dec 01		M234-78
Fr 1831 Dec 01*		18-1537
Fr 1836 Dec 14		32-1143
Jolly John et al		
Fr 1831 Jun 02#		M234-77
Fr 1836 Apr 16		M234-79
Joly Jean Batiste		
Re 1831 Sep 19	par	18-0846
Jones Albert		
To 1835 Oct 29		DLC-73
Jones Alexander		
Fr 1831 Feb 04		M639-12
Jones Anson		
Fr 1845 Jun 23		37-0259
Jones Atlas		
Fr 1830 Nov 20#		16-0809
Jones Augustus		
Fr 1836 cMay 19		M639-21
Jones Ben B		
Fr 1814 Nov 07		DLC-13
Fr 1814 Dec 23		DLC-14
Jones Benjamin et al		
Fr 1835 Dec 29		M639-27
Jones Branch		
Fr 1818 Mar	fin	6-0062
Jones Calvin		
Fr 1829 Jan 15		DLC-36
Jones Catesby ap Roger		
Fr 1836 Mar 28		30-0907
Jones Edward		
To 1804 Apr 22#	fin	1-1317
Fr 1815 Sep 05		DLC-19
Fr 1820 Dec 08	fin	DLC-29
Fr 1821 Mar 02		DLC-29
Jones Eliza M		
Fr 1833 Nov 14		M688-74
Jones Frederick		
Fr 1833 May 14		M567-84
Jones George		
Fr 1816 Feb 06		DLC-20
To 1816 Mar 15		DLC-20
Fr 1836 Mar 12		DLC-47
Jones George Wallace		
Fr 1836 Apr 13		M179-82
Fr 1836 Apr 21		M687-12
Fr 1836 Apr 21		M687-4
Fr 1836 Apr 21		M687-3
Fr 1836 Apr 21		M687-19
Fr 1836 Apr 26		M639-7
Fr 1836 Apr 26		30-1355
Fr 1836 Apr 27		M687-16
Fr 1836 May 27		31-0167
Fr 1836 Jun 01		31-0264
Fr 1836 Dec 16		M567-122
Fr 1837 Jan 04		32-1486
Fr 1837 Feb 01		M687-30
Jones Henry H et al		
Fr 1833 Feb		M639-24

Jones James Chamberlain			
	To 1844 Jun 06		36-0588
	Fr 1844 Jun 10		36-0596
Jones Joel W			
	Fr 1829 Aug 11		13-1104
Jones John			
	Fr 1831 Jun 06		17-1533
	To 1831 Jun 16		18-0032
Jones John Rice			
	Fr 1794 Nov 30		DLC-1
Jones Joseph			
	Re 1832 Nov 19	par	21-0464
Jones Joshua			
	Fr 1813 Oct 10	fin	DLC-61
Jones Leonard			
	Fr 1838 Dec 05		DLC-51
Jones Levi			
	Fr 1831 Apr 04		DLC-39
	Fr 1831 Apr 18		DLC-39
	To 1831 Apr 21		17-1202
	Fr 1831 Dec 12		DLC-40
	Fr 1832 Apr 09		DLC-40
Jones M M			
	Fr 1844 Jun 05		36-0582
	To 1844 Jun 25		36-0648
Jones Nelson P			
	Re 1819	fin	DLC-58
	Re 1820 Nov 04	leg	7-1402
	To 1820 Nov 25		DLC-72
Jones Peter			
	Fr 1835 Oct 12#	fin	DLC-47
Jones Richard H			
	To 1808 Feb 06	lnd	2-0613
Jones Robert Jackson			
	Fr 1840 Apr 28		DLC-52
Jones Robert Tignall			
	Re 1836 Oct 20		M22-41
Jones Roger			
	Fr 1832 Feb 29		19-1262
	To 1834 Oct 27#		M567-98
	Fr 1834 Oct 30		M222-32
	Re 1835 Feb 24		M221-115
	Re 1835 Feb 24*		27-0605
	Fr 1836 Feb 27#		M221-116
	To 1836 Sep 13*		M567-124
	Fr 1836 Nov 09#		M567-118
Jones Rolling			
	Fr 1832 Nov 14		M567-72
Jones S			
	Fr 1829 Mar 19		M639-12
Jones Samuel et al			
	Fr 1829 Apr 06		M639-1
Jones Thomas			
	Re 1830 May 04	par	15-0896
	Fr 1833 Jan 28#		DLC-42
Jones Thomas ap Catesby			
	Fr 1830 Mar 20		M273-25
	Fr 1830 Oct 11		16-0367
	Fr 1837 Feb 22		33-0823
Jones Thomas B			
	Fr 1843 cJan		35-1079
Jones Thomas H			
	Fr 1836 Mar 29		M124-152
Jones Thomas R			
	Fr 1842 May 30		DLC-54
Jones W S			
	Fr 1837 Jan 30		M688-104
Jones Walter			
	Fr 1835 Dec 17#		M179-81
Jones Walter et al			
	Fr 1835 Apr 06		DLC-46
Jones William			
	Fr 1830 Jan 01#	fin	14-1263
	Fr 1837 Mar 03	fin	DLC-74
Jones William et al			
	To 1817		5-0664
	Fr 1836 Nov 16		M567-135
Jones William A et al			
	Fr 1834 Feb 21		M639-24
Jones William D			
	Fr 1831 Jun 28#		DLC-39
	Fr 1836 Sep 07		M296-1
	Fr 1837 Jun 01		DLC-50
	Fr 1839 Oct 30		34-1028
Jones William Gwynn			
	Re 1837 Feb 21		
Jones William H			
	Fr 1832 Jan		19-0543
	Fr 1835 Apr 09		DLC-46
	Fr 1836 May 30		M639-12
Jones William H et al			
	Fr 1833 Nov 04		23-1188
Jones Wood			
	Fr 1817 Feb 16	fin	DLC-22
Jordan John Jr			
	Re 1804 Oct 22	fin	DLC-3
Jordan Thomas			
	Re 1805 Nov 29	fin	DLC-3
	Fr 1832 Jul 23		20-1225
Jordy Frederick			
	Fr 1814 Sep 12		DLC-12
Jouet Joel W			
	Fr 1829 Jul 20		M567-44
Jouett John			
	Fr 1813 May 11		DLC-71
Journeay Henry P			
	Fr 1844 Jan 04		DLC-56
Journey William			
	Re 1800 Jun 23	leg	1-0773
Judah Samuel et al			
	Fr 1829 Jan		12-0416
Judson Andrew Thompson			
	Fr 1829 Jan 29		M639-26
Judson Andrew Thompson et al			
	Fr 1833 Feb 05		22-0266
	To 1833 Mar 07		22-0684
Judson P E et al			
	Fr 1835 cJan		DLC-59
Judson Roswell			
	To 1836 Dec 26		32-1322
	Fr 1844 Oct 07		DLC-57
Judson William A			
	Fr 1834 Nov 13#	fin	DLC-45
	Fr 1835 Sep 29	fin	DLC-47
Jugneal E B			
	Fr 1832 Sep 06#		20-1486
Jung Jacob			
	Re 1837 Jan 14	par	32-1583
Justice Samuel			
	To 1814 Jul 26		3-1172
Kahkeshegahseng et al			
	Fr 1836 May 10		M234-387
Kahl Frederick			
	Re 1829 May 14		13-0320
Kalb Baron de			
	Fr 1829 May 09		DLC-37

Kane Elias			
	Fr 1836 Apr 09		M639-3
Kane Elias Kent			
	Fr 1829 Mar 09		M639-26
	Fr 1831 Feb 23		DLC-39
	Fr 1834 Dec 11		M639-10
Kane John Kintzing			
	Fr 1829 Sep 29		DLC-37
	Fr 1829 Sep 29		DLC-37
	To 1829 Oct 02		14-0090
	To 1829 Oct 02*		DLC-37
	Fr 1833 Oct 10		DLC-43
	Fr 1836 Jan 14		30-0009
	Fr 1836 Jun 27		M639-18
	Fr 1839 Aug 28		DLC-52
Karamanli Ali			
	Fr 1832 Nov 27		M179-76
Karamanli Yusuf ibn Ali			
	To 1831 Aug 23		18-0581
Karns William			
	Fr 1843 Feb 07		DLC-55
	Fr 1843 Oct 30		DLC-55
Kaskaskia and Peoria treaty			
	Re 1833 Feb 12		M668-7
Kaushkawnonew			
	Fr 1831 Oct 24		18-1115
Kaushkawnonew et al			
	Fr 1831 Apr 09		M234-315
	Fr 1831 Apr 09		M234-315
	Fr 1831 Apr 09		M234-315
Kavanagh Edward			
	Fr 1835 May 11		28-0340
	Fr 1836 Jul 09		M873-89
Kavanaugh Charles			
	To 1814 Feb 08		DLC-62
	Fr 1814 Feb 14		DLC-9
	Fr 1814 Feb 20		DLC-9
	Fr 1815 Apr 05		DLC-18
	Re 1815 May	fin	DLC-68
	Fr 1815 May 01		4-1021
	Fr 1815 May 01		DLC-68
	Fr 1815 May 01		DLC-68
	Fr 1815 May 07		DLC-68
	Fr 1815 May 13		4-1030
	Fr 1815 Jul 02		DLC-18
	Fr 1815 Jul 14		DLC-68
	Fr 1816 Mar 06		DLC-20
Kawgagosh et al			
	Fr 1836 Jul 14		T494-3
	Fr 1836 Jul 14*		31-1065
	Fr 1836 Jul 14*		M234-402
Kay Reuben L			
	Fr 1840 May 14		DLC-52
Kay & Thomas			
	Fr 1836 Jul 16#	fin	DLC-50
	Fr 1840 Mar 07	fin	DLC-52
Kean Nathaniel B et al			
	Fr 1831 cJan 28		M639-1
Kean Stephen R			
	Fr 1829 Mar 03	fin	DLC-72
Keane John			
	To 1815 Feb 04		DLC-16
	Fr 1815 Feb 08		DLC-16
Kearby John			
	To 1801 Oct 08	lnd	1-0928
Kearney James			
	Fr 1832 Dec 24		21-1151
	To 1834 Jan 06		DLC-44
Kearney John A			
	Re 1834 Dec 03	par	26-1386
Kearny Alfred			
	Fr 1838 Apr 23	fin	DLC-51
Kearny Lawrence			
	Fr 1830 Apr 10		15-0660
Kearsley Jonathan			
	Fr 1802 Feb 28		DLC-2
	Fr 1835 Nov 20		M639-9
Kearsley Jonathan et al			
	Fr 1830 Jan 29		M639-27
	Fr 1833 Feb 12		M639-8
Keeble Edwin Augustus			
	Fr 1844 Mar 14		DLC-56
Keefel James			
	Fr 1835 Feb 11		M179-79
Keene Richard Raynal			
	Fr 1829 Apr 27		DLC-37
Keene W R			
	To 1827 Jun 16		DLC-34
Keener C & D & S			
	Fr 1831 Apr 04		M124-127
Keeton G W			
	Fr c1829 May 02		13-0240
Kegwater Richard			
	Fr 1834 Dec 06#		DLC-45
Keichline William H			
	Fr 1844 Mar 22		DLC-56
Keim Daniel J et al			
	Fr 1829 cMar		M639-5
Keiper Jacob			
	Fr 1830 Dec 15		M22-27
Keiser Christopher			
	Fr 1818 Feb 10		DLC-24
Keith Timothy et al			
	Fr 1836 Jun 03		31-0286
Keller John et al			
	Fr 1832 cJul 10		20-1013
Kelley Joshua			
	Fr 1807 May 06	fin	DLC-4
Kelley Nathaniel J			
	Fr 1836 Jan 21		M179-81
Kellogg Daniel			
	Fr 1837 Feb		M687-20
Kellogg Josiah et al			
	Fr 1834 Oct		DLC-44
Kellogg Miner Kilbourne			
	Fr 1840 Jul 16		34-1480
	Fr 1840 Dec 30		DLC-53
Kelly Samuel			
	Fr 1814 Apr 26	fin	DLC-61
	Fr 1814 Apr 26*	fin	M221-65
Kelly William			
	Fr 1830 Apr 15#		15-0721
	Re 1835 Feb 11	par	27-0492
Kelly William C			
	Fr 1829 May 28		M221-109
Kelso Charles W			
	Fr 1835 Apr 13		28-0065
Kempe James			
	To 1814 Nov 14		DLC-62
Kemper Nathaniel et al			
	Fr 1815 Jan		DLC-16
Kemper Reuben			
	Fr 1815 Nov 17		4-1236
	Fr 1819 Apr 06		DLC-26
Kenadnunk et al			
	Fr 1833 Oct 20		M234-421
Kendall Amos			
	Fr 1827 Aug 22		11-0814
	Fr 1827 Aug 27		11-0825

Kendall Amos (cont)

To	1827 Sep 04		DLC-78
Fr	1828 Nov 19		12-0277
To	1828 Nov 25		DLC-78
To	1828 Nov 25*		DLC-35
Re	1829 Mar 21		12-1070
To	1829 Apr 28		M124-140
To	1829 Jul 02		13-0806
Fr	1829 Nov 20		14-0526
Fr	1829 Dec 06#		DLC-72
Fr	1830 Jan 05		14-1334
Fr	1830 Mar 10#		15-0324
To	1830 May 10		DLC-38
To	1830 Dec 06		DLC-38
Fr	1830 Dec 20		16-1505
Fr	1831 Jan 26		M639-1
To	1832 Jan 26		19-0871
To	1832 Mar 05		DLC-40
To	1832 Jul 23		DLC-78
To	1832 Aug 28		DLC-78
Fr	1832 Nov		21-0247
To	1832 Dec 03	chk	DLC-41
Fr	1833 Jan 23		M179-75
Fr	1833 Mar 20		DLC-42
Re	1833 Mar 20	mem	22-0838
Fr	1833 May 09		DLC-42
To	1833 Jul 12		DLC-43
Fr	1833 Aug 02		DLC-43
Fr	1833 Aug 11		DLC-43
Fr	1833 Aug 14		DLC-43
Fr	1833 Aug 25		DLC-43
To	1833 Sep 05		23-0652
Fr	1833 Sep 12		DLC-43
To	1833 Nov 18		23-1251
Fr	1834 cApr		25-0521
To	1834 Apr 01		25-0539
To	1834 Apr 01		25-0545
Fr	1834 Jul 19		DLC-73
To	1834 Aug 08		DLC-44
Fr	1834 Aug 21		DLC-44
To	1834 Oct 25		DLC-73
Fr	1834 Nov 25		DLC-45
Fr	1835 Feb 26		DLC-78
To	1835 May 01		28-0209
To	1835 May 05		DLC-46
Fr	1835 May 05		28-0289
To	1835 May 21		DLC-78
To	1835 Jul 19		DLC-78
To	1835 Jul 31		28-1213
Fr	1835 Aug 07		DLC-46
To	1835 Aug 09		DLC-78
Fr	1835 Aug 31		DLC-73
To	1835 Oct 31		DLC-73
Fr	1835 Nov 24		DLC-73
Fr	1835 Dec 01		29-0710
Fr	1836 Jan 07		29-1496
Fr	1836 Jun 08		M601-50
Fr	1836 Jun 08*		M234-225
To	1836 Jun 24		DLC-78
To	1836 Jun 27		31-0601
To	1836 Jun 28		31-0625
To	1836 Jul 05		DLC-74
Fr	1836 Jul 05		DLC-74
To	1836 Jul 08		31-0960
Fr	1836 Jul 30		31-1171
Fr	1836 Jul 30*		DLC-74
Fr	1836 Jul 30		M601-50
Fr	1836 Jul 30		M601-50
Fr	1836 Aug 03		31-1222
To	1836 Aug 05		31-1228
Fr	1836 Aug 07		31-1247
To	1836 Aug 12		DLC-78
To	1836 Sep 05		DLC-78
To	1836 Nov 24		DLC-78
Fr	1836 Dec 05		32-0844
To	1836 Dec 08		DLC-78
Fr	1836 Dec 20		32-1208
Fr	1836 Dec 20*		M601-50
Fr	1836 Dec 27		32-1355
To	1837 Jan 22		DLC-78
To	1837 Jan 23		DLC-78
To	1837 Jan 23#		33-0109
Fr	1837 Jan 31		33-0275
To	1837 Feb 10		DLC-50
Fr	1837 Feb 13		33-0652
To	1837 Mar 28		DLC-78
To	1837 May 22		DLC-78
To	1837 May 26		DLC-78
Fr	1837 Jun 06		DLC-50
To	1837 Jun 23		DLC-78
Fr	1837 Aug 11		DLC-50
To	1837 Aug 26		DLC-78
To	1838 Jan 16		34-0194
Fr	1838 Mar 06		DLC-74
To	1838 Mar 23		DLC-78
To	1838 Mar 27		DLC-78
Fr	1838 Nov 28		DLC-51
Fr	1839 Jan 29		34-0616
To	1839 Feb 11		DLC-78
To	1839 Apr 18		DLC-78
To	1839 Apr 19		DLC-78
To	1839 May 29		34-0800
To	1839 Aug 13		DLC-78
Fr	1839 Aug 28		DLC-75
To	1839 Oct 10		DLC-78
Fr	1839 Nov 12		DLC-52
To	1839 Nov 26		DLC-78
To	1839 Dec 23		34-1107
To	1840 Feb 05		DLC-78
To	1840 Feb 27		DLC-78
Fr	1840 Mar 04		DLC-52
To	1840 Apr 06		34-1285
To	1840 Jun 02		DLC-78
Fr	1840 Sep 12		DLC-74
To	1840 Sep 23		35-0022
To	1840 Sep 23*		DLC-53
To	1841 Jan 02		DLC-74
To	1841 Feb 17		DLC-53
Fr	1841 May 05		DLC-53
To	1841 May 15		DLC-78
Fr	1841 May 28		35-0310
Fr	1841 Oct 20		DLC-53
Re	1841 Nov	leg	35-0464
To	1841 Dec 15		DLC-78
Fr	1841 Dec 28		35-0544
To	1842 May 23		DLC-78
Fr	1842 Jun 05		DLC-54
To	1842 Jun 17		35-0807
To	1842 Jun 17*		DLC-54
To	1842 Jun 18		DLC-78
Fr	1842 Sep 19		DLC-54
To	1842 Sep 29		DLC-78
Fr	1842 Oct 09		DLC-54
Fr	1842 Oct 12		DLC-54
To	1842 Oct 18#		DLC-54
To	1842 Oct 26		DLC-78
To	1842 Nov 03		35-0986
Fr	1842 Nov 23		DLC-54
To	1842 Nov 25		DLC-78

Fr 1842 Nov 29 DLC-54
To 1842 Dec 12 DLC-78
Fr 1842 Dec 13 DLC-75
To 1842 Dec 21 DLC-74
Fr 1842 Dec 23 DLC-74
To 1842 Dec 29 35-1069
To 1843 Jan 02 35-1086
To 1843 Jan 03# DLC-55
To 1843 Jan 03# DLC-74
To 1843 Jan 10 35-1102
To 1843 Jan 26 35-1150
To 1843 Jan 26# DLC-74
Fr 1843 Jan 27 DLC-74
To 1843 Feb 06 35-1172
Fr 1843 Feb 07 35-1192
To 1843 Feb 08 35-1195
To 1843 Feb 08# DLC-55
To 1843 Feb 13 DLC-74
To 1843 Feb 14# DLC-74
Fr 1843 Feb 15 DLC-55
Fr 1843 Feb 17 DLC-74
Fr 1843 Feb 23 DLC-74
To 1843 Feb 27 35-1259
To 1843 Mar 03 35-1272
To 1843 Mar 08# 35-1276
To 1843 Mar 13# DLC-74
To 1843 Mar 15# DLC-74
Fr 1843 Mar 19 DLC-55
To 1843 Mar 20 DLC-78
To 1843 Mar 24 DLC-78
Fr 1843 Mar 28 DLC-55
Fr 1843 Apr 10 DLC-55
To 1843 Apr 19 DLC-74
To 1843 May 10 DLC-78
To 1843 May 15 35-1351
To 1843 May 15* DLC-74
To 1843 Sep 29 DLC-78
Fr 1843 Oct 21 DLC-55
To 1843 Nov 02 DLC-78
To 1843 Nov 13 DLC-78
To 1843 Nov 16 DLC-56
Fr 1843 Nov 20 36-0013
To 1843 Dec 04 DLC-78
To 1843 Dec 04* 36-0040
To 1843 Dec 25# DLC-56
To 1844 Jan 09 DLC-78
To 1844 Feb 12 DLC-78
To 1844 Mar 18 DLC-78
Fr 1844 Mar 31 36-0412
To 1844 Apr 12 DLC-78
Fr 1844 Aug 28 DLC-57
To 1844 Sep 10 DLC-78
Fr 1844 Sep 22 DLC-57
To 1844 Oct 07 36-0939
To 1844 Oct 07* DLC-74
Fr 1844 Nov 12 DLC-74
Fr 1844 Nov 18 DLC-74
To 1844 Nov 23 DLC-78
To 1844 Nov 28 DLC-78
Fr 1844 Dec 02 36-1115
Fr 1845 Jan 05 36-1314
To 1845 Jan 15 DLC-78
To 1845 Jan 15 DLC-78
To 1845 May 20 DLC-78
Fr 1845 May 31 DLC-74

Kendrick E P et al
Fr 1833 Sep M639-21

Kennan Charles
Fr 1829 Nov 30 M22-28

Kennedy A
Fr 1835 Feb 26# fin DLC-45
Fr 1835 Apr 01# fin DLC-46

Kennedy Edmund Pendleton
Fr 1827 Jun 09 DLC-34
To 1827 Jun 30 11-0718
To 1827 Jun 30* DLC-34
Fr 1830 Apr 11 15-0671

Kennedy James
Fr 1814 Jul 24 3-1164
Fr 1838 May 19 DLC-51

Kennedy James Lenox
Re 1829 Oct 15 14-0165

Kennedy John
Fr 1829 Apr 18 M639-11
Fr 1836 Jul 25 add 31-1156
Re 1836 Oct 25 32-0345
Fr 1836 Dec 18 32-1185

Kennedy John et al
To 1836 Jul 25 add 31-1157

Kennedy John S
Fr 1842 Oct 04 DLC-54

Kennedy Joseph Pulaski
Fr 1814 Sep 15 DLC-12
Fr 1814 Oct 08 DLC-13
Fr 1816 Dec 21 DLC-22

Kennedy Lucas
Fr 1825 Sep 11 add DLC-33
To 1825 Sep 20 DLC-33
Fr 1825 Sep 27 add 11-0006
To 1825 Oct 01 add 11-0011

Kennedy Sam
Fr 1821 Feb 20 DLC-29

Kennedy Thomas
Fr 1826 Mar 19 DLC-33
Fr 1829 Feb 28 M639-13
Fr 1829 Mar 02 M639-22
Fr 1830 May 31 DLC-38
Fr 1830 Jun 05 DLC-38
Fr 1830 Jun 26 DLC-38
Fr 1831 Mar 15 M639-13

Kennedy Thomas S
Fr 1830 Dec 04 M688-72

Kennedy William
Re 1832 Dec 24 par T967-1

Kennedy William Edmiston et al
Fr 1834 Sep 03 26-0418
To 1834 Sep 05 26-0423

Kenner William
To 1821 Feb 15 8-0118
Fr 1823 Jun 02 DLC-32

Kenner William & Co
Fr 1819 Jan 08 DLC-26

Kennon William
Fr 1833 Feb 12 M639-24
Fr 1833 Jul 25 23-0223

Kensett George
Re 1832 Oct 30 par T967-1

Kentucky Democratic Society
Fr 1793 Dec 31 DLC-1

Ker David C
Fr 1814 Sep 08 DLC-12
Fr 1815 Jul 28 M222-16
Fr 1815 Jul 28* DLC-19
Fr 1816 Jan 05 DLC-15
To 1821 Feb 15 8-0122
Fr 1824 Nov 23 DLC-33
Fr 1828 Nov 06 DLC-35
Fr 1828 Nov 11 DLC-35

Ker David C (cont)
Fr 1828 Nov 15 DLC-35
To 1828 cNov 16 DLC-35
Fr 1830 Jan 14 M639-4
Kercheval Samuel
Fr 1822 Nov 07 DLC-31
Kern Jacob
Fr 1835 Jan 30 M639-4
Kern Jacob et al
Fr 1835 Feb 15 M639-17
Kerns James
Fr 1815 Feb 22 DLC-71
Kerr Aaron et al
Fr 1829 Mar 04 M639-6
Kerr Andrew
Re 1838 Mar lnd 34-0258
Re 1840 Jun 08# leg 34-1399
Kerr James
Fr 1794 Feb 06 1-0191
Kerr John Leeds
Fr 1833 Apr 26 22-1183
Kerr Thomas J
Re 1836 Jul 06 par 31-0871
Kerr William R & Co
Fr 1837 Mar 01 DLC-50
Kerr Wilson
Re 1813 Dec 22 DLC-61
Kerr & Co
Fr 1820 Apr 20 fin DLC-29
Ketcham Thomas
Fr 1829 May 14# 13-0321
Fr 1829 Oct 12# M124-121
Key Francis Scott
Fr 1829 Oct 15 14-0167
Fr 1831 Jan 26 M639-1
Fr 1832 Jul 10 M639-5
Re 1835 cApr mem 27-1411
Fr 1836 Jan 13 30-0005
Fr 1836 Mar 15 30-0793
Fr 1837 Jan 16 32-1589
Key Francis Scott et al
Fr 1832 May 28 M22-29
Fr 1834 Mar 29 M688-88
Key H G
Fr 1829 Jul 30 M688-64
Key Philip Barton
Fr 1844 Dec 01 DLC-57
Key West FL soldiers
Re 1835 May 28 mem 28-0510
Keyser George
Fr 1830 Apr 23# DLC-38
Keyworth Mary
Fr 1836 Jun 18# fin DLC-48
Keyworth Robert
Fr 1829 Dec 10# fin DLC-72
Fr 1834 Dec 08# fin DLC-45
Fr 1835 Jan 16# fin DLC-45
Fr 1835 Nov 02 fin DLC-47
Fr 1836 May 18# fin DLC-48
Fr 1836 Jul 05# fin DLC-48
Kickapoo treaty
Re 1833 Feb 13 M668-7
Kidd William
Fr 1830 Sep 28 16-0262
Kiler James M
Fr 1837 Feb 08 fin DLC-50
Fr 1837 Feb 21# fin DLC-50
Fr 1837 Mar 04# fin DLC-50
Kille Joseph
Fr 1831 May M639-12
Kille Joseph et al
Fr 1829 Mar 25 M873-19
Killer David
Fr 1829 Jun 13 M639-4
Killiam Joseph
Re 1840 Mar 12# leg 34-1255
Killogh David
Fr 1809 Jan 19 fin DLC-4
Kimansa et al
Fr 1831 Nov 22 18-1472
Kimbro James
Fr 1816 Jun 13# DLC-20
Kincaid John et al
Fr 1830 May 15-0867
Kincaid Joseph
Fr 1830 Dec 23 M234-774
Fr 1830 Dec 23* 16-1548
Kincanon Matthew
Fr 1792 Aug 20# fin 1-0131
Kinchy Paul
Fr 1834 May 01# fin DLC-44
Fr 1834 Aug 11# fin DLC-44
Fr 1834 Nov 04# fin DLC-45
Fr 1834 Dec 01# fin DLC-45
Fr 1835 Jan 01# fin DLC-45
Fr 1835 Apr 01# fin DLC-46
Fr 1835 Jun 01# fin DLC-46
Fr 1835 Jul 01# fin DLC-46
Fr 1835 Aug 11# fin DLC-46
Fr 1835 Oct 02# fin DLC-47
Fr 1835 Nov 04# fin DLC-47
Fr 1835 Dec 03# fin DLC-47
Fr 1836 Feb 01# fin DLC-47
King Adam
Fr 1831 Dec 20 M22-29
King Benjamin
Re 1836 Oct 18 32-0222
Fr 1836 Oct 22 32-0324
Fr 1836 Nov 11 32-0481
King Edward
Fr 1829 Jul 16 M639-16
King Edward et al
Fr 1829 Jun 01 M639-10
King Elisha W et al
Fr 1834 Feb 05 M639-24
King F & C et al
Fr 1835 Aug M639-15
King Gamaliel
Re 1829 Dec 26 par 14-1126
King Hiram
Fr 1834 Dec 24# DLC-45
King James
To 1795 May 13# 1-0256
King John
Fr 1842 Feb 12 DLC-54
King John et al
Fr 1831 Dec 12 M639-24
King John Pendleton
Fr 1835 Apr 16 28-0090
Fr 1835 Apr 16* M234-242
Fr 1836 Feb 29 30-0623
Fr 1836 Feb 29* M234-436
King John Pendleton et al
Fr 1836 Feb 29 M124-151
King Martin
Re 1830 May 14 par T967-1
King Miles
Re 1830 cJan 14-1253

King Mulatto
    Fr 1821 Oct 27 8-1307
    Fr 1821 Dec 24 M116-10
King Mulatto et al
    Fr 1821 Nov 11 M221-93
    Fr 1821 Nov 11* M221-96
King Robert
    Re 1792 Oct 11 fin 1-0133
    Fr 1793 Oct 23 DLC-1
    Fr 1795 Jul 08 DLC-1
King Rufus
    Fr 1820 Feb# mem DLC-28
King S
    Fr 1829 Aug 18 M639-18
King S et al
    Fr 1829 Aug 12 M639-18
    Fr 1829 Aug 12 M639-18
King Samuel D
    Fr 1836 Jul 09 31-1017
    Re 1836 Jul 09 31-1019
King Wigton
    Fr 1814 Sep 26 DLC-12
    Fr 1814 Sep 30 DLC-12
    Fr 1814 Oct 14 DLC-13
    Fr 1814 Nov 04 DLC-13
    Fr 1816 Feb 12 DLC-20
    Fr 1816 Feb 12* M271-1
King William (AL)
    Fr 1818 Oct 15 M221-81
    Fr 1818 Oct 15* 6-1361
    Fr 1819 Feb 04 7-0231
    Fr 1819 Feb 04* M221-80
    Fr 1819 Feb 10 7-0249
    To 1819 Apr 13 7-0470
    To 1819 Apr 18 DLC-63
    To 1820 Nov 29 8-0001
    Fr 1821 Nov 23 DLC-31
King William Mrs (AL)
    Fr 1831 Dec 17 M22-28
King William (ME)
    Fr 1831 Dec 01 M639-11
King William (TN)
    Fr 1809 Apr 25 fin 2-0801
King William (TN) et al
    To 1814 Feb 11 DLC-62
King William Rufus DeVane
    Fr 1832 Feb 29 19-1266
    Fr 1834 Mar 14 M234-241
    Fr 1834 Mar 14* 25-0210
    Fr 1835 Apr 28 DLC-46
    Fr 1835 Jul 25 M639-14
    Fr 1836 Feb 29 30-0623
    Fr 1836 Feb 29* M234-436
    Re 1837 Jan 28 33-0197
    Fr 1837 Feb 25 33-0893
    Fr 1837 Feb 28 M234-81
    Fr 1843 Dec 19 DLC-56
King William Rufus DeVane et al
    Fr 1835 Feb 24 M234-242
King & Co
    Re 1792 Dec 10 fin DLC-1
King Carson & King
    Fr 1809 Jun 02 fin DLC-4
Kingsbury Cyrus
    Fr 1820 Oct 18 M271-3
    Fr 1820 Oct 18* 7-1385
    Fr 1835 Oct 30 M234-778
Kingsley Alpha
    Fr 1812 Aug 24 2-1233
    To 1812 Dec 23 DLC-5
    To 1812 Dec 23* DLC-61
    To 1812 Dec 24 DLC-5
    To 1812 Dec 24* DLC-61
    Fr 1812 Dec 24 DLC-5
    Fr 1812 Dec 24* DLC-61
    Fr 1812 Dec 30 2-1311
    To 1813 Mar 21 3-0346
    To 1813 Mar 21* DLC-61
    To 1813 Mar 21 3-0348
    To 1813 Mar 21* DLC-6
    To 1813 Mar 21* DLC-61
    Fr 1813 Apr 25 DLC-6
    Fr 1814 Mar 13 DLC-9
    To 1814 May 27 DLC-10
    Fr 1814 Jun 04 DLC-10
    To 1816 Oct 25 chk DLC-21
    Fr 1818 Jun 15 fin 6-1055
Kingsley Eliza
    Fr 1821 May 15# DLC-30
    To 1821 Jun 21# 8-0644
    To 1821 Jul 23# 8-0893
    To 1824 Dec 23# 10-0996
Kingston A B
    Fr 1836 Oct 20 M567-132
Kinnard George L
    Fr 1833 Dec 03 24-0176
    Fr 1833 Dec 03 24-0192
    Fr 1835 Jun 06 28-0592
    Fr 1835 Jun 15 28-0683
    Fr 1835 Jun 15 M234-435
    Fr 1836 Jan 23 M639-26
    Fr 1836 Jan 23 M234-355
    Fr 1836 Jan 26 M639-26
Kinney Chesley et al
    Fr 1831 cNov M639-18
Kinney Simon
    Fr 1829 Oct 24 M639-14
Kinney Simon et al
    Fr 1829 Oct 24 M639-14
Kinney William
    Fr 1829 Oct 08 DLC-37
    Fr 1835 Jan 15 M639-13
    Fr 1835 Jan 15 M639-26
    Fr 1835 Nov 16 DLC-47
Kinney William et al
    Fr 1829 Mar 06 M639-26
Kinney William Jr
    Fr 1831 Dec 01 M639-18
Kinsley Zebina James Duncan
    Fr 1834 Apr 19 M688-88
Kintner James H et al
    Fr 1834 Jun 30 M234-354
Kintzing William Frederick
    Fr 1841 Apr 26 DLC-56
Kinzer E E
    Fr 1840 Apr 06 DLC-52
Kinzey Solomon
    Fr 1838 Sep 07 DLC-51
Kirby Edmund
    Fr 1834 Oct 27# M567-98
Kirby William M
    Fr 1814 Jan 04 DLC-61
    To 1814 Jan 05 DLC-61
Kirkhane John
    Fr 1818 Jun 09 fin DLC-69
    Fr 1818 Jun 09* fin 6-1040
Kirkman Ellen (Jackson)
    To 1820 Dec 16 8-0025

Kirkman H and J & Co
Fr 1836 Apr 26 fin DLC-48
Kirkman Thomas
Fr 1808 May 21 fin DLC-4
To 1817 Sep 16# DLC-23
To 1818 Oct 20 DLC-25
Fr 1819 Jul 29 DLC-27
Kirkman & Erwin
Fr 1813 Sep 04 fin DLC-11
Fr 1819 Jul 29 fin DLC-27
Fr 1821 Jan 01 fin DLC-31
Kirkman & Jackson
Fr 1815 Apr 17 fin DLC-18
Fr 1818 Dec 01 7-0017
Fr 1819 Jan 11 fin 7-0127
Kirkman Jackson & Erwin
Fr 1815 Jun 08 fin DLC-22
Kirkman & Livingston
Fr 1827 May 11# fin DLC-34
Kirkpatrick Alexander
To 1801 Oct 08 lnd 1-0931
To 1802 Mar 26 lnd 1-0958
Kirkpatrick Jabez
Fr 1837 Feb 01 33-0348
Kirkpatrick Littleton et al
Fr 1830 Feb 10 M639-24
To 1833 Jun 09 23-0006
Kittera Thomas
Fr 1829 Mar 30 M639-13
Kizer David
Fr 1829 Apr 22 M639-13
Fr 1829 May 02 M639-13
Klaer Elizabeth
Fr 1836 Jan 19 M124-151
Klendgen John D
Fr 1834 Jun 02 M639-21
Klopfer Christian
Re 1833 Oct 28 par 23-1097
Knaggs James
Fr 1836 Jun 13 31-0447
Knapp Jacob
Fr 1821 May 12 DLC-30
Knapp Thomas S et al
Fr 1831 Dec 19 19-0354
Kneass Dallas A
Fr 1845 Feb 01 36-1430
Knight Alfred
Re 1831 Jan 11 par 17-0236
Knight Jacob et al
Fr 1833 Apr M639-4
Knight Simeon
Re 1815 Mar 29 4-0912
To 1815 cMar 31 4-0918
To 1815 Apr 04 DLC-18
Fr 1815 Apr 04 M221-63
To 1815 Apr 04 M221-63
To 1815 Apr 04* DLC-18
Fr 1815 May 24 DLC-18
Fr 1815 May 24* M221-63
To 1815 Jun 08 DLC-68
Fr 1815 Jul 03 M221-63
To 1815 Jul 18 M221-63
To 1815 Jul 18* DLC-62
To 1829 cJul DLC-60
Knight William
Fr 1831 Feb 18 M22-27
Knowles James D
Fr 1832 Mar 08 M234-775
Knowles L & Co
Fr 1836 Jun 01 DLC-74
Fr 1836 Sep 10 DLC-49
Knowles & Thayer
Fr 1833 Nov 22 23-1293
Knowlton J R
Fr 1838 May 26 DLC-51
Kncx David
Re 1809 Oct 17 leg 2-0859
Knox Mary (Caffery)
Fr 1822 Jan 06 fin DLC-32
Fr 1822 Mar 29 fin DLC-31
Knox Robert
Fr 1796 Nov 01 fin 1-0456
Fr 1803 Apr 17# DLC-2
Kochus Hadjo
Re 1834 Apr 30 25-0942
Koepper C
Fr 1825 Mar 18 fin DLC-72
Kowelocco
Re 1835 Feb 01 lnd 27-0363
Kremer George
Fr 1824 May 05 10-0702
To 1824 May 06 10-0705
Fr 1825 Mar 08 DLC-33
Fr 1834 Oct 03 26-0496
Krems John
Fr 1831 May 09 M567-62
Krepps James S
To 1831 Jan 29# 17-0375
Krepps Solomon G
Fr 1830 Jun 18 M234-433
Fr 1830 Sep 27 M234-433
Fr 1832 Mar 29 M22-29
Kridelbaugh S H
Fr 1845 Feb 10 DLC-57
Kuhn Joseph L
Fr 1829 Oct 16 M273-27
To 1829 Oct 17# M273-27
Fr 1830 Sep 27 M273-27
Re 1830 Oct 07 M273-27
Fr 1830 Oct 11 M273-27
Fr 1831 May 07 M273-27
Re 1832 Apr 05 M273-27
Kurtz Daniel
Re 1833 May 06 22-1308
Re 1833 Jul 20 23-0165
To 1835 Apr 27 28-0141
To 1835 Jul 03 28-0891
To 1835 Oct 31 29-0399
Re 1836 Aug 22 31-1345
Kurtz William
Re 1836 Jul 08 par 31-0963

L J M
Fr 1828 Sep 26 DLC-35
L P
Fr 1828 Oct 20 DLC-35
Labatut Jean Baptiste
Fr 1836 Mar 22 30-0876
Labatut Jean Baptiste et al
Fr 1827 Dec 03 DLC-35
Fr 1827 Dec 03* 11-0944
Fr 1827 Dec 10 DLC-35
To 1827 Dec 18 DLC-35
Labory Pierre Joseph
Fr 1832 Feb 10 M179-72

Lacock Abner
Fr 1832 Jun 25 DLC-40
Fr 1832 Jun 25* 20-0809
Lacoste Casimir et al
Fr 1836 Jan 23 M639-4
Lacoste Emilie
Fr 1815 cFeb 4-0672
Lacoste Pierre
To 1814 Dec 25 DLC-62
To 1821 Feb 16 8-0131
To 1825 Oct 28 11-0048
Lacoste Pierre et al
Fr 1832 Mar 15 M639-4
Lacy Thomas J
Fr 1831 Mar 24 17-0961
Fr 1833 Apr 13 DLC-42
Fr 1834 Apr 14 25-0704
Fr 1834 Jun 04 DLC-44
Fr 1835 Mar 17 DLC-45
Fr 1836 Jul 14# 31-1074
Fr 1836 Oct 06 32-0087
Ladd Ira et al
Fr 1831 Aug 29 18-0620
Lafayette George Washington
Fr 1834 Jun 15 25-1378
Fr 1834 Jun 15* DLC-44
To 1834 Jun 27 25-1574
Fr 1834 Oct 21 26-0672
To 1839 Apr 04 34-0719
Lafayette Marquis de
To 1824 Sep 10 DLC-33
Fr 1824 Oct 18 DLC-33
Re 1825 May 04 add 10-1257
Fr 1825 Aug 21 DLC-33
Re 1826 Jul 08 add 11-0304
To 1828 Apr 09 11-1208
Re 1828 Jul 02 add 12-0041
Fr 1829 Feb 26 12-0597
To 1829 Apr 17 DLC-37
To 1829 Oct 08 14-0122
To 1830 Oct 01 16-0290
To 1830 Oct 01* DLC-38
To 1830 Dec 23 16-1549
To 1830 Dec 23* DLC-38
Fr 1830 Dec 28 17-0031
To 1831 Jan 19 17-0296
To 1831 Jan 19* DLC-38
To 1831 Aug 10 18-0495
To 1831 Oct 14 18-0995
Fr 1832 Feb 05 19-0969
Fr 1832 Jun 16 DLC-40
Fr 1832 Jun 16 DLC-40
Fr 1832 Jul 17 20-1121
Fr 1833 Mar 15 22-0773
Fr 1833 Apr 06 M179-76
To 1833 Jun 05 22-1579
To 1833 Sep 21 23-0818
To 1833 Sep 28 23-0891
To 1833 Sep 28 23-0895
To 1834 Jun 04 25-1256
Re 1834 Jun 21 M567-93
Re 1834 Jun 21* 25-1456
Lafferty John
Re 1808 Jun 18 leg 2-0677
Lafloeur Lewis
Re 1816 Sep 06 5-0457
LaFosse Jacques
Re 1829 Mar 19 par 12-1037
Re 1829 Mar 19* par T967-1
Laframboise Claude
Fr 1831 Nov 11 18-1243
Lagarde G
Fr c1834 37-0322
Laighton Samuel
Fr 1830 Jun 23 DLC-38
Laighton Thomas B
Fr 1829 Aug 31 13-1211
To 1829 Sep 05# 13-1258
Fr 1829 Oct 21 14-0225
Fr 1829 Nov 14 14-0462
Lally James L
Fr 1840 Jul 24 DLC-53
Lamar Gazaway Bugg
To 1842 Feb 28 35-0637
Lamar Henry Graybill et al
Fr 1831 Dec 07 19-0236
Lamb George
To 1836 Apr 04 chk DLC-47
To 1837 Mar 01 chk DLC-50
Lamb J B
Fr 1843 Sep 18 DLC-55
Lambert Edward John
Fr 1823 Aug 04 DLC-32
Lambert John
To 1815 Jan 08 DLC-62
To 1815 Jan 08 DLC-15
To 1815 Jan 08* DLC-62
Fr 1815 Jan 08 DLC-15
Fr 1815 Jan 08 DLC-15
To 1815 Jan 09 DLC-15
Fr 1815 Jan 09 DLC-15
To 1815 Jan 10 DLC-16
To 1815 Jan 10* DLC-62
To 1815 Jan 11 DLC-15
Fr 1815 Jan 11 DLC-15
Fr 1815 Jan 12 DLC-15
To 1815 Jan 12 DLC-62
To 1815 Jan 13 DLC-62
Fr 1815 Jan 13 DLC-15
To 1815 Jan 16 DLC-62
To 1815 Jan 16* DLC-15
Fr 1815 Jan 16 DLC-15
To 1815 Jan 17 DLC-15
To 1815 Jan 17* DLC-62
To 1815 Jan 17 DLC-62
Fr 1815 Jan 20 DLC-15
To 1815 Jan 23 DLC-15
To 1815 Feb 04 DLC-16
Fr 1815 Feb 08 DLC-16
Fr 1815 Feb 19 DLC-16
To 1815 Feb 20 DLC-16
To 1815 Feb 26 DLC-62
Fr 1815 Feb 27 DLC-17
To 1815 Mar 04 DLC-17
To 1815 Mar 06 4-0822
To 1815 Mar 06* DLC-17
To 1815 Mar 07 DLC-17
To 1815 Mar 13 DLC-17
To 1815 Mar 16 DLC-17
Fr 1815 Mar 16 DLC-17
Fr 1815 Mar 18 DLC-17
Fr 1815 Mar 18* M221-63
Fr 1815 Mar 19 DLC-17
Fr 1815 Mar 19* M221-63
To 1815 Mar 24 DLC-68
Lambert William
Fr 1836 Sep 30 M567-128
Lamme S C
Fr 1829 Jun 05 13-0574

Lamont W H
Fr 1844 Sep 16 DLC-57
Lamouth N L
Fr 1835 Dec 22# 29-1295
Lamprey Uri
Fr 1844 Feb 26 DLC-56
Lancaster Joseph
Fr 1829 12-0372
Lance William
To 1837 Feb 03 33-0382
Land sales
Re 1829 Jun 23 mem 13-0704
Lane Albert G
Fr 1837 Feb 04 M639-14
Lane Amos
Fr 1833 Dec 03 24-0176
Fr 1833 Dec 03 24-0192
Fr 1835 Jan 07 27-0121
Fr 1835 Sep 08 M639-11
Fr 1835 Dec 01 M639-11
Fr 1835 Dec 21 M639-11
Fr 1836 Apr 25 M639-6
Fr 1837 Jan 25 M221-117
Lane Daniel et al
Fr 1836 cFeb 01 M639-2
Lane Garrett
To 1814 Feb 09 DLC-62
Lane Henry
Re 1790 May 06 leg 1-0075m
Lane Isaac
Fr 1830 Feb 15 M639-22
Lane John F
Re c1829 mem 12-0376
Re 1835 cApr mem 27-1424
Fr 1836 Jul 20 DLC-48
Fr 1836 Jul 28 DLC-48
Lane Marcus
Fr 1836 Oct 31-1546
Fr 1836 Oct* M179-82
Lane Robert Carr
Fr 1818 Apr 28 DLC-24
Lane Samuel et al
Fr c1836 29-1398
Lang John
Fr 1831 Apr 13 M639-6
Fr 1833 Nov 19 M639-25
Langdon Elam P
Fr 1835 Mar 21 M639-1
Fr 1837 Mar 18 add DLC-74
To 1837 Mar 18 add DLC-74
Fr 1840 May 02 34-1337
Langdon John P
Re 1836 Mar 08 par 30-0710
Fr 1836 Jun 04 31-0323
Langdon Richard C
Fr 1825 Nov 09 DLC-33
To 1825 Nov 18 DLC-33
Fr 1826 Apr 12 DLC-33
Fr 1827 Nov 05 DLC-34
Langham Elias T
Fr 1832 Jul 24 20-1237
Langley Henry G
Fr 1844 Oct 16 DLC-57
Langlois Paul
Fr 1834 Jan 22 24-1025
Langstroth James N
To 1840 Jan 08# fin DLC-52
To 1840 Jul 21 chk DLC-53
Langtree & O'Sullivan
To 1837 Mar 06 M567-149
Fr 1839 May 08 fin DLC-52
Langworthy Asahel
Fr 1829 May 14 M639-13
Fr 1830 Mar 21 M639-13
Langworthy Augustus
Fr 1834 Mar 25 25-0355
Lanier Churchill
To 1840 Jul 21 chk DLC-53
Lanier James
Re 1789 May leg DLC-1
Lanier James W
Fr 1824 Apr 28 DLC-32
To 1824 May 15 DLC-32
Lansing Abraham
Fr 1836 Jun 10 31-0426
Lansing George
Re 1832 Jun 14 M273-28
Re 1832 Jun 14* 20-0754
To 1832 Jun 14# DLC-40
Lansing Gerrit Yates
Fr 1837 Jan 30 M639-5
Lantern Joseph
To 1807 Mar 05 fin DLC-4
Laporte Eugene
Re 1835 Oct 13 par 29-0280
Laporte John et al
Fr 1830 Feb 25 M639-23
Fr 1835 Oct 05 M639-18
Lapsley Joseph B
Fr 1836 Nov 09# fin DLC-50
Fr 1837 Nov 09# fin DLC-50
Lapsley Robert Armstrong
Fr 1844 Sep 14 DLC-57
Fr 1844 Oct 02 DLC-57
Fr 1845 Feb 05 DLC-57
Larimor Samuel et al
Fr 1836 Jan M639-5
Larned James
Fr 1835 Feb 21 M179-79
Fr 1836 Oct 06 32-0089
Larned Joseph
Re 1836 Jan 22 par 30-0164
Larned & Torrey
Fr 1832 Aug 20 20-1371
LaRonde Pierre Denis de
Fr 1815 Jan 26 DLC-15
Fr 1815 Jan 26 DLC-15
Fr 1815 Jan 27 DLC-16
Fr 1815 Feb 01 DLC-16
Fr 1815 Feb 05 DLC-16
To 1815 Apr 03 4-0964
To 1815 Apr 03* DLC-18
Fr 1815 Jul 28 DLC-19
Re 1821 Jan 10 8-0058
Larue J F
Fr 1835 Jun 01 DLC-46
Larwill Joseph H
Re 1829 Apr 16 12-1365
Fr 1834 Dec M639-9
Lasley Samuel C
Fr 1832 Feb 21 M22-29
Lasselle Hyacinthe
Fr 1829 Aug 27 13-1206
Latapie Anthony
Fr 1822 Oct 28 fin DLC-32
Fr 1823 Mar 22 fin DLC-32
Fr 1824 Feb 20 fin DLC-33

Fr 1826 May 18 fin DLC-33
Fr 1826 Oct 17 fin DLC-34
Latham Allen et al
Fr 1835 Jan 01 M639-27
Latham Bela
Fr 1835 Jan 07 M639-27
Fr 1835 Mar 24 M639-3
Fr 1837 Oct 30 37-0532
Fr 1837 Oct 30* 34-0011
Latham R W
Fr 1843 Dec 10 DLC-56
Fr 1844 Mar 13 DLC-56
Latimer Nathaniel
Fr 1840 Jul 18 DLC-53
Latour Arsene Lacarriere
To 1815 Jan 27# 4-0638
To 1815 Jan 27* DLC-16
Fr 1815 Jan 30 4-0645
Fr 1829 May 22 M639-13
Latrobe Benjamin Henry
To 1815 Aug 14 DLC-62
Lattimore ______
To 1838 Nov 01# fin DLC-51
Laub Andrew M
Re 1831 Jul 12 mem 18-0198
Laub John
Re 1832 Jul 21 20-1214
Lauderdale James
Re 1827 Oct 01 add 11-0885
Lauderdale William
To 1814 Oct 18 4-0272
To 1814 Oct 18* DLC-62
To 1814 Oct 22 DLC-62
Fr 1828 Jun 04 DLC-35
To 1828 Jun 04 DLC-35
Laughlin H H
Fr 1844 Jun 14 36-0610
Laughlin Samuel Hervey
Fr 1828 Mar 15 add 11-1169
To 1828 Mar 15 add 11-1171
Fr 1828 Apr 02# DLC-72
Fr 1835 Mar 01 27-0672
To 1837 Apr 04 33-1152
To 1837 Jun 13 33-1293
To 1837 Jun 13* DLC-74
Fr 1844 Jan 22 DLC-56
Fr 1844 May 23# DLC-56
Fr 1845 Mar 15 DLC-57
Laughlin Samuel Hervey et al
Fr 1829 Apr 08 M639-2
Laurenson James
Fr 1835 Sep 08 DLC-46
Laurie James et al
Fr 1830 Jan 05# M124-122
Fr 1833 Jan 31 22-0165
Laveaux Charles
Fr 1828 Jan 10 DLC-35
Lavender George M
Fr 1836 May 03# M234-80
Lavergne Hughes de
To 1815 Feb 20 DLC-16
Law John
To 1842 Aug 24 lnd 35-0899
Law Thomas
Fr 1830 Jan 07# DLC-37
Law case (federal)
Re c1831 mem 17-0088
Lawler Joab
Fr 1836 Jun 28 31-0626
Lawrence Abbott et al
Fr 1836 Apr M687-28
Lawrence Cornelius Van Wyck
Fr 1834 Jan 08 M639-18
To 1835 Jul 13 28-1007
Lawrence Cornelius Van Wyck et al
Fr 1837 Jan 08 32-1543
Fr 1837 Jan 08* DLC-49
Lawrence John
Re 1805 May 22 leg 2-0044
Lawrence John B
Re 1835 Jul 04 par 28-0901
Lawrence R
Fr 1829 Mar 31 M639-13
Lawrence Richard
Re 1835 Feb 04 27-0396
Lawrence William
To 1814 Sep 12 DLC-62
To 1814 Sep 15 DLC-62
Fr 1814 Sep 15 M221-63
To 1814 Oct 16 DLC-62
To 1814 Dec 19 DLC-62
Fr 1815 Feb 12 DLC-16
Fr 1815 Feb 12* M221-63
To 1815 Apr 06 4-0977
Fr 1831 Jun 16# M567-62
Lawrence William D
Fr 1831 Mar 11 M639-13
Lawrence William Pitt
To 1838 Aug 24 34-0435
Lawrence Wolcott et al
Fr 1834 Feb 14 24-1336
Lawrenson Philip
Fr 1831 Nov 09 M22-28
Lawson Stephen
Fr 1833 Mar 08 M639-13
Lawton Job G
Re 1832 Jul 02 par 20-0858
Lea David
Fr 1841 Nov 22 DLC-54
Lea Franklin W
Fr 1834 Apr 25-0526
Lea James N
Fr 1831 Mar 11 DLC-39
Lea Luke
Fr 1834 Jun 11# M179-78
Fr 1835 Mar 07 M688-89
Leach Joseph et al
Fr 1832 May 28 20-0614
Leak F T et al
Fr 1835 Apr 16 DLC-46
Leak Walter F
Fr 1835 Jul 07 M234-136
Leak William H
Fr 1835 Jul 07 M22-36
Leake Joseph S
Fr 1832 Jun 14 M639-14
Fr 1835 Aug 09 28-1265
Fr 1835 Oct 24 29-0338
Leake Samuel
Fr 1829 Aug 11 M639-14
Leamy John et al
Fr 1829 Nov 09 14-0440
Lear Clinton W
Fr 1844 Nov DLC-57
Lear Tobias
Fr 1814 Dec 06 DLC-14
Fr 1814 Dec 06* 4-0381
To 1815 Jan 13# 4-0527

Lear Tobias (cont)
To 1815 Jan 17 4-0560
To 1815 Jan 17* DLC-62
To 1815 Jan 20 4-0583
To 1815 Feb 03 4-0683
To 1815 Feb 03* DLC-16
Fr 1815 Apr 07 DLC-18
Fr 1815 Apr 07* 4-0979
Fr 1815 Apr 15 4-0992
Fr 1815 Jun 09 DLC-18
Fr 1815 Jun 09* 4-1076
To 1815 Jul 02 DLC-62
Fr 1815 Aug 18 DLC-19
Fr 1815 Aug 18* 4-1161
To 1815 Sep 04 DLC-62
Fr 1815 Sep 22 DLC-19
Fr 1815 Sep 22* 4-1188
Fr 1815 Nov 27 DLC-19
To 1815 Nov 27 DLC-62
Fr 1815 Nov 28 DLC-19
Fr 1815 Dec 19 DLC-19
Fr 1815 Dec 19* 4-1292
Fr 1815 Dec 22 DLC-20
Fr 1815 Dec 22* 4-1299
Fr 1815 Dec 23 DLC-20
Fr 1815 Dec 23* 4-1305
Fr 1816 Jun 25 DLC-21
Fr 1816 Jun 25* 5-0242
Fr 1816 Jul 08 DLC-21
Fr 1816 Jul 08* 5-0294
Fr 1816 Jul 16 DLC-21
Fr 1816 Jul 16* 5-0304
To 1816 Jul 27 5-0330
Fr 1816 Aug 03 DLC-21
Fr 1816 Aug 03* 5-0342
Fr 1816 Aug 12 5-0351
Fr 1816 Sep 19 DLC-21
Fr 1816 Sep 19* 5-0493
Fr 1816 Oct 03 DLC-21
Fr 1816 Oct 03* 5-0529
Fr 1816 Oct 08 DLC-21
Fr 1816 Oct 08* 5-0533
L'eaumont Nicolas-Marie Vicomte de
Fr 1832 Sep 12 M179-74
Fr 1832 Sep 14 M179-74
Fr 1834 Feb 11 M179-77
Fr 1834 Jul 04 M179-78
Leavitt Humphrey Howe
Fr 1833 Oct 07 M639-24
Leavitt Humphrey Howe et al
Fr 1829 Feb 11 M639-10
Leavitt Thomas
Fr 1833 Jul 17 M639-14
Fr 1834 Oct 04 M639-14
Leavitt Lord & Co
Fr 1836 Mar 30-0643
LeClair Pierre
Fr 1836 Jun 15 31-0490
LeClere Margarette
Fr 1831 Sep 30 18-0902
Lecompte Joseph
Fr 1829 Feb 20 M639-2
Fr 1830 Sep 02 M639-3
Ledbetter Wiley et al
Fr 1832 cJan 19-0553
Ledwith Michael
Fr 1831 Jan 03 17-0164
Lee Charles Carter
Fr 1838 Jan 05 34-0165

Lee Corbin
Fr 1806 Feb 22 2-0182
Fr 1806 Jul 03# 2-0291
Fr 1824 Dec 14 DLC-33
Lee Edmund J
Fr 1830 Jan 15 M639-10
Lee Elizabeth (Blair)
To 1844 Mar 25 36-0405
Lee Gideon
Fr 1833 Jan 04 21-1319
Fr 1833 Jan 16 21-1446
Fr 1833 Feb 08 22-0324
Fr 1833 May 01 22-1253
Fr 1833 Dec 12 M639-24
Fr 1833 Dec 12* 24-0459
Fr 1834 Jan 28 24-1091
Fr 1834 Oct 27 26-0749
Fr 1834 Nov 19 26-0955
Fr 1834 Dec 10 26-1464
Fr 1835 Feb 05 27-0412
Fr 1836 Oct 22 32-0327
Lee Gideon et al
Fr 1834 Mar M639-5
Lee Henry
To 1815 Dec 01 4-1270
Fr 1825 Sep 11 add DLC-33
To 1825 Oct 07 DLC-33
Fr 1826 Jul 01 DLC-34
Fr 1826 Sep 14 DLC-34
Fr 1826 Oct 02 DLC-34
Fr 1826 Nov 18 DLC-34
To 1826 Dec 25 11-0442
To 1826 Dec 25* DLC-34
Fr 1827 Mar 12 DLC-34
To 1827 Jun 16 11-0703
To 1827 Nov 17 11-0924
To 1827 Dec 01 11-0941
To 1827 Dec 17 DLC-35
To 1828 Mar# 11-1155
Fr 1828 May 08 DLC-35
Re 1828 Jun 22 DLC-35
To 1828 Jun 22 DLC-35
Fr 1828 Jun 26 DLC-35
Fr 1828 Aug 12 DLC-35
Fr 1828 Aug 15 DLC-35
Fr 1828 cNov 20 DLC-59
Fr 1829 Mar 11# M639-20
Fr 1829 Mar 30 12-1184
Fr 1829 Apr 05 M639-20
Fr 1829 Apr 07 M639-11
To 1829 Apr 14# M23-13
Fr 1829 May 30 M639-11
Fr 1829 cAug 15 13-1136
Fr 1829 Aug 20 DLC-37
Fr 1830 Aug 22 DLC-38
Fr 1830 Aug 29 DLC-38
Fr 1830 Dec 16 DLC-38
Fr 1830 Dec 24 DLC-38
Fr 1831 Sep 07 M22-28
Fr 1831 Dec 05 19-0078
Fr 1832 Sep 04 DLC-41
Fr 1832 Sep 05 DLC-41
Fr 1833 Jan 06 DLC-42
Fr 1833 Jan 14 M179-75
Fr 1833 Feb 10 22-0329
Fr 1833 Apr 04 DLC-42
Fr 1833 Jun 28 DLC-43
Fr 1833 Dec 27 DLC-43
Fr 1835 Jul 30 DLC-46

Lee John
Re 1834 Oct 16 par 26-0654
Fr 1835 Feb 09 M639-11
Lee John Fitzgerald
Fr 1834 Jun 13 M567-95
Lee Richard Bland
Fr 1816 Sep 11 DLC-21
Fr 1816 Sep 11* 5-0471
Lee Roswell
Fr 1829 Feb 17 12-0527
Fr 1829 Jul 22 13-0911
Fr 1833 Feb 27 22-0530
Lee Thomas
Fr 1816 Jul 18 DLC-21
Lee Thomas Jefferson
Fr 1836 Jul 14 M567-127
Lee William
Fr 1817 Jan 22 DLC-22
Fr 1817 Jan 22* 5-0712
Fr 1817 Feb 07 5-0721
To 1817 Oct 21 5-1115
Fr 1817 Nov 06 5-1126
Fr 1817 Dec 10 5-1173
Fr 1819 Jan 28 7-0208
Fr 1820 Jun 10 DLC-29
Fr 1820 Jun 10* 7-1111
Fr 1820 Jun 10 DLC-29
Fr 1820 Jun 10* 7-1112
To 1820 Jul 08 7-1138
To 1820 Jul 08* DLC-63
Fr 1820 Jul 10 DLC-29
Fr 1820 Jul 10* 7-1148
To 1820 Jul 28 DLC-63
Fr 1820 Aug 25 DLC-29
Fr 1820 Aug 29 DLC-29
To 1820 Sep 13 7-1356
Fr 1820 Dec 28 DLC-29
Fr 1820 Dec 28* 8-0030
Fr 1821 Jan 13 8-0071
To 1821 Jan 21 DLC-63
To 1821 Feb 12 DLC-63
Fr 1821 Feb 19 DLC-29
To 1821 Mar 14 DLC-63
Fr 1821 Mar 16 8-0230
Fr 1821 Apr 04 DLC-30
Fr 1821 Apr 04* 8-0286
To 1821 Apr 14 DLC-63
Fr 1821 Apr 26 DLC-30
Fr 1821 Apr 26* 8-0375
Fr 1821 May 01 DLC-30
Fr 1821 May 01* 8-0415
To 1821 Jul 15 DLC-63
Fr 1821 Aug 07 DLC-30
Fr 1821 Aug 07* 8-1039
Fr 1821 Aug 11 DLC-30
Fr 1821 Aug 11* 8-1042
Fr 1822 Jan 12 DLC-31
Fr 1822 Jan 12* 8-1398
To 1824 Jan 07 9-0902
To 1824 Jan 07 37-0496
Fr 1824 Jan 09 9-0909
Fr 1824 Jan 14 9-0926
Fr 1824 Feb 12 10-0455
Fr 1825 Jan 05 10-1041
Fr 1836 Mar 17 M639-14
Leech Samuel E et al
Fr 1836 Dec 17 DLC-49
Leet G J
Fr 1836 Nov 09 32-0422
Leet Isaac
Fr 1834 Oct 20 M639-1
Leet Isaac et al
Fr 1836 Mar 17 M639-18
Fr 1836 Jun M687-25
Lefever Jacob et al
Fr 1835 Apr 08 27-1566
Leflore Greenwood
Fr 1830 Mar 18 15-0391
Leflore Greenwood et al
Fr 1831 Sep 05 18-0667
Legate T C
Fr 1844 Jan 12 DLC-56
Leggett Aaron
Fr 1829 Jun 02 M639-4
Fr 1833 Dec 25 M303-1
Legrand Nash
Fr 1832 May 23# M124-133
Lehigh Coal & Navigation Co
Fr 1833 Jul 13# fin DLC-43
Fr 1835 Jun 01 fin DLC-46
Lehmanowsky John Jacob
Re 1833 Aug 31 23-0567
Leib Thomas
Fr 1827 Aug 25 DLC-34
Leibert John S
Fr 1844 Nov 28 DLC-57
Leiper George Gray
Fr 1829 Feb 17 M639-13
Fr 1829 Nov 06 M639-15
To c1830 DLC-40
Fr 1831 Feb 19 17-0587
Leiper George Gray et al
Fr 1830 Dec 20 16-1507
Leiper Matthew
Fr 1832 Sep 06 20-1495
Leiper William J
Fr 1829 Nov 05 M639-15
Fr 1831 Sep 27 M639-13
Fr 1833 Jul 01 23-0092
Fr 1833 Jul 30# M639-6
Fr 1833 Aug 07 DLC-43
To 1835 Feb 11# M567-111
Fr 1837 Mar 18# DLC-50
Leland Henry
Re 1836 Feb 24 par 30-0513
Leland James
Re 1837 Jan 30 par 33-0247
Leland Joseph W
Fr 1837 Jan 20 M687-16
Lemmon Richard
Fr 1833 Apr 12# M639-20
Lemon John M
Fr 1837 May 10 DLC-50
Lemond Edmund H et al
Fr 1837 Jan 26 33-0183
LeMonnier Ives
To 1829 Oct 13 14-0151
LeMoyne A
Fr 1833 Apr 25 M639-16
Lenox Robert et al
Fr 1834 Sep 06 26-0424
Lentilhon Anthony & Co
Fr 1833 Apr 25 M639-16
Lentz William
Fr 1815 Oct 02 fin DLC-69
Leonard John
Fr 1829 Nov 25 M639-14
Fr 1830 Jan 18 M639-14

Leonard John (cont)
Re 1830 Mar 03 M639-14
Fr 1830 May 15 M639-14
Fr 1832 Jun 12 M639-14
Fr 1832 Jun 20 M179-73
Fr 1832 Jun 22 M179-73
Fr 1832 Jun 22 M179-73
Re 1832 Aug 31 20-1436
Fr 1834 Dec 06 M639-14
Fr 1834 Dec 06# M639-14
Fr 1840 Jan 29 DLC-58

Leonard L
Fr 1840 Jun 13 34-1413

Leonard Stephen Banks
Fr 1837 Feb 09 M687-21

Leopold Grand Duke of Baden
Fr 1830 Oct 17 16-0430
Fr 1830 Nov 10 16-0705
Fr 1830 Nov 10* M34-28
To 1831 Mar 01 17-0702
To 1831 Mar 01 17-0703
Fr 1832 Mar 10 19-1391
To 1832 Jun 02 20-0688
Fr 1832 Jul 22 20-1220
Fr 1833 May 07 22-1310
To 1833 Jul 25 23-0225
Fr 1834 Aug 07 26-0285
Fr 1834 Oct 22 26-0679
To 1834 Oct 23 26-0689
Fr 1834 Nov 21 26-0974
To 1834 Dec 17 26-1527
To 1835 Jan 22 27-0277
Fr 1835 Dec 19 29-1238
To 1836 Mar 07 30-0705
Fr 1837 Feb 23 33-0843

Leopold I King of Belgium
Fr 1832 Apr 10 20-0179

LeRoy Daniel
Fr 1834 Mar 27 25-0436

Leroy Pierre
Fr 1821 Mar 31 fin DLC-70

Lescure Joseph M G
Fr 1834 Jul 28 DLC-44

Leslaier Joseph
Re 1833 Nov 23 par 23-1301
Re 1833 Nov 23* par T967-1

Lester John
Fr 1845 Jan 01 36-1287

Letourno Joseph
Fr 1845 Apr 28 DLC-58

Levis Samuel
Fr 1829 Apr 11 M639-22

Levy Chapman
Fr 1832 cDec DLC-41
Fr 1834 Jan 15# DLC-44
Fr 1836 Jul 09 M234-145

Levy L J
Fr 1834 Dec 09# fin DLC-47
Fr 1835 Apr 16 fin DLC-46
Fr 1835 Sep 03# fin DLC-46
Fr 1836 Oct 31# fin DLC-50
Fr 1836 Nov 12# fin DLC-49

Levy Uriah Phillips
Fr 1836 May 04 M639-14

Levy Uriah Phillips et al
Fr 1833 Apr M639-25

Lewis Addin
To 1814 Aug 29 DLC-62
Fr 1821 May 19 DLC-30
Fr 1821 May 19* 8-0485

Lewis C
Fr 1836 Oct 19 DLC-49
To 1836 Oct 31 DLC-49

Lewis Cadwallader
Fr 1844 Dec 16 DLC-57

Lewis Charles
Fr 1834 Oct 07 26-0529

Lewis David M
Fr 1834 Feb 02 24-1140

Lewis Dixon Hall
To 1831 Jan 26# M222-29
Fr 1836 May 30 M567-126

Lewis Dixon Hall et al
Fr 1830 Feb 09 M688-66

Lewis E
Fr 1824 Dec 30 fin 10-1018

Lewis Edwin
Fr 1829 Nov 03 14-0400
Fr 1829 Nov 05 14-0412

Lewis Eleanor Parke (Custis)
To 1826 cMar 09 DLC-33

Lewis Emily Rushbrook
Fr 1843 Jul 18 DLC-55

Lewis Henderson
Fr 1825 Sep 11 add DLC-33
To 1825 Sep 20 DLC-33

Lewis John
Fr 1844 Nov 23 DLC-57

Lewis John et al
Fr 1835 cMay 14 28-0378

Lewis John H
To 1826 Jun 30 11-0263
To 1826 Jul 18 11-0323

Lewis Jonathan
Re 1833 Mar 08 par 22-0698

Lewis Joseph S
Fr 1830 Jun 05 M639-5

Lewis Levi
Fr 1835 Feb 03 DLC-45

Lewis Lew
Fr 1840 Nov 20 fin DLC-53

Lewis Mary Ann
see also Pageot M A L
Re 1821 Mar 07 leg 8-0160

Lewis Micajah Green
Fr 1844 Dec 21 DLC-57

Lewis Morgan
Fr 1829 Apr 27 M639-19
Fr 1829 May 02 M639-24
Fr 1832 Mar 05# 19-1306

Lewis Robert M
Fr 1829 Sep 29 DLC-37
To 1829 Oct 02 14-0090
To 1829 Oct 02* DLC-37

Lewis Samuel
To 1802 Apr 09 lnd 1-0988
To 1831 Oct 06 18-0930
To 1832 Oct 20 21-0125
To 1833 Sep 23 23-0839
To 1834 Jul 08 26-0192
To 1835 Aug 29 28-1455
To 1835 Sep 26 29-0111

Lewis Seth
Fr 1801 Dec 09 DLC-2
Fr 1803 Oct 08 1-1196
Fr 1803 Nov 11 DLC-3
Fr 1804 Dec 21 DLC-3
Fr 1821 Feb 19 DLC-29

Lewis William
Fr 1837 Dec 05 DLC-50

Lewis William Berkeley

To	1812 Nov 21		2-1275
Fr	1812 Dec 31		DLC-61
To	1813 Jan 01	fin	2-1320
To	1813 Jan 05		2-1327
To	1813 Jan 05*		DLC-61
Re	1813 Jan 07		3-0003
To	1813 Jan 09		3-0242
To	1813 Jan 09*		DLC-61
To	1813 Jan 09	fin	DLC-6
To	1813 Jan 13		3-0246
To	1813 Jan 16		3-0252
To	1813 Jan 17		3-0253
Fr	1813 Feb 08		DLC-6
To	1813 Feb 15		3-0276
To	1813 Feb 21		DLC-6
Fr	1813 Mar 02		DLC-6
To	1813 Mar 04		3-0288
To	1813 Mar 04*		DLC-75
To	1813 Mar 13		3-0302
To	1813 Mar 15		3-0317
To	1813 Mar 21		3-0349
To	1813 Apr 09		37-0409
To	1813 May 26	leg	3-0400
To	1813 Sep 25		3-0478
To	1813 Sep 25*		DLC-61
To	1813 Sep 25		DLC-61
To	1813 Sep 27		DLC-61
To	1813 Sep 27		DLC-61
To	1813 Oct 04	fin	DLC-65
To	1813 Oct 20		3-0538
To	1813 Oct 24		DLC-7
To	1813 Oct 29		3-0555
Fr	1813 Nov 12		DLC-7
Fr	1813 Nov 12*		DLC-61
Fr	1813 Nov 21		DLC-7
To	1813 Nov 22		DLC-61
To	1813 Dec 14		3-0669
To	1813 Dec 14*		DLC-61
To	1813 Dec 18		3-0683
To	1813 Dec 19		3-0687
Fr	1813 Dec 23		DLC-8
Fr	1813 Dec 23		DLC-8
Fr	1813 Dec 27		DLC-8
Fr	1814 Jan 26		DLC-8
To	1814 Jan 29		3-0824
To	1814 Feb 15		3-0870
To	1814 Feb 17		DLC-9
To	1814 Feb 21		3-0886
To	1814 Mar 05		3-0900
To	1814 May 23		M222-12
To	1814 May 24		3-1065
To	1814 Jun 20	chk	DLC-10
To	1814 Jun 24		3-1102
To	1814 Jun 25		3-1110
To	1814 Aug 06		3-1232
To	1814 Aug 27		M221-59
To	1814 Aug 27		DLC-11
To	1814 Aug 27		4-0155
To	1814 Aug 27*		M221-59
To	1814 Sep 02		DLC-62
To	1815 May 08		4-1025
To	1815 May 08		4-1026
Fr	1815 May 14		DLC-18
To	1815 May 15		4-1037
To	1815 May 20		4-1048
To	1815 May 23		4-1056
To	1815 May 23*		DLC-68
To	1815 Jun 27		DLC-18
To	1815 Jun 29		4-1100
To	1815 Jul 17	chk	DLC-18
Fr	1815 Jul 17	fin	DLC-18
Fr	1815 Jul 20		M222-16
To	1815 Jul 25		4-1133
To	1816 Jul	fin	DLC-69
Fr	1816 Jul 20	fin	DLC-22
To	1817 Dec 08		5-1169
Fr	1818 Jan 13		DLC-71
To	1818 Oct 09		DLC-62
To	1818 Oct 09*		T494-1
Fr	1818 Oct 10		DLC-62
Fr	1818 Oct 10*		T494-1
To	1819 Jan 12		7-0132
To	1819 Jan 25		7-0193
To	1819 Jan 30		7-0214
To	1819 Mar 26		7-0442
To	1819 Jul 30		7-0588
To	1819 Aug 17		7-0613
Fr	1819 Aug 20		DLC-27
To	1819 Nov 23		7-0895
To	1820 Jul 14		7-1153
Fr	1820 Jul 15		7-1154
To	1820 Jul 15		7-1158
To	1820 Jul 16		7-1162
To	1821 Apr 28		DLC-30
To	1821 Sep 21		8-1199
To	1821 Sep 22		8-1204
To	1821 cNov		8-1322
To	1822 Mar 15		9-0054
To	1822 Mar 19		9-0056
To	1822 Jul 01		9-0206
To	1823 Dec 07		9-0790
To	1823 Dec 22		9-0825
Re	1823 Dec 23		M222-23
To	1824 Feb 22		10-0471
To	1824 Mar 31		10-0612
To	1824 May 07		10-0713
To	1824 cSep 13		10-0891
To	1824 Nov 07		DLC-72
To	1824 Dec 08		10-0965
To	1824 Dec 27		10-1005
To	1825 Jan 11		10-1069
To	1825 Jan 21		10-1078
To	1825 Jan 24		10-1084
To	1825 Jan 29		10-1090
To	1825 Feb 07		10-1098
To	1825 Feb 14		10-1110
To	1825 Feb 20		10-1134
To	1825 Feb 27		10-1187
To	1825 Apr 27		10-1248
To	1826 Jul 15		11-0320
To	1826 Dec 12		11-0427
To	1827 Feb 08		11-0484
Fr	1827 Feb 10		DLC-34
To	1827 Apr 05		11-0556
Fr	1827 Apr 09#		11-0563
To	1827 May 05		11-0577
To	1827 Jun 13		11-0696
To	1827 Jul 16		11-0751
To	1827 Jul 23		11-0766
To	1827 Jul 27		11-0772
To	1827 Aug 16		11-0796
To	1827 Aug 22		11-0819
To	1827 Sep 01		11-0838
To	1827 Nov 25		11-0931
To	1827 Dec 18		11-0964
To	1827 Dec 19		11-0967
Fr	1827 Dec 24		DLC-35

Lewis William Berkeley (cont)

To	1827 Dec 25		11-0978
To	1827 Dec 26		11-0984
To	1828 Mar 03		11-1157
To	1828 Mar 08		11-1164
To	1828 Mar 22		11-1188
To	1828 Jun 19		12-0020
To	1828 Jun 22		12-0024
To	1828 Jun 28		12-0035
To	1828 Jul 01		12-0037
To	1828 Jul 10		12-0045
To	1828 Jul 16		12-0051
To	1828 Jul 28		12-0059
To	1828 Jul 29		12-0062
To	1828 Aug 05		12-0120
To	1828 Aug 13		12-0131
To	1828 Aug 15		12-0144
To	1828 Aug 16		12-0160
To	1828 Aug 19		12-0169
To	1828 cSep 01		12-0179
Fr	1828 Sep 13		DLC-35
To	1828 Sep 14		12-0196
To	1828 Sep 26		12-0217
To	1828 Oct 15		12-0230
To	1828 Oct 19		12-0237
To	1828 cNov 01		12-0257
To	1828 cNov 15		12-0270
To	1828 Nov 27		12-0291
Re	1829 Mar 21		12-1071
To	1829 Apr 07	chk	DLC-36
To	1829 May 29#		M124-118
To	1829 Jun 18	chk	DLC-37
Fr	1829 Jul 02		DLC-37
Re	1829 Jul 07		M221-110
Re	1829 Jul 07*		13-0822
Re	1829 Jul 07*		M124-119
Re	1829 Jul 08	mem	13-0829
To	1829 Aug 19		13-1177
To	1829 Aug 19*		M124-120
Fr	1829 Sep 08		DLC-37
Fr	1829 Sep 08*		13-1282
To	1829 Sep 10		13-1294
To	1829 Sep 10*		DLC-37
To	1829 Sep 16#		DLC-75
To	1829 Sep 22#		DLC-75
Fr	1829 Oct 05#		DLC-75
To	1829 Oct 05#		DLC-75
To	1829 Nov 13	chk	DLC-37
To	1829 Nov 15#		14-0468
To	1829 Dec 19#		DLC-75
To	1829 Dec 20#		DLC-37
Fr	1830 Feb 10		15-0119
Fr	1830 Feb 10*		M222-28
To	1830 Mar 27	chk	DLC-38
To	1830 Apr 01	chk	DLC-38
To	1830 May 24	chk	DLC-38
To	1830 May 28	chk	DLC-38
To	1830 Jun 21		15-1519
To	1830 Jun 26		15-1532
To	1830 Jun 28		15-1546
To	1830 Jul 18		16-0026
To	1830 Jul 21		16-0035
To	1830 Jul 28		16-0061
To	1830 Aug 07		16-0081
Fr	1830 Aug 07	mem	DLC-38
To	1830 Aug 10		16-0091
To	1830 Aug 15		16-0110
To	1830 Aug 17		16-0119
To	1830 Aug 25		16-0145
To	1830 Aug 31		16-0191

To	1830 Sep 18		16-0250
To	1830 Dec 07	chk	16-1351
To	1830 Dec 24#		DLC-38
Fr	1831 Jan 13#		17-0252
To	1831 Mar 29		17-1003
To	1831 Apr 04	chk	DLC-39
To	1831 May 07		17-1308
To	1831 May 26	chk	DLC-39
To	1831 Jun 22		18-0075
To	1831 Jun 22*		DLC-39
Fr	1831 Jun 22		18-0081
To	1831 Jun 26		18-0109
Fr	1831 Jun 27		18-0114
To	1831 Jun 28#		DLC-39
Fr	1831 Jun 29		DLC-39
Fr	1831 Jul 01		DLC-39
To	1831 Jul 19	chk	DLC-39
To	1831 Aug 15#		DLC-39
To	1831 Sep 30#		DLC-40
To	1831 Dec#		DLC-43
To	1831 Dec 09	chk	DLC-40
Fr	1831 Dec 09	fin	DLC-40
To	c1832		19-0519
To	1832 Feb 28#		DLC-40
To	1832 Jun 28#		DLC-41
To	1832 Jul 05	chk	DLC-41
Fr	1832 Jul 24	mem	20-1239
Fr	1832 Jul 28		DLC-41
To	1832 Aug 09		20-1268
To	1832 Aug 18		20-1328
To	1832 Aug 28		20-1403
To	1832 Dec 26	chk	DLC-41
To	c1833		21-1236
To	1833 Feb 18#		DLC-42
To	1833 Mar 19#		DLC-42
To	1833 Apr 03		22-0931
Fr	1833 Apr 03		DLC-42
Fr	1833 Apr 03*		22-0932
To	1833 Apr 14		22-1020
Fr	1833 Apr 17		DLC-42
To	1833 Apr 19		22-1056
Fr	1833 Apr 21		DLC-42
Fr	1833 Apr 26		DLC-42
To	1833 Apr 29		22-1201
Fr	1833 May 03		DLC-73
Fr	1833 May 03		DLC-73
To	1833 May 04		22-1294
Fr	1833 May 16		DLC-43
To	1833 Jun 05	leg	22-1577
To	1833 Jun 21	chk	DLC-43
To	1833 Jul 13		23-0128
Fr	1833 Aug 13		DLC-43
To	1833 Aug 17#		23-0362
Fr	1833 Sep 10		23-0680
To	1833 Nov 07		23-1195
To	1833 Dec 16#		DLC-43
To	1834 Jan 06#		DLC-44
To	1834 Jan 08	chk	24-0795
To	1834 Jan 11#		DLC-44
To	1834 Feb 03	chk	DLC-44
To	1834 Jul 09		26-0205
To	1834 Jul 15		26-0223
Fr	1834 Jul 25		DLC-73
To	1834 Jul 26		26-0252
Fr	1834 Aug 18		DLC-44
Fr	1834 Aug 20		DLC-44
To	1834 Sep 08		26-0425
To	1834 Sep 14		26-0434
To	1834 Sep 19		26-0446

To	1834	Oct	02#		DLC-44
Fr	1834	Oct	04		DLC-44
To	1834	Oct	13		26-0624
To	1834	Oct	25		26-0726
Fr	1834	Nov	02		DLC-45
Fr	1834	Nov	16		DLC-45
To	1834	Dec	20#	fin	DLC-45
To	1834	Dec	22#	fin	DLC-45
Fr	1835	Apr	16		DLC-73
To	1835	Apr	27		28-0142
Fr	1835	May	03		DLC-46
Fr	1835	May	10		DLC-46
Fr	1835	May	17		DLC-46
To	1835	Jul	18		28-1040
To	1835	Jul	29		28-1206
Fr	1835	Sep	17		29-0063
Fr	1836	Feb	13		M639-27
To	1836	Jun	13#		DLC-48
Fr	1836	Jul	06#		DLC-48
Fr	1836	Nov	15		DLC-49
To	1836	Nov	15	mem	32-0507
Fr	1836	Nov	28		DLC-49
To	1837	Jan		mem	32-1464
Fr	1837	Feb	28		33-0924
To	1837	May	23	mem	DLC-50
Fr	1837	Jun	27		DLC-50
To	1837	Aug	03		33-1403
Fr	1837	Oct	02		DLC-50
To	1837	Oct	19		33-1533
Fr	1837	Oct	26#		DLC-50
To	1838	Jan	01		34-0157
Fr	1838	Jan	16		34-0195
To	1838	Jan	23		34-0205
To	1838	Jun	21		34-0385
Fr	1838	Jul	13		DLC-51
Fr	1838	Nov	26		DLC-51
To	1838	Dec	10		34-0565
Fr	1839	Jan	08		DLC-74
Fr	1839	Feb	18		DLC-52
To	1839	Mar	04		34-0672
Fr	1839	Mar	16		DLC-74
Fr	1839	Mar	25		DLC-52
To	1839	Apr	18		34-0752
To	1839	May	29		34-0801
Fr	1839	Jun	18		DLC-52
Fr	1839	Jun	25		DLC-52
To	1839	Aug	13		34-0865
Fr	1839	Aug	30		DLC-52
Fr	1839	Aug	30*		34-0877
To	1839	Sep	09		34-0932
Fr	1839	Oct	06		DLC-52
Fr	1839	Oct	06*		34-0978
To	1839	Oct	19		34-1010
Fr	1839	Nov	05		DLC-52
Fr	1839	Nov	05*		34-1035
To	1839	Nov	10		34-1053
To	1839	Dec	19		34-1094
To	1839	Dec	21		34-1105
Fr	1840	Mar	21		DLC-52
To	1840	May	22		34-1378
To	1840	Oct	27		35-0083
Fr	1840	Nov	16		DLC-74
To	1840	Dec	26		35-0137
Fr	1841	Feb	06		DLC-53
Fr	1841	Aug	09		35-0361
To	1841	Aug	19		35-0379
To	1841	Aug	24		35-0387
Fr	1841	Sep	04		DLC-53
Fr	1841	Sep	11		DLC-53
Fr	1841	Sep	20		DLC-53
To	1841	Sep	23		35-0405
To	1841	Sep	30		35-0423
To	1841	Oct	01		35-0439
Fr	1841	Oct	11		DLC-74
To	1841	Oct	25		35-0457
To	1841	Nov	18		35-0493
Fr	1841	Nov	23		DLC-54
To	1841	Dec	03#		DLC-54
Fr	1841	Dec	06		35-0522
Fr	1841	Dec	20		35-0539
To	1841	Dec	28		35-0545
To	1841	Dec	28		35-0551
To	1842	Jan	01		35-0583
To	1842	Jan	15		35-0600
To	1842	Feb	12		35-0621
Fr	1842	Feb	19		35-0628
To	1842	Feb	27		35-0635
To	1842	Feb	28		35-0638
Fr	1842	Mar	01		DLC-54
To	1842	Mar	15		35-0649
Fr	1842	Mar	15		DLC-74
To	1842	Mar	26		35-0655
To	1842	Mar	30		35-0661
To	1842	Mar	31		35-0665
To	1842	Apr	02		35-0671
Fr	1842	Apr	07		DLC-54
To	1842	Apr	23		35-0682
To	1842	May	23		35-0725
To	1842	Jun	02		35-0759
To	1842	Jun	15		35-0791
Fr	1842	Jun	28		35-0823
Fr	1842	Jul	21		DLC-54
To	1842	Aug	03		35-0869
To	1842	Sep	01		35-0919
Fr	1842	Nov	30		DLC-54
Fr	1842	Dec	08		35-1023
Fr	1842	Dec	12		DLC-54
To	1842	Dec	15		35-1034
To	1842	Dec	20		35-1048
To	1842	Dec	21		DLC-54
Fr	1843	Jan	07		DLC-55
Fr	1843	Jan	12		DLC-55
To	1843	Jan	17		35-1128
To	1843	Jan	20		35-1131
To	1843	Jan	24		35-1143
Fr	1843	Jan	26		DLC-55
To	1843	Feb	06		35-1183
Fr	1843	Feb	08		DLC-55
To	1843	Feb	13		35-1224
Fr	1843	Feb	15		DLC-74
To	1843	Feb	20		35-1242
To	1843	Feb	20*		DLC-74
To	1843	Feb	27		35-1263
Fr	1843	Feb	27		DLC-55
To	1843	Mar	24		35-1290
Fr	1843	Apr	16		DLC-55
Fr	1843	Jul	10		DLC-74
To	1843	Jul	19		35-1424
To	1843	Jul	25		35-1432
Fr	1843	Jul	30		DLC-55
To	1843	Aug	09		35-1447
To	1843	Aug	11		35-1456
Fr	1843	Aug	29		DLC-55
To	1843	Sep	12		35-1484
To	1843	Sep	18		35-1494
To	1843	Oct	23		35-1561
To	1843	Oct	31		35-1577
To	1843	Nov	02		35-1583

Lewis William Berkeley (cont)			
	To 1843 Nov 16		36-0007
	To 1843 Nov 27		36-0027
	Fr 1843 Dec 04		DLC-56
	Fr 1843 Dec 06		DLC-74
	To 1843 Dec 15		36-0058
	Fr 1844 Jan 09		DLC-56
	To 1844 Jan 18		36-0136
	Fr 1844 Feb 15		DLC-56
	To 1844 Feb 22		36-0332
	To 1844 Feb 24		36-0338
	Fr 1844 Feb 26		36-0341
	To 1844 Feb 27		36-0348
	Fr 1844 Mar 04		36-0364
	To 1844 Mar 11		36-0374
	To 1844 Mar 22		36-0392
	Fr 1844 Mar 28		DLC-56
	To 1844 Apr 05		36-0424
	To 1844 Apr 08		36-0428
	To 1844 Apr 08*		DLC-56
	Fr 1844 Apr 18		DLC-56
	Fr 1844 Apr 19		DLC-56
	Fr 1844 Apr 26		DLC-56
	Fr 1844 Apr 27		DLC-56
	Fr 1844 Apr 30		36-0461
	Fr 1844 May 01		DLC-56
	To 1844 May 03		36-0484
	To 1844 May 07		36-0502
	To 1844 May 11		36-0524
	Fr 1844 May 15		DLC-56
	Fr 1844 May 22		DLC-56
	Fr 1844 Jun 24		DLC-57
	To 1844 Jun 28		36-0655
	To 1844 Jul 12		36-0700
	Fr 1844 Jul 19		DLC-57
	To 1844 Jul 26		36-0751
	To 1844 Aug 01		36-0760
	To 1844 Aug 15		36-0793
	Fr 1844 Sep 06		DLC-57
	Fr 1844 Sep 16		DLC-57
	To 1844 Sep 17		36-0884
	To 1844 Sep 27		36-0909
	To 1844 Oct 09		36-0944
	Fr 1844 Oct 22		DLC-57
	Fr 1844 Nov 20		DLC-57
	To 1844 Dec 18		36-1216
	Fr 1844 Dec 21		DLC-57
	To 1845 Jan 01		36-1291
	Fr 1845 Jan 01		DLC-57
	Fr 1845 Jan 04		DLC-57
	Fr 1845 Jan 06		DLC-57
	Fr 1845 Jan 14		36-1329
	To 1845 Jan 15		36-1336
	To 1845 Jan 15		36-1340
	To 1845 Jan 15		36-1343
	Fr 1845 Jan 15		DLC-57
	To 1845 Jan 18		DLC-57
	Fr 1845 Jan 22		DLC-57
	To 1845 Jan 25		36-1406
	To 1845 Feb 04		36-1451
	To 1845 Feb 05		36-1455
	To 1845 Feb 11		36-1482
	To 1845 Feb 12		36-1485
	Fr 1845 Feb 17		36-1496
	Fr 1845 Feb 21		DLC-74
	To 1845 Feb 28		36-1519
	To 1845 Feb 28*		DLC-57
	To 1845 Mar 03		36-1534
	Fr 1845 Mar 13		DLC-57
	To 1845 Mar 22		37-0019
	Fr 1845 Mar 31		DLC-57
	Fr 1845 Apr 01		DLC-58
	To 1845 Apr 08		37-0121
	To 1845 Apr 10		37-0136
	To 1845 Apr 11		37-0140
	Fr 1845 Apr 24		DLC-58
Lewis William Henry			
	Fr 1838 Jan		DLC-51
	Fr 1842 Jun 09		DLC-54
Lewis William Terrell			
	Re c1790	leg	1-0075a
	Fr 1796 Mar 11	lnd	1-0361
	Re 1805 Nov 19	mem	DLC-3
	Re 1810 Jan 15	leg	2-0869
	Re 1810 May 10	leg	2-0904
	Re 1813 May 22		3-0399
	Re 1813 Jul 26		3-0428
	Re 1814 Apr 26	leg	3-0997
	Re 1814 Aug	leg	3-1202
	Re 1814 Nov	leg	4-0313
	Re 1816 Jan 15	leg	4-1363
	Re 1816 May 23	leg	5-0088
	Re 1816 Jun 21	leg	5-0187
	Re 1817 Jan 27	leg	5-0713
	Re 1818 Apr 18	leg	6-0401
	Re 1825 Feb 25	leg	10-1157
	Re 1833 Dec 03	leg	24-0200
	Re 1836 Jan 05	leg	29-1465
Lewis v Lewis			
	Re 1808 Nov 29	leg	2-0742
Lewis & Co et al			
	Fr 1831 Dec 10		M639-15
Lewright John S			
	Fr 1833 Jan 06		DLC-41
Lexington KY citizens			
	To 1819	add	DLC-23
Liddell James			
	Fr 1838 Dec 03		DLC-51
Liebenan Henry			
	Fr 1844 Feb 19		DLC-56
Lientz William			
	Fr 1816 Oct 05	fin	DLC-22
Liggett John			
	Fr 1829 Sep 07		DLC-37
	Fr 1829 Oct 20#		DLC-37
	Fr 1829 Dec 16#		DLC-37
Lillard William			
	To 1813 Dec 17		DLC-61
	Fr 1813 Dec 24		DLC-61
	To 1813 Dec 26		DLC-61
	To 1813 Dec 26		3-0722
	To 1813 Dec 26*		DLC-61
	Fr 1813 Dec 26		DLC-8
	Fr 1813 Dec 26*		DLC-61
	To 1814 Jan 03		DLC-61
	Fr 1814 Jan 03		DLC-8
	Fr 1814 Jan 03*		DLC-61
	Fr 1814 Jan 07		DLC-61
	To 1814 Jan 08		DLC-8
Lillibridge David			
	Fr 1834 Jan 10		DLC-44
Limbaugh Christian			
	Fr 1814 Jul 10		DLC-11
	To 1814 Oct 31		DLC-62
Limricks T			
	Fr 1822 Aug 01	fin	DLC-31
	Fr 1822 Nov 02	fin	DLC-31
Lincoln Enoch			
	Fr 1829 May 02		M639-4

Lincoln J M			
	Fr 1837 Feb 03		M639-14
Lincoln Joshua			
	Fr 1837 Feb 04		M687-20
Lincoln Levi			
	Fr 1831 Apr 27		M179-70
	Fr 1833 Jun 22	add	23-0050
Lindley George T			
	To 1828 Nov 12		DLC-35
Lindsay Adam et al			
	Fr 1830 Oct 16		M639-3
Lindsay George F			
	Fr 1832 Feb 10#		19-1054
Lindsay William			
	Fr 1816 Feb 12		DLC-20
	Fr 1818 Apr 27		DLC-24
	Fr 1818 Aug 09		DLC-25
	Fr 1820 Dec 16		DLC-29
	To 1821 Jan 14#		DLC-63
Lindsley Adrian Van Sinderen			
	Fr 1843 Aug 12		DLC-55
	Fr 1843 Aug 29		DLC-55
	Fr 1844 May 18		DLC-56
	To 1844 Jun 04		36-0578
Lindsley E			
	Fr 1837 Mar 06	fin	DLC-50
Lindsley Philip			
	Fr 1825 May 05	add	10-1258
	Fr 1825 Dec 20	fin	11-0075
	Fr 1828 Dec 24		DLC-36
	Fr 1829 Apr 16		DLC-36
	To 1829 May 03		13-0242
	To 1832 Oct 26		21-0163
	Fr 1835 Dec 01		M639-14
	Fr 1836 Aug 08		DLC-48
Lineberger William			
	To 1827 May 31		DLC-34
Link Edward Jackson			
	Fr 1836 Apr 27		M567-126
Linn Elizabeth A (Relfe)			
	Fr 1841 Sep 16		DLC-53
	To 1842 Jun 14		35-0789
	To 1843 Nov 15		36-0005
	Fr 1844 Jan 25		DLC-56
Linn John E			
	Fr 1820 Nov 23	fin	7-1418
	Fr 1822 Feb 14	fin	9-0027
Linn Lewis Fields			
	Fr 1833 Nov 28#		23-1323
	Fr 1834 Sep 05		M639-19
	Fr 1836 Mar 10		M639-6
	Fr 1836 May 17		M567-124
	Fr 1836 Jul 25		31-1158
	Fr 1836 Sep 08		31-1435
	Fr 1837 Feb 18		M687-23
	To 1837 Feb 23#		33-0845
	To 1837 Nov 22		DLC-50
	Fr 1841 Aug 02		DLC-53
	Fr 1842 Feb 28		DLC-54
	To 1842 Mar 14		35-0648
	To 1842 Mar 14*		DLC-54
	To 1842 Jun 02		DLC-74
	To 1842 Jun 02*		35-0764
	Fr 1842 Jun 21		DLC-54
	To 1842 Jul 04		DLC-54
	Fr 1842 Dec 21		DLC-54
	Fr 1843 Feb 20		DLC-55
	Fr 1843 Jul 04		DLC-55
Linn Lewis Fields et al			
	Fr 1836 Jun 24		31-0574
Linsey James			
	Fr 1829 Mar 12		DLC-36
Linton Benjamin F			
	Fr 1835 Aug 25		28-1365
Linton John F			
	Fr 1840 Jul 22		34-1495
Lintz William			
	To 1814 Jun 20	chk	DLC-10
Lippincott Joseph et al			
	Fr 1829 Mar		M639-12
Lippincott Samuel W			
	Fr 1843 Nov 24#		37-0544
List Frederick			
	Fr 1830 Aug 04		DLC-38
	Fr 1830 Oct 20		M639-14
	Re 1830 Nov 08		16-0699
	Fr 1832 Oct 16		M639-14
Lister William			
	Re 1833 Aug 30	par	23-0535
	Re 1833 Sep 16	par	23-0723
Litle Charles L			
	Fr 1837 Jan 12		M567-146
Littell Eliakim			
	Fr 1826 May 12		DLC-33
	To 1826 Jun 04		DLC-34
Little John			
	Fr 1829 Mar 21		M639-6
Littlefield Cornelia L			
	Fr 1845 Feb 18		M873-63
Littlefield Nathaniel Swett			
	Fr 1837 Feb 26		M687-16
Littlefield William			
	Fr 1835 Mar 26#		27-1384
Litton Joseph			
	Fr 1821 Mar 31#	fin	DLC-30
	To 1845 Jun 06	chk	37-0255
Livermore Harriet			
	To 1833 Feb 25		22-0469
Livingston Charles L et al			
	Fr 1832 Mar		M639-6
	Fr 1834 Dec 26		M639-2
Livingston Edward			
	Fr 1814 Sep 21		DLC-71
	To 1814 Sep 30		DLC-62
	To 1814 Oct 23		DLC-62
	Fr 1814 Nov 05		DLC-13
	Fr 1814 Nov 21		DLC-71
	Fr 1814 Dec 14		DLC-71
	Fr 1814 Dec 25		DLC-15
	Fr 1815 cMar 27		DLC-17
	Fr 1815 Apr 20		DLC-71
	To 1815 May 01		4-1022
	To 1815 May 17		DLC-18
	To 1815 Jun 12		DLC-18
	To 1815 Jul 05		4-1103
	To 1815 Sep 05		4-1184
	Fr 1815 Sep 15		DLC-71
	Fr 1816 Jan 04		DLC-15
	Fr 1816 Jan 04		DLC-20
	Fr 1816 Feb 02		DLC-71
	To 1816 Apr 19		5-0038
	To 1816 Oct 24		5-0547
	Fr 1816 Nov 07		DLC-21
	To 1816 Dec 05		5-0595
	Fr 1818 Aug 18		DLC-71
	To 1818 Aug 31		6-1272
	Fr 1819 Jun 05		DLC-72
	Fr 1819 Jun 17		DLC-27
	To 1819 Jul 20		7-0583

Livingston Edward (cont)

Fr 1819 Aug 08		DLC-72
To 1819 Aug 23		7-0634
To 1820 Jan 07		7-0981
Fr 1821		DLC-31
Fr 1821 May 14		DLC-30
To 1823 Mar 24		9-0504
To 1824 Jul 05		DLC-33
Fr 1826 Aug 03		DLC-72
Fr 1827 May 21		DLC-72
Fr 1827 Nov 11		DLC-72
To 1828 Jan 12		11-1056
Fr 1828 Jan 16		DLC-72
Fr 1828 Mar 07		DLC-72
Fr 1828 Jun 20		DLC-72
To 1828 Aug 02		12-0114
Fr 1828 Aug 12		DLC-35
Fr 1829 Jan 03		12-0435
To 1829 Feb 26	chk	DLC-36
Fr 1829 Mar 07		M639-17
Fr 1829 Mar 23		M639-17
Fr 1829 Apr 04		M639-12
Fr 1829 Apr 04		M639-27
Fr 1829 Apr 13		M639-21
Fr 1829 Apr 17		12-1380
Fr 1829 May 03		13-0244
To 1830 Mar 02		15-0287
Fr 1830 Apr 05		M639-14
Fr 1830 May 13		15-0992
Fr 1830 Dec 21		16-1522
Fr c1831#		17-0090
To 1831 Apr 09#		17-1109
Fr 1831 Apr 20		DLC-39
Re 1831 May 24		17-1418
To 1831 May 26#		17-1450
Fr 1831 Jun 20		18-0066
Fr 1831 Jun 20*		M40-22
To 1831 Jun 24		T1-6
To 1831 Jun 24		18-0097
Fr 1831 Jun 25		18-0104
To 1831 Jun 28		18-0133
To 1831 Jun 28#		DLC-39
Fr 1831 Jun 30		DLC-39
Fr 1831 Jul 01		18-0142
To 1831 Jul 08		18-0168
To 1831 Jul 24#		DLC-39
To 1831 Jul 25		M179-70
To 1831 Aug 01		M179-71
To 1831 Aug 01*		DLC-39
To 1831 Aug 01		M179-71
To 1831 Aug 06		M179-71
To 1831 Aug 07		18-0477
Fr 1831 Aug 09		M179-71
Fr 1831 Aug 16		18-0550
Fr 1831 Aug 22		DLC-39
To 1831 Sep 03		18-0664
Fr 1831 Sep 22#		M77-9
To 1831 Oct 15		M179-71
To 1831 Oct 20		M179-71
Fr 1831 Oct 20		M40-22
Fr 1831 Nov 07		18-1217
Fr 1831 Nov 07*		M40-22
To 1831 Nov 10		18-1234
To 1831 Nov 19#		M219-2
Fr 1831 Nov 21		M40-22
Fr 1831 Dec 02		18-1542
Fr 1831 Dec 05		19-0083
Fr 1831 Dec 05*		M40-22
Fr 1831 Dec 06		19-0204
Fr 1831 Dec 06*		M40-22
To 1831 Dec 08		19-0261
To 1831 Dec 17		M639-15
Fr 1831 Dec 17		19-0329
To 1831 Dec 21		M179-71
Fr 1831 Dec 28		19-0432
To 1831 Dec 28#		DLC-40
To c1832		DLC-41
To 1832 Jan 05#		M179-70
Fr 1832 Jan 09		19-0644
Fr 1832 Jan 09		M40-22
Re 1832 Jan 12		DLC-40
To 1832 Jan 13#		19-0678
Fr 1832 Jan 13#		M38-5
Fr 1832 Jan 17		19-0738
Fr 1832 Jan 26		19-0872
Fr 1832 Jan 26		M639-24
To 1832 Feb 05		19-0971
Fr 1832 Feb 06		19-0978
To 1832 Feb 06#		M179-72
To 1832 Feb 08		M179-72
Fr 1832 Feb 13		19-1077
Fr 1832 Feb 13*		M40-23
To 1832 Feb 24		M179-72
To 1832 Feb 25#		M179-72
Fr 1832 Feb 26		19-1248
Fr 1832 Feb 29		19-1268
Fr 1832 Mar 01		19-1291
To 1832 Mar 02		M179-72
To 1832 Mar 05		19-1308
Fr 1832 Mar 05		M179-72
Fr 1832 Mar 05*		19-1312
To 1832 Mar 07		M179-72
Fr 1832 Mar 16		19-1481
To 1832 Mar 19		M179-72
To 1832 Mar 19*		DLC-40
To 1832 Mar 22		M179-72
Fr 1832 Mar 22		M124-132
Fr 1832 Mar 22*		19-1534
Fr 1832 Mar 29		20-0044
Fr 1832 Mar 29*		M77-152
To 1832 Mar 31		M179-72
Fr 1832 Mar 31		20-0073
Fr 1832 Apr 02		20-0093
Fr 1832 Apr 03		20-0117
Fr 1832 Apr 03		20-0120
To 1832 Apr 06		M179-73
Fr 1832 Apr 09		20-0171
Fr 1832 Apr 09		20-0173
To 1832 Apr 11		M179-73
Fr 1832 Apr 12		20-0191
Fr 1832 Apr 19		20-0299
Fr 1832 Apr 21		20-0337
Fr 1832 Apr 23		M40-23
To 1832 May 01		M179-73
Fr 1832 May 01		20-0451
Fr 1832 May 01		20-0453
To 1832 May 03		M179-73
Fr 1832 May 04		M40-23
Fr 1832 May 23		20-0581
Fr 1832 May 25		20-0592
Fr 1832 Jun 13		M40-23
Fr 1832 Jun 22		20-0801
Fr 1832 Jun 23		20-0804
Fr 1832 Jul 05		M40-23
Fr 1832 Jul 14		20-1088
To 1832 Jul 21		20-1215
To 1832 Jul 21#		M179-74
To 1832 Jul 21*		M221-112
To 1832 Jul 23		M179-74

Fr 1832 Aug 07 M40-23
Fr 1832 Sep 01 DLC-41
To 1832 Sep 08 20-1505
Fr 1832 Oct 24 21-0147
Fr 1832 Nov 09 T206-4
To 1832 Nov 13# 21-0395
To 1832 Nov 17 M179-74
Fr 1832 Nov 17 M40-23
Fr 1832 Nov 20 21-0474
Fr 1832 Nov 22 M40-23
Fr 1832 Nov 22* 21-0496
Fr 1832 Nov 23 M281-1
Fr 1832 Nov 23* M40-23
Fr 1832 Nov 23 M639-26
Fr 1832 Nov 23* M40-23
To 1832 Nov 25 M179-74
To 1832 Dec 04 21-0851
To 1832 Dec 07 21-0925
Fr 1832 Dec 15 M40-23
Fr 1832 Dec 19 21-1090
To 1832 Dec 20# M179-74
To 1832 Dec 21 M179-74
Fr 1832 Dec 22 21-1117
To 1832 Dec 24 M179-74
To 1832 Dec 26 M179-74
Fr 1832 Dec 26 21-1170
Fr 1833 Jan 01 21-1290
To 1833 Jan 01# M281-1
Fr 1833 Jan 05 21-1329
To 1833 Jan 07# M179-72
Fr 1833 Jan 10 21-1397
Fr 1833 Jan 23 22-0031
Fr 1833 Jan 31 22-0168
To 1833 Feb 03# T1-7
To 1833 Feb 03# 22-0256
To 1833 Feb 05 M179-75
Fr 1833 Mar 02 22-0595
To 1833 Mar 02 22-0627
Fr 1833 Mar 07# M40-23
To 1833 Mar 07# 22-0682
To 1833 Mar 12 M179-75
To 1833 Mar 14 M179-75
To 1833 Mar 15 M97-7
To 1833 Mar 21 M179-75
To 1833 Apr 09 22-0978
To 1833 Apr 13 M179-76
To 1833 May 01 22-1255
To 1833 May 01* M40-23
Fr 1833 May 28 M639-24
To 1833 May 29 M639-24
Fr 1833 May 29 22-1510
To 1833 May 29 DLC-73
Re 1833 May 29 22-1512
Fr 1833 Jul 28 DLC-73
Fr 1833 Aug 10 DLC-73
Fr 1834 May 06 25-0969
Fr 1834 Jun 23 DLC-44
To 1834 Jun 27 25-1582
Fr 1834 Jul 14 DLC-44
Fr 1834 Oct 12 DLC-44
Fr 1834 Oct 13 DLC-44
To 1834 Nov 08 26-0848
Fr 1834 Nov 26 DLC-45
Fr 1834 Dec 20# DLC-45
Fr 1835 Jan 15 DLC-45
Fr 1835 Jan 16 DLC-45
Re 1835 Jan 20 mem 27-0260
Fr 1835 Jan 29# 27-0317
Fr 1835 Jan 31 DLC-45
Re 1835 Feb 20 mem 27-0578
Fr 1835 Feb 28 DLC-73
Re 1835 cMar mem 27-0669
To 1835 Mar 10 27-1077
Fr 1835 Mar 30 27-1394
Fr 1835 Apr 12 DLC-46
Re 1835 Apr 30 DLC-46
Fr 1835 May 02 DLC-73
To 1835 May 22 28-0492
Fr 1835 Jun 22 DLC-46
Fr 1835 Jul 11 DLC-46
Fr 1835 Jul 24 M179-80
Fr 1835 Sep 05# DLC-51
Fr 1835 Dec 05 DLC-47
Fr 1835 Dec 27 DLC-47
To 1835 Dec 31 29-1370
Fr 1836 Jan 11 29-1547
Fr 1836 Feb 16 DLC-47
Fr 1836 Feb 24 DLC-47
To 1836 Feb 27 30-0614
Fr 1836 Mar 09 DLC-47
To 1836 May 03 chk 30-1495
Livingston Edward P
Fr 1832 Jul 02 20-0873
Livingston James
Fr 1829 Nov 08 M688-63
Fr 1842 Apr 18# fin DLC-54
Livingston John Philip
Fr 1844 Oct 03 36-0924
Livingston Lewis
Fr 1819 Sep 07 DLC-27
Livingston Louise (Davezac)
Fr 1835 Feb 24 DLC-73
To 1836 May 26 31-0123
Fr 1840 Sep 23 DLC-74
To 1840 Nov 12 35-0100
Livingston Ridley
Fr 1831 Dec 09 M639-14
Livingston William
Fr 1829 Jun 13-0521
Livingston William P
Re 1829 Jul 08 M273-23
Lloyd Harriet M
Re 1835 Nov 09 par 29-0478
Lloyd Henry
Re 1835 Mar 02 par 27-0694
Lloyd James
Fr 1826 May 23 DLC-33
To 1826 Jul 14 11-0317
To 1826 Jul 14* DLC-34
Lloyd John
Fr 1833 Apr 22 M639-16
Lloyd Richard B
Re 1835 Jan 23 par 27-0279
Lochart Hamilton
Fr 1825 cMar 10-1194
Fr 1826 Apr 27 DLC-33
Locke Frank
Re 1799 May 17 leg 37-0488
Locke Hall Jackson
Fr 1829 Dec 04 14-0798
Locke John
Fr 1823 Dec 01 9-0774
Locke Joseph L
Fr 1836 Mar 09 DLC-47
Locke Joseph Lorenzo
Fr 1835 Dec M567-127
Lockwood James H
Fr 1836 May M200-6

Lockwood Thomas P
To 1832 Sep 03 20-1480
Logan Andrew
Fr 1835 Nov 05 M639-27
Logan Henry et al
Fr 1830 Feb 26 M639-23
Logan James
Re 1791 Feb 23 leg DLC-1
Logan John
Fr 1840 Jun 20 DLC-74
Logan Samuel
Re 1788 Nov leg 1-0051
Lohse & Kayser
Fr 1833 Apr 24 M639-16
Lomax Mann Page
Fr 1834 Mar 12 M567-98
Lombard Albert
Fr 1845 Mar 04 DLC-57
Lombarden Francisco
Fr 1815 Feb 13 DLC-16
London William
Fr 1804 Aug 31 fin DLC-3
Re 1807 Apr leg 2-0483
Long Burgess Ball
Fr 1829 Aug 04# M639-14
Long James
Fr 1813 Sep 08 DLC-6
Long John B
To 1814 Dec 22 DLC-62
To 1814 Dec 22* 4-0444
Long Medicus A et al
To 1839 Sep 28 34-0972
Long P W
Fr 1825 May 06 fin DLC-33
Long Robert A
Fr 1831 May 02 M22-28
Long Stephen Harriman
Re 1817 cApr 22 mem 5-0829
Longacre James Barton
Fr 1837 Jan 26 fin DLC-49
To 1837 Jan 26 chk DLC-49
Fr 1839 Feb 28 fin DLC-52
Loomis ____
Fr 1835 Feb 22 M22-36
Loomis J C et al
Fr 1835 Jan 08 DLC-45
Lord Melvin
Re 1833 Dec 16 par 24-0531
Lord Nathan
Fr 1833 Jun 26 23-0058
Loring Alonzo
Fr 1844 Mar 20 DLC-56
Lorman William & Son et al
Fr 1829 Sep 24 M639-18
Lorumier Charles V
Fr 1804 Jul 14 fin DLC-3
Fr 1804 Jul 14 1-1346
Louallier Louis
Fr 1815 Mar 05 DLC-17
Re 1815 Mar 11 4-0831
Re 1815 Mar 14 leg 4-0847
Louallier v A Jackson
Re 1815 Sep 15 leg DLC-19
Loubat Alphonse
Fr 1833 Apr 25 M639-16
Loudan Jeremiah
Fr 1821 Sep 07 fin DLC-70
Loughborough Preston S
Fr 1828 Dec 05 DLC-36
Fr 1829 Feb M639-2
Fr 1844 Oct 12 DLC-57
Loughmiller James
Fr 1814 Apr 27 DLC-10
Louis Grand Duke of Baden
Fr 1829 Feb 19# 12-0534
To 1829 Apr 30 13-0191
Fr 1829 Dec 18 14-1067
To 1830 Apr 08 15-0643
Louis Philippe King of France
Fr 1830 Aug 22 16-0135
Fr 1830 Sep 10 16-0230
To 1830 Sep 27 16-0260
To 1830 Nov 20 16-0811
To 1830 Nov 20 16-0815
Fr 1830 Dec 15 16-1444
To 1831 Mar 07 17-0816
Fr 1832 Aug 11 20-1276
To 1832 Oct 25 21-0149
To 1833 Jun 04 22-1568
To 1836 Oct 04 32-0058
Fr 1836 Dec 10 32-1082
Fr 1836 Dec 14 32-1144
Louisiana General Assembly
Fr 1829 Jan 28 M567-42
Louisiana citizens
Fr 1843 Aug 11 DLC-55
Louisiana free blacks
To 1814 Sep 21 add DLC-62
To 1814 Sep 21 4-0235
To 1814 Dec 18 DLC-14
Louisiana legislator
To 1828 Feb 09 11-1104
Louisiana militia
To 1814 Dec 18 DLC-14
To 1815 Mar 07 add DLC-62
Love Alexander
To 1821 Jul 24 DLC-63
Love Charles Jones
Fr 1798 Jan 31 1-0598
Re 1806 Jan 28 leg 2-0128
Fr 1829 Apr 04 M639-2
Fr 1829 Apr 04 M639-2
Fr 1829 Apr 15 DLC-36
Fr 1829 May 20 DLC-37
Fr 1829 Jul 09 DLC-37
To 1829 Jul 27 DLC-37
To 1829 Dec 17 DLC-37
Fr 1830 Jan 15 DLC-37
To 1830 Feb 28 DLC-37
Fr 1830 May 08 DLC-38
Fr 1830 Jun 08 DLC-38
To 1831 Mar 07 DLC-39
Fr 1833 Feb 03 DLC-42
Fr 1833 Apr 21 DLC-42
Fr 1833 Sep 14 M639-3
Fr 1835 Jan 19 M639-9
Fr 1835 Jan 28 27-0304
To 1835 Sep 07 28-1587
Fr 1837 Jan 20# DLC-49
Love Charles Jones et al
Fr 1836 Aug 09 31-1271
To 1836 Aug 10 31-1283
Love David
Fr 1813 Dec 02 DLC-7
Love Elizabeth Dixon
Fr 1839 Mar 05 DLC-52
Love Frances Peyton (Dixon)
Fr 1833 Mar 27 DLC-42

Name	Date	Type	Location
Love Henry et al			
	Fr 1836 Sep 26		31-1520
Love John			
	Fr 1800 Apr 02	lnd	1-0764
	Fr 1800 Apr 02*	lnd	DLC-2
	Fr 1800 Apr 02	lnd	1-0766
	Fr 1800 Apr 02*	lnd	DLC-2
	To 1802 Apr 07	lnd	1-0974
Love Robert			
	Fr 1830 Aug 19		DLC-38
	Fr 1831 Nov 17		DLC-40
	To 1831 Dec 10		DLC-40
	Fr 1832 Sep 01		DLC-41
	Fr 1832 Dec 06		DLC-41
	Fr 1833 Nov 19		DLC-43
	Fr 1836 Jul 06		DLC-48
Love Thomas			
	Fr 1840 Jul 02		34-1459
Love Thomas Cutting			
	Fr 1836 Sep 14		M567-123
Love & Lanier			
	Fr 1823 Nov 06	fin	DLC-34
Lovejoy & Denham			
	Fr 1832 Apr 26	fin	DLC-40
Lovell Joseph			
	Fr 1833 Nov 19#		23-1252
	Fr 1835 Mar 09		T168-14
Lovell Josiah			
	Fr 1833 Oct 02		M639-12
Lovell Warren			
	Fr 1833 Jun 28	add	23-0065
Lovely Persis			
	Fr 1830 Jan 09		14-1360
Lovely William L			
	Fr c1798 Oct	mem	DLC-60
	Fr 1816 Jan 20		DLC-20
Loving John			
	Fr 1827 Jun 16		DLC-34
Low William H			
	Fr 1829 Mar 31		M639-14
Lowber James C			
	Fr 1833 Aug 19		23-0425
	To 1833 Aug 30		23-0545
Lowe Bradley S A			
	Fr 1845 Mar 07		M873-54
Lowe David			
	Fr 1825 Apr 03	fin	10-1233
	Fr 1827 Mar 13	fin	11-0501
	Fr 1828 Sep 20	fin	12-0209
Lowell Henry C			
	Fr 1837 Jan 21		33-0088
Lowell Joshua Adams			
	Fr 1836 Dec 26		32-1323
	Re 1837 Jan 16		M687-20
Lowery Alexander			
	Fr 1814 Nov 07		DLC-13
Lowman Nicholas			
	Re 1834 Dec 09	par	26-1451
Lownds Oliver M			
	Fr 1829 Mar 25		12-1108
Lowrey Charles F et al			
	Re 1836 Jul 21	par	31-1145
Lowrey George et al			
	Fr 1830 Feb 25		M234-74
	Fr 1830 Feb 25*		15-0249
	Fr 1830 Mar 26		M234-74
	Fr 1830 Mar 26*		15-0463
Lowrie Walter			
	To 1831 Dec 20		19-0369
	To 1834 Jul 08#		26-0187
Lowry Heman			
	Fr 1835 Nov 30		29-0690
Lowry John			
	Fr 1813 Nov 07		DLC-7
	Fr 1813 Nov 07		DLC-7
	Fr 1813 Nov 07*		DLC-61
	To 1813 Nov 07		DLC-61
	To 1814 Jan 07		DLC-61
	To 1814 Jan 08		DLC-61
	To 1814 Mar 15		DLC-9
	Fr 1817 Aug 15		5-0984
Loyall George			
	Fr 1831 Sep 07		M124-129
	Fr 1832 Jun 12		20-0742
	Fr 1833 Dec 12		24-0461
	Fr 1834 Oct 10		26-0577
	Fr 1836 Jan 15		M124-151
	Fr 1836 cOct 07		M22-41
Loyd Alexander et al			
	Fr 1836 May		M687-27
Lucas Edward			
	Fr 1834 Jan 13		M639-21
	Fr 1836 Sep		M22-40
	Fr 1837 Feb 23		M688-111
Lucas F Jr			
	To 1823 Oct 08		9-0684
	To 1823 Dec 10		9-0796
Lucas James			
	Fr 1830 Feb 15		DLC-37
Lucas Robert			
	Fr 1830 Feb 04		M639-2
	Fr 1832 Dec 08		M639-6
	Fr 1833 Aug 02		23-0260
	Fr 1835 Mar 20#		27-1238
	Fr 1835 Jun 25		28-0787
	To 1835 Jul 04		28-0908
	Fr 1836 Jan 20		T494-3
	Fr 1836 Apr 25		M639-16
	Fr 1838 Oct 11		DLC-51
Lucas Robert et al			
	Fr 1830 Feb 14		M639-13
	Fr 1834 Dec 26		M639-27
	Fr 1835 Mar 22		M639-3
Lucas T			
	To 1828 Oct 08		12-0229
Luckett Craven P			
	Fr 1829 Feb 21		M639-18
Ludlo John			
	Re 1787 Oct 28	leg	1-0029
Ludwig Jacob			
	Fr 1837 Feb		M687-20
Ludwig Moses R			
	Fr 1837 Jan 28		33-0199
Ludwig Newell R			
	Fr 1837 Feb		M687-20
Lufborough Nathan			
	Fr 1831 Jun 25		M688-76
	Fr 1832 Jul 09		M639-5
	Fr 1836 Aug 23		M124-154
Lukey Francis			
	Fr 1844 Jul 18		DLC-57
Luma Desiderio			
	Fr 1821 Aug 09	fin	DLC-70
	Fr 1821 Oct 07	fin	DLC-70
Lummus Aaron et al			
	Fr 1829 May 22		13-0377
Lumpkin Wilson			
	Fr 1828 Mar 06		DLC-35
	Fr 1832 Jan 02		19-0588

Lumpkin Wilson (cont)
Fr 1832 Jan 02 M234-75
Fr 1832 Jan 02* 19-0593
To 1832 Jun 22 DLC-40
To 1832 Jun 22* DLC-41
Fr 1832 Jul 12 20-1050
Fr 1833 Apr 22 22-1143
To 1833 Apr 30 22-1216
Fr 1834 Dec 10 DLC-45
Fr 1835 Jan 12# M221-115
Fr 1835 Feb 09 DLC-45
Fr 1835 May 20 DLC-46
Fr 1835 May 20* 28-0487
To 1835 May 29 28-0521
Fr 1835 Sep 17 M639-4
Fr 1836 Aug 21 31-1333
Fr 1836 Aug 22 DLC-48
Fr 1836 Sep 24 31-1493
Fr 1836 Sep 24* M234-80
Fr 1836 Dec 01 32-0611
Fr 1836 Dec 18 32-1185
Lundy Benjamin
Fr 1823 Sep 04 DLC-32
Luqueer Robert S
Fr 1842 Jan 11 DLC-54
Lusk Robert & Co
Fr 1826 Dec 23 fin DLC-34
Lutz John
Fr 1829 Dec 15 DLC-37
Fr 1830 Mar 05 fin DLC-37
Fr 1835 May 04 fin DLC-46
Fr 1835 Aug 04 fin DLC-48
To 1836 Apr 11 chk DLC-48
Lyle William C et al
Fr 1835 Apr 28 DLC-46
Lyles Thomas W
Re 1834 Nov 20 par 26-0962
Lyman Robert
To 1820 Jan 04 DLC-63
To 1820 Jan 30# DLC-63
Fr 1820 Feb 29 DLC-28
Lynch Charles
To 1836 Aug 07 M179-82
To 1836 Aug 07* 31-1251
To 1836 Aug 07* DLC-48
To 1836 Aug 07* M567-122
Lynch D
Fr 1829 Apr 23 M639-14
Lynch D L
To 1832 Aug 28 chk DLC-41
Lynch Daniel et al
Fr c1836 29-1400
Lynch David et al
Fr 1834 Nov M639-1
Lynch Dominick
Re 1835 Apr 07 27-1560
Lynch James
Fr 1838 Aug 18 DLC-51
Lynch Jasper
Fr 1829 Mar 25 M639-14
Fr 1829 May 22 M639-14
Lynchburg VA citizens
To 1828 Dec 09 12-0308
Lyncoya
Fr 1823 Dec 29 9-0857
Lyon Aaron W
Fr 1836 Aug 10 31-1275
Lyon Chittenden
Fr 1831 Jun 23 M639-16
Fr 1832 Feb 27 M22-29
Lyon Chittenden et al
Fr 1830 Apr 09 M639-14
Lyon Francis Strother
Fr 1836 Jun 28 31-0628
Lyon Francis Strother et al
Fr 1836 May 13 31-0008
Fr 1837 Feb 10 33-0592
Lyon James
Fr 1805 Jan 25 DLC-71
Fr 1813 Oct 27 DLC-7
Fr 1813 Oct 31 DLC-7
Lyon James G
Fr 1823 Aug 18 DLC-32
Lyon Lucius
Re 1831 Aug 15 18-0541
Fr 1833 Jan 29 M179-75
Fr 1833 Jan 29* 22-0093
Fr 1833 Jan 29 M179-75
Fr 1833 Jan 29* 22-0091
Fr 1834 Apr 21 M639-9
Fr 1835 Feb 12 M639-15
Fr 1835 Feb 12* 27-0504
Fr 1835 Dec 09 M200-6
Fr 1836 Apr 12 M639-6
Fr 1836 Apr 20 M639-6
Fr 1837 Jan 27 M234-422
Lyon Matthew
Fr 1800 Feb 28 DLC-71
Fr 1814 Jun 02 DLC-10
Fr 1816 Aug 20 DLC-21
Fr 1818 Aug 10 DLC-25
Fr 1819 Jun 08 DLC-27
Lyon W H
Fr 1845 Jan 19 36-1376
Lyon Washington H
Fr 1829 Jul M639-14
Lyon William
To 1817 Jan 15 lnd 5-0707
Fr 1836 Nov 19 32-0564
Fr 1837 Jan 05 M639-14
Fr 1841 Aug 01 DLC-53
Lyon William W
Fr 1829 Jun 12 DLC-37
Lytle John S
Fr 1829 Mar 26 M639-11
Lytle Robert Todd
Fr 1831 Mar 19 DLC-39
Fr 1832 Mar 13# 19-1433
Fr 1834 Jul 28 26-0267
Fr 1835 Jan 22 DLC-45
Fr 1835 Apr 02 DLC-46
Fr 1835 Aug 15 M639-17
Fr 1836 Jan 16 M639-12
Fr 1837 Feb 26 DLC-50
Lytle William (OH)
Fr 1829 May 17 DLC-37
Re 1829 May 25 13-0422
Fr 1829 Jun 03 M639-3
Fr 1830 May 08 M477-4
Fr 1830 May 08* M478-8
Lytle William (OH) et al
Fr 1829 Feb 16 M639-17
Fr 1830 Jun 27 add 15-1543
To 1830 Jun 27 add 15-1544
Lytle William (TN)
Re 1805 Nov 19 mem DLC-3
Fr 1807 Dec 17 fin DLC-4

Mabry _____ (Gen)
Re 1836 cFeb 12 mem 37-0347
Mabry Jesse
Fr 1839 Nov 16 DLC-52
Mabson Samuel C
Fr 1814 Jul 17 DLC-11
Fr 1814 Jul 28 DLC-11
Macalester Charles
Fr 1834 Oct 29 26-0767
Fr 1835 Dec 14 DLC-47
Fr 1835 Dec 15 DLC-47
Macarty Auguste
Fr 1819 Dec 30 DLC-28
To 1820 Jan 27 7-1015
Macauley Patrick
Re 1833 Aug 08 23-0299
Maccracken Samuel F
Fr 1830 Apr 03 M639-27
Fr 1833 Sep 28 M639-12
MacCulloch Arthur
Fr 1835 Jun 21 M639-15
MacDonald A
Fr 1829 Apr 06 M639-15
Macdonald J
Fr 1815 Dec 01# fin DLC-19
Mace Thomas
Re 1832 May 08 par 20-0490
MacEwen Duncan
Fr 1837 Mar 04 DLC-50
Machen Edward
Fr 1814 Jul 30 DLC-11
Machen Lewis H
Fr 1832 Jul 19# 20-1151
Mack A
Fr 1825 Apr 08 fin DLC-33
Mack Andrew
Fr 1834 Apr 09 M639-9
Fr 1835 Nov 30 M639-9
Fr 1836 Mar 30 DLC-47
Mack Andrew et al
Fr 1829 Feb 03 M639-17
Mackenzie William Lyon
Fr 1844 Feb 21 DLC-56
Mackey M
Fr 1820 Oct 06 M271-3
Macky William Thomas et al
Fr 1835 cJan DLC-59
Fr 1835 Jan 08 DLC-45
Maclin Sackfield
Fr 1844 Dec 04 M873-4
Macneven William J
Fr 1828 Sep 20 DLC-35
Macomb Alexander
Fr 1819 May 31 7-0532
Fr 1824 Apr 17 10-0653
Fr 1824 Jun 10 10-0776
Fr 1824 Dec 18 DLC-33
Fr 1824 Dec 18* 10-0987
Fr 1829 Oct 29 14-0260
Fr 1829 Oct 30 14-0271
To 1831 Jul 28# M567-61
Fr 1832 Jul 24 20-1240
Fr 1832 Aug 11 20-1281
Fr 1833 Mar 26 M567-85
Fr 1833 Mar 26* 22-0897
Fr 1833 Apr 12 22-0999
Fr 1835 Apr 14 28-0083
Fr 1835 Jul 23 28-1123
Fr c1836 29-1402
Fr 1836 Jun 17# 31-0498
Fr 1836 Jun 25# M567-125
Fr 1836 Aug 11 31-1284
Fr 1836 Sep M22-41
Fr 1836 Oct 12 M567-126
Fr 1836 Oct 12* 32-0165
Fr 1836 Oct 18 32-0223
Macomb David B
Re 1830 Jan 16 14-1442
Macon Edgar
Fr 1829 Sep 28 M639-15
Macon Nathaniel
Fr 1794 Dec 22 DLC-71
To 1795 Oct 04 DLC-1
Fr 1796 Jan 17 DLC-1
Fr 1796 Feb 29 DLC-71
Fr 1797 Feb 21 1-0493
Fr 1797 May 24 1-0512
Fr 1800 Feb 14 DLC-2
Fr 1801 Jan 12 DLC-2
To 1833 Aug 17 DLC-43
Fr 1833 Aug 26 DLC-43
To 1833 Sep 02 23-0591
To 1833 Sep 02* DLC-43
Fr 1833 Sep 25 DLC-43
Fr 1835 May 12 28-0368
Macon Thomas
Fr 1827 Aug 15 DLC-34
Macpherson Alexander M
Fr 1835 Jan 28 M639-10
Fr 1835 Jan 28* M179-79
Fr 1835 Sep 03 M639-15
Macpherson R H
Fr 1816 Mar 03 DLC-20
MacRea William
Fr 1814 Jul 12 DLC-11
Fr 1814 Aug 10 DLC-11
Fr 1814 Aug 15 DLC-11
To 1814 Aug 27 4-0156
To 1814 Aug 27* DLC-62
To 1814 Aug 30 DLC-62
Fr 1814 Sep 03 DLC-12
Fr 1814 Sep 06 DLC-12
Fr 1814 Sep 09 DLC-12
Fr 1814 Sep 10 DLC-12
Fr 1814 Sep 10 DLC-12
Fr 1814 Sep 19 DLC-12
Fr 1814 Sep 22 DLC-12
Fr 1814 Sep 27 DLC-12
Fr 1814 Oct 12 DLC-13
Fr 1814 Oct 12 DLC-13
To 1814 Oct 14 DLC-62
Fr 1814 Oct 17 DLC-13
Fr 1814 Oct 17 DLC-13
Fr 1814 Oct 20 DLC-13
Fr 1814 Oct 21 DLC-13
Fr 1814 Oct 25 DLC-13
Fr 1814 Oct 27 DLC-13
Fr 1814 Oct 28 DLC-13
Fr 1814 Nov 07 DLC-13
Fr 1814 Nov 17 DLC-14
Fr 1814 Dec 03 DLC-14
Fr 1815 Jan 06 4-0493
To 1815 Dec 16 DLC-62
Fr 1816 Jul 25 DLC-21
Macrery Andrew
Fr 1838 Jun 27 DLC-51
Macrery Andrew et al
Fr 1834 Nov DLC-45

Macy John B
Fr 1844 Sep 28 36-0915
Maddox Ellis
Re 1806 Jul leg 2-0288
Madison Dolly (Payne)
To 1836 Jul 09 31-1020
To 1836 Jul 09* M179-82
Fr 1836 Aug 20 M179-82
Fr 1836 Aug 20* 31-1327
Fr 1836 Oct 31-1544
Fr 1836 Nov 15 32-0509
Fr 1836 Nov 15* M179-82
To 1836 Nov 26 32-0587
Madison James
To 1813 Mar 15 DLC-6
To 1814 Aug 08 M200-20
To 1814 Aug 08* 3-1247
Fr 1814 Dec 18 37-0414
To 1815 cAug 14 4-1160
Fr 1816 Jul 20 DLC-21
Fr 1816 Jul 20* 5-0320
Fr 1833 Jul 19 23-0162
Fr 1835 Oct 11 29-0275
Fr 1835 Dec 15# DLC-47
Re 1836 Jun 30 M179-82
Madwolf
Re 1814 Aug 10 3-1293
To 1820 Dec 11 8-0015
Magenis Arthur L
Fr 1844 Mar 16 DLC-56
To 1844 Mar 28 36-0408
Magruder Mary
Re 1832 Jan 04 par 19-0612
Maguire Bernard
Fr 1839 Jul 04 DLC-52
Fr 1843 Jul 04 DLC-55
Fr 1844 Jan 08 DLC-56
Fr 1844 Jan 31 DLC-56
Fr 1844 Mar 01 DLC-56
Maguire Patrick
To 1822 Jan 26 9-0005
Fr 1823 Jan 30 fin 9-0437
Mahan Dennis Hart
Fr 1834 May 26 M567-96
Fr 1836 Mar 03# 30-0663
Mahan James
Re 1835 Oct 09 par 29-0248
Mahan M
Re 1835 cJul 06 mem M688-100
Maher James
Fr 1837 Oct 23 DLC-50
Fr 1845 Feb 21 DLC-57
Maher Richard
To 1818 May 07 6-0676
Mahmud II Sultan of Turkey
To 1831 Apr 15 17-1179
Mahon Martin H W
Re 1829 Apr 01 par 12-1228
Re 1829 Apr 01* par T967-1
Mahon Michael
Fr 1834 Aug 25 M639-15
Re 1835 Apr 30 28-0199
Major John
Re 1830 Nov 20 par 16-0818
Majors John and David
Re 1833 Apr 06 par 22-0953
Maker Ebenezer
Fr 1844 Dec 02 DLC-57
Malibran Eugene
Re 1830 Oct 16 par 16-0401
Mallett Edward James
To 1833 Jun 14# 23-0032
Fr 1843 Jan 12 DLC-55
Mallory W W
To 1818 May 07 6-0676
Mangum Willie Person
Fr 1832 Jun 19 M639-27
Mann Abijah Jr
Fr 1834 Dec 30 M639-22
Fr 1835 May 30 28-0531
Fr 1836 Apr 26 M687-16
Fr 1836 May 09# 30-1575
Fr 1837 Feb 06# DLC-50
Mann Job et al
Fr 1836 Apr 27 M639-24
Mann Joel Keith
Fr 1834 Dec 18 M639-1
Mann Joel Keith et al
Fr 1834 Dec 18 M639-1
Mann Joseph et al
Fr 1832 May 17 M639-16
Mann Milo
Fr 1821 Apr 11 fin DLC-70
Manning John et al
Fr 1829 May M639-24
Manning Randolph et al
Fr 1835 Nov 16 M639-9
Manning Richard Irvine
To 1834 Jan 15# DLC-44
Fr 1836 Jan 06 M688-106
Fr 1836 Mar 19 30-0832
To 1836 Mar 21 30-0848
Fr 1836 Apr 07 M567-128
Fr 1836 Apr 27 DLC-48
Manor Levi W
Fr 1814 Jan 01 DLC-8
Manrique Mateo Gonzalez
To 1814 Jul 12 3-1122
Fr 1814 Jul 21 DLC-11
Fr 1814 Jul 21* M200-9
Fr 1814 Jul 21* 3-1160
Fr 1814 Jul 26 DLC-11
Fr 1814 Jul 26* M200-9
Fr 1814 Jul 26* 3-1174
To 1814 Aug 24 3-1320
To 1814 Aug 24* M200-9
To 1814 Aug 24* M221-63
To 1814 Aug 24* DLC-62
Fr 1814 Aug 30 DLC-11
Fr 1814 Aug 30* M200-9
Fr 1814 Aug 30* 4-0165
Fr 1814 Sep 07 DLC-12
To 1814 Sep 09 4-0193
To 1814 Sep 09* M221-63
To 1814 Sep 09* DLC-62
To 1814 Sep 09* M200-9
To 1814 Sep 11 4-0211
To 1814 Sep 11* DLC-62
To 1814 Sep 12 DLC-62
To 1814 Nov 06 DLC-62
To 1814 Nov 06* M221-63
To 1814 Nov 06* M200-9
To 1814 Nov 06* 4-0317
To 1814 Nov 06 DLC-62
To 1814 Nov 06* M221-63
To 1814 Nov 06* M200-9
To 1814 Nov 06* 4-0319
Fr 1814 Nov 06 DLC-13
Fr 1814 Nov 06* M221-63

Marshall William (cont)
Fr 1834 Mar 22 25-0319
Fr 1835 Feb 17 DLC-45
Fr 1835 Feb 18 DLC-45
Marshall William et al
Fr 1829 Mar 04 12-0851
Marshall & Watkins
Fr 1817 Jan 23 fin DLC-22
Fr 1818 Dec 28 fin DLC-26
Fr 1820 Sep 29 fin DLC-29
Marsteller Lewis H
Re 1836 Dec 20 32-1225
Martin Barkley et al
Fr 1815 Mar add 4-0805
Martin Brice
Fr 1812 Oct 06 DLC-5
Fr 1813 Sep 25 DLC-6
Fr 1813 Sep 25* DLC-61
Martin Brice et al
Fr 1813 Dec 08 DLC-61
To 1813 Dec 08 DLC-7
To 1813 Dec 08* DLC-61
Fr 1813 Dec 09 DLC-61
Martin Catherine (Donelson)
To 1822 Jul 10 DLC-72
To 1834 Mar 17# 25-0251
Martin Daniel
Fr 1831 Jan 27 M222-30
Fr 1831 Jan 27* 17-0372
Martin Elizabeth Anderson
see also Randolph E A M
and Donelson E A M
Fr 1834 Mar 17# 25-0251
Martin George M
Fr 1830 Jul 31 16-0070
Martin George Washington
To 1815 Jun 13 chk DLC-18
To 1816 Nov 19 DLC-22
To 1816 Dec 27 5-0643
To 1817 Dec 17 5-1180
Fr 1823 Aug 14 DLC-32
To 1823 Oct 15 9-0699
To 1823 Oct 18 9-0706
To 1823 Oct 30 9-0723
To 1824 Jan 02 9-0883
To 1825 Jun 18 10-1314
To c1826# 11-0095
To 1827 Mar 25 11-0514
Fr 1828 Dec 27 DLC-36
Fr 1829 Jun 30 M639-4
To 1832 Mar 05 19-1314
To 1833 Feb 25 22-0470
To 1833 Sep 03 23-0616
Fr 1833 Sep 11 M234-188
Fr 1833 Sep 11* 23-0687
Fr 1833 Oct 03 M234-188
Fr 1834 Jun 12 25-1325
To 1843 Aug 11 35-1459
Re 1843 Aug 11 35-1461
To 1843 Oct 30 35-1572
Martin James
Fr 1814 Dec 27 fin DLC-17
Martin James Glasgow
Fr 1818 May fin DLC-25
To 1822 May 10 9-0146
To 1836 May 01 30-1481
Martin J G & Co
Fr 1821 Dec 01 fin DLC-31
Martin James Monroe
Fr 1829 Apr 13 M639-15
Martin John F
Fr 1835 Jan 08 DLC-45
Martin John H
Fr 1813 Oct 06 DLC-6
Fr 1828 Jul 02 DLC-35
To 1828 Jul 02 DLC-36
Fr 1829 Apr 15 M639-15
Martin John P
Fr 1832 Apr 28 M22-29
Martin Joshua Lanier
Fr 1836 Jun 28 31-0630
Fr 1839 Jul 15 DLC-52
Fr 1841 Jul 07 DLC-53
Martin Joshua Lanier et al
Fr 1837 Mar 03 M639-15
Martin Matt
To 1807 Oct 06 lnd 2-0562
To 1809 May 15 lnd 2-0816
To 1809 Jun 15 lnd 2-0837
Martin Morgan Lewis et al
Fr 1835 Mar 23 27-1317
To 1835 Apr 02# 27-1510
Martin Mortimer A
Fr 1829 Apr 20 M639-5
Martin Patrick H
Fr 1814 Jul 13 DLC-11
Fr 1814 Oct 10 DLC-13
Martin Peter H
Fr 1818 Jan 09 fin DLC-23
Martin Samuel
Fr 1823 Jun 17 DLC-32
Fr 1823 Aug 12 DLC-32
Re 1831 Jun 08 par 17-1566
Martin Samuel N
Fr 1844 Jul 03 DLC-57
Martin T H
Fr 1836 Jan 27 M639-13
Martin Thomas
Re 1790 May leg 1-0075i
Martin William (stagedriver)
Re 1837 Mar 01 par 33-0959
Martin William (TN; 1765-1846)
To 1796 Oct 05 lnd 1-0447
To 1796 Oct 05* lnd DLC-1
Fr 1796 Nov lnd 1-0455
Fr 1809 Jan 04 DLC-4
Fr 1813 Sep 23 DLC-6
Fr 1813 Nov 02 DLC-7
Fr 1813 Nov 14 DLC-7
Fr 1813 Nov 14* DLC-61
Fr 1813 Dec 04 DLC-61
To 1813 Dec 06 DLC-61
To 1813 Dec 06* DLC-7
To 1813 Dec 08 DLC-61
Fr 1813 Dec 08 3-0641
Fr 1813 Dec 08* DLC-61
To 1813 Dec 08 DLC-61
Fr 1813 Dec 08 3-0643
Fr 1813 Dec 10 DLC-61
To 1813 Dec 10 DLC-61
Fr 1816 Oct 31 DLC-21
Fr 1816 Nov 14 DLC-21
Fr 1822 Jul 09 DLC-31
Fr 1822 Nov 28 DLC-31
Fr 1824 Sep 09 DLC-33
Fr 1826 Mar 23 DLC-33
Fr 1826 Apr 19 DLC-33
Re 1829 mem DLC-37
Martin William (1765-1846) et al
Fr 1813 Nov 15 3-0605

Martin William (TN militia Maj)
Fr 1814 Apr 18 DLC-10
Fr 1814 Apr 24 DLC-10
Martin William (US Army)
Fr 1836 Jan 30 M567-127
Martin William Dickinson
Fr 1829 Mar 17 M639-4
Fr 1829 May 11 13-0308
Martin William P
Fr 1826 Jul 05 add 11-0271
To 1826 Jul 05 add 11-0276
Martin Wyly
Fr 1814 Nov 10 DLC-14
Martin Y E
To 1840 Sep 22 35-0015
Martin Zadoc
Fr 1831 Jul M234-749
Martin & Williams
Fr 1822 Sep 23 fin DLC-31
To 1823 Sep 08 9-0654
Fr 1824 Mar 18 fin DLC-32
Mary Hope (bark)
Re 1831 Jun 06 par 17-1542
Mary Jane (schooner)
Re 1833 Dec 16 par 24-0536
Maryland General Assembly
Fr 1834 Jan 28 M222-32
Masi F & Co
Fr 1830 Mar 10# fin DLC-39
Fr 1831 Apr 06 fin DLC-39
Fr 1831 Aug 16 fin DLC-40
To 1832 Jun 11 chk DLC-40
Mason ______
To 1836 Jan 02 29-1450
Mason Catherine
Fr 1839 Jan 16 37-0535
Mason David
Fr 1812 Jun 11 DLC-5
Fr 1812 Jul 01 M221-42
Fr 1812 Jul 22 DLC-5
Fr 1815 May 15 add 4-1039
Mason George
Fr 1829 Mar 23 M639-15
Mason James
Fr 1832 Nov 24 DLC-41
Mason John
Fr 1815 Jan 10 M221-64
Fr 1815 Jan 10* M16-3
Fr 1815 Nov 19 DLC-19
Fr 1830 Mar 12 M273-25
Mason John Thomson
Fr 1831 Apr 18 DLC-39
Fr 1831 Jul 12 18-0199
To 1832 Dec 16# M639-2
Fr 1832 Dec 24 21-1153
Fr 1834 Oct 14 DLC-44
Fr 1834 Dec 04 26-1410
Fr 1835 Feb 14 DLC-45
Fr 1844 Feb 21 DLC-56
Mason John Young
Fr 1835 Apr 11 M124-147
Fr 1836 Mar 21 M687-33
Fr 1836 Mar 28 30-0910
Fr 1836 Apr 24 M687-22
Fr 1844 Feb 12 DLC-56
Fr 1844 Jul 23 DLC-57
To 1844 Aug 01 DLC-74
Mason Milo
To 1818 Jan 22 fin 5-1334
Fr 1818 Jun 23 DLC-25
Fr 1818 Jun 25 DLC-25
To 1819 Jun fin 7-0538
Fr 1820 Feb 01 DLC-28
Fr c1829 DLC-37
Fr 1834 Jun 27 M22-35
Mason Moses Jr
Fr 1836 Jun 03 31-0289
Mason Richard B
Fr 1829 Mar 17 M639-15
Mason Richard C
Fr 1830 Mar 29 M273-25
Fr 1836 Mar 18 30-0815
Mason Samson et al
Fr 1836 Jul 01 31-0741
Mason Sidney
Re 1829 Sep 08 13-1284
Mason Stevens Thomson (1760-1803)
Fr 1798 Apr 27 DLC-2
Fr 1798 May 25 DLC-2
Fr 1799 Jan 18 DLC-2
Mason Stevens Thomson (1811-1843)
Re 1831 Jul 12 18-0201
Fr 1834 Apr 06 M639-9
Fr 1835 Mar 05# 27-1018
Fr 1835 Mar 05# 27-1020
Fr 1835 Mar 05# 27-1022
Fr 1835 Mar 06# 27-1030
Fr 1835 Mar 06# 27-1035
Fr 1835 Mar 09# DLC-45
Fr 1835 Mar 21 27-1275
Fr 1835 Mar 23 27-1368
Fr 1835 Apr 25# 28-0130
Mason Thomson
Fr 1829 Jun 12 M639-15
Mason Thomson F
Fr 1829 cMar M639-11
Fr 1830 Mar M273-25
Mason William S
Fr 1838 Nov 06 DLC-51
Masonic Hall
Re 1818 Jan 15 5-1286
Masot Jose
Fr 1817 Nov 03 DLC-23
Fr 1818 Feb 16 DLC-24
To 1818 Mar 25 6-0151
To 1818 Mar 26 6-0177
Fr 1818 Apr 15 DLC-24
Fr 1818 Apr 15* 6-0352
To 1818 Apr 27 6-0482
Fr 1818 May 18 6-0712
To 1818 May 23 6-0784
Fr 1818 May 23 6-0841
Fr 1818 May 23* DLC-25
To 1818 May 24 6-0862
Fr 1818 May 24 6-0874
Fr 1818 May 24* DLC-25
Fr 1818 May 24* M116-4
To 1818 May 25 DLC-25
To 1818 May 25* 6-0924
Fr 1818 May 28 DLC-25
Fr 1818 May 29 DLC-25
Fr 1818 May 29 DLC-25
Mass Samuel et al
Fr 1834 Dec 26-1109
Massachusetts arsenal
Re c1829 mem 12-0355
Massachusetts militia expenses
Re 1829 cApr mem 12-1211
Re 1829 cJul mem 13-0768

Massey James
Fr 1828 Aug 18 12-0166
Massey Matthew Strong
To 1820 Jun 30# DLC-63
To 1820 Aug 24 DLC-63
Massias Abraham A
Fr 1832 Dec 19# M222-31
Massingill Henry
Fr 1814 Mar 24 DLC-9
Masten Thomas
To 1804 Jul 17 DLC-3
Masterson Christiana (Roane)
Fr 1845 May 28 37-0233
Matheys Robert E
Fr 1841 Apr 07 DLC-53
Matlock Thomas Jefferson et al
Fr 1829 Jan M639-15
Matthews James
Re 1836 Apr 16 par 30-1195
Re 1836 Apr 27 par 30-1380
Matthews John D
Fr 1844 Dec 25 DLC-57
Fr 1845 Feb 01 36-1433
Fr 1845 May 05 DLC-58
Mattingly George
To 1830 Jun 12 chk DLC-38
Mattson Joseph S et al
Fr 1835 cJan DLC-59
Maul John
Fr 1818 Jun 04 fin DLC-69
Fr 1818 Jun 10 DLC-25
Fr 1829 May 23 13-0401
Maund Thomas
To 1823 Dec 22 9-0828
To 1823 Dec 27 9-0851
Fr 1824 Sep 06 DLC-33
Fr 1829 Dec 18 M567-42
Maury Abram Poindexter
To 1813 Dec 03 3-0637
To 1815 Jan 13# 4-0529
Fr 1816 Feb 08 DLC-20
Fr 1816 Feb 17 DLC-20
To 1817 Apr 22 DLC-71
To 1819 Sep 12 7-0657
Fr 1823 Sep 20 9-0672
To 1823 Sep 21 9-0673
Fr 1830 May 21 M688-68
Fr 1836 Oct 24# DLC-49
To 1836 Oct 29# DLC-49
Maury Fontaine
Fr 1821 Sep 22 DLC-30
Fr 1821 Sep 22* M40-17
Fr 1821 Sep 22* 8-1206
To 1821 Nov 17 M40-17
To 1821 Nov 17* DLC-63
Fr 1821 Dec 01 DLC-70
Fr 1822 Jan 25 DLC-31
Fr 1822 Jan 25* M40-17
To 1822 Feb 13 M179-53
Fr 1822 Mar 05 DLC-31
Fr 1822 Mar 05* M40-17
To 1822 Mar 16 DLC-72
To 1822 Mar 21 M179-53
To 1822 Mar 25 M179-53
To 1822 Mar 25* DLC-63
To 1822 May 19 M179-54
To 1822 May 19* DLC-63
Fr 1822 Jun 05 DLC-31
Fr 1822 Jun 05* M40-17
Fr 1824 Jan 06 M40-18
Maury Thomas W et al
Fr 1837 Feb 06 DLC-50
To 1837 Feb 14 DLC-50
Maxcy Virgil
Fr 1829 Mar 30 M639-3
Fr 1830 Jun 15 15-1459
Fr 1830 Oct 15 16-0391
To 1830 Nov 06 16-0655
To 1830 Nov 06 16-0657
To 1831 Mar 10 17-0835
To 1831 Sep 01 18-0650
Fr 1832 May 14 20-0506
Fr 1832 Jul 13 20-1068
To 1833 Oct 09 23-0993
Fr 1833 Oct 26 23-1092
To 1833 Oct 28 23-1107
Fr 1833 Nov 07 23-1197
To 1833 Nov 09 23-1213
Fr 1833 Nov 23 23-1307
Fr 1834 Apr 10 25-0669
Fr 1834 Apr 17 25-0827
Fr 1834 Nov 08# 26-0852
To 1836 Feb 09# 30-0340
Fr 1836 Apr 07 30-1109
Fr 1836 Jun 20# 31-0524
Fr 1836 Oct 05 32-0064
Fr 1836 Oct 17 M639-19
Fr 1836 Oct 17* 32-0217
Fr 1837 Feb 07 33-0469
Fr 1837 Feb 11 33-0625
Maxey Powhatan Wooldrige
To 1840 Jul 21 chk DLC-53
Fr 1844 Mar 23 36-0397
To 1844 Mar 23 36-0398
Maxey & Hagen
Fr 1839 Aug 08# fin DLC-52
Maxwell George P
Fr 1831 cJan 28 M639-1
Maxwell Lewis
Fr 1829 Jul 25 M639-2
Maxwell William
Fr 1836 May 30 31-0205
May Andrew Jackson
To 1842 Dec 35-1016
Fr 1842 Dec 14 DLC-54
May Dulce
To 1813 Sep 04 chk DLC-6
May Francis
Re 1798 Jan 22 mem 1-0585
To 1806 Apr 15 DLC-3
May Frederick
Fr 1829 Dec 22 M639-21
May George
To 1844 Jun 06 36-0589
May Leroy
To 1814 Mar 07 DLC-9
May William L
Fr 1829 Nov 20 14-0540
Fr 1836 Mar 30 30-0916
Fr 1836 Oct 01 31-1572
To 1837 Jun 01 33-1270
Mayer Brantz
Fr 1838 Mar 08 DLC-51
Mayer Charles F et al
Fr 1833 Jan 21-1262
Mayer George Louis
Fr 1833 Feb 12 DLC-42
Fr 1833 Feb 12* DLC-73
Mayfield Catherine
Fr 1836 Sep 24 31-1505

Mayfield George
To 1814 Aug 11 chk DLC-11
Fr 1814 Oct 10 DLC-13
To 1814 Oct 22 DLC-62
Fr 1814 Nov 02 DLC-13
To 1816 Oct 31 chk DLC-21
Mayfield James S
Fr 1834 Nov 19 26-0957
Maynard Otis G
Fr 1842 Feb 02 DLC-54
Mayo Robert
Fr 1829 Aug 13# 37-0503
Fr 1830 Dec 02 16-0974
Fr 1831 Jun 03 17-1496
To 1831 Jun 23# DLC-40
Fr 1833 Feb 28 22-0547
Fr 1833 Mar 09 M222-31
Fr 1834 Jul 03 M639-15
Fr 1835 Feb 12 M639-15
Re 1835 Sep 18 par 29-0077
Fr 1835 Oct 09 M639-15
Fr 1836 Oct 03 32-0047
Re 1839 May 15 leg DLC-52
Re 1839 May 15* leg 34-0791
Mayrant Robert P
Re 1830 Mar 25 M273-23
Mayson Charles C et al
Fr 1835 Apr 06 M639-11
Maywood R C
To 1835 Dec 07 29-0782
Mazzuchelli Samuel Charles
Fr 1835 May 10 M234-777
McAdams William R
Fr 1836 Nov M22-41
McAfee Robert Breckinridge
Fr 1816 Feb 26 DLC-71
Fr 1829 Apr 22 M639-15
Fr 1830 Aug 23 DLC-38
Fr 1831 Mar 22 DLC-73
Fr 1836 Jun 03 DLC-48
Fr 1836 Jun 30 31-0664
Fr 1843 Jan 07 DLC-55
To 1843 Jan 14 DLC-55
Fr 1844 Feb 06 DLC-56
To 1844 Feb 20 36-0322
To 1844 Feb 20* DLC-56
Fr 1844 Nov 23 36-1046
McAfee Robert Breckinridge et al
Fr 1829 Feb 19 M639-2
Fr 1844 Dec 12 DLC-57
McAlester A et al
Fr 1829 Sep 17 13-1344
McAllister John & Co
Fr 1831 Oct 13 fin DLC-40
Re 1831 Nov 10 fin 18-1237
McAllister Matthew
Fr 1815 Feb 27 DLC-17
McAllister Matthew Hall
Fr 1834 Oct 12# 26-0600
Fr 1844 Dec 02 36-1116
McAlpin James
Fr 1798 Mar 15 fin 1-0639
McBee Silas
Fr 1820 May 01 M221-21
McBride William
Fr 1829 Jan 24 M639-15
McCahen John J
Fr 1841 Jun 17 35-0333
Fr 1844 May 01 DLC-56
McCaleb James
To 1811 Dec 28 fin 2-1030
McCall ______ (Dr)
To 1824 Oct 14 10-0942
McCall George Archibald
Fr 1836 Sep 13# M567-124
McCall William
Fr 1814 Jan 03 DLC-8
McCalla John M
To 1830 Oct 11 16-0369
To 1837 Apr 01 33-1137
McCalla John M et al
To 1840 Jul 02 34-1460
McCallum A T K
Fr 1836 Dec 23 32-1287
Fr 1836 Dec 23 DLC-49
To 1836 Dec 26 DLC-49
To 1836 Dec 26* 32-1325
McCalpin Robert
Fr 1814 Jan 05 DLC-8
To 1814 Jan 07 DLC-61
McCandless William
To 1814 Jan 02 DLC-61
McCanter Amos
Re 1813 Jan 25 DLC-61
McCaraher Alexander
Fr 1832 Nov 17 M222-31
McCarney Thomas
To 1819 Mar 08 7-0416
McCarrick William
Fr 1831 Jan 08 M22-27
McCarthy Michael
Re 1833 Jun 01 par 22-1547
McCarty Abner
Fr 1835 Jul 04 28-0927
Fr 1835 Nov 09 DLC-47
McCarty Benjamin
Fr 1828 Oct 07 12-0226
McCarty Jonathan
Fr 1835 Dec 19 M639-11
McCarty William Mason
Fr 1829 Jun 10 13-0619
McCauley Daniel Smith
Fr 1829 Nov 23 M639-15
Re 1831 Jul 29 18-0311
McCausland Robert
Fr 1815 Jan 13 4-0533
Fr 1815 Jan 27 4-0640
To 1815 Jan 27# 4-0627
Fr 1815 Jan 28 4-0643
Fr 1815 Feb 16 DLC-16
Fr 1815 Feb 20 DLC-16
Fr 1815 Feb 24 DLC-17
Fr 1815 Mar 02 DLC-17
McClary Benjamin
Fr 1835 Oct 24 29-0342
McClean Hackett
To 1801 Oct 09 lnd 1-0934
McCleary Samuel
Fr 1844 Dec 23 DLC-57
McCleary Samuel F
Fr 1833 Jun 22# 23-0051
McCleland James A
Fr 1837 Jan 16 M687-21
McClellan David
Fr 1814 Jul 05 DLC-11
Fr 1814 Aug 16 DLC-11
Fr 1814 Sep 13 DLC-12
Fr 1814 Nov 01 DLC-13

McClellan David (cont)
Fr 1816 Jun 17 DLC-21
Fr 1829 Dec 02 M234-184
Fr 1831 Aug 01 DLC-39
Fr 1836 Jun 30 31-0666
McClellan George et al
Fr 1836 Jun 25 M567-122
McClellan John
Fr 1808 Feb 08 DLC-4
McClellan William
Fr 1813 Oct 09 DLC-61
Fr 1813 Oct 13 DLC-6
Fr 1813 Oct 14 3-0529
Fr 1813 Oct 14* DLC-61
To 1813 Oct 18 DLC-7
Fr 1814 Jul 10 DLC-11
Fr 1814 Aug 26 DLC-11
Fr 1814 Oct 28 DLC-13
Fr 1814 Nov 22 DLC-14
Fr 1821 Jun 27 DLC-30
Fr 1823 Oct 18 DLC-32
McClelland John
Fr 1814 Jul 12 DLC-11
McClintock John et al
Fr 1830 Nov 27 16-0894
McClung Charles
To 1801 Apr 1-0859
Fr 1806 Dec 14 DLC-4
Fr 1809 DLC-75
Fr 1814 Nov 01 DLC-13
Fr 1817 Sep 08 DLC-23
Fr 1822 Jun 03 DLC-31
To 1832 Aug 10 lnd 20-1273
McClung James W et al
Fr 1829 Jun M639-21
Fr 1829 Oct 17 M639-3
Fr 1836 Jan 08 M639-5
Fr 1836 Nov 30 M687-33
McClure Charles
Fr 1837 Jan 25 33-0154
McClure Charles et al
Fr 1836 Mar 23 M639-18
McClure Robert et al
Fr 1829 Feb 20 M639-14
McClure William
Fr 1840 Feb 06# fin DLC-53
McCluskey George
Fr 1812 Jan 02 M221-42
McClusky ______
Fr 1831 Nov 19 M22-28
McCollum Joel
Fr 1844 Dec 20 DLC-57
McComb Sophiah
Fr 1815 May 29 DLC-18
McCombs & Robinson
Fr 1828 Dec 23 12-0332
Fr 1836 Jul 18# fin DLC-48
McConnell Alexander E
Fr 1829 Oct 15 M567-54
McConnell Richard
Fr 1844 Dec 11 36-1169
McConnell Robert
Re 1798 Aug 18 leg 1-0673
Re 1799 May 28 leg 1-0717
McCook George
Fr 1828 Jan 04 DLC-35
McCord James
Fr 1835 Oct 09 29-0262
McCorkle Miles Blythe
Fr 1823 Nov 05 fin DLC-33
Fr 1824 Aug 03 10-0841
To 1826 Jan 21 fin 11-0112
Fr 1827 Jul 17 fin DLC-34
Fr 1829 Jan 06 fin DLC-36
Fr 1832 Feb 17 fin DLC-44
Fr 1833 Apr 19 DLC-42
Fr 1845 May 30 DLC-58
McCorry Thomas
To 1821 Jan 11 8-0061
Fr 1821 Feb 27 DLC-29
To 1821 Mar 06 8-0155
McCoun William T et al
Fr 1834 Jun 03 M639-9
Fr 1834 Jun 03* M687-13
McCown John Porter
Fr 1836 Oct M22-41
McCoy A
Fr 1816 Nov 08 DLC-21
Fr 1817 Jun 26 M208-7
McCoy Ananias
To 1795 Nov 01 fin 1-0326
McCoy Isaac
Fr 1829 Feb 09# 12-0488
Re 1831 Feb 11 M234-300
Fr 1832 Apr 07 M22-29
McCoy William
Fr 1829 May 23 M639-18
Fr 1829 Jul 24 M639-18
Fr 1830 Dec 25 M22-27
Fr 1831 Mar 19 M639-18
To 1831 Dec 01# M639-18
Fr 1831 Dec 08 M639-18
McCoy & Co
Fr 1822 Dec 13 DLC-31
McCoy & Scallan
Fr 1821 Dec 12 DLC-31
McCracken Henry F
Fr 1831 Mar 13 M22-27
Fr 1831 Jul 23 18-0251
Fr 1831 Dec 03 M22-28
McCrate John D
Fr 1836 Jun 01 M687-20
McCrea John
Fr 1819 Apr 15 DLC-26
McCrea John et al
Fr 1834 Sep 01 M639-10
McCreary Robert et al
Fr 1835 cJan DLC-59
McCreery William
Fr 1829 Mar 28 M639-6
Fr 1831 Nov 02 M639-1
McCreery William W
Fr 1836 Aug 15 M567-128
McCrory James
Fr 1829 Aug 10 13-1066
McCrory Thomas
Fr 1812 Jun 22 DLC-5
McCullers William
Fr 1833 Aug 21 M234-223
McCulloch John
To 1807 Feb 07 fin DLC-4
To 1807 Feb 07 fin DLC-4
McCulloh Alexander H
Fr 1833 Dec 10 24-0441
McCullough James
Fr 1834 Jan 10 DLC-44
McCullough Samuel D
Fr 1845 May 05 DLC-58
McCully James
To 1825 Oct 21 fin DLC-33

McCully James & Mary
Fr 1826 Jul 11 fin DLC-33
McCully William
Fr 1821 Sep 29 DLC-72
McCurdy Dennis
Fr 1835 Jun 11 28-0641
McCutchings Samuel
Re 1845 May 12# leg 37-0201
McCutchon Samuel
Fr 1824 Feb 08 M688-29
Fr 1828 Jun 20 DLC-35
McDaniel Collin
Fr 1814 Dec 04 DLC-14
Fr 1815 Sep 10 DLC-71
Fr 1829 May 21 M688-68
McDaniel George
Re 1836 Jul 09 par 31-1024
McDaniel James
Re 1831 May 19 par 17-1396
McDaniel Mary
Fr 1815 Dec 24# fin DLC-68
McDonald Charles James
Fr 1844 Feb 03 DLC-56
McDonald James
Fr 1816 Jul 16 DLC-21
Fr 1817 Apr 01 DLC-22
McDonald John et al
Fr 1831 cFeb 01 M639-2
McDonald Joshua P
Fr 1835 Jun 27 M234-136
McDonald Moses
Fr 1837 Feb 13 M687-16
McDonald William
Fr 1816 Jul 22 DLC-21
McDonell John
Fr 1832 Jul 26 DLC-41
McDonnell John
Fr 1838 Mar 11 DLC-51
McDonough Anthony A
Fr 1834 Jan 25 DLC-44
McDonough Margaret
Fr 1832 May 13 M688-83
Fr 1832 Dec 05 21-0869
McDowell James
Fr 1840 Feb 26 DLC-52
To 1840 Mar 10 DLC-52
To 1840 Mar 10* 34-1254
McDowell John
Fr 1831 Nov 05 M639-18
McDowell Joseph
Fr 1798 Apr 26 DLC-2
Fr 1799 Feb 03 DLC-2
McDuell George
Fr 1837 Feb 18 fin DLC-50
McDuffie George
Fr 1829 Mar 17 M639-4
McElderry Hugh
Fr 1830 cNov 06 M639-12
Fr 1833 Nov 11 M688-88
Fr 1836 Nov 18 32-0557
McElhenney James A
Fr 1828 Jun 30 DLC-35
To 1828 Aug 06 DLC-35
McEllroy William et al
Fr 1829 Apr 04 M639-6
McElroy Joseph
Fr 1835 Feb 18 DLC-45
McElvain John
Fr 1829 Apr 02 M222-26
Fr 1835 Mar 24 M639-3
McElyea Patrick
To 1807 Jan 17 fin DLC-4
To 1807 Jan 31 fin DLC-4
McEvers LeRoy
Fr 1836 Feb 07 M639-15
McEwen Alexander
Fr 1829 Feb 12-0478
McEwen James
Fr 1813 Mar 08 DLC-6
McFaddin Elias
To 1804 Dec 20 fin DLC-3
McFall Henry
Fr 1807 Jun 15 fin DLC-4
Fr 1808 Apr 15 DLC-4
McFarland Alexander
Fr 1834 Nov 15 DLC-45
McFarland John
Fr 1824 Aug 14 DLC-72
McFarland Samuel
Fr 1830 Jun 24 15-1522
To 1830 Jun 24 15-1523
McFarlane J S
Fr 1845 Jan 21 36-1389
McGahey Daniel
Fr 1814 Aug 02 DLC-11
Fr 1814 Aug 07 DLC-11
McGavock David
Fr 1823 Nov 03 DLC-32
McGavock David & Randal
Fr 1797 Nov 18 fin DLC-2
McGavock Frank et al
Fr 1835 Jan 17 M639-9
McGavock Jacob
Fr 1835 Jan 08 M639-9
McGavock John et al
Fr 1838 Sep 14 DLC-51
To 1838 Sep 18 34-0457
McGavock Randal
Fr 1806 Aug 23 2-0317
McGhee Barclay H
To 1814 Feb 02 DLC-61
Fr 1814 Apr 11 DLC-10
McGilvery William
Fr 1835 Nov 10 29-0490
Fr 1844 Jun 16 DLC-74
McGinnis Polly
Re 1803 Sep 29 leg 1-1173
McGirk Andrew S
Re 1830 mem DLC-38
McGirtt Zachariah
Fr 1819 Apr 24 DLC-26
To 1819 May 24 DLC-63
McGown James
Re 1829 Jul 29 par 13-0993
Re 1829 Jul 29* par T967-1
McGregor Flowers
To 1807 Feb 26 fin DLC-4
McGregor John
Fr 1821 May 12 DLC-30
McGriffin Joseph
Re 1801 Oct 09 mem DLC-60
McGuire Bernard
Fr 1841 Jan 08 DLC-53
McGuire James
Fr 1844 Dec 03 36-1119
McGuire Margaret
Fr 1836 Apr 25 M567-127
McHatton Robert Lytle
Fr 1829 Feb 20 M639-2

McHatton Robert Lytle et al
Fr 1829 Mar 04 M639-23
McHenry James (1753-1816)
Fr 1796 Jan 05 1-0339
To 1798 Feb 12 1-0613
Fr 1798 Feb 13 1-0617
Fr 1798 Mar 07 1-0637
McHenry James (1785-1845)
Fr 1832 Jan 16 M639-15
McHenry John
Fr 1841 Sep 18 DLC-53
McHenry Robert W
Fr 1832 Jun 30 20-0843
McIlvaine John
Fr 1831 Jun 12 17-1576
McIlvaine Joseph B
Fr 1832 Nov 08# fin DLC-41
McIntire Rufus
Fr 1835 Sep 16 M639-17
Fr 1836 Apr 18 30-1235
Fr 1837 Feb 21 M687-16
McIntire Rufus et al
Fr 1832 Jan 19 M639-26
McIntosh George
Fr 1833 Jul 31 DLC-43
To 1833 Jul 31 DLC-43
McIntosh James Simmons
Fr 1836 Jan 22 30-0181
McIntosh John
To 1814 Nov 16 DLC-62
Fr 1814 Dec 18 4-0418
To 1815 Feb 22 DLC-17
Fr 1815 Feb 23 4-0783
To 1815 Mar 13 DLC-17
Fr 1815 Mar 19 DLC-17
McIntosh John H Jr et al
Fr 1832 Jan 25 M567-76
McIntosh John N
Fr 1818 Mar 14 DLC-24
Fr 1818 Mar 15 DLC-24
Fr 1818 Mar 16 DLC-24
Fr 1818 Mar 19 DLC-24
Fr 1818 Mar 25 DLC-24
Fr 1818 Mar 25 DLC-24
Fr 1818 Mar 26 DLC-24
Fr 1818 Mar 27 DLC-24
Fr 1818 Apr 06 DLC-24
Fr 1818 Apr 08 DLC-24
McIntosh Lachlan
Fr 1798 Nov 06 DLC-2
McIntosh Mary M
Fr 1836 Aug 22 DLC-48
McIntosh Roley
Fr 1830 Feb 25 M234-236
Fr 1830 Feb 27 M234-236
Fr 1830 Mar 22 M234-236
McIntosh Roley et al
Fr 1829 Mar 07 M234-236
Fr 1829 Jun 22 M234-236
Fr 1831 Oct 25 M234-236
Fr 1831 Oct 25* M234-237
Fr 1831 Oct 25* 18-1123
Fr 1831 Oct 29 M234-236
Fr 1831 Oct 29* 18-1145
Fr 1834 Jul 08 M234-236
McIntosh William
To 1814 Feb 17 DLC-61
To 1815 Mar 03 DLC-62
Fr 1816 Aug 22 5-0439
Re 1816 Oct 04 5-0530
Fr 1818 Feb 23 DLC-24
Fr 1818 Feb 26 DLC-24
Fr 1818 Feb 27 DLC-24
Fr 1818 Mar 16 DLC-24
Fr 1818 Mar 19 DLC-24
To 1818 Mar 22 6-0085
Fr 1818 Mar 24 DLC-24
To 1818 Apr 14 6-0349
Fr 1818 Apr 24 DLC-24
Fr 1818 May 05 6-0644
To 1818 Jul 08 6-1116
To 1818 Jul 08* M221-78
To 1821 Sep 19 M221-93
To 1821 Sep 19* DLC-63
Fr 1821 Nov 02 M221-93
McJilton & Cannon
Fr 1831 May 22 M124-128
McKain Alexander
To 1813 Feb 19 DLC-61
Re 1813 Feb 20 DLC-61
McKain James
Fr 1793 Jul 02 fin 1-0160
Fr 1793 Jul 02 fin 1-0161
Re 1807 Sep 15 leg 2-0555
McKain Joseph
Re 1807 Mar leg 2-0469
McKamey Alexander D
Fr 1814 Jan 31 DLC-8
Fr 1814 Feb 25 DLC-62
McKean Joseph W
Fr 1822 Dec 02 DLC-31
McKean Maria P
Fr c1814# 3-0777
Fr 1814 Mar 08# 3-0905
Fr 1814 Nov 01# DLC-13
Fr c1815# 4-0479
McKean Samuel
Fr 1830 Jan 18# 14-1460
McKean Samuel et al
Fr 1835 cNov M639-27
McKean Samuel M
Fr 1835 Jun 11 mem 28-0651
McKee James S
Fr 1843 Jul 13 DLC-55
McKee John
To 1793 Jan 30 1-0138
To 1794 May 16 1-0232
To 1813 Oct 24 DLC-61
Fr 1813 Dec 24 3-0710
Fr 1814 Jan 06 DLC-8
Fr 1814 Jan 06 DLC-8
Fr 1814 Jan 26 DLC-8
To 1814 Feb 03 DLC-61
Fr 1814 Feb 26 DLC-9
Fr 1814 Aug 09 DLC-11
To 1814 Aug 23 DLC-62
To 1814 Aug 25 DLC-62
To 1814 Aug 26 DLC-62
Fr 1814 Aug 27 DLC-11
Fr 1814 Sep 09 DLC-12
Fr 1814 Sep 13 DLC-12
To 1814 Sep 15 DLC-62
Fr 1814 Sep 15 DLC-12
Fr 1814 Sep 21 DLC-12
Fr 1814 Sep 27 DLC-12
To 1814 Oct 19 DLC-62
To 1814 Oct 31 DLC-62
Fr 1814 Nov 19 DLC-14

Fr 1814 Nov 22 DLC-14
Fr 1814 Nov 30 DLC-14
Fr 1814 Dec 06 DLC-14
To 1814 Dec 22 DLC-62
Fr 1814 Dec 22 DLC-14
Fr 1814 Dec 22 DLC-14
Fr 1814 Dec 28 DLC-15
Fr 1815 Jan 14 4-0544
Fr 1815 Jan 24 4-0610
Fr 1815 Mar 01 4-0809
To 1815 Sep 08 DLC-62
Fr 1816 Jul 20 DLC-21
To 1818 Oct 20 6-1377
To 1819 Apr 22 DLC-63
To 1819 Apr 22* M271-2
To 1819 Apr 22* 7-0493
Fr 1819 Jul 31 7-0591
To 1819 Aug 04 DLC-63
Fr 1819 Aug 13 M271-2
Fr 1819 Aug 13* 7-0605
Fr 1820 Jun 09 DLC-29
To 1820 Jul 21 7-1175
To 1820 Aug 24 7-1216
To 1820 Aug 31 7-1224
Fr 1820 Oct 24 DLC-29
To 1823 Apr 14 9-0520
Fr 1823 Oct 14 DLC-32
McKee Thomas et al
Fr 1835 cApr 27-1426
McKeever Isaac
To 1818 Mar 25 M125-58
To 1820 Aug 19 DLC-29
To 1826 Feb 03 DLC-33
Fr 1827 Oct 12 DLC-34
Fr c1829 12-0377
Fr 1830 Apr 14 15-0694
Fr 1830 Nov 07 16-0675
Fr 1832 Oct 17 DLC-41
Fr 1836 Nov 08 M639-27
McKeever M F
Fr 1845 Jan 06 DLC-57
McKeige William
Re 1834 Jun 11 mem 25-1299
McKelden William P
Fr 1834 May 31 fin DLC-44
Fr 1834 Aug 02 fin DLC-44
Fr 1834 Aug 09 fin DLC-44
Fr 1834 Aug 16 fin DLC-44
Fr 1834 Aug 23 fin DLC-44
Fr 1834 Aug 30 fin DLC-44
Fr 1834 Oct 04 fin DLC-44
Fr 1834 Oct 11 fin DLC-44
Fr 1834 Oct 18 fin DLC-44
Fr 1834 Oct 25 fin DLC-44
Re 1834 Nov 01 fin DLC-44
Fr 1834 Nov 08 fin DLC-45
Fr 1834 Nov 15 fin DLC-45
Fr 1834 Nov 22 fin DLC-45
Fr 1834 Nov 29 fin DLC-45
Fr 1834 Dec 06 fin DLC-45
Fr 1834 Dec 13 fin DLC-45
Fr 1834 Dec 20 fin DLC-45
Fr 1834 Dec 27 fin DLC-45
Fr 1835 Jan 03 fin DLC-45
Fr 1835 Jan 10 fin DLC-45
Fr 1835 Jan 17 fin DLC-45
Fr 1835 Jan 24 fin DLC-45
Fr 1835 Jan 31 fin DLC-45
Fr 1835 Apr 04 fin DLC-46
Fr 1835 Apr 11 fin DLC-46
Fr 1835 Apr 18 fin DLC-46
Fr 1835 Apr 25 fin DLC-46
Fr 1835 Jun 06 fin DLC-46
Fr 1835 Jun 13 fin DLC-46
Fr 1835 Jun 20 fin DLC-46
Fr 1835 Jun 27 fin DLC-46
Fr 1835 Jul 04 fin DLC-46
Fr 1835 Jul 11 fin DLC-46
Fr 1835 Jul 18 fin DLC-46
Fr 1835 Jul 25 fin DLC-46
Fr 1835 Aug 08 fin DLC-46
Fr 1835 Aug 16 fin DLC-46
Fr 1835 Aug 22 fin DLC-46
Fr 1835 Aug 29 fin DLC-46
Fr 1835 Oct 03 fin DLC-47
Fr 1835 Oct 10 fin DLC-47
Fr 1835 Oct 17 fin DLC-47
Fr 1835 Oct 24 fin DLC-47
Fr 1835 Oct 31 fin DLC-47
Fr 1835 Nov 07 fin DLC-47
Fr 1835 Nov 14 fin DLC-47
Fr 1835 Nov 21 fin DLC-47
Fr 1835 Nov 28 fin DLC-47
Fr 1835 Dec 05 fin DLC-47
Fr 1835 Dec 12 fin DLC-47
Fr 1835 Dec 19 fin DLC-47
Fr 1835 Dec 26 fin DLC-47
Fr 1836 Feb 06 fin DLC-47
Fr 1836 Feb 13 fin DLC-47
Fr 1836 Feb 20 fin DLC-47
Fr 1836 Feb 27 fin DLC-47
Fr 1836 Apr 02 fin DLC-47
Fr 1836 Apr 09 fin DLC-48
Fr 1836 Apr 16 fin DLC-48
Fr 1836 Apr 23 fin DLC-48
Fr 1836 Apr 30 fin DLC-48
Fr 1836 May 07 fin DLC-48
Fr 1836 May 14 fin DLC-48
Fr 1836 May 21 fin DLC-48
Fr 1836 May 28 fin DLC-48
McKellup James
Re 1836 Apr 27 par 30-1395
McKenney Thomas Loraine
Fr 1829 Apr 23 M21-5
McKennie C P
To 1832 Mar 22 chk DLC-40
McKenzie Hugh
Re 1833 Aug 30 par 23-0547
McKenzie J
Fr 1814 Aug 10 DLC-11
McKenzie James
Fr 1829 Jun 27 13-0735
McKeon John
Fr 1836 Mar 26 30-0905
McKeon John et al
Fr 1836 Oct M22-41
McKibbin Joseph
Fr 1838 Mar 09 34-0271
To 1838 Mar 13 34-0274
McKiernan & Stout
To 1811 Mar 01 fin DLC-6
Fr 1814 Jul 25 fin DLC-68
To 1815 Feb 07 chk DLC-16
Fr 1815 Jun 15 fin 4-1080
To 1815 Jun 15 chk DLC-18
To 1815 Sep 27 chk DLC-19
Fr 1816 Oct 17 DLC-69
Fr 1817 May 15 fin DLC-28

McKillian Joseph			
	Re 1839 Sep#	leg	34-0894
McKim Alexander			
	Fr 1829 Mar 16		M639-3
McKim Isaac			
	Fr 1833 Apr 03		M639-2
	Fr 1833 Apr 17		M124-137
	Fr 1834 Mar 27		M688-79
	Fr 1834 Dec 24		M639-11
	Fr 1835 Oct 20		M124-149
	Fr 1836 Feb 17		M639-17
	Fr 1836 Mar 14		M687-15
McKim Isaac et al			
	Fr 1829 Mar		M639-15
	Fr 1830 Sep 27		M639-1
	Fr 1832 Mar		M639-18
	Fr 1835 Mar		M639-8
	Fr 1836 Nov		M22-41
McKim John			
	Fr 1829 Feb 23		M222-26
	Fr 1831 Jan 22		M124-126
	Fr 1831 Jan 28		M124-126
McKinley John			
	Fr 1829 Aug 15		M639-16
	Fr 1832 Feb 14		M688-85
	Fr 1833 Jul 08		M639-26
	Fr 1835 Nov 17		M639-9
	Fr 1837 Apr 14		DLC-50
McKinney Henry			
	To 1802 May 10		DLC-2
McKinney Hinton			
	Re 1829 Jul 01	par	13-0776
	Re 1829 Jul 03	par	13-0810
	Re 1829 Jul 03*	par	T967-1
McKinney John A			
	Fr 1834 Aug 09		DLC-44
	To 1834 Aug 10		26-0304
McKinney John V			
	Fr 1813 Aug 28		DLC-6
McKinser M			
	Fr 1814 Aug 31		DLC-12
McKinsey James			
	Fr 1804 Feb 22	fin	1-1284
	Re 1804 Sep 21	leg	1-1388
McKinsey Michael			
	Fr 1819 May 01		M439-11
McKinstry David C et al			
	Fr 1831 Jul 26		M639-15
McKissack William D et al			
	Fr 1835 Oct		M639-9
McKissick James			
	Fr 1826 Jul 07	add	11-0291
	To 1826 Jul 07	add	11-0296
McKnew Z W			
	Fr 1832 Jul 23		M639-15
McKnight John			
	Fr 1838 Apr 19		DLC-51
McKnight Samuel B			
	Re 1814 Jan 29		DLC-8
	Fr 1818 Jun 14	fin	DLC-69
	Fr 1818 Jun 14*	fin	6-1051
McKnight William			
	Fr 1817 Nov 24	fin	5-1147
	Fr 1818 May 11	fin	6-0689
	Fr 1821 Nov	fin	8-1326
	Fr 1821 Nov 07	fin	DLC-29
McLanahan James J			
	Fr 1829 Mar 06		M639-15
McLane Allen			
	Fr 1819 Jan 28		DLC-26
	Fr 1831 Jun 23#		DLC-40
McLane Louis			
	Re 1829 Apr 18		13-0068
	To 1829 Jun 02		13-0549
	Fr 1830 Jan 22		DLC-37
	Fr 1830 Feb 06		DLC-37
	To 1830 Mar 17		DLC-38
	Fr 1830 Apr 17		M639-9
	To 1830 Jun 01		15-1246
	To c1831		17-0092
	To 1831 Mar 08		DLC-73
	Fr 1831 Jun 06		17-1550
	Fr 1831 Jul 28		M30-33
	Fr 1831 Aug 02		18-0397
	Re 1831 Aug 08		18-0479
	Fr 1831 Sep 08#	fin	18-0702
	To 1831 Sep 13		M221-111
	To 1831 Sep 13*		18-0719
	To 1831 Oct 05		M234-74
	Fr 1831 Oct 17		M639-24
	Fr 1831 Oct 28		18-1144
	To 1831 Nov 14		DLC-40
	Fr 1831 Nov 14		DLC-40
	Fr 1831 Dec 26		19-0422
	Fr 1832 cJan 01		M179-72
	Fr 1832 Feb 28		19-1252
	Fr 1832 Apr 16		20-0249
	Fr 1832 Apr 23		20-0351
	Fr 1832 Apr 23		20-0353
	Fr 1832 May 05		DLC-40
	Fr 1832 Jul 19		M179-74
	Fr 1832 Aug 03		DLC-41
	Fr 1832 Aug 22		20-1378
	Fr 1832 Oct 23		21-0137
	To 1833 Jan 07#		21-1348
	To 1833 Jan 22#		22-0019
	To 1833 Jan 22*		M733-1
	Fr 1833 Jan 23		22-0034
	Fr 1833 Jan 25		22-0068
	To 1833 Jan 30#		DLC-42
	To 1833 Feb 08#		M221-113
	To 1833 Feb 15#		22-0388
	To 1833 Feb 15*		M733-1
	Fr 1833 Mar 25#	fin	22-0893
	Fr 1833 Apr 05		22-0946
	Fr 1833 Apr 05*		M733-1
	Fr 1833 Apr 06#	fin	22-0959
	Fr 1833 Apr 08		M733-1
	Fr 1833 Apr 09		M415-1
	Fr 1833 Apr 12		22-1002
	Fr 1833 Apr 12*		M415-1
	Fr 1833 Apr 13		22-1009
	To 1833 Apr 16#		22-1032
	Fr 1833 Apr 18		M415-1
	Fr 1833 Apr 20		M415-1
	Fr 1833 Apr 20*		22-1063
	Fr 1833 Apr 22		M415-1
	Fr 1833 Apr 22*		22-1145
	Fr 1833 Apr 26		22-1185
	Fr 1833 Apr 29		22-1211
	Fr 1833 Apr 29*		M415-1
	Fr 1833 May 01		22-1257
	Fr 1833 May 07		22-1315
	Fr 1833 May 07*		M415-1
	Re 1833 May 13		22-1360
	Fr 1833 May 18		M415-1
	Fr 1833 May 20		DLC-42

Re 1833 May 29 22-1513
Fr 1833 Jul 08 23-0095
To 1833 Jul 16# M179-76
To 1833 Jul 30# M639-6
Fr 1833 Jul 31 23-0244
Fr 1833 Aug 01 23-0256
Fr 1833 Aug 18 23-0367
Fr 1833 Aug 29 M179-77
Fr 1833 Aug 29* M40-24
Fr 1833 Oct 09 23-0995
Fr 1833 Oct 28 T20-6
Fr 1833 Oct 28* 23-1109
To 1833 Nov 09# M639-19
To 1833 Nov 16 M179-75
Fr 1833 Nov 19 23-1256
To 1834 Jan 07# T1-7
Fr 1834 Jan 11 24-0860
Fr 1834 Jan 20 24-1005
Fr 1834 Jan 22 24-1028
Fr 1834 Jan 25 24-1058
Fr 1834 Feb 12 24-1293
Fr 1834 Feb 12 24-1295
To 1834 Feb 14 M179-77
Fr 1834 Feb 21 M40-24
Fr 1834 Feb 22 24-1445
Fr 1834 Mar 05 24-1576
Fr 1834 Mar 13 25-0205
Fr 1834 Mar 13* 25-0149
Fr 1834 Mar 14 25-0211
Fr 1834 Mar 19 25-0275
Fr 1834 Mar 20 25-0292
To 1834 Mar 24 M639-5
To 1834 Mar 24* 25-0346
Fr 1834 Mar 28 M179-77
To 1834 Mar 29# M179-77
Fr 1834 Mar 31 25-0513
Fr 1834 Apr 03 25-0580
Fr 1834 Apr 04 M124-142
Fr 1834 Apr 04* 25-0586
To 1834 Apr 07# M179-78
Fr 1834 Apr 10 25-0671
Fr 1834 Apr 10 M179-82
Fr 1834 Apr 10* 25-0675
Fr 1834 Apr 10 25-0677
To 1834 Apr 10 25-0679
To 1834 Apr 10 M179-78
To 1834 Apr 18# DLC-44
Fr 1834 Apr 22 25-0859
To 1834 Apr 22 M179-78
Fr 1834 Apr 23 M179-78
Fr 1834 Apr 24 25-0882
To 1834 Apr 30# M179-78
To 1834 May 05# M179-78
To 1834 May 07# M179-78
To 1834 May 29# M179-78
To 1834 Jun 10# M639-15
To 1834 Jun 11# M179-78
Fr 1834 Jun 13 25-1331
To 1834 Jun 14 DLC-44
Fr 1834 Jun 21 M639-2
Fr 1834 Jun 21* 25-1473

McLannahan Samuel
Fr 1840 Oct 08 add 35-0057

McLaughlin James A
Re 1842 Dec 21 mem DLC-74
Re 1842 Dec 21 mem DLC-64
Fr 1843 Jan 03# DLC-55
Fr 1843 Jan 03# DLC-74
Fr 1843 Jan 26# DLC-74
Fr 1843 Feb 08# DLC-55
Fr 1843 Feb 14# DLC-74
To 1843 Feb 25# DLC-74
Fr 1843 Mar 08# 35-1276
Re 1843 Mar 11 35-1277
Fr 1843 Mar 13# DLC-74
Fr 1843 Mar 15# DLC-74
Fr 1843 Apr 17 35-1308
Fr 1843 Apr 20 DLC-55
Fr 1843 May 27 DLC-55

McLaughlin Robert K
Fr 1835 Feb 14 DLC-45

McLaughlin William H et al
Fr 1825 Jul 01 10-1331
To 1825 Jul 01 10-1333

McLean Alexander Clinton
Fr 1833 May 08# 22-1321

McLean Charles D
To 1818 Oct 19 6-1376
Fr 1836 Aug 25 DLC-49

McLean John (IL)
Fr 1829 Mar 09 M639-26

McLean John (OH)
To 1824 Mar 22 DLC-32
To 1824 Mar 22* 10-0571
Fr 1825 Jan 25 M601-30
Fr 1825 Jan 26 M601-30
Fr 1827 Feb 03 DLC-34
Fr 1827 Feb 03* M601-34
To 1827 Mar 06 DLC-34
To 1827 Aug 21 DLC-34
To 1827 Aug 21* 11-0806
Fr 1827 Sep 22 DLC-34
Fr 1827 Sep 22* 11-0869
Fr 1829 Mar 09 12-0912
Fr 1829 Mar 31 M639-21
Fr 1829 Apr 16 M639-13

McLean M et al
Fr 1835 Apr 27-1500

McLean Nathaniel
Fr 1829 Apr 02 M222-26

McLean Thomas M
Re 1836 Apr 21 par 30-1284

McLemore ______
Re 1834 May 07 leg 25-0986

McLemore Charles
Fr 1835 Apr 07 27-1561
Fr 1835 Apr 07* M234-242

McLemore Charles et al
Fr 1835 Apr 08 27-1568

McLemore John Christmas
Fr 1822 Mar 29 DLC-31
To 1822 Apr 11 9-0106
Fr 1822 Apr 28 DLC-31
Fr 1822 Jun 25 DLC-31
Re 1823 Oct 13 mem DLC-32
To 1823 Oct 13 lnd 9-0686
Fr 1823 Oct 13 lnd DLC-32
Fr 1823 Oct 13* lnd 9-0693
To 1823 Nov 08 9-0740
Fr 1824 Jan 13 9-0922
To 1824 Jan 30 10-0417
Fr 1827 Nov 30 DLC-35
Fr 1829 Apr 09# M639-4
To 1829 Apr 26 DLC-37
To 1829 Apr 26* 13-0156
To 1829 May 03 13-0247
Fr 1829 May 11 M639-2
Fr 1829 Jun 25# M639-8

McLemore John Christmas (cont)
To 1829 cSep 15 13-1314
To 1829 Sep 28 13-1440
To 1829 Oct 04 14-0103
Fr 1829 Oct 06# M639-1
To 1829 Nov 24 14-0587
To 1830 Apr 30 15-0862
To 1830 Dec 25 16-1562
To 1831 Jun 27 18-0117
Fr 1831 Jul 29 18-0312
Fr 1831 Aug 19 DLC-39
To 1831 Oct 20# 18-1070
Fr 1832 Sep 25 DLC-41
To 1832 Sep 29 21-0052
To 1832 Sep 29* DLC-41
Fr 1835 Apr 06 27-1531
Fr 1835 Aug 14 28-1284
Fr 1835 Nov 25# DLC-47
To 1835 Dec 23 29-1316
Fr 1836 Jan 01# DLC-47
Fr 1837 Jul 07# DLC-50
McLemore John Christmas et al
Fr 1829 Jun 25 M639-8
Fr 1836 Apr 05 M234-137
McLemore John Coffee
Fr 1840 Apr 10 34-1299
McLene Jeremiah
Fr 1835 Mar 23 M639-3
McMahon J Ponte Coulant
Fr 1831 Mar 24 M22-27
McMahon John Van Lear
Fr 1829 Mar 16 M639-3
Fr 1830 Jan 23 M639-12
Fr 1830 Nov 06 M639-12
McMahon William
Fr 1834 Dec 30 M639-8
Fr 1836 Apr 08 M234-137
McMahon William et al
Fr 1836 Mar 21 M639-15
McMeans James R
Fr 1833 Sep 26 M639-3
McMillan John
Fr 1835 Nov 05 M639-18
McMinn Joseph
To 1815 Nov 22 DLC-19
To 1815 Nov 22* DLC-62
To 1816 Feb 13 4-1406
Fr 1816 Mar 29 DLC-20
Fr 1816 May 27 DLC-20
Fr 1816 May 27 DLC-20
Fr 1816 Jun 27 DLC-21
Fr 1816 Jun 27 DLC-21
Fr 1816 Jul 25 DLC-21
Fr 1816 Jul 30 DLC-21
Fr 1816 Aug 06 DLC-21
To 1816 Aug 12 5-0352
Fr 1816 Aug 30 DLC-21
Fr 1816 Aug 30 DLC-21
Fr 1816 cSep 01 DLC-23
Fr 1816 cSep 01 DLC-23
Fr 1816 Sep 02 DLC-21
Fr 1816 Sep 06 DLC-21
To 1816 Sep 15 5-0483
Fr 1816 Sep 25 DLC-21
To 1816 Oct 16 5-0536
Fr 1816 Oct 21 DLC-21
Fr 1816 Oct 25 DLC-21
Fr 1817 Jan 10 DLC-22
Fr 1817 Aug 25 5-0995
Fr 1817 Aug 29 DLC-23
Fr 1817 Sep 01 DLC-23
Fr 1817 Dec 31 5-1214
To 1818 Jan 11 5-1244
To 1818 Jan 19 DLC-24
To 1818 Jan 19* 5-1295
Fr 1818 Jun 20 DLC-25
Fr 1818 Jun 20* 6-1067
Fr 1818 Aug 27 DLC-25
Fr 1819 Apr 06 DLC-26
Fr 1819 Apr 06* 7-0463
Fr 1819 Apr 30 DLC-26
Fr 1819 Jun 07 DLC-27
To 1819 Aug 20 DLC-27
To 1819 Aug 25 DLC-27
Fr 1819 Sep 09 DLC-27
To 1819 Sep 13 DLC-27
To 1819 Sep 29 DLC-27
Fr 1824 Feb 09 M221-97
McMurtree David
Fr 1828 Sep 29 DLC-35
McNair Alexander
Fr 1816 Jan 05 DLC-20
McNair David D
Fr 1830 Nov 25 M22-27
McNairy Andrew
To 1793 Dec 16 leg 1-0178
McNairy Boyd
Fr 1819 Aug 23 leg DLC-27
Fr 1819 Aug 23* leg DLC-28
McNairy John
Fr c1794 1-0181
Fr 1797 May 04 DLC-2
To 1797 May 09 DLC-2
To 1797 May 12 DLC-2
Fr 1797 May 12 DLC-2
Fr 1802 Nov 15 1-1061
Fr 1806 Jan 17 DLC-71
Re 1807 Mar 20 mem DLC-4
Re 1807 Sep 15 mem DLC-4
Fr 1807 Nov DLC-60
To 1808 Jan 20 DLC-4
Fr 1808 Jan 22 DLC-4
Fr 1808 Jan 23 DLC-4
To 1808 Feb 13 DLC-4
Fr 1808 Mar 11 DLC-4
Re 1808 May 18 leg 2-0657
Re 1809 Jun 01 leg 2-0823
Re 1810 Sep 22 leg 2-0965
Fr 1813 Jul 30 DLC-6
Fr 1818 Dec 30 DLC-26
Fr 1823 Sep 01 DLC-32
To 1823 Sep 06 DLC-32
Fr 1826 Jul 19 DLC-34
Fr 1833 Aug 08 23-0300
McNairy Nathaniel A
Fr 1806 Jan 17 DLC-71
Fr 1806 Feb 15# 2-0178
Fr 1806 Feb 21# 2-0180
Fr 1835 Jan 17 M639-9
McNairy William H
Fr 1834 Oct 25 26-0731
McNally William
Re 1836 Dec 29 M273-33
McNamara Michael
Fr 1832 Mar 21 19-1521
McNeal John Harris
Re 1832 Jul 03 par 20-0878
McNeil John
Fr 1829 May 13 M639-13
Fr 1829 Dec 24 14-1108

Fr 1830 Mar M273-25
Fr 1839 May 27 34-0799
McNeilly Robert et al
Fr 1840 Jul 02 34-1461
McPhail Leonard Cassell
Fr 1828 Aug 28 DLC-35
To 1828 Sep 12 DLC-35
McPheeters Hugh et al
Fr 1829 Jan 22 M639-15
McRae Daniel et al
Fr 1831 Dec 31 19-0483
McReynolds Robert
Fr 1802 Aug 30 fin DLC-2
McReynolds Samuel
Fr 1836 Jul 21 M234-80
McReynolds William
Fr 1813 Sep 10 DLC-6
McRoberts Andrew
Fr 1796 Jul 01 fin DLC-1
McRoberts Samuel
Fr 1829 Jan 24# M639-26
Fr 1829 Nov 20 14-0540
Fr 1835 Dec 14 M639-18
Fr 1842 Apr 25 DLC-54
McSweeney John
To 1792 Aug 20# fin 1-0131
Fr 1843 Sep 30 DLC-55
McWhirter Samuel Caldwell
Fr 1838 Mar 14 DLC-51
Fr 1838 Aug 14 DLC-51
Fr 1838 Oct 08 DLC-51
Mead Cowles
Fr 1814 Sep 17 DLC-12
Mead John
Fr 1823 Jun 09 DLC-32
Mead Lemuel
Fr 1829 Mar 16 M639-16
Fr 1829 Jul 23# M639-21
Mead Whitman
Fr 1824 May 10 10-0720
Meade Richard Worsam
Re 1832 May 12 M273-28
Meader John B
Fr 1844 Dec 20 36-1230
Meagher Patrick
To 1823 Feb 06 lnd 9-0445
Meares William B
Fr 1834 Mar 29 M179-77
Mears John
Fr 1825 Mar 29 fin DLC-33
Mease James
Fr 1825 Jan 03 10-1026
To 1825 Jan 08 10-1046
Fr 1832 Dec 28 21-1195
Meaux John G
Fr 1841 Nov 29 DLC-54
Mechlin Joseph
Re 1829 Sep 22 M205-1
To 1833 May 30 22-1528
Mecklenburg-Schwerin Grand Duchy of
Re 1835 Apr 28 28-0171
Medicis Francisco M et al
Fr 1831 Oct 12 M639-21
Meehan John Sylva
Re 1829 May 28 13-0470
To 1832 Feb 04 19-0954
Meeker Moses
Fr 1836 Apr 02 30-0982
Meeker N C
Fr 1843 Jan 31 DLC-55
Meeker Samuel
To 1803 May 05 fin DLC-2
Fr 1803 May 07 fin DLC-3
Fr 1803 May 07 fin DLC-3
Fr 1803 May 07 fin DLC-3
Fr 1803 May 07 fin DLC-3
Fr 1803 Oct 10 1-1209
Fr 1803 Nov 26 DLC-3
Re 1804 May 07 mem DLC-3
Fr 1804 Oct 22 1-1402
Fr 1804 cDec DLC-75
Fr 1805 May 10 DLC-3
Fr 1805 Jul 27 DLC-3
Fr 1821 Jul 05 DLC-30
Meeker William P
Fr 1805 Jan 31 DLC-3
Re 1807 Jul 29 leg 2-0523
Meeker Cochran & Co
Fr 1795 Aug 11 DLC-1
Fr 1797 May 19 DLC-2
Meeker Denman & Co
Fr 1802 May 12 fin 1-0996
Meeker Williamson & Patton
Fr 1805 Jul 29 DLC-3
Fr 1805 Aug 03 DLC-3
Fr 1806 Feb 27 DLC-3
Fr 1806 Mar 26 DLC-4
Fr 1806 Apr 03 DLC-4
Fr 1806 May 08 fin 2-0235
To 1807 Apr 29 DLC-4
Meeks Joseph et al
Fr 1834 Jan M639-24
Fr 1834 Feb 01 24-1129
Meigs Clara (Benjamin)
Fr 1835 Apr 02 27-1511
Meigs Henry
Fr 1835 Apr 30# M179-80
Meigs John B
Fr 1837 Feb 18 33-0771
Fr 1843 May 15 DLC-55
Meigs Josiah
Fr 1819 Oct 19 7-0718
Fr 1820 May 06 DLC-29
Meigs Return Jonathan (1740-1823)
Fr 1813 Sep 30 DLC-61
Fr 1814 Jan 12 DLC-8
Fr 1814 Feb 11 DLC-8
To 1814 Mar 15 DLC-61
Fr 1814 Jul 06 DLC-11
Fr 1814 Oct 27 DLC-13
Fr 1814 Nov 10 DLC-14
Fr 1815 Jan 04 DLC-15
Fr 1815 Aug 08 M208-6
Fr 1815 Aug 30 DLC-19
Fr 1815 Aug 30* M208-6
Fr 1815 Oct 09 DLC-75
To 1815 Oct 18 DLC-62
Fr 1816 Jun 17 DLC-21
Fr 1816 Jun 17* M208-7
To 1816 Jun 25 5-0243
Fr 1816 Jul 05 DLC-21
Fr 1816 Jul 06 DLC-21
Fr 1816 Jul 06* 5-0289
Fr 1816 Aug 06 DLC-21
Fr 1816 Aug 06* M208-7
Fr 1816 Aug 07 DLC-21
Fr 1816 Aug 07* M208-7
Fr 1816 Aug 08 DLC-21
Fr 1816 Aug 08* 5-0348

Meigs Return Jonathan (cont)		
Fr 1816 Aug 08*		M208-7
Fr 1816 Aug 19		DLC-21
Fr 1816 Aug 21		DLC-21
Fr 1816 Aug 30		DLC-21
Fr 1816 Aug 30*		M208-7
Fr 1816 Sep 27		M208-7
Fr 1817 Mar 25		DLC-22
Fr 1817 Mar 25*		M208-7
Fr 1817 May 24		DLC-22
Fr 1817 Jun 27		DLC-23
To 1817 Aug 26		5-0999
Fr 1817 Sep 09		M208-7
Fr 1818 Aug 12		DLC-25
Fr 1819 May 29		DLC-27
Fr 1820 Feb 17		DLC-28
To 1820 Feb 28		DLC-28
Fr 1820 Mar 11		DLC-28
Fr 1820 Mar 15		DLC-70
Fr 1820 Jun 15		DLC-29
To 1820 Jun 28#		M208-8
To 1820 Jun 28*		DLC-63
To 1820 Aug 06		7-1190
To 1821 Jan 02		DLC-63
To 1821 Feb 26#		M208-9
Fr 1821 Mar 04		DLC-29
Meigs Return J (1740-1823) et al		
Fr 1814 Aug 04		DLC-11
Meigs Return Jonathan (1801-1891)		
Fr 1834 Aug 24		26-0355
Meircken John S		
Re 1829 Aug 21		13-1180
Melcher William Fullerton		
Re 1832 May 28	par	20-0647
Meldrum David et al		
Fr 1830 Mar		M639-27
Mellen John		
To 1821 Aug 29		8-1114
Mellon Michael		
Re 1830 Dec 11	par	16-1398
Melton David		
Fr 1816 Nov 22	lnd	DLC-22
Melton Eliza		
Fr 1816 Nov 22	fin	DLC-22
Melton Nancy		
Fr 1816 Nov 22	fin	DLC-22
Melton's Bluff farm		
Re 1816 Dec 14	fin	5-0602
Melville Gansevoort		
Fr 1844 Sep 15		DLC-57
Melvin Edmon		
To 1806 Nov 24	fin	DLC-4
To 1806 Dec 20	fin	DLC-4
Melvin James & Co		
Fr 1815 Nov 27	fin	4-1265
Menard Peter et al		
Fr 1834 Feb 24		24-1461
Menees James		
Fr 1802 Apr 19	lnd	1-0991
Fr 1802 Apr 19*	lnd	DLC-2
Menominee treaty		
Re 1832 Jul 09		M668-6
Re 1833 Mar 13		M668-7
Re 1837 Feb 15		M668-8
Mercein Thomas R		
Fr 1817 Oct 03#		DLC-23
Fr 1830 Feb 24		15-0239
Mercein Thomas R et al		
Fr 1832 Jan 31		19-0914
Mercer Charles Fenton		
Fr 1824 Jan 08		9-0903
To 1824 Jan 08		9-0904
Fr 1825 Feb 28		10-1189
Fr 1829 Mar 05		M639-24
Merchant Charles Spencer		
Fr 1835 Dec		M567-127
Meredith Jonathan et al		
Fr 1834 Dec		M639-8
Meredith William		
Fr 1831 Feb 09		M639-14
Merg Thomas A		
Fr 1824 Dec 07		DLC-33
Meriwether David		
Fr 1816 Nov 30		DLC-22
Merkle _____ (Gen)		
To 1829 Mar 24		12-1099
Mero District Superior Court		
To 1795 Nov 17	leg	1-0327
To 1803	leg	1-1068
Merriford John A		
Fr 1842 Mar 08		DLC-54
Merrill Ayers P		
To 1820 Sep 08		7-1312
Merrill Benjamin		
Fr 1829 Apr 06		M639-1
Merrill J		
Fr 1825 Mar 11	fin	DLC-73
Merrill Richard E		
Fr 1843 Jun 16		DLC-55
Merrill Sewall		
Fr 1840 Apr 07		DLC-52
Merrow Josiah		
Fr 1837 Feb 23		M687-20
Merry Samuel		
Fr 1831 Oct 10		M639-9
Messengers		
Re 1830 Mar	mem	15-0271
Messersmith Samuel		
Re 1835 Jun 09	par	28-0612
Messinger John		
Fr 1833 Jan 29		M179-75
Fr 1833 Jan 29*		22-0093
MeTaiWah et al		
Fr 1836 Nov 25		M234-362
Metcalf Anthony		
Re 1813 Oct 17		DLC-61
Metcalfe Hai		
Fr 1817 Mar 08	fin	DLC-22
Metoxin John et al		
Fr 1829 Dec 04#		M234-315
Mexico boundary		
Re 1829 cMay	mem	13-0225
Re 1830 cNov 01	mem	DLC-73
Re 1831 Feb 10		T1223-1
Mexico treaty		
Re 1832 Apr 05		20-0141
Re 1832 Apr 05		20-0144
Re 1832 Apr 05		20-0146
Re 1836 Feb 02		30-0271
Re 1836 Apr 21		30-1295
Meyer & Hupeden et al		
Fr 1830 May 15		M9-6
Michigan Legislative Council		
Fr 1830 Jul 30		16-0067
Fr 1832 Jun 29		DLC-41
Mickleham Septemia (Randolph)		
To 1840 Oct 31		35-0086
Middleswarth Ner et al		
Fr 1829 Mar		12-0682

Middleton Arthur Jr
Re 1833 Apr 10 22-0981
Middleton B F
Fr 1834 May 28 fin DLC-44
Fr 1834 Oct 01 fin DLC-44
Fr 1834 Oct 29 fin DLC-44
Fr 1834 Nov 28 fin DLC-45
Fr 1834 Dec 01 fin DLC-45
Fr 1834 Dec 08 fin DLC-45
Fr 1834 Dec 13 fin DLC-45
Fr 1835 Apr 04 fin DLC-46
Fr 1835 Jun 04 fin DLC-46
Fr 1835 Jul 07 fin DLC-46
Fr 1835 Jul 30 fin DLC-46
Fr 1835 Oct 03 fin DLC-47
Fr 1835 Nov 03 fin DLC-47
Fr 1835 Nov 21 fin DLC-47
Fr 1835 Nov 28 fin DLC-47
Fr 1835 Dec 11 fin DLC-47
Fr 1835 Dec 19 fin DLC-47
Fr 1835 Dec 22 fin DLC-47
Fr 1835 Dec 29 fin DLC-47
Fr 1836 Feb 29 fin DLC-47
Middleton W C
Fr 1814 Aug 22 DLC-11
Middleton & Beall
Fr 1836 May 01 fin DLC-48
Fr 1836 May 30 fin DLC-48
Mifflin Benjamin
Fr 1836 Oct 03 M639-19
Mifflin John R
Fr 1824 Apr 20 DLC-32
Miguel Dom of Portugal
Fr 1830 Jan 14 14-1425
To 1830 Apr 08 15-0644
Milburn Thomas
Re 1831 Mar 26 par 17-0982
Milburn Timothy
Re 1832 Dec 13 par 21-1037
Miles Edward
Re 1830 Nov 20 par 16-0818
Miles John
Fr 1828 Jul 28 DLC-35
To 1828 Aug 22 DLC-35
Fr 1829 Mar 11 M639-16
Miles John Jr et al
Fr 1832 Dec DLC-41
Miles William
Fr 1832 May 07 M639-16
Fr 1835 Dec 09# T330-1
Military courier
Fr 1812 Nov 21 fin DLC-5
Re 1814 May 08 3-1014
Military road
Re 1819 Jul DLC-27
Miller (sloop)
Fr 1834 Aug 23 fin DLC-44
Fr 1834 Nov 28 fin DLC-45
Miller ______ (Capt)
To 1844 Jul 12 36-0703
Miller Abraham K
Fr 1835 Mar 14 27-1207
Miller Adam
Re 1804 May 11 fin DLC-3
Miller Daniel B
Fr 1834 Jul 22 M639-27
Miller Daniel H
Fr 1829 Apr 17 M639-3
Fr 1829 Aug 05 13-1038
Fr 1829 Nov 17 M639-1
Miller Daniel H et al
Fr 1829 Mar M639-19
Fr 1830 Mar 09 M639-11
Miller E S Mrs
Fr 1830 Jun 20 15-1518
Miller George A
Fr 1838 Jan 22 DLC-51
Fr 1838 Apr 07 DLC-51
Miller George D
Fr 1831 May 04 M22-28
Miller J H
Fr 1835 Jun 03 28-0561
Miller Jack
Fr 1829 May M639-24
Miller James
Fr 1814 Dec 29 DLC-15
Fr 1832 Jan 24 19-0838
Fr 1834 Oct 06 fin DLC-44
Fr 1834 Oct 17 fin DLC-45
Miller James D
To 1817 Aug 23 DLC-23
Fr 1817 Aug 23 fin DLC-23
Miller James R
Fr 1829 Apr 14 12-1345
Fr 1836 May 23 31-0082
Miller Jesse
Fr 1830 Feb 27 M639-23
To 1833 Dec 26 24-0589
Fr 1834 Aug 26 M639-4
Fr 1835 Mar 19 27-1233
Re 1836 Nov 01 32-0385
Fr 1836 Nov 29 M687-25
Fr 1836 Dec 27 M639-9
Fr 1837 cFeb 17 M22-41
Fr 1837 Jun 23 DLC-50
Fr 1837 Jun 23* 33-1332
Miller Joel
Fr 1835 Jun 03 28-0564
Fr 1837 Jan M687-20
Miller John
Fr 1812 Mar 15 M221-42
Fr 1814 Nov 08 DLC-14
Fr 1816 Feb 17 DLC-20
Miller John (FL)
To 1821 Jul 24 DLC-63
To 1821 Aug 21 DLC-63
To 1821 Aug 22 8-1082
Fr 1821 Aug 22 M116-7
Fr 1821 Aug 22* DLC-63
To 1821 Oct 01 8-1247
Fr 1821 Oct 22 M116-9
Fr 1821 Oct 22* DLC-63
Fr 1821 Nov 26 DLC-31
Miller John (ME)
Fr 1829 May M639-24
Miller John (MO)
Fr 1829 Aug 08 M567-45
Miller John F
Fr 1821 May fin DLC-31
Miller Joseph
To 1814 Jan 31 DLC-62
Miller Pleasant Moorman
To 1801 May 03 1-0871
Fr 1813 Sep 28 3-0486
Fr 1819 Sep 23 DLC-27
Fr 1819 Sep 23* 7-0676
Fr 1820 Aug 09 DLC-29
To 1821 Mar 31 8-0278
To 1823 Jun 09 9-0590

Miller Pleasant Moorman (cont)
Fr 1823 Jul 01 DLC-32
Fr 1823 Oct 21 DLC-32
Fr 1824 Apr 11 DLC-32
Miller R H
Fr 1833 Oct 10 M639-24
Miller Samuel
To 1806 Jul 10# 2-0295
To 1806 Jul 26# 2-0305
Re 1830 Feb 04 M567-51
Fr 1836 Sep 29 M567-128
Miller Samuel et al
Fr 1829 Apr 02 M639-8
Miller Silvanus
Fr 1827 Dec 04 DLC-35
Miller Stephen Decatur
Fr 1829 Dec 15 14-1045
Fr 1832 Jun 13 M639-7
Miller Sylvester
Fr 1830 Jan 26 M639-15
Miller Sylvester et al
Fr 1833 Jan M639-16
Miller Thomas
Fr 1828 Dec 03 DLC-35
Fr 1829 Sep 09 M639-16
Miller Thomas L
To 1829 May 13 DLC-37
Miller Washington D
Fr 1844 Apr 07 DLC-56
Mills Alexander
Fr 1830 Jan 05 M124-122
Mills Benjamin et al
To 1825 Nov DLC-33
Mills Elijah Hunt
Fr 1829 Mar 25 12-1111
Mills George et al
Fr 1835 Mar 11 DLC-46
Mills Isaac
Fr 1829 Mar 02 M639-16
Mills John
Fr 1829 Nov 21 14-0544
Fr 1834 Dec 04 fin DLC-45
Fr 1835 Jun 19# fin DLC-46
Fr 1835 Oct 03# fin DLC-47
Fr 1835 Nov 28# fin DLC-47
Fr 1835 Dec 10# fin DLC-47
Fr 1835 Dec 31# fin DLC-47
Fr 1836 Feb 13# fin DLC-47
Fr c1836 Apr 16# fin 30-1216
Fr c1836 May 28# fin 31-0185
Fr 1836 Jun 14 31-0477
Mills Robert
To 1827 Jul 08 11-0734
Fr 1829 Aug 15 13-1138
Re 1836 Jul 06 31-0885
Fr 1836 Aug 03 DLC-48
Fr 1844 Dec 07 36-1128
Mills Silvester H
Fr 1832 Feb 22 DLC-40
Mills William J et al
Fr 1831 Oct 17 M639-6
Milner John et al
Fr 1829 Jul 17 M179-67
Milroy Samuel
Re 1829 Jul 27 13-0942
To 1833 Apr 08 22-0967
Milton Homer Virgil
Fr 1814 Mar 25 DLC-9
To 1814 Apr 05 DLC-10
Fr 1814 Apr 28 DLC-10
Fr 1814 Jul 22 DLC-11
Fr 1814 Aug 24 DLC-11
Fr 1814 Aug 24* 3-1343
Fr 1814 Sep 13 DLC-12
Fr 1814 Oct 20 DLC-13
Fr 1818 Mar 16 DLC-24
Mims John et al
Fr 1831 Feb 04 17-0436
Miner Asher et al
Fr 1831 Oct 03 18-0915
Mingo King et al
Fr 1829 Nov 14 M234-135
Minh-Mang Emperor of Vietnam
To 1833 Jan 26 M37-10
To 1835 Mar 20 M77-152
To 1835 Mar 20* M37-10
To 1835 Mar 20* 27-1243
Minor Charles Landon Carter
Re 1832 Apr 28 mem 20-0399
Minor D
Fr 1829 Jun 15 M639-11
Minor Garrit
Fr 1830 Oct 12 M688-69
Minor Theodore P
Fr 1835 Sep 29 DLC-47
Minor W G
Fr 1842 Dec 15 DLC-54
Miranda Jane
Fr 1833 Feb 27 22-0532
Mississippi delegates
To 1828 Jan 08 DLC-36
Mississippi General Assembly
Fr 1814 Jan 21 DLC-8
Fr 1821 Feb 09 DLC-29
To 1828 Jan 20 11-1065
Fr 1828 Jan 20 add 11-1066
Mississippi gentleman
To 1823 Mar 23 add 9-0502
Missroon John S
Re 1833 Oct 22 M124-140
Mitchel John
Fr 1808 Jun 21 fin 2-0681
Fr 1828 Nov 10 fin 12-0259
Mitchell A H
Fr 1844 Dec 24 36-1261
Mitchell Charles
Re 1793 Jun 15 leg DLC-1
Mitchell Charles A
Re 1835 May 04 par 28-0268
Fr 1837 Feb 05 par 33-0405
Fr 1837 Feb 06 par 33-0424
Mitchell Charles Halsey
Fr 1844 Nov 26 DLC-57
Mitchell David
Fr 1845 Apr 08 DLC-58
Mitchell David Brydie
To 1813 Oct 10 3-0519
To 1813 Oct 10* DLC-6
To 1813 Oct 10* M221-55
Fr 1813 Oct 19 DLC-61
Fr 1813 Oct 19* DLC-75
Fr 1813 Oct 19* 3-0537
Fr 1816 May 23 5-0090
Re 1818 Mar 15 6-0076
Fr 1818 Mar 22 DLC-24
To 1818 Jul 08 M221-78
Fr 1818 Aug 10 M221-78
Mitchell David R
Fr 1829 Jun 16 M234-222

Fr 1829 Jun 21 M234-222
Fr 1829 Dec 30 M234-222
Mitchell Edward
Fr 1815 May 13 4-1032
Fr 1816 Jan 12 DLC-20
Fr 1821 Feb 07 DLC-29
Mitchell George M
Fr 1844 Jan 12 DLC-56
Mitchell James
Fr 1813 Nov 06 DLC-75
Fr 1813 Nov 08 DLC-75
To 1813 Dec 21 3-0695
To 1813 Dec 22 DLC-61
Fr 1813 Dec 24 3-0711
Fr 1814 Jan 11 DLC-8
Fr 1814 Jan 26 DLC-8
Fr 1814 Feb 18 DLC-9
Mitchell James Coffield
Fr 1827 Jan 28 DLC-34
Fr 1829 Apr 04 M639-16
Fr 1829 Jun 04 M639-21
Fr 1829 Jun 29 M639-16
Mitchell John
Fr 1814 Jan 09 DLC-8
Fr 1829 Feb 09 12-0493
Fr 1829 cMar 01 M639-17
Mitchell John C
Fr 1821 Oct 24 DLC-31
Mitchell Mark
Fr 1795 Oct 12 1-0322
Fr 1795 Nov 21 DLC-1
Fr 1798 Jun 04 DLC-2
Re 1803 Dec 12 leg DLC-3
Fr 1804 Jan 30 leg DLC-3
Fr 1806 May 19 DLC-71
Mitchell Martha A
To 1825 Feb 16 10-1118
Mitchell Mary
Re 1791 Aug leg 1-0101
Mitchell Morris
To 1803 Oct 22 fin DLC-3
Mitchell N
Fr 1818 Oct 18 fin 6-1363
Mitchell Nathaniel
Fr 1833 Jan 24 M639-1
Mitchell Richard
Fr 1804 Nov 18# fin DLC-3
Mitchell Robert
Fr 1833 Oct 02 M639-24
Fr 1844 Dec 24 DLC-57
Fr 1844 Dec 24* 36-1264
Mitchell Robert et al
Fr 1834 cJun 15 25-1384
Mitchell Samuel
Fr 1811 Nov 04 lnd DLC-5
Fr 1825 Mar 11 fin DLC-33
Fr 1838 Jan 20 DLC-51
Mitchell Samuel L
To 1822 Jun 03 9-0188
Mitchell T & W
Fr 1826 Mar 10 fin DLC-33
Mitchell Thomas
Fr 1795 Sep 10 1-0315
Mitchell Thomas Rothmaler
Fr 1831 Dec 23 19-0404
Fr 1832 Jun 02 M639-11
Mitchell William
To 1813 Dec 22 DLC-61
Fr 1820 Jul 14 M688-15
Mitchell William D et al
Fr 1840 Sep 10 DLC-53
Mitchell William G
Fr 1829 Jun 30 M639-16
Mitchell William S
Fr 1818 Apr 13 DLC-24
Fr 1818 Apr 16 DLC-24
Moad Henry
Re 1834 Mar 13 par 25-0151
Moffat John L
Fr 1837 Jan 07 32-1523
Moffat Thomas
Re 1835 Jun 30 par 28-0849
Molton Michael
Fr 1814 Oct 25 DLC-25
Monges John A
Fr 1835 Dec 26 M639-16
Monitawquah et al
Re 1836 Apr 26 30-1358
Monoquet
Fr 1835 Nov 28 29-0623
Monroe James
To 1813 Jan 04 DLC-61
Fr 1814 Sep 07 DLC-12
Fr 1814 Sep 07* M6-7
Fr 1814 Sep 07* 4-0185
Fr 1814 Sep 27 DLC-12
Fr 1814 Sep 27* M6-7
Fr 1814 Sep 27* 4-0243
To 1814 Oct 10 M221-63
To 1814 Oct 10* DLC-62
To 1814 Oct 10* M200-9
Fr 1814 Oct 10 DLC-13
Fr 1814 Oct 10* M6-7
Fr 1814 Oct 10* 4-0264
To 1814 Oct 14 M221-63
To 1814 Oct 14* DLC-62
To 1814 Oct 17 M221-63
To 1814 Oct 17* DLC-62
Fr 1814 Oct 19 DLC-13
Fr 1814 Oct 19* 4-0276
Fr 1814 Oct 21 DLC-13
Fr 1814 Oct 21* M6-7
Fr 1814 Oct 21* M200-9
Fr 1814 Oct 21* 4-0287
To 1814 Oct 26 M221-63
To 1814 Oct 26* DLC-62
To 1814 Oct 26* M200-9
To 1814 Oct 26* 4-0293
To 1814 Oct 31 DLC-62
To 1814 Oct 31 M221-63
To 1814 Oct 31* DLC-62
To 1814 Oct 31* 4-0308
To 1814 Nov 4-0312
To 1814 Nov 14 M221-63
To 1814 Nov 14* M200-9
To 1814 Nov 14* DLC-62
To 1814 Nov 20 M221-63
To 1814 Nov 20* DLC-62
To 1814 Nov 20* DLC-14
To 1814 Nov 21 4-0367
To 1814 Nov 21* DLC-62
To 1814 Dec 02 M221-63
To 1814 Dec 02* DLC-62
To 1814 Dec 02* M200-9
Fr 1814 Dec 07 DLC-14
Fr 1814 Dec 07* M6-7
Fr 1814 Dec 07* M200-9
Fr 1814 Dec 07* 4-0382

Monroe James (cont)

Fr 1814 Dec 10		DLC-14
Fr 1814 Dec 10*		M6-7
Fr 1814 Dec 10*		4-0386
To 1814 Dec 13		M221-63
To 1814 Dec 13*		DLC-62
To 1814 Dec 13*		4-0398
To 1814 Dec 16		M221-63
To 1814 Dec 16*		DLC-62
Fr 1814 Dec 20		DLC-14
Fr 1814 Dec 20*		4-0431
To 1814 Dec 26		M221-63
To 1814 Dec 27		M221-63
To 1814 Dec 27*		DLC-62
To 1814 Dec 29		M221-63
To 1814 Dec 29*		DLC-62
Fr 1814 Dec 31		DLC-15
To 1815 Jan 02		M858-1
To 1815 Jan 03		4-0488
To 1815 Jan 03*		DLC-62
Fr 1815 Jan 05		DLC-15
Fr 1815 Jan 05*		M7-1
To 1815 Jan 09		M221-63
To 1815 Jan 09*		DLC-62
To 1815 Jan 13		4-0534
To 1815 Jan 13*		DLC-15
To 1815 Jan 13		4-0537
To 1815 cJan 15		4-0548
To 1815 Jan 19		M222-16
To 1815 Jan 19*		DLC-62
To 1815 Jan 19*		DLC-15
To 1815 Jan 25		DLC-15
Fr 1815 Feb 04		DLC-16
Fr 1815 Feb 04*		4-0695
Fr 1815 Feb 05		DLC-16
Fr 1815 Feb 05*		M7-1
Fr 1815 Feb 05*		4-0698
To 1815 Feb 13		4-0720
To 1815 Feb 13*		DLC-16
Fr 1815 Feb 13		DLC-16
Fr 1815 Feb 13*		M6-8
Fr 1815 Feb 13*		4-0735
Fr 1815 Feb 14		DLC-16
To 1815 Feb 16		M222-16
Fr 1815 Feb 16		DLC-16
Fr 1815 Feb 16*		M6-8
Fr 1815 Feb 16*		4-0751
To 1815 Feb 17		M221-63
To 1815 Feb 17		4-0757
To 1815 Feb 17*		DLC-62
To 1815 Feb 17		4-0761
To 1815 Feb 18		DLC-16
To 1815 Feb 18*		DLC-63
To 1815 Feb 24		M221-63
To 1815 Feb 24*		DLC-62
To 1815 Mar 06		M221-63
To 1815 Mar 06*		DLC-17
To 1815 Mar 10		M222-16
To 1815 Mar 10*		4-0828
To 1815 Mar 10		4-0829
Fr 1815 Mar 13		DLC-17
Fr 1815 Mar 13*		M6-8
To 1815 Mar 16		M221-63
To 1815 Mar 16*		DLC-62
To 1815 Mar 19		DLC-17
Fr 1815 Mar 20		DLC-17
To 1815 Apr 06		DLC-71
To 1815 Apr 28		M221-63
To 1815 Apr 28*		DLC-18
To 1815 Apr 28*		4-1018

To 1816 Feb 21		M179-33
Fr 1816 Mar 24		DLC-20
To 1816 May 08		5-0075
To 1816 May 12		5-0079
Fr 1816 Jun 18		DLC-21
Fr 1816 Jul 03		DLC-21
To 1816 Jul 08		DLC-21
To 1816 Jul 09		5-0296
To 1816 Jul 27		5-0331
Fr 1816 Aug 14		DLC-21
To 1816 Oct 23		DLC-21
To 1816 Oct 23*		5-0545
To 1816 Nov 12		DLC-21
To 1816 Nov 12*		DLC-71
Fr 1816 Dec 14		DLC-22
Fr 1816 Dec 14*		5-0615
To 1817 Jan 06		DLC-22
To 1817 Jan 06*		DLC-71
To 1817 Jan 10		5-0677
To 1817 Jan 10		5-0678
To 1817 Jan 12		5-0689
Fr 1817 Mar 01		DLC-22
To 1817 Mar 04		5-0749
Re 1817 Mar 04	mem	5-0770
To 1817 Mar 18		5-0781
To 1817 Mar 18*		DLC-22
Fr 1817 May 16		DLC-22
Fr 1817 May 16*		5-0859
Fr 1817 May 21		5-0867
Fr 1817 Jun 02		DLC-22
To 1817 Jun 11		DLC-22
To 1817 Jun 12		5-0895
To 1817 Jun 12*		DLC-22
To 1817 Jun 23		DLC-23
To 1817 Jul 09		5-0923
Fr 1817 Aug 04		DLC-23
Fr 1817 Aug 04*		5-0956
To 1817 Aug 12		5-0969
To 1817 Sep 02		5-1004
To 1817 Sep 09		M222-19
To 1817 Sep 10		5-1013
Fr 1817 Sep 27		DLC-23
Fr 1817 Oct 05		DLC-23
Fr 1817 Oct 05*		5-1079
To 1817 Oct 22		5-1118
To 1817 Oct 22*		DLC-23
Fr 1817 Dec 02		DLC-23
To 1817 Dec 20		5-1193
To 1817 Dec 20*		DLC-23
To 1817 Dec 23		5-1196
Fr 1817 Dec 28		5-1209
To 1818 Jan 06		5-1231
To 1818 Jan 06*		DLC-23
To 1818 Jan 21		5-1323
Fr 1818 Apr 17		DLC-24
Fr 1818 Apr 17*		6-0399
To 1818 Jun 02		6-1014
Fr 1818 Jul 19		DLC-71
Fr 1818 Jul 19*		DLC-25
To 1818 Aug 10		6-1213
To 1818 Aug 19		6-1247
To 1818 Aug 19*		DLC-71
To 1818 Aug 19*		DLC-25
To 1818 Aug 19*		DLC-26
To 1818 Aug 21		6-1255
Fr 1818 Oct 20		6-1378
Fr 1818 Oct 20*		DLC-25
To 1818 Oct 30		6-1396
To 1818 Nov 15		6-1423

To 1818 Nov 15*		DLC-71
To 1818 Nov 29		7-0009
To 1818 Dec 07		7-0037
To 1818 Dec 07*		DLC-26
Fr 1818 Dec 21		DLC-26
Fr 1818 Dec 21*		7-0065
To 1819 Feb 25		M439-10
To 1819 Mar 07		7-0413
To 1819 Mar 08		7-0417
To 1819 Mar 18		M439-14
Fr 1819 May 31		DLC-27
Fr 1819 May 31*		7-0534
Re 1819 Jun 09	add	7-0546
To 1819 Jun 12		M688-10
To 1819 Jul 05		7-0567
To 1819 Sep 10		7-0655
To 1819 Sep 13		7-0658
To 1819 Sep 22		M439-13
To 1819 Sep 29		7-0689
To 1819 Sep 29*		DLC-27
To 1819 Oct 02		7-0701
To 1819 Oct 07		7-0707
To 1819 Oct 08		7-0710
To 1819 Nov 16		7-0867
To 1819 Nov 16		7-0871
To 1819 Nov 22		7-0881
To 1819 Nov 29		7-0899
To 1819 Nov 29*		DLC-72
To 1819 Dec 10		7-0914
Fr 1819 Dec 12		DLC-28
To 1819 Dec 30		7-0956
To 1820 Jan 15		7-0993
To 1820 Mar 14		7-1043
To 1820 Apr 15		7-1070
To 1820 Apr 15*		DLC-28
Fr 1820 May 23		7-1098
To 1820 Jun 20		7-1117
Fr 1820 Jul 13		DLC-29
Fr 1820 Jul 13*		7-1152
To 1820 Aug 11		DLC-29
To 1820 Nov 13		7-1410
Fr 1820 Dec 12		8-0017
To 1821 Jan 01		8-0034
To 1821 Jan 12		DLC-29
To 1821 Jan 12*		8-0063
To 1821 Jan 22		8-0091
Fr 1821 Jan 24		DLC-29
To 1821 Feb 11		8-0103
To 1821 Feb 22		M439-8
To 1821 Mar 06		8-0157
Fr 1821 May 23		DLC-72
Fr 1821 May 23*		8-0513
To 1821 Jun 13		8-0601
To 1821 Aug 04		8-1019
To 1821 Aug 04*		DLC-63
Fr 1821 Sep 16	fin	DLC-72
To 1821 Oct 05		8-1272
To 1821 Oct 05*		DLC-63
To 1821 Nov 13		8-1340
To 1821 Nov 13*		DLC-63
To 1821 Nov 13		M116-9
To 1821 Nov 13*		DLC-63
To 1821 Nov 14		8-1354
To 1821 Nov 14*		DLC-63
To 1821 Nov 30		M439-10
Fr 1821 Dec 31		M40-17
Fr 1821 Dec 31*		8-1375
To 1822 Jan 22		M116-10
To 1822 Jan 22*		DLC-63

To 1822 Jan 29		9-0014
To 1822 Jan 29*		DLC-63
To 1822 Mar 19		9-0059
To 1822 Mar 19*		DLC-63
To 1822 Apr 02		M116-10
Fr 1822 May 30		9-0175
To 1822 Jul 02		M688-63
To 1822 Jul 26		9-0228
To 1822 Jul 26*		DLC-31
To 1822 Oct 04		M221-96
To 1822 Oct 04*		9-0282
To 1822 Dec 12		9-0351
To 1822 Dec 30		M439-5
Fr 1823 Jan 20#		9-0407
To 1823 Jan 21		9-0419
Fr 1823 Jan 27		DLC-32
Fr 1823 Jan 27*		9-0434
Fr 1823 Jan 30		DLC-72
To 1823 Feb 19		9-0459
To 1823 Feb 19*		DLC-72
To 1823 May 12		9-0555
To 1823 May 18		9-0563
To 1823 Aug 19		9-0641
To 1823 Sep 25		9-0674
To 1823 Oct 10		DLC-32
To 1823 Dec		9-0770
To 1823 Dec 30		M439-16
To 1824 Jan 15		9-0930
To 1824 Jan 16		9-0937
Fr 1824 Jan 16		9-0939
To 1824 Feb		10-0427
To 1824 Feb 22		10-0474
Fr 1824 Feb 22		10-0477
To 1824 Feb 27		10-0495
To 1824 Feb 28		10-0497
To 1824 Feb 28*		DLC-32
Fr 1824 Mar 01		10-0506
To 1824 Mar 16		10-0561
To 1824 Mar 16		M221-98
To 1824 Mar 16*		10-0564
Fr 1824 Mar 16	add	M221-98
To 1824 Apr 09		10-0633
To 1824 Apr 09*		DLC-32
To 1824 Apr 10		10-0636
Fr 1824 Apr 10		DLC-32
To 1824 May 20		10-0739
To 1824 May 22		10-0747
To 1824 Jun 11		DLC-32
To 1824 Jul 12		10-0825
To 1825 Jan 22		M439-9
Fr 1825 Feb 26		DLC-33
To 1825 Feb 28		10-1189
Fr 1825 Jul 03		DLC-33
Fr 1825 Jul 03*		10-1335
To 1830 Dec 09		16-1359
To 1830 Dec 09*		DLC-38
Fr 1831 Mar		17-0689
To 1831 Jun 03#		17-1507
To 1831 Jun 03*		DLC-39
To 1831 Jun 03*		DLC-73
Monroe Joseph		
Fr 1816 Feb 10		DLC-20
Monroe Thomas		
Fr 1836 May 16		M567-122
Monroe Thomas Bell		
Fr 1836 Dec 22		M639-15
Montague George R		
Fr 1830 Nov 15		DLC-38
Montandon T		
Fr 1831 Mar 24	fin	DLC-39

Montgomery Alexander et al			
	Fr 1840 Jun 07		34-1398
Montgomery Chesod P			
	Fr 1829 Aug 18		13-1149
	Fr 1829 Aug 18		13-1151
	To 1829 Aug 19		DLC-72
	Fr 1829 Aug 21#		13-1181
	Fr 1829 Sep 01		13-1223
	Fr 1829 Sep 05		13-1259
	Fr 1829 Sep 16		13-1322
	To 1829 Sep 19		13-1365
	Fr 1829 Sep 26		13-1429
	Fr 1829 Sep 30		13-1457
	Fr 1829 Oct 01		14-0086
	Fr 1831 Apr 08		DLC-39
Montgomery Elijah			
	Fr 1820 Jun 26		DLC-29
Montgomery George Washington			
	Re 1835 Sep 17		29-0075
Montgomery Hugh			
	Re 1787 Oct 28	leg	1-0029
	To 1830 Jul 27#		DLC-38
	To 1834 Sep 03		DLC-44
	To 1834 Sep 03*		M208-9
	To 1834 Sep 03*		26-0413
Montgomery James M C			
	Fr 1814 Mar 20		DLC-9
	Fr 1814 Jul 24		DLC-11
	Fr 1814 Jul 24		DLC-11
	Fr 1831 Aug 13		18-0519
Montgomery John			
	Fr 1829 Apr		M639-5
Montgomery Lemuel Purnell			
	Fr 1813 Jul		3-0405
Montgomery Samuel			
	Re 1809 Aug 29	leg	DLC-4
Montgomery William			
	Fr 1836 Jun 30		31-0668
	Fr 1836 Jun 30*		M234-113
Montgomery William et al			
	Fr 1835 Dec 16		M639-21
Montim ______ (Capt)			
	Fr 1831 cOct		M234-601
	Fr 1831 cOct *		18-0908
Mooklar William T			
	Fr 1831 Oct 20		M22-28
	To 1831 Nov 07		18-1218
Mooney Thomas			
	Fr 1842 May 14		35-0690
	To 1842 May 23		35-0730
Mooney William			
	Fr 1819 Feb 15		7-0276
	To 1819 Feb 18	add	7-0284
	Fr 1829 Mar 04		12-0853
Moontail et al			
	Fr 1836 May 10		M234-697
Moor Henry			
	Fr 1835 Jan 27		M124-146
Moor Samuel			
	Fr 1803 Oct 29		1-1244
	To 1803 Dec 02	fin	DLC-3
Moore Alfred			
	Fr 1836 Mar 12		DLC-47
Moore Andrew			
	Fr 1818 Jun 09	fin	DLC-69
	Fr 1818 Jun 09*	fin	6-1041
Moore Anna			
	Fr 1809 Jul 22		DLC-4
Moore Brice M			
	Fr 1844 Nov 19		DLC-57
Moore David			
	To 1814 Mar 08		DLC-61
	Fr 1814 Mar 13		DLC-9
Moore Emmet			
	Fr 1845 Jan 08		DLC-57
Moore Gabriel			
	Fr 1829 Sep 06		M639-16
	Fr 1829 Oct 20		M639-3
Moore J			
	Fr 1812 Jan 22		DLC-5
Moore James			
	Fr 1821 Dec 22		DLC-31
Moore James B			
	Fr 1838 Nov 03#		DLC-51
Moore James F			
	Fr 1806 Feb 19		DLC-3
Moore James F & Co			
	Re 1805 Apr 08	leg	DLC-3
	To 1805 Jul 08	fin	DLC-3
Moore Jesse			
	Re 1829 Jun 18		13-0678
Moore John M			
	To 1830 Jun 12#		15-1357
	To 1830 Jun 15		15-1461
	Fr 1830 Jun 16		15-1471
	Re 1830 Oct 01		16-0292
	Fr 1830 Oct 14		M25-26
	To 1831 Apr 01		17-1062
	Fr 1831 Apr 25		17-1236
	Fr 1831 Apr 25*		M25-26
	Fr 1831 Apr 25		M25-26
	Fr 1831 May 12		M25-26
	To 1832 Dec 15		21-1054
	Fr 1832 Dec 20		M25-28
	Re 1833 Jun 05		22-1582
	Fr 1833 Jul 10		23-0099
	Fr 1833 Jul 12		23-0119
	Fr 1833 Jul 13		M25-28
	Re 1833 Sep 05		23-0653
	Fr 1833 Sep 05		23-0654
	Fr 1833 Sep 05*		M25-28
	Fr 1833 Sep 10		23-0682
	Fr 1833 Sep 11		23-0688
	Fr 1833 Sep 20		23-0800
	Fr 1833 Sep 30		M25-28
	Fr 1833 Sep 30		23-0907
	Fr 1833 Oct 01		M25-28
	Re 1834 Jul 07		26-0182
	To 1834 Jul 08#		26-0190
	To 1834 Oct 03#		26-0488
	Fr 1835 Jun 20		28-0756
	To 1835 Jun 22		28-0762
	Fr 1835 Jun 23		28-0766
	Fr 1835 Jun 23		28-0769
	Fr 1835 Jun 30		28-0858
	Fr 1835 Jun 30*		M25-30
	Fr 1835 Jul 01#		28-0868
	Fr 1835 Jul 03#		M234-435
	Fr 1835 Jul 10		28-0994
	To 1835 Jul 25#		28-1167
	To 1835 Jul 28		28-1188
	Fr 1835 Aug 03		28-1232
	Fr 1835 Aug 03*		M234-136
	Fr 1835 Aug 05		M25-30
	Fr 1835 Aug 20		28-1333
	Fr 1835 Aug 20		28-1337
	Fr 1835 Aug 22		28-1352
	Fr 1835 Aug 22		28-1357
	Fr 1836 Jul 09		31-1029

Re 1836 Jul 09		31-1031
Fr 1836 Nov 01		32-0386
Fr 1836 Nov 14		32-0494
Fr 1836 Nov 15		32-0528
Fr 1836 Nov 24		M25-31
Fr 1836 Nov 25		32-0581
Moore John P		
Fr 1830 May 11#	fin	DLC-38
Fr 1830 Nov 25#		DLC-38
Moore Joseph		
Re 1802 Nov	leg	1-1049
Fr 1835 Feb 11#		M567-111
Moore Joseph et al		
Fr 1837 Feb 20		M234-189
Moore Joseph J et al		
Fr 1834 Dec 27		M234-188
Moore Joseph M		
Fr 1839 Jan 29		DLC-51
Moore Joseph Scott		
Fr 1843 Oct 23		DLC-55
Moore L H		
Fr 1836 Mar 23		30-0887
Moore R		
Fr 1814 Jan 04		DLC-8
Moore Robert G		
Fr 1836 Jul 15		31-1089
Fr 1836 Aug 12		31-1287
Moore Samuel		
Fr 1830 Jan 01		14-1286
Fr 1831 Jan 01		17-0125
Fr 1832 Jan 01		19-0571
Fr 1833 Jan 15		21-1433
Fr 1834 Jan 01		24-0728
Fr 1834 Aug 01		26-0276
Fr 1835 Jan 01		27-0066
Fr 1835 Mar 23		27-1373
Fr 1835 May 16		28-0448
Fr 1835 Nov 25		M639-18
Moore Samuel B		
Fr 1829 May 01		M639-21
Fr 1829 Sep 16		13-1326
Moore Samuel B et al		
Fr 1836 Jan 08		M639-5
Moore Susan		
Re 1838 Aug 04		34-0418
Moore Thomas		
Fr 1819 Nov 02	leg	DLC-28
Moore Thomas I et al		
Fr 1820 Jun 03	add	7-1108
To 1820 Jun 03	add	7-1109
Moore Thomas P		
Fr 1829 May 28		M639-7
Fr 1829 Jul 23		M639-12
Moore Thomas Patrick		
Fr 1826 Jun 19		DLC-34
To 1826 Jun 28		DLC-34
Fr 1826 Jul 21		DLC-34
To 1826 Jul 31		DLC-34
To 1826 cAug 31		11-0345
Fr 1827 Jun 13		DLC-34
To 1827 Jun 16		DLC-34
Fr 1829 Nov 28		14-0606
Fr 1834 Aug 28		DLC-44
Fr 1836 Aug 23		DLC-49
Fr 1836 Aug 23#		DLC-49
Fr 1837 Jan 06		32-1510
Moore Thomas Patrick et al		
Fr 1829 cJan		12-0418
Fr 1829 cMar 01		M639-20
To 1844 Jun 25		36-0650
Moore William		
Fr 1814 May 22		DLC-10
To 1814 Jun 25		DLC-11
Fr 1826 Jun 10		DLC-34
To 1826 Jun 15		DLC-34
To 1827 Jan 04		11-0460
To 1833 Nov 15		23-1237
Moore William M A		
Re 1830 Mar 06		M273-22
Moore William W		
To 1833 Apr 27#		22-1190
Moore & Adams		
To 1842 May 21		DLC-54
Fr 1842 Aug 01	fin	35-0867
Mooring William S et al		
Fr 1835 Jan 29		M639-1
Moors Thomas		
Fr 1807 Sep 30		DLC-4
Moran Isidore		
Fr 1835 Sep 07		29-0001
Morazan Francisco		
Fr 1830 Sep 18		T34-1
To 1831 Jul 20		18-0239
Mordecai Alfred		
Fr 1830 Jun 02		DLC-38
Moreau & Low et al		
Fr 1829 Apr 09		M639-1
Morehead James Turner		
To 1836 Aug 07		M179-82
To 1836 Aug 07*		31-1251
To 1836 Aug 07*		DLC-48
To 1836 Aug 07*		M567-122
Morel Pierre Louis		
Fr 1815 Mar 05		4-0818
Fr 1815 Mar 05#	leg	DLC-17
Morell George		
Fr 1835 Dec 20#		M639-16
Morell John D et al		
Fr 1829 Aug 15		M639-9
Morfit Henry Mason		
Fr 1829 Apr 02		M639-3
Fr 1829 Apr 18		M639-16
Fr 1829 May 08		13-0265
To 1833 May 28#		M639-16
Fr 1833 Jul 13		M639-16
Fr 1836 Mar 02		M639-15
Morgan Alexander G		
Fr 1829 Jul 16#		M639-15
Fr 1837 Feb 23#		33-0845
Morgan Benjamin		
To 1813 Jan 05		DLC-61
Fr 1814 Oct 17		DLC-13
To 1821 Jan 04		8-0045
To 1821 Feb 15		8-0126
Re 1836 May 16	par	T967-2
Morgan Benjamin et al		
Fr 1815 cFeb 25		4-0790
Morgan Charles S		
Fr 1829 Aug 03		M639-6
Fr 1829 Aug 24		M639-6
Fr 1836 Mar 21		M639-6
Fr 1836 Mar 22		M639-6
Fr 1836 Mar 23		M639-6
Morgan Charles S et al		
Fr 1829 May 29		M639-10
Fr 1829 Jul		M639-6
Morgan Charles S Mrs		
Fr 1836 Mar 22		M639-6
Morgan Charles W		
Fr 1831 Feb 05		17-0444

Morgan David Bannister
Fr 1814 Dec 18 DLC-14
To 1814 Dec 22 DLC-62
Fr 1814 Dec 22 DLC-14
To 1814 Dec 23 4-0450
Fr 1814 Dec 24 DLC-15
Fr 1814 Dec 24 DLC-15
Fr 1814 Dec 25 DLC-15
To 1814 Dec 26 DLC-62
Fr 1814 Dec 26 DLC-15
To 1815 Jan 02 4-0483
To 1815 Jan 07 4-0496
To 1815 Jan 07* DLC-62
Fr 1815 Jan 07 DLC-71
To 1815 Jan 08 4-0498
To 1815 Jan 08* DLC-62
To 1815 Jan 08 DLC-62
To 1815 Jan 08* 4-0501
Fr 1815 Jan 08 DLC-71
To 1815 Jan 08 DLC-62
To 1815 Jan 08* 4-0502
To 1815 Jan 10 4-0515
To 1815 Jan 10 4-0517
To 1815 Jan 10* DLC-62
Fr 1815 Jan 10 4-0520
Fr 1815 Jan 11 DLC-15
Fr 1815 Jan 12 4-0524
Fr 1815 Jan 12 4-0526
Fr 1815 Jan 13 4-0539
Fr 1815 Jan 13 4-0541
Fr 1815 Jan 14 4-0546
To 1815 Jan 17 4-0562
To 1815 Jan 17* DLC-62
To 1815 Jan 18 4-0571
To 1815 Jan 18* DLC-62
To 1815 Jan 18 4-0573
Fr 1815 Jan 21 4-0588
Fr 1815 Jan 22 4-0595
Fr 1815 Jan 26 4-0621
To 1815 Feb 13 DLC-16
To 1815 Feb 13* 4-0737
Fr 1815 Mar 08 4-0824
Fr 1815 Mar 28 DLC-17
To 1821 May 19 8-0487
Fr 1829 Aug 30 M124-120
Fr 1830 Jan 15 M639-4
Morgan George Washington
Fr 1839 Jul 29 DLC-52
Morgan Gideon
Fr 1813 Nov 02 DLC-61
Fr 1813 Nov 02* DLC-75
Fr 1813 Nov 04 3-0568
Fr 1813 Nov 04* DLC-61
To 1813 Dec 18 DLC-61
Fr 1814 Jan 16 DLC-8
To 1814 Feb 01 DLC-62
Fr 1814 Feb 05 DLC-8
Fr 1814 Feb 09 DLC-8
To 1814 Feb 17 DLC-61
To 1814 Feb 21 DLC-61
Fr 1814 Feb 22 DLC-9
To 1814 Feb 26 DLC-61
Fr 1814 Feb 27 DLC-9
Fr 1814 Feb 28 DLC-9
To 1814 Apr 03 DLC-10
Fr 1814 Oct 18 DLC-13
Fr 1814 Oct 27 DLC-13
Fr 1814 Nov 10 DLC-14
Fr 1817 Jul 17 M208-7
Fr 1836 Feb 20 M234-80
Fr 1836 Aug 14 DLC-48
Fr 1836 Oct M22-41
Morgan John et al
Fr 1829 Nov 16 14-0478
Morgan John H
Fr 1826 Jul 06 add 11-0279
To 1826 Jul 06 add 11-0285
Morgan John Jordan
Fr 1829 Mar 25 12-1118
Fr 1829 Mar 28 M639-6
Fr 1829 Nov 19 M639-6
Fr 1835 Jul 21 M124-148
Morgan John Jordan et al
Fr 1833 Dec 23 M639-18
Morgan Katherine (Duane)
To 1825 May 18# 10-1271
To 1829 Jan 03 12-0438
Fr 1829 Mar 11 DLC-36
Fr 1833 May 27 22-1464
Re 1844 Mar 22 mem DLC-56
Fr 1845 Mar 22 DLC-57
Morgan Rufus
Fr 1814 Jan 11 DLC-8
To 1814 Feb 01 DLC-61
Morgan Thomas
To 1828 May 24 12-0015
Fr 1829 Feb 10 12-0499
To 1837 Mar 10 DLC-50
Fr 1839 Jul 28 DLC-52
Morgan William Stephen
Fr 1837 cJan 27 M22-41
Morgan & Smith
Fr 1813 Dec 10 DLC-61
Morganton NC citizens
Fr 1831 Jul 28 M22-28
Morisete Joseph
Fr 1833 Sep 12 M124-139
Morison David
Fr 1831 Dec 06 19-0205
Fr 1832 Jun 10# 20-0732
Morocco treaty
Re 1837 Jan 30 33-0259
Morphy Diego
Fr 1814 Dec 12 DLC-14
Fr 1815 Jan 18 4-0574
Fr 1815 Feb 17 4-0762
Morrell Benjamin
Fr 1833 Jan 30 M124-136
Morrell John & Son
Fr 1803 May 04 fin 1-1118
To 1803 May 07 fin DLC-2
To 1804 May 14 fin DLC-3
Fr 1805 Jan 08 DLC-3
Fr 1805 Feb 22 DLC-3
Fr 1806 Aug 29 fin DLC-4
Fr 1807 Apr 10 DLC-4
Fr 1807 Jun 23 DLC-4
Fr 1807 Dec 16 fin DLC-4
Morris Absalom
Fr 1827 Dec 28 DLC-35
Morris Philip
Fr 1824 Jul 14 fin DLC-33
Morris R
Fr 1831 Aug 15# DLC-39
Morris Thomas et al
Fr 1834 Feb 03 M639-17
Morris William E
Fr 1813 Dec 12 DLC-7

Morris William W
To 1816 Feb 09 DLC-20
Morrison Andrew
To 1839 May 11 chk DLC-52
Morrison E D
Fr 1816 Nov 14 M124-77
Morrison James
Fr 1815 Jun 17 DLC-18
Morrison James J
Re 1840 Feb 04# mem DLC-52
To 1840 Feb 06 fin DLC-52
Re 1841 Apr 27 fin DLC-53
Re 1841 May 10 mem 35-0303
Morrison Robert et al
Fr 1829 Jan 12 M639-2
Morrison Sarah Jane (Smith)
Fr 1844 Feb 05 DLC-56
Morrow Alexander S
To 1825 Jul 22 10-1360
Morrow John
Re 1833 Mar 26 22-0904
Morse Elihu
Fr 1829 M222-28
Morse Isaac
Fr 1829 M222-28
Morse Isaac Edward
Fr 1843 Jan 17 DLC-55
Morse N B
Fr 1835 Aug 27 M273-31
Morse Nathan
To 1828 Feb 09 11-1106
Fr 1830 Jan 20 M639-4
Fr 1831 Oct 11 18-0951
Morse Richard E et al
Fr 1835 Nov M639-9
Morse Samuel A
Fr 1836 Dec 05 32-0882
Fr 1837 Feb 22 M687-20
Morsell Benjamin K
Re 1830 Sep 29 16-0270
Fr 1835 Dec 17 DLC-73
Morsell Benjamin K et al
Fr 1831 May 26 17-1457
Morton _____ et al
Re 1835 May 21 mem DLC-46
Morton George
To 1823 Jul 15 9-0614
Morton J
Fr 1829 Nov 10 M222-27
Fr 1829 Nov 10* 14-0447
Morton Jackson et al
Fr 1837 Feb 09 33-0576
Fr 1837 Feb 11 M687-9
Morton John
Fr 1815 Oct 07 4-1207
Morton Joseph
Fr 1804 Apr 17 fin DLC-3
Morton Marcus
Fr 1829 Sep 19 13-1367
Fr 1830 Feb 22 M639-21
Fr 1833 Sep 30 23-0909
Fr 1835 Apr 01 27-1508
Fr 1836 Jun 06 31-0351
Fr 1844 Dec 21 36-1235
Moseley Peter
Fr 1817 Dec 30 DLC-23
Fr 1828 Feb 25 fin DLC-35
To 1828 Sep 19 12-0208
Fr 1830 Feb 18 lnd DLC-38
Fr 1830 Feb 18* lnd 15-0176
Fr 1831 Jun 27 lnd DLC-40
Fr 1831 Jun 27* lnd 18-0125
To 1831 Jun 27# fin DLC-39
To 1831 Jul 09 chk DLC-39
Moseley & Bondurant
Fr 1839 Jan 07# fin DLC-52
Moser Joseph
Fr 1833 Dec 27 M639-18
Moses Israel
Re 1829 Dec 24 par 14-1109
Moses Reuben
Re 1833 Mar 14 par 22-0754
Mosher George R
Fr 1835 Feb 03 DLC-45
Mosher James
Fr 1830 Jan 09 M639-12
Fr 1830 Nov 06 M639-12
Fr 1834 Dec 15 26-1511
Mosher T
Fr 1815 Nov 20 fin 4-1252
Mosquera Joaquin
Fr 1831 Sep 23 M51-2
Moss Samuel R
Fr 1835 Apr 08 28-0001
Fr 1835 Apr 08* M234-242
Motheral Samuel
To 1823 May 23 9-0566
Moulder Andrew Jackson
Fr 1841 Dec 18 DLC-54
Moulder John Nicholson
To 1830 Mar 27 15-0470
Re 1834 Apr 09 25-0656
Re 1834 Jul 08 26-0194
Re 1835 May 30 28-0534
Fr 1835 Jun 26 28-0820
To 1836 Jun 18 31-0511
Re 1836 Oct 01 31-1580
Moulder John Nicholson et al
Fr 1824 Jan 08 9-0905
To 1824 Jan 08 9-0906
Fr 1825 Jan 08 add 10-1048
To 1825 Jan 08 add 10-1050
Fr 1831 Jan 17-0108
To 1832 Dec 05 21-0871
Moulder John U
Fr 1839 Aug 27 DLC-52
Mountflorence James Cole
Fr 1789 Nov 27# leg 1-0074
Fr 1790 Jul 23 1-0076
Mountjoy Arthur Dobbs
Fr c1829 12-0379
Mount Vernon
Re 1815 cNov 20 mem 4-1253
Mount Vernon AL arsenal
Re 1830 Mar 10 15-0328
Mountz George W
To 1821 Aug 22 DLC-63
To 1821 Aug 22* M116-7
Fr 1821 Aug 23 DLC-63
Fr 1821 Aug 24 M116-9
Fr 1821 Aug 24 M116-9
To 1821 Sep 22 DLC-63
Fr 1821 Sep 24 M116-9
Mouton A E
Fr 1844 Nov 27 36-1058
Mouton Alexander
Fr 1835 Nov 27 M639-9
Fr 1837 Feb 24 33-0862

Mouton Alexander (cont)
Fr 1843 May 05 DLC-55
Fr 1843 May 05 DLC-55
To 1843 Jun 05 35-1363
Mouton Alexander et al
Fr 1844 Dec 07 36-1131
To 1844 Dec 28 36-1271
Mower Thomas Gardner
Fr 1836 Oct 21 32-0313
Muhlenberg Henry Augustus Philip
Fr 1832 Mar 27 19-1563
Fr 1835 Feb 16 M639-17
Fr 1835 Apr 03 27-1515
Re 1835 Jun 28-0545
Muhlenberg Henry Augustus Philip et al
Fr 1828 Dec 08 M639-12
Fr 1832 May M639-14
Fr 1833 Mar 03 M124-137
Fr 1834 Dec 24 M639-22
Fr c1836 Dec M639-9
Fr 1837 Jan 07 M687-21
Fr 1837 Jan 07* 32-1525
Muir Alexander M
Fr 1828 Dec 20 DLC-72
Muir Charles
Fr 1814 Jul 28 DLC-11
Fr 1814 Jul 28* M221-63
Muir Mary
Fr 1831 Jul 13 18-0206
Mulhollan George Jr
Fr 1829 Mar 21 M639-1
Mulledy Thomas F
Fr 1829 Dec 01 fin 14-0793
Muller ______ (Rev)
Re 1843 Nov 17 mem DLC-56
Mullikin John B
Fr 1836 Nov 09 M567-134
Mullowny John
Fr 1829 Feb 05 M639-16
Fr 1829 Feb 05 M639-16
Fr 1829 May 12 T61-4
Fr 1829 Oct 15# T61-4
Mulvany Patrick
Fr 1829 Oct 05 M639-3
Mumford Gurdon Saltonstall
Fr 1819 Jan 28 7-0209
To 1819 Feb 02 7-0223
Fr 1825 Mar 31 DLC-33
Mumford John I
Fr 1834 Mar 12 25-0136
Mumford Thomas
Fr 1838 Jan 04 DLC-51
Fr 1838 Aug 06 DLC-51
Fr 1838 Oct 29 DLC-51
Mumford William C
Fr 1803 Dec 07 DLC-3
Mundy Edward
Fr 1835 Nov 19 M639-9
Mundy Edward et al
Fr 1836 Mar M687-9
Munford William P
Fr 1835 Jun 04 M22-36
Muniz Joas Braulio
To 1831 Oct 24 18-1119
Munks & Bellsnyder
Re 1840 Aug 20 mem DLC-53
Munn David
Fr 1833 Oct 20# fin DLC-43
Munn Jeptha B et al
Fr 1836 Jan 11 29-1548
Munro H
Fr 1821 Apr 29 fin DLC-30
Murat Lucien
Fr 1836 Mar 28 M179-81
Fr 1836 Apr 03 M179-82
Murdock S et al
Fr 1831 Nov 28 M639-1
Murphy John et al
Fr 1833 Jun 04 M639-6
Murphy Nicholas
Fr 1814 Sep 16 DLC-12
Murphy Thomas B M
To 1840 Jul 03 34-1465
Murray George
To 1821 Jul 24 M116-5
To 1821 Jul 27 M116-5
Murray Thomas C
Fr 1814 Oct 17 DLC-13
Murrell John
To 1807 Jan 02 DLC-4
Fr 1807 Jan 08 2-0448
Murrey John
Fr 1812 Jun 15 DLC-5
Murry Bland
Fr 1814 Mar 05 DLC-9
Fr 1814 Mar 24 DLC-9
Mushat John
Fr 1828 Jul 28 DLC-35
Fr 1834 Jan 06 24-0757
Mushulatubbe
Fr 1829 May 16 M234-169
Fr 1832 Mar 27 19-1566
Mushulatubbe et al
Fr 1830 Aug 16 M234-169
Fr 1830 Dec 23 M234-774
Fr 1830 Dec 23* 16-1381
Fr 1831 Mar 24 M234-185
Fr 1831 Mar 24* 17-0967
Mustafa Bascha Bey of Tunis
Fr 1835 May T303-5
Myerle David
Fr 1837 Mar 16 DLC-50
Myers Abraham G
Re 1833 Nov 11 par 23-1217
Myers M
Fr 1844 Dec 11 36-1172
Myers Mark
Re 1836 Oct 19 par 32-0243
Myers Mordecai et al
Fr 1833 Jan M639-16
Myers Moses
Re 1829 Oct 05 mem 14-0109
Myers Willis et al
Fr 1834 Feb 24-1119
Myott Catherine
Fr 1835 Nov 09 29-0486
Myrick Josiah
Fr 1837 Feb 04 M687-20

Nagle Patrick G C
Fr 1828 Nov 18 DLC-72
Naglee John
Fr 1834 Oct 28 26-0761
Fr 1835 Jan 02 M639-9
Fr 1836 Jun 28 DLC-48
Nancrede Joseph Guerard
Fr 1829 Sep 22 M639-17
Nancy (ship)
Re 1836 May 28 leg 31-0170

Napier D
Fr 1831 Dec 15 M22-29
Napier Richard C
Fr 1804 Aug 30 DLC-3
Re 1807 May 01 leg 2-0492
To 1814 Feb 17 DLC-62
Nash Francis R
Re 1805 May 22 leg 2-0044
Nash Sylvester
Fr 1831 Feb 10 M22-27
Fr 1831 Mar 28 M22-27
Nash Travis C
To 1812 Dec 21 DLC-61
To 1813 Jan 01 DLC-61
Nashee George
Fr 1822 Nov 29 DLC-72
To 1822 Dec 17 DLC-31
To 1822 Dec 17* 9-0363
Nashville Bank
Re 1808 Oct 24 fin DLC-4
To 1814 Oct 11 DLC-62
To 1815 Oct 02 4-1205
To 1816 Jul 25 fin DLC-69
Nashville citizens
To 1809 Jan 16 add 2-0763
Fr 1819 Apr 01 add 7-0449
To 1819 Apr 01 add 7-0451
To 1824 Jun 10 add 10-0780
To 1828 cDec 15 DLC-36
Nashville Inn
Fr 1817 Mar 27 fin DLC-69
Nashville Republican
To 1828 11-1000
Nashville spokesman
Fr 1828 cDec 15 DLC-36
Nashville University
Re 1827 Nov 08 11-0918
Nashville University Alumni Society
Fr 1834 Dec 24 26-1588
Nashville Whig editors
To 1816 Jul 07 5-0293
Natchez Expedition
Re 1812 Nov 16 2-1274
Natchez mayor
To 1815 cApr 20 add 4-1008
Natchez citizens
To 1840 cJan 15 add 34-1174
Nathans Nathan
Fr 1835 Feb 13 M639-17
National bank
Re c1833 37-0311
Re c1833 mem 37-0318
National Portrait Gallery
of Distinguished Americans
Re 1834 Jun 26 fin 25-1570
Natt ______
To 1816 Oct 19 chk DLC-21
NawKaw
Fr 1829 Mar 14 T494-2
Naylor F J
To 1829 Aug 07 DLC-60
Naylor Henry et al
Fr 1830 Jan 07 M567-54
Neah Micco et al
Fr 1830 Feb 01 M234-222
Fr 1830 Apr 20 M234-222
Fr 1833 Jan 20 22-0005
Fr 1833 Jul 01 M234-223
Fr 1835 Aug 25 28-1399
Fr 1835 Aug 25* M234-242
Fr 1836 Feb 06 M234-225
Neal Michael W
Fr 1842 Sep 23 DLC-54
Neal Moses L et al
Fr 1829 Dec 14-0714
Neal William
To 1834 Jun 23 chk DLC-44
Neale Charles
Fr 1836 Mar 29 M639-3
Neale Henry C
Fr 1829 Apr 20 M639-16
Neale Julien
Fr 1826 Jul 29 fin 11-0329
Neamathla
Fr 1821 Nov 23 M221-93
Fr 1821 Nov 23* M221-96
Ned (slave)
Re 1815 Sep 12 4-1185
Neely James S
To 1814 Jan 31 DLC-62
Neely Joseph
Re 1807 Nov leg 2-0582
Negrin Paul
Fr 1827 May 14 fin DLC-34
To 1839 Jul 03# fin DLC-52
Fr 1839 Aug 31# fin DLC-52
Neilson William et al
Fr 1835 Mar M639-8
Neisler Hugh
Fr 1831 Oct 28 M22-28
Nelson Charles H
Fr 1836 Jul 10 M567-128
Nelson David
Re 1800 Oct 06 leg 1-0795
Nelson Hugh
Fr 1829 Apr 18 M639-15
Nelson Jane
Fr 1817 Jul 29 DLC-23
Nelson Jeremiah et al
Fr 1831 Sep 18-0645
Nelson John
Re 1831 Oct 24 18-1114
Fr 1834 Oct 20 26-0667
Nelson Joshua
Re 1830 Nov 09 M639-17
Re 1830 Nov 12 16-0717
Nelson Matthew
Fr 1845 Feb 24 DLC-57
Nelson Samuel et al
Fr 1829 Oct 15 M639-6
Neptune Sabattis
Fr 1829 Nov 18 14-0495
Nesmith James
Fr 1832 May 28 M639-12
Netherlands minister to
Re 1829 Apr mem 12-1212
Nevels William
To 1804 Jan 11 fin DLC-3
Nevill George
To 1796 Mar 17 DLC-1
Neville Morgan
Fr 1828 Dec 18 DLC-36
To 1828 Dec 29 12-0341
Fr 1829 Apr 13 M639-17
Fr 1829 Apr 27 M639-3
Fr 1834 Jul 25 26-0239
Fr 1835 Oct 18 29-0316
Fr 1836 Feb 11 M639-12

Neville Nancy
Fr 1830 Jun 01 15-1249
Fr 1838 Sep 21 DLC-51
Nevilles Joseph B
Fr 1796 Mar 08 lnd 1-0353
New Hampshire congressmen
Fr 1834 Feb 06 24-1246
New Jersey General Assembly
Fr 1836 Feb 12 30-0368
New Orleans citizens and soldiers
To 1814 Dec 15 4-0404
To 1814 Dec 16 4-0406
To 1815 Jan 01 DLC-71
Fr 1815 Jan 03 DLC-15
To 1815 Jan 08 add 4-0505
To 1815 Jan 08* add DLC-62
To 1815 Jan 10 add DLC-71
To 1815 Jan 21 add 4-0590
To 1815 Jan 21 add 4-0593
To 1815 Jan 31 4-0663
To 1815 Feb 02 add 4-0677
To 1815 Feb 02* add DLC-16
To 1815 Feb 19 add 4-0766
Re 1815 Feb 28 add DLC-17
Re 1815 Feb 28* add M179-31
To 1815 Mar 05 add 4-0819
To 1815 Mar 08 4-0826
To 1815 Mar 13 add 4-0843
To 1815 Mar 14 add DLC-17
To 1815 Mar 14* add 4-0867
To 1815 Mar 31 add 4-0920
To 1815 Apr# DLC-71
New Orleans Jackson Monument Committee
Re 1840 cJan 10 34-1167
New Orleans Young Hickory Club
Fr 1844 Dec 13 36-1192
New York City Common Council
Fr 1819 Feb 23 DLC-26
Fr 1819 Feb 23 7-0313
Fr 1829 Jan 12 12-0455
New York Democratic meeting
Re 1834 cApr mem 25-0532
New York General Assembly
Fr 1815 Apr 04 DLC-18
New York Indians of Green Bay
Fr 1831 Mar 04 17-0810
Newcom Joseph
To 1807 Jan 15 fin DLC-4
To 1807 Jan 16 fin DLC-4
To 1807 Feb 10 fin DLC-4
Newell George
Fr 1828 Nov 20 DLC-35
Newell P
Fr 1824 Mar 30 DLC-32
Newell William
Fr 1804 Jul 11 fin 1-1345
Newlin Henry M
To 1812 Dec 21 DLC-61
Newlon Johnson F et al
Fr 1829 Jul 17 M639-19
Fr 1829 Jul 20 M639-2
Newman Francis
Fr 1814 Jul 10 3-1118
Fr 1814 Dec 20 4-0432
Fr 1814 Dec 20 4-0433
Fr 1814 Dec 21 4-0441
To 1814 Dec 22 DLC-62
Fr 1814 Dec 24 4-0455
Fr 1815 Jan 15 DLC-15
Newnan Daniel
Fr 1832 Jun 25 DLC-40
Newnan John
To 1814 Apr 12 fin DLC-10
Fr 1820 Dec 12 fin 8-0019
Newnan L
Fr 1841 Nov 02 fin DLC-53
Newsom Ansel B
Fr 1839 Jan 27# DLC-51
Re 1839 Oct 07# leg 34-0989
Newton David et al
Fr 1836 Jun 04 31-0326
Newton N Jr
Fr 1843 Oct 18 DLC-55
Newton Robert
Fr 1818 Jun 12 fin DLC-69
Newton William L
Fr 1828 Aug 30 DLC-35
To 1828 Sep 09 DLC-35
Niagara Falls canal
Re 1835 cMar M22-36
Niccolo Giorgio (brig)
Re 1831 Oct 17 par 18-1011
Nichol Charles M
To 1832 Mar 05# fin DLC-40
To 1834 Aug 18 DLC-44
To 1835 Nov 19# fin DLC-47
Fr 1837 Apr 10 fin DLC-50
Nichol James
Re 1839 Jan 23 leg 34-0605
Fr 1839 Aug 24 DLC-52
To 1842 Jan 06 chk DLC-54
Fr 1842 Jan 07 35-0588
Fr 1844 Jan 02 fin DLC-57
Nichol James & Co
Fr 1837 Jan 18 fin DLC-51
Fr 1837 Oct 02 fin DLC-51
Nichol John
Fr 1823 Dec 17 fin DLC-32
Fr 1838 May 29# fin DLC-51
Nichol John & Co
Fr 1828 Oct 03 fin 12-0225
Nichol Josiah
To 1814 Jun 09 DLC-10
To 1814 Jun 21 chk DLC-10
Fr 1819 Apr 05 DLC-26
Fr 1825 May 26 fin DLC-33
Fr 1825 May 27 fin DLC-33
Fr 1825 May 30 fin 10-1293
Fr 1825 Jun 11 fin DLC-33
Fr 1826 Jan 12 fin 11-0106
Fr 1826 Apr 05 fin DLC-33
Fr 1826 Nov 21 fin 11-0398
Fr 1827 Oct 25 fin 11-0895
Fr 1827 Oct 26 fin 11-0897
Fr 1827 Dec 05 fin 11-0950
Re 1829 Dec 29 fin 14-1157
Fr 1831 Jan 11 DLC-38
Fr 1831 Oct 19 DLC-40
Fr 1831 Dec 30 DLC-40
Fr 1832 Jan 05 DLC-40
Fr 1832 Jan 07 DLC-40
Fr 1832 Mar 03 DLC-40
Fr 1832 Mar 12 DLC-40
Fr 1832 Jun 21 DLC-40
Nichol Josiah et al
To 1828 Dec 04 12-0298
Fr 1828 Dec 04 12-0300
Fr 1832 Aug 16 DLC-41
To 1832 Aug 16 DLC-41

Nichol Josiah & Co
Fr 1824 Apr 09 fin DLC-33
Fr 1833 Oct 31# fin DLC-44
To 1836 Aug 22 fin DLC-48
Fr 1839 Jan 01 fin DLC-52
Fr 1839 Jan 09# fin DLC-52
To 1839 Jun 08 34-0813
Nichol Josiah & Son
Fr 1829 Nov 27 fin DLC-38
Fr 1831 Sep 29 fin DLC-40
Nichol William
To 1835 Jun 18# fin DLC-53
To 1839 Apr 18 fin DLC-53
To 1839 Dec 24# fin DLC-53
To 1839 Dec 24# fin DLC-53
To 1839 Dec 24# fin DLC-53
To 1840 Jan 01# fin DLC-52
To 1840 May 18# fin DLC-53
To 1840 Jul 11# fin DLC-53
To 1840 Jul 11# fin DLC-53
Fr 1840 Jul 13 DLC-53
Fr 1841 Mar 11 DLC-53
Fr 1845 Feb 17 DLC-57
Nichol & Hill
To 1829 Aug 04 chk DLC-37
Fr 1830 Jun 07 fin DLC-38
Fr 1830 Jul 24 fin DLC-40
To 1830 Aug 20 chk DLC-38
Nicholas ______ (Col)
Re 1832 Mar 22 mem 19-1537
Nicholas Cary
To 1818 Jan 06 5-1236
To 1818 Dec 07 7-0041
Fr 1820 Feb 25 M221-86
Fr 1820 Feb 29 M566-130
Fr 1820 Sep 14 M221-89
To 1821 Oct 03# 8-1267
Fr 1821 Oct 08 fin DLC-70
Nicholas John
Fr 1829 Mar 07 M639-17
Nicholas N
Fr 1835 Apr 23 28-0116
Nicholas Philip Norborne
Fr 1833 Dec 05 M639-17
Nicholas Robert Carter (d 1836)
Fr 1815 Jun 17 DLC-18
To 1815 Jul 03 DLC-62
Fr 1815 Jul 13 DLC-75
To 1816 Feb 03 DLC-62
Fr 1816 Oct 29 M221-70
Fr 1818 Aug 01 DLC-25
Re 1830 Mar 20 par 15-0413
Nicholas Robert Carter (1793-1857)
Fr 1836 Apr 21 30-1297
Nicholas & Tunstall
Fr 1821 Oct 08 fin DLC-70
Nicholas I Emperor of Russia
To 1830 Jun 16 15-1472
To 1830 Jun 18 15-1512
Fr 1831 Jan 12 17-0243
Fr 1831 Jan 12* M39-2
To 1831 May 23 17-1411
Fr 1831 Jun 24 18-0098
Fr 1831 Aug 10 18-0496
Fr 1831 Aug 28 18-0610
To 1831 Nov 16 18-1285
To 1831 Nov 16 18-1286
To 1832 Mar 26 19-1555
Fr 1832 Oct 15 21-0094
Fr 1832 Oct 15* M39-2
To 1833 Apr 05 22-0950
Fr 1833 Jul 31 23-0248
Fr 1833 Jul 31* M39-2
To 1834 Jun 03 25-1237
To 1834 Jul 02 26-0069
Fr 1836 Mar 19 30-0835
To 1836 Mar 30 30-0930
Nicholls William S
Fr 1829 Jul 09 M639-7
Nichols Ann (Romaine)
Fr 1845 Mar 14 M873-63
Nichols Asaph R
Fr 1837 Feb 23 M687-16
Nichols George W Mrs
Fr 1844 Nov 23 DLC-57
Nichols Humphrey
Re 1834 Mar 11 par 25-0038
Nichols Rowland et al
Fr 1835 Jan 08 DLC-45
Nichols Thomas
Re 1832 Jan 18 par 19-0758
Nicholson Alfred Osborn Pope
Fr 1835 Nov 04 29-0444
To 1835 Dec 18 DLC-47
To 1835 Dec 18* 29-1225
Fr 1836 Jan 26 DLC-47
Fr 1836 Aug 20 M234-189
Fr 1836 Oct 03 DLC-49
To 1836 Oct 17 DLC-49
Fr 1837 Nov 22 34-0036
Fr 1840 Feb 17 DLC-52
Fr 1844 Mar 16 DLC-56
Nicholson George
Fr 1841 Feb 13 DLC-53
Nicholson James
Fr 1821 Apr 24 DLC-30
Nicholson John
Fr 1829 Mar 07 M639-15
Fr 1833 Apr 08 M179-76
Fr 1834 May 14 25-1041
Fr 1836 May 16 M567-122
Nicholson Malachi
Re 1819 Aug 12 leg 7-0603
Fr 1819 Dec 22 fin 7-0933
To 1820 Oct 03 fin 7-1383
Fr 1821 Jan 04 fin 8-0042
Fr 1821 Jan 17 fin 8-0079
Fr 1821 Mar 11 DLC-30
Fr 1821 Apr 05 DLC-29
Fr 1821 Apr 18 fin 8-0357
Fr 1821 Dec 29 fin 8-1373
Fr 1822 Jan 01 fin 8-1379
Fr 1822 Jun 13 fin 9-0189
Fr 1822 Sep 21 9-0267
Fr 1822 Sep 21 fin 9-0269
Fr 1822 Nov 11 fin 9-0302
Fr 1822 Nov 17 fin 9-0309
Fr 1823 Jan 08# fin 9-0395
Fr 1823 Jan 27 fin 9-0435
Fr 1824 Jul 15 fin 10-0829
Fr 1825 Jan 01 fin 10-1021
Nicholson William et al
Fr 1835 cJan DLC-59
Nicks John
Fr 1814 Aug 08 DLC-11
To 1814 Dec 25 DLC-62
To 1814 Dec 25 4-0460
Fr 1815 Jan 08 DLC-15

Nicks John (cont)
To 1815 Jan 09 DLC-62
To 1815 Jan 14 DLC-62
Fr 1817 DLC-59
Fr c1817 DLC-59
Fr 1821 Feb 05 DLC-29
Fr 1829 Jun 15 M222-26

Nicolet Theodore
Fr 1835 Dec 01 M567-104
Fr 1835 Dec 01* M179-81

Nicoll Francis H
Fr 1834 Oct 16 M639-10

Nicolson John B
Fr 1841 Nov 20 DLC-54

Nicolus Louis et al
Fr 1815 Jan 21 DLC-15

Nicoson John
To 1814 Mar 05 DLC-9

Niles George Washington
Fr 1837 Apr 18 DLC-50

Niles Henry
To 1823 Dec 19 9-0813

Niles Hezekiah
Fr 1817 Jul 31 DLC-23
To 1817 Aug 26 5-1000
To 1822 Aug 09 9-0245
Fr 1823 Jul 23 DLC-32

Niles John Milton
Fr 1832 Jan 19 19-0784
Fr 1835 Dec 25 M639-17
Fr 1836 Jul 02 31-0761
To 1838 Jan 24 34-0212
Fr 1840 Sep 22 DLC-53
Fr 1840 Sep 22* 35-0016

Niles John Milton et al
Fr 1836 Jan 19 M124-153

Niles Nathaniel
Re 1830 Nov 09 16-0704

Nisbet Archibald
Fr 1829 Dec M567-46

Nisbet Mary
Fr 1829 Dec M567-46

Niswanger C
Fr 1835 Mar 24 M639-3

Nixon George H
Fr 1814 Jul 19 3-1152
Fr 1814 Jul 27 3-1183
Fr 1814 Jul 28 3-1186
Fr 1814 Sep 06 4-0178
To 1814 Sep 22 DLC-62
To 1814 Sep 24 DLC-62
Fr 1814 Sep 29 DLC-12
To 1814 Oct 06 DLC-62
Fr 1814 Oct 09 4-0260
Fr 1814 Oct 28 4-0301
To 1815 Feb 03 DLC-16
Fr 1815 Feb 17 4-0763
To 1815 Mar 04 4-0813
To 1815 Mar 04* DLC-62
Fr 1817 Aug 30 DLC-23

Nixon Lewis A
Re 1837 Jan 30 par 33-0239

Noah Mordecai Manuel
Fr 1829 Mar 25 12-1120
Fr 1829 Jul 06 M639-20
To 1830 May 20# 15-1056
Fr 1831 Sep 07 M639-18
Fr 1832 Mar 30 20-0060
Fr 1833 Jan 07 21-1345
Fr 1833 May 01 M124-138

Noahquagephik et al
Fr 1836 Jan 27 M234-422

Noble James
Fr 1829 Feb 25 M639-13
Fr 1829 Feb 25 M639-22
Fr 1829 Feb 25 M639-10
Fr 1829 Mar 02 M639-15
Fr 1829 Mar 04 M639-15
Fr 1829 Mar 05 M639-6
Fr 1829 Mar 05 12-0859
Fr 1829 Mar 06 12-0866

Noble Noah
Fr 1834 Jan 15 M234-354

Nock Tobias
Fr 1830 Jun 28 M124-124

Noel Matthew
Fr 1835 Sep 06 M639-11

Noel Silas M
Fr 1821 Apr 03 DLC-30

Noels Reuben
Fr 1806 Jan 27 fin DLC-3

Noland Charles Fenton Mercer
Fr 1834 Apr 14 M567-100

Noland William
Fr 1828 Feb 17 DLC-35
Fr 1830 May 18 15-1047
Re 1836 Jul 06 31-0885
To 1836 Jul 09 31-1032
Fr 1836 Jul 26 DLC-48
To 1836 Oct 18 32-0225
Fr 1836 Oct 26 32-0348
Fr 1836 Dec 03 32-0834
Fr 1837 Jan 23 33-0110
To 1837 Mar 04# 33-1065
To 1837 cMar 06# 33-1072
To 1837 Mar 06# mem 33-1074
To 1837 Mar 11 33-1075
To 1837 Apr 27 33-1187
To 1837 May 14# 33-1226
Fr 1837 May 19 DLC-50
To 1837 May 23# 33-1246
To 1837 Aug# 33-1402
To 1837 Dec 01# 34-0066
To 1837 Dec 18 34-0132
To 1838 Feb 14 34-0242
To 1838 Apr 09 34-0312
Fr 1838 Apr 30 DLC-51
Fr 1838 Apr 30# DLC-51
Fr 1838 May 14 DLC-51
To 1838 May 24 34-0348
Fr 1839 Apr 22 DLC-52
Fr 1840 May 26 DLC-52
Fr 1842 Feb 03 DLC-54

Nolin Berry
To 1803 Aug 12 fin 1-1148

Norfolk Volunteer Corps
To 1831 Jul 01 18-0144

Noridge William
To 1814 Jun 24 3-1104

Norman G W
Fr 1836 Mar 06 DLC-47

Norman Thomas
Fr 1830 Apr 22 M124-123

Norris H Ariel
To 1833 Sep 12 23-0702

North Carolina General Assembly
To 1789 Nov leg 1-0071
To 1789 Nov 27# leg 1-0074

Northeastern boundary
Re 1831 Mar mem DLC-40
Re 1832 cJun 23 mem DLC-43
Northrop Lucius Ballinger
Fr 1836 May 14 M567-128
Fr 1836 May 15 M567-128
Northrup Claudian B
Fr 1836 Mar 25 M567-128
Fr 1836 Mar 26 M567-128
Norton C A et al
Fr 1830 Dec 16-0912
Norton John P
Fr 1845 Mar 06 36-1538
Norton John P et al
Fr 1829 May 05 13-0256
Fr 1829 Nov 20 14-0535
Norton Joseph et al
Fr 1829 Mar M873-19
Norvell John
Fr 1829 Mar 17 M639-19
Fr 1831 Jun 20 M639-19
Fr 1835 Dec 09 M200-6
Fr 1836 Feb 05 M639-26
Fr 1836 Apr 01 M687-34
Fr 1836 Apr 20 M639-6
Fr 1836 Jun 20 M687-34
Fr 1837 Jan 27 M234-422
Norvell Joseph
To 1822 Nov 25 9-0316
Norvell Moses & Joseph
Fr 1814 Jun 11 fin DLC-18
Nott Henry Junius
Fr 1836 Jul 04 M639-17
Nourse Charles J
Fr 1823 Dec 20 M565-6
Fr 1829 Mar 18 M234-808
Nourse Michael
Fr 1820 Jun 08 DLC-29
To 1820 Jul 05 7-1135
To 1830 Feb 16 15-0148
To 1830 Apr 17 15-0749
Re 1831 Aug 19 18-0572
Re 1832 Jul 18 20-1136
Re 1832 Dec 31 21-1214
Re 1833 May 02 22-1264
Re 1833 Jun 13 23-0023
Re 1833 Oct 12 23-1018
Re 1834 Jul 07 26-0183
To 1835 Sep 23 29-0102
To 1836 Apr 20 30-1274
Re 1836 Jul 09 31-1034
Novell Joseph
Fr 1824 Jan 15 9-0932
Nowland Rebecca
Fr 1823 Feb 08 fin DLC-72
Nowlin & Weaver
Fr 1841 Apr 13 fin DLC-53
Fr 1841 Apr 14 fin DLC-53
Fr 1842 Jan 29 DLC-54
Nuckolls William Thompson
Fr 1829 May 11 13-0308
Fr 1832 19-0509
Nullification
Re 1832 Nov mem 21-0251
Re 1832 Nov 07 mem 21-0346
Re 1832 Dec 10 T1223-1
Re 1832 Dec 10* 21-0935
Re 1832 Dec 10* DLC-77
Re 1833 cJan 01 mem 21-1296
Nun (sloop)
Re 1830 Jun 14 par 15-1392
Nute Levi Monroe
Fr 1835 Aug 07# M567-112
Nuttall Elijah F
Fr 1830 Aug 20 M639-2
Nye Shadrach
Fr 1808 Mar 20 DLC-71
Nye Shadrach et al
Fr 1804 Dec 18 lnd 1-1426
Nye William C
Fr 1830 Jun 04 M179-68
Fr 1830 Jun 08 M179-68
Fr 1830 Jun 08 M179-68
Nye William C et al
Fr 1830 Jun 03 M179-68

Oakey S W
Fr 1836 Oct 24 32-0339
Oakford John et al
Fr 1829 cMar M639-5
Fr 1839 Oct 23 34-1022
Oakford Richard
Fr 1834 May 31 M639-2
Oakley Charles
Re 1836 Dec 10 par 32-1086
Oakley Henry A
Fr 1844 Dec 17 DLC-57
O'Brien David
Fr 1837 Feb 04 M687-20
O'Brien James
Fr 1834 Jan 21 M639-17
O'Brien John
Fr 1837 Jan 30 M687-20
O'Brien William
Re 1836 Jul 07 par 31-0937
O'Connor John Michael
Fr 1818 Feb 15 DLC-24
Octe Achee Emathla
Fr 1831 Feb 18 M234-222
Odam James
Re 1808 Sep 21 leg 2-0723
Odell Jacob
Fr 1829 M639-11
Odlin Woodbridge
Re 1829 Jun 25 13-0713
Offley David
Fr 1829 Mar 17 M46-2
Fr 1829 Mar 17* 12-1022
Fr 1829 Mar 21 M46-2
Fr 1829 Mar 21* 12-1072
Fr 1829 Aug 09 T238-1
Fr 1829 Aug 09* 13-1057
Fr 1830 Jun 08 M46-3
Fr 1830 Jun 08* 15-1318
Fr 1831 Aug 17 M639-17
Ogden Francis Barber
Fr 1829 Mar 06 M639-17
To 1829 Apr 16# 12-1367
To 1829 Apr 17# 12-1374
To 1829 Apr 18# 13-0064
Re 1829 Jun 18 13-0679
Fr 1829 Nov 22# DLC-75
To 1829 Nov 26# DLC-75
Fr 1829 Nov 30# DLC-75
Fr 1835 Aug 30 28-1462
Fr 1836 Dec 12 32-1097
Fr 1844 Nov 30 M873-64

Name	Date	Note	Reference
Ogden George M			
	Fr 1815 Feb 03		DLC-16
Ogden James D P			
	Re 1842 cSep 05	mem	35-0922
Ogden Lewis			
	Re 1832 May 31		M273-28
Ogden Peter G			
	To 1815 Mar 11		DLC-62
Ogden Rebecca Cornell			
	Fr 1843 Sep 21#		DLC-55
Ogden W B et al			
	Fr 1836 Jun		M687-14
Ogden Ferguson & Co et al			
	Fr 1834 Mar 24		M639-14
Ogle Alexander			
	Fr 1830 Apr 07		15-0637
Oglesby William W			
	Fr 1841 Apr 29#		DLC-53
O'Hanlon James			
	Fr 1832 Nov 30		DLC-41
	To 1832 Dec 06		DLC-41
	Fr 1832 Dec 20		DLC-41
	Fr 1834 Apr 24		DLC-44
O'Hara James			
	Fr 1805 May 13		DLC-3
	Fr 1805 Dec 02		2-0095
	Fr 1809 Mar 25		2-0797
O'Hara Michael			
	Fr 1836 May 30		31-0207
	Fr 1836 Jun 03		31-0291
Ohio canal			
	Re 1806 Mar 22		2-0193
Ohio General Assembly			
	Fr 1842 Mar 07		DLC-54
Ohio legislators			
	Fr 1831 Dec 16		M22-29
Okie A			
	Fr 1833 Apr 22		M639-20
Old soldier (pseudonym)			
	Fr 1830 Aug 23		16-0141
Oldenburg shipping			
	Re 1830 Sep 18		T1223-1
	Re 1830 Sep 18*		16-0252
Oldfields & Co			
	Fr 1820 Aug 08#	fin	DLC-29
Oldham John P			
	Fr 1830 Jan 25		15-0015
	Fr 1830 Jan 31		M639-14
Oldham S			
	Fr 1834 Mar 10#		M688-94
Olds Joseph et al			
	Fr 1833 Oct 01		M639-12
Oliphant Samuel			
	To 1801 Jun 09	lnd	1-0880
Oliver Henry			
	Fr 1836 May		30-1444
Oliver Isaac			
	Fr 1828 Sep 18		DLC-35
Oliver James D et al			
	Fr 1834 Jan		M639-18
Oliver Peter			
	To 1840 Oct 25	fin	DLC-53
Oliver Robert			
	To 1830 Sep 27		16-0261
	Fr 1830 Oct 19		M639-10
	Fr 1830 Oct 20		M639-26
	To 1830 Oct 26		16-0553
	Fr 1830 Nov 22		16-0832
	Fr 1831 Oct 18		M639-10
Oliver Robert et al			
	Fr 1831 Oct		M639-17
	Fr 1831 Nov 02		M639-11
	Fr 1833 Apr 03		M639-2
	Fr 1834 Dec 09		M179-79
Oliver Walter et al			
	Fr 1830 Dec 15		M22-27
Oliver William Morrison et al			
	Fr 1830 Mar 15		M639-13
Oliver Y N			
	Fr 1835 Oct 03	fin	DLC-47
	To 1835 Oct 03	chk	DLC-47
Olivier Marie			
	Fr 1815 Apr 04		DLC-18
	Fr 1815 Apr 04*		M221-63
	Fr 1815 Apr 04	mem	DLC-18
	Fr 1815 Apr 04*	mem	M221-63
Olivier Marie et al			
	Fr 1814 Dec 20		DLC-14
Olmsted Charles G			
	Fr 1833 Mar 25		22-0895
Olmsted Charles G et al			
	Fr 1832 Apr 03		20-0124
Olney G W			
	Fr 1834 Jul 24		DLC-44
Olney J			
	Fr 1841 Nov 18		DLC-54
O'Maher Timothy			
	Fr 1836 Nov 09#		32-0426
Ompablongah et al			
	Fr 1833 Oct 03		M234-883
	Fr 1833 Oct 03*		23-0940
One of the People (pseudonym)			
	Fr 1828 Sep 24		DLC-36
O'Neal Edward Asbury			
	Fr 1844 Jul 09		DLC-57
O'Neal Timothy			
	To 1806 Jul 17	lnd	2-0296
O'Neal William			
	Fr 1834 Apr 15		25-0709
O'Neale John H P			
	Re 1837 Feb 17		M567-149
O'Neale Rhoda			
	Fr 1845 Mar 08		DLC-57
O'Neale William			
	To 1797 Aug 25#	fin	DLC-1
	Fr 1825 Feb 12	fin	10-1109
	Fr 1825 Mar	fin	10-1196
	Fr 1829 Feb 10	fin	DLC-36
	To 1830 Apr 23#		DLC-38
	Re 1831 Mar 02		17-0717
	Re 1832 Mar 13		19-1417
	Fr 1835 Mar 31#	fin	DLC-46
	Fr 1835 Aug 22	fin	DLC-47
	Fr 1835 Nov 18#	fin	DLC-47
	To 1836 Oct 03#		DLC-49
	To 1836 Oct 11#	fin	DLC-49
	To 1836 Oct 26#		DLC-49
O'Neall John Belton			
	Fr 1834 Oct 13		DLC-44
O'Neill Barnard			
	Fr 1829 Jun 13#		M124-119
	Fr 1829 Aug 03		M124-120
	Fr 1829 Sep 12		M124-120
Opothleholo et al			
	Fr 1835 Jun 13		M234-224
	Fr 1835 Oct 25		29-0349
	Fr 1835 Oct 25*		M234-242
	Fr 1836 Jan 07		M234-243

Fr 1836 Jan 14 30-0029
Fr 1836 Jan 14* M234-225
Fr 1836 Apr 14 30-1171
Fr 1836 Apr 14* M234-243
Oppenheimer C T & Co et al
Fr 1836 Jul 08 M687-12
Orator (schooner)
Fr 1834 Dec 05# fin DLC-45
Orbegoso Luis Jose
Fr 1836 Mar 04 T802-1
Ord P
To 1836 Dec 08 chk DLC-49
Ore James
To 1797 Mar 04 1-0501
Fr 1797 May 01 DLC-2
O'Reilly John A et al
Fr 1835 Dec 24 29-1338
Orme Jeremiah et al
Fr 1831 cJan 01 M639-3
Orme W C et al
Fr 1836 Apr 04 M687-28
Orr Benjamin G
Fr 1817 Jan 17 DLC-22
Orr John
Fr 1805 Feb 25 fin DLC-3
Orton J B
Fr 1833 Oct 02 M639-12
Orton Richard
Re 1810 Apr 14 leg 2-0882
Osborn George L
Fr 1843 Aug 30 DLC-55
Osborn J & Gardner
To 1816 Dec 07 fin DLC-22
Osborne T A et al
Fr 1836 cAug 02 31-1209
Osbourne Samuel M
Fr 1829 Jul 10 13-0835
Osbrooks Michael
Re 1806 Jul 04 leg 2-0292
Osgood Gayton Pickman
Fr 1834 Dec 24 27-0002
Osgood S H
Fr 1836 Jun 11 31-0432
Osgood Walter F
Re 1835 cDec 19 par 29-1242
Oshkosh
Fr 1831 Oct 24 18-1115
Osterhout Lucas
Fr 1831 Jan 25 M22-27
O'Sullivan William R
Re 1830 Dec 10 M273-25
Otey James Hervey
Fr 1835 Mar 21 M22-36
Fr 1836 Aug 02 M124-154
Otis Amos
Re 1834 Nov 14 par 26-0906
Re 1834 Dec 09 par 26-1458
Otis George Alexander
Fr 1839 May 06 DLC-52
Fr 1845 Mar 17 36-1577
Otis Harrison Gray
Fr 1833 Oct 15 23-1036
Otis John Alexander
Re 1833 Dec 11 par 24-0448
Otis Oran Gray et al
Fr 1831 cDec M639-24
Otis Samuel Allyne
To 1798 Feb 05 1-0603
Otis William
Re c1835 Oct mem 37-0345
Fr 1835 Oct 05 29-0203
Fr 1835 Dec 19 29-1250
Fr 1836 Oct 05 32-0070
Oto and Missouri treaty
Re 1834 Apr 12 M668-7
OtoCho et al
Fr 1831 May 28 M234-136
Fr 1831 May 28* 17-1464
Ottawa treaty
Re 1832 Apr 06 M668-6
Re 1833 Mar 22 M668-7
Ottawa and Chippewa treaty
Re 1836 May 27 M668-8
Otto I King of Greece
Fr 1832 Oct 05 M34-29
To 1836 Oct 01 31-1581
Ouilmett Michell
Fr 1831 Nov 21 18-1465
Outlaw Alexander
Fr 1801 Mar 22 DLC-2
Fr 1808 Oct 10 2-0732
Re 1814 Aug leg 3-1209
Overstreet G M
Fr 1843 Mar 23 DLC-55
Overton Archibald Waters
Fr 1828 Jul 04 DLC-59
To 1828 Jul 04 DLC-35
Overton James
Fr 1805 Sep 08 DLC-3
Fr 1837 Mar 11 DLC-50
Fr 1837 Mar 13 DLC-50
Fr 1837 Mar 25 add 33-1115
To 1837 Mar 25 add 33-1116
Overton John
Re 1794 Jan 04 leg DLC-1
Re 1794 May 12 leg DLC-1
Re 1794 Nov 15 leg 1-0242
Fr 1795 Feb 20 leg 1-0249
Fr 1795 Mar 08 mem DLC-1
To 1795 Jun 09 1-0300
To 1795 Jun 18 1-0308
Re 1795 Sep 22 leg 1-0320
Fr 1796 Feb 28 lnd 1-0340
Fr 1796 Mar 10 DLC-1
Fr 1796 Mar 12 DLC-1
Fr 1796 Dec 18 DLC-1
Fr 1796 Dec 20 DLC-1
To 1798 Jan 22 1-0586
To 1798 Feb 03 1-0599
To 1798 Feb 03 1-0602
To 1798 Feb 23 1-0627
To 1798 Jun 09 1-0663
Fr 1799 May 02 fin DLC-2
To 1799 Jun 23 1-0722
To 1799 Nov 30 1-0748
Re 1800 Nov 24 leg 1-0824
To 1801 Jul 10 1-0886
Fr 1802 May 27 fin DLC-2
To 1802 Jul 14 1-1027
Fr 1802 Jul 14 DLC-2
To 1802 Sep 1-1039
Fr 1802 Sep 24 DLC-2
Fr 1804 Jul 20 DLC-75
To 1806 Feb 03 fin 2-0146
To 1806 Mar 08# 2-0188
Fr 1806 May 29 lnd 2-0251
Fr 1806 Jun 01 2-0269

Overton John (cont)

Fr 1806 Sep 12		2-0338
Fr 1808 Mar 18		2-0621
Re 1810 Sep 22	leg	2-0967
To 1811 Jan 21		2-0987
Fr 1812 Jan 19		DLC-5
Re 1812 Jul	leg	2-1111
To 1812 Dec 12	lnd	2-1293
To 1813 Jul 21	lnd	3-0424
Fr 1814 Feb 12		DLC-9
Fr 1814 May 08		DLC-10
To 1814 Aug 10		3-1296
To 1816 cFeb 02		4-1380
Fr 1818 Dec 21		DLC-26
Re 1819 Jan 06	leg	7-0121
Fr 1819 Oct 21		7-0721
Fr 1821 Feb 19		M439-8
To 1821 Dec 09		8-1360
Fr 1822 Mar 29		9-0078
To 1822 Apr 02	leg	9-0095
Fr 1822 Apr 05		9-0099
Fr 1822 Apr 17	lnd	DLC-31
To 1822 Apr 19	lnd	9-0118
To 1822 Apr 19	lnd	9-0126
To 1823 Oct 24		9-0715
To 1823 Nov 04		9-0729
To 1823 Nov 08		9-0744
To 1823 Dec 05		9-0783
To 1823 Dec 21		9-0821
To 1824 Mar 23		10-0580
To 1824 Nov 06		10-0952
To 1824 Dec 09		10-0972
To 1824 Dec 19		10-0988
To 1825 Jan 10		10-1062
To 1825 Feb 10		10-1102
Fr 1825 Apr 16	add	10-1236
To 1825 Apr 16	add	10-1238
To 1825 Sep 10		10-1417
To 1825 Sep 13		10-1419
To 1826 Jan 22		11-0115
To 1826 Feb 06		11-0139
To 1826 Feb 15		11-0141
Fr 1826 Nov 26		11-0409
To 1826 Dec 07		11-0423
Fr 1827 May 14		DLC-34
To 1827 Jun 16		11-0704
Fr 1827 Jun 23		11-0706
Fr 1827 Jun 23		11-0709
To 1827 Jun 24		11-0712
To 1827 Aug 15		11-0793
To 1827 Aug 18		11-0803
Fr 1827 Aug 25		DLC-34
To 1827 Sep		11-0835
To 1827 Nov 07		11-0916
Fr 1828 Aug 15		12-0148
Fr 1829 Feb 22		M639-4
Fr 1829 May 10		M639-2
To 1829 Jun 08		13-0595
To 1829 Jul 05		13-0817
To 1829 Dec 31		14-1192
To 1830 May 13		15-0994
To 1830 May 27		15-1162
Fr 1830 Jun 16		DLC-38
To 1830 Sep 30		16-0277
To 1831 Jan 16		17-0277
Fr 1831 Feb 03		17-0421
To 1831 Feb 08		17-0474
To 1831 Feb 12		17-0505
To 1831 Feb 28		17-0673
Fr 1831 Jun 02		DLC-39
Fr 1831 Jun 02*		DLC-73
Fr 1831 Jun 04#		17-1520
Fr 1831 Jul 27	fin	18-0292
To 1831 Aug 27#		18-0608
To 1831 Sep 13		18-0720
To 1831 Sep 16		18-0796
To 1831 Dec 05		19-0085
Fr 1832 May 09		20-0496
Fr 1832 Oct 30		M639-4
Fr 1832 Nov 05		DLC-41

Overton John et al

Re 1819 Jan 12	leg	7-0134

Overton John Holmes

Fr 1825 Jan 07		M688-38
Fr 1836 Mar 31		DLC-47
Fr 1837 Mar 12		DLC-50

Overton John Holmes et al

Fr 1835 Dec 05		M639-8

Overton John W

Fr 1813 cSep		3-0442
Fr 1817 May 04		DLC-22
Fr 1820 Jan 22	fin	7-1010
Fr 1830 Nov 11		16-0711
Fr 1833 Apr 01#		DLC-42
Re 1833 Aug 11		23-0314
Re 1833 Aug 17		23-0365
Fr 1836 Aug 04		DLC-48
Fr 1838 Dec 18		DLC-51
Fr 1839 Aug 24		34-0870

Overton Patrick Henry

Fr 1834 Oct 07		DLC-44

Overton Samuel Ragland

Re 1820 Aug 24		T494-1
Re 1820 Aug 24*		7-1221
Fr 1821 Jan 30		DLC-29
Fr 1821 Feb 10		DLC-29
Fr 1821 Mar 11		DLC-30
Fr 1821 Aug 01		DLC-30
Fr 1822 Mar 21		DLC-31
To 1822 Apr 11	lnd	9-0108
Fr 1822 Jun 09		DLC-31
Fr 1822 Jul 05		DLC-31
Fr 1822 Sep 02		DLC-31
Fr 1822 Sep 10		DLC-31
Fr 1822 Sep 22		DLC-31
Fr 1822 Oct 15		DLC-31
Fr 1822 Nov 30		DLC-31
Fr 1823 Jan 09		DLC-31
Fr 1823 Jan 28		DLC-32
Fr 1823 Mar 19		DLC-72
Fr 1823 Apr 15		DLC-32
Fr 1823 May 24		DLC-32
Fr 1823 Jun 08		DLC-32
Fr 1823 Jun 27		DLC-32
Fr 1823 Jun 29		DLC-32
Fr 1823 Jul 22		DLC-32
Fr 1823 Aug 15		DLC-32
Fr 1823 Aug 26		DLC-32
Fr 1823 Sep 26		DLC-32
Fr 1823 Oct 01		DLC-32
Fr 1825 Jan 28		DLC-33
Fr 1825 Mar 05		DLC-33
Fr 1825 Apr 12		DLC-33
Fr 1826 Feb 05		DLC-33
Fr 1826 Jul 05		DLC-34
Fr 1826 Aug 28		DLC-34
Fr 1826 Sep 17		DLC-34
Fr 1826 Nov 07		DLC-34
Fr 1827 May 31		DLC-34

Name	Date	Note	Source
Overton Thomas			
	To 1798 Mar 06		1-0634
	Fr 1806 Mar 04		DLC-3
	Fr 1806 Jun 25		2-0279
	Fr 1810 Oct 08		DLC-71
	Fr 1812 Oct 08		DLC-71
	Fr 1815 Jan 17		4-0564
	Fr 1823 Mar 10	fin	DLC-32
Overton Thomas Jefferson			
	Re 1805 cJul 28	mem	DLC-60
	Fr 1805 Aug 01		DLC-3
Overton Thomas W			
	Fr 1834 Jun 11		25-1313
Overton Walter Hampden			
	Fr 1810 Sep 26		DLC-4
	Fr 1811 Jun 04		DLC-5
	Fr 1814 Dec 17		4-0413
	To 1815 Jan 07		DLC-62
	To 1815 Jan 09		DLC-62
	Fr 1815 Jan 09		DLC-75
	Fr 1815 Jan 19		DLC-15
	Fr 1815 Jan 19*		M221-63
	Fr 1815 Jan 19		DLC-15
	Fr 1815 Jan 21		DLC-15
	Fr 1815 Jan 30		DLC-16
	Fr 1815 Feb 05		DLC-16
	To 1815 Feb 15		DLC-16
	Fr 1829 Dec 13		M639-9
	Fr 1834 Dec 14		26-1497
Owen Arthur			
	To 1807 Jan 05	fin	DLC-4
	To 1807 Feb 02	fin	DLC-4
	To 1807 Feb 14	fin	DLC-4
Owen Benjamin Rush			
	Fr 1845 Mar 28		DLC-57
	To 1845 Mar 28	chk	37-0056
Owen Edward			
	Fr 1836 Apr 20	fin	DLC-48
	To 1836 May 17	chk	DLC-48
Owen George Washington			
	Fr 1829 Mar 23		M639-6
	Fr 1834 Apr 19		M688-92
	Fr 1836 Jun 14		31-0480
Owen John			
	Fr 1829 Dec 11		14-1011
Owen Richard B			
	Fr 1814 Jun 21	fin	DLC-9
	Fr 1816 Jul 08	fin	DLC-22
Owen Samuel			
	Fr 1813 Dec 05		DLC-61
	To 1813 Dec 05		DLC-61
Owen Thomas J V			
	Fr 1831 Nov 21		18-1467
	Fr 1831 Dec 31		19-0486
	Fr 1832 Mar 14		19-1464
	Fr 1833 Feb 28		22-0548
	Fr 1844 Nov 20		DLC-57
Owens George Welshman et al			
	Fr 1836 Jan 12		M639-23
Owens John			
	Re 1832 Jul 23	par	20-1231
Owens Theodore			
	Fr 1829 Aug 08		13-1046
	Fr 1832 May 28		M639-17
Owens William			
	To 1825 Oct 17		DLC-33
	Fr 1827 Jul 22		DLC-34
	To 1827 Jul 26		DLC-34
Owings Thomas Deye			
	To 1829 Jun 01#		DLC-37
	Fr 1829 Sep 30		M639-17
Owner William			
	Fr 1833 Feb 06		M124-136
Oxnard Thomas			
	Fr 1829 Mar 13		M639-17
Ozias George			
	Fr 1843 Dec 23		DLC-56
Pablo Juan			
	Fr 1815 Feb 15		4-0744
Pace Alfred E			
	Fr 1832 Nov 02		21-0271
Pacolet (horse)			
	Re 1814 Feb 09		3-0858
	Re 1815 Feb 28		4-0800
Pacquetol Francis			
	Fr 1814 Dec 28	fin	DLC-15
Page Francis			
	Fr 1845 Mar 24		DLC-57
Page James			
	Re 1832 Apr 19		20-0303
	Fr 1833 Jul 29		23-0236
	Fr 1834 Mar 03		M639-3
	Fr 1834 Oct 29		DLC-44
	Fr 1836 Aug 18		31-1318
	Fr 1843 Nov 09		DLC-56
Page James et al			
	Fr 1842 Jun 21		DLC-54
Page Jery L et al			
	Fr 1835 Feb 26		M639-17
Page Jessee			
	To 1840 Jul 21	chk	DLC-53
Page John			
	Fr 1836 Dec 21		M639-5
Page Sherman et al			
	Fr 1836 Apr 06		M639-6
Pageot Alphonse Joseph Yves			
	To 1833 Oct 05		23-0964
	Fr 1835 Apr 25		DLC-46
	To 1836 Jul 06#		DLC-48
	Re 1836 Nov 15	mem	DLC-48
	Re 1836 Nov 15	mem	32-0507
Pageot Mary Ann (Lewis) see also Lewis M A			
	To 1833 Nov 26		23-1311
	To 1834 Jun 12#	fin	DLC-44
	To 1834 Aug 30		26-0404
Pahuska et al			
	Fr 1832 Jan		M234-631
	Fr 1832 Jan*		19-0557
Paimboeuf Louis			
	Fr 1834 Jul 16		M639-17
	Fr 1836 Jul		M22-40
	Fr 1836 Dec		32-0603
	To 1837 Feb 01	chk	DLC-50
Paine Amasa			
	Fr 1829 Aug 20		DLC-75
Paine John T et al			
	Fr 1837 Jan 13		M687-16
Paine Matthew			
	To 1807 Apr 08		DLC-4
Paine William			
	Fr 1802 Feb 06		DLC-2
Paithuckoosaw et al			
	Fr 1831 Nov 20		M234-300
	Fr 1831 Nov 20*		18-1331

Paithuckoosaw et al (cont)
Fr 1832 Jul 20 M234-300
Fr 1832 Jul 20* 20-1197
Palao Severino
Fr 1821 Aug 11 8-1043
Fr 1821 Aug 29 M116-7
Palfrey Henry William
Fr 1838 Oct 24 DLC-51
Fr 1839 Aug 10 DLC-52
Fr 1840 Jan 06 34-1139
Fr 1843 May 25 DLC-55
Palmer Barnabas
Fr 1837 Jan 26 M687-16
Palmer Barnabas et al
Fr 1832 Jan 10 M639-26
Palmer Charles S
Fr 1843 Jan 30 DLC-55
To 1843 Oct 19 35-1551
Palmer Daniel et al
Fr 1829 Dec 08 14-0981
Palmer Dudley S
Fr 1829 Nov 06 14-0421
Palmer John J
Fr 1835 May 16# DLC-46
Palmer brothers
Fr 1831 Feb 21 DLC-39
Re 1831 Mar 15 par DLC-39
Re 1831 Mar 15* par T967-1
Re 1831 Mar 15* par 17-0845
Pamar R
Fr 1821 May 17# fin DLC-30
Panic of 1837
Re 1837 Jul mem DLC-74
Re 1837 Jul mem DLC-74
Pannell Edward Jr
Fr 1829 Nov 02 M639-2
Paquett Peter
Fr 1835 Jul 29 28-1208
Paquette Pierre
Fr 1834 May 14 25-1047
Pardee Jared W
Fr 1836 Jun 10 M639-17
Pardue W M
Fr 1829 Jul 16 M639-17
Paris George
Re 1832 May 25 par 20-0594
Parish E M
Fr 1821 Feb fin DLC-58
Parish Richard Charles
Fr 1836 Jun 01 M567-129
Park James
Fr 1836 Sep 01 DLC-49
Park James & William
Fr 1815 Jun 30 DLC-18
Fr 1815 Jul 11 M222-16
Park William
To 1815 Jun 26 DLC-62
Park William et al
Fr 1830 Sep 07 16-0216
To 1830 Sep 07 16-0217
Parker A W P et al
Fr 1836 May 18 DLC-48
Parker Benjamin
Re 1802 Jul 15 leg 1-1029
Parker Daniel
Fr 1815 Feb 07 DLC-16
Fr 1815 Feb 18 DLC-16
Fr 1815 Feb 18* M565-5
Fr 1815 Mar 19 DLC-17
Fr 1815 Mar 31 DLC-17
Fr 1815 Mar 31* M565-5
To 1815 May 18 4-1046
To 1815 May 18* DLC-62
Fr 1815 Jun 05 M565-5
Fr 1815 Jul 11 DLC-18
Fr 1815 Jul 11* M565-51
Fr 1815 Jul 11 DLC-18
Fr 1815 Jul 11* M565-5
Fr 1815 Jul 18 DLC-18
Fr 1815 Jul 18* M565-5
Fr 1815 Aug 10 M565-5
Fr 1815 Sep 15 DLC-19
Fr 1815 Sep 15* M565-5
Fr 1816 Feb 13 DLC-20
Fr 1816 May 06 DLC-20
Fr 1816 May 06* M565-5
Fr 1816 May 31 DLC-20
Fr 1816 May 31* M565-5
Fr 1816 Jul 09 M222-19
Fr 1816 Jul 09* DLC-23
Fr 1816 Jul 20 DLC-21
Fr 1816 Jul 20* M565-5
Fr 1816 Jul 25 M565-5
Fr 1816 Aug 09 M565-5
Fr 1816 Sep 18 DLC-21
Fr 1816 Dec 07 DLC-22
To 1816 Dec 09 5-0598
To 1816 Dec 10 DLC-22
To 1816 Dec 27 5-0646
Fr 1817 Jan 06 DLC-22
Fr 1817 Feb 10 DLC-22
Fr 1817 May 28 M565-5
Fr 1817 Oct 04 DLC-23
Fr 1817 Oct 16# DLC-23
Fr 1817 Oct 16* M565-5
To 1818 Jan 07# M221-78
Fr 1818 Mar 26 DLC-24
Fr 1818 May 11 M565-5
Fr 1818 Jul 10 DLC-25
Fr 1818 Jul 27 DLC-25
Fr 1818 Jul 27* M565-5
Fr 1818 Sep 24 DLC-25
Fr 1818 Sep 24* M565-6
Fr 1818 Oct 30 M565-6
Fr 1818 Nov 12 DLC-70
Fr 1818 Nov 26 DLC-26
Fr 1818 Nov 26* M565-6
Fr 1818 Dec 03 DLC-26
Fr 1818 Dec 03* M565-6
Fr 1818 Dec 05 M565-6
Fr 1818 Dec 07 DLC-26
Fr 1818 Dec 07* M565-6
Fr 1818 Dec 28 DLC-26
Fr 1819 Jan 29 DLC-26
Fr 1819 Feb 04 DLC-26
Fr 1819 Feb 04* 7-0233
Fr 1819 Mar 20 DLC-26
Fr 1819 Mar 20* 7-0430
Fr 1819 Mar 28 DLC-26
Fr 1819 Jul 16 DLC-27
Fr 1819 Jul 16* 7-0580
Fr 1819 Aug 06 DLC-27
Fr 1819 Aug 06* M565-6
Fr 1819 Aug 11 7-0600
Fr 1819 Aug 18 DLC-27
Fr 1819 Aug 18* 7-0620
Fr 1819 Aug 19 7-0621
Fr 1819 Sep 25 7-0679
Fr 1819 Dec 01 DLC-28

Fr 1819 Dec 01* 7-0903
Fr 1819 Dec 07 DLC-28
Fr 1819 Dec 07* 7-0913
Fr 1820 Feb 18 7-1030
Fr 1820 Feb 21 M565-6
To 1820 Apr 12# DLC-63
Fr 1820 Apr 18 7-1077
To 1820 May 01# DLC-70
Fr 1820 May 03# DLC-29
Fr 1820 May 03* M565-6
Fr 1820 May 08# DLC-29
Fr 1820 May 08* M565-6
Fr 1820 May 29 M565-6
Fr 1821 May 08 DLC-30
Fr 1821 May 08* 8-0465
Fr 1821 Jul 10 DLC-30
Fr 1829 Sep 22# DLC-75
Fr 1831 Apr 15# DLC-39
Fr 1834 Dec 24# 27-0011
Fr 1835 Jan 23 27-0285

Parker Isaac et al
Fr 1829 Apr 11 M639-1

Parker James
Fr 1833 Feb 05 22-0268
Fr 1834 Jun 27 M639-3
Fr 1835 Dec 21 29-1269
Fr 1840 Jul 04 DLC-52

Parker James et al
Fr 1836 Jun 22 M567-132

Parker James M
Re 1841 Jan 01 35-0169
Fr 1841 Feb 21 DLC-53
To 1841 May# 35-0296
Fr 1841 May 02 DLC-53
To 1844 May 11 DLC-56
Fr 1844 Jul 21 DLC-57
Fr 1844 Aug 02 DLC-57

Parker John
Fr 1836 Oct 24 32-0339

Parker John A
Fr 1830 Dec 08 DLC-38
Re 1835 Jun 24 28-0772
Fr 1836 Nov 02 M687-25

Parker John A et al
Fr 1830 Apr 27 M639-19

Parker Leonard M
To 1834 Dec 12# 26-1490
Fr 1835 Jan 15 27-0236

Parker Richard Elliott
Fr 1835 Jul 01 28-0871
Fr 1836 Feb 26 DLC-47
Fr 1837 Feb 23 M688-111

Parker Shivers et al
Fr 1833 Jun 13# 37-0517
Fr 1833 Jun 13* 23-0027

Parker Thomas H
Fr 1836 Mar 09# M687-27

Parker William
Re 1813 Oct 30 DLC-61

Parker William C
Fr 1835 Feb 26 DLC-45

Parkhurst Jabez
To 1821 Apr 30 M566-143

Parks Gorham
Fr 1835 Jan 07 M639-17
Fr 1836 Jan 30# 30-0228
Fr 1836 Apr 24 M567-130
Fr 1837 Jan M687-28

Parks Gorham et al
Fr 1836 Jun 06 M639-26

Parks Marshall
Fr 1829 Aug 21 fin DLC-37
To 1831 Jul 14 chk DLC-39
Fr 1833 Jul 27 fin DLC-43

Parks Pleasant
Fr 1832 Jan 30 19-0912

Parks Simeon C
Re 1837 Feb 04 par 33-0392

Parr J W
Fr 1836 Feb 03 30-0277

Parrish David W
Fr 1836 Mar 12 M234-436
Fr 1836 Mar 12 M234-436

Parrish Joel
Re 1814 Jan 31 DLC-62

Parrott William S
Fr 1830 Oct 27 16-0568
Fr 1844 Dec 14 DLC-57

Parshall John
Fr 1835 Apr 18 28-0097
Fr 1835 Dec 15 29-1113

Parsons A V
Fr 1833 Jun 08 M639-6

Parsons A V et al
Fr 1831 Feb 08 M639-11

Parsons Benjamin S
Fr 1833 Jan 22 M234-223

Parsons Enoch
Fr 1814 Apr 08 3-0963
Fr 1815 Jun 17 DLC-18
Fr 1819 Mar 25 DLC-26
To 1819 Mar 25 add 7-0436
Fr 1823 Sep 15 DLC-32
Fr 1829 Apr 08 M639-4
Fr 1829 May 25 13-0424
Fr 1829 Sep 18 13-1364
Fr 1832 Oct 12 M234-223
Fr 1833 Jan 22 M234-223
Fr 1833 Sep 21 M234-223
Fr 1833 Sep 21* 23-0819
Fr 1835 Sep 19 M639-5

Parsons George et al
Fr 1833 cOct 01 23-0929

Parsons Joseph Jr
Re 1837 Jan 25 par 33-0156

Parsons Peter
Fr 1828 Dec 02 12-0295
To 1828 Dec 13 12-0324
Fr 1829 Apr 28 M639-15
Fr 1831 Mar 18 DLC-39

Parsons Solomon
Fr 1836 Jun 06 31-0357
Fr 1836 Jun 07 31-0380

Partridge Alden
To 1817 Jan 12 5-0691
Fr 1829 Feb 26 12-0598
Fr 1834 Feb 01# 24-1134
Fr 1834 Feb 08 M639-17
Fr 1836 Nov 02 M124-155
Fr 1837 Jan 29 M124-156

Partridge C et al
Fr 1836 Nov 09 M124-155

Partridge Edward et al
Fr 1834 Apr 10 25-0681

Pascal John
To 1829 May 19 DLC-37

Pashpoho et al
Fr 1836 Oct 18 M234-355

Pasquier F
Fr 1821 Aug 28# fin DLC-30

Passon Thomas
Fr 1818 Mar 31 DLC-24
Patch George Q
Re 1829 Mar 18 par T967-1
Patchell Edward
Fr 1824 Aug 07 DLC-33
Fr 1825 Mar 04 DLC-33
Fr 1828 Sep 30 DLC-35
Fr 1829 Nov 05 14-0416
Fr 1834 Jun 18 25-1430
Pathkiller
Fr 1813 Oct 22 DLC-7
Fr 1813 Oct 22* DLC-61
Fr 1813 Oct 23 DLC-7
Fr 1813 Oct 23* DLC-61
To 1813 Oct 23 DLC-61
To 1813 Oct 23* 3-0543
To 1813 Oct 23 3-0545
Fr 1813 Oct 29 DLC-7
Fr 1813 Oct 30 DLC-7
To 1813 Nov 02 DLC-7
Fr 1813 Dec 28 DLC-8
To 1814 Jan 03 DLC-61
To 1814 Jan 07 DLC-61
To 1814 Feb 18 DLC-61
Fr 1818 Feb 17 DLC-24
Fr 1818 Dec 13 DLC-26
Fr 1820 Dec 11 M221-89
Pathkiller et al
To 1821 Jan 18 M221-89
To 1821 Jan 18* 8-0086
Patrick John
Fr 1834 May 16# 25-1072
Patten William
Fr 1826 Jul 06 DLC-34
Patterson Andrew et al
Fr 1813 Nov 12 DLC-7
Fr 1813 Nov 12* DLC-61
Patterson Charles W
Fr 1830 Mar 17 fin 15-0388
Patterson Daniel Todd
To 1814 Aug 27 DLC-62
To 1814 Oct 14 DLC-62
To 1814 Oct 23 DLC-62
Fr 1814 Dec 26 4-0470
To 1815 Jan 07 DLC-62
Fr 1815 Jan 07 DLC-15
Fr 1815 Jan 07* 4-0497
Fr 1815 Jan 07 DLC-15
Fr 1815 Jan 18 DLC-15
To 1815 Jan 19 add 4-0576
To 1815 Jan 19 4-0580
Fr 1815 Jan 31 DLC-16
To 1815 Feb 03 4-0685
Fr 1815 Feb 09 DLC-16
Fr 1815 Feb 11 DLC-16
Fr 1815 Feb 11 DLC-16
To 1815 Feb 11 DLC-16
To 1815 Feb 13 DLC-71
Fr 1815 Feb 13 DLC-16
Fr 1815 Feb 17 DLC-16
Fr 1815 Feb 18 DLC-16
To 1815 Feb 20 4-0772
To 1815 Feb 22 4-0780
Fr 1815 Feb 27 DLC-17
Fr 1815 Feb 27 DLC-17
Fr 1815 Feb 27 DLC-17
Fr 1815 Mar 01 DLC-17
To 1815 Apr 02 4-0926
Fr 1815 Apr 03 DLC-18
Fr 1815 Apr 03* M222-16
Fr 1817 Jun 19 DLC-22
To 1818 Jan 12 M125-58
To 1818 Apr 08 M125-58
Fr 1818 May 05 DLC-24
Fr 1829 Oct 27# M179-67
To 1830 Feb 11 15-0130
Fr 1830 Apr 10 15-0663
To 1831 May 11 chk DLC-39
To 1832 Apr 02 DLC-40
Fr 1832 Oct 15 DLC-41
Fr 1833 Aug 05 M179-77
Patterson Daniel Todd et al
Fr 1821 DLC-31
Patterson E M
Fr 1841 Dec 06 DLC-54
Fr 1842 Jul 06 DLC-54
Fr 1844 Nov 24 DLC-57
Patterson Edmund
Fr 1841 Aug 28 DLC-53
Patterson J & J
To 1835 May 08# 28-0326
Fr 1835 Jun 22 fin 28-0765
Patterson J B
Fr 1834 Oct 02 M234-729
Patterson J W
Fr 1821 Oct 05 DLC-30
Patterson James
Fr 1835 Jan 06 27-0105
Patterson John
Fr 1835 Jan 06 M639-27
Fr 1835 Mar 23 M639-1
Patterson John et al
Fr 1829 Jul 30 M873-19
Fr 1831 Apr 26 M22-28
Fr 1833 Sep M639-14
Patterson John B
Fr 1829 Apr 20 13-0076
Patterson John S
Re 1835 Jun 16 M273-32
Patterson R
Fr 1834 Dec 18 26-1528
Patterson Robert
To 1823 May 17 9-0558
To 1823 May 18# 9-0562
Fr 1836 Mar 29 M639-5
Patterson Robert et al
Fr 1834 Dec M639-1
Patterson Robert Maskell
Fr 1832 Feb 09 DLC-40
To 1835 May 26 28-0505
Fr 1835 May 29 DLC-47
Fr 1835 May 29* 28-0525
Fr 1835 Nov 27 M639-18
Fr 1835 Nov 27* 29-0605
Fr 1836 Jan 01 29-1433
Fr 1836 Jan 08 29-1509
Fr 1837 Jan 19 33-0036
Fr 1842 Jan 08 35-0592
To 1842 Aug 20 35-0895
Patterson Sarah Ann (Eagle)
To 1843 May 15 35-1352
Patterson William
Fr 1833 Apr 17 M124-137
Fr 1835 Mar 24 M234-601
Patterson William & Sons et al
Fr 1832 Jan 21 M639-8
Patterson William Daniel
Re 1829 Jul 27 13-0943

Name	Date	Type	Location
Patteson Benjamin			
	Fr 1837 Nov 15		M687-7
Patteson Bernard M			
	Fr 1815 Mar 08		DLC-17
Patteson Nelson			
	Fr 1813 Dec 23		3-0704
Pattison Mary			
	Fr 1837 Feb 11		33-0634
Patton Benjamin Jr			
	Fr 1830 May 25		15-1085
	Fr 1844 Dec 13		36-1194
Patton Benjamin Jr et al			
	Fr 1835 Sep 07		M639-13
Patton James C			
	Fr 1829 May 29		M639-10
Patton John			
	Fr 1831 Jun 27		M124-128
Patton Robert Miller			
	Fr 1836 Jan 30		30-0239
Patton Samuel B			
	Fr 1814 Feb 03		DLC-61
Patton Thomas et al			
	Fr 1830 Dec 17		M639-12
Patton Thomas T			
	Re 1836 May 05	par	30-1506
Patton W H			
	Fr 1840 Jul 24		DLC-53
Patton William			
	Fr 1841 Aug 10		DLC-53
	Fr 1841 Oct 13		35-0446
Paulding James Kirke			
	To 1830 Jan 07		14-1352
	To 1834 Jan 01		24-0735
	Fr 1834 Mar 28		M22-34
	Fr 1837 Mar 25		33-1117
	To 1839 May 10		34-0788
	To 1840 Apr 10		DLC-74
	Fr 1840 Apr 30		M209-10
	To 1840 May 25		34-1386
	To 1840 Jul 02		34-1463
	Fr 1840 Jul 17		M209-10
	To 1840 Aug 26		34-1581
	Fr 1842 Sep 22		DLC-54
	Fr 1843 Jan 21		DLC-55
	Fr 1843 Feb 27		35-1266
	Fr 1843 Mar 15		35-1278
	To 1843 Mar 30		35-1293
	Fr 1843 Jun 01		DLC-55
	Fr 1843 Sep 02		DLC-55
	Fr 1843 Oct 04		DLC-55
	Fr 1844 Jan 08		DLC-56
	Fr 1844 Nov 15		DLC-57
Paulding William			
	To 1828 Feb 01		11-1088
Paulding William et al			
	Fr 1829		M639-11
Paup John W et al			
	Fr 1844 Feb 15		DLC-56
Pawnee treaty			
	Re 1834 Apr 12		M668-7
Paxton John A			
	Fr 1817 Feb 18		DLC-22
Payne Matthew			
	To 1807 Feb 27	fin	DLC-4
	Fr 1810 Oct 25	fin	DLC-5
Payne Matthew Mountjoy			
	Fr 1835 Nov 25		M567-112
Payne Robert et al			
	Fr 1826 Sep 25		DLC-34
	To 1826 Sep 30		DLC-34
Payne William Winter			
	Fr 1843 Feb 13		DLC-55
	Fr 1845 Feb 10		M873-96
Payton Ephraim			
	Re 1790 May	leg	1-0075i
	Re 1790 May	leg	1-0075k
	Re 1794 Nov 15	leg	1-0242
	Re 1802 Jul 15	leg	1-1029
Peabody George et al			
	Fr 1832 Jan 23		M639-26
Peabody J			
	Fr 1838 Apr 10#	fin	DLC-51
	To 1840 Jan 29#	fin	DLC-52
Peabody Joseph et al			
	Fr 1830 Oct 29		M179-69
	Fr 1831 Jul 21		M124-129
	Fr 1832 Jan 23		M639-26
	Fr 1832 Dec		M639-4
	Fr 1833 Apr 16		M639-4
	Fr 1834 Dec 24		M179-79
Peabody & Chamberlain			
	Fr 1821 Apr 23	fin	DLC-70
Peacock James			
	Fr 1834 Jul 19		26-0235
	Fr 1838 Mar 19#	fin	DLC-51
Peacock John			
	Fr 1808 Oct 04		2-0728
	Fr 1809 Jan 23		DLC-4
	To 1809 Jul 22	lnd	2-0851
Peacock William			
	Fr 1814 Jul 14		DLC-75
	Fr 1821 Jun 21		DLC-30
Peairs Isaac			
	Fr 1820 Jul 07	fin	DLC-24
Peake Humphrey			
	Re 1829 Jul	mem	13-0769
Pearce Dutee Jerauld			
	Fr 1835 Apr 03		27-1517
	Fr 1835 Apr 20		M639-26
	Fr 1835 Sep 15		29-0050
	Fr 1835 Nov 11		M639-11
	Fr 1836 Jun 29		31-0644
	Fr 1836 cJun 29		31-0647
	Fr 1836 Oct 05		32-0073
	Fr 1837 Feb 14		M124-156
Pearce Dutee Jerauld et al			
	Fr 1836 Dec		M639-5
Pearce William			
	To 1814 Aug 30		DLC-62
Pearce Winsor			
	Re 1788 Dec	leg	1-0055
Pears Joshua			
	Fr 1836 May 12		30-1607
Pearson Henry			
	Fr 1829 Oct 17		M179-67
Pearson John L			
	Fr 1836 Oct 24		M567-129
Pearson P F & Co			
	Fr 1827 Apr 02	fin	11-0550
Pease John & Son			
	To 1842 Nov 12		35-0989
	Re 1842 Dec 16	mem	DLC-54
	To 1843 Apr 07		35-1299
	Fr 1843 Apr 18		DLC-55
Peck John			
	Fr 1820 Jul 01	fin	7-1133
Peck Moses L			
	To 1813 Dec 16		DLC-61
Peck Nathaniel			
	Fr 1816 Nov 22	fin	DLC-22

Peck W H
Fr 1837 Feb 27 DLC-50
To 1837 Mar 04 33-1066
Fr 1841 Mar 15 DLC-53
Pedro I Emperor of Brazil
Fr 1829 Jun 19 M49-1
Fr 1829 Jun 19* 13-0686
To 1830 Jan 23 15-0008
Peebles & Graham
Fr 1835 Jul 01 M22-36
Peebly Albert
Fr 1830 May 08 M179-68
Peirce Charles et al
Fr 1829 May 14 13-0323
Peire Henry D
To 1814 Nov 06 DLC-62
To 1814 Nov 07 DLC-62
Fr 1814 Nov 07 4-0325
To 1814 Nov 08 DLC-62
Fr 1815 Jan 11 DLC-15
Fr 1815 Jan 25 DLC-15
Fr 1815 Jan 31# 4-0664
Fr 1815 Feb 16 4-0754
To 1821 Jul 23 DLC-63
Fr 1829 May 16 M124-119
Fr 1829 Jun 19 M639-18
Fr 1843 Jan 09 DLC-55
Fr 1843 Aug 35-1445
Peirsol J North
Fr 1845 Apr 21 DLC-58
Pelham William
Re 1830 Jun 08 15-1323
Pellerz Louis
Fr 1815 Feb 20 DLC-16
Pemberton John
To 1824 Dec 20 10-0991
Fr 1825 Feb 15 DLC-33
Fr 1829 Mar 10 12-0926
Fr 1829 Mar 23 M639-6
Fr 1829 Mar 23* 12-1090
Fr 1829 Apr 06 12-1281
Fr 1829 May 26 13-0439
Fr 1829 Jun 22 M639-18
Fr 1829 Jun 22* 13-0697
Fr 1829 Sep 01 M639-8
Fr 1829 Sep 01* 13-1227
Fr 1829 Sep 28 13-1448
Fr 1829 Oct 04 14-0104
Fr 1829 Oct 22 14-0235
Fr 1829 Nov 03 14-0408
Fr 1829 Nov 07 M639-15
Fr 1829 Nov 07* 14-0423
Fr 1829 Nov 17 M639-1
Fr 1829 Nov 17* 14-0485
Fr c1830 37-0298
Fr 1830 Jan 07 M639-11
Fr 1830 Jan 07* 14-1354
Fr 1830 Apr 06 15-0621
Fr 1830 Oct 18 16-0436
Fr 1830 Oct 26 16-0557
Fr 1830 Oct 28 16-0570
Fr 1831 Mar 24 17-0969
Fr 1831 Jul 06 DLC-39
Fr 1831 Jul 06* 18-0153
Fr 1831 Aug 09 DLC-39
Fr 1831 Aug 09* 18-0487
To 1831 Aug 13 18-0523
Fr 1831 Aug 16 18-0553
To 1831 Aug 17 18-0558
Fr 1831 Aug 19 18-0573
Fr 1831 Sep 20 18-0858
Fr 1831 Oct 19 18-1063
Fr 1831 Nov 03 18-1194
Fr 1831 Nov 17 18-1323
Fr 1831 Dec 15 19-0309
Fr 1831 Dec 17 19-0339
Fr 1831 Dec 24 19-0412
Fr 1832 Jan 03 19-0594
Fr 1832 Jan 07 19-0635
Fr 1832 Jan 07 19-0638
Fr 1832 Jan 17 19-0740
Fr 1832 Feb 12 19-1072
Fr 1832 Mar 05 19-1321
Fr 1832 Mar 30 20-0063
Fr 1832 Apr 20 20-0330
Fr 1832 Jul 18 20-1137
Fr 1832 Aug 25 20-1380
Fr 1832 Oct 23 21-0138
Fr 1832 Oct 27 21-0176
Fr 1832 Nov 05 21-0332
To 1832 Dec 10 21-0981
Fr 1832 Dec 13 21-1043
Fr 1832 Dec 14 21-1050
Fr 1832 Dec 15 21-1055
Fr 1832 Dec 29 21-1203
To 1833 Feb 19 22-0409
Fr 1833 Feb 20 22-0430
Fr 1833 Feb 22 22-0446
Fr 1833 Apr 05 M639-2
Fr 1833 Apr 05* 22-0951
Fr 1833 Apr 18 22-1052
Fr 1833 May 28 22-1469
Fr 1833 Jul 11 23-0100
To 1833 Sep 01 23-0584
Fr 1833 Oct 21 23-1072
Fr 1833 Oct 22 23-1079
Fr 1833 Dec 07 24-0423
Fr 1834 Jan 09 24-0824
Fr 1834 Jan 10 M639-7
Fr 1834 Jan 10* 24-0851
Fr 1834 Jan 31 24-1115
Fr 1834 Feb 06 24-1248
Fr 1834 Feb 19 24-1430
Fr 1834 Mar 04 M639-3
Fr 1834 Mar 04* 24-1569
Fr 1834 Mar 26 25-0371
Fr 1834 May 10 25-1010
Fr 1834 Jun 13 25-1341
Fr 1834 Oct 28 26-0763
Fr 1834 Oct 29 26-0771
Fr 1834 Nov 18 26-0945
Fr 1834 Dec 03 26-1395
Fr 1835 Feb 01 27-0365
Fr 1836 Mar 31 30-0956
Fr 1836 Jun 27 31-0603
Fr 1836 Dec 12 M639-15
Fr 1836 Dec 12* 32-1100
Fr 1837 Feb 07 33-0556
To 1837 Feb 10 33-0597
To 1837 Feb 27 chk DLC-50
Fr 1845 Mar 06 36-1541
Pemberton John T
Fr 1814 Nov 21 DLC-75
Fr 1815 Feb 13 DLC-16
Fr 1815 Feb 14 DLC-16
Fr 1815 Mar 02 DLC-17
Fr 1815 Mar 04 DLC-17
Fr 1815 Mar 06 DLC-17

Fr 1815 Mar 11 DLC-17
To 1815 Mar 17 DLC-68
Fr 1815 Mar 21 DLC-17
Fr 1815 Mar 26 DLC-17
To 1815 Apr 04 DLC-18
Fr 1815 Apr 04 DLC-18
To 1815 May 30 4-1072
Pemberton Rebecca (Clifford)
Fr 1829 cMar 10 12-0928
Penalton Jacob
Re 1794 Jan 16 leg 1-0185
Pendleton Benjamin
Fr 1829 Mar 12 M124-117
Pendleton Edmund Henry
Fr 1832 Feb 20 M639-22
Pendleton James et al
Fr 1832 Jan 15 M639-9
Penfield Charles
Fr 1835 Dec 22 fin DLC-47
Penieres Jean A
Fr 1821 Jul 15 M221-93
Fr 1821 Jul 15* 8-0832
Fr 1821 Aug 24 M221-92
Fr 1821 Aug 27 8-1107
To 1821 Nov 21 DLC-63
Penington Fredus
Fr 1844 Nov 24 DLC-57
Penn Alexander Gordon
Fr 1830 Dec 08 16-1352
Penn James et al
Fr 1830 Dec 26 M639-5
Penn Shadrach Jr
Fr 1822 Dec 28 DLC-31
Fr 1825 Nov 14 DLC-33
Fr 1825 Dec 09 DLC-33
Fr 1827 Jul 05 DLC-34
Fr 1831 Mar 20 17-0913
To 1835 Jun 10 chk 28-0632
Fr 1836 Apr 26 DLC-48
Fr 1836 Jun 02 M567-120
Fr 1836 Nov M22-41
Fr 1844 Sep 10 DLC-57
Fr 1845 Jan 31 36-1426
Penn Thomas H
To 1821 Jul 27 8-0915
Pennsylvania congressmen
Fr 1832 Jan 21 M22-29
Pennsylvania Democratic committee
To 1835 cJul 25 DLC-73
Pennsylvania legislators
Fr 1830 Mar 20 15-0423
Fr 1837 Jan 19 DLC-49
To 1837 Feb 11 33-0637
Penny James
Fr 1825 Mar 11 fin 10-1224
Penrose Charles Bingham
To 1830 Oct 09 16-0354
Fr 1834 Aug 18 26-0333
Fr 1834 Oct 03 M639-4
Fr 1835 Jan 30 M639-4
Fr 1835 Feb 03 M639-17
Fr 1835 May 04 28-0285
Pensacola FL
Re 1821 Jul M116-6
Re 1821 Jul 18 M116-6
Re 1821 Jul 18* DLC-63
Re 1821 Jul 18* 8-0873
Re 1821 Jul 19 M116-6
Re 1821 Jul 19* DLC-63
Re 1821 Jul 19* 8-0879
Re 1821 Jul 20 DLC-63
Re 1821 Sep 06 M116-7
Pension commissioner
Re 1833 May 04 22-1303
Pension laws
Re 1829 Nov mem 14-0332
Pension office
Re c1829 mem 12-0385
Pentland Joseph
Re 1830 Apr 02 15-0566
Pepin Ferdinand Fayette
Fr 1830 May 02 M688-70
Pepper Abel C
Fr 1835 Jan 17# 27-0248
Fr 1835 Feb 23 27-0590
Fr 1835 Aug 06 28-1257
Fr 1835 Nov 26 29-0598
Fr 1836 Jan 13 30-0007
Fr 1836 Mar 19 30-0844
Percival Mary A
Fr 1841 Sep 29 DLC-53
Perkins Bishop
Fr 1834 May 18# 25-1079
Perkins Charles
To 1813 Dec 05 DLC-61
Perkins Isaac et al
Fr 1831 May 21 M639-21
Perkins Nicholas T
Re 1814 Jan 27 3-0800
Re 1814 Jan 27* DLC-8
Re 1814 Jan 27* DLC-61
Perkins Peter
Fr 1812 Jul 05 DLC-5
Fr 1813 Oct DLC-75
Fr 1813 Oct 03 DLC-61
Fr 1813 Oct 06 3-0499
Fr 1813 Oct 06* DLC-61
Fr 1813 Oct 19 DLC-61
To 1813 Oct 20 DLC-7
Fr 1813 Oct 27 DLC-61
To 1813 Oct 29 DLC-61
Fr 1813 Nov 03 DLC-61
Fr 1813 Nov 08 DLC-75
Fr 1813 Nov 18 DLC-75
Fr 1813 Dec 16 DLC-75
Fr 1813 Dec 16* DLC-61
To 1813 Dec 18 DLC-61
To 1814 Jan 13 DLC-61
To 1814 Feb 08 DLC-61
To 1814 Mar 10 DLC-9
To 1814 Apr 01 3-0948
Fr 1814 Apr 09 DLC-10
Fr 1814 Apr 25 DLC-10
Fr 1814 Oct 30 4-0303
Fr 1814 Nov 09 4-0326
Fr 1815 May 23 DLC-18
Perkins Virginia Fontaine
Fr 1839 Nov 12 DLC-52
Perkins William
Fr 1821 Dec 08 fin DLC-31
Fr 1824 Jun 22 fin DLC-32
Perpall Gabriel William
Fr 1818 Jun 16 DLC-25
Fr 1818 Jun 16* 6-1057
Perrault Paul Hyacinte
Fr 1818 Aug 28 DLC-25
Fr 1820 May 09 DLC-29
To 1820 Jun 23# DLC-63

Perrin Joseph
Re 1801 Oct 09 mem DLC-60
Perry Henry
Fr 1815 Jul 28 DLC-71
Perry Isaac et al
Fr 1834 cMar 10 25-0028
Perry James H
Fr 1835 Dec 21 M179-81
Fr 1835 Dec 21 M179-81
Perry Samuel
Fr 1815 Feb 12 DLC-16
Perry William D
Fr 1815 Jan 27 DLC-16
Fr 1815 Feb 17 DLC-16
Pershapaho et al
Fr 1829 Jul 30 M234-728
Person Benjamin P
Fr 1822 Nov 01 fin DLC-32
Fr 1825 Feb 22 fin 10-1144
Re 1825 May 13 mem DLC-33
To 1826 Apr 13 chk 11-0193
Fr 1826 Apr 13 fin DLC-33
Re 1827 cMar mem DLC-58
To 1827 Mar 19 DLC-33
Pessenger George
Fr 1835 Apr 10 DLC-46
Pessenger George et al
To 1835 Apr 15 DLC-46
Petchaka Elisabeth
Fr 1830 Jan 12 14-1386
Peters John R
Fr 1828 Nov 24 DLC-35
Peters Osmond
Fr 1835 Sep 19 29-0086
Fr c1836 29-1409
Fr 1836 Apr 05 30-1012
Peters Samuel J
Fr 1834 Jul 28 26-0269
To 1834 Oct 07 26-0531
Peters William
Re 1832 Mar 08 par 19-1350
Peterson Erasmus N
Fr 1843 Dec 13 DLC-56
Peterson H W
Fr 1823 Feb 03 DLC-32
To 1823 Feb 23 9-0466
Peterson Henry H et al
Fr 1830 cNov M567-51
Fr 1834 May 20 25-1101
Peterson Isaac Z
Fr 1839 Feb 26 DLC-52
Petit G
Fr 1825 Jan 08 fin DLC-33
Petriken David et al
Fr 1835 Apr 15 28-0088
Petrikin Henry
Fr 1830 Apr 02 DLC-38
Fr 1835 Jan 30 M639-4
Pettigru William
Fr 1835 Jun 01 M22-36
Pettis F H
Fr 1829 Mar 13 M639-18
Fr 1829 May 14 M639-18
Pettis Fontain H
Re 1831 Nov 16 par 18-1287
Pettis Spencer Darwin
Fr 1828 Oct 08 DLC-35
Fr 1829 Feb 25 M639-18
Fr 1829 Feb 25 M639-20
Fr 1830 Feb 02 M234-300
Fr 1830 Mar 15 15-0366
Fr 1830 Mar 27 15-0471
Fr 1830 Mar 27 15-0473
Fr 1831 Mar 18 M234-434
Fr 1831 Mar 20 M234-434
Fr 1831 Mar 24 M234-434
Fr 1831 Apr 17-1032
Pettit Thomas McKean
Fr 1836 Jan 29 30-0223
Pettit William V
Fr 1835 Mar 14 DLC-45
Fr 1837 Jan 04 M639-18
Fr 1840 Jun 04 DLC-52
Pettway Hinchey
To 1808 Dec 05 fin 2-0746
Peyton Balie
Fr 1834 May 17 M688-92
To 1834 Sep 04 26-0419
To 1835 Dec 08 chk DLC-47
Re 1836 cOct 14 mem 37-0352
Fr 1837 Feb 16 DLC-50
Fr 1837 Feb 23 DLC-50
To 1837 Feb 24 DLC-50
Peyton Francis
Fr 1836 Jun 17 M22-40
Peyton John Howe
Fr 1829 Jul 21 M639-18
Fr 1831 Nov 30 M639-18
Fr 1831 Dec 01# M639-18
Fr 1835 Oct 09 M639-18
Pfeiffer Henry H et al
Fr 1829 Mar 31 M639-6
Phagan John
Fr 1832 Feb 04 19-0955
Phelps Cicero
Fr 1844 Sep 17 DLC-57
Phelps Lancelot
Fr 1836 May 23 31-0083
Fr 1836 Jun 03 M687-3
Phelps Lancelot et al
Fr 1836 Jun 16 M639-11
Phelps Myron et al
Fr 1831 Jul 29 18-0316
Phelps Noah A
Fr 1832 Jan 19 19-0788
Fr 1834 Jun 14 M639-24
Fr 1836 Mar 14 M687-17
Phelps Oliver et al
Fr 1835 Jun 02 M639-15
Phelps Orrin S
Fr 1835 Aug 24 M639-18
Philadelphia Aurora
Re 1798 Apr 12 fin 1-0660
Philadelphia cabinetmakers
To 1834 Mar 17 25-0249
Philadelphia citizens
To 1819 Feb 18 add 7-0283
To 1835 Apr 12 28-0028
To 1835 Jun DLC-73
Fr 1836 Oct 01 31-1582
Re 1840 Jan mem 34-1124
Re 1843 Dec mem DLC-56
Philadelphia marine barracks
Re 1832 Jun 08 M124-133
Re 1832 Jun 08* 20-0721
Philadelphia merchants
Re c1803 mem DLC-75
Re 1803 May fin DLC-71

Re 1804 cApr mem DLC-60
Re 1804 cJul 01 mem DLC-3
Philbrick B Morgan
Fr 1845 May 17 DLC-58
Philippart John
Fr 1822 May 01 DLC-31
Philips David
Re 1791 Feb 23 leg DLC-1
Philips George et al
Fr 1832 Nov 13 M639-5
Philips Joseph
Fr 1815 Aug 07 DLC-19
Fr 1822 Nov 10 DLC-31
Philips Joseph et al
Fr 1825 Apr 14 DLC-33
To 1825 Apr 14 DLC-33
Phillips Asher
Fr 1831 Jul 16 M22-28
Phillips Benjamin
Fr 1830 Jun 08 M124-124
Fr 1831 Mar 20 17-0918
Fr 1834 Oct 07 M124-145
Phillips George
To 1814 Aug 06 3-1235
Phillips Isaac
Fr 1833 Sep 26 23-0874
Phillips J Allamont
Fr 1836 Jun 27 M639-18
Phillips James
Fr 1835 cApr 06 M639-11
Phillips John
Fr 1814 Jul 22# DLC-11
Fr 1816 May 31 DLC-20
Phillips John W
Re 1826 Nov 21 leg 11-0401
Fr 1827 Dec 13 fin 11-0958
Phillips John Walter
Fr 1818 Mar 03 DLC-24
Phillips Jonathan
Fr 1831 Aug 12 DLC-39
Phillips Lewis
Fr 1829 Sep 06 M222-25
Phillips Richard
Fr 1839 Jan 23 DLC-51
Phillips Samuel
Fr 1829 May 08 13-0267
Phillips William et al
Fr 1830 Nov 13 M639-5
Phillips Zalegman
Fr 1829 Feb 21 M639-18
Fr 1833 Aug 27 M639-18
Fr 1834 Jan 19 M639-18
Fr 1837 Feb 20 M639-18
Philo Jackson (pseudonym)
Fr 1833 21-1238
Fr 1833 21-1242
Physick Philip Syng
To 1835 cMay 28-0202
Piankeshaw and Wea treaty
Re 1833 Feb 12 M668-7
Piatt William
Fr 1814 Aug 22 3-1306a
Fr 1814 Sep 10 4-0210
Fr 1814 Sep 28 M222-13
To 1814 Dec 16 DLC-62
Fr 1814 Dec 18 DLC-62
To 1814 Dec 19 DLC-62
To 1814 Dec 21 DLC-62
To 1815 Jan 09 DLC-62
Fr 1815 Feb 05 DLC-16
To 1815 Feb 12 DLC-16
Fr 1815 Feb 12 DLC-16
To 1815 Feb 22 DLC-17
Fr 1815 Feb 22 DLC-17
To 1815 Mar 11 DLC-62
Fr 1815 Mar 16 DLC-17
To 1815 Mar 16 DLC-17
To 1815 Mar 19 DLC-17
To 1815 Mar 20 DLC-17
Fr 1815 Mar 27 DLC-17
Fr 1815 Apr 03 DLC-18
Fr 1826 Feb 05 11-0134
Fr 1830 Feb 12 15-0138
Piatt William M
Fr 1844 Sep 23 DLC-57
Pickell John
Fr 1837 Feb 07# M567-149
Pickens Andrew et al
Fr 1833 Feb 11 M639-24
Pickens James B
Fr 1814 Feb 03 DLC-61
Pickering William
Fr 1834 Feb 22 24-1449
Pickett George C
Fr 1832 Sep 16 21-0001
Pickett James Chamberlayne
Fr 1829 Mar 10 M639-18
Re 1829 Jun 09 13-0604
To 1835 May 01 28-0210
Fr 1836 Jun 14 DLC-48
Fr 1836 Nov 08 M687-2
Fr 1836 Nov 29 M687-25
Pickett William D
Fr 1835 Feb 25 M639-24
Pickman Benjamin et al
Fr 1832 Dec M639-4
Pickman Dudley L
Fr 1831 Jul 20 M124-129
Fr 1831 Jul 23 M124-129
Pickman Dudley L et al
Fr 1830 Oct 14 M639-20
Pickrell John et al
Fr 1829 Sep 21 13-1399
Pierce Benjamin
Fr 1829 Jan 12 DLC-36
Fr 1834 Dec 01 DLC-45
Pierce Benjamin et al
Fr 1829 Jun 24 13-0708
Pierce Everett H
Fr 1829 Aug 21 M234-73
Pierce Franklin
Fr 1836 Dec 21 M639-5
Fr 1844 Feb 02 DLC-56
To 1844 Feb 19 36-0299
Pierce George W
Fr 1835 May 27 28-0508
Pierce Josiah
Fr 1835 May 27 28-0508
Piercy Andrew Jackson
Fr 1844 Aug 11 36-0788
Pierie John G
Fr 1835 Aug 07 M639-15
Pierie John G et al
Fr 1835 Aug M639-15
Pierie William L
Fr 1835 Aug 15 M639-15
Piernas Luis
To 1818 May 24 DLC-25

Pierse James
Re 1796 Feb 19 leg DLC-1
Pierson Job
Fr 1834 Jan 13 M639-7
Pike Albert
Re 1837 Jan 23 33-0120
Pilcher William S
Fr 1836 May 21 31-0071
Pilegar Louis and Catharine
Fr 1833 Nov 12 23-1228
Pillar William English
Fr 1814 Apr 03 3-0954
To 1814 May 10 3-1024
Pillavoine Alexander
Fr 1829 Sep 13 DLC-37
To 1829 Sep 15# DLC-37
Pillow Gideon
Fr 1836 Aug 25 add 31-1364
Pillow Gideon et al
To 1836 Aug 25 add 31-1367
Pillow William
Re 1818 Sep 19 6-1312
Pillow William et al
Fr 1813 Nov 15 DLC-7
Fr 1813 Nov 15* DLC-61
Pilsbury Timothy
Fr 1836 Feb 12 30-0364
Fr 1837 Jan 02 M687-3
Pinckney Henry Laurens
Fr 1829 Apr 25 13-0153
Fr 1836 Jun 04# 31-0330
Fr 1845 Jan 29 36-1416
Pinckney Thomas
Fr 1813 Nov 16 DLC-7
Fr 1813 Nov 16* M221-56
Fr 1813 Nov 16* 3-0609
Fr 1813 Nov 16 DLC-7
Fr 1813 Nov 16* 3-0616
Fr 1813 Nov 29 DLC-7
Fr 1813 Nov 29* 3-0626
Fr 1813 Nov 29* M221-56
Fr 1813 Dec 02 DLC-7
Fr 1813 Dec 02* 3-0629
To 1813 Dec 03 DLC-61
To 1813 Dec 03* M221-54
To 1813 Dec 08 DLC-61
To 1813 Dec 11 DLC-7
To 1813 Dec 11* M221-56
Fr 1813 Dec 12 DLC-7
Fr 1813 Dec 12* 3-0658
Fr 1813 Dec 12* M221-56
To 1813 Dec 13 M221-56
To 1813 Dec 13* DLC-8
Fr 1813 Dec 23 DLC-8
Fr 1813 Dec 23* 3-0705
Fr 1813 Dec 23* M221-56
Fr 1813 Dec 24 DLC-8
Fr 1813 Dec 24* 3-0712
To 1813 Dec 27 DLC-61
To 1813 Dec 27* M221-56
To 1813 Dec 31 DLC-61
To 1813 Dec 31* 3-0765
To 1814 Jan 02 3-0780
Fr 1814 Jan 09 DLC-8
Fr 1814 Jan 09* M222-13
Fr 1814 Jan 09* 3-0785
Fr 1814 Jan 10 DLC-8
Fr 1814 Jan 10* 3-0790
Fr 1814 Jan 10* M221-56
Fr 1814 Jan 26 DLC-8
Fr 1814 Jan 26* 3-0796
Fr 1814 Jan 26* M221-56
Fr 1814 Jan 26 DLC-8
Fr 1814 Jan 26* M221-56
Fr 1814 Jan 26* 3-0798
To 1814 Jan 29 M222-13
To 1814 Jan 29* DLC-61
To 1814 Jan 29 DLC-8
To 1814 Jan 29* M221-56
To 1814 Jan 29* DLC-61
To 1814 Jan 31 DLC-61
To 1814 Jan 31* M221-56
To 1814 Feb 04 DLC-61
To 1814 Feb 05 DLC-61
To 1814 Feb 05* M221-56
Fr 1814 Feb 05 DLC-8
Fr 1814 Feb 05* 3-0856
Fr 1814 Feb 09 DLC-8
Fr 1814 Feb 09* 3-0859
Fr 1814 Feb 10 DLC-8
Fr 1814 Feb 10* 3-0864
To 1814 Feb 12 DLC-61
To 1814 Feb 16 DLC-61
To 1814 Feb 16* M221-56
To 1814 Feb 17 DLC-61
To 1814 Feb 17* M221-56
Fr 1814 Feb 17 DLC-9
Fr 1814 Feb 17* 3-0880
Fr 1814 Feb 17* M221-56
Fr 1814 Feb 17 3-0876
Fr 1814 Feb 20 DLC-9
Fr 1814 Feb 20* 3-0881
Fr 1814 Feb 20* M221-56
To 1814 Feb 26 DLC-61
To 1814 Feb 26* M221-56
Fr 1814 Feb 26 DLC-9
Fr 1814 Feb 26* 3-0892
Fr 1814 Feb 26* M221-56
To 1814 Feb 28 DLC-61
To 1814 Feb 28* M221-56
To 1814 Mar 02 DLC-61
To 1814 Mar 04 DLC-61
To 1814 Mar 04* M221-56
To 1814 Mar 06 M221-56
Fr 1814 Mar 08 DLC-9
Fr 1814 Mar 08* 3-0907
Fr 1814 Mar 11 M221-56
Fr 1814 Mar 11* 3-0910
Fr 1814 Mar 11* DLC-9
Fr 1814 Mar 13 DLC-9
Fr 1814 Mar 13* 3-0913
Fr 1814 Mar 13* M221-56
To 1814 Mar 14 DLC-61
To 1814 Mar 14* M221-56
To 1814 Mar 22 M221-56
To 1814 Mar 22* DLC-9
To 1814 Mar 23 DLC-9
To 1814 Mar 23* M221-56
Fr 1814 Mar 23 DLC-9
Fr 1814 Mar 23* M221-56
Fr 1814 Mar 23* 3-0917
Fr 1814 Mar 23 DLC-9
Fr 1814 Mar 23* M221-56
Fr 1814 Mar 23* 3-0921
To 1814 Mar 28 M221-56
To 1814 Mar 28* DLC-9
Fr 1814 Mar 28 DLC-9
Fr 1814 Mar 28* M221-56

Fr 1814 Mar 28*	3-0931
To 1814 Apr 05	M221-56
To 1814 Apr 05	M221-56
To 1814 Apr 05*	DLC-10
Fr 1814 Apr 07	DLC-10
Fr 1814 Apr 07*	M221-56
Fr 1814 Apr 07*	3-0960
To 1814 Apr 13	DLC-10
To 1814 Apr 14	M221-56
To 1814 Apr 14*	DLC-10
Fr 1814 Apr 14	DLC-10
Fr 1814 Apr 14*	M221-56
Fr 1814 Apr 14*	3-0968
To 1814 Apr 15	DLC-10
Fr 1814 Apr 16	DLC-10
Fr 1814 Apr 16*	M221-56
Fr 1814 Apr 16*	3-0969
To 1814 Apr 17	DLC-10
Fr 1814 Apr 17	DLC-10
Fr 1814 Apr 17*	M221-56
Fr 1814 Apr 17*	3-0971
To 1814 Apr 18	DLC-10
To 1814 Apr 18	M221-56
Fr 1814 Apr 18	DLC-10
Fr 1814 Apr 18*	3-0978
Fr 1814 Apr 18	DLC-10
Fr 1814 Apr 18*	3-0980
To 1814 Apr 19	DLC-10
To 1814 Apr 21	DLC-10
To 1814 Apr 21*	M221-56
Fr 1814 Apr 21	DLC-10
Fr 1814 Apr 22	DLC-10
Fr 1814 Apr 22*	M221-56
Fr 1814 Apr 22*	3-0982
Fr 1814 Apr 24	DLC-10
Fr 1814 Apr 24*	M221-65
Fr 1814 Apr 24*	3-0986
To 1814 Apr 25	DLC-10
To 1814 Apr 25*	M221-63
To 1814 Apr 26	M221-65
Fr 1814 May 03	DLC-10
Fr 1814 May 03*	3-1001
Fr 1814 May 04	3-1003
To 1814 May 08	3-1015
To 1814 May 08*	DLC-10
Fr 1814 May 19	3-1037
Fr 1814 Jun 18	DLC-10
To 1814 Jul 19	DLC-62
Fr 1814 Jul 19	DLC-11
To 1814 Jul 25	M221-65
To 1814 Jul 25*	DLC-62
To 1814 Jul 27	DLC-62
To 1814 Jul 27*	M221-65
Fr 1814 Aug 03	DLC-11
To 1814 Aug 04	DLC-62
Fr 1814 Aug 11	DLC-11
Fr 1814 Aug 30	DLC-11
To 1814 Sep 02	DLC-62
Fr 1814 Sep 05	DLC-11
To 1814 Sep 12	DLC-62
To 1814 Sep 12*	M221-65
To 1814 Oct 04	DLC-62
To 1814 Oct 31	DLC-62
Fr 1814 Nov 02	DLC-13
To 1814 Nov 16	4-0359
To 1814 Nov 16*	DLC-62
Fr 1814 Nov 20	DLC-14
Fr 1814 Dec 30	DLC-15
To 1828 Apr 22	DLC-35
Fr 1828 May 26	DLC-35

Pinckney William		
Fr 1820 Feb#	mem	DLC-28
Pinkley Frederick		
Fr 1817 May 01	fin	DLC-22
Pintard C		
Fr 1834 Dec#	fin	DLC-45
Pintard J A		
Fr 1835 Sep 08#	fin	DLC-46
Pinto Francisco Antonio		
To 1829 Jun 02		13-0550
Piomingo (pseudonym)		
Fr 1824 Aug		DLC-33
Pipe ______ (Capt)		
Fr 1831 cOct		M234-601
Fr 1831 cOct*		18-0908
Pipkin Philip		
Fr 1814 Sep 04		DLC-12
To 1814 Sep 12		4-0215
Fr 1814 Oct 31		4-0311
Fr 1814 Nov 11		4-0327
Pitcher Nathaniel		
Fr 1829 Sep 25		13-1427
Pitchlynn James		
Fr 1818 Dec		M221-81
Fr 1819 Jun 22		M271-2
Fr 1819 Jun 22*		7-0558
Fr 1819 Sep 13		M221-86
Fr 1820 Jan 28		M221-98
To 1820 cFeb 04		M221-98
Fr 1820 Apr 27		M222-22
Pitchlynn John		
Fr 1815 Aug 20		DLC-19
To 1830 Apr 06		15-0623
To 1830 Aug 05		DLC-38
To 1830 Aug 05#		DLC-38
Fr 1830 Aug 11		DLC-38
Fr 1831 Aug 18		M234-169
Fr 1831 Aug 18*		18-0566
Pitman John		
Fr 1834 Jan 01		M639-9
Pitot James		
Fr 1815 Jan 04		DLC-15
Pittsburgh citizens		
Re 1844 Jan 03	mem	DLC-56
Planters' Bank of Tennessee		
To 1839 Jan 30#	chk	DLC-52
To 1840 Jan 27#	chk	DLC-52
To 1840 Jul 22	chk	DLC-53
Platt F A		
Fr 1839 Oct 20		DLC-52
Platt James et al		
Fr 1832 May 28		20-0669
Platt Job		
Re 1836 Apr 16	par	30-1195
Platt William		
Fr 1829 Sep 29		DLC-37
To 1829 Oct 02		14-0090
To 1829 Oct 02*		DLC-37
Plauche Jean Baptiste		
Fr 1814 Dec 19		4-0423
Fr 1815 Feb 03		DLC-16
To 1815 Apr 03		4-0965
To 1821 Feb 16		8-0134
Fr 1822 Jun 08		DLC-31
Fr 1822 Nov 11		DLC-31
To 1825 Oct 28		DLC-33
Fr 1828 Nov 15		DLC-35
To 1828 Dec 27		12-0338
Fr 1829 Apr 03		M688-63

Entry	Note	Reference
Plauche Jean Baptiste (cont)		
Fr 1830 Jan 21		M639-4
Fr 1837 Feb 16		33-0719
Fr 1840 Jan 08	add	34-1153
To 1840 Jan 08	add	34-1154
Fr 1841 Jun 01		DLC-53
Fr 1841 Sep 16		DLC-53
To 1841 Oct 25		35-0461
To 1841 Nov 22		35-0498
To 1841 Nov 23		35-0500
Fr 1841 Dec 21		DLC-54
Fr 1842 Jan 10		DLC-54
Fr 1842 Mar 25		DLC-54
To 1842 Jun 21		35-0812
Fr 1842 Sep 19		DLC-54
Fr 1842 Oct 19		DLC-54
Fr 1842 Nov 02		DLC-54
Fr 1842 Nov 29		DLC-54
Fr 1843 Jan 23		DLC-55
Fr 1843 Apr 01		DLC-55
Fr 1843 Apr 08		DLC-55
Fr 1843 Nov 25		DLC-56
Fr 1844 Jan 24		DLC-56
Fr 1844 Feb 27		DLC-56
Fr 1844 Jun 02		DLC-57
To 1844 Jun 14		36-0614
Fr 1844 Jul 12		DLC-57
Fr 1844 Nov 12		DLC-57
Fr 1844 Nov 21		36-1040
Fr 1844 Nov 30		36-1085
Fr 1844 Nov 30		M873-90
Fr 1844 Dec 11		36-1179
Fr 1845 Jan 06		36-1318
To 1845 Feb 03		36-1442
Fr 1845 Feb 15		DLC-57
Plauche Jean Baptiste et al		
Fr 1814 Dec 16		DLC-14
Fr 1815 Mar 16	add	4-0873
To 1815 Mar 16	add	4-0875
To 1826 May 26		11-0219
Plauche Jean Baptiste & Co		
Fr 1842 Nov 03		DLC-54
Fr 1843 Jan 06		DLC-55
Fr 1843 Jan 24	fin	DLC-55
Fr 1843 Feb 19		DLC-55
Fr 1843 Mar 27		DLC-55
Fr 1843 May 24	fin	DLC-56
Fr c1844		36-0089
Fr 1844 Jan 24		DLC-56
Fr 1844 Feb 12		DLC-56
Fr 1844 Apr 29	fin	DLC-56
Fr 1844 May 30		DLC-56
Fr 1844 Nov 12		DLC-57
Fr 1845 Feb 08		DLC-57
Fr 1845 Mar 18		DLC-57
Fr 1845 May 22		DLC-58
To 1845 Jun 06		37-0256
Plauche Urban		
Fr 1815 Feb 15		4-0743
To 1815 Feb 18		DLC-62
Pleasonton Stephen		
Fr 1822 Aug 14		DLC-31
Fr 1822 Aug 14*		9-0247
Fr 1823 Dec 17		9-0812
To 1823 Dec 22		9-0829
Fr 1823 Dec 23		9-0843
To 1823 Dec 24		9-0848
Fr 1823 Dec 27		9-0853
Fr 1829 May 08		13-0269
Fr 1829 May 08		13-0270
Fr 1829 May 13		13-0311
Fr 1829 May 14		13-0325
To 1829 May 14		13-0334
To 1829 May 20		DLC-37
To 1829 May 27		13-0445
Fr 1829 May 27		13-0447
Fr 1829 May 28		13-0471
To 1830 Jan 19		14-1468
Fr 1830 Feb 10		15-0121
Fr 1830 Apr 29		15-0859
To 1832 Apr 23		20-0364
Fr 1833 Jan 07#		21-1348
To 1833 Apr 27		22-1194
Fr 1834 Jun 13		M234-435
Fr 1834 Jun 13*		25-1343
Fr 1834 Dec 30		27-0041
Fr 1835 Sep 26#		29-0113
Fr 1836 Mar 30#		30-0932
Fr 1839 Dec 19		DLC-52
Pletcher R		
Fr 1832 Jan 24		M22-29
Plichy Joseph		
To 1834 Jun 03	chk	DLC-44
Plitt George		
Fr 1836 Nov		M22-41
Fr 1841 Dec 11		DLC-54
Plitt George et al		
Fr 1843 Mar 31		DLC-55
Plumer Eliza (Garden)		
To 1838 Dec 21		DLC-51
Plumer William L		
Fr 1845 May 19		DLC-58
Plumer William Swan		
Fr 1838 Dec 06		DLC-51
Plummer Franklin E		
Fr 1834 Sep 17		M234-188
To 1835 Mar 03#		27-0702
Fr 1835 Mar 22		27-1308
Fr 1835 Apr 13		DLC-46
Poindexter George		
Fr 1814 Dec 26		DLC-71
Fr 1818 Dec 12		DLC-26
Fr 1819 Jul 22		DLC-27
To 1820 Oct 02		7-1375
Fr 1820 Oct 25		DLC-29
Fr 1820 Oct 25*		7-1395
Fr 1820 Oct 25*		DLC-72
To 1821 Jun 09		8-0557
Fr 1823 May 04		DLC-32
To 1823 Jul 14		DLC-32
Fr 1830 Dec 14		M22-27
To 1830 Dec 20		16-1509
Fr 1831 Feb 15		17-0533
Fr 1835 Jan 31		27-0357
Poinsett Joel Roberts		
Fr 1823 Jan 31		DLC-32
To 1829 Aug 27		13-1208
Fr 1830 Oct 23		16-0481
Fr 1832 May 09		M639-11
Fr 1832 Oct 16		DLC-41
To 1832 Nov 07		21-0347
Fr 1832 Nov 16		DLC-41
Fr 1832 Nov 24		DLC-41
Fr 1832 Nov 25		DLC-73
Fr 1832 Nov 26		M222-31
Fr 1832 Nov 28		M639-5
Fr 1832 Nov 29		DLC-41
To 1832 Dec 02		21-0654
To 1832 Dec 09		21-0931

To 1832 Dec 09* DLC-41
To 1832 Dec 09* DLC-73
Fr 1832 Dec 17 DLC-41
Fr 1832 Dec 24 21-1155
Fr 1833 Jan 07 DLC-41
To 1833 Jan 16 21-1448
Fr 1833 Jan 16 DLC-42
Fr 1833 Jan 19 DLC-42
Fr 1833 Jan 20 DLC-42
To 1833 Jan 24 22-0055
Fr 1833 Jan 27 DLC-73
Fr 1833 Jan 28 DLC-42
Fr 1833 Jan 30 DLC-42
To 1833 Feb 07 22-0313
Fr 1833 Feb 09 DLC-42
To 1833 Feb 17 22-0402
To 1833 Feb 17* DLC-73
Fr 1833 Feb 22 DLC-42
Fr 1833 Feb 28 DLC-42
To 1833 Mar 06 22-0676
To 1833 Mar 06* DLC-73
Fr 1833 Mar 21 DLC-42
Fr 1833 Mar 23 22-0889
Fr 1833 Dec 20 24-0569
To 1833 Dec 26# M124-141
Fr 1834 Jan 19 M124-141
Fr 1834 Jan 19* 24-1000
Fr 1834 Sep 12 26-0432
Fr 1834 Sep 12* DLC-44
Fr 1834 Oct 02 M688-83
Fr 1834 Oct 20 DLC-44
Fr 1835 Feb 13 DLC-45
Fr 1835 Jun 02 M688-53
Fr 1835 Jun 17 28-0730
Fr 1836 Jun 09 DLC-48
Fr 1836 Dec 02 32-0620
Fr 1837 Jan 18 33-0016
Fr 1837 Aug 19 33-1422
Fr 1837 Aug 21 33-1427
To 1837 Aug 27 DLC-74
To 1837 Aug 27* 33-1444
To 1837 Aug 28 33-1452
To 1837 Sep 04 33-1465
Fr 1837 Sep 06 DLC-50
To 1837 Sep 14 DLC-50
Fr 1837 Sep 17 33-1488
Fr 1837 Sep 23 DLC-50
To 1837 Sep 28 33-1495
To 1837 Oct 01 33-1499
To 1837 Oct 04 M567-147
To 1837 Oct 14 33-1524
To 1837 Oct 19 33-1538
To 1837 Oct 24 33-1541
Fr 1837 Nov 10 34-0019
To 1837 Nov 22 34-0038
Fr 1837 Dec 02 34-0068
To 1837 Dec 13 34-0088
To 1838 Jan 10 34-0180
To 1838 cAug 20 34-0427
To 1838 Aug 29 34-0442
Fr 1838 Sep 12# DLC-51
To 1838 Oct 29 34-0505
Fr 1838 Nov 11 34-0515
To 1838 Dec 03 34-0540
Fr 1839 Mar 21 DLC-52
To 1839 Apr 04 34-0721
To 1839 May 18 34-0794
To 1839 May 30 34-0809
Fr 1839 Jun 14 34-0820
Fr 1839 Oct 12# DLC-52
To 1840 Apr 10 34-1303
Fr 1840 Apr 25 DLC-52
To 1840 Jul 21 34-1491
Fr 1840 Aug 28 34-1583
Fr 1842 Oct 24 DLC-54
Fr 1844 Oct 28 DLC-57
To 1844 Nov 12 36-1017

Points James
Fr 1834 Aug 01 DLC-44

Poishick et al
Fr 1834 Aug 26 M234-729
Fr 1834 Aug 26 M234-729

Pokegan et al
Fr 1835 Jan 26 M234-777

Polari Constant
Re 1832 cSep par 20-1447

Polk Ezekiel
Fr 1813 Sep 02 DLC-6
Re 1844 cSep 04 mem DLC-57

Polk James Knox
Fr 1826 Apr 03 DLC-33
To 1826 May 03 11-0206
Fr 1826 Dec 04 DLC-34
To 1826 Dec 24 11-0439
To 1828 Mar 23 11-1192
Fr 1828 Apr 13 DLC-35
Fr 1828 Apr 15 DLC-35
Fr 1828 May 03 11-1234
Fr 1828 Jun 29 DLC-37
To 1828 Aug 28 12-0176
Fr 1828 Sep 08 12-0190
To 1828 Sep 16 12-0202
Fr 1828 Dec 01 DLC-35
Fr 1828 Dec 05 DLC-36
Fr 1829 Apr 22 M639-27
Fr 1830 Aug 14 16-0106
To 1830 Aug 18 16-0132
To 1830 Aug 31 16-0197
Fr 1830 Aug 31 16-0201
Fr 1831 Mar 28 17-1000
To 1832 cDec 04 21-0854
To 1832 Dec 16 21-1064
To 1833 Aug 31 23-0569
To 1833 Dec 18 24-0559
Fr 1833 Dec 23 24-0574
To 1833 Dec 23 24-0575
To 1834 May 18 25-1085
Fr 1834 Aug 23 DLC-44
Fr 1834 Aug 23* 26-0348
Fr 1834 Sep 01 DLC-44
Fr 1835 Jan 28 M639-3
Fr 1835 Apr 29 DLC-73
To 1835 May 03 28-0245
To 1835 May 12 28-0370
Fr 1835 May 15 DLC-46
Fr 1835 May 16 M688-98
Fr 1835 May 27 DLC-46
To 1835 Aug 03 28-1233
Fr 1835 Aug 14 DLC-46
Fr 1835 Sep 10 29-0016
To 1835 Sep 15 29-0052
To 1835 cSep 16# 37-0343
Fr 1835 Sep 22# DLC-73
Fr 1835 Oct 10 DLC-47
Fr 1835 Oct 10 DLC-47
To 1835 Oct 20 29-0322
To 1836 Jan 20 30-0151
To 1836 Jan 28 30-0221

Polk James Knox (cont)

Fr 1836 Mar 04		30-0676
Fr 1836 Apr 14		30-1175
Fr 1837 cJan 03		M22-41
To 1837 Feb 06		33-0429
Fr 1837 Feb 25		33-0894
Fr 1837 Feb 25#		33-0898
Fr 1837 Mar 03		M687-4
Fr 1837 May 19		DLC-50
To 1837 May 22		33-1235
Fr 1837 May 29		DLC-50
Fr 1837 Jun 14		33-1300
Fr 1837 Jun 16		33-1309
To 1837 Jun 19		33-1316
Fr 1837 Jun 21		33-1324
Fr 1837 Jun 22		33-1328
To 1837 Aug 06		33-1415
To 1837 Oct 29		34-0002
Fr 1838 Jan 07		DLC-74
Fr 1838 Jan 07		DLC-51
Fr 1838 Jan 18		DLC-51
To 1838 Feb 01		DLC-51
To 1838 Feb 02		34-0231
Fr 1838 Feb 04#		DLC-51
Fr 1838 Mar 07		DLC-51
To 1838 Mar 23		34-0287
Fr 1838 Apr 03		DLC-51
To 1838 May 21		DLC-51
Fr 1838 Jun 11		34-0368
Fr 1838 Aug 07		DLC-51
Fr 1838 Sep 02		DLC-74
Fr 1838 Sep 23		DLC-51
Fr 1838 Oct 29#		DLC-51
Fr 1839 Feb 07		DLC-51
Fr 1839 Feb 07*		34-0630
To 1839 Feb 11		34-0634
Fr 1839 Aug 12		DLC-52
To 1839 Aug 13		34-0867
Fr 1839 Aug 15		34-0869
Fr 1839 Aug 31		DLC-52
To 1840 May 09		34-1343
To 1840 May 15		34-1354
To 1840 Dec 19		35-0127
To 1840 Dec 20		35-0130
To 1841 Feb 08		35-0224
To 1841 Mar 06		35-0240
To 1841 Mar 20		35-0260
Fr 1841 Aug 02#		DLC-53
To 1841 Oct 14		35-0448
To 1841 cOct 15		35-0451
Fr 1841 Oct 30		DLC-53
To 1841 Oct 31		35-0462
Fr 1841 Dec 31		35-0555
To 1842 Jan 07		35-0589
Fr 1842 Jul 01		DLC-54
Fr 1843 Aug 07#		DLC-55
Fr 1843 Dec 25		DLC-56
Fr 1844 Feb 22		DLC-56
Fr 1844 Mar 15		DLC-56
To 1844 Jun 29		36-0660
Fr 1844 Jul 22		36-0732
To 1844 Jul 23		36-0735
Fr 1844 Jul 23		DLC-57
To 1844 Jul 26		36-0755
Fr 1844 Aug 03		DLC-57
To 1844 Sep 02		36-0838
Fr 1844 Sep 09		36-0856
To 1844 Sep 17		36-0852
To 1844 Sep 26		36-0904
To 1844 cOct		36-0919
To 1844 Oct 03		36-0895
To 1844 Oct 04		36-0915
To 1844 Oct 05		36-0928
To 1844 Oct 06#		36-0934
To 1844 Oct 29#		36-0964
To 1844 Oct 31#		36-0972
To 1844 Nov 04#		36-0984
To 1844 Nov 05#		36-0989
To 1844 Nov 06#		36-0993
To 1844 Nov 06#		36-0996
To 1844 Nov 08#		36-1006
To 1844 Nov 09#		36-1010
To 1844 Nov 09#		36-1013
To 1844 Nov 16		DLC-57
To 1844 Nov 24#		36-1052
Re 1844 Nov 29		36-1078
To 1844 Dec 08		36-1134
To 1844 Dec 10		36-1139
To 1844 Dec 10		M873-21
To 1844 Dec 11		M873-21
To 1844 Dec 13		36-1202
To 1844 Dec 13		M873-6
To 1844 Dec 16		36-1211
To 1844 Dec 23		36-1254
To 1845 Jan 10		36-1321
To 1845 Jan 25		36-1408
To 1845 Jan 29		36-1420
To 1845 Feb 03		36-1444
To 1845 Feb 05		36-1457
To 1845 Feb 07		36-1459
To 1845 Feb 07		36-1461
To 1845 Feb 08		36-1465
To 1845 Feb 15		36-1489
To 1845 Feb 22		36-1506
To 1845 Feb 28		36-1521
To 1845 Mar 06		36-1545
To 1845 Mar 11		36-1528
To 1845 Mar 12	mem	36-1568
To 1845 Mar 17		36-1579
Fr 1845 Mar 17		DLC-57
Fr 1845 Mar 17*		36-1581
Fr 1845 Mar 26		DLC-57
Fr 1845 Mar 26*		37-0027
To 1845 Apr 07		37-0117
To 1845 Apr 11		37-0142
Fr 1845 Apr 27		DLC-58
To 1845 Apr 30		37-0164
To 1845 May 02		37-0174
Fr 1845 May 12		DLC-58
To 1845 May 16		37-0206
Fr 1845 May 22		DLC-58
To 1845 May 26		37-0221
Fr 1845 Jun 05		37-0251
To 1845 Jun 06		DLC-58
To 1845 Jun 08#		DLC-58
To 1845 Jun 30#		37-0261
To 1845 Oct 10#		DLC-58

Polk Lucius Junius

To 1836 Oct 16		32-0187
To 1838 Mar 12		34-0272
To 1838 Mar 12		37-0369
To 1839 Apr 11		34-0738
Fr 1839 Jul 28		DLC-52
To 1841 Mar 06		35-0243
To 1842 Jan 20		35-0611
To 1842 Jan 21	chk	DLC-54
To 1843 May 08		35-1345
Fr 1843 May 16		35-1355

Polk Mary Ann (Eastin)			
see also Eastin M A			
	Fr 1832 Jun 24		DLC-40
	To 1832 Nov 26		21-0580
	Fr 1832 Dec 18		DLC-41
	To 1833 Mar 18		22-0794
	To 1836 Mar 14		30-0771
	To 1836 Dec 22		32-1270
	To 1838 Mar 12		37-0369
	To 1841 Aug 12		35-0368
	Fr 1843 May 15		35-1353
Polk Samuel			
	Fr 1815 Aug 17		DLC-19
	To 1815 Aug 19		DLC-19
Polk William			
	Fr 1800 Sep 18		DLC-2
	Fr 1823 Sep 20		DLC-32
	Fr 1825 Jan 17		M439-9
	To 1825 Oct 25		11-0045
	To 1827 Oct 11		11-0890
	To 1829 Jan 05		12-0447
	To 1829 Sep 21		13-1402
	To 1830 Mar 12		15-0350
	To 1830 Aug 25		16-0159
	To 1832 Apr 11		20-0184
	Fr 1833 Dec 07		DLC-43
Polk William et al			
	Fr 1829 Mar 04	add	12-0854
	To 1829 Mar 04	add	DLC-36
Polk & Walker			
	Fr 1816 Aug 15		DLC-21
Polkinhorn Charles			
	Fr 1830 Mar 16	fin	DLC-38
Pollard ______ (Capt) et al			
	Fr 1834 Mar 19		M234-832
Pollard Richard			
	To 1833 Nov 04#		M688-89
	Re 1833 Nov 09		23-1215
	Fr 1833 Dec 30		M296-1
	Fr 1834 Mar 26		M688-89
Polydore (slave)			
	Re 1822 Apr 12		DLC-31
Pomar Anthony			
	To 1835 Aug 19	fin	28-1331
Pomare Queen of Tahiti			
	Fr 1836 Dec 31		T953-4
Poole William Laurens			
	Fr 1829 May 07		M639-18
	Fr 1836 Oct 08		32-0117
Pooley Samuel J			
	Fr 1834 Jan 16		DLC-44
Poor Edward et al			
	Fr 1837 Feb 03		M687-20
Pope A			
	Fr 1829 Dec 07		14-0811
Pope Daniel N			
	Re 1831 Oct 20		18-1087
Pope Frances (Walton)			
	Fr 1829 May 30		13-0509
	To 1829 Jun 08		DLC-37
Pope John			
	Fr 1829 Feb 19		DLC-36
	Fr 1829 May 11		M639-21
	Fr 1829 Jun 05		13-0578
	Fr 1829 Jun 12		M639-20
	Fr 1830 Apr 26		M222-28
	Fr 1830 Aug 26		DLC-38
	Fr 1830 Oct 04		M179-69
	Fr 1831 Nov 12		18-1256
	Fr 1832 Nov 08		21-0363
	Re 1833 Aug	mem	DLC-43
	Re 1833 Sep 02		23-0598
	Fr 1836 Jun 20		DLC-48
Pope Leroy			
	To 1813 Oct 28		DLC-61
	To 1813 Oct 28*		M221-56
	To 1813 Oct 29		DLC-61
	To 1813 Oct 31		DLC-7
	To 1813 Nov 01		DLC-61
	Fr 1813 Nov 02		DLC-61
	To 1813 Nov 04		DLC-61
	Fr 1813 Nov 04		DLC-61
	Fr 1813 Nov 05		DLC-75
	To 1813 Nov 07		DLC-61
	Fr 1813 Nov 09		DLC-61
	To 1813 Nov 12		DLC-61
	To 1813 Nov 16		DLC-61
	To 1813 Nov 20		DLC-61
	Fr 1813 Dec 05		DLC-75
	To 1813 Dec 15		DLC-61
	To 1813 Dec 18		DLC-61
	Fr 1814 Nov		DLC-75
	Fr 1815 Feb 13		DLC-16
	To 1815 Mar 20		DLC-62
	Fr 1816 May 29		DLC-20
	Fr 1816 Nov 26		DLC-22
Pope Leroy et al			
	To 1813 Oct 23		DLC-61
	To 1813 Oct 23*		M221-56
	To 1818 Jul 22	fin	6-1149
Pope Maria			
	Fr 1814 Apr		3-0999
	To 1814 May 07#		DLC-10
Pope Worden			
	Fr 1829 Feb 08		M639-20
	Fr 1829 Feb 21		M639-18
	Fr 1829 May 31		DLC-37
	Fr 1829 Dec 25		DLC-37
	Fr 1831 Jun 19		DLC-39
	Fr 1831 Aug 06		DLC-39
	Fr 1833 Apr 21		DLC-42
	Fr 1836 cFeb		30-0253
	Fr 1836 Dec 30		M639-15
Pope Worden et al			
	Fr 1828 Dec 29		DLC-36
Pope & Brahan			
	To 1813 Dec 08		DLC-7
	To 1814 Feb 06		DLC-61
	To 1814 Feb 18		DLC-61
	To 1814 Mar 22		DLC-9
	To 1814 Mar 22		DLC-9
	Fr 1814 May 12		DLC-10
	To 1814 May 18		DLC-10
Poree Alexander W			
	Fr 1834 Mar 18		M688-89
Porter Alexander			
	Fr 1818 Oct 26	fin	DLC-28
	Fr 1831 Jan 26		M22-27
Porter Alexander et al			
	Fr 1836 Apr 25		M567-129
Porter Benjamin			
	To 1814 Jun 20	chk	DLC-10
Porter Calvin et al			
	Re 1835 Jun 17		M273-32
Porter D C et al			
	Fr 1829 Aug 28		M639-17
Porter David			
	Re 1829 Aug 18		M179-67

Porter David (cont)
Fr 1830 Jan 22 M179-68
Re 1831 Apr 15 17-1184
Fr 1831 Oct 07 18-0934
Fr 1832 Dec 05 DLC-41
Fr 1832 Dec 21 M124-137
Fr 1832 Dec 22 M124-137
Fr 1834 Jul 02 26-0071
Fr 1835 Apr 24 M46-9
Porter E et al
Fr 1829 Feb 27 M179-67
Porter Eveline (Anderson)
Fr 1828 Nov 29 DLC-35
Fr 1834 Nov 11 M688-73
Fr 1836 Jan 19 30-0148
Porter Frederick W
Fr 1830 Nov 27 16-0897
Fr 1838 Nov 27 34-0537
To 1838 Dec 34-0539
Porter George Bryan
Fr 1829 Feb 16 12-0520
Fr 1829 Jul 21 M639-7
Re 1831 Aug 06 18-0466
Fr 1832 Feb 09 M567-75
To 1833 Dec 02 23-1516
Fr 1833 Dec 15 M234-421
Fr 1833 Dec 15* 24-0507
Porter James
Fr 1812 Oct 23 fin DLC-10
Fr 1830 May 28 15-1189
Fr 1832 Aug 12 M639-12
Porter James Madison
To 1843 Jul 19 M688-147
Fr 1843 Aug 19 35-1469
Fr 1843 cSep 30 35-1518
To 1843 Oct 03 35-1523
Porter Joseph B
Fr 1816 Aug 14 DLC-21
Fr 1816 Aug 22 DLC-21
Porter Penelope
To 1824 Jun 19 10-0799
Porter Peter Buell
Re 1829 Nov 13 mem 14-0459
Porter Reece
Fr 1796 Mar 19 lnd 1-0366
Porter Samuel Humes
Fr 1843 Apr 28 DLC-55
To 1843 Dec 18 36-0068
Porter Thomas J
Fr 1836 Jul 30 DLC-48
To 1836 Aug 03# DLC-48
Porter William G et al
Fr 1835 Nov 12 par 29-0507
Porter William N
Fr 1845 Jan 27 M873-69
Porter & Rolling
Fr 1825 Nov 16 fin DLC-33
Portsmouth (ship)
Re 1832 Nov 28 M179-74
Portsmouth naval officers' quarters
Re 1832 Jun 12 M124-133
Post Henry E Jr
Fr 1828 Feb 25 DLC-35
Fr 1829 Apr 05# DLC-36
Post Isaac et al
Fr 1829 Apr 06 M639-19
Post Reuben
Fr 1829 Feb 25 12-0587
Fr 1831 May 03 M873-55
Post Russel H
Re 1836 Dec 12 par 32-1102
Potawatomi Ottawa and Chippewa Indians
Fr 1835 cSep 28-1477
Potawatomi treaty
Re 1833 Jan 21 M668-7
Re 1833 Jan 21* 22-0009
Re 1833 Jan 21 M668-7
Re 1833 Jan 21 M668-7
Re 1835 Mar 16 M668-7
Re 1835 Mar 16 M668-7
Re 1835 Mar 16 M668-7
Re 1835 Mar 16 M668-7
Re 1836 Mar 21 30-0855
Re 1836 May 25 M668-8
Re 1836 Jun 04 M668-8
Re 1836 Jun 04 M668-8
Re 1837 Feb 16 M668-8
Re 1837 Feb 18 M668-8
Potomac bridge
Re 1833 Apr 03 22-0933
Re 1833 May 23 22-1436
Potter _____ (Dr)
To 1810 Aug 30 DLC-4
Potter Archibald
To 1814 Jan 10 DLC-61
To 1814 Jan 11 DLC-61
Fr 1814 Feb 01 3-0848
To 1814 Feb 04 DLC-62
To 1814 Feb 23 DLC-61
Fr 1814 Feb 23 DLC-61
Re 1816 Jul 11 fin 5-0300
Potter Benjamin Jr
Fr 1838 Oct 13 DLC-51
Potter Elisha Reynolds
Fr 1831 Jun 20 M639-10
Fr 1833 Feb 18 22-0405
Potter L C
To 1835 Jan 02# M639-10
Potts Joseph C
Fr 1834 May 23 DLC-44
Potts Stacy Gardner
Fr 1832 May 16 20-0532
Poulson Robert J
Fr 1836 Jul 15 31-1093
Poultney John
Fr 1815 Jan 27 DLC-16
Poulton William
Fr 1835 Sep# fin DLC-47
Poursine William
Fr 1815 Jan 15 DLC-15
Poussin William Tell
Fr 1832 Jun 07 M567-75
Powel Baxter A
Re 1830 Feb 18 par 15-0181
Powel Samuel
To 1803 Sep 15 leg 1-1163
Powel William
Fr c1833 Apr 26 22-1187
Powell Addison
Fr 1830 Oct 23 16-0487
To 1830 Oct 23 16-0495
Fr 1830 Oct 23 16-0499
To 1830 Nov 13 16-0721
Powell G W J
Fr 1832 Jun 16 M221-112
Powell John
Fr 1843 Jan 24 DLC-55
Powell N B
Fr 1844 Feb 29 DLC-56
Powell Sampson
Fr 1804 Mar 15 fin DLC-3

Powell Theophilus
Fr 1814 Sep 07 fin DLC-12
To 1814 Sep 07 fin DLC-14
Power Manley
Fr 1815 Mar 30 DLC-17
Fr 1815 Mar 30* M222-16
Power Samuel
Fr 1831 May 17 M567-63
Powers Hiram
To 1835 Dec 07 29-0783
Powers William H
Re 1835 Apr 29 par 28-0184
Poyzer George
Fr 1807 Mar 01 DLC-4
Fr 1807 Aug 17# 2-0538
Fr 1807 Sep 25# 2-0559
Fr 1812 Dec 17 2-1299
Prather Leonard
Re 1836 Feb 25 par 30-0575
Pratt Luther
Fr 1836 Aug 10 DLC-48
Pratt S
Fr 1836 Jan 18# fin DLC-47
Pray P Rutilius R
Fr 1836 Sep 15# 31-1450
Preble William Pitt
Fr 1829 May 06 DLC-37
Re 1829 Jun 01 13-0545
To 1829 Jun 20 13-0690
Fr 1830 Dec 25 16-1579
Fr 1831 Jan 17 17-0282
Fr 1831 Jul 14 M42-13
Fr 1834 Mar 07 M639-22
Fr 1834 Mar 07* 24-1599
Prentis Ebenezer
Fr 1830 Oct 22 16-0465
Prentis John
Fr 1830 Oct 22 16-0465
Prentiss Henry et al
Fr 1836 cMay 30-1446
Prentiss Samuel
To 1834 cDec 22 37-0519
Prescott Joseph N
Fr 1835 Jun 30 28-0860
Prescott William
Fr 1844 May 27 DLC-56
To 1844 Jun 10 36-0597
Fr 1844 Nov 07 DLC-57
To 1844 Nov 30 36-1088
Pressley John B
Fr 1831 Nov 04 M639-6
Pressly John S
Fr 1835 Oct 15 29-0299
Fr 1836 Feb 06 30-0294
Prestage William
Re 1831 Oct 13 par 18-0976
Re 1832 Nov 02 par 21-0273
Preston Francis
Re 1803 Apr 11 leg DLC-2
To 1803 Sep 13 1-1161
To 1804 Apr 15 1-1316
Fr 1804 Dec 18 DLC-3
To 1805 Jan 06 2-0004
To 1805 Jan 23 2-0007
To 1806 Aug 10 2-0312
Fr 1807 Dec 17 DLC-4
Fr 1807 Dec 17* 2-0597
To 1810 May 03 2-0900
To 1819 Feb 02 7-0224
To 1822 Feb 19 9-0029
To 1824 Jan 27 10-0402
Fr 1825 Jan 22 DLC-33
Fr 1828 Dec 09 DLC-36
To 1828 Dec 18 12-0326
Fr 1829 Feb 23 M639-18
Fr 1829 Aug 17 M639-18
To 1830 Mar 06 15-0311
To 1830 Mar 09 15-0317
Fr 1830 Mar 16 DLC-37
To 1830 Jun 16 15-1473
To 1831 Mar 18 17-0906
Fr 1832 Jul 02 M688-83
Fr 1834 Sep 27 26-0459
Preston Isaac Trimble
Fr 1829 Feb 13 M639-18
Fr 1829 Oct 31# 14-0282
Fr 1831 Apr 16 M639-22
Fr 1836 Jan 24 M639-4
Fr 1839 Aug 10 DLC-52
Preston John
Fr 1824 Mar 20 M688-32
Preston Sarah P
Fr 1829 Jan 05 12-0450
Preston Thomas
Fr 1814 Mar 07 3-0903
Preston Warren et al
Fr 1829 May M639-24
Preston William Campbell
Fr 1815 Oct 25 4-1220
To 1815 Oct 25 4-1221
Prevaux John
Re 1832 Dec 22 leg 21-1123
Price Augustus
Re 1833 Dec 11 fin DLC-43
Price Chandler
Fr 1821 Oct 06 DLC-31
To 1824 Jan 06 9-0898
To 1824 Jan 20 10-0385
To 1824 Feb 07 DLC-75
To 1825 Jan 09 10-1051
Price Thomas K
Fr 1844 Dec 04 36-1123
Fr 1844 Dec 28 36-1272
Price William
Fr 1836 Feb 27 M639-17
Price William Harrison
Fr 1836 Oct 11 M567-129
Price William M
Fr 1829 Mar 26 12-1152
Fr 1829 Apr 16# 12-1367
Fr 1831 Sep 27 M639-18
Fr 1831 Oct 14# M639-24
Fr 1832 Dec 10 M639-16
Fr 1833 Feb 06 DLC-42
Fr 1835 Jul 15 28-1024
Priestly James
To 1810 Jun 06 fin 2-0957
To 1811 Jun 26 lnd 2-1005
Fr 1816 Jan mem DLC-60
Priestly Joseph
Fr 1814 May 14 add 3-1026
Priestly Philander et al
Fr 1844 Aug 26 36-0825
Prieur Denis
Fr 1840 Nov 03 DLC-53
Fr 1844 Dec 21 36-1241
Prime Ruth H
Fr 1839 Jul 10 DLC-52
To 1839 Sep 21 34-0948

Prime Samuel			
	Re 1813 Oct 29		DLC-61
Prince Bayliss E			
	To 1813 Dec 13		DLC-61
Prince Ezekiel et al			
	Fr 1835 Jul 02		28-0878
Prince Henry			
	Fr 1835 Jul 05		M22-36
Pringle James R			
	To 1830 Dec 24		16-1556
Pringle John Julius et al			
	Fr 1834 Aug 12		M639-18
Pritchett & Shall			
	Fr 1814 Mar 08	fin	DLC-20
	Fr 1815 May 23	fin	DLC-69
	To 1815 Oct 08	fin	DLC-19
	Fr 1816 Feb 19		DLC-20
	To 1816 Feb 19	chk	DLC-20
	Fr 1816 Feb 22	fin	DLC-69
	To 1816 Aug 19	chk	DLC-21
Privat Theodore			
	Re 1829 Sep 26		13-1432
Proctor John			
	Fr 1834 Jul 24		26-0236
Proli Maximilian Ludwig			
	Fr 1831 Sep 07		M179-71
	To 1831 Sep 14		18-0756
Provensal Joaquin et al			
	Fr 1815 Feb 17		DLC-16
Provest Alexander et al			
	Fr 1831 Jan 29		M639-1
Providence RI citizens			
	To 1844 Aug 22		36-0820
Prussia treaty			
	Re 1829 Mar 12		12-0975
	Re 1829 Mar 14		12-1010
Pryor Cincinnatus			
	Re 1832 May 12		M273-27
Pryor James			
	Fr 1829 May 15		M639-2
Pryor Norton			
	To 1805 Dec 12		2-0098
Pryor Samuel			
	To 1806 Jun		2-0262
	Fr 1807 Jan 01	fin	DLC-4
	Fr 1807 Mar 05		DLC-4
	Fr 1807 Aug 19	fin	DLC-4
	Fr 1807 Dec 31	fin	DLC-4
	Fr 1808 Jan 06	fin	2-0603
	Re 1808 Jan 08	mem	DLC-4
	Re 1808 Jan 24	leg	2-0609
	Re 1808 Jan 29	leg	2-0610
	To 1808 Sep 23	fin	DLC-4
	Re 1810 Jan 15	leg	2-0869
	Re 1812 Jul 29	leg	2-1137
Pryor Samuel et al			
	Re 1805 Dec 30	leg	DLC-71
Public debt			
	Re 1833 Mar	mem	22-0582
Public lands			
	Re c1829	add	37-0280
Puckett Ann			
	Fr 1819 Sep 30		DLC-27
Puckett Benjamin			
	Fr 1830 Sep 05		16-0208
Puckett J A			
	Fr 1841 Dec 11	mem	DLC-54
Puckett John			
	Fr 1831 Sep 06	fin	DLC-40
Puckett Shippey Allen			
	To 1806 Mar 28	fin	DLC-4
Puckett Thomas			
	Fr 1819 Sep 30		DLC-27
Puckett William			
	Fr 1831 Sep 06	fin	DLC-40
Puett Austin Montana			
	Fr 1835 Sep 06		M639-11
Pugett Frederick			
	Fr 1830 Jun 17		15-1492
Pulaski TN citizens			
	Fr 1826 Jul 04	add	11-0266
Pulis John			
	Fr 1830 Sep 02		M639-18
Pulis Joseph			
	Fr 1830 Sep 02		M639-18
Pumfrey Jonathan			
	Fr 1806 Jul 18	fin	DLC-4
Punch John Smith			
	Re 1834 Jul 02		M273-30
Punomo			
	Fr 1835 Nov 28		29-0623
Punshon Robert			
	Fr 1829 Feb 06		12-0485
	Fr 1829 Mar 28		12-1159
Purcell John Baptist			
	Fr 1832 May 07		M688-83
Purdy Elijah F			
	Fr 1841 Feb 27		DLC-53
	To 1841 Mar 16		35-0258
	Fr 1843 Nov 29		36-0034
Purdy Robert			
	Fr 1803 Sep 08		1-1157
	Fr 1806 Jan 06		DLC-3
	Fr 1806 Jan 31		2-0130
	Fr 1806 Feb 08		2-0163
	Fr 1806 Mar 06#		2-0187
	Fr 1808 Feb 15		DLC-71
	Fr 1808 Jun		2-0675
	Fr 1809		DLC-75
	Fr 1809		2-0759
	Fr 1810 Feb 20		2-0874
	Fr 1810 Apr 20		DLC-75
	Fr 1810 May 24		DLC-4
	Fr 1810 Jul 20		DLC-4
	Fr 1810 Nov		DLC-75
	Fr 1810 Dec 16		DLC-5
	Fr 1811 May 28		DLC-5
	Fr 1815 Feb 17		DLC-16
	Fr 1815 Feb 26		DLC-17
	Fr 1815 Mar 26		DLC-17
	Fr 1815 May 01		DLC-18
	Fr 1815 May 26		DLC-18
	Fr 1815 Jun 24		DLC-18
	Fr 1815 Jul 18		M221-63
	Fr 1815 Sep 24		DLC-19
	Fr 1824 Sep 29		DLC-33
	Fr 1829 Mar 02		M639-15
	Fr 1829 Apr 06		M639-2
Purnell William			
	To 1809 Nov 18#		2-0861
	Fr 1809 Nov 19		2-0863
	Fr 1810 Dec 14		2-0972
Pursell Thomas			
	Fr 1836 Jan 07#	fin	DLC-47
Pushmataha et al			
	Fr 1820 Oct 20		M271-3
Putnam Benjamin A			
	Fr 1831 Oct 12		M639-2

Putnam Joshua et al
Fr 1837 Feb 08 M639-14
Putnam Lewis et al
Fr 1835 Sep 28-1486

Qualls James
To 1814 Apr 25 DLC-61
Fr 1814 Apr 25 fin DLC-10
Quapaw treaty
Re 1818 Aug 24 DLC-25
Re 1834 Apr 12 M668-7
Quarles John B
Re 1814 Jan 28 DLC-62
Quarles Randolph
Fr 1814 Sep 06 DLC-12
Quarles Tunstall
Fr 1829 Jan 06 M639-22
Quarles W H
Fr 1816 Jan 30 fin DLC-69
Quarles William
Fr 1813 Jul 21 3-0426
Fr 1825 Aug 25 DLC-33
Queen William
Re 1788 Mar leg 1-0037
Quertier N
Fr 1836 Oct 24 32-0339
Quimby Amos
Fr 1836 Jun 07 31-0386
Quin John
Fr 1836 Mar 13 30-0759
Quincy Abraham H
Fr 1819 Feb 05 DLC-26
Quincy Charles Edmund
Fr 1835 Apr 30# M639-5
Quincy Josiah
Fr 1833 Jun 26 add 23-0064
To 1833 Jun 29# 23-0075
Quinney John W
Fr 1830 Dec 14 M234-315
Fr 1830 Dec 14* 16-1431
Quinney John W et al
Fr 1831 Jan 20 M234-315
Fr 1831 Jan 20* 17-0308
Quintana Luis
Fr 1829 Dec 31 M54-1
QuishQuehLah
Fr 1835 Nov 20 29-0542
Fr 1835 Nov 20* M234-355
Fr 1835 Nov 20* M234-642
Quitman John Anthony et al
Fr 1840 cJan 14 34-1170

Rabiou Charles
To 1821 Jul 19 M116-6
Rabun William
To 1818 Jan 12 5-1279
Fr 1818 Feb 09 DLC-24
Fr 1818 Feb 09* 5-1445
To 1818 Feb 10 6-0011
Fr 1818 Mar 21 DLC-24
Fr 1818 Mar 21* 6-0079
Fr 1818 Mar 21* M271-2
Fr 1818 Mar 21* M221-79
To 1818 Apr 20 6-0459
To 1818 May 07 6-0677
To 1818 May 07* M271-2
To 1818 May 07* M221-78
To 1818 May 07* M221-79
Fr 1818 Jun 01 DLC-25
Fr 1818 Jun 01* 6-0945
Fr 1818 Jun 01* M271-2
Fr 1818 Jun 01* M221-79
To 1818 Aug 01 6-1175
Fr 1818 Sep 01 DLC-25
Fr 1818 Sep 01* 6-1275
Radford Edward
Re 1806 Jul 08 leg 2-0294
Raffles Thomas
Fr 1829 Oct 13 14-0153
Ragan John
Fr 1825 Feb 22 10-1146
Fr 1845 Apr 08 DLC-58
Raggi ______
Re c1829 mem 37-0281
Raguet Henry
Fr 1836 Feb 13 M234-436
Rahn George
Fr 1830 Feb 26 M639-23
Raines Austin J
Re 1833 Oct 17 23-1056
Rainey Winfield S
Re 1839 Nov 30 mem 34-1065
Rains ______
To 1837 Jan# DLC-49
Rains Felix Robertson
Fr 1840 Jan 11 fin DLC-52
Fr 1842 fin 35-0574
Fr 1842 Jun 03 fin DLC-54
Re 1842 Jun 04 mem DLC-54
Ralli John
Re 1831 Jun 02 17-1494
Ralls John
Fr 1844 Apr 24 36-0444
Ralston Alexander
Fr 1814 Sep 24 DLC-12
Fr 1814 Oct 10 DLC-13
Ralston John et al
Fr 1835 cJan DLC-59
Ralston Matthew C et al
Fr 1832 Nov M639-9
Ralston Robert et al
Fr 1831 Jan 15 M639-11
Rama III King of Siam
To 1835 Mar 20 M77-152
To 1835 Apr 17 M77-152
Ramage James
Fr 1821 May 26 DLC-30
Fr 1821 Aug 20 DLC-30
Fr 1821 Aug 22 DLC-30
Fr 1829 May 24# DLC-37
Re 1829 Sep 16 M273-23
Re 1831 Sep 23 M273-26
Ramirez Angel
Fr 1815 Feb 13 DLC-16
Ramsay Charles R
Fr 1834 May 30 25-1173
Ramsay Samuel et al
Fr 1829 Jan 07 12-0453
Ramsey James Gettys McGready
To 1823 Jun 14 9-0597
To 1827 Jan 15 11-0466
Ramsey James Gettys McGready et al
Fr 1831 Sep 10 M22-28
Fr 1840 May 14 34-1348
Ramsey John
Fr 1829 Sep 15 M639-3

Random J M			
	Fr 1835 Mar 31	fin	DLC-46
Rankin Christopher			
	Fr 1820 May 16		DLC-29
	To 1820 Jun 19		DLC-29
Rankin Eliza C			
	Fr 1834 Oct 25		26-0733
	Fr 1837 Aug 08		DLC-50
Rankin Henry et al			
	Fr 1837 Feb 23		M687-6
Rankin Joseph et al			
	Fr 1829 Mar		M639-12
Rankin Robert			
	Fr 1835 Mar 31		DLC-46
Rankin William			
	Fr 1836 Jan 06		DLC-73
Ransom Robert			
	Fr 1837 Apr 07		DLC-50
Rapier Richard			
	Fr 1814 Oct 28		DLC-13
	To 1816 Jul 03	chk	DLC-21
	Fr 1822 Oct 01		DLC-31
Rapier & Simpson			
	Fr 1819 Dec 21	fin	7-0931
	Fr 1821 Nov 08	fin	8-1331
	Fr 1822 Jan 02	fin	8-1381
	Fr 1822 Jan 08	fin	DLC-31
	Fr 1822 Nov 14	fin	9-0304
Rasch Anthony			
	Fr 1821 May 23#	fin	DLC-30
Ratell Paul et al			
	Fr 1829 Dec		M639-20
Rathbun John W			
	Fr 1829 Feb 02		M639-19
Raum John et al			
	Fr 1833 cFeb		M639-27
Rawle William			
	Fr 1830 Jun 07#		15-1314
Rawles John			
	Fr 1820 Jan 25		DLC-28
Rawlings Benjamin			
	Fr c1798		DLC-74
	Fr 1806 Feb 18#	fin	DLC-3
	Fr 1808 Mar 22		DLC-71
	Re 1816 Apr 01	leg	5-0001
Rawlings Daniel			
	Fr 1813 Feb 21		DLC-6
	Fr 1814 Feb 09		DLC-8
	Fr 1816 Apr 26		DLC-20
	Fr 1818 Aug 22	fin	6-1258
Rawlings James S			
	Re 1806 Aug 19	leg	DLC-71
	To 1809 May 04	lnd	2-0803
	Fr 1810 Jun 10		DLC-4
Rawls Benjamin			
	Fr 1845 Mar 17		DLC-57
Raworth & Biddle			
	Fr 1812 Dec 14	fin	DLC-5
Rawson S S			
	Fr 1836 Dec 16		32-1179
	Fr 1837 Feb 23		M687-20
Ray James Brown			
	Fr 1828 Jan 30		11-1078
	To 1828 Feb 23		11-1130
	Fr 1828 Dec 27		M639-15
	Fr 1829 Jan 22		M639-13
	Fr 1831 Nov 15		M639-13
	Fr 1832 Jan 16		19-0720
Ray Joseph			
	Re 1829 Apr 18	mem	13-0070
	Fr 1833 Nov 09#		M639-19
	Fr 1836 Oct 06		M639-19
	Re 1836 Oct 07		32-0107
Raymond A L et al			
	Fr 1837 Feb 20		M687-20
Raymond Sands			
	Fr 1831 May 20		M22-28
Rayner John Jr			
	Re 1829 Sep 30	par	13-1459
	Re 1829 Sep 30*	par	T967-1
Rea John			
	Fr 1836 Jun 29#	fin	DLC-48
	Fr 1837 Feb 24#	fin	DLC-50
	Fr 1837 Feb 24#	fin	DLC-50
Read Almon Heath			
	Fr 1829 Apr 18		M639-19
Read Amasa			
	Fr 1842 Jan 12		DLC-54
Read Clement Nash			
	Fr 1813 Jan 05		DLC-5
	Fr 1813 Dec 30		DLC-8
	Fr 1814 Jan 08		DLC-8
	Fr 1814 Aug 24		DLC-11
	Fr 1814 Oct 13		DLC-13
Read George Jr et al			
	To 1831 Sep 13		18-0721
Read James Gray			
	Fr 1831 Jan 09		M639-6
	Fr 1831 Sep 18		M639-13
	Fr 1832 Aug 23		DLC-41
Read John			
	Fr 1813 Aug 28		M222-8
	Fr 1830 Nov 29		16-0898
Read Leigh			
	Fr 1837 Feb 20		M567-151
Read Sion S			
	Fr 1840 Apr 28		DLC-52
Read Thomas J			
	Fr 1843 May 26		DLC-55
	Fr 1845 Jan 18		M873-71
Read Thomas J & Co			
	Fr 1816 Dec 10	fin	DLC-30
Read Thomas J & Son			
	Fr 1839 Jan 09		DLC-51
	Re 1840 Jul 20#	leg	34-1489
Read W M			
	Fr 1829 Mar 13		12-0999
Read William T			
	Fr 1834 Nov 05		M639-19
Read Mitchell & Co			
	To 1813 Oct 13		DLC-61
	Fr 1813 Oct 18		DLC-7
	Fr 1813 Oct 18*		DLC-61
	Fr 1814 Mar 28		DLC-9
Reaves Elijah			
	Fr 1827 May 10	fin	11-0580
Reckless Joseph W			
	Re c1834	mem	37-0324
Records Susan			
	Fr 1832 Jan 14		M124-131
Rector Thompson M			
	Fr 1829 Apr 29		M639-21
Rector Whorton			
	To 1836 Aug 15		31-1294
	Fr 1836 Aug 15		M567-130
Rector William			
	Fr 1836 Aug 22		31-1346

Redfern Samuel
Fr 1834 May 08# fin DLC-44
Fr 1834 Sep 15# fin DLC-44
Redington Alfred
Fr 1837 Feb 27 M687-20
Fr 1844 Feb 19 DLC-56
Reed Charles M
Fr 1842 Aug 17 DLC-54
Reed Edward Cambridge
Fr 1832 Mar 24 19-1542
Reed Garret B
Re 1836 Oct 11 par 32-0148
Reed Ira D
Fr 1840 Jun 05 34-1393
To 1840 Jun 26 34-1449
Reed J H
Fr 1814 Aug 01 DLC-11
Reed James
Fr 1814 Dec 13 DLC-14
Reed John
Fr 1836 Dec 31 M639-11
Reed Joseph Jr
Fr 1844 Jan DLC-56
Fr 1844 May 01 36-0470
Reed Lumon
Fr 1835 Feb 21 DLC-45
Reed Philip
Fr 1829 Mar 18 M639-19
Fr 1829 May 20 M639-15
Reed Rufus S et al
Fr 1832 Dec 31 DLC-41
To 1833 Jun 13 23-0030
Reed Thomas Buck
Fr 1828 Jan 03 DLC-35
To 1828 Jan 03 mem DLC-58
Fr 1828 Jan 04 add 11-1006
To 1828 Jan 04 add 11-1008
Reed William et al
Fr 1832 Feb M639-5
Reeder Benjamin
Fr 1829 Jul 27 M639-19
Rees Ebenezer
Fr 1804 Oct 03 DLC-75
Fr 1815 Jun 07 DLC-18
Rees John
Re 1830 Oct 25 par 16-0526
Re 1830 Nov 13 par 16-0723
Rees Thaddeus B
Fr 1840 Jun 12 34-1410
Reese Frederick
Fr 1834 Jul 07 DLC-44
Reese George et al
Fr 1831 Jun 10 17-1574
Reese Jacob
Re 1807 Jul 29 leg 2-0521
Re 1809 Oct 17 leg 2-0858
Reese Samuel
Fr 1830 Feb 02 15-0092
Reeside James
To 1830 Mar 03 15-0290
Fr 1830 Apr 17# 15-0751
Fr 1831 Jul 06 18-0155
Fr 1832 Feb 29 DLC-40
To 1832 May 06 chk DLC-40
Fr 1832 Jul 23 fin DLC-41
To 1832 Jul 23 chk DLC-41
Fr 1833 Mar 30 DLC-42
To 1833 May 28 chk DLC-43
To 1833 Nov 26 23-1312
To 1834 Jan 06 chk DLC-44
Fr 1834 Sep 05 M639-10
Fr 1835 Nov 04 M639-27
Fr 1840 Dec 04 DLC-53
Reeside James et al
Fr 1830 Oct 13 add 16-0375
To 1830 Oct 13 add DLC-73
Reeves Moses G et al
Fr 1844 Jun 10 36-0600
To 1844 Jun 15 36-0620
Reid Daniel
Fr 1835 Aug 10 M639-16
Reid George C
To 1821 Jul 16 M116-6
To 1821 Jul 16* 8-0846
To 1821 Jul 16* DLC-63
Reid James
Fr 1813 Dec 30 DLC-8
Fr 1814 Jan 02 DLC-8
To 1814 Jan 03 DLC-61
Fr 1814 Jan 11 DLC-8
Fr 1814 Feb 01 DLC-8
Fr 1814 Mar 06 DLC-9
Fr 1814 Apr 03 DLC-10
Reid John
To 1812 Dec 11 DLC-71
To 1812 Dec 11* DLC-61
Fr 1812 Dec 11 DLC-61
Fr 1812 Dec 11* DLC-71
Fr 1812 Dec 30 DLC-5
Fr 1812 Dec 30* DLC-71
To 1812 Dec 30 2-1313
To 1812 Dec 30* DLC-5
Fr 1812 Dec 31 DLC-71
Fr 1813 Jan 05 DLC-71
To 1813 Jan 08 DLC-71
To 1813 Sep 25 DLC-64
To 1813 Oct 02 3-0496
Fr 1814 Jan 31 DLC-8
To 1814 Feb 08 DLC-71
Fr 1814 May 07# add DLC-10
To 1814 May 08 mem DLC-71
To 1814 May 27 3-1070
To 1814 Jun 08 DLC-10
To 1814 Jun 13 DLC-71
To 1814 Aug 09 3-1270
Fr 1814 Aug 23 DLC-11
To 1814 Aug 27 4-0158
To 1814 Sep 18 4-0227
Fr 1814 Oct 05 DLC-13
To 1814 Oct 11 DLC-71
Fr 1814 Oct 31 DLC-13
Fr 1815 Jan 13# 4-0529
To 1815 Feb 09# DLC-16
To 1815 May 12 DLC-71
Fr 1815 Jun 12 4-1077
To 1815 Jun 13 DLC-71
To 1815 Jun 22 4-1090
Re 1815 Aug 21 4-1164
To 1816 Jan 02 4-1319
To 1816 Jan 02 DLC-69
To 1816 Jan 15 4-1360
To 1816 Jan 23 DLC-71
Reid John Jr
To 1839 Sep 21 34-0953
Reid Nathan
To 1816 Feb 08 4-1386
To 1816 Jun 23 DLC-71
Fr 1829 Apr 13 12-1334
To 1830 Nov 16 16-0740

Reid Nathan Jr		
Fr 1821 Apr 09		DLC-30
Fr 1829 Jan 28		M639-25
Fr 1842 Aug 01		DLC-54
Reid Samuel Chester		
Fr 1829 Mar 12		M639-19
Fr 1834 Feb 10		24-1283
Reid Sophia		
To 1816 Apr 27#		DLC-71
Reilly Philip et al		
Fr 1829 Aug 12		M639-18
Reily Philip Barr		
Fr 1845 Jan 20		36-1380
Reily Thomas B		
Fr 1829 Aug 11		M639-1
Reinder S		
Fr 1821 Jun 15	fin	DLC-70
Remsen Peter		
Fr 1830 May 20#		15-1056
Renshaw Benjamin		
Re 1834 Oct 16		26-0658
Re 1835 Mar 24		27-1381
Renshaw Isaiah et al		
Fr 1813 Nov 13		DLC-7
Fr 1813 Nov 13*		DLC-61
Reynolds Benjamin Franklin		
Fr 1830 Aug 11#		DLC-38
Fr 1835 Aug 29		28-1458
Reynolds Enoch		
To 1829 May 13		13-0314
To 1830 May 25		15-1088
To 1830 Jun 01		15-1252
Re 1830 Oct 09		16-0356
Re 1831 Jun 15		18-0029
Re 1831 Jul 26		18-0278
To 1832 Jan 12		19-0671
Re 1832 Oct 19		21-0110
To 1833 Apr 22		22-1146
Re 1833 Jun 06		22-1597
To 1833 Jul 24		23-0214
Reynolds John		
Fr 1831 Apr 15		M179-70
Fr 1831 Apr 29		M179-70
Fr 1831 Jun 04		M179-70
To 1831 Jul 16		18-0226
Fr 1831 Aug 02		M234-757
Fr 1831 Aug 02*		18-0401
Fr 1831 Aug 15		18-0542
To 1831 Aug 31		18-0627
Fr 1831 Oct 06		18-0931
Fr 1831 Nov 23		18-1482
Fr 1832 Dec 12		M221-113
Fr 1832 Dec 12*		21-1032
Fr 1832 Dec 17		M234-132
Fr 1832 Dec 17*		21-1081
Fr 1832 Dec 27		M221-113
Fr 1832 Dec 27*		21-1178
Fr 1833 Jan 07		21-1361
Fr 1833 May 14		22-1361
Fr 1834 Dec 02		M639-10
Fr 1835 Oct 17		29-0312
Fr 1836 Mar 31		30-0959
Fr 1836 May		M639-19
Fr 1836 Oct 01		31-1572
Fr 1844 Apr 22		36-0440
Reynolds John et al		
Fr 1825 Dec 31		11-0082
To 1826 Feb 02		11-0130
Fr 1836 May 23		31-0085
Reynolds John N		
Fr 1834 Sep 29#		M124-144
Reynolds Joseph et al		
Fr 1836 Jun 11		M687-32
Reynolds L		
Fr 1831 Jan 28#		DLC-73
Reynolds Lyman		
Fr 1845 Jan 17		DLC-57
Reynolds Michael		
To 1814 Dec 22		DLC-62
To 1814 Dec 22*		4-0445
Fr 1814 Dec 24		DLC-15
Fr 1815 Jan 26		4-0623
Fr 1815 Mar 11		DLC-17
Reynolds Sharp S		
Fr 1842 Apr 25		DLC-54
Reynolds Thomas		
Fr 1843 Jan 08		DLC-55
To 1843 Jan 31		35-1160
To 1843 Jan 31*		DLC-55
Fr 1843 Feb 06		DLC-55
Reynolds William		
To 1813 Dec 14		DLC-61
Fr 1821 Nov 13		M116-10
Fr 1821 Nov 13*		8-1343
Rhea Daniel		
Re 1830 Nov 13	par	16-0727
Rhea John		
To 1801 Apr 06	lnd	1-0860
Fr 1803 Jun 25		1-1125
Fr 1804 Jan 14		DLC-3
To 1814 Oct 10		4-0266
Fr 1815 Feb 05		4-0708
Fr 1815 Aug 23		4-1172
Fr 1817 Sep 02		DLC-23
Fr 1817 Nov 27		DLC-23
Fr 1817 Dec 24		DLC-23
Fr 1818 Jan 12		DLC-23
Fr 1818 Dec 18		DLC-26
Fr 1819 Sep 08		DLC-27
Fr 1822 Feb 10		DLC-31
Fr 1823 Mar 07		DLC-32
Fr 1823 Apr 02		DLC-32
Fr 1823 Jun 13		DLC-32
To 1831 Jan 04		17-0196
Fr 1831 Feb		DLC-39
Fr 1831 Mar 30		DLC-39
To 1831 Apr 23		DLC-73
To 1831 Jun 02		DLC-39
Fr 1831 Jun 03#		17-1507
Fr 1831 Jun 03*		DLC-39
Fr 1831 Jun 03*		DLC-73
Rhea Samuel		
Fr 1831 Apr 04		DLC-39
Rhind Charles		
Fr 1829 Jul 17		M639-20
Fr 1829 Jul 21		M639-20
Re 1829 Aug 07		13-1041
Fr 1830 Mar 18		M639-3
Fr 1830 Apr 23		M46-3
Fr 1830 May		15-0869
Fr 1830 May 10		M46-3
Fr 1830 May 10*		15-0973
Fr 1830 Jun 21		M46-3
Fr 1830 Dec 10		16-1384
Fr 1831 May 30		M46-3
Rhinelander John R et al		
Fr 1833 Feb 01		22-0232
To 1833 Feb 23		22-0459

Rhinn John et al
To 1835 Jun 29 DLC-73
Rhodes Francis B et al
Fr 1829 Aug 28 M639-17
Riano Jose Antonio de
Fr 1815 Jan 22 4-0597
Rice ______
Re 1791 Aug leg 1-0117
Rice Elisha
Fr 1795 Mar 13 DLC-1
Fr 1795 May 15 lnd 1-0298
To 1796 Oct 02 fin DLC-1
Rice Elisha et al
Fr 1796 Sep 15 lnd 1-0445
Rice J W
Fr 1829 Jul 04 M639-4
Rice Joel
To 1792 May 29 fin DLC-1
Fr 1795 Apr 05 leg 1-0253
Fr 1795 cMay 14 lnd 1-0287
Rice John
To 1800 May 12 lnd 1-0767
Fr 1804 Jun 25 fin DLC-3
Rice Martin
Fr 1835 Apr 23 fin DLC-46
Fr 1837 Feb 20 fin DLC-50
Rice R R
Fr 1842 May 18 fin DLC-54
Rice T W
Fr 1844 Jul 03 DLC-57
Rice Theodorick B
Fr 1813 Nov 17 DLC-7
Fr 1814 Sep 30 DLC-12
Rice William
Re 1831 Dec 14 par 19-0304
Re 1831 Dec 30 par 19-0459
Rich Obadiah
Re 1834 Oct 06 26-0524
Richards Benjamin W
Fr 1833 cJul 12 23-0120
Richards Benjamin W et al
Fr 1832 Jul 26 M639-10
Richards George
Fr 1829 Apr 04 12-1268
Richards Philamon
Re 1802 Jul 21 DLC-2
Richards Samuel
Fr 1829 Nov 11 M639-15
Richards Stephen
Fr 1821 Oct 27 8-1307
Fr 1821 Dec 24 M116-10
Richards William Smith
Fr 1814 Dec 05 DLC-14
Richardson Alexander
Re 1816 Jan 15 4-1363
Richardson Christopher
Fr 1831 cDec M50-16
Richardson James et al
Fr 1835 Mar M639-5
Richardson John
Fr 1831 Mar 17 DLC-73
Re 1831 Mar 21 17-0922
Richardson John Peter et al
Fr 1837 cFeb 08 M22-41
Richardson John S
Fr 1816 Jul 18 DLC-21
Richardson N S
Fr 1845 Mar 09 DLC-57
Richardson Origen D
Fr 1836 Oct 31-1546
Fr 1836 Oct* M179-82
Richardson Robert D
Fr 1829 May 05 13-0258
Fr 1829 Jun 01# DLC-37
Richardson Turner H
Fr 1835 Oct 07 29-0231
Richardson William B
Fr 1837 Mar fin 33-0946
Richardson William Merchant
Fr 1830 Aug 05 M639-7
Richmond Barton
Fr 1826 Jul fin DLC-34
Fr 1826 Jul fin DLC-34
Richmond Joseph
Re 1835 Oct 30 par 29-0381
Richmond & Flint
Fr 1819 Mar 06 fin DLC-28
Fr 1819 Aug 30# fin DLC-27
Fr 1820 Nov 18 fin DLC-29
Rickard William
Fr 1795 DLC-1
Fr c1795 Jul 11 DLC-71
Re 1812 Dec 17 DLC-61
Riddell Thomas & Sons et al
Fr 1836 Dec 06 M639-11
Riddle James
Fr 1816 Jul 18 DLC-21
To 1816 Oct 22 5-0544
Riddley John
Fr 1836 Sep 30 31-1535
Ridge John
To 1836 May 03# M234-80
Fr 1836 Jun 30 31-0669
Fr 1836 Jun 30* M234-80
Fr 1836 Aug 30 DLC-49
Ridge Major
Fr 1825 Jan 10 10-1066
Fr 1833 cJan 21-1274
Fr 1836 Jun 30 31-0669
Fr 1836 Jun 30* M234-80
Ridge Major et al
Fr 1835 Dec 01 29-0728
To 1836 Aug 26# DLC-49
Ridgely Charles
Fr 1823 Dec 30 9-0860
To 1823 Dec 31 9-0872
Ridgely George Goodwin
Re 1835 cMay mem DLC-46
Ridgely Henry Moore
Fr 1829 Nov 19 M639-10
Ridgely Nicholas Greenberry
Fr 1829 Apr 22 13-0102
Fr 1829 Nov 18 14-0488
Ridgely Richard H
Fr 1833 May 29 22-1514
Fr 1833 Aug 18 23-0378
Ridley George
Fr 1806 Jun 25 2-0280
Ridley James
Fr 1813 Dec 02 3-0631
To 1813 Dec 11 DLC-61
Ridley Moses et al
To 1838 Aug 20 34-0428
Ridley Samuel J
Fr 1814 Jan 31 DLC-8
Ridley Thomas E et al
Fr 1836 cSep 25 31-1512

Ridley Vincent
To 1813 Dec 11 DLC-61
Fr 1813 Dec 11 DLC-61
To 1813 Dec 11 DLC-61
Ridley William M L
Fr 1835 Mar 14 27-1211
Rieff Joseph
Fr c1835 fin DLC-49
Fr 1835 cJan 01 mem 27-0074
Rieff & Hume
Fr 1835 Jan 01 mem DLC-45
Fr 1835 May 01 fin DLC-48
Fr 1835 Jul 29# fin DLC-46
Fr 1835 Dec 18 fin DLC-47
Fr 1836 Mar 26 fin DLC-47
Fr 1836 May 04 fin DLC-48
Fr 1836 Jun 24 fin DLC-48
Riell Henry E
Fr 1842 Aug 04 DLC-54
Rigden Henry J
Fr 1829 Feb 23 12-0575
Fr 1830 Jun 18 M234-433
Fr 1830 Sep 27 M234-433
Rigden Henry J et al
Fr 1837 Mar 14 DLC-50
To 1837 Mar 17 33-1081
To 1837 Mar 17* DLC-50
Rigdon Thomas et al
Fr 1831 Jan 17-0111
To 1831 Feb 09 17-0482
Rigel Jacob
Fr 1836 Oct 07 32-0108
Rigny Henri Gauthier Comte de
To 1835 Jan 29# 27-0317
Rigsby James
Re 1834 Oct 30 par 26-0785
Riker Ephraim
Fr 1843 Feb 24 DLC-55
Riker Richard
Fr 1819 Mar 09 DLC-26
Fr 1829 Mar 25 12-1122
Fr 1829 Jul 01 M639-20
To 1830 Feb 25 DLC-72
Fr 1831 Sep 08 M639-18
Fr 1833 Dec 30 M639-18
Fr 1836 Feb 12 DLC-47
Riley Bennet
To 1835 May 25 28-0500
Riley John
Fr c1837 Dec 28 34-0151
Riley & Van Amringe
Fr 1836 Oct 08 M179-82
Rine John
Re 1832 Dec 22 par 21-1125
Ringgold James G et al
Fr 1829 Jun 05 M639-7
Ringgold Tench
Fr 1814 Dec 04 DLC-14
Fr 1814 Dec 04* M6-7
To 1829 Oct 15 DLC-37
Ringgold Thomas Lee
Fr 1832 Jun 22# M688-79
Ringland Thomas
Fr 1834 Oct M639-1
Ringland Thomas et al
Fr 1829 Mar M639-7
Fr 1830 cDec 16-0915
Fr 1832 Dec 20 M639-27
Ringold Thomas G
Re 1835 cApr mem 27-1410
Rip Raps VA
Re c1829 mem 37-0283
Ripeto William
To 1801 Aug 25 lnd 1-0908
Ripley Eleazar Wheelock
Fr 1816 Jun 29 DLC-21
Fr 1816 Dec 09 DLC-22
Fr 1816 Dec 21 DLC-22
Fr 1817 Feb 28 DLC-22
Fr 1817 Mar 31 DLC-22
Fr 1817 Nov 09 DLC-23
Fr 1817 Nov 13 DLC-23
To 1817 Dec 02 DLC-23
Fr 1817 Dec 22 DLC-23
Fr 1817 Dec 30 DLC-23
Fr 1818 Jun 11 DLC-25
Fr 1818 Aug 15 DLC-25
Fr 1818 Oct 22 DLC-25
Fr 1818 Oct 31 M221-81
Fr 1818 Nov 01 DLC-26
To 1818 Nov 15 M221-81
To 1818 Nov 27 M221-81
Fr 1818 Nov 30 DLC-26
Fr 1818 Dec 19 DLC-26
Fr 1819 Apr 08 DLC-26
Fr 1819 Apr 19 DLC-26
Fr 1819 Jul 10 DLC-27
Fr 1819 Jul 10* M221-86
Fr 1819 Jul 12 M221-86
Fr 1819 Jul 12* M221-87
Fr 1819 Jul 12* 7-0570
To 1819 Jul 24 DLC-63
To 1819 Jul 24* M221-86
To 1819 Jul 31 M221-86
To 1819 Jul 31* DLC-63
To 1819 Aug 04 DLC-63
To 1819 Aug 17# DLC-63
Fr 1819 Aug 19 DLC-27
Fr 1819 Aug 20# 7-0622
To 1819 Aug 24 M271-2
To 1819 Aug 24* DLC-63
To 1819 Sep DLC-63
Fr 1819 Sep 01 DLC-27
Fr 1819 Sep 01* M221-86
Fr 1819 Sep 11 DLC-27
Fr 1819 Sep 11* M221-86
Fr 1819 Sep 24 DLC-27
Fr 1828 Jan 04 DLC-35
To 1828 Jan 04 11-1010
Fr 1828 May 01 DLC-35
Fr 1833 Dec 24 M639-4
Fr 1834 Nov 11 M639-10
Fr 1835 Oct 20# 29-0327
Fr 1836 Apr 21 30-1297
Fr 1837 cJan 19 M22-41
Ripley Eleazar Wheelock et al
Fr 1837 cFeb 28 M22-41
Ripley James Wheelock
Fr 1829 Mar 09 12-0914
Fr 1829 Mar 12 M639-15
Ripley S W
Fr 1844 Aug 08 DLC-57
Risque James B
Fr 1808 Oct 09 DLC-4
Fr 1809 Nov 08 DLC-75
Ritchie J & C
Fr 1838 Apr 19# fin DLC-51
Ritchie Thomas
Fr 1835 Nov 28# DLC-47

Ritchie William F		
To 1840 Jan 02	add	34-1128
Fr 1840 Jan 02	add	34-1131
Riter George W		
Fr 1834 Oct 07		M639-20
Ritscher Adam et al		
Fr 1834 Jul 31		DLC-44
Ritter A & J B		
Fr 1837 Feb 18	fin	DLC-50
Ritter David		
To 1829 May 07		13-0264
Rivers Myra		
Fr 1842 Jun 14		DLC-54
Rivery Peter		
Fr 1814 Aug 20		DLC-11
Fr 1814 Oct 05		DLC-13
Fr 1814 Oct 22		DLC-13
Fr 1814 Nov 14		DLC-14
Fr 1815 Feb 21		DLC-17
Rives John Cook		
Fr 1842 Apr 04#		DLC-54
Re 1842 Apr 04	mem	35-0675
Fr 1842 May 21		DLC-54
To 1842 Jun 27		35-0817
To 1843 Feb 06		35-1164
To 1843 Apr 04		35-1298
Fr 1843 Apr 19		DLC-55
Fr 1843 Jul 27		DLC-55
Fr 1843 Sep 11		DLC-55
To 1843 Sep 22		35-1506
Fr 1844 Oct 28		DLC-57
Fr 1845 Mar 12		36-1569
Rives Judith Page (Walker)		
To 1829 Jun 26		13-0717
To 1829 Jun 28		13-0737
Rives William Cabell		
Fr 1829 Feb 28		12-0606
Fr 1829 Mar 04		M639-24
Re 1829 Apr 18		13-0071
Fr 1829 Apr 25		M639-15
To 1829 Jun 23		13-0705
Fr 1829 Aug 12		13-1108
To 1830 Jun 09		15-1335
Fr 1830 Dec 29		17-0037
Fr 1831 Jan 19		17-0300
Fr 1831 Jan 19		17-0301
Fr 1831 Jun 29		18-0134
Fr 1831 Sep 28		18-0883
Fr 1831 Oct 05		18-0928
Fr 1831 Oct 05*		M22-28
To 1831 Oct 07		18-0938
To 1831 Oct 14		18-0998
To 1831 Dec 06		19-0210
Fr 1832 Mar 09		M639-9
Fr 1832 Mar 09*		19-1371
To 1832 Apr 23		20-0366
Fr 1832 Nov 18		21-0415
Fr 1833 Mar 05		22-0669
Fr 1833 Apr 25		M688-89
Fr 1833 Oct 04		M124-140
Fr 1833 Dec 09		M639-17
Fr 1834 Jan 13		M639-21
Fr 1834 Feb 18		24-1423
To 1834 Feb 22		24-1451
To 1834 Feb 22*		DLC-44
Fr 1834 Feb 23		DLC-44
Fr 1834 Mar 26		M688-89
Fr 1834 May 17		25-1075
Fr 1834 Dec 29		M639-17
Fr 1835 Jan 14		DLC-45
Fr 1835 Feb 10		27-0472
Fr 1835 May 13		DLC-46
Fr 1835 May 14		28-0429
To 1835 Jun 03		28-0568
Fr 1836 Jan 04		DLC-47
To 1836 Mar 18#		30-0807
Fr 1836 Oct 05		32-0075
Rives William Cabell et al		
Fr 1829 Mar 05		M639-16
Rix James M		
Fr 1837 Jun 23		DLC-50
Roach Jesse		
Fr 1805 Dec 03		DLC-3
Roads John		
Fr 1832 Mar 10		M22-29
Roane Archibald		
To 1801 Aug 27	lnd	1-0911
Fr 1802		1-0950
To 1802 Feb 08		1-0952
Fr 1803 Jul 10		DLC-2
Fr 1803 Jul 15		1-1133
Fr 1803 Jul 22		DLC-2
Fr 1806 Apr 21		DLC-4
Re 1807 Apr 15	leg	2-0489
Fr 1810 Dec 25		2-0983
Roane John		
Fr 1828 Aug 08		12-0127
Fr 1828 Sep 14		DLC-35
Fr 1830 May 26		M639-24
Roane John Jones		
Fr 1832 Dec 08		M688-73
Roane Samuel C		
Fr 1832 Oct 05		21-0070
Robards Lewis		
Re 1785 Mar 01#	leg	1-0023
Fr 1790 Mar 04#		1-0075g
Re 1790 Dec 20	leg	1-0079
Robarts J W L et al		
Fr 1830 Dec 25		16-1584
Robb David R		
Fr 1837 May 10		DLC-50
Robb James		
Fr 1823 Apr 15		DLC-32
Robb John		
Fr 1827 Aug 28		DLC-34
Fr 1829 Mar 10		M639-20
Fr 1830 Nov 02		M22-27
Fr 1830 Dec 22		DLC-38
To 1831 Oct 11		M222-30
To 1831 Oct 21		M222-30
To 1831 Nov 24		M222-30
To 1831 Nov 24*		DLC-40
Fr 1831 Nov 25		DLC-40
Fr 1831 Nov 25*		M222-30
Re 1832 Jun 08		M221-112
Re 1832 Jun 08*		20-0727
Fr 1832 Jun 12		M222-31
Re 1832 Jul 16		M221-112
Re 1832 Jul 16*		20-1108
To 1832 Jul 17#		M688-83
Fr 1832 Jul 25		DLC-41
Fr 1832 Aug 03		DLC-41
Fr 1832 Aug 07		DLC-41
Fr 1832 Aug 08		DLC-41
Fr 1832 Aug 08*		M127-2
To 1832 Aug 13#		M567-66
To 1832 Aug 17		M234-603
To 1832 Aug 17*		20-1322

To 1832 Aug 18 M22-32
Fr 1832 Aug 30 DLC-41
Re 1832 Nov 12 21-0393
Re 1833 May 06 22-1309
Fr 1833 May 28 22-1473
Re 1833 Jun 06 22-1599
Fr 1833 Jul 20 23-0166
Re 1833 Sep 28 23-0896
Fr 1835 Oct 04 29-0188
Fr 1842 Mar 31 DLC-54
Fr 1843 Apr 29 DLC-55

Robb Joshua
Fr 1831 Jul 04 DLC-39

Robbins Asher
Fr 1831 Feb 13 17-0509
Fr 1831 Sep 28 M639-11

Robbins Asher et al
Fr 1831 Feb 13 17-0511
Fr 1831 Mar 28 M124-127

Robert William
Fr 1836 Sep M22-40

Roberts A M
Fr 1837 Feb 04 M687-20

Roberts Charles B
Fr 1837 Feb 20 33-0783

Roberts Edmund
Re 1832 Jan 31 19-0917
Fr 1834 Jul 03# M37-10

Roberts Edward
To 1804# 1-1267
To 1806 DLC-1
Fr 1806 Apr 04# fin 2-0205
To 1806 Sep 10# 2-0336
To 1806 Oct 21# 2-0366
To 1806 Dec 12 DLC-4
To 1806 Dec 25# 2-0412

Roberts Isaac
Fr 1804 Jul 15 DLC-3
To 1806 Jan 01 DLC-3
To 1806 Jan 02 DLC-3
Fr 1806 Jan 03 DLC-3
Fr 1807 May 11 DLC-4
Fr 1812 Jul 04 DLC-5
To 1812 Aug 10 2-1227
Fr 1812 Sep 13 2-1245
Fr 1813 Oct 16 3-0531
To 1813 Dec 28 DLC-61
To 1813 Dec 28* 3-0727
Fr 1813 Dec 28 DLC-61
Fr 1813 Dec 28* 3-0729
To 1813 Dec 29 DLC-61
Fr 1813 Dec 30 DLC-61
To 1813 Dec 31 3-0770
To 1813 Dec 31* DLC-61
Re 1814 Jan 03 DLC-61
To 1814 Jan 06 DLC-61
Fr 1814 Jan 30 DLC-8
Fr 1814 Jan 30* 3-0828
To 1814 Jan 31 3-0841
To 1814 Jan 31* DLC-62
To 1814 Feb 04 DLC-62
To 1814 Feb 17 DLC-62
Re 1814 Feb 19 DLC-62
To 1814 Feb 19 DLC-62
Re 1814 Feb 22 DLC-62
To 1814 Mar 05 DLC-9

Roberts Isaac H
Fr 1837 Nov 22 34-0036

Roberts J H
Fr 1838 Apr 24 DLC-51

Roberts John M
Fr 1836 Jan 05 M639-5

Roberts Lewis P
Fr 1838 May 29 34-0352
To 1838 Jun 04 34-0362

Roberts William Y et al
Fr 1836 Jan M639-5

Robertson David
Fr 1815 Aug 30 DLC-19

Robertson Felix
Fr 1805 Mar 25 DLC-3
Fr 1813 Aug 05 DLC-6
Fr 1814 May 14 fin 3-1027
Fr 1829 Apr 06 M639-3
Fr 1829 Apr 06 M639-10
To 1832 Aug 21 20-1373
Fr 1839 Mar 21 DLC-52
Fr 1840 Jul fin DLC-54

Robertson Felix et al
Fr 1838 Oct 24 34-0504
To 1838 Nov 03 34-0506

Robertson James
To 1798 Jan 11 1-0580
To 1799 May 02 fin 1-0712
Fr 1803 Sep 07 DLC-3
Fr 1806 Feb 01 DLC-71
Re 1807 Mar 20 mem DLC-4
Fr 1813 Mar 15 DLC-6
Fr 1813 Aug 13 DLC-6
Fr 1813 Sep 16 DLC-6

Robertson James et al
Fr 1793 Apr 13 lnd 1-0158
Fr 1807 cJan 07 2-0435
To 1807 cJan 07 2-0436

Robertson James (DC)
Re 1829 Jul 16 par 13-0853

Robertson James H et al
Fr 1833 Aug 15 DLC-43
To 1833 Aug 17 DLC-43

Robertson John
To 1807 Feb 09 fin DLC-4

Robertson John & Son et al
Fr 1835 Jun 10 M639-11

Robertson John T
Re 1814 Feb 12 DLC-61

Robertson William
Re 1831 Jun 07 par 17-1558

Robertson William H
Fr 1814 Jul 28 DLC-11
Fr 1814 Jul 28* M221-63

Robertson William R
Fr 1840 Nov 01# fin DLC-53

Robertson Wyndham Jr
Fr 1844 Jun 19 36-0628

Robertson & Elliot
Fr 1827 Jan 23 fin 11-0478

Robeson William L
Fr 1815 Feb 25 DLC-17
Fr 1815 Mar 02 DLC-17

Robinson Alexander et al
Fr 1832 Mar 14 19-1467

Robinson David Jr et al
Fr 1835 Oct 27 M639-22

Robinson E W
Fr 1836 Sep M22-41

Robinson Edward
Re 1830 Jun 17 par 15-1496

Robinson Edwin W
Fr 1834 Mar 07 24-1601

Robinson G
Fr 1831 Oct 17 M124-130
Robinson James
Fr 1814 Jul 07 DLC-11
Re 1834 May 30 par 25-1176
Robinson James et al
Fr 1835 Jan 31 M234-583
Robinson James W
Fr 1832 Sep 14 20-1527
Robinson Jeremy
Fr 1833 Dec 12 24-0462
Re 1834 Feb 08 24-1260
Robinson John
Fr 1837 Jan 27 33-0188
Robinson John McCracken
Fr 1831 Jun 13 M639-16
Fr 1834 Dec 02 M639-10
Robinson John McCracken et al
Fr 1834 Mar 10 25-0030
Fr 1836 Jan 04 M639-13
Robinson Jonathan et al
Fr 1829 Feb 24 M639-4
Robinson Peter
Fr 1829 Jul 15 M639-10
Robinson Solon
Fr 1836 Jul M22-40
Robinson William
Fr 1824 Jan 08 9-0907
To 1824 Jan 08 9-0908
To 1828 Feb 03 11-1091
Fr 1829 Mar 12 M639-20
Fr 1829 May 11 DLC-37
Fr 1830 Jan 24 15-0011
To 1830 Jun 12 chk DLC-38
Fr 1830 Aug 09 DLC-38
Fr 1835 May 06 M22-36
Fr 1835 Jun 18 28-0743
Rodgers Ann Maria (Perry)
Fr 1833 Dec 27 M124-140
Rodgers John
Fr 1833 Mar 11 22-0741
Fr 1833 Dec 31 M124-140
Fr 1837 Jan 19 33-0045
Rodman Benjamin
Fr 1833 Apr 16 M639-6
Rodman Gilbert Jr
Fr 1829 Oct 02 M639-14
Rodman Samuel et al
Fr 1829 Dec 20 14-1081
Rodman William M
Fr 1842 Jan 04 DLC-54
Rodriquez John
Fr 1815 Feb 11 DLC-16
Roenunas
Fr 1834 Apr 26 25-0900
Roenunas et al
Fr 1832 Feb 04# M234-601
Roffignac Louis Philippe Joseph
To 1821 Jan 16 8-0072
Rogers A et al
Fr 1834 Apr 10 M286-1
Rogers Benjamin Robert
Re 1829 Apr 21 DLC-72
Rogers George
Fr 1837 Feb 22 M687-20
Rogers James
Fr 1814 Oct 03 DLC-13
Fr 1819 May 17 DLC-27
To 1819 Jul 14 DLC-27
Rogers John
Fr 1820 Jun 07 M221-89
Fr 1820 Aug 07 M271-3
To 1820 Sep 02 DLC-63
Rogers John et al
Fr 1834 Apr 24 M234-79
Rogers John A
Fr 1814 Jun 04 DLC-10
Fr 1815 May 10 DLC-18
Fr 1816 Feb 01 DLC-20
Rogers Joseph et al
Fr 1832 Apr 17 M639-3
Fr 1832 Dec 05 21-0872
Fr 1835 Jun 13 DLC-46
Rogers Molten C
Fr 1829 Mar 08 M639-18
Fr 1829 Mar 16 M639-6
Rogers Samuel
Fr 1829 Mar 05 M124-117
Fr 1836 Sep M22-40
Rogers Thomas et al
Fr 1829 cMar 07 12-0882
Rogers Thomas A
Fr 1814 Nov 17 DLC-14
Rogers Thomas S
Fr 1816 Mar 31 DLC-20
Rogers William
Fr 1836 Aug 30 DLC-49
Rogers William T et al
Fr 1836 Mar M639-8
Role O B
Fr 1827 Jun 20 DLC-34
Rolland James S
Fr 1831 May 26 fin DLC-39
Ronaldson James
To 1827 Dec 18 DLC-75
Fr 1828 Dec 07 M639-7
To 1829 Jan 04 12-0442
Fr 1829 Feb 26 12-0601
Fr 1829 Mar 09 M639-7
Fr 1829 Mar 18 M639-7
Fr 1829 Apr 09 M639-7
Fr 1829 Aug 03 13-1036
Fr 1829 Sep 20 M639-17
Fr 1829 Sep 20* 13-1390
Fr 1830 Jun 09 DLC-38
Fr 1831 Mar 19 M639-14
Fr 1831 Sep 30# DLC-40
Ronaldson James et al
Fr 1831 Feb 09 M639-14
Roney Thomas et al
Fr 1832 Sep M639-18
Roosevelt Clinton
Fr 1839 Jul 08 DLC-52
Roosevelt James I
Fr 1841 Oct 18 DLC-53
Root Chester
To 1821 Apr 29# DLC-30
To 1821 May 12# DLC-63
To 1821 May 12# DLC-63
To 1821 May 13# DLC-63
Fr 1821 Nov 30 DLC-31
Root Erastus
Fr 1832 Apr 27 M639-18
Root James E
Fr 1838 Nov 22 DLC-51
Root Jeriel
Fr 1831 Jul 02 M234-434
Roper James W
Fr 1829 Aug 10 13-1070

Name	Date	Note	Reference
Ropes Henry			
	Fr 1830 Oct 14		M639-20
Rorer David			
	Fr 1832 Oct 31		21-0229
Rose Alexander R			
	Re 1836 May 20		M273-33
Rose George W			
	Fr 1838 Jun 20		DLC-51
Rose Howell et al			
	Fr 1819 Nov 02		DLC-20
	To 1819 Nov 09		7-0848
Rose J B			
	Fr 1832 Nov 30		DLC-41
	To 1832 Dec		DLC-41
Rose Leland B			
	Re 1833 Nov 30	par	23-1394
Rose Neil B			
	Fr 1813 Feb 25	fin	DLC-6
	To 1813 Mar 15		DLC-61
	To 1813 Mar 15*		3-0319
	To 1813 Oct 24		DLC-61
	Fr 1813 Oct 25		DLC-7
	Fr 1813 Oct 25*		DLC-61
	Fr 1813 Oct 27		DLC-7
	Fr 1813 Oct 27*		DLC-61
	Fr 1813 Nov 16		DLC-7
	Fr 1814 Feb 04		DLC-8
	Fr 1814 Feb 16		DLC-9
	Fr 1814 Mar 28		DLC-9
	To 1814 Apr 01		3-0949
	Fr 1814 Apr 09		DLC-10
	Fr 1814 Apr 20		DLC-10
	Fr 1814 Apr 25		DLC-10
	Fr 1815 Feb 07		DLC-16
	To 1815 Mar 15		DLC-17
	Fr 1829 May 10		M639-20
	Fr 1829 Jul 24		13-0927
	Fr 1837 Aug 17		DLC-50
Rose Samuel			
	To 1833 May 27#		M567-87
Rose Y S			
	Fr 1833 May 27#		M567-87
Rosier John			
	Re 1835 May 16		M273-31
Ross Andrew			
	Fr 1815 Jan 11		4-0522
	Fr 1817 Apr 07		DLC-22
Ross Ann J			
	Fr 1838 Feb 23		DLC-51
	To 1838 Jul 08		34-0399
	Fr 1841 Oct 16		DLC-53
Ross Daniel			
	Fr 1818 Jul 27		M221-78
Ross Ely K			
	Fr 1814 Oct 14		DLC-62
Ross George P et al			
	Fr 1829 Aug 10		M639-18
Ross George Thompson			
	Fr 1814 Aug 15		DLC-11
	Fr 1814 Oct 03		DLC-13
	Fr 1814 Dec 11		DLC-14
	Fr 1814 Dec 18		DLC-14
	Fr 1814 Dec 31		DLC-15
	Fr 1815 Jul 17		DLC-18
	Fr 1815 Jul 17*		M221-63
Ross J Marion			
	Fr 1844 Jun 29		DLC-57
Ross Jack Ferrell			
	Fr 1816 Feb 04		DLC-20
	Fr 1816 May 15		DLC-20
Ross Jesse S			
	Fr 1844 Nov 28		M873-75
Ross John			
	Fr 1820 Jun 19		DLC-29
	Fr 1829 Jun 24		13-0711
	Fr 1834 Feb 03		DLC-44
	To 1834 Feb 03		DLC-44
	Fr 1834 Mar 12		M234-76
	Fr 1834 Mar 12*		25-0138
	Fr 1834 Apr 17		M234-76
	Fr 1834 Apr 17*		25-0828
	Fr 1834 Sep 01		M234-776
	Fr 1834 Sep 01*		26-0410
	Fr 1834 Sep 15		DLC-44
	Fr 1834 Sep 15*		26-0443
	Fr 1836 Aug 26#		DLC-49
Ross John et al			
	To 1824 May 01		M234-71
	Fr 1829 Mar 06		12-0868
	Fr 1829 Apr 06		M234-73
	Fr 1829 Apr 06*		12-1283
	Fr 1834 Mar 12		M234-76
	Fr 1834 Mar 12*		25-0141
	Fr 1834 Mar 17		25-0255
	Fr 1834 Mar 28		25-0454
	Fr 1834 Mar 28*		M234-76
	Fr 1835 Jan 23		DLC-45
Ross John M			
	Fr 1833 Sep 17		23-0734
Ross John W			
	Fr 1841 May 25		DLC-53
Ross Robert et al			
	Fr 1832 Jan 29		19-0905
Rossell William			
	Fr 1831 May 26		M639-12
Rossignol-Grandmont Chevalier de			
	Fr 1832 Sep 12		M179-74
Roszel Stephen G et al			
	Fr 1830 Sep 24		M639-16
Rotch William Jr et al			
	Fr 1829 Mar		12-0691
Roth Volkert W			
	Fr 1842 Oct 31		DLC-54
Rothschild Nathan Meyer & Sons			
	Re 1835 Jun 27		28-0825
Rouget P A			
	Re 1831 Sep 14	par	18-0757
Roulston James			
	Fr 1813 Oct 18		DLC-7
Roulstone George			
	Fr 1796 May 09	fin	1-0409
	To 1801 Sep 29		1-0921
	Fr 1803 Sep 27		DLC-3
	To 1803 Oct 08		1-1199
Roumfort Augustus Louis			
	Fr 1834 Nov 10		26-0875
	To 1835 Jan 08		27-0157
Roumfort Augustus Louis et al			
	Fr 1835 Jan 01		27-0077
Rouse Casper M et al			
	Fr 1835 Jan 08		DLC-45
Rouse John R et al			
	Fr 1835 cJan		DLC-59
	Fr 1835 Jan 08		DLC-45
Roux de Rochelle Jean Baptiste Gaspar			
	Fr 1830 Sep 01		M53-8
	Fr 1830 Sep 01*		16-0206
	Fr 1831 Mar 05		M53-8

Rowan John
Fr 1826 Aug 20 DLC-34
To 1826 Sep 05 DLC-34
Fr 1829 Feb 25 M639-10
Fr 1829 Mar 11 M639-1
Fr 1829 Mar 12 M639-16
Fr 1830 May 27 15-1165
Fr 1830 Jul 05 M639-16
Fr 1832 Oct 10 DLC-41
Rowland Reuben
To 1841 May 10 DLC-53
Rowland Thomas et al
Fr 1830 Mar M639-27
Rowles William Penn
Fr 1840 Aug 22 DLC-53
To 1840 Aug 24 DLC-74
To 1840 Aug 24* 34-1576
Fr 1842 Sep 19 35-0947
Rowley N W
Fr 1845 Jan 16 DLC-57
Roy Beverley
Fr 1814 Sep 24 DLC-12
Fr 1829 Jul M639-20
Fr 1829 Aug 18 M639-20
Fr 1834 Apr 16 25-0820
Royall R R
Fr 1823 Jul 20 DLC-32
Roysdon De La F
Fr 1830 Jul 26 M222-28
Rucker Samuel Reade
Fr 1845 Jan 17 M873-75
Rucker Western T
Fr 1827 Mar 22 fin 11-0509
Rucker Western T et al
Fr 1824 Aug 27 DLC-33
To 1824 Aug 27 DLC-33
Rucker & Powell
Fr 1827 Jul 24 fin 11-0768
Rucks James
Fr 1829 Apr 08 M639-5
Ruffin James et al
Fr 1829 Nov 19 M234-135
Ruggles Benjamin
Fr 1829 May 27 DLC-37
Fr 1844 Feb 05 DLC-56
Ruggles James
Fr 1829 Aug 01 fin DLC-72
Ruggles John
Fr 1835 Mar 03 DLC-45
Fr 1836 Mar 04 30-0677
Ruggles John et al
Fr 1836 Jun 27 31-0605
Ruiz Francisco
Re 1835 Jun 07 par 28-0596
Re 1835 Jul 06 par 28-0962
Ruiz Jose Aranero
Fr 1830 Oct 19 DLC-73
Runnels Hiram G
Fr 1834 Nov 09 26-0870
Fr 1835 Jan 05 M639-20
Fr 1840 Jan 20# fin DLC-52
Fr 1840 Jan 20# fin DLC-52
Fr 1840 Jan 22# DLC-52
Fr 1840 Apr 21# DLC-52
Fr 1845 Apr 11# DLC-58
Runnels Hiram G et al
Fr 1832 Oct 23 21-0140
Ruple James
To 1829 Jan 09 12-0454
Fr 1830 Jun 24 15-1522
To 1830 Jun 24 15-1523
Fr 1837 Feb M22-41
Rush Benjamin
Fr 1836 Oct 18 DLC-49
Fr 1838 Mar 30 DLC-51
Fr 1839 Oct 16 34-1001
Rush Richard
Fr 1815 Aug 25 DLC-19
Fr 1822 May 07 DLC-31
To 1829 Feb 17 DLC-60
Fr 1836 Jan 11 DLC-47
Fr 1836 Feb 17 DLC-47
Re 1836 Jul 08 31-0969
Fr 1836 Sep 26 DLC-49
Fr 1836 Nov 23 DLC-49
Fr 1837 Jul 08 DLC-50
Fr 1837 Aug 12 DLC-50
Fr 1838 May 15 DLC-74
Fr 1839 Apr 15 DLC-52
To 1839 May 02 34-0777
Fr 1839 May 24 DLC-52
Fr 1839 Aug 21 DLC-52
Fr 1839 Oct 22 DLC-52
Fr 1839 Nov 21 DLC-52
Fr 1840 Jan 04 DLC-52
Fr 1840 Mar 01 DLC-52
Fr 1840 May 26 DLC-52
Rusk Thomas Jefferson
Fr 1831 Jun 25 M234-113
Fr 1831 Jun 25* 18-0107
Russel Samuel et al
Fr 1831 Dec 31 M639-4
Russell Abraham
Re 1830 May 04 par 15-0902
Russell Benjamin et al
To 1833 Jun 23 23-0052
Russell Charles
Fr 1835 Jun 18 DLC-46
Russell Charles et al
Fr 1829 Nov 24 14-0590
Fr 1830 Jun 04 M179-68
Russell Eliza C
Fr 1842 Jun 22 DLC-54
Russell G E et al
Fr 1836 May 30 31-0211
Russell Gilbert Christian
Fr 1804 Oct 20 DLC-3
To 1814 Apr 16 DLC-10
Re 1814 Jul 24 DLC-11
Re 1814 Jul 24* 3-1166
Fr 1814 Jul 24 M221-65
To 1814 Jul 25 DLC-62
Russell James
To 1813 Sep 27 DLC-6
To 1813 Oct 09 DLC-6
Fr 1813 Oct 09 fin DLC-61
Russell James McPherson et al
Fr 1829 cFeb M639-14
Russell John
Fr 1814 Oct 18 DLC-13
Fr 1814 Oct 31 DLC-13
Russell Jonathan
Fr 1830 Jun 02 15-1267
Russell Judson
Re 1830 May 04 par 15-0908
Re 1832 May 14 par 20-0520
Russell Thomas C et al
Fr 1835 Apr 08 M234-242

Russell Thomas S		
Re 1833 Apr 13		22-1012
Russell William (AR)		
Fr 1844 Jun 10		DLC-57
To 1844 Jul 08		36-0693
Russell William (OH)		
Fr 1829 Feb 23		M639-4
Fr 1829 Mar 03		M639-4
Russell William (TN)		
To 1813 Oct 08		DLC-6
To 1814 Jan 05		DLC-61
To 1814 Mar 05		DLC-9
Fr 1814 Apr 01		DLC-9
To 1814 Apr 01		DLC-9
Fr 1815 Jan 28		DLC-16
Fr 1818 Jun 21	fin	DLC-69
Fr 1818 Jun 21*	fin	6-1075
Fr 1830 Dec 16		M22-27
Fr 1835 Sep 16		M567-115
Russia treaty		
Re 1833 Apr 08		22-0969
Re 1833 May 11		22-1345
Rutherford William		
Fr 1829 Jun 15		DLC-37
Rutherford County TN		
Re 1808 May 18	lnd	2-0660
Re 1808 May 21	lnd	2-0665
Re 1808 May 21	lnd	2-0668
Re 1808 Jul 20	lnd	2-0695
Re 1808 Jul 20	lnd	2-0699
Re 1808 Jul 20	lnd	2-0704
Re 1808 Jul 20	lnd	2-0708
Re 1809 Mar 22	lnd	2-0789
Re 1809 Jun 17	lnd	2-0839
Re 1809 Jun 17	lnd	2-0846
Re 1816 Aug 16	lnd	5-0359
Rutherford County TN Court		
To 1831 Aug 19	leg	18-0575
Rutledge Edward A		
To 1821 May 12		DLC-63
Fr 1821 Aug 16	mem	DLC-63
Fr 1821 Aug 24	fin	DLC-70
Fr 1821 Sep 03		M116-7
Fr 1821 Sep 03*		DLC-63
Fr 1821 Sep 30		8-1244
Fr 1822 Aug 24		DLC-31
Rutledge George		
To 1803 Oct 07		1-1193
Rutledge Henry Middleton		
To 1821 May 15		8-0476
Fr 1822 May 09		DLC-31
Fr 1822 Jun 30		DLC-31
To 1823 Oct 13		9-0698
To 1824 Mar 11		10-0548
Fr 1830 Oct 14		16-0385
To 1830 Nov 07		16-0677
Fr 1843 Mar 21		DLC-55
Rutledge Henry Middleton et al		
Fr 1837 Apr 01		33-1138
To 1837 Apr 01		33-1140
Ryerson John		
To 1801 Jul 05		1-0884
Fr 1803 Oct 11		DLC-3
Ryland John F		
Fr 1830 Jan 09		14-1363
Fr 1836 Mar 21		M639-20
Ryland William		
Fr 1829 Sep 28		DLC-75
Fr 1832 May 24		M22-29
Sac and Fox treaty		
Re 1831 Feb 24		M668-4
Re 1833 Feb 13		M668-6
Re 1837 Feb 15		M668-8
Sacket Edward et al		
Fr 1833 Nov		23-1163
Sadberry Peter		
Fr 1832 Nov 13#		21-0395
Saffaran David		
Fr 1835 Dec 29	fin	DLC-47
Saffold Addison J		
Fr 1838 Jun 01		DLC-51
Saffold Reuben		
Fr 1835 Oct 06		M639-4
Sage E et al		
Fr 1831 Nov 07		M179-71
Sage William L		
Fr 1836 May 07		30-1563
St Clair Arthur		
Fr 1831 Aug 29		M639-13
Fr 1833 Oct 30		23-1137
Fr 1835 Jul 01#		28-0873
St Clair Arthur et al		
Fr 1829 Jan		12-0419
St Francisville railroad commissioners		
Fr 1831 Jun 09		M22-28
St Geme Henri de		
To 1815 Mar 16		DLC-17
Re 1816 Apr 15		5-0037
St Germain Pierre de		
Fr 1815 Feb 11		DLC-16
St John Ellen Francis (Gaines)		
Fr 1844 Feb 19		DLC-56
St John Thomas		
Fr 1840 Jan #	fin	DLC-52
St John's Church (DC)		
Fr 1833 Dec 31	fin	DLC-44
To 1834 Mar 18	chk	DLC-44
Fr 1834 Mar 31	fin	DLC-44
Fr 1834 Sep 30	fin	DLC-44
To 1834 Oct 13	chk	DLC-44
Salem NJ Hickory Club		
Fr 1832 Nov 23		DLC-41
Salisbury Stephen Jr		
Fr 1841 Apr 10		DLC-53
Salle Dominique		
Fr 1816 Dec 21		DLC-22
Salomon E		
Fr 1821 Aug 01		DLC-30
To 1821 Aug 23		DLC-63
Fr 1821 Sep 03		DLC-70
Salsbury Elias et al		
Fr 1835 Jan 08		DLC-45
Saltonstall Leverett		
Fr 1829 Apr 06		M639-1
Saltonstall Nathaniel		
Fr 1829 Apr 06		M639-1
Saltonstall Rosewell		
Fr 1829 May 25		DLC-37
Fr 1829 Jun 01		DLC-37
Fr 1833 Sep 20		23-0802
Sample Jared J		
Fr 1829 Mar 09		M639-21
Fr 1829 Mar 25#		M639-21
Sample William		
To 1805 Aug 05	fin	2-0076
Sanborn J E		
Fr 1844 Aug 20		36-0804

Sanchez Joseph Simeon
Fr 1831 Oct 12 M639-21
Sanders Alexander
Fr 1832 Mar 16 M234-78
Fr 1832 Mar 16* 19-1494
Sanders Edward
Re 1805 Jun 22 2-0067
Sanders Francis
To 1806 Nov 10 lnd 2-0383
Sanders James
Fr 1802 Jun 27 DLC-2
Fr 1806 Mar 09 DLC-4
To 1807 cJan 13 2-0452
Fr 1807 Jan 13 DLC-71
Fr 1809 Mar 26 2-0799
Fr 1817 Dec 30 DLC-23
To 1819 DLC-59
Sanders Lewis
Fr 1832 Jun 25 20-0817
Sanders Lewis Jr
Fr 1835 Aug 01 M639-24
Fr 1835 Nov 28 M639-24
Fr 1836 Jan 25 M567-130
Fr 1837 Jan 18 33-0019
Sanders Lewis Jr et al
Fr 1829 Feb 25 M639-2
Sanders Mary (Smith)
see also Donelson M S
To 1817 Feb 28 5-0747
Sanders & Sewell
To 1816 Feb 24 chk DLC-20
Sanderson G
Fr 1832 Apr M22-29
Sanderson Henry S
Fr 1829 Nov 03 M639-2
Sanderson Joseph M
Fr 1838 Apr 19 DLC-51
Sanderson Joseph M et al
Fr 1829 Nov 17 M639-17
Sanderson & White
Fr 1806 Jan 09 DLC-3
Sandiford Vincent
Fr 1832 Feb 06 M22-29
Sands Abraham L
Fr 1814 Sep 04 DLC-12
Fr 1815 Aug 12 DLC-19
Fr 1819 Dec 26 DLC-28
Sankanosh
Fr 1831 Oct 03 M234-775
Fr 1831 Oct 03* 18-0916
Sankanosh et al
Fr 1836 Nov 23 M234-362
Sanse Richard
Fr 1832 Apr 14 M22-29
Santa Anna Antonio Lopez de
Fr 1832 Nov 04# DLC-41
To 1833 Apr 24 22-1163
To 1834 Feb 08 24-1258
Fr 1836 Jul 04 31-0804
Fr 1836 Jul 04* DLC-48
Fr 1836 Jul 04* M179-82
To 1836 Sep 04 DLC-49
To 1836 Sep 04* M179-82
To 1836 Sep 04* 31-1414
Fr 1840 Oct 31 DLC-53
To 1843 Feb 27 DLC-55
Fr 1843 Apr 19 35-1318
To 1844 Mar 01 DLC-56
To 1844 Mar 01* 36-0358
Fr 1844 Apr 17 DLC-56
Santa Cruna A G de
Fr 1837 Jan 24 DLC-49
Santander Francisco de Paula
Fr 1829 May 19 DLC-37
To 1833 Mar 30 22-0918
Santee Augustus
Fr 1819 DLC-59
Sappington Mark Brown
Fr 1836 Jan 25 DLC-47
Sappington Thomas
Fr 1814 Nov 18 DLC-14
Sargent John Hersey
Fr 1832 Nov 26 DLC-41
Fr 1832 Dec 01 DLC-41
Fr 1832 Dec 02 21-0660
Sargent Temple
Fr 1844 Dec 07 M873-6
Sargent Winthrop
Fr 1815 Apr 10 DLC-18
Sartori John Baptist
Fr 1829 Dec 05 M639-21
Sathliegy
Re 1834 Oct 25 26-0737
Satorios Catalina
Fr 1822 Apr 12 fin DLC-31
Fr 1822 Apr 16 DLC-31
Fr 1822 cApr 16 9-0117
To 1822 May 16 DLC-31
To 1822 May 22 DLC-31
Fr 1822 Jun 07 DLC-31
Fr 1822 Jun 25 fin DLC-31
Fr 1822 Jul 08 DLC-31
Saul Joseph
To 1815 Feb 16 4-0756
Fr 1815 May 12 M221-63
Fr 1815 May 12 M221-63
To 1818 Aug 07 6-1200
Fr 1818 Aug 28 DLC-25
To 1818 Sep 21 DLC-63
Fr 1829 Jan 29 M639-21
Fr 1829 Mar 31 DLC-72
Fr 1829 May 16 M639-21
Fr 1830 Jul 13 DLC-38
Re 1831 Mar 02 17-0740
Saul William McFarland
Fr 1829 Jun 12 DLC-37
Saulneir John
Fr 1829 May 14 M639-21
Saunders Cyrus
Fr 1814 Nov 30 DLC-14
Saunders David et al
Fr 1836 Apr 04 M687-28
Saunders David M
Fr 1832 Dec 12 DLC-41
To 1832 Dec 30 DLC-41
Fr 1833 Jan 15 DLC-42
Fr 1833 Nov 28 M639-13
Saunders Francis
Fr 1820 Sep 04 M688-22
To 1823 Jan 31 9-0439
To 1823 Dec 23 fin 9-0846
To 1824 Feb 24 fin 10-0480
To 1824 Apr 27 fin 10-0692
Fr 1824 Jul 13 fin DLC-33
Saunders Harrison
Fr 1821 Apr 05# fin DLC-30
Saunders Henry
Fr 1829 Sep 10 M222-26
Fr 1829 Sep 10* M222-31
Fr 1829 Sep 10* M567-55

Saunders J B
Fr 1835 Jan 14 M124-151
Saunders Lafayette
Fr 1823 Jul 23 DLC-32
Fr 1828 Jul 18 DLC-35
Fr 1829 Jan 30 M639-21
Saunders R G
Fr 1843 Sep 07 DLC-55
Saunders Romulus Mitchell
Re 1833 May 01 22-1261
Fr 1836 Apr 10 DLC-48
Saunders Samuel Hyde
Fr 1830 May 08 15-0964
Saunders William
Fr 1822 May 22 fin 9-0173
Fr 1822 Jul 23 M688-26
Fr 1825 Nov 10 M688-38
Saunders & Chandler
Fr 1817 Nov 22 fin DLC-69
Fr 1818 May 27# fin DLC-26
Fr 1819 Jan 15# fin DLC-26
Fr 1819 Jan 15# fin DLC-28
Fr 1819 Jan 30 fin 7-0218
Saunderson James
Re 1813 Oct 30 DLC-61
Savage John et al
Fr 1832 Feb 22 M687-12
Savary Charles
Fr 1840 Jan 12 34-1168
Savary Charles Mrs
Fr 1841 Apr 09 DLC-53
Savell Jeremiah et al
Fr 1832 Jan 19-0561
Savoury Phineas et al
Fr 1824 Jun 24 DLC-32
Sawyer J Jay
Fr 1844 May 10 DLC-56
Sawyer Lemuel
Fr 1829 Feb 28 M639-21
Fr 1835 Jan 08 M639-21
Sawyer Thomas Jr
Fr 1837 Feb 09 M687-20
Sawyers William
Re 1806 Jan 30 leg 2-0129
Sayers Foster
Re 1806 Nov 01 leg 2-0377
Sayle W P
To 1834 Jan 30# DLC-44
Fr 1837 Jan 23# fin DLC-51
Sayre Daniel
Fr 1805 Nov 30 DLC-3
Fr 1810 Oct 24 DLC-5
Sayyid Said Sultan of Muscat
To 1832 Jan 31 19-0919
Fr 1832 Feb 10 M179-72
Fr 1833 Oct 07 M37-10
To 1835 Mar 20 M77-152
To 1835 Apr 17 M77-152
To 1836 Apr 05 30-1016
To 1836 Apr 05 30-1017
Scales ______
Re 1791 Aug leg 1-0117
Scallan James
Fr 1820 Feb 27 DLC-70
Fr 1820 Mar 19 M221-86
Fr 1820 Mar 22 DLC-28
Fr 1820 Jul 07 M221-89
Fr 1820 Jul 08 M221-89
Fr 1820 Oct 02 DLC-29
Fr 1820 Dec 18 DLC-29
Fr 1821 Aug 18# 8-1069
Fr 1822 Aug 10 DLC-31
Fr 1822 Aug 19 DLC-31
Scammon John Fairfield
Fr 1837 Jan 20 M687-16
Schaumburgh Bartholomew
To 1813 Jan 05 2-1332
To 1821 Aug 03 8-1016
Schaumburgh James Wilkinson
Re 1832 Oct 20 M273-28
Fr 1836 Sep 25 31-1514
To 1843 Jan 12 35-1110
Fr 1843 Mar 23 DLC-55
Scheerer John L
Fr 1844 Mar 23 DLC-56
Schenck Ferdinand Schureman
Fr 1836 May 24 M639-26
Schenck Ferdinand Schureman et al
Fr 1832 Dec 06 21-0889
Schermerhorn John Freeman
Fr 1813 Jun 18 DLC-6
Fr 1824 May 14 DLC-32
Fr 1827 Jul 10 11-0742
Fr 1829 Mar 24 M639-7
Fr 1831 Jun 23 DLC-39
Fr 1831 Jul 12 18-0202
Fr 1832 May 12 DLC-40
To 1832 Jun 12 DLC-73
Fr 1833 Oct 24 23-1082
Fr 1834 Mar 02# M234-921
Fr 1835 Oct 20 M567-109
To 1836 Jan 19# DLC-47
Fr 1836 Aug 29 M234-583
Fr 1836 Aug 30 M234-583
Fr 1836 Oct 29 DLC-49
Fr 1837 Oct 27 33-1548
Schielin Henry
Re 1831 Jun 02 17-1495
Schillow Frederick
Re 1829 Sep 26 13-1433
Schlatter William
Fr 1825 Jul 20 fin 10-1358
Schley William
Fr 1835 Nov 11 29-0500
Fr 1836 Feb 13 30-0375
Fr 1836 Feb 13* M234-76
Fr 1836 Jul 07 M567-131
To 1836 Aug 07 31-1257
Schmoele William
Fr 1835 Mar 09 DLC-45
Schmuck Jacob
Fr 1834 Mar 19 M567-101
Schnebly William
Fr 1830 Jun 19 fin DLC-73
Schoolcraft Henry Rowe
Fr 1833 Feb 08 22-0326
Fr 1835 Nov 18 M639-9
Fr 1836 Feb 10 M179-81
Fr 1836 Feb 10* 30-0349
Fr 1836 Feb 22 M179-81
Fr 1836 Feb 22* 30-0455
Schoolfield J
Fr 1835 Feb 03 27-0373
Fr 1835 Mar 13 DLC-45
Schott B
Fr 1842 Jun 08 DLC-54
To 1842 Jun 21 DLC-54
Schumman William
Fr 1844 Dec 08 DLC-57

Schwarz John George
Re 1829 Oct 10 14-0145
Scivally John
To 1810 Apr 03 lnd 2-0877
Scobey Joseph
Fr 1814 Dec 07 DLC-14
Scoby David
Re 1796 Apr 05 fin 1-0369
Scott Alexander
Fr 1829 Mar 01# DLC-36
Scott Alexander et al
Fr 1835 Jan 09 27-0172
Scott Charles et al
Fr 1830 Jan 15 M639-10
Scott Christopher
Re 1834 Oct 10 par 26-0579
Scott David
Fr 1819 May 20 DLC-27
Scott David et al
Fr 1830 Jan 27 M639-22
Fr 1833 Apr 14 M639-22
Scott Edward
Fr 1803 Nov 10 DLC-3
Scott Elizabeth D
Fr 1838 Feb 03 DLC-51
Scott Francis T
Fr 1834 May 19 M234-188
Scott John
Re 1835 Oct 05 par 29-0207
Fr 1838 Feb 17 DLC-51
Scott John M
Fr 1825 Mar 11 DLC-72
Scott Joseph
Fr 1829 May 04 M639-21
Scott Joseph W
Fr 1829 Mar 06 M639-21
Scott M
Fr 1831 Apr 30 M22-28
Scott Samuel
Fr 1823 Mar 04 fin DLC-32
Scott T Parkin
Fr 1841 Oct 15 DLC-53
Scott Thomas
Fr 1829 May 10 M234-77
Fr 1829 Jul 01 M639-24
Scott Thomas et al
Fr 1829 Jul 01 M639-24
Scott Victor
Fr 1815 May 11 DLC-18
Scott William Anderson
Fr 1838 Nov 18 DLC-51
To 1838 Nov 19 34-0526
Fr 1838 Nov 19 DLC-51
Fr 1839 Mar 18 DLC-52
To 1839 Jul 06 chk DLC-52
To 1839 Sep 05 34-0918
Fr 1839 Sep 13 DLC-52
Fr 1839 Nov 09 34-1049
Fr 1840 May 28 DLC-52
To 1840 Jun 09 34-1405
Fr 1840 Sep 02 DLC-53
Fr 1840 Dec 09 DLC-53
To 1840 Dec 16 35-0117
Fr 1840 Dec 28 DLC-53
Fr 1841 Apr 21 DLC-53
To 1841 May 08 35-0299
Fr 1841 Jun 21 DLC-53
Fr 1841 Jun 21 DLC-53
Fr 1841 Jul 08 DLC-53
To 1841 Sep 28 35-0414
Fr 1841 Nov 22 DLC-54
To 1841 Nov 29 35-0515
To 1841 Dec 03 35-0517
Fr 1842 Apr 16 DLC-54
To 1842 Jun 16 35-0799
Fr 1842 Jul 19 DLC-54
To 1843 Feb 02 35-1162
Fr 1843 Mar 31 DLC-55
To 1843 Apr 21 35-1333
To 1844 Feb 06 36-0159
Fr 1844 Apr 19 DLC-56
To 1844 May 06 36-0495
To 1845 Feb 03 36-1447
Scott Winfield
Fr 1817 Jul 30 5-0947
To 1817 Sep 08 5-1008
Fr 1817 Oct 04 DLC-23
Fr 1817 Oct 04* 5-1075
To 1817 Dec 03 5-1153
Fr 1818 Jan 02 DLC-23
Fr 1818 Jan 02* 5-1224
Fr 1823 Dec 11 DLC-72
Fr 1823 Dec 11* 9-0801
To 1823 Dec 11 DLC-32
To 1823 Dec 11* 9-0803
Fr 1832 Mar 02# 19-1297
Fr 1832 Aug 16# DLC-41
Fr 1832 Aug 19# DLC-41
Fr 1832 Aug 24 DLC-41
Fr 1836 Jan 16 30-0130
Scudder Charles & Co et al
Fr 1829 Mar 19 M639-8
Scull John W
Re 1831 Sep 05 par T967-1
Seabrook Whitemarsh B
Fr 1844 May 27 DLC-56
Seal William et al
Fr 1829 Jun 26 M639-10
Seale Arnold
Fr 1835 Apr 10 28-0018
Fr 1835 Apr 10* M234-242
Seale William
Fr 1818 Jun 14 fin DLC-69
Fr 1818 Jun 14* fin 6-1053
Searcy Bennett
Re 1803 Feb 28 leg 1-1090
Searcy H
To 1814 Jun 21 chk DLC-10
Searcy Isham G
Fr 1830 May 20 15-1058
Searcy Jesse
Fr 1813 Nov 12 3-0592
Searcy Robert
Re 1797 Sep 26 leg 1-0528
Re 1799 Sep 24 leg 1-0734
Re 1801 Oct 03 leg 1-0922
Re 1803 Oct 12 1-1234
Re 1805 Oct 01 leg 2-0086
Fr 1813 Oct 07 DLC-6
Fr 1813 Oct 07* DLC-61
Fr 1813 Dec 09 DLC-7
Fr 1813 Dec 27 DLC-8
To 1814 Feb 19 DLC-62
To 1814 Feb 23 DLC-62
To 1815 Sep 27 chk DLC-19
Fr 1817 Jan 06 DLC-22
Seargeantes L W
Fr 1843 May 29 DLC-55

Searle Nathaniel et al
Fr 1831 Sep 15 M639-11
Sears Alfred F
Fr 1844 Oct 16 DLC-57
Sears J H
Fr 1841 Jul 24 DLC-53
Seaver Ebenezer
Fr 1835 Apr 03 M639-16
Seawell Benjamin
Re 1807 Apr 28 leg 2-0491
Seawell Joseph
To 1806 Dec 17 fin DLC-71
Seay Samuel
Fr 1836 Aug 20 fin DLC-50
Fr 1839 Apr 10# fin DLC-52
Seay & Shepherd
Fr 1843 Dec 29 DLC-56
Secrest John
Fr 1822 Sep 30# fin DLC-31
Sedgwick Theodore
Fr 1834 Nov 01 26-0802
Fr 1843 May 27 35-1357
Sedilla Antonio de
To 1828 Jan 08 add DLC-36
To 1828 Jan 08* add 11-1017
Seelottee
Fr 1814 Nov 02 DLC-13
Seely Jonas et al
Fr 1830 Dec 04 M639-9
Seely Morris
Fr 1835 Aug M22-36
Seesahhow et al
Fr 1836 Nov 21 M234-729
Seignouret S
Fr 1821 May 16 fin DLC-30
Fr 1821 May 16* fin DLC-30
Selby Lloyd
Fr 1844 Mar 03 DLC-56
Selden Cary
Fr 1836 Feb 02 M124-149
Selden William
Fr 1844 Feb 19 36-0300
Fr 1844 Feb 19 36-0302
Sellers W H
Fr 1843 Feb 04 DLC-55
Seminole campaign controversy
Re c1830 mem 14-1229
Re 1831 DLC-41
Seminole Indians
To 1835 Feb 16 27-0521
Seminole treaty
Re 1834 Apr 12 M668-6
Re 1834 Apr 12 M668-7
Seminole War
Re 1836 Feb 03 M567-126
Re 1836 Jul 25 DLC-48
Re 1836 Oct 14 32-0175
Re 1836 Oct 14* M567-125
Senacheewane
Fr 1829 Nov 17 M234-749
Seneca Indians
Re 1829 Apr mem 12-1213
Seneca treaty
Re 1831 Mar 24 M668-6
Seneca and Shawnee treaty
Re 1832 Apr 06 M668-6
Re 1833 Mar 22 M668-7
Seney Joseph
Fr 1832 Jul 10 20-1017
Serurier Louis Barbe Charles
Fr 1831 Mar 05 M53-8
Fr 1833 Mar 05 add M53-8
Serwener John
To 1829 Nov 02 chk DLC-37
Seryczynski John N
Fr 1837 Jan 32-1466
Seton Charles et al
Fr 1834 Apr 25-0533
Sevier Ambrose Hundley
Fr 1829 Jun 10 13-0621
Fr 1829 Dec 07 14-0816
Fr 1830 Apr 03 15-0576
Fr 1831 Mar 06 M22-27
Fr 1831 Aug 23 M22-28
Fr 1832 Feb 03 M639-14
Fr 1832 Feb 06 M567-75
Fr 1833 Dec 12 M639-8
Fr 1834 May 01 M567-100
Fr 1835 May 10 28-0334
Fr 1835 May 11 DLC-46
To 1836 Feb 15# 30-0392
Fr 1836 Apr 04 M687-27
Fr 1836 Jul 14 31-1086
Fr 1836 Sep M22-41
Fr 1836 cSep M22-41
Fr 1836 Sep 29 31-1529
Sevier Charles Robertson
Fr 1813 Dec 09 DLC-7
Fr 1814 Jan 02 DLC-8
Fr 1814 Jan 03 DLC-8
Fr 1814 Jan 03* DLC-61
To 1814 Jan 03 DLC-61
To 1814 Jan 05 DLC-61
To 1814 Apr 01 DLC-9
Sevier James
Fr 1796 Jul 13# fin 1-0442
Sevier John
To 1796 Jul 05# 1-0440
Fr 1796 Dec 12 1-0461
Fr 1797 Jan 17 1-0474
Fr 1797 Jan 17* DLC-71
To 1797 Jan 18 1-0476
Fr 1797 Jan 29 1-0482
To 1797 Feb 24 1-0495
Fr 1797 Apr 05 DLC-71
To 1797 May 08 1-0503
To 1797 May 08* DLC-2
Fr 1797 May 08 DLC-2
To 1797 May 10 1-0507
To 1797 May 10* DLC-2
Fr 1797 May 11 DLC-2
To 1797 May 13 1-0510
To 1797 May 13 1-0511
Fr 1797 May 13 DLC-2
Fr 1797 Nov 19 1-0537
Fr 1797 Nov 27 1-0541
Fr 1798 Jan 08 1-0573
Fr 1798 Jan 12 1-0582
Fr 1798 Jan 22 1-0594
Fr 1798 Feb 05 1-0605
Fr 1798 Feb 07 1-0607
Fr 1798 Mar 20 1-0640
Fr 1798 Mar 28 1-0650
Fr 1798 Apr 05 1-0651
Fr 1798 Apr 05 1-0655
Fr 1798 Jun 14 1-0665
To 1798 Jun 24 1-0667
To 1798 Jul 06# 1-0670

Sevier John (cont)
Fr 1798 Aug 29 1-0675
Fr 1799 Mar 27 DLC-2
Fr 1799 May 01 1-0707
To 1802 Mar 27 DLC-2
Re 1803 Oct 1-1177
Fr 1803 Oct 01 1-1179
To 1803 Oct 02 1-1185
To 1803 Oct 02* DLC-3
To 1803 Oct 03 1-1186
Fr 1803 Oct 03 1-1188
To 1803 Oct 09 1-1200
Fr 1803 Oct 09 1-1208
Re 1803 Oct 10 add DLC-71
To 1803 Oct 10 1-1212
Fr 1803 Oct 10 1-1215
Fr 1803 Oct 10 1-1219
To 1803 Oct 11 1-1226
To 1804 Sep 15 1-1363
To 1804 Oct 15 fin DLC-3
Fr 1805 Nov 29 DLC-3
Fr 1805 Nov 29* 2-0093
To 1805 Dec 30 DLC-3
To 1806 Jan 02 DLC-3
To 1806 Jan 06 DLC-3
Fr 1807 May 15 DLC-4
To 1808 Apr 20 DLC-4
To 1808 Apr 20* M221-30
Fr 1809 Jan 12 DLC-4
Fr 1815 Jul 30 4-1137
To 1815 Aug 08 DLC-62
Sevier Sarah (Knox)
Fr 1843 May 27 35-1360
Fr 1844 Feb 03 DLC-56
Fr 1845 Feb 07 DLC-57
Fr 1845 May 27 DLC-58
Sewall Joseph
Fr 1836 Apr 15 30-1185
Sewall Rufus
Fr 1830 Sep 17 DLC-38
Sewall Rufus et al
Fr 1830 Nov 04 16-0644
Sewall Thomas
Re 1834 May 31 par 25-1197
Sewall Kendrick & Co et al
Fr 1829 cApr M639-1
Sewell James H et al
Fr 1831 Apr 09 M22-27
Sewell John & Newton
To 1817 Apr 04 fin DLC-22
Sexsmith John
Fr 1837 Feb 21# fin DLC-50
Sexton Lester
Fr 1840 Jan 12# fin DLC-52
Shabanie
Fr 1831 Jul 30 M234-749
Shackelford Thomas
To 1807 Jan 09 fin DLC-4
To 1807 Jan 10 fin DLC-4
Shackleford H L et al
Fr 1836 Apr 29 M234-189
Shackleford Richard
Re 1829 May 20 par 13-0355
Re 1829 May 20* par T967-1
Fr 1831 May 03 M22-28
Shain Benjamin Jones
Fr 1830 Mar 05 15-0297
Shakers of Alfred ME
Fr 1833 Jul 15 23-0147
Shaler Charles
To 1835 Aug 29 28-1461
Shaler Ephraim
Fr 1831 Sep 08 18-0705
Shaler William
Fr 1829 Mar 25 M639-21
Fr 1829 cApr 12-1214
Re 1829 Sep 08 13-1285
Fr 1830 Feb 10# T20-5
Fr 1830 Sep 15 16-0243
Fr 1831 Apr 26 M688-72
Re 1832 May 07 20-0487
Shannon David
To 1821 Jul 24 DLC-63
Fr 1821 Oct 29 DLC-31
Fr 1821 Nov 24 DLC-31
Shannon David et al
Fr 1821 Oct M116-8
Shannon George
Fr 1830 Jan 17 14-1448
Shannon James
Fr 1828 Nov 15 DLC-35
Fr 1829 Mar 02# M639-11
Shannon John
Fr 1796 Mar 10 lnd 1-0358
Fr 1796 Mar 10* lnd DLC-1
Shannon Lindsay
Fr 1814 Dec 18 DLC-14
Sharp Daniel
Fr 1832 Mar 08 M234-775
Sharp F C
Fr 1839 Oct 25 34-1025
Sharp J T
Fr 1840 Jan 28 DLC-52
Sharp James S
To 1838# fin DLC-51
Fr 1839 Aug 03 DLC-52
Sharp John
To 1803 Apr 17# DLC-2
Fr 1833 cMay 12 22-1349
Sharp M D L F
Fr 1828 Jun 28 DLC-35
To 1828 Jul 05 DLC-35
Sharp Richard et al
Fr 1840 Sep 12 DLC-53
Sharp Solomon P
Fr 1817 Apr 19 5-0827
Sharrock Stephen
Fr 1822 Mar 23 fin DLC-31
Sharrock William
Fr 1829 Jul 01 M688-60
Shaw Basil
Fr 1807 Nov 02 DLC-65
Fr 1814 Mar 27 DLC-9
Shaw Benjamin et al
Fr 1829 May 20 M639-24
Shaw George L
Fr 1844 May 22 DLC-56
Shaw James et al
Fr c1832 19-0522
Shaw John
Fr 1829 Mar 07 12-0884
Fr 1829 cMar 07 12-0885
Shaw Joseph
Fr 1835 Apr 04 DLC-46
Shaw Joshua
Fr 1831 Nov 01 M234-434
Shaw Robert
Fr 1843 Jul 17 DLC-55
Shaw Robert G
Fr 1836 Oct 13# 32-0172

Shaw Robert G et al
Fr 1830 Jan 22 M639-17
Fr 1836 Jan 26 M639-27
Shaw Robert G & Co
Fr 1835 Aug 14 M639-15
Shaw Samuel
Fr 1817 May 20 DLC-22
Shaw T D
Fr 1836 Jul 05# DLC-48
Shaw Z
Fr 1814 Dec 28 DLC-15
Shawnee treaty
Re 1832 Apr 06 M668-6
Shawnee and Delaware treaty
Re 1833 Feb 12 M668-7
Shearman Orrin
Re 1829 Dec 11 par 14-1016
Re 1829 Dec 12 par T967-1
Re 1830 Feb 02 par 15-0096
Sheckells John T
Re 1836 Jun 13 par 31-0449
Sheerwood John
Fr 1835 Jun 07 M124-148
Sheid James G
Fr 1825 Jan 15 10-1072
Fr 1825 Mar 01 10-1200
Fr 1825 Mar 16 fin 10-1226
Shelby ______
Re 1834 May 07 leg 25-0986
Shelby Anthony B
To 1811 Mar 2-0994
To 1816 Jun 17 lnd 5-0170
Fr 1829 Jul 13 M124-119
Re 1830 Aug 16 16-0117
To 1831 Oct 16# 18-1006
Shelby David (c1763-1822)
Fr 1797 Aug 04 DLC-2
Re 1805 Dec 16 2-0101
Re 1805 Dec 16 leg 2-0103
Fr 1806 Jul 25 DLC-4
Shelby David
Fr 1831 May 11 17-1347
To 1832 Apr 23 20-0370
Shelby Isaac
To 1814 Sep 26 DLC-62
Fr 1814 Oct 20 DLC-13
To 1814 Oct 31 DLC-62
Fr 1815 Feb 08 DLC-16
To 1815 Apr 21 DLC-18
To 1815 Jun 27 4-1094
To 1815 Jun 27* DLC-61
To 1815 Jun 27* DLC-18
Fr 1815 Aug 27 DLC-19
Fr 1818 Jun 27 DLC-25
Fr 1818 Jun 27* 6-1083
To 1818 Jul 07 6-1108
Fr 1818 Jul 22 6-1151
To 1818 Jul 31 6-1167
To 1818 Aug 11 6-1217
To 1818 Aug 25 6-1263
Fr 1818 Aug 25 6-1266
To 1818 Nov 24 6-1441
To 1818 Nov 29 7-0012
Fr 1818 Dec 08 DLC-26
Fr 1818 Dec 14 7-0059
To 1818 Dec 31 7-0100
Fr 1824 Sep 01 DLC-72
Re 1824 Nov 16 add 10-0956
Re 1829 Sep 23 mem 13-1414
Shelby James
Fr 1828 Sep 19 DLC-72
Fr 1828 Oct 06 DLC-72
Shelby John
To 1806 Jul 29 lnd 2-0307
Fr 1813 Dec 23 DLC-8
Fr 1813 Dec 29 DLC-8
Fr 1813 Dec 30 DLC-8
Fr 1814 Feb 17 DLC-9
Fr 1826 Apr 05 fin 11-0182
Shelby John et al
Fr 1815 Nov 17 4-1242
Shelby Moses
To 1794 Jan 22 fin 1-0190
To 1794 Oct 29 fin 1-0238
Shelby & McCall
Fr 1825 Sep 15 fin 10-1421
Shelby & Pugsley
Fr 1826 Jan 08 fin DLC-34
Fr 1826 Nov 04 fin 11-0388
Shelby County TN
Re 1822 Dec 05 lnd 9-0335
Sheldon Henry L
Fr 1840 Sep 15 DLC-53
Fr 1842 Mar 09 DLC-54
Fr 1842 Aug 15 DLC-54
Sheldon John P
Fr 1830 Jan 13# M639-20
Sheldon Josiah
Re 1830 Nov 16 par 16-0742
Sheldon Luther H
Fr 1838 Dec 15 DLC-51
Sheldon Sylvester W
Re 1836 Oct 16 par 32-0192
Sheldon Thomas C
Fr 1835 Nov 23 M639-9
Shelley R
Fr 1838 May 06 DLC-51
To 1838 May 21 DLC-51
Shelocta
Re 1814 Aug 10 3-1298
Shelton Jesse
Fr 1823 Feb 02 fin DLC-32
Shelton Moses
To 1833 Jan 15 fin DLC-42
Shepherd John
Fr 1833 Nov 16 23-1241
Shepherd M
Fr 1840 Jun 13 34-1413
Shepherd Sampson
Fr 1825 Aug 13 DLC-33
To 1825 Aug 14 DLC-33
Shepherd Thomas
Fr 1829 Feb 24 M639-7
Shepley Ether
Fr 1835 Feb 03 M124-146
Fr 1835 Mar 03 DLC-45
Fr 1835 Aug 07 M639-3
Shepley Ether et al
Fr 1836 Feb 27 30-0616
Fr 1836 Mar 01 M639-27
Shepley John
Fr 1836 Apr 25 30-1345
Fr 1837 Feb M687-16
Sheppard Benjamin H
Fr 1841 Dec 24 DLC-54
Shepperd Augustine Henry
Fr 1835 Jan 12# 27-0197

Sherburne Henry
Fr 1818 Jul 28 DLC-25
To 1818 Aug 18 6-1246
To 1818 Oct 02 fin DLC-25
Fr 1818 Dec 12 DLC-26
Fr 1818 Dec 30 DLC-26
Fr 1819 Apr 21 DLC-26
Sherburne John Henry
To 1829 Mar 16 12-1020
Sherburne John Henry et al
Fr 1829 Feb 05 12-0481
Sheridan E
Re 1837 Feb 25 par 33-0901
Sherman John
Fr 1837 Jan 19 M567-117
Sherman Mary M
To 1838 Nov 03 34-0507
Sherrard John
Fr 1837 Feb M22-41
Sherrill Archibald
To 1815 Sep 22 lnd 4-1189
Shields Thomas
Fr 1815 Feb 12 DLC-16
Fr 1815 Feb 15 4-0746
Fr 1815 Feb 15* M221-63
Fr 1815 Feb 27 4-0796
Fr 1815 May 31 DLC-71
Shields William B
Fr 1813 Aug 15 DLC-75
To 1814 Mar 10 DLC-61
Shillaber John
Fr 1834 Apr 20 M101-1
Shillaber Jonathan
Re 1835 May 02 28-0242
Shinn William Norton
Fr 1829 Jul 03 M873-19
Fr 1832 Oct 01 fin DLC-41
Shoemaker Lewis
Re 1831 Mar 02 17-0741
Shomo J
Fr 1821 Oct 04 fin DLC-70
Short Aaron
Fr 1818 Jun 08 fin DLC-69
Fr 1818 Jun 08* fin 6-1037
Short Thomas
Fr 1836 Jan 04 29-1460
Short Thomas (Shawnee)
Fr 1836 Jul 04 M234-422
Shorter Tarver & Co et al
Fr 1835 Nov 18 29-0523
Fr 1835 Nov 18* M234-242
Shreve Henry Miller
Fr 1829 Oct 13 M124-121
To 1832 Sep 10 20-1510
Fr 1836 Apr 29 30-1415
Fr 1836 Apr 29* M234-31
Shrout Richard et al
Fr 1835 Jan 08 DLC-45
Shumate James
To 1796 May 02 lnd 1-0381
Shunk Francis Rawn
Fr 1845 Mar 26 DLC-57
Shurlds Henry
Fr 1836 Dec 22# M179-82
Shurtleff Roswell et al
Fr 1834 Jan 17 M639-17
Shushiyu
Re 1834 Apr 16 25-0823
Shute John A
Fr 1826 Aug 06 DLC-34
Fr 1826 Aug 06 fin DLC-34
To 1838 Nov 25 DLC-51
Fr 1838 Nov 25 DLC-51
To 1839 Jan 03 DLC-51
To 1841 Dec 09 fin DLC-54
Shute Philip
To 1842 Jan 18 chk DLC-54
To 1844 Sep 05 DLC-57
Sibley John
Fr 1814 Sep 13 DLC-12
Fr 1814 Nov 09 DLC-14
Fr 1814 Nov 22 DLC-14
Sibley Jonas
Fr 1830 Feb 18 M639-21
Sieber Silvanous et al
Fr 1829 Jul 14 M639-14
Sifford W W
Fr 1840 Jul 04 DLC-53
Silas Edward
Fr 1833 Jan 03 21-1312
Silkman Charles Henry
Fr 1843 Feb 06 DLC-55
Silliman Benjamin
To 1821 Jul 14 8-0819
Silliman N et al
Fr 1836 Sep 09 M639-3
Silliman Wyllis
Fr 1835 May 18# 28-0461
Silsbee Nathaniel
Fr 1830 Nov 15 M179-69
To 1830 Dec 03# M639-11
Fr 1831 Jul 20 M124-129
Silva Francisco de Lima
To 1831 Oct 24 18-1119
Silvertooth John
To 1815 Jun 15 lnd 4-1082
Sim Thomas
To 1830 May 14# M639-3
Simmons Anthony
Fr 1829 Mar 06 M639-11
Simmons Daniel et al
Fr 1831 Dec 28 19-0435
Simms Edward et al
Fr 1836 Jul 05 DLC-48
Simms Henry
Re 1833 Apr 20 par 22-1074
Simms James
Re 1831 Apr 28 par 17-1248
Simon M et al
To 1815 Feb 18 DLC-62
Simonds Johnson
Re 1830 Apr 10 par 15-0665
Simonds Joseph C
Fr 1835 Jan 02 M688-83
Simons Richard
Re 1831 Nov 08 par 18-1222
Simons Samuel
Fr 1835 Feb 11 DLC-45
Simons William Troost
Re 1829 Sep 17 13-1348
Simonton J W
Fr 1844 Nov 07 36-1002
Simonton James
To 1829 Oct 15 14-0170
Simonton John W
Fr 1829 Dec 19# DLC-75
Fr 1830 May 07 M124-124

Simpson Charles
Fr 1813 Oct 06 DLC-6
Fr 1813 Oct 06* DLC-61
Simpson Henry
Fr 1835 Feb 10 M639-11
To 1836 Jun 29 31-0642
Simpson Henry et al
Fr 1830 Dec 08 M639-11
Fr 1836 Dec 30 DLC-49
To 1837 Jan 04 32-1490
To 1837 Jan 04* DLC-49
Simpson John
Fr 1829 cMar 12-0696
Fr 1829 Mar 28 M639-21
Fr 1829 Jun 11 DLC-37
Simpson John & Co
Fr 1823 Jul 18 fin 9-0616
Fr 1824 Feb 26 fin 10-0488
Fr 1825 Jan 01 fin 10-1023
Simpson John & Thomas
Fr 1826 Jan 04 fin 11-0097
Fr 1827 Jan 20 fin 11-0476
Fr 1828 Jan 01 fin 11-1004
Simpson John K
Fr 1834 Dec 13 26-1492
Simpson John K et al
Fr 1829 Mar 19 M639-8
Fr 1833 Mar 11 22-0743
To 1833 May 21 22-1423
Simpson Josias
Re 1831 May 06 par 17-1298
Simpson Michael T
Fr 1829 Apr 01 M639-21
Simpson Robert
Fr 1807 Apr 03 fin DLC-4
Simpson Stephen
Fr 1823 Jul 05 DLC-32
To 1823 Aug 13 9-0630
To 1824 May 20 10-0742
To 1824 Aug 18 10-0856
Fr 1825 Nov 03 DLC-33
To 1825 Nov 23 DLC-33
To 1827 Dec 27 11-0988
Fr 1828 Feb 18 DLC-35
To 1828 Apr 14 DLC-35
Fr 1829 Feb 28 DLC-36
Fr 1829 Mar 07 M639-11
Fr 1829 Mar 26 M639-11
Fr 1829 Jun 18 DLC-37
To 1829 Jun 27 DLC-37
Fr 1829 Jul 01 13-0786
Fr 1829 Dec 17 DLC-37
Fr 1830 Jan 20 DLC-37
Fr 1830 Nov 17 M639-21
Fr 1834 Oct 21 DLC-44
Simpson T
Fr 1816 Feb 06 DLC-20
To 1816 Mar 15 DLC-20
Simpson Thomas
Fr 1793 Nov 21 fin 1-0171
Fr 1839 Dec 10 DLC-52
Sims Henry
Re 1829 Mar 25 par 12-1125
Re 1829 Mar 25* par T967-1
Re 1830 Jun 17 par T967-1
Sims John G
To 1815 Dec 18 DLC-19
Sims Leonard Y
Fr 1844 Mar 26 DLC-56
Sims Thomas
To 1832 Jan 03 chk DLC-40
Simson Robert et al
Fr 1815 Feb 15 DLC-16
To 1815 Feb 16 DLC-16
To 1815 Feb 16* DLC-62
Sinclair William
Fr 1813 Dec 09 3-0652
Sing John
Fr 1829 Sep 19 13-1384
Singleton A R
Fr 1836 Sep M22-41
Singleton M R
Fr 1836 Sep M22-40
Singleton Washington G
Re 1829 mem 37-0498
Fr 1829 Apr 28 13-0171
Fr 1829 Jun 27 M639-21
Fr 1834 May 07# M179-78
Fr 1834 Nov 13 M688-92
Fr 1835 Oct 16 M639-18
Singleton & Mezick et al
Fr 1833 Apr 11 M639-20
Sioux treaty
Re 1837 Feb 15 M668-8
Re 1837 Feb 15 M668-8
Re 1837 Feb 18 M668-8
Sisk Thomas et al
Fr 1829 Sep 16 13-1337
Sisters of the Visitation
Fr 1829 Jul 28 13-0950
Sittler James W
Fr 1813 Sep 05 leg DLC-6
To 1813 Dec 08 3-0650
To 1813 Dec 08* DLC-61
Fr 1813 Dec 08 DLC-61
To 1813 Dec 09 DLC-61
To 1813 Dec 22 DLC-61
To 1813 Dec 28 3-0732
To 1814 Jan 04 DLC-66
To 1814 Jan 04* DLC-61
To 1814 Jan 09 DLC-8
To 1814 Jan 09* DLC-61
Fr 1814 Feb 16 3-0874
Fr 1814 Mar 01 DLC-9
Fr 1814 Mar 03 DLC-9
Fr 1814 Mar 10 3-0909
To 1814 Apr 24 DLC-10
Sizer Nelson
Fr 1844 Feb 12 DLC-56
Skinker Samuel W
Fr 1838 Oct 16 DLC-51
Skinner J L et al
Fr 1833 Aug 28 M639-14
Skinner John Stuart
Fr 1823 Aug 15 fin DLC-32
Fr c1829# 37-0284
Fr 1829 Jul 21 M222-26
Fr 1831 Oct 17 M639-8
To 1831 Oct 24 18-1120
To 1833 Jan 09# DLC-41
Fr 1833 Jan 17 DLC-42
To 1834 Apr 21 25-0845
To 1834 Jun 04 chk DLC-44
To 1834 Jun 13 chk DLC-44
Fr 1835 Nov 07# 29-0472
Skinner Thomas Harvey
Fr 1830 Jun 11 15-1427

Skinner Usher		
Fr 1830 Apr 16		DLC-38
Fr 1830 Apr 26		DLC-38
Skinner & Grant		
Fr 1821 May 25#	fin	DLC-30
Skipwith Fulwar		
Fr 1827 May 15		11-0587
Skipwith Gary		
Fr 1845 Jan 24		DLC-57
Slacum William A		
Fr 1836 Mar 10#		DLC-47
Slade Charles		
Fr 1829 Nov 20		14-0540
Slade William		
Fr 1838 Jan 17		DLC-51
Slamm Levi D et al		
Fr 1837 Oct 03		DLC-50
Slatter H R		
To 1840 May 14#	fin	DLC-55
Slaughter N F		
Fr 1829 Feb		M639-21
Slaughter R F		
Fr 1829 May 27		M639-10
Slaughter Thomas S		
Fr 1829 Dec 14		14-1028
Slaughter William A		
Fr 1814 Sep 23		DLC-12
Slaughter William B		
Fr 1829 May 11		M639-21
Fr 1833 Mar 19#		DLC-42
Slaves		
see also names		
of individual slaves		
Re 1804 Sep 26		1-1395
Re 1821 Feb	fin	DLC-58
Re 1825 Jan 01		DLC-33
Sleeper William		
To 1827 Aug 15		DLC-34
Sletor Thomas		
Fr 1842 Jan 08		DLC-54
Slicer Samuel		
Fr 1825 Mar	fin	10-1197
Slicer W		
Fr 1825 Mar	fin	10-1199
Slidell John		
Fr 1830 Jan 13		M639-4
Fr 1843 Jan 23		DLC-55
Fr 1843 Mar 01		DLC-55
Fr 1843 Jul 12		DLC-55
Fr 1844 Feb 13		36-0254
Fr 1844 Dec 15		DLC-57
Sloan G L & F		
Fr 1841 Aug 15	fin	DLC-54
To 1842 Jan 05	chk	DLC-54
Sloan John		
Fr 1835 Jun 08#		28-0607
Sloan Thomas		
Fr 1830 Jun 18		M234-433
Fr 1830 Sep 27		M234-433
Slocum Charles		
Fr 1816 Jan 19		DLC-20
Slocum George W		
To 1835 Dec 17#		M179-81
Slye Benjamin S		
Re 1830 Mar 12		M273-22
Small Samuel		
Fr 1837 Feb 17		M687-16
Small William et al		
Fr 1832 Dec 26		M639-16
Smedley Lemuel		
Fr 1835 Feb 18		DLC-45
Smiley _____ (Mrs)		
Fr 1837 Jan		M22-41
Smiley James		
Fr 1829 Feb 10		M639-27
Smiley Robert		
Fr 1816 Jul 22	fin	DLC-21
To 1816 Aug 19	chk	DLC-21
Fr 1817 Aug 30	fin	DLC-24
Fr 1818 Sep 17	fin	6-1310
Fr 1819 May 10	fin	7-0512
Smiley Robert estate		
Fr 1823 Jun 18	fin	DLC-32
Smiley William		
Fr 1814 Aug 26	fin	DLC-11
Smith _____		
Fr 1833 Sep 05#		23-0655
Smith (slave)		
Re 1840 Aug 02		DLC-74
Smith Abraham Russel		
Fr 1830 Mar		M639-22
Smith Albert		
Fr 1833 Nov 18		M179-77
Fr 1834		24-0703
Fr 1834 Mar 19		25-0280
Fr 1836 Apr 23		30-1332
Smith Albert et al		
Fr 1829 cMar 01		M639-15
Fr 1829 Mar 18		M639-15
Smith Alexander		
Fr 1803 Sep 12	lnd	1-1159
Fr 1803 Sep 12*	lnd	DLC-3
Smith Alexander H		
Fr 1831 Jan 21		17-0328
Smith Andrew Jackson		
Fr 1844 Jun 12		DLC-57
Fr 1845 May 23		DLC-58
Smith Asa		
Re 1834 Mar 13	par	25-0151
Smith Benjamin Fort		
Fr 1818 May 06	fin	DLC-70
Fr 1818 Jun 30		M221-78
Re 1827 Jul 18		11-0765
Fr 1828 Dec 10		DLC-36
Smith Bennett		
Fr 1810 May 01		DLC-4
To 1814 Jun 27	chk	DLC-11
Fr 1814 Dec 23		DLC-14
To 1815 Jan 31	chk	DLC-16
To 1824 Sep 22	fin	10-0897
Re 1825 Jun 01		10-1299
Smith Bernard		
Fr 1829 Jul 01#		13-0772
Fr 1832 Nov 01		21-0262
Smith Bernard et al		
Fr 1834 Oct 29		M639-27
Smith Bird		
To 1812 Aug 13		DLC-5
To 1812 Sep 08		DLC-5
Fr 1813 Dec 15		DLC-7
Smith Charles		
Fr 1831 Oct 13		18-0984
Smith Charles G		
Fr 1843 Jan 27		DLC-55
Smith Charles Henry		
Fr 1831 Aug 19		18-0576
Smith Conrad		
Fr 1829 Jul 15		M222-26

Smith Constantine		
Fr 1830 Jan 02		M222-26
Fr 1830 Jun 05#		M567-55
Smith Daniel		
To 1789 Feb 13		1-0061
To 1791 Jan 20		1-0081
To 1795 Oct 29		1-0324
To 1796 Dec 18		DLC-75
Fr 1806 Feb 19		DLC-3
Fr 1806 Apr 12		DLC-4
To 1806 Nov 12		DLC-4
To 1806 Nov 17		2-0389
To 1806 Nov 27		2-0392
Fr 1806 Dec 19		DLC-4
Fr 1806 Dec 29		DLC-4
Fr 1807 Jan 03		DLC-4
To 1807 Feb 11		2-0464
To 1807 Nov 28		DLC-4
Fr 1808 Jan 27		DLC-4
Fr 1814 Dec 28		DLC-15
Fr 1816 Apr 05		5-0024
To 1817 Mar 27		5-0794
Smith Daniel W		
Fr 1829 Jul 04		M639-22
Re 1832 Aug 29		20-1410
Fr 1833 Jan 01#		M281-1
Fr 1835 Dec 20#		M281-1
Smith David		
Fr 1812 Sep 28		2-1250
Fr 1813 Mar 13		DLC-61
Fr 1813 Sep 17		DLC-6
Fr 1813 Dec 23		DLC-8
Fr 1814 Feb 05		DLC-8
Fr 1814 Feb 26		DLC-9
To 1814 Apr 02		DLC-10
Fr 1814 Apr 04		DLC-10
Fr 1814 Apr 05		DLC-10
Fr 1835 Apr 06		M639-11
Smith David et al		
Fr 1830 May		15-0870
Smith Delazon et al		
Fr 1842 May 18		DLC-54
Smith Ebenezer		
Fr 1831 Dec 28		M22-29
Smith Edwin		
Fr 1837 Jan 18		33-0022
Smith Edwin et al		
Fr 1829 May		M639-24
Smith Ephraim Kirby		
Re 1830 Oct 01		16-0293
Smith Fleet		
Fr 1830 Jan 22		M639-22
Smith Francis		
To 1817 Mar 29		5-0799
To 1829 May 19		13-0354
Smith Francis Ormand Jonathan		
Fr 1836 Mar 01		30-0654
Fr 1837 Feb 22		M687-20
Smith George		
Fr 1813 Nov 22		DLC-7
Fr 1813 Nov 23		DLC-7
To 1813 Dec 19		DLC-61
Fr 1814 Feb 15		DLC-62
To 1814 Apr 01		DLC-9
Fr 1814 Apr 18		M221-56
Fr 1814 Nov 23		DLC-14
Smith George W		
Fr 1832 Mar 14		M688-82
Fr 1833 Jan 17		M688-82
Smith Guy		
Fr 1814 Apr 05		DLC-10
Smith H Y		
Fr 1844 Feb 14		DLC-56
Smith Hugh et al		
Fr 1831 Dec 24		M639-15
Smith J K		
Fr 1829 Oct 05		14-0110
Fr 1830 May 06		15-0925
Smith James		
Re 1832 Oct 27	par	21-0178
Smith James & Son		
Fr 1804 Oct 15		DLC-75
Fr 1805 Jun 15		DLC-3
Smith James R et al		
Fr 1831 Aug 02		DLC-39
Smith Jeremiah		
Fr 1834 Dec 26		M639-22
Smith Joel M		
Fr 1839 Jun 26		DLC-52
Fr 1839 Oct 15#	fin	DLC-52
Smith John		
To 1814 Mar 03		DLC-62
To 1814 Mar 03*		3-0895
To 1814 Aug 03		DLC-62
Fr 1814 Aug 30		DLC-11
Fr 1814 Sep 29		DLC-12
Fr 1814 Oct 13		DLC-13
To 1814 Oct 28		DLC-62
Fr 1822 Sep 09		DLC-31
Fr 1823 Jan 07	fin	DLC-31
Re 1829 Jun 30	par	DLC-37
Re 1829 Jun 30*	par	13-0748
Re 1829 Jun 30*	par	T967-1
Re 1829 Jul 18	par	13-0893
Re 1829 Jul 18*	par	T967-1
Re 1834 Jun 02	par	25-1230
Smith John Adams		
Re 1829 Jul 16		13-0858
Smith John H		
Fr 1812 Aug 10	fin	DLC-6
Fr 1812 Nov 18	fin	DLC-6
To 1812 Dec 30	fin	DLC-5
To 1813 May 19	fin	DLC-6
Fr 1813 Jun 13		DLC-6
To 1813 Jun 23	fin	DLC-6
Fr 1813 Aug 10	fin	DLC-12
To 1813 Aug 25	fin	DLC-6
To 1814 Apr 13	fin	DLC-10
To 1814 Jun 21	chk	DLC-10
Fr 1826 Dec 17	lnd	11-0430
Smith John H & Co		
Fr 1805 Apr 08		DLC-3
Fr 1805 Apr 30	fin	2-0033
Smith John L		
Fr 1836 Jun 12		M567-130
Smith John Lind		
To 1822 Sep 06		DLC-31
Smith John N		
Re 1836 Dec 10	par	32-1086
Smith John Spear		
Fr 1829 Mar 14		M639-3
Fr 1829 May 05		M639-2
Smith John Speed		
Fr 1828 Sep 16		DLC-35
To 1828 Sep 26		DLC-35
Fr 1829 Jul 14		M688-59
Smith John T		
Re 1830 Dec 17	par	16-1467
Fr 1845 May 09		DLC-58

Smith John W N A
Fr 1816 DLC-22
Smith Jonathan B
Fr c1833 37-0319
Smith Jonathan S
Fr 1831 Apr 16 M639-22
Smith Joseph
Fr 1814 Dec 30 DLC-15
Smith Joseph Dickson
Fr 1813 Sep 26 DLC-10
Fr 1821 May 14 DLC-30
Smith Joseph Lee
Fr 1829 Jul 30 13-1008
Fr 1829 Nov 18 14-0489
Fr 1831 Apr 11 17-1121
Fr 1832 Feb 13 19-1078
Smith Joseph W
Re 1835 Oct 03 par 29-0179
Smith Kenderton et al
Fr 1832 Jul 20 M639-10
Smith Lemuel
Fr 1829 Apr 11 12-1321
Smith Lucius E
Fr 1844 Jul 11 DLC-57
Smith M
Fr 1832 Oct 31 M124-135
Smith Matthew
Fr 1835 Jan 08 DLC-45
Smith Meriwether
Fr 1803 Nov 14 DLC-3
Smith Morgan L
Fr 1834 Jan 22 M639-24
Fr 1834 May 26 M639-21
Smith Morgan L et al
Fr 1834 Jan 06 M639-24
Smith Oliver Hampton
Fr 1829 Feb M639-6
Fr 1829 Feb M639-15
Smith Oliver Hampton et al
Fr 1835 Jul 30 M639-23
Smith P P
Fr 1842 Aug 08 DLC-54
Smith Persifor Frazer
Fr 1836 Aug 08 31-1266
Smith Richard (cabinetmaker)
Fr 1821 Dec 03 fin 8-1359
Smith Richard (Capt)
Re 1830 Feb 22 M273-23
Smith Richard (DC)
To 1829 Mar 19 leg 12-1063
To 1830 Mar 18 chk DLC-38
To 1832 Jul 21 20-1217
To 1832 Oct 29 chk DLC-41
To 1834 Oct 13 chk DLC-44
To 1834 Oct 31 chk DLC-44
To 1834 Nov 26 chk DLC-45
To 1835 Dec 05 chk DLC-47
Smith Richard (overseer)
To 1841 Aug 12# 35-0371
Re 1841 Aug 17 leg 35-0377
Re 1843 Sep 12# leg 35-1489
Smith Robert (PA)
Fr 1829 Mar 09 M639-22
Fr 1829 Mar 16 M639-22
Fr 1829 Jun 29 DLC-37
Fr 1829 Jun 29 DLC-37
Fr 1829 Jul 13 DLC-37
Smith Robert (TN)
Fr 1810 Nov 10 DLC-5
Fr 1810 Nov 10* M40-14
Fr 1825 May 29 DLC-33
Smith Robert R
Fr 1804 Apr 23 fin DLC-3
Smith S S et al
Fr 1829 Jun 01 M639-25
Smith Samuel (MD)
Fr 1829 Feb 21 12-0566
Fr 1829 Mar 07 12-0887
Fr 1829 May 11 M639-3
Fr 1829 Jun 15 M688-70
To 1830 Apr 28 15-0830
To 1830 Jun 14 15-1404
To 1831 Jan 08# M179-70
Fr 1831 Apr 25 17-1240
Fr 1831 Oct 27 M567-61
Fr 1832 Jan 03 19-0599
Fr 1832 Jan 28 19-0898
Fr 1832 Mar 31 20-0076
Fr 1832 Jun 17 DLC-40
Fr 1833 Feb 20 DLC-42
To 1833 Sep 21 23-0827
Fr 1833 Dec 04 24-0381
Fr 1834 Mar 11 25-0081
Smith Samuel (MD) et al
Fr 1828 Dec 04 DLC-36
Fr 1832 Apr 15 M22-29
Fr 1833 Jan 22 M639-2
Smith Samuel (NY) et al
Fr 1829 May 30 M124-118
Smith Samuel (TN)
Re 1791 Aug leg 1-0101
Smith Samuel Emerson
Fr 1831 Mar 02 17-0742
Fr 1831 Mar 26 17-0988
Fr 1831 Jun 23 18-0087
Fr 1832 May 10 20-0501
Smith Samuel Granville
Fr 1828 Dec 27# DLC-36
Fr 1835 Feb 06 DLC-45
Smith Samuel Harrison
To 1815 Aug 28 DLC-19
To 1836 Jun 06 fin 31-0360
To 1837 Feb 09 chk DLC-50
Smith Samuel Harrison et al
Re 1829 May 01 13-0237
Re 1833 Apr 30 22-1220
Smith Sarah (Michie)
Fr 1826 Dec 10 DLC-4
Smith Thomas
Fr 1789 Apr 09 fin 1-0063
To 1817 Mar 11 5-0774
Fr 1817 Mar 22 5-0789
To 1817 Apr 11 5-0809
Fr 1825 Feb 24 fin 10-1154
To 1827 Jul 25 11-0770
Smith Thomas Adams
Fr 1815 Sep 08 M222-16
Fr 1815 Oct 01 DLC-19
Fr 1815 Oct 01* 4-1202
To 1815 Oct 04 DLC-62
Fr 1815 Nov 05 4-1222
Fr 1815 Nov 12 4-1230
To 1815 Nov 25 DLC-62
To 1815 Nov 28 DLC-19
Fr 1815 Dec 01 DLC-19
Fr 1815 Dec 01* 4-1271
To 1816 Jan 23 DLC-62
To 1816 Feb 02 DLC-62

Fr 1816 Feb 04 4-1382
Fr 1816 Feb 04 4-1384
Fr 1816 Feb 11 DLC-20
Fr 1816 Feb 11* 4-1389
Fr 1816 Feb 18 M221-70
Fr 1816 Jul 08 DLC-21
Fr 1816 Jul 08* M222-19
Fr 1816 Jul 08 DLC-21
Fr 1816 Jul 13 DLC-21
Fr 1816 Oct 20 DLC-21
Fr 1817 Aug 30 5-1002
Fr 1818 Oct 10 DLC-25
Fr 1818 Oct 10* 6-1351
Fr 1818 Oct 10 6-1352

Smith Thomas Jefferson
Fr 1839 Nov 27 DLC-52

Smith Thomas L
Re 1829 May 30 13-0512
Fr 1829 Jun 04# 13-0572
Fr 1830 May 03 DLC-38
Fr 1830 Jun 11 DLC-38
To 1831 Apr 05 DLC-39
To 1831 Jun 22 18-0075
To 1831 Jun 22* DLC-39
Fr 1831 Jun 22 18-0083
Fr 1831 Nov 10 M639-25
To 1832 Mar 31# DLC-40
To 1832 Aug 13 chk DLC-41
Fr 1832 Dec 13 M639-6
Fr 1833 Mar 18 22-0798
Fr 1833 Dec 21 M639-18
Fr 1834 Jan 03 M639-18
Fr 1834 Jan 14 M639-18
Fr 1834 Feb 25# 24-1475
To 1834 Mar 08 24-1605
Fr 1834 Dec 26-1112
Fr 1834 Dec 26-1116
Fr 1835 Feb 12 M179-79
Fr 1835 Jun 11# 28-0663
Fr 1836 Oct 22# 32-0329

Smith Thomas L et al
Fr 1843 Jan 11 DLC-55

Smith Thomas P
Fr 1814 Aug 10 DLC-11

Smith Walter
Fr 1829 12-0387

Smith Walter et al
Fr 1815 Nov 20 add DLC-19
To 1815 Nov 20 add 4-1255
To 1815 Nov 20* add DLC-62
To 1815 Nov 20* add DLC-19
Fr 1815 Nov 21 DLC-19
Fr 1815 Nov 28 add DLC-20

Smith Waters
Fr 1831 Jan 05 M639-22
Fr 1831 Feb 12 M124-126

Smith William
To 1806 Dec 30 2-0413

Smith William (1762-1840)
Fr 1831 Oct 28 M639-6
Fr 1835 Sep 28 M639-10
Re 1837 Aug 29 mem DLC-50
Fr 1837 Oct 01 DLC-50
Fr 1837 Nov 08 M687-7
Fr 1838 May 06 DLC-51
Fr 1838 Nov 30 DLC-51
Re 1840 Jul 01 mem 34-1458

Smith William (1762-1840) et al
Fr 1834 Aug 14 26-0314
To 1834 Aug 19 26-0337
Fr 1839 cSep 04 DLC-52
To 1839 Sep 04 34-0912
To 1839 Sep 14 34-0938

Smith William (1797-1887)
Fr 1834 Jun 24 M639-17

Smith William (1797-1887) et al
Fr 1835 cFeb 27-0361

Smith William B
Re 1834 Mar 28 par 25-0466

Smith William H
Fr 1834 Mar 14 M639-22

Smith William J
To 1813 Jan 06 DLC-61
Fr 1813 Dec 24 DLC-8

Smith William Rudolph
Fr 1845 Jan 18 36-1368

Smith Zachariah
Re 1835 Aug 18 par 28-1303
Re 1835 Aug 18* par T967-1
Re 1835 Oct 06 par 29-0219
Re 1835 Oct 06* par T967-1

Smith & Chisholm
Fr 1820 Oct 23 fin 7-1392

Smithson Bryan H
Fr 1832 Nov 28 21-0587

SmithT John
Fr 1804 Jul 30 DLC-3
Re 1805 Feb 24 mem DLC-3
Fr 1805 Feb 24 fin 2-0019
To 1805 May 21 fin 2-0043
To 1806 Apr 04# fin 2-0205
Re 1806 May 20 leg 2-0237
Re 1806 Jun leg 2-0263
Re 1808 Apr 19 fin DLC-4
Re 1818 May 15 leg 6-0695

Smoot Benjamin S
Fr 1816 Mar 11 add DLC-20

Smoot George C
Fr 1831 Jan 27 M639-1

Smoot Walter
To 1836 Nov 08 chk DLC-49
Fr 1836 Dec 10 fin DLC-49
To 1836 Dec 10 chk DLC-49

Smuggling
Re 1829 Jun 20 mem 13-0693

Smyth Alexander
Fr 1829 Mar 05 M639-22

Smyth Harold
Fr 1815 Feb 07 DLC-16

Snelling Joseph
Fr 1829 Nov 24# 14-0594

Snoddy Andrew
Re 1798 Aug 18 1-0673

Snodgrass William
Fr 1813 Dec 21 DLC-61
To 1813 Dec 24 3-0715
To 1813 Dec 24* DLC-61
Fr 1813 Dec 24 DLC-61
To 1814 Jan 03 DLC-61
To 1814 Jan 05 DLC-61
Fr 1814 Jan 16 DLC-8
Fr 1814 Jan 31 DLC-8
To 1814 Feb 02 DLC-61
Fr 1814 Jul 18 DLC-11
To 1815 Jun 29 DLC-62

Snodgrass William et al
Fr 1830 Dec 17 M22-27

Snow Johnson & Moore
Fr 1826 Jan 12 fin DLC-34

Snowden Arthur H
Fr 1829 Feb 27 M639-3
Snowden Edgar
Fr 1829 Dec 04# 14-0796
Snowden Jacob
Re 1813 Jan 20 DLC-61
Snowden James Ross
To 1844 Feb 07 36-0237
Snowden James Ross et al
Fr 1844 Jan 19 36-0144
Snowden John M
Fr 1829 Mar 12 12-0978
Fr 1835 Nov 05 M639-27
Snowden Samuel B
Fr 1833 May 25 22-1458
Fr 1838 Dec 04 34-0541
Snowden Thomas J
Fr 1831 Dec 27 19-0427
Snyder Henry
Fr 1816 Feb 06 DLC-20
To 1816 Mar 15 DLC-20
Fr 1841 Oct 15 DLC-53
Snyder John
Re 1830 Jun 16 par 15-1475
To 1832 Sep 20 21-0035
Snyder Nicholas
To 1835 May 12 M179-80
Snyder Simon et al
Fr 1835 cApr 27-1502
Sockbason Deacon
Fr 1829 Nov 18 14-0495
Solis Lewis
Fr 1814 Sep 26 DLC-12
Solliday Samuel
Re 1836 Jul 16 par 31-1100
Solomon Isaac
Fr 1829 Apr 06 M639-10
Somers James
Re 1828 Aug 29 DLC-35
Somerville A & Co
Fr 1821 Mar 20 fin DLC-30
Sommerville John
Fr 1807 Nov 17 DLC-4
Fr 1815 Sep 24 DLC-19
Fr 1821 Jul 20 DLC-30
Fr 1822 Feb 04 DLC-31
Fr 1822 Feb 15 fin DLC-31
Fr 1822 Mar 19 M179-53
Fr 1822 Apr 17 M116-10
To 1826 Aug 23 11-0344
Fr 1827 Jun 06 fin DLC-72
Fr 1829 Mar 09# M639-22
To 1830 Aug 28 chk DLC-38
Sommerville John et al
Fr 1821 Nov 05 DLC-31
To 1821 Nov 06 8-1330
Sommerville John H
Fr 1832 Jun 20 20-0778
Sommerville Maxwell
Fr 1829 Jun 05# M639-22
Fr 1829 Jun 06 M639-10
Son of Liberty (pseudonym)
Fr 1824 Oct 30 DLC-33
Soule Pierre
Fr 1844 Nov 27 36-1060
Soule Rufus
Fr 1837 Feb M687-20
Sousa Domingo
Re 1821 Aug 22 mem DLC-63
Re 1821 Aug 22 M116-7
Re 1821 Aug 22* DLC-63
Re 1821 Aug 22 M116-7
Re 1821 Aug 22* DLC-63
Re 1821 Aug 23 M116-7
Re 1821 Aug 23* DLC-63
South George W
Fr 1833 Jun 29 fin 23-0080
To 1833 Jun 29 chk DLC-43
Fr 1836 Jan 02# fin DLC-47
To 1836 Jan 09 chk DLC-47
To 1836 Jan 19 chk DLC-47
Southall J J B
To 1842 Apr 01 35-0667
Southard Samuel Lewis
Fr 1824 Jan 19 10-0379
To 1824 Jan 21 10-0391
To 1824 Mar 09 10-0540
To 1824 Mar 25 10-0584
Fr 1825 Mar 07 10-1218
Fr 1825 Mar 08 10-1222
To 1825 Mar 09 M124-101
To 1826 Feb 20 11-0144
Fr 1826 Mar 18 M209-5
To 1827 Jan 05 DLC-34
To 1827 Jan 05* DLC-72
Fr 1827 Feb 09 DLC-72
Fr 1827 Feb 09* DLC-34
To 1827 Feb 15 DLC-72
Fr 1827 Feb 16 DLC-72
To 1827 Mar 06 DLC-72
To 1827 Mar 06* DLC-34
To 1827 Mar 06* 11-0493
Fr 1834 May 08 M286-1
Southgate Wright
Fr 1836 Jul 04 31-0831
Southwick George
Fr 1835 Mar 05 leg DLC-45
Southworth M
Fr 1832 Oct 17 21-0104
Southworth Sylvester S
Fr 1830 Dec 18 16-1486
Fr 1834 Oct 06 DLC-44
Sowell Arenton
Fr 1812 Nov 18 fin DLC-6
Spaight Richard Dobbs Jr
Fr 1836 Apr 30 M688-104
Spaight Richard Dobbs Jr et al
Fr 1834 Dec 31 M639-27
Spain spoliation claims
Re 1831 cAug mem 18-0389
Re 1831 Sep 08 mem 18-0704
Spain treaty
Re 1834 May 15 25-1055
Re 1834 Nov 01 26-0805
Spalding Bela P
Fr 1829 Jan 28 M639-26
Spalding Ignatius B
Re 1836 Jul 06 par 31-0887
Re 1836 Jul 08 par 31-0972
Spalding J W
Fr 1844 Apr 24 36-0447
Spalding Rufus P et al
Fr 1836 Sep 28 M639-3
Spangler Samuel et al
To 1840 May 11 34-1347
Spanish officers
To 1821 Sep 29 8-1242
Fr 1821 Oct 03# 8-1267

Sparks John			
	To 1807 cSep 01#	fin	2-0552
Sparks Richard			
	Fr 1814 Jan 14		DLC-8
	Fr 1814 Jul 09		DLC-66
	Fr 1814 Jul 20		DLC-11
	To 1814 Jul 26		DLC-62
	Fr 1814 Aug 09		DLC-11
	Fr 1814 Aug 16		DLC-11
	To 1814 Aug 27		DLC-62
	Fr 1814 Oct 30		DLC-13
	To 1814 Nov 09		DLC-62
	Fr 1814 Nov 14		DLC-14
Spaulding Azel			
	Fr 1835 Nov 14		M639-22
Speaker et al			
	Fr 1819 Jun 10		DLC-27
Spear William T			
	Fr 1836 Jun 07		31-0386
Specie circular			
	Re c1836 Dec	mem	32-0598
	Re 1837 cMar 01	mem	DLC-50
	Re 1837 Mar 03		33-1033
	Re 1837 Mar 03*		DLC-50
Speer Alexander			
	Fr 1829 Dec 23		14-1102
	Fr 1830 Jan 02		14-1306
Speers William B			
	Fr 1829 Jan 12		M688-61
Speight Jesse			
	Fr 1830 Apr 29		T431-1
	Fr 1834 Oct 12#		26-0604
	Fr 1836 Jun 25		M687-15
	Fr 1836 Jun 29		31-0639
	Fr 1840 Jan 18	add	34-1184
	To 1840 Jan 18	add	34-1188
	Fr 1840 May 26		DLC-52
Spencer John Canfield			
	Fr 1844 Feb 17		36-0292
Spencer Lucina			
	Fr 1844 Feb 01		DLC-56
Spering Charles F			
	Re 1831 Sep 23		M273-26
Sperry Charles			
	Re 1831 Apr 21		M273-26
	Re 1832 Dec 13		21-1045
Spicer Elizabeth			
	Fr 1833 Dec 26		24-0592
Spicer Peter W			
	Fr 1829 Apr 19		DLC-37
	Fr 1830 Oct 29#		16-0580
	To 1831 May 02		17-1272
	Fr 1833 Apr 13		22-1014
Spicer Thomas			
	Re 1834		24-0705
Spicer Thomas Young			
	Fr 1829 Jun 22		M639-22
Spinks John et al			
	Fr 1835 Jul 05#		28-0940
Splane Alexander R			
	Fr 1835 Oct 07		29-0234
Spooner A M			
	Fr 1842 Jul 29		DLC-54
	Fr 1842 Aug 24		DLC-54
	Fr 1844 Nov 06		DLC-57
Spooner Jane E			
	Fr 1844 Apr 08		DLC-56
Spooner Stillman			
	Fr 1838 Jan 15		DLC-51
Spoor Abraham			
	Fr 1832 Mar 06		M688-67
Spoor C T			
	Fr 1814 Feb 02		DLC-8
Spotts Samuel			
	Fr 1815 Jan 05		DLC-15
	Fr 1821 Jan 16		DLC-29
Sprague Joshua			
	Fr 1829 Jun 23		DLC-37
Sprague Norman S			
	Fr 1830 Mar		M639-27
Sprague Peleg			
	Fr 1830 Apr 26		M179-68
Sprague William Buell			
	To 1829 Apr 07		DLC-75
Sprigg James Cresap			
	Fr 1829 May 25		M639-2
Sprigg Michael Cresap			
	Fr 1829 Dec 21		14-1085
Sprigg Robert			
	To 1812 Oct 04		DLC-5
	Fr 1812 Nov 03		DLC-5
	Fr 1815 Jan 08	fin	4-0508
	Fr 1815 Jan 24		DLC-15
Springs Sedgwick			
	To 1827 Dec 01		DLC-35
Squire (slave)			
	Re 1839 Jan 28	leg	34-0607
Staats Cuyler			
	Fr 1828 Apr 28		11-1223
	Fr 1828 Apr 30		DLC-35
	Fr 1828 Aug 12		DLC-35
Stabler James P			
	To 1828 Aug 28		12-0177
Stafford Stephen M			
	Fr 1835 Jan 08		DLC-45
Stambaugh Samuel C			
	Fr 1829 Mar		12-0620
	Fr 1830 Sep 08		M234-315
	Fr 1830 Sep 08*		16-0218
	To 1831 Feb 01		T494-2
	To 1831 Feb 01*		17-0398
	Fr 1836 Oct 08		M234-422
Stanard Caroline M			
	Fr 1837 Feb 22		M688-105
Stanbery Henry et al			
	Fr 1833 Sep 28		M639-12
Standifer James			
	Fr 1814 Oct 01		DLC-12
	Fr 1816 Aug 22		5-0441
	To 1834 Feb 15#		M234-76
	Fr 1836 Jan 25		DLC-47
	To 1836 Jan 26		DLC-47
Standifer William			
	To 1801 Nov 25	lnd	1-0947
Stansbury James W			
	Fr 1835 Aug 15		M639-15
Stanton Henry			
	Fr 1821 Apr 23		M116-5
	Fr 1821 Apr 25		8-0369
	Fr 1821 Apr 25*		8-0369
	To 1821 May 07#		DLC-63
	To 1821 May 10#		DLC-63
	To 1821 May 26#	fin	DLC-30
	To 1821 Jun 20		M116-6
	To 1821 Jun 20*		DLC-30
	To 1821 Jun 20*		DLC-63
	To 1821 Jun 20*		8-0641
	Fr 1821 Jun 20		M116-6

Stanton Henry (cont)		
To 1821 Jun 23		M116-6
To 1821 Jun 23*		DLC-30
To 1821 Jun 23*		DLC-63
To 1821 Jun 23*		8-0667
Fr 1821 Jun 26		M116-6
Fr 1821 Jun 27		DLC-30
Fr 1821 Jul 01		DLC-30
Fr 1821 Jul 02		DLC-30
Fr 1821 Jul 05		DLC-30
To 1821 Jul 06		M116-6
To 1821 Jul 06*		DLC-30
To 1821 Jul 06*		DLC-63
To 1821 Jul 06*		8-0774
To 1821 Jul 10		DLC-30
Fr 1821 Jul 17	fin	DLC-70
To 1821 Jul 27		8-0916
Fr 1821 Jul 30		M116-6
Fr 1821 Aug 02		DLC-30
Fr 1821 Aug 02*		DLC-63
Fr 1821 Aug 02*		M116-6
Fr 1821 Aug 02*		8-0994
To 1821 Aug 03		DLC-30
To 1821 Aug 03*		M116-6
To 1821 Aug 03*		DLC-63
To 1821 Aug 03*		8-0998
Fr 1821 Aug 03		DLC-30
Fr 1821 Aug 03*		M116-6
Fr 1821 Aug 03*		DLC-63
Fr 1821 Aug 03*		8-1001
To 1821 Aug 08		DLC-30
To 1821 Aug 08*		DLC-63
Fr 1821 Aug 08		DLC-30
Fr 1821 Aug 08*		DLC-63
To 1821 Aug 20		DLC-63
Fr 1821 Aug 24		DLC-70
Staples Charles H		
Fr 1834 Jan 08		24-0797
Staples Josiah		
Fr 1837 Feb		M687-20
Starboard George et al		
Fr 1835 Sep		28-1498
Stark ______ (Misses)		
Fr 1829 Jun 12		DLC-37
Stark C Jr et al		
Fr 1832 Feb 02		M639-24
Stark Caleb		
Fr 1828 Oct 20		DLC-35
Fr 1829 Jan 08		DLC-36
Stark Henry		
Fr 1829 Jun 19		DLC-37
Fr 1829 Jun 25		DLC-37
Stark John		
Fr 1836 Jun 28		DLC-48
Stark Robert B		
Fr 1829 May 18		DLC-37
Fr 1832 Jun 13		20-0749
Fr 1833 Feb 09		M688-87
Fr 1834 Jun 01		25-1222
Fr 1835 Dec 14		M124-150
Stark Robert B et al		
Fr 1829 Jul 09		13-0832
Starkey Jonathan		
Fr 1831 Aug 12		M22-28
Starkey Joshua		
To 1826 Nov 05	fin	DLC-34
Starks William et al		
Fr 1816 Mar 22		DLC-20
Starkweather George Anson et al		
Fr 1832 Dec 26		M639-16
Starr Caleb		
Fr 1831 Sep 05		M234-113
Fr 1837 Nov 01		M234-114
Starr James		
Fr 1832 Mar 04		M234-113
Fr 1832 Mar 04*		19-1303
Stearns Christopher H		
Re 1831 Jan 25	par	17-0348
Re 1831 Jan 25*	par	T967-1
Stearns William Jr		
Fr 1836 Jul 12		31-1062
Steck Joseph Michael et al		
Fr 1829 Mar		M639-12
Stedman Jefferson		
Re 1831 Mar 30	par	17-1011
Steed ______ (Rev)		
Re 1835 cMay	mem	28-0203
Steed William		
Fr 1844 Jan 13		DLC-56
Steel J		
Re 1815 Mar	mem	DLC-17
Steele Andrew		
Fr 1805 Dec 30	fin	DLC-3
Steele Graves W		
To 1829 Jan 19	leg	12-0463
To 1829 Nov 07		DLC-37
Fr 1830 Aug 20	fin	DLC-38
Fr 1830 Dec 30		DLC-38
To 1832 Feb 04		DLC-40
Fr 1832 Apr 11		DLC-40
Fr 1832 Apr 25		DLC-40
Fr 1832 May 25		DLC-40
Fr 1832 Jun 26		DLC-41
Fr 1832 Jul 06		DLC-41
Steele Horace		
Fr 1844 Dec 12		DLC-57
Steele J et al		
Fr 1835 Mar		DLC-46
Steele John J		
Fr 1827 Dec 28		DLC-35
To 1828 Feb 17		DLC-35
Fr 1829 Apr 22		M639-6
Steele Robert		
To 1814 Mar 16		DLC-62
Fr 1814 Mar 20		DLC-9
To 1814 Mar 22		DLC-9
Fr 1814 Mar 22		DLC-9
To 1814 Mar 23		DLC-9
To 1814 Mar 23		DLC-9
Fr 1814 Mar 26		DLC-9
To 1814 Apr 02		DLC-10
Fr 1814 Apr 04		DLC-10
Steenrod Daniel		
Fr 1827 Mar 08		DLC-34
To 1827 Mar 29		DLC-34
Fr 1829 Mar 06		M234-432
Fr 1829 Aug 10		M639-18
Fr 1829 Aug 12		M639-18
Fr 1836 Oct 12		M22-41
Fr 1837 Nov 08		DLC-50
Fr 1838 Jan 25		DLC-51
Steiger William T		
Re 1835 Jul 06	mem	DLC-46
Re 1836 Jul 09		31-1035
Stephens Charles		
Fr 1829 Dec 10		14-0994
Fr 1833 Nov 27		23-1316
Stephens Philander		
To 1831 Dec 10#		M567-58

Name / Date		Note	Reference
Stephens Philander et al			
	Fr 1831		M639-11
Stephensburg VA citizens			
	To 1815 Dec 26		DLC-20
Stephenson B F et al			
	Fr 1835 Oct 01		29-0164
Stephenson James			
	To 1804 Mar 11		DLC-3
Sterett Samuel et al			
	Fr 1832 Aug 14		M639-25
Sterigere John Benton			
	Fr 1833 Feb 26		M639-20
	Fr 1835 Jul 27		M567-109
Sterrett James			
	Fr 1814 Dec 02		DLC-14
Sterrett James M et al			
	Fr 1835 cJan		DLC-59
Sterrett Robert et al			
	Fr 1835 cJan		DLC-59
Sterrett William			
	Fr 1829 May 13		DLC-37
Stettinius Samuel			
	Re 1833 Sep 24		23-0860
Steuart George H			
	Fr 1827 Feb 03		DLC-34
	Fr 1830 Nov 06		16-0660
	Fr 1832 Aug 13		M639-25
	Fr 1833 Feb 25		DLC-42
	Fr 1833 Sep 23		23-0840
Stevens Edward			
	Fr 1831 Dec 08		M639-18
Stevens Hestor Lockhart			
	Fr 1830 Apr 10		M222-28
Stevens Hestor Lockhart et al			
	Fr 1830 Apr 07		M222-28
Stevens John			
	Fr 1830 Apr 07		15-0640
Stevens Levi			
	Fr 1832 Feb 28		M22-29
Stevens Moses			
	Fr 1824 Nov 15	fin	10-0954
Stevens Samuel			
	Fr 1829 Mar 30		12-1185
Stevens Stephen C			
	Fr 1835 Jul 24		M639-23
Stevenson Andrew			
	Fr 1828 Dec 08		DLC-36
	To c1829		12-0391
	Fr 1829 Mar 04		M639-24
	Fr 1830 Mar 20		M639-10
	To 1830 Nov 10		DLC-38
	Fr 1831 Mar 31		17-1027
	To 1831 May 26		DLC-39
	Fr 1833 Feb 28		22-0551
	Fr 1835 Jun 09		28-0629
	To 1837 Jan 12		32-1578
	To 1839 Mar 26		34-0696
	To 1840 Mar 14		34-1257
Stevenson Andrew et al			
	Fr 1829 cMar 01		M639-24
Stevenson Daniel			
	Fr 1831 Feb 21		M22-27
	Fr 1831 May 09		M22-28
Stevenson James			
	Fr 1814 Dec 17		DLC-14
Stevenson Vernon King			
	Fr 1845 Jan 07		DLC-57
Stevenson Volney S			
	To 1842 Jan 12	chk	DLC-54
Stewart Andrew			
	Fr 1825 Mar 10		DLC-33
Stewart Andrew et al			
	Fr 1829 Feb 16		M639-14
	Fr 1830 Dec		16-0918
Stewart David			
	Fr 1831 Apr 01	fin	DLC-39
	Fr 1835 Feb 13	leg	DLC-73
Stewart Duncan			
	Re 1831 Sep 09		18-0709
Stewart Edmund			
	Fr 1835 Jul 01	fin	DLC-46
Stewart Isaac			
	Fr 1844 Jul 17		DLC-57
Stewart James			
	Fr 1806 Oct 28	fin	DLC-4
	Fr 1823 Oct 09	fin	DLC-32
	Fr 1830 Aug 26		16-0176
Stewart James & Co			
	Fr 1821 Mar 29	fin	DLC-31
	Fr 1822 Jul 22	fin	9-0220
	Fr 1822 Dec 10		DLC-31
	Fr 1822 Dec 17		DLC-31
	Fr 1822 Dec 25		DLC-31
	Fr 1822 Dec 31	fin	DLC-32
	Fr 1823 Jan 03		DLC-31
	Fr 1823 Jan 03	fin	DLC-32
	Fr 1823 Jan 12	mem	DLC-31
	To 1823 Apr 01#	fin	DLC-32
	Fr 1823 Jun 04	fin	DLC-32
Stewart John H			
	Fr 1841 Jan 15		DLC-53
Stewart Robert T et al			
	Fr 1830 Apr 12		M639-3
Stewart Thomas C et al			
	Fr 1836 Jan 18		M639-26
	Fr 1836 Feb 02		DLC-47
Stewart William et al			
	Fr 1831 cJan 28		M639-1
Stewart William M			
	Fr 1829 Mar 29		M639-23
Stickney J C			
	Fr 1835 Mar 31		DLC-46
Stickney Lyman D			
	Fr 1840 Jan 27		DLC-52
Stickney Samuel			
	Re 1833 Feb 23	par	22-0460
	Fr 1836 Aug 15		31-1296
Stiggins Susannah			
	Fr 1818 Jun 02		DLC-25
Stiles George C			
	Fr 1834 Apr 26		M688-101
Stiles John S			
	Fr 1831 Jul 18		M124-129
	Fr 1831 Nov 16		M124-130
	Fr 1832 Jan 25		19-0845
Still George W			
	Fr 1814 Mar 14		DLC-9
Stillman Truman			
	Fr 1840 Jan 08		DLC-52
Stilwell Richard E			
	Fr 1841 Sep 16		DLC-53
	Fr 1844 Feb 26		DLC-56
Stinson Abner P			
	Fr 1832 Feb 16		M639-18
	Fr 1835 Jan 22		M639-23
	Fr 1843 Sep 18		DLC-55
	Fr 1844 Aug 20		36-0806
	Fr 1844 Sep 11		36-0865

Stirling William
Re 1829 Sep 12 13-1313
Stith Anna
To 1828 Oct 29# 12-0252
Stith Fernando
To 1841 Jul 31 35-0355
Stitt Alfred G
Fr 1845 May 12 DLC-58
Stockbridge Mark
Fr 1838 Feb 06 DLC-51
Stockton Lucius W
To 1836 Dec 27 32-1363
Stockton Robert Field
Fr 1835 cMar 27-0670
Fr 1844 Apr 04 DLC-56
Stoddard Ebenezer
Fr 1836 Mar 15 M687-17
Stoddard Henry et al
Fr 1833 Oct 04 M639-12
Stoddard Jonathan et al
Fr 1836 May 31 M687-17
Stoddert John Truman
Fr 1834 Jun 11 25-1315
Stoddert John Truman et al
Fr 1834 Jun 17 M687-15
Stoddert William
Fr 1825 Sep 19 add 10-1428
To 1825 Sep 19 add 10-1432
Stokely John
Fr 1807 Dec 14 DLC-4
Fr 1815 Feb 13 DLC-71
Fr 1815 May 04 DLC-71
Stokes Montfort
Fr 1831 Jul 01 18-0145
Fr 1832 Jan 30 M124-131
Fr 1834 Apr 14 M234-776
Fr 1836 Aug 02 31-1215
Fr 1836 Aug 02* M234-236
Stokes Robert
Fr c1836 Aug 30 31-1377
Stokes William A
Fr 1844 Nov 17 DLC-57
Stollings G
Fr 1832 Oct 25 21-0150
Stone A J
Fr 1837 Feb 16 M687-20
Stone Benjamin W
Fr 1836 Aug 27 31-1373
Stone George
Fr 1843 Aug 10 DLC-55
Stone H B
Fr 1842 Mar 08 DLC-54
Stone J
Fr 1833 Mar 01 DLC-42
Stone John
Fr 1798 Oct 15 1-0686
Stone R
Fr 1841 Jun 21 DLC-53
Stone Robert
Fr 1831 Jul 20 M124-129
Stone S B et al
Fr c1836 29-1413
Stone Thomas J
To 1839 Apr 01 34-0711
Stone William
Fr 1818 Jun 03 6-1020
Stone William J
Fr 1836 Jan 01# fin DLC-47
Stoney John et al
Fr 1831 Jun 05 17-1524
To 1831 Jun 14 18-0018
Stoney Joshua
Fr 1829 Jun 03 13-0563
Storrow Samuel A
Fr 1816 Aug 12 DLC-21
Storrs Henry Randolph
Re 1820 Mar mem DLC-59
Re 1820 Mar mem DLC-60
Storrs William Lucius
Fr 1829 Jun 09 13-0605
Fr 1829 Aug 12 13-1110
Stothart Robert & Co
Re 1798 May 28 fin DLC-2
Stothart William
Fr 1804 May 24 DLC-3
Re 1804 Jul 04 mem DLC-3
Fr 1804 Jul 15 DLC-3
Fr 1804 Jul 22 DLC-3
Fr 1804 Nov 10 1-1409
Stothart & Bell
Re 1804 cJul mem DLC-60
Stott Elizabeth
Fr 1833 Oct 02# fin DLC-43
Fr 1834 Dec 03# fin DLC-45
Fr 1835 Feb 24# fin DLC-46
Fr 1835 Jun 29# fin DLC-46
Fr 1835 Aug 21# fin DLC-46
Fr 1835 Oct 20# fin 29-0331
Fr 1836 Feb 15# fin DLC-48
Stout John C
Re 1834 Jun 04 par 25-1259
Stout Samuel V D
Fr 1824 Feb 23 fin DLC-32
Stout Samuel V D & Co
Fr 1819 Feb 10 fin DLC-28
Fr 1821 Apr 11 DLC-30
Fr 1821 Apr 14 fin DLC-30
Stout Samuel V D & Son
Fr 1839 Jun 15 fin DLC-53
Stout & Pope
Fr 1826 Jun 09 fin 11-0240
Stow Edward
Fr 1833 Aug 09 DLC-43
Stow John et al
Fr 1836 Feb M639-11
Stow Joshua
Fr 1832 Jan 20 19-0800
Fr 1836 May 30 M639-12
Stower John G
Fr 1830 Mar 22 15-0430
Stower John G et al
Fr 1832 Feb 10 M687-12
Strange Robert
Fr 1836 Dec 26 32-1327
Fr 1837 Feb 15 M687-17
Fr 1837 Feb 16 M688-107
Fr 1840 Jun 17 DLC-52
Stras Emily C
Fr 1829 Feb 16 DLC-36
Stratton Thomas
Fr 1827 Jun 18 fin DLC-34
Straughan Joseph L
Re 1833 Jul 23 par 23-0198
Street Joseph Montfort
Fr 1833 Jul 10 M234-947
Street S A
Fr 1836 Apr 15 DLC-48

Name	Date	Note	Location
Street Thomas P			
	Fr 1836 May		M200-6
Streeter Squire			
	Fr 1829 Jun 24		M639-23
Stribling Erasmus			
	Fr 1831 Dec 02		M639-18
Stringer D			
	Fr 1829 Jul 30		M639-2
Strobel George			
	Re 1831 Apr 14		17-1165
Strode J M			
	Fr 1836 Nov 16		M567-135
Strohecker John			
	Fr 1834 Feb 28		24-1502
Strohecker John et al			
	Fr 1834 Feb 28		24-1505
Strong George D et al			
	Fr 1830 Feb 11		15-0132
	To 1830 Mar 12		15-0351
Strong Harvey			
	Fr 1831 Aug 30		M639-23
	Fr 1831 Sep 06		M179-71
	Fr 1831 Oct 10		M639-23
Strong Henry W et al			
	Fr 1833 Dec 27		M639-7
Strong John W			
	Fr 1831 Dec 01		M688-76
Strong Joseph C et al			
	Fr 1832 Aug 09		DLC-41
	To 1832 Aug 09		DLC-41
Strong N T			
	Fr 1836 cApr 15		30-1183
Strong William K			
	Fr 1836 Oct 05		32-0077
Strong William K et al			
	Fr 1834 Jan		M639-18
Strother David Hunter			
	Fr 1831 Jan 12		M22-27
Strother George French			
	Fr 1829 Aug 25		13-1199
Strother John			
	Fr 1806 Jan 04		DLC-3
	To 1812 May 01		DLC-5
	To 1812 Jul 12		DLC-5
	To 1813 Sep 28		3-0489
	Fr 1813 Oct 05		DLC-6
	Fr 1813 Oct 05*		DLC-61
	Fr 1813 Oct 09		DLC-6
	Fr 1813 Oct 09*		DLC-61
	To 1813 Dec 08		DLC-61
	Fr 1814 Feb 20		DLC-9
	To 1814 Feb 23		DLC-61
	Fr 1814 Mar 01		DLC-9
	Fr 1814 Mar 02		DLC-9
	Fr 1814 Mar 10		3-0909
	Fr 1815 Jun 06		DLC-18
	Fr 1815 Jun 10		DLC-18
	Fr 1815 Jun 23		M222-16
	Fr 1819 Feb 12	fin	7-0264
Stuart _____ (Capt)			
	Fr 1837 Mar 30		DLC-50
Stuart J P et al			
	Fr 1829 Mar 01		M639-10
Stuart Jacob W et al			
	Fr 1831 Nov 04		18-1197
Stuart James			
	Re 1796	mem	DLC-60
	Fr 1796 Apr 17		1-0378
	Fr 1840 Dec 20		DLC-53
Stuart James P et al			
	Fr 1835 Oct 05		M639-27
Stuart John G			
	To 1831 Dec 08	chk	DLC-40
Stuart P P			
	Fr 1814 Nov 29		DLC-14
Stuart Thomas			
	To 1807 Jan 02		2-0429
	To 1808 Feb 13		DLC-4
	To 1810 Jun 06	fin	DLC-4
	Fr 1815 Mar 13		DLC-17
	Fr 1833 Nov 25		M639-15
Stubling Robert			
	Fr 1814 Jul 30		DLC-11
Stump Frederick			
	Re 1795 Nov	leg	DLC-1
	Re 1795 Nov*	leg	DLC-71
	Fr 1807 Mar 03		DLC-4
	Re 1818 Apr 18	leg	6-0401
Stump John			
	Re 1814 Jan 27		3-0800
	Re 1814 Jan 27*		DLC-8
	Re 1814 Jan 27*		DLC-61
	Fr 1814 Jan 31		DLC-8
Stump John F			
	Fr 1834 Sep 15		M639-15
	Fr 1835 Feb 06		M639-15
Stump John F et al			
	Fr 1834 Nov 13		M179-79
Stump William Henry			
	Fr 1836 Mar 14		M567-130
Stump the Dealer (horse)			
	Re 1812 Aug 11		DLC-5
Sturgeon Daniel			
	Fr 1831 Jan 25		17-0358
	Fr 1843 Feb 28		DLC-55
	To 1843 Mar 20		35-1285
Sturgeon Daniel et al			
	To 1828 Dec 30		12-0351
	To 1828 Dec 30*		DLC-36
Sturges Benjamin B			
	Fr 1836 Aug 04		M567-131
Suarez Peter et al			
	Fr 1831 Dec 31		19-0488
Suffern Thomas			
	Fr 1833 Nov 09#		DLC-43
Sugg George Augustus			
	Fr 1791 Dec 21	fin	1-0120
	Fr 1791 Dec 21*	fin	DLC-71
Sullivan Daniel F			
	Fr 1818 May 03		DLC-24
	Fr 1818 May 03*		6-0563
Sullivan George et al			
	Fr 1830 Aug 05		M639-7
Sullivan John T			
	Fr 1833 Apr 08		DLC-42
	To 1833 Apr 14		22-1022
	To 1833 Apr 14*		DLC-42
	Fr 1833 Apr 22		22-1110
	To 1833 Aug 03		DLC-43
	To 1833 Aug 03*		23-0262
	Fr 1833 Aug 06		DLC-43
	Fr 1833 Aug 14		DLC-43
	Fr 1833 Nov 02		M639-19
	Fr 1833 Dec 03		DLC-43
	Fr 1835 Sep 01		M639-14
	Fr 1836 Jun 07	fin	DLC-48
	Fr 1836 Jun 17	fin	DLC-48
	To 1837 Mar 03	chk	DLC-50

Sullivan L
Fr 1800 Jan 03 fin DLC-2
Sullivan Samuel et al
Fr 1829 Mar 13 M639-11
Sulzman Charles H
Fr 1844 Feb DLC-56
Summerlin Jacob et al
Fr 1831 Dec 22 19-0397
Sumner County TN
Re 1819 Jul 20 lnd 7-0582
Re 1832 Dec 22 lnd 21-1130
Sumner County TN citizens
To 1824 cDec 10-0963
Re 1827 Mar 15 add 11-0503
Sumter Thomas
Fr 1807 Mar 24 2-0478
Sutherland Jacob et al
Fr 1833 Jun 14 23-0034
To 1833 Jun 30 23-0088
Sutherland Joel Barlow
To 1829 May 25 13-0428
Fr 1829 May 25 DLC-37
Fr 1829 May 26 DLC-37
Fr 1829 May 30 DLC-37
Fr 1829 Oct 28 14-0256
To 1834 Oct 16 DLC-73
Fr 1836 Jun M639-18
Fr 1840 Nov 04 35-0088
Fr 1844 Aug 20 36-0809
To 1844 Sep 02 36-0842
Fr 1844 Sep 17 36-0888
Fr 1844 Nov 04# 36-0984
Fr 1844 Nov 06# 36-0993
Fr 1844 Nov 08 36-1008
Fr 1844 Nov 09# 36-1013
Fr 1845 Jan 25 36-1409
To 1845 Feb 10 36-1475
Fr 1845 Mar 20 DLC-57
To 1845 Mar 21 37-0004
Fr 1845 Apr 08 DLC-58
Sutherland Joel Barlow et al
Fr 1834 cDec 01 M639-1
Fr 1836 Jul 04# 31-0835
Fr c1836 Dec M639-6
Sutherland Thomas J
Fr 1829 May 17 M124-118
Sutherland William
Re 1832 Jul 16 par T967-1
Sutton John
Re 1834 Apr 12 par 25-0688
Sutton Richard
Fr 1834 May 20# M124-142
Swackhamer C
Fr 1843 Jul 28 DLC-55
Swain David Lowry
Fr 1833 Jan 15 21-1441
Fr 1834 Jan 19 24-1002
Fr 1835 Jan 12 M179-79
Swain David Lowry et al
Fr 1835 Jul 18 M22-36
Swan G
To 1838 Nov 03# DLC-51
Swan James
To 1801 Oct 23 lnd 1-0937
Swan James et al
Fr 1830 May 15-0871
Swan Joshua A
Fr 1842 Mar 10 DLC-54
Swaney James A
Fr 1829 Jan 25 M639-23
Swaney John et al
Fr 1832 cJul 10 20-1019
Swann Thomas
Fr 1829 Mar 28 12-1168
Fr 1832 Feb 25 M639-6
Fr 1835 Feb 02# 27-0370
Swann Thomas et al
Fr 1829 Apr 13 12-1336
Swann Thomas Jr
Fr 1831 Dec 18 M639-23
Fr 1831 Dec 18 M639-23
Fr 1833 Mar 08 M639-13
Swann Thomas (TN)
Fr 1806 Jan 03 2-0110
To 1806 Jan 07 2-0116
Fr 1806 Jan 12 2-0121
Fr 1806 Feb 01 2-0139
Fr 1806 Feb 19 2-0179
Fr 1806 Feb 28 2-0183
Fr 1806 May 20# 2-0240
Fr 1809 May 26 DLC-71
Swann William P
Fr 1833 Mar 09 22-0728
Swanson James
Fr 1805 Sep 07 2-0083
Swartwout Robert
Fr 1835 May 21 M567-113
Swartwout Samuel
Fr 1819 Apr 26 DLC-72
Fr 1819 Aug 28 DLC-72
To 1819 Sep 25 DLC-75
To 1823 Dec 16 9-0806
To 1824 Mar 04 10-0516
Fr 1824 Mar 16 M688-35
To 1824 Mar 25 10-0586
To 1824 Sep 27 10-0902
To 1824 Dec 14 10-0981
To 1824 Dec 14* DLC-33
Fr 1825 Feb 18 10-1125
To 1825 Feb 22 10-1148
To 1825 Mar 05 DLC-33
Fr 1825 Apr 02 DLC-33
To 1825 May 16 10-1268
To 1825 May 26 10-1284
Fr 1825 Nov 20 DLC-33
To 1825 Dec 15 DLC-33
Fr 1826 Oct 24 DLC-34
Fr 1827 Jul 20 DLC-34
Fr 1829 Mar 18 M639-5
Fr 1829 Mar 20 M639-22
Fr 1829 Mar 22 M639-3
Fr 1829 Apr 08# M639-15
Fr 1829 Apr 29 13-0184
Fr 1829 Jun 03 M639-4
Fr 1829 Jun 04 DLC-37
Fr 1829 Aug 15 M639-7
To 1829 Sep 27 DLC-37
Fr 1829 Oct 02 14-0094
Fr 1829 Nov 25 DLC-37
Fr 1829 Dec 07# M639-14
Fr 1830 Mar 27 DLC-38
Fr 1830 Jun 14 M639-3
Fr 1831 Apr 19 17-1197
Fr 1831 Oct 14 M639-24
Fr 1832 Mar 31# DLC-40
Fr 1832 Jun 13 M639-5
Fr 1832 Dec 04 M688-56
Fr 1832 Dec 09 M639-6
Fr 1832 Dec 10 M639-16

To 1833 Jan 12 chk DLC-41
Fr 1833 Jan 30 M124-136
Fr 1833 Mar 01 M688-88
Fr 1833 Aug 16 M639-2
To 1833 Nov 26 23-1314
Fr 1833 Nov 28 DLC-43
Fr 1833 Dec 03 DLC-43
Fr 1833 Dec 18 M639-18
Fr 1834 Mar 08 DLC-47
Fr 1834 Mar 08 DLC-47
To 1834 Mar 15 DLC-44
Fr 1834 Mar 17 DLC-44
Fr 1834 Apr 22 M179-78
To 1834 Nov 10 26-0880
Fr 1835 Feb 01 DLC-45
To 1835 Sep 14 29-0043
Fr 1835 Nov 03 29-0427
To 1836 Feb 21 DLC-73
Fr 1836 Oct 31 DLC-49
Fr 1837 Mar 04 DLC-50
Swartwout Samuel et al
Fr 1825 Feb 10 10-1103
To 1825 Feb 10 10-1104
Fr 1829 Jun 11 M639-25
Fr 1829 Nov 24 M639-8
Swasey Horatio J
Fr 1836 Dec 19 M639-11
Swayne Noah Haynes
Fr 1835 Jan 03 M639-27
Fr 1835 Mar 23 M639-1
Sweitzer Lewis et al
Fr 1836 Jan 11 M639-5
Swift Jonathan
Fr 1837 Feb 14 M687-20
Swift Joseph Gardner
To 1817 Jan 12 5-0692
Fr 1817 Apr 02 DLC-22
To 1817 Apr 22 5-0833
To 1825 Mar 08 10-1223
Fr 1827 Jun 07 DLC-34
Fr 1829 Mar 30 DLC-36
Swift William Henry
Fr 1832 Jan 26 M22-29
Swift William R
Fr 1828 Apr 08 DLC-35
To 1828 Jun 02 DLC-35
Fr 1828 Jul 26 DLC-35
Fr 1828 Oct 30 DLC-35
Swiler ______ (Capt)
To 1821 May 13# DLC-63
Swiler Joseph
Fr 1833 Dec 27 24-0612
Fr 1833 Dec 27# 24-0615
Swinton Henry
Fr 1834 Mar 17 25-0256
Symington John
To 1819 Dec 13# DLC-63

Tabor Isaac J
Fr 1837 Feb 08 M639-14
Tait David
Fr 1836 Sep 29 M639-3
Tait John
To 1819 Aug 04 lnd 7-0593
Tait Richard
To 1815 Jun 17 lnd 4-1085
Tait William
Re 1793 Mar 10# leg 1-0154
To 1797 Dec 22 DLC-2
Re 1805 Jul 10 mem DLC-3
Fr 1807 Nov 23 DLC-4
Tait & Deaderick
Fr 1793 Jul 08 mem DLC-1
Talbert James
Fr 1827 Aug 10 DLC-34
Talbot Clayton
Fr 1815 May 26 fin 4-1067
Fr 1829 Oct 25 M688-64
Fr 1836 Apr 30 DLC-48
Talbot Green
Fr 1838 Nov 04 DLC-51
Talbot J C
Fr 1837 Jan 30 33-0264
Talbot J C et al
Fr 1837 Jan 17 M687-3
Talbot James H
Fr 1844 Feb 27 DLC-56
Talbot Joseph H
Fr 1825 May 30 DLC-33
To 1825 Jun 18 add 10-1312
Talbot M J
Fr 1837 Feb 10 M687-20
Talbott Joseph
Fr 1825 Jan 15 10-1072
Fr 1825 Jan 18 fin DLC-72
Fr 1825 Mar 01 10-1200
Fr 1825 Mar 16 fin DLC-72
Talcott George
Fr 1831 Jan 08 M22-27
Re 1835 Sep 02 28-1512
Talcott Samuel A
Fr 1829 Mar 13 12-1001
Taliaferro John
Fr 1829 Mar 10 12-0929
Taliaferro Sarah F
Fr 1835 Oct 08 DLC-47
Tallahassee Railroad Co
Re 1835 Jun 25 28-0806
Talley Alexander
Fr 1829 Sep 18# M222-26
Tallmadge James
Fr 1824 Mar 06 DLC-32
To 1824 Mar 12 DLC-32
Fr 1831 Dec 31# DLC-40
To 1835 Apr 29 28-0192
Tallmadge Nathaniel Pitcher
Fr 1834 Feb 24 M639-24
Fr 1834 Sep 23 DLC-44
Tallmadge Nathaniel Pitcher et al
Fr 1832 Feb 09 19-1027
To 1832 Feb 23 19-1207
Tallmadge Stephen et al
Fr 1835 cJan DLC-59
Tammany Hall
Fr 1829 Jan 08 DLC-36
Taney Roger Brooke
Fr 1829 Apr 20 M639-23
Fr 1829 May 22 M639-11
To 1831 Jul 20 M221-111
To 1831 Jul 20* 18-0240
Re 1831 Jul 20 18-0241
To 1831 Jul 21 M234-728
To 1831 Jul 25 M22-28
To 1831 Jul 28 M222-30
Fr 1831 Jul 28# DLC-39
To 1831 Jul 31 M22-28
Fr 1831 Aug 05 18-0426

Taney Roger Brooke (cont)

Fr	1831	Aug 05*		M127-2
To	1831	Aug 06		M567-62
To	1831	Aug 06*		M234-434
To	1831	Aug 06*		18-0467
Fr	1831	Aug 19		T412-3
To	1831	Sep 07#		18-0698
Fr	1831	Sep 09		T412-3
Fr	1831	Sep 09*		18-0710
Fr	1831	Sep 09*		M234-169
To	1831	Sep 12		M221-111
To	1831	Sep 12*		18-0717
Fr	1831	Nov 01		T412-3
Fr	1831	Nov 01*		18-1170
Fr	1831	Nov 01*		M234-169
Fr	1831	Nov 03		M699-1
Fr	1831	Nov 03*		M699-2
Fr	1831	Nov 30		T412-3
Fr	1831	Dec 02		T412-3
Fr	1831	Dec 14		T412-3
Fr	1831	Dec 28#		DLC-40
Fr	1832	Jan 04		T412-3
To	1832	Mar 19#		19-1503
To	1832	Mar 19*		M733-1
Fr	1832	Mar 22		M699-1
Fr	1832	Mar 22*		M699-2
To	1832	Mar 29		20-0051
Fr	1832	Apr 05		20-0148
Fr	1832	Jun 07		M699-1
Fr	1832	Jun 07*		M699-2
Fr	1832	Jun 14		20-0755
Fr	1832	Jun 27		DLC-41
Fr	1832	Jul 19		20-1153
To	1832	Jul 23		M179-74
Fr	1832	Oct 29		21-0217
Fr	1832	Oct 31		21-0232
Fr	1832	Dec 14		21-1052
Fr	1832	Dec 14*		M699-1
Fr	1832	Dec 14*		M699-2
Fr	c1833			21-1247
To	1833	Jan 19		21-1573
Fr	1833	cMar		DLC-42
To	1833	Mar 12		22-0746
Fr	1833	Mar 22		22-0862
Fr	1833	Apr 29		DLC-42
Fr	1833	May 10		DLC-43
Fr	1833	May 16		22-1370
Fr	1833	Aug 05		DLC-43
To	1833	Aug 11		23-0317
Fr	1833	Aug 30		DLC-43
Fr	1833	Sep 10#		23-0684
Fr	1833	Sep 11		23-0689
Fr	1833	Sep 12		23-0704
To	1833	Sep 15		DLC-43
Fr	1833	Sep 17		DLC-43
Fr	1833	Sep 21		DLC-43
Re	1833	cSep 22	mem	23-0829
To	1833	Sep 23		23-0843
To	1833	Sep 23*		DLC-43
Fr	1833	Sep 23		23-0845
Re	1833	Sep 23		23-0849
Fr	1833	Sep 23		DLC-42
Fr	1833	Oct 05		23-0965
Fr	1833	Oct 05*		M567-81
Fr	1833	Oct 05*		M415-1
Fr	1833	Oct 05*		M179-77
Fr	1833	Oct 05*		M124-140
Fr	1833	Oct 05*		M234-435
Fr	1833	Oct 07		23-0989
Fr	1833	Oct 07*		M733-1
Fr	1833	Oct 09		23-0998
To	1833	Oct 22		23-1081
To	1833	Oct 28		23-1111
Fr	1833	Nov 07		M415-1
Fr	1833	Nov 14		23-1233
Fr	1833	Nov 16		23-1243
To	1833	Nov 22		23-1295
To	1833	Nov 22		23-1297
Fr	1833	Nov 27		23-1322
To	1833	Dec 05#		DLC-43
Fr	1833	Dec 10		24-0444
Fr	1833	Dec 10*		M415-1
To	1833	cDec 20		DLC-43
Fr	1833	Dec 20#		DLC-43
To	1834	Jan 04		M179-77
Fr	1834	Jan 06		24-0761
Fr	1834	Jan 15		24-0968
Fr	1834	Jan 15*		M415-1
To	1834	Jan 19#		24-0996
Fr	1834	Jan 29		24-1102
Fr	1834	Jan 29*		M415-1
Fr	1834	Feb 03		24-1220
Fr	1834	Feb 03*		M415-1
Fr	1834	Mar 01		24-1519
Fr	1834	Mar 03		24-1527
Fr	1834	Mar 03*		M415-1
Fr	1834	Mar 03		24-1531
Fr	1834	Mar 03		24-1537
Fr	1834	Mar 03		24-1542
Fr	1834	Mar 05		24-1579
Fr	1834	Mar 05*		M415-1
Fr	1834	Mar 11		25-0083
Fr	1834	Mar 11*		M415-1
Fr	1834	Mar 20		25-0297
Fr	1834	Mar 27		25-0438
Fr	1834	Apr 11		25-0686
Fr	1834	Apr 11*		M415-1
Fr	1834	Apr 22		25-0860
Fr	1834	Apr 22*		M733-1
To	1834	May 07		25-0987
To	1834	May 19#		25-1087
To	1834	May 26		25-1150
Re	c1834	Jun	mem	25-1217
To	1834	Jun 11		25-1317
To	1834	Jun 12#		M639-27
Fr	1834	Jun 17		25-1399
Fr	1834	Jun 17*		M733-1
Fr	1834	Jun 24		M415-1
Fr	1834	Jun 25		25-1539
To	1834	Jun 25		25-1540
Fr	1834	Jun 27		M733-1
Fr	1834	Jul 18		DLC-44
Fr	1834	Oct 12		DLC-44
To	1834	Oct 13		26-0627
Fr	1834	Oct 20		DLC-44
To	1834	Nov 08		26-0857
Fr	1834	Nov 20		DLC-45
Fr	1835	Jan 12		DLC-45
Fr	1835	Feb 03		27-0378
Fr	1835	Nov 21		DLC-47
Fr	1836	Mar 15		M687-15
Fr	1836	Mar 17		DLC-47
Re	1836	Mar 22		30-0878
Fr	1836	Jun	mem	31-0241
Fr	1836	Jun 20		DLC-48
Fr	1836	Jun 27		DLC-48
To	1836	Oct 13		DLC-49
Fr	1836	Oct 15		DLC-49
Fr	1836	Oct 27		DLC-49

Fr 1836 Nov 19 DLC-49
To 1836 Dec 06 32-1029
Fr 1836 Dec 08 DLC-49
Fr 1837 Jan 27 DLC-49
To 1837 Feb 09 33-0580
Fr 1837 Feb 09 33-0582
Fr 1837 Jul 03 DLC-50
Fr 1837 Oct 09 DLC-50
Fr 1837 Dec 19 DLC-50
To 1838 Apr 14 34-0320
Fr 1838 May 28 DLC-51
Fr 1838 Sep 12 DLC-51
Fr 1839 Jan 10 DLC-51
Fr 1839 Aug 31 DLC-52
To 1839 Oct 10 34-0993
Fr 1839 Nov 04 DLC-52
Fr 1840 Mar 23 34-1261
Fr 1840 Sep 04 DLC-53
Fr 1841 Apr 24 DLC-53
Fr 1841 Sep 30 DLC-53
To 1841 Nov 27 35-0511
Fr 1842 May 22 DLC-54
To 1842 Jun 15 35-0794
Fr 1842 Oct 24 DLC-54
Fr 1843 Apr 28 DLC-55
Fr 1843 Oct 18 DLC-55
Fr 1844 Jan 04 DLC-56
Fr 1844 Mar 15 36-0390
Fr 1844 Jun 19 36-0631
Fr 1844 Nov 20 DLC-57
Fr 1845 Jan 01 DLC-57

Tannehill Wilkins
Fr 1825 Apr 28 DLC-33
Fr 1825 Aug 13 DLC-33
To 1825 Aug 14 10-1410

Tanner Jonas C
Fr 1821 Oct 04 fin DLC-70

Tappan Benjamin
Fr 1829 Apr 06 M639-8
Fr 1830 cFeb M639-27
Re 1833 Oct 12 23-1019
Fr c1834 Dec M639-27
Fr 1835 Jan 06 M639-27
Fr 1845 Jan 13 DLC-57

Tappan Benjamin S
Fr 1825 Jul 04 add 10-1344

Tappan John et al
Fr 1829 Feb M639-8

Tarascon L A
Fr 1836 Oct 20 DLC-49

Targee John
Fr 1829 M639-11
Fr 1829 Mar 26 12-1154
Fr 1831 cSep M639-18
Fr 1833 Feb 20# DLC-42

Targee John et al
Fr 1829 Mar 12-0699
Fr 1832 Dec 27 21-1179

Tariff
Re 1824 cApr 10-0617
Re 1829 Nov mem 14-0334

Tarlton Lewis A
Re 1836 Jul 06 par 31-0887
Re 1836 Jul 08 par 31-0972

Tarr A DeKalb
Fr 1836 Oct 20 M567-132

Tarrant Carter
Fr 1815 Apr 25 DLC-18
Fr 1815 Jun 17 DLC-18

Tarrant Edward H
To 1825 Sep 20 DLC-33

Tarshar et al
Fr 1835 Jan M234-31

Tate Adam
Re 1788 Mar 12 leg 1-0039

Tate David
Fr 1814 Nov 15 DLC-11
Fr 1814 Nov 15 DLC-14

Tate Martha
To 1807 Jan 03 fin DLC-4

Tate Paul
Fr 1834 May 22 25-1136

Tate Richard
To 1807 Jan 24 fin DLC-4

Tate William H
Fr 1823 Feb 03 fin DLC-32
Fr 1823 May 14 fin DLC-32

Tate Z
Fr 1819 Nov fin 7-0726

Tate Zachariah
To 1807 Feb 14 fin DLC-4

Tatum Howell
Re 1791 May 11 lnd 1-0095
Fr 1793 Dec 13 fin 1-0172
Fr 1802 Sep 14 DLC-2
Fr 1803 Aug 22 1-1149
Fr 1803 Nov 08# 1-1248
Re 1813 Nov 07 DLC-65
To 1814 Jan 15 DLC-61
To 1814 Feb 25 DLC-62
To 1815 Jan 27# 4-0638
To 1815 Jan 27* DLC-16
Fr 1815 Feb 15 DLC-16
Re 1815 May 26 4-1069
To 1816 Jul 18 5-0310
Fr 1816 Jul 26 DLC-21

Tatum James
To 1814 Feb 09 DLC-62
To 1814 Feb 09 DLC-62
To 1814 Feb 22 DLC-61
To 1815 Jun 13 DLC-62

Tatum & Wiggin
To 1796 Dec 19 fin DLC-1

Taul Thomas P
Fr 1827 Jul 18 DLC-34

Taxes
Re 1815 May 19 fin 4-1047

Tayloe Benjamin Ogle
Fr 1836 Aug 27 DLC-49

Tayloe Julia Maria (Dickinson)
Fr 1842 Jan 23 DLC-54

Taylor Benjamin
To 1813 Sep 26 DLC-6
Fr 1814 Feb 17 DLC-9
Fr 1814 May 03 DLC-10
Fr 1815 May 03 DLC-18
Fr 1827 Aug 29 DLC-34
To 1827 Sep 11 DLC-34
Fr 1829 Mar 07 M639-11
Fr 1829 Mar 25 M639-24
Fr 1832 Aug 18 DLC-41
Fr 1845 Jan 06 DLC-57

Taylor Daniel
Fr 1818 Jun 14 fin DLC-69
Fr 1818 Jun 14* fin 6-1054

Taylor E D
Fr 1835 Oct 27 M639-18

Taylor E W
Fr 1835 Nov 27 M639-9

Taylor Frank			
	To 1837 Apr 01	fin	DLC-50
Taylor George			
	Fr 1845 Apr 21		DLC-58
Taylor Gilbert D			
	Fr 1813 Dec 14		DLC-7
Taylor Grant			
	Re 1814 Mar 07		3-0904
Taylor James			
	Fr 1792 Aug 16	fin	1-0130
	Fr 1829		12-0393
	Fr 1829 Feb 23		M639-2
	Fr 1829 Jun 08		M222-26
	Fr 1830 Jan 03		DLC-37
	Fr 1830 May 22		M639-24
	Fr 1831 Jan 31		17-0384
	Fr 1831 Jan 31		17-0385
	Fr 1831 Jan 31#		17-0387
	Fr 1836 Aug 17#		DLC-48
Taylor James Jr			
	Fr 1829 Feb 23#		M639-2
Taylor James (AL)			
	Fr 1835 Apr 06		27-1543
Taylor James G			
	Fr 1844 Jun 05		36-0585
Taylor Jeremiah			
	Fr 1844 Nov 21		36-1043
Taylor John			
	Fr 1831 Feb 04		M22-27
Taylor John et al			
	Fr 1834 Dec 31		M688-105
Taylor John K			
	Fr 1835 Jul 21		28-1099
	Fr 1835 Aug 14		28-1286
Taylor John M			
	Fr 1829 Feb 17		12-0530
	Fr 1829 Mar		12-0702
	Fr 1829 Aug 08		M639-16
	Fr 1829 Oct 22		M639-3
Taylor Jones et al			
	Fr 1837 Feb		M687-20
Taylor Joseph			
	To 1809 Jul 08	lnd	2-0849
Taylor Joseph et al			
	Fr 1831 Dec 01		M639-20
Taylor Joshua			
	To 1806 Dec 31	fin	DLC-4
Taylor Keturah L			
	Fr 1845 Feb 20		DLC-57
Taylor Nathaniel			
	Fr 1814 Jan 31		3-0845
	To 1814 Feb 02		DLC-61
	To 1814 Mar 08		DLC-61
	Fr 1814 Sep 28		DLC-12
	Fr 1814 Nov 05		DLC-75
	Fr 1814 Nov 12		4-0328
	Fr 1815 Jun 30		DLC-18
Taylor R J et al			
	Fr 1829 Apr 02		M639-11
Taylor Richard et al			
	Fr 1819 Jun 23		7-0560
	To 1819 Jun 24		7-0562
	Fr 1834 Aug 22		M234-776
Taylor Samuel			
	Fr 1814 Mar 15		DLC-9
Taylor Thomas			
	Fr 1804 Sep	fin	DLC-3
Taylor Waller			
	Fr 1805 Aug 11		DLC-3
	Fr 1807 Feb 21		DLC-71
Taylor Ward			
	Fr 1835 Sep 20		M639-5
	Fr 1836 Apr 10		M639-6
Taylor William			
	Fr 1843 Oct 18		DLC-55
	Fr 1843 Nov 28		DLC-56
Taylor Zachary			
	Fr 1819 Nov 12		DLC-28
	Fr 1834 Aug 06		26-0281
Taylor Zachary et al			
	Fr 1821 Jul 28		DLC-30
	Fr 1835 Dec		M639-3
Tazewell Henry			
	Fr 1798 Jul 20		DLC-2
Tazewell Littleton Waller			
	Fr 1828 Aug 26		DLC-35
	Fr 1829 Feb 11	add	12-0501
	To 1829 Feb 11		12-0502
	To 1829 Mar 12		12-0982
	Fr 1829 Mar 30		DLC-36
	To 1829 Apr 06		12-1288
	To 1829 Apr 06*		DLC-60
	Fr 1830 Feb 17		M124-122
	Fr 1830 Feb 17*		15-0166
	To 1830 Feb 19		15-0206
	To 1830 Feb 20		15-0211
	Fr 1830 Feb 20		15-0213
	To 1830 Feb 22		15-0231
	To 1830 Feb 24		15-0242
	Fr 1830 Feb 24		15-0245
	Fr 1830 Feb 25		15-0259
	To 1830 Mar 11		15-0341
	Fr 1835 Oct 10		29-0267
Tazewell Littleton Waller Jr			
	To 1829 Jul 16		13-0859
Tazewell William			
	Fr 1835 Jun 10		28-0633
Tead Peter W			
	Re 1814 Jan 31		DLC-62
Tebbs William P			
	Fr 1807 Jul 10		2-0516
Tefft Israel Kerch			
	Fr 1839 Aug 13		DLC-52
	Fr 1840 Jul 27		DLC-53
	To 1843 Mar 20		35-1287
Telford James			
	Re 1824 May 20		DLC-32
Telford James Jr			
	Fr 1840 Oct 29#	leg	DLC-53
Teller Henry et al			
	Fr 1835 cJan		DLC-59
Temperance pledge			
	Re 1834 Oct		26-0463
Temple F M			
	Fr 1824 Oct 20#	fin	DLC-33
Temple H			
	Fr 1823 Dec 29	fin	DLC-32
	Fr 1826 Sep 15#	fin	DLC-33
Temple John			
	Fr 1831 Apr 02		M22-28
Templeman George			
	Fr 1832 Aug 03	fin	DLC-42
	To 1833 Apr 15	chk	DLC-42
	Fr 1834 May 24		25-1144
Templeman & Denham			
	Fr 1833 Dec 14	fin	24-0504
	Fr 1833 Dec 16	fin	DLC-44
	To 1834 Apr 04	chk	DLC-44
	Fr 1834 Apr 10	fin	DLC-45

To 1834 Nov 12 chk DLC-45
Fr 1834 Nov 12 fin DLC-45
Fr 1835 Mar 12 fin DLC-46
To 1835 Sep 01 chk 28-1506
Fr 1835 Sep 28 fin DLC-47
Fr 1835 Oct 10 fin DLC-47
Fr 1835 Dec 03 fin DLC-46
To 1836 Apr 04 chk DLC-47
Tenant Thomas
Fr 1829 Apr 01 M639-15
Tenant Thomas et al
Fr 1829 Sep 10 M179-67
Fr 1829 Sep 10* M124-120
Ten Eyck Abraham
Fr 1844 Jun 07 36-0592
Tennessee citizens
Fr 1815 cMay 15 add 4-1040
Tennessee congressmen
Fr 1832 Mar 28 M22-29
Fr 1834 Mar 08 M22-34
Tennessee Gazette
To 1803 Dec 14 1-1256
Tennessee General Assembly
To 1796 Apr 11 DLC-1
To 1798 Dec 12 1-0691
To 1819 Mar 7-0388
To 1824 Sep 10-0882
To 1825 Oct 14 add 11-0041
Tennessee land fraud
Re 1797 Dec 06 1-0553
Tennessee legislators
To 1832 Sep DLC-41
Tennessee militia
Re 1798 Dec 08 1-0689
Re 1812 Dec 31 DLC-64
To 1815 cMay 13 add 4-1028
--detached
To 1812 Nov 11 2-1270
To 1814 Feb 04 add DLC-8
To 1814 Feb 04 add 3-0852
--first division
To 1813 Dec 19 add DLC-7
To 1813 Dec 19* add DLC-61
To 1813 Dec 19* add DLC-8
To 1814 Jan 05 DLC-61
To 1814 Mar 14 DLC-61
Re 1814 Apr 04 DLC-10
--second division
To 1807 Jan 10 2-0450
To 1807 Apr 10 2-0486
Re 1807 Jun 01 DLC-4
To 1809 Feb 20 DLC-4
Re 1810 Jul 02 DLC-4
To 1812 Feb 03 2-1048
To 1812 Mar 07 add DLC-5
To 1812 Mar 07* add 2-1052
To 1812 Apr 24 2-1085
To 1812 Jun 05 DLC-8
To 1812 Jun 19 2-1108
To 1812 Jul 09 2-1128
To 1812 Sep 08 2-1243
Re 1814 Mar 14 DLC-9
To 1814 May 24 DLC-10
--second division officers
To 1806 Oct 04 2-0353
To 1807 Jan 05 DLC-4
To 1808 Apr 20 DLC-4
To 1808 Dec 19 2-0751
To 1808 Dec 19 DLC-4
Re 1809 Jan 16 2-0766
Fr 1809 Jan 16 DLC-4
To 1811 Nov 28 DLC-5
To 1812 Apr 24 2-1087
To 1813 Aug 20 3-0441
To 1814 Apr 25 DLC-10
Tennessee penitentiary
Fr 1834 Nov 14# fin DLC-51
Tennessee politics
Re 1836 Aug 20 add 31-1332
Tennessee volunteers
Re 1812 Jun 17 M221-42
To 1812 Jul 31 DLC-5
To 1812 Nov 14 add DLC-61
To 1812 Nov 24 DLC-61
To 1812 Nov 24* DLC-65
To 1812 Dec 12 DLC-61
To 1812 Dec 13 DLC-61
To 1812 Dec 18 DLC-5
To 1812 Dec 18* DLC-61
To 1812 Dec 18* 2-1302
Re 1812 Dec 19 2-1304
To 1812 Dec 27 DLC-5
To 1812 Dec 27* DLC-61
Re 1812 cDec 27 mem DLC-5
To 1812 Dec 31 add DLC-64
To 1812 Dec 31* add DLC-61
To 1813 Jan 06 DLC-5
To 1813 Jan 06* DLC-61
To 1813 Feb 16 DLC-61
To 1813 Mar 16 add DLC-6
To 1813 Mar 16* add DLC-61
To 1813 Mar 16* add 3-0330
To 1813 Mar 24 DLC-6
To 1813 Apr 03 3-0367
To 1813 Apr 24 3-0381
To 1813 Jul 20 add 3-0423
To 1813 Sep 14 add 3-0474
To 1813 Sep 24 DLC-61
To 1813 Sep 24* 3-0475
To 1813 Oct 07 add 3-0501
To 1813 Oct 07* add DLC-71
To 1813 Oct 07* add DLC-61
To 1813 Oct 08 DLC-61
To 1813 Oct 08* 3-0508
To 1813 Oct 24 add DLC-61
To 1813 Oct 24* add 3-0548
To 1813 Oct 24* add DLC-7
Re 1813 Nov mem DLC-58
Re 1813 Nov 13 3-0596
To 1813 Nov 13 DLC-61
To 1813 Nov 14 add DLC-6
To 1813 Nov 15 DLC-61
To 1813 Nov 15* 3-0607
To 1813 Dec 02 add DLC-7
To 1813 Dec 02* add DLC-61
To 1813 Dec 15 DLC-71
To 1814 Jan 02 DLC-8
To 1814 Jan 13 DLC-61
Re 1814 Jan 17 3-0792
To 1814 Apr 02 add DLC-10
To 1814 Apr 02* add 3-0952
Re 1814 Apr 05 DLC-10
To 1814 Apr 27 DLC-10
To 1814 Apr 28 add DLC-10
To 1814 Apr 28* add DLC-71
To 1814 May 10 add DLC-10
To 1818 Jan 31 add 5-1419
To 1818 Jun 26 add 6-1081
To 1818 Jun 26* add DLC-25

Tennessee volunteers (cont)
--cavalry brigade
To 1813 Sep 26 DLC-6
To 1813 Sep 26* DLC-61
To 1813 Nov 06 add DLC-61
To 1813 Nov 06* add 3-0576
To 1813 Nov 06* add DLC-7
To 1813 Nov 21 DLC-61
To 1813 Nov 21* DLC-7
--first brigade
To 1813 Dec 09 DLC-61
To 1813 Dec 09* 3-0654
To 1813 Dec 13 3-0662
To 1813 Dec 13* DLC-61
To 1813 Dec 13 add 3-0665
To 1813 Dec 13* add DLC-61
To 1813 Dec 13* DLC-8
--second brigade
To 1813 Dec 29 add DLC-61
To 1813 Dec 29* add 3-0740
To 1813 Dec 29 add DLC-61
To 1813 Dec 29* add 3-0741
Tennille William A et al
Fr 1840 Jun 05 34-1394
To 1840 Jun 22 34-1434
Tenny Jonathan Jr
Fr 1841 Jul 26 DLC-53
Terrass Henry
Fr 1816 Jul 31 fin DLC-69
Fr 1819 Apr 14 fin 7-0478
Fr 1819 Jun 08 fin DLC-27
Terrell George Whitfield
Fr 1837 Oct 16 M687-32
Fr 1842 Mar 10 DLC-54
Terrell George Whitfield et al
To 1836 Sep 06 31-1426
Terrell William
Fr 1795 Sep 16 DLC-71
Terrett William H
Re 1831 Dec 15 par 19-0311
Terrill James
Fr 1812 Sep 01 DLC-5
To 1813 Nov 14 3-0599
To 1813 Nov 14* DLC-61
Fr 1813 Nov 17 DLC-7
Fr 1831 Nov 28 M179-71
Fr 1831 Dec 08 M179-71
Terrill John D
To 1826 Jul 29 11-0331
Fr 1832 Dec 20 M234-136
Terry Garland B
Fr 1831 May 31 M234-222
Terry Nathaniel
Fr 1843 Sep 05 DLC-55
Fr 1844 Aug 16 DLC-57
Terry Nathaniel et al
Fr 1844 Jan 30 DLC-56
Test John
Fr 1829 Nov 14-0335
To 1829 Dec 24 14-1116
Fr 1831 Jan 28 17-0373
Test John Jr
Fr 1834 Dec 20 M639-6
Texas
Re 1836 cNov 32-0372
Re 1837 cJan 32-1468
Tharp William
Fr 1803 Sep 06 1-1153
Fr 1804 Nov 08 DLC-3
To 1829 Jul 02 13-0807
Fr 1829 Jul 26 13-0937
Thatcher Stephen
Re 1830 Mar mem 15-0272
Thayer Bezabel et al
Re 1836 Nov 09 par 32-0429
Thayer Jonathan et al
Fr 1837 Jan 27 M687-20
Thayer Joseph et al
Fr 1830 Feb 15 M639-21
Thayer Juliet
Fr 1844 Feb 23 DLC-56
Thayer Sylvanus
To 1819 Aug 06 7-0599
Fr 1822 Feb 04 DLC-70
To 1822 Mar 09 DLC-31
To 1823 Apr 14 9-0521
To 1823 May 26 9-0576
Fr 1823 Aug 04 DLC-32
To 1824 Jun 26 10-0815
To 1830 May 24 15-1079
To 1830 Jun 01 15-1253
To 1830 Jun 16 15-1482
Fr 1832 Mar 14# 19-1469
Fr 1832 Mar 18# 19-1501
To 1836 Feb 27# M221-116
Thibault Jean Pierre
Fr 1816 Apr 11# DLC-20
Thistle Hezekiah L
Fr 1836 cJul DLC-47
Tholen J A
Re 1832 Nov 05 par 21-0334
Thomas Benton A
Fr 1841 Apr 07 DLC-53
Thomas David
Fr 1829 Dec 17 M639-9
Fr 1831 Nov 06 M639-10
Thomas David B
Fr 1842 Jun 27 DLC-54
Thomas Francis
Re c1831 mem 17-0093
Thomas Francis et al
Fr 1835 Feb 14 M639-13
Fr 1836 Jan 14 30-0037
Thomas George
To 1833 Oct 04 leg 23-0960
To 1834 Dec 08 chk 26-1438
To 1835 Jan 07 chk DLC-44
To 1835 Jun 01 chk 28-0560
To 1835 Sep 14 chk DLC-46
To 1835 Oct 03 chk DLC-47
To 1835 Oct 22 chk DLC-47
Fr 1835 Oct 22 fin DLC-47
To 1836 May 25 DLC-48
To 1836 Jul 10 31-1037
To 1836 Oct 21 chk DLC-49
To 1836 Oct 28 chk DLC-49
To 1836 Nov 07 chk DLC-49
To 1837 Feb 18 chk DLC-50
Fr 1837 Mar 06 DLC-50
Re 1839 Sep# leg 34-0896
Thomas George Cummins Jr
Fr 1836 Jul 15 M567-132
Thomas Isaac
Re 1791 Apr 18 leg DLC-1
Fr 1791 Aug 17 leg 1-0119
To 1816 Jul 24 DLC-21
Fr 1816 Aug 12 DLC-21
Thomas Isaac Jetton
Fr 1831 Dec 07 19-0237
Thomas J M
To 1832 Nov 13 chk DLC-41

Fr 1833 Mar 27# fin DLC-42
Fr 1833 Aug 27# DLC-43
To 1833 Aug 27 chk DLC-43
Fr 1833 Dec 31 fin DLC-45
To 1834 Jan 03 chk DLC-43

Thomas James
Fr 1828 Dec 10 12-0312
Fr 1833 May 08 22-1324
Fr 1834 Jan 28 M222-32
Fr 1835 Aug 10 M567-114

Thomas Jesse Burgess
Fr 1831 Jun 05 M688-77

Thomas John (KY)
Fr 1814 Dec 08 DLC-14
Fr 1815 Feb 06 DLC-16
To 1815 Feb 07 DLC-16
Fr 1815 Feb 10 DLC-16
To 1815 Feb 10 DLC-16
To 1815 Mar 11 DLC-62
To 1815 Mar 11* DLC-17
Fr 1815 Apr 01 DLC-17

Thomas John (NY)
Fr 1829 May 29# M124-118

Thomas John (TN)
Fr 1805 May 01 fin 2-0035
To 1814 Feb 17 DLC-62

Thomas John Addison
Fr 1835 Mar 07 M22-36

Thomas Martin
Fr 1833 Mar 21 M567-85

Thomas Philemon
To 1814 Dec 22 DLC-62
To 1815 Jan 08 DLC-62
Fr 1815 Jan 09 DLC-15
Fr 1815 Jan 22 DLC-15
Fr 1815 Jan 26 DLC-15
Fr 1815 Feb 17 DLC-16
Fr 1815 Mar 22 DLC-17

Thomas Rowland M
Fr 1829 May 15 M639-2
Fr 1830 Aug 20 M639-2

Thomas Seth J
Fr 1836 Apr 25 30-1347

Thomas William
Fr 1844 Oct 08 DLC-57

Thomason Edward
To 1833 Mar 09 22-0730

Thompson A B
Fr 1836 Jan 01 M567-131

Thompson Benjamin
Re 1832 Aug 19 par 20-1359

Thompson Charles C B
To 1815 Feb 22 M179-31
To 1815 Feb 22* DLC-17

Thompson D L
Fr 1827 Jan 10 fin DLC-34

Thompson E
Fr 1821 Jun 15 fin DLC-70

Thompson George W
Fr 1815 May 16 DLC-18

Thompson Giles
Fr 1833 Dec 24 24-0583

Thompson Gillies
Re 1832 Jan 20 19-0803
Fr 1832 Oct 22 M124-135

Thompson Henry
To 1807 Jan 06 fin DLC-4
To 1807 Jan 31 fin DLC-4
To 1827 Sep 15 fin 11-0861
Re 1833 Feb 25 par 22-0472
Re 1836 Apr 27 par 30-1395

Thompson Henry A
Fr 1836 Feb 08# DLC-47

Thompson J L N
Fr 1842 Jun 26 DLC-54

Thompson James (DC)
Fr 1818 Aug 25 DLC-25
Fr 1818 Aug 25* 6-1268
To 1830 Jun 12 15-1366
To 1831 Jun 09 17-1573
Re 1832 Jun 12 20-0744
Re 1833 May 17 DLC-75
To 1835 Aug 17 28-1292
Re 1836 Aug 15 31-1299

Thompson James (PA)
Fr 1835 Jan 29 M639-4

Thompson James B
Re 1810 Apr 14 leg 2-0882

Thompson John
Fr 1817 Aug 01 DLC-23
Fr 1821 Feb 08 M208-9
Fr 1830 Jul 04 DLC-38
Re 1834 Apr 15 mem 25-0712

Thompson John et al
To 1835 Jul 02 28-0882

Thompson John W
Fr 1828 Oct 09 DLC-35

Thompson Jonah et al
Fr 1830 Jan 14 M639-10

Thompson Jonas
Fr 1831 Feb 20 M22-27

Thompson Jonathan
Fr 1812 Jul 03 DLC-71
Fr 1812 Sep 30 2-1253

Thompson Lewis G
Fr 1831 Jan 28 M234-354
Fr 1831 Jan 28 M234-354

Thompson Pishey
Fr 1829 Sep 02 fin DLC-37
To 1830 Jan 28 chk DLC-37
Fr 1837 Mar 06# fin DLC-50

Thompson Richard Wigginton
Fr 1830 Jan 14 DLC-72

Thompson Samuel
Fr 1805 Oct 04 fin DLC-3

Thompson Samuel H
Fr 1833 Jul 23 M639-24
Fr 1833 Oct 14 M639-24
Fr 1834 Nov 17 M639-24

Thompson Smith
To 1819 May 01 7-0503
To 1820 Jan 07 7-0983
To 1820 Aug 11 DLC-29
Fr 1821 Mar 11 DLC-30
To 1822 Jan 22 M124-92
To 1822 Sep 24 9-0271

Thompson Stephen
Fr 1836 Jul 25 M22-40

Thompson Waddy Jr
Fr 1842 Jun 22 35-0813
To 1843 Jul 12 35-1409
To 1843 Jul 12* DLC-55
Fr 1843 Sep 24 35-1510

Thompson Wiley
Fr 1831 Mar 01 17-0704
Fr 1831 Jul 18 M22-28
Fr 1832 Feb 01 19-0930
Fr 1834 Oct 28 M234-806

Name / Date	Note	Reference
Thompson Wiley (cont)		
Fr 1835 Jun 14		28-0682
Fr 1835 Jun 14*		M234-806
Thompson William et al		
Fr 1835 Jan 16		M639-9
Thompson William M		
Fr 1831 May 04		M22-28
Thompson & Homans		
Fr 1830 Nov 08	fin	DLC-39
Fr 1831		17-0094
To 1832 Jul 05	chk	DLC-41
To 1833 May 11	chk	DLC-43
Thomson Alexander		
Fr 1831 Jan 07		17-0211
Re 1831 Oct 20		18-1088
Thomson Henry		
To 1810 Aug 18	fin	DLC-4
Thomson John		
Fr 1829 Feb 11		M639-17
Fr 1830 Jan 11		DLC-37
Fr 1833 Sep 30		M639-14
Fr 1833 Oct 03		M639-24
Thomson William et al		
Fr 1829 Mar 09		M639-19
Fr 1835 Oct		M639-9
Thorndike Edward et al		
Fr 1836 May		30-1453
Fr 1836 Jun 08		31-0407
Thorndike Israel et al		
Fr 1830 cNov		16-0627
Fr 1832 Feb		M639-5
Thorndike P L		
Fr 1843 May 01		DLC-55
Thornton George W		
Fr 1824 Jun 26		DLC-32
Thornton James B		
Fr 1831 Mar 12#		DLC-39
To 1831 May 12		17-1356
Fr 1831 May 25		M639-21
To 1831 Sep 29		18-0901
Fr 1834 Dec 14		DLC-45
Fr 1834 Dec 14*		26-1501
Thornton John et al		
Fr 1830 Jun 08		15-1324
Thortan William		
Fr 1814 Oct 29		DLC-13
Throop Enos Thompson		
Fr 1832 Mar 22		19-1539
Fr 1834 Feb 12#		DLC-44
Fr 1834 Sep 26		DLC-44
Fr 1834 Nov 08		DLC-45
Throop George B et al		
Fr 1833 Feb 06		M639-8
Throop J V N		
To 1836 Nov 01	chk	DLC-49
Throop John		
To 1834 May 31	chk	DLC-44
Thruston Alfred		
Fr 1820		DLC-60
Thruston Algernon S		
To 1826 Mar 15		11-0167
Thumlert William		
Fr 1830 Jan 01	fin	DLC-37
Fr 1830 Apr 08#	fin	DLC-40
Fr 1832 May 05	fin	DLC-41
Fr 1832 Jul 20	fin	DLC-41
Fr 1834 Dec 13	fin	DLC-47
Fr 1835 Jan 11#	fin	DLC-45
Thurlow Carr		
Fr 1844 Dec 02		DLC-57
Thursby Edward		
Fr 1808 Feb 26	fin	DLC-4
Thurston C M		
Fr 1834 Dec 13#		26-1495
Thustin Luther T		
Fr 1844 Jul 09		DLC-57
Tibault Joseph		
Fr 1836 Jun 20		31-0532
Tibbits Elisha et al		
Fr 1831 Mar 01		M639-3
Tiefield Avery et al		
Fr 1836 Mar 04		30-0681
Tierce Charles		
Re 1831 Sep 13	par	18-0722
Tiernan M et al		
Fr 1833 May 14		M222-31
Tierney Richard		
Fr 1825 Mar 25	fin	DLC-72
Tifford H W		
Fr 1838 Jun 22		DLC-51
Tilford Jamie		
Fr 1839 Aug 06		DLC-52
Tilghman Edward		
Fr 1824 Jan 17		M439-17
Tillinghast John Charles		
Fr 1829 Dec 07		M639-24
Tilly B		
Fr 1838 Oct 12		DLC-51
Timberlake John Bowie		
Re 1829 Sep 02	mem	13-1233
Tinley Alexander		
Re 1834 May 13	par	25-1029
Tinley John		
Fr 1815 Jul 20		4-1125
Fr 1816 Apr 27		DLC-20
Tippatt Thomas J N et al		
Fr 1831 cJan 28		M639-1
Tipton Jacob		
Fr 1816 Nov 04		DLC-21
Tipton John (IN)		
Fr 1829 Feb 26		M639-15
Fr 1831 Dec 31		M234-354
Re 1832 Jun 12	mem	DLC-40
Fr 1832 Jul 05		M221-112
Fr 1834 Feb 20		24-1434
Re 1834 Apr 14		25-0706
Fr c1836 Mar 19		30-0845
Fr 1836 Aug		31-1178
Fr 1836 Sep 01		31-1397
Fr 1837 Jan 18		33-0014
Tipton John (IN) et al		
Fr 1832 Jun 16		20-0761
Tipton John (TN)		
To 1803 Oct 07		1-1193
Tipton John (TN) et al		
Fr 1803 Oct 05		DLC-3
Tishomingo		
Fr c1817		DLC-59
Fr 1817 Nov 08		DLC-23
Tissot ______		
Fr nd	fin	DLC-60
Titus James		
Fr 1816 Dec 05		DLC-22
Fr 1823 Sep 07		DLC-32
Titus Peter S et al		
Fr 1829 Mar		12-0706
Tochaler		
Fr 1817 Sep 30		M222-19
Todd John Pain		
To 1817 Jan 12		5-0694

Todd Samuel
Fr 1830 Aug 20 M639-2
Todd Stephen
Fr 1834 Jul 06 26-0172
Todd Thomas et al
Fr 1836 Apr 16 30-1217
Todd William B
Fr 1836 Jan 26# fin DLC-47
Tohopeka (battle)
Re 1814 Mar 27 3-0927
Toland Henry
To 1829 Dec 08 chk DLC-37
To 1830 May 05# fin DLC-38
To 1830 Jul 20 chk DLC-38
Fr 1830 Nov 27 M639-12
To 1832 Mar 13 chk DLC-40
Fr 1832 Mar 16 19-1496
Fr 1832 Apr 08 DLC-40
To 1832 Apr 10 20-0181
Fr 1832 Apr 16 DLC-40
Fr 1832 Apr 16 fin 20-0250
To 1832 Apr 18 chk DLC-40
Fr 1832 Jul 16 DLC-41
To 1832 Jul 18 chk DLC-41
To 1832 Sep 12 20-1514
To 1832 Nov 03 21-0303
Fr 1832 Nov 05 fin DLC-41
To 1832 Nov 08# fin DLC-41
Fr 1832 Nov 12 21-0394
To 1832 Dec 03 chk DLC-41
Fr 1833 Mar 02 DLC-42
To 1833 Mar 17 DLC-42
Fr 1833 Mar 20 22-0839
Fr 1833 Apr 02 M639-20
To 1833 May 02 22-1265
Fr 1833 May 09 DLC-42
Fr 1833 May 16 DLC-43
To 1833 May 17 22-1388
Fr 1833 Jun 28# 23-0066
To 1833 Jul 13# fin DLC-43
Fr 1833 Aug 22 M639-27
Fr 1833 Aug 24 M639-18
Fr 1833 Sep 02 M639-20
To 1833 Sep 13# fin DLC-43
Fr 1833 Oct 09# 23-1000
Fr 1833 Oct 10 DLC-43
To 1833 Oct 14 23-1035
Fr 1833 Oct 25 fin DLC-44
Fr 1833 Oct 31 M639-19
Fr 1834 Jan 06# DLC-44
Fr 1834 Jan 11# DLC-44
Fr 1834 Mar 04 M639-3
Fr 1834 Mar 17 M639-3
Fr 1834 May 31 M639-2
To 1834 Sep 26 chk DLC-44
Fr 1834 Sep 26 fin DLC-45
Fr 1834 Oct 08 DLC-44
Fr 1835 Jan 03 M639-2
Fr 1835 May 29 28-0527
Fr 1835 Jul 10 DLC-46
To 1835 Jul 22 28-1120
To 1835 Jul 22 chk 28-1118
To 1835 Sep 09 DLC-75
Fr 1835 Sep 11 fin 29-0035
Fr 1835 Oct 27 DLC-47
To 1835 Oct 29 chk DLC-47
To 1835 Nov 12# fin DLC-47
Fr 1835 Nov 12 fin DLC-47
Fr 1835 Dec 14 DLC-47
To 1836 Jan 09 29-1534
Fr 1836 Jan 09 DLC-47
To 1836 Jan 09 chk DLC-47
Fr 1836 Jan 14 DLC-47
Fr 1836 Jan 27 M639-3
To 1836 Feb 20 chk DLC-47
Fr 1836 Apr 02 M639-3
Fr 1836 Jun 17 M124-153
Fr 1836 Oct 03 M639-19
Fr 1836 Oct 08 fin 32-0120
To 1836 Oct 14 chk DLC-49
Fr 1836 Nov 01 DLC-49
To 1836 Nov 20 32-0573
To 1836 Nov 29 32-0591
To 1836 Nov 29 chk DLC-49
To 1837 Feb 04 33-0404
Fr 1837 Feb 09 fin DLC-50
Fr 1837 Feb 09# DLC-50
To 1837 Feb 13 chk DLC-50
Re 1837 cFeb 13 fin 33-0683
Fr 1837 Apr 30 fin DLC-50
To 1837 Jun 08 33-1288
Fr 1837 Jun 20 DLC-50
Fr 1837 Oct 04 33-1510
Fr 1838 Mar 27 DLC-51
Toland Henry et al
Fr 1829 cJun M639-25
Fr 1830 Nov 13 M639-5
Fr 1833 May 30 22-1531
Fr 1834 Jan 13 M639-7
Toland Henry Jr
Fr 1835 Nov 14# DLC-47
Toland Nathaniel
Fr 1805 Dec 13 fin 2-0100
Toland & Magoffin
Fr 1832 Sep 26 fin DLC-41
Fr 1834 Oct 17 fin DLC-44
Toledo Jose Alvarez de
Fr 1815 Feb 09 DLC-16
Toler Hopeful
Fr 1844 Dec 12 36-1181
Tolls Reuben M
To 1842 Apr 23 35-0686
Tomlin Allan
Fr 1844 Jan 12 DLC-56
Tommy Micco
Re 1834 Nov 01 26-0801
Tompkins Daniel D
Fr 1815 Apr 21 DLC-18
To 1815 Nov 18 DLC-19
To 1815 Nov 18* DLC-62
To 1820 cJan DLC-59
To 1820 Apr DLC-59
Fr 1821 Mar 15 DLC-30
Fr 1821 May 18 DLC-30
Tompkins William
Re 1832 Feb 19-0928
Toomer John D et al
Fr 1830 Dec 13 16-1420
To 1831 Jan 15 17-0265
Topp John S et al
Fr 1830 Feb 27 M639-1
Torrence Hugh
To 1803 Apr 17# DLC-2
Totten Joseph Gilbert
Fr 1844 Feb 19 36-0304
Touard Francisco
Fr 1814 Sep 07 fin DLC-12

Toulmin Harry		
Fr 1814 Jun 22		DLC-11
Fr 1814 Jul 09		DLC-75
To 1814 Jul 18		DLC-62
Fr 1814 Jul 21		DLC-11
Fr 1814 cAug		DLC-75
Fr 1814 Sep 01		DLC-12
Fr 1814 Sep 06		DLC-12
Fr 1814 Sep 20		DLC-12
To 1814 Oct 27		DLC-62
Fr 1815 Jul 03		DLC-18
Fr 1818 Nov 16		DLC-25
Tousard Louis de		
Fr 1815 Jan 18		DLC-15
Fr 1815 Jan 18		DLC-15
To 1815 Mar 04		DLC-17
Fr 1815 Mar 06		DLC-17
To 1815 Mar 06		DLC-17
To 1815 Mar 06		DLC-62
Tower James M		
Fr 1842 Feb 21		DLC-54
Townsend Mary Ann		
Fr 1830 Feb 07		M567-56
Townsend Peter S		
Fr 1829 Mar 11		M639-24
Fr 1829 May 22		M639-24
Towson Nathan		
Fr 1820 May 01#		DLC-70
Re c1829	mem	37-0285
Fr 1829 Oct 14		14-0159
To 1836 Oct 25#		M567-125
Trabue West & Co		
To 1839 May 28#	fin	DLC-54
Fr 1839 Sep 06#	fin	DLC-52
Fr 1842 Jan 06		DLC-54
To 1842 Jan 11	chk	DLC-54
Fr 1842 Feb 10#	fin	DLC-54
Tracy George D		
Fr 1823 Jan 11	fin	9-0401
Tracy Henry D		
Fr 1832 Jan 19		M179-72
Fr 1832 Jan 19*		19-0790
Tracy Horatio N et al		
Fr 1835 Jun		28-0546
Tracy John et al		
Fr 1833 Dec 26		M639-7
Trafton Jacob		
Fr 1837 Feb 08		33-0569
Trafton William		
Fr 1837 Feb 08		33-0569
Fr 1837 Feb 13		M687-16
Travers John		
Fr 1829 Apr 06		M873-19
Fr 1835 Mar 09		M124-147
Treadwell Jacob C		
Fr 1829 May 09		13-0273
Treasury department		
Re 1830 cMar	mem	15-0273
Treat James		
Fr 1833 Apr 01		M179-76
Treat Samuel		
Fr 1834 Feb 22		24-1453
Fr 1844 Mar 18		DLC-56
Tremper Lawrence		
Fr 1829 May 20		M639-18
Trevitt William		
Fr 1843 Jan 06		35-1098
Trigg William & Will		
Fr 1799 Apr 15	fin	1-0701

Trigg William Jr		
Fr 1799 May 02	fin	1-0713
Fr 1819 Apr 27		DLC-26
Trimble William Allen		
Fr 1817 Jun 04		DLC-22
Fr 1817 Jun 11		DLC-22
Fr 1818 Jan 15		DLC-23
Fr 1818 Feb 04		DLC-24
Fr 1818 Feb 12		DLC-24
Fr 1818 Feb 16		DLC-24
Fr 1818 Mar 24		DLC-24
Trimble William L		
Fr 1834 Aug 25		DLC-44
Fr 1836 Mar 18		30-0818
Triplett Robert		
Fr 1824 Feb 18		M688-28
Triplett Thomas		
Re 1836 Mar 24	par	30-0890
Triplett William		
Fr 1818 Nov 22		DLC-26
Trist Hore Browse		
Re 1831 Jun 15		18-0030
Trist Nicholas Philip		
Fr c1829		37-0286
To 1829 Dec 14		14-1031
Fr 1830 Jan 12#		M639-3
Fr 1830 Apr 12		15-0682
To 1831 Feb 10#		M179-70
To 1831 Mar 29		17-1005
To 1831 Apr 12		17-1148
To 1831 May 19		17-1401
Fr 1831 Jul 07#		DLC-39
To 1831 Aug 12		18-0515
To 1831 Aug 31		18-0633
To 1831 Sep 15		18-0795
To 1831 Oct 21		18-1093
Fr 1831 Nov 16		M639-19
To 1832 Jan 03	chk	DLC-40
To 1832 Nov 13		21-0398
Fr 1832 Dec 04		21-0861
To 1832 Dec 15	chk	DLC-41
To 1833 Mar 20		22-0842
Fr 1833 Mar 20		22-0843
Re 1833 Apr 24		22-1166
To 1833 May 27		22-1465
Fr 1833 Dec 22		DLC-43
Re 1834 Feb 08		24-1260
Fr 1834 Oct 14#		26-0643
Fr 1834 Dec 27#		T20-6
Fr 1835 Jan 04		27-0082
Fr 1835 May 15		28-0434
Fr 1835 May 15		28-0438
Fr 1835 May 18		28-0479
To 1835 Nov 17		29-0521
To 1835 Dec 16		29-1191
Fr 1835 Dec 18		DLC-73
Fr 1836 Apr 23		M639-10
Fr 1836 Oct 06#		32-0093
To 1836 Oct 27		32-0356
To 1837 Jan 23		33-0122
To 1837 Mar 02		33-1000
To 1838 Feb 06		34-0234
To 1838 Sep 19		34-0466
Fr 1839 Apr 03		34-0713
Fr 1840 Jun 15		DLC-52
To 1840 Oct 05		35-0041
Fr 1842 Dec 01		DLC-54
Fr 1842 Dec 01*		35-1017
To 1843 May 08		35-1348

To 1844 Sep 09 36-0858
Fr 1844 Nov 28 36-1063
Fr 1844 Nov 30 36-1089
Trist Virginia Jefferson (Randolph)
To 1838 Jan 15 34-0192
Trotter Thomas L
Fr 1818 Feb 11 DLC-24
Troup George Michael
Fr 1829 Dec 17 14-1059
Fr 1830 Apr 15-0553
Fr 1830 Apr 27 M222-28
Fr 1830 May 12 M124-124
Fr 1831 Mar 03 M124-127
Fr 1831 Dec 26 M234-236
Fr 1832 Mar 17 19-1500
Trousdale John
Fr 1804 Jun 19 lnd 1-1340
Trousdale Robert
Re 1806 Nov leg 2-0367
Trousdale William
Fr 1837 Jun 04 DLC-50
To 1837 Jun 05 33-1276
Trout Henry et al
Fr 1835 cJan DLC-59
Trowbridge Charles C et al
Fr 1835 Mar 07 27-1048
Trudeau _____ (Maj)
To 1836 May 06 30-1527
Trudeau Rene
To 1814 Dec 17 DLC-62
To 1814 Dec 20 DLC-62
Fr 1815 Jan 02 DLC-15
True John
Fr 1804 Feb 22 fin DLC-3
True Jackson Man (pseudonym)
Fr 1831 Jul 30 M124-129
Trufant Betsy
Fr 1834 Jan 27 M567-102
Truman Joseph et al
Fr 1835 Jul 04 28-0936
Truxton (horse)
Re 1805 mem DLC-71
Re 1805 May 11 mem DLC-3
Re 1805 May 25 mem 2-0056
Re 1806 Mar 01 2-0185
Re 1806 Apr 08 2-0210
Re 1807 Mar 12 2-0474
Re 1808 Mar 06 2-0618
Re 1809 Feb 23 2-0777
Re 1814 Mar 09 mem DLC-9
Re 1814 Mar 30 fin DLC-9
Tuchebahu et al
Fr 1830 Apr 20 M234-222
Tuckabachee Hadjo
Fr 1831 Feb 18 M234-222
Tucker Enoch
To 1834 Oct 21 chk DLC-44
Fr 1835 Jan 21# fin DLC-47
Fr 1835 Apr 28 fin DLC-46
To 1835 May 27 chk DLC-46
Fr 1835 Oct 29 fin DLC-47
Fr 1836 Oct 03 fin DLC-49
To 1836 Oct 27 chk DLC-49
Fr 1836 Dec 07 fin DLC-49
To 1836 Dec 31 chk DLC-49
Fr 1837 Feb 27 fin DLC-50
To 1837 Mar 03 chk DLC-50
Tucker Enoch & Co
To 1836 Jan 04 chk DLC-47
Tucker Henry C
Fr 1831 Apr 23 M22-28
Tucker Henry St George
Fr 1832 Mar 24 DLC-40
Tucker Lemuel
Fr 1822 May 22 DLC-20
Fr 1834 Sep 15 T690-1
Tucker Nathaniel Beverley
Fr 1833 Mar 01 22-0587
Tucker Thomas Tudor
To 1815 Jul 02 DLC-62
To 1816 Jul 12 fin DLC-21
Fr 1817 Aug 19 DLC-23
Tucker & Thompson
Fr 1824 Dec 07 fin DLC-33
Fr 1829 Feb 12 fin DLC-72
Fr 1829 May 22# fin DLC-37
Fr 1829 May 25 fin DLC-37
Fr 1829 May 25 fin DLC-37
Fr 1829 Jul 30 fin DLC-72
Fr 1829 Nov 05 fin 14-0418
Fr 1829 Nov 13 fin DLC-37
Fr 1830 Jan 11 fin DLC-72
Fr 1830 Jan 11# fin 14-1382
Fr 1830 Jan 15 fin DLC-37
Fr 1830 Jun 08 fin DLC-73
Fr 1831 Jan 15 fin DLC-39
Fr 1831 Feb 02# fin DLC-39
Fr 1831 Feb 02# fin DLC-40
Fr 1831 Aug 16 fin DLC-40
To 1831 Dec 22 chk 19-0401
Fr 1832 Jan 23# fin DLC-43
Fr 1832 Mar 22# fin DLC-40
To 1832 Jun 26 chk DLC-41
Fr 1832 Jul 18 fin DLC-41
Fr 1832 Oct 20 fin DLC-41
Fr 1833 Feb 28 fin DLC-42
To 1833 May 16 chk DLC-43
Fr 1833 Jul 11 fin DLC-43
To 1833 Dec 06 chk DLC-43
Tuckerman William Shaw
Fr 1838 Feb 09 DLC-51
Tuel Peter
Re 1833 Jul 17 par 23-0150
Tunstall George
To 1818 Oct 19 6-1376
Fr 1821 Aug 24 fin DLC-70
Tunstall Richard C
Fr 1828 Mar 12 DLC-35
Tunstall Thomas B
Fr 1829 Jul 07 M639-4
Turk A R
Fr 1836 Jun 13 31-0460
Fr 1836 Jun 13* M234-76
Turkey treaty
Re 1830 mem DLC-38
Re 1831 Feb 02 17-0414
Re 1832 Feb 04 19-0957
Turnbull Alexander
Fr 1832 Oct 18 22-0764
Turner Abel
Re 1833 Sep 20 par 23-0804
Turner Anthony J
Fr 1813 Dec 24 DLC-61
Fr 1814 Jan 02 DLC-8
To 1814 Jan 05 DLC-61
Turner Daniel
Re 1829 Apr 15 M179-67
Re 1829 Apr 15* DLC-60

Turner Daniel (cont)
Re 1829 cMay 18 mem 13-0349
Fr 1830 Apr 15-0555
Re 1830 Apr 17 M273-23
Turner Daniel B
Fr 1838 Feb 01 DLC-51
Fr 1844 Feb 07 DLC-56
Turner James H
Fr 1838 Jan 01 DLC-50
Turner James P
To 1829 May 04 DLC-60
Fr 1830 Apr 06# 15-0625
Turner Joshua
Fr 1837 Mar 02 DLC-50
Turner Mary C
Fr 1832 Feb 08 M688-56
Turner R B
Fr 1836 Sep 05 M688-104
Turner William
Fr 1831 Oct 31 M234-728
Turney Hopkins Lacy et al
Fr 1830 Feb 10 M639-1
To 1839 Sep 14 34-0940
Turpin White
Fr 1813 Mar 22 3-0353
Tuscany Grand Dukedom
Re 1836 Sep 01 31-1400
Tuskenahan
Fr 1831 May 21 M234-222
Tuskenahan et al
Fr 1829 Mar 20 M234-222
Fr 1829 Oct 12 M234-222
Fr 1829 Nov 20 M234-222
Fr 1829 Dec 10 M234-222
Fr 1830 Apr 25 M234-222
Tustanucke Ninnehomala
Fr 1821 Nov 23 M221-93
Fr 1821 Nov 23* M221-96
Tuston Ferdinand
Fr 1836 cJun 30 fin 31-0675
Tustunnugee Opou
Fr 1818 Feb 26 DLC-24
Fr 1818 Mar 19 DLC-24
Tustunnugee Thlucco
Re 1814 Aug 10 3-1299
Tutt Ann M
Fr 1830 Oct 27 M124-125
Tutt Charles Pendleton
Fr 1823 Jun 24 DLC-32
Fr 1824 Jun 12 DLC-32
To 1825 Jan 08 DLC-33
Fr 1825 Jan 09 DLC-33
Fr 1825 Jun 01 DLC-33
To 1825 Jul DLC-33
Fr 1826 Apr 02 DLC-33
Fr 1827 Jun 06 DLC-34
To 1827 Jun 30 DLC-34
Fr 1828 Jan 04 DLC-35
To 1829 DLC-37
Fr 1829 Mar 03 12-0836
Fr 1829 Mar 08 M639-24
Fr 1829 Aug 15 13-1140
Fr 1829 Dec 14 DLC-37
Fr 1830 Jun 29 M639-27
Fr 1831 May 30 M124-128
Fr 1832 Feb 10 M124-131
Tuttle Stephen
Fr 1834 Aug 13 26-0305
Re 1834 Oct 13 26-0634
Re 1834 Nov 08 26-0859

Twiggs David Emanuel
Fr 1818 May 03 DLC-24
Fr 1818 May 03* 6-0580
Fr 1821 Feb 15 DLC-29
Fr 1836 Aug 11 31-1285
Fr 1844 Nov 30 36-1098
Twitty Allen
Re 1836 Apr 04 par 30-0988
Two Sicilies Kingdom
Re 1831 Sep 08 mem 18-0704
Re 1831 cSep 10 mem 18-0716
Re 1835 Dec 26 29-1342
Two Sicilies treaty
Re 1833 Jan 19 21-1574
Re 1833 Aug 27 23-0463
Twopence David
Fr 1829 Aug 24 DLC-37
Tyack William
Fr 1836 May 08 DLC-48
Fr 1844 Jan 08 DLC-56
Fr 1845 Feb 03 DLC-57
Tybout Andrew
Fr 1797 Dec 13 fin DLC-2
Tyler Benjamin Owen
Fr 1824 Feb 22 DLC-32
Fr 1833 Sep 05 23-0657
Tyler Charles
Fr 1835 Mar 17# 27-1227
Tyler George
Re 1832 Jan 18 par 19-0765
Tyler Henry B
Fr 1834 Nov 19 M625-78
Tyler John
Fr 1829 Mar 11 M639-8
Fr 1832 Jun 15 M22-29
To 1835 Dec 17 29-1211
To 1842 Sep 09 35-0937
Fr 1842 Sep 20 DLC-54
Re 1842 Dec 20 mem 35-1051
To 1843 Jan 31 DLC-55
To 1843 Oct 03 35-1525
To 1843 Oct 12 35-1535
To 1843 Dec 26 M873-64
Fr 1844 Feb 16 DLC-56
To 1844 Feb 27 36-0352
Fr 1844 Apr 18 DLC-56
Fr 1844 Aug 18 DLC-57
Fr 1844 Sep 17 DLC-57
Tyler John et al
Fr 1832 Jul 02 M688-83
Tyler William
Fr 1826 May 06 DLC-33
Fr 1829 Nov 27 DLC-37
Tyler William et al
Fr 1830 Jun 18 15-1514
To 1830 Jun 18 15-1516
Tyndale Robinson
Fr 1835 Sep 01# fin DLC-46
Fr 1836 Nov 09# fin 32-0474
Tyrrill John et al
Fr 1834 Jan 24 24-1051

Underwood Abner
To 1820 Feb 26 DLC-28
Underwood Thomas
Fr 1829 Jun 09 13-0609
Fr 1829 Oct 18 14-0190
Re 1833 Jan 09 par 21-1381
Re 1833 Feb 12 par 22-0338

U S Congress--message (cont)

To 1836 May 10 30-1589
To 1836 Jun 30 31-0677
To 1836 Jun 30* DLC-77
To 1836 Jun 30 31-0682
To 1836 Dec 06 32-1032
To 1836 Dec 06* DLC-49
To 1836 Dec 20 32-1212
To 1836 Dec 21 32-1227
To 1836 Dec 21* DLC-49
To 1836 Dec 26 32-1330
To 1837 Jan 19 33-0047
To 1837 Feb 06 33-0455
To 1837 Feb 09 33-0584
To 1837 Mar 04 DLC-64

--report

To 1830 Feb 08 15-0113
To 1830 Apr 23 15-0778
To 1830 May 14 15-1010
To 1831 Jan 12 17-0248
To 1831 Feb 19 17-0591
To 1831 Dec 21 19-0392
To 1832 Jan 16 19-0722
To 1832 Apr 23 20-0371
To 1833 Jan 19 21-1577
To 1833 Jan 19 22-0001
To 1833 Feb 07 22-0318
To 1834 Jan 15 24-0893
To 1835 Jan 12 27-0199
To 1835 Feb 25 27-0614
To 1835 Dec 08 29-1034
To 1835 Dec 09 29-1057
To 1835 Dec 09* M200-6
To 1835 Dec 09 29-1064
To 1835 Dec 09* M200-6
To 1835 Dec 17 29-1199
To 1835 Dec 17* M37-12
To 1835 Dec 22 29-1308
To 1836 Jan 11 29-1552
To 1836 Feb 23 30-0490
To 1836 Dec 06 32-1038
To 1836 Dec 30 32-1414
To 1837 Jan 17 32-1598
To 1837 Jan 17 33-0001
To 1837 Jan 20 33-0067
To 1837 Jan 27 33-0190

--unsent message

To 1832 cJun 28 DLC-73
To 1832 cJun 28* 20-0831
To 1834 Jun 25-1209

United States government bureau heads

Re c1832 mem 37-0301

United States House of Representatives

Re 1797 Jan 17 DLC-1
Re 1797 Jan 17 DLC-1
To 1818 Jan 27 5-1350
Fr 1819 Dec 14 7-0918
Fr 1820 May 11# DLC-29

--message

To 1829 Dec 15 DLC-37
To 1830 Jan 05 14-1337
To 1830 Feb 12 15-0141
To 1830 Mar 09 15-0319
To 1830 Mar 09 15-0321
To 1830 Mar 31 15-0537
To 1830 May 13 15-1000
To 1830 May 27 15-1166
To 1830 May 29 15-1209
To 1831 Jan 07 17-0213
To 1831 Jan 15 17-0266
To 1831 Jan 25 17-0360
To 1831 Feb 15 17-0535
To 1831 Feb 28 17-0675
To 1831 Dec 29 19-0450
To 1832 Jan 23 19-0819
To 1832 Mar 01 19-1293
To 1832 Apr 02 20-0096
To 1832 Jul 12 20-1053
To 1832 Dec 28 21-1198
To 1833 Jan 03 21-1315
To 1833 Jan 23 22-0037
To 1833 Jan 24 22-0059
To 1833 Jan 29 22-0109
To 1833 Feb 22 22-0448
To 1833 Dec 06 24-0411
To 1833 Dec 11 24-0456
To 1833 Dec 23 24-0578
To 1834 Jan 25 24-1062
To 1834 May 01 25-0954
To 1834 May 19 25-1094
To 1834 May 21 25-1107
To 1834 Jun 20 25-1445
To 1834 Dec 12 26-1485
To 1836 Feb 10 30-0355
To 1836 Jun 30 31-0685
To 1836 Jun 30* 31-0253
To 1837 Jan 07 32-1529
To 1837 Jan 30 33-0266
To 1837 Feb 11 33-0638
To 1837 Feb 14 33-0701
To 1837 Feb 24 33-0874

--report

To 1829 Dec 15 14-1051
To 1829 Dec 15* DLC-37
To 1829 Dec 30 14-1161
To 1829 Dec 30* DLC-37
To 1830 Feb 18 15-0192
To 1830 Mar 15 15-0368
To 1830 Mar 18 15-0395
To 1830 Apr 02 15-0571
To 1830 Apr 13 15-0692
To 1830 Apr 22 15-0770
To 1830 May 13 15-1002
To 1830 May 25 15-1089
To 1831 Jan 05 17-0206
To 1831 Jan 25 17-0362
To 1831 Feb 03 17-0426
To 1832 Jan 24 19-0841
To 1832 Jan 26 19-0879
To 1832 Jan 31 19-0920
To 1832 Feb 06 19-0981
To 1832 Feb 10 19-1056
To 1832 Mar 12 19-1406
To 1832 Mar 12 19-1408
To 1832 Mar 16 19-1497
To 1832 May 02 20-0462
To 1832 May 29 20-0671
To 1832 May 29 20-0673
To 1832 Jul 14 20-1091
To 1833 Jan 02 21-1300
To 1833 Jan 07 21-1363
To 1833 Jan 10 21-1398
To 1833 Jan 17 21-1566
To 1833 Jan 25 22-0073
To 1833 Dec 06 24-0409
To 1834 Jan 07 24-0792
To 1834 Jan 28 24-1093
To 1834 Feb 12 24-1299
To 1834 Feb 12 24-1301

To 1830 Mar 19	15-0402
To 1830 Mar 24	15-0448
To 1830 Mar 25	15-0461
To 1830 Mar 27	15-0478
To 1830 Mar 29	15-0529
To 1830 Mar 29	15-0531
To 1830 Mar 30	15-0535
To 1830 Mar 31	15-0540
To 1830 Mar 31	15-0542
To 1830 Mar 31	15-0544
To 1830 Mar 31	15-0546
To 1830 Mar 31	15-0548
To 1830 Apr 05	15-0584
To 1830 Apr 05	15-0586
To 1830 Apr 08	15-0645
To 1830 Apr 09	15-0654
To 1830 Apr 09*	M472-1
To 1830 Apr 10	15-0669
To 1830 Apr 12	15-0683
To 1830 Apr 14	15-0707
To 1830 Apr 21	15-0765
To 1830 Apr 22	15-0772
To 1830 Apr 22	15-0774
To 1830 Apr 24	15-0806
To 1830 Apr 24	15-0808
To 1830 Apr 27	15-0828
To 1830 May 01	15-0874
To 1830 May 04	15-0912
To 1830 May 05	15-0924
To 1830 May 06	15-0933
To 1830 May 06	15-0935
To 1830 May 06	15-0937
To 1830 May 07	15-0945
To 1830 May 07	15-0947
To 1830 May 12	15-0987
To 1830 May 13	15-1004
To 1830 May 13	15-1006
To 1830 May 15	15-1034
To 1830 May 20	15-1061
To 1830 May 21	15-1067
To 1830 May 22	15-1072
To 1830 May 24	15-1080
To 1830 May 25	15-1091
To 1830 May 25	15-1093
To 1830 May 26	15-1105
To 1830 May 26*	M472-1
To 1830 May 28	15-1193
To 1830 May 28	15-1195
To 1830 May 28	15-1197
To 1830 May 29	15-1212
To 1830 May 29	15-1214
To 1830 May 29	15-1216
To 1830 May 29	15-1218
To 1830 May 29*	M472-1
To 1830 May 29	15-1220
To 1830 May 29	15-1222
To 1830 May 29	15-1224
To 1830 May 30	15-1230
To 1830 Dec 09	16-1363
To 1830 Dec 11	16-1408
To 1830 Dec 14	16-1435
To 1830 Dec 14	16-1438
To 1830 Dec 15	16-1450
To 1830 Dec 15	16-1452
To 1830 Dec 15	16-1454
To 1830 Dec 17	16-1481
To 1830 Dec 17	16-1483
To 1830 Dec 18	16-1490
To 1830 Dec 18	16-1492
To 1830 Dec 20	16-1517
To 1830 Dec 23	16-1552
To 1830 Dec 23	16-1554
To 1830 Dec 27	17-0018
To 1830 Dec 28	17-0032
To 1830 Dec 28	17-0034
To 1830 Dec 29	17-0040
To 1830 Dec 30	17-0044
To 1830 Dec 31	17-0057
To 1830 Dec 31	17-0059
To 1830 Dec 31	17-0061
To 1830 Dec 31*	M472-1
To 1831 Jan 05	17-0208
To 1831 Jan 07	17-0215
To 1831 Jan 15	17-0268
To 1831 Jan 18	17-0284
To 1831 Jan 18	17-0286
To 1831 Jan 25	17-0364
To 1831 Jan 25*	M472-1
To 1831 Jan 31	17-0389
To 1831 Feb 01	17-0402
To 1831 Feb 01	17-0404
To 1831 Feb 04	17-0440
To 1831 Feb 04	17-0442
To 1831 Feb 07	17-0455
To 1831 Feb 07*	M472-1
To 1831 Feb 07	17-0458
To 1831 Feb 07	17-0460
To 1831 Feb 07	17-0462
To 1831 Feb 07*	M472-1
To 1831 Feb 08	17-0478
To 1831 Feb 08	17-0480
To 1831 Feb 09	17-0483
To 1831 Feb 10	17-0495
To 1831 Feb 10	17-0497
To 1831 Feb 11	17-0503
To 1831 Feb 14	17-0517
To 1831 Feb 16	17-0550
To 1831 Feb 16	17-0551
To 1831 Feb 17	17-0574
To 1831 Feb 18	17-0583
To 1831 Feb 18	17-0585
To 1831 Feb 19	17-0594
To 1831 Feb 21	17-0603
To 1831 Feb 22	17-0623
To 1831 Feb 22	17-0625
To 1831 Feb 22	17-0627
To 1831 Feb 22	17-0629
To 1831 Feb 22	17-0631
To 1831 Feb 22	17-0633
To 1831 Feb 23	17-0639
To 1831 Feb 23	17-0641
To 1831 Feb 23	17-0643
To 1831 Feb 24	17-0651
To 1831 Feb 28	17-0677
To 1831 Feb 28	17-0679
To 1831 Feb 28	17-0681
To 1831 Mar 01	17-0711
To 1831 Mar 01	17-0713
To 1831 Mar 01*	M472-1
To 1831 Mar 02	17-0762
To 1831 Mar 02	17-0764
To 1831 Mar 02	17-0766
To 1831 Mar 02	17-0768
To 1831 Mar 02	17-0770
To 1831 Mar 02	17-0772
To 1831 Mar 02	17-0774
To 1831 Mar 02	17-0776
To 1831 Mar 02	17-0778

U S Senate--nomination (cont)

To 1832 Jul 14	20-1104
To 1832 Jul 14	20-1106
To 1832 Dec 05	21-0874
To 1832 Dec 05*	M472-2
To 1832 Dec 06	21-0919
To 1832 Dec 06	21-0921
To 1832 Dec 06	21-0923
To 1832 Dec 10	21-0984
To 1832 Dec 11	21-0994
To 1832 Dec 11	21-0996
To 1832 Dec 11	21-1000
To 1832 Dec 17	21-1083
To 1832 Dec 19	21-1094
To 1832 Dec 19	21-1096
To 1832 Dec 20	21-1102
To 1832 Dec 24	21-1158
To 1832 Dec 28	21-1201
To 1832 Dec 31	21-1215
To 1832 Dec 31	21-1217
To 1832 Dec 31	21-1220
To 1832 Dec 31	21-1222
To 1832 Dec 31	21-1224
To 1833 Jan 02	21-1302
To 1833 Jan 02	21-1304
To 1833 Jan 05	21-1332
To 1833 Jan 07	21-1367
To 1833 Jan 08	21-1378
To 1833 Jan 10	21-1400
To 1833 Jan 10	21-1402
To 1833 Jan 11	21-1404
To 1833 Jan 18	21-1571
To 1833 Jan 21	22-0017
To 1833 Jan 22	22-0024
To 1833 Jan 24	22-0064
To 1833 Jan 26	22-0083
To 1833 Jan 28	22-0089
To 1833 Jan 30	22-0118
To 1833 Jan 31	22-0222
To 1833 Jan 31	22-0226
To 1833 Feb 01	22-0233
To 1833 Feb 01	22-0235
To 1833 Feb 01	22-0237
To 1833 Feb 02	22-0252
To 1833 Feb 02	22-0254
To 1833 Feb 06	22-0290
To 1833 Feb 06*	M472-2
To 1833 Feb 06	22-0292
To 1833 Feb 07	22-0322
To 1833 Feb 09	22-0327
To 1833 Feb 12	22-0354
To 1833 Feb 12	22-0356
To 1833 Feb 12*	M472-2
To 1833 Feb 12	22-0358
To 1833 Feb 13	22-0370
To 1833 Feb 13	22-0372
To 1833 Feb 19	22-0422
To 1833 Feb 19	22-0424
To 1833 Feb 25	22-0478
To 1833 Feb 25*	M472-2
To 1833 Feb 26	22-0524
To 1833 Feb 28	22-0553
To 1833 Feb 28	22-0555
To 1833 Feb 28	22-0557
To 1833 Feb 28	22-0559
To 1833 Feb 28	22-0561
To 1833 Mar 02	22-0631
To 1833 Mar 02	22-0633
To 1833 Mar 02*	M472-2
To 1833 Mar 02	22-0635
To 1833 Mar 02	22-0637
To 1833 Mar 02	22-0647
To 1833 Mar 02	22-0649
To 1833 Mar 02	22-0651
To 1833 Mar 02	22-0653
To 1833 Mar 02	22-0655
To 1833 Mar 02	22-0658
To 1833 Mar 02	22-0660
To 1833 Dec 05	24-0405
To 1833 Dec 09	24-0425
To 1833 Dec 09*	M472-2
To 1833 Dec 09	24-0428
To 1833 Dec 10	24-0446
To 1833 Dec 16	24-0546
To 1833 Dec 17	24-0555
To 1833 Dec 17	24-0557
To 1833 Dec 18	24-0561
To 1833 Dec 19	24-0563
To 1833 Dec 19	24-0565
To 1833 Dec 19	24-0567
To 1833 Dec 23	24-0580
To 1833 Dec 23*	M472-2
To 1834 Jan 02	24-0737
To 1834 Jan 02	24-0739
To 1834 Jan 03	24-0741
To 1834 Jan 10	24-0853
To 1834 Jan 13	24-0877
To 1834 Jan 14	24-0884
To 1834 Jan 15	24-0901
To 1834 Jan 15	24-0903
To 1834 Jan 16	24-0959
To 1834 Jan 16	24-0961
To 1834 Jan 16	24-0963
To 1834 Jan 18	24-0994
To 1834 Jan 20	24-1017
To 1834 Jan 20	24-1019
To 1834 Jan 22	24-1030
To 1834 Jan 23	24-1042
To 1834 Jan 23	24-1044
To 1834 Jan 23*	M472-2
To 1834 Jan 27	24-1085
To 1834 Jan 27	24-1087
To 1834 Jan 28	24-1095
To 1834 Jan 30	24-1111
To 1834 Jan 30	24-1113
To 1834 Feb 03	24-1223
To 1834 Feb 06	24-1250
To 1834 Feb 06*	M472-2
To 1834 Feb 07	24-1252
To 1834 Feb 11	24-1288
To 1834 Feb 11	24-1290
To 1834 Feb 11*	M472-2
To 1834 Feb 13	24-1321
To 1834 Feb 14	24-1338
To 1834 Feb 14	24-1340
To 1834 Feb 14*	M472-2
To 1834 Feb 14	24-1342
To 1834 Feb 17	24-1404
To 1834 Feb 17	24-1408
To 1834 Feb 18	24-1425
To 1834 Feb 18	24-1427
To 1834 Feb 18*	M472-2
To 1834 Feb 19	24-1432
To 1834 Feb 19*	DLC-77
To 1834 Feb 20	24-1435
To 1834 Feb 20	24-1437
To 1834 Feb 21	24-1443
To 1834 Feb 24	24-1464
To 1834 Feb 24	24-1466

U S Senate--nomination (cont)

To 1834 Feb 24*	M472-2
To 1834 Feb 25	24-1478
To 1834 Feb 28	24-1509
To 1834 Mar 03	24-1552
To 1834 Mar 04	24-1571
To 1834 Mar 04	24-1573
To 1834 Mar 04*	M472-2
To 1834 Mar 10	25-0032
To 1834 Mar 10*	M472-2
To 1834 Mar 11	25-0122
To 1834 Mar 15	25-0224
To 1834 Mar 15	25-0226
To 1834 Mar 15	25-0232
To 1834 Mar 17	25-0258
To 1834 Mar 17	25-0260
To 1834 Mar 18	25-0267
To 1834 Mar 19	25-0286
To 1834 Mar 19	25-0288
To 1834 Mar 20	25-0298
To 1834 Mar 20	25-0301
To 1834 Mar 20	25-0303
To 1834 Mar 21	25-0315
To 1834 Mar 25	25-0366
To 1834 Mar 26	25-0373
To 1834 Mar 27	25-0448
To 1834 Mar 28	25-0487
To 1834 Apr 02	25-0569
To 1834 Apr 02	25-0571
To 1834 Apr 08	25-0642
To 1834 Apr 09	25-0659
To 1834 Apr 09	25-0661
To 1834 Apr 16	25-0825
To 1834 Apr 16*	M472-2
To 1834 Apr 18	25-0837
To 1834 Apr 21	25-0846
To 1834 Apr 22	25-0864
To 1834 Apr 25	25-0891
To 1834 Apr 28	25-0908
To 1834 Apr 29	25-0923
To 1834 Apr 30	25-0944
To 1834 Apr 30	25-0946
To 1834 May 01	25-0956
To 1834 May 01	25-0958
To 1834 May 03	25-0960
To 1834 May 03*	M472-2
To 1834 May 06	25-0978
To 1834 May 08	25-0996
To 1834 May 08	25-0998
To 1834 May 10	25-1012
To 1834 May 13	25-1039
To 1834 May 19	25-1098
To 1834 May 20	25-1103
To 1834 May 20	25-1105
To 1834 May 21	25-1114
To 1834 May 22	25-1140
To 1834 May 26	25-1152
To 1834 May 26	25-1154
To 1834 May 26	25-1156
To 1834 May 26*	M472-2
To 1834 May 27	25-1162
To 1834 May 29	25-1168
To 1834 May 29	25-1170
To 1834 May 30	25-1190
To 1834 Jun 09	25-1295
To 1834 Jun 11	25-1318
To 1834 Jun 13	25-1351
To 1834 Jun 13	25-1353
To 1834 Jun 13	25-1355
To 1834 Jun 13*	M472-2
To 1834 Jun 13	25-1357
To 1834 Jun 14	25-1376
To 1834 Jun 14*	M472-2
To 1834 Jun 16	25-1397
To 1834 Jun 20	25-1449
To 1834 Jun 20	25-1451
To 1834 Jun 21	25-1480
To 1834 Jun 21	25-1482
To 1834 Jun 23	25-1514
To 1834 Jun 23	25-1516
To 1834 Jun 23*	M472-2
To 1834 Jun 23	25-1518
To 1834 Jun 24	25-1526
To 1834 Jun 24	25-1528
To 1834 Jun 25	25-1541
To 1834 Jun 25	25-1543
To 1834 Jun 25	25-1545
To 1834 Jun 27	25-1584
To 1834 Jun 27	25-1586
To 1834 Jun 27	25-1588
To 1834 Jun 28	25-1594
To 1834 Jun 28	25-1596
To 1834 Jun 28	25-1598
To 1834 Jun 28	25-1600
To 1834 Jun 28	25-1602
To 1834 Jun 28	25-1604
To 1834 Jun 28	25-1606
To 1834 Jun 28	25-1608
To 1834 Jun 28	25-1610
To 1834 Jun 28	25-1613
To 1834 Jun 30	26-0015
To 1834 Jun 30	26-0016
To 1834 Jun 30	26-0026
To 1834 Jun 30	26-0028
To 1834 Jun 30	26-0030
To 1834 Jun 30	26-0032
To 1834 Jun 30*	M472-2
To 1834 Jun 30	26-0034
To 1834 Jun 30	26-0036
To 1834 Jun 30	26-0038
To 1834 Jun 30	26-0040
To 1834 Jun 30	26-0042
To 1834 Jun 30	26-0044
To 1834 Jun 30	26-0046
To 1834 Dec 03	26-1397
To 1834 Dec 03	26-1399
To 1834 Dec 03	26-1401
To 1834 Dec 03	26-1403
To 1834 Dec 03	26-1405
To 1834 Dec 03	26-1407
To 1834 Dec 04	26-1418
To 1834 Dec 06	26-1423
To 1834 Dec 08	26-1439
To 1834 Dec 09	26-1462
To 1834 Dec 10	26-1470
To 1834 Dec 12	26-1488
To 1834 Dec 15	26-1516
To 1834 Dec 15	26-1518
To 1834 Dec 16	26-1523
To 1834 Dec 16	26-1525
To 1834 Dec 18	26-1529
To 1834 Dec 22	26-1556
To 1834 Dec 22*	M472-2
To 1834 Dec 23	26-1570
To 1834 Dec 23	26-1572
To 1834 Dec 24	27-0015
To 1834 Dec 29	27-0035
To 1834 Dec 29	27-0037
To 1834 Dec 29	27-0039

To 1834 Dec 31	27-0048
To 1835 Jan 02	27-0080
To 1835 Jan 05	27-0099
To 1835 Jan 06	27-0110
To 1835 Jan 06	27-0112
To 1835 Jan 07	27-0130
To 1835 Jan 07	27-0132
To 1835 Jan 08	27-0159
To 1835 Jan 09	27-0173
To 1835 Jan 10	M472-2
To 1835 Jan 10	27-0179
To 1835 Jan 12	27-0201
To 1835 Jan 13	27-0219
To 1835 Jan 14	27-0229
To 1835 Jan 15	M472-2
To 1835 Jan 15	27-0242
To 1835 Jan 17	27-0251
To 1835 Jan 17	27-0253
To 1835 Jan 19	27-0257
To 1835 Jan 19	37-0520
To 1835 Jan 20	27-0262
To 1835 Jan 21	27-0272
To 1835 Jan 24	27-0287
To 1835 Jan 24	27-0289
To 1835 Jan 27	27-0299
To 1835 Jan 27*	M472-2
To 1835 Jan 28	27-0307
To 1835 Jan 28	27-0309
To 1835 Jan 28	27-0311
To 1835 Jan 29	27-0349
To 1835 Feb 02	27-0371
To 1835 Feb 03	27-0385
To 1835 Feb 04	27-0398
To 1835 Feb 05	27-0414
To 1835 Feb 05*	M472-2
To 1835 Feb 06	27-0443
To 1835 Feb 11	27-0502
To 1835 Feb 12	27-0507
To 1835 Feb 21	27-0581
To 1835 Feb 21	27-0584
To 1835 Feb 23	27-0593
To 1835 Feb 23	27-0595
To 1835 Feb 25	27-0621
To 1835 Feb 27	27-0656
To 1835 Feb 27	27-0658
To 1835 Feb 27	27-0660
To 1835 Mar 02	27-0700
To 1835 Mar 03	27-0997
To 1835 Mar 03	27-0999
To 1835 Mar 03	27-1001
To 1835 Mar 03*	M472-2
To 1835 Mar 03	27-1003
To 1835 Mar 03	27-1005
To 1835 Mar 03	27-1007
To 1835 Mar 03	27-1009
To 1835 Mar 03	27-1011
To 1835 Mar 03	27-1013
To 1835 Dec 10	29-1075
To 1835 Dec 11	29-1085
To 1835 Dec 11	29-1087
To 1835 Dec 11	29-1090
To 1835 Dec 14	29-1105
To 1835 Dec 14	29-1107
To 1835 Dec 15	29-1115
To 1835 Dec 15	29-1117
To 1835 Dec 16	29-1192
To 1835 Dec 17	29-1207
To 1835 Dec 17	29-1209
To 1835 Dec 18	29-1226
To 1835 Dec 19	29-1265
To 1835 Dec 21	29-1271
To 1835 cDec 21	29-1273
To 1835 cDec 21	29-1276
To 1835 Dec 22	29-1305
To 1835 Dec 22*	M472-2
To 1835 Dec 23	29-1319
To 1835 Dec 23	29-1321
To 1835 Dec 24	29-1340
To 1835 Dec 28	29-1349
To 1835 Dec 28	29-1351
To 1835 Dec 30	29-1360
To 1835 Dec 31	29-1374
To 1836 Jan 06	29-1483
To 1836 Jan 06	29-1485
To 1836 Jan 06	29-1488
To 1836 Jan 08	29-1511
To 1836 Jan 12	29-1570
To 1836 Jan 12*	M472-2
To 1836 Jan 12	29-1572
To 1836 Jan 12	29-1574
To 1836 Jan 14	30-0040
To 1836 Jan 15	30-0116
To 1836 Jan 18	30-0144
To 1836 Jan 27	30-0219
To 1836 Jan 27*	M472-2
To 1836 Feb 01	30-0257
To 1836 Feb 01	30-0259
To 1836 Feb 02	30-0273
To 1836 Feb 03	30-0282
To 1836 Feb 11	30-0362
To 1836 Feb 22	30-0479
To 1836 Feb 22	30-0481
To 1836 Feb 22	30-0483
To 1836 Feb 23	30-0494
To 1836 Feb 29	30-0635
To 1836 Feb 29	30-0637
To 1836 Mar 04	30-0684
To 1836 Mar 05	30-0688
To 1836 Mar 07	30-0708
To 1836 Mar 08	30-0731
To 1836 Mar 08	30-0734
To 1836 Mar 09	30-0739
To 1836 Mar 10	30-0745
To 1836 Mar 11	30-0749
To 1836 Mar 15	30-0795
To 1836 Mar 16	30-0801
To 1836 Mar 17	30-0805
To 1836 Mar 17*	M472-2
To 1836 Mar 18	30-0819
To 1836 Mar 18	30-0821
To 1836 Mar 21	30-0856
To 1836 Mar 21	30-0858
To 1836 Mar 30	30-0942
To 1836 Mar 30	30-0944
To 1836 Mar 30	30-0946
To 1836 Apr 01	30-0976
To 1836 Apr 02	30-0985
To 1836 Apr 04	30-1010
To 1836 Apr 05	30-1018
To 1836 Apr 06	30-1022
To 1836 Apr 06	30-1024
To 1836 Apr 07	30-1119
To 1836 Apr 11	30-1138
To 1836 Apr 11	30-1140
To 1836 Apr 15	30-1187
To 1836 Apr 18	30-1238
To 1836 Apr 22	30-1330
To 1836 Apr 26	30-1362

U S Senate--nomination (cont)

To 1836 Apr 26 30-1364
To 1836 Apr 26 30-1366
To 1836 Apr 27 30-1387
To 1836 Apr 27 30-1389
To 1836 Apr 27 30-1391
To 1836 Apr 27 30-1393
To 1836 Apr 28 30-1409
To 1836 Apr 28 30-1411
To 1836 May 06 30-1535
To 1836 May 09 30-1569
To 1836 May 14 31-0025
To 1836 May 17 31-0050
To 1836 May 17* M472-2
To 1836 May 25 31-0114
To 1836 May 28 31-0189
To 1836 Jun 01 31-0269
To 1836 Jun 03 31-0297
To 1836 Jun 04 31-0335
To 1836 Jun 06 31-0362
To 1836 Jun 10 31-0430
To 1836 Jun 10* M472-2
To 1836 Jun 11 31-0434
To 1836 Jun 11 31-0436
To 1836 Jun 13 31-0462
To 1836 Jun 13* M472-2
To 1836 Jun 13 31-0464
To 1836 Jun 14 31-0482
To 1836 Jun 15 31-0492
To 1836 Jun 16 31-0494
To 1836 Jun 18 31-0512
To 1836 Jun 18 31-0514
To 1836 Jun 21 31-0545
To 1836 Jun 22 31-0549
To 1836 Jun 23 31-0557
To 1836 Jun 23 31-0559
To 1836 Jun 27 31-0608
To 1836 Jun 27 31-0610
To 1836 Jun 27 31-0612
To 1836 Jun 27 31-0614
To 1836 Jun 27 31-0617
To 1836 Jun 28 31-0635
To 1836 Jun 28 31-0637
To 1836 Jun 29 31-0651
To 1836 Jun 30 31-0690
To 1836 Jun 30 31-0692
To 1836 Jul 01 31-0745
To 1836 Jul 02 31-0762
To 1836 Jul 02 31-0764
To 1836 Jul 02 31-0768
To 1836 Jul 02 31-0770
To 1836 Jul 02 31-0772
To 1836 Jul 02 31-0774
To 1836 Jul 02 31-0776
To 1836 Jul 02 31-0778
To 1836 Jul 02 31-0780
To 1836 Jul 04 31-0839
To 1836 Jul 04 31-0841
To 1836 Jul 04 31-0843
To 1836 Jul 04 31-0845
To 1836 Jul 04 31-0847
To 1836 Jul 04 31-0849
To 1836 Dec 07 32-1056
To 1836 Dec 07 32-1058
To 1836 Dec 07* M472-3
To 1836 Dec 08 32-1063
To 1836 Dec 08 32-1067
To 1836 Dec 08* M472-3
To 1836 Dec 12 32-1113
To 1836 Dec 12 32-1116
To 1836 Dec 12 32-1118
To 1836 Dec 12 32-1121
To 1836 Dec 19 32-1193
To 1836 Dec 19 32-1195
To 1836 Dec 20 32-1220
To 1836 Dec 20 32-1222
To 1836 Dec 24 32-1310
To 1836 Dec 26 32-1345
To 1836 Dec 27 32-1368
To 1836 Dec 28 32-1379
To 1836 Dec 28* M472-3
To 1836 Dec 28 32-1382
To 1836 Dec 28 32-1384
To 1836 Dec 29 32-1400
To 1837 Jan 02 32-1476
To 1837 Jan 02 32-1478
To 1837 Jan 03 32-1481
To 1837 Jan 06 32-1512
To 1837 Jan 06 32-1514
To 1837 Jan 07 32-1536
To 1837 Jan 07 32-1538
To 1837 Jan 09 32-1560
To 1837 Jan 10 32-1566
To 1837 Jan 11 32-1572
To 1837 Jan 11 32-1574
To 1837 Jan 12 32-1580
To 1837 Jan 17 33-0009
To 1837 Jan 21 33-0091
To 1837 Jan 24 33-0133
To 1837 Jan 24 33-0135
To 1837 Jan 26 33-0185
To 1837 Feb 01 33-0350
To 1837 Feb 02 33-0364
To 1837 Feb 02 33-0366
To 1837 Feb 03 33-0384
To 1837 Feb 03 33-0386
To 1837 Feb 03 33-0388
To 1837 Feb 03* M472-3
To 1837 Feb 06 33-0462
To 1837 Feb 06* M472-3
To 1837 Feb 09 33-0585
To 1837 Feb 09* M472-3
To 1837 Feb 09 33-0587
To 1837 Feb 09* M472-3
To 1837 Feb 10 33-0600
To 1837 cFeb 14 33-0704
To 1837 Feb 16 M472-3
To 1837 Feb 17 33-0745
To 1837 Feb 17 M472-3
To 1837 Feb 20 33-0786
To 1837 Feb 20 33-0788
To 1837 Feb 22 33-0826
To 1837 Feb 22 33-0829
To 1837 Feb 24 33-0876
To 1837 Feb 24 33-0878
To 1837 Feb 25 33-0906
To 1837 Feb 25* M472-3
To 1837 Feb 27 33-0911
To 1837 Feb 27 33-0913
To 1837 Feb 27 33-0915
To 1837 Feb 27 33-0917
To 1837 Feb 27 33-0919
To 1837 Feb 27 33-0921
To 1837 Feb 27* M472-3
To 1837 Feb 28 33-0926
To 1837 Feb 28 33-0928
To 1837 Feb 28 33-0930
To 1837 Mar 01 33-0965
To 1837 Mar 01* M472-3

To 1837 Mar 01 33-0967
To 1837 Mar 02 33-1006
To 1837 Mar 02 33-1008
To 1837 Mar 03 33-1042
To 1837 Mar 03 33-1045
To 1837 Mar 03 33-1047
To 1837 Mar 03* M472-3
To 1837 Mar 03 33-1049
To 1837 Mar 03 33-1057
--report
To 1829 Dec 14 14-1032
To 1829 Dec 14* DLC-60
To 1830 Jan 05 14-1339
To 1830 Feb 05 15-0106
To 1830 Apr 06 15-0630
To 1830 Apr 23 15-0780
To 1830 May 29 15-1210
To 1830 Dec 20 16-1513
To 1830 Dec 20 16-1515
To 1831 Jan 15 17-0270
To 1831 Jan 24 17-0344
To 1831 Feb 26 17-0661
To 1831 Dec 13 19-0301
To 1832 Jan 18 19-0768
To 1832 Feb 08 19-1019
To 1832 Feb 08 19-1021
To 1832 Feb 13 19-1086
To 1832 Feb 29 19-1277
To 1832 Feb 29 19-1279
To 1832 Mar 01 19-1295
To 1832 Mar 02 19-1301
To 1832 Mar 12 19-1410
To 1832 Mar 29 20-0054
To 1832 Apr 04 20-0134
To 1832 Apr 09 20-0175
To 1832 Apr 18 20-0254
To 1832 Apr 20 20-0332
To 1832 Apr 23 20-0373
To 1833 Jan 04 21-1321
To 1833 Mar 02 22-0629
To 1834 Jan 22 24-1032
To 1834 Mar 20 25-0306
To 1834 Apr 08 25-0644
To 1834 Apr 10 25-0683
To 1834 Dec 27 27-0031
To 1835 Jan 10 27-0177
To 1835 Feb 14 27-0518
To 1835 Feb 21 27-0586
To 1835 Feb 28 27-0662
To 1835 Dec 10 29-1077
To 1835 Dec 23 29-1323
To 1836 Jan 08 29-1513
To 1836 Jan 18 30-0146
To 1836 Feb 09 30-0338
To 1836 Feb 15 30-0395
To 1836 Feb 25 30-0585
To 1836 Feb 29 30-0639
To 1836 Apr 12 30-1144
To 1836 Jun 14 31-0484
To 1836 Jul 01 31-0747
To 1836 Dec 26 32-1347
To 1836 Dec 29 32-1402
To 1837 Jan 09 32-1562
To 1837 Jan 13 32-1582
To 1837 Jan 18 33-0024
To 1837 Jan 18 33-0028
To 1837 Feb 13 33-0684
To 1837 Feb 15 33-0713

--unsent message
To 1830 May DLC-72
To 1831 Dec DLC-73
To 1831 Dec* 18-1530
To 1832 Jan 16 DLC-40
To 1832 Jan 16* 19-0726
--veto
To 1830 May 31 15-1243
To 1832 Jul 10 20-0916
To 1832 Jul 10* DLC-41
To 1832 Jul 10* DLC-76
To 1832 Dec 06 21-0891
To 1833 Dec 04 24-0333
To 1833 Dec 04* DLC-43
To 1833 Dec 04* DLC-73
To 1835 Mar 03 27-1015
To 1836 Jun 09 31-0416
United States senators
To 1836 Dec 20 32-1224
United States v A Jackson
Re 1815 Mar 21 leg DLC-17
Re 1815 Mar 24 leg DLC-17
Re 1815 Mar 31 leg DLC-17
Re 1815 Apr 02 leg 4-0928
Re 1815 Apr 02* leg DLC-18
Re 1815 Apr 05 leg 4-0968
Re 1815 Apr 05* leg DLC-17
Unknown
To nd 37-0273
Fr 1799 Mar 04 fin 1-0698
To 1802 Mar 11 M22-1
To 1803 1-1069
To 1803 Oct 1-1178
To 1805 Nov 26 fin 2-0092
Fr 1809 Jan 29 DLC-75
To 1811 Oct 16 chk DLC-5
To 1812 Mar 20 2-1057
Fr 1813 Apr 18 DLC-75
Fr 1813 Oct DLC-75
Fr 1814 Jan 15 DLC-8
Fr 1815 Jan 10 DLC-16
To 1815 Feb 21 DLC-71
To 1815 cMar 31 4-0921
Fr 1815 Sep 24 4-1190
To 1816 Jul 5-0245
Fr 1817 Aug 14 5-0982
Fr c1817 Sep 25 5-1022
To 1818 Apr 09 6-0342
To 1819# 7-0111
To 1820 Apr 03 DLC-28
To 1820 Sep 08 7-1314
Fr 1821 May DLC-75
To 1823 May 06 DLC-32
To 1823 Oct 04 DLC-72
To 1823 Oct 11 DLC-72
To 1823 Nov 04 9-0732
To 1824 Oct 19 10-0944
Fr 1825 Mar fin DLC-72
Fr 1825 Mar fin DLC-72
Fr 1825 Mar fin DLC-72
To 1825 Jul 09 10-1355
Fr 1827 DLC-35
To 1827 Apr 09# 11-0563
To 1827 Sep 02 11-0841
To 1828 11-1003
To 1828 cFeb 28 DLC-35
Fr 1828 cMay 01 11-1232
To 1829 Mar 12 12-0996
To 1829 Apr 05# DLC-36

Unknown (cont)

Fr 1829 May 28		13-0484
Fr c1829 Jul 28		37-0293
To 1829 Sep 03		13-1253
Fr 1829 Oct 26		14-0247
To 1829 Nov 20	chk	DLC-37
To 1829 Dec 21	chk	DLC-37
To 1830 Feb 18		15-0194
Fr 1830 cMar		15-0275
Fr 1830 Mar 15		15-0370
Fr 1830 May 07		15-0949
To 1830 May 10		15-0979
Fr 1830 Aug 18		16-0128
To 1830 Oct 09	chk	DLC-38
To 1830 Oct 12		16-0373
To 1830 Nov 06	chk	DLC-38
To 1830 Nov 20	chk	DLC-38
To 1830 Dec 07	chk	DLC-38
To 1830 Dec 09	chk	DLC-38
To c1831		17-0096
To c1831		17-0099
To 1831 Jan 05	chk	DLC-38
To 1831 Jan 06	chk	DLC-38
To 1831 Feb 06	chk	DLC-39
To 1832 Mar 25		19-1545
To 1832 Apr		20-0088
Fr 1832 May 30		20-0680
Fr 1832 Jun 22		DLC-40
To 1832 Oct 08	chk	DLC-41
To 1832 Nov 13	chk	DLC-41
To 1833	chk	21-1250
To 1833 Jan		21-1288
Fr 1833 Jan 07		21-1372
To 1833 Feb 05	chk	DLC-42
To 1833 Apr 10		DLC-73
Fr 1833 Jun	add	22-1545
To 1833 Jun 13		23-0031
Fr 1833 Jul 15#		DLC-73
Fr 1833 Aug 23		DLC-43
To 1833 Aug 30		23-0557
To 1833 Sep 10		23-0686
Fr 1833 Oct 10		DLC-43
To 1833 Oct 19		23-1067
Fr 1833 Nov 04		23-1191
Fr 1833 Nov 23#		23-1308
Fr 1834 Feb 08		24-1272
Fr 1834 Feb 09		24-1274
Fr 1834 Feb 17		24-1410
Fr 1834 Apr 02		DLC-44
Fr 1834 Apr 05		25-0596
Fr 1834 May 02		M124-142
Fr 1834 Oct 07		26-0540
To 1834 Dec 20#		DLC-45
Fr 1835 Feb 24		DLC-45
Fr 1835 Mar 04		DLC-45
To 1835 cJul 25		28-1169
Fr 1835 Oct 29		29-0379
Fr 1835 Dec 17		DLC-47
To c1836	add	DLC-49
Fr 1836 Jan		29-1432
Fr 1836 cJan 03		M639-9
To 1836 Feb 25		30-0588
Fr 1836 cMar 12		DLC-48
Fr 1836 May 26		31-0127
To 1836 Jul 01		31-0749
To 1836 Jul 10		31-1039
Fr 1836 cJul 20		DLC-48
Fr 1836 Aug 15		DLC-48
Fr 1836 Oct		M22-41
Fr 1836 Oct 15		32-0184
Fr 1836 Nov		32-0373
Fr 1836 Nov 11		32-0484
To 1836 Nov 19		32-0566
Fr 1836 Dec 20		32-1225
Fr c1837		37-0360
Fr 1839 May 23#	fin	DLC-52
To 1839 cJul		34-0833
Fr 1839 Jul 29		DLC-52
To 1840 Jun		37-0394
Fr 1840 Jun 04		34-1391
Fr 1840 Jul 04		34-1466
To 1840 Dec 26		35-0141
Fr 1841 Jun 10		35-0320
To 1842 Jul		35-0829
To 1842 Dec 16		35-1040
Fr 1844 Apr 25		DLC-56
To 1844 Jun 24		36-0643
Fr 1844 Aug 09	add	36-0781
To 1845 Mar 06	chk	36-1550

Upchurch Stephen

Fr 1822 Nov 02	fin	DLC-31

Upham Freeman et al

Fr 1836 Jun 03		31-0299

Upton David

Fr 1840 Jul 26		DLC-53

Upton James

Fr 1814 Aug 04		DLC-11

Urdaneta Rafael

Fr 1829 Oct 13#		T33-5

Urquhart D

Fr 1829 Jul 27		M639-21

Urquhart Thomas

Fr 1814 Sep 07		DLC-12

Urquhart Thomas et al

Fr 1834 Oct 04		M124-145

Usher John

Re 1830 May 06	par	15-0939

Utica NY Young Men's Committee

Fr 1828 Aug 19		DLC-72

Utter Samuel et al

Fr 1831 Aug 08		M179-71

Uzzell Jordan

Fr 1828 Sep 04	fin	DLC-35

Vail Aaron

Fr 1831 May 30		M567-65
Re 1831 Aug 01		18-0393
Fr 1832 May 29		M30-35
Fr 1833 Feb 25		22-0480
Fr 1833 Jun 21		DLC-43
To 1833 Aug 15		23-0340
To 1833 Aug 15*		DLC-43
To 1834 Mar 27		25-0451
To 1834 Jun		25-1218
To 1834 Jun 05		25-1269
Fr 1834 Aug 20#		M30-38
Fr 1835 Mar 06		DLC-45
To 1835 Apr 16		28-0092
To 1835 Apr 16*		DLC-73
Fr 1835 May 06		M30-39
Fr 1835 May 22		DLC-46
Fr 1835 Jul 18		DLC-46
Fr 1836 Jan 14		30-0042

Vail Eugene A

Fr 1832 Apr 02		M179-73

Vail Joel H et al

Fr 1820 Oct 19		7-1389

Valdor Joseph			
Fr	1832 Aug 14		M639-25
Fr	1832 Nov 14		M639-25
Valence Peter			
Re	1834 Mar 13	par	25-0151
Valentine Samuel L			
Re	1830 Feb 20	par	15-0224
Re	1830 Feb 20*	par	T967-1
Vallette Elie A F			
Fr	1829 Apr 18#		DLC-75
Van Arsdall W K et al			
Fr	1837 Feb 19		M687-3
Van Buren John			
Re	1833 Jan 04	par	21-1323
Van Buren Martin			
Fr	1827 Sep 14		11-0853
Fr	1827 Nov 04		11-0907
To	1828 Jun 23		12-0028
Fr	1828 Nov 16		12-0272
To	1829		M531-5
Fr	c1829#		12-0396
To	c1829		12-0400
Fr	c1829		12-0401
Fr	c1829		12-0403
Fr	c1829		12-0406
To	c1829		37-0287
Fr	c1829		37-0289
To	1829 Feb 15		12-0514
To	1829 Feb 15*		DLC-60
Fr	1829 Feb 20		12-0543
Fr	1829 Feb 23		DLC-36
Fr	1829 Feb 27		12-0602
To	1829 Mar		M179-67
To	1829 Mar 06#		DLC-60
To	1829 Mar 20#		DLC-60
To	1829 Mar 27		12-1157
Fr	1829 Mar 31		12-1189
Fr	1829 Mar 31*		DLC-36
To	1829 Mar 31		12-1198
To	1829 Mar 31*		DLC-36
Fr	1829 Apr	mem	12-1218
Fr	1829 Apr 05		12-1273
To	1829 Apr 07		12-1297
To	1829 Apr 07		12-1300
To	1829 Apr 08		12-1305
To	1829 Apr 08		12-1307
To	1829 Apr 09		12-1309
To	1829 Apr 11		M179-67
Fr	1829 Apr 14		12-1349
To	1829 Apr 20		13-0080
To	1829 Apr 20		13-0082
To	1829 Apr 20		13-0083
Fr	1829 Apr 21		13-0087
To	1829 Apr 23		13-0111
Fr	1829 Apr 23		13-0114
To	1829 Apr 24		DLC-60
To	1829 Apr 24		13-0136
Fr	1829 Apr 24		13-0138
To	1829 Apr 24		13-0144
To	1829 Apr 28		13-0175
To	1829 Apr 30		13-0192
To	1829 May 03		13-0251
Fr	1829 May 07		M639-4
To	1829 May 14#		M639-5
Fr	1829 May 14		DLC-72
Fr	1829 May 18		M124-118
To	1829 May 18		13-0351
To	1829 May 18		DLC-37
To	1829 May 18*		DLC-60
Fr	1829 May 20		13-0363
Fr	1829 May 21		13-0368
To	1829 May 23		13-0405
To	1829 May 23		13-0411
To	1829 May 23		13-0409
To	1829 May 26		13-0441
To	1829 May 26		13-0443
To	1829 May 28		13-0488
To	1829 May 28		13-0490
To	1829 May 30		M179-67
To	1829 May 30		M179-67
To	1829 Jun 01		13-0546
To	1829 Jun 02		13-0553
Fr	1829 Jun 02		M179-67
To	1829 Jun 02		M179-67
To	1829 Jun 04		M179-67
To	1829 Jun 04		M179-67
To	1829 Jun 04		M179-67
To	1829 Jun 04		M179-67
To	1829 Jun 05		M179-67
To	1829 Jun 06		13-0585
To	1829 Jun 06		M179-67
Fr	1829 Jun 09		DLC-72
To	1829 Jun 09		M179-67
To	1829 Jun 11#		13-0631
To	1829 Jun 15		M639-18
To	1829 Jun 15		M639-6
To	1829 Jun 15		13-0668
To	1829 Jun 15*		DLC-60
To	1829 Jun 16		13-0672
Fr	1829 Jun 17		M40-21
To	1829 Jun 18		13-0680
To	1829 Jun 18		13-0682
To	1829 Jun 25		13-0714
To	1829 Jun 30		13-0756
To	1829 Jul 15		M179-67
To	1829 Jul 21		13-0910
To	1829 Jul 22		13-0914
To	1829 Jul 27		13-0944
To	1829 cAug 01		13-1032
To	1829 Aug 12		13-1113
To	1829 Aug 13		13-1123
To	1829 Aug 13*		DLC-60
To	1829 Aug 14		13-1131
To	1829 Aug 14		13-1134
To	1829 cAug 15		13-1142
To	1829 Aug 15#		M179-67
To	1829 Aug 17		13-1147
To	1829 Aug 18		13-1169
To	1829 Aug 18*		DLC-60
To	1829 Aug 18		M179-67
To	1829 Aug 19#		M179-67
To	1829 Sep		M639-14
Fr	1829 Sep 03		13-1254
To	1829 Sep 08		13-1287
To	1829 Sep 15		M179-67
To	1829 Sep 16		13-1342
Fr	1829 Sep 17		13-1349
To	1829 Sep 17		13-1351
To	1829 Sep 26		13-1434
Fr	1829 Sep 28		13-1450
To	1829 Oct 06		14-0113
To	1829 Oct 13#		T33-5
To	1829 Oct 14		M179-67
To	1829 Oct 15#		T61-4
To	1829 Oct 17		14-0186
To	1829 Oct 29		M179-67
Fr	1829 Oct 31		14-0286
To	1829 Oct 31		14-0290

Van Buren Martin (cont)

To 1829 Nov 26	14-0596
Fr 1829 Nov 28	14-0608
To 1829 Nov 28	14-0615
Fr 1829 Dec 10	14-1002
Fr 1829 Dec 14	14-1042
To 1829 Dec 18#	M179-67
To 1829 Dec 22#	14-1088
To 1829 Dec 29	14-1160
Fr 1829 Dec 30	DLC-37
Fr 1829 Dec 30#	DLC-37
To 1829 Dec 31	14-1218
To c1830	14-1244
Fr 1830 Jan 02	14-1308
To 1830 Jan 12	14-1390
To 1830 Jan 13#	M639-20
Fr 1830 Jan 20	14-1493
Fr 1830 Jan 21	14-1494
To 1830 Jan 22#	M639-3
To 1830 Jan 24	15-0014
To 1830 Jan 24#	M639-14
To 1830 cJan 25	15-0024
To 1830 Jan 28	M179-68
To 1830 Feb 10#	T20-5
Fr 1830 Feb 16	15-0152
To 1830 Feb 18#	M639-4
To 1830 Mar 04	15-0296
Fr 1830 Mar 15	15-0371
Fr 1830 Mar 20	M40-21
Fr 1830 Mar 20	15-0425
To 1830 Mar 22	15-0432
Fr 1830 Mar 23	M40-21
To 1830 Mar 31	M639-27
Fr 1830 Apr	15-0559
To 1830 Apr 08#	M179-68
To 1830 Apr 10	DLC-38
To 1830 Apr 15	15-0727
To 1830 Apr 15	M531-1
To 1830 Apr 20#	M179-68
Fr 1830 May 04	15-0915
To 1830 May 04	15-0919
To 1830 May 04	15-0921
Fr 1830 May 04	15-0922
To 1830 May 15	15-1036
To 1830 May 22#	15-1069
To 1830 May 25	M179-68
Fr 1830 May 27	15-1175
To 1830 Jun 01	15-1255
To 1830 Jun 05	M124-124
Fr 1830 Jun 05	M40-21
To 1830 Jun 07#	15-1310
To 1830 Jun 07#	15-1314
Fr 1830 Jun 15	15-1464
To 1830 Jun 15#	15-1455
Fr 1830 Jun 23	M40-21
Fr 1830 Jun 25	15-1527
To 1830 Jun 26	15-1539
To 1830 Jul 08	M179-69
To 1830 Jul 09	M179-69
To 1830 Jul 12	16-0017
Fr 1830 Jul 25	16-0050
To 1830 Aug 12	16-0099
To 1830 Sep 05#	M179-69
To 1830 Oct 03	16-0307
To 1830 Oct 04	16-0314
To 1830 cOct 05	16-0320
To 1830 Oct 15	M179-69
To 1830 Oct 15*	DLC-38
To 1830 Oct 18	16-0439
To 1830 Oct 23	16-0504

To 1830 Oct 23		16-0506
To 1830 Oct 23		M179-69
To 1830 Oct 23*		M40-21
To 1830 Nov 01		16-0633
To 1830 Nov 01		16-0637
To 1830 Nov 15		16-0733
To 1830 Nov 18		16-0802
To 1830 Nov 21#		DLC-38
To 1830 Nov 29		M179-69
To 1830 Dec 11		M179-69
Fr 1830 Dec 18		16-1494
To 1830 Dec 18#		M179-69
Fr 1830 Dec 22		M179-69
Fr 1830 Dec 29		M179-69
To 1830 Dec 29		M179-69
To 1830 Dec 31		M639-7
To 1831 Jan		17-0113
To 1831 Jan 07		M179-70
Fr 1831 Jan 07		17-0217
Fr 1831 Jan 15		17-0272
To 1831 Jan 15#		M639-15
To 1831 Jan 31		M179-70
To 1831 Feb 09		M179-70
To 1831 Feb 10		T1223-1
Fr 1831 Feb 15		17-0539
To 1831 Feb 24		17-0652
To 1831 Mar 06		17-0812
Fr 1831 Mar 29		17-1007
To 1831 Apr 04		M639-14
Fr 1831 Apr 07		M40-22
To 1831 Apr 08		17-1089
To 1831 Apr 08#		DLC-39
Fr 1831 Apr 09#		17-1109
Fr 1831 Apr 11		DLC-39
Fr 1831 Apr 11*		17-1126
Fr 1831 Apr 11		17-1145
To 1831 Apr 11#		17-1117
To 1831 Apr 12		17-1151
To 1831 Apr 12*		DLC-39
To 1831 Apr 12		17-1156
To 1831 Apr 28		17-1257
To 1831 Apr 28*		M77-152
To 1831 May 20		17-1403
Fr 1831 May 21		DLC-73
To 1831 May 23		17-1414
To 1831 Jun 02	chk	DLC-39
To 1831 Jun 23		18-0092
To 1831 Jul 11		18-0191
Fr 1831 Jul 16		18-0228
To 1831 Jul 23		18-0255
To 1831 Jul 25		18-0269
Fr 1831 Jul 29		18-0319
Fr 1831 Jul 30		18-0329
Re 1831 Aug 01		18-0394
Fr 1831 Aug 03		18-0417
Fr 1831 Aug 04		M30-34
To 1831 Aug 08		18-0481
To 1831 Aug 08*		DLC-39
To 1831 Aug 10		18-0504
To 1831 Aug 12		18-0517
Fr 1831 Aug 12		M639-5
Fr 1831 Aug 14		18-0527
Fr 1831 Aug 15		18-0545
Fr 1831 Aug 15		18-0546
Fr 1831 cSep		18-0647
To 1831 Sep 05		18-0670
To 1831 Sep 18		18-0815
Fr 1831 Sep 21		18-0860
Fr 1831 Sep 22		18-0869

Fr 1831 Sep 28	18-0884
Fr 1831 Sep 28	18-0893
Fr 1831 Oct 11	18-0953
Fr 1831 Oct 14	18-1000
Fr 1831 Oct 21	18-1094
Fr 1831 Oct 29	18-1153
To 1831 Nov 14	18-1275
To 1831 Nov 14*	DLC-40
Fr 1831 Nov 25	18-1489
To 1831 Dec 06	19-0212
To 1831 Dec 17	19-0343
To 1831 Dec 19	19-0365
Fr 1832 Jan 13	19-0682
Re 1832 Jan 13	DLC-40
Fr 1832 Feb 11	19-1070
To 1832 Feb 12	19-1074
Fr 1832 Feb 20	19-1171
Fr 1832 Mar 06	19-1329
Fr 1832 Mar 06	19-1337
Fr 1832 cMar 09	19-1372
Fr 1832 Mar 13	19-1440
Fr 1832 Mar 28	20-0001
Fr 1832 Apr 02	20-0099
To 1832 Jun 14	20-0758
To 1832 Jul 07	20-0903
Fr 1832 Aug 26#	20-1392
Fr 1832 Aug 29	20-1411
To 1832 Aug 30	20-1431
Fr 1832 Aug 31	20-1438
To 1832 Sep 16	21-0004
Fr 1832 Sep 20	21-0037
To 1832 Oct 23	21-0143
To 1832 Nov 03	21-0305
Fr 1832 Nov 14	21-0401
To 1832 Nov 18	21-0426
To 1832 Nov 18*	DLC-41
Fr 1832 Nov 18	21-0430
To 1832 Nov 25	21-0574
Fr 1832 Nov 29	21-0615
Fr 1832 Dec 05	21-0876
To 1832 Dec 10	21-0986
Fr 1832 Dec 10	21-0988
To 1832 Dec 15	21-1058
Fr 1832 Dec 22	21-1131
To 1832 Dec 23	21-1147
To 1832 Dec 25	21-1162
Fr 1832 Dec 27	21-1183
Fr 1833	21-1251
Fr c1833	21-1252
Fr 1833 Jan 03	21-1317
Fr 1833 Jan 09	21-1391
To 1833 Jan 13	21-1410
To 1833 Jan 25	22-0075
Fr 1833 Feb 06	22-0294
Fr 1833 Feb 20	22-0434
To 1833 Feb 20#	DLC-42
Fr 1833 Mar	M639-22
To 1833 Mar 12#	DLC-42
Fr 1833 Apr 21	22-1081
To 1833 Apr 25	22-1179
Fr 1833 May 02	22-1266
Fr 1833 May 07	22-1317
Fr 1833 May 09	22-1326
To 1833 May 12	22-1353
Fr 1833 May 16	22-1382
To 1833 May 19	22-1409
Fr 1833 May 25	22-1462
To 1833 Jun 06	22-1602
Fr 1833 Jul 22	23-0193
To 1833 Jul 24	23-0215
To 1833 Jul 25	23-0226
To 1833 Jul 27	23-0232
Fr 1833 Jul 29	23-0238
To 1833 Jul 30	23-0241
Fr 1833 Aug 06	23-0286
Fr 1833 Aug 08	23-0302
To 1833 Aug 12	23-0323
To 1833 Aug 16	23-0344
Fr 1833 Aug 19	DLC-43
To 1833 Aug 20	23-0438
Fr 1833 Aug 30	DLC-43
Fr 1833 Sep 04	DLC-43
Fr 1833 Sep 04*	23-0623
Fr 1833 Sep 07	DLC-43
To 1833 Sep 08	23-0666
Fr 1833 Sep 11	DLC-43
Fr 1833 Sep 11*	23-0694
Fr 1833 Sep 14	DLC-43
To 1833 Sep 15	23-0719
To 1833 Sep 19	23-0788
To 1833 Sep 22	23-0833
Fr 1833 Sep 22	DLC-73
To 1833 Sep 23	23-0852
To 1833 Sep 24	23-0862
To 1833 Sep 25	23-0864
To 1833 Sep 26	23-0877
Fr 1833 Sep 26	23-0879
Fr 1833 Sep 27	23-0889
Fr 1833 Sep 28	23-0897
To 1833 Sep 29	23-0903
Fr 1833 Oct 02	23-0936
Fr 1833 Oct 04	M639-14
To 1833 Oct 05	23-0978
Fr 1833 Oct 12	23-1027
Fr 1833 Nov	23-1167
To 1833 Nov 09#	DLC-43
To 1833 Nov 16	23-1247
To 1833 Nov 19	23-1259
To 1834 Jan 03	24-0743
To 1834 Jan 27	24-1089
To 1834 Feb 12#	DLC-44
To 1834 Feb 13#	DLC-44
Fr 1834 Feb 21#	M124-141
Fr 1834 Feb 25	24-1480
Fr 1834 Jul 22	DLC-73
Fr 1834 Jul 25	26-0241
Fr 1834 Aug 07	26-0288
To 1834 Aug 08	26-0295
To 1834 Aug 16	26-0323
Fr 1834 Aug 20	26-0339
To 1834 Sep 14	26-0439
Fr 1834 Oct 02	26-0475
To 1834 Oct 05	26-0504
Fr 1834 Oct 13	26-0637
Fr 1834 Oct 18	26-0659
Fr 1834 Oct 23	26-0690
To 1834 Oct 27	26-0751
Fr 1834 Nov 05	26-0820
Fr 1834 Dec 06	26-1425
To 1834 Dec 13#	26-1495
To 1834 Dec 24#	DLC-45
To 1835 cFeb 25#	27-0623
Fr c1835 May	28-0204
Fr 1835 May	28-0206
To 1835 cMay 01	28-0211
Fr 1835 cMay 10	DLC-46
To 1835 May 16#	DLC-46
Fr 1835 Sep 05	28-1574

Van Buren Martin (cont)

Fr	1835	Nov 28			29-0627
To	1835	Nov 28#			DLC-47
To	1835	Dec 15#			DLC-47
To	1835	Dec 17			29-1211
Fr	1835	cDec 19			29-1267
Fr	1835	Dec 19			DLC-47
Fr	1836	cMar 10			30-0747
Fr	1836	Mar 29			M567-127
Fr	1836	cJun			37-0348
Fr	1836	Jun 04			31-0337
Fr	1836	Aug 05			31-1229
To	1836	Aug 22			31-1347
Fr	1836	Sep 01			31-1402
To	1836	Sep 19			31-1470
To	1836	Oct 02			31-1592
To	1837	Mar 03			M124-156
To	1837	Mar 22			33-1095
Fr	1837	cMar 25			33-1119
To	1837	Mar 30			33-1125
To	1837	Mar 30*			DLC-50
Fr	1837	Apr 24			33-1180
To	1837	May			33-1200
To	1837	May 12			33-1219
To	1837	May 20			33-1232
Fr	1837	May 22			33-1238
To	1837	Jun 06			33-1280
Fr	1837	Jun 30			33-1353
Fr	1837	Jul 28			33-1395
To	1837	Aug 07			DLC-50
To	1837	Aug 12			33-1420
To	1837	Sep 14			33-1477
To	1837	Sep 14			33-1482
To	1837	Sep 28			33-1496
Fr	1837	Oct 03			33-1505
Fr	1837	Oct 17			33-1529
To	1837	Oct 24			33-1542
To	1837	Oct 29			34-0005
Fr	1837	Nov 18			34-0027
To	1837	Nov 20			M687-7
To	1837	Nov 27			34-0047
To	1837	Dec 02			34-0071
Fr	1837	Dec 05			34-0079
To	1837	Dec 18			34-0136
Fr	1838	Jan 08			34-0169
Fr	1838	Jan 10			34-0181
Fr	1838	Jan 13			34-0188
To	1838	Jan 23			34-0208
To	1838	Feb 13			34-0239
Fr	1838	Mar 02			34-0261
Fr	1838	Mar 17			34-0280
To	1838	Mar 26			34-0289
To	1838	Apr 04			34-0302
Fr	1838	Apr 15			34-0327
Fr	1838	Apr 24			34-0336
Fr	1838	Apr 29			34-0339
To	1838	May 01			34-0344
To	1838	Jun 01			34-0357
To	1838	Jun 04			34-0364
Fr	1838	Jun 17			34-0376
To	1838	Jul 06			34-0390
To	1838	Jul 08			34-0402
Fr	1838	Jul 22			34-0403
Fr	1838	Aug 11			34-0420
To	1838	Oct			34-0480
Fr	1838	Oct 08			34-0481
Fr	1838	Oct 17			34-0490
To	1838	Oct 22			34-0498
Fr	1838	Nov 16			34-0518
To	1838	Nov 19			34-0529
To	1838	Dec 04			34-0543
Fr	1838	Dec 04			37-0372
To	1838	Dec 06			34-0548
To	1838	Dec 18			34-0577
To	1839	Jan 17			34-0598
Fr	1839	Feb 17			34-0648
To	1839	Mar 04			34-0676
To	1839	Mar 04			M687-35
Fr	1839	Mar 23			34-0691
To	1839	Apr 04			34-0726
Fr	1839	Apr 14			34-0742
To	1839	May 02			34-0782
Fr	1839	May 29			34-0805
To	1839	Jun 13			34-0816
Fr	1839	Jul 30			34-0850
To	1839	Aug 12			34-0861
To	1839	Oct 05			34-0974
To	1839	Oct 18			34-1006
To	1839	Nov			34-1034
To	1839	Dec 23			34-1108
Fr	1840	Feb 02			34-1191
To	1840	Feb 15			34-1219
To	1840	Feb 17			34-1236
To	1840	Apr 03			34-1272
To	1840	Apr 10			34-1305
To	1840	Apr 15			34-1310
Fr	1840	Apr 17			DLC-74
To	1840	Apr 29			34-1330
To	1840	May			34-1334
To	1840	May 21			34-1368
Re	1840	cJun		mem	34-1387
Fr	1840	Jun 17			34-1418
To	1840	Jun 27			34-1453
To	1840	Jul 13			34-1473
Fr	1840	Jul 16			34-1482
To	1840	Jul 31			34-1548
To	1840	Jul 31			34-1551
Fr	1840	Sep 05			34-1587
To	1840	Sep 21			35-0013
To	1840	Sep 22			35-0017
Fr	1840	Nov 10			35-0096
To	1840	Nov 12			35-0102
To	1840	Nov 24			35-0104
Fr	1840	cDec 10			35-0108
To	1840	Dec 26			35-0142
To	1841	Mar 04			35-0236
Fr	1841	Mar 12			35-0248
Fr	1841	Mar 30			35-0263
To	1841	Mar 31			35-0269
Fr	1841	May 15			35-0304
To	1841	May 31			35-0317
Fr	1841	Jul 30			35-0350
To	1841	Aug 16			35-0373
Fr	1841	Oct 12			35-0442
Fr	1841	Nov 09			35-0486
To	1841	Nov 25			35-0504
Fr	1842	Feb 07			35-0618
To	1842	Feb 22			35-0630
Fr	1842	Mar 26			35-0659
Fr	1842	May 27			35-0744
To	1842	Jun 03			35-0772
Fr	1842	Jul 30			35-0862
To	1842	Sep 15			35-0943
Fr	1842	Oct 19			35-0976
To	1842	Nov 22			35-0996
To	1842	Dec 15			35-1036
Fr	1843	Jan 05			35-1093
Fr	1843	Apr 13			35-1302
To	1843	Apr 21			35-1336

Fr 1843 Sep 08 35-1480
To 1843 Sep 22 35-1507
Fr 1843 Nov 10 35-1585
To 1843 Nov 29 36-0036
Fr 1844 Jan 03 DLC-56
Fr 1844 Jan 13 36-0124
To 1844 Feb 07 36-0238
Fr 1844 Feb 21 36-0324
To 1844 Mar 08 36-0370
Fr 1844 Mar 23 36-0399
Fr 1844 Mar 29 36-0409
Fr 1844 Sep 16 36-0871
To 1844 Oct 02 36-0921
To 1844 Oct 22 36-0955
Fr 1844 Nov 02 36-0977
Fr 1844 Nov 14 M873-21
Fr 1845 Jan 28 DLC-74
Fr 1845 Feb 03 DLC-74
To 1845 Feb 10 36-1477
Fr 1845 Apr 27 37-0157

Van Buren Smith Thompson
Fr 1836 Nov 16 DLC-49

Van Campen Moses
Fr 1830 Jan 06 M222-28

Vance Elijah et al
Fr 1835 Dec 29 M639-27

Vance Joseph
Fr 1831 Feb 26 17-0666
Fr 1831 Mar 23 17-0938

Vance Joseph C
Fr 1835 Sep 21 M567-115

Van Cortlandt Philip
Fr 1829 Feb 20 12-0561

Van Court Alexander
Fr 1844 Mar 07 DLC-56
To 1844 Mar 12 36-0381

Vandegriff William
Fr 1829 Jul 22 M639-25
Fr 1829 Jul 26 M639-25

Vanderlyn Levi E
Fr 1840 Sep 07 DLC-53
To 1840 Sep 22 DLC-53
To 1840 Sep 22* 35-0021

Vanderpoel Aaron
Fr 1831 Oct 03 M639-23
Fr 1832 Dec 15 M179-74
Fr 1834 Jan 26 M639-7
Fr 1836 Aug 19 M687-1
To 1840 Apr 14 34-1306

Vanderpoel J et al
Fr 1837 Jan 25 M639-5

Vandeventer Christopher
Fr 1818 Jun 02 DLC-25
Fr 1818 Jun 02* M6-10
Fr 1818 Jun 02* 6-1018
Fr 1818 Aug 28 6-1271
Fr 1818 Aug 28* M6-10
Fr 1819 Nov 22 DLC-28
Fr 1819 Nov 22* M222-21
Fr 1819 Nov 22* 7-0883
Fr 1819 Nov 22* M7-1
Fr 1820 Aug 21 DLC-29
Fr 1820 Aug 21* M15-5
Fr 1820 Aug 21* 7-1214
Fr 1826 Aug 14 M6-12
Fr 1830 Dec 10 M22-27

Van Deventer John
Fr 1845 Jan 15 36-1346

Van Dorn Peter Aaron
Fr 1823 Jun 17 DLC-32
Fr 1823 Jun 28 DLC-32
Fr 1829 Mar 20 M639-25

Vandyke Thomas John
Fr 1803 Nov 05 DLC-3
Fr 1803 Nov 26 DLC-3
Fr 1811 Dec 09 DLC-5
To 1813 Dec 24 3-0717
To 1813 Dec 24* DLC-61

Van Horne James
Fr 1830 Dec 06 M639-25

Van Kleeck Laurance L
To 1831 Jul 20 DLC-39

Vanleer & Co
Fr 1823 Jan 26 fin DLC-32
Fr 1824 Feb 26 fin DLC-32
Fr 1824 Apr 10 fin DLC-32

Van Ness Cornelius
Fr 1834 Dec 17# DLC-45
Fr 1837 Jan 05 32-1501

Van Ness Cornelius Peter
Fr 1829 May 14 M639-13
Re 1829 Jun 01 13-0548
Re 1829 Nov 13 mem 14-0459
Re 1834 May 29 25-1172
Fr 1836 Sep 07 M31-32
Fr 1837 Feb 10 M31-32

Van Ness John Peter
Fr 1828 Nov 29 DLC-35
Fr 1829 Mar 06 M639-25
Fr 1829 Apr 04 12-1270
Fr 1829 Apr 24 13-0146
To 1829 cJun 13-0528
Fr 1829 Jul 15 M639-7
Fr 1830 Oct 17 M22-27
To 1830 Oct 22 16-0468
Fr 1830 Dec 17 M639-8
Fr 1831 Jul 01 M639-7
Fr 1832 Feb 20 M639-6
Fr 1832 Nov 23 DLC-41
Fr 1833 May 08 add 22-1325
Fr 1833 Sep 20 M639-23
To 1834 May 03 25-0962
Fr 1834 Nov 10 DLC-45
Fr 1834 Dec 03 26-1344
To 1834 Dec 17# DLC-45
To 1835 Feb 21 M179-79
Fr 1836 Mar 29 M687-23
Fr 1836 Jun 24 M687-33
Fr 1836 Jul 09 M639-4
Fr 1836 Nov 18 32-0560

Van Ness John Peter et al
Fr 1832 Dec 05# 21-0879

Vannoy Mason et al
Fr 1844 Sep 06 36-0843
To 1844 Sep 10 36-0860

Van Pelt Peter J
Fr 1830 Nov 30 DLC-38

Van Rensselaer Solomon
Fr 1832 Feb 25 M687-12

Vansant Joshua
Fr 1837 Mar 02 DLC-50

Van Santvoord Abraham
Fr 1836 Apr 15 fin DLC-48

Van Schaick Myndert
Fr 1833 Dec 12 M639-24

Van Schaick Myndert et al
Fr 1834 Feb 25 M639-18

Van Sickle Green
Re 1835 Dec 15 par 29-1119
Re 1835 Dec 29 par 29-1356
Van Sinderen A et al
Fr 1835 Oct 13 29-0287
Vanskie John
Fr 1835 Jan 26 DLC-45
Van Voorhis Daniel
Fr 1830 Apr 20 M124-123
Fr 1833 Dec 27 M639-18
Van Wyck William
Fr 1833 Dec 23 M639-24
Van Zandt Nicholas B
Re 1830 Sep 29 16-0270
Varian William P
Fr 1835 Apr 10 DLC-46
Varnum John
Fr 1830 Apr 28 15-0832
Vashon George
Fr 1818 Apr 09 DLC-24
Re 1825 Feb 19 10-1132
Fr 1829 Mar 02 12-0824
Fr 1829 Oct 27 14-0250
Fr 1830 Sep 12 M234-77
Fr 1830 Sep 12* 16-0239
Fr 1830 Nov 21 M234-77
Fr 1830 Nov 21* 16-0828
Fr 1834 Feb 10 M234-79
Vaughan Charles Richard
To c1829# 12-0396
To 1829 Apr 14 12-1351
To 1830 Jul DLC-73
Fr 1831 May 09 17-1321
To 1831 May 09 17-1330
To 1831 Sep 16 18-0799
Fr 1833 Jul 14 23-0131
Fr 1835 Sep 14# M50-18
Vaughn ______ (Sgt)
To 1814 Mar 23 DLC-9
Vaux Roberts
Fr 1835 Apr 21 28-0112
Veazie Samuel
Re 1831 Sep 17 par 18-0802
Veening Isaac Gerard
Re 1832 Nov 02 par 21-0283
Velez Pedro
Fr 1829 Dec 31 M54-1
Venable William Edward et al
Fr 1840 Jun 10 34-1407
To 1840 Jun 22 DLC-74
Venezuela treaty
Re 1836 Jun 20 31-0535
Verell John
Fr 1801 Feb 27 leg DLC-2
Re 1805 May 11 mem DLC-3
To 1805 Nov 29 fin DLC-3
Re 1806 Jan 24 2-0123
Fr 1806 Jan 29 fin DLC-71
Verell Robert N
Fr 1829 Mar 07 12-0889
Veritas (pseudonym)
Fr 1803 Dec 14 1-1256
Veron Lewis & Co
To 1829 Nov 13 chk DLC-37
Fr 1836 Nov 02# fin DLC-50
Verplanck Gulian Crommelin
Fr 1829 May 09 M639-14
Fr 1829 May 22 13-0381
Fr 1830 Apr 12 15-0685
Fr 1832 Feb 25# M179-72
Vickers Joel
Fr 1830 Jan 09 M639-12
Vickrey Albert
Fr 1817 Feb 02 DLC-22
Victoria Princess
To 1834 Mar 12 25-0145
Vicuna Francisco Ramon de
Fr 1829 Oct 15 M73-1
Vidal Mercedes
Fr 1821 Aug 23 DLC-63
Fr 1821 Aug 28 8-1112
Fr 1821 Aug 29 M116-7
Vidal N M (heirs of)
Re 1821 Sep 06 leg 8-1156
Re 1821 Sep 17 leg 8-1174
Re 1821 Oct 08 leg 8-1295
Re 1821 Dec 10 leg DLC-31
Vigue Francisco
Re 1829 Jul 29 par 13-1001
Re 1829 Jul 29* par T967-1
Villere Jacques Philippe
To 1814 Dec 19 4-0427
To 1814 Dec 22 4-0447
To 1815 Jan 10 4-0521
Fr 1815 Jan 20 DLC-15
To 1815 Jan 23 4-0606
To 1815 Jan 24 4-0611
To 1815 Jan 25 4-0614
To 1815 Feb 08 DLC-16
To 1821 Feb 15 8-0129
To 1827 Mar 01 11-0490
Villiers Marcos de et al
Fr 1821 Aug 23 8-1092
Vincent Anthony et al
Fr 1831 Feb 10 17-0499
Vincent B B et al
Fr 1835 cJan DLC-59
Vining John
Fr 1829 Mar 19 M639-16
Vinson Isabella (Fowler)
see also Butler I F
Fr 1810 Sep 10 DLC-4
To 1817 May 09 5-0847
Vinson Stokely
Fr 1837 Nov 02# DLC-50
To 1837 Nov 03 DLC-50
Vinson William B
Re 1813 Jan 18 mem DLC-6
Re 1813 Jan 18 leg 3-0254
Visger Harman
Fr 1833 Jun 19 T185-3
Viverett Micajah
Re 1809 Feb 02 leg 2-0771
Volant (brig)
Re 1830 Mar 20 par T967-1
Von Scholten P
Fr 1830 Nov 16 M52-1
To 1830 Nov 16 16-0795
Voorhees John V D
To 1821 Jul 21 DLC-63
Fr 1821 Oct 07 fin DLC-70
Vought John G
Fr 1826 Dec 04 11-0419
Vroom Peter Dumont
Fr 1831 Jun 25 M567-59
Fr 1834 Feb 21 M639-3
Fr 1834 Mar 20 25-0309

Name	Type / Date	Note	Reference
W J			
	Fr 1829 May		M639-14
W R			
	Fr 1843 Jul 04		35-1401
Wabash & Erie Canal			
	Re 1836 Oct 31		32-0368
Wabashaw et al			
	Fr 1834 May 02		M234-697
Wabsai et al			
	Fr 1835 Dec		29-0704
	Fr 1835 Dec*		M234-133
Waddell Pemberton			
	Fr 1831 Jun 26		M22-28
	Fr 1836 Dec 26		M567-134
Waddell William Coventry H			
	Re 1831 Nov 07		18-1221
	Fr 1831 Nov 17		M639-7
	Fr 1833 Nov 23		23-1309
	Fr 1836 Oct		M22-41
Waddill A			
	Fr 1836 Aug 09		31-1272
Wade ______			
	Re c1829		37-0290
Wade William			
	Fr 1817 Mar 17		DLC-22
Wade Winslow W			
	Fr 1826 Dec 07	fin	DLC-34
Wadsworth Daniel			
	Fr 1833 Mar 28		22-0906
Wadsworth Decius			
	Fr 1818 Aug 25		6-1269
	Fr 1818 Sep 05		DLC-25
	Fr 1818 Sep 05*		6-1284
Wagener David Douglas			
	Fr 1833 Apr 14		M639-22
	Fr 1836 Jan 25		M639-27
Wagener David Douglas et al			
	Fr 1830 Apr 19		M688-73
	Fr 1836 Jun		M639-3
Wager G B			
	Fr 1830 Nov 11		M22-27
Wager Peter			
	Fr 1821 Aug 24		M116-7
	Fr 1821 Aug 24*		DLC-63
	Fr 1833 Apr 08		DLC-42
	To 1833 Apr 14		22-1022
	To 1833 Apr 14*		DLC-42
	Fr 1833 Apr 22		22-1110
	To 1833 Aug 03		DLC-43
	To 1833 Aug 03*		23-0262
	Fr 1833 Sep 13#	fin	DLC-43
	Fr 1835 Jul 15		M124-148
	Fr 1835 Nov 12#	fin	DLC-47
	Fr 1844 Dec 04		36-1125
Waggaman George Augustus			
	Fr 1815 Jun 24		DLC-18
Waggaman Thomas E			
	Fr 1806 Apr 16	fin	DLC-4
	To 1809 Mar 11	leg	2-0778
	To 1809 Mar 20	lnd	2-0783
Waggener Edmund M			
	To 1825 Oct 17		DLC-33
Waggoner (horse)			
	Re 1812 Mar 23		2-1058
Wail William S			
	Re 1833 Dec 16	par	24-0531
Wainwright Edward			
	Re 1836 Apr 18	par	30-1240
Wait Samuel Jr			
	Fr 1839 Apr 18#	fin	DLC-52
Wait William S			
	Fr 1845 Jan 18		DLC-57
Waite William			
	To 1808 Jul 09	lnd	2-0683
Wakazo Joseph			
	Fr 1836 Apr 29		30-1419
Wakefield W			
	Fr 1815 Feb 23		DLC-17
Walden Nathan et al			
	Fr 1829 Nov		14-0339
Walker ______ (Maj)			
	To 1824 Aug 03		DLC-33
Walker ______ (Maj; AL)			
	To 1814 cMay 08	add	DLC-10
Walker Catherine (Caffery)			
	To 1819 Mar 18#		7-0428
	To 1823 May 05		9-0547
Walker Charles H			
	Fr 1836 cSep		M22-40
Walker David			
	Fr 1813 Dec 10		DLC-7
	Fr 1816 Jun 15		DLC-21
Walker David et al			
	Fr 1834 Nov 22		26-0978
Walker David T			
	Fr 1814 Jan 09		DLC-8
	To 1814 Jan 14		DLC-61
Walker Gabriel			
	Fr 1831 Sep 14		M639-25
Walker George			
	Fr 1813 Aug 23		DLC-6
	Fr 1814 Feb 20#		DLC-9
	Fr 1814 Feb 22#		3-0889
	Fr 1814 Jun 04		DLC-10
	Fr 1815 Aug 07		DLC-19
	Fr 1842 Oct 18#		DLC-54
Walker George K			
	Fr 1835 Jul 15		M179-80
	Fr 1835 Nov 08		M639-25
	Fr 1836 May 16		M179-82
Walker George W			
	Fr 1837 Feb 14		33-0706
Walker J W			
	Fr 1837 Nov 05		DLC-50
Walker James			
	Fr 1818 Jun 25	fin	DLC-69
	Fr 1818 Jun 30		DLC-25
	Fr 1835 Apr 05		DLC-46
	Re 1835 Nov 03	par	29-0429
	Fr 1843 Apr 03		DLC-55
Walker James M			
	Fr 1821 Jan 08		DLC-29
Walker John			
	Fr 1834 May 21	fin	DLC-44
	Fr 1834 Jul 28	fin	DLC-44
	Fr 1834 Aug 04	fin	DLC-44
	Fr 1834 Aug 11	fin	DLC-44
	Fr 1834 Aug 18	fin	DLC-44
	Fr 1834 Aug 25	fin	DLC-44
	Fr 1834 Sep 29	fin	DLC-44
	Fr 1834 Oct 06	fin	DLC-44
	Fr 1834 Oct 13	fin	DLC-44
	Fr 1834 Oct 20	fin	DLC-44
	Fr 1834 Oct 27	fin	DLC-44
	Fr 1834 Nov 01	fin	DLC-45
	Fr 1834 Nov 10	fin	DLC-45
	Fr 1834 Nov 11	fin	DLC-45
	Fr 1834 Nov 24	fin	DLC-45
	Fr 1834 Dec 01	fin	DLC-45

Walker John (cont)
Fr 1834 Dec 08 fin DLC-45
Fr 1834 Dec 15 fin DLC-45
Fr 1834 Dec 22 fin DLC-45
Fr 1834 Dec 29 fin DLC-45
Fr 1835 Jan 05 fin DLC-45
Fr 1835 Jan 12 fin DLC-45
Fr 1835 Jan 19 fin DLC-45
Fr 1835 Jan 26 fin DLC-45
Fr 1835 Mar 30 fin DLC-46
Fr 1835 Apr 13 fin DLC-46
Fr 1835 Apr 20 fin DLC-46
Fr 1835 Apr 27 fin DLC-46
Fr 1835 May 04 fin DLC-46
Fr 1835 May 11 fin DLC-46
Fr 1835 May 25 fin DLC-47
Fr 1835 Jun 01 fin DLC-46
Fr 1835 Jun 08 fin DLC-46
Fr 1835 Jun 15 fin DLC-46
Fr 1835 Jun 22 fin DLC-46
Fr 1835 Jun 29 fin DLC-46
Fr 1835 Jul 06 fin DLC-46
Fr 1835 Jul 13 fin DLC-46
Fr 1835 Jul 21 fin DLC-46
Fr 1835 Jul 27 fin DLC-46
Fr 1835 Aug 03 fin DLC-46
Fr 1835 Aug 11 fin DLC-46
Fr 1835 Aug 17 fin DLC-46
Fr 1835 Aug 24 fin DLC-46
Fr 1835 Sep 28 fin DLC-47
Fr 1835 Oct 06 fin DLC-47
Fr 1835 Oct 12 fin DLC-47
Fr 1835 Oct 19 fin DLC-47
Fr 1835 Nov 02 fin DLC-47
Fr 1835 Nov 09 fin DLC-47
Fr 1835 Nov 16 fin DLC-47
Fr 1835 Nov 23 fin DLC-47
Fr 1835 Dec 04 fin DLC-47
Fr 1835 Dec 14 fin DLC-47
Fr 1835 Dec 21 fin DLC-47
Fr 1836 Feb 01 fin DLC-47
Fr 1836 Feb 08 fin DLC-47
Fr 1836 Feb 15 fin DLC-47
Fr 1836 Feb 22 fin DLC-47
Fr 1836 Mar 28 fin DLC-47
Fr 1836 Apr 04 fin DLC-47
Fr 1836 Apr 11 fin DLC-48
Fr 1836 Apr 19 fin DLC-48
Fr 1836 Apr 25 fin DLC-48
Fr 1836 May 02 fin DLC-48
Fr 1836 May 09 fin DLC-48
Fr 1836 May 16 fin DLC-48
Fr 1836 May 23 fin DLC-48
Fr 1836 Jul 04 fin DLC-48
Walker John Jr
Fr 1832 Mar 04 M234-113
Fr 1832 Mar 04* 19-1303
Fr 1834 Feb 15# M234-76
Walker John M
Fr 1845 Feb 17 DLC-57
Walker John U et al
Fr 1826 Sep 16 DLC-34
To 1826 Sep 17 DLC-34
Walker John Williams
Fr 1819 Aug 08 DLC-27
Walker Joseph et al
Fr 1836 Feb 05 M567-133
Walker Joseph Marshall
Fr 1834 Dec 14 26-1497
Walker Joseph W
Re 1839 Sep# leg 34-0903
Walker Lyman B
Fr 1828 Nov 04 DLC-35
Fr 1841 Nov 20 DLC-54
Walker Patience
To 1803 Aug 23 fin DLC-71
Walker Philip
To 1830 Sep DLC-38
Fr 1830 Sep 20 DLC-38
Walker Robert
Re 1832 Jun 13 par 20-0750
Walker Robert John
Fr 1831 Nov 14 M222-30
Fr 1836 Mar 08# DLC-47
Fr 1836 Mar 11 M234-189
Fr 1836 Apr 11 M639-8
Fr 1836 Jun 23 31-0563
Fr 1837 Mar 01 DLC-50
Fr 1837 Mar 01 33-0969
Fr 1844 Jan 10 DLC-56
To 1844 Jan 19 36-0148
Fr 1844 Feb 13 DLC-56
Fr 1844 Feb 14 DLC-56
To 1844 Mar 11 36-0377
Walker Samuel P Jr
Fr 1833 May 22 22-1426
Walker Tandy
Fr 1830 Mar 04 M234-222
Walker William
To 1814 Sep 22 4-0237
To 1814 Sep 22* DLC-62
Fr 1814 Sep 22 DLC-12
Fr 1814 Sep 26 DLC-12
Fr 1814 Oct 04 4-0258
Fr 1815 Jun 23 DLC-18
Fr 1815 Jun 27 DLC-18
Fr 1815 Jul 10 DLC-18
Fr 1815 Aug 18 DLC-19
Wall Garret Dorset
Fr 1829 Mar 11 M873-19
Fr 1829 May 20 M639-25
Fr 1829 Jul 01 M873-19
Fr 1831 Jun 28 M567-59
Fr 1834 Feb 25 M639-3
Fr 1834 Nov 03 26-0814
Fr 1834 Nov 24 26-0990
Fr 1835 Sep 24 29-0106
Fr 1835 Nov 27 29-0612
Fr 1836 May 21 M639-26
Fr 1837 Jan 31 M124-156
Wall Garret Dorset et al
Fr 1829 Feb 26 M873-19
Wall Noah
Fr 1834 Apr 25-0535
Wall William H
Re 1833 Jun 05 par 22-1585
Wallace D C
Fr 1815 Feb DLC-17
Wallace Isaac
Re 1832 Jan 04 par 19-0617
Wallace John H
Fr 1830 Jun 11 M124-124
Wallace Joseph Washington Elliot
Fr 1829 Mar 20 M639-25
Re 1829 Oct 27 14-0252
Wallace William
Fr 1845 Jan 03 DLC-57
Wallace William et al
Fr 1834 Jan 31 M639-19
Wallach J W
To c1829 12-0408

Waller William S
Fr 1830 Feb 12 M639-16
Walmsley Jane
Fr 1833 Sep 10 M567-90
Fr 1833 Dec 30 M567-90
Walmsley Robert McGregor
Fr 1818 Nov 15 DLC-26
Waln Jesse
Fr 1831 May 05 M639-25
Walsh Michael
Fr 1815 Mar 13 DLC-17
Fr 1815 Jun 23 DLC-18
Fr 1815 Jun 26 DLC-18
Walsh Michael et al
Fr 1815 Jan 23 DLC-15
Walter Jacob
Fr 1844 Feb 08 DLC-56
Fr 1844 Dec 29 DLC-57
Walters Henry
Re 1836 Nov 04 par 32-0400
Walthall Richard B
To 1814 Feb 19 DLC-62
Fr 1814 Feb 23 DLC-9
Walton Azariah
Fr 1837 Jul 16 DLC-50
Walton George
Fr 1821 Aug 20 fin DLC-70
To 1821 Aug 21 DLC-63
Fr 1821 Aug 22 M116-7
Fr 1821 Aug 22* DLC-63
To 1821 Aug 23 M116-7
Fr 1821 Sep 27 fin DLC-70
To 1821 Oct 05 DLC-63
Fr 1821 Oct 08 fin DLC-70
Fr 1821 Oct 08 fin DLC-70
Fr 1821 Oct 15 DLC-31
Fr 1821 Oct 22 DLC-31
To 1821 Oct 29 8-1315
Fr 1821 Oct 29 DLC-31
Fr 1821 cNov DLC-59
Fr 1821 Nov 05 DLC-31
Fr 1821 Nov 09 DLC-31
Fr 1821 Nov 12 DLC-31
To 1821 Nov 13 8-1345
To 1821 Nov 13* DLC-63
To 1821 Nov 17 DLC-63
Fr 1821 Nov 26 DLC-31
Fr 1821 Dec 03 DLC-31
To 1821 Dec 06 DLC-63
Fr 1821 Dec 10 DLC-31
To 1821 Dec 12 DLC-63
Fr 1821 Dec 17 DLC-31
Fr 1821 Dec 23 DLC-31
Fr 1822 Jan 07 DLC-31
Fr 1822 Jan 07* M116-10
Fr 1822 Jan 07* 8-1384
Fr 1822 Jan 28 M116-10
Fr 1822 Feb 04 DLC-31
Fr 1822 Feb 24 DLC-31
Fr 1822 Oct 10 DLC-31
To 1822 Nov 26 9-0317
Fr 1823 Apr 18 DLC-32
To 1823 Oct 28 9-0718
Walton George et al
Fr 1821 Aug 23 M116-7
Fr 1821 Aug 23* DLC-63
Walton Ira
To 1827 Jan 29 fin DLC-34
To 1827 May 12 fin DLC-32
Walworth Reuben Hyde
Fr 1844 Feb 26 DLC-56
Walworth Thomas P
Fr 1834 Apr 24 25-0870
Wankewauk
Fr 1835 Nov 28 29-0623
War department
Re 1807 Jun 01 fin 2-0498
War department funds
Re 1829 Jul 08 13-0830
Re 1829 Oct 28 mem M222-26
War secretary
To c1829 mem 12-0409
Ward Aaron
Fr 1829 Mar 26 12-1155
To 1831 Dec 31# DLC-40
Fr 1834 Jan 05 DLC-44
Fr 1835 Feb 20 M639-2
Fr 1836 May 27 31-0167
Fr 1836 Oct M22-41
Ward Albert G
To 1828 Sep 26 fin 12-0219
To 1838 fin DLC-52
Re 1839 Jan 23 leg 34-0605
Fr 1840 Feb 06 DLC-52
To 1840 Jul 17# fin DLC-53
To 1840 Nov 30 fin DLC-53
Re c1841 mem 35-0160
Re 1843 cOct leg 35-1520
Ward Alexis et al
Fr 1832 Dec 26 M639-16
Ward Edward
To c1804 DLC-59
To 1804 Jul 06 lnd DLC-3
To 1805 May 07 2-0037
Fr 1805 Jun 10 2-0063
To 1805 Jun 10 DLC-71
To 1810 Oct 26 DLC-21
To 1813 Aug 06 chk DLC-6
Fr 1814 Aug 30 DLC-11
Fr 1817 Dec 30 DLC-23
Fr 1821 Mar 23 DLC-30
Fr 1823 Aug 25 DLC-32
Fr 1823 Sep 20 DLC-32
Ward Edward C
Re 1834 Oct 15 M273-31
Ward Emily
To 1836 Dec 24 DLC-49
Ward George T
Fr 1836 Feb 12 M567-133
Ward Giles
Fr 1832 Nov 28 DLC-41
Ward Henry et al
Fr c1836 29-1416
Ward John
Re 1829 Aug 15 13-1146
Fr 1833 Dec 31 M234-241
Ward John W
Fr 1835 Jun 15# fin DLC-46
Ward L
Fr 1843 Jan 31 DLC-55
Ward Lauriston
Fr 1837 Jan 20 M687-16
Ward Maria J (Baker) et al
Re 1842 May 14 leg 35-0691
Re 1844 Feb 06 leg 36-0162
Ward Richard
Fr 1829 Sep 11 M179-67
Fr 1831 Nov 13 18-1259

Name	Date	Note	Reference
Ward Robert J			
	Fr 1828 Aug 29		DLC-35
	To 1828 Sep 09		DLC-35
	Fr 1832 Dec 12		M567-68
	Fr 1845 Feb 05		DLC-57
Ward Robert J et al			
	Fr 1832 Dec 12		M567-68
Ward Sarah			
	To 1840 Nov 30	fin	DLC-53
	Re 1842 Jan 03	mem	DLC-54
Ward Thomas			
	Re 1831 May 25	par	17-1432
	Re 1831 Jun 03	par	17-1512
Ward William			
	Fr 1810 Apr 11	lnd	DLC-4
	Fr 1810 Apr 11*	lnd	2-0880
	To 1810 Apr 11	lnd	2-0881
	Fr 1814 Jul 20	fin	3-1158
	Fr 1830 Oct 11		M234-169
Ward & Lippincott			
	Fr 1826 Nov 15	fin	DLC-34
Ward & Panton			
	Fr 1809 Oct 14	fin	DLC-5
Ward & Taylor			
	Fr 1813 Mar 30	fin	DLC-6
	Fr 1813 Nov 06		DLC-7
	Fr 1813 Nov 08		DLC-7
	Fr 1813 Nov 08*		DLC-61
Wardell Robert			
	Fr 1834 Jun 23		25-1520
	Fr 1834 Aug 06		26-0283
Wardell Zebulon P			
	Re 1830 cOct		M273-25
Warden David Bailie			
	Fr 1829 Jan 01		M639-25
	Fr 1832 Mar 25		DLC-40
	Fr 1833 Mar 14		M639-25
Wardwell Daniel et al			
	Fr 1832 Mar 02		M639-16
Ware Betsy			
	Re 1831 May 11	par	17-1351
Ware Nicholas			
	Fr 1821 May 16		DLC-30
Ware Robert J			
	Fr 1837 Dec 26		DLC-50
Warfield William Henry			
	Fr 1832 Aug 31		M567-77
Waring John E			
	Fr 1834 Jun 12#	fin	DLC-44
Waring Morton A			
	Fr 1833 Jan 02		M639-25
Warner David			
	Fr 1835 Jan 11		DLC-45
Warner Marshal			
	Fr 1829 Nov 24		M688-64
Warner Thomas			
	Fr 1834 Apr 04		25-0589
	Fr 1835 Apr 17		M22-36
Warpole et al			
	Fr 1835 Jan 14		M234-601
Warren Benjamin			
	Fr 1844 Feb 27		DLC-56
Warren H			
	Fr 1831 Aug 29		18-0623
Warren James Cogan			
	Fr 1814 Sep 03		DLC-12
	Fr 1814 Oct 10		DLC-13
Warren John			
	Fr 1835 Apr 13		28-0069
	Fr 1836 Jul 10		M567-134
Warren John et al			
	Fr 1831 Dec 09		19-0284
Warren John G			
	Fr 1830 Feb 24		15-0239
Warren Lyman M			
	Re 1835 Jan	mem	M234-421
Warrington Lewis			
	Fr 1830 Apr 12		15-0687
Wasaonoquet			
	Fr 1836 May 10		30-1594
	Fr 1836 May 10*		M234-422
Wasdell John			
	Fr 1815 Jan 26		DLC-15
Washington George			
	To 1797 Feb 08		M179-15
	Re 1826 Jul 04		11-0270
Washington George Corbin			
	Fr c1830 Feb 19		15-0210
Washington J M			
	Fr 1820 Apr 07		DLC-28
Washington Jane C			
	Fr 1833 May 26		DLC-43
Washington Mary (Ball)			
	Re 1833 May 07	add	22-1319
	Re 1833 May 07*	add	DLC-73
Washington Peter Grayson			
	To 1830 Dec 22		16-1543
	To 1831 Aug 03		18-0418
	To 1832 Jul 18		20-1139
	To 1833 Jan 16		21-1564
	To 1833 Mar 02		22-0662
	To 1833 Apr 23		22-1162
	To 1833 May 29		22-1518
	To 1833 Jul 20		23-0170
	To 1833 Sep 12		23-0706
	To 1833 Oct 16		23-1053
	To 1834 Feb 18		24-1429
	To 1834 Jul 07		26-0184
	To 1835 Mar 24		27-1382
	To 1835 Jul 03		28-0893
	To 1836 Feb 17	chk	DLC-47
	Fr 1836 Feb 17	fin	DLC-47
	To 1836 Jul 05		31-0870
Washington Richard C			
	Fr 1835#	fin	DLC-47
Washington Richard C & Co			
	Fr c1832#	fin	19-0524
	Fr 1832 Feb 07#	fin	DLC-40
	To 1832 Dec 29	chk	DLC-41
Washington S P			
	Fr 1840 Feb 04		DLC-52
Washington Samuel George			
	Fr 1830 Jun 05		15-1299
Washington Spotswood A			
	Re 1832 May 12		M273-27
Washington Thomas			
	Re 1812 Apr 23		2-1076
	Fr 1822 Feb 23		DLC-31
	Fr 1822 Feb 23*		9-0033
	Fr 1823 Oct 31		DLC-32
	Fr 1824 Jun 26		DLC-32
	To 1842 Jul 06		35-0840
Washington (schooner)			
	Re 1835 Oct 04	fin	DLC-47
Washington Academy students			
	Fr 1815 Apr 22	add	4-1013
	To 1815 Apr 22	add	4-1014
Washington Alexandria & Georgetown Steam Packet Co			
	Fr 1834 Dec 05	fin	DLC-45

Weademann Philip			
	Fr 1836 Apr 03		M221-116
Weakley James H			
	Fr 1833 Jul 08		M639-26
	Re 1833 Jul 20		23-0173
Weakley Robert			
	Fr 1804 Jul 25		DLC-3
	Fr 1804 Aug 16		DLC-3
	Fr 1804 Aug 17		DLC-3
	To 1828 Aug 05		12-0123
	To 1836 Aug 27#		DLC-49
	Fr 1837 Mar 11		DLC-50
	Fr 1843 Feb 25#		DLC-74
	Fr 1845 Jan 29		36-1422
Weakley Robert et al			
	Fr 1836 Feb		M639-9
Weakley County TN citizens			
	To 1840 Sep 01		34-1586
Weatherford William			
	To 1814 Mar 28		3-0933
	Fr 1814 Mar 28		3-0935
Weathers Sarah Ann			
	Fr 1830 Nov 15		M221-111
Weaver George et al			
	Re 1836 Apr 21	par	30-1300
Weaver John et al			
	Fr 1835 cMar 01		M639-16
Weaver William A			
	Fr 1829 Oct 31		M639-13
	Fr 1832 Jun 28		20-0839
Webb Charles			
	To 1831 Sep 05		DLC-40
Webb Elizabeth			
	Fr 1836 Nov		M22-41
Webb James			
	Re 1829 Jun 06	mem	13-0588
	Fr 1837 Jan 23		M687-9
	Fr 1837 Feb		M687-9
Webb James Watson			
	Fr 1831 Dec 29		19-0455
Webb Quartus Morgan			
	Re 1831 Oct 25	par	18-1127
	Re 1831 Nov 08	par	18-1227
Webb Thomas T			
	Re 1835 Jan	mem	M124-146
Webb William			
	Fr 1815 Jan 31		DLC-16
Webber John A			
	Fr 1835 Apr 28		M639-26
Webster Daniel			
	Fr 1833 Mar 02#		M639-24
	Fr 1836 Apr 13		M687-28
	Re c1837 Jan	mem	DLC-49
Webster John D			
	Fr 1837 Mar 09	fin	DLC-50
Webster Naylor			
	Re 1830 Nov 26	par	16-0887
Wedderburn Alexander J			
	Fr 1835 Sep 02		28-1513
Weed John S et al			
	Fr 1831 Nov		M639-1
Weedon F			
	Fr 1831 Sep 28		M639-21
	Fr 1832 Dec 16		M639-26
Weeks Henry			
	Re 1829 Jul 31	par	13-1024
	Re 1829 Jul 31*	par	T967-1
Weeks John Wingate			
	Fr 1832 Jan 23		M639-5
Weems James J			
	Fr 1829 Jan 30		M639-21
Weems John Crompton			
	Fr 1829 Jun 09		M222-26
Weida John et al			
	Fr 1833 Jan 10		M639-7
Weightman Roger C			
	Fr 1825 Jul 26		10-1377
Weights and measures			
	Re 1829 cJun	mem	13-0530
Weirich Christian			
	Re 1834 Mar 26	par	25-0375
Welch Elizabeth (Ouilmett)			
	Fr 1831 Nov 21		18-1469
Welch Michael P			
	Fr 1831 Nov 21		18-1469
Welch William H			
	Fr 1831 May 09		M22-28
Welch Macomber & Co			
	Fr 1835 Jan 27		M179-79
Weller John B			
	Fr 1843 Dec 19		DLC-56
Welles Gideon			
	Fr 1832 Feb 04		19-0966
	Fr 1842 Feb 17		DLC-54
Welles & Co			
	Re 1834 Apr 15		25-0817
	To 1836 Feb 22		30-0485
Wells Charles			
	Fr 1833 Jun 21	add	23-0049
Wells Haydon			
	Fr 1794 Jul 12	fin	DLC-1
Wells James			
	Re 1794 Jan	leg	1-0182
Wells John Jr			
	Re 1835 May 30		28-0540
Wells John D			
	Fr 1839 Sep 07		DLC-52
Wells Joseph et al			
	Fr 1835 Jan 08		DLC-45
Wells Lemuel			
	Re 1831 Mar 02		17-0780
Wells Robert William			
	Fr 1830 Jan		14-1255
Wells Samuel A			
	Fr 1830 Dec 03#		M639-11
Wells Samuel A et al			
	Fr 1830 Nov 29		M639-11
	Fr 1830 Nov 29*		T239-2
Wells Thomas			
	Fr 1826 Nov 09	fin	DLC-34
	Fr 1826 Nov 09	fin	DLC-34
	Fr 1835 Aug 27	fin	28-1428
	Fr 1836 Apr 25#	fin	DLC-48
	Fr 1836 Jun 11	fin	DLC-48
	Fr 1836 Oct 06	fin	DLC-49
	Re 1838 Mar	mem	34-0259
	To 1838 Jul 20#	fin	DLC-51
	Re 1839	fin	DLC-52
Wells W			
	Fr 1815 Dec 29	fin	4-1309
Welsh Henry R			
	Fr 1830 Feb 27		M639-23
Welsh & Patterson			
	Fr 1835 Jan 30		M639-4
Weltberger Peter			
	Fr 1802 May 12	fin	DLC-2
Wentworth John et al			
	Fr 1830 Feb		M639-22

Wertz Henry
    Re 1831 May 26   17-1460
    Fr 1832 Nov 15   M639-5
West Cato
    Fr 1801 Jun 26   DLC-2
    To 1801 Aug 08   1-0904
West Charles S
    To 1822 Feb 14   M179-53
    To 1822 Feb 14*   DLC-31
    Fr 1822 Feb 26   fin   DLC-70
    Fr 1822 Feb 27   DLC-31
    Fr 1822 Mar 02   DLC-31
West Emanuel J
    Re 1829 Oct 22   14-0237
West George
    Fr 1813 Oct 30   DLC-7
    Fr 1813 Nov 05   DLC-7
    To 1813 Dec 08   DLC-61
    Fr 1818 May 30   DLC-25
West John B
    Fr 1839 Feb 20   fin   DLC-52
    Fr 1839 Mar 07   fin   DLC-52
West John K
    Fr 1836 Aug 08   M639-26
    Fr 1836 Sep 30   M124-154
West Nathaniel
    Fr 1834 Dec 23   26-1574
    Fr 1836 Feb 12   M639-26
West Robert
    Fr 1830 May 05#   fin   DLC-38
West Point
    Re 1830   mem   DLC-38
West Point cadets
    Re 1831 Aug 05   DLC-39
Westcott James Diament Jr
    Fr 1829 Jun 12   M639-26
    Re 1829 Jun 15   13-0670
    Fr 1831 Sep 25   M639-7
    Fr 1836 Dec 06   32-1041
Westcott James Diament Jr et al
    Fr 1831 Sep 25   M639-7
Westcott John Jr
    Fr 1832 Dec 15   M639-26
Weston Nathan et al
    Fr 1836 Feb 26   M639-27
Weston Thomas
    Fr 1821 Feb 26   fin   DLC-29
    Fr 1824 Jul 20   fin   DLC-33
Wetherald & Yeatman
    To 1811 May 22   fin   DLC-5
    Fr 1811 May 30   fin   DLC-5
Wetherbee John
    Fr 1843 Jan 09   DLC-55
Wetherill Samuel M
    To 1834 Dec 30   chk   DLC-45
    To c1835   27-0057
    Fr 1835 Jul 08   M639-16
    To 1836 Jan 14   chk   DLC-47
Wetherill Samuel M Mrs
    To 1834 Dec 09#   fin   DLC-47
Wetmore Alphonso
    Fr 1829 Jul 01   M639-26
    Fr 1829 Jul 11   13-0839
    Fr 1829 Jul 21   M222-26
    Fr 1829 Jul 28   M222-26
    Fr 1831 Jul   M234-749
    Re 1832 Oct 27   21-0199
Wetmore Prosper M
    Fr 1833 Apr 06   22-0961
    Fr 1837 Feb 11#   DLC-50
    Fr 1837 Feb 22#   DLC-74
Wewelino et al
    Fr 1829 Jun 29   M234-300
Whann Adam et al
    Fr 1829 May 05   M639-23
Whartenby Richard
    Fr 1818 Jun 21   DLC-25
    To 1821 Feb 16   8-0138
Wharton Charles H W
    Fr 1829 Mar 30   M639-26
    Fr 1831 Jan 26   M639-1
    Fr 1831 Jan 29   M639-27
    Fr 1833 Aug 31   M639-14
    Fr 1835 Jan 29   27-0351
Wharton Clifton
    Fr 1833 Sep   M567-82
Wharton Jesse
    Fr 1815 Feb 16   DLC-16
    Fr 1822 Apr 17   lnd   DLC-31
    Fr 1828 Dec 24   DLC-36
    To 1832 May 25   20-0600
Wharton John Overton
    Fr 1832 Dec 21#   21-1108
Wharton William Henry
    Fr 1822 Apr 30   fin   DLC-31
    Fr 1837 Feb 08   33-0571
    Fr 1837 Mar 03   DLC-50
Whatman G
    Fr 1839 Jul 15   fin   34-0845
Wheaton Henry
    Re 1831 Jan 08   17-0224
Wheeler Andrew C
    Fr 1834 Apr 24   25-0870
Wheeler John Hill
    Fr 1835 May 22   DLC-46
    To 1835 Jun 15   28-0687
    To 1842 Sep 09   35-0939
    Fr 1842 Dec 10   DLC-54
    To 1842 Dec 21   35-1052
    Fr 1843 Feb 01   DLC-55
Wheeler Samuel et al
    Fr 1835 Oct   29-0160
Wheelock Clarendon et al
    Fr 1836 Jun 04   31-0339
Wheelock Thompson B
    Fr 1832 Mar 09   19-1384
Whelpley Peter et al
    Fr 1835 Sep   28-1504
Whight Alvin Thomas
    Fr 1840 May 18   34-1367
Whipple George
    Fr 1839 Apr 04   DLC-52
Whitaker W H
    Fr 1829 Jul 02   M639-4
Whitcomb James
    Fr 1832 Jan 17   19-0749
    Re 1836 Oct 21   32-0317
    Fr 1836 Dec 12   M25-31
    Fr 1836 Dec 20   M25-31
    Fr 1836 Dec 23   32-1291
    Fr 1837 Jan 04   32-1491
    Fr 1837 Jan 04   32-1497
    Fr 1837 Jan 19   33-0057
    Fr 1837 Jan 20   33-0081
    Fr 1837 Jan 21   33-0103
    Fr 1837 Jan 31   33-0332
    Fr 1837 Feb 06   33-0464
    Fr 1837 Feb 08   33-0572

Whitcomb James (cont)
Fr 1837 Feb 10 33-0602
Fr 1837 Feb 10 33-0603
Fr 1837 Feb 11 33-0646
Fr 1837 Feb 16 33-0722
Fr 1837 Feb 17 33-0747
Fr 1837 Feb 17 33-0749
Fr 1837 Feb 21 33-0819
Fr 1837 Feb 28 33-0932
Fr 1837 Mar 03 33-1059
Whitcombe John B
To 1838 Jul 26# DLC-51
White A
Fr 1808 Nov 18 fin DLC-4
White Alexander A
Fr 1814 Dec 19 DLC-14
Fr 1819 Nov 10 DLC-28
Fr 1824 Dec 10 DLC-33
White Andrew
Fr 1803 Oct 10 1-1223
To 1803 Oct 13 1-1237
White Benjamin F
Re 1835 Jun 05 par 28-0582
White Campbell Patrick
Fr 1829 Mar 04 M639-5
Fr 1829 Mar 25 12-1132
Fr 1829 Apr 04 M639-25
Fr 1829 Apr 06 M639-22
Fr 1829 Apr 06* 12-1291
Fr 1829 Apr 18 M639-14
Fr 1830 Apr 20 15-0763
Fr 1831 Oct 14 M639-24
Fr 1832 Feb 25# M179-72
Fr 1833 Feb 22 22-0452
To 1833 Feb 23 22-0467
Fr 1833 May 24 DLC-43
Fr 1834 Jan 13 M639-18
Fr 1834 Jan 16 M639-18
Fr 1834 Mar 07 M639-18
Fr 1835 Nov 06 29-0466
To 1836 Feb 21 DLC-73
Fr 1836 Nov 15 32-0531
Fr 1837 Feb M22-41
White Chapman
To 1815 May 11 DLC-18
White Edward Douglass
To 1836 Aug 07 M179-82
To 1836 Aug 07* 31-1251
To 1836 Aug 07* DLC-48
To 1836 Aug 07* M567-122
White Edward Douglass et al
Fr 1832 Jan 04 M639-24
White Hays G
Fr 1815 Jan 23 DLC-15
Fr 1815 Feb 07 DLC-16
Fr 1815 Feb 26 DLC-17
Fr 1815 Apr 21 DLC-18
Fr 1815 Apr 23 DLC-18
White Hugh
Fr 1797 Sep 09 DLC-2
White Hugh Lawson
Fr 1812 Nov 16 DLC-5
Fr 1813 Sep 22 DLC-75
To 1814 Jan 06 DLC-61
Fr 1814 Jan 14 DLC-8
To 1819 Mar 25 add 7-0438
Fr 1819 Mar 25 add 7-0440
Fr 1821 Jan 29 8-0095
To 1824 Jan 22 10-0392
To 1826 Mar 16 11-0170
Fr 1827 Jan 17 DLC-34
Fr 1827 Feb 02 DLC-34
To 1827 Feb 07 DLC-34
To 1827 Feb 16 DLC-34
Fr 1827 Apr 07 DLC-34
Fr 1827 Jun 19 DLC-34
Fr 1827 Jun 20 DLC-34
Fr 1828 Feb 22 DLC-35
Fr 1828 Mar 02 DLC-72
To 1828 Mar 30 DLC-35
Fr 1828 Oct 04 DLC-35
To 1828 Oct 17 12-0235
To 1829 Oct 12 14-0150
To 1831 Apr 09 DLC-39
Fr 1831 Apr 20 DLC-39
To 1831 Apr 29 17-1264
To 1831 Apr 29* DLC-39
To 1831 Jun 01 17-1491
To 1831 Jun 01* DLC-39
Fr 1831 Jun 15 DLC-39
Fr 1832 Jan 16 19-0731
To 1832 Feb 06 DLC-73
Fr 1832 Dec 05 M639-4
To 1833 Mar 24 DLC-42
Fr 1833 Apr 11 DLC-42
Fr 1833 Nov 29# M234-75
To 1834 cJan 20 24-1024
Fr 1834 Feb 27 24-1490
Fr 1834 Dec 15 DLC-45
Fr 1835 Feb 14 DLC-45
Fr 1835 Feb 20 DLC-45
Re 1835 cAug mem DLC-73
Re 1835 cOct 10 mem 29-0272
To 1836 Jan 23 DLC-73
Re 1837 May mem 33-1201
Re 1837 cJul 21 mem 33-1386
Re 1837 Jul 27 DLC-74
White J C
Fr 1835 Aug 22# fin DLC-46
Fr 1835 Dec 12# fin DLC-47
White James
Fr 1813 Oct 06 DLC-61
Fr 1813 Oct 13 DLC-61
To 1813 Oct 23 DLC-61
To 1813 Oct 23* 3-0540
To 1813 Oct 31 DLC-61
To 1813 Oct 31* 3-0556
Fr 1813 Nov 01 DLC-61
Fr 1813 Nov 01* 3-0559
To 1813 Nov 04 DLC-61
To 1813 Nov 04* 3-0570
Fr 1813 Nov 05 DLC-61
Fr 1813 Nov 05* 3-0575
To 1813 Nov 07 DLC-61
To 1813 Nov 07* 3-0578
Fr 1813 Nov 07 DLC-61
Fr 1814 Jul 17 DLC-11
White James L Jr
Fr 1836 Mar 26 M687-17
White John
Re 1835 Jun 30 par 28-0849
White John Blake
Fr 1819 Apr 29 DLC-26
Fr 1844 Feb 29 36-0355
White John Campbell
Fr 1829 Apr 05 M639-25
White John Campbell et al
Fr 1829 Apr 05 M639-25

White Joseph		
Fr 1831 Jan 08#		M179-70
Fr 1834 May 29#		M179-78
Fr 1836 Nov 15		32-0534
Fr 1836 Nov 16		32-0542
White Joseph M		
Fr 1825 Dec 03		DLC-33
To 1825 Dec 29		11-0081
To 1825 Dec 29*		DLC-33
Fr 1829 Feb 24		M639-4
Fr 1831 Oct 12		M639-24
Fr 1831 Oct 27		M639-21
Fr 1832 Jan 19		M234-800
Fr 1832 Nov 16		21-0411
Fr 1834 Mar 25		M179-77
Fr 1835 Mar 10		M639-7
Fr 1836 Jan 13		M124-151
Fr 1836 Feb 13		M124-151
Fr 1836 May 03		M639-27
Fr 1836 May 14		DLC-48
Fr 1836 May 26		31-0129
Fr 1836 May 28		M567-133
Fr 1836 May 28*		31-0191
Fr 1836 Jul 29		DLC-48
Re 1837 Jun 02		33-1271
White Joseph M et al		
Fr 1837 Feb 11		M687-9
White Joseph W		
Fr 1829 Jul 04		M639-26
Fr 1829 Aug 06		M639-26
White Maunsel		
Fr 1815 Feb 03		DLC-16
Fr 1815 Feb 20		DLC-16
Fr 1815 Nov 27		DLC-19
Fr 1826 Feb 16		DLC-33
Fr 1826 Mar 18		DLC-33
Fr 1826 Mar 22		DLC-33
Fr 1827 Apr 07		DLC-34
Fr 1827 Jun 14		DLC-34
Fr 1827 Jun 14	fin	DLC-34
Fr 1827 Aug 04		DLC-34
To 1827 Dec 17		11-0963
Fr 1828 Jan 26		11-1075
To 1828 Dec 12		12-0321
Fr 1830 May 14		DLC-38
Fr 1831 Jan 29		DLC-39
Fr 1832 Jun 09		DLC-40
Fr 1832 Dec 14		DLC-41
To 1832 Dec 22		21-1135
Fr 1833 Jan 12		21-1407
Fr 1834 Apr 18		DLC-44
Fr 1834 Nov 29		DLC-45
Fr c1835		37-0338
To 1836 Jan 24		30-0194
To 1836 Dec 02		32-0622
To 1837 Jan 27		33-0194
Fr 1837 May 30		DLC-50
To 1837 Jul 12		33-1370
To 1837 Aug 23		33-1434
Re 1837 Dec 13	mem	DLC-50
Fr 1837 Dec 29		DLC-50
To 1838 Jan 27		34-0223
Fr 1838 Mar 03		DLC-51
To 1838 Apr 07		34-0306
To 1838 Apr 20		34-0335
Fr 1838 May 30		DLC-51
To 1838 Jun 15		34-0374
Fr 1839 Aug 10		DLC-52
Fr 1839 Nov 03		DLC-52
To 1840 Apr 07		34-1292
To 1840 Apr 20		34-1314
Fr 1840 Jun 03		DLC-52
To 1841 Jan 01		35-0191
Fr 1841 Jan 06		DLC-53
Fr 1841 Mar 20		DLC-53
Fr 1841 Jun 22		DLC-53
Fr 1841 Dec 08		DLC-54
Fr 1841 Dec 17		35-0536
To 1842 Feb 28		35-0642
Fr 1842 Apr 07		DLC-54
Fr 1842 Apr 07*		35-0676
Fr 1842 Jun 06		DLC-54
To 1843 Sep 29		35-1515
Fr 1843 Nov 27		36-0030
Fr 1843 Dec 14		36-0047
To 1844 Jan 12		36-0123
Fr 1844 Feb 13		DLC-56
To 1844 Mar 04		36-0368
Fr 1845 Jan 26		36-1411
Fr 1845 Mar 12		DLC-57
Fr 1845 Mar 12*		36-1571
To 1845 Mar 27		37-0052
Fr 1845 May 01		37-0173
White Maunsel & Co		
To 1826 Feb 26	fin	11-0147
To 1838 Jan 29		34-0228
Fr 1838 Feb 24	fin	34-0256
Fr 1839 Mar 02		DLC-52
Fr 1839 Apr 01		DLC-52
To 1839 Apr 25#	fin	DLC-52
Fr 1840 Jan 28	fin	34-1190
Fr 1840 Mar 18	fin	DLC-53
Fr 1840 Mar 31	fin	DLC-52
Fr 1840 Apr 07		DLC-52
Fr 1840 May 09		DLC-52
Fr 1840 Nov 21		DLC-53
Fr 1840 Nov 25	fin	DLC-53
Fr 1840 Nov 30		DLC-53
Fr 1840 Dec 23		DLC-53
Fr 1840 Dec 28	fin	DLC-53
Fr 1840 Dec 29		DLC-53
Fr 1841 May 24		DLC-53
Fr 1842 Feb 05		DLC-54
Fr 1842 Feb 28		DLC-54
Fr 1842 Jun 06		DLC-54
To 1843 Mar 30		35-1294
To 1843 Mar 30	fin	35-1295
To 1843 Apr 21		35-1340
Fr 1843 Nov 25		DLC-56
Fr 1844 Jan 20		DLC-56
Fr 1844 Feb 10		DLC-56
Fr 1844 Feb 13		DLC-56
Fr 1844 May 07		DLC-56
Fr 1844 Nov 20		DLC-57
White Peter		
Fr 1835 Oct 08		29-0237
White Seneca		
Fr 1831 Jan 11		M234-808
Fr 1831 Jan 11*		17-0231
White Seth et al		
Fr 1835 cJan		DLC-59
White Thomas et al		
Fr 1829 Mar 02		M639-1
White William		
Fr 1814 Jan 16		DLC-8
Fr 1814 Mar 30		DLC-9
To 1814 Apr 02		DLC-10
Fr 1832 Oct 31		M639-4

White William F
Fr 1833 Oct 09 M639-3
White William J
Fr 1835 Apr 16 M179-80
White County TN
Re 1808 May 21 lnd 2-0671
Whitecar William B
Fr 1844 Oct 29# 36-0964
Fr 1844 Nov 06# 36-0996
Whitehead John
Fr 1829 May 25 M639-26
Fr 1834 May 23 M639-24
Whitehead William Adee
Fr 1833 Apr 20 22-1079
Whiteley William et al
Fr 1829 Feb 26 M639-4
Whiteside A G
Fr 1836 Oct 20 M567-132
Whiteside Jenkin
Fr 1802 Jun 14 DLC-2
Fr 1807 Feb 09 DLC-4
Fr 1810 Jan 26 DLC-4
To 1810 Feb 10 DLC-4
To 1810 Feb 10 DLC-4
Fr 1810 Mar 11 DLC-75
To 1810 Jun 16 fin DLC-4
To 1811 Jul 03 chk DLC-58
Re 1813 Jan 09 leg 3-0240
Fr 1815 Aug 12 mem DLC-60
To 1815 Aug 22 DLC-19
To 1816 Jul 08 chk DLC-21
Fr 1820 Mar 21 lnd 7-1058
To 1820 Mar 21 fin 7-1056
Fr 1820 Nov 13 fin 7-1412
Fr 1821 Apr 09 DLC-70
Re 1821 Apr 13 leg 8-0316
Re 1821 Apr 13* leg DLC-30
Whitesides David
Fr 1820 Oct 02# fin DLC-29
Whiteworth Jeremiah
To 1807 May 11 lnd 2-0493
Whitfield E H et al
Fr 1832 cJan 19-0564
Whitfield Newton L
Fr 1836 Feb 11 M234-189
Whiting Levi
Fr 1818 Oct 31 DLC-26
Fr 1818 Oct 31* 6-1399
Fr 1820 Jul 28 7-1179
Re 1835 Jun 17 M567-109
Whitlock E D
Re 1832 May 22 M273-28
Fr 1832 Jun 20 M124-133
Whitlock James
Fr 1835 Oct 27 M639-18
Whitlock William et al
Fr c1833 21-1254
Whitney C F
Fr 1842 Sep 28 DLC-54
Whitney J
Fr 1824 Dec 15# fin DLC-33
Whitney James
Re 1832 Aug 25 par 20-1382
Whitney Joel et al
Fr 1829 Jun 13 M639-24
Whitney Marshall H
Fr 1837 Feb 21 M687-20
Whitney Reuben M
Fr 1833 Mar 18 DLC-42
Fr 1833 Apr 03 DLC-42
Fr 1833 Apr 03 22-0934
Fr 1833 Apr 30 22-1222
Fr 1834 Oct 06 DLC-44
Fr 1835 Jan 21 M639-10
Fr 1835 Feb 11 M639-10
Fr 1836 Mar 24 DLC-47
Fr 1836 Mar 25 DLC-47
Fr 1836 Oct 27 DLC-49
Fr 1837 May 31 DLC-50
Fr 1844 Apr 09 DLC-56
Whitney & Ford
Fr 1835 Aug 22# fin DLC-46
Fr 1835 Sep# fin DLC-47
Fr 1836 Feb# fin DLC-47
Whitsell William D
Re 1814 Nov 17 4-0362
Whitsett John C
Fr 1834 Oct 25 M234-188
Fr 1834 Oct 25* 26-0739
Whitson Elizabeth
Fr 1803 Sep 02 fin DLC-3
To 1805 Sep 02 fin DLC-3
Whittemore Bernard B
Fr 1835 Mar 01 DLC-45
Whittier Ebenezer et al
Fr 1830 Aug M639-4
Whittle William A
Fr 1836 Jun 07 31-0398
Whittlesey Charles
Fr 1832 Jul 04 M567-77
Whittlesey Elisha
Fr 1832 Jan 28 M639-10
Fr 1834 Jan 29 24-1103
To 1834 Feb 04 24-1237
Fr 1834 Jun 21 25-1483
To 1834 Jun 21 25-1485
Fr 1836 Jan 07 29-1500
To 1836 cJan 07 29-1504
Whyte J A
Fr 1830 Aug 12 DLC-38
Whyte Robert
To 1806 Mar 18 2-0191
To 1806 Aug 23 2-0320
Wickham A
Fr 1838 Apr 02 DLC-51
Fr 1838 Jun 09 DLC-51
Wickham James McClung
Fr 1833 Dec 04 M639-27
Wickliffe Charles Anderson
Fr 1826 Jul 08 DLC-34
Fr 1829 cMar 01 12-0816
Fr 1844 Sep 26 DLC-57
Wickliffe Charles Anderson et al
Fr 1829 cMar 01 12-0815
Wickliffe Robert
Fr 1820 Apr 13 M439-15
Wiggin George S et al
Fr 1837 Jan 30 M687-20
Wiggins ______
Fr 1825 Mar 20 fin DLC-72
Wilber Reuben et al
Fr 1831 Dec 07 M639-20
Wilcher William W
Re 1831 Feb 16 par 17-0553
Wilcox John
Fr 1836 Feb 09 M567-133
Wilder M A et al
Fr 1837 Feb 14 M687-20

Wiley John S
Re 1834 Oct 15 M273-31
Wilie ______
Fr 1825 DLC-33
Wilkes John
Fr 1807 Jan 29 DLC-4
Wilkeson Meredith
Fr 1826 Sep 27 fin DLC-34
Fr 1826 Sep 27 fin DLC-34
Wilkins Henry F
Fr 1830 Jun 14 15-1405
Wilkins James C
Fr 1817 May 13 DLC-22
Fr 1817 May 14 DLC-22
Wilkins Lewis M
Re 1835 Jun 16 M273-32
Wilkins Ross
Fr 1829 May 26 M688-60
Fr 1829 Sep 08 M639-3
Fr 1830 Apr 03# DLC-38
Fr 1830 May 05 DLC-38
Fr 1830 May 06# DLC-38
Fr 1835 Oct 25 M639-27
Wilkins William
Fr 1831 Sep 24 M639-13
Fr 1832 Jun 13 M84-2
Fr 1832 Jul 06 M567-67
Fr c1834# 37-0327
Fr 1834 Jul 02 M639-1
Fr 1834 Aug 05 26-0278
Fr 1834 Aug 16 DLC-44
Fr 1835 Dec 24 DLC-47
To 1843 Nov 22 36-0018
To 1844 May 20 36-0561
Wilkins William et al
Fr 1832 M639-18
Fr 1832 Feb 03 19-0952
Wilkinson James
Fr 1806 Dec 19 2-0407
Fr 1813 Jan 06 DLC-5
Fr 1813 Jan 06* DLC-61
Fr 1813 Jan 22 DLC-6
Fr 1813 Jan 22* DLC-61
Fr 1813 Jan 22* 3-0257
Fr 1813 Jan 25 DLC-6
Fr 1813 Jan 25* DLC-61
Fr 1813 Jan 25* 3-0261
To 1813 Feb 16 DLC-61
To 1813 Feb 16* M222-8
To 1813 Feb 20 DLC-61
To 1813 Feb 20* M222-8
To 1813 Feb 20* 3-0277
Fr 1813 Feb 22 DLC-6
Fr 1813 Feb 22* DLC-61
Fr 1813 Feb 22* M222-9
To 1813 Mar 01 DLC-61
Fr 1813 Mar 01 DLC-6
Fr 1813 Mar 01* DLC-61
Fr 1813 Mar 01* M222-9
Fr 1813 Mar 08 DLC-6
Fr 1813 Mar 08* 3-0294
Fr 1813 Mar 08* DLC-61
To 1813 Mar 08 DLC-61
To 1813 Mar 08* M222-9
To 1813 Mar 15 DLC-6
To 1813 Mar 15* 3-0320
To 1813 Mar 15* DLC-61
Fr 1813 Mar 16 DLC-61
Fr 1813 Mar 16* M222-9
Fr 1813 Mar 16* 3-0335
Fr 1813 Mar 20 3-0341
To 1813 Mar 22 DLC-61
Wilkinson James A et al
Fr 1829 Mar 12-0710
Wilkinson Jesse
To 1797 Jan 06 1-0473
Fr 1829 Mar 10 M625-405
Wilkinson John et al
Fr 1834 Dec 23 M639-7
Wilkinson Kinchen T
Fr 1812 May 28 DLC-5
Fr 1814 Nov 06 DLC-13
Fr 1816 Jul 24 DLC-21
To 1816 Aug 12 chk DLC-21
Wilkinson Nathaniel G
Fr 1815 Jun 05 DLC-18
Wilkinson William Jasper
Re 1836 Jan 25 par 30-0197
Willard F et al
Fr 1836 Jun 03 31-0302
Willard William Tell
Fr 1843 Mar 18 DLC-55
Willcox Norris
Fr 1832 Jan 19 19-0784
Fr 1833 Nov 04 23-1193
Fr 1836 May 27 M687-17
Willey William J et al
Fr 1836 Mar 21 M639-6
William Ewing (bark)
Re 1833 Jul 20 par 23-0179
William I King of the Netherlands
To 1829 Oct 31 14-0292
Fr 1830 Sep 15 16-0246
To 1830 Nov 18 16-0804
Fr 1832 Sep 06 20-1496
Fr 1833 Jul 06 23-0093
Fr 1833 Jul 06* M56-1
To 1833 Oct 01 23-0935
Fr 1834 Nov 02 26-0811
Fr 1834 Nov 02* M56-1
To 1834 Dec 30 27-0045
Fr 1836 Apr 25 M56-1
Fr 1836 Aug 25 31-1369
To 1836 Oct 19 32-0247
William IV King of Great Britain
Fr 1830 Jun 29 15-1554
Fr 1830 Jun 30 15-1558
Fr 1830 Jun 30* M50-15
To 1830 Aug 12 16-0103
To 1830 Sep 29 16-0271
To 1830 Sep 29 16-0272
Fr 1830 Dec 16 16-1462
To 1831 Aug 01 18-0396
To 1834 Mar 17 25-0263
Fr 1834 Dec 05 26-1421
To 1835 Jan 19 27-0259
Fr 1835 Sep 22 29-0094
Fr 1835 Oct 02 29-0170
To 1836 Apr 01 30-0978
To 1836 Apr 01 30-0979
Williams ______ (Col)
Fr 1831 Dec 15 M639-6
Williams Benjamin
Fr 1832 Mar 05 M179-72
Williams Daniel Jr
Fr 1814 Jun 30 DLC-11
Williams David C
Fr 1806 Jul 26 2-0306
Fr 1814 Sep 10 DLC-12

Williams David Rogerson			
	Fr 1815 Dec 22		DLC-20
	To 1816 Feb 09		DLC-62
Williams E D et al			
	To 1837 Feb 16		33-0731
Williams Edward			
	Re 1813 Sep 07	leg	3-0454
Williams Elijah			
	To 1828 Jan 29	fin	DLC-35
Williams Elizabeth			
	Fr 1829 May 03		M179-67
Williams Ethelred			
	Fr 1802 Mar 28	fin	DLC-2
	Re 1806 Jul 09	mem	DLC-4
	To 1807 Feb 10	lnd	2-0462
	Re 1807 May	mem	DLC-75
	Re 1807 Oct 17		DLC-4
Williams G B			
	Fr 1837 Apr 10		DLC-50
Williams George G			
	Fr 1829 Jun 15		M639-4
Williams George W			
	Fr 1842 Feb 04		DLC-54
Williams Henry			
	Re 1831 Jan 29	par	17-0376
Williams Henry J			
	Fr 1835 Sep 15		DLC-47
	To 1835 Sep 18		DLC-47
Williams Hezekiah et al			
	Fr 1836 Dec 05		M687-3
Williams J			
	Fr 1845 Feb 08		M873-7
Williams J et al			
	Fr 1845 Feb 08		M873-7
Williams James			
	Fr 1833 Aug 27		23-0471
	Re 1833 Oct 15	par	23-1039
	Fr 1834 May 09		M639-17
	Re 1836 Apr 27	par	30-1395
Williams James Glasgow			
	Fr 1834 Apr 16		M234-76
Williams James L			
	Re 1836 Oct 11		M273-33
Williams John			
	Fr 1810 Feb 17		DLC-4
	Fr 1810 Dec 15	fin	DLC-71
	Fr 1812 Jun 16		DLC-5
	To 1812 Aug 25		2-1234
	To 1812 Aug 25*		DLC-5
	To 1814 Jan 07		DLC-61
	To 1814 Jan 15		DLC-61
	Fr 1814 Jan 22		DLC-8
	To 1814 Feb 04		DLC-61
	Fr 1814 Feb 04		DLC-61
	To 1814 Feb 09		DLC-62
	To 1814 Feb 09*		3-0863
	Fr 1814 Feb 10		3-0866
	To 1814 Feb 19		DLC-62
	To 1814 Feb 23		DLC-62
	Fr 1814 Mar 13		DLC-9
	To 1814 Mar 13		DLC-62
	To 1814 Mar 14		DLC-9
	Fr 1814 Mar 22		DLC-9
	Fr 1814 cMay 08		DLC-10
	To 1814 May 18		3-1031
	To 1814 May 18*		DLC-10
	To 1814 May 26		3-1066
	Fr 1814 Jul 15		DLC-11
	Fr 1814 Aug 21		DLC-11
	To 1814 Sep 26		DLC-62
	To 1814 Oct 17		DLC-62
	Fr 1814 Oct 23		DLC-13
	Fr 1814 Nov 01		DLC-13
	Fr 1815 Feb 19		DLC-16
	Fr 1815 May 31		DLC-18
	Fr 1815 Jun 18		DLC-18
	Fr 1815 Jun 20		DLC-18
	To 1815 Jun 30		DLC-18
	Fr 1815 Aug 14		DLC-19
	Re 1836 cNov 15	mem	DLC-49
Williams John & Co			
	Fr 1828 May 24#	fin	DLC-35
	Fr 1828 Dec 04#	fin	DLC-36
Williams John I			
	Fr 1829 Mar 10		12-0937
Williams John R			
	Fr 1836 Dec 15		32-1147
Williams John W			
	Fr 1837 Jun 07		DLC-50
Williams Lewis			
	Fr 1833 Feb 02		DLC-42
Williams Lewis et al			
	Fr 1829 Mar 03		M639-3
Williams Micajah Terrell			
	Re 1831 Mar 29		17-1009
	Fr 1833 Oct 03		M639-24
	Fr 1835 Mar 19		27-1236
	Fr 1835 Mar 20		M639-1
	Fr 1836 Feb 26		M639-27
Williams Nathan			
	Fr 1840 Sep 08	fin	DLC-53
Williams Nathaniel			
	Re 1806 Oct 20	leg	2-0363
	Fr 1829 Jun 03		M179-67
	To 1829 Oct 13		DLC-37
	Fr 1836 Dec 31		M639-27
Williams Nathaniel W			
	To 1828 Feb 23		11-1139
	Fr 1828 Feb 27		11-1150
Williams O			
	Fr 1828 Sep 04		DLC-35
Williams Peter			
	Re 1834 Nov 08	par	26-0863
	Re 1836 Jan 22	par	30-0160
Williams R			
	Fr 1824 Dec 02#	fin	DLC-33
	Fr 1825 Jan 28	fin	DLC-33
Williams Reuel			
	Fr 1835 Oct 26		M639-27
	Fr 1837 Feb 16		M687-28
Williams Robert W			
	Fr 1830 Apr 26		15-0816
	Fr 1833 Jan 09#		DLC-41
Williams Rosetta			
	Re 1829 Sep 11	par	13-1305
	Re 1829 Sep 11*	par	T967-1
Williams S			
	Fr 1840 Jan 28#	fin	DLC-52
Williams Sampson			
	Fr 1794 Feb 12	lnd	1-0222
	Fr 1794 Feb 12*	lnd	DLC-1
	To 1794 Jul 19	fin	1-0237
	Fr 1801 Feb 18	lnd	1-0849
	Fr 1803 Jul 20		DLC-2
	Fr 1808 Apr 25		DLC-4
	Fr 1810 Jan 17		DLC-4
	Fr 1810 Jul 03		DLC-4
	Fr 1823 Sep 04		DLC-32

Williams Samuel H
Fr 1812 Jul 27 DLC-5
Williams Thomas Hickman
Fr 1842 Jan 08 DLC-54
To 1842 Jan 14 35-0598
Fr 1842 Jan 17 DLC-54
Williams Thomas Hill
Fr 1819 Mar 29 DLC-26
To 1821 Jan 01 8-0037
Fr 1821 Jan 29 DLC-29
To 1831 Apr 07 17-1079
Williams Turner
Fr 1791 Jul 07 fin 1-0097
Fr 1791 Jul 07* fin DLC-71
Williams W
Re c1829 mem 12-0411
Williams Wallace M
Fr 1834 Nov 04 M639-1
Williams William
Fr 1818 Jun 21 fin DLC-69
Fr 1818 Jun 21* fin 6-1076
To 1819 Sep 25 7-0681
Fr 1823 Apr 24 M688-32
Fr 1824 Dec 03 DLC-33
Re 1829 Dec 22 par 14-1096
Williams William A
Fr 1836 Feb 10 fin DLC-50
Fr 1836 Jun 06 fin DLC-48
Fr 1836 Jun 21 fin DLC-48
To 1836 Dec 17 chk DLC-49
Fr 1836 Dec 29# fin DLC-49
To 1836 Dec 30 chk DLC-49
Williams William Trumbull
Fr 1829 Feb 06 M639-26
Fr 1829 Aug 25 13-1201
Williams Willoughby
Fr 1835 Nov 11# fin DLC-47
Williams Young
Fr 1815 Feb 27 DLC-17
Williamson A J
Fr 1835 Oct 07 M221-115
Williamson Frances H
Fr 1829 Nov 30 M22-28
Fr 1831 Jul 27 M688-59
Fr c1832 Jan 03 19-0600
Fr 1835 Sep 26 29-0123
Williamson John
Fr 1805 Jun 03 DLC-3
Fr 1805 Sep 09 DLC-3
Fr 1805 Nov 07 DLC-3
Fr 1805 Dec 12 DLC-3
Fr 1806 May 29 2-0255
To 1806 Dec 06 fin DLC-4
To 1807 Jan 16 fin DLC-4
Re 1832 May 16 20-0535
Williamson John et al
Fr 1833 Nov 16 M639-8
Williamson Matthias
Fr 1835 27-0058
Williamson N G et al
Fr 1836 Nov 03 M639-2
Williamson Robert
Fr 1808 Mar 22 DLC-71
Williamson Russell M
Fr 1835 Feb 18 M639-7
Fr 1835 Apr 14 M639-11
Fr 1840 Jan 08 34-1151
Williamson Thomas
To 1807 Dec 15 fin DLC-59
Fr 1812 Mar 19 DLC-5
To 1813 Dec 17 DLC-61
Fr 1814 Feb 11 DLC-8
Fr 1818 Feb 14 DLC-24
Fr 1818 Apr 20 DLC-24
Fr 1823 Sep 20 DLC-32
To 1823 Sep 27 DLC-32
Williamson William Durkee
Fr 1829 Jun 22 M639-24
Williamson William S et al
Fr 1836 Nov 03 M567-131
Williamson County TN citizens
To 1815 May 15 add 4-1044
Willink R
Fr 1834 Oct 07 M179-78
Willis Abel
To 1814 Feb 02 DLC-61
Willis David P
Fr 1815 Feb 02 DLC-16
Willis Lewis B
Fr 1817 Jun 26 DLC-23
Fr 1817 Jul 08 DLC-23
Fr 1817 Dec 04 M222-19
Fr 1833 Jul 14 M639-27
Willis Nathan
Fr 1836 Oct 27 32-0354
Willis Perrin
Fr 1815 Dec 21# fin DLC-19
Fr 1820 Feb 21 DLC-28
Fr 1820 Feb 21* 7-1034
Willis W
Fr 1815 Feb 25 DLC-17
Willis William
Re 1832 Nov 27 par 21-0583
Wills Andrew et al
Fr 1826 Sep 27 DLC-34
To 1826 Oct 15 11-0383
Wills W R B
Fr 1844 Dec 28 DLC-57
Willson James et al
Fr 1835 Jul 14 28-1022
Willson Thomas D et al
Fr 1836 Dec 28 M639-15
Wilmer Simon
Fr 1831 Sep 05 18-0678
Wilson Aaron
Fr 1807 Sep 05 fin 2-0554
Wilson Aaron B et al
Fr 1836 Mar 05 30-0690
Wilson Andrew
Fr 1830 Dec 18 16-1501
Wilson Charles John Stuart
Fr 1831 May 17 M567-65
Wilson E
Fr 1832 Sep 06 fin DLC-41
Wilson Ephraim King et al
Fr 1830 Feb M639-11
Wilson George
Fr 1807 Feb 17 DLC-4
To 1824 Apr 17 10-0656
To 1824 Aug 11 10-0843
To 1824 Aug 13 10-0850
Fr 1824 Dec 18 DLC-33
To 1825 Feb 20 10-1139
To 1827 Jan 04 11-0463
Re 1830 Jun 14 par 15-1412
Wilson Henry
Fr 1829 Sep 12 M639-27
Fr 1829 Dec 07 M639-27

Wilson James
To 1807 Jan 02 fin DLC-4
Wilson James & Co
Fr 1840 Jan 14 fin 34-1173
Wilson James A
Re 1801 May 12 leg 1-0876
Wilson John
Fr 1831 Sep 08 M124-129
Fr 1831 Oct 10 M124-130
Wilson John G
Fr 1827 Mar 20 fin DLC-34
Wilson John Lyde
Fr 1828 Jan 27 DLC-72
Fr 1832 May 15 M639-11
Wilson Louis D
Fr 1843 Jan 28 DLC-55
Wilson Mason
Fr 1822 Mar 07 DLC-31
Wilson N & Co
Fr 1809 Dec 08 fin DLC-4
Wilson Nathaniel
Fr 1844 Jun 11 36-0602
Wilson Nel
Fr 1829 Apr 11 M639-27
Fr 1829 May 18 M639-27
Wilson S F
Fr 1844 Feb 14 DLC-56
Wilson Samuel
To 1821 Apr 08 lnd DLC-32
Wilson Thomas
Fr 1825 Dec 23 fin DLC-33
Wilson Thomas P
Fr 1829 Apr 10 M639-22
Wilson Thomas W
Fr 1838 Dec 03 DLC-51
Wilson William
Fr 1817 Jan 20 5-0709
Fr 1832 Dec 16 M639-26
Wilson & Peterson et al
Fr 1835 Aug 18 M639-18
Wilson County TN
Re 1802 Aug 16 lnd 1-1032
Re 1802 Aug 16* lnd DLC-2
Re 1816 Feb 28 lnd 4-1412
Wiltbank James
Fr 1835 Sep 26 29-0127
Fr 1837 Feb 07 33-0561
Re 1837 Feb 25 33-0908
Fr 1837 Mar 30 DLC-50
Winand Caroline B
Fr 1843 Aug 29 DLC-55
To 1843 Sep 14 35-1490
Fr 1843 Sep 29 35-1516
Winant Bornt P
Fr 1844 Jun 21 36-0638
Winborne Jesse
Fr 1827 Sep 24 fin 11-0877
Fr 1827 Dec 27 fin 11-0990
Fr 1828 Jan 14 fin 11-1059
Winborne William
Fr 1826 Jun 10 fin 11-0246
Winchester Benjamin
Fr 1829 Feb 05 M639-21
Winchester George
Fr 1825 Dec 21 DLC-33
To 1826 Jan 15 DLC-33
Fr 1831 Jul 14 18-0210
Fr 1832 Mar 16 M639-18
Fr 1832 Aug 16 M639-25

Winchester James
Fr c1797 Jan 1-0471
Fr 1797 Feb 08 DLC-1
Fr 1797 Sep 12 fin 1-0526
Fr 1802 Feb 08# 1-0952
To 1802 May 10 DLC-2
Fr 1803 Aug 23 1-1151
To 1805 Feb 17 2-0016
Fr 1805 Jun 22 DLC-3
Fr 1805 Aug 23 2-0079
To 1806 Jan 01 DLC-3
Fr 1806 Jun 29 DLC-4
To 1806 Oct 04 2-0358
To 1807 Jan 01 2-0423
To 1807 Jan 01 2-0427
To 1807 Jan 01 DLC-4
Fr 1807 Jan 06 DLC-4
Fr 1807 Jan 15 DLC-4
Fr 1807 Jul 16 DLC-4
Fr 1809 Mar 04 DLC-4
To 1809 Mar 15 DLC-4
Fr 1809 Aug 20 DLC-75
Fr 1811 Sep 19 2-1008
Fr 1812 Mar 19 2-1056
Fr 1812 Mar 23 DLC-5
Fr 1812 cApr 23 DLC-71
To 1812 Apr 23 2-1081
Fr 1814 Oct 20 DLC-13
Fr 1814 Nov 17 DLC-14
To 1814 Nov 18 DLC-71
To 1814 Nov 18* DLC-62
To 1814 Nov 21 DLC-71
To 1814 Nov 22 4-0371
To 1814 Nov 22* DLC-14
Fr 1814 Dec 01 DLC-14
Fr 1814 Dec 02 DLC-14
Fr 1814 Dec 05 DLC-14
Fr 1814 Dec 08 DLC-14
Fr 1814 Dec 09 DLC-14
To 1814 Dec 11 DLC-62
To 1814 Dec 16 DLC-62
To 1814 Dec 17 DLC-14
Fr 1814 Dec 17 DLC-14
To 1814 Dec 19 DLC-71
To 1814 Dec 19* DLC-62
Fr 1814 Dec 24 DLC-15
Fr 1814 Dec 26 DLC-15
Fr 1814 Dec 29 DLC-15
Fr 1815 Jan 03 DLC-15
To 1815 Jan 10 DLC-62
Fr 1815 Jan 15 4-0550
To 1815 Jan 19 DLC-15
Fr 1815 Jan 22 4-0598
Fr 1815 Jan 27 DLC-16
To 1815 Jan 31 4-0667
To 1815 Jan 31* DLC-16
Fr 1815 Feb 03 DLC-16
To 1815 Feb 10 DLC-16
To 1815 Feb 13 4-0738
To 1815 Feb 13* DLC-16
Fr 1815 Feb 16 DLC-16
Fr 1815 Feb 17 DLC-16
Fr 1815 Feb 20 DLC-16
Fr 1815 Feb 20 DLC-16
To 1815 Feb 22 4-0781
To 1815 Feb 22* DLC-17
To 1815 Feb 23 DLC-62
Fr 1815 Feb 25 DLC-17
Fr 1815 Feb 25 DLC-17

Fr 1815 Mar 02 DLC-17
To 1815 Mar 03 DLC-17
Fr 1815 Mar 06 DLC-17
Fr 1815 Mar 07 DLC-17
Fr 1815 Mar 09 DLC-17
Fr 1815 Mar 12 DLC-17
Fr 1815 Mar 18 DLC-17
Fr 1815 May 12 DLC-18
Fr 1815 May 19 DLC-18
Fr 1815 May 28 DLC-18
Fr 1815 Jun 05 DLC-18
Fr 1815 Jun 09 DLC-18
To 1815 Jun 14 4-1078
Fr 1815 Jul 09 4-1105
To 1817 May 11 5-0850
Fr 1817 May 24 5-0870
To 1818 Dec 12 lnd 7-0048
Re 1819 Jan 06 leg 7-0121
To 1819 Apr 13 7-0475
Fr 1821 Mar 11 DLC-30
Fr 1821 Mar 18 DLC-30

Winchester Marcus Brutus
Fr 1818 Oct 12 DLC-62
Fr 1818 Oct 12* T494-1
Fr 1841 May 23# fin DLC-53

Winchester Richard
To 1797 Jul 03 lnd 1-0515

Winchester Stephen
To 1797 Jul 03 lnd 1-0521

Winchester Thomas
Fr 1836 Aug 18 M221-116

Winchester & Cage
Fr 1805 Apr 30 DLC-3
Fr 1806 Aug 23 DLC-59

Windle Joseph A
Fr 1815 Dec 16 DLC-19

Wing Austin Eli
Fr 1833 Feb 18 22-0407
Fr 1836 Oct 31-1546
Fr 1836 Oct* M179-82

Wingate Harrison
Fr 1835 Mar 03 M124-147

Wingate Joseph Ferdinand
To 1831 Feb 08# 17-0888
To 1831 Feb 08* M40-22

Winn John W
Fr 1815 Apr 19 fin DLC-18

Winn Richard
Fr 1812 Jun 18 2-1106
Fr 1815 Feb 01 DLC-16
Fr 1838 Feb DLC-51

Winn Thomas M
Fr 1816 Jan 10 DLC-20

Winnebago treaty
Re 1830 Jan 02 M668-6
Re 1833 Feb 13 M668-6

Winslow Joshua
Re 1829 Apr 30 par 13-0195
Re 1829 Apr 30* par T967-1

Winston Anthony
Re 1807 Aug 01 leg 2-0537
Fr 1823 Feb 18 fin 9-0455
To 1826 Dec 11 fin 11-0426
Fr 1829 Jun 11 M639-4

Winston Anthony et al
Fr 1824 Aug 28 DLC-33
To 1824 Aug 29 DLC-33

Winston Isaac
Fr 1844 Nov 19 M687-34

Winston John
To 1805 May 01 fin DLC-3

Winston John J
To 1807 Jan 27 fin DLC-4
To 1807 Mar 30 fin DLC-4
Fr 1833 Feb 01 22-0239
Fr 1837 Nov 08 M687-7
Fr 1844 Jan 29 DLC-56
Fr 1845 Mar 07 M873-96

Winston John J et al
Fr 1829 Jun M639-4

Winston Louis
To 1813 Dec 18 DLC-61
Fr 1813 Dec 18 DLC-7
Fr 1816 Jul 02 5-0256

Winston Thomas B
Fr 1842 Mar 12 DLC-54

Winston W
Fr 1803 Dec 30 fin DLC-3

Winston William O
Fr 1814 Sep 21 DLC-12
Fr 1816 May 28 DLC-20
Fr 1816 Jul 18 DLC-21
Fr 1816 Sep 01 DLC-21
Fr 1819 Mar 12 DLC-72
Fr 1819 May 12 DLC-27

Winter Gabriel
Fr 1844 Dec 01 DLC-57

Winthrop Grenville T
Fr 1834 Oct 11 M639-27

Wirt Elizabeth Washington
Fr 1834 Feb 27 24-1496

Wise Henry Alexander
Fr 1829 Apr 04 M639-7
Fr 1834 Jan 11 M639-21
Fr 1834 Jan 14 24-0886
Fr 1834 Jan 31 DLC-73
Re 1837 DLC-50
Re 1837 mem 32-1458
Re 1837 DLC-50
Fr 1837 Jan 24 DLC-49
To 1837 Jan 26 DLC-49
To 1837 Jan 31 DLC-49
Fr 1837 Feb 16 33-0733

Wise Jacob M et al
Fr 1829 Mar M639-12
Fr 1831 Feb 03 17-0430
To 1831 Feb 09 17-0485

Wishart John et al
Fr 1831 Nov M639-1

Witherell Benjamin F H
Fr 1830 Apr 24 M639-27

Witherell Benjamin F H et al
Fr 1829 Dec M639-20

Withers Alexander S
Fr 1829 Aug 07 M639-12

Witherspoon James H
To 1824 Aug 11 DLC-33
Fr 1825 Apr 16 DLC-33
To 1829 May 25 13-0429
To 1836 Dec 12 32-1125

Witherspoon James H et al
Fr 1828 May 12 DLC-35
To 1828 Jun 02 12-0016
To 1828 Jun 02* DLC-35

Witherspoon John
To 1795 Dec 14 fin 1-0331
To 1795 Dec 14 lnd 1-0332

Witte William H
Fr 1844 Apr 18 DLC-56

Wofford W B et al
Fr 1837 cFeb 24 33-0864
Wolbert Frederick G
Fr 1829 Aug 29 M124-120
Wolf George
Fr 1830 Jan 18# 14-1460
To 1834 Mar 01 DLC-43
To 1834 Mar 10 25-0034
Fr 1835 Apr 18 DLC-46
Fr 1836 Jan 14 DLC-47
Fr 1836 Feb 08 M639-8
Fr 1836 Oct M22-41
Wolf George et al
Fr 1836 Nov 24 M687-25
Wolfe Daniel et al
Fr 1842 Nov 28 DLC-54
WolfeTone William Theobald
Fr 1819 Jun 16 DLC-27
Wollstonecraft Charles
Fr 1814 Jul 19 DLC-11
Fr 1814 Aug 16 DLC-11
Fr 1814 Aug 26 DLC-11
Fr 1814 Sep 13 DLC-12
Fr 1814 Sep 27 DLC-12
Fr 1814 Oct 03 DLC-13
Fr 1814 Dec 16 DLC-14
Fr 1814 Dec 18 DLC-14
Fr 1815 Feb 20 DLC-16
Fr 1815 Feb 20 DLC-16
To 1815 Feb 21 DLC-17
Fr 1815 Feb 24 DLC-17
To 1815 Feb 26 DLC-62
To 1815 Feb 26 DLC-62
Fr 1815 Feb 28 DLC-75
Fr 1815 Mar 02 DLC-17
Fr 1815 Mar 05 DLC-17
Fr 1815 May 05# DLC-18
Fr 1815 Jun 26 DLC-18
Womack Abner
Fr 1815 Jun 17 DLC-18
Womack Jacob B
Fr 1836 Jan 18 M639-27
Womack John W
Fr 1835 Nov 18 29-0531
Womer William M
Fr 1825 Mar 04 fin 10-1213
Wood Abiel et al
Fr 1829 May 30 M639-24
Wood Ann
Re 1844 Jul 02 mem 36-0679
Wood Charlotte
Fr 1834 Mar 13 M688-79
Wood Ephraim
Fr 1831 May 11 M22-28
Wood Ingham
Fr 1836 Nov 27 M567-134
Wood James B
Re 1834 Jul 01 par 26-0061
Wood John
Re 1814 Feb 23 DLC-62
To 1814 Mar 14 DLC-62
Fr 1832 Apr 06 M22-29
Wood William
To 1834 Apr 14 chk DLC-44
Fr 1835 Jul 04 DLC-46
Wood William P M
Fr 1829 Aug 16 M639-27
Woodbury Levi
To 1828 Jun 23 12-0030
Fr 1829 Mar 03 12-0839
Fr 1829 May 02 M639-4
Fr 1829 Jun 20 13-0694
To c1831 17-0100
Fr 1831 Feb 05 17-0446
To 1831 Apr 21 DLC-39
Fr 1831 Apr 27 DLC-39
To 1831 May 01 DLC-39
Re 1831 May 23 17-1416
Fr 1831 May 24 M472-2
To 1831 May 25 17-1440
Fr 1831 Jun 13 M472-2
Fr 1831 Jun 24 M472-2
Fr 1831 Jun 27 18-0126
Fr 1831 Jun 27* M472-2
Fr 1831 Jun 27 M273-25
Fr 1831 Jun 27* M472-2
Fr 1831 Jun 28 DLC-39
Fr 1831 Jun 28 M472-2
Fr 1831 Jun 28 M472-2
Fr 1831 Jun 30 M472-2
Fr 1831 Jul 08 M472-2
Fr 1831 Jul 12 M472-2
Fr 1831 Jul 16 M472-2
Fr 1831 Jul 25 M472-2
To 1831 Jul 29 18-0327
Fr 1831 Aug 02 M472-2
Fr 1831 Aug 03 M472-2
To 1831 Aug 06 M124-129
Fr 1831 Aug 06 M472-2
Fr 1831 Aug 25 18-0589
Fr 1831 Sep 22 M472-2
Fr 1831 Sep 24 M472-2
Fr 1831 Oct 04 M472-2
Fr 1831 Oct 08 M472-2
Fr 1831 Oct 10 M472-2
Fr 1831 Oct 10 M472-2
Fr 1831 Oct 11 M472-2
Fr 1831 Oct 15 M472-2
To 1831 Oct 18 M221-111
To 1831 Oct 18* 18-1021
Fr 1831 Oct 18 M472-2
Fr 1831 Oct 18 18-1022
Fr 1831 Oct 19 M472-2
Fr 1831 Oct 20 M472-2
Fr 1831 Oct 26# 18-1136
Fr 1831 Nov 01 M472-2
Fr 1831 Nov 05 M472-2
Fr 1831 Nov 08 M472-2
Fr 1831 Nov 09 M472-2
Fr 1831 Nov 14 M124-130
Fr 1831 Nov 14* M472-2
Fr 1831 Nov 17 M472-2
Fr 1831 Nov 18 M472-2
Fr 1831 Nov 19 M472-2
Fr 1831 Nov 22 M472-2
Fr 1831 Nov 22 M472-2
Fr 1831 Nov 28 M472-2
Fr 1831 Dec 02 M472-2
Fr 1831 Dec 03 19-0010
Fr 1831 Dec 03* DLC-76
Fr 1831 Dec 09 M472-2
Fr 1831 Dec 15 M472-2
Fr 1831 Dec 30 M472-2
To 1832 Jan 04# 19-0611
Fr 1832 Jan 05 M472-2
Fr 1832 Jan 06 M472-2
Fr 1832 Jan 09 M472-2
Fr 1832 Jan 12 19-0676

Fr 1832 Jan 12*	M472-2
Fr 1832 Jan 12	M472-2
Fr 1832 Jan 12	M472-2
Fr 1832 Jan 12	M472-2
Fr 1832 Jan 14	M472-2
Fr 1832 Jan 16	M472-2
Fr 1832 Jan 20	M472-2
Fr 1832 Jan 21	M472-2
Fr 1832 Jan 25	19-0864
Fr 1832 Jan 25*	M472-2
Fr 1832 Jan 26	M472-2
Fr 1832 Jan 27	M472-2
Fr 1832 Jan 27	M472-2
Fr 1832 Jan 30	M472-2
Fr 1832 Feb 01	M472-2
Fr 1832 Feb 03	M472-2
To 1832 Feb 03#	M124-131
Fr 1832 Feb 04	M472-2
Fr 1832 Feb 06	M472-2
To 1832 Feb 07	19-0999
Fr 1832 Feb 08	M472-2
To 1832 cFeb 08	19-1023
Fr 1832 Feb 10	M472-2
Fr 1832 Feb 11	M472-2
Fr 1832 Feb 13	M472-2
Fr 1832 Feb 14	M472-2
Fr 1832 Feb 15	M124-131
Fr 1832 Feb 15*	M472-2
To 1832 Feb 16	M124-131
Fr 1832 Feb 16	M472-2
To 1832 Feb 20	19-1195
To 1832 Feb 20*	DLC-40
Fr 1832 Feb 20	M472-2
Fr 1832 Feb 29	M472-2
Fr 1832 Mar 02	M472-2
To 1832 Mar 09	19-1387
Fr 1832 Mar 09	M472-2
Fr 1832 Mar 20	19-1514
Fr 1832 Mar 20*	M472-2
Fr 1832 Mar 27	M472-2
Fr 1832 Mar 28	M472-2
To 1832 Mar 29	20-0059
Fr 1832 Mar 30	M179-72
Fr 1832 Mar 30*	M472-2
Fr 1832 Mar 30*	20-0065
To 1832 Apr#	M124-132
Fr 1832 Apr 04	M472-2
Fr 1832 Apr 13	M124-132
Fr 1832 Apr 13*	M472-2
To 1832 Apr 19	M124-132
Fr 1832 Apr 23	20-0380
Fr 1832 Apr 23*	M472-2
Fr 1832 Apr 23	M472-2
Fr 1832 Apr 26	M472-2
Fr 1832 Apr 30	M179-73
Fr 1832 Apr 30*	M472-2
Fr 1832 May 02	M472-2
Fr 1832 May 09	M472-2
Fr 1832 May 18	M179-73
Fr 1832 May 18*	M472-2
Fr 1832 May 21	M472-2
Fr 1832 May 22	20-0562
Fr 1832 May 22*	M472-2
Fr 1832 May 22	M472-2
To 1832 May 23#	M124-133
Fr 1832 May 24	M472-2
Fr 1832 May 25	M472-2
Fr 1832 Jun 01	M472-2
To 1832 Jun 09#	M179-73

Fr 1832 Jun 11	M472-2
Fr 1832 Jun 14#	DLC-40
Fr 1832 Jun 15	M472-2
Fr 1832 Jun 22	M472-2
Fr 1832 Jun 22	M472-2
Fr 1832 Jun 23	M472-2
Fr 1832 Jun 26	M124-133
Fr 1832 Jun 26*	M472-2
Fr 1832 Jun 27	M472-2
Fr 1832 Jun 27	M472-2
Fr 1832 Jul 12	M472-2
Fr 1832 Jul 14	M472-2
Fr 1832 Jul 16	M472-2
Fr 1832 Jul 17	20-1122
Fr 1832 Jul 17*	M472-2
Fr 1832 Jul 17	M472-2
Fr 1832 Jul 24	20-1245
Fr 1832 Jul 24*	M472-2
Fr 1832 Aug 25	M472-2
To 1832 Sep 01	20-1476
Fr 1832 Sep 03	M472-2
To 1832 Sep 05	20-1483
To 1832 Sep 11	DLC-41
Fr 1832 Sep 17	21-0028
Fr 1832 Sep 17*	M472-2
Fr 1832 Oct 20	M472-2
Fr 1832 Oct 23	M472-2
Fr 1832 Oct 23	M472-2
To 1832 Oct 27	21-0203
To 1832 Nov 06	M273-24
Fr 1832 Nov 08	M472-2
Fr 1832 Nov 10	M472-2
Fr 1832 Nov 10	M472-2
To 1832 Nov 13	21-0399
Fr 1832 Nov 15	M472-2
Fr 1832 Nov 28	21-0589
Fr 1832 Nov 28*	M472-2
To 1832 Nov 29	21-0616
Fr 1832 Nov 29	M472-2
Fr 1832 Dec 03	21-0665
To 1832 Dec 05#	21-0879
To 1832 Dec 12	M222-31
To 1832 Dec 12*	DLC-41
Fr 1832 Dec 13	M472-2
Fr 1832 Dec 15	M472-2
Fr 1832 Dec 22	21-1139
Fr 1832 Dec 22*	M472-2
Fr 1832 Dec 22	M472-2
Fr 1832 Dec 29	M472-2
Fr 1832 Dec 29	M472-2
Fr 1833 Jan 02	M472-2
Fr 1833 Jan 02	M472-2
Fr 1833 Jan 08	M472-2
Fr 1833 Jan 11	M472-2
Fr 1833 Jan 18	M472-2
Fr 1833 Jan 23	M472-2
Fr 1833 Jan 23	M472-2
To 1833 Jan 24#	M124-136
Fr 1833 Jan 25	M472-2
Fr 1833 Jan 26	M472-2
Fr 1833 Jan 31	M472-2
Fr 1833 Feb 05	22-0270
Fr 1833 Feb 05*	M472-2
Fr 1833 Feb 05	M472-2
Fr 1833 Feb 06	22-0296
Fr 1833 Feb 06*	M472-2
Fr 1833 Feb 12	M472-2
To 1833 Feb 22	22-0453
Fr 1833 Feb 26	M472-2

Woodbury Levi (cont)

Fr 1833 Mar 01		M472-2
Fr 1833 Mar 01		M472-2
Fr 1833 Mar 01		M472-2
Fr 1833 Mar 02		M472-2
Fr 1833 Mar 06		M472-2
Fr 1833 Mar 19		M472-2
Fr 1833 Mar 19		M472-2
Fr 1833 Mar 19*		22-0828
Fr 1833 Apr 02		DLC-42
To 1833 May 08#		22-1321
Fr 1833 May 10		22-1334
Fr 1833 May 25		M472-2
Fr 1833 May 27		M472-2
To 1833 May 28		M124-138
Fr 1833 May 28		M639-13
Fr 1833 May 28*		M472-2
Fr 1833 Jun 03		M472-2
Fr 1833 Jun 04		M472-2
Fr 1833 Jun 05		M472-2
Fr 1833 Jul 08		M472-2
Fr 1833 Jul 12		M472-2
To 1833 Jul 23		23-0210
Fr 1833 Jul 25		M472-2
Fr 1833 Jul 25		M472-2
To 1833 Sep 14		M124-139
Fr 1833 Sep 14		M472-2
Fr 1833 Sep 17		M472-2
Fr 1833 Sep 26		M472-2
To 1833 Sep 28		23-0901
Fr 1833 Sep 30		M472-2
Fr 1833 Oct 01		M472-2
To 1833 Oct 07		M124-140
Fr 1833 Oct 10		M472-2
Fr 1833 Oct 12		M472-2
Fr 1833 Oct 19		M472-2
Fr 1833 Nov 09		M472-2
Fr 1833 Nov 12		M472-2
Fr 1833 Nov 19		M472-2
Fr 1833 Nov 29		23-1370
Fr 1833 Nov 29*		M127-3
Fr 1833 Nov 29*		M472-2
Fr 1833 Nov 30		23-1414
Fr 1833 Dec 06		24-0413
Fr 1833 Dec 06*		M472-2
Fr 1833 Dec 09		M472-2
Fr 1833 Dec 21		24-0571
Fr 1833 Dec 21*		M472-2
Fr 1833 Dec 26		M472-2
Fr 1833 Dec 30		M472-2
To c1834#		24-0694
To 1834 Jan 04		M124-141
Fr 1834 Jan 04		M472-2
Fr 1834 Jan 08		M472-2
Fr 1834 Jan 09		24-0831
Fr 1834 Jan 09		M472-2
Fr 1834 Jan 11		M472-2
To 1834 Jan 26		M124-141
Fr 1834 Jan 28		M472-2
To 1834 Feb 01#		24-1134
Fr 1834 Feb 03		M472-2
Fr 1834 Feb 08		M472-2
Fr 1834 Feb 19		M472-2
To 1834 Feb 21#		M124-141
Fr 1834 Feb 26		M472-2
To 1834 Feb 28		24-1512
To 1834 Mar 07		24-1603
Fr 1834 Mar 07		M472-2
Fr 1834 Mar 18		M472-2
Fr 1834 Mar 21		M472-2
Fr 1834 Mar 29		M472-2
Fr 1834 Apr 01		M472-2
Fr 1834 Apr 08		M472-2
Fr 1834 Apr 12		M472-2
Fr 1834 Apr 16		M472-2
To 1834 Apr 16		M124-142
Fr 1834 Apr 17		M472-2
Fr 1834 Apr 19		M472-2
Fr 1834 Apr 23		M472-2
To 1834 Apr 26		M124-142
To 1834 Apr 30		25-0947
Fr 1834 May 02		M472-2
Fr 1834 May 05		M472-2
Fr 1834 May 10		M472-2
Fr 1834 May 16		M472-2
To 1834 May 17		M124-142
Fr 1834 May 17		M472-2
Fr 1834 May 20		M472-2
To 1834 May 20#		M124-142
Fr 1834 May 21		25-1117
To 1834 May 25		25-1148
Fr 1834 May 29		M472-2
Fr 1834 Jun 02		M472-2
Fr 1834 Jun 05		M472-2
Fr 1834 Jun 05		M472-2
To 1834 Jun 06		DLC-44
To 1834 Jun 13		M124-142
Fr 1834 Jun 13		M472-2
Fr 1834 Jun 17		M472-2
Fr 1834 Jun 18		M472-2
Fr 1834 Jun 24		M472-2
Fr 1834 Jun 24		M472-2
To 1834 Jun 25		25-1547
Fr 1834 Jun 25		M472-2
Fr 1834 Jun 26		M472-2
Fr 1834 Jun 28		M472-2
To 1834 Jul 03		26-0132
Fr 1834 Jul 05		26-0164
Fr 1834 Jul 05*		M415-1
To 1834 Jul 08		26-0197
Fr 1834 Jul 08		26-0199
Fr 1834 Jul 08*		M415-1
Fr 1834 Jul 08#	fin	26-0202
Fr 1834 Jul 10		26-0211
Fr 1834 Jul 10		26-0215
Fr 1834 Jul 11		DLC-44
Fr 1834 Jul 11		M415-1
Fr 1834 Jul 11*		26-0219
Fr 1834 Jul 12		M415-1
Fr 1834 Jul 12*		26-0220
To 1834 Jul 15		26-0228
Fr 1834 Jul 15		M415-1
Fr 1834 Jul 15*		26-0232
Fr 1834 Jul 17		26-0233
Fr 1834 Jul 18		DLC-73
To 1834 Jul 26		26-0263
Fr 1834 Jul 28		DLC-44
Fr 1834 Aug 02		DLC-44
Fr 1834 Aug 05		DLC-44
To 1834 Aug 08		26-0301
Fr 1834 Aug 12		M415-1
To 1834 Aug 15		26-0317
Fr 1834 Aug 18		DLC-44
Fr 1834 Aug 23		26-0353
Fr 1834 Aug 27		M415-1
Fr 1834 Aug 28		26-0367
Fr 1834 Aug 29		26-0398
To 1834 Sep 29#		M124-144
To 1834 Oct 06		26-0525

To	1834	Oct 09			26-0548
To	1834	Oct 12#			26-0604
Fr	1834	Oct 14			26-0645
Fr	1834	Oct 14*			M415-1
To	1834	Oct 22			26-0684
To	1834	Nov 08#			26-0852
To	1834	Nov 17			DLC-73
Fr	1834	Nov 18			26-0949
Fr	1834	Nov 28			M415-1
Fr	1834	Nov 28*			26-1051
Fr	1834	Dec 12#			26-1490
To	1834	Dec 24#			27-0011
To	1835	Jan 05			27-0101
Fr	1835	Jan 12			27-0203
Fr	1835	Jan 12*			M415-1
To	1835	Jan 14#			27-0231
To	1835	cJan 15			27-0244
Fr	1835	Jan 24#			M179-79
To	1835	cFeb 05			27-0417
To	1835	Feb 25			27-0629
To	1835	Mar 03		mem	27-0995
Fr	1835	Mar 11#			M179-79
To	1835	Mar 26#			27-1384
To	1835	Apr 07#			DLC-46
Fr	1835	Apr 08			28-0003
Fr	1835	Apr 08*			M415-1
Fr	1835	Apr 12			28-0030
To	1835	Apr 23#			DLC-46
Fr	1835	Apr 28			28-0173
Fr	1835	Apr 28*			M415-1
To	1835	Apr 30#			M639-5
To	1835	May 05			28-0287
Fr	1835	May 05			28-0289
To	1835	May 12			28-0376
To	1835	May 14			28-0431
Fr	1835	May 14			28-0433
Fr	1835	May 14*			M415-1
To	1835	May 18#			28-0461
To	1835	May 21			28-0490
To	1835	May 23			28-0496
Fr	1835	May 23			28-0497
To	1835	May 25			28-0501
To	1835	May 29#			28-0518
To	1835	Jun 16#			28-0720
To	1835	Jun 24			28-0773
To	1835	Jul			28-0866
To	1835	Jul 01#			28-0873
To	1835	Jul 01#			28-0868
To	1835	Jul 02			28-0883
To	1835	Jul 03			28-0896
To	1835	Jul 03#			M234-435
To	1835	Jul 05			28-0944
To	1835	Jul 05#			28-0940
To	1835	Jul 06			28-0968
Fr	1835	Jul 06			28-0973
Fr	1835	Jul 10			28-0998
Fr	1835	Jul 11			M639-18
To	1835	Jul 13			28-1008
Fr	1835	Jul 13			28-1013
Fr	1835	Jul 13			28-1019
Fr	1835	Jul 13*			M415-1
To	1835	Jul 17			28-1034
Fr	1835	Jul 18			28-1048
Fr	1835	Jul 20			28-1094
Fr	1835	Jul 20*			M415-1
Fr	1835	Jul 21			28-1103
Fr	1835	Jul 24			M415-1
Fr	1835	Jul 24*			28-1153
Fr	1835	Jul 25			DLC-46

Fr	1835	Jul 25*			28-1176
Fr	1835	Jul 25*			M415-1
Fr	1835	Jul 26			DLC-46
Fr	1835	Jul 27			28-1185
Fr	1835	Jul 27*			M415-1
To	1835	Jul 28			28-1192
To	1835	Aug 07			M567-112
To	1835	cAug 26			28-1407
Fr	1835	Aug 27			M415-1
Fr	1835	Aug 27*			28-1429
Fr	1835	Aug 27*			M234-355
Fr	1835	Sep 10			29-0019
Fr	1835	Sep 10*			M415-1
To	1835	Oct 20#			29-0327
Fr	1835	Nov 03			29-0435
Fr	1835	Nov 03*			M733-1
Fr	1835	Nov 04			29-0457
Fr	1835	Nov 04*			M415-1
Fr	1835	Nov 10			29-0496
Fr	1835	Nov 10*			M415-1
Fr	1835	Nov 10			M733-1
Fr	1835	Nov 10*			29-0499
To	1835	Nov 13#		mem	29-0511
To	1835	Dec 03#			29-0734
Fr	1835	Dec 07			29-1027
Fr	1835	Dec 07*			M415-1
Fr	1835	Dec 08			29-1038
Fr	1835	Dec 08*			M415-1
Fr	1835	Dec 15			29-1177
Fr	1835	Dec 15*			M415-1
Fr	1835	Dec 23			29-1328
Fr	1836	cJan#			29-1424
Fr	1836	Jan		mem	DLC-49
Fr	1836	Jan 15			30-0113
Fr	1836	Jan 15*			M415-1
To	1836	Jan 21#			DLC-47
To	1836	Jan 30#			30-0228
To	1836	Feb 03			30-0284
Fr	1836	Feb 09#			30-0340
Fr	1836	Feb 13#			30-0384
Fr	1836	Feb 15			30-0397
Fr	1836	Feb 19			30-0413
Fr	1836	Feb 19			30-0417
Fr	1836	Feb 19*			M733-1
To	1836	Feb 19#			30-0420
To	1836	Mar 08#			DLC-47
Fr	1836	Mar 11#			DLC-47
To	1836	Mar 22#			30-0871
Fr	1836	Apr 13			M415-1
Fr	1836	Apr 13*			30-1148
To	1836	Apr 15		mem	30-1189
To	1836	Apr 18#			30-1227
Fr	1836	Apr 27			M415-1
Fr	1836	Apr 27*			30-1400
To	1836	Apr 30			30-1426
Fr	1836	May 03			30-1496
Fr	1836	May 03*			M415-1
To	1836	May 04			30-1501
To	1836	May 05#			30-1520
Fr	1836	May 06			30-1537
To	1836	May 07#			30-1551
Fr	1836	May 11			30-1601
Fr	1836	May 11*			M415-1
To	1836	May 19			31-0060
Fr	1836	May 20			31-0062
Fr	1836	May 20*			M733-1
Fr	1836	May 20*			M234-436
Fr	1836	May 26			M415-1
Fr	1836	May 26*			31-0133

Woodbury Levi (cont)

To 1836 May 26#		31-0131
Fr 1836 Jun 03		31-0305
Fr 1836 Jun 03*		M415-1
To 1836 Jun 05#		31-0341
Fr 1836 Jun 06	mem	DLC-48
To 1836 Jun 07		31-0401
To 1836 Jun 12#		31-0438
To 1836 Jun 13		31-0466
To 1836 Jun 20#		31-0524
To 1836 Jun 22#		31-0547
Fr 1836 Jun 27		31-0619
Fr 1836 Jun 27*		M415-1
Fr 1836 Jun 30		31-0694
To 1836 Jul 04		31-0852
To 1836 Jul 04#		31-0835
To 1836 Jul 08		31-0986
Fr 1836 Jul 08		31-0993
Fr 1836 Jul 11		31-1061
Fr 1836 Jul 11*		M415-1
Fr 1836 Jul 12		DLC-48
Fr 1836 Jul 18		31-1131
Fr 1836 Jul 18*		M415-1
Fr 1836 Jul 22		M733-1
Fr 1836 Jul 23		31-1153
Fr 1836 Jul 23*		M415-1
Fr 1836 Jul 26		31-1167
Fr 1836 Jul 26*		M415-1
Fr 1836 Jul 26		31-1168
Fr 1836 Jul 26*		M415-1
Fr 1836 Jul 27		31-1169
Fr 1836 Jul 27*		M415-1
Fr 1836 Jul 28		31-1170
Fr 1836 Jul 28*		M415-1
Fr 1836 Jul 30		31-1175
Fr 1836 Jul 30*		M415-1
Fr 1836 Aug 02		31-1219
Fr 1836 Aug 02*		M415-1
Fr 1836 Aug 02#		31-1193
To 1836 Aug 05#		31-1234
Fr 1836 Aug 06#		31-1236
Fr 1836 Aug 19		DLC-48
Fr 1836 Aug 30		31-1381
Fr 1836 Aug 30*		M415-1
To 1836 Sep 15#		31-1450
Fr 1836 Sep 18		31-1456
Fr 1836 Sep 18*		M415-1
Fr 1836 Oct 06		32-0101
Fr 1836 Oct 11#		32-0158
To 1836 Oct 13#		32-0172
To 1836 Oct 18		32-0227
To 1836 Oct 22#		32-0329
Fr 1836 Oct 27		32-0357
Fr 1836 Oct 27*		M415-1
Fr 1836 Nov 25		32-0583
Fr 1836 Nov 25*		M415-1
Fr 1836 Nov 29		32-0594
Fr 1836 Nov 29*		M415-1
To 1836 Dec		32-0604
To 1836 Dec 03		32-0843
To 1836 Dec 06		32-1043
To 1836 Dec 12		32-1127
Fr 1836 Dec 24		32-1312
Fr 1836 Dec 24*		M415-1
To 1836 Dec 27	mem	32-1365
Fr 1837 Jan 07		DLC-49
Fr 1837 Jan 07*		32-1540
To 1837 Jan 11		32-1576
Fr 1837 Feb 01		M221-117
Fr 1837 Feb 01*		33-0352
Fr 1837 Feb 02		33-0368
Fr 1837 Feb 02*		M415-1
Fr 1837 Feb 09		33-0591
Fr 1837 Feb 14		33-0709
Fr 1837 Feb 14*		M415-1
Fr 1837 cFeb 14		M415-1
Fr 1837 Feb 20		33-0790
Fr 1837 Feb 20*		M415-1
Fr 1837 Feb 28		33-0938
Fr 1837 Apr 06		DLC-50
To 1837 Apr 27		33-1191
Fr 1837 May 10		DLC-50
To 1837 May 16		DLC-50
To 1837 May 17		M234-853
To 1837 May 23		33-1249
Fr 1837 May 29		33-1257
Fr 1837 Jun 04		DLC-50
To 1837 Jun 16		33-1312
Fr 1837 Jun 28		DLC-50
Fr 1837 Jul 03		DLC-50
To 1837 Oct 30		34-0012
Fr 1837 Nov 13		DLC-50
Fr 1837 Nov 13*		34-0024
To 1837 Nov 24		34-0041
Fr 1837 Dec 09		34-0085
To 1838 Mar 27		34-0293
Fr 1838 Apr 09		DLC-51
Fr 1838 Apr 09*		34-0315
Fr 1838 Jun 02		34-0360
To 1838 Jun 21		34-0387
Fr 1839 Jul 06		DLC-52
To 1839 Jul 20		34-0846
Fr 1840 Nov 08		DLC-53

Woodbury N L		
Fr 1837 Feb 22		M687-3
Woodbury Phineas		
Fr 1815 Sep 27		DLC-19
Woodcock John H		
Fr 1827 Jan 10	fin	11-0464
Woodcock & Sledge		
Fr 1824 Jul 10	fin	10-0821
Wooden William D		
Fr 1843 Jan 30		DLC-55
Wooding Robert Sterling		
Fr 1834 Nov 24	fin	DLC-45
Woodruff Joseph		
Fr 1814 Jul 29		3-1188
Fr 1814 Aug 06		DLC-11
Fr 1814 Aug 29		DLC-11
To 1814 Sep 08		DLC-62
To 1814 Sep 16		DLC-12
Fr 1814 Sep 18		DLC-12
Fr 1814 Sep 26		DLC-12
Fr 1814 Oct 22		DLC-13
Fr 1814 Nov 08		M221-63
Fr 1814 Nov 21		DLC-14
Fr 1815 Jan 29		DLC-16
To 1815 Mar 13		DLC-17
Fr 1815 Mar 23		DLC-17
Fr 1815 Mar 23*		M221-63
Fr 1815 Jun 01		DLC-18
Fr 1815 Sep 15		DLC-19
Fr 1816 Apr 18		DLC-20
Fr 1816 Oct 25		DLC-21
Fr 1821 Feb 16		DLC-29
Woodruff Thomas M		
Fr 1833 Dec 28		M639-24
Woodruff & Smiley		
Fr 1823 Nov 06	fin	DLC-32

Woods J et al			
	Fr 1829 Aug 10		M639-18
Woods James & Robert			
	Fr 1822 Jan 19		DLC-31
	Fr 1822 Jan 31		DLC-31
Woods Joseph			
	Fr 1813 Feb 05	fin	3-0266
	To 1813 Aug 10	chk	DLC-6
Woods Richard M			
	Fr 1837 Aug 23		DLC-50
Woods Stephen			
	Fr 1829 Apr 13		M639-6
Woodside James D			
	Fr 1835 Oct 29	fin	DLC-47
	To 1835 Oct 29	chk	DLC-47
	Fr 1835 Nov 04	fin	DLC-47
Woodside Jane Isabelle			
	Fr 1844 Jul 15		DLC-57
Woodson Philip Jr			
	Fr 1829 Jun 29		M639-21
Woodson Thomas J			
	Re 1836 Apr 25#	fin	30-1350
Woodward Alfred L			
	Fr 1844 Jan 08		DLC-56
	To 1844 Mar 23		36-0403
	Fr 1845 Jan 08		DLC-57
Woodward C C			
	Fr 1829 Jun 10		M639-27
Woodward Elbert			
	Fr 1819 Nov 03		M221-21
Woodward Nathaniel A			
	Fr 1832 Nov 16		DLC-41
Wool John Ellis			
	To 1828 Feb 26		11-1149
	Fr 1834 Oct 22		26-0685
	Fr 1835 Jul 20		M221-115
	Fr 1836 Jun 17#		31-0498
	To 1836 Aug 07		DLC-48
	Fr 1836 cAug 15		DLC-48
	Fr 1836 Aug 16		DLC-48
	To 1836 Aug 23		DLC-49
	Fr 1836 Aug 30		DLC-49
	Fr 1836 Aug 30*		31-1382
	To 1836 Sep 07		31-1431
	To 1836 Sep 07*		M234-80
Woolf John L et al			
	Fr 1829 Jan 24		M639-12
Woolley Abram R			
	Fr 1814 Nov 08		DLC-14
	Fr 1814 Nov 15		DLC-14
	Fr 1814 Dec 10		DLC-14
	Fr 1814 Dec 20		DLC-14
	Fr 1815 Jan 01		DLC-15
	Fr 1815 Jan 11		DLC-15
	Fr 1815 Jan 18		DLC-67
Woolley Melling			
	Fr 1790 Mar 01	fin	DLC-1
Woolridge Thomas			
	Re 1833 Oct 17		23-1057
Woolverton John D et al			
	Fr 1829 Mar 12		M639-26
Wootten William			
	Fr 1814 Sep 04		DLC-12
	Fr 1814 Nov 03		DLC-13
Work George			
	Fr 1839 Feb 21		M687-35
Workman James et al			
	Fr 1828 Nov 15		DLC-35
Workman S			
	Fr 1834 Jul 19		26-0235
Workman S et al			
	Fr 1836 Oct		M688-104
Wormeley Hugh Wallace			
	Fr 1821 Apr 02		DLC-30
Worrall John			
	To 1829 Sep 15		13-1316
Worrell ______ (Maj Gen; PA)			
	To 1819 Feb 19	add	DLC-28
Worrell Edward			
	Fr 1830 Nov 07		M222-28
Worsley William W			
	To 1817 Mar 11		5-0774
	Fr 1817 Mar 22		5-0789
	To 1817 Apr 11		5-0809
Wortham Robert			
	Fr 1830 Nov 03		M22-27
Worthington Asa			
	Re 1829 Oct 21		14-0226
Worthington Edward			
	Fr 1830 Dec 21#		DLC-73
Worthington Erastus et al			
	Fr 1836 May 24		31-0092
Worthington John Tolley Hood			
	Fr 1832 Mar 31		20-0078
Worthington Thomas			
	Fr 1815 Apr 03		DLC-18
Worthington William G D			
	To 1821 Jun 25		M116-10
	To 1821 Jul 01		DLC-63
	To 1821 Jul 25		DLC-63
	To 1821 Jul 26		DLC-63
	To 1821 Jul 27		DLC-63
	To 1821 Aug 09		M116-7
	To 1821 Aug 13		M116-10
	To 1821 Aug 13*		DLC-63
	To 1821 Aug 13*		8-1045
	Fr 1821 Aug 28		M116-7
	To 1821 Sep 18		DLC-63
	To 1821 Sep 21		DLC-63
	To 1821 Oct 01		DLC-63
	Fr 1821 Oct 04		M116-10
	Fr 1821 Oct 04*		M221-94
	Fr 1821 Oct 04*		8-1269
	Fr 1821 Oct 06		M116-10
	Fr 1821 Oct 26		DLC-31
	Fr 1821 Oct 31		DLC-31
	Fr 1821 Nov 09		M116-10
	Fr 1821 Nov 09*		8-1334
	Fr 1821 Dec 11		M116-9
	Fr 1821 Dec 18		M116-9
	To 1822 Jan 18		DLC-63
	Fr 1822 Feb 18		M116-10
	Fr 1822 Feb 20		DLC-31
	To 1824 Jan 17		9-0941
	Fr 1824 Feb 04		M688-30
Wortz David			
	Fr 1838 Apr 02		DLC-51
Wotwood George			
	Re 1794 Apr	leg	1-0224
Wourt William			
	Fr 1843 Apr 06		DLC-55
Wray William			
	To 1838 Jun 07#		DLC-51
Wray & Judson			
	Fr 1836 Apr 30	fin	DLC-48
Wrifford Allison			
	Fr 1837 Jan 08		32-1546
Wright Alfred			
	Fr 1841 Apr 16		DLC-53

Wright Benjamin
Fr 1845 Jan 03 DLC-57
Wright Charles
Fr 1803 Jan 12 DLC-2
Wright Clinton
Fr 1816 Sep 07 DLC-21
Fr 1818 Feb 08 DLC-24
Wright Daniel W
Fr 1829 Mar 04 M234-432
Fr 1830 Apr 11# 15-0673
Fr 1830 Jul 26 M222-28
Fr 1831 Jan 23 M234-169
Fr 1831 Jan 23* 17-0339
Wright David
To 1821 Jul 20 DLC-63
Wright Francis B
Fr 1835 Aug 31 28-1465
Fr 1835 Nov 23 29-0553
Fr 1836 Feb 19# 30-0420
Fr 1836 Jun 05# 31-0341
Wright James
Fr 1833 Apr 17 22-1040
Wright Joel
Fr 1832 Jan 17 fin 19-0752
Wright John
Fr 1815 Mar 03 DLC-17
Fr 1823 Nov 06 fin DLC-33
Wright John A
Fr 1844 Apr 24 36-0444
Wright Joseph
Fr 1820 Jan 25 fin DLC-28
Wright Silas
Fr 1831 Oct 13 M639-23
Fr 1834 Jan 08 M639-7
Fr 1834 Feb 14 M639-7
Fr 1834 Feb 22 M124-141
Fr 1834 Mar 01 M639-14
Fr 1834 Jun 09 M639-24
Fr 1835 May 22 28-0493
Fr 1842 Apr 02 DLC-54
To 1843 Feb 08 35-1199
Fr 1843 Mar 02 DLC-55
To 1843 Sep 21# DLC-55
Wright Silas et al
Fr 1836 Apr 20 30-1275
Wright Thomas
Re 1832 Oct 27 21-0199
Wright Thomas et al
Fr 1820 Aug 09 7-1200
Wright William
Fr 1830 Jan 10 14-1370
Fr 1835 May 28 DLC-46
To 1835 Jun 04 DLC-46
Wright William & Co
Fr 1806 Dec 22 fin DLC-4
Wright William H D C
Fr 1829 Nov 28 14-0618
Wurts John
Fr 1829 Nov 17 M179-67
Wyandot Indians
Fr 1832 Mar 10 M22-29
Wyandot treaty
Re 1832 Apr 06 M668-6
Re 1836 May 16 M668-8
Wyatt Thomas E
Re 1814 May 27 3-1072
Wyatt Tod R
Fr 1844 Dec 12 DLC-57
Wyer Edward
Fr 1829 Sep 15 DLC-37
Wylie Theodore
Fr 1844 Jul 03 DLC-57
Wyly James W
Fr 1845 Jan 26 M873-97
Wyly James W et al
Fr 1836 Jul 23 DLC-48
To 1836 Jul 25 DLC-48
Wynn John L
To 1828 Feb 10 11-1109
Wynne John Knibb
To 1812 Aug 25 2-1236
To 1813 Dec 19 3-0691
To 1813 Dec 19* DLC-61
To 1813 Dec 26 DLC-61
To 1813 Dec 26* 3-0722
To 1814 Jan 05 DLC-61
To 1814 Jan 05* DLC-8
Wynne Lewis B
Fr 1845 Feb 07 DLC-57
Wynne William W
To 1814 Jun 26 3-1112
Fr 1814 Jul 17 DLC-11
Fr 1814 Jul 17* M6-7
To 1814 Jul 22 DLC-62
Wynns Thomas
Fr 1833 Oct 01 DLC-43
Wyse John M
Fr 1836 Jul 06# 31-0898
Fr 1836 Jul 10 DLC-48

Yancey Joel
Fr 1835 Jan 05 M234-76
Fr 1835 Feb 14 DLC-45
Fr 1836 Dec 18 32-1189
Fr 1836 Dec 29# DLC-49
Fr 1838 Apr 25 DLC-51
Fr 1838 Jul 30 DLC-51
Yancey Joel et al
Fr 1836 Dec 17 32-1183
Yandell John
To 1814 Mar 14 DLC-62
Yandell Wilson
Fr 1812 Aug 18 DLC-5
Yeatman Thomas
Fr 1816 Jan 02 fin DLC-69
Fr 1817 Oct 01 fin DLC-70
Fr 1822 Feb 11 DLC-31
Yell Archibald
Fr 1826 Jul 08 add 11-0305
To 1826 Jul 08 add 11-0308
Fr 1834 Feb 13 24-1324
Fr 1835 Aug 06 28-1259
Fr 1836 Feb 10 DLC-47
Fr 1836 Jul 19 M22-40
Fr 1836 Aug 07 31-1259
Fr 1838 Jan 13 DLC-51
Yellowhair John et al
Fr 1833 Nov 10 M234-806
Yerby William
Fr 1815 Aug 05 DLC-19
To 1815 Aug 15 DLC-62
Yerger George S
Fr 1832 Oct 29 M639-4
Yoholo Micco et al
Fr 1835 Aug 27 28-1443
York Jonathan
Re 1809 Aug 29 leg DLC-4
To 1809 Dec 14 fin DLC-4

Name	Date	Type	Reference
York Thomas			
	Re 1809 Aug 29	leg	DLC-4
	To 1809 Dec 14	fin	DLC-4
You Dominique			
	To 1828 Jan 10		11-1054
Young E			
	Fr 1836 Jun 04#	fin	DLC-49
	To 1836 Jul 04	chk	DLC-48
	Fr 1836 Jul 05	fin	DLC-48
	To 1836 Jul 08	chk	DLC-48
	To 1837 Jan 02	chk	DLC-49
Young E & A H			
	Fr 1835 Jul 01#	fin	DLC-47
Young Guilford D			
	To 1829 Jan 05		12-0451
Young Hugh			
	Fr 1816 Nov 29		DLC-22
	Fr 1816 Dec 04		DLC-22
	Fr 1816 Dec 22		DLC-22
	Fr 1817 Jan 19		DLC-22
	Fr 1817 Mar 14		DLC-22
	Fr 1817 Mar 14*		M221-74
	Fr 1817 Mar 14*		5-0775
	Fr 1817 Apr 25		DLC-22
	Fr 1817 Jun 07		DLC-22
	Fr 1817 Jul 06		DLC-23
	Fr 1817 Sep 14		5-1014
	Fr 1817 Sep 30		5-1032
	Fr 1817 Oct 09		5-1103
	Fr 1818 May 05		6-0645
	Fr 1818 Sep 01		DLC-25
	Fr 1818 Oct 12		M222-20
	Fr 1819 Sep 23		M221-11
	Fr 1819 Nov 17		DLC-28
	Fr 1820 Jul 19		DLC-29
	To 1821 Feb 20		8-0144
Young John S et al			
	Fr 1836 Dec 21		32-1268
Young Joshua			
	Fr 1830 Jan 05		M124-122
Young L Huntington			
	Fr 1831 Feb 01		17-0406
Young McClintock			
	To 1834 Jun 25		25-1549
	Re 1834 Jul 02		26-0077
	To 1834 Dec 06#		DLC-45
	Fr 1835 Jan 14#		27-0231
	To 1835 Jul 01		28-0877
	To 1835 Oct 20		29-0332
	Fr 1835 Nov 13#	mem	29-0511
	Fr 1837 Jan 28		33-0201
	Fr 1844 Feb 17		36-0294
	Fr 1845 Jan 24		36-1397
Young Nathan			
	Re 1836 Jul 07	par	31-0943
Young Richard Montgomery			
	Fr 1829 Feb 14		M639-3
	Fr 1837 Feb 22		33-0834
Young Robert			
	Fr 1814 Dec 30		DLC-15
	Fr 1815 Jan 01		DLC-15
	Fr 1815 Feb 10		DLC-16
Young Sandy			
	Re 1831 Nov 25	par	18-1498
Young Thomas et al			
	Fr 1831 Jan 26		M639-1
Young Thomas M W			
	Fr 1827 Nov 06		DLC-34
Young William			
	Fr 1815 Nov 06		DLC-19
	Fr 1820 Apr 04		DLC-28
Young Citizen (horse)			
	Re c1831	mem	17-0078
Young King et al			
	Fr 1829 Jul 20		M234-832
	Fr 1830 Jan 18		M234-832
Young Truxton (horse)			
	Re 1822 Mar 20		9-0069
	Re 1822 Mar 25		DLC-75
Youngs White			
	Fr 1818 May 19		DLC-25
Zane Noah et al			
	Fr 1829 Aug 10		M639-18
Zanesville OH citizens			
	Fr 1832 Apr 12		M22-29
Zantzinger William P			
	To 1830 Oct 08#		16-0338
Zeilin Jacob Jr			
	Fr 1831 Jul 06		18-0157
Zeilin John K			
	Fr 1831 Jul 07		18-0160
	Fr 1832 Feb 11		M221-112
Zeylstra Focke Hiddes			
	Re 1833 Jan 30	par	22-0120
Ziegler F L			
	Fr 1838 May 16		DLC-51
Zuniga Mauricio de			
	To 1816 Apr 23		5-0045
	To 1816 Apr 23*		M221-70
	Fr 1816 May 26		5-0091
	Fr 1816 May 26*		DLC-20

/E337.8.J3P31987>C1/